Welcome to the 20th Edition of MedStudy's *Internal Medicine Core*!

This 20th edition represents the knowledge, expertise, and labor of love of superb physician educators from internal medicine residencies and teaching hospitals across the U.S. This edition has been extensively rewritten to ensure that the information is tightly focused and clearly explains what you need to know, reflects current standards of care, and references the most recent practice guidelines.

This Core is the foundation of the entire Study Strong System and is tightly integrated with MedStudy Internal Medicine Q&As, Core Scripts® Flashcards, Audio Pearls, our Review Courses and Videos, and our new Personal Trainer. Think of your Internal Medicine Core as a series of well-crafted lectures given by the best teachers you've ever had—those teachers who had a knack for connecting with you and for clearly explaining obtuse concepts. These lectures are casual, yet concise, and focus on the medical knowledge needed to have a strong internal medicine practice and to easily pass your exams.

But casual, concise, and focused content is not enough—there's still a lot of material! How can you determine what, out of all this content, is the most important to know? And how in the world do you get it into your long-term memory?

First: How do you identify what's most important?

For both exams and clinical practice, our writers and editors know what you need to know and teach it every day. They've identified the must-know, most-asked information from each topic and have highlighted it in yellow. The Preview | Review questions at the beginning of each main topic are based on some of this highlighted material.

Second: How do you get this must-know information into long-term memory?

The answer is the **MedStudy Method**, our evidence-based approach to learning. All MedStudy products are built from the ground up with features that work optimally with this method.

> Read more about the MedStudy Method in the *StudyWise* guide, which you can access at any time in the **Helpful Stuff** area of your myMedStudy account. Review this guide thoroughly before you jump into the Core! It covers how memory works, learning myths and truths, and the best brain-hacking techniques to learn, retain, and easily recall the must-know information.

NEW! Personal Trainer, our super-smart adaptive learning guide, uses the techniques from the MedStudy Method to build personalized, adjustable study plans that align with your goals. Weekly Core and Q&A assignments combine the content with the MedStudy Method to move what you need to know into your long-term memory. Log into your myMedStudy account and set up your study goals. We'll do the rest!

We are truly honored to be a part of your medical education. We wish you more balance in your life, more confidence in your practice, and a whole lot more fun.

Study Strong,

Tony

Robert A . "Tony" Hannaman, MD
MedStudy's Founder and Editor in Chief

Core Features Bring the Reading to Life

While you're reading these pages, it's meant to feel like you're sitting in a live lecture from your favorite professor.

Highlighted text

Indicates must-know content—including answers to Preview | Review Questions

Bold text

Denotes important lists and defined terms

Preview | Review Questions

Contain the highest-yield questions for you to preview, study, and review

Burgundy text

Emphasizes certain words the same way a great teacher would

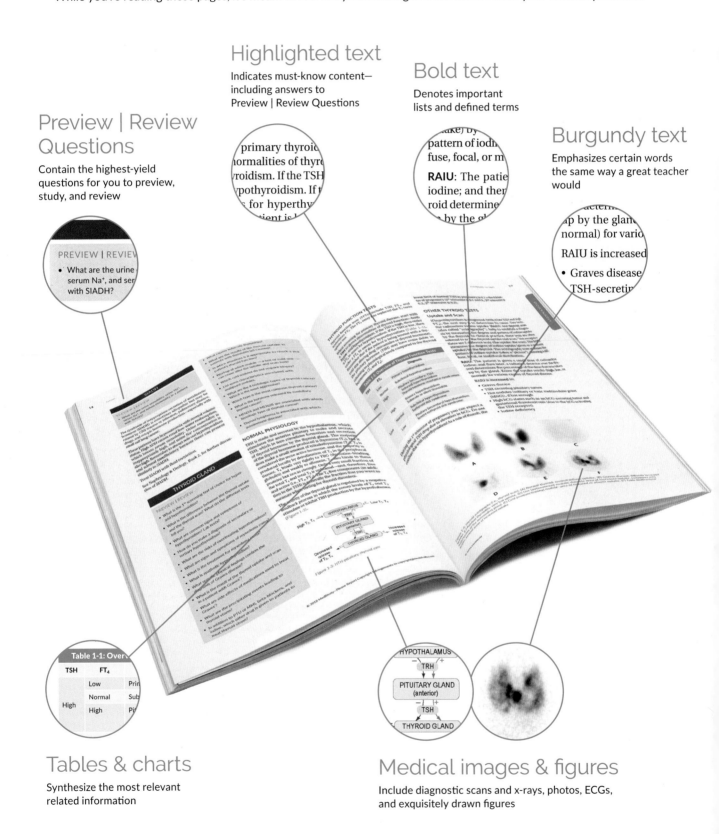

primary thyroid
normalities of thyro
yroidism. If the TSH
ypothyroidism. If t
s for hyperthy
tient is h

RAIU: The patie
iodine; and ther
roid determine
by the gl

p by the glan
normal) for vario

RAIU is increased

- Graves disease
- TSH-secretin

PREVIEW | REVIEW
- What are the urine
  serum Na⁺, and ser
  with SIADH?

Table 1-1: Over		
TSH	**FT₄**	
	Low	Prin
High	Normal	Sub
	High	Pi

Tables & charts

Synthesize the most relevant related information

Medical images & figures

Include diagnostic scans and x-rays, photos, ECGs, and exquisitely drawn figures

Truly **Learn** Medicine with Personal Trainer

Your interactive Personal Trainer guides you through the 3 phases of learning for each topic in the Core, locking the information you must know into your long-term memory.

3 ESSENTIAL PHASES OF LEARNING

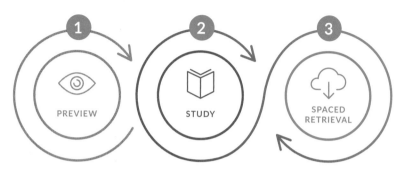

1 PREVIEW

2 STUDY

3 SPACED RETRIEVAL

You get a continuously updated, personalized study plan based on the content you need to learn and how much time you have. Your super-smart Personal Trainer creates weekly assignments and displays them on your study board.

STUDY BOARD

Your home base for daily interaction with all of your assignments.

Your Personal Trainer adapts to any changes in your schedule, keeps track of what you accomplish, and provides encouraging feedback along the way.

Personal Trainer works with both the print and digital Core. Set up your Personal Trainer at my.MedStudy.com!

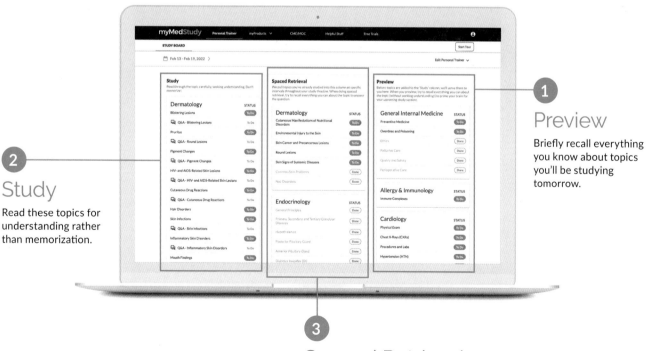

2

Study

Read these topics for understanding rather than memorization.

1

Preview

Briefly recall everything you know about topics you'll be studying tomorrow.

3

Spaced Retrieval

Practice recall of the same study material over progressively longer intervals. This moves information into easily accessible long-term memory!

MedStudy 20th Edition *Internal Medicine Core*

CME START DATE:
November 1, 2022

CME EXPIRATION DATE:
November 1, 2025

Eligible for a maximum 150 CME Credits and 150 ABIM MOC Credits

CME ACCREDITATION

MedStudy is accredited by the Accreditation Council for Continuing Medical Education (ACCME) to provide continuing medical education for physicians.

MedStudy designates this enduring material for a maximum of 150 *AMA PRA Category 1 Credits*™. Physicians should claim only the credit commensurate with the extent of their participation in the activity.

This credit may be submitted to the American Osteopathic Association (AOA) for category 2 credit. All other health care professionals completing this continuing education activity will be issued a certificate of participation.

AMERICAN BOARD OF INTERNAL MEDICINE (ABIM) MOC POINTS

Successful completion of this CME activity, which includes participation in the evaluation component, enables the participant to earn 150 Medical Knowledge MOC points in the American Board of Internal Medicine's (ABIM) Maintenance of Certification (MOC) program. Participants will earn MOC points equivalent to the amount of CME credits claimed for the activity. It is the CME activity provider's responsibility to submit participant completion information to ACCME for the purpose of granting ABIM MOC credit.

HOW TO APPLY FOR CME CREDIT AND ABIM MOC POINTS

CME and MOC credits are available only to the original purchaser of this product (directly from MedStudy), and issuance of credit is subject to verification of product ownership. CME and MOC credits will be available only after passing the required online posttest with a score of at least 70%. All credits should be claimed by the expiration date.

To claim your CME credits and/or MOC points:

1. Log into your myMedStudy account with your email address and password.
2. Follow the instructions for completing the CME credit application and posttest.
3. Return to your Eligible Credits page to claim the ABIM MOC credits (optional).
4. MedStudy will report claimed MOC credits directly to the ABIM within 1–2 business days.

For any questions, please email us at cme@medstudy.com or call 1-800-841-0547.

LEARNING OBJECTIVES

As a result of participation in this activity, learners will be able to:

- integrate and demonstrate increased overall knowledge of internal medicine,
- identify and remedy areas of weakness (gaps) in knowledge and clinical competencies,
- describe the clinical manifestations and treatments of diseases encountered in internal medicine and effectively narrow the differential diagnosis list by utilizing the most appropriate medical studies, and
- apply the competence and confidence gained through participation in this activity to both a successful board exam–taking experience and daily practice.

TARGET AUDIENCE

Participants in this MedStudy educational activity are those physicians seeking to assess, expand, and reinforce their knowledge and clinical competencies in internal medicine, focusing their learning on subjects that are directly relevant to clinical scenarios that will be encountered on the ABIM Certification board exam or the Maintenance of Certification (MOC) board exam and the American Osteopathic Board of Internal Medicine (AOBIM) board exams, as well as in the contemporary clinical setting. The content of this activity is intended to help learners assess their own key knowledge and clinical competencies with evidence-based standards of care, as reflected on the board exams, and remedy any potential competency gaps that may exist.

METHOD OF PARTICIPATION

The content of this CME activity is intended to help learners assess their key knowledge and clinical competencies with evidence-based standards of care, which are reflected on the board exams and in day-to-day practice. Internists or other physicians preparing for the ABIM certification or MOC exam—or who simply want to update their knowledge of internal medicine—should:

- Preview the section material the day before a study session by reading the Preview | Review questions and recalling whatever knowledge they might already have.
- Read the Core, paying special attention to yellow-highlighted text, which is the must-know material for the ABIM certification and MOC exams, based on ABIM content outlines. Review tables and figures to reinforce study and to see concise summaries of interrelated facts and clinical examples in key topic areas. Self-test again later by answering Preview | Review questions.
- One to two days after reading the Core, go back to the Preview | Review questions again, and try to recall as much as possible. Repeat this again in 7–10 days, 1–2 months, and 4–6 months to improve knowledge and proficiency and, ultimately, to ensure mastery of the material.

The learner will be required to complete a posttest as part of the requirements for receiving CME or MOC credit for this product.

> Without these people,
> the 20th Edition *Internal Medicine Core* wouldn't exist.
> Thank You.

EDITOR IN CHIEF

Robert A. Hannaman, MD
MedStudy
Colorado Springs, CO

SENIOR MEDICAL EDITORS

Catherine A. Hatchell, MD
MedStudy
Colorado Springs, CO

Eileen Scott Yale, MD
Assistant Professor
Department of Internal Medicine
Division of General Internal Medicine
Gainesville, FL

CONTRIBUTORS

Diego F. Belardi, MD
Cardiologist
Kaiser Permanente Colorado
Denver, CO

Theresa A. Buck, MD
Pulmonary/Critical Care
C.W. Bill Young VA Medical Center
Bay Pines, FL

Lynn Bullock, MD
MedStudy
Colorado Springs, CO

Marius M. Commodore, MD
Medical Director
Campus Health, Tulane University
New Orleans, LA

Hasmukh Jain, MD*
Professor, Medical Oncology
Tata Memorial Centre
Mumbai, Maharashtra, India

Rachel Lucille Kelly, DO
Internal Medicine
Hickory, NC

Robert G. Kowalski, MD, MS*
Clinical Instructor, Department of Neurology
Research Instructor, Department of
 Neurosurgery
University of Colorado School of Medicine
Aurora, CO

Angela Ryan Lee, MD
Cardiologist
Dallas, TX

Jasbir K. Matharu, MD*
Family Medicine
Los Angeles, CA

Sharon E. Maynard, MD
Associate Professor of Medicine
Division of Nephrology
Lehigh Valley Health Network
Allentown, PA

Mary Regina Olsovsky, MD
Seattle, WA

Melba I. Ovalle, MD
Professor & Medical Director
Nova Southeastern University
Orlando, FL

Brandy A. Panunti, MD
System Chair of Endocrinology
Ochsner Health System
New Orleans, LA

Kashif J. Piracha, MD
Clerkship Director, Department of Internal
 Medicine
Adjunct Assistant Professor of Clinical
 Medicine
Texas A&M University College of Medicine,
 Methodist Willowbrook Site
Houston, TX

Thanai Pongdee, MD*
Assistant Professor, Division of Allergic
 Diseases
Mayo Clinic College of Medicine and Science
Mayo Clinic
Rochester, MN

Vijay R. Pottathil, MD, MME
Medical Director, Gastroenterology &
 Hepatology
San Mateo Medical Center
San Mateo, CA

Rishi Sawhney, MD
Medical Director
Bayhealth Cancer Institute
Dover, DE

Sussan K. Sutphen, MD, MEd
Atlanta, GA

James A. Vitarius, MD, PhD*
Leonia, NJ

Austin D. Williams, MD, MSEd
Memorial Sloan Kettering Cancer Center
New York, NY

Touqir Zahra, MD
Academic Hospitalist & Associate Program
 Director,
Internal Medicine Residency Program
Florida Atlantic University / Boca Raton
 Regional Hospital
Boca Raton, FL

Fred Arthur Zar, MD
Professor of Clinical Medicine
Program Director, Internal Medicine Residency
Director of Academic Affairs
University of Illinois at Chicago
Chicago, IL

Note: Those contributors with an asterisk (*) after their names have disclosed relationships with entities producing, marketing, reselling, or distributing health care goods or services consumed by, or used on, patients. All others have documented they have no relationships with such entities.

MEDSTUDY DISCLOSURE POLICY

It is the policy of MedStudy to ensure balance, independence, objectivity, and scientific rigor in all its educational activities. In keeping with all policies of MedStudy and the ACCME, any contributor to a MedStudy CME activity is required to disclose all relevant relationships with any entity producing, marketing, reselling, or distributing health care goods or services consumed by, or used on, patients. Failure to do so precludes acceptance by MedStudy of any material by that individual. All contributors are also required to submit a signed Clinical Content Validity Agreement, affirming that their contribution is based upon currently available, scientifically rigorous data that is free from commercial bias and that any clinical practice and patient care recommendations offered are based on the best available evidence for these specialties and subspecialties. All content is carefully reviewed by MedStudy's in-house physician editors, as well as on-staff copyeditors, and any perceived issues or conflicts are resolved prior to publication of an enduring product or the start of a live activity.

MEDSTUDY DISCLOSURE STATEMENT

As the provider of this continuing medical education activity, MedStudy Corporation, including all its employees, has no financial interest, arrangement, or affiliation with any commercial entity producing, marketing, reselling, or distributing health care goods or services consumed by, or used on, patients. Furthermore, MedStudy complies with the AMA Council on Ethical and Judicial Affairs (CEJA) opinions that address the ethical obligations that underpin physician participation in CME: 8.061, "Gifts to physicians from industry," and 9.011, "Ethical issues in CME," and 9.0115, "Financial Relationships with Industry in CME."

FOR FURTHER STUDY

For both review articles and current internal medicine practice guidelines, visit the MedStudy Hub:

medstudy.com/hub

The Hub contains an online consolidated list of all current guidelines focused on internal medicine. Guidelines on the Hub are easy to find, continually updated, and linked to the published source.

BECOME OUR NEXT STAR CONTRIBUTOR

Are you a great writer? Want to teach? Looking for an opportunity for a side hustle? We're looking for contributors who are able to translate their rich experience as physicians and teachers into writing or presenting concise, engaging, and clearly explained concepts. If you'd like to be a part of MedStudy's team, we'd like to hear from you!

Email: medstudy.com/become-a-contributor

WE WANT TO HEAR FROM YOU

Have feedback about the 20th Edition *Internal Medicine Core*? Have a burning question? We'd love to hear it!

Email: support@medstudy.com

Phone: 800-841-0547 (Monday–Friday, 8:00am–5:00pm MST)

PRODUCTION STAFF

Sarah Bearden
Production Director

Melanie Herd
Production Manager / Product Owner

Carla Breidenbach
Product Lead Internal Medicine Core

Joyce Linder
Senior Development Editor

Tom Champe
Medical Development Editor

George Yaksick
Medical Development Editor

Vidya Ford
Medical Development Editor

Deborah Turner
Product Lead Medical Student Core

Kathleen Rowland
Contract Medical Copyeditor

Allison Esposito
Contract Medical Copyeditor

Deborah Hughes
Contract Medical Copyeditor

Ashley Dreyer
Marketing Director

Lauren Wilson
Marketing Manager

Katie Converse
Content Marketing Manager

Dorie Hopkins
Creative Lead

Emily Acanfora
Digital Design Lead

Gabriele Ewerts
Medical Illustrator

Rebecca Gelertner
Medical Illustrator

Mark Fender
Publishing Production Artist

Toly Melinkov
Software Engineering Director

Shannon Bomar
Senior Product Owner

Ted Doss
Content Engineer

Gregory Ramsey
Content Engineer

Jason Botwick
Dev Manager / Architect

Joe Luciano
Systems Engineer

Charles Marquez
IT Support Engineer

Lawan Agbedor
Senior Software Engineer

Jared Youtsey
Dev Manager / UI Architect

Alicia Pino
Head Unicorn Wrangler

Sherry Snyder
CME Manager

ADDRESSING DIVERSITY, EQUITY, & INCLUSION

As we strive toward a future that is more diverse, equitable, and inclusive, we acknowledge that there is still work to be done within our products. To that end, you will begin to notice changes in both our text and images as we broaden the spectrum of respectful and accurate inclusion in order to enhance medical education, and thus patient treatment and experience. For example, in this edition we are using person-first language when describing patients with diseases or conditions; e.g., "a person with diabetes" rather than "a diabetic." We are also no longer using the terms "African American" and "Caucasian" unless a study we are referencing specifically used those descriptors for race and ethnicity.

Since the print editions are representative of where we were at the time of printing, you will see evolutions in the content first in our digital editions, which receive ongoing updates.

Not only are we working to reflect current standards of care and reference the most recent practice guidelines, but we are also working to respect the diversity of human experience. If you have comments, thoughts, or suggestions, we encourage you to please send them to us at support@medstudy.com. We'd love to hear from you.

Endocrinology

SECTION EDITOR

Brandy A. Panunti, MD
System Chair of Endocrinology
Ochsner Health System
New Orleans, LA

CONTENT CONTRIBUTORS

Touqir Zahra, MD
Academic Hospitalist & Associate Program Director,
Internal Medicine Residency Program
Florida Atlantic University/Boca Raton Regional Hospital
Boca Raton, FL

Eileen Scott Yale, MD
Assistant Professor, Department of Internal Medicine
University of Florida
Gainesville, FL

Table of Contents

GENERAL PRINCIPLES

PREVIEW | REVIEW

- What is meant by positive and negative feedback regulation in endocrine diseases? Which is most common: positive or negative feedback?

If you want to test for hyposecretion of a hormone, try to stimulate it. Example: In adrenal insufficiency, adrenocorticotropic hormone (ACTH) fails to stimulate cortisol production (the ACTH stimulation test).

If you want to test for hypersecretion of a hormone, try to suppress it. Example: In Cushing syndrome, dexamethasone fails to suppress production of cortisol (the dexamethasone suppression test).

Laboratory findings must always be interpreted within a clinical context. Example: In primary hyperparathyroidism, parathyroid hormone (PTH) is expected to be high but may be inappropriately normal for the lab range; this inappropriately normal PTH level is consistent with PTH hypersecretion because the proper PTH response to hypercalcemia is suppression to a very low level.

Biochemical confirmation of hormonal disease (with labs and dynamic testing) always precedes imaging because benign, nonfunctional masses are common in all endocrine glands (incidentalomas). Know what you are looking for before you image!

Important characteristics to know about a hormone:

- What is its function?
- Where is it produced and secreted?
- What stimulates and inhibits its release?
- Where are these controls?
- How is it secreted? Is it diurnal, pulsatile, or under tonic inhibition?

Note: Many endocrine glands respond to feedback mechanisms that regulate hormone secretion by negative and/or positive feedback. Positive feedback stimulates hormone release, whereas negative feedback inhibits or suppresses hormone release. Feedback is important in maintaining homeostasis. Most endocrine glands are under negative feedback control. Example: Excess cortisol inhibits both corticotropin-releasing hormone (CRH) and ACTH production.

Note on plasma vs. serum: Plasma is the liquid component of blood that has no cells. Serum is plasma with the clotting factors removed. In the body, the liquid component of the blood is plasma. Serum is the liquid in a red-top tube after clotting occurs. You will see these terms used interchangeably, and it is okay because it usually doesn't matter. For example, you are actually measuring plasma osmolality by doing a serum osmolality test. In this section, we generally stick with the term plasma when talking about the body and serum for lab tests.

PRIMARY, SECONDARY, AND TERTIARY GLANDULAR DISEASES

PREVIEW | REVIEW

- What are the definitions of primary, secondary, and tertiary glandular diseases?

With regard to glandular abnormalities:

Primary glandular disease refers to disease of the gland that secretes the hormone.

Secondary glandular disease refers to disease of the gland that controls the primary gland.

Tertiary glandular disease refers to disease of the gland that controls the secondary gland that controls the primary gland.

Let's look at some examples:

Primary hypothyroidism results from a diseased thyroid gland underproducing thyroid hormone.

Secondary hypothyroidism is caused by a diseased pituitary gland underproducing thyroid-stimulating hormone (TSH). Consequently, the thyroid underproduces thyroid hormone.

Tertiary hypothyroidism begins with a diseased hypothalamus underproducing thyroid-releasing hormone (TRH). Because of this, the pituitary underproduces TSH. As a result, the thyroid underproduces thyroid hormone.

Here are 2 more examples:

Primary aldosteronism (a.k.a. primary hyperaldosteronism) results from a diseased adrenal gland overproducing aldosterone. This condition is caused by an aldosterone-secreting tumor or adrenal hyperplasia.

Secondary hyperaldosteronism originates with a diseased kidney overproducing renin. As a consequence, adrenal glands overproduce aldosterone. So, disease is at the level of the kidney: renovascular disease or a renin-secreting tumor.

HYPOTHALAMUS

PREVIEW | REVIEW

- How does the hypothalamus control output of the anterior pituitary? Of the posterior pituitary?

The hypothalamus sits in the forebrain just below the thalamus and above the pituitary gland. It controls the endocrine function in the body by assessing many bodily and external environmental signals and then using hormones and nerves to output new control signals to the pituitary gland.

Input to the hypothalamus is from the cortex, autonomic nervous system, peripheral endocrine system, and external environment (e.g., temperature and light).

The hypothalamus controls output of the anterior pituitary by means of releasing hormones, such as CRH and TRH, and inhibiting hormones, such as dopamine. It controls the output of the posterior pituitary (i.e., neurohypophysis) by direct nerve stimulation.

POSTERIOR PITUITARY GLAND

PREVIEW | REVIEW

- What hormones synthesized in the hypothalamus are stored in the posterior pituitary gland?
- What is the main effect of antidiuretic hormone (ADH)?

The pituitary gland is considered the master gland. Functionally, it is composed of the anterior pituitary and the posterior pituitary, which participate in different hormonal axes. Each axis has different positive and negative feedback controls.

It helps to think of the posterior pituitary as an extension of the hypothalamus. The antidiuretic hormone (ADH; a.k.a. vasopressin) and oxytocin synthesized in the hypothalamus are transported and stored in the posterior pituitary. (All other pituitary hormones are made in and secreted by the anterior pituitary gland.) The posterior pituitary secretes these hormones in response to nerve stimuli from the hypothalamus.

ADH regulates plasma osmolality. Normal plasma osmolality is 285–295 mOsm/kg (285–295 mmol/kg), and it can be either measured directly or estimated. Be familiar with the formula:

$$\text{Osmolality} = (2 \times [Na^+]) + (\text{glucose}/18) + (BUN/2.8)$$

Plasma osmolality is the most important determinant of ADH secretion and the main effect of ADH is decreasing renal free water excretion in the late distal tubule and cortical collecting duct. Osmoreceptors of the hypothalamus are exquisitely sensitive to small changes in plasma osmolality; small increases in the plasma osmolality sensed in the hypothalamus lead to large increases in ADH secretion, increased renal water retention, and a concentrated urine.

ADH secretion causes the kidneys to conserve water and concentrate the urine (antidiuresis), which prevents hyperosmolarity from getting worse. However, free-water intake is needed to correct hyperosmolarity, even when the urine is maximally concentrated. Hence, high plasma osmolality also stimulates thirst. Thirst produces the needed increase in free-water intake.

The osmotic threshold (i.e., set point) for ADH release is decreased (ADH is released at a lower osmolality) in pregnancy, leading to mild physiologic hyponatremia.

ADH also is released in response to nonosmotic factors; the most potent of these is nausea, which increases ADH levels to several hundred times normal. Other factors that stimulate ADH include pain, medications, lung disorders (including lung cancer), and central nervous system disorders. In these states, ADH impairs free-water excretion, causing hyponatremia—this is termed the syndrome of inappropriate antidiuretic hormone (SIADH). ADH release is also triggered by severely decreased effective arterial blood volume (e.g., true hypovolemia, heart failure, liver cirrhosis).

For more on SIADH, see Disorders of Water Balance in the Nephrology section.

ANTERIOR PITUITARY GLAND

PREVIEW | REVIEW

- What are the hormones of the anterior pituitary?
- What are the signs and symptoms of a pituitary tumor?
- What is the workup for a pituitary tumor?
- Aside from a prolactinoma, what are the other causes of hyperprolactinemia?
- What is the best initial medical therapy for hyperprolactinemia?
- How do you test for acromegaly?
- Which cancers most commonly metastasize to the pituitary?
- What is the clinical presentation of pituitary apoplexy? What is the treatment?

OVERVIEW

The anterior pituitary produces 6 hormones (and without them, you feel like a **FLAT PiG**):

1) **F**ollicle-stimulating hormone (FSH)
2) **L**uteinizing hormone (LH)
3) **A**drenocorticotropic hormone (ACTH)
4) **T**hyroid-stimulating hormone (TSH)
5) **P**rolactin (PRL)
6) **G**rowth hormone (GH)

It secretes these hormones in response to releasing and inhibiting hormones that are made in the hypothalamus and released into the hypophyseal portal system (a specialized portal system that connects the hypothalamus with the anterior pituitary).

The anterior pituitary hormones are controlled by both positive and negative feedback. High plasma hormone levels inhibit hormone production and low plasma hormone levels stimulate hormone production. This feedback system is termed the hypothalamus-pituitary-target gland axis.

With positive feedback, low hormone levels cause the hypothalamus to produce releasing hormones (e.g., TRH, corticotropin-releasing hormone [CRH]) that induce pituitary hormone secretion (e.g., TSH, ACTH), which, in turn, stimulates target gland hormone production (e.g., thyroxine, cortisol).

With negative feedback, higher-than-normal levels of the target gland hormones inhibit hormone production in both the pituitary and the hypothalamus. The exception to the rule is prolactin, which is continuously inhibited by dopamine from the hypothalamus. When there is a decrease in dopamine, prolactin increases.

ACTH has a diurnal variation with a peak at 6 a.m. and a nadir at midnight. ACTH stimulates the adrenal gland to produce corticosteroids and adrenal androgens, and it has a regulatory effect on production of mineralocorticoids. ACTH increases in response to CRH from the hypothalamus and to physical or psychological stresses; ACTH is suppressed in response to high cortisol levels.

GH is secreted in a pulsatile fashion and is regulated by 2 hypothalamic hormones: growth hormone–releasing hormone (GHRH) and somatostatin (a.k.a. growth hormone–inhibiting hormone). **GHRH** causes release of GH from the pituitary, and somatostatin tonically inhibits release of GH from the pituitary. Note: Somatostatin can also inhibit the release of TSH from the pituitary and regulate other neuroendocrine cell activity. Because the release of GH is pulsatile, a random GH level is not useful. As a screen for GH excess or deficiency, measure the more stable GH product, insulinlike growth factor 1 (**IGF-1**).

LH and **FSH** regulate sex hormone production. LH and FSH production is regulated by pulsatile secretion of gonadotropin-releasing hormone (GnRH) from the hypothalamus. **Inhibin**, produced in the ovary and testis, inhibits only FSH secretion.

PRL is different from the other hormones because it is under tonic inhibition by hypothalamic dopamine sent down the pituitary stalk. This is an important concept because stalk compression is a cause of hyperprolactinemia.

TSH secretion is stimulated by hypothalamic TRH and inhibited by thyroid hormone and somatostatin. When thyroid hormone levels are high (i.e., primary hyperthyroidism), TSH levels will be low.

PITUITARY TUMORS

Pituitary tumors can present with symptoms of hormonal hypersecretion, hypopituitarism, and vision loss. They can also be detected as an incidental finding (after imaging of the brain for unrelated symptomatic complaints, such as headache). These are sometimes called incidentalomas. Pituitary tumors are due to the abnormal proliferation of cells of the anterior pituitary.

The **1st step in evaluating** a pituitary tumor is to determine its size and if it is functional (secreting hormones). The **2nd step** is to determine if it is causing a mass effect leading to anterior pituitary hormone hyposecretion or to vision loss. The size of the tumor determines the evaluation process. A pituitary adenoma > 1.0 cm (macroadenoma) is evaluated

for hormonal hypersecretion, hyposecretion, and vision loss, and those < 1.0 cm (microadenoma) are evaluated only for hypersecretion as they are generally not large enough to cause hormone hyposecretion or vision loss.

Clinical presentation depends on the type of adenoma:

- **Lactotrophs (prolactinomas):** hyperprolactinemia, resulting in amenorrhea and galactorrhea in women, hypogonadism in men, and infertility in both; the most common functioning adenoma
- **Gonadotrophs:** mostly clinically silent until they become macroadenomas and cause mass effect and/or pituitary hypofunction; the most common nonfunctioning adenoma
- **Thyrotrophs (TSHoma):** hypersecretion of TSH, resulting in hyperthyroidism; least common adenoma (Labs show a normal/high TSH and high free T_4 [FT_4].)
- **Somatotrophs:** hypersecretion of GH, resulting in acromegaly (best screen = IGF-1)
- **Corticotrophs:** hypersecretion of ACTH, resulting in Cushing disease
- **Mixed cell type:** most often combines somatotrophs + lactotrophs, called **somatomammotrophs**, with cosecretion of both GH and prolactin

Remember: Mixed cell type tumors exist; therefore, it is important to always check a prolactin level in somatotroph tumors and IGF-1 in lactotroph tumors because prolactin- and GH-producing cells are from a common cell line.

Typical mass effect symptoms include headaches, diplopia, or visual field defects (e.g., bitemporal hemianopsia). Less commonly, adenomas can extend and cause CSF rhinorrhea.

Acute hemorrhage into an adenoma causes **apoplexy**, manifesting as acute severe headache, nausea, vomiting, vision impairment and loss, and altered mental status. This is an endocrine emergency and requires immediate corticosteroids and a neurosurgical consult. Although all types of pituitary hormonal deficiencies can occur, only the sudden loss of ACTH production is life threatening; it stops cortisol production and precipitates an adrenal crisis, which can rapidly progress to shock.

Suspect a pituitary adenoma when a patient presents with multiple hormone abnormalities or a mixture of symptoms, such as low libido, weight loss, anorexia, weakness, and (in women) amenorrhea.

When interpreting FSH and LH levels, always consider whether the levels are appropriate for the reproductive stage of the female (pre- vs. postmenopausal). For example, if a postmenopausal female patient has low or inappropriately normal FSH and LH levels, there is a gonadotropin deficiency. (Remember: Postmenopausal women should have an elevated FSH level, so a normal level is inappropriately normal.)

Diagnosis: MRI is the imaging of choice for the tumor. When a patient presents with an incidental pituitary tumor, the size of the tumor determines biochemical evaluation.

If < 1 cm, check the following for hypersecretion:

- Prolactin level
- IGF-1 to screen for GH excess
- TSH and FT_4 (TSH helps in evaluation if FT_4 is high.)
- Screen for cortisol excess with:
  - 24-hour urine free cortisol,
  - low-dose (1 mg) overnight dexamethasone suppression test, or
  - midnight salivary cortisol.
- LH, FSH, and α subunit tests are generally not done.

If > 1 cm, do formal visual field testing and check for both hypersecretion (with these same tests) and hyposecretion. To work up for hyposecretion, do the following:

- ACTH stimulation test (screening for cortisol deficiency)
- LH and FSH in postmenopausal women (both are normally high) and testosterone in men to screen for hypogonadism
- IGF-1 to screen for GH deficiency
- TSH and FT_4 (TSH helps in evaluation if FT_4 is low.)
- In premenopausal women, ask about changes in menses. A regular menstrual cycle off OCPs excludes gonadotrophin deficiency.

If the hormone labs are normal, the tumor is nonfunctional and is likely a gonadotroph tumor that is inefficient in making the active hormone β subunit.

Remember: Gonadotropins (LH and FSH), TSH, and human chorionic gonadotrophin (hCG) have an α and a β subunit. The β makes it unique, whereas α subunits are just inactive glycoprotein. Finding high levels of α subunits supports a diagnosis of gonadotroph or nonfunctional tumor.

If the tumor is nonfunctional, it does not impinge on the optic nerve or chiasm, and there is no hypersecretion of hormones, then the tumor can be reimaged in about 6 months if it's a macroadenoma or in 1 year if it's a microadenoma. If there is no change in size, then repeat yearly for macroadenomas, and for microadenomas repeat every 1–2 years for the following 3 years.

Indications for surgical removal of a pituitary tumor include:

- visual field or other ophthalmologic defects,
- a lesion in or abutting the optic chiasm or compressing the optic nerve,
- apoplexy, or
- hypersecretion of ACTH, GH, or TSH.

Prolactinomas have their own criteria for surgical removal, which we will cover in Hyperprolactinemia and Prolactinomas.

On MRI, other sellar masses can be seen, including craniopharyngiomas, which often present as calcified cystic suprasellar lesions. They are considered benign, but they can cause symptoms secondary to mass effect and impingement on the optic nerve.

Radiologists may occasionally report an empty sella, which is a description of an imaging finding and not a diagnosis, because the majority of people have normal hormonal function. In empty sella, the pituitary has been displaced and squished by CSF but still functions normally; it has been described in multiparous women. No treatment is needed for empty sella syndrome if there are no associated hormone deficiencies.

Hyperprolactinemia and Prolactinomas

A serum PRL concentration that is repeatedly elevated (> 20 ng/mL) is termed hyperprolactinemia. This is the most frequent functional abnormality of the pituitary gland.

When hyperprolactinemia is not caused by a prolactinoma, prolactin levels are generally < 200 ng/mL.

Nonprolactinoma causes of hyperprolactinemia:

- Drugs that are dopamine antagonists; i.e., certain antipsychotics (e.g., phenothiazines, haloperidol, risperidone), metoclopramide, and verapamil
- Diseases of the hypothalamus and/or pituitary stalk that interfere with production or transport of dopamine, thus removing the negative inhibition on prolactin production (e.g., sarcoidosis, stalk compression, trauma). Stalk compression is when a pituitary tumor pushes on the stalk and interferes with transport of dopamine.
- Pregnancy or estrogen use—pregnancy is the most common cause of physiologic hyperprolactinemia (refer to the Women's and Men's Health section under Gynecology).
- Nipple stimulation (e.g., due to lactation)
- Orgasm: Recommend patients abstain from sexual activity for 24 hours prior to test.
- Chest wall injuries, including skin lesions (e.g., piercing, herpes zoster)
- Hypothyroidism (Always check a TSH.)
- Chronic kidney disease

Prolactinoma is the most common functional pituitary tumor. Prolactinomas are usually < 1 cm (microadenomas), but they can also be macroadenomas causing visual field defects. PRL levels generally correlate with tumor size (> 200 ng/mL for macroadenomas). Elevated PRL level inhibits the release of GnRH, decreasing LH and FSH. Therefore, hyperprolactinemia of any cause results in hypogonadism and erectile dysfunction in men and amenorrhea and galactorrhea in women.

If you see a macroadenoma with only mild hyperprolactinemia (prolactin < 200 ng/mL), then it is not a prolactinoma—the prolactin elevation is likely due to pituitary stalk compression. In this case, dopamine delivery to the lactotrophs is impaired, removing the tonic inhibition of prolactin production.

Note: Watch for the following pitfall in the lab! A markedly elevated prolactin can be masked (falsely low) due to a lab artifact called the hook effect. If the tumor is ≥ 1 cm and the PRL level is < 100 ng/mL, check a diluted prolactin test before diagnosing stalk effect.

Due to amenorrhea, prolactinomas are diagnosed earlier in women than in men. Decreased libido is the earliest symptom of a prolactinoma in males but is often ignored, so men tend to present later and with larger masses and visual field defects. Galactorrhea occurs in most women with prolactinomas but rarely in men. Longstanding hypogonadism is associated with decreased skeletal bone mineralization in both men and women.

Management options for prolactinomas include medical treatment, surgical resection, and observation. Indications for medical or surgical treatment include:

- Tumor size > 1 cm
- Hypogonadal symptoms (e.g., amenorrhea, infertility, erectile dysfunction)
- Galactorrhea affecting the patient's quality of life
- Women with impaired fertility

Always check TSH and pregnancy test (in women) before deciding to treat.

Microadenomas usually do not grow to > 1 cm, so observation alone can be an appropriate option for certain groups: postmenopausal women, premenopausal women who do not desire fertility and do not have or are not troubled by galactorrhea, and men who are not interested in fertility. Conservative management should include estrogen replacement in premenopausal women (oral contraceptive pills [OCPs]), testosterone replacement in men, and observation in postmenopausal women. Follow with serial MRIs and prolactin levels to assess any change in size. Stable prolactin levels predict a stable tumor size.

Prolactinomas are extremely sensitive and responsive to medical treatment. For most patients, treatment with dopamine agonists is the best initial option. Dopamine agonists decrease both the PRL level and tumor size. **Cabergoline** is 1st line because of its efficacy and safety profile. Cabergoline can cause increased cardiac valvulopathy when administered at a very high dosage, as in the treatment of Parkinson's. Cabergoline is contraindicated in patients with known lung, heart valve, and retroperitoneal fibrotic disease. **Bromocriptine** is the 2nd line agent; it causes more nausea and orthostatic hypotension than cabergoline.

Transsphenoidal surgery is only used when the patient cannot tolerate drug therapy, or when it is ineffective. Postoperatively, an elevated PRL level is indicative of persistent or recurrent disease, particularly in the case of macroadenomas. **Radiation** is usually reserved for postsurgical cases to eradicate any remaining tumor.

When a woman on drug therapy for a prolactinoma becomes pregnant, stop the medication and monitor clinically for symptoms, physical exam, and visual field testing. Do not check prolactin levels; they are expected to increase with pregnancy. About 1/3 of macroadenomas enlarge during pregnancy; however, a normal pituitary also enlarges during pregnancy. MRI is only recommended if there is clinical evidence of growth, such as new headaches or visual field changes. If the tumor enlarges enough to cause symptoms, cabergoline or bromocriptine can be restarted. If vision is threatened, surgery is a therapeutic option. Both bromocriptine and cabergoline appear to be safe in early pregnancy, but data on fetal effects with long-term exposure are limited.

Acromegaly

Growth hormone (GH) is required for normal growth. GH production is suppressed by hyperglycemia and somatostatin and is stimulated by hypoglycemia.

When excess GH presents in childhood before growth plates are closed, it is termed **gigantism**. When it occurs in adulthood, it is termed **acromegaly** because the growth plates are closed; there is not excessive linear growth, but there is acral growth (i.e., hands, feet).

> 99% of acromegaly cases are due to a benign, well-defined adenoma, which is recognized on CT or MRI. Affected patients typically become symptomatic in their late 30s to mid 40s. Signs and symptoms of acromegaly include:

- Enlarging hands and feet
- Coarsening of the facial features
- Deepening of the voice
- Carpal tunnel syndrome, often bilateral
- Acanthosis nigricans
- Skin tags
- Pronounced jaw growth (which leads to multiple dental problems)
- Excessive sweating, body odor

Acromegaly has an insidious onset associated with an increased mortality when untreated. The most important long-term problem associated with acromegaly is cardiovascular disease. Patients have increased risk of:

- Ischemic heart disease
- Cardiomyopathy
- Diastolic dysfunction
- Hypertension
- Left ventricular hypertrophy
- Stroke

Acromegaly is also associated with obstructive sleep apnea, insulin resistance/diabetes mellitus, colon polyps, and colorectal cancer.

Screen for acromegaly by checking an IGF-1 level. Do not order a random GH level because a single value of GH is not useful in diagnosing acromegaly; its secretion is pulsatile, and levels in the blood can vary greatly in a healthy individual. IGF-1 is produced by the liver and mediates the growth-promoting effect of GH. Unlike GH, IGF-1 levels are stable throughout the day. A normal age-adjusted IGF-1 level almost always excludes the diagnosis of acromegaly. If the IGF-1 level is elevated, confirm the diagnosis by demonstrating a failure of GH to suppress after a 75-g oral glucose load (via an oral glucose tolerance test [OGTT]). A post-OGTT GH level > 1 ng/mL (1 µg/L) is diagnostic of acromegaly. Also check prolactin levels (elevated due to cosecretion in 25% of GH tumors). If the tumor is > 1 cm, check for visual field deficits and for other hormonal deficiencies.

Order a screening colonoscopy and echocardiogram on all patients diagnosed with acromegaly, regardless of age.

Treat all patients with transsphenoidal surgery, even if they are asymptomatic. Some experts recommend medical therapy with somatostatin analogs as initial therapy prior to surgery for a better chance for a cure and possibly safer intubation.

Radiation is used as initial therapy only in poor surgical candidates.

Medical treatment may be used as adjuvant therapy in patients with residual tumor after surgical resection and in poor surgical candidates. Options include somatostatin analogs (e.g., octreotide) +/− dopamine agonists (e.g., cabergoline or bromocriptine), and GH receptor antagonists (i.e., pegvisomant).

Other Pituitary Tumors

We mentioned **gonadotroph adenomas** under Pituitary Tumors on page 1-3. Recall that they are the most common type of nonfunctioning adenomas, usually macroadenomas. Gonadotroph tumors can present variably:

- Incidentally on imaging and hormonally silent
- Mass effect and hormonally silent
- Mass effect with symptoms of hypogonadism/partial panhypopituitarism
- Mass effect with symptoms of gonadotropin excess (very, very rare)

A diagnosis of gonadotroph adenoma is usually supported by finding an increase in free α subunits (inactive) or rarely, high levels of FSH and/or LH.

Transsphenoidal surgery is indicated for symptomatic nonfunctioning or functional gonadotroph adenomas.

For asymptomatic patients with preserved endocrine function and a normal visual field assessment, observation with serial imaging studies is appropriate.

Radiation is an option for certain types of tumors but primarily is used postsurgically to contain residual tumor mass. Patients who have had pituitary radiation need lifelong monitoring of anterior pituitary function for adrenal insufficiency and secondary hypothyroidism.

Pituitary hyperplasia is expected in pregnancy and can mimic a pituitary tumor if imaging is done (for more on pituitary adenoma during pregnancy, see the Women's and Men's Health section under Obstetrics). Severe primary hypothyroidism (disease of the thyroid gland) can also cause pituitary hyperplasia as the pituitary thyrotrophs become hyperplastic from the overdemand for TSH; imaging shows a pituitary mass. Clinically, the patient is hypothyroid; biochemically, the FT_4 is low and the TRH and the TSH are high. The elevated TRH suppresses dopamine, causing an increase in PRL; thus, the patient can be mistakenly diagnosed with a prolactinoma.

Treatment with thyroxine replacement causes the thyrotrophs to shrink and PRL levels to normalize.

Metastatic cancer can be seen in the pituitary; the posterior part of the gland is most often involved. These metastases can present as isolated central diabetes insipidus (DI; absent or deficient ADH production). Breast and lung cancer metastases are most common. Infiltrative diseases, such as sarcoidosis, can also cause isolated DI. Lymphoma and leukemia can present as primary cancer of the pituitary.

Acquired Hypopituitarism

Pituitary apoplexy is a neurosurgical emergency caused by hemorrhage into a pituitary mass, usually an adenoma. Suspect apoplexy in the patient who presents with severe headache, N/V, diplopia, +/− altered mental status. Symptoms can begin suddenly ("mule kick in the head" or "the worst headache of my life") or can develop over 1–2 days. Diabetes with microvasculature changes, radiation therapy, and current warfarin use are risk factors. The patient's history may include indications or a diagnosis of an adenoma causing hormone excess or deficiency.

Pituitary hormones are abnormal in apoplexy. Apoplexy causes hypopituitarism, which can cause a decrease in all the pituitary hormones, the most life-threatening of which is ACTH. No ACTH means no cortisol (i.e., secondary adrenal insufficiency), shock, and death. Apoplexy can be difficult to distinguish from subarachnoid hemorrhage (SAH) occurring in the same area; however, in SAH, pituitary hormones are normal.

Suspect pituitary apoplexy when the patient has the acute symptoms mentioned above; the diagnosis is confirmed by finding a dense pituitary mass on CT or MRI. Test pituitary hormones (remember: the most critical one is ACTH), along with a cortisol level. Again, urgent recognition and treatment of secondary adrenal insufficiency is necessary to prevent life-threatening hypotension.

Treatment: If the symptoms are mild, only corticosteroids are necessary. Edema can cause a mass effect and require emergent decompression. Consult a neurosurgeon to make the call on whether to use corticosteroids alone or take the patient to surgery.

Sheehan syndrome (1/10,000 deliveries) is postpartum hypopituitarism. It always involves the anterior pituitary and sometimes also affects the posterior pituitary, but it rarely causes central diabetes insipidus (i.e., low ADH from posterior pituitary).

Severe cases can manifest with symptoms of adrenal insufficiency and/or hypothyroidism (e.g., weakness, lethargy, anorexia, hypotension).

Sheehan syndrome results from hypovolemic shock following severe obstetrical bleeding that causes necrosis of the enlarged anterior pituitary of pregnancy. This classic form of Sheehan syndrome nowadays occurs rarely in medical resource-rich countries. Instead, patients may present with failure to lactate, postpartum amenorrhea, or chronic hypopituitarism.

Acute postpartum hypopituitarism may indicate underlying unsuspected pituitary disease, e.g., autoimmune hypophysitis with resulting cortisol deficiency, growth hormone deficiency, and hypoglycemia (especially seen with growth hormone deficiency). Confirm cortisol deficiency by measuring the serum cortisol level. Hypoglycemia can also be due to the sudden increase in insulin sensitivity that occurs immediately postpartum.

Treat all causes of acute hypopituitarism emergently with high doses of hydrocortisone as well as IV glucose as needed to correct any hypoglycemia. If the patient is hypothyroid, delay thyroid therapy until the patient has been stabilized with hydrocortisone. Treating with thyroid hormone first can precipitate an adrenal crisis.

Other causes of hypopituitarism include pituitary and parasellar tumors, radiation, infections, inflammation, and infiltrative processes, such as sarcoidosis, hemochromatosis, and histiocytosis X.

Remember: If one anterior pituitary hormonal deficiency is found (independent of the etiology), all other anterior pituitary hormones should be assessed for concomitant deficiencies.

DIABETES INSIPIDUS (DI)

PREVIEW | REVIEW

- What happens to the urine osmolality and serum Na⁺ during water deprivation in a patient with diabetes insipidus?

DI occurs when the kidneys are unable to retain free water, causing a dilute urine despite progressively increasing plasma osmolality. It is characterized by thirst (with polydipsia) and the production of large volumes of dilute urine (usually > 3 L/day). Serum Na⁺ is normal if the patient has access to water, but hypernatremia occurs if access to water is limited. Nocturia typically is the 1st symptom of DI. Volume depletion rarely occurs, as long as there is an intact thirst mechanism and patients have access to water. Infants, nursing home patients, and those who are unconscious are vulnerable to these complications.

DI can be **central** (decreased ADH production) or **nephrogenic** (renal resistance to the effect of ADH).

Central DI (a.k.a. neurogenic DI) is either acquired or congenital. Acquired central DI occurs when there is disease or damage to the posterior pituitary. It can be caused by brain cancer or metastases, trauma, neurosurgery, or systemic infiltrative diseases (e.g., eosinophilic granuloma, sarcoidosis, granulomatosis with polyangiitis). When caused by surgery or trauma, acquired central DI is generally transient and is part of the triphasic response, which is immediate diabetes insipidus due to hypothalamic trauma followed by SIADH due to unregulated release of ADH from the posterior pituitary, with the expectation of recovery.

Figure 1-1 shows what's going on with ADH and plasma osmolality in central DI. Normally, as plasma osmolality increases (e.g., when there is lack of access to water), plasma ADH increases. In central DI, plasma ADH does not increase with rising plasma osmolality. The kidneys do not get the signal (ADH) to conserve water, urine osmolality stays low, and, unless the patient drinks, hypernatremia will get worse.

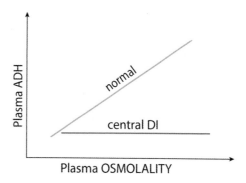

Figure 1-1: Central diabetes insipidus (DI)

Nephrogenic DI (a.k.a. ADH-resistant DI) can be acquired or due to gene mutations in the ADH receptor or in an aquaporin. (Aquaporins are transmembrane proteins that increase water permeability of the renal collecting tubule in response to ADH.) Important causes of acquired nephrogenic DI:

- Drugs (especially lithium)
- Hypercalcemia (serum Ca^{2+} > 11 mg/dL)
- Chronic hypokalemia (serum K⁺ < 3 mEq/L)
- Intrinsic renal disease (especially Sjögren syndrome)

Figure 1-2 illustrates the pathogenesis of nephrogenic DI. Normally, as plasma ADH rises in response to rising plasma osmolality, ADH acts on the kidneys to increase urine osmolality. High urine osmolality means high renal water reabsorption, which helps correct the hypernatremia. With nephrogenic DI, ADH increases appropriately; however, the kidney does not respond, and the urine osmolality remains low.

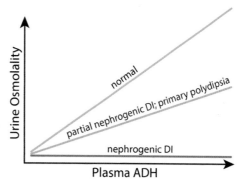

Figure 1-2: Nephrogenic diabetes insipidus (DI)

Both central and nephrogenic DI can be complete or partial. In partial central DI, the ADH release in response to hyperosmolarity is present but inadequate. In partial nephrogenic DI, there is a blunted renal response to the effects of ADH. In both cases, disease is milder than in the complete forms.

Diagnose central vs. nephrogenic DI with the **water restriction test**. This test ideally should be done in the hospital; it can be done in the office only when there is access to phlebotomy and quick turnaround on lab results.

Note: Do not restrict water if the serum Na$^+$ is already high (> 145 mEq/L)! These patients have already self-restricted; measure plasma and urine osmolality and skip to desmopressin administration.

If serum Na$^+$ is not already high, the first step is to restrict water/fluid intake. Then measure the urine osmolality, plasma osmolality, and serum Na$^+$ every 2 hours. If the urine osmolality rises to > 600 mOsm/L, you are done: the patient does not have DI, so there is no need to give desmopressin. If the urine osmolality remains < 600 mOsm/L, wait until the serum Na$^+$ rises to 144–145 mEq/L, then give desmopressin (i.e., synthetic ADH). Assess the renal response to desmopressin by measuring the urine osmolality every 30 minutes for 2 hours.

When interpreting the results of the water restriction test, refer to Figure 1-1 and Figure 1-2 on page 1-7.

In central DI, ADH does not increase in response to a rising plasma osmolality, so the urine osmolality remains low (i.e., the urine remains dilute). However, the kidneys respond normally to exogenous desmopressin with an increase in urine osmolality. Therefore, diagnose central DI when the urine does not concentrate with water deprivation but does concentrate after desmopressin administration.

In nephrogenic DI, exogenous desmopressin has no (or little) effect. So, diagnose nephrogenic DI if the urine does not concentrate with water restriction or desmopressin administration.

Primary polydipsia (a.k.a. psychogenic polydipsia) mimics DI; consider it in patients with polydipsia and polyuria +/– psychiatric illness. The water restriction test quickly differentiates psychogenic polydipsia from DI because patients with psychogenic polydipsia concentrate the urine normally with water restriction. Also, psychogenic polydipsia patients will never have hypernatremia; in fact, they are at risk for hyponatremia due to excessive water ingestion.

Treat central DI with either subcutaneous or intranasal desmopressin, a synthetic vasopressin analog. Desmopressin effectively reduces polyuria and nocturia. Because the kidneys immediately respond to ADH, giving desmopressin results in a quick increase of the urine concentration and reduction in urine output. The intranasal preparation is more potent than the oral; injectable is the most potent. Be careful to titrate the dose properly and counsel the patient to drink only when thirsty because hyponatremia can easily occur (i.e., drug-induced SIADH). Mild cases of partial central DI can occasionally be managed with an oral drug that stimulates ADH (e.g., chlorpromazine, carbamazepine) or with thiazides and salt restriction, but desmopressin acetate (DDAVP) is preferred.

In nephrogenic DI, the urine is persistently dilute, even when ADH is high. Giving desmopressin does not increase the concentration of the urine. Treat nephrogenic DI with a low-solute diet first, then add thiazide diuretics or amiloride if needed. NSAIDs are used to treat rare hereditary forms.

Note: In central DI, if the thirst center and ADH osmoreceptors are damaged, which can occur with a hypothalamic lesion (e.g., craniopharyngioma), the patient can have recurrent hypernatremic dehydration without thirst (adipsic hypernatremia). These patients are often very difficult to treat.

Remember: DI typically presents as polyuria/polydipsia, with or without hypernatremia, with normal volume status. SIADH usually presents as hyponatremia, also with normal volume status.

SYNDROME OF INAPPROPRIATE SECRETION OF ANTIDIURETIC HORMONE (SIADH)

PREVIEW | REVIEW

- What are the urine osmolality, urine Na$^+$, serum Na$^+$, and serum osmolality in a patient with syndrome of inappropriate secretion of antidiuretic hormone?

SIADH is sometimes idiopathic but may be caused by CNS trauma or infection, pulmonary disease, drugs, and ectopic hormone production, especially with small cell lung cancer.

These patients have hyponatremia with normal volume status. High ADH causes renal free-water reabsorption, which lowers serum osmolality. Urine osmolality is inappropriately high, and urine Na$^+$ concentration is also high. Remember to always rule out hypothyroidism and adrenal insufficiency, because these can present similarly to SIADH.

Treat SIADH with fluid restriction.

For further discussion of SIADH, see Disorders of Water Balance in the Nephrology section.

THYROID GLAND

PREVIEW | REVIEW

- What is the 1st screening test of choice for hyper- and hypothyroidism?

- What is the difference between the thyroid uptake and the thyroid scan? What do the different tests tell you?

- What are common signs and symptoms of hypo-thyroidism? Lab tests?

- How do you make a diagnosis of secondary or ter-tiary hypothyroidism?

- What are the risks of overtreating hypothyroidism?

- What are signs and symptoms of myxedema coma?

- What is the treatment for myxedema coma?

- What is apathetic hyperthyroidism?

- What specific physical findings confirm the diag-nosis of Graves disease?

- What is the result of the thyroid uptake and scan in a patient with Graves disease?

- What are side effects of medications used to treat Graves disease?

- What are the precipitating events leading to thyroid storm?

- In addition to propylthiouracil or methimazole, β-blockers, and iodine, which other drug is given to patients to treat thyroid storm?

- What is the presumptive cause of subacute thyroiditis?

- What are the results of the thyroid uptake in patients with thyroiditis (all causes)?

- In which situations is it appropriate to check a sick patient's thyroid function?

- Workup of which nodule—a hot or cold one— can cease after the uptake and scan test?

- List some characteristics associated with malig-nant nodules.

- Which cold nodules do not require biopsy?

- What are the 4 histologic types of thyroid cancer?

- Which type is the most common thyroid cancer?

- Which is the most aggressive type of thyroid cancer?

- What is the hormone released by medullary thyroid cancer?

- Multiple endocrine neoplasia 2A (MEN2A) and MEN2B are associated with which histologic type of thyroid cancer?

- Thyroid lymphoma is associated with which auto-immune disease?

NORMAL PHYSIOLOGY

TRH is made and secreted by the hypothalamus, which stimulates the anterior pituitary to make and secrete TSH, which in turn stimulates formation and secretion of thyroid hormone by the thyroid gland. The majority of the thyroid hormone produced is thyroxine (T_4), but it does make a small amount of triiodothyronine (T_3). T_3 is considered the more active hormone, and the majority is produced locally by deiodination of T_4 in the peripheral tissues. T_4 binds very tightly to TBG (thyroxine-binding globulin) and weakly to albumin. T_3 also binds to these proteins but not as strongly. Only a very small fraction of the total T_4 and total T_3 is unbound and, therefore, free and active (i.e., FT_4, FT_3). The FT_4 free component (in addition to the TSH) is generally the fraction that you want to measure when testing for thyroid disorders.

The activity of the thyroid gland is regulated by a negative feedback process in which the serum levels of T_4 and T_3 stimulate or inhibit TRH production by the hypothalamus (Figure 1-3).

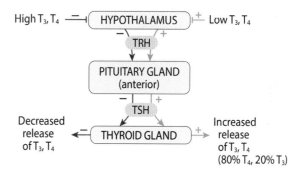

Figure 1-3: Hypothalamic-pituitary-thyroid axis

THYROID FUNCTION TESTS (TFTs)

Thyroid function tests (TFTs) include TSH, FT_4, and some-times FT_3. The FT_4 assay has replaced the T_3 resin uptake test.

When screening for primary thyroid disease, start with a **TSH** to detect abnormalities of thyroid function–both hyper- and hypothyroidism. If the TSH is high, then order a FT_4 to assess for hypothyroidism. If the TSH is low, then order a FT_4 to assess for hyperthyroidism (Table 1-1 on page 1-10). Remember that 80% of the thyroid hormone production by the thyroid is T_4, whereas the majority of T_3 is production is by extrathyroidal deiodination of T_4 peripherally. Note: If the patient is being treated with a thyroid axis–altering drug (thioamides or thyroid hor-mone), the pituitary hormone (TSH) may have some delay in returning to physiological levels compared to the thy-roid hormones (T_3 and T_4).

Table 1-1: Overview of Thyroid Function Tests		
TSH	**FT₄**	**Diagnosis**
High	Low	Primary hypothyroidism
	Normal	Subclinical hypothyroidism
	High	Pituitary (secondary; TSH-induced) hyperthyroidism Thyroid hormone resistance syndromes
Low	High	Primary hyperthyroidism Subacute or silent thyroiditis
	Normal	Subclinical hyperthyroidism Euthyroid sick syndrome
	Low	Pituitary (secondary) hypothyroidism Severe euthyroid sick syndrome

During the 1st trimester of pregnancy, you can expect a physiological TSH drop due to elevation in hCG (remember, they both have a common α subunit so HCG can stimulate the receptor). Do not confuse this with hyperthyroidism! As a rule of thumb, the lower limit of normal TSH in pregnancy is 0.1 × the trimester of pregnancy (1st trimester is 0.1 mU/L; 2nd trimester is 0.2; 3rd trimester is 0.3). For more information on TFTs in pregnancy, see the Women's and Men's Health section under Obstetrics.

OTHER THYROID TESTS

Uptake and Scan

If primary hyperthyroidism is diagnosed (with a low TSH and high FT₄), the next step is to determine its cause. Two tests, the radioactive iodine uptake (RAIU) and thyroid scan (also called scintigraphy), help to establish a diagnosis by measuring the degree and pattern of iodine uptake by the thyroid. In clinical practice, these tests are often referred to as "the thyroid uptake and scan," but recognize these are 2 different tests (the uptake; the scan). The RAIU measures the degree of iodine uptake (given as a percent uptake) by the thyroid. The scintigraphy scan assesses the pattern of iodine uptake (creates picture), showing a diffuse, focal, or multifocal distribution.

RAIU: The patient is given a small dose of radioactive iodine; and then later, a radiation detector over the thyroid determines the percentage of the dose that was taken up by the gland. Know the uptake results (high, low, or normal) for various causes of thyroid disease.

RAIU is increased in:

- Graves disease
- TSH-secreting pituitary tumor
- Hot nodules (solitary or toxic multinodular goiter [MNG]), if hot enough
- High hCG states, such as an hCG-secreting tumor and gestational thyrotoxicosis (due to the hCG activating the TSH receptor)
- Iodine deficiency

RAIU is decreased in:

- Thyroiditis ("dumping" of thyroid hormone)
- Excess exogenous T₄ or T₃
- Iodine excess (e.g., contrast dye, diet, amiodarone)
- Factitious hyperthyroidism

Thyroid scan (scintigraphy): The patient is given a dose of technetium-99m or radioactive iodine and a scintillation scanner produces a rough picture indicating how these isotopes localize in the thyroid (Figure 1-4). The scan gives information on the size, shape, and overall activity of the gland and shows hot (hyperfunctioning) and cold

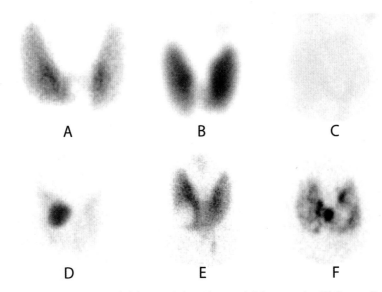

Figure 1-4: Thyroid scintigraphy (i.e., thyroid scan). (A) Normal thyroid: normal diffuse uptake. (B) Graves disease: diffusely increased uptake. (C) Painless thyroiditis: very low uptake. (D) Hot (autonomous) nodule: discrete area of increased uptake, sometimes with suppression of the surrounding gland. (E) Cold (nonfunctioning) nodule: area of reduced or absent uptake. (F) Toxic multinodular goiter: several areas of increased uptake.

(underfunctioning) spots. In Graves disease, the scan shows diffuse increased uptake; in a hot nodule, it's local.

The thyroid RAIU and scintigraphy scan are essential in determining the cause of hyperthyroidism and are never used in the workup of a hypothyroid or euthyroid patient. Thyroid scintigraphy can be used in the evaluation of thyroid nodules, but only if the TSH is low. (If the TSH is normal, then ultrasound is the best way to determine if a thyroid nodule biopsy is needed.) Hyperfunctioning (hot) nodules are rarely malignant and do not require biopsy.

Ultrasound (U/S)

Thyroid U/S is used to:

- Determine the size and number of nodules.
- Determine whether a nodule is cystic or solid.
- Stratify a nodule's malignancy risk by U/S characteristics (low, medium, or high).
- Localize a nodule for fine needle aspiration.
- Follow up a nodule's size over time.
- Follow up in a patient after thyroid cancer resection.

When a patient presents with a palpable nodule and is hyperthyroid, an RAIU and scintigraphy should always precede a thyroid U/S. If the palpable nodule is "hot" (functional), then no biopsy is needed; consider radioactive iodine (^{131}I) therapy. When a patient presents with a palpable nodule and is hypothyroid or euthyroid, the next step in the workup is to go directly to U/S to see if the nodule meets criteria for a biopsy. This is discussed further under Nodule Workup on page 1-17.

Biopsy

Fine needle aspiration (FNA) is a biopsy method used to evaluate a thyroid nodule (also discussed under Nodule Workup on page 1-17) and results dictate the next step.

HYPOTHYROIDISM

Findings

Symptoms of hypothyroidism are nonspecific but include:

- Cold intolerance
- Weight gain
- Fatigue
- Menstrual irregularities; infertility
- Mental slowness and concentration issues
- Depressed mood
- Constipation
- Puffiness in the face
- Extremity swelling
- Hoarseness
- Coarse hair/alopecia
- Brittle nails
- Dry skin
- Decreased tolerance to exercise
- Carpal tunnel syndrome

Signs on physical exam include:

- Goiter
- Cool/pale skin
- Coarse hair
- Periorbital and nonpitting edema
- Tongue enlargement (severe cases)
- Bradycardia
- Delayed reflexes

In addition to a high TSH and a low FT$_4$, abnormal labs/studies include:

- Hyponatremia (euvolemic)
- Macrocytic anemia
- Hyperlipidemia (increased total cholesterol and LDL)
- Pericardial effusion on echocardiograms (rare)
- Increased prolactin level

Hypothyroidism is a cause of hyperprolactinemia, amenorrhea, and galactorrhea. If a woman has an elevated prolactin and amenorrhea, check thyroid function after confirming that she is not pregnant. If symptoms are due to hypothyroidism, the elevated prolactin, amenorrhea, and galactorrhea resolve with thyroxine treatment.

Diagnosis

The best screening test for hypothyroidism is the TSH, which is elevated. Add an FT$_4$ if secondary (pituitary) or tertiary (hypothalamic) hypothyroidism is suspected:

- High TSH and low FT$_4$ = primary hypothyroidism.
- High TSH and normal FT$_4$ = subclinical hypothyroidism.
- Low or inappropriately normal TSH and low FT$_4$ = secondary (problem with pituitary) or tertiary (problem with hypothalamus) hypothyroidism or euthyroid sick syndrome.

Our understanding of subclinical hypothyroidism is still evolving. We know TSH normally drifts up with age. Patients with TSH 5–10 mU/L (mildly elevated) develop overt hypothyroidism at a rate of about 4% per year, which is low, so not everybody needs to be treated. A family history of autoimmune thyroid disease and positive anti-thyroid peroxidase (anti-TPO) antibodies are risk factors for subclinical disease.

Low or inappropriately normal TSH with a low normal FT$_4$ is secondary or tertiary hypothyroidism except in hospitalized, sick patients who may have euthyroid sick syndrome. (See Euthyroid Sick Syndrome on page 1-16.) Less than 1% of those with hypothyroidism have central hypothyroidism (i.e., secondary or tertiary). Secondary hypothyroidism is due to TSH deficiency and tertiary hypothyroidism is due to TRH deficiency. Suspect secondary/tertiary disease when you see a deficiency of multiple hormones (e.g., adrenal insufficiency and hypothyroidism occurring in the same patient) or in patients with a history of pituitary mass, pituitary surgery, or traumatic brain injury. (Isolated hypothyroidism due to pituitary or hypothalamic dysfunction is very rare and is usually genetic in nature.)

Secondary and tertiary hypothyroid diseases are differentiated by imaging the sella. Routine TRH stimulation test is not done because management is the same: Replace thyroid hormone to achieve a normal FT_4 level (not a TSH level).

Treatment

Treatment for hypothyroidism is levothyroxine (T_4) alone. Adding T_3 might help with some neuropsychological symptoms, but multiple randomized trials have shown no benefit of combined T_3/T_4 beyond that achieved with T_4 monotherapy. In addition, T_3 therapy is harder to regulate due to its short half-life and may cause hyperthyroid effects, such as atrial fibrillation and bone loss. T_3 is not recommended in the treatment of hypothyroidism.

T_4 has a long half-life and takes weeks to equilibrate. In most cases, you can start patients on 50–100 mcg/day or 1.6 mcg/kg/day while fasting (an hour before breakfast). For patients with the potential for coronary artery disease, especially older patients, start low (50 mcg/day) and slowly titrate up. Adjust the dose of levothyroxine every 6 weeks in increments of 12.5–25 mcg.

For primary hypothyroidism, the main treatment target is the TSH: Keep the level within the lower half of the normal reference range for your laboratory. Allow enough time for the blood level to come to a steady state, so do not check the TSH again until a full 6–8 weeks after a dose adjustment. Do not overtreat because you risk inciting complications of hyperthyroidism, such as atrial fibrillation and osteoporosis.

Know that a TSH elevation > 10 µU/mL (10 mU/L) in a patient prescribed > 200 mcg/day of T_4 is most commonly due to nonadherence.

Watch out for food, drinks, and drugs that interfere with absorption of thyroxine (e.g., iron/calcium/aluminum supplements, bile acid sequestrants), raise TBG levels (estrogens), or increase the metabolism of T_4. These, in addition to malabsorption (think celiac), cause persistently elevated TSH despite therapeutic dosages of T_4.

If a patient is hypothyroid and needs emergent surgery for another reason, do it! Otherwise, try to restore euthyroidism before surgery.

Always treat pregnant hypothyroid patients and follow their TSH levels every 4 weeks during pregnancy because their requirements increase (the dose needs to be adjusted upwards ≥ 50% over the prepregnancy dose). The goal in pregnancy is to keep TSH in the lower half of the trimester-specific reference range (approximately < 2.5 µU/mL [2.5 mU/L]). Failure to treat maternal hypothyroidism during pregnancy can adversely affect the baby. For more on hypothyroidism during pregnancy, see the Women's and Men's Health section under Obstetrics.

Treating subclinical hypothyroidism is controversial. In clinical practice, the decision to treat is individualized. American Association of Clinical Endocrinologists/American Thyroid Association guidelines (2012) generally recommend treatment for patients with a TSH > 10 µU/mL (10 mU/L) and no treatment for patients with TSH < 10 µU/mL. When to start thyroid hormone for a TSH < 10 µU/mL: in pregnancy, in those attempting pregnancy, in the presence of a large goiter, and, most controversially, when symptoms suggest hypothyroidism + anti-TPO antibodies.

Myxedema Coma

Myxedema coma is 1 of 2 thyroid emergencies (the other being thyroid storm). Mortality is 30–40% and is higher in older patients and in those with heart disease. It is a clinical and not a biochemical diagnosis, so the diagnosis depends on recognition of the classic signs and symptoms—not on the absolute value of T_4 or elevation of TSH.

Any cause of hypothyroidism can lead to myxedema coma. Undiagnosed, longstanding hypothyroidism can progress to myxedema coma. In patients with known but inadequately treated hypothyroidism, myxedema coma can be precipitated by infection, exacerbation of heart disease, opiates, or cold temperature.

Patients usually present with a history of progressive hypothyroid symptoms. Decreased mentation, bradycardia, and hypothermia (even body temperatures down to 74°F [23.3°C]!) are classic findings. Other signs indicate a generalized slowing of systemic processes: hypoventilation, hypoglycemia, and hypotension.

For the patient who presents to the emergency department obtunded with multisystem failure, quiz relatives for possible antecedent signs and symptoms of thyroid dysfunction.

Other symptoms depend on why the patient has thyroid disease:

- If the disease is primary, there may be no other symptoms, but be aware that rarely, primary autoimmune processes can affect both the thyroid and the adrenal, called Schmidt syndrome.
- If the disease is secondary, the patient may have symptoms of other hormone deficiencies; adrenal insufficiency is especially important.
- Patients may have a pericardial effusion.
- Up to 25% of patients have seizures.

Other lab abnormalities include hyponatremia, hypoglycemia, anemia, and hyperlipidemia.

Diagnose myxedema coma by history and physical examination in combination with hypothyroidism on labs. If the patient is stable, assess for adrenal insufficiency with an ACTH stimulation test prior to treating with thyroid hormone. (See Steroid Synthesis on page 1-20.) If the patient is unstable, just empirically treat with glucocorticoids without doing the ACTH stimulation test.

Give empiric stress-dose glucocorticoids until adrenal insufficiency is excluded by ACTH stimulation testing. Note: This should always be done prior to giving thyroid hormones because giving thyroid hormones first can precipitate adrenal crisis.

Treat myxedema coma with thyroid hormone. Optimal treatment is controversial; options include:

- T_3 (advantages: rapid onset and decreased conversion of T_4 to T_3 during acute illness), or
- intravenous T_4 (due to reduced absorption with oral), or
- combined T_3 and T_4 (preferred by most experts) using a loading dose and a smaller daily dose thereafter.

Give empiric broad-spectrum antibiotics until infection is excluded. Pay particular attention to gradually warming the body temperature, maintaining adequate blood pressure with IVF and/or vasopressors, and normalizing the serum Na^+.

Know that the mortality of myxedema coma is directly related to the degree of hypothermia and that passive rewarming (i.e., with blankets) is one of the most important elements of supportive care. Active rewarming can worsen hypotension (due to vasodilation) and should be avoided.

HYPERTHYROIDISM

Etiology

The most common cause of hyperthyroidism is autoimmune Graves disease (see Graves Disease). Most other causes occur in the context of nodular disease or thyroiditis and are discussed under Thyroid Nodules and Cancer on page 1-17 and Thyroiditis on page 1-15, respectively. Causes of hyperthyroidism:

- Toxic multinodular goiter (MNG)
- Toxic adenomas
- Thyrotoxicosis due to autoimmune thyroiditis (a.k.a. Hashitoxicosis)
- Factitious thyrotoxicosis (exogenous thyroid hormone ingestion)
  - Thyroglobulin is a protein made by thyroid cells. Thyroglobulin levels are used mainly for thyroid cancer surveillance but can also be used when factitious thyrotoxicosis is suspected. Thyroglobulin is elevated in all endogenous hyperthyroidism etiologies (including thyroiditis) and low in factitious thyrotoxicosis.
- Iodine-induced hyperthyroidism (e.g., amiodarone, contrast)
- Subacute (i.e., painful) thyroiditis
- Postpartum thyroiditis
- TSH-producing adenoma (rare)

A good history and a thyroid scan and uptake will often get you the right diagnosis.

Findings

Symptoms of hyperthyroidism, regardless of cause, include:

- Anxiety and restlessness
- Irritability
- Insomnia
- Impaired concentration (even confusion or psychosis)
- Weight loss
- Diarrhea/hyperdefecation (increased frequency of stools with normal consistency)
- Heat intolerance
- Alopecia
- Onycholysis
- Dyspnea
- In women: menstrual irregularities (oligomenorrhea or amenorrhea, impaired fertility)
- In men: gynecomastia, decreased libido, infertility, and/or erectile dysfunction

Exam may reveal:

- Goiter
- Warm skin
- Exophthalmos (the "hyperthyroid stare") in patients with Graves disease
- Lid lag
- Tremor
- Tachycardia
- Atrial fibrillation or ectopy in up to 20% of patients (more common in older patients)

Note: β-Blockade (propranolol) is indicated in the setting of symptomatic hyperthyroidism, even prior to establishing the cause of hyperthyroidism, because β-blockade can control the symptoms of thyrotoxicosis (palpitations/anxiety) and decrease peripheral T_4 to T_3 conversion.

Abnormal general labs/studies (in addition to a low TSH and elevated FT_4):

- Low total cholesterol and LDL
- Normochromic, normocytic anemia
- Hypercalcemia with increased bone alkaline phosphatase
- Osteopenia/osteoporosis
- Dilated cardiomyopathy

Consider the diagnosis of hyperthyroidism in older patients with new-onset atrial fibrillation or depression without classic symptoms of hyperthyroidism—this is termed apathetic hyperthyroidism. Hyperthyroidism in older patients can look like failure to thrive with apathy, anorexia, and weight loss. You may need to distinguish thyroid disease from polymyalgia rheumatica and clinical depression or adjustment disorder.

Graves Disease

Graves disease is the most common cause of thyrotoxicosis. It is caused by thyroid-stimulating immunoglobulins, IgG antibodies that bind to and stimulate the TSH receptors in the thyroid gland.

Physical findings specific for Graves disease (in addition to those listed in Findings on page 1-13; also see Figure 1-5):

- A diffuse, soft, symmetric goiter (See Nontoxic Goiter on page 1-19.)
- Presence of bruit on thyroid auscultation
- Ophthalmopathy: proptosis and periorbital edema with impaired extraocular movements → diplopia, corneal ulcerations, visual impairment. Know that the risk of Graves ophthalmopathy (GO) is increased in both active and passive smokers and after radioactive iodine (RAI) therapy. Smoking is also associated with progression of GO after RAI therapy and adversely affects the course of GO during treatment with steroids and orbital radiotherapy. Know that 90% of patients with Graves disease have ocular involvement on MRI or CT. Clinically apparent GO requires formal eye testing and imaging to determine the degree of eye inflammation. If a patient with mild-to-moderate GO decides on RAI treatment, pretreatment with steroids is warranted in order to prevent the progressions of GO. RAI is contraindicated in patients with severe eye inflammation.
- Dermopathy: Pretibial myxedema is a thickening and redness of the dermis due to a lymphocytic infiltrate that gives it a peau d'orange appearance (looks different from the myxedema seen in hypothyroid patients).

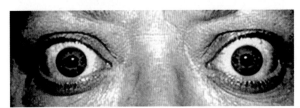

Figure 1-5: Graves disease: proptosis and lid retraction

Diagnosis

To diagnose Graves disease, use a good clinical exam (GO +/− goiter with a bruit) + TFTs + thyroid uptake and scan. TSH is low (usually < 0.01 μU/mL [0.01 mU/L]), FT_3 and FT_4 are elevated (rarely, only FT_3 is increased with normal or low FT_4), and the thyroid uptake and scan shows an enlarged gland with diffusely increased uptake (see Figure 1-4 on page 1-10). Other common lab abnormalities: elevated alkaline phosphatase, hypercalcemia, anemia, and thrombocytopenia. Autoantibodies are generally not measured unless the diagnosis is unclear or a thyroid uptake and scan cannot be done (e.g., pregnant, recent contrast), but TSI (thyroid-stimulating immunoglobulins, a.k.a. thyroid receptor antibodies) are specific for and positive in > 90% of cases of Graves disease.

Treatment

Treatment options for Graves disease are antithyroid drugs (i.e., methimazole [**MMI**] or propylthiouracil [**PTU**]), radioactive iodine, or surgery.

MMI is the preferred drug in nonpregnant patients because of a lower toxicity than PTU. PTU received an FDA black box warning for increased risk of death due to acute liver failure or severe liver injury, so PTU is no longer the 1st line therapy in nonpregnant patients and children. Vasculitis and lupus-like side effects have also been reported. PTU is still the 1st line treatment for thyroid storm and in the 1st trimester of pregnancy.

The most serious side effects of PTU and MMI are hepatic toxicity and agranulocytosis, which are rare and unpredictable. LFTs and CBCs do not require monitoring. Check only if the patient becomes symptomatic (e.g., jaundice, dark urine, prolonged fever/sore throat), and discontinue the drug at that time. Side effects almost always disappear when the drug is discontinued. Mild side effects include skin rash and polyarthritis.

β-Blockers can be used independent of the etiology of the hyperthyroidism to help with adrenergic symptoms, including tremor, tachycardia, and anxiety, while waiting for PTU or MMI to take effect.

Remission is seen in 30% of patients after 1–2 years on antithyroid medication; relapse is common. Relapse is much less likely if thyroid stimulating immunoglobulins disappear with treatment, but this happens in a small minority of cases—usually young, female patients with relatively small thyroid glands.

In the U.S., most patients with Graves disease receive definitive treatment with thyroid ablation using [131]I. Pretreat virtually all patients with β-blockers, and many with MMI (or PTU), prior to radioactive iodine ablation. Remember to rule out pregnancy in female patients (as radioiodine is contraindicated in pregnancy), and counsel patients to avoid pregnancy for 6 months to 1 year after thyroid ablation. Most patients become hypothyroid in response to ^{131}I therapy; it can take several months for the TSH to normalize and then become elevated.

Surgery may be indicated in patients who are pregnant (2nd trimester is optimal; for more on hyperthyroidism during pregnancy, see the Women's and Men's Health section under Obstetrics), in patients with an associated cold nodule and a concerning FNA, relapse after radiation, or severe allergic reactions to antithyroid drugs and in some young patients with a large goiter. Complications of surgery include loss of all parathyroids and damage to recurrent laryngeal nerves. Remember, all patients need lifelong thyroid hormone therapy after surgery.

Thyroid Storm

Thyroid storm is the 2nd thyroid emergency that carries a high mortality rate (the other is myxedema coma). Thyroid storm is often precipitated in patients with undiagnosed or inadequately treated hyperthyroidism. Precipitating events include surgery, infections, or an iodine load, such as amiodarone or contrast dye.

Symptoms of thyroid storm are similar to symptoms of hyperthyroidism, only more severe: tachycardia, heart failure, fever, psychosis, or delirium. Some patients have GI symptoms of nausea, vomiting, and diarrhea. As with myxedema coma, thyroid storm is a clinical rather than a biochemical diagnosis, so the diagnosis depends on recognition of the classic signs and symptoms, not on the severity of T_4 or TSH abnormalities. Suspect thyroid storm with clinical presentation of fever, tachycardia, and altered mental status in the context of overt hyperthyroidism. In virtually all cases, TSH is very low and FT_4 is markedly increased.

Thyroid storm is characterized by severe metabolic stress that the patient can no longer tolerate. This severe stress results in a relative adrenal insufficiency, even though the adrenal glands may be functioning perfectly and secreting a large amount of cortisol. Patients in thyroid storm die from cardiovascular collapse. A very important aspect of treatment is supraphysiologic doses of glucocorticoids.

Treatment of thyroid storm includes the following:

- Glucocorticoids, as described above
- Interrupt the physiologic response to excess thyroid hormone: IV propranolol or esmolol
- Block new hormone synthesis: high-dose thioamide (PTU preferred)
- Block release of preformed hormone from the gland: stable iodide
- Block peripheral conversion of T_4 to T_3: iodinated contrast agent, propranolol, and corticosteroids. PTU—but not MMI—also does this, although the clinical relevance of this is unknown.
- Give empiric broad-spectrum antimicrobial coverage until infection is excluded.
- Provide supportive care in the ICU with diligent attention to volume status, temperature, and heart rate.

THYROIDITIS

Thyroiditis (thyroid inflammation) can be the result of multiple disease processes, each causing a different type of inflammation in the thyroid gland. All causes of thyroiditis that completely resolve follow a typical pattern of changes in thyroid function: from hyperthyroidism (caused by inflammation-induced cell death) to euthyroidism (as the inflammation resolves) to hypothyroidism and then back to euthyroidism again at the end of the healing process (Figure 1-6). Some types do not completely resolve and lead to persistent hypothyroidism (mainly Hashimoto's).

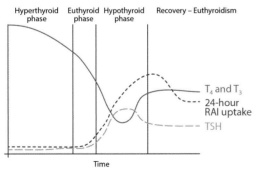

Figure 1-6: Normal course of a thyroiditis that completely resolves

Review of the labs during the phases of thyroiditis:

1) Hyperthyroidism: High FT_4 and FT_3; TSH is suppressed; high ESR; RAIU is low, because low TSH is suppressing production. (High FT_4 and FT_3 are due to thyroid destruction.)

2) Euthyroid: all labs normal

3) Subclinical hypothyroidism: normal FT_4, high TSH (typically 5–10 mU/L)

4) For those that go to overt hypothyroidism: low FT_4, high TSH (typically > 10 mU/L)

5) Back to euthyroid state: all labs normal

The most inflammatory disease processes cause the most pain and tenderness and indicate a need for a quicker workup. So let's review thyroiditis from this standpoint—painful vs. painless.

Painful and Tender

Subacute thyroiditis (a.k.a. granulomatous or de Quervain thyroiditis) is a common problem in 30- to 50-year-olds and in females > males (~4:1) and is the most common cause of a painful and tender thyroid. Subacute thyroiditis is presumed to be caused by a viral infection. Pathology shows thyroid inflammation and granulomas; fibrosis can occur but eventually resolves with a return to normal histology. Patients complain of a tender and painful anterior neck with pain that can radiate to the ear; they also often have constitutional symptoms including fever, chills, sweats, and malaise. On occasion, constitutional symptoms dominate the presentation.

Subacute thyroiditis follows the typical pattern of changes in thyroid function: from hyperthyroidism to euthyroidism to subclinical hypothyroidism to either complete normalization with euthyroidism (~ 85%) or long-term overt hypothyroidism (~15%).

Subacute thyroiditis is typically (85%) self-limited and usually does not require treatment other than NSAIDs for the inflammatory symptoms. When NSAIDs are not sufficient, give glucocorticoids as an 8-week taper. Occasionally, a patient may need β-blockers for thyrotoxic symptoms or levothyroxine for overt hypothyroidism. Reevaluate periodically until the patient's thyroid function normalizes.

Infectious thyroiditis (a.k.a. suppurative thyroiditis) is a rare problem that is most commonly the result of a staph or strep infection, and much less commonly, fungal or other bacterial infections. It usually occurs in children and can have an acute or chronic presentation. With the acute presentation, patients typically have severe pain, fever, and unilateral swelling. Do an ultrasound and fine needle aspiration with a Gram stain and C+S. Treat with the appropriate antibiotic.

Radiation thyroiditis can develop shortly (7–10 days) after exposure to radiation, which may be in the form of radioactive iodine treatment, radiotherapy of head and neck cancer, or accidental exposure (e.g., nuclear accident). Note that radiation thyroiditis is painful, but it resolves without therapy.

Painless and Nontender

Hashimoto thyroiditis (a.k.a. chronic autoimmune thyroiditis) is the most common thyroiditis (4% of the population, women:men 8:1) and the most common cause of hypothyroidism in the U.S. (Worldwide, iodine deficiency is the most common cause.) Both genetic and environmental factors are part of Hashimoto's; however, this is not well understood. Cases are clustered in families, and the thyroiditis is sometimes associated with other autoimmune diseases, such as Type 1 diabetes, primary adrenal insufficiency, pernicious anemia, and vitiligo.

Hashimoto thyroiditis is characterized by a painless, chronic, lymphocytic infiltration of the gland causing a firm and often irregular goiter, which sometimes is confused for multiple nodules (ultrasound helps distinguish).

Up to 95% of patients with Hashimoto's have measurable anti-TPO antibodies. Immune-mediated thyroid cell apoptosis is the ultimate cause of hypothyroidism, but how these antibodies specifically cause cell death is unclear.

Virtually all patients become hypothyroid over time as the gland is gradually destroyed, but some present with thyrotoxicosis (what some call Hashitoxicosis). Presenting symptoms, therefore, are variable and depend on what phase of the disease they have on presentation. Most patients present with persistent hypothyroidism and are treated with levothyroxine.

Painless thyroiditis (a.k.a. silent thyroiditis, subacute lymphocytic thyroiditis) can present as hyper- or hypothyroidism. The disease process generally starts with a hyperthyroid stage (2–4 weeks), which progresses to a hypothyroid stage (4–12 weeks). Most patients recover. The gland is nontender and may be enlarged. Thyroid scans done during the hyperthyroid phase show diffusely low uptake (see Figure 1-4 on page 1-10). This is helpful in distinguishing painless thyroiditis from Graves disease, in which uptake is high. 50% of these patients later develop chronic autoimmune hypothyroidism associated with anti-TPO antibodies.

Postpartum thyroiditis is fairly common, affecting up to 10–15% of postpartum women within 1 year of delivery. Patients present with hyper- or hypothyroid symptoms and a painless goiter. ESR is normal, but many patients do have anti-TPO antibodies. RAIU is decreased. Treat symptomatic hypothyroidism with low-dose levothyroxine, and treat symptomatic hyperthyroidism with β-blockers. Patients usually recover completely, although some stay hypothyroid. Those that recover need annual follow-up because of the risk of overt hypothyroidism later.

Because many of those with anti-TPO antibodies progress to overt hypothyroidism, painless thyroiditis and postpartum thyroiditis are considered variants of Hashimoto's.

See Table 1-2 for a comparison.

Remember: RAIU helps distinguish Graves disease from thyroiditis as a cause for hyperthyroidism. RAIU is high in Graves disease and low in patients who are hyperthyroid due to thyroiditis, iodine excess, exogenous T_4 or T_3 ingestion, and struma ovarii (thyroid tissue in an ovarian teratoma).

EUTHYROID SICK SYNDROME

Euthyroid sick syndrome (a.k.a. nonthyroidal illness syndrome) is seen in seriously ill or starving patients and can be confused with secondary hypothyroidism. In states of significant illness, the body does not need much FT_3 (the active hormone). Instead, the body converts FT_4 to reverse T_3 (rT_3), an inactive compound. The FT_3 is very low while both the FT_4 and TSH are low or low-normal. In addition to low T_4 and T_3, thyroid-binding globulins are also decreased.

Clinically, you see a severely ill, hospitalized patient with a mildly decreased FT_4 and low-normal TSH.

Patients with euthyroid sick syndrome are not given thyroid supplementation. Do not check TFTs in sick patients unless their acute illness is possibly due to a thyroid emergency (i.e., thyroid storm or myxedema coma).

Table 1-2: Types of Thyroiditis and Their Treatments				
Symptoms	**Type**	**Antibody**	**T₄ Levels**	**Treatment**
Painful and tender	Subacute	–	Hyper- to hypo- to euthyroid	Resolves without therapy; NSAIDs for pain
	Infectious	–	Variable	Resolves after infection treated; NSAIDs prn
	Radiation	±	Hyper- to hypo- to euthyroid	Resolves without therapy; NSAIDs prn
Painless and nontender	Hashimoto's	Anti-TPO	Hypo!	Levothyroxine
	Painless	Anti-TPO, anti-Tg	Hyper- to hypo- to euthyroid	Treat hyper with β-blockers; hypo with low-dose thyroxine.
	Postpartum	Anti-TPO	Hyper- to hypo- to euthyroid	Treat hyper with β-blockers; hypo with low-dose thyroxine.

Generally, the diagnosis of euthyroid sick syndrome is presumptive because central hypothyroidism is a very rare entity. In the recovery phase, the TSH can be elevated, but a TSH level > 20 µU/mL (20 mU/L) makes it very unlikely to be a finding in euthyroid sick recovery and more likely to indicate overt hypothyroidism.

THYROID NODULES AND CANCER

Thyroid nodules are common, especially in females and in older patients. Incidental thyroid nodules are seen in > 50% of patients who undergo ultrasound, CT, or MRI to evaluate anterior carotid disease! < 10% of these nodules are malignant; however, these incidentalomas require the same evaluation as nodules that present clinically (see below). Incidental thyroid nodules can also be found on PET scan; up to 40% of nodules found on PET scan in patients with a normal TSH are malignant, and workup is indicated. (Note: Diffuse thyroid uptake on PET is more suggestive of Hashimoto's than malignancy.)

Nodules can be multiple or single, hot or cold. Most solitary nodules are cold, and most of those are benign. Virtually all hot or purely cystic nodules are benign.

A malignant nodule can be primary thyroid carcinoma or a metastasis. Neck radiation as a child (especially with > 100 rads) is a major risk factor for malignant nodules (mostly papillary carcinoma), as well as nonmalignant nodules (colloid adenomas).

So, the task for the internist is to determine which nodules are malignant and which ones aren't, keeping in mind that most nodules are not malignant.

Basic evaluation of thyroid nodules: First, check TSH and ultrasound. If the TSH is low, do a thyroid scan (scintigraphy) to see if the nodule is hyperfunctioning (i.e., hot). If TSH is normal or high possibly do a fine needle aspiration to rule out malignancy based on U/S results. More on this is found in Nodule Workup.

Here are some helpful generalities:

- Autonomously functioning nodules (hot nodules) are rarely malignant, so a single hot nodule does not require a biopsy if U/S is low suspicion. Histology from a hot thyroid nodule can be indistinguishable from a follicular thyroid malignancy, which can lead to false-positive biopsies and unnecessary surgery or RAI. In general, hot nodules should not be biopsied!
- The majority of nodules are cold, and the majority of these are benign, but thyroid malignancies also present as cold nodules.
- Cold nodules in a patient with Graves disease are still evaluated with a biopsy because they can be malignant.
- Multinodular goiters (MNGs) can have both hot and cold nodules. As with solitary nodules, do a thyroid scan only if the TSH is low. If the thyroid scan shows cold areas use the thyroid U/S to determine if a biopsy is warranted. If the TSH is normal or high, a thyroid

scan is not needed, and the U/S alone will dictate if an FNA is needed. See also Multinodular Goiter – Nontoxic and Toxic on page 1-19.
- Purely cystic nodules may appear as cold nodules on a thyroid scan but do not need a biopsy because they have a low malignancy risk. Always confirm cold nodules with a thyroid ultrasound prior to biopsy.
- All nodules should have an U/S to evaluate for suspicious characteristics and help determine if FNA is needed.

Risk Factors for Thyroid Cancer

The following risk factors increase the likelihood that a nodule is malignant:

- History of head/neck irradiation
- Family history of thyroid cancer
- New nodules in those < 20 or > 70 years of age
- Male
- Growing nodule (If the rate of growth is rapid, you must rule out a thyroid lymphoma.)
- Firm or hard consistency
- Lymphadenopathy
- Fixed
- Symptoms of compression in a patient without comorbid goiter: dysphonia, dysphagia, and cough
- Suspicious U/S features (See Nodule Workup.)
- Hypermetabolic nodule detected by PET scan (focal uptake; diffuse thyroid uptake is consistent with autoimmune thyroiditis)

Nodule Workup

Thyroid nodules can be discovered by the patient, by routine physical examination, or incidentally during imaging done for another indication (incidentaloma). Nodules can be solitary, or with multinodular goiter. The 2015 American Thyroid Association (ATA) thyroid nodule guidelines determine the need for FNA based on risk factors, U/S features, and nodule size. General rule: If a thyroid nodule (single, multiple, or within an MNG) has any suspicious characteristics by U/S or there is clinical concern, refer for FNA.

Know the workup for thyroid nodules. Start with a good history and physical exam with focus on risk factors for malignancy, including prior neck radiation and a family history of thyroid cancer. Then, check the TSH and thyroid U/S:

- **Normal or high TSH:** Check a thyroid U/S (even if the nodule was found on CT or MRI). If the nodule has suspicious ultrasound features (see below), perform an FNA. Patients with high TSH also require evaluation for hypothyroidism (see Hypothyroidism on page 1-11).
- **Low TSH** indicates that the nodules may be hyperfunctioning. In addition to U/S do a thyroid scan (scintigraphy; see Figure 1-4 on page 1-10). Patients

with low TSH should also be evaluated for hyperthyroidism (see Hyperthyroidism on page 1-13).

- In the context of a low TSH, hot nodules with low suspicion U/S are rarely malignant and do not require FNA. Histologically, hot nodules can look very similar to cancer, and biopsies often lead to false-positive results.
- If the nodule is cold and U/S criteria are met, proceed with FNA.

Ultrasound criteria for biopsy (FNA) are as follows:

- High-risk U/S findings (biopsy high-risk nodules if they are ≥ 1 cm in size):
  - Solid or hypoechoic
  - Irregular margins
  - Microcalcifications
  - Taller-than-wide shape
  - Rim calcifications
  - Extrathyroidal extension
- Low-risk U/S findings:
  - Partially cystic, hyperechoic, or isoechoic
  - None of the high-risk U/S features above

Biopsy low-risk nodules only if ≥ 1.5–2 cm in size.

Purely cystic nodules (i.e., with no solid component) are benign and generally not biopsied/drained unless there are compressive symptoms or for cosmetic reasons.

What you do after FNA of thyroid nodules depends on what the pathology shows. Malignant or suspicious pathology goes to surgery. Nondiagnostic and follicular lesion of undetermined significance (FLUS) pathology goes for repeat FNA. Follicular neoplasm generally gets a hemithyroidectomy or repeat FNA with molecular markers. Benign nodules are followed with repeat U/S.

Benign Nodular Disease

In euthyroid patients with nodules and/or an MNG established as benign on FNA, consider surgery only if compressive symptoms develop, such as difficulty breathing or swallowing. Consider repeat biopsy if there is significant growth or development of high-risk U/S features. Recurrence of a cystic nodule after several aspirations is considered to be an indication for surgical excision, as is persistent patient anxiety and concern about cosmetic appearance.

Toxic Adenoma

A toxic thyroid adenoma is a benign area of autonomous hyperfunctioning thyroid tissue. Most occur as a single hyperfunctioning nodule within normal tissue that grows slowly, eventually becoming large enough to suppress TSH production. The end result is an autonomous, hyperfunctioning nodule in the midst of suppressed thyroid tissue (i.e., a hot nodule). These are usually diagnosed by TFTs, which demonstrate overproduction of FT_3 and FT_4 with

suppression of TSH, and are confirmed on thyroid scan (focal uptake in hot nodule; see Figure 1-4 on page 1-10).

Treatment of thyroid adenomas: If the patient is hyperthyroid, 1st line therapy is radioactive iodine for ablative treatment or surgical resection. If the thyroid adenoma is compressing underlying structures or is cosmetically problematic, surgery is the best treatment.

Antithyroid drugs work but are not curative, so they generally are not offered.

For the euthyroid patient with a thyroid adenoma, do not use suppressive therapy with thyroxine because the risks of overt hyperthyroidism outweigh the benefits of mild shrinkage.

Percutaneous ethanol injection of autonomous functioning thyroid nodules is an alternative to surgery and RAI (e.g., in patients who are not a candidate for either), with restoration of normal thyroid function in the majority of cases. This treatment is not routinely done in the U.S.

To review RAIU and scan findings in hyperthyroid disorders:

- Hyperthyroidism with high RAIU: Distinguish these 3 with a thyroid scan!
  - Graves disease
  - Toxic multinodular goiter
  - Toxic adenoma
- Hyperthyroidism with a decreased RAIU:
  - Thyroiditis
  - Overmedication with thyroxine supplements
  - Medications containing iodine (e.g., amiodarone)

Thyroid Carcinoma

Thyroid cancer is the most common endocrine cancer and incidence rates are increasing. There are 4 histologic types of carcinoma:

1) **Papillary:** most common; well-differentiated; usually indolent; spreads via lymphatics to local lymph nodes, and later to bone/lungs
2) **Follicular:** less common; differentiated; spreads hematogenously to bone/lungs/CNS. Capsular and/or vascular invasion is crucial in differentiating a follicular carcinoma from a benign adenoma. This is why a hemithyroidectomy is necessary after a biopsy showing follicular neoplasm. If surgical pathology confirms carcinoma, then a completion thyroidectomy is performed.
3) **Anaplastic:** rare; highly undifferentiated and highly malignant; death within 6 months of diagnosis; no good treatment available
4) **Medullary:** associated with hyperplasia of parafollicular C cells and elevated serum calcitonin. Medullary thyroid cancer can be sporadic or inherited with ~ 15% occurring as a component of multiple endocrine neoplasia syndromes (i.e., MEN2A and MEN2B) and familial medullary thyroid cancer (FMTC) syndrome.

MEN cases are associated with point mutations in the *RET* protooncogene. If *RET*+, always screen for pheochromocytoma; if confirmed, resect the pheo before resecting the medullary thyroid cancer.

Note: You do not need to know the specific staging systems of the various thyroid cancers.

Treatment of the thyroid cancer is usually a near-total thyroidectomy, which always leaves part of the posterior capsule around the recurrent laryngeal nerve intact. A thyroid lobectomy can be done as treatment for papillary cancer that is very small and limited to one lobe.

Frequently, a small amount of residual thyroid tissue also remains after near-total thyroidectomy. Postoperative RAI therapy can be given to higher-risk patients to destroy any remaining normal cells (remnant ablation) and any thyroid cancer cells.

There is higher risk of recurrence with:

- Incomplete tumor resection
- Extrathyroidal extension
- Distant metastases
- Poor tumor differentiation or advanced tumor grade
- Mediastinal or bilateral cervical lymph node metastases (if papillary cancer)
- Extensive capsular and vascular invasion (if follicular cancer)

The decision to treat with RAI, as well as the dose of ^{131}I used, is individualized, but patients with risk factors for recurrence definitely should receive postoperative RAI. Following surgery, thyroxine therapy is necessary but sometimes is not started immediately after thyroidectomy if RAI is going to be given. Instead, the TSH is allowed to rise over several weeks; once the TSH level is > 25 µU/mL (25 mU/L), RAI is given. After RAI, thyroid hormone is started. If thyroid hormone withdrawal is not the best option (mostly for patients with comorbidities), then increase the TSH with recombinant human thyrotropin alfa. If thyrotropin alfa is used, then thyroid hormone therapy can be started immediately after surgery—even if RAI is going to be given.

Once thyroid hormone is started, use suppressive doses of thyroxine in higher-risk cancers Most differentiated thyroid cancers remain responsive to TSH, so keeping the TSH suppressed slightly below the lower limit of normal helps prevent recurrence. Suppression of TSH can increase the risk of hyperthyroid complications (e.g., atrial fibrillation, dilated cardiomyopathy, osteoporosis); therefore, target the TSH to be around 0.1 µU/mL (0.1 mU/L) for cancers with higher risk of recurrence while maintaining a normal FT$_4$.

Long-term follow-up usually involves one or more of the following: neck ultrasound, total body scans, and/or thyroglobulin levels (as long as the patient does not have antithyroglobulin antibodies to interfere with the assay). Thyroglobulin is only expressed by thyroid tissue (both cancer and noncancerous cells), so thyroglobulin levels following surgery and RAI therapy should be undetectable. Any rise in thyroglobulin levels suggests recurrent disease. Do not check the thyroglobulin immediately after surgery, as it has a long half-life (> 60 hours) and levels can be elevated up to 25 days post-op.

Thyroid lymphoma is associated with chronic autoimmune thyroiditis. Think about this in a patient with chronic autoimmune thyroiditis who develops a fast-growing thyroid mass. The most common tumor type is a diffuse large B-cell lymphoma, which is treated with chemotherapy and external beam radiation. Surgery is used only for biopsy and diagnosis.

Nontoxic Goiter

Simple, nontoxic goiter is a diffuse enlargement of the thyroid gland with a normal TSH and FT$_4$. It can be caused by a lack of iodine or ingestion of a goitrogen (e.g., cassava root, Brussels sprouts, cauliflower, cabbage), but many cases are idiopathic. Diagnose nontoxic goiter with thyroid function tests; FT$_4$ and TSH are normal.

Treatment: Remove any goitrogens from the diet. If the cause is low iodine, iodine supplements help.

Multinodular Goiter — Nontoxic and Toxic

Nontoxic multinodular goiter (MNG) is fairly common and occurs more often in women. Cause is multifactorial. Nodules of varying sizes are distributed throughout the gland, but patients are generally asymptomatic and euthyroid with a normal TSH. They come to attention because of the size of their gland or because (rarely) the gland gets large enough to compress surrounding structures.

Suspect this diagnosis when various-sized nodules are palpated in a goiter. After obtaining a normal TSH, perform U/S to look for any nodules with features suspicious for malignancy. If concerning features are present, do a biopsy (see the U/S criteria for FNA biopsy under Nodule Workup on page 1-17). If no biopsy is needed or the results of the FNA are benign, then nontoxic MNG is generally managed conservatively but has 2 main indications for treatment:

1) Symptomatic compression of key structures (e.g., trachea or esophagus)

2) Cosmetic: surgical correction of a disfiguration

Standard surgical treatment of nontoxic MNG, if indicated, is bilateral subtotal thyroidectomy. If the patient is not a surgical candidate, radioiodine therapy can be used for goiter shrinkage. These nodules are typically benign. Benign nodules remain benign, and they do not change size. Thyroxine suppressive therapy is not used because it is not very effective and long-term thyroxine therapy increases the risk of osteoporosis and atrial fibrillation.

Toxic MNG refers to an MNG with thyrotoxicosis. TSH is suppressed, and FT$_3$ and FT$_4$ are often increased. The thyroid scan (see Figure 1-4 on page 1-10) usually shows ≥ 1 hot nodule.

Toxic MNG can be treated with antithyroid medications (e.g., methimazole) in urgent or emergent clinical situations to control the hyperthyroidism, but 1st line treatment is usually ablative therapy with radioactive iodine since it is curative. This does not destroy all the nodules, but it does destroy those that are hyperfunctioning. Most patients end up euthyroid after RAI. Surgery is used in cases that are refractory or in symptomatic cases when compression symptoms are present.

ADRENAL GLAND

PREVIEW | REVIEW

- Name 3 different hormones that are produced in the adrenal cortex. (Also see Figure 1-8.)
- What is produced in the adrenal medulla?
- Which genes control steroid synthesis in the adrenal cortex? Which cortical hormones are increased and decreased when there is a defect in 21-hydroxylase?
- What do mineralocorticoid hormones do?
- What are the mineralocorticoid effects of excess cortisol?
- How does a woman who overproduces adrenal androgens present?
- Which gene defect is most commonly associated with congenital adrenal hyperplasia?
- What is the difference between Cushing syndrome and Cushing disease?
- What is the adrenocorticotropic hormone level in Cushing disease?
- What are your choices for initial tests to evaluate a patient who may have Cushing syndrome?
- In which clinical situations does pseudo-Cushing syndrome occur?
- How does adrenal insufficiency (both primary and secondary) present?
- Abnormal K+ levels occur in which type of adrenal insufficiency? Why?
- How does aldosterone affect serum Na+ and K+?
- Which syndrome should you be concerned about in a patient with difficult-to-treat hypertension and low K+?
- What is the best screening test for aldosteronism? How do you interpret it?
- Hypoaldosteronism is usually due to which acquired problem?
- Which screenings are employed to test for pheochromocytoma?
- What are the 1st steps in working up adrenal incidentalomas?

OVERVIEW

Aldosterone, cortisol, and adrenal androgens are made in the cortex of the adrenal gland from cholesterol.

The adrenal cortex has 3 zones (remember **GFR** as the sequence and "the deeper you go, the sweeter it gets"):

1) The outer zona **glomerulosa** (aldosterone = salt)

2) The middle zona **fasciculata** (cortisol = sugar)

3) The inner zona **reticularis** (androgens = sex)

The adrenal medulla makes epinephrine in chromaffin cells.

Hypothalamic corticotropin-releasing hormone (CRH) is secreted in response to a low serum cortisol, stress, and circadian rhythm. CRH causes the release of adrenocorticotropic hormone (ACTH) from the anterior pituitary, which stimulates the adrenal gland to release glucocorticoids (cortisol and precursors), adrenal androgens (mainly dehydroepiandrosterone sulfate [DHEAS]), and to a lesser extent, mineralocorticoids (aldosterone and precursors), because aldosterone production is mostly regulated by the renin-angiotensin system. ACTH has no effect on epinephrine production from the adrenal medulla. See Figure 1-7.

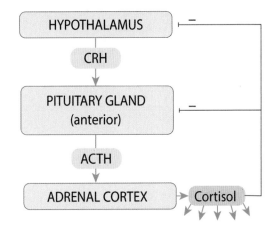

Figure 1-7: Hypothalamic-pituitary-adrenal (HPA) axis

STEROID SYNTHESIS

Refer to the adrenal steroid synthesis diagram (Figure 1-8). It gives you all you need to know for those mind-boggling conditions of congenital adrenal hyperplasia.

Remember: In response to ACTH, the adrenal gland takes cholesterol and forms 3 products—mineralocorticoids (aldosterone), cortisol, and androgens (DHEAS)—through a series of enzyme actions.

In Figure 1-8, the solid green line represents normal pathways of steroid synthesis. The ovals are the genes that code for important enzymes:

- *CYP17* → 17-α-hydroxylase
- *CYP21A2* → 21-hydroxylase
- *CYP11B1* → 11-β-hydroxylase

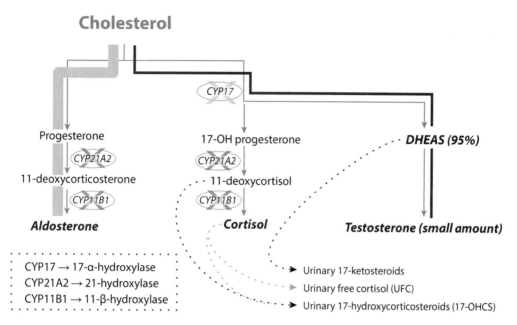

Figure 1-8: Adrenal steroid synthesis pathways

An X over the oval represents a defect in the gene, with subsequent impairment of the enzyme for that step of synthesis. The color of the X matches the color of the pathway that increases if that enzyme is blocked. For example, a defect in either *CYP11B1* or *CYP21A2* results in increased DHEAS and decreased aldosterone and cortisol. Not only that, but it causes a buildup in the hormone right before it. For example, a defect in *CYP11B1* causes a buildup of 11-deoxycortisol, and a defect in *CYP21A2* causes a buildup of 17-hydroxyprogesterone.

Recognize that whenever a pathway is blocked, precursors to the blocked point build up. Levels of these precursor hormones are measured clinically to diagnose the particular enzyme deficiency. If you know the effects of the final product of each pathway, then you can easily deduce the clinical presentation of deficiencies and excesses that arise when any pathway is blocked and rerouted into other pathways.

Now, let's go over the actions of the 3 ultimate products and their effects:

1) Mineralocorticoids (e.g., **aldosterone**) increase renal Na⁺ reabsorption and K⁺/H⁺ excretion, so high levels cause hypertension, hypokalemia, and metabolic alkalosis. Although ACTH does stimulate aldosterone production, the major regulator is angiotensin II.

2) Glucocorticoids (e.g., cortisol) stimulate lipolysis and gluconeogenesis by the liver, and they release amino acids from the muscles. They also weaken bones by decreasing the protein matrix. Cortisol inhibits all stages of the inflammatory process. Its immunosuppressive effect is on T cells and their associated cell-mediated immunity and delayed hypersensitivity. Excess cortisol can also stimulate mineralocorticoid receptors with the clinical appearance of aldosterone excess (i.e., hypertension, hypokalemia, and alkalosis) even though the aldosterone level is low!

3) The main androgen produced by the adrenals is DHEAS, but there are sex-based differences:

   • In normal males, adrenal androgens are overshadowed by the production of testicular androgens.

   • Normally, in females, the adrenals contribute half of the circulating testosterone (ovaries contribute the other 50%). Together with adrenal DHEAS, these androgens slightly virilize the normal female (e.g., pubic and axillary hair). In excess, the clinical effects depend on whether exposure occurs in utero (causing ambiguous genitalia in females) or postnatally (causing virilization, hirsutism, and abnormal menses). Bottom line: Anytime virilization is noted in a female, think about overproduction of androgens by either the adrenals or ovaries. You can tell where androgens are coming from by the DHEAS level because DHEAS is only produced by the adrenal gland; this is unlike testosterone, which can be from either adrenals or ovaries. So, high DHEAS = adrenal origin!

Virilization is the development of male secondary sex characteristics (e.g., male hair growth, male pattern baldness, increased muscle bulk) in a female.

Refer again to the synthesis diagram (Figure 1-8) and note the following:

• With defective *CYP21A2* and *CYP11B1*, the increased precursors force the reactions along the purple line with enhanced production of adrenal androgens (DHEAS).

• If *CYP17* is defective, the reaction is forced along the pink line, and more mineralocorticoids are produced.

CONGENITAL ADRENAL HYPERPLASIA (CAH)

CAH is a congenital, autosomal recessive mutation that causes a decrease in cortisol production. CAH is caused by defects in 1 of the 3 genes previously mentioned:

- *CYP21A2* (enzyme = 21-hydroxylase)
- *CYP11B1* (enzyme = 11-β-hydroxylase)
- *CYP17* (enzyme = 17-α-hydroxylase)

95% of all CAH is due to mutations in **CYP21A2**, causing a deficiency of 21-hydroxylase such that 17-OH progesterone is not converted to 11-deoxycortisol (and thus 17-OH progesterone accumulates and is the screening test). This mutation/deficiency blocks cortisol (and aldosterone) production and the high precursors lead to increased androgen production. These mutations have variable expression and can result in severe, moderate, or mild clinical syndromes. The elevated ACTH that occurs in response to the low cortisol causes adrenal hyperplasia. Note: These patients will require long-term glucocorticoid and mineralocorticoid therapy.

Severe 21-hydroxylase deficiency causes the classic **salt-wasting** form of CAH. The newborn can present in adrenal crisis with hyponatremia and hyperkalemia. Females with this type are born with ambiguous genitalia. This occurs because the impairment of 21-hydroxylase during gestation forces an increase in DHEAS and testosterone (purple line on diagram), which causes not only the ambiguous genitalia in newborn girls but also subsequent virilization in boys and girls.

Moderate 21-hydroxylase deficiency causes the classic **simple virilizing** form of CAH. These patients have 1–2% of normal 21-hydroxylase enzyme activity. This is just enough to make sufficient cortisol and aldosterone, but there is still a buildup of precursors that cause an elevated DHEAS so females have prepubertal virilization and males have precocious puberty.

Mild 21-hydroxylase deficiency causes the nonclassic **late onset** form of CAH. Females have postpubertal virilization. Labs show an early morning elevation of blood 17-hydroxyprogesterone, and increased blood DHEAS. Late-onset CAH must be differentiated from polycystic ovary syndrome (PCOS). Confirm with a markedly elevated 17-hydroxyprogesterone level after ACTH stimulation. Combination estrogen-progesterone oral contraceptive pills (OCPs) are first-line therapy, similar to polycystic ovary syndrome (PCOS) management. Spironolactone can be added. Glucocorticoids are effective but are not used as first-line agents for late-onset CAH due to the need for long-term therapy and the possible side effects of long-term glucocorticoid use. However, glucocorticoids can be used for a short time to assist with infertility/anovulation in late-onset CAH when fertility is desired.

Less commonly, CAH is due to a genetic defect in **CYP11B1** with 11-β-hydroxylase deficiency. This leads to elevated 11-deoxycortisol and 11-deoxycorticosterone (DOC). DOC is a mineralocorticoid precursor but it also has its own mineralocorticoid activity. As with 21-hydroxylase deficiency, cholesterol is shunted along the purple line of the diagram into producing excess DHEAS and testosterone. As a result, patients with 11-β-hydroxylase deficiency have both virilization and signs of mineralocorticoid excess, even though aldosterone levels are low! Thus, the clinical presentation is hypertension, hypokalemia, and metabolic alkalosis due to DOC and hirsutism and menstrual irregularities from the elevated DHEAS.

Mutations in **CYP17** are the rarest of all, accounting for < 1% of all CAH. Here, deficiency in 17-α-hydroxylase pushes the pathway into formation of only mineralocorticoids (primarily DOC). Clinical features are hypertension, hypokalemia, alkalosis (due to DOC), and hypogonadism (due to androgen deficiency). Aldosterone is suppressed by the hypokalemia and renin is low, due to the hypervolemic state. Diagnose with a high DOC and corticosterone with low cortisol, androgens, and estrogens.

CUSHING SYNDROME

Cushing syndrome occurs when there is an excess of glucocorticoid in circulation causing easy fatigability, proximal muscle weakness, easy bruising, weight gain, and emotional lability (sometimes frank psychosis). In women, it additionally causes amenorrhea, hirsutism, and acne. Physical exam reveals facial plethora (a.k.a. moon facies; i.e., a round, red face); thin skin; thick (at least 1.0 cm), bright purplish striae (Figure 1-9); cervicodorsal fat pad ("buffalo hump"); and truncal obesity. Cortisol in high concentrations can stimulate mineralocorticoid receptors, leading to edema, hypertension, hypokalemia, and metabolic alkalosis in some patients. Comorbid diagnoses include insulin resistance (20% have Type 2 diabetes) and osteoporosis.

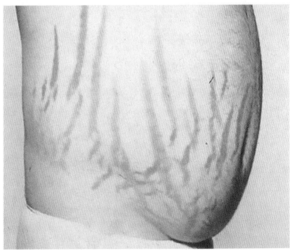

Figure 1-9: Abdominal striae in Cushing syndrome

Causes of Cushing syndrome:

- Iatrogenic glucocorticoid administration (e.g., prednisone); the most common cause
- ACTH-secreting pituitary adenoma (Cushing disease); the most common cause of ACTH-dependent cortisol excess

- **Ectopic ACTH-secreting tumor:** bronchogenic, pancreatic, or thymic carcinoma (Small cell lung cancer is the most common cause of ectopic Cushing's syndrome in patients > 60 years of age!)
- Bilateral adrenal hyperplasia
- Adrenal adenomas or carcinomas

Cushing syndrome caused by pituitary adenomas is termed Cushing disease. Next to exogenous steroids, Cushing disease is the most common cause of Cushing syndrome.

Know the following about ACTH levels in Cushing disease:

- The ACTH level is elevated or inappropriately normal in Cushing disease.
- Recall that ACTH increases the synthesis of not only cortisol, but also adrenal androgens (see Figure 1-8 on page 1-21). So, in Cushing disease (pituitary disease) and ectopic ACTH production, elevated ACTH stimulates production of adrenal DHEAS, and females can present with hirsutism, virilization, and acne. This is in contrast to non-ACTH-mediated cortisol excess, in which the ACTH and DHEAS are both low.

In clinical practice, Cushing's can have subtle nuances, but typical exam question scenarios are straightforward when you use the following workup.

Workup

The suspicion of Cushing syndrome comes from recognizing the typical clinical features (i.e., moon facies, buffalo hump, and central obesity).

Before starting the following workup for hypercortisolism, be sure to exclude exogenous glucocorticoid administration, including factitious (i.e., surreptitious) ingestion. Patients on glucocorticoids should not be worked up for Cushing syndrome because you cannot assess for endogenous cortisol excess while on glucocorticoids. All glucocorticoids, including steroid inhalers, topical steroids, and injectable steroids will suppress ACTH and endogenous cortisol secretion.

Step 1: Document the presence of cortisol excess with 1 of the following initial tests:

- 24-hour urinary free cortisol (UFC),
- late-night salivary cortisol, and/or
- low-dose (1 mg) dexamethasone suppression test (DST).

Confirm an abnormal test either by repeating it or with 1 of the other 2 tests. A random cortisol is affected by multiple factors and is not useful to evaluate for cortisol excess.

The majority of plasma cortisol is bound to cortisol-binding globulin (CBG), and < 5% is free and physiologically active. Be aware that estrogen (OCPs) raises CBG, which raises serum cortisol and can give a false-positive DST. The urinary and salivary cortisol tests measure free cortisol and do not result in false-positives with estrogen use.

If the patient has depression, obesity, alcohol use disorder, or has uncontrolled diabetes, think pseudo-Cushing's before attributing the clinical scenario to true Cushing syndrome. Identify pseudo-Cushing's with the low-dose DST or salivary cortisol levels. Patients with pseudo-Cushing's usually have normal cortisol suppression after treatment with dexamethasone and they maintain their diurnal rhythm on salivary cortisol testing. Do not use a UFC because it can often be elevated in pseudo-Cushing's. If a screen for excess cortisol production is abnormal, make an endocrine referral.

Remember: Cushing syndrome is the general description for any state of excess cortisol and includes the specific diagnosis of Cushing disease, which refers to an ACTH-secreting pituitary tumor.

Step 2: Determine if the Cushing syndrome is ACTH-dependent or ACTH-independent.

Once you have identified a patient with true Cushing syndrome with a Step 1 test, check the ACTH level. Normally, a high cortisol state completely suppresses ACTH production. Thus, any measurable ACTH indicates ACTH-dependent Cushing syndrome—either Cushing disease or ectopic ACTH production. Go to Step 3a.

A suppressed ACTH indicates ACTH-independent Cushing syndrome—adrenal hyperplasia, adrenal nodule, or adrenal carcinoma. Go to Step 3b.

Step 3a (ACTH-dependent Cushing syndrome):

ACTH-dependent Cushing syndrome means the cause is either a pituitary tumor (Cushing disease) or an ectopic, ACTH-secreting tumor. Again, ACTH level is elevated or inappropriately normal in both, but Cushing disease is much more common.

See the algorithmic approach for ACTH-dependent vs. ACTH-independent workup (Figure 1-10 on page 1-24).

As Cushing disease is more common than ectopic secreting tumors in ACTH-mediated cortisol excess, the next step is to image the pituitary with a gadolinium-contrasted MRI and refer the patient to a neurosurgeon if you see a pituitary tumor.

Some ACTH-producing microadenomas are not visible on MRI due to their very small size, so pituitary etiology of cortisol excess is verified with inferior petrosal sinus venous sampling (IPSS; detects local production of ACTH). If the IPSS does not confirm a pituitary source, the patient likely has an ectopic ACTH-producing tumor, such as primary lung or carcinoid tumor; look for these with high-resolution CT of the chest and abdomen.

Step 3b (ACTH-independent Cushing syndrome):

When the patient has a high cortisol and low ACTH, there is most likely an adrenal tumor (hyperplasia, adenoma or carcinoma) that is secreting cortisol. Image the adrenals with a contrast-enhanced CT. If a mass is found, refer to a surgeon for adrenalectomy.

Consider ordering DHEAS concentration. Since patients with cortisol-producing adrenal adenomas have low

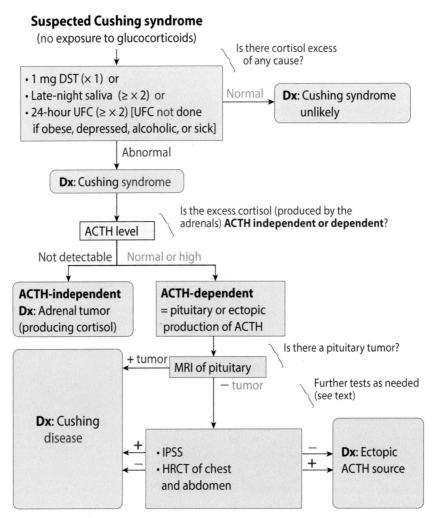

Suspected Cushing syndrome
(no exposure to glucocorticoids)

Is there cortisol excess of any cause?

- 1 mg DST (× 1) or
- Late-night saliva (≥ × 2) or
- 24-hour UFC (≥ × 2) [UFC not done if obese, depressed, alcoholic, or sick]

Normal → **Dx**: Cushing syndrome unlikely

Abnormal ↓

Dx: Cushing syndrome

↓

ACTH level — Is the excess cortisol (produced by the adrenals) **ACTH independent or dependent?**

Not detectable / Normal or high

ACTH-independent
Dx: Adrenal tumor (producing cortisol)

ACTH-dependent
= pituitary or ectopic production of ACTH

Is there a pituitary tumor?

+ tumor → MRI of pituitary

− tumor

Further tests as needed (see text)

Dx: Cushing disease

+ / −
- IPSS
- HRCT of chest and abdomen

− / + → **Dx**: Ectopic ACTH source

Figure 1-10: Cushing syndrome workup

ACTH, the DHEAS level will also be low. In contrast, carcinomas can make all adrenal products, and they can have high DHEAS, cortisol, aldosterone, and urine 17-ketosteroids despite a low ACTH.

ADRENAL INSUFFICIENCY (AI)

AI can be primary (a.k.a. Addison disease; dysfunction of the adrenal gland itself) or secondary (pituitary) disease. When AI presents acutely, it is an endocrine emergency (adrenal crisis).

In industrialized countries, **primary** AI is most often the result of autoimmune adrenalitis (which is sometimes seen in polyglandular autoimmune syndromes 1 and 2), but it can also be caused by granulomatous and infiltrative diseases (e.g., HIV/AIDS, CMV, TB, amyloidosis, sarcoidosis). The most common cause of **secondary** AI is rapid withdrawal of chronic exogenous glucocorticoids.

Polyglandular autoimmune syndrome 1 is autosomal recessive (defective *AIRE* gene). Key manifestations include chronic mucocutaneous candidiasis, hypoparathyroidism, and adrenal insufficiency. Other findings can include malabsorption/pernicious anemia, hepatitis, alopecia, chronic autoimmune thyroiditis, and premature gonadal failure.

Polyglandular autoimmune syndrome 2 includes ≥ 2 of the following: primary AI, chronic autoimmune thyroiditis, premature ovarian failure, and Type 1 diabetes. Less common findings include pernicious anemia, vitiligo, alopecia, sprue, and myasthenia. Schmidt syndrome is the Type 2 syndrome with primary adrenal insufficiency and autoimmune thyroid disease (and often Type 1 diabetes). Know that you must replace cortisol first because giving thyroid replacement prior to glucocorticoid replacement can precipitate an adrenal crisis.

Remember that autoimmune diseases often occur together.

Signs and symptoms of AI: The preeminent symptom of adrenal insufficiency is weakness. As the disease worsens, patients can become bed-bound. Other symptoms include anorexia, weight loss, N/V, vague abdominal pain, hypoglycemia, and moodiness. Hypercalcemia occurs in 20% of patients (mechanism is unknown). Eosinophilia is unusual but, if present, can be a clue.

Since primary AI affects the entire cortex in addition to cortisol deficiency and low DHEAS level, there is aldosterone deficiency leading to hyperkalemia. Hyponatremia is often seen in primary AI. Hyperpigmentation may be evident on physical exam and is due to cosecretion of ACTH and melanin precursor.

Secondary AI (disease of the pituitary; e.g., postpartum hypopituitarism [a.k.a. Sheehan syndrome]): Low cortisol is not due to diseased adrenal glands; thus, because aldosterone is normal and hyponatremia and hyperkalemia are not seen, the zona glomerulosa can still make aldosterone in response to the renin-angiotensin system. The renin-angiotensin system is the major regulator of aldosterone production, not ACTH. It is not associated with hyperpigmentation. Here, the DHEAS is low due to lack of ACTH stimulation.

Diagnosis and treatment of AI: If the patient has acute adrenal insufficiency, it needs to be treated immediately. Your first task is simply to recognize that AI exists and treat it. You can sort out etiology later.

Treatment of adrenal crisis: If the patient is in shock and you suspect adrenal shock, check a random cortisol, give IV fluids with glucose if the patient is hypoglycemic and dexamethasone. Perform an ACTH stimulation test after the patient stabilizes. Dexamethasone is potent, does not interfere with the cortisol assay, and does not cause endogenous adrenal suppression for a few hours, so the ACTH stimulation test is reliable. Dexamethasone does suppress the ACTH level, so if you have time, draw a serum ACTH prior to instituting treatment.

Treatment of stable patients with AI: In patients who are hemodynamically stable, perform an ACTH stimulation test: First, draw a baseline cortisol and ACTH level, then give cosyntropin (synthetic ACTH) 0.25 mg IM/IV, and recheck cortisol at 30 and 60 minutes. Normally, the cortisol level increases with cosyntropin stimulation. If the stimulated cortisol is < 18–20 µg/dL (496–552 nmol/L), your patient has AI. The ACTH level determines whether the disease is in the adrenals (primary; high ACTH level) or the pituitary (secondary; low ACTH level).

You may not need the cosyntropin (ACTH) test in 2 types of patients when AI is suspected: those whose 8 a.m. cortisol is < 3 µg/dL (83 nmol/L) with clear-cut clinical findings of adrenal insufficiency and those with chronic glucocorticoid use or recent high-dose glucocorticoid therapy. In these cases, the test is impossible to interpret.

Note: The cosyntropin stimulation test is abnormal (lower than expected increase in cortisol) in both primary and secondary adrenal insufficiency. In primary AI, endogenous ACTH levels are already high and administration of cosyntropin has little effect. In longstanding secondary/tertiary AI (disease in pituitary or hypothalamus), the adrenal glands do not respond to ACTH stimulation even though they are not diseased (because they are atrophied).

If the cosyntropin test is abnormal, you can check an ACTH level and a serum aldosterone. In primary AI, the ACTH level is high while the serum aldosterone is low.

Summary of interpretation of labs in AI:

- Primary AI = abnormal cosyntropin stimulation, high ACTH level, and low aldosterone (because multiple layers of adrenal are affected by the disease process). Hyperkalemia occurs in > 20% of cases, but its absence does not rule out primary AI. Low DHEAS.
- Secondary/Tertiary AI = abnormal cosyntropin stimulation, low or low-normal ACTH level, and normal aldosterone. Low DHEAS. Image the pituitary (sella) with MRI if no history of steroid use.

Although longstanding secondary/tertiary AI causes an abnormal cosyntropin stimulation test, acute causes of central adrenal insufficiency (e.g., after pituitary surgery, intracranial trauma/bleeding) can have a normal cosyntropin test because the adrenal glands haven't had time to atrophy (so they respond normally to ACTH stimulation). Consider treating empirically and wait several weeks before checking the cosyntropin test in these patients.

After the acute phase of treatment of AI, these patients need long-term glucocorticoid therapy. Remember to instruct the patient about stress dosing (doubling their baseline steroid therapy in case of illness) and the importance of having a medical ID form with them at all times describing their disease. Also, remember that in primary AI, there is usually an associated mineralocorticoid deficiency, so for long-term care you need to also replace mineralocorticoids with fludrocortisone.

MINERALOCORTICOIDS

Aldosterone is discussed extensively in the Nephrology section under Renal Physiology and Diuretics and Acid-Base Disorders. Aldosterone increases Na^+ resorption and, hence, K^+ and H^+ excretion in the distal tubules, causing hypokalemia and a metabolic alkalosis. Increased Na^+ resorption means increased water retention and the tendency for hypertension. The release of aldosterone is mainly controlled by both the renin-angiotensin system and the K^+ level, but ACTH does have some effect.

To recap, renin is released by the healthy kidney from the juxtaglomerular apparatus in response to at least 3 independent factors:

1) Perceived volume depletion, as measured by the juxtaglomerular cells. These are specialized myoepithelial cells cuffing the afferent arteriole.

2) Decreased levels of filtered Na^+, as measured by the efferent macula densa cells

3) Sympathetic nervous system stimulation, which stimulates release of renin in response to assuming the upright posture

Renin converts angiotensinogen to angiotensin I, which is then converted to angiotensin II by the angiotensin-converting enzyme (ACE)—mainly in the lungs. Angiotensin II has pressor effects and stimulates aldosterone release from the zona glomerulosa in the adrenal glands.

Primary and Secondary Aldosteronism

Primary aldosteronism (a.k.a. primary hyperaldosteronism) is caused by disease in the adrenal gland(s). Clinical features include hypertension, hypokalemia, and metabolic alkalosis. Renin levels are suppressed.

Secondary hyperaldosteronism is caused by high levels of renin, driven by disease outside the adrenals—in the kidneys or elsewhere. One cause is renal artery stenosis: decreased renal blood flow (from either atherosclerotic renovascular disease or fibromuscular dysplasia) → increased renin → increased angiotensin II → increased aldosterone.

Some conditions can resemble aldosterone excess (i.e., hypertension and hypokalemia); however, aldosterone levels are low. Examples include licorice ingestion and Cushing syndrome.

Figure 1-11 summarizes the diagnostic approach to a patient with suspected primary aldosteronism.

The best **screening test** for primary aldosteronism is a paired plasma aldosterone concentration (PAC) and plasma renin activity (PRA). Use these results to calculate the PAC:PRA ratio. Interpret the results this way:

- **Primary aldosteronism**—aldosterone (PAC) elevated and renin (PRA) suppressed → elevated PAC:PRA ratio (> 20:1). Causes include aldosterone-producing adenoma and bilateral adrenal hyperplasia.
- **Secondary hyperaldosteronism**—PAC and PRA both elevated, with PAC:PRA usually < 10. Think renovascular disease (common) or renin-secreting tumor (rare).
- **Cushing** syndrome (cortisol activates mineralocorticoid receptor) and chronic consumption of **black licorice** (increases mineralocorticoid effect of normal endogenous cortisol)—PAC and PRA both low, with PAC:PRA either normal or elevated

Know that aldosterone blockers (e.g., spironolactone, eplerenone) will increase aldosterone levels and must be stopped 4 weeks prior to performing this test. All

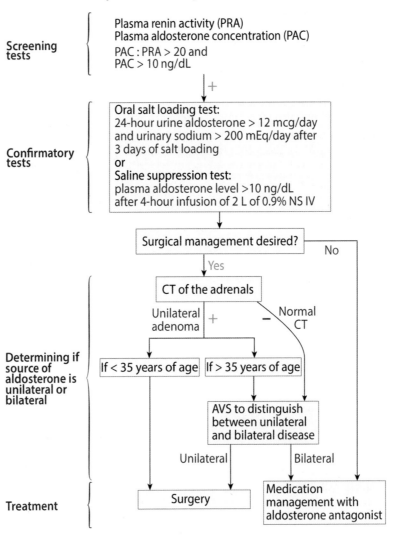

Suspected Primary Aldosteronism

Screening tests
Plasma renin activity (PRA)
Plasma aldosterone concentration (PAC)
PAC : PRA > 20 and
PAC > 10 ng/dL

+

Confirmatory tests
Oral salt loading test:
24-hour urine aldosterone > 12 mcg/day
and urinary sodium > 200 mEq/day after
3 days of salt loading
or
Saline suppression test:
plasma aldosterone level >10 ng/dL
after 4-hour infusion of 2 L of 0.9% NS IV

Surgical management desired?   No

Yes

CT of the adrenals

Unilateral adenoma   +   −   Normal CT

Determining if source of aldosterone is unilateral or bilateral
If < 35 years of age   If > 35 years of age

AVS to distinguish between unilateral and bilateral disease

Unilateral   Bilateral

Treatment
Surgery   Medication management with aldosterone antagonist

Figure 1-11: Primary aldosteronism workup

other antihypertensive medications can be continued. Hypokalemia decreases aldosterone production and can give a false-negative PAC:PRA ratio, so correct hypokalemia with oral K+ before testing.

Confirmatory tests: If the labs support primary aldosteronism (PAC high, PRA low, and PAC:PRA high), confirm the diagnosis by trying to suppress aldosterone production. In saline suppression testing, give 2 L normal saline IV over 3–4 hours to the recumbent patient. Nonsuppression of PAC (PAC > 10 ng/dL) indicates primary aldosteronism. Alternatively, you can give an oral Na+ load for 3 days, then measure the 24-hour urine aldosterone excretion. Again, nonsuppression suggests adrenal disease. These tests are not as easy as they seem. In patients with significant hypertension, giving saline or a high-salt diet runs the risk of dangerously increasing blood pressure.

Remember, if the aldosterone level is not high (at least > 10 ng/dL [277.4 pmol/L]), it is not primary aldosteronism, even if the PAC:PRA ratio is high. The renin activity can be very low for other reasons (e.g., high salt consumption, essential hypertension), giving a misleadingly high PAC:PRA ratio.

Once primary aldosteronism is confirmed, the next step is to determine if it is due to an aldosterone-producing adenoma (APA) or primary adrenal hyperplasia (PAH). With this workup, keep in mind that while only APA can be treated surgically, both APA and PAH can be treated medically. If the patient is not a surgical candidate, or surgical treatment is not preferred, you can stop here—just treat with an aldosterone antagonist!

If the patient is a surgical candidate and wishes to pursue surgical treatment, proceed as follows. First, image the adrenals with either high-resolution CT or MRI to see if there is an adrenal adenoma.

If there is a unilateral adrenal nodule on CT/MRI, the next step depends on the age of the patient:

- < 35 years of age: Go straight to surgical adrenalectomy. Nonfunctioning adrenal adenomas are rare in this age group.
- > 35 years of age: Perform adrenal vein sampling (AVS) to prove the adenoma is functional (i.e., an APA). If AVS is consistent with APA (lateralization of high aldosterone to the side with the tumor), proceed to surgical adrenalectomy.

If imaging does not reveal an adrenal nodule, there still may be an APA that is too small to detect on imaging. Regardless of age, perform AVS. If there is lateralization of aldosterone production, you can proceed with adrenalectomy.

If AVS shows no lateralization (i.e., no APA), the primary aldosteronism is due to PAH and treatment is with aldosterone antagonists (i.e., spironolactone, eplerenone). As with PAC and PRA screening, AVS cannot be done while a patient is taking a mineralocorticoid antagonist. Stop these at least 4 weeks prior to the study.

Hypoaldosteronism

The most common cause of hypoaldosteronism is decreased production of renin in patients with diabetes with mild renal failure (hyporeninemic hypoaldosteronism, a.k.a. Type 4 renal tubular acidosis [RTA]). It is also seen in patients with chronic interstitial nephritis, chronic NSAID use, and heparin therapy. More severe hypoaldosteronism is seen with primary adrenal insufficiency.

Suspect hypoaldosteronism in patients with hyperkalemia and normal anion gap metabolic acidosis out of proportion to the kidney disease (low aldosterone leads to failure to excrete H+/K+ in the distal tubule). Patients are unable to retain Na+ in states of volume contraction, and they develop postural hypotension.

Start the workup by excluding AI as a cause of the hyperkalemia and hypotension because, clinically, they can look similar; perform an ACTH stimulation test. Next, measure renin and aldosterone levels during upright posture and salt restriction (renin is low in this diagnosis but high in AI). Treat with a mineralocorticoid (fludrocortisone). If hypertension and edema are present, do not use fludrocortisone; treat with a low-potassium diet and a loop diuretic.

PHEOCHROMOCYTOMA

In 2014 the Endocrine Society published the 1st clinical practice guidelines for pheochromocytoma. Our discussion is based on these guidelines.

Pheochromocytoma (pheo) is a rare catecholamine-secreting tumor that arises from chromaffin tissue of the adrenal medulla. They are called paragangliomas when they arise in extraadrenal sympathetic ganglia. Symptoms are due to secretion of catecholamines: epinephrine, norepinephrine, and dopamine. Symptoms are typically paroxysmal and described as "spells." The classic triad is headaches, sweating, and tachycardia. Rule of thumb: 10% are extraadrenal, 10% are bilateral, 10% are malignant, and 10% are genetic/familial.

The risk of malignancy is higher in extraadrenal pheo and in certain genetic mutations. 5–15% of patients with these tumors do not present with hypertension and many have sustained, not paroxysmal hypertension.

The differential diagnosis includes labile essential hypertension, anxiety, hyperthyroidism, hypoglycemia, and menopausal flushing—all are more common than pheo. Medications and drugs (e.g., cocaine, pseudoephedrine, amphetamines) can also cause similar symptoms. Carcinoid tumor can mimic pheo but is quite rare.

Suspect a pheo in patients who have spells of headaches, sweating, and tachycardia. The likelihood of a pheo increases with these risk factors:

- Orthostatic hypotension (volume depletion)
- Refractory HTN
- HTN in a young person without a family history
- Adrenal incidentaloma

- Dilated cardiomyopathy of unknown cause
- HTN during procedures or with ingestion of tyramine-containing foods
- Paroxysmal HTN
- Atypical results when using certain classes of medications (e.g., MAO inhibitors, sympathomimetics, opioids, dopamine receptor antagonists, β-blockers)
- Family history of pheochromocytoma (particularly high risk)
- Family history of MEN2, neurofibromatosis (NF), or von Hippel-Lindau (VHL) disease (particularly high risk)

Start the pheo workup with the following biochemical screening tests:

- **24-hour urinary fractionated metanephrines:** This screening test is very sensitive and specific but cumbersome. It's usually the best test in patients with low pretest probability of pheo. Wean patients off tricyclic antidepressants and cyclobenzaprine 2 weeks before testing because these meds interfere with the results. (SSRIs are okay.)
- **Plasma free metanephrines:** Simple to do, and sensitivity is high, so a negative test excludes disease. However, specificity is lower, and false-positive results are common, especially in patients with low pretest probability of disease. Plasma free metanephrines is most appropriate in high-risk patients: those with MEN2/NF/VHL, incidentaloma with characteristics of pheo, or family history of pheo.
- Do not measure plasma catecholamines or vanillylmandelic acid (VMA)—these tests have proven to be less accurate than the above tests.
- If screening test confirms pheo (> 3× ULN) then image; if not, then confirmatory testing needs to be done with a clonidine suppression test.

If the biochemical tests confirm a pheo, perform CT or MRI to localize the tumor.

If imaging does not show a tumor and you still suspect one given the screening tests and history, look for the tumor using a PET scan, total body MRI, or radioactive tracer (^{123}I-metaiodobenzylguanidine [MIBG] scintigraphy, a norepinephrine analog that concentrates in adrenals and pheos).

Discuss genetic testing with all patients with pheochromocytoma, but prioritize the following patient groups:

- Young age (< 45 years)
- Paraganglioma: familial paragangliomas due to germline mutations of genes encoding succinate dehydrogenase subunits B, C, and D (SDHB, SDHC, SDHD), which increase malignancy risk
- Those with a family history of pheo or paraganglioma
- Those with multifocal, bilateral, or metastatic disease

Always treat pheos with surgical resection. Laparoscopic adrenalectomy is usually appropriate, but open resection should be considered for large (> 6 cm) or invasive tumors. Treat all patients with preoperative α-adrenergic receptor blockade (phenoxybenzamine or doxazosin) for at least 7–14 days prior to resection. A CCB or β-blocker can be added if blood pressure cannot be controlled with α-blockade alone.

Remember to never to use a β-blocker without first treating with an α-blocker, because it leads to unopposed α stimulation, which can cause hypertensive crisis. Patients with pheo tend to have depleted intravascular volume; replace preoperatively using intravenous saline or a high-sodium diet.

Although most pheos are benign, approximately 10% are malignant. For those with malignant, metastatic disease and positive ^{123}I-MIBG scintigraphy, treatment with ^{131}I-MIBG can be effective. For rapidly expanding lesions or those with negative ^{123}I-MIBG scintigraphy, a chemotherapy regimen of cyclophosphamide, vincristine, and dacarbazine can provide up to 50% tumor regression.

Patients with an undiagnosed pheo who go to surgery for an unrelated condition have a high mortality rate. Severe adverse reactions to anesthesia include hypertensive crisis, cardiac arrhythmia, and death.

OTHER ADRENAL MASSES

Many adrenal masses are "incidentalomas"—masses > 1.0 cm and discovered by accident on an imaging study done for another reason, such as abdominal pain. Prevalence of incidentalomas increases with age and can reach 10%. Up to 15% of patients with an incidentaloma have bilateral masses.

90% of incidentalomas are nonfunctioning adenomas. < 3% are cancerous unless the patient has a known diagnosis of malignancy, in which case the mass has a 50% chance of being malignant.

Without a history of malignancy, the 2 questions to ask yourself are:

1) Is it making hormones?
2) Is it cancerous (primary adrenocortical carcinoma [ACC] or metastatic)? ACC is suspected with lesions > 4–6 cm.

All patients with adrenal incidentaloma should have the following tests:

- Low-dose **overnight dexamethasone suppression test** for all patients; this test evaluates for subclinical Cushing syndrome, the most common hormonal abnormality.
- **Plasma free** or **urinary fractionated metanephrines** for all patients; this test evaluates for pheochromocytoma, the most dangerous hormonal abnormality.
- **Blood pressure** and **serum K⁺** for all patients. Only check PAC:PRA if hypertension or hypokalemia is present. These tests evaluate for primary aldosteronism.
- Only check adrenal sex hormones if females have virilization (DHEAS) or males have feminization (estradiol).

If the results of these tests are normal and the mass is < 4 cm, observation is appropriate with repeat imaging in 6–12 months and repeat hormonal testing for cortisol excess yearly for a few years, depending on the clinical setting. Know that FNA is never used to determine whether an adrenal mass is an adenoma or an ACC because cytologic features may not distinguish between them. However, FNA may be used to differentiate an adenoma from metastatic disease. Remember to rule out pheochromocytoma before doing any procedure on an adrenal mass!

There are 3 indications for adrenalectomy of an incidentaloma:

1) Tests indicate a functioning tumor (namely cortisol or catecholamine production, because aldosterone excess can be treated medically or surgically).

2) Mass is > 4–6 cm.

3) Imaging characteristics are suspicious for malignancy (e.g., irregular margins, calcifications, inhomogeneous density, growth over time).

HORMONES OF REPRODUCTION

PREVIEW | REVIEW

- What is the definition of primary amenorrhea? What are the common causes?

- A female patient with short stature, primary amenorrhea, and little or no breast development probably has which genetic defect?

- What is the definition of secondary amenorrhea, and what are the common causes?

- What are the initial labs for the workup of secondary amenorrhea, once pregnancy is excluded?

- What do elevated follicle-stimulating hormone (FSH) and luteinizing hormone (LH) levels in an amenorrheic woman tell you?

- What testing is done for a woman with secondary amenorrhea who has low FSH and LH levels?

- What is the most common cause of primary hypogonadism in males?

- Differentiate Kallmann syndrome from Klinefelter syndrome.

- In which situations do you see gynecomastia as a normal finding? As part of a disease state?

FEMALES

Normal Physiology

Follow along in Figure 1-12 on page 1-30.

The menstrual cycle is a complex series of changes required for the production of an oocyte and for the preparation of the uterus for pregnancy. The cycle is divided into 2 phases: follicular and luteal. The follicular phase begins with the onset of menses (day 1 of the menstrual cycle) and ends at ovulation (some say it ends on the day before the LH surge). The follicular phase can last 14 to 21 days. The luteal phase, which consistently lasts 14 days, begins after ovulation (some say on the day of the LH surge) and ends at the onset of the next menses.

The hypothalamus secretes gonadotropin-releasing hormone (GnRH) in a pulsatile fashion (60- to 90-minute cycle), which stimulates the anterior pituitary to then pulse out 2 gonadotropins, luteinizing hormone (LH) and follicle-stimulating hormone (FSH).

LH stimulates androgen formation within the theca cells. FSH regulates the new ovarian follicle granulosa cells to produce 2 hormones: estrogen from the androgen precursors (builds up the lining of the uterus) and inhibin (suppresses secretion of FSH). Estrogen normally inhibits FSH and LH production; however, at midcycle, estrogen has a positive feedback effect causing a surge in the LH and FSH, which then stimulates ovulation.

After ovulation, the follicle becomes a corpus luteum that secretes estradiol (main estrogen) and progesterone. Progesterone, in turn, prepares the lining of the uterus for possible implantation and suppresses gonadotropin release.

In women, the ovaries and adrenals share the task of producing testosterone—each producing 50%. Differentiate where androgen excess is from by checking DHEAS, because sulfation of DHEA only occurs in the adrenal glands (not the ovaries). The major effect of testosterone in females is androgenization with normal hair development in the pubic and axillary regions.

Amenorrhea

Amenorrhea is the absence of menses and can be intermittent or permanent, depending on the etiology.

Primary Amenorrhea

Primary amenorrhea is the absence of menses by 16 years of age in the presence of normal growth and secondary sexual characteristics. It is commonly the result of a genetic cause or an anatomical problem.

To determine etiology, think of the organs affecting the menstrual cycle:

- Hypothalamus (e.g., anorexia, constitutional delay of puberty, GnRH deficiency)
- Pituitary (e.g., hypopituitarism, hyperprolactinemia, hypothyroidism)
- Ovary (e.g., PCOS, Turner syndrome gonadal dysgenesis)
- Uterus (e.g., Müllerian agenesis)
- Vagina (e.g., transverse vaginal septum)

An abnormality at any one of these locations can cause primary amenorrhea.

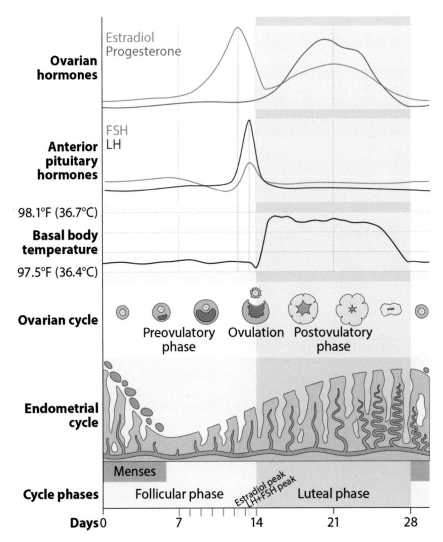

Figure 1-12: Menstrual cycle

Primary amenorrhea is rare, and evaluation is often undertaken by pediatricians; however, know the following important diagnoses:

- If a patient with primary amenorrhea has short stature, widely spaced nipples, little breast development, webbed neck, and decreased pubic and axillary hair, think of Turner syndrome (karyotype 45,X).
- If you see a female with no palpable cervix and no uterus, but there are normal secondary sex characteristics, including breasts and pubic and axially hair, consider congenital absence of the uterus.
- If you see a female with no palpable cervix, no uterus, and no pubic and axillary hair, but there are breasts, consider androgen insensitivity syndrome (an insensitivity to androgens in a karyotypic 46,XY). In this condition, testosterone levels are in the normal male range.

Secondary Amenorrhea

Secondary amenorrhea is the absence of menses for:

- ≥ 3 months in a woman who previously had regular menstrual cycles or
- ≥ 6 months in a woman who has had irregular menses.

The most common causes of secondary amenorrhea are pregnancy, PCOS, and functional hypothalamic amenorrhea.

Know that erratic menstrual cycles are common in the 1st years after menarche and in the last years prior to menopause. Secondary amenorrhea is most often caused by pregnancy; once that is excluded, think about the other causes.

In initial labs, include a pregnancy test (always!), FSH, LH, prolactin (PRL), and thyroid-stimulating hormone (TSH). If the woman is hirsute, and particularly if she is virilized (e.g., deepening voice, balding), measure serum total testosterone and DHEAS. Also consider 17-OH progesterone.

Increased FSH and LH levels in the amenor-rheic woman tell you that there is ovarian failure. See Figure 1-13. If the woman is < 40 years of age, this is called primary ovarian insufficiency (POI), and, if the woman is > 40 years of age, it is called menopausal ovarian failure. (The median age of menopause is 51 years.) In POI cases, consider mosaic Turner syndrome (get a karyotype), fragile X, or autoimmune polyglandular syndrome. Note, though, that POI does occur idiopathically in many women.

Low FSH and LH levels in the amenorrheic woman tell you that the pituitary is not making the hormones, either because it is diseased or because the hypothalamus is not sending out GnRH. This is called **hypogonadotropic hypogonadism**, and it has several causes. Etiologies include hyperprolactinemia, hypothyroidism, infiltrative disorders, celiac disease, and functional hypothalamic amenorrhea.

Functional hypothalamic amenorrhea (FHA) is caused by stress from an eating disorder and/or prolonged, intense exercise; e.g., long-distance running. FSH/LH and estrogen are decreased. Measure PRL and TSH to exclude hyperprolactinemia and hypothyroidism before making this diagnosis.

So, check the following for the secondarily amenorrheic woman with low FSH and LH:

• Prolactin level
• TSH level
• MRI of the pituitary gland

If there is a question as to the estrogen status (LH and FSH are normal with secondary amenorrhea), a progesterone challenge test can be done. If withdrawal bleeding occurs, it signifies the presence of endogenous estrogen exposure—consider adding progesterone for endometrial protection. Absence of menses after progesterone withdrawal confirms a low or absent estrogen state. Order a brain MRI and consider starting estrogen to prevent long-term complications.

Amenorrhea with Hirsutism

The amenorrheic woman with virilizing signs needs a good history (duration of symptoms), physical exam, and labs: DHEAS, testosterone, and 17-OH progesterone levels.

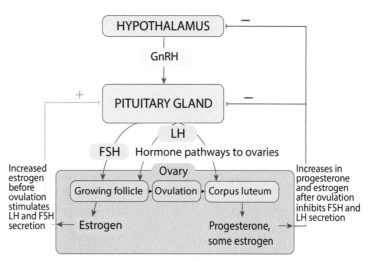

Figure 1-13: Hypothalamic-pituitary-gonadal axis in women

The major diagnoses that cause amenorrhea and virilization are polycystic ovary syndrome (PCOS), congenital adrenal hyperplasia, and, rarely, tumors of the adrenal or ovary. Recall from the discussion in Steroid Synthesis on page 1-20 that, in the female, both the ovaries and the adrenals contribute to androgen production, almost equally. Usually, normal androgen production causes only growth of pubic and axillary hair. Excess growth of hair in these areas and/or other virilizing signs prompt concern about either PCOS or adrenal/ovarian tumors.

Polycystic Ovary Syndrome

For a discussion of polycystic ovary syndrome, see the Women's and Men's Health section under Gynecology.

Hirsutism

This topic is simply a more targeted discussion of hirsutism—a specific virilizing sign (Table 1-3). Hirsutism is when a woman grows coarse hair in places they typically either do not grow hair or only have very fine hair (e.g., moustache area, chin, torso, back). The history and physical exam are keys to evaluating a hirsute woman. Rapid onset and progression are always more worrisome for a tumor. Always ask the patient about the hair distribution in family members (mother/sister) to distinguish from normal ethnic/genetic hirsutism. Objectively assess hair growth and distribution during the physical.

Idiopathic hirsutism refers to hirsutism with no identifiable cause in a woman with no other signs of virilization

Table 1-3: Hirsutism Workup — Laboratory Findings				
Disorder	Testosterone	DHEAS	LH:FSH Ratio	17-OH Progesterone
Adrenal carcinoma	Normal/↑	↑↑↑	Normal	Normal/↑
Ovarian carcinoma	↑↑↑	Normal	Normal	Normal
Congenital adrenal hyperplasia	Normal/↑	Normal/↑	Normal	↑↑↑
Polycystic ovary syndrome	Normal/↑	Normal/↑	> 2	Normal

(e.g., clitoromegaly, deepening of the voice, male-pattern balding, increased muscle mass) and with normal menstrual cycles, hormone levels, and weight. The best treatment to slow hair growth is spironolactone, which is an aldosterone and androgen receptor antagonist. Birth control pills may also slow hair growth and should be used in conjunction with spironolactone (since spironolactone is contraindicated in pregnancy!).

A scoring system (Ferriman-Gallwey) can be useful to determine whether a patient truly has worrisome features. The scale shows photos of hair growth in parts of the body subject to androgens: upper lip, chin, chest, abdomen, pelvis, upper arms, thighs, upper back, and lower back. For each location, the amount of hair is assessed and graded on a scale of 0 to 4. A score > 8 merits further evaluation, especially when the hirsutism is associated with other virilizing signs/symptoms (e.g., deepening of the voice, increased muscle bulk).

In truth, the scoring system is not used much in practice, as hirsutism is not typically pathologic. It's the presence of virilization and rapidly worsening hirsutism that are concerning.

The workup for the virilized female includes evaluation of ovarian and adrenal androgens: testosterone, DHEAS, the LH:FSH ratio, and 17-OH progesterone (see Table 1-3 on page 1-31).

Recognize the following lab results, which are seen in the virilized woman:

- Mild elevations of DHEAS and/or testosterone are consistent with PCOS.
- Elevated testosterone and very high DHEAS are consistent with an adrenal carcinoma.
- Very high testosterone with normal DHEAS is consistent with an ovarian stromal tumor (e.g., Sertoli-Leydig tumor = < 1% of ovarian cancers).

Remember that hirsutism can also be due to late-onset, partial congenital adrenal hyperplasia, which is usually caused by a *CYP21A2* gene defect (→ 21-hydroxylase deficiency). Labs show elevated blood 17-hydroxyprogesterone and blood DHEAS.

Cushing disease (in the pituitary) and prolactinoma are uncommon causes of hirsutism. Drugs causing hirsutism include minoxidil, cyclosporine, and phenytoin.

MALES

In men, luteinizing hormone stimulates Leydig cells (**L stimulates L**) to produce testosterone, which in turn inhibits FSH and LH secretion. FSH stimulates the Sertoli cells to secrete inhibin B and also secrete androgen-binding protein (ABP), which in turn binds to testosterone and moves into the seminiferous tubules. ABP-testosterone is less lipophilic and concentrates within the luminal fluid of the seminiferous tubules, enabling spermatogenesis in these tubules and sperm maturation in the epididymis. Hence, both FSH and LH are required for spermatogenesis. See Figure 1-14 for the hypothalamus-pituitary-gonadal axis in men.

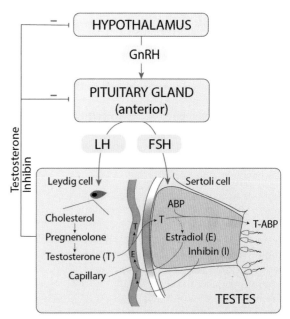

Figure 1-14: Hypothalamic-pituitary-gonadal axis in men

Primary hypogonadism (testicular failure) is usually due to Klinefelter syndrome (47,XXY or mosaic 46,XY/47,XXY). The genetic abnormality results in defective testosterone synthesis by the Leydig cells. The testes do not grow properly, and they fail to adequately produce androgens. Clinical features include small testes, long arms and legs, infertility, lack of virilization (sparse hair growth and muscle mass), and gynecomastia. Some patients have learning disabilities. The expression of this genetic abnormality is variable. Occasionally, mosaic individuals are fertile. Testosterone is decreased, and serum LH and FSH are markedly elevated. Diagnose with a karyotype. Treat Klinefelter syndrome with testosterone. Infertility can be addressed with in vitro techniques harvesting spermatozoa from the testes.

Secondary hypogonadism is due to an abnormal hypothalamic-pituitary-gonadal axis, so testosterone level is low and FSH and LH are low or inappropriately normal. Causes of secondary hypogonadism are acquired or congenital.

Acquired causes are more common and include:

- Hyperprolactinemia
- Longstanding use of exogenous testosterone or misuse of anabolic steroids
- Excessive glucocorticoids from any source
- Infiltrative disorders
- Chronic opioid use
- Aging
- Obesity

The workup for hypogonadism in men is summarized in Figure 1-15.

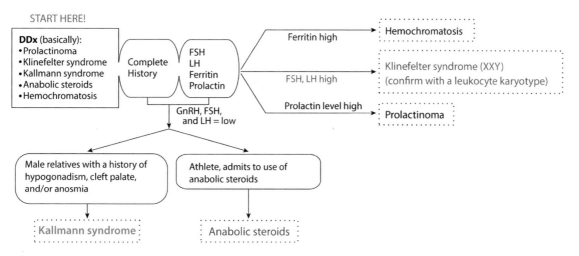

Figure 1-15: Hypogonadism workup for men

Kallmann syndrome is an example of a congenital gonad-otropin deficiency. It is characterized by GnRH deficiency + anosmia (inability to smell). It is associated with midline defects, such as cleft palate and horseshoe kidney. It is X-linked recessive, so male relatives on the maternal side may be affected. In Kallmann syndrome, FSH and LH levels are low (distinguishing it from Klinefelter syndrome, where LH and FSH are high).

Erectile dysfunction is discussed in the Women's and Men's Health section under Erectile Dysfunction (ED).

Gynecomastia results from an increased estrogen-to-androgen ratio. Unilateral or bilateral gynecomastia is normal at puberty and tends to regress after 1–2 years. It is found in males who have increased aromatization of circulating androgens into estrogen. Also, conditions that produce excess testosterone (such as DHEAS-secreting adrenal adenoma) can result in excess estradiol because of peripheral aromatization.

Gynecomastia is also seen in advanced age, obesity, renal failure, cirrhosis, hyperthyroidism, Klinefelter syndrome, germ cell tumors, and hyperprolactinemia. It can be brought on by certain drugs (think spironolactone!), including anabolic steroids (additional clues to anabolic steroid use include a very muscular physique, small testes, and infertility), and certain supplements. A healthy male with chronic stable nontender gynecomastia and a normal history and physical exam does not require further workup.

Labs for gynecomastia include TSH, estradiol, prolactin, testosterone, LH:FSH, and hCG levels. In males with gynecomastia and an elevated hCG and/or high estradiol levels, check a testicular ultrasound for a tumor. Testicular cancers are discussed further in the Oncology section under Testicular Cancer.

GENDER TERMINOLOGY

Information about gender terminology and gender dysphoria is in the Psychiatry section under Gender Dysphoria.

DIABETES MELLITUS (DM)

OVERVIEW

The U.S. is seeing an epidemic of metabolic syndrome and DM that parallels the epidemic of U.S. obesity. For those born in 2000, the lifetime risk of developing any kind of DM is 33% (males) and 39% (females)! Patients with diabetes have a 2× higher death rate from cardiovascular disease (CVD) than patients without diabetes. The lifespan of patients with diabetes is reduced by 12 years (males) and 19 years (females), when compared with individuals without diabetes. Early initiation of excellent glycemic control reduces the risk of CVD and microvascular complications in patients with Type 1 and Type 2 diabetes.

Classification of diabetes is based on the mechanism of dysfunction (Type 1 or 2), not on whether the patient requires insulin for treatment.

The American Diabetes Association (ADA) and the American Association of Clinical Endocrinologists (AACE) have practice guidelines for management.

CLASSIFICATION

PREVIEW | REVIEW

- What are the categories of diabetes mellitus?

- List 3 medications that can induce diabetes or impair insulin action.

- Define maturity-onset diabetes of the young and latent autoimmune diabetes in adults.

Know these categories of diabetes mellitus:

- **Prediabetes** includes both impaired glucose tolerance (IGT) and impaired fasting glucose (IFG).
- **Type 1 DM** (T1DM; < 10% of DM): previously called insulin-dependent DM (IDDM) and juvenile-onset

DM. The term IDDM is not used anymore. T1DM is most commonly immune mediated but can be idiopathic (antibody negative).

- **Type 2 DM** (T2DM; > 90% of DM): previously non-insulin-dependent DM (NIDDM) and adult-onset DM. The term NIDDM is not used anymore.
- **Gestational DM:** diabetes or glucose intolerance with pregnancy
- Specific types of DM due to **other causes:**
  - Drug-induced or chemical: Certain drugs can induce T2DM in patients with insulin resistance or impair the action of insulin (especially niacin, steroids, thiazides, oral contraceptives, β-blockers, statins, and immune checkpoint inhibitors).
  - Endocrinopathy-induced: Cushing syndrome, acromegaly, pheochromocytoma
  - Exocrine pancreas-induced: trauma, surgery, pancreatitis, cystic fibrosis (termed cystic fibrosis–related diabetes [CFRD])
  - Posttransplant diabetes
  - Genetic defects of the β-cells: Maturity-onset diabetes of the young (MODY) is a group of rare monogenetic autosomal dominant defects that cause ineffective production and or release of insulin by the β-cells in the pancreas. If the patient does not have evidence of T1DM (negative T1DM antibody test), consider MODY if there is a strong family history of diabetes and the patient does not have risk factors for T2DM (obesity, acanthosis, HTN).
  - Latent autoimmune diabetes in adults (LADA): A late onset of an immune-mediated diabetes mellitus, LADA is also referred to as Type 1.5 DM. These patients are generally > 30 years of age and often nonobese adults. LADA can be initially controlled on orals but will require insulin over time. Distinguish from T2DM with a positive T1DM antibody test.

DIAGNOSIS AND SCREENING

PREVIEW | REVIEW

- What are the criteria for the diagnosis of prediabetes?
- Which diseases can result in a misleading value of hemoglobin A1c?
- When are finger stick glucoses useful? When should they not be used?

The recommendations in this section are based on the 2022 American Diabetes Association's Standards of Medical Care in Diabetes.

Normal fasting plasma glucose (FPG) is < 100 mg/dL (5.6 mmol/L).

Diagnosis of prediabetes (use 1 of the following):

1) Impaired fasting glucose (IFG) = FPG 100–125 mg/dL (5.6–6.9 mmol/L)

2) Impaired glucose tolerance (IGT) = 2-hour plasma glucose of 140–199 mg/dL (7.8–11.0 mmol/L) after a 75-g oral glucose load; i.e., during an oral glucose tolerance test (OGTT)

3) HbA1c of 5.7–6.4%

The OGTT is more sensitive than FPG for diagnosing prediabetes, but it is rather impractical in most offices—and the screening guidelines take this into account.

Diagnosis of diabetes (use 1 of the following):

1) FPG ≥ 126 mg/dL (7.0 mmol/L)

2) Random plasma glucose ≥ 200 mg/dL (11.1 mmol/L) with symptoms (polyuria, polydipsia)

3) HbA1c ≥ 6.5%

4) 2-hour plasma glucose ≥ 200 mg/dL after a 75-g OGTT

Confirm diagnosis by retesting at least once unless there are clear signs of metabolic decompensation (i.e., diabetic ketoacidosis [DKA], hyperosmolar coma).

Approximately 20% of patients screened with the HbA1c have false-negative tests, compared to using the FPG or OGTT.

Additionally, the HbA1c result can be misleading in some patient groups, such as those with hemoglobinopathies (e.g., sickle cell disease, thalassemias, iron deficiency or hemolytic anemias, hepatic or renal diseases).

Finger stick (capillary whole blood) glucoses are not equivalent to serum/plasma glucoses. Finger sticks obtain whole blood from capillaries, and capillary whole blood glucoses are subject to much variability. Finger sticks are acceptable for self-monitoring of patients with known diabetes, but only use plasma or serum for diagnosis of diabetes.

Screen all patients for DM or pre-DM at a minimum of 3-year intervals, beginning at 35 years of age, and screen younger patients if overweight (2022 ADA guidelines define overweight as a BMI ≥ 25 kg/m^2 or BMI ≥ 23 kg/m^2 in Asian American people) with any of the following risk factors:

- 1st degree relative with diabetes
- CVD
- Acanthosis nigricans, PCOS, nonalcoholic fatty liver disease
- Sedentary
- High-risk ethnicity (e.g., Black, Latin American, Native American, Asian American, Pacific Islander)
- Metabolic syndrome
- HTN or on therapy for HTN
- Dyslipidemia (HDL < 35 mg/dL [0.9 mmol/L]; triglycerides [TG] > 250 mg/dL [2.8 mmol/L])
- Hx of gestational diabetes or of delivery of infant > 9 lb
- Antipsychotic therapy (for schizophrenia or bipolar disorder)
- Chronic glucocorticoid exposure

PREDIABETES

> **PREVIEW | REVIEW**
> - What is the significance of diagnosing prediabetes?

Patients with prediabetes have a 6-fold increased risk of developing overt T2DM; 1/3 of them do, 1/3 stay prediabetic, and 1/3 normalize. The condition is quite important to discover because some patients with prediabetes develop microvascular disease. Also, overt diabetes increases a patient's risk of CVD by 50%!

Goals and Types of Treatment

Promoting a healthy lifestyle is your best bet for helping the patient with prediabetes. Weight loss of 5–10% decreases the risk of developing overt diabetes by 50%, as do regular exercise (30–60 minutes, moderate intensity, 5 days/week) and a low-sodium/high-fiber diet (low in saturated and trans fats) with moderation of alcohol.

No drugs are FDA approved yet for the treatment of prediabetes, although metformin, acarbose, glitazones, and GLP-1 agonists have been studied, with strong evidence in their favor. Per the ADA and other experts, metformin should be considered for the prevention of prediabetes in high-risk patients (25–59 years of age with BMI $\geq$ 35 kg/m^2, higher fasting plasma glucose [e.g., $\geq$ 110 mg/dL], or higher HbA1c [e.g., $\geq$ 6%]; women with prior gestational DM) to decrease the rate of progression to T2DM by 30%. (Note: there was a 50% decrease with 5–7% weight loss!).

Lipid and blood pressure goals and aspirin therapy should be the same as for the patient with diabetes (see Ancillary Management on page 1-43).

The 2022 ADA guidelines recommend yearly screening of patients with prediabetes for the development of diabetes and assessment of modifiable CVD risk factors.

TYPE 1 DIABETES MELLITUS (T1DM)

> **PREVIEW | REVIEW**
> - Which autoimmune diseases are associated with Type 1 diabetes mellitus (T1DM)?
> - What is the primary treatment for T1DM?
> - Explain the honeymoon effect and the dawn phenomenon.
> - What is the best way to treat morning hyperglycemia?

T1DM accounts for 5–10% of diabetes and is caused by cell-mediated β-cell destruction that leads to an absolute insulin deficiency. 90% of patients have autoantibodies against:

- islet cells,
- insulin,
- glutamic acid decarboxylase [GAD], and/or
- tyrosine phosphatases IA-2 and IA-2β.

Test patients with prediabetes, IGT, or IFG yearly.

95% of patients with T1DM have HLA DR3 or DR4, indicating a genetic predisposition. Certain environmental factors, such as viruses, may also be important.

The rate of β-cell destruction is quite variable, being rapid in some individuals (mainly infants and children) and slow in others (mainly adults). When there is slowly progressive autoimmune diabetes with an adult onset, it is often called latent autoimmune diabetes in adults (LADA).

T1DM patients are prone to ketosis, depending on how much insulin is being produced or taken. Do not forget that T1DM is associated with other autoimmune diseases. Autoimmune diseases associated with T1DM include Hashimoto thyroiditis, primary adrenal insufficiency, celiac disease, vitiligo, pernicious anemia (B$_{12}$ deficiency due to autoantibodies), and myasthenia gravis. (Note: In T2DM, screen for B$_{12}$ deficiency if on long term metformin.)

Treatment

Treatment of hyperglycemia in T1DM reduces micro- and macrovascular complications.

Treat with insulin. Oral hypoglycemics are ineffective. See Table 1-4 on page 1-36.

Multiple daily injection (MDI) insulin regimens include agents in 2 main groups:

1) Basal—long-acting insulin to cover fasting needs (about 50% of the daily insulin):
   - Glargine
   - Detemir (Levemir)
2) Bolus or prandial—short-acting insulin to cover meals (about 50% of the daily insulin):
   - Regular (HumuLIN R, NovoLIN R)
   - Lispro (Humalog)
   - Aspart (NovoLOG)
   - Glulisine (Apidra)

Intermediate-acting insulin can also be used to cover fasting and meals: NPH (neutral protamine Hagedorn; HumuLIN N, NovoLIN N) is not used as much as the basal and bolus insulins in the above list. It is generally only used when cost is an issue. Timing of the evening NPH dose can be tricky and is generally given with dinner. If there is nocturnal hypoglycemia or early morning hyperglycemia, the evening NPH dose can be changed from dinner to bedtime to shift the insulin peak from overnight to morning.

Premixed insulin combinations (e.g., 70/30 of NPH/R) are generally not recommended to treat patients with T1DM.

Fixed daily doses of each type of insulin do not always correct hyperglycemia, especially in patients whose intake of carbohydrates varies dramatically. The approach is to use nutritional counseling to teach patients how to effectively carbohydrate count (i.e., estimate the grams of carbohydrate in their next meal). Then, they use a preestablished

Table 1-4: Insulin Preparations

Type	Duration of Action	Drug (Brand Name)	Onset	Peak	Duration	Relative Cost	Miscellaneous
Human insulin preparations	Intermediate	NPH (HumuLIN N, NovoLIN N)	2 hours	4–10 hours	10–16 hours	$	Peaks and duration do not simulate natural basal and post-meal insulin activity as well as insulin analogs.
	Short	Regular (HumuLIN R, NovoLIN R)	30–60 minutes	2–4 hours	5–8 hours	$	
Insulin analogs	Long	Glargine	2 hours	None!	20–24 hours	$$$	Less nocturnal hypoglycemia compared to NPH
		Detemir (Levemir)	2 hours	3–9 hours	6–24 hours*	$$$	
	Short	Lispro (Humalog)	5–15 minutes	30–75 minutes	3–5 hours	$$$	Less hypoglycemia compared to Regular
		Aspart (NovoLOG)	5–15 minutes	30–75 minutes	3–5 hours	$$$	
		Glulisine (Apidra)	5–15 minutes	30–75 minutes	3–5 hours	$$$	

*Duration of action for detemir is dose dependent.

insulin:carbohydrate (I:C) ratio to calculate the dose of their premeal short-acting insulin. For example, if using rapid acting insulin and the patient's individualized I:C ratio is 1:15, then when the intake is estimated at 60 g of carbs, the dose is 60/15, or ~ 4.0 units of short-acting insulin premeal. This dosing method gives patients a little more dietary flexibility and still prevents hyperglycemia. The counseling aspect is important because it is difficult to estimate the carbohydrate content of most meals. The use of mobile device apps has greatly improved patients' ability to accurately count carbohydrates. Counseling should emphasize the consumption of high-quality, nutrient-dense carbohydrates which contain a high fiber content. The source of carbohydrates should be vegetables, legumes, fruits, dairy (e.g., milk, yogurt), and whole grains and eliminate, to the extent possible, those that are refined and contain added sugar, fat, and sodium. At least 14 g of fibers/1,000 kcal, with at least half of those containing whole intact grains, should be routinely incorporated into their nutritional plan. Patients should be encouraged to refrain from consuming sugar-sweetened beverages and processed foods containing high amounts of refined grains and added sugars.

Alternatively, patients can be treated with a continuous pump that provides rapid-acting insulin at a basal rate throughout the day. Patients then enter a premeal glucose level and the amount of carbs to be eaten. The pump then delivers a bolus that provides an appropriate insulin correction and the meal dose of insulin. The pumps appear to slightly improve glucose control over MDI injections, decrease hypoglycemic events, and allow for greater flexibility in timing of meals.

Pumps and intensive insulin regimens carry a danger of hypoglycemia, and this can be fatal if it occurs at night or is otherwise unrecognized. Malfunction of the pump can result in quick ketoacidosis.

Continuous glucose monitoring (CGM) is also a useful tool in diabetes care. It is considered standard of care for most patients with T1DM. Real-time and intermittently scanned CGM devices are available for patient use. Studies show that the more the patient used real-time CGM or scanned the sensor in intermittently scanned CGM, the better the outcomes of lower HbA1c and decreased hypoglycemic events in T1DM.

Know that nocturnal hypoglycemia is a problem, not only because it is potentially lethal, but also because episodes lead to feeling poorly the next day with marked fatigue and a measurable decrease in productivity.

Notes

Labile DM: T1DM is a difficult condition to manage because so many factors impact glucose levels (e.g., food, exercise, stress, sleep). Labile DM (a.k.a. brittle diabetes) reflects very hard-to-control diabetes with marked variability in glucose reading, which leads to overt hyper and hypoglycemia. Labile DM is so unstable that patients are often unable to maintain a normal life and have frequent hospitalizations. Female patients tend to have complicated pregnancies. Labile T1DM occurs in 3/1,000 patients with T1DM, most of whom are young women. Hypoglycemia and DKA seem unpredictable. Contributing causes include defective insulin action or delayed food absorption. For example, increased growth hormone in puberty causes increased insulin resistance. An important cause is delayed gastric emptying (a.k.a. gastroparesis; from autonomic neuropathy). Malabsorption, antipsychotic meds, and alcohol use can also contribute to labile diabetes. Factitious (i.e., self-induced) lability is sometimes seen, resulting from some combination of cognitive, behavioral, and psychosocial factors. Management depends on etiology, but those with profound recurrent hypoglycemia without a modifiable cause may benefit from pancreas transplantation.

The **honeymoon effect** refers to an improvement of hyperglycemia after diagnosis and institution of treatment. Sometimes, patients can be removed from insulin entirely for a short while. Eventually, however, they require reinstitution of treatment. The **dawn phenomenon** refers to increased blood glucose between 4:00 and 7:00 a.m. with no preceding hypoglycemia. It also can occur in healthy people without diabetes. The cause is transient, mild insulin resistance due to the normal early-morning rise in cortisol and growth hormone (GH).

In patients with diabetes, early-morning hyperglycemia can also be due to the evening long-acting insulin dose wearing off. Increase the basal (long-acting) insulin in the evening to target a normal fasting glucose level.

The **Somogyi effect**: It was hypothesized that nocturnal hypoglycemia causes early morning hyperglycemia and the suggested treatment had previously been to decrease the evening insulin to prevent the nocturnal hypoglycemia. This theory has been disproven! Thus, it is incorrect to reduce the evening basal insulin in patients with morning hyperglycemia.

TYPE 2 DIABETES MELLITUS (T2DM)

PREVIEW | REVIEW

- Which mechanisms lead to the development of Type 2 diabetes mellitus (T2DM)?
- Which conditions are associated with acanthosis nigricans?
- What are the mechanisms of action of the main classes of oral hypoglycemics?
- What are the initial drugs used to treat newly diagnosed T2DM?
- What are the metformin side effects and contraindications?
- What are the side effects and contraindications of thiazolidinediones?
- In which T2DM situations should patients be prescribed insulin early in treatment?

Etiology

More than 90% of diabetes cases are due to T2DM. T2DM is characterized by impaired glucose handling at many sites. The disease has a strong hereditary component (multifactorial and polygenic), and several candidate genes have emerged in various populations. Concordance of T2DM in monozygotic twins is 70–90%. Obesity increases insulin resistance, and ~ 80% of patients with T2DM have obesity. Patients with T2DM with central obesity, HTN, and dyslipidemia are said to have metabolic syndrome. For more information, see Obesity on page 1-47.

Know the mechanisms that lead to T2DM:

- Insulin resistance in muscle and fat tissues
- Gradual reduction in insulin secretion by the pancreas
- Dysregulated hepatic gluconeogenesis and glucagon secretion
- Reduction in gastrointestinal incretins (glucagon-like peptide 1 and glucose-dependent insulinotropic polypeptide)

Note: Insulin resistance is also associated with acanthosis nigricans. This velvety, dark rash in flexural areas occurs in conditions associated with insulin resistance, such as PCOS, Cushing's, medications (e.g., niacin, corticosteroids), and acromegaly. Rapid onset of widespread acanthosis nigricans in the older patient suggests paraneoplastic GI malignancy.

Treatment

Oral and injectable medications used in the treatment of T2DM are reviewed in Table 1-5 on page 1-38 and Table 1-6 on page 1-39.

For general competency and for exam questions, it is important to know the mechanisms of action of each class of oral hypoglycemic drugs. Note the maximum efficacy in lowering HbA1c for metformin and sulfonylureas is 1–2%; the efficacy is lower for the other medications.

The sulfonylureas and meglitinides are insulin secretagogues: they both increase insulin secretion but do so by different, although similar, mechanisms of action.

Metformin monotherapy, in addition to therapeutic lifestyle changes (TLC; i.e., diet and exercise, weight loss) is recommended as initial treatment for most patients with T2DM, unless there are contraindications (e.g., glomerular filtration rate [GFR] < 30 mL/minute). Glucagon-like peptide-1 receptor agonists (GLP-1) and sodium-glucose cotransport (SGLT2) inhibitors, with or without metformin, can be considered initial therapy for a patient with, or at high risk for, atherosclerotic coronary artery disease, heart failure, and/or chronic kidney disease.

Agents from other classes are added later as needed to achieve glycemic control. Use a patient-centered approach to guide the choice of add-on pharmacologic agents. Consider cardiovascular comorbidities and hypoglycemia risk, as well as impact on weight, cost, risk for side effects, and patient preferences. Additional information on when and how to initiate these agents is covered under Approach to Drug Therapy on page 1-41. First, we will go over the different agents and their classes. In the following, focus particularly on metformin, GLP-1 receptor agonists, and insulin.

Sulfonylureas

Second-generation sulfonylureas include **glipizide, glyburide,** and **glimepiride.** Glyburide's half-life is very long, and patients (especially older ones) are at risk for severe hypoglycemia. The use of glyburide is no longer preferred by the ADA; use glipizide and glimepiride instead. Sulfonylureas are rarely used, except when cost is an issue.

Table 1-5: Oral Antihyperglycemic Drugs for Type 2 Diabetes Mellitus

Drug Class	Examples	HbA1c Reduction	Effect on Weight	Hypoglycemia (Monotherapy)	Advantages	Contraindications	Adverse Drug Effect
α-Glucosidase inhibitors	Acarbose Miglitol	0.5–1%	Neutral	None	Lowers postprandial glucose	Liver cirrhosis, inflammatory bowel disease, colonic ulceration	Diarrhea, flatulence, abdominal distention
Biguanide	Metformin	1–1.5%	Neutral–modest	None	Inexpensive; reduced risk of microvascular and MACE	eGFR < 30 mL/minute/1.73 m², decompensated heart failure, and/or acute or chronic metabolic acidosis	Nausea, diarrhea, abdominal pain, metallic taste, vitamin B_{12} deficiency, lactic acidosis
Dopamine agonist*	Bromocriptine	0.5%	Neutral	None	Reduced risk of MACE	Avoid with ergot-related derivatives	Nausea, vomiting, headache, somnolence, syncope
Bile-acid sequestrant*	Colesevelam	0.5%	Neutral	None	Decreased LDL concentration	May interfere with the absorption of oral drug, including statins and ezetimibe	Constipation, dyspepsia, elevated serum triglyceride concentration
DPP4 inhibitors	Alogliptin Linagliptin Saxagliptin Sitagliptin Vildagliptin	0.5–1%	Neutral	Rare	Well-tolerated; neutral effect on ischemic cardiovascular events	None	Possible hepatic failure, worsening heart failure, severe skin reactions (blistering, angioedema, anaphylaxis)
Meglitinides	Nateglinide Repaglinide	0.5–1%	Gain	Yes	Short-acting	Severe renal impairment; caution when used with sulfonylurea	Minimal other than hypoglycemia
SGLT2 inhibitors	Canagliflozin Dapagliflozin Empagliflozin Ertugliflozin	0.5–1%	Loss	None	Reduces systolic blood pressure, MACE, heart failure, and nephropathy	eGFR < 45 mL/minute/1.73 m²	Genital mycotic infection, volume depletion, AKI, hypotension, Fournier gangrene, euglycemic DKA, increased risk of amputation (canagliflozin)
Sulfonylureas	Glimepiride Glipizide Glyburide	1–1.5%	Gain	Yes	Inexpensive; reduces microvascular/macrovascular complication and albuminuria	Reduce dose in patients with hepatic or renal disease; caution when used with meglitinides	Hypoglycemia, asthenia, dizziness, headache, nausea
Thiazolidinediones	Pioglitazone Rosiglitazone	1–1.5%	Gain	Low risk	No significant increased risk for MACE	Increased risk of heart failure, osteoporosis	Heart failure, increased fracture risk, bladder cancer (pioglitazone)
GLP-1 receptor agonist	Semaglutide	1–1.5%	Loss	Rare	Reduced rate of MACE	Gastroparesis, AKI in patients with severe GI adverse effects, medullary thyroid carcinoma, MEN Type 2	Nausea, vomiting, abdominal pain, diarrhea, constipation

*Not recommended as monotherapy

AKI = acute kidney injury
DKA = diabetic ketoacidosis
DPP4 = dipeptidyl-peptidase 4
eGFR = estimated glomerular filtration rate
GI = gastrointestinal

GLP-1 = glucagon-like peptide-1
LDL = low-density lipoprotein
MACE = major adverse cardiovascular events
MEN Type 2 = multiple endocrine neoplasia syndrome Type 2
SGLT2 = sodium-glucose cotransport

Table 1-6: Injectable Noninsulin Antihyperglycemic Drugs for Type 2 Diabetes Mellitus								
Drug Class	**Examples**	**HbA1c Reduction**	**Effect on Weight**	**Hypoglycemia (Monotherapy)**	**Advantages**	**Contraindications**	**Adverse Drug Effect**	
GLP-1 receptor agonists	Albiglutide Dulaglutide Exenatide Liraglutide Lixisenatide Semaglutide	1–1.5%	Loss	None	Reduced rate of MACE	Rare AKI, worsening chronic renal failure, personal or family history of medullary thyroid carcinoma and MEN Type 2. Avoid exenatide in GFR < 30 mL/ minute/1.73 m².	Nausea, vomiting, diarrhea, abdominal pain, constipation	
Amylin analog*	Pramlintide	0.5%	Loss	Yes	Weight loss, reduced postprandial glucose excursion	Severe hypoglycemia when given with insulin, gastroparesis	Nausea, vomiting, headache, anorexia	

*Not recommended as monotherapy

AKI = acute kidney injury
GFR = glomerular filtration rate
GI = gastrointestinal

GLP-1 = glucagon-like peptide-1
MACE = major adverse cardiovascular events
MEN Type 2 = multiple endocrine neoplasia syndrome Type 2

Sulfonylureas are approved for use in combination with most other drugs except meglitinides. Weight gain and hypoglycemia are common side effects of sulfonylureas.

Hypoglycemia can persist for several days in states of overdose or renal impairment. Severe hypoglycemia caused by an overdose of sulfonylureas mandates an admission to the hospital because the resultant persistent hypoglycemia may require:

- close observation for several days,
- IV dextrose initially to reverse the hypoglycemia, and
- octreotide (usually IM or SQ, q 6 hours × 24 hours).

Octreotide is a long-acting somatostatin analog that markedly inhibits insulin secretion.

Use sulfonylureas with caution in older patients and in patients with declining renal function; glipizide has a relatively shorter half-life and is safer in these conditions.

Meglitinides

Meglitinides are also insulin secretagogues. These are rapid-acting drugs with a very short half-life. Examples are **repaglinide** and **nateglinide**. The major effect is on postprandial glucose.

As with sulfonylureas, weight gain is a common side effect of the meglitinides. As a group, there is less evidence of their effect with regard to macro- or microvascular outcomes.

Use secretagogues with caution in patients with chronic kidney disease. Rarely used, because they need to be taken with each meal.

Biguanides

Biguanides are insulin sensitizers and reduce hepatic glucose production.

Metformin is the only biguanide on the market in the U.S. It is a 1st line medication along with lifestyle modifications in most patients with diabetes, unless the patient has an indication for immediate insulin (more information is under Insulins on page 1-41). Patients at high risk for cardiovascular disease or who have heart failure and/or chronic kidney disease should be prescribed either glucagon-like peptide 1 receptor agonists, sodium-glucose cotransporter 2 inhibitors, with or without metformin, depending on glycemic needs.

Start with 500 mg bid and gradually increase to a maximum of 2,000 mg/day in divided doses. Many other formulations are available, such as extended-release metformin and metformin in combination with glyburide as a single tablet.

There are fewer side effects with metformin monotherapy than with sulfonylureas. There is no weight gain, and hypoglycemia is rare.

Also favorable: Metformin decreases LDL and TGs and may decrease cardiovascular events, according to the United Kingdom Prospective Diabetes Study (UKPDS).

Be aware of side effects and conditions that sometimes limit the use of metformin:

- Dose-related abdominal pain and diarrhea
- Metformin is contraindicated in patients with severe renal dysfunction (GFR < 30 mL/minute/1.73 m²), decompensated heart failure (HF), and acute or chronic metabolic acidosis.

- In acutely ill patients and in those scheduled for contrast procedures or surgery, hold the metformin due to the increased risk of lactic acidosis. (The supposed propensity of metformin to cause lactic acidosis is not supported by evidence; however, it is still in the package insert, and you may be tested on it.)
- Potential for B_{12} deficiency

Thiazolidinediones (TZDs)

TZDs (a.k.a. glitazones) are also insulin sensitizers. They act on adipose, muscle, and liver to increase glucose utilization and decrease glucose production and may help preserve some function of pancreatic β-cells. There are 2 approved in the U.S.: **rosiglitazone** and **pioglitazone**.

Favorable effects: modest reduction in blood pressure, increased HDL, and decreased TGs.

Serious adverse effects include fluid retention, exacerbation of stable heart failure, and weight gain, so avoid thiazolidinediones in those with or at risk for HF. (There is an FDA black box warning of HF for these medications.) There is also an increased risk of fractures (definitely in women, probably in men). Pioglitazone may be associated with bladder cancer. Rare hepatotoxicity has been reported, so obtain baseline liver tests and monitor periodically. There is low risk of hypoglycemia.

α-Glucosidase Inhibitors (AGIs)

AGIs (**acarbose** and **miglitol**) delay carbohydrate absorption in the gut. They are not used often. The biggest effect is on postprandial glucose. Common side effects are flatulence, diarrhea, and abdominal bloating. AGIs are approved as monotherapy and in combination with sulfonylureas.

Amylin Analogs

Amylin is a hormone secreted by pancreatic β-cells, along with insulin, which regulates glucose influx by suppressing glucagon and slowing stomach emptying.

Pramlintide is an amylin analog given as an injection before meals. It is intended to be used with prandial insulin because it helps insulin work more effectively. Based on the complexity of the regimen, it is not used often.

Cut the insulin dose by 50% when initiating treatment with pramlintide. Gastroparesis and insensitivity to hypoglycemia are contraindications.

Glucagon-Like Peptide-1 (GLP-1) Receptor Agonists

GLP-1 drugs are called incretin mimetics. Incretin hormones are secreted by the gut (GLP-1 is an example) and regulate glucose by stimulating insulin release, inhibiting postprandial glucagon release, slowing nutrient absorption, and accelerating satiety.

Exenatide was the 1st GLP-1 injection approved for diabetes treatment, with injections 2 times a day.

Extended-release exenatide is available for once-weekly injection. It can be combined with MET, sulfonylureas, and TZDs as well as basal insulin. Other GLP-1 receptor agonists are **liraglutide**, **dulaglutide**, **albiglutide**, **semaglutide**, and **lixisenatide** injections.

Side effects include vomiting and diarrhea, which can be significant.

Acute pancreatitis has been reported in association with GLP-1 receptor agonist treatment, but there is not sufficient data to know if there is a causal relationship.

There is an FDA black box warning of the risk of thyroid C-cell tumors. All GLP-1 receptor agonists are contraindicated in patients with a family history of medullary thyroid cancer, including MEN2 syndromes, because of C-cell hyperplasia (seen only in rodents so far and not in humans). Exenatide should not be used in patients with GFR < 30 mL/minute/1.73 m², but other GLP-1 can be used cautiously in CKD.

GLP-1 receptor agonists are useful add-ons to metformin to promote weight loss and to minimize hypoglycemia risk.

GLP-1 receptor agonists with demonstrated cardiovascular disease benefit (liraglutide, semaglutide, dulaglutide) should also be strongly considered, independent of A1c, in those who have established atherosclerotic cardiovascular disease or indicators of high risk, established kidney disease, or heart failure.

Dipeptidyl-Peptidase 4 Inhibitors (DPP4Is)

DPP4Is slow the breakdown of endogenous incretins, such as GLP-1, thereby increasing their concentration. Representative drugs are: **sitagliptin**, **saxagliptin**, **vildagliptin**, **linagliptin**, and **alogliptin**. They can be used alone or in combination with metformin or TZD.

The biggest effect is on decreasing postprandial hyperglycemia. DPP4Is do not tend to cause hypoglycemia. The glycemic lowering is less than GLP-1 agonists. DPP4Is are effective in patients with chronic kidney disease; some will need dose adjustments. Rarely, these drugs cause severe skin reactions, such as blistering, angioedema, and anaphylaxis. The concerns about increased pancreatitis with DPP4Is seem not to have panned out, similar to the situation with GLP-1 agonists.

Like GLP-1 agonists, DPP4Is are useful add-ons to metformin, sulfonylureas, or TZDs to minimize weight gain and minimize hypoglycemia risk.

Sodium-Glucose Cotransport (SGLT2) Inhibitors

SGLT2 inhibitors are an important class of oral hypoglycemic agents. They block renal reabsorption of Na^+ and glucose in the proximal tubule, increasing urinary excretion of glucose. These drugs do not cause hypoglycemia and they lead to modest weight loss.

ENDOCRINOLOGY

Canagliflozin was the 1st agent in this class. It is an oral agent approved as monotherapy and in combination with metformin, sulfonylureas, glitazones, and insulin. **Empagliflozin**, **ertugliflozin**, and **dapagliflozin** are other approved SGLT2 inhibitors. They are not approved for use in Type 1 diabetes or in patients with a GFR < 45 mL/minute/1.73 m². Common side effects are dehydration, renal impairment, urinary tract infections, and genital mycotic infections. This class of drugs may increase the risk of euglycemic DKA in patients with T2DM! There is an FDA black box warning about the risk of amputation with canagliflozin.

Strongly consider SGLT2 inhibitors, independent of A1c, in patients who have ASCVD to reduce the risk of major adverse cardiovascular events in those with T2DM. In patients with ASCVD, multiple risk factors for ASCVD, or diabetic kidney disease, SGLT2 inhibitors appear to reduce risk of heart failure hospitalization and progression of kidney disease.

Insulins

Most patients with T2DM eventually require insulin therapy. The same insulins used in T1DM are used in T2DM. Although they may cause less nocturnal hypoglycemia, the insulin analogs (long- and short-acting) are not more effective at lowering HbA1c than the older human insulins (NPH and regular); however, human insulin is much less expensive for patients. The fixed insulin preparations (e.g., 70/30 of NPH/regular) are also used in patients with T2DM. (See Table 1-4 on page 1-36.)

As in patients with T1DM, patients with T2DM who take insulin can sometimes benefit from using the carbohydrate:insulin ratio to calculate premeal insulin doses.

Nocturnal hypoglycemia can lead to poor daytime functioning in patients with T2DM, just as in patients with T1DM.

Add insulin to the treatment regimen when there is persistent hyperglycemia on oral drugs, except in the following special situations, in which you should institute insulin initially:

- Consistently high random plasma glucoses (≥ 300 [16.7 mmol/L])
- HbA1c > 10
- Severe symptoms of hyperglycemia (e.g., polyuria and polydipsia) or evidence of catabolism (e.g., weight loss)

In these situations, oral agents can be added later, after the glucoses have stabilized with insulin—and, eventually, you may be able to stop the insulin entirely.

Both the ADA and the AACE suggest waiting to add insulin (i.e., use oral agents 1st), except in the above groups, because of the side effects of weight gain (~ 2–4 kg) and hypoglycemia associated with insulin use.

The ADA-preferred regimen for insulin is basal-bolus dosing, where patients are given a long-acting insulin that keeps glucoses controlled during the fasting state, and short-acting insulin is given preprandially (just before meals) or a continuous subcutaneous insulin infusion. In patients who are hospitalized, or are fasting for whatever reason, do not discontinue their basal insulin simply because they are not eating. Stop the rapid-acting prandial (mealtime) insulins, but continue the basal insulin because its function is to deal with the hyperglycemia that occurs regardless of whether food is present or not, though the dose might need to be reduced by 30–50%.

Approach to Drug Therapy

Initial therapy is personalized based on comorbidities, treatment factors (e.g., medication intolerance), and management needs and may include metformin, a GLP-1 agonist, or SGLT2 inhibitor. Intensify treatment if the HbA1c is ≥ 7% (6.5% per the AACE) after 3–6 months.

The 2022 ADA Standards of Medical Care in Diabetes recommends the following treatment approach:

- First-line therapy = metformin plus comprehensive lifestyle modification in most patients. GLP-1 agonist or SGLT2 inhibitor monotherapy with or without metformin plus comprehensive lifestyle modifications is the initial therapy in patients at high risk for atherosclerotic cardiovascular disease, heart failure, or chronic kidney disease unless contraindicated.
- Initial HbA1c >1.5% above target = many patients will require dual therapy: metformin + one of the following: sulfonylurea, GLP-1 agonist, DPP4I, TZD, SGLT2 inhibitor, or basal insulin to achieve target HbA1c.
- HbA1c > 10%, blood glucose > 300 mg/dL (16.65 mmol/L), or marked symptoms = combination injectable therapy (usually basal insulin + rapid-acting insulin) + metformin, GLP-1 agonist, or SGLT2 inhibitor.

If the HbA1c is not at goal after 3–6 months, intensify therapy with an additional agent from another class. Add-on medication choice is governed by comorbidities, as well as hypoglycemia, weight gain, and cost concerns.

If ASCVD or multiple risk factors for ASCVD, choose a GLP-1 receptor agonist with demonstrated cardiovascular benefit. If CKD or heart failure, consider an SGLT2 inhibitor with demonstrated heart failure reduction and/or CKD progression benefit.

If hypoglycemia is a concern, consider GLP-1 agonist, DPP4I, TZD, or SGLT2 inhibitor. To minimize weight gain or promote weight loss, consider GLP-1 agonist or SGLT2 inhibitor. Only choose SU or TZD if cost is a major issue.

Insulin pumps are not a quick fix but are good for patients who require multiple injections and are motivated to learn carbohydrate counting. Insulins are described under Treatment on page 1-35.

Keep in mind that bariatric surgery is an option with a BMI > 35 kg/m², per the ADA.

GLYCEMIC TREATMENT GOALS

PREVIEW | REVIEW

- What are the treatment goals for glucose and hemoglobin A1c (HbA1c)?

- Describe the relationship between HbA1c and pre- and postprandial blood glucoses.

For both T1DM and T2DM, keep the glucose level as close to normal as possible while avoiding significant hypoglycemia. Recommendations between the advisory groups differ only slightly in targets. The ADA recommends a target HbA1c < 7% for many nonpregnant adults; the AACE recommends < 6.5%. However, treatment targets should be individualized.

Note: Data has emerged (ADVANCE, VADT, and ACCORD studies) showing that intensive glycemic control (compared to standard control) may have no long-term benefit or actually cause harm in some groups of patients. Therefore, the target HbA1c may be loosened to < 8% for the following groups:

- History of severe hypoglycemia or hypoglycemic unawareness
- Limited life expectancy
- Advanced vascular complications
- Extensive comorbidities
- Longstanding DM with difficulty attaining low HbA1c despite optimal and aggressive management attempts.

If the HbA1c remains elevated but the FPG are controlled, start checking postprandial glucose levels.

Also know that preprandial hyperglycemia contributes more to high average blood glucose when the HbA1c is elevated. Once the HbA1c is < 7.5–8%, postprandial hyperglycemia contributes more to high average blood glucose and is linked to macrovascular complications.

When using insulin to treat DM, consider checking the postprandial glucose periodically, even when the HbA1c is at target, so you do not miss periods of hyperglycemia.

Some patients who are hospitalized get worse when their blood glucoses are tightly controlled (80–110 mg/dL [4.4–6.1 mmol/L]); therefore, these are the recommendations:

- Noncritically ill patients: Basal insulin or a basal plus bolus correction insulin regimen is the preferred regimen for patients who are NPO. Basal, prandial, and correction components are the preferred treatment for hospitalized patients with good nutritional intake. For those on insulin, use the patient's typical basal regimen and a titrated prandial regimen. A corrective dose of insulin is appropriate if needed to correct prandial hyperglycemia.
- Critically ill patients: Use a continuous IV insulin infusion.
- Use of sliding scale is strongly discouraged.

DIABETIC COMPLICATIONS

PREVIEW | REVIEW

- Name 3 diabetic microvascular complications and characterize their screening and treatment.

- Which microvascular complication usually occurs first in patients with diabetes, retinopathy or nephropathy?

- Discuss the major diabetes studies that show a correlation between reducing blood glucoses and subsequent micro- and macrovascular complications.

- Which tests make up the annual monitoring for a patient with known diabetes?

Diabetes causes microvascular disease (e.g., retinopathy, nephropathy, neuropathy) and macrovascular disease (e.g., coronary and peripheral atherosclerosis → CVD, stroke, and PAD). Tobacco use greatly accelerates macrovascular complications.

Start screening for microvascular complications immediately at diagnosis because T2DM may already have been present for 5–10 years. The following 3 microvascular complications usually appear 10–15 years after the onset (not diagnosis) of DM:

1) **Retinopathy** correlates with duration and control of DM. Early findings include dot hemorrhages. Macular edema and neovascularization (proliferative retinopathy) are late findings. Treatment options include intravitreal anti-vascular endothelial growth factor (anti-VEGF) and photocoagulation (laser treatment). Retinopathy can worsen transiently with initiation of tight glycemic control.

2) **Nephropathy** is usually heralded by persistent albuminuria (urine albumin:creatinine ratio > 30 mg/g). Note: Albuminuria in the range of 30–300 mg/g was previously called microalbuminuria. Treat with either ACEI or ARB to decrease the rate of nephropathy progression (by decreasing intraglomerular pressure). Retinopathy almost universally precedes nephropathy. If a patient with diabetes without retinopathy develops nephrotic-range proteinuria, evaluate the patient for other causes of nephrotic syndrome.

3) **Neuropathy** includes autonomic neuropathy, axonal (Schwann cell) degeneration, distal symmetric polyneuropathy ("stocking and glove" distribution), erectile dysfunction, and gastroparesis. Both alcohol and tobacco use increase the risk and severity of neuropathy. Diabetic mononeuropathy usually affects the 3rd and 6th cranial nerves, the peroneal nerve (foot drop), and the radial nerve (wrist drop). Strict glycemic control decreases the risk of neuropathy and improves nerve conduction. The pain associated with diabetic sensory dysfunction is difficult to treat. Recommended drugs include amitriptyline, venlafaxine, duloxetine, gabapentin, and pregabalin. Remember: Before diagnosing a neuropathy due to diabetes, check B_{12} levels if on metformin.

Know the major diabetes studies and how glycemic control affects diabetic complications:

- Tight blood glucose control reduces microvascular complications in both T1DM and T2DM. This was demonstrated for T1DM by the Diabetes Control and Complications Trial (DCCT) and for T2DM by the UKPDS, the Japanese Kumamoto study, and the ACCORD study.
- A reduction in macrovascular complications (cardiovascular disease) has been harder to show, particularly for T2DM. A 10-year follow-up of intensively treated (HbA1c ~ 7%) UKPDS and DCCT patients (the EDIC trial) showed improved cardiovascular outcomes. Although the difference was not statistically significant at the time of the original studies, the benefit emerged as the patients aged. However, ACCORD, ADVANCE, and VADT did not show any benefit of tighter glycemic control on cardiovascular outcomes in patients with T2DM.

Monitoring

All patients with diabetes need annual evaluations for microvascular complications (5 years after diagnosis in T1DM and immediately at diagnosis in T2DM).

Be sure to do the following:

- Urine spot albumin:creatinine ratio as a test for nephropathy. Normal is < 30 mg of albumin per gram of creatinine. Moderately increased albuminuria is 30–300 mg/g. Severely increased albuminuria is > 300 mg/g.
- Check creatinine and estimated GFR.
- Refer patient to an ophthalmologist for a retinal exam and rapidly refer macular edema or proliferative retinopathy. Macular edema can lead to vision loss if not treated. It is acceptable to use fundus photography in clinical situations when experienced ophthalmologists are unavailable.
- Inspect the feet and perform a sensory evaluation using 10-g monofilament, pinprick, temperature, and vibration. Know that loss of vibratory sense and sensation to the 10-g monofilament predicts foot ulcers.
- Do not routinely screen asymptomatic patients with diabetes for ischemic heart disease. Outcomes are unchanged with intervention in asymptomatic patients, provided you are treating their CVD risk factors.

ANCILLARY MANAGEMENT

PREVIEW | REVIEW
- Which antihypertensives are recommended for patients with diabetes with hypertension?

Hypertension

Although blood pressure targets are individualized in hypertensive patients with diabetes, the 2022 ADA Standards of Medical Care recommends medication in addition to lifestyle changes for those with blood pressures ≥ 140/90 mmHg and low risk for atherosclerotic cardiovascular disease (ASCVD) or 10-year ASCVD risk ≤ 15%. For patients at high CVD risk (existing ASCVD or 10-year ASCVD risk ≥15%), a target of < 130/80 mmHg may be appropriate if it can be safely attained.

The 2022 ADA Standards of Medical Care in Diabetes, which are consistent with the 2019 ACC/AHA High Blood Pressure guidelines, say to treat patients with diabetes with albuminuria (albumin:creatinine ratio > 30 mg/g) 1st with an ACEI or an ARB. Next, add a thiazide diuretic (e.g., chlorthalidone)—and/or dihydropyridine calcium channel blocker (e.g., amlodipine) if needed—to reach the BP target. Remember: Avoid combination ACEI + ARB! ONTARGET (2008) showed this combo increases risk of hypotensive symptoms, hyperkalemia, and acute kidney injury, with no cardiovascular benefit.

For the rare patient with DM who is not hypertensive, use an ACEI or an ARB if albuminuria is present. There is no evidence to support the use of ACEI or ARB for primary prevention in patients with diabetes without albuminuria or hypertension.

Dyslipidemia

The 2022 ADA guidelines include recommendations on statin initiation. Recommendations are risk based, not LDL based; i.e., they are directed to the statin benefit group rather than the treat to target group.

Treat patients with diabetes who are 40–75 years of age with:

- A moderate-intensity statin (atorvastatin 10–20 mg, rosuvastatin 5–10 mg, simvastatin 20–40 mg, pravastatin 40–80 mg, lovastatin 40 mg, extended-release fluvastatin 80 mg, pitavastatin 1–4 mg)
- A high-intensity statin if at high risk (atorvastatin 40–80 mg, rosuvastatin 20–40 mg)

Every 39 mg/dL (1.0 mmol/L) LDL-C decrease causes a 21% decrease in major vascular events. Treatment of dyslipidemia is discussed in detail in the Cardiology section under Hyperlipidemia.

Know that triglyceride levels are very dependent upon glycemic control. The worse the diabetes control, the higher the triglycerides. Also know that even if the triglycerides are high and the LDL is normal, the initial lipid therapy is a statin (statin benefit group).

Aspirin

Aspirin use in patients with diabetes is controversial because not all patients with diabetes have the same risk for heart disease, despite DM being listed as a CVD risk-equivalent. Per the 2022 ADA recommendation, aspirin therapy (75–162 mg/day) may be considered as a primary prevention strategy in those with diabetes who are at increased cardiovascular risk, after a comprehensive discussion with the patient on the benefits versus the comparable increased risk of bleeding. Give patients with diabetes with known cardiovascular disease a daily aspirin as secondary prevention. ASA-allergic patients can take clopidogrel.

HYPERGLYCEMIC EMERGENCIES

PREVIEW | REVIEW

- List the symptoms of diabetic ketoacidosis (DKA).

- Which lab abnormalities occur in the patient with DKA?

- What is the formula used for correction of pseudohyponatremia due to hyperglycemia?

- When is HCO_3^- given to treat DKA?

Diabetic Ketoacidosis (DKA)

DKA is sometimes the initial presentation of T1DM, but it can also occur in T2DM.

It is caused by a state of complete or partial insulin deficiency leading to massive lipolysis. Lipolysis causes a release of free fatty acids and ketone bodies (β-hydroxybutyrate and acetoacetate). These products, high anion gap acidosis (because ketones are acids), and the associated hyperglycemia cause volume depletion from massive osmotic diuresis.

Symptoms include nausea, vomiting, abdominal pain, polyuria, and lethargy. Ask about symptoms of infection (e.g., pneumonia, UTI) and nonadherence with diabetes medications, the two most frequent precipitating conditions for DKA.

On clinical exam, hypotension can occur due to severe volume depletion. Fruity breath and a Kussmaul (deep and rapid breathing) pattern suggest ketoacidosis. Severe cases are marked by confusion or obtundation.

Diagnosis: DKA is diagnosed by a high anion gap acidosis, ketosis, and, most of the time, hyperglycemia (Table 1-7). Secondary derangements include deficits in total body K^+ and phosphorus (even though both can be normal in serum measurements at presentation because of the acidosis and hemoconcentration). Serum Na^+ is usually decreased because of the osmotic shift of water from inside cells to the intravascular space caused by the hyperglycemia, a phenomenon referred to as pseudohyponatremia. Correct for this by adding 2.0 mEq/L (2 mmol/L) to the measured serum Na^+ for every 100 mg/dL (5.6 mmol/L) increase in blood glucose over 100 mg/dL.

Treatment:

- Treat precipitating causes (e.g., infection, infarction).
- Start aggressive volume replacement; give normal saline (~ 2–3 L), then either continue the normal saline or switch to 0.45% saline if the corrected serum Na^+ is > 135 mEq/L (135 mmol/L).
- Start IV insulin at 0.1 units/kg/hour. When glucose is < 200 mg/dL (11.1 mmol/L), add D5 (5% dextrose) to the IV fluids to avoid hypoglycemia while insulin is infusing. Keep the IV insulin going until the acidosis is resolved and the anion gap is normal; the insulin is required to stop production of the ketoacids.
- If the K^+ is < 5.0 mEq/L (5.0 mmol/L) at the start of treatment, give potassium chloride (KCl) immediately because there is usually a several-hundred mEq K^+ deficit despite normal serum K^+ concentration.
- In cases of very low K^+ (< 3.3 mEq/L [3.3 mmol/L]), give KCl and hold insulin until the K^+ is ≥ 3.3 mEq/L.

More on K^+: It falls with treatment of DKA because of shifting into the cells from both the reversal of acidosis and the action of insulin. This can further aggravate hypokalemia and lead to cardiac arrest or respiratory muscle weaknesses. Also monitor the heart-wave morphology and rhythm for any hypokalemic changes, such as T-wave amplitude flattening (1st change), ST-segment depression, T-wave inversions, PR-interval prolongation, and, finally, an increase in amplitude of U waves.

Bicarbonate (HCO_3^-) is controversial but can be given when pH is < 7.0, especially if the patient is having respiratory or hemodynamic collapse.

The standard urine ketone test (and older plasma tests) react with acetoacetate, but not β-hydroxybutyrate. With severe ketoacidosis, β-hydroxybutyrate levels can be much higher than acetoacetate levels. In this situation, urine ketone testing can underestimate the presence or severity of the DKA.

If the patient is being treated for DKA and seems to be getting better but the ketones start rising, the β-hydroxybutyrate is being converted to acetoacetate as the acidosis resolves. Clinically, you can follow resolution by monitoring the pH and anion gap. The anion gap reflects both types of ketones. Plasma β-hydroxybutyrate concentration can be checked directly with point of care testing, and it is sensitive and more specific than the urine tests.

Hyperglycemic Hyperosmolar State (HHS)

HHS is one of the most serious acute complications of T2DM. It can lead to coma and death and has many precipitating factors, including volume depletion, infection, drugs (e.g., glucocorticoids), and any serious illness.

HHS is caused by partial insulin deficiency and decreased intake of fluids. The patient is usually older and has a preceding history of lethargy, weight loss, and polyuria.

Exam is consistent with severe volume depletion and confusion, stupor, or coma. These patients are not severely acidotic, so they do not have fruity breath or Kussmaul respirations.

Labs show severe hyperglycemia (typically > 600 mg/dL [33.3 mmol/L]) and evidence of azotemia, dehydration, and volume depletion. If an anion gap metabolic ketoacidosis is present, it is generally mild.

See Table 1-7 for a comparison of diagnostic criteria in DKA vs. HHS.

Treat HHS similarly to DKA, with IV fluid resuscitation and insulin bolus + infusion. Be sure to correct the serum Na^+ for the hyperglycemia to determine if a free-water deficit exists, then replace it gradually over the next 24–48 hours. K^+ replacement is usually required.

Table 1-7: Diagnostic Criteria for Diabetic Ketoacidosis (DKA) vs. Hyperglycemic Hyperosmolar State (HHS)

Parameter	DKA	HHS
Usual glucose at diagnosis	> 250 mg/dL (13.88 mmol/L)	> 600 mg/dL (33.3 mmol/L)
Arterial pH	< 7.3	> 7.3
Serum HCO₃⁻	< 18 mEq/L (18 mmol/L)	> 18 mEq/L (18 mmol/L)
Urine ketones	Positive	Small value or negative
Serum ketones	> 3 mmol/L	< 0.6 mmol/L
Effective serum osmolality	Variable	> 320 mOsm/kg (320 mmol/kg)
Anion gap	> 10 mEq/L (10 mmol/L)	Variable
Mental status	Varies with severity	Stupor/Coma

Adapted from: Kitabchi, A. E., G. E. Umpierrez, J. M. Miles, and J. N. Fisher. 2009. Hyperglycemic crises in adult patients with diabetes. *Diabetes Care.* 32(7):1335–1343.

DIABETES IN PREGNANCY

For information on diabetes in pregnancy, see the Women's and Men's Health section under Obstetrics.

HYPOGLYCEMIA

PREVIEW | REVIEW

- What is the Whipple triad?
- Which laboratory tests help you determine if someone is factitiously self-injecting insulin to induce hypoglycemia?

OVERVIEW

The diagnosis of hypoglycemia is not based on a low blood glucose level alone; it requires fulfillment of the **Whipple triad**:

1) Signs and symptoms consistent with hypoglycemia
2) Associated low plasma glucose level (< 55 mg/dL [3.0 mmol/L]—do not measure with a home glucose monitor.)
3) Relief of symptoms with supplemental glucose

Symptoms are autonomic (e.g., palpitations, tremor, sweating, paresthesias) and neuroglycopenic due to CNS glucose deprivation (e.g., confusion, impaired consciousness, seizures). Usually, autonomic symptoms happen first. Signs of hypoglycemia are nonspecific (e.g., hunger, sweating, anxiety, tremor, altered mental status).

Divide your patients into 2 groups—hypoglycemic patients without diabetes and hypoglycemic patients with diabetes—and then treat accordingly. For details, see

Hypoglycemia in Patients without Diabetes below, and Hypoglycemia in Patients with Diabetes on page 1-47.

HYPOGLYCEMIA IN PATIENTS WITHOUT DIABETES

Etiology

Causes of hypoglycemia in patients without diabetes include:

- **Drugs:** insulin, insulin secretagogues (e.g., glyburide), oral hypoglycemic agents, alcohol. Be sure to think about accidental, surreptitious, and malicious ingestion of sulfonylureas or insulin, especially in patients in the health care field or in those who have a family member with diabetes (see Genetic Causes on page 1-50).
- **Hormone deficiencies:** cortisol, glucagon, epinephrine
- **Critical illness:** heart failure, renal failure, liver failure, sepsis, severe malnutrition
- **Islet cell tumors:** insulinoma, insulinlike growth factor (IGF)-secreting tumor
- **Non-islet cell tumors:** Rarely, other tumors (e.g., hepatocellular carcinoma, fibrosarcomas) can cause hypoglycemia via overproduction of insulinlike growth factor-2 (IGF-2).
- **Functional B-cell disorders:** post gastric bypass, non-insulinoma pancreatogenous hypoglycemia (usually postprandial hypoglycemia)
- **Autoimmune:** endogenous antibodies to insulin or insulin receptor (rare)

Diagnostic Approach

After the diagnosis of hypoglycemia has been established (using Whipple's triad), begin your diagnostic evaluation. First, do a careful history (especially medications) and physical exam, looking for clues to one of the causes listed in Etiology. If the patient is seemingly well, always evaluate for exogenous, accidental, surreptitious, or malicious ingestion or administration of sulfonylureas (SUs) or insulin before doing any further testing. Consider adrenal insufficiency, even though it is rare that this would cause hypoglycemia without other clinical features. Finding an isolated low cortisol during a hypoglycemic event does not necessarily mean the patient has primary adrenal insufficiency because recurrent hypoglycemia lowers the baseline of cortisol secretion; i.e., the hypoglycemia may be causing the low cortisol. If the etiology is not apparent, proceed with laboratory testing.

There are 2 classifications of hypoglycemia: reactive (sometimes called postprandial) and nonreactive (sometimes called fasting).

Reactive Hypoglycemia

Reactive hypoglycemia (a.k.a. postprandial hypoglycemia) develops in response to a nutrient challenge. Significant postprandial hypoglycemia has been documented in postoperative gastric bypass patients due to islet cell hypertrophy. This must be distinguished from traditional dumping syndrome in postoperative bariatric surgery patients, where there are hypoglycemic-type symptoms but no hypoglycemia after a meal. Initial treatment for both includes small, frequent meals that are high in protein and fiber and low in carbs. Postoperative bariatric surgery patients with refractory severe hypoglycemia due to abnormal islet cells may require surgery (pancreatectomy or reversal of the bypass).

Postprandial hypoglycemia in patients without gastric bypass also needs to be evaluated. The test of choice is a nonliquid mixed meal that the patient believes will trigger the hypoglycemia. In the past, postprandial hypoglycemia was diagnosed based on hypoglycemia after an OGTT. This diagnosis has been discredited over time due to poor reproducibility and poor correlation between hypoglycemic symptoms and documented low blood glucose. Never order an OGTT to work up hypoglycemia. On exams, OGTT is a typical distractor from the correct answer.

All reactive hypoglycemia requires fulfillment of the Whipple triad to be a true diagnosis warranting additional evaluation.

Nonreactive Hypoglycemia

In nonreactive hypoglycemia (a.k.a. fasting hypoglycemia), the patient is unable to maintain glucose levels with fasting. The most common causes in hospitalized patients are alcohol misuse, drugs (e.g., oral hypoglycemics, pentamidine), and sepsis.

The causes of nonreactive hypoglycemia in seemingly healthy patients—and that are most commonly tested on exams—are causes of hyperinsulinism. The workup for nonreactive hypoglycemia is summarized in Figure 1-16.

Factitious Hypoglycemia

Factitious hypoglycemia is hypoglycemia in a patient without diabetes caused by ingestion of antidiabetes medications. Insulin and insulin secretagogues are the typical culprits; other classes of antidiabetic medications do not usually cause hypoglycemia. Ingestion can be accidental, surreptitious, and/or malicious. Evaluate for and exclude this diagnosis before any imaging to look for an insulinoma. Review the patient's medication list, and search for pharmacy/medication errors. Suspect surreptitious or malicious etiologies if a patient or family members are in the health care fields or have knowledge/access to glucose-lowering medications.

Endogenous Hyperinsulinism

Endogenous hyperinsulinism is a group of diseases that includes insulinomas, β-cell disorders (such as may occur after gastric bypass), antiinsulin antibodies, and the use of secretagogues in those without diabetes.

If the patient has a spontaneous hypoglycemic event, first confirm the hypoglycemic value with a plasma glucose (capillary/fingerstick glucose values are unreliable and should not be used for hypoglycemia diagnosis), and pair the glucose with a C-peptide, proinsulin, insulin level, and a sulfonylurea (SU) screen.

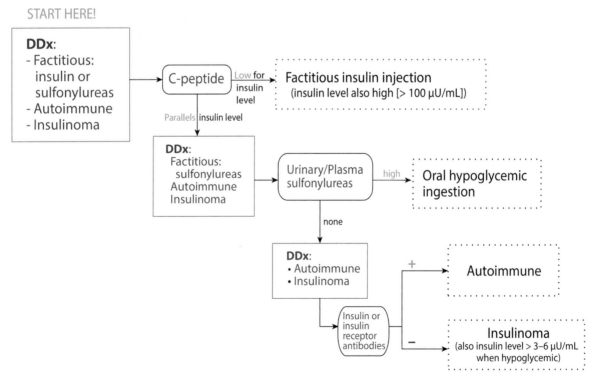

Figure 1-16: Nonreactive hypoglycemia workup

If insulinoma is suspected but Whipple's triad has not yet been documented, it can be induced by a supervised fast (gold standard: 72-hour fast). The following labs should be obtained at the time of hypoglycemic symptoms (prior to treatment):

1) Serum proinsulin (always paired with a glucose)

2) C-peptide (always paired with a glucose)

3) Urinary/Plasma SU screen

4) Serum insulin (always paired with a glucose)

Proinsulin (the precursor of insulin): Insulinomas tend to cause a high ratio of proinsulin to total insulin in the serum. The normal level is 10% of total insulin. With insulinomas the level is > 20%, and often 30–40%. With exogenous insulin use, it is low.

C-peptide is produced in a 1:1 ratio with insulin when they are both cleaved from proinsulin. Therefore, with endogenous insulin production (sulfonylurea-induced and insulinoma), the C-peptide level parallels serum insulin values and is high or inappropriately normal during a hypoglycemic event. C-peptide is low with exogenous insulin injection.

A **urinary/plasma sulfonylurea** test rules in or out factitious hypoglycemia from SU use. Do not proceed to any imaging for insulinoma until a negative SU screen is documented.

Insulin is high or inappropriately normal during the hypoglycemic episode in the following situations:

- Exogenous insulin administration: Insulin levels can be high (sometimes > 100 μU/mL [694.4 pmol/L]) due to self-administration, but the C-peptide is low!
- SU ingestion: Insulin, C-peptide, and proinsulin levels are all high, but the SU screen is positive.
- Insulinoma: Insulin, proinsulin, and C-peptide levels are usually high during an episode of hypoglycemia; SU screen is negative.
- Autoimmune etiologies (antibodies to insulin and insulin receptors): These conditions can cause hypoglycemia or hyperglycemia.

HYPOGLYCEMIA IN PATIENTS WITH DIABETES

Hypoglycemia caused by medications is by far the most frequent cause of hypoglycemia in patients with diabetes. Do not test patients with diabetes for rare causes of hypoglycemia until after extensively reviewing diabetes management and adjusting antidiabetic medications appropriately.

Remember that in T1DM, other comorbidities (e.g., adrenal insufficiency, celiac disease) can increase the risk of hypoglycemia. In longstanding T2DM and patients with diabetes with comorbidities (e.g., heart failure, renal failure, liver failure), agents that are not typically associated with hypoglycemia (i.e., biguanides, TZDs, GLP-1 analogs,

DPP4 inhibitors) can still be the cause of hypoglycemia, especially if they are combined with insulin therapy.

Treatment of hypoglycemia, regardless of the etiology, is generally oral carbs (15–20 g) if the patient is able to take them. If not, options are IV dextrose if an IV is in place, or IM/SQ/nasal glucagon if the patient does not have an IV.

OBESITY

PREVIEW | REVIEW
- Which patients should be screened for obesity, and how should they be screened?

OVERVIEW

The prevalence of obesity has increased significantly in the U.S. over the last 30 years: 40% of adults in the U.S. are now obese (BMI > 30 kg/m²), and 7.7% are severely obese (BMI > 40 kg/m²). Obesity is associated with the development of diabetes, hypertension, fatty liver, dyslipidemia, cardiovascular disease, degenerative joint disease, and obstructive sleep apnea.

EVALUATION AND CLASSIFICATION

Screen every patient for obesity by measuring their body mass index (BMI, in kg/m²). Normal BMI is 18.5–24.9 kg/m², BMI 25.0–29.9 kg/m² is overweight, and BMI ≥ 30 kg/m² is obese. Note that BMI will overestimate obesity in individuals with high muscle mass (e.g., bodybuilders) and underestimate obesity in individuals with low muscle mass (e.g., older adults).

Measure waist circumference—it's an additional cardiovascular risk factor if > 102 cm for men and > 88 cm for women.

MANAGEMENT

Most obesity-associated diseases and complications improve with only a 5–10% weight reduction. Remember to manage the patient's weight loss expectations and focus on healthy lifestyle, not on weight loss alone.

Every patient with overweight/obesity should be offered a lifestyle management plan consisting of 3 components:

- Meal plan: Recommend a diet 500–750 kcal/day less than the daily requirement, and individualize the plan to the patient's preference and culture.
- Physical activity: Recommend aerobic exercise that progresses to 150 minutes/week on 3–5 separate days, with 2–3 resistance exercise sessions 2–3×/week.
- Behavioral modification: Recognize and control environmental cues and stimuli that promote unhealthy eating and sedentary lifestyle. Include self-monitoring, education, stress reduction, and goal setting that requires participation of others.

For patients with obesity, and patients with overweight with ≥ 1 weight-related disease or complication, offer weight-loss medications if lifestyle management therapy has failed.

Weight-loss medications, which can be used alone or in combination, include serotonin agonists (lorcaserin), diabetes medications (liraglutide), sympathomimetics (phentermine), antidepressants (bupropion), anticonvulsants (topiramate), and inhibitors of fat digestion (orlistat). Most of them produce an average of 6–8 kg of weight loss, with around 50–60% of patients reaching a 5% weight loss. All weight-loss medications are contraindicated in pregnancy.

Consider bariatric surgery in patients with BMI > 40 kg/m^2 or BMI > 35 kg/m^2 with ≥ 1 severe weight-related diseases/complications who have not met weight-loss goals with exercise, diets, and meds.

BONE / CALCIUM DISORDERS

PREVIEW | REVIEW

- A normal intact parathyroid hormone level in the setting of hypercalcemia suggests which diagnosis?
- How can you differentiate familial hypocalciuric hypercalcemia from primary hyperparathyroidism?
- What are the indications for surgical treatment of primary hyperparathyroidism?
- What monitoring is needed in patients with primary hyperparathyroidism who are being medically managed?
- What are the common causes of secondary hyperparathyroidism?
- Define tertiary hyperparathyroidism. When is it likely to be seen?
- Which vitamins and medications can cause hypercalcemia?
- Which malignancies are associated with hypercalcemia?
- What is the treatment for hypercalcemia?
- What is osteomalacia? How does it present?
- What is the most common cause of vitamin D deficiency?
- Which lab value is used to measure vitamin D levels?

NORMAL CALCIUM PHYSIOLOGY

Ca^{2+} is absorbed from the duodenum, stored in the bone, and excreted by the kidneys. Ca^{2+} levels are tightly regulated by multiple hormones to keep serum Ca^{2+} in a normal range.

When serum Ca^{2+} is low, 2 endogenous hormones are responsible for increasing serum Ca^{2+} levels: parathyroid hormone (PTH) and 1,25-$(OH)_2$-vitamin D (a.k.a. 1,25-$(OH)_2$-D, calcitriol).

PTH increases Ca^{2+} in the blood through the following:

- Stimulates release of bone Ca^{2+} stores by indirect stimulation of osteo**c**lasts (**c** = **c**hew bone)
- Increases renal tubular Ca^{2+} reabsorption and renal tubular phosphorus excretion
- Increases activity of kidney 1-α-hydroxylase, which increases the production of 1,25-$(OH)_2$-D, thereby increasing Ca^{2+} and phosphorus absorption from the gut

Vitamin D is either ingested or is made in the skin after a reaction with sunlight, but it is inert until it is sequentially hydroxylated, first in the liver to form 25-OH-D, and then in the kidney to form 1,25-$(OH)_2$-D. 1,25-$(OH)_2$-D increases Ca^{2+} and phosphorus absorption from the gut. 25-OH-D is the stored (measured) vitamin D, and 1,25-$(OH)_2$-D is the active vitamin D, which acts as a hormone.

High serum free Ca^{2+} feeds back to suppress PTH secretion and subsequently, 1,25-$(OH)_2$-D. Low serum Ca^{2+} and vitamin D deficiency increase PTH production.

Calcitonin, from the thyroid parafollicular cells (C cells), can be considered a PTH antagonist. It slows down the osteoclasts, causing a decrease in bone resorption and increase in renal Ca^{2+} clearance (calciuria).

Other hormones can also influence Ca^{2+} levels and bone health. Normal levels of glucocorticoids help maintain osteo**b**last (**b** = **b**uild bone) function, but excess levels increase bone resorption, decrease bone formation, and cause calciuria.

HYPERCALCEMIA

Hyperparathyroidism

Primary hyperparathyroidism (PHPT) is often found incidentally after noting high serum Ca^{2+} on screening laboratory studies. 80% of cases are caused by solitary parathyroid adenomas. Complications of untreated PHPT include low bone density (measured in the distal radius), fractures, kidney stones, and hypercalcemia.

Although most patients are asymptomatic, the classic signs and symptoms of PHPT have been described as "bones, stones, abdominal moans, and psychic groans." Bones refer to both increased risk of fractures and the presence of bone aches and pains. There is an increased risk of calcium-containing kidney stones and nephrocalcinosis. Abdominal moans refer to the multiple GI symptoms (e.g., constipation, nausea, anorexia, abdominal pain, peptic ulcer) linked to hypercalcemia. Psychic groans can include confusion, memory loss, and delirium. As helpful as this mnemonic is, remember that most symptomatic patients have mostly vague, nonspecific symptoms, like generalized fatigue, attention/concentration deficits, depression, and weakness.

On the ECG, expect to find a shortened ST segment.

Subperiosteal bone resorption (a.k.a. osteitis fibrosa cystica) with a moth-eaten appearance to the radial side of phalangeal cortices on finger radiographs is the classic finding, indicating prolonged PTH excess. This finding is now rare, probably due to earlier recognition. If an exam question shows you radiographs of a patient's hands, think about primary hyperparathyroidism.

The diagnosis of PHPT is made by finding an elevated or inappropriately normal intact PTH (iPTH) with an elevated Ca^{2+} (Table 1-8). A normal iPTH in the setting of hypercalcemia is compatible with the diagnosis of primary hyperparathyroidism because normally, high Ca^{2+} suppresses iPTH. Serum phosphorus is usually low-normal to low (Table 1-8).

Know that patients with drug-induced hypercalcemia caused by lithium or thiazides may present with PTH levels above normal; ask about these meds, and stop thiazides for 3 months before the hypercalcemia evaluation is done.

Differentiate hypercalcemia due to PHPT from benign familial hypocalciuric hypercalcemia (FHH) by measuring 24-hour urinary Ca^{2+} and Cr excretion and calculating the Ca^{2+}/Cr clearance ratio:

$$\frac{Ca^{2+}}{Cr\ clearance} = \frac{[24h\ urine\ Ca^{2+} \times serum\ Cr]}{[24h\ urine\ Cr \times serum\ Ca^{2+}]}$$

Urinary Ca^{2+} excretion is very low in FHH (Ca^{2+}/Cr clearance ratio < 0.01) and normal to high in PHPT. FHH does not need treatment (see Genetic Causes on page 1-50).

Remember: If a patient with PHPT is taking hydrochlorothiazide (HCTZ) or lithium or has coexisting vitamin D deficiency, the 24-hour urine Ca^{2+} (and the Ca^{2+}/Cr clearance ratio) can be low. Screen patients with PHPT for vitamin D deficiency by checking the 25-OH-D level (not 1,25-$(OH)_2$-D).

PHPT is a biochemical diagnosis (made by labs); imaging is not necessary for the diagnosis but is often done to localize the adenoma. Imaging can include sestamibi scans and ultrasound.

Once the diagnosis of PHPT has been established biochemically, determine if parathyroidectomy is indicated. Indications for surgical parathyroidectomy include:

- Symptomatic PHPT (remember "bones, stones, abdominal moans, psychic groans")
- eGFR < 60 mL/minute/1.73 m^2 (CKD Stage 3 or higher)
- Serum Ca^{2+} > 1 mg/dL (0.25 mmol/L) above the upper limit of normal
- T-score of ≤ –2.5 at lumbar spine, femoral neck, total hip, or distal 1/3 radius; Z-score of ≤ –2.0 in premenopausal women and men < 50 years of age
- < 50 years of age
- Vertebral fracture by x-ray, CT, MRI, or dual energy x-ray absorptiometry.
- Kidney stone, either clinically or on imaging, or nephrocalcinosis
- 24-hour urine Ca^{2+} > 400 mg (> 10 mmol) and increased stone risk by urine biochemical stone risk profile

Monitoring and management of asymptomatic PHPT patients who do not undergo surgery includes:

- Measure serum Ca^{2+} and creatinine yearly.
- Obtain bone density scans every 1–2 years.
- Check 25-OH-D level, and supplement if < 20 ng/dL (480 pmol/L).
- Measure 24-hour urinary Ca^{2+}. If the urinary Ca^{2+} is > 400 mg/day, then do a complete urinary biochemical stone profile.
- Diet advice is the same as for patients without primary hyperparathyroidism (i.e., goal = Ca^{2+} intake of 1,000 mg/day). Do not tell patients to restrict their Ca^{2+} intake—just avoid excessive supplementation.

No specific drug is recommended by the 2014 Guidelines for the Management of Asymptomatic Primary Hyperparathyroidism because long-term efficacy data are

Table 1-8: Labs in Diseases Affecting Calcium						
Calcium-Related Diseases	Ca^{2+}	PO_4^{3-}	Alkaline Phosphatase	iPTH	25-OH-D	1,25-$(OH)_2$-D
Primary hyperparathyroidism	↑	Normal/↓	Normal/↑	Normal/↑	Normal/↓	N/A
Hypercalcemia of malignancy due to lytic bone lesions	↑	Normal/↑	↑	↓	Normal	Normal (except in lymphoma, where it is ↑)
Humoral hypercalcemia of malignancy (i.e., due to PTHrp)	↑	Normal/↓	↑	↓ (but PTHrp is ↑)	Normal	Normal
Chronic kidney disease	Normal/↓	↑	N/A	↑	Normal/↓	Do not check (but it is ↓).
Osteomalacia from vitamin D deficiency	↓	↓	↑	↑	↓	Do not check.

scarce. However, cinacalcet is approved for the medical management of PHPT. Cinacalcet can be useful in patients who are not candidates for, or refuse, surgical parathyroidectomy. Note that this agent controls hypercalcemia alone and does not address bone loss or hypercalciuria. Bisphosphonates can be used to build bone in the lumbar spine and hips, but they do not decrease serum Ca^{2+} or urine Ca^{2+} excretion in the long term. Therefore, the clinical situation determines whether and which medication to use. A patient with fractures or severe osteoporosis requires bisphosphonates, while symptomatic hypercalcemia requires cinacalcet. If neither of these situations apply, do not give these medications. Hypercalciuria and kidney stones can only be addressed by parathyroid surgery.

Secondary hyperparathyroidism is the overproduction of parathyroid hormone secondary to a chronic abnormal stimulus inducing its production. Ca^{2+} is usually normal. Typically, this is due to chronic kidney disease and/or vitamin D deficiency. In chronic kidney disease, there is reduced renal 1-hydroxylation (i.e., activation) of 25-OH-D, leading to low levels of active $1,25\text{-}(OH)_2\text{-}D$. This leads to lower Ca^{2+} and high PTH. Phosphate (PO_4^{3-}) is high due to poor renal excretion. For further discussion, see Table 1-8 on page 1-49 and the Nephrology section under Chronic Kidney Disease (CKD).

Tertiary hyperparathyroidism is seen in patients with end-stage kidney disease (ESKD; a.k.a. end-stage renal disease [ESRD]) and chronic, poorly controlled secondary hyperparathyroidism. There is progression from 4-gland hyperplasia to autonomous PTH production. It can persist after renal transplantation if the autonomous, hypertrophied parathyroid glands continue to oversecrete parathyroid hormone, causing elevated serum Ca^{2+} levels. In the setting of ESKD +/− transplant, labs show a markedly elevated PTH and high Ca^{2+}. Surgery is generally needed for severe tertiary hyperparathyroidism.

Summary: Hypercalcemic patients with elevated or normal iPTH and low phosphorus = primary hyperparathyroidism. If symptomatic (e.g., kidney stones, CKD, low bone density), do surgery. Secondary hyperparathyroidism with a normal Ca^{2+} = consider vitamin D deficiency and CKD as the cause. Tertiary hyperparathyroidism = ESKD or kidney transplant with hyperparathyroidism + hypercalcemia.

Other Causes

Vitamins and Medications

Vitamin D excess, vitamin A excess (causes Ca^{2+} release from bones), thiazide diuretics (decreases Ca^{2+} excretion), and lithium (increases PTH threshold by requiring Ca^{2+} to be at a higher level to shut off PTH production) can cause hypercalcemia.

Genetic Causes

Benign familial hypocalciuric hypercalcemia (FHH) is autosomal dominant with normal or slightly elevated iPTH and elevated serum Ca^{2+}—the same laboratory pattern as in primary hyperparathyroidism. The problem is in the calcium-sensing receptor, which requires a higher Ca^{2+} level before turning off PTH secretion. FHH requires no treatment, so it is important to differentiate from other causes of hypercalcemia (especially primary hyperparathyroidism). If FHH is suspected, measure Ca^{2+} and creatinine in the serum and urine, then calculate the Ca^{2+}/Cr clearance ratio. If the ratio is < 0.01, the diagnosis is FHH; if > 0.02, FHH is excluded, and the diagnosis is most likely primary hyperparathyroidism. Remember that this is a very rare disease, so verify that there are no factors that are causing a falsely low urine Ca^{2+} (especially vitamin D deficiency, malabsorption, celiac disease). Also recognize that FHH is genetic and not acquired. Thus, if there were normal calcium levels in the past, it is not FHH.

Hypercalcemia of Malignancy

Mechanisms of hypercalcemia of malignancy (non-PTH mediated) are:

- osteolytic bone lesions,
- PTH-related protein (PTHrP) production, or
- extrarenal 1-α-hydroxylase production to make $1,25\text{-}(OH)_2\text{-}D$ (active vitamin D).

Types of cancer that cause hypercalcemia: myeloma, some solid tumors, tumors with bone metastases, and lymphoma.

Some solid tumors (e.g., breast, renal, squamous cell) secrete a PTHrP, in which the *N*-terminal (amino) end is identical to iPTH. But the mid- and carboxy-terminal portions are different, so it is not measured by the iPTH assay. The elevated Ca^{2+} inhibits production of PTH by the parathyroid glands, so PTH levels are suppressed. Make the diagnosis by measuring PTHrP levels.

Bone metastases (e.g., breast cancer, multiple myeloma) account for 1/2 of all patients with elevated Ca^{2+} and malignancy; they produce local osteoclast activation substances, causing breakdown of bone.

Lymphoma can have macrophages and lymphocytes with unregulated production of 1-α-hydroxylase, the enzyme that normally converts 25-OH-D into $1,25\text{-}(OH)_2\text{-}D$ in the kidney. This extrarenal source of 1-α-hydroxylase causes an increase in $1,25\text{-}(OH)_2\text{-}D$ and hypercalcemia. Make the diagnosis by measuring $1,25\text{-}(OH)_2\text{-}D$ (calcitriol) levels.

More information can be found in the Oncology section under Hypercalcemia of Malignancy.

Granulomatous Diseases

Several granulomatous diseases, including sarcoidosis, tuberculosis, berylliosis, histoplasmosis, and leprosy, can cause hypercalcemia by stimulating macrophages to increase $1,25\text{-}(OH)_2\text{-}D$ production (similar to lymphoma). Macrophages (and lymphocytes) have unregulated 1-α-hydroxylase activity, which converts 25-OH-D into $1,25\text{-}(OH)_2\text{-}D$. If suspected, measure $1,25\text{-}(OH)_2\text{-}D$ (calcitriol) levels.

Immobilization

Immobilization can cause elevated Ca^{2+}. High bone turnover states (e.g., hyperthyroidism, Paget disease, adolescence) increase the risk, but immobilization-induced hypercalcemia can occur without those comorbidities. The high Ca^{2+} level causes a decrease in iPTH.

Treatment

For severe hypercalcemia, immediately give 3–4 L of **normal saline** to treat volume depletion (remember, hypercalcemia causes renal salt wasting and nephrogenic DI). **Calcitonin** is added to increase renal calcium excretion and inhibit bone turnover. **Loop diuretics** should be used only if the patient develops fluid overload from saline resuscitation (monitor electrolytes and volume status).

Bisphosphonates inhibit bone resorption in areas of high turnover, such as sites of malignancy, and usually are used in conjunction with saline infusions and calcitonin to treat moderate-to-severe hypercalcemia.

Pamidronate and zoledronic acid are the bisphosphonates favored by most because of their rapid onset of action (48 hours) and intravenous formulation. Know that these drugs can cause osteonecrosis of the jaw in patients with multiple myeloma and metastatic bone disease.

Give glucocorticoids to treat hypercalcemia caused by sarcoidosis and other granulomatous diseases (see Granulomatous Diseases), myeloma, and lymphoma.

Mobilize patients as much as possible with physical therapy, home health assistance, and help of family.

HYPOCALCEMIA

Signs and Symptoms

Hypocalcemia can cause nonspecific symptoms, including fatigue, anxiety, and depression. The hallmark of hypocalcemia is neuromuscular irritability (i.e., tetany). Patients report paresthesias, especially in the fingers and toes and around the mouth, and muscle cramps. On physical exam, try to elicit Trousseau sign (inflate a blood pressure cuff above systolic BP for 3 minutes; the muscles of the hands will spasm) and Chvostek sign (tap the facial nerve just in front of the ear; the facial muscles will spasm).

Severe hypocalcemia can cause seizures. Know that alkalosis exacerbates hypocalcemic seizures, and acidosis is protective. In a patient with hypocalcemia and metabolic acidosis, always correct the hypocalcemia before you correct the acidosis!

Causes

Low serum Ca^{2+} is caused by the following:

- Hypoparathyroidism—decreased PTH secretion (clue: high PO_4^{3-} + low Ca^{2+}):
  ◦ Primary hypoparathyroidism
  ◦ Thyroid surgery with loss of parathyroid glands

  ◦ Severe hypomagnesemia ($Mg^{2+} < 0.8$ mEq/L [0.4 mmol/L]); Mg^{2+} is required for PTH release and its effect on target organs. This can be seen in patients with bowel disease or excessive use of alcohol.
- Vitamin D deficiency
- Severe, acute pancreatitis: precipitation of Ca^{2+} salts in the abdominal cavity
- Acute, severe hyperphosphatemia, whereby Ca^{2+} is chelated by the phosphorus
- "Hungry bone" after parathyroidectomy (clue: low PO_4^{3-} + low Ca^{2+} + high pre-op alkaline phosphatase)
- Pseudohypoparathyroidism (Types Ia, Ib, Ic, II) is due to PTH resistance. It is a rare genetic disease due to a mutation in a gene involved in PTH receptor function. These patients have an appropriately elevated PTH (in response to the hypocalcemia). In addition to hypocalcemia, patients with Type Ia have short 4th metacarpals and short stature.

When patients with shortened 4th metacarpals and short stature have a normal serum Ca^{2+}, they may have pseudo-pseudohypoparathyroidism. These patients are heterozygous for the Ia mutation, and have the physical phenotype of pseudohypoparathyroidism Type Ia, but normal Ca^{2+} homeostasis.

Osteomalacia

Osteomalacia is a condition of decreased mineralization of normal bone at sites of bone turnover. It typically presents with symptoms of bone pain, but occasionally presents with hypocalcemia (see Table 1-8 on page 1-49). It is most commonly caused by vitamin D deficiency. In children, osteomalacia is called rickets; it causes listlessness, irritability, and bowing of the legs. Older patients present with bone pain and proximal muscle weakness. Patients of all ages have diffuse decreased bone mineral density.

These patients have an elevated alkaline phosphatase due to compensatory osteoblastic activity. This is a good lab clue!

In adults, bilateral symmetric pseudofractures (i.e., narrow radiolucent lines, most commonly in the femoral neck and femoral shaft) establish the diagnosis. An iliac crest bone biopsy with tetracycline double-labeling can provide a definitive pathologic diagnosis, but usually osteomalacia is diagnosed clinically without a biopsy.

Once the diagnosis is established, work up the cause (many possibilities). Again, vitamin D deficiency is the most common case in adults. The usual cause of vitamin D deficiency is inadequate intake and/or malabsorption. It's quite common in older persons and in those who live in higher latitudes. Vitamin D deficiency is also more typical in people who use a lot of sunscreen, have darker skin, and/or avoid sunlight.

Studies link vitamin D deficiency with falls, fractures, cancer, and CVD. Look for osteomalacia in older patients with prolonged hospitalizations, who develop bone pain with radiographs that show hairline fractures.

If you suspect vitamin D deficiency, check the 25-OH-D level, not the 1,25-$(OH)_2$-D level! In osteomalacia due to vitamin D deficiency (the most common cause), the 25-OH-D level will be low.

Renal osteodystrophy and adynamic bone disease are discussed in the Nephrology section under Chronic Kidney Disease (CKD). Osteoporosis is discussed in the General Internal Medicine section under Osteoporosis.

MULTIPLE ENDOCRINE NEOPLASIA (MEN)

MEN syndromes: All are autosomal dominant but with varying expression! See Table 1-9. The types are categorized as MEN1, MEN2A, and MEN2B.

Table 1-9: Multiple Endocrine Neoplasia Syndromes

Type	Clinical
MEN1	Primary hyperparathyroidism Pituitary adenomas Pancreatic islet cell tumors
MEN2A	Primary hyperparathyroidism Medullary thyroid cancer Pheochromocytoma
MEN2B	Medullary thyroid cancer Pheochromocytoma Developmental abnormalities*

*Marfanoid body type, skeletal deformations, mucosal neuromas (especially lips and tongue ["blubbery lips"])

MEN1: Symptoms are caused by hyperplasia, adenomas, and/or cancers of the **p**arathyroid, **p**ituitary, or the islet cells of the **p**ancreas (think **PPP**). Primary hyperparathyroidism due to multiple parathyroid adenomas is typical. Prolactinoma is the most common pituitary tumor, and gastrinoma is the most common symptomatic pancreatic tumor. Suspect MEN1 in a patient with hyperprolactinemia and hypercalcemia. There is often a strong family history of peptic ulcer disease (undiagnosed gastrinoma) or primary hyperparathyroidism. Phenotypic expression within a family might be quite variable.

Aside from gastrinomas, the pancreatic tumors in MEN1 can also be insulinomas, VIPomas (which secrete vasoactive intestinal peptide), or glucagonomas. Insulinomas can cause hypoglycemic episodes and are diagnosed by documenting inappropriately high serum insulin levels. VIPomas present with secretory diarrhea. Diagnose with a high serum VIP level.

Glucagonoma is a very rare malignant tumor of pancreatic islet cells that produces glucagon and can cause a blistering dermatitis, hyperglycemia +/– diabetes, cheilitis (inflammation of the lips), diarrhea, weight loss, and cognitive impairment. The skin and tongue changes are due to a glucagon-induced amino acid deficiency. Think about it in patients with a family history of MEN1 who present with a triad of mild hyperglycemia, glossitis with a beefy red tongue, and a distinctive blistering erythematous rash that is often found in the groin region (termed migratory necrolytic erythema).

Diagnose glucagonoma by measuring a glucagon level—one of the rare instances when it is useful to perform a randomly timed hormone assay! A level > 500 pg/mL (500 ng/L) is supportive. Image the pancreas with a helical CT if glucagon levels are high. In the majority of patients, glucagonoma is metastatic (to liver, lymph nodes, bone, adrenals, kidney, and/or lung) at diagnosis.

MEN2A: Medullary thyroid cancer occurs in virtually all patients with MEN2A (and MEN2B) and often occurs early in life. Pheochromocytoma occurs frequently; primary hyperparathyroidism occurs in 25–50%.

MEN2B: Like MEN2A, patients have medullary thyroid carcinoma, and 1/2 of patients have pheochromocytoma. Unlike MEN2A, they do not have primary hyperparathyroidism. This type is easy to differentiate from the others because of the mucosal neuromas seen on physical exam.

Remember: Both MEN2A and MEN2B have medullary thyroid cancer and pheochromocytoma.

Table 1-9 summarizes the classic clinical findings in MEN1, MEN2A, and MEN2B. Remember:

- **Primary hyperparathyroidism** (parathyroid hyperplasia) causes hypercalcemia but generally no symptoms.
- **Pituitary adenomas** can cause prolactinomas, acromegaly, or Cushing disease but can also be nonfunctional.
- **Pancreatic islet cell tumors** can present with hypoglycemic episodes (insulinoma) or peptic ulcer disease (gastrinoma).
- **Medullary thyroid cancer** is characterized by a high calcitonin level; diagnosis is with fine needle aspiration (FNA) biopsy.
- **Pheochromocytoma** can present with episodes of headache, palpitations, sweating, and hypertension but usually is asymptomatic.

Question: If a patient with an elevated iPTH has a family history of one brother having medullary cancer and another having a parathyroid tumor, what tests do you run on the patient?

Answer: Think MEN2A. Check calcitonin and free plasma metanephrines. In an exam setting, you may see only one of these in the answer choices.

The *RET* protooncogene test for hereditary medullary thyroid cancer (MTC) can also be very useful and offers the potential for prophylactic surgical intervention prior to the development of MTC in family members who are at risk. Calcitonin elevation correlates with tumor burden and may be the 1st sign of recurrent disease. Calcitonin doubling time is accurate in predicting prognosis. Elevated calcitonin levels can cause symptoms, such as flushing, diarrhea, and weight loss.

Treatment of MTC is surgical resection. For disease persistence or recurrence options, include observation, surgery, external beam radiation, and tyrosine kinase inhibitors.

THE MEDSTUDY HUB: YOUR GUIDELINES AND REVIEW ARTICLES RESOURCE

For both review articles and current internal medicine practice guidelines, visit the MedStudy Hub at

medstudy.com/hub

The Hub contains the only online consolidated list of all current guidelines focused on internal medicine. Guidelines on the Hub are easy to find, continually updated, and linked to the published source. MedStudy maintains the Hub as a service to the medical community and makes it available to anyone and everyone at no cost to users.

FIGURE SOURCES

Figure 1-1: MedStudy illustration
Figure 1-2: MedStudy illustration
Figure 1-3: MedStudy illustration
Figure 1-5: Jonathan Trobe, CC BY 3.0
Figure 1-6: MedStudy illustration
Figure 1-7: MedStudy illustration
Figure 1-8: MedStudy illustration
Figure 1-10: MedStudy illustration
Figure 1-11: MedStudy illustration
Figure 1-12: MedStudy illustration
Figure 1-13: MedStudy illustration
Figure 1-14: MedStudy illustration
Figure 1-15: MedStudy illustration
Figure 1-16: MedStudy illustration
The remaining figures are from the MedStudy archives.

Allergy & Immunology

SECTION EDITOR

Thanai Pongdee, MD
Assistant Professor, Division of Allergic Diseases
Mayo Clinic College of Medicine and Science
Mayo Clinic
Rochester, MN

Table of Contents

HYPERSENSITIVITY REACTIONS

IMMUNOLOGIC HYPERSENSITIVITY REACTIONS

PREVIEW | REVIEW

- What mediates immediate hypersensitivity reactions?
- When does the late phase of a Type 1 hypersensitivity reaction occur? Why does it occur?
- What is the difference between the late phase of Type 1 hypersensitivity reaction and the delayed Type 4 hypersensitivity reaction?
- What is the treatment for anaphylaxis?
- Which antihypertensive medication is relatively contraindicated in someone at risk for anaphylaxis? Why?
- Which diseases are mediated by Type 3 immune complex hypersensitivity reactions?

OVERVIEW

Immunologic hypersensitivity reactions reflect immune-mediated tissue injury seen in allergies, autoimmune disease, and other inflammatory diseases. These immune responses are the staggeringly important basis for disease prevention in the body, and are the normal reaction to a foreign antigen. There are 2 general dysfunctions in which these normal defense mechanisms cause disease:

1) An overexuberant response to a foreign antigen

2) Autoimmune disease develops, in which the body sees a self-antigen as foreign

So, as we go through the following mechanisms of immunologic hypersensitivity responses, remember that these are also the mechanisms of our normal immune responses to foreign antigens. We tend to forget that!

There are 4 types of immunologic hypersensitivity reactions (per Gell and Coombs):

- **Type 1:** IgE-mediated—immediate (anaphylactic, atopic)
- **Type 2:** IgG- or IgM-mediated cytotoxic
- **Type 3:** Immune complex–mediated (i.e., antibody–antigen-mediated)
- **Type 4:** T-cell-mediated—delayed, 4 subtypes (a, b, c, d)

TYPE 1 — IgE-MEDIATED IMMEDIATE HYPERSENSITIVITY REACTION

The "classic" allergies are IgE-mediated Type 1 immediate hypersensitivity reactions. Almost all of these reactions are triggered by foreign allergens. Examples include hives/urticaria, allergic rhinitis, allergic asthma, and reactions to insect stings, drugs (e.g., penicillin [PCN]), or foods (e.g., eggs, peanuts, tree nuts, shellfish, soy).

Acute Response

The acute phase of an immediate hypersensitivity reaction occurs within minutes to hours after exposure. Mast cell degranulation (especially producing histamine) is the cause of the symptoms. This reaction is IgE mediated. The IgE reaction is antigen-specific and occurs only in response to previous exposure to the same allergen.

The base (Fc portion; see Antibodies on page 2-18) of IgE binds to a receptor on mast cells. This receptor is not specific, so there are many IgEs (each with its own antigen specificity) bound to a mast cell. Typically, no reaction occurs when IgE binds to a mast cell; however, when IgE attaches to its specific allergen, the same antigen reacts with 2 or more IgE molecules, interlinking them. Degranulation of the mast cell occurs with this complicated activation process, releasing histamine and stimulating the synthesis and secretion of other mediators like leukotriene, prostaglandin D2 (PGD2), and cytokines. Histamine is responsible for most of the acute symptoms. Mast cells also release other products that have chemotactic effects, and some of them are enzymes (e.g., chymase, tryptase). We can measure tryptase levels to confirm anaphylactic reactions because unlike histamine, which is broken down rapidly after release, tryptase is stable for up to a few hours after mast cell degranulation. See Mastocytosis on page 2-25.

A quick review—histamine interacts with 4 receptors:

- H_1 activation causes the wheal and flare, bronchoconstriction, and pruritus.
- H_2 activation results in increased gastric acid secretion.
- H_3 activation causes decreased histamine synthesis and release (negative feedback).
- H_4 activation is immunomodulatory and affects eosinophil and mast cell chemotaxis.

Late-Phase Response

The late-phase response (LPR) occurs 3–12 hours after the acute response in < 25% of cases and can last from hours to days. The LPR is caused by the initial immediate IgE reaction that stimulates the synthesis of cytokines and the subsequent cellular recruitment of eosinophils and basophils. This results in an eosinophilic inflammatory infiltrate.

In the airways, the LPR is a cause of airway hypersensitivity seen in patients with asthma.

Anaphylaxis

Anaphylaxis is a potentially life-threatening allergic reaction that presents with symptoms such as urticaria, angioedema, abdominal pain, hypotension, and respiratory compromise. It is rapid in onset and can cause death. Anaphylaxis may begin within 5–30 minutes after antigen exposure; however, anaphylaxis can be delayed up to 2 hours.

ALLERGY & IMMUNOLOGY

The term "anaphylaxis" was traditionally associated only with the IgE-mediated set of symptoms we discuss under Acute Response on page 2-1, and the term "anaphylactoid" was used for all other causes of this same set of symptoms. As detailed by the Joint Task Force on Practice Parameters, anaphylaxis is now the only term used for this set of symptoms. Anaphylaxis, as with hypersensitivity reactions, is further categorized as immunologic or nonimmunologic.

Immunologic anaphylaxis includes:

• IgE-mediated reactions
• Complement activation with the release of anaphylatoxins C3a, C4a, and C5a

Nonimmunologic anaphylaxis includes all those previously termed "anaphylactoid," in which the medication or substance itself directly triggers histamine and tryptase release from mast cells. Examples of nonimmunologic anaphylaxis are:

• Radiocontrast media reactions
• Certain drug reactions
  ◦ Vancomycin flushing syndrome
  ◦ Opioids—especially codeine or meperidine

Immunologic anaphylaxis is usually the result of an extreme IgE-mediated form of an immediate hypersensitivity reaction and this is the focus of the rest of this topic. IgE causes the release of the cytoplasmic granules with histamine and tryptase from mast cells (and maybe basophils). These released cytoplasmic granules cause an immediate reaction that results in anaphylactic symptoms.

There are many causes of IgE-mediated anaphylaxis. The most common include:

• Drugs—especially penicillins and non-ASA NSAIDs
• Insect stings—especially bees, wasps, and yellow jackets
• Foods—especially peanuts, tree nuts, and shellfish

A person may be sensitive to insect stings/bites and sustain a large, local reaction. However, this does not increase the risk of anaphylaxis and further workup is not necessary. Of course, insect-sting anaphylaxis requires further evaluation with venom skin testing and serum venom-specific IgE. Refer to Stinging-Insect Allergy on page 2-11.

The diagnosis of anaphylaxis is solely based on blood pressure and the patient's symptoms—as outlined in Table 2-1. It involves at least 2 organ systems. Recognition and timely treatment of anaphylaxis are essential. Remember: Hypotension is not necessary for the diagnosis of anaphylaxis!

Biphasic phase of anaphylaxis (late phase): Up to ~ 20% of patients experiencing IgE-mediated anaphylaxis have a 2nd episode within 1–30 hours after the initial event. This 2nd phase is believed to be caused by recruitment of inflammatory cells, including eosinophils, lymphocytes, and basophils, which is similar to the LPR of Type 1 hypersensitivity. Patients treated for anaphylaxis must

Table 2-1: Anaphylaxis Diagnosis
Anaphylaxis is diagnosed when 1 of the following 3 criteria is fulfilled:
1) Sudden onset with involvement of the skin or mucosal tissue and either: • Sudden respiratory symptoms or • Hypotension
2) ≥ 2 of the following occur suddenly after exposure to a likely allergen: • Skin or mucosal tissue involvement • Respiratory involvement • Hypotension • GI symptoms
3) Hypotension after exposure to a known allergen

be observed for the biphasic response or provided with emergency self-medications (e.g., epinephrine autoinjectors) if discharged. While difficult to predict, certain factors may increase the likelihood of the biphasic phase:

• Delayed initial epinephrine administration
• Severe initial symptoms
• Delayed resolution of initial symptoms
• Coexistence of asthma
• Oral ingestion of allergens
• β-Blocker medication

Treatment

Treatment for immediate hypersensitivity includes avoidance of the **a**llergen, **a**ntihistamine therapy (occasionally glucocorticoids), and **a**llergen-specific immunotherapy (**3 As**). Advise all patients who have had prior anaphylaxis—especially those at high risk for recurrent exposure to its cause such as beekeepers—to get an epinephrine autoinjection kit. Provide an anaphylaxis action plan and instructions on how/when to use epinephrine. Immunotherapy can take up to 1 year to show an effect and is not available for all causes of anaphylaxis. Effective immunotherapy causes an increase in regulatory T-cell secretion of interleukin-10 (IL-10) and blocking antibodies of the IgG isotype, among many other effects. Only IgE-mediated reactions benefit from immunotherapy treatment.

Anaphylaxis treatment encompasses:

• Administer 0.2–0.5 mL IM of epinephrine (1:1,000 dilution) in the lateral thigh muscle (fastest site of systemic absorption). The maximum dosage is 0.5 mg (0.5 mL of 1:1,000). Do not give the dose by IV due to adverse cardiovascular effects, and do not give SQ because absorption is slower compared to IM. Repeat dosing can be given every 10–20 minutes as needed. Note: Do not use the IV solution for IM treatment. Giving 0.5 mL of the 1:10,000 IV solution of epinephrine would grossly underdose the patient, resulting in the administration of 0.05 mg (in 0.5 mL), 10× less than the intended dose of 0.5 mg.

- H₁ and H₂ antagonists (commonly diphenhydramine and cimetidine, respectively) can also be given for urticaria and pruritus.
- Give inhaled albuterol if bronchospasm develops.
- Ensure that the patient remains recumbent until they are completely asymptomatic. Deaths have occurred from patients being prematurely raised to a sitting position.
- For refractory hypotension: Administer 0.5 mg of epinephrine (5 mL of the 1:10,000 dilution) by IV every 5–10 minutes. Use caution and hemodynamic monitoring whenever using IV epinephrine due to risk of cardiac arrhythmia. Intravascular volume expansion (normal saline preferred) should also be given to patients who do not respond initially to IM epinephrine. Lastly, vasoactive agents such as dopamine, norepinephrine, and vasopressin may be needed for anaphylaxis refractory to epinephrine.

IV or PO glucocorticoids should be administered as part of the initial treatment. They are not effective for acute cases but may decrease likelihood of delayed response. Do not send patients home without making provisions for emergency self-treatment of the biphasic phase, even if they are given systemic glucocorticoids. Intramuscular epinephrine is 1ˢᵗ line treatment for all causes of anaphylaxis! The failure to recognize the symptoms of anaphylaxis and to promptly administer epinephrine has led to preventable fatalities.

Epinephrine affects the α- and β-adrenergic systems, resulting in bronchial relaxation, vasoconstriction, and decreased vascular permeability. The effect of epinephrine is blunted in patients on β-blockers. Therefore, in patients at risk for anaphylaxis (primary treatment is epinephrine), the use of β-blockers is relatively contraindicated. Glucagon slow infusion (5 mg slow IV bolus over 5 minutes) can be used in patients on β-blockers with anaphylaxis refractory to epinephrine; however, epinephrine should always be used first, even for patients on β-blockers. Again: Epinephrine is always 1ˢᵗ line treatment! At discharge, refer patients to an allergist and prescribe epinephrine autoinjector.

TYPE 2 — IgG- OR IgM-MEDIATED CYTOTOXIC HYPERSENSITIVITY

Type 2 cytotoxic hypersensitivity is the main mechanism of autoimmune diseases that cause tissue or cell damage. Type 2 reactions occur when IgG or IgM binds to a fixed target tissue antigen or cell receptor, causing either dysfunction or inflammatory destruction. Most of Type 2 reactions are autoimmune—that is, directed at self-antigens. Extrinsic allergens can cause this reaction when they attach to cell surfaces. Penicillin is an example of an extrinsic agent that can cause both immediate IgE-mediated reactions and delayed IgG-mediated reactions.

The binding of the antibody results in target cell destruction by various means:

- Complement activation causes cells to be lysed by membrane attack complexes (MACs). This is discussed under The 3 Complement Pathways on page 2-19.
- Complement activation may result in opsonization from the production of C3b. Phagocytes have a receptor for C3b and readily attack opsonized C3b-coated cells.
- Phagocytes also have a receptor for the Fc portion of the antibodies and readily attack opsonized antibody-coated cells.

Examples of target cell receptors are:

- Platelets (immune thrombocytopenia; formerly immune thrombocytopenic purpura)
- RBCs (autoimmune hemolytic anemia)
- RBCs when penicillin binds to them, causing them to be recognized as foreign
- Foreign RBCs (hemolytic disease of the newborn)

Examples of Type 2 reactions targeting fixed tissue antigens are:

- Anti-GBM disease with pulmonary hemorrhage (involving the basement membrane of the kidney and lung [formerly Goodpasture syndrome]; see the Nephrology section under Glomerular Diseases.)
- Bullous pemphigoid, pemphigus vulgaris
- Rheumatic fever
- Graves disease (TSH receptor)
- Myasthenia gravis (acetylcholine receptor on muscle cells)

Do not get Type 2 cytotoxic hypersensitivity mixed up with the T-cell-mediated cytotoxic damage seen in Type 4 hypersensitivity reactions.

TYPE 3 — IMMUNE COMPLEX HYPERSENSITIVITY

Anytime you see a vasculitis, think of Type 3 hypersensitivity reactions. Type 3 reactions are seen in autoimmune diseases and in reactions to drugs. Immune complexes (ICs) form when antibodies combine with an antigen (self or foreign). A hypersensitivity reaction occurs when antibody (usually IgG) reacts with a target antigen to form ICs, which, in certain conditions, precipitate and activate complement with subsequent small vessel inflammation and necrosis.

Remember: Just because an antibody reaction occurs and ICs are formed, it does not necessarily mean there is precipitation. Significant precipitation occurs only when there is slight antigen excess in relation to the antibody.

Review: When the antibody response initiates, there is a huge excess of antigens compared to antibodies (Ag : Ab >> 1). The ICs that are formed are small, soluble, and quickly cleared.

Within 1–2 weeks, as exceedingly more antibodies are produced, a point is reached when there is only slight antigen excess. This allows the ICs to interlace and become bigger and less soluble. These large ICs precipitate in the small vessels and activate complement, which starts a cascade—causing the release of more cytokines and the gathering of more inflammatory cells. This process ultimately results in necrosis of the small vessels in any organ. This small vessel vasculitis is also termed hypersensitivity vasculitis and leukocytoclastic vasculitis.

The pathologic hallmark skin finding in a patient with leukocytoclastic vasculitis is palpable purpura (Figure 2-1). See more on leukocytoclastic vasculitis in the Rheumatology section under Vasculitis.

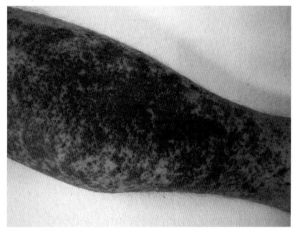

Figure 2-1: Confluent palpable purpura in severe leukocytoclastic (small vessel) vasculitis

As the antigen is cleared, there comes a point when there is antibody excess. The formed ICs are large, and are quickly cleared by circulating phagocytes (e.g., monocytes, macrophages).

There are 2 possible clinical consequences:

1) **Serum sickness** is a systemic reaction in which a large amount of antigen is injected into a nonimmunized host and within 1–2 weeks, you see a necrotic vasculitis similar to the one just discussed. Other symptoms include fever and joint pain.

2) **Arthus reaction** is a local reaction that occurs when a patient is first hyperimmunized (so there are many circulating IgGs) and then given a small intradermal injection of the target antigen. Many ICs are made at the injection site and they induce the complement cascade and inflammation. Within 4–12 hours, a painful, indurated lesion appears and may progress to a sterile abscess.

Serum sickness and Arthus reaction are generally self-limited, and patients usually fully recover. Occasionally, glucocorticoids are given.

Type 3 reactions play a role in the following autoimmune diseases and their associated antigen(s):

- SLE—nuclear materials such as dsDNA and Smith antigen
- Chronic autoimmune thyroiditis (a.k.a. Hashimoto thyroiditis, chronic lymphocytic thyroiditis)—thyroglobulin
- Pernicious anemia—intrinsic factor
- Rheumatoid arthritis—rheumatoid factor

External antigens:

- Hepatitis antigen-associated serum sickness
- Tetanus and diphtheria immunization
- Local insulin reactions
- Treat external antigen reaction by stopping the exposure to the antigen.

TYPE 4 — DELAYED T-CELL-MEDIATED HYPERSENSITIVITY

Type 4 delayed T-cell-mediated hypersensitivity is a CD4+ helper-cell-driven response and is not mediated by antibodies, unlike the other 3 hypersensitivity reactions. Previously sensitized CD4+ helper cells migrate to, and interact with a foreign antigen, and overproduce cytokines (signaling proteins) which initiate an inflammatory reaction with an overabundance of macrophages, eosinophils, cytotoxic T8+ cells, or neutrophils. The reaction peaks in 24–72 hours—hence, the common name of "delayed-type hypersensitivity."

Gell and Coombs classification further divides delayed cell-mediated hypersensitivity into 4 subtypes dependent upon the effector cells that cause tissue damage and specific disease:

- **Type 4a:** monocytes/macrophages (seen in contact dermatitis and granulomatous reactions like tuberculin skin test, tuberculosis, and leprosy)
- **Type 4b:** eosinophils (seen in chronic asthma, chronic allergic rhinitis, maculopapular exanthema with eosinophilia, and drug reaction with eosinophilia and systemic symptoms [DRESS])
- **Type 4c:** cytotoxic T8+ cells (seen in contact dermatitis and skin sloughing reactions such as Stevens-Johnson syndrome/toxic epidermal necrolysis)
- **Type 4d:** neutrophils (seen in pustular exanthema reactions such as Behçet disease)

Clinically, hypersensitivity reactions can be a combination of types:

- Contact dermatitis often has Type 4a and Type 4c features.
- Chronic allergic asthma and chronic allergic rhinitis can have Type 1 (i.e., IgE) and Type 4b mechanisms.
- Allergic bronchopulmonary aspergillosis has components of Types 1, 3, and 4.
- Hypersensitivity pneumonitis starts out as a Type 3 reaction and then becomes more of a Type 4 reaction.

Do not confuse the delayed-type hypersensitivity reaction of Type 4 with the late-phase response of Type 1!

URTICARIA

PREVIEW | REVIEW

- What is the difference between acute and chronic urticaria?
- What precipitates cholinergic urticaria?
- What is the difference between acute urticaria and urticarial vasculitis?

Acute urticaria presents as superficial, blanching, transient, pruritic wheal-and-flare reactions (hives) that last < 6 weeks (Figure 2-2). Common causes include allergies to food, insects, latex, and drugs. If the patient has isolated urticaria, treat with antihistamines. Look for other systemic symptoms (i.e., respiratory, cardiovascular, GI) that indicate more severe anaphylaxis. Allergy testing is guided by the clinical history. Refer to Skin vs. Serum Allergy Testing on page 2-12.

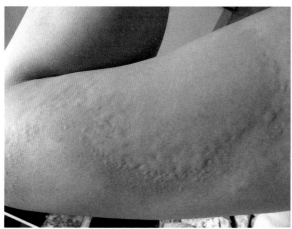

Figure 2-2: Acute urticaria

Chronic urticaria (CU) is hives that last ≥ 6 weeks. Up to 50% of patients with CU are allergic to their own IgE receptors, 10% are allergic to their own IgE, and 10% have antithyroid antibodies. Although there is an association between CU and autoimmune disorders, routine tests to diagnose autoimmune diseases are not recommended in the absence of a clinical history suggestive of autoimmune disease.

No diagnostic testing is required for most patients with CU. However, limited routine laboratory testing can be performed to provide reassurance and to exclude underlying causes. These may include a CBC with differential, erythrocyte sedimentation rate (ESR), and/or C-reactive protein, liver enzyme, and thyroid-stimulating hormone measurement.

Treatment of urticaria involves addressing pruritus and swelling. Use H_1 antihistamines (e.g., hydroxyzine) or newer 2nd generation H_1 antihistamines (e.g., cetirizine), which are less sedating. H_2 antihistamines and glucocorticoids are reserved for refractory urticaria or angioedema.

There are also several non-allergen-mediated causes of urticaria:

- **Dermatographism** (a.k.a. dermatographia) simply means "writing on the skin." Exaggerated wheals and flares arise after the skin is stroked or gentle pressure is applied (Figure 2-3).
- **Acquired cold urticaria** is mediated by either cryoglobulins or IgE. Shock can occur if the patient is immersed in cold water! Diagnose with a 5-minute skin ice-cube challenge.
- **Familial cold urticaria** is an autosomal dominant inflammatory disease characterized by urticaria, myalgias, fever, and joint pain after cold exposure.
- **Cholinergic urticaria** is precipitated by heat (e.g., hot showers, a hot day, exercise). It usually presents as punctate lesions that are very pruritic. The exact etiology is unknown; mast cell hypersensitization is most likely. Treat symptoms with a 1st generation antihistamine such as hydroxyzine, or a 2nd generation antihistamine such as cetirizine.
- **Pressure urticaria** commonly causes swelling and burning of areas exposed to heavy pressure. Diagnose by placing 15 pounds (6.8 kg) of weight suspended over a patient's shoulder for 15 minutes and monitoring for development of swelling.
- **Urticarial vasculitis (UV)** can clinically resemble acute urticaria. However, patients report hives lasting ≥ 24 hours in a fixed location (in contrast to acute urticaria, which resolves in minutes to hours or migrates to other areas). Patients often complain that the hives are nonpruritic, burn, and are painful. Other red flags include skin ecchymosis, purpura, petechiae, or elevated ESR, which are not seen in acute urticaria. Diagnose UV by skin biopsy. Although the mainstay of UV treatment is glucocorticoids, other agents are options depending on the severity of clinical signs and symptoms:
  - Pruritus—H_1 antihistamines
  - Arthralgia/Arthritis—NSAIDs
  - Mild/Moderate—dapsone, hydroxychloroquine, colchicine
  - Severe—methotrexate, azathioprine, cyclosporine A

Figure 2-3: Dermatographism

ATOPIC DERMATITIS (AD)

PREVIEW | REVIEW

- What is the 1st line treatment for atopic dermatitis?

- What do you do if you encounter an adult patient with new-onset recalcitrant eczema?

AD (a.k.a. eczema, atopic eczema) is the most common type of eczema, so the terms AD and eczema are often used interchangeably. AD occurs in ~ 1–3% of adults and is due to dysfunctions in the innate and adaptive immune systems and skin barrier abnormalities. It typically presents as a very pruritic, dry, thickened, scaly rash on the flexural skin surfaces (Figure 2-4). When severe, the rash becomes thick scaling plaques. Symptoms are lifelong and there is no known cure.

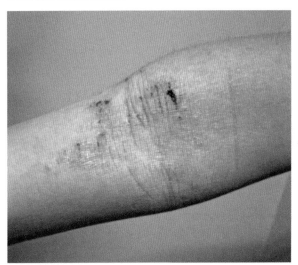

Figure 2-4: Atopic dermatitis

There is a layered treatment approach:

- **Moisturizers** are the 1st layer of therapy. There should be aggressive application of emollients multiple times a day and every time after the patient gets wet (e.g., showers, baths, sweating, swimming). Moisturizers are less effective if applied to dry skin.

- **Immunomodulatory creams** are the 2nd layer of therapy. Topical corticosteroids or topical calcineurin inhibitors (i.e., pimecrolimus, tacrolimus) should be applied to problem areas of the skin to decrease inflammation. Although topical corticosteroids are the 1st line antiinflammatory agents, they can cause skin atrophy. Use on the face, axilla, and genitalia should be avoided. Topical calcineurin inhibitors do not cause skin atrophy.

- **Antihistamines** are the 3rd layer of therapy. 1st generation antihistamines are more effective than the later generations; however, they have some degree of sedation. This can be useful for patients who are unable to sleep because they are constantly scratching their skin at night. It is important to break the scratch-itch-scratch cycle. Avoidance of common irritant triggers such as harsh soaps, detergents, wool, and chemicals is recommended.

Oral corticosteroids should only be used for temporary control of an acute flare. They should not be used for chronic control because cessation can lead to rebound disease. **Antibiotics** are used if the patient shows signs of infection. Treat these infections with topical or oral antibiotics. Most patients with AD are colonized with *Staphylococcus aureus*, and superinfection is fairly common.

Know! For new-onset adult eczema that is recurrent and refractory to conventional therapy, refer the patient to a dermatologist to rule out cutaneous T-cell lymphoma (e.g., mycosis fungoides).

For more information on AD and other types of eczema, see the Dermatology section under Common Skin Problems.

CONTACT DERMATITIS

PREVIEW | REVIEW

- What should you do if you have a patient with a linear itchy rash just below the umbilicus where the belt buckle touches the abdomen?

Poison oak and poison ivy cause contact dermatitis in most individuals (Figure 2-5). Other agents, such as nickel (found in some jewelry), rubber components, perfumes, hair products, and makeup, can cause contact dermatitis in sensitized individuals. Remember: Contact dermatitis often has features of hypersensitivity Types 4a and 4c.

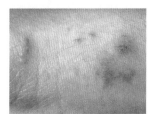

Figure 2-5: Poison ivy contact dermatitis

Order patch testing if the patient has a rash in a pattern that suggests their makeup, hair product, nickel-containing jewelry, or a belt buckle caused the rash. Once the allergen or irritant is identified, recommend avoidance of the offending agent.

For additional information on contact dermatitis, see the Dermatology section under Common Skin Problems.

RHINITIS

PREVIEW | REVIEW

- What are the 1st line therapies for mild vs. moderate-to-severe allergic rhinitis?

- Which class of medication for the treatment of allergic rhinitis is avoided during the 1st trimester of pregnancy?

- What is rhinitis medicamentosa? How is it treated?
- What is atrophic rhinitis? How is it treated?

NOTE

There are 2 broad categories of rhinitis: allergic and nonallergic. The most common type of rhinitis is viral rhinitis, followed by allergic rhinitis.

ALLERGIC RHINITIS

There are 2 main types of **allergic rhinitis**:

1) Seasonal—provoked by seasonally present pollens
2) Perennial (year-round)—provoked by dust mites, molds, or animal dander

Symptoms of allergic rhinitis include congestion, sneezing, rhinorrhea, and nasal itching. Once initiated, patients have nonspecific hypersensitivity to many irritating stimuli. Patients demonstrate sensitization to allergens when tested by skin prick or a serum assay for specific IgE antibodies. See Skin vs. Serum Allergy Testing on page 2-12.

Eosinophils appear on nasal smear only when the patient is symptomatic. Patients with perennial allergic rhinitis can have a high nasal eosinophil count year-round. In patients with a positive allergen testing, a nasal eosinophil count > 3/HPF is very specific but not very sensitive for allergic rhinitis.

Treatment of allergic sinusitis: Intranasal glucocorticoids are the 1st line therapies for mild allergic rhinitis. For moderate-to-severe symptoms or symptoms not controlled with intranasal glucocorticoids alone, use an intranasal antihistamine or a combination of intranasal glucocorticoid plus intranasal antihistamine.

Other drugs include the oral form of the 2nd generation less-sedating antihistamines. Of these 2nd generation antihistamines, fexofenadine and bilastine (not available in the U.S.) do not cross the blood–brain barrier and are completely nonsedating. The other 2nd generation antihistamines (e.g., cetirizine, levocetirizine, loratadine, desloratadine) are somewhat sedating because they partially cross the blood–brain barrier.

The 1st generation antihistamines (e.g., diphenhydramine, chlorpheniramine, hydroxyzine) are generally not used and are never given to older patients. They easily cross the blood–brain barrier and cause sedation, blurry vision, dry mouth, and urinary retention.

Cromolyn sodium is sometimes used for mild symptoms.

Treatment of allergic sinusitis during pregnancy:

- For mild symptoms not controlled by avoidance, cromolyn ophthalmic drops are the treatment of choice.
- For moderate-to-severe symptoms, an intranasal glucocorticoid spray is the treatment of choice; budesonide is preferred.
- If intranasal budesonide is not effective enough, chlorpheniramine is commonly added on. It has a long safety record in pregnant women. If sedation is an issue with chlorpheniramine, use 2nd generation antihistamines—especially loratadine or cetirizine.
- Allergy shots are not started during pregnancy; however, if a woman has already started allergy shots and becomes pregnant, she can continue without dose escalation.
- Avoid oral decongestants in the 1st trimester of pregnancy! They increase the risk of congenital malformations such as gastroschisis and atresia of the small intestine.

NONALLERGIC RHINITIS

There are many nonallergic categories of rhinitis: infectious, vasomotor, noninfectious with eosinophilia, medicamentosa, and atrophic. Unless there is an overlap, patients with nonallergic rhinitis do not demonstrate sensitization to allergen when tested by skin prick or serum assay (i.e., IgE is not involved).

Infectious rhinitis is an acute rhinitis caused by a viral, bacterial, or fungal infection. Viral infections (e.g., common cold, flu) are by far the most common cause of any type of rhinitis. Classic symptoms are self-limited with sneezing and a watery nasal drainage.

Vasomotor rhinitis (a.k.a. idiopathic rhinitis) is the usual noninfectious cause of nonallergic rhinitis. It tends to occur in middle age. It is thought to be neurogenic—a reaction to a specific stimulus. Patients have sneezing attacks, followed by nasal congestion and rhinorrhea when exposed to cold, sunlight, certain foods, or various other stimuli. Treatment is with intranasal glucocorticoids; intranasal anticholinergic sprays are effective when rhinorrhea is the predominant symptom. As with all the other causes of nonallergic rhinitis, these patients do not demonstrate sensitization to allergen when tested by skin prick or a serum assay.

NARES—**n**onallergic **r**hinitis with **e**osinophilia **s**yndrome—is an inflammatory rhinitis that causes year-round symptoms of rhinorrhea, sneezing, and occasionally, loss of smell. NARES is not a Type 1 hypersensitivity reaction. Eosinophils are found in nasal secretions. Negative allergy screening along with a nasal smear showing 5–20 eosinophils/HPF makes NARES likely.

Rhinitis medicamentosa is rebound congestion caused by prolonged use of vasoconstricting nasal drops (i.e., phenylephrine, oxymetazoline). A beefy, red nasal mucosa is the diagnostic finding in the setting of persistent nasal congestion and continued use of an α-adrenergic nasal spray. Treat by stopping use of adrenergic nasal sprays. Use intranasal glucocorticoids when necessary to help with recovery.

Atrophic rhinitis is characterized by atrophy of the nasal mucosa, crusting, dryness, fetor, and loss of smell. Patients are typically younger and from warmer climates. Some are colonized with *Klebsiella ozaenae*. Secondary causes include excessive nasal/sinus surgeries, granulomatous disease, and exposure to radiation. Treat atrophic rhinitis with nasal saline lavage.

Other causes of chronic nasal congestion rhinitis include:

- Deviated septum
- Foreign body—typically unilateral and with malodorous discharge
- Tumors
- Drug reactions—especially with propranolol and α-methyldopa

Persistent nasal symptoms may accompany pregnancy, hypothyroidism, or testosterone deficiency (hormonal rhinitis).

RHINOSINUSITIS

PREVIEW | REVIEW

- What are the characteristic symptoms and the duration of acute rhinosinusitis?
- When are antibiotics used to treat acute rhinosinusitis?
- How long must symptoms last before the diagnosis of chronic rhinosinusitis (CRS) can be made?
- How is CRS treated?

The term "rhinosinusitis" is now used instead of sinusitis because inflammation of the sinuses is almost always accompanied by inflammation of the nasal mucosa. **Acute rhinosinusitis** is defined as rhinorrhea, nasal congestion, facial pain, and sinus tenderness lasting < 4 weeks. Diagnosis is made clinically. Do not order a sinus CT or other imaging for uncomplicated acute rhinosinusitis. Sinus CT or x-rays cannot distinguish between bacterial and viral infections. The vast majority of cases are caused by viral infections, which do not require antibiotics.

Initially treat acute rhinosinusitis symptomatically with NSAIDs or acetaminophen for pain, nasal saline washes, and intranasal glucocorticoids.

Give antibiotics only in the following scenarios:

- Severe initial symptoms with high fever (> 102.0°F [38.9°C]), purulent nasal discharge, and facial pain
- Worsening symptoms after initial improvement (a.k.a. "double sickening")
- Persistent symptoms with no improvement after 7–10 days

The 1st line treatment is amoxicillin + clavulanic acid. Use doxycycline for penicillin allergy.

Remember: Recurrent episodes of acute sinusitis, may indicate a selective IgA deficiency. Check an IgA level in these patients.

Chronic rhinosinusitis (CRS) occurs when symptoms last > 12 weeks. It can occur with or without nasal polyps and can have eosinophils, neutrophils, or both in the nasal mucosa. Depending on the H&P, workup can include evaluation for allergens, immunodeficiency, cystic fibrosis, sinus CT, and referral to an ENT specialist for possible surgery in recalcitrant cases.

CRS diagnosis requires all the following history and findings:

- Duration of disease for > 12 weeks
- Presence of 2 of the following (MOPS):
  - **M**ucopurulent discharge
  - **O**bstruction/Congestion
  - **P**ain over paranasal sinus areas of face
  - Loss of **s**mell
- Evidence of sinusitis on CT scan or evidence of mucopurulent discharge from ostiomeatal complex (visualized by rhinoscope) in posterior area of nasal cavity

Manage CRS by restoring ostiomeatal patency/drainage of sinuses with topical glucocorticoids and nasal saline lavage.

Know! Do not obtain sinus x-rays. They are not helpful in the workup of acute rhinosinusitis or CRS.

ASTHMA

Asthma is an important disease in the Allergy & Immunology subspecialty. However, for the sake of concision, asthma is extensively covered solely in the Pulmonary Medicine section under Obstructive Lung Diseases.

DRUG HYPERSENSITIVITY REACTIONS

PREVIEW | REVIEW

- When is drug desensitization indicated? Give 2 examples of when penicillin desensitization is required.
- What is DRESS syndrome? Name a few drugs that commonly cause this reaction.
- What is the difference between Stevens-Johnson syndrome and toxic epidermal necrolysis?

OVERVIEW

Here we talk about drug hypersensitivity reactions. Remember that these are quite different from drug side effects, listed on the drug information sheet, and from the effects of a drug overdose. The timing and type of reaction provide clues as to which type of drug reaction is occurring. If a drug is given intravenously and an immediate reaction with urticaria develops within minutes to an hour, a Type 1 immediate IgE-mediated reaction has most likely occurred.

If a reaction is delayed up to 24–72 hours, a Type 4 delayed hypersensitivity reaction is likely. An exanthematous (maculopapular or morbilliform) eruption also suggests a delayed hypersensitivity reaction.

More severe skin manifestations include Stevens-Johnson syndrome (SJS), toxic epidermal necrolysis (TEN), and DRESS syndrome. See more on these three manifestations under Stevens-Johnson Syndrome (SJS) and Toxic Epidermal Necrolysis (TEN) on page 2-10 and under DRESS Syndrome. These manifestations usually appear > 72 hours after exposure to the drug. For more details on SJS and TEN, see the Dermatology section under Blistering Lesions.

Besides skin manifestations, other problems can occur, including fever, arthritis, and vasculitis, as well as GI, neurologic, and pulmonary findings. Prior exposure to the drug is necessary for an immunologic reaction to occur.

Laboratory testing is generally not helpful. Peripheral blood eosinophilia is suggestive but not conclusive of a drug allergy. Penicillin (PCN) skin testing is helpful if you suspect an IgE-mediated mechanism (i.e., Type 1 hypersensitivity reaction).

Also see Immunologic Hypersensitivity Reactions on page 2-1.

β-LACTAM ANTIBIOTICS

β-lactam antibiotics are the most common cause of drug allergy, and penicillin (PCN) is by far the most common of these. Despite this, PCN allergy is exceedingly overdiagnosed. ~ 5–10% of patients report a history of PCN allergy. However, 80–95% of patients with a reported PCN allergy are found not to be allergic, leaving us with an actual prevalence between 0.25% and 2%.

Confirm PCN allergy with skin testing; a negative skin test has a negative predictive value of > 95% and thus makes a future anaphylactic reaction to PCN very unlikely. For those who are confirmed PCN allergic by skin testing and require treatment with PCN, desensitization is available. See Drug Desensitization for more information.

PCN itself does not cause an allergic reaction. It is the degradation products when linked to self-proteins (i.e., when tissue-bound) that are allergenic. The major determinant used in skin testing reagents is penicilloyl-polylysine. ~ 75% of those with a PCN allergy react to this reagent.

Other skin testing reagents, to which fewer people react, are called minor determinants. These are:

- Benzylpenicillin (penicillin G)
- Penicilloate
- Penilloate

One study suggests that those who react to minor determinants are more likely to have more severe reactions. It is ideal to include both the major and minor determinants when testing for PCN allergy. Unfortunately, in the U.S., only penicillin G is available.

A negative allergy test does not rule out an allergic reaction to PCN because it is only about 75% sensitive. Remember: All allergy skin testing (PCN testing included) checks only for IgE-mediated reactions (i.e., Type 1 only; not Types 2, 3, and 4).

Like PCN allergy, PCN cross-reactivity also appears to be overdiagnosed. In the past, PCN was thought to cross-react with cephalosporins at a rate of as much as 20%. However, data shows that cross-reactivity between PCN and 3rd generation cephalosporins is extremely low (< 2%). Cross-reactivity between PCN and 1st and 2nd generation cephalosporins may be higher as cross-reactivity involves similarities of side chains. Cross-reactivity between β-lactams and carbapenems is very low. Aztreonam does not cross-react with other β-lactams except for ceftazidime. (They both share a common R-group side chain.)

To treat any drug allergy, stop the drug. For anaphylaxis, give epinephrine without delay and ensure that the patient is in a recumbent position until recovered and asymptomatic. See Treatment on page 2-2 for more information.

DRUG DESENSITIZATION

Adhering to a drug desensitization protocol in the appropriate situation allows for a temporary state of tolerance to the drug, as long as the person continues to take the specific drug.

Desensitization can be done for any patient with a Type 1 IgE-mediated hypersensitivity reaction to a medication. It is effective in this group for those with immediate or late-phase reactions. Common antibiotics that can cause this reaction are the β-lactams, quinolones, and clindamycin.

Know! Desensitization is necessary if the drug is the only known clinically effective therapy or all other effective treatments are unavailable.

Desensitization is contraindicated for serious non-IgE-mediated reactions such as SJS, TEN, or DRESS syndrome.

A typical desensitization procedure (e.g., for PCN allergy) starts with very tiny oral or IV doses of ~ 1/10,000 of the full therapeutic dose—with increased dosage every 15 minutes. After 4–8 hours, a full dose is reached, and a temporary tolerance to the drug is achieved. The patient can then be given the full course of the antibiotic. This tolerance is rapidly lost once the drug is stopped, so the procedure must be repeated if the drug is ever given again.

Generally, oral doses are the preferred method; however, even with oral doses, the patient must be in a monitored setting where treatment for anaphylaxis (injectable epinephrine and other drugs) is available at the bedside.

Scenarios where drug desensitization is required:

- A pregnant woman with syphilis who has a PCN allergy
- A patient with neurosyphilis who has a PCN allergy

Both cases require desensitization because PCN is the only known effective therapy. After desensitization, give PCN for the duration of therapy. Again, if PCN is required in the future, desensitization therapy must be repeated.

DRESS SYNDROME

DRESS stands for drug rash with eosinophilia and systemic symptoms. DRESS syndrome is a Type 4b (i.e., with eosinophils) hypersensitivity reaction. Patients typically develop a polymorphic drug rash, peripheral eosinophilia, and systemic symptoms—which include fever, lymphadenopathy, and multiorgan involvement (e.g., liver, kidney, heart). It commonly occurs 2–8 weeks after exposure to the offending drug, usually aromatic antiseizure medications, minocycline, and allopurinol. Reactivation of human herpesvirus 6 and other viruses has been implicated.

Treat DRESS by stopping the offending drug. (Symptoms may initially worsen or persist.) Treatment is with glucocorticoids and IVIG. The disease may be progressive even after discontinuation of the offending agent. When there is organ involvement, such as cardiac myopathy, corticosteroids must be weaned with extreme caution. These patients are at risk for cardiac failure and should be managed by clinicians experienced with DRESS syndrome.

STEVENS-JOHNSON SYNDROME (SJS) AND TOXIC EPIDERMAL NECROLYSIS (TEN)

SJS and TEN are part of a single disease spectrum. It is a Type 4c (i.e., with cytotoxic CD8+ T cells) hypersensitivity reaction. There is severe sloughing of the skin, equivalent to a 3rd degree burn! Mucosal involvement of the eyes, mouth, and lips almost always occurs (Figure 2-6). Nikolsky sign is positive and refers to the removal of the epidermis with slight tangential pressure.

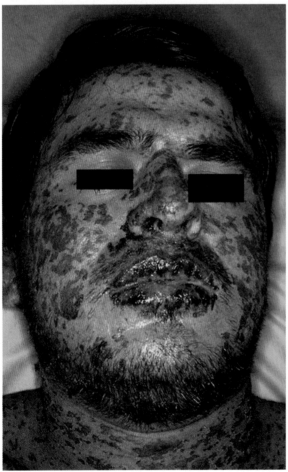

Figure 2-6: Stevens-Johnson syndrome

Diagnosis depends on the extent of epidermal detachment according to body surface area (BSA):

- SJS (< 10% BSA)
- Overlap syndrome (10–30% BSA)
- TEN (> 30% BSA)

Treat SJS and TEN with supportive care in a burn unit. Of course, stop the offending drug. IVIG may be beneficial. Glucocorticoids are contraindicated in TEN; use of glucocorticoids in SJS is controversial. Mortality is high.

For more information on SJS and TEN, see the Dermatology section under Blistering Lesions.

RADIOCONTRAST MEDIA (RCM) REACTIONS

RCM reactions are almost always nonimmunologic reactions to parenteral iodine or gadolinium contrast media. These reactions are caused by the direct interaction of contrast with mast cells; i.e., they are not immunoglobulin-mediated or cell-mediated. Incidence of this reaction has decreased recently with the use of nonionic and hypoosmolar contrast media. Symptoms are usually mild; however, they can be severe. Symptoms range from flushing, hives, and laryngeal edema to angioedema and outright anaphylaxis. Onset of symptoms can occur quickly—within 1 hour—or be delayed for days.

Immediate, severe symptoms are indistinguishable from those of an IgE-mediated anaphylactic reaction and are termed nonimmunologic anaphylaxis. For more on this recent change in terminology, see Anaphylaxis on page 2-1. Rather than an IgE mediation of effects, this nonimmunologic anaphylactic reaction is caused by the media directly activating mast cells, basophils, or both. The resulting release of mediators such as histamine and tryptase cause the severe clinical reaction. Rarely, RCM causes an IgE-mediated immediate allergic response.

Know that RCM reactions are not associated with seafood or iodine allergies. Risk factors for RCM reactions include female gender, asthma, and prior reaction to RCM. Use of β-blockers or underlying cardiovascular disease increases the risk for more serious RCM reactions.

Decrease the likelihood of RCM reactions by giving nonionic or hypoosmolar radiocontrast and pretreat with the following regimen:

- Prednisone (50 mg): 13, 7, and 1 hour prior to procedure
- Diphenhydramine (50 mg): 1 hour prior to procedure

The nonimmunologic anaphylaxis category includes all those previously termed "anaphylactoid" in which the medication or substance itself directly triggers the release of histamine and tryptase from mast cells. Other causes of nonimmunologic anaphylaxis are vancomycin (vancomycin flushing syndrome) and opioids (especially codeine and meperidine). For a dermatologic discussion of radiocontrast media cutaneous drug reaction, see the Dermatology section under Cutaneous Drug Reactions.

VANCOMYCIN HYPERSENSITIVITY

Vancomycin flushing syndrome (VFS) is the most common vancomycin hypersensitivity reaction and is caused by nonimmunologic, direct mast cell degranulation (release of histamine from mast cells). Treat by decreasing the infusion rate, not by decreasing the dose.

Although vancomycin can also cause an IgE-mediated immediate hypersensitivity reaction, this is rare.

STINGING-INSECT ALLERGY

PREVIEW | REVIEW

- What type of hypersensitivity reactions are stinging-insect allergies?
- True or false? A large local reaction to a sting represents an allergic reaction?

Stings from the order Hymenoptera (e.g., bees, wasps, yellow jackets, hornets, fire ants) are the most common cause of insect allergy. These allergic reactions are a Type 1 IgE-mediated immediate hypersensitivity reaction.

A large local reaction to a sting or bite is not an allergic reaction and needs no workup. Even generalized hives do not increase the risk of anaphylaxis and need no workup. Of course, anaphylaxis itself does require workup with allergy skin tests and serum allergy tests. Identifying the correct stinging insect by history is notoriously unreliable.

Give venom immunotherapy (venom allergy shots) to patients with anaphylaxis with confirmed positive insect allergy tests. This treatment has a success rate of 98%! Prescribe an epinephrine autoinjector and recommend insect avoidance.

FOOD ALLERGY

PREVIEW | REVIEW

- What type of hypersensitivity reactions are food allergies?

The prevalence of food allergies is ~ 4% in the adult population. The most common food allergens are peanuts, tree nuts, fish, shellfish, and soy. Food allergies are a Type 1 IgE-mediated immediate hypersensitivity reaction.

Patients need to learn how to avoid the food(s) they are allergic to. Teach patients how to ask the right questions in restaurants and how to read food labels to avoid exposure. Patients with severe food allergies should receive an epinephrine autoinjector and receive training on its proper administration.

LATEX ALLERGY

PREVIEW | REVIEW

- What type of hypersensitivity reaction is a latex allergy?
- Which fruits and vegetables have proteins that are cross-reactive with latex allergens?

Latex is natural rubber tapped from the sap-like fluid of rubber trees. Latex allergy is due to sensitization to highly allergenic proteins—primarily hevein—on the surface of the latex products. This is a true allergic reaction, like those to stinging insects and food, and is a Type 1 IgE-mediated immediate hypersensitivity reaction.

Before latex alternatives were available, latex allergy was a frequent cause of anaphylaxis in patients in hospitals and among health care workers. Now, development of latex allergy is uncommon unless patients have a condition that gives them an increased exposure to latex-containing products (e.g., spina bifida, urologic problems).

The main risk factors for development of latex allergy in patients with spina bifida are the number of surgeries, total serum IgE, presence of a ventriculoperitoneal shunt, and a personal history of atopy. The greatest risk factor for patients (not just those with spina bifida) is multiple surgeries at an early age.

Interestingly, several fruits and vegetables have proteins that are cross-reactive with latex allergens. While these patients can show a high IgE level to multiple fruits, vegetables, and nuts, the main ones that show clinical relevance are **PKB PACT** (peekaboo **PACT**):

- **P**apaya, **k**iwi, **b**anana (fruits)
- **P**otato, **a**vocado, **c**hestnut, **t**omato (vegetables, fruits, and nuts)

Patients with spina bifida have more cross-reactivity to potatoes, and health care workers have more cross-reactivity to kiwis, bananas, and avocados.

Evaluate for latex allergy by inquiring about a history of prior reactions and getting a latex-specific IgE antibody immunoassay. A negative immunoassay essentially rules out latex allergy.

Skin test reagents (for skin prick tests) are not commercially available in the U.S. They are used successfully in many places outside the U.S.

Treat by providing a latex-free environment, which many hospitals and clinics have adopted.

ALLERGY & IMMUNOLOGY

HYPERSENSITIVITY LUNG DISEASE

PREVIEW | REVIEW

- What are the symptoms for acute, subacute, and chronic presentation of hypersensitivity pneumonitis (HP)?
- Why are skin tests not helpful in the diagnosis of HP?
- Allergic bronchopulmonary aspergillosis (ABPA) is seen in which 2 disease processes?
- How are severe exacerbations of ABPA treated?

NOTE

Both hypersensitivity pneumonitis and allergic broncho-pulmonary aspergillosis are discussed in more detail in the Pulmonary Medicine section under Interstitial Lung Diseases (ILDs).

HYPERSENSITIVITY PNEUMONITIS (HP)

HP (a.k.a. extrinsic allergic alveolitis) is a very complex disease with variable presentation that can be caused by many organic agents—as suggested by its many common names, including ventilation pneumonitis, farmer's lung, bird fancier's lung, maltworker's lung, and mushroom worker's lung. Thermophilic *Actinomyces* spp are thought to be the culprit in many instances, especially farmer's lung. HP is initiated by a Type 3 immune complex–mediated hypersensitivity reaction, with an IgG precipitin developing against a specific allergen, and eventually develops a Type 4 cell-mediated hypersensitivity reaction (again, HP = Types 3 and 4).

Presentation of HP:

- **Acute**—Symptoms start within hours of exposure and include chest tightness, dyspnea without wheezing, fever, and chills.
- **Subacute**—gradual onset of cough and dyspnea with fatigue and weight loss
- **Chronic**—insidious onset of cough and dyspnea with fatigue and weight loss

Diagnosis of HP is usually made with a suggestive history, an HRCT of the lung that reflects the presentation, and results of antigen avoidance. Occasionally bronchoalveolar lavage (BAL) or lung biopsy is done. Skin tests are not a helpful diagnostic test. (This is not an IgE-mediated reaction!) HRCT findings encompass:

- Acute—infiltrates with a ground glass pattern of attenuation (may be fleeting)
- Subacute—ground glass infiltrates, centrilobar nodules, darker lobar areas due to decreased attenuation and vascularity
- Chronic—spotty ground glass infiltrates, centrilobular nodules, larger upper lobe decreased attenuation (darker areas) mainly due to air trapping. Eventually HRCT looks more like idiopathic pulmonary fibrosis.

Treatment of HP is mainly allergen avoidance. Consider a trial of glucocorticoids in chronic disease with an inflammatory component (ground glass infiltrates or BAL with > 20% lymphocytosis).

ALLERGIC BRONCHOPULMONARY ASPERGILLOSIS (ABPA)

ABPA is almost exclusively limited to patients with asthma (prevalence 1–2%) or cystic fibrosis (prevalence 2–9%). There are 3 hypersensitivity reactions involved in the reaction of atopic individuals to aspergillus: Type 1 IgE-mediated, a Type 3 immune complex–mediated (with IgG), and Type 4 cell-mediated (again, ABPA = Types 1, 3, and 4).

ABPA manifests as asthma symptoms with recurrent, sometimes severe exacerbations. Early symptoms are mild fever, wheezing, dyspnea, and coughing up sputum with brownish flecks. With severe exacerbations, the patient can have fever, bronchial plugging, dyspnea, hemoptysis, and coughing with expectoration of the brownish bronchial plugs.

Treatment for severe exacerbations includes glucocorticoids and antifungal therapy with itraconazole or voriconazole. A typical dosing regimen with prednisone is 0.5 mg/kg/day for 2 weeks followed by gradual tapering over 4–6 weeks.

Immunotherapy treatments such as allergy injections do not work with ABPA; they actually worsen it. APBA involves multiple types of hyperreactivity to multiple proteins of *Aspergillus fumigatus*, and can also involve IgE to other related allergens—so specific immunotherapy cannot hit all the targets.

SKIN vs. SERUM ALLERGY TESTING

PREVIEW | REVIEW

- What are the benefits of skin testing?
- When is serum antigen-specific IgE testing indicated?

Skin testing is quicker and has a slightly better negative predictive value (NPV) than serum-specific IgE testing. When testing for **food allergens**, both serum and skin tests have only 50–60% positive predictive value (PPV). A positive test only demonstrates sensitization to a particular allergen and does not guarantee clinical reactivity. Only order food allergy testing when there is a compatible history of food allergy.

For the serum specific IgE test, scoring is done with either a radioallergosorbent assay or the newer fluorescent enzyme immunoassay, which uses the College of American Pathologists scoring scheme. There are cut-off levels that have a high PPV for a limited number of foods (Table 2-2).

Table 2-2: Serum-Specific IgE Cut-Off Levels		
Food	IgE Concentration (kU/L)	PPV
Egg	7	95%
Milk	15	95%
Peanut	14	100%
Codfish	20	100%
Soy	30	73%
Wheat	26	74%

IgE = immunoglobulin E
PPV = positive predictive value

Regarding inhalant allergens, skin testing has high PPV and NPV, especially when combined with positive history of reactions to inhalants. There is less data on accuracy of using antigen-specific serum IgE tests for inhalant allergies. They have good PPV; however, their NPV is not as good as skin testing.

Serum testing is often done in lieu of skin testing for both food and inhalant allergens when there is:

- Extensive skin disease
- Dermatographism
- Anaphylactic sensitivity to the allergen
- Ongoing antihistamine use that cannot be withheld for 1–2 weeks (Antihistamines depress the skin test response.)

Remember: Positive results on both allergy skin testing and a serum allergy testing only suggest sensitivity to a potential allergen; a negative test is strong evidence against allergy to that substance.

VACCINES

INFLUENZA VACCINE AND EGG ALLERGY

PREVIEW | REVIEW

- What should be done if your patient needs the influenza vaccine but gets hives with egg ingestion?

Large trials have proven that even confirmed egg-allergic patients can safely receive the injectable inactivated influenza vaccine as a single dose. The recommendation is the same for those with an egg allergy and for everybody else. The previously recommended staggered dosing of 10% then 90% is no longer done; nor is vaccine skin testing; nor is the 30-minute postvaccination observation period.

IMMUNODEFICIENCY AND LIVE VACCINES

PREVIEW | REVIEW

- Know when live vaccines are contraindicated.

Live viral vaccines include the following:

- Rotavirus
- Measles, mumps, rubella (MMR)
- Live attenuated influenza vaccine (LAIV)
- Varicella
- Zoster
- Yellow fever (YF)
- Smallpox
- Oral polio vaccine (OPV)
- Live oral typhoid vaccine (LOTV)
- Bacille Calmette-Guérin (BCG; a.k.a. Calmette-Guérin bacillus)

Live vaccines are contraindicated in the following conditions:

- HIV—CD4 < 200 cells/μL (0.20 × 10⁹/L)—all live vaccines
- B-cell deficiency—all live vaccines
- T-cell deficiency—all live vaccines
- Complement deficiency—no vaccine contraindications
- Phagocyte dysfunction—LOTV and BCG (the live bacterial vaccines), LAIV, OPV, YF, MMR
- Chemotherapy or high doses of immunosuppressive therapy—all live vaccines
- Chronic glucocorticoid use (i.e., prednisone > 20 mg/day)

PREGNANCY AND VACCINES

PREVIEW | REVIEW

- Which vaccines are contraindicated in pregnancy? Which should be given?

Vaccines should be given before conception when possible. When administered during pregnancy, vaccine benefit to the mother and fetus should outweigh any risk. Most toxoid, inactivated vaccines are safe, while live virus vaccines may be harmful and are contraindicated.

Know the following vaccines that are recommended and contradicted in pregnancy:

- Vaccines recommended in pregnancy: Tdap (tetanus, diphtheria, and acellular pertussis); inactivated influenza vaccine—give with each pregnancy
- Vaccines contraindicated in pregnancy: All live attenuated vaccines including varicella, MMR, zoster live virus vaccine, intranasal live influenza vaccine, rotavirus, and yellow fever. Note that

recombinant zoster vaccine (an inactivated vaccine) has replaced zoster live vaccine, but because sufficient testing has not been done, the CDC recommends that pregnant patients who have had shingles wait until after pregnancy and breastfeeding to take the vaccine.

For more information about vaccines and pregnancy, see the Women's and Men's Health section under Obstetrics.

IMMUNOGLOBULIN THERAPY AND LIVE VACCINES

PREVIEW | REVIEW
- How long should you wait to give the measles, mumps, and rubella vaccine after your patient has received a transfusion of packed red blood cells?

Only 2 vaccines have been shown to have a significant interaction with immunoglobulin (IG) products:

1) Measles-containing vaccines (MMR and MMRV)

2) Varicella-containing vaccines (varicella and MMRV)

The following are the recommended intervals between administering measles or varicella vaccine and IG-containing products:

- IVIG—8–11 months, depending on dose
- Whole blood—7 months
- Plasma, platelets, packed red blood cells (PRBCs)—6 months
- Measles IG—6 months
- Varicella IG—5 months
- Rabies IG—4 months
- Tetanus, hepatitis A, and hepatitis B IGs—3 months

THE IMMUNE SYSTEM

THE INNATE IMMUNE SYSTEM

PREVIEW | REVIEW
- What is the 1st line of defense of the immune system?
- Which part of the immune system is rapid and nonspecific?

The innate immune system is the 2nd line of defense against pathogens after the skin, which is the 1st line of defense.

Characteristics of the innate immune system include:

- Rapid acting
- Nonspecific
- No memory

Components of the innate immune system include:

- Complement
- Macrophages
- Natural killer (NK) cells

THE ADAPTIVE IMMUNE SYSTEM

PREVIEW | REVIEW
- Which part of the immune system is slow and specific?

The adaptive immune system is the 3rd line of defense against pathogens and is activated by the innate immune system. Unlike the innate immune system, the adaptive system is much slower to get started, is very specific, and has memory.

The adaptive immune system can be broken down into 2 main components:

1) **Humoral**—B cells, plasma cells, and immunoglobulins (IGs). Activated B cells become plasma cells, which make IG.

2) **Cell-mediated**—T cells

INNATE vs. ADAPTIVE IMMUNITY

PREVIEW | REVIEW
- How is cellular messaging used oppositely in innate and adaptive immunity?
- How do innate and adaptive immune systems overlap?

OVERVIEW

The innate immune system is the foundation on which the more sophisticated adaptive immune system sits. The innate system not only protects the body while the adaptive system gears up, it also helps direct the response. The innate immune system, in general, needs messages to prevent it from killing pathogens; the adaptive immune system needs messages, usually from the innate immune system, to allow it to kill pathogens.

The key difference between the 2 systems can be found in their receptors:

- **Innate** immune system receptors are generic, ready-made receptors (e.g., Toll-like receptors). These receptors allow a quick but nonspecific response—one that is rapid but does not recognize distinct pathogens. Think of these as "first responders" to a new attack. The cells that carry out most innate immune functions are myeloid cells.
- **Adaptive** immune system receptors are custom-made receptors (T-cell receptors [TCRs] and IGs) that are refined to be as specific as possible for the pathogen. They provide the immune system with the ability to recognize a seemingly infinite variety of pathogens.

Once these custom-made receptors have served their purpose, the body keeps a few of them around in case it needs them again in the future, enabling a quicker reaction based on memory. The cells that carry out most adaptive immune functions are lymphoid cells.

Summary: The innate immune system provides a quick, generic response, while the adaptive provides a slower—but more powerful and specific—response to the foreign pathogen. Thanks to immunologic memory, if the pathogen is encountered again in the future, the adaptive system can mount a quicker and more robust response.

INNATE AND ADAPTIVE OVERLAP

There is significant overlap between the innate and adaptive immune systems:

- The classical pathway of the innate complement system requires C1 to bind to an immune (antibody-antigen) complex formed by the adaptive immune system to initiate its activity.
- C3b, made by all pathways of the innate complement system and continuously generated by the alternative pathway, opsonizes pathogens and immune complexes—coating and tagging them for phagocytosis. Phagocytes like macrophages and dendritic cells are also professional antigen-presenting cells (APCs) and present these antigens to the helper T cells (T_H cells), which in turn initiate or accelerate the adaptive immune response of B cells. (Whew!)
- Macrophages and NK cells initially function as part of the innate system; when they become further activated by T cells, they can subsequently act as part of the adaptive immune system.

INNATE-LIKE CELLS

There are cells that are part of the adaptive immune system but are innate-like. They show overlap because they are more rapid-acting and less specific than the other lymphocytes. Examples of innate-like immune cells are:

- γδ T cells
- Natural killer T (NKT) cells
- B-1 cells (an innate-like version of B cells)

CELLS OF THE IMMUNE SYSTEM

PREVIEW | REVIEW
- What are the major cell types in the immune system?

There are 2 major cell types in the immune system:

1) **Lymphoid cells**
   - Lymphocytes
     ◦ T cells
       – αβ T cells
       – CD4+ helper T cells (T_H cells)
       – CD8+ cytotoxic T cells (T_C cells)
       – γδ T cells (innate-like)
       – Natural killer T cells (NKT cells; innate-like)
     ◦ B cells
       – B-1 cells (innate-like, found mainly in peritoneal and pleural cavities)
       – B-2 cells (a.k.a. conventional B cells; the workhorses of the immune system that produce all IGs)
       – Marginal B cells (innate-like, found mainly in the spleen)
   - Natural killer cells (NK cells; do not confuse with the similarly named T cells!)
2) **Myeloid cells**
   - Granulocytes
     ◦ Neutrophils
     ◦ Eosinophils
     ◦ Basophils
   - Professional antigen-presenting cells (APCs)
     ◦ Monocytes/Macrophages
     ◦ Dendritic cells
     ◦ B cells are APCs that are not myeloid
   - Other
     ◦ Mast cells
     ◦ Erythrocytes
     ◦ Megakaryocytes/Platelets

HUMAN LEUKOCYTE ANTIGENS (HLAs)

PREVIEW | REVIEW
- What are Class I human leukocyte antigens (HLAs)? What type of cells do they appear on?
- What are Class II HLAs? What type of cells do they appear on?
- What is major histocompatibility complex restriction?

The HLA complex is a group of genes that code for unique proteins, specific for that individual, that are expressed on cell surfaces. The immune system uses a class of these proteins (Class I) to determine if the cell is self (okay) or nonself (not okay—terminate!). It uses another class, Class II, to make sure that a cell presenting foreign antigen is a professional antigen-presenting cell (APC). Many species have this system, and it is identified as the major histocompatibility complex; HLA complex is the same system in humans. The HLA gene complex is located on the short arm of chromosome 6. There are 3 classes of HLA. In the following, remember only the **class**—not any of the subclasses.

Class I HLAs (HLA-A, -B, and -C) are expressed on all nucleated cells and are used to determine if the cell is self or nonself. The Class I HLA protein on these cells complex with and present foreign antigens to the cytotoxic CD8+ (killer) T cells. Class I HLAs play a major role in transplant rejection, neoplasms, and viral infections.

In contrast to these "generalist" APCs, there are other specialized cell types that present antigen as a main function. These are called professional APCs.

Class II HLAs (HLA-DP, -DQ, and -DR) are expressed on the surface of the professional APCs, which include monocytes/macrophages, dendritic cells (including Langerhans cells), and B cells. The expressed Class II HLAs complex with foreign antigens and present them to CD4+ T_H cells. Class II HLAs mediate the reactions among macrophages, T cells, and B cells.

Class III HLAs code for peptides involved with inflammation such as tumor necrosis factor (TNF), heat shock proteins, and certain complement proteins.

T cells can recognize antigens only if the antigen is complexed with the proper HLA protein. HLA I presents antigen to CD8+ T cells, and HLA II presents antigen to CD4+ T cells (mnemonic: $8 \times 1 = 8$ and $4 \times 2 = 8$). This is the key concept of MHC restriction.

LYMPHOID CELLS

PREVIEW | REVIEW
- What are the functions of T cells?
- Which antigens do CD4+ T_H cells recognize? CD8+ T cells?
- What is the important distinction between the way natural killer cells and natural killer T cells kill other cells?
- Which immunoglobulins are present on the surface of mature B cells?

LYMPHOCYTES

T Cells

Clusters of differentiation (CD) markers are like "ID tags" that can be identified by monoclonal antibodies in labs. They are useful in immunophenotyping lymphocytes, which allows us to differentiate one immune cell from another. For example:

- CD45+: all nucleated hematopoietic cells and their precursors (i.e., granulocytes, monocytes, lymphocytes)
- CD3+: T_H cells and T_C cells
- CD4+: T_H cells and natural killer T cells
- CD8+: T_C cells and suppressor T cells
- CD19+ and CD20+: mature B cells
- CD16+ and CD56+: natural killer cells

ILs are the "language of the immune system" and allow immune cells to communicate with one another. For example:

- Secretion of IL-17 causes an inflammatory response.
- Secretion of IL-4, IL-5, and IL-13 causes an allergic response.
- Secretion of IL-10 causes immune suppression.

Functions of T cells:

- Destroy intracellular and other bacteria (especially gram-negatives), viruses, fungi, parasites, and mycobacteria
- Regulate IG production by B cells
- Activate other immune cells, such as macrophages, by secreting cytokines

All T cells have T-cell receptors (TCRs), which are antigen-specific binding sites composed of 2 subunits (the majority being α and β, and a minority being the innate-like γ and δ). The TCR is always complexed with CD3, which allows intracellular signaling.

Again: CD4 cells recognize antigen only if it is presented along with a Class II HLA molecule. CD8+ T cells recognize an antigen only if it is presented with a Class I HLA, whereas CD4+ T cells recognize an antigen only if it is presented with a Class II HLA. This is the key concept of MHC restriction.

CD4+ T Cells

CD4+ T_H cells are the primary defense against extracellular threats. They are divided into several subsets:

- T_H activates macrophages and CD8+ T_C cells, leading to a cell-mediated immune reaction.
- T_H2 activates mature B cells to produce antibody, resulting in a humoral immune reaction.
- T_H17 induces local inflammation by secreting IL-17 which stimulates local tissue cells to express chemokines and attract inflammatory cells.

Again: T_H cells are activated only by antigen presented in association with Class II HLAs, which only appear on professional APCs such as B cells, monocytes/macrophages, and dendritic cells (including Langerhans cells).

How are CD4+ T cells activated? An APC, such as a macrophage, ingests an extracellular foreign pathogen. This foreign particle is ingested, processed, and presented along with the Class II HLA to CD4+ T_H cells. These T cells, after being activated, induce B cells to convert to plasma cells and produce specific antibodies against that foreign particle.

How does HIV affect the immune system? HIV targets all CD4+ cells, including CD4+ T_H cells, macrophages, monocytes, and microglial cells. By targeting and attacking CD4+ cells, HIV severely weakens the immune system, allowing opportunistic infections to occur.

CD8+ T Cells

The CD8+ cells are T_C cells and are important in the defense against intracellular threats such as viruses and neoplastic cells. When a cell is infected by a virus or becomes neoplastic, these viral or neoplastic antigens are processed by the infected cell and presented on its surface in combination with Class I HLAs. This marks the cell for destruction by the T_C cells. All nucleated cells have Class I HLAs, so most cell types can present antigen to CD8+ T cells!

Regulatory T Cells

Regulatory T cells are a specialized subpopulation of T cells that modulate the activity of the immune system. The expression of the transcription factor FOXP3 controls the development and function of Treg cells. These cells secrete immunosuppressive cytokines such as IL-10 and transforming growth factor β (TGF-β). Treg cells can down-regulate both Th1 and Th2 responses, thereby, reducing allergic inflammation and inducing tolerance against self-antigens. Genetic mutations in *FOXP3* cause an overwhelming systemic autoimmunity known as **IPEX** (**i**mmune dysregulation, **p**olyendocrinopathy, **e**nteropathy, **X**-linked).

Natural Killer T Cells

Name alert! Do not confuse natural killer T (NKT) cells with natural killer (NK) cells—the innate lymphoid cells with a very similar name.

NKT cells are so named because they share several features with NK cells such as granzyme production and CD16 and CD56 expression. Unlike NK cells, NKT cells have TCRs and require a signal to kill. They are restricted to a type of MHC-like molecules called CD1, which primarily recognize lipids and glycolipids. This is in contrast to the MHC molecules, which primarily recognize protein antigens.

B Cells

B cells not only produce all the immunoglobulins in the body, they also use these same antibodies as receptors bound to the surface of the B cell. These are called B-cell receptors (BCRs). In a naive, mature B cell (one that has never seen antigen), these receptors are ready to interact with antigen presented by a T_H cell or with an antigen itself. A single B cell has about 100,000 of each class of surface IGs that cover its surface.

Progenitors to B cells develop in the bone marrow and become immature B cells (with surface IgM; IgM only = immature), which then migrate from the bone marrow to the lymph nodes, where they express surface IgD in addition to the surface IgM—and now are naive mature B cells (IgM + IgD = naive mature). These naive, mature B cells wait to become activated by T_H cells presenting an antigen, or by an antigen itself. The activated B cell—now with a B-cell receptor (BCR = activated B cell) whose variable region contains changes due to the antigen DNA—then moves to the germinal center of the lymph node and starts proliferating wildly, while continuously mutating and producing different variable regions to the BCR. Most of the resulting BCRs have low affinity for the antigen and the B cell dies (apoptosis). Occasionally, one will have a receptor with increased affinity for the antigen, and this "high-affinity" BCR+ B cell survives.

When a T_H cell connects to this high-affinity BCR on this mature B cell, it will induce the B cell to transform into:

- a plasma cell that will then produce the antigen-specific IgM antibodies at a rate of thousands per second or
- a memory B cell that will "class-switch" the receptors on its surface (e.g., to IgG, IgA, IgE) but keep the same variable region. It (or its clones) hangs around for years. When a memory B cell meets that same antigen, it will immediately proliferate and differentiate into plasma cells that will produce that new class of antibody.

B cells can be stimulated to convert to plasma cells by activated CD4+ T cells or, if there are sufficiently large quantities, by antigen alone. Plasma cells produce specific antibodies that coat the surface of a particular foreign organism. This coating identifies it as edible to the macrophages (opsonization) and initiates the complement cascade. Specific antibodies can also neutralize bacterial toxins and viruses.

B cells are also APCs and have Class II HLAs on their surfaces, enabling them to present foreign antigens to CD4+ T_H cells. The activated T cells can then induce other B cells to convert to plasma cells and produce antibodies.

NATURAL KILLER CELLS

Name alert! Do not confuse these cells of the innate immune system with NKT cells.

Natural killer (NK) cells are lymphoid cells that play a major role in the immune system response to tumors and viruses. They express CD16 and CD56 but not TCRs or their associated CD3 molecules. This is an important difference between NK and NKT cells!

NK cells are called natural killers because they are always in kill mode. Cells encountered by the NK cells must present themselves appropriately to avoid getting killed. For example, all cells (except mature RBCs) must display Class I HLA-E on their cell surfaces in order to avoid getting killed by NK cells. This is in contrast to T cells and NKT cells that require a signal in order to kill.

NK cells are an important component of the immune system because some viruses have evolved to reduce Class I HLA expression on the host cell, protecting them from recognition and destruction by T cells. It is precisely this absence or reduction of Class I HLA expression that causes the NK cell to kill the infected cell, typically by inducing apoptosis, which would have been missed by the T cells.

MYELOID CELLS

PREVIEW | REVIEW

- Which 3 types of cells are considered professional antigen-presenting cells?

Granulocytes are WBCs with identifiable granules within their cytoplasm.

Neutrophils are also known as polymorphonuclear leukocytes, polys, PMNs, segs (mature), and bands (immature). They have a multilobed nucleus with 3–5 lobes. PMNs phagocytize microorganisms, especially those coated with antibodies. If PMNs are absent, patients get overwhelming pyogenic infections.

Eosinophils are involved in the pathology of allergic reactions and in the immunologic defense against parasites.

Basophils are involved with the late-phase response of IgE-mediated Type 1 hypersensitivity. See Type 1 — IgE-Mediated Immediate Hypersensitivity Reaction on page 2-1.

Professional antigen-presenting cells (APCs) are cells that express Class II HLAs, and, like all nucleated cells, also express HLA I. This is an exclusive group of cells consisting of 3 cell types:

1) **B cells:** the most specific APCs

2) **Monocytes/Macrophages** phagocytose opsonized microorganisms, process and present antigens, and secrete interleukin-1 (IL-1; stimulates T cells).

3) **Dendritic cells** are scavengers; they change conformation (when they ingest a pathogen), travel to a lymph node, and activate lymphocytes.

Note that phagocytic cells consist of neutrophils, monocytes/macrophages, and dendritic cells. The monocytes/macrophages and dendritic cells together form the mononuclear phagocyte system.

Others:

- Mast cells are involved with the early-phase response of IgE-mediated Type 1 hypersensitivity. See Type 1 — IgE-Mediated Immediate Hypersensitivity Reaction on page 2-1.

- Erythrocytes directly participate in the immune complex reaction (bacteria, complement, and antibody) for enhanced phagocytosis; their primary functions are in oxygenation, balancing blood pH balance, and transporting nutrients and electrolytes. More information on RBC function is in the Hematology section under Normal Red Blood Cell (RBC) Function.

- Megakaryocytes/Platelets are recognized for their clotting properties; they also are active participants in immune defense (with recruitment of neutrophils and cytokine signaling in the lysis of microorganisms). Refer to the Hematology section under Hemostasis and Disorders of the Bone Marrow, respectively, for more information on megakaryocyte and platelet functions.

ANTIBODIES

PREVIEW | REVIEW

- Characterize the various immunoglobulins: G, A, M, E, and D.

- Which antibody crosses the placenta?

- Which antibody is produced first during an infection?

All antibodies (a.k.a. immunoglobulins [IGs]) have the same basic structure (Figure 2-7). Each monomer is composed of 2 heavy and 2 light chains that are held together by disulfide bonds. There are 5 immunoglobulin isotypes: G, A, M, E, and D. These isotypes are determined by differences in the structure of the constant regions of the heavy chains. All antibodies have 1 of 2 types of light chains, κ or λ.

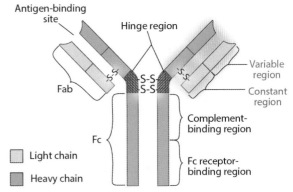

Figure 2-7: Antibody structure

Remember the following key points about immunoglobulins G, A, M, E, and D:

- **IgG** is simplest, smallest, and most abundant IG in the serum. It is the smallest antibody and the only IG that can pass through the placental barrier. ~ 75% of IGs in the serum are IgG. Mechanisms used by IgG to fight pathogens:
  - Immobilize pathogen by mediating their agglutination
  - Opsonize pathogens, making them more susceptible to phagocytosis
  - Activate the classical complement pathway
  - Bind and neutralize bacterial exotoxins and viruses

  A single plasma cell can make IgGs tailored to a specific antigen at a rate of thousands per second! IgG antibodies can cross the placental barrier and provide passive immunity to the fetus (and for the child's first 6 months of life). IgG is involved with Type 2 IgG-mediated cytotoxic hypersensitivity and Type 3 immune complex hypersensitivity reactions.

- **IgA** is the most abundant IG produced in the body. It is produced by surface IgA+ plasma cells and is the main IG in secretions. It is considered the 1st line of defense against pathogens. IgA also is ~ 15% of IG in the serum. It is usually in a dimer configuration (2 IGs) with a J (joining) chain connecting the 2 bases. This dimer configuration automatically attaches to a secretory component, which allows IgA to exit the body via exocrine glands and become part of seromucous secretions. IgA is found in tears, saliva, sweat, and secretions of the sinuses, respiratory tract, digestive tract, and GU tract. It is the main IG secreted in breast milk, and is especially high in colostrum. IgA works with the same mechanisms as IgG, but does not activate complement.

- **IgM** is the 1st immunoglobulin to develop in the fetus, appearing at ~ 20 weeks. IgM is also the 1st surface IG on a developing B cell and the 1st IG released by B cells when converted to plasma cells after the initial encounter with a pathogen. IgM is secreted as a pentamer (5 immunoglobulins) in which each monomer is connected at its base by a J chain. Checking for IgM can be useful in diagnosing a current illness and can help distinguish acute vs. chronic infection. IgM has the same mechanisms as IgG, but it is the most effective IG for complement activation.

- **IgE** is the IG with the lowest concentration in normal serum (0.05% of IGs); however, it is a major factor in many allergic conditions, including asthma, allergic rhinitis, atopic dermatitis, and food allergies. It is also used to fight off parasitic infections. In all these cases, plasma IgE levels can be elevated.

- **IgD** is a surface IG found on B cells and identifies a B cell as mature. It is involved with the formation of B-cell receptors on B cells that are fundamental in their activation. A tiny amount is found in the serum (~ 0.25% of IGs); however, its function in this expressed form is uncertain.

The variability in IG specificity is responsible for the immune system's ability to encounter and then remember an almost limitless number of pathogens. The rearrangement of several regions within the antibody gene makes this possible. Most of the variability is located in the complementarity determining regions, also known as hypervariable regions.

IGs bind specific antigens in the Fab region and then activate either cells or complements (see Complement Cascade), by means of the Fc region, to destroy the antigen-bearing material.

COMPLEMENT CASCADE

PREVIEW | REVIEW

- What is the cause of hereditary angioedema (HAE)?
- What is the clinical presentation of HAE?
- Which infection is most often seen with terminal complement deficiency?
- What does the CH50 assay measure, and when is it used?

OVERVIEW

The 3 Complement Pathways

The complement system (follow along with Figure 2-8) is a group of about 30 known plasma factors important in host defense. It has 3 pathways: classical, lectin, and alternative. Through these different pathways, they ultimately perform the same functions:

- Opsonizing target cells with C3b
- Inducing more inflammation with anaphylatoxins C3a, C4a, and C5a
- Building and activating the C5b–C9 membrane attack complex (MAC)

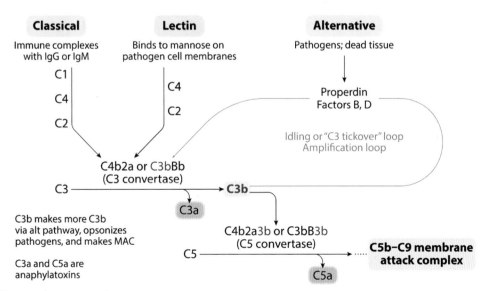

Figure 2-8: The complement cascade

Classical Pathway

IgM and IgG immune complexes (IG + antigen) activate the classical pathway. In this system, we have both the innate (complement) and adaptive (IG) systems working together. The C1 complex is activated when it attaches to the antibody of an immune (Ag-Ab) complex. Activated C1 cleaves many C2s and C4s, subcomponents of which (C4b and C2a) combine and form C4b2a (a C3 convertase). C4b2a, in turn, cleaves many C3s.

One IgM pentamer can initiate the classical pathway; however, it generally takes at least 2 IgGs or even greater quantities of antigen to perform the same initiation process.

Lectin Pathway

Lectins bind mannose on the surface of pathogens. Lectins are also called mannose-binding lectins (MBLs) or mannose (mannan)-binding proteins. These MBL complexes are produced by an acute phase response and are fairly nonspecific. Associated proteases then cleave many C2s and C4s, and subsequent steps are similar to the classical pathway.

Alternative Pathway

The alternative pathway is very nonspecific; however, it acts extremely fast when it is activated by a pathogen or dead tissue to make more C3b to opsonize the pathogen. C3b goes on to stimulate the production of the terminal complement components (C5–C9) which form the membrane attack complex (MAC) on the cell surface of the pathogenic bacteria. C3, the pivotal piece of the complement system, slowly dissociates due to protein factors in the alternative pathway that combine with C3b to make a C3 convertase. The newly produced C3b feeds back into the alternative pathway to repeat the process. This process loop is like an idling motor, and is called C3 tick-over—keeping just enough C3b around to immediately opsonize an invading pathogen.

Common Terminal Pathway — C3b Opsonization

Opsonins coat pathogens and mark them for destruction by the immune system. This is typically carried out by macrophages like the Kupffer cells in the liver. The 2 most important opsonins are IgG of the adaptive immune system and C3b of the innate immune system. So, while the slower and more specific adaptive immune system's IgG takes days to mount an appropriate response, the quicker and less specific C3b fulfills this important role more rapidly.

Membrane Attack Complex (MAC)

C3, when combined with either C4b2a or Factor B, activates C5 and forms the C5-6-7-8-9 MAC. This complex forms transplasma membrane channels on the surface of pathogenic bacteria, causing lysis.

COMPLEMENT DEFICIENCIES

Hereditary Angioedema (HAE)

HAE is an autosomal dominant disorder characterized by recurrent attacks of angioedema caused by a decrease in C1 esterase inhibitor (C1-INH; a.k.a. C1 inhibitor) production or function. While C1-INH is a key inhibitor of the 1st complex in the complement cascade, it is also the principal regulator of bradykinin expression. Lack of C1-INH results in unchecked production of bradykinin, the key mediator in HAE attacks. Patients can have either a decreased C1-INH level (Type I; 85% of HAE patients) or a nonfunctioning C1-INH (Type II; 15% of HAE patients). Anything that causes an increase in kinins/bradykinins unmasks HAE and precipitates angioedema. Drugs such as ACEIs are recognized causes of angioedema due to the accumulation of bradykinin.

Patients have recurrent angioedema with each episode, lasting 1–3 days. Unlike angioedema/urticaria caused by immediate hypersensitivity reactions, hereditary angioedema is not associated with urticaria or itching. Even minor trauma from dental procedures can precipitate attacks! Most patients experience facial swelling, especially lip swelling. The cutaneous symptoms can also affect extremities (Figure 2-9) and genitalia and are rapid in onset. Attacks can include laryngeal swelling with possible stridor and potentially life-threatening obstruction. GI tract attacks are caused by bowel wall swelling and can produce severe abdominal pain, often leading to inappropriate surgeries.

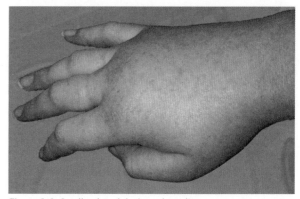

Figure 2-9: Swollen hand during a hereditary angioedema attack

Diagnosis: Screen by checking for low C4 levels. A normal C4 level during an acute episode of angioedema rules out HAE. A C1-INH functional assay provides definitive diagnosis of HAE:

- If the C1-INH level is low, it is **Type I HAE**.
- If the C1-INH level is normal, it is **Type II HAE**.

Treat acute attacks as early as possible with 1 of the following (in order of preference):

- C1-INH (plasma-derived or recombinant)
- Bradykinin receptor antagonist (icatibant; competes for the bradykinin B receptor)
- Kallikrein inhibitor (ecallantide; decreases bradykinin production)

Trigger avoidance is the 1st step to prevent acute attacks. Common triggers are trauma to facial and throat areas, oral and dental infections, and certain medications—especially angiotensin-converting enzyme inhibitors and estrogens. If this is not sufficient, then one of the following is given:

- IV or SQ plasma-derived C1 inhibitor replacement (best overall; best if pregnant or lactating)
- Tranexamic acid (limited effect; often tried first because it is given orally)

Epinephrine, glucocorticoids, and antihistamines are not effective in any HAE therapy.

Acquired Angioedema

Acquired angioedema is clinically similar to HAE, but is defined by low C1-INH (as in HAE) and also a low C1q. Synthesis of complement components in the liver and macrophages are inhibited by myelo- and lymphoproliferative diseases like lymphoma. In addition, autoimmune disease can result in the formation of C1-INH autoantibodies. Both instances result in decreased C1-INH and C1q levels. Again, C1q levels are normal in HAE. Acquired angioedema is found in older patients with underlying disease, and treatment is similar to HAE.

C1, C2, and C4 Deficiencies

C1, C2, or C4 deficiencies cause decreased activation of complement via the classical pathway. C2 deficiency is the most common complement deficiency in White people in North America. Most of the complement proteins are inherited as autosomal recessive genes. Although the alternative pathway takes up some of the slack, these patients are likely to have recurrent sinopulmonary disease due to encapsulated bacteria such as *Streptococcus pneumoniae*, *Haemophilus influenzae* Type b, and *Neisseria meningitidis*. Patients must undergo prophylactic vaccinations against encapsulated organisms. In patients with 1 abnormal gene, serum complement levels are ~ 1/2 normal. In these patients, there is an increased incidence of rheumatoid diseases—especially systemic lupus erythematosus!

C3 Deficiency

C3 deficiency (complete absence of its function) is heritable and results in severe pyogenic (bacterial) infections.

C5–C9 Deficiency

C5–C9 deficiency (a.k.a. terminal complement deficiency) is an autosomal recessive disorder that affects the MAC.

A very rare deficiency of Factor D or properdin in the alternative pathway also decreases the production of terminal complex components and the MAC.

It results in increased *Neisseria* meningococcal/gonococcal infections, especially meningitis or septicemia. Screen for terminal complement deficiency with a CH50 assay. Specific diagnosis is made by assay of these complement components.

CH50 ASSAY

The CH50 (a.k.a. CH100) screening assay measures the total complement activity of the classical pathway. A normal test shows that all factors of the classical pathway (C1–C9) are present. A CH50 is done on meningococcemia patients as a screen for terminal complement deficiency (C5–C9). CH50, C3, and C4 are sometimes used to follow the disease activity of SLE. If the CH50 is very low, check individual complement components (C1–C9 levels) for specific deficiencies. Know that CH50 activity can be normal even when an individual component is 50–80% decreased. For this reason, if the index of suspicion is high for a complement disorder and the CH50 is normal, it may still be necessary to measure individual components.

IMMUNE COMPLEXES (ICs)

PREVIEW | REVIEW
- Name 3 conditions that cause increased levels of immune complexes in the serum.

ICs or antigen-antibody complexes form during normal day-to-day immune surveillance and are then removed from the serum. As they form, complement is usually activated and a C3 component (C3b) attaches to the complex.

The C3b-IC entity is recognized by and attaches to the complement receptor (CR). The main CR1 is found in abundance on RBCs.

ICs are scrubbed off the RBCs by the Kupffer cells in the liver. Remember: Kupffer cells also remove and destroy C3-coated gram-positive and gram-negative bacteria; for more information, see Common Terminal Pathway — C3b Opsonization. If there are any defects in this elimination process, ICs increase in the serum, as in the following conditions:

- **Hepatic vein thrombosis** (a.k.a. Budd-Chiari syndrome) and cirrhosis cause a decreased clearance of ICs.
- **Paroxysmal nocturnal hemoglobinuria** causes decreased binding of ICs; for more information, see the Hematology section under Anemia.
- **SLE** causes a decreased amount of CR1 on RBCs.

Note that each of these disorders causes an increase in ICs in the serum.

Immune complexes activate complement to form C3b, which attaches to the Fc portion of IgG. This maintains the solubility of the complexes in the serum and prevents them from cross-connecting and precipitating. IgA does not activate the classical complement pathway and is therefore more susceptible to precipitation. This causes ICs to deposit in small blood vessels and tissues when high levels build up.

See Type 3 — Immune Complex Hypersensitivity on page 2-3 for more information.

IMMUNODEFICIENCIES

HIGHLIGHTS

PREVIEW | REVIEW
- What are the characteristics and associations of inherited selective deficiency of IgA?

Know the characteristics and associations of the following inherited and acquired immunodeficiencies.

Inherited humoral immune deficiency (deficiency of B-cell differentiation and antibody production):

- Recurrent sinopulmonary infections with encapsulated organisms
- Enteroviral infections
- Giardiasis
- Increased risk of autoimmune disease
- Increased risk of malignancy

Inherited selective deficiency of IgA (the most common type of humoral immunodeficiency):

- Mostly asymptomatic
- Food and respiratory allergies
- False-positive serum pregnancy tests
- Anaphylaxis with blood transfusion and IVIG
- Association with autoimmune diseases

Acquired humoral deficiencies can be seen in patients as a result of splenectomy, leukemias, lymphomas, myeloma, and HIV/AIDS. Infections typically involve encapsulated organisms.

Classical early complement deficiencies may result in sinopulmonary infections with encapsulated organisms. C2 deficiency is also associated with SLE.

Terminal complement deficiencies may result in infections with encapsulated organisms and *Neisseria meningococcus.*

T-cell defects can be seen in patients as a result of HIV/AIDS, after transplantation, or after treatment with glucocorticoids. Resulting infections from T-cell defects typically involve fungi, acid-fast bacteria, viruses, and/or parasites.

Note: The most important thing when thinking of immunodeficiency is to remember that HIV is not the only cause. If you see a patient with severe, recurrent, or atypical infections who does not have HIV, you are not done with your workup. Consider other diagnoses such as common variable immunodeficiency, uncontrolled

diabetes, cystic fibrosis, and 22q11.2 deletion syndrome (a.k.a. DiGeorge syndrome).

Also see Complement Deficiencies on page 2-20.

IMMUNOGLOBULIN (IG) DEFICIENCIES

PREVIEW | REVIEW
- Which immune deficiency has no mature B cells? What are its symptoms?
- What is the most common IG deficiency? How frequently does it occur?
- With what disorders do symptomatic IgA-deficient patients present?
- What is Wiskott-Aldrich syndrome?

NOTE

IG deficiencies can be inherited (e.g., agammaglobulinemia, CVID, IgA deficiency) or acquired (e.g., multiple myeloma, acute lymphoblastic leukemia, chronic lymphocytic leukemia, HIV/AIDS, asplenia).

INHERITED IG DEFICIENCIES

X-linked agammaglobulinemia (XLA) (a.k.a. Bruton agammaglobulinemia, congenital agammaglobulinemia) patients have increased susceptibility to pyogenic and encapsulated organisms (e.g., *Staphylococcus*, *Streptococcus*, meningococcus, *Haemophilus*); hence, they have recurrent sinopulmonary and ear infections. Some may also develop bacteremia with *Ureaplasma*, *Mycoplasma*, *Helicobacter*, *Campylobacter jejuni*, and *Pseudomonas* species. Enteroviral infections with echovirus are suggestive of agammaglobulinemia.

Diagnosis: IG assay shows very low or no IGs. There are also no B cells (i.e., no SmIg+ cells, CD19+ cells).

Prognosis is good if the condition is caught early. Test all the patient's brothers and male cousins on the mother's side.

Treatment: exogenous IVIG or SQIG. Prophylactic antibiotics are required for some patients.

Common variable immunodeficiency (CVID) is the most clinically significant immunodeficiency in adults after HIV, yet it is highly underdiagnosed! CVID is a deficiency of IgG accompanied by deficiencies of IgA and/or IgM. Like XLA, patients have increased susceptibility to encapsulated organisms (e.g., *S. pneumoniae, H. influenzae*). Patients have recurrent sinopulmonary infections and bronchiectasis; they also tend to get giardiasis and enterovirus infections. Multiple pulmonary symptoms are common and are the leading cause of death in patients with CVID. Diarrhea is the most common presenting symptom for related GI disease. Giardiasis and enteritis with *Campylobacter jejuni* and salmonellosis are common enteric infections.

There is an increased incidence of autoimmune disease and malignancy, especially lymphoma.

Diagnosis: IG assay shows low IgG with low IgA and/or low IgM. Unlike XLA, CVID patients have mature B cells present (CD19+).

Treatment: exogenous IVIG or SQIG. Some patients may require prophylactic antibiotics. Monitor for signs of disease-associated autoimmune complications and malignancy.

Selective IgA deficiency is the most common IG deficiency, with an incidence as high as 1/300! Fortunately, ~ 2/3 of patients are asymptomatic. The ~ 1/3 of patients with symptoms present with 1 or more of the following:

- Autoimmune disorders (e.g., rheumatoid arthritis, lupus, celiac disease, chronic autoimmune thyroiditis)
- Allergies
- Recurrent sinopulmonary infections (e.g., rhinosinusitis, pneumonia; often caused by encapsulated organisms [e.g., *S. pneumoniae*, *H. influenzae*])
- GI infections—especially giardiasis
- Celiac disease

Know these 4 important facts about selective IgA deficiency:

1) Women can have false-positive serum pregnancy tests. (Urine pregnancy test is normal.)

2) In patients with celiac disease, IgA deficiency can cause false negative results in the 2 standard serologic tests for celiac disease—tissue transglutaminase (TTG) IgA antibody and antiendomysial IgA antibody. Thus, it is essential to also order a total serum IgA level at the same time either of these markers is checked. If the patient is IgA deficient, check for IgG TTG antibody.

3) Blood transfusion is associated with a higher-than-normal risk of anaphylaxis and should be avoided if possible. These patients have anti-IgA antibodies, and transfused blood contains small amounts of IgA. For more on anaphylactic reactions to transfused blood, see the Hematology section under Hemostasis.

4) IVIG and plasma infusions are contraindicated for the same reason as blood transfusion.

Treat patients who have recurrent infections with prophylactic antibiotics.

Wiskott-Aldrich syndrome (WAS) presents with low IgM and IgG, elevated IgA, and elevated IgE. The triad of findings is **e**czema, **i**mmunodeficiency, and **t**hrombocytopenia. Remembering that it is **X**-linked makes for a helpful mnemonic: "Wisk" through the **EXIT**. Leukemia and B-cell lymphoma (associated with Epstein-Barr virus) are malignancies found in young males with WAS. Infection with bacteria having polysaccharide capsules (e.g., *Streptococcus pneumoniae*) is dangerous in patients with WAS. Bone marrow transplantation may be a successful cure.

ACQUIRED IG DEFICIENCIES

Acquired IG deficiencies secondary to malignancy, collagen vascular disease, and chemotherapy, such as rituximab, are common clinical scenarios for the general internist. Infections arise because either effective antibodies are not produced, or B and T lymphocytes are not communicating effectively with one another. Most of these diseases are associated with hypogammaglobulinemia (reduction in levels of specific IgA, IgM, and IgG) but with a relative polyclonal increase in the gammaglobulin fraction. That is, patients produce an excess of fairly useless antibodies not specific for an antigen, are usually ineffective, and may cross-react with normal body components such as RBCs and platelet surface receptors.

Patients with acquired humoral deficiencies are predisposed to infections with encapsulated organisms and giardiasis. See The Adaptive Immune System on page 2-14 for more information.

The spleen clears out bacteria and is the site for formation of opsonizing antibodies. Opsonizing antibodies are important in defending the host from infection with encapsulated organisms, especially pneumococcus. Splenectomy and functional asplenia increase the risk of overwhelming pneumococcal, malarial, and babesial infections. The latter 2 are intra-RBC protozoan parasites.

IgA blocks viral attachment to mucosal surfaces, and IgG blocks viral attachment to host cells.

Other secondary immunodeficiency states to consider include diabetes mellitus, liver failure, renal failure, chronic glucocorticoid use, and malnutrition.

T-CELL DEFICIENCIES

PREVIEW | REVIEW
- Know the infections associated with solid organ transplants and when each is likely to occur.

ETIOLOGY

T-cell-deficient patients have decreased cellular immunity. These patients present with opportunistic infections (OIs); infections that do not usually present in immunocompetent patients such as *Pneumocystis jiroveci* pneumonia, CMV colitis, and cryptococcal meningitis. Patients are found to have either low T-cell levels or poor T-cell function.

T-cell defects occur in the following:

- HIV/AIDS
- 22q11.2 deletion syndrome (a.k.a. DiGeorge syndrome)
- Hodgkin lymphoma (if T-cell derived)
- T-cell variant of acute lymphoblastic leukemia
- Prolonged glucocorticoid use
- Solid organ transplantation (because of immunosuppressant medications)

ASSOCIATED INFECTIONS

Patients with T-cell defects are more susceptible to routine community-acquired bacteria and viruses (e.g., pneumococcus, *Mycoplasma*, *Legionella*, *Listeria*, *Salmonella*, influenza, respiratory syncytial virus [RSV]), as well as OIs with the following pathogens:

- Bacteria (e.g., *Nocardia*, *Rhodococcus equi*, mycobacteria)
- Viruses—especially new infections with cytomegalovirus (CMV), herpes simplex virus (HSV), or varicella-zoster virus
- Fungi (e.g., *Pneumocystis*, *Cryptococcus*, *Aspergillus*, endemic fungi)
- Parasites (e.g., *Strongyloides*)

Patients also frequently reactivate protozoal and viral diseases that they have previously held in check (e.g., *Toxoplasma gondii*, HSV).

HIV/AIDS is an acquired T-cell deficiency, discussed in the Infectious Disease section under Human Immunodeficiency Virus (HIV) and Acquired Immunodeficiency Syndrome (AIDS).

22q11.2 deletion syndrome (a.k.a. DiGeorge syndrome, congenital thymic hypoplasia) is a T-cell deficiency due to an early intrauterine malformation of the embryo that can affect several tissues and organs, including the thymus, parathyroids, heart and great cardiac vessels, and face. A mnemonic for these findings is **CATCH-22** (**c**ardiac, **a**bnormal facies, **t**hymic hypoplasia, **c**left lip, **h**ypocalcemia, chromosome **22**).

There is a wide range of symptoms and variable decrease in T-cell function related to the variable decrease in thymic tissue. In many patients, a microdeletion in chromosome 22q11.2 is demonstrated. In rare circumstances, severely affected infants (complete DiGeorge syndrome = no thymus and no T cells!) receive thymic transplantation. Some patients reach adulthood. Most adults with DiGeorge syndrome have fewer cardiac anomalies; however, they have more craniofacial defects and psychiatric illnesses.

SOLID ORGAN TRANSPLANTATION

Patients who have received a solid organ transplant are at risk for infections carried by the donor organ, as well as nosocomial infections. Additionally, they can reactivate infections that had been previously controlled by their immune system. Some of these infections are mentioned in Associated Infections; they also include endemic fungi and mycobacteria.

Infections caused by immunosuppressive drugs tend to arise predictably, based on the length of treatment.

Know the following classic 3 posttransplantation time periods and their associated infection risks:

- **Month 1**—infections from the donor; nosocomial infection (i.e., specific to the type of surgery performed)

- **Months 2–6**—Immunosuppressant medication is starting to take effect, and patients are at risk for the OIs described in Associated Infections (e.g., CMV from donor+ and recipient– solid organ transplant recipients).
- **> 6 months**—community-acquired infections

However, the use of routine prophylaxis with trimethoprim/sulfamethoxazole and valganciclovir has shifted the time of onset for some OIs. For instance, CMV may not occur until after valganciclovir is stopped in these patients.

COMBINED T- AND B-CELL DEFICIENCIES

PREVIEW | REVIEW

- Name 2 examples of combined T- and B-cell deficiencies.

Combined T- and B-cell deficiencies present with infections—usually opportunistic infections. It is difficult to separate this group from the T-Cell Deficiencies on page 2-23 because you cannot have normally functioning B cells without normally functioning T cells. These patients are found to have both low IG and low T-cell numbers (or low T-cell function). These defects usually present in infancy and are universally fatal without stem cell transplantation.

Severe combined immunodeficiency (SCID) is a deficiency in both T- and B-cell numbers or function. SCID is either autosomal recessive or X-linked. It is always fatal in infancy unless treated with stem cell transplantation.

Ataxia telangiectasia is an autosomal recessive disorder that causes both cellular and IG deficiency. This results in recurrent sinopulmonary infections, bronchiectasis, and progressive telangiectasias. Patients also have a progressive neurologic deterioration of uncertain etiology, characterized by cerebellar ataxia and progressive mental deterioration. Survival into adulthood is not common.

NEUTROPENIA

PREVIEW | REVIEW

- Name some factors that affect whether a patient with neutropenia develops an infection.

In neutropenia, the absolute neutrophil count (ANC) is < 1,500 cells/μL (1.5×10^9/L). Neutropenia occurs in the following scenarios:

- Normal low-variant populations who are asymptomatic (Only 4% of the Black population in the U.S. have ANC > 1,500.)
- Decreased bone marrow production due to medications, nutritional deficits, collagen vascular disease, or malignancy

- Congenital neutropenias, such as neutrophil elastase and HAX1 deficiency, usually present in childhood; however, they may be seen in adults during initial presentation in rare cases.
- A shift from general circulation to other organs like the spleen (e.g., hypersplenic conditions)
- Immune destruction of neutrophils (e.g., autoimmune disease)

Neutrophils help to fight disease by disrupting or consuming disease-producing cells and microorganisms. Neutropenia can hinder the body's ability to fight disease, resulting in infection. Most often, sepsis is caused by flora that colonize the patient and enter the bloodstream across disrupted gut mucosa (via an IV catheter) or through the oropharynx into the lungs and/or sinuses. Neutropenic infections can be caused by both gram-negative and gram-positive bacteria.

The most common gram-positive organisms causing neutropenic infections are *S. aureus*, *S. epidermidis*, and streptococcal spp. More and more infections are caused by the less common gram-positive organisms such as *Corynebacterium* spp, *Cutibacterium acnes* (formerly *Propionibacterium acnes*), *Bacillus* spp, and *Leuconostoc*. These are important to remember because some are not effectively treated with vancomycin.

Common gram-negative infections include *Pseudomonas* spp and Enterobacteriaceae (e.g., *E. coli*, *Klebsiella* spp, *Enterobacter*).

Fungi, including yeasts such as *Candida* and molds such as *Aspergillus* spp, are important pathogens in patients with prolonged neutropenia. Infections with *Fusarium* spp and agents of mucormycosis are especially deadly and are being seen more frequently. Not all fungi are equally susceptible to all antifungal drugs. When a patient with neutropenia develops fever and/or an infection while receiving an empiric antifungal drug, it is very important to know which organisms are resistant to that antifungal. See the discussion of antifungal agents in the Infectious Disease section under Antifungal Agents for more information.

The risk for infection in the patient with neutropenia is directly proportional to the degree and duration of neutropenia.

Other factors that increase risk are:

- Comorbidities
- Presence of catheters
- Concomitant use of immunosuppressive drugs such as monoclonal antibodies and glucocorticoids (increases risk of *Pneumocystis* and tuberculosis)

A patient with severe neutropenia (< 500 neutrophils/μl) is at a much higher risk than a patient with mild neutropenia (500–1,500 neutrophils/μl); however, function of cells is as important as number of cells in resisting infection. Even with an adequate number of cells, patients can develop infection if the granulocytes that are present do not function properly. Suspect granulocyte dysfunction (e.g., chronic granulomatous disease) if the patient has an adequate ANC but has a history of recurrent staphylococcal skin infections, lung infections, and/or lymphadenitis. The duration of neutropenia is also key: An ANC < 500 for > 7 days greatly increases the risk of infection.

For febrile neutropenia, see the Infectious Disease section under Febrile Neutropenia.

OTHER

MASTOCYTOSIS

PREVIEW | REVIEW

- Which physical finding is pathognomonic for urticaria pigmentosa?

Mastocytosis is a rare disorder characterized by abnormal mast cell proliferation and accumulation in various organs. The degree of involvement determines the extent of the disease.

There are 3 types of mastocytosis:

1) **Cutaneous mastocytosis** results from increased mast cells only in the dermis. There are characteristic brownish macules called urticaria pigmentosa. Formation of a wheal upon gentle stroking of the macule (**Darier sign**) is pathognomonic.
2) **Systemic mastocytosis** is caused by increased mast cells in tissues, organs, and skin. These patients have generalized symptoms dependent upon the degree of involvement.
3) **Malignant mastocytosis** causes severe systemic symptoms; however, there are often no skin changes. Physical exam may reveal hepatosplenomegaly and lymphadenopathy.

Screen with elevated tryptase ≥ 20 ng/mL. Remember: Mast cells secrete tryptase. Therefore, if you have a lot of mast cells, the tryptase levels are high. Diagnosis of systemic mastocytosis is based on the presence of the major criterion plus 1 minor criterion, or the presence of 3 of the 4 minor criteria (Table 2-3).

Table 2-3: Diagnosis of Systemic Mastocytosis	
Major Criterion (plus 1 minor)	**Minor Criteria (3 of 4 required)**
Mast cell aggregates in bone marrow and/or extracutaneous organs	1) Atypical/Spindle-shaped cells in bone marrow or other extracutaneous tissue 2) Tryptase level > 20 ng/mL 3) Presence of *c-kit* gene point mutation 4) Expression of surface markers CD2, CD25, or both

ALLERGY & IMMUNOLOGY

Advise patients to stay away from cold, heat, alcohol, aspirin (a.k.a. acetylsalicylic acid [ASA]), and opiates. Oral cromolyn may help GI symptoms. Various chemotherapy regimens have been used in the treatment of systemic and malignant mastocytosis. Unfortunately, chemotherapy has not been particularly successful.

EOSINOPHILIC ESOPHAGITIS (EoE)

PREVIEW | REVIEW

- How does eosinophilic esophagitis present?

EoE is characterized by persistent eosinophil infiltration of the esophagus. **Solid food dysphagia and food impaction** are the most common presenting symptoms. Other symptoms include chest pain, heartburn, and upper abdominal pain. Patients often have other allergic conditions, including asthma, allergic rhinitis, and atopic dermatitis.

Diagnose by endoscopy and biopsy of the esophagus looking for > 15 eosinophils/HPF.

Treatment is individualized and involves ≥ 1 of the following:

- Proton pump inhibitors
- Swallowed inhaled glucocorticoids
- 6-food elimination diet—milk, eggs, soy, wheat, fish/shellfish, peanuts/tree nuts

For additional information on EoE, see the Gastroenterology section under Esophagus.

HUMAN LEUKOCYTE ANTIGEN (HLA) DISEASES

PREVIEW | REVIEW

- Which rheumatologic disorders have a positive human leukocyte antigen B27?

There are many diseases associated with certain HLAs; this makes sense, as the HLA complex is the **backbone** of immune surveillance. Autoimmune disease arises when there is immune dysfunction. Many **rheumatic** disorders are accompanied by HLA-B27. They include ankylosing spondylitis, acute anterior uveitis, reactive arthritis, **psoriatic spondyloarthropathy**, and **juvenile idiopathic arthritis**; however, **not** adult rheumatoid arthritis (RA).

RA is associated with the HLA-DR4 antigens. See the Rheumatology section under Rheumatoid Arthritis (RA) for more information.

THE MEDSTUDY HUB: YOUR GUIDELINES AND REVIEW ARTICLES RESOURCE

For both review articles and current internal medicine practice guidelines, visit the MedStudy Hub at

medstudy.com/hub

The Hub contains the only online consolidated list of all current guidelines focused on internal medicine. Guidelines on the Hub are easy to find, continually updated, and linked to the published source. MedStudy maintains the Hub as a service to the medical community and makes it available to anyone and everyone at no cost to users.

FIGURE SOURCES

Figure 2-1: James Heilman, MD; CC BY-SA 3.0
Figure 2-2: john, CC BY-SA 3.0
Figure 2-3: R1carver; CC BY-SA 3.0
Figure 2-4: James Heilman, MD; CC BY-SA 3.0
Figure 2-5: Britannic124, CC BY-SA 3.0
Figure 2-6: Thomas Habif, MD; CC BY-SA 3.0
Figure 2-7: MedStudy illustration
Figure 2-8: MedStudy illustration
Figure 2-9: LucyHAE, CC BY-SA 3.0

Dermatology

SECTION EDITOR

Jasbir K. Matharu, MD
Los Angeles, CA

Table of Contents

COMMON SKIN PROBLEMS

PREVIEW | REVIEW

- What bacterium most commonly infects patients with atopic dermatitis? What virus?
- What is the clinical presentation of seborrhea?
- What is the clinical presentation of intertrigo?
- Allergic contact dermatitis is an example of what type of hypersensitivity reaction?
- What are the serious side effects of isotretinoin?
- How do you distinguish rosacea from acne vulgaris?
- What inflammatory scarring disease affects the axilla, groin, and perianal areas?

OVERVIEW

As the largest organ of the human body, it is no surprise that the skin serves numerous functions that are essential in the maintenance of human health. More specifically, the skin functions to prevent infection using both innate and adaptive immunity, repair injury, protect the integrity of DNA, provide circulation, maintain a barrier for water and temperature regulation, provide sensory communication, and provide nutrition.

The skin is composed of 3 main layers: the epidermis, the dermis, and the subcutaneous tissue. The epidermis is the body's 1st line of defense and comprises a semipermeable, laminated surface that acts as a barrier to chemical penetration, microbiologic invasion, and fluid and solute loss. The dermis provides structural and nutritional support and is populated by nerves and vasculature. At the dermal-epidermal interface is the basement membrane, which is an area of great interest, because genetic defects of this zone may lead to significant disease. It is also a target of autoimmune attack. The subcutaneous tissue provides thermoregulation and cushioning to prevent injury to underlying structures, such as bone and muscle. Any failure of the skin to function in these capacities can lead to substantial morbidity and mortality.

Eczema is a general term for an inflammatory condition of the skin characterized by dryness, redness, itching, and oozing vesicular lesions, which can become scaly, leathery, crusted, or hardened. The most common type of eczema is atopic dermatitis. Other types of eczema include contact dermatitis, stasis dermatitis, dyshidrotic eczema, nummular eczema, and neurodermatitis. Some types of eczema will be discussed here because they are common skin problems.

MedStudy Skin Signs (available at medstudy.com/products/skin-signs) provides additional images and examples of various dermatologic conditions.

ATOPIC DERMATITIS (AD)

AD (a.k.a. eczema, atopic eczema) is the most common type of eczema, so the terms atopic dermatitis and eczema are often used interchangeably. AD is a chronic inflammatory skin condition with a relapsing and remitting course (Figure 3-1). Typically, 60% of cases present in infancy, with > 90% of all cases presenting at < 5 years of age; in 10–30%, the condition persists to adulthood. Onset is rare after 30 years of age, and the disease generally becomes less severe with increasing age.

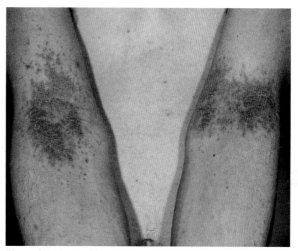

Figure 3-1: Antecubital fossa with atopic dermatitis

AD is characterized by dry skin and pruritus. Subsequent scratching leads to more inflammation and lichenification (i.e., thickening and hardening of the skin, with exaggeration of its normal markings), as well as more itching and scratching (i.e., "itch-scratch" cycle). In adults, the most commonly involved areas are the wrists and the antecubital and popliteal fossae. Patients can also develop erythematous and edematous pruritic patches on the head and neck, which can crust and then "weep," at least partially as a result of scratching.

There is often a personal or family history of eczema, allergic rhinitis, or asthma, as well as laboratory findings of elevated serum IgE levels and eosinophilia. The combination of AD, allergies, and asthma is referred to as the atopic triad.

Flares can be precipitated by clothing (particularly wool), changes in weather, emotional stress, aeroallergens (dust mites and pollen), and infections. *Staphylococcus aureus* infection, appearing as honeycombing and weeping, is often present in severe cases. Diluted bleach baths can decrease *S. aureus* colonization but have not been shown to reduce flares. Give oral antibiotics or topical mupirocin cream for secondary infections.

Most treatments for AD focus on avoiding exacerbating factors, maintaining a good moisturizing regimen, and using medications when the first 2 methods do not suffice. Hydration, moisture-trapping agents with low water content (emollients), ointments, and topical corticosteroids are the mainstays of treatment for AD. Lotions (high water content) can actually worsen the condition by drying the area through dehydration. Lotions or gels with alcohol are even more drying.

Topical steroids are the mainstay of AD treatment. Use a step-up or step-down strength method depending on the results of treatment. Use mid- or high-potency topical corticosteroids for the trunk and extremities and low-potency topical corticosteroids for the face. However, topical corticosteroids are not recommended for prolonged use especially on the face or intertriginous areas, because they can cause striae, atrophy, telangiectasias, pigmentary changes, and acneiform skin eruptions. Instruct patients to use steroids twice daily until their skin returns to baseline or up to 2 weeks at a time, whichever occurs first.

Tacrolimus and pimecrolimus are topical immunosuppressants (calcineurin inhibitors) that are effective alternatives to topical corticosteroids. Because these do not cause skin atrophy, they are especially good for facial lesions. There is a theoretical risk of skin cancer or T-cell lymphoma (FDA black box warning due to risk with systemic use; no significant topical data yet), so these agents are 2nd line for intermittent treatment of AD. These agents should be avoided in HIV+ patients or anyone with a weakened immune system or if the skin is infected. Counsel patients about this risk; the risk of severe local side effects from topical steroids may outweigh the risk of calcineurin inhibitors for lesions involving the face.

AD is a chronic condition, so patients will need to follow this protocol with each flare. Because patients with AD have a defective skin barrier, they need to use a bland emollient not only during but also after flares to help prevent recurrences. AD can run a much more chronic and severe course, which may necessitate a referral to a dermatologist.

Also, educate patients on the avoidance of rubbing or scratching the skin lesions.

Pruritus is a significant component of AD, and controlling the itch tends to improve the rash. Oral antihistamines (H$_1$ blockers) can be very helpful but generally work at night as a sedative to reduce itching. Topical antihistamines should be avoided as they can cause contact sensitization.

Avoid soap. It can be drying and strips the skin of natural oils.

Crisaborole, which is a phosphodiesterase inhibitor, can be used topically for mild and moderate AD. It is rarely used because it is expensive, but it is a nonsteroidal choice and safe for long-term use on the face and for anyone > 2 years old. Use oral cyclosporine, azathioprine, mycophenolate mofetil, or methotrexate for severe AD that does not respond to conservative therapy. Dupilumab is an injectable biologic medication that inhibits interleukin-4 (IL-4) and is indicated for severe or refractory AD. JAK inhibitors ruxolitinib and upadacitinib have recently been approved (2021) for treatment in those not responding to topical therapy. Ultraviolet (UV) light therapy is also used

in this setting. Oral corticosteroids are rarely indicated for acute flares and often cause rebound flares when tapered.

Eczema herpeticum is caused by herpes simplex virus, and it can cause a severe disseminated infection. Suspect eczema herpeticum in patients who develop fever and pustular or punched-out lesions that do not respond to oral antibiotics. It is more common in patients who are taking immunosuppressants and needs to be addressed quickly to limit systemic effects. If suspected, treat with oral antivirals or, if the patient is unable to swallow, intravenous acyclovir while establishing the diagnosis.

SEBORRHEIC DERMATITIS

Seborrheic dermatitis affects 2–5% of the population and is a chronic condition that manifests as a yellow, greasy scale overlying erythematous patches or plaques (Figure 3-2). Pruritus is variable. It affects areas where sebaceous glands are most active and particularly involves the scalp (dandruff), eyebrows, paranasal area, and external auditory canals; however, the chest, axilla, and groin areas can also be involved. There is a strong association with *Malassezia furfur*, although the relationship between the resident yeast and seborrheic dermatitis is not entirely clear.

Figure 3-2: Seborrheic dermatitis

Seborrheic dermatitis is common in patients with HIV/AIDS, Parkinson disease and other neurologic disorders, and mood disorders.

Treatment of seborrheic dermatitis encompasses frequent washing and an antidandruff shampoo. The active ingredient in these shampoos is selenium sulfide, zinc pyrithione, or salicylic acid. The antimicrobial shampoos include ketoconazole or ciclopirox.

Use low-potency topical corticosteroids in combination with ketoconazole cream for skin disease. Topical calcineurin inhibitors, such as tacrolimus and pimecrolimus, can be used as steroid-sparing agents. Sulfur/sulfacetamide cleansers or lotions are effective adjunctive or maintenance therapy for skin disease, especially for the face.

INTERTRIGO

Intertrigo is an irritant dermatitis found in intertriginous areas: warm and moist skin folds that rub together and have little air circulation (e.g., inframammary fold, axilla, interdigital, groin). Intertrigo presents as tender, pruritic, macerated, brightly erythematous plaques. Contributing factors include obesity, hyperhidrosis, diabetes, alcohol, and smoking. Skin microbiomes cause secondary infections (e.g., *Candida*, a yeast). Suspect *Candida* when satellite papules extend beyond the main eruption. Tinea cruris and erythrasma can mimic nonspecific intertrigo. These can be ruled out with a potassium hydroxide (KOH) test and Wood lamp, respectively. The KOH test shows hyphae with dermatophytes and pseudohyphae with candidal infection. Wood lamp shows green with pseudomonal infection and coral red with erythrasma, which is an infection with the bacterium *Corynebacterium* that is treated with erythromycin.

Treat intertrigo with topical antifungals and drying agents (e.g., antifungal powders, aluminum sulfate products, corn starch). Avoid the use of talcum powder in the genital area of women because of the potential increased risk of ovarian cancer.

CONTACT DERMATITIS

Contact dermatitis does not have a single presentation. Its manifestations can vary from slightly dry and erythematous skin to the development of edema, oozing vesicles, or chronic eczema or dermatitis.

Contact dermatitis (Figure 3-3) can be caused by irritant contact dermatitis (80% of cases), or it can be of allergic origin (20% of cases).

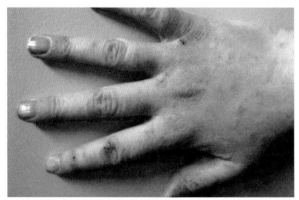

Figure 3-3: Contact dermatitis of the hand

The most typical **chemical irritants** are soapy water, rubbing alcohol, and common household cleaners. Sufficient exposure to these irritants causes dermatitis in every individual. For irritant contact dermatitis, prior sensitization is not required. **Dyshidrotic eczema** is common in individuals who wash their hands frequently. The finding of highly pruritic vesicles on the sides of the fingers is helpful in making this diagnosis.

The **allergic** type of contact dermatitis is due to a T-cell-mediated, delayed-type hypersensitivity reaction (Type 4 hypersensitivity) in the skin. Patients must become sensitized to the antigen with 1 or many exposures. After sensitization and upon reexposure, the skin develops a pruritic lesion within 12 hours to 2 days. The most common allergens are nickel, chromium, neomycin, bacitracin, and oleoresin urushiol such as found in poison oak, poison ivy, and poison sumac. Linear and geometric eruptions often reflect an external cause. The distribution can also provide a clue such as an allergy to nickel in jewelry that occurs on the earlobes or an allergy to jeans buttons that occurs on the abdomen.

Identify and remove the offending allergen or irritant as 1st line treatment. Symptomatic treatment includes cool compresses, topical corticosteroids, and Burow solution (aluminum acetate dissolved in water, 1:40). If the reaction is severe or involves the face, give systemic corticosteroids, usually as a reducing dose over 2 weeks. A shorter course can precipitate rebound reaction. Patch testing is the gold standard to identify contact allergens, especially if there is no obvious precipitating exposure. In patch testing, multiple suspected allergens are applied to the patient's back under occlusive dressings. After 48 hours, the dressings are removed and the area is examined for evidence of delayed hypersensitivity reactions.

STASIS DERMATITIS

Stasis dermatitis is 1 of the clinical manifestations of chronic venous insufficiency of the lower extremities. Venous hypertension is exacerbated by gravity and valvular incompetence in leg veins and causes distention of capillaries. This distention allows leakage of fluid and plasma into tissue, as well as deposition of hemosiderin and erythrocyte extravasation.

Clinical features include pitting edema of the shin and calf that is more pronounced at the end of the day and resolves overnight, rusty hemosiderin deposition, and eczematous findings such as itchy and dry skin. Over time, the legs start to develop signs of lipodermatosclerosis, characterized by induration and a firm circular cuff that creates an inverted wine bottle appearance. Venous ulcers can develop and increase risk of secondary infection. Scratching may lead to oozing and crusting. Edema and superimposed contact sensitization to self-treatments may lead to blistering.

The mainstay of treatment is management of venous hypertension. Elevation of the legs and compression with stockings or bandaging can improve venous return. Encourage exercise and lifestyle changes. Surgical

DERMATOLOGY

strategies can be pursued in more severe cases. For symptom control and management of skin changes, topical therapy such as that used for atopic dermatitis is indicated, including topical corticosteroids and emollient use.

ACNE AND ROSACEA

Acne Vulgaris

Presentation

Acne vulgaris is divided into inflammatory and noninflammatory lesions. Noninflammatory lesions consist of open comedones (blackheads) and closed comedones (whiteheads). Inflammatory acne includes papules, pustules, and nodules (cysts).

Noninflammatory acne develops in early adolescence. It is caused by occlusion of the follicles.

Inflammatory acne occurs as a reaction to several factors, including *Cutibacterium acnes* (previously known as *Propionibacterium acnes*) within the follicle, ruptured follicular epithelium with leaking of sebum, and the immunologic response to these factors.

Acne severity is determined by genetic and hormonal factors, with an imbalance between estrogens and androgens. However, most patients with acne do not overproduce androgens. Rather, sebaceous glands are locally hyperresponsive to androgens. Very severe nodular acne with the development of sinus tracts is called acne conglobata. It usually occurs in young males on the chest and back.

In women with polycystic ovary syndrome (PCOS), increased serum androgens contribute to the development of acne. PCOS occurs in 5–10% of all women, and ~ 1/3 of women with acne have PCOS. Women with oligomenorrhea and hirsutism plus acne can be investigated for PCOS with tests for luteinizing hormone (LH), follicle-stimulating hormone (FSH), free and total testosterone, dehydroepiandrosterone sulfate (DHEAS), a lipid profile, glucose tolerance test, and insulin sensitivity. See more on PCOS in the Women's and Men's Health section under Gynecology.

Factors that can exacerbate acne include:
- Cosmetics
- Skin and hair oils
- Repetitive mechanical trauma (e.g., scrubbing)
- Clothing (e.g., turtlenecks, bra straps, sports helmets)
- High humidity
- Heavy sweating
- Diet (controversial): low-fat milk consumption, high glycemic load diets
- Stress

Rosacea is distinguished from acne vulgaris by the presence of telangiectasia and the absence of comedones.

Treatment

Minimize friction in acne-prone areas (e.g., chin straps, baseball caps), and discontinue aggravating factors (e.g., topical corticosteroids, industrial compounds, certain oral contraceptives, lithium, phenytoin, phenobarbital).

Noninflammatory acne: Topical retinoids are the drugs of choice for comedonal acne. These include adapalene, tretinoin, and tazarotene. Retinoids (except adapalene) are deactivated by sunlight, so they should be applied at night. Retinoids also are keratolytic agents.

Side effects are mainly skin irritation and photosensitivity. Start at a low concentration and apply 2–3×/week, increasing to daily application as tolerated. Remember: Topical retinoids are contraindicated in pregnancy! Other agents for comedonal acne include topical salicylic acid, benzoyl peroxide, azelaic acid, and glycolic acid. All have anticomedonal activity. In addition, benzoyl peroxide has antibacterial properties.

Mild inflammatory acne (Figure 3-4): Use benzoyl peroxide in conjunction with topical erythromycin or clindamycin to treat the *C. acnes* of inflammatory acne. This combination therapy decreases development of antibiotic resistance; combination preparations are available commercially. Topical retinoids are also useful adjuncts. Topical dapsone, an antimicrobial agent, can be used as a 2nd line agent. Spironolactone is also effective for inflammatory acne in adult women; however, it is not approved by the FDA.

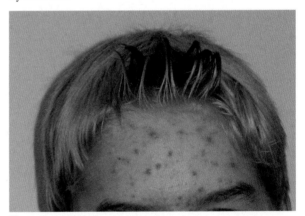

Figure 3-4: Mild inflammatory acne

Moderate-to-severe inflammatory acne (Figure 3-5) often responds to oral antibiotics such as tetracycline, doxycycline, and minocycline. Topical and oral antibiotics should not be used together. Oral antibiotics should be used only for 3 months. The high prevalence of *C. acnes* resistance to erythromycin has led to decreased use of this agent. Trimethoprim/sulfamethoxazole (TMP/SMX) is recommended for short-term treatment in selected refractory cases.

Oral isotretinoin (1 mg/kg/day) is highly effective in severe nodulocystic, scarring, or resistant cases. However, it is also a powerful teratogen. The use of isotretinoin is restricted to physicians who have registered with the

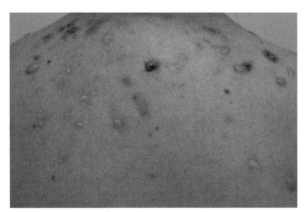

Figure 3-5: Moderate-to-severe inflammatory acne

FDA's electronic iPLEDGE program and requires multiple steps to prescribe. Some of the common birth defects it causes are hearing and visual impairments, facial dysmorphism, and intellectual disabilities. Because of these risks, female patients must have 2 negative pregnancy tests before beginning the medication and must use 2 forms of birth control while taking it. Additionally, women of childbearing potential are required to undergo monthly pregnancy tests prior to obtaining their next prescription.

Patients should be counseled on these risks and advised that conception is safe beginning 1 month after the last dose of isotretinoin.

Male patients are also advised not to impregnate a woman while taking isotretinoin, although there have been no reports of fetal abnormalities in this circumstance.

In addition to teratogenicity, there are serious side effects associated with the use of isotretinoin:

- Idiopathic intracranial hypertension (formerly pseudotumor cerebri), especially if used in conjunction with tetracyclines
- Aggression
- Alopecia
- Anemia
- Arthralgias
- Bronchospasm
- Colitis
- Depression and psychosis
- Dry eyes
- Elevated glucose
- Elevated triglycerides
- Increased cholesterol
- Inflammatory bowel disease
- Hair loss
- Headache
- Hearing loss
- Marked hypertriglyceridemia
- Myalgias
- Night vision loss
- Pancreatitis
- Skeletal abnormalities

- Syncope
- Stroke
- Suicidal ideation

There is a controversial association between isotretinoin and depression as well as inflammatory bowel disease. Prescribers of isotretinoin must be familiar with its side effects. A careful history is essential to identify potential contraindications.

Hypertriglyceridemia, if severe, warrants discontinuation of isotretinoin and monitoring of triglyceride levels, which should return to normal off the medication. Fenofibrate may be used to treat mild-to-moderate hypertriglyceridemia.

Isotretinoin can cause palpitations, vascular thrombotic disease, and stroke, but aspirin is not routinely recommended.

If oral isotretinoin is used, all other acne treatments must be stopped.

Oral estrogen-based contraceptive therapy is used in patients with PCOS to decrease androgen excess and to regulate menstrual cycles. Spironolactone, which has antiandrogen effects, may be used alone or in combination with oral contraceptives. Avoid spironolactone in pregnancy, due to the potential for feminization of male fetuses.

Rosacea

Rosacea (Figure 3-6) is a relapsing and remitting lifelong condition that primarily affects fair-skinned, middle-aged patients and presents with erythema, phymas, telangiectasias, papules, and pustules (acne-like lesions) on the central face. It occurs more frequently in women; however, it is more severe in men.

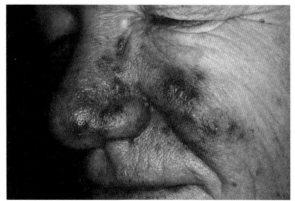

Figure 3-6: Rosacea

According to the Global Rosacea Consensus (ROSCO) Panel, rosacea is defined according to diagnostic features and major and secondary symptoms and signs. Diagnostic features are central facial erythema and phymatous changes. Major features—any 2 of which make a diagnosis— include pustules and papules, flushing, telangiectasias, and ocular changes. Minor features are burning, stinging, swelling, and dryness.

Ocular symptoms and signs occur in 50% but may predate or occur in the absence of rosacea. Symptoms include dryness, burning and stinging, light sensitivity, blurred vision, and foreign body sensation. Signs include lid margin and conjunctival telangiectasias, blepharitis, plugging of the meibomian glands, chalazia, corneal inflammation, keratitis, iritis, scarring, and loss of visual acuity.

Know how to distinguish acne vulgaris from rosacea. Unlike acne vulgaris, rosacea can have telangiectasias and does not have comedones.

Rhinophyma is more common in older men and may require surgical therapy.

Patients with rosacea can have a flushing reaction to various stimuli (e.g., alcohol, stress, spicy foods) even before the lesions appear. Once the rosacea manifests, the flush can become permanent. Trigger avoidance is recommended. Sun protection is important.

Treatment depends on diagnostic features, symptoms, and signs but can be topical or oral and light therapy based.

Phymas can be treated topically with brimonidine, oxymetazoline, and retinoids. Oral therapies are carvedilol, doxycycline, minocycline, tetracycline, isotretinoin, azithromycin, and TMP/SMX. Intense pulsed light and laser therapies can be used. Papules respond to topical ivermectin, metronidazole, azelaic acid, ivermectin, retinoids, or sulfur/sulfacetamide preparations or oral antibiotics (e.g., tetracycline, doxycycline, azithromycin, minocycline, oral isotretinoin, TMP/SMX).

Treat ocular symptoms with topical azithromycin or cyclosporine or oral cyclosporine, azithromycin, doxycycline, and minocycline; refer to an ophthalmologist.

Telangiectasias can be treated with laser therapy or retinol; persistent erythema and flushing can be treated with brimonidine topical gel and oxymetazoline.

Steroids should be avoided as they exacerbate the disease.

Periorificial dermatitis (Figure 3-7) is a rosacea-like rash that presents with grouped superficial papulovesicular or papulopustular lesions and erythema located around the mouth, chin, nasolabial, and periocular areas with vermillion sparing. It is also referred to as perioral dermatitis. Patients report intolerance to sunlight, cosmetics, topical moisturizers, water, and soaps. Steroids can worsen the condition. Treatment is generally the same as for rosacea.

HIDRADENITIS SUPPURATIVA

Hidradenitis suppurativa (a.k.a. acne inversa), which affects ~ 1% of the population, is a chronic inflammatory scarring process involving apocrine gland–bearing areas such as the groin/perianal and the axillary regions (Figure 3-8). It typically develops after puberty and manifests as painful, deep-seated nodules, sinus tracts, and abscesses. The presentation is symmetric. The abscesses are usually sterile but can become secondarily superinfected. Although it occurs in both sexes (women > men, 4:1), axillary and

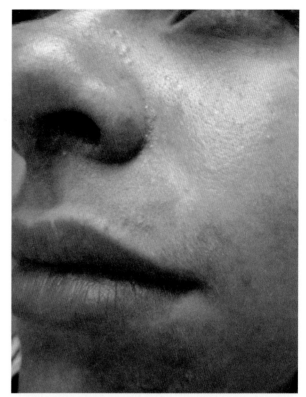
Figure 3-7: Periorificial dermatitis

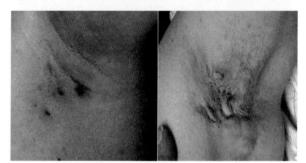
Figure 3-8: Hidradenitis suppurativa; mild vs. severe

vulvar involvement is more common in women and perianal involvement is more common in men. Smoking and obesity correlate with severity of disease.

The disease process begins with dilated, occluded follicles (comedones) that often have multiple openings. Subsequently, the disease can range from mild to severe (induration, scarring, pitting, and draining abscesses). There is often an association with severe acne, dissecting cellulitis of the scalp, and pilonidal cysts, known as the follicular occlusion tetrad.

Treatment for hidradenitis suppurativa should be guided by disease severity and often is challenging. If applicable, recommend smoking cessation and weight loss. Patients should avoid deodorants (antiperspirants are okay), tight synthetic clothing, and prolonged exposure to hot, humid environments. Treat early disease with 1% topical clindamycin and intralesional steroids. Treat acute infections with incision, drainage, and packing.

Treat late disease with either oral tetracycline or oral clindamycin + rifampin. Corticosteroids can be injected into the nodules or used orally for severe cases. Treat more severe disease with immunosuppressants, such as the tumor necrosis factor inhibitor adalimumab, which is approved by the FDA for treatment of moderate to severe hidradenitis suppurativa. Infliximab is also effective; however, it is not approved by the FDA. Etanercept is not effective. Oral retinoids can improve severe cases (3rd line). Antiandrogens, such as cyproterone acetate and finasteride, and zinc gluconate can be beneficial nonsurgical alternatives. For severe refractory lesions, definitive therapy is complete surgical excision, but laser therapy is also increasingly being used.

For females, estrogen-containing birth control pills may help, as may spironolactone. Metformin can be beneficial depending on comorbid conditions.

MOUTH FINDINGS

PREVIEW | REVIEW

- What finding on the buccal mucosa can be seen with measles? Describe and name the finding.
- What viral infection causes oral hairy leukoplakia?
- A beefy red tongue is seen with what underlying disease states?
- What are the "4 Ds" that patients with glucagonomas may develop?
- If you see macroglossia, what underlying diseases should you consider?

NOTE

Know all mouth findings outlined here!

ORAL BLISTERS AND ULCERS

Recurrent aphthous stomatitis is a common and multifactorial disorder with an unclear etiology, but it is thought to be secondary to a dysfunction of the immune system. Minor aphthae are the most common presentation and are round, shallow, and painful ulcerations that heal without scarring. Major aphthae are larger and deeper lesions that are more persistent and may heal with scarring. Herpetiform aphthae are uncommon and consist of groups of small, numerous, and painful ulcerations that are mostly limited to nonkeratinized surfaces (i.e., lining of mouth), a feature that helps to distinguish these lesions from herpes simplex virus (HSV).

Herpes simplex infections consist of painful, grouped vesicles on an erythematous base that are often preceded by tingling, burning, or pain. Outbreaks are often recurrent, and recurrent lesions are commonly on the vermillion border of the lips and less commonly on the nose, perioral skin, or cheek (Figure 3-9).

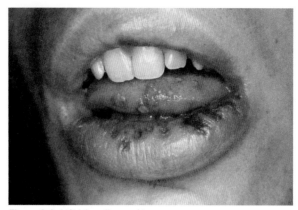

Figure 3-9: HSV-1 on lips and tongue

Squamous cell carcinoma is the most common malignancy of the oral cavity and is associated with tobacco and alcohol use. It can manifest as an ulcer, an exophytic mass, or an endophytic, indurated lesion. These lesions are more aggressive than their counterparts on the skin.

Pemphigus vulgaris presents as painful oral erosions that may be scattered throughout the oral mucosa but are most typically found on the buccal and palatine mucosa. The presence of ulceration can lead to decreased oral intake, and patients presenting solely with oral lesions may experience a delay in diagnosis compared to those patients with cutaneous lesions. For more information on pemphigus vulgaris, see Blistering Lesions on page 3-30.

WHITE ORAL LESIONS

Koplik spots (Figure 3-10) are small, painless, white papules on an erythematous base found on the buccal mucosa in patients with measles. Even though the rash is not present yet, these patients are highly contagious. The oral spots usually precede the skin lesions by several days.

Figure 3-10: Koplik spots

Oral leukoplakia (Figure 3-11) is an adherent plaque found on the mucosal surface of the mouth. It is diagnosed only after ruling out other similar lesions with an identifiable cause such as oral candidiasis, smoker's keratosis, and oral hairy leukoplakia. These are considered precancerous lesions.

Figure 3-11: Oral leukoplakia

Oral hairy leukoplakia (Figure 3-12) is a type of leukoplakia that most commonly occurs in patients with HIV/AIDS. It is due to opportunistic Epstein-Barr virus infection in the superficial layers of the tongue's squamous epithelium. It manifests as asymptomatic, white, corrugated (or "hairy") plaques along the sides of the tongue. In contrast to *Candida*, it cannot be scraped off!

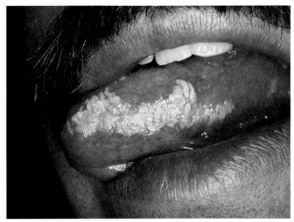

Figure 3-12: Oral hairy leukoplakia

Oral candidiasis, or thrush, causes white semiadherent plaques on the tongue and mucosa. Unlike hairy leukoplakia, these can be scraped off.

Lichen planus (LP) can have up to 7 presentations, including erosive, bullous, and atrophic. The most common presentation is a lacelike pattern of white, raised lines, called Wickham striae. Oral LP, particularly the erosive type, has a reported association with hepatitis C.

TONGUE LESIONS

Beefy red tongue (glossitis) is seen in pernicious anemia and various vitamin B deficiencies. B_{12} deficiency can present with glossitis but also shows anemia, fatigue, and neurologic symptoms. Beefy red tongue can also be associated with glucagonomas.

Glucagonomas (pancreatic α-cell tumors) secrete excessive amounts of glucagon and can cause a beefy red tongue (think **GL**ucagonoma = **GL**ossitis), angular cheilitis, and a necrolytic migratory erythematous rash. Patients with glucagonomas may develop the **4 Ds: d**iabetes, **d**eep venous thrombosis, **d**epression, and **d**ermatitis. Weight loss is characteristic. Erosions of the skin primarily affecting the groin, buttocks, and lower legs and sometimes affecting the face characterize the glucagonoma syndrome. When glucagonoma syndrome is diagnosed, it is important to rule out a zinc or magnesium deficiency because the presentations can be similar. The sooner the glucagonoma is found and treated, the better is the prognosis.

Macroglossia ("big tongue") is associated with multiple myeloma, primary amyloidosis, lymphoma, hemangioma, acromegaly, hypothyroidism, angioedema, and trisomy 21 (a.k.a. Down syndrome). Macroglossia associated with pinch purpura (i.e., purpura and ecchymoses that develop after mild trauma such as pressure or rubbing), especially around the eyes, strongly suggests amyloidosis. Amyloid deposits present as waxy nodules around the face, neck, scalp, and hands.

"Geographic" tongue is an idiopathic inflammatory condition that results in the loss of filiform papillae. It has the appearance of migratory, denuded, erythematous patches with serpiginous, raised, white borders that resemble a map (Figure 3-13). It is asymptomatic and benign but is associated with psoriasis.

Figure 3-13: Geographic tongue

"Strawberry" tongue is due to inflamed tongue papillae and is associated with scarlet fever, toxic shock syndrome, and Kawasaki disease, which is a mucocutaneous lymph node syndrome typically seen in children.

"Bald" tongue is atrophy of the lingual papillae associated with pellagra, iron deficiency anemia, pernicious anemia, and xerostomia (dry mouth; commonly seen in Sjögren syndrome, lymphoma, mumps, and sarcoidosis; occasionally idiopathic).

CUTANEOUS DRUG REACTIONS

PREVIEW | REVIEW

- What adverse cutaneous reactions are associated with phenytoin?

- What is gadolinium? What adverse reaction can it have?

- What drug class is the most common cause of isolated angioedema?

PRESENTATIONS

DRESS syndrome (**d**rug **r**eaction with **e**osinophilia and **s**ystemic **s**ymptoms) carries a mortality rate of ~ 10%. Patients typically present with a morbilliform rash, facial swelling, fever, lymphadenopathy, elevated liver enzymes, and hepatomegaly. The majority of cases have associated eosinophilia. Antiseizure medications and allopurinol are the most commonly implicated drugs. Treat by removing the offending medication. Of note, corticosteroids can improve the cutaneous and visceral (e.g., liver, lung, heart) manifestations of DRESS and can be lifesaving; however, relapses are often observed when the corticosteroids are tapered. In the months following DRESS resolution, monitor for long-term sequelae, which include autoimmune diseases such as Type 1 diabetes mellitus, hypothyroidism, and anemia.

Fixed drug eruption: This is a specific type of cutaneous drug reaction that recurs in the same location every time the offending drug is given. Most often, it will present in the mucosal sites of the vulva or penis, lips, hands, face, or feet and is a round or oval erythematous patch with some swelling and/or a blister. In time, it fades to purple/brown; the blister shrinks and peels off, but it can ulcerate. Treatment consists of discontinuing the offending drug.

SPECIFIC DRUGS

The following are the most frequently seen drug-associated skin changes. Know all of them.

Penicillin (PCN):

- Immediate hypersensitivity reaction; anaphylaxis (IgE)
- Delayed hypersensitivity reaction; immune complex reaction such as vasculitis or morbilliform eruption

Tetracyclines: photosensitivity (demeclocycline > doxycycline > tetracycline > minocycline). Other drugs that commonly cause photosensitivity include fluoroquinolones (e.g., ofloxacin, ciprofloxacin), sulfonamides, furosemide, thiazides, phenothiazines, amiodarone, and retinoids.

Nonsteroidal antiinflammatory drugs (NSAIDs): urticaria/angioedema in 1% and asthma in 0.5%; can cause photosensitivity or toxic epidermal necrolysis (TEN).

Phenytoin:

- Hypersensitivity syndrome—rash, facial edema, lymphadenopathy, and hepatitis
- Various skin reactions, including erythema multiforme—an eruption of well-demarcated erythematous, targetoid papules (usually without scale) that commonly appear on palms and soles. It is often associated with drugs (e.g., NSAIDs, PCN), as well as underlying infection such as HSV and *Mycoplasma*.
- Gingival hyperplasia is caused by 3 groups of drugs—immunosuppressants (e.g., cyclosporine), calcium channel blockers (e.g., nifedipine, verapamil, diltiazem, amlodipine), and anticonvulsants (e.g., phenytoin). It is also seen in M3 and M4 subtypes of acute myeloid leukemia.
- Hirsutism

Corticosteroids: skin changes, including striae, atrophy, telangiectasia, pigmentary changes, and acne-like lesions.

Warfarin: necrotic patches of skin appearing 3–10 days after starting warfarin, typically occurring in patients with previously undiagnosed protein C deficiency. Lesions classically affect areas with the highest fat deposition such as the breasts, buttocks, thighs, and abdomen.

Radiocontrast media: This can cause urticaria/erythema (1:15 incidence) and, rarely, a severe anaphylactoid reaction (1:1,000 incidence; not IgE mediated). It is caused by the release of mast cells. With a prior reaction to contrast media, there is a 30% chance of a subsequent reaction; often, the recurrence is more severe. For the prevention of radiocontrast media cutaneous drug reaction, see the Allergy & Immunology section under Drug Hypersensitivity Reactions.

Gadolinium is a contrast material used for magnetic resonance imaging. It can cause nephrogenic systemic fibrosis, a fibrotic disease of the skin and internal organs similar to, but distinct from, systemic sclerosis (scleroderma) in that it typically spares the face. It is a disease exclusive to end-stage kidney disease (a.k.a. end-stage renal disease). There is no good treatment, so prevention is paramount. Do not give gadolinium to a patient with Stage 4 or higher chronic kidney disease!

Angiotensin-converting enzyme inhibitors (ACEIs): Angioedema occurs in only 0.5% of patients treated with an ACEI. However, because so many patients receive an ACEI, it is 1 of the most common causes of isolated angioedema (i.e., no concurrent urticaria [hives] or anaphylaxis). ACEI-associated angioedema usually involves the lips, tongue, mouth, and pharynx. Angioedema can occur at any time during treatment with ACEIs. Angiotensin receptor blockers (ARBs) rarely cause angioedema. However, use ARBs cautiously in patients who have a previous history of angioedema with ACEI use. Make sure that the benefit outweighs the risk (e.g., systolic heart failure, significant proteinuria).

INFLAMMATORY SKIN DISORDERS

PREVIEW | REVIEW

- Nail pitting with onycholysis is a fairly specific finding for what dermatologic disorder?
- What drugs should be added to the regimen for patients with psoriatic arthritis?
- Characterize the malar rash of systemic lupus.
- What are the manifestations of limited cutaneous systemic sclerosis?
- What skin findings are associated with sarcoidosis?
- What are the skin manifestations of dermatomyositis?
- Pyoderma gangrenosum is associated with which systemic illnesses?

PSORIASIS

Psoriasis is a response triggered by T lymphocytes in the skin. The epidermis becomes hyperproliferative, producing skin cells at a faster rate than normal. Trauma or irritation of normal skin commonly induces lesions of psoriasis at the site (Koebner phenomenon).

All types of psoriasis can be precipitated/exacerbated by β-blockers, stress, sunburn, lithium, and infection (e.g., virus, streptococcal pharyngitis). Obesity is associated with psoriasis, and significant weight loss may lead to clinical improvement. (Additional information on psoriasis is under Seronegative Spondyloarthritis in the Rheumatology section.)

DERMATOLOGY

Types

Plaque psoriasis is the most common type of psoriasis (Figure 3-14). It presents with well-defined, stable, slow-growing, erythematous skin lesions with distinctive mica-like (silvery) scales. Pruritus is variable (absent to severe), with patients usually having mild itching. It is typically symmetric and occurs on extensor surfaces of the knees and elbows, the sacral area, and the scalp.

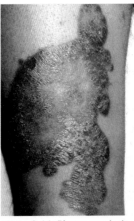
Figure 3-14: Plaque psoriasis

Guttate (eruptive) psoriasis is an abrupt eruption of multiple small salmon-pink or red lesions (3–10 mm in diameter) and typically occurs on the trunk of children or young adults with no previous history of psoriasis (Figure 3-15). Streptococcal pharyngitis is a known trigger of guttate psoriasis.

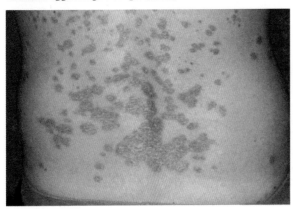
Figure 3-15: Guttate psoriasis

Flexural (inverse) psoriasis affects skin fold areas. It is called inverse because it is not on the extensor surfaces.

There are 2 rare, especially severe types of psoriasis:

1) Erythrodermic psoriasis
2) Pustular psoriasis

Erythrodermic psoriasis is an exfoliative reaction in which the entire surface of the skin becomes red, warm, and scaly—and the patient is unable to control body temperature (hypo-/hyperthermia is typical). Dehydration, hypoalbuminemia, and anemia of chronic disease are common sequelae. Erythrodermic psoriasis is an uncommon psoriasis subset but can be life-threatening.

In patients with stable psoriasis, erythroderma (involvement of > 90% body surface area) can be precipitated by certain medications. Potential offenders exacerbating psoriasis include β-blockers, NSAIDs, antimalarials, TMP/SMX, gold, and lithium, as well as the rebound effect of topical and oral steroids. If possible, β-blocker use should be avoided in patients with psoriasis.

Pustular psoriasis has many small pustules, often coalescing to form "psoriatic lakes of pus." There are 2 forms:

1) The localized form affects only the palms and soles. It is associated with distal interphalangeal joint (DIP) joint arthritis.

2) The rare, generalized form (von Zumbusch type) is the most severe form of psoriasis and can occur with the erythrodermic type. Sudden withdrawal of systemic corticosteroids is a well-described inciting event.

Exfoliative dermatitis (erythroderma) is not associated with herpes simplex or herpes zoster. It is frequently seen as an allergic reaction to drugs such as sulfonamides, antimalarials, penicillin, phenytoin, and barbiturates. It has also been associated with psoriasis, atopic dermatitis, or malignancy (especially cutaneous T-cell lymphoma). Up to 30% of cases are idiopathic. No matter what the etiology, skin biopsy is often nonspecific. The course and prognosis of exfoliative dermatitis are related to the course of the underlying process. Drug-induced exfoliative dermatitis has the best prognosis, whereas cases associated with malignancy have the highest mortality.

Nail Changes

50% of patients with plaque psoriasis and 80% of those with psoriatic arthritis have fingernail changes. These can cause significant functional impairment, pain, and distress.

Psoriatic changes of the nails differ in the fingernails and the toenails. The toenail changes seen in psoriasis can be difficult to distinguish from onychomycosis.

Know the following about these fingernail findings:

• The most common nail change in psoriasis is "ice-pick" pitting; these pits are usually in small irregular groups on the nail (in contrast to a gridlike pattern of pitting seen in alopecia areata). Pitting is an expression of disease activity; normal nails between the groups of pits indicate disease-free activity.

• The most specific psoriatic nail finding is a yellow or salmon-colored "oil spot" beneath the nail plate.

• Any of these fingernail changes in a psoriasis patient are a predictor of psoriatic arthritis; a strong predictor is pitted nails in association with onycholysis (separation of distal nail plate from the nail bed; Figure 3-16). For more on psoriatic arthritis, see the Rheumatology section under Seronegative Spondyloarthritis.

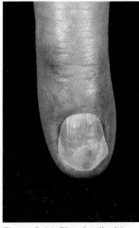
Figure 3-16: Pitted nail with onycholysis

Treatment

Treatment of psoriasis depends on the severity of disease, percentage of body surface area (BSA) involved, and involvement of the hands, feet, facial, or genital regions. Involvement of these locations can interfere significantly with activities of daily living, irrespective of the amount of BSA involved.

Limited/mild disease (psoriasis covering < 3% BSA): Use emollients plus topical high-potency or ultra-high-potency corticosteroids. Taper to a topical mid-potency agent for maintenance.

For scalp involvement, use topical corticosteroid solutions, foams, or lotions. Other options include topical vitamin D analogs (e.g., calcipotriene or calcitriol), tar, and topical retinoids (e.g., tazarotene). Combinations of steroids/vitamin D and steroid/tazarotene are often used.

For the face and intertriginous areas, use:

- low-potency corticosteroids,
- topical tacrolimus or pimecrolimus,
- calcitriol, or
- topical retinoids (tazarotene).

If the patient fails to respond, consider ultraviolet (UV) phototherapy or short-term systemic therapy.

Moderate disease (3–10% BSA): Treatment is the same as for limited disease except that UV phototherapy (typically narrow band ultraviolet B [NB-UVB]) is routinely used. PUVA can be used for those who fail UVB therapy. Adverse effects from PUVA include skin damage and squamous cell carcinoma in individuals who have fair skin. Avoid using PUVA in young people, women who are pregnant or nursing, and in individuals with a history of skin cancer, photosensitivity, ionizing radiation exposure, arsenic exposure, or use of immunosuppressants or phytotoxic medications.

Depending on morbidity associated with the disease, consider treatment with systemic agents, such as MTX, apremilast, acitretin, or a biologic agent (e.g., etanercept, infliximab). Apremilast is a phosphodiesterase inhibitor and is an oral drug for psoriasis; reduce the dosage in patients with kidney disease. Apremilast is metabolized in the liver by cytochrome P450 (CYP450) and can be affected by concomitant use of CYP450-inducing drugs. Other side effects include depression, weight loss, and dehydration. Acitretin is a systemic retinoid. Because it is not an immunosuppressant, it is safe to use in patients with HIV infection. It can be used alone, with NB-UVB or PUVA, or with systemic biologic agents. Acitretin is contraindicated in pregnancy and in patients with severe liver or kidney disease or hyperlipidemia. Tofacitinib, a JAK inhibitor not approved by the FDA, can be considered in moderate to severe cases.

Widespread/severe disease (> 10% BSA): NB-UVB is the 1st line treatment, with consideration of PUVA if NB-UVB is ineffective. Other treatment options include MTX, cyclosporine, a biologic, or a combination of these therapies. Cyclosporine can be used for short-term treatment of severe recalcitrant psoriasis. Do not use cyclosporine with NB-UVB, due to an increased risk of skin cancer and lymphoma. Side effects of cyclosporine include kidney damage, hypertension, hypertrichosis, gingivitis, seizures, hypertriglyceridemia, and increased susceptibility to infection. Cyclosporine, like apremilast, is metabolized by CYP450; avoid using it with other medications that induce CYP450; these will reduce cyclosporine's effectiveness. For severe psoriasis, biologics such as TNF inhibitors (e.g., adalimumab, infliximab), IL-17 inhibitors (e.g., secukinumab), and IL-23 inhibitors (e.g., ustekinumab) are often used.

Guttate psoriasis: Treat with UVB +/– topical steroids and/or NB-UVB. Identify and treat superimposed bacterial infection (e.g., *Streptococcus*).

Flexural psoriasis: Treat with low-potency topical corticosteroids or with topical tacrolimus or pimecrolimus.

Targeted phototherapy with excimer laser or light is better than generalized phototherapy in psoriasis with < 10% involvement, especially in patients with palmoplantar pustulosis or scalp psoriasis. A sunny climate may help; however, improvement is not long lasting.

Nail psoriasis: Treat with pulsed dye laser, tazarotene, or a biologic.

Drugs Used to Treat Psoriasis

Know all of these.

Topical corticosteroids are the primary treatment for plaques. To increase their effectiveness, topical steroids can be occluded with cellophane or plastic wrap. Long-term use of high-potency steroids causes striae and thinning of the skin, and their use is especially avoided on the face and intertriginous areas (i.e., skin-to-skin areas, such as the axillae, under the breasts, the anogenital area, and between digits). Oral corticosteroids are not used, because they cause "rebound flares." (See pustular psoriasis under Types.)

Tar is a traditional treatment that is safe and moderately effective. It is often combined with a corticosteroid in a compounded preparation. Application is time consuming, odorous, and messy, but tar is well tolerated and reasonably priced.

Calcineurin inhibitors: topical tacrolimus and topical pimecrolimus. These are often used for facial and intertriginous areas where high-potency steroid use is avoided. Be aware of the FDA black box warning for a potential increased risk of lymphoma and skin malignancy with calcineurin inhibitors.

Phosphodiesterase-4 inhibitor: Apremilast is a systemic medication that suppresses inflammatory cytokines and mediators.

Retinoids (vitamin A derivatives):

- Tazarotene gel decreases the hyperkeratosis or thick scales associated with psoriasis; the main side effect is skin irritation.
- Acitretin, a 2nd generation oral retinoid, is used for severe psoriasis of all types. Because of its potentially toxic effects, it must be monitored closely and used with

caution. Acitretin has a side-effect profile similar to that of isotretinoin, although its potential for teratogenicity can last up to 3 years after discontinuing the medication; this is in contrast to isotretinoin, which has potential teratogenicity for 1 month following discontinuation of the medication. See moderate-to-severe inflammatory acne discussed in Treatment on page 3-4.

Do not use acitretin in women with childbearing potential who use unreliable contraceptive prevention. Important: The FDA has warned against the use of acitretin in women who are pregnant or who intend to become pregnant in the 3 years following treatment.

Vitamin D₃ analogs: These agents are less effective than high-potency topical steroids but do not cause thin skin or striae.

Immunosuppressants: Both methotrexate (MTX) and cyclosporine are very effective for extensive severe psoriasis:

- MTX can cause severe liver and pulmonary toxicity, as well as bone marrow suppression. Do not give MTX to patients with a history of excessive alcohol use, liver disease, or severe kidney impairment. (The drug is excreted renally.)
- Cyclosporine can cause renal toxicity and hypertension and is recommended only for short-term "rescue" use.

Biologic immunomodulators: These effective treatments for psoriasis have provided safe options for patients with moderate to severe psoriasis. The biologic immunomodulators include:

- Tumor necrosis factor (TNF) inhibitors: etanercept, infliximab, adalimumab, certolizumab
- IL-12 and IL-23 blockers—ustekinumab
- IL-17A blocker—secukinumab, ixekizumab, brodalumab
- IL-23 inhibitor—guselkumab, tildrakizumab, ustekinumab

Ultraviolet (UV) light can be added to the above treatments or used as monotherapy. UVB (290–320 nm) therapy is often used. Narrow-band UVB (NB-UVB; 311 nm) is possibly more effective than the broader-spectrum treatment and generally is the treatment of choice, but it requires more expensive equipment and a longer duration of therapy per session.

PUVA (psoralen + long-wave UVA [320–400 nm]) is also very effective and is usually given to those who fail UVB. UVA penetrates more deeply than UVB and is less likely to burn (hence, the photosensitizing psoralen), but it is associated with accelerated photoaging, an increased likelihood of skin cancer (squamous cell carcinoma), and possibly melanoma in fair-skinned White individuals. Future treatment with cyclosporine increases this risk.

Any patient with psoriatic arthritis is at risk for permanent joint damage. Treat with a disease-modifying oral/injectable agent (cyclosporine, MTX, or the biologics). Classic presentation of psoriatic arthritis is symmetric DIP arthritis, but asymmetric arthritis can also be seen with a "sausage digit"; 1/3 of patients with psoriasis will get arthritis. For more information on psoriatic arthritis see the Rheumatology section under Seronegative Spondyloarthritis.

LUPUS

Systemic lupus erythematosus (SLE): Malar (a.k.a. "butterfly") rash occurs in ~ 1/2 of acute SLE patients and rarely occurs in patients without systemic symptoms. Classically, this rash involves both cheeks and extends across the bridge of the nose, sparing the nasolabial fold (Figure 3-17). The malar rash is erythematous and either flat or slightly edematous, and it often occurs after sunlight exposure (photosensitivity); there is no scarring.

Figure 3-17: Classic systemic lupus erythematous rash

Rosacea can mimic a malar rash but can be distinguished by prominent telangiectasias, papules/pustules, and the lack of systemic symptoms. Likewise, seborrheic dermatitis can mimic a malar rash but can be distinguished by involvement of the nasolabial folds, which are spared with the malar rash of SLE.

SLE patients can get a red, scaly rash on the backs of the hands and fingers, often sparing the knuckles. This is in contrast to the Gottron papules of dermatomyositis, in which the rash occurs over the knuckles.

Patchy nonscarring alopecia is typical in SLE. See the Rheumatology section under Systemic Lupus Erythematosus (SLE) for more information on SLE.

Subacute cutaneous lupus erythematosus (SCLE) is a distinct subset of lupus characterized by erythematous macules/papules that evolve into papulosquamous plaques on sun-exposed areas. Like the acute rash of SLE, but in contrast to discoid lupus, these lesions heal without scarring. Many patients are seropositive for SSA and/or SSB antibodies. Patients uncommonly have significant systemic manifestations.

Chronic cutaneous lupus erythematosus (discoid lupus): Discoid lesions are erythematous and raised with tightly adherent scales. They cause atrophic scarring. They typically occur on sun-exposed areas, including the face, scalp, neck, and ear canals. Only 5% of discoid lupus patients develop SLE. However, patients with SLE who develop discoid lupus lesions tend to have a very good prognosis, devoid of significant renal manifestations.

Intralesional corticosteroids are especially effective for discoid lupus. 1st line oral therapy includes antimalarials, such as hydroxychloroquine. More aggressive systemic therapy with immunosuppressants (e.g., MTX, azathioprine, mycophenolate mofetil) is used in severe cases or for treatment of SLE with significant systemic involvement.

SYSTEMIC SCLEROSIS (SSc)

Scleroderma means "hard skin." It is a connective tissue disorder that always involves the skin but may additionally have systemic involvement. Skin (and subadjacent tissues) involvement is called morphea (a.k.a. localized scleroderma). Disease with systemic involvement is called systemic sclerosis.

Morphea is characterized by plaques that become sclerotic with a hypopigmented center and erythematous border. It usually occurs in children or young adults. It can be just a few lesions (localized morphea) or widespread with some confluence (generalized morphea).

SSc has systemic involvement, and patients commonly have associated fatigue, weakness, stiff joints, and pain. It has 2 major subtypes, depending on the extent of skin sclerosis:

- Limited cutaneous systemic sclerosis (lcSSc) is a grouping of symptoms that has limited systemic involvement, most commonly manifesting as skin thickening distal to the elbows and knees but sometimes affecting the face and neck. Patients classically present with several to all of the CREST features: calcinosis cutis (small tender nodules on the fingers), Raynaud syndrome, esophageal dysmotility, sclerodactyly of the fingers, and telangiectasias. Anticentromere antibody (ACA) is specific and is seen in ~ 50% of patients. Patients who are ACA+ tend to develop more severe digital ischemia and pulmonary hypertension.
- Diffuse cutaneous systemic sclerosis (dcSSc) is the progressive form of SSc that leads to diffuse skin thickening and is more likely to have multiorgan involvement. Rapid skin involvement of the trunk, face (Figure 3-18), upper arms, and thighs characterizes this subset. It is frequently associated with antitopoisomerase I (anti-Scl-70) or anti-RNA polymerase III antibodies, and patients are more likely to develop interstitial lung disease and scleroderma renal crisis.

Raynaud phenomenon eventually develops in almost all patients with SSc. In lcSSc, Raynaud's usually occurs several years before other signs and symptoms become apparent, whereas in (dcSSc), Raynaud's typically occurs simultaneously with the other manifestations.

Nail-fold capillary changes are commonly seen in both subtypes and correlate with severity of disease.

Immune modulation is the usual treatment. See Systemic Sclerosis (SSc) in the Rheumatology section for more information on SSc.

SARCOIDOSIS

Sarcoidosis is a noncaseating granulomatous disease, of unknown etiology. It often affects the lungs, lymph nodes, eyes, and skin. It is most common in northern European countries (e.g., Denmark, Finland, Sweden). In the U.S., sarcoidosis affects Black individuals 3–4× more often than White individuals. Skin involvement is seen in ~ 25% of patients. Sarcoidosis is a great mimicker of other disorders, including many dermatologic diseases.

Lesions are divided into 2 categories:

1) Specific sarcoid skin lesions are characteristically noncaseating granulomas on biopsy and are most commonly found on the head, neck, and upper back. Specific lesions include:
   - Erythematous papules, mainly around the face, which rarely present as a micropapular variant
   - Scar sarcoidosis presenting as granulomatous changes in a healing skin wound or scar tissue (e.g., laceration, tattoo)
   - Plaquelike lesions
   - Nodules
2) Nonspecific skin lesions do not have granulomas and are considered reactive. They include:
   - Erythema nodosum is the most typical nonspecific skin lesion seen in sarcoidosis and is a marker of good prognosis. Sarcoidosis is one of the most common causes of erythema nodosum. Do not biopsy erythema nodosum in sarcoidosis for the diagnosis of sarcoidosis—the histopathology shows just a panniculitis (inflammation of the fat) and not granulomas (see Erythema Nodosum on page 3-14).
   - Löfgren syndrome is an acute form of sarcoidosis that presents with erythema nodosum, bilateral hilar adenopathy, and arthritis. It is frequently accompanied by fevers. It is usually self-limiting and requires only supportive care.

Lupus pernio is a type of sarcoidosis that has skin changes ranging from violaceous (purple) lesions on the tip of the nose and earlobes to large purple nodules/tumors on the face and fingers. It has a slow onset and almost never resolves! It is associated with chronic disease and extrapulmonary involvement.

Treat cutaneous sarcoidosis with topical corticosteroids, intralesional steroid injections, antimalarials, and MTX. Lesions typically respond to treatment for pulmonary sarcoidosis.

For more information on sarcoidosis, see the Pulmonary Medicine section under Interstitial Lung Diseases (ILDs).

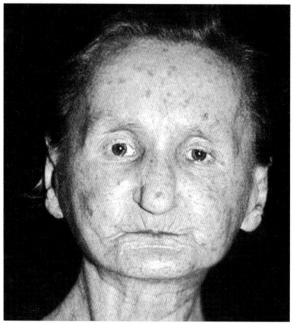

Figure 3-18: Diffuse systemic sclerosis

ERYTHEMA NODOSUM

Erythema nodosum (Figure 3-19) consists of red, warm, very tender nodules that are usually bilateral, symmetric, and classically located on the shins. It is more common in women than in men and is generally idiopathic. Know! Erythema nodosum is associated with:

- Sarcoidosis (common)
- Inflammatory bowel disease
- Infection (e.g., tuberculosis, streptococcal, deep fungal, hepatitis B, *Coccidioides immitis*, *Histoplasma capsulatum*)
- Drugs (especially oral contraceptives, sulfas, and penicillins)
- Pregnancy
- Löfgren syndrome when arthralgia/arthritis and hilar adenopathy are also present

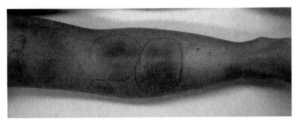

Figure 3-19: Erythema nodosum

Worldwide, **streptococcal infection** pharyngitis is probably the **most common cause** of erythema nodosum. Treatment consists of treatment of the underlying disorder and supportive therapy including NSAIDs.

DERMATOMYOSITIS

Buzzwords: **Gottron papules** and **periorbital heliotropic rash** (a violaceous, sometimes scaly rash around the eyes; Figure 3-20) +/– periorbital edema.

Patients also manifest photodistributed, itchy, erythematous, scaly plaques on the chest, face, neck, and upper extremities—similar to psoriasis. Gottron sign is macular erythema over the dorsal aspects of the interphalangeal/metacarpophalangeal (MCP) joints or over the elbows and knees.

Gottron papules, an extension of Gottron sign, are flat-topped, reddish-to-violet, sometimes scaling papules; sometimes they just look like "cigarette paper" crinkling of the skin over the knuckles (MCP, proximal interphalangeal [PIP], and/or DIP). Gottron papules are the most specific finding with dermatomyositis and proximal muscle weakness. They may be described only as a "rash" or "eruption" over the knuckles (Figure 3-21) in contrast to the finger rash in SLE, which spares the knuckles. "Mechanic's hands" are bilateral, symmetric areas of hyperkeratotic scale most typically on the lateral fingers or on the palm in dermatomyositis. This finding is associated with antisynthetase syndrome, anti-Jo-1 antibodies, and interstitial lung disease.

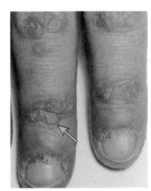

Figure 3-21: Gottron papules

Patients have symmetric proximal muscle weakness but may present solely with cutaneous disease, termed amyopathic dermatomyositis.

Remember: In older patients, dermatomyositis may be a **paraneoplastic** phenomenon. (Genitourinary [GU]/ovarian, gastrointestinal [GI], and lung cancers and lymphomas are most common.) Offer all patients age-appropriate cancer screening. Patients who test positive for anti-p155/p140 are at particularly high risk of cancer.

Treatment of dermatomyositis is **corticosteroids**. This is usually given for 1 year in a slowly tapering dose. A steroid-sparing drug (azathioprine, MTX, or mycophenolate mofetil) is sometimes started with initial treatment; other clinicians start it when there is failure to respond to prednisone.

Antimalarials (hydroxychloroquine is 1st line) help with the skin disease but do **nothing** for the muscle disease. IV gamma globulin may be effective in patients who do not respond to the other medications. Rituximab is an effective 2nd line treatment for systemic disease and 3rd line treatment for cutaneous disease.

More information on dermatomyositis is provided in the Rheumatology section under Inflammatory Myopathies.

REACTIVE ARTHRITIS

Reactive arthritis is an immunologic reaction to an infection elsewhere in the body and typically occurs 1–4 weeks after a GU or GI infection. The classic triad of urethritis, conjunctivitis, and asymmetric arthritis is seen in < 1/3 of patients. Cutaneous manifestations are common and

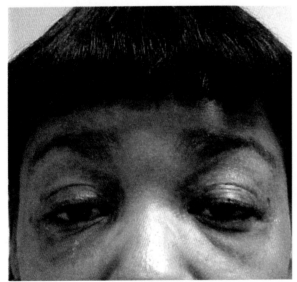

Figure 3-20: Periorbital heliotropic rash

include keratoderma blennorrhagicum and mucocutaneous genital lesions and/or mouth ulcers.

Keratoderma blennorrhagicum (Figure 3-22) classically presents as papules/pustules with central erosion and characteristic crusting on the palms and soles. It can be indistinguishable from pustular psoriasis.

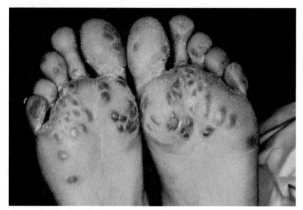

Figure 3-22: Keratoderma blennorrhagicum

Circinate balanitis presents as an erythematous pustular or plaquelike lesion on the glans or shaft of the penis.

For more information on reactive arthritis, see the Rheumatology section under Seronegative Spondyloarthritis and Infectious Arthritides.

VASCULITIS

Vasculitis presents most classically as palpable purpura, usually starting on the legs. Palpable purpura is the extravasation of red blood cells into the skin and is commonly caused by a small vessel vasculitis. Skin biopsy typically displays leukocytoclastic vasculitis. There are many causes of cutaneous vasculitis, including infection (e.g., viral, bacterial), collagen vascular disease, and drug reactions. Up to 50% of self-limited cutaneous cases may be idiopathic. Always look for extracutaneous manifestations, especially kidney involvement. If a young patient presents with arthralgias, abdominal pain, kidney disease, and palpable purpura, think IgA vasculitis.

For more information on small vessel vasculitides, see the Rheumatology section under Vasculitis.

PETECHIAE / PURPURA / ECCHYMOSIS

Defined as hemorrhage into the skin or mucosal membranes, purpura has a vast and complicated differential diagnosis. Classifying the patient's physical findings by morphology can facilitate the evaluation of a patient with primary purpura.

Petechiae (≤ 4 mm): The etiology of petechiae can be further broken down into 3 types of pathophysiology: hemostatically relevant thrombocytopenia (e.g., immune thrombocytopenia, thrombotic thrombocytopenia, disseminated intravascular coagulation), abnormal platelet function (congenital or acquired platelet dysfunction), and nonplatelet etiologies (e.g., trauma, scurvy, benign pigmented purpura).

Macular purpura (5–9 mm): The differential diagnosis of macular purpura includes hypergammaglobulinemic purpura of Waldenström, infection or inflammation in patients with thrombocytopenia, scurvy, and small vessel vasculitis that is minimally inflamed.

Macular ecchymosis (≥ 1 cm): Like petechiae, ecchymosis can be further broken down into 3 types of pathophysiology: procoagulant defect (especially anticoagulant use, hepatic failure, and vitamin K deficiency), poor dermal support (as with solar purpura, systemic steroid therapy, Ehlers-Danlos, and scurvy), and platelet problems (usually thrombocytopenia or von Willebrand disease).

Palpable purpura: The potential etiologies of palpable, or inflammatory, purpura are vast. It may be triggered by the deposition of immune complexes, such as those caused by infection or drugs. It may be due to small or medium vessel vasculitis, such as that seen on biopsy in mixed cryoglobulinemias, rheumatic vasculitis, and antineutrophil cytoplasmic antibody (ANCA)-associated vasculitis. Leukocytoclastic vasculitis (LCV) is a nonspecific inflammatory neutrophilic infiltration in the setting of a small vessel vasculitis. Non-LCV causes may include erythema multiforme and benign pigmented purpura.

PYODERMA GANGRENOSUM

Pyoderma gangrenosum is an inflammatory (not infectious and not a vasculitis) ulcer typically occurring on the legs (Figure 3-23). It is most commonly associated with inflammatory bowel disease but also can be seen with rheumatoid arthritis, ankylosing spondylitis, and hematologic malignancy. However, it is idiopathic in 25–50% of patients. Although a skin biopsy is not diagnostic (i.e., would reveal nonspecific neutrophilic infiltrate), it serves to exclude other

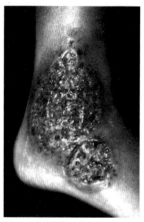

Figure 3-23: Pyoderma gangrenosum

causes of ulceration. The classic presentation is a deep ulceration with an inflamed and violaceous border that overhangs the ulcer. Treating the colonized bacteria usually does not help. Patients often complain of pain out of proportion to the clinical appearance of the lesion. Pathergy, the appearance of ulcers or lesions at sites of cutaneous trauma, is a common phenomenon. Avoid wound debridement.

In idiopathic cases, 1st line treatment is corticosteroids. Otherwise, treat the underlying disorder. Patients may still require pulse dose steroids.

SWEET SYNDROME

Sweet syndrome is an inflammatory disorder that is also referred to as acute febrile neutrophilic dermatosis. It can be:

- Idiopathic (50%)
- Drug induced
- Postinfectious
- Pregnancy related
- Seen with inflammatory or autoimmune disorders
- Seen with underlying hematologic malignancy (e.g., acute myeloid leukemia)

Patients have high fever and painful red plaques, ~ 1 inch in diameter, typically on the upper extremities, trunk, neck, and face. These plaques may be bullous in nature. A skin biopsy shows a dense but benign neutrophilic infiltrate. The lesions respond dramatically to corticosteroids. Potassium iodide, dapsone, and colchicine are also 1st line agents.

NAIL DISORDERS

PREVIEW | REVIEW

- What nutrient deficiency is associated with spooned nails?
- What do dark red lines on a nail bed in a person who uses IV drugs suggest?

Koilonychia is characterized by thin, concave (spoon-shaped) nails. It resolves spontaneously in children but often is secondary to occupational demands or severe iron deficiency in adults.

Psoriatic changes of the nails are covered in Nail Changes on page 3-10.

Clubbing of the nails is common. See the Pulmonary Medicine section under Obstructive Lung Disease and Interstitial Lung Diseases (ILDs) for more information.

Onychomycosis has varied clinical findings depending on its cause. The most commonly observed pattern is the distal or lateral subungual type with invasion of the hyponychium. This is characterized by nail thickening, subungual debris, and yellow or brown discoloration.

The superficial white type is caused by direct invasion into the nail plate and may have white patches or white linear striations. This pattern may be associated with immuno-suppression such as that seen in AIDS.

The proximal subungual type may also be associated with immunosuppression and caused by invasion of the proximal nail fold.

Diagnosis of onychomycosis can be confirmed with KOH scraping, periodic acid–Schiff, and/or culture of a nail clipping and should be done before treating as 50% of suspected cases do not have a fungal infection and treatment with oral antifungals, although most efficacious, can be toxic. Psoriasis and nail dystrophy can mimic fungal infection. Terbinafine is given for 12 weeks for toenail infections and 6 weeks for fingernail infections. Terbinafine is associated with hepatic failure, Stevens-Johnson syndrome/toxic epidermal necrolysis, and pancytopenia.

Onycholysis frequently involves the fingernails, and affected nails are detached from the nail bed. Idiopathic onycholysis may be due to exposure to irritants or water exposure. White or green discoloration may accompany changes. Onycholysis also can be secondary to trauma, psoriasis, tetracyclines, hypothyroidism, or fungal infections. As mentioned previously, onycholysis with pitting is a strong predictor of psoriatic arthritis (see Nail Changes on page 3-10).

Paronychia can be acute or chronic. Acute paronychia is characterized by swelling, redness, and pus of the proximal nail fold. It is most commonly caused by bacterial infection following trauma. If it is recurrent, consider HSV and perform culture or polymerase chain reaction. Treatment includes drainage of the abscess and appropriate antimicrobial treatment–antibiotics for bacterial etiology and antivirals for those cases due to HSV. Clinical features of chronic paronychia include erythema and edema of the proximal nail fold and absence of the cuticle (Figure 3-24). It is thought to be secondary to exposure to irritants or allergens and has a prolonged course. Treatment is avoidance of exacerbating factors, topical steroids, and antiseptics. Do not confuse a paronychia with a felon, which causes a painful infection involving the finger pad and nail bed, or a herpetic whitlow with an associated herpetic vesicular lesion (contagious).

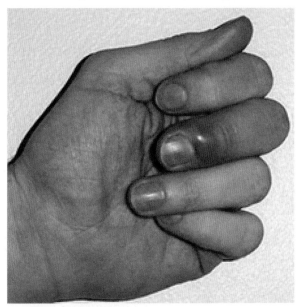

Figure 3-24: Paronychia

Splinter hemorrhages are dark red, thin lines usually located to the distal portion of the nail (Figure 3-25). They are most commonly due to trauma, psoriasis, or onychomycosis. They may also indicate underlying systemic disease such as endocarditis, vasculitis, and antiphospholipid syndrome. Splinter hemorrhages can be seen in people who use IV drugs, who are also at risk of endocarditis.

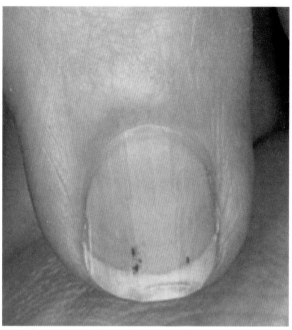

Figure 3-25: Splinter hemorrhage

Nail-fold telangiectasias are common in patients with connective tissue disorders. Patients with dermatomyositis and scleroderma may have reduced capillary density with avascular areas that alternate with dilated capillary loops. Patients with lupus may have normal capillary density with dilated capillary loops.

CUTANEOUS MANIFESTATIONS OF NUTRITIONAL DISORDERS

PREVIEW | REVIEW

- What vitamin deficiency causes a photosensitivity dermatitis?
- What are the dermatologic manifestations of zinc deficiency?
- What vitamin deficiency causes follicular hyperkeratosis?

Deficiency of B_{12}, folate, or niacin may cause diffuse hyperpigmentation, as well as hair and nail changes.

Niacin deficiency results in pellagra (remember the **3 Ds: d**ermatitis [photosensitive areas], **d**iarrhea, and **d**ementia). Isoniazid and carcinoid syndrome (which is characterized by flushing of the skin) can also induce pellagra. Isoniazid is a competitive inhibitor of nicotinamide adenine dinucleotide (niacin precursor) and impairs pyridoxine functioning, which is essential for niacin synthesis from tryptophan.

Tryptophan can be metabolized to niacin or serotonin by 2 separate pathways. In carcinoid syndrome, most of the L-tryptophan is diverted to the production of serotonin, leaving the patient at risk for niacin deficiency.

Zinc deficiency causes an irritant eczematous red rash that has a predilection for periorificial (e.g., perioral, periocular, anogenital) and acral (i.e., hands and feet) areas.

Iron deficiency is usually associated with hair loss, fragile longitudinal nail ridges, and koilonychia (spoon-shaped nails).

Vitamin C deficiency can result in follicular hyperkeratosis, especially on the posterolateral aspect of the arms, resembling keratosis pilaris. The hairs within these plugged follicles become curled, resulting in "corkscrew" hairs. Perifollicular purpura and petechiae develop as the disease advances.

ENVIRONMENTAL INJURY TO THE SKIN

PREVIEW | REVIEW

- What is the treatment for frostbite?

Thermal burns are categorized by depth:

- **Superficial** (formerly **1st degree**)—limited to epidermis; red, blanches with pressure, dry, minor swelling, and minor pain. Commonly resolves in 5–7 days.
- **Partial-thickness** (formerly **2nd degree**) is divided into superficial and deep:
  - Superficial partial-thickness—papillary dermis; blistering, pink, moist, much more painful. Typically heals in 2–3 weeks without scarring.
  - Deep partial-thickness—reticular dermis; blistering, red and/or white with poor blanching and capillary refill, moist or dry, typically painful with variable sensation to light touch. Can take 3–9 weeks to heal, often with scarring.
- **Full-thickness** (formerly **3rd degree**)—entire epidermis and dermis; dry, leathery, waxy, and painless. Requires skin grafting unless small. When fully circumferential, a full-thickness burn can form a strangulating eschar that causes ischemia distally.
- **4th degree** involves skin, subcutaneous tissue, and underlying structures (i.e., fascia, muscle, bone).

General treatment of superficial or superficial partial-thickness burns includes cool compresses for pain relief and infection prevention with application of topical antimicrobial agents such as silver sulfadiazine. Deep partial-thickness, full-thickness, and 4th degree burns often require surgical debridement and skin flaps.

Frostbite (FB) occurs when skin temperature falls below 28.0°F (−2.0°C). It can be divided into 4 categories of severity:

- 1st degree FB is characterized by edema, erythema, and transient pain. Patients have full recovery.
- 2nd degree FB is characterized by severe erythema, edema, and blistering. Patients may have lasting neuropathy.

DERMATOLOGY

- 3rd degree FB is characterized by full-thickness loss of the dermis with hemorrhagic bullae and waxy, dull skin.
- 4th degree FB can result in loss of skin, as well as loss of underlying structures such as muscle and bone. Damage of this degree may require amputation.

Treatment includes rapid rewarming and reestablishment of circulation.

SKIN INFECTIONS

PREVIEW | REVIEW

- What is the significance of finding a lesion of ecthyma gangrenosum on physical exam?
- What 2 organisms can cause impetigo?
- Characterize the lesions of disseminated gonorrhea.
- How does staphylococcal scalded skin syndrome differ from toxic epidermal necrolysis?
- Characterize the rash of erythema migrans.
- What antibiotic is used to treat a cat bite?
- What tinea infections require oral therapy?
- Molluscum contagiosum, if seen in an adult, should raise your suspicion for what immunodeficiency?
- How does the dose of acyclovir differ when the drug is used to treat varicella and herpes simplex infections in the immunocompromised?
- What are the treatments for head lice? What topical treatment is not pesticide based? What drug is the most potent for head lice?
- What type of lice is sexually transmitted?
- How do the effects of the venoms of the brown recluse and black widow spiders differ?
- What spider bite has a longer recovery time?

BACTERIAL INFECTIONS OF THE SKIN AND SOFT TISSUES

Many of the following infections and treatments are covered more fully in the Infectious Disease section under Bacteria.

Cellulitis and Abscesses

Erythrasma is a well-defined, red lesion with some slight scaling. It is usually found in the axilla, groin, and toe webs. In patients with obesity, it is seen under the breasts. Gram-positive *Corynebacterium minutissimum* is frequently isolated from the lesion (especially after it has become scaly or macerated). Differential diagnosis: tinea cruris, *Candida*, and intertrigo—an irritant dermatitis typically found in the skin folds of individuals with obesity (see Intertrigo on page 3-3). Diagnosis: Erythrasma fluoresces bright red (attributed to coproporphyrin III) with a Wood lamp (UV light). Treat with benzoyl peroxide or topical erythromycin +/– an "-azole" antifungal cream. In severe cases, oral erythromycin or tetracycline may be used.

Folliculitis

Folliculitis inflammation of hair follicles usually caused by *Staphylococcus aureus*. **Furuncles** (deep folliculitis or "boils") are a folliculitis that extends deep into the dermis. **Carbuncles** are collections of furuncles that have coalesced under the skin, forming a networked, single mass. Treatment includes oral or parenteral antibiotics and moist heat. Consider surgical drainage of fluctuant lesions.

Be cognizant that folliculitis associated with hot tubs is often caused by *Pseudomonas*, not *Staphylococcus*, and is acquired in hot tubs with inadequate chlorination. The resulting pustules usually occur around the buttocks and thighs or in occluded skin areas such as skinfolds or under a swimsuit. Pseudomonal folliculitis resolves without treatment in ~ 1 week. 5% acetic acid (i.e., vinegar) compresses can be used for symptomatic relief.

A much more serious infection is *Pseudomonas* septicemia with the initial dermatologic finding of small, dark-centered (necrotic) papules. In a very ill, neutropenic patient, this papule progresses and becomes the pathognomonic ecthyma gangrenosum, a necrotic ulcer with an erythematous rim (Figure 3-26).

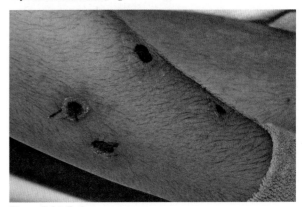

Figure 3-26: Ecthyma gangrenosum

Impetigo

S. aureus is by far the most common cause of impetigo; however, it also may be caused by group A *Streptococcus*. It starts as an erythematous, vesicular lesion that quickly becomes pustular and crusty (a honey-colored crust). Impetigo is highly contagious, and patients generally do not appear systemically ill. The face and exposed areas are most commonly affected. Methicillin-resistant *S. aureus* (MRSA) causes many community outbreaks. When impetigo—an infection of the epidermis—extends into the dermis, it is called ecthyma.

Limited skin lesions can be treated with topical mupirocin for 5 days. Extensive lesions and ecthyma require oral treatment with antibiotics that cover both *S. aureus* and streptococci. These include dicloxacillin or cephalexin with erythromycin as an alternative for allergic patients. If MRSA is suspected by history or culture, use clindamycin, trimethoprim/sulfamethoxazole (TMP/SMX), or doxycycline. The usual course of treatment with oral agents is 7 days.

Note: Bullous impetigo usually occurs in young children < 2 years of age and presents with the acute onset of large, loose bullae (Figure 3-27). An exotoxin/exfoliatin toxin causes cleavage of the epidermis.

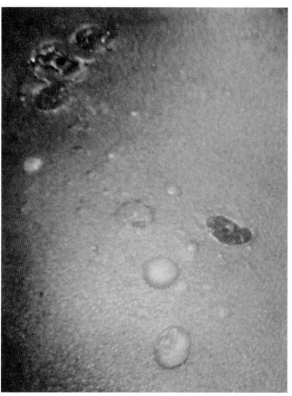

Figure 3-27: Bullous impetigo

Erysipelas

Erysipelas is an explosive superficial infection (often caused by group A *Streptococcus*) that is confined to the dermis and spreads quickly through skin lymphatics (Figure 3-28). The area of infection is clearly demarcated, red, and palpable. It usually starts from a superficial abrasion, typically around the central face, with erythema and swelling. Lymphangitic spread with red streaking is seen. Initial treatment is IV antibiotics followed by oral therapy.

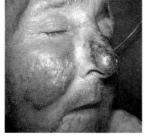

Figure 3-28: Erysipelas

Necrotizing Fasciitis (NF)

NF is a deep soft tissue infection involving planes of subcutaneous fat and fascia. This area contains the nerve bundles, which, when damaged, cause extreme pain followed by anesthesia. Blood supply can also be damaged, so antibiotic response is poor and necrosis of the overlying tissue occurs. Unlike erysipelas, NF does not have a distinct border and can be difficult to diagnose early. NF can be hard to distinguish from cellulitis in the early stages, but in NF, the pain is usually out of proportion to the physical signs and there are signs of sepsis. Ask about any history of skin trauma. Cellulitis is characterized by erythema, swelling, and lymphangitis. Lymphadenopathy is absent in NF, and skin changes rapidly progress with violaceous discoloration and sometimes blisters (necrosis) and crepitus. NF should be treated urgently with antibiotics and surgical exploration. If suspecting NF, it is imperative to act rapidly. Surgical intervention is often necessary before a full diagnostic work-up is completed (e.g., skin biopsy, blood cultures, CPK indicating muscle damage, imaging [including CT and MRI]).

There are 3 types of NF. **Type I**, the most common type, is a polymicrobial infection (including anaerobes) seen in immunocompromised patients, such as those with diabetes. **Type II** is generally caused by group A *Streptococcus* or MRSA and most commonly affects healthy individuals. If NF is suspected, obtain cultures, start antibiotic therapy, and consider emergent surgery, as there is a high mortality rate even with appropriate medical and surgical intervention. Avoid wasting time with computed tomography scans if NF diagnosis is suspected. **Type III** occurs as a result of infection from deep penetrating trauma and typically involves clostridial species.

Gonococcus and Meningococcus

Disseminated gonococcal infection causes a few (commonly < 12) hemorrhagic pustules on the extremities, often around the joints. Culture of the skin lesions is typically negative. Swab for cultures from the initial site of infection (e.g., oral mucosa, cervix, urethra, rectum) because there is a much higher yield.

Meningococcemic skin signs start as macular or petechial lesions and evolve to large purpura. Purpura fulminans consists of purpura, ecchymoses, and confluent maplike, gray-to-black, necrotic skin lesions. It is associated with severe infection and diffuse intravascular coagulation.

Staphylococcal Scalded Skin Syndrome (SSSS)

SSSS primarily affects newborns and children < 5 years of age. Rarely, it affects immunocompromised adults. Patients with SSSS present with tender, red, peeling skin—due to circulating toxins from localized *Staphylococcus* infection or colonization that generally is initiated at a nonskin site (e.g., sinuses, umbilicus in infants). Skin changes are similar to those seen in toxic epidermal necrolysis (TEN), which is noninfectious (e.g., a side effect of drugs like allopurinol, NSAIDs, or trimethoprim/sulfamethoxazole), so consider

DERMATOLOGY

it during the workup. The skin in SSSS separates much more superficially than in TEN. The peeling skin is caused by a similar exotoxin or exfoliatin toxin, as seen in bullous impetigo (a localized form of SSSS); however, it circulates systemically in SSSS. Treatment includes debridement of necrotic superficial epidermis, topical antibiotics for bullous impetigo lesions, and systemic antibiotics for more severe and/or widespread disease.

Toxic Shock Syndrome (TSS)

TSS is caused by *S. aureus* and *Streptococcus pyogenes*. First described in 1978 in association with the use of highly absorbent tampons in menstruating women, today > 50% of cases are not associated with menstruation.

Staphylococcal TSS presents with abrupt development of fever, shock, and multiorgan system failure. In the acute phase, patients develop a diffuse, painless, macular erythrodermic rash ("sunburn") followed by desquamation of the palms and soles during the convalescent phase. Patients are commonly < 30 years of age, and mucosal involvement is typical. Treatment includes supportive care and systemic antibiotics.

Streptococcal TSS causes symptoms similar to those of staphylococcal TSS. Treatment is with IV penicillin (PCN) + clindamycin +/– intravenous immunoglobulin. In contrast to staphylococcal TSS, blood cultures are usually positive in streptococcal TSS.

For more information on TSS see the Infectious Disease section under Bacteria.

Scarlet Fever

Scarlet fever primarily presents in children with streptococcal pharyngitis and a rash known as "scarlatina"—a fine, red, sandpaper-like rash that is more prominent in skin folds (Pastia lines) and involves the trunk and extremities but spares the palms and soles. "Strawberry tongue" also commonly presents in the acute phase. During the convalescent stage, desquamation of the palms and soles occurs.

Strep Throat

PCN is by far the best treatment for group A *Streptococcus* throat infection. Give oral PCN (× 10 days) or intramuscular benzathine PCN. Give erythromycin for PCN-allergic patients. Clindamycin is often added to PCN when there is serious infection to decrease toxin production such as necrotizing fasciitis or toxic shock.

Rocky Mountain Spotted Fever (RMSF)

RMSF is usually heralded by several days of fever. Then, small lesions develop that progress from peripheral to central (centripetal) distribution and from macular to petechial to purpuric type. As you can see in Figure 3-29, the skin findings can be deceivingly nondescript. Treat with doxycycline or chloramphenicol.

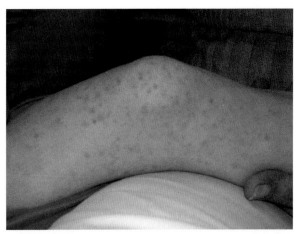

Figure 3-29: Rocky Mountain spotted fever

Spirochetal Skin Infections

Lyme disease: The first stage of Lyme disease is often associated with erythema migrans (Figure 3-30). Typically, this is a slowly enlarging (over ~ 1 week), annular, erythematous rash with a clear center (looks like a bull's-eye). Occasionally, the center is not clear. Treat early Lyme disease with oral antibiotics—including doxycycline, amoxicillin, or cefuroxime axetil—to reduce the signs and symptoms and decrease the risk of late Lyme disease development.

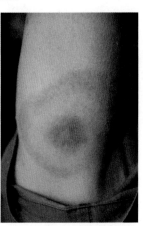

Figure 3-30: Erythema migrans

Syphilis: A chancre (painless ulcer at site of inoculation) indicates primary syphilis. This is commonly on the penis or vagina but can present on the pharynx or anus depending on sexual practices. A few weeks after the chancre appears, a diffuse scaling nonitchy macular papular rash is seen on the palms and soles. This rash is a hallmark of secondary syphilis but it also can be found on the trunk, head and neck, genitals, and mucosal surfaces. White, thickened plaques (condylomata lata) are additional secondary syphilis signs. There is lymphadenopathy. Gummas occur in tertiary syphilis. These are painless, indurated, nodular, or ulcerative lesions.

Animal Bites

Dog and cat bites can both cause infection with *S. aureus* and *Pasteurella multocida*, but cat bites more commonly cause *P. multocida* infection. Human bites can cause severe infection by bacteria such as *Eikenella corrodens*, *Streptococcus* and *Staphylococcus*, and corynebacterium.

Clean and lavage well and give amoxicillin/clavulanate as prophylaxis and treatment. Doxycycline can be given alone to patients who are allergic to PCN. Trimethoprim/sulfamethoxazole, cefuroxime, or ciprofloxacin do have coverage against *Pasteurella*, but they need to be combined with clindamycin or metronidazole to provide adequate anaerobic coverage.

Macrolides (erythromycin), clindamycin, and antistaphylococcal penicillins (dicloxacillin) lack activity against *P. multocida*.

Use antibiotic prophylaxis in the following situations:

- Immunocompromised host
- Bites on the face, hand, or near a bone or joint
- Significant tissue destruction
- Presenting edema
- Crush injuries

Bites on the hand are prone to deep infection due to the relative paucity of soft tissue above bones and joints.

All animal bites are considered as contaminated wounds due to saliva, so review tetanus status.

Give a tetanus vaccine if:

- The patient has received < 3 doses of vaccine in lifetime
- The wound is dirty and it has been > 5 years since the last tetanus vaccine

In addition, give tetanus immunoglobulin if the wound is contaminated, and the patient has had < 3 tetanus vaccines in their lifetime or if the patient does not know their status.

The animal should be observed for 10 days if possible. Rabies postexposure immunization is necessary only if the animal shows signs of illness or if the animal cannot be observed.

FUNGAL INFECTIONS OF THE SKIN

Superficial Fungal Infections

Dermatophytes (*Microsporum*, *Epidermophyton*, and *Trichophyton*) cause superficial fungal infections (outer layer of skin) and are named according to the site involved:

- Tinea capitis (scalp ringworm)
- Tinea corporis (common ringworm on torso or extremities; Figure 3-31)
- Tinea cruris (jock itch)
- Tinea unguium/onychomycosis (nails; Figure 3-32)
- Tinea pedis (athlete's foot; Figure 3-33)

The diagnosis is often made clinically but can be

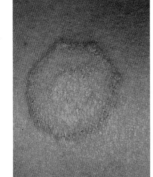

Figure 3-31: Tinea corporis

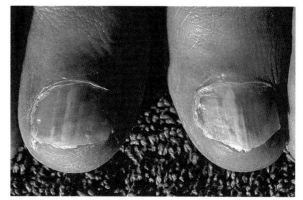

Figure 3-32: Tinea unguium

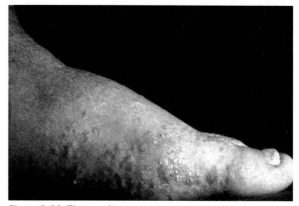

Figure 3-33: Tinea pedis

confirmed with potassium hydroxide (KOH) test on skin scrapings, which reveals branching filamentous hyphae.

Topical antifungal creams, such as ketoconazole, miconazole, clotrimazole, and terbinafine, control most fungal skin infections. Systemic therapy (the same as is used for tinea capitis) is required for those who fail topical therapy or who have extensive skin involvement. Due to the potential for liver toxicity with terbinafine, liver function tests should be done at baseline and periodically throughout therapy.

Tinea unguium (onychomycosis) can be treated with either topical or oral antifungal agents.

Use topical treatments when < 1/2 of the distal nail plate is affected. Topical options include ciclopirox 8% and efinaconazole 1% nail solutions, as well as tavaborole 5% solution. Duration of topical treatment is 48 weeks.

Oral therapy may be needed for topical therapy failures and generally is more efficacious. Oral treatment for tinea unguium is terbinafine, itraconazole, or fluconazole.

Obtain a nail clipping sample and send it to the lab. Up to 50% of patients with suspected onychomycosis do not have a fungal nail infection. Common conditions, such as psoriasis or a nail dystrophy, can mimic onychomycosis. Given the potentially severe toxicity of terbinafine, confirmation of a fungal infection is recommended prior to initiation of therapy. Terbinafine is rarely associated with hepatic failure, Stevens-Johnson syndrome (SJS)/toxic epidermal necrolysis (TEN), and pancytopenia. The

DERMATOLOGY

diagnosis can be confirmed with a nail clipping with KOH scraping, periodic acid–Schiff, and/or culture.

Oral terbinafine is prescribed for 12 weeks when toenails are involved. It is prescribed for 6 weeks for fingernails. Check transaminases at baseline and consider repeating at 6 weeks.

Tinea capitis must always be treated with oral antifungals such as griseofulvin, terbinafine, fluconazole, or itraconazole for 8 weeks. Tinea capitis is a superficial fungal infection caused by dermatophytes: *Microsporum*, *Epidermophyton*, and *Trichophyton*. This is an infection of the scalp and causes erythema, scale, pruritus, and localized alopecia. KOH scraping shows branching (filamentous hyphae).

Tinea corporis is spread primarily by direct skin-to-skin contact or secondarily from other sites of fungal infection. Classic presentation is an annular, scaly rash with raised, advancing erythematous margin and scale that is clear toward the center with a history of pet contact. A differential diagnosis includes the herald patch of pityriasis rosea and granuloma annulare (GA). Itch is a differentiating factor (present in tinea), and GA lacks scales. Nummular eczema is similar. Microscopically, these demonstrate long, narrow hyphae; spores are not seen. Tinea corporis can be treated with topical antifungals or oral antifungals. Oral treatment is the same as for tinea capitis.

Tinea versicolor (pityriasis versicolor) is caused by *Malassezia globosa* or *M. furfur*. Skin infection results in hypopigmented or hyperpigmented (depending on the patient's skin tone/color) spreading macules, usually on the upper torso and upper arms, but the infection can spread over the body. Microscopic KOH skin scraping reveals "spaghetti and meatballs" (Figure 3-34). Treatment is topical such as imidazole creams, selenium sulfide, or

Figure 3-34: Tinea versicolor (KOH prep)

ketoconazole shampoo and/or oral such as itraconazole or fluconazole. Always consider secondary syphilis when evaluating disseminated rashes on the body although the hallmark sign for syphilis is on the palms and soles.

Deeper Fungal Infections

Candidiasis intertrigo is a deeper skin fungal infection that causes red patches in intertriginous areas. These sites are often chronically moist with lack of circulation. A variant occurs in the interdigital spaces of the hands, especially for persons in occupations where hands are frequently in water such as dishwashers or nurses. Candidiasis of the mouth (thrush) causes white semiadherent plaques on the tongue and mucosa. Unlike hairy leukoplakia, these can be scraped off. Vaginal candidiasis has similar plaques with cheesy discharge. Other presentations are perleche and diaper dermatitis. Treatment can be with topical formulations or systemic agents, depending on the area affected and patient's comorbidities. Visualization demonstrates pseudohyphae and yeast cells. Treatment is topical imidazoles (e.g., clotrimazole).

Cutaneous mucormycosis is a rare infection caused by extremely common fungus of the class *Mucorales*. Infection can occur after inoculation of the fungal spores, usually by trauma, into the dermis of an immunocompromised person, most commonly a patient with poorly controlled diabetes. It first appears as a single tender and painful indurated area that quickly spreads, causing tissue necrosis. Cutaneous mucormycosis usually remains cutaneous and does not spread to the deeper dermis tissues or become systemic.

VIRAL INFECTIONS OF THE SKIN

Human Papillomavirus (HPV)

Warts are caused by any 1 of > 100 types of HPV. They often resolve spontaneously, but this can take up to 2 years. However, because of their appearance, patients may request treatment, which typically involves some form of tissue destruction:

- Verruca vulgaris is the common wart. Treatments include liquid nitrogen, topical acids, and CO_2 laser.
- Verruca plana is the flat wart. Treatment is the same as that for verruca vulgaris, but note that these lesions do exhibit koebnerization (i.e., spread) with trauma to the skin.
- Verruca plantaris is the plantar wart (Figure 3-35). Initial treatment may consist of a strong acid (i.e., trichloroacetic acid), concentrated (40%) salicylic acid plaster, liquid nitrogen, or laser.

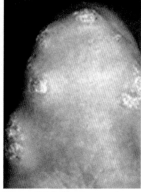

Figure 3-35: Plantar warts

- Condylomata acuminata are anogenital warts. 90% are caused by HPV-6 or -11. They are sometimes coinfected by HPV-16, -18, or -31—the oncogenic HPV types (associated with cancer of the cervix and anus). If unsure of diagnosis, do a shave biopsy. Treat with topical podophyllin, trichloroacetic acid, imiquimod, liquid nitrogen, or CO_2 laser. Podophyllin is teratogenic, so do not give it to pregnant patients.

Molluscum Contagiosum

Know: Molluscum contagiosum is caused by a poxvirus. It consists of smooth, umbilicated, pearly papules

(Figure 3-36). It usually occurs in children (anywhere on the body except the palms and soles), but you may also see it in the pelvic area of sexually active young adults—and it is common in AIDS patients (can be sexually transmitted). Although molluscum contagiosum often resolves spontaneously, except in immunosuppressed patients (e.g., AIDS), treatment options include cryotherapy with liquid nitrogen, surgical curettage, and cantharidin application. Antiretroviral treatment imiquimod is used to treat molluscum associated with HIV infection.

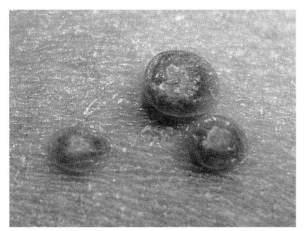

Figure 3-36: Molluscum contagiosum

Measles and Rubella

Know: **Measles** (rubeola) has several stages. The prodromal stage lasts 3–4 days with fever, malaise, sinus discharge, and a hacking cough. Koplik spots often appear on the palate from 1 to several days before the onset of rash. As the Koplik spots begin to disappear, a red maculopapular rash starts on the face and behind the ears and quickly spreads downward and outward, with the densest concentration of lesions from the face to the shoulders. The palms and soles are affected last. Lesions gradually fade in order of appearance and may have some desquamation.

Rubella (a.k.a. German measles and 3-day measles) is benign except when it occurs in pregnant women. The rash is similar to measles but lasts only 3 days. Rubella has been eradicated in the Americas, but there are still ~ 120,000 cases/year worldwide. Congenital rubella results in a variety of serious birth defects:

- Heart malformations
- Ocular defects
- Microcephaly
- Intellectual disability
- Deafness
- Thrombotic thrombocytopenic purpura
- Bone problems

Varicella-Zoster Virus (VZV)

VZV causes 2 diseases: chickenpox and herpes zoster (shingles). Both diseases present with vesicles on an erythematous base. Herpes zoster is reactivation of VZV in a person who has had chickenpox.

Chickenpox (Figure 3-37) has decreased in incidence with routine childhood vaccination. Rash is initially maculopapular and rapidly progresses to vesicles and then to scabbed lesions. These tend to come in "crops" over 2–4 days.

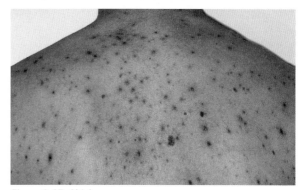

Figure 3-37: Chickenpox

Herpes zoster (a.k.a. shingles; Figure 3-38) manifests as grouped vesicles along a dermatome with focal pain and is unilateral. Affected dermatomes can include the regions of the eye (herpes zoster ophthalmicus; Figure 3-39 on page 3-24) and ear (herpes zoster oticus). Older age and immunosuppression (e.g., HIV) are risk factors. Zoster occurring along the 1st branch of the trigeminal nerve (V1) affecting the nasal tip is known as Hutchinson sign. Zoster in this pattern runs the risk of zoster ophthalmicus, a sight-threatening condition, and requires an evaluation by an ophthalmologist. Treatment of herpes zoster is 800 mg oral acyclovir 5×/day for 7–10 days, but if the patient has an immunocompromised status, such as an HIV-infected patient, then intravenous acyclovir is needed at 10 mg/kg 5×/day for 7 days. Adjust dose for chronic kidney disease.

If started within 72 hours of onset, antiviral therapy with acyclovir, famciclovir, or valacyclovir decreases disease duration. Systemic steroids can help reduce acute pain, but use is controversial, whereas gabapentin can reduce the likelihood of progression to postherpetic neuralgia.

More information on the VZV and herpes zoster vaccine is in the Infectious Disease section under Viruses.

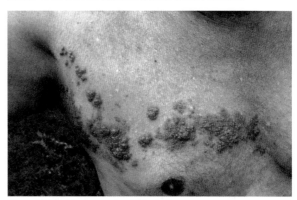

Figure 3-38: Herpes zoster (shingles)

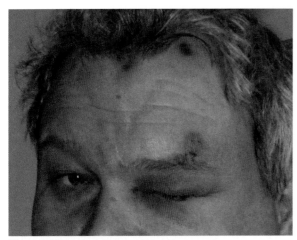

Figure 3-39: Herpes zoster ophthalmicus

Herpes Simplex Virus

See herpes simplex infections in Oral Blisters and Ulcers on page 3-7.

INFESTATIONS AND BITES

Note: Parasitic skin infection outbreaks typically occur in schools, nursing home communities, and camps.

Lice

Head lice (*Pediculus humanus capitis*) have a 1-month lifespan, during which time the females lay ~ 10 eggs per day and firmly attach them to the base of hair strands. Transmission is through direct contact with hair on the head of an infected person. Diagnosis is made by direct visualization of live lice in the hair; nits (eggs) alone do not confirm active infestation because nits can persist after successful treatment. A Wood lamp examination can be performed in difficult cases. Live nits are fluorescent pale blue/white when illuminated with a Wood lamp. Empty nits are fluorescent gray.

Most treatments are neurotoxic to the lice. Benzyl alcohol causes asphyxiation. Chemical treatment should be followed by nit removal manually with a comb. Chemical treatments include:

- Topical ivermectin is the strongest drug. It requires a single application and has an effectiveness of ~ 95%. Oral ivermectin can also be effective; however, it has not been approved by the FDA for this treatment.
- Malathion is a pesticide-based treatment that kills both lice and eggs. Effectiveness of malathion is ≥ 90%, but it is expensive and flammable (!) and must be left on for 8 hours.
- Spinosad is derived from a soil bacterium, *Saccharopolyspora spinosa*. It overexcites the central nervous system (CNS) of the lice, interacting with their acetylcholine receptors. Second application is done only if live lice are seen 7 days later. It has an effectiveness of ~ 85%.

- Benzyl alcohol lotion 5% contains no neurotoxic pesticides. It kills by suffocating the lice. It is safe in children > 6 months of age. Retreatment after 7 days is required. It has an effectiveness of ~ 75%.
- Over-the-counter treatments include permethrin cream 1% and a lotion with permethrin + piperonyl butoxide. Unfortunately, in the U.S., resistance is growing against permethrin and malathion. Effectiveness of permethrin treatments is not very high (< 50% overall and even lower in areas of high resistance).
- 1% lindane shampoo is a 2nd line treatment because of neurotoxicity to humans.

Remove nits with a fine-toothed comb following treatment. There are professional services that will, for a fee, remove lice in their clinics or in the patient's home. Although transmission by fomites is controversial, treat infested close contacts and bedmates at the same time; disinfect brushes, combs, and hats.

Body lice (*Pediculus humanus corporis*; Figure 3-40) live in clothes and are on the body only when feeding. Treatment is bathing and discarding or carefully laundering clothes and bed linens, using hot water. Clothes can also be ironed

Figure 3-40: Body louse

with focus on the seams. If the patient has a few nits on body hair, additionally treat with permethrin 5% cream.

Pubic lice (*Pthirus pubis*): The crab louse is sexually transmitted and can also infect the eyelashes. Fomites rarely transmit crab lice. Itching in the groin area is the most common manifestation of infection. Physical examination may reveal bluish macules (maculae ceruleae) in the groin area, usually in patients who have been infested for a prolonged period. Treatment is similar to that of head lice. Use topical permethrin or pyrethrin + piperonyl butoxide. Wash bedding and clothing in hot water, and use a hot dryer.

Scabies

Scabies is caused by a the tiny (0.2–0.4 mm) (*Sarcoptes scabiei*) mite that tunnels into the skin to lay eggs (Figure 3-41). It is spread by skin-to-skin contact—the mites do not live > 48 hours without a host! Consider it in anyone with unexplained, intense itching in areas of erythematous papules that is worse at night and after a hot shower, particularly in hospitalized or institutionalized patients. Classically, scabies is associated with itching of the flexor aspects of wrists, axilla, and interdigital spaces. Diagnosis is made by microscopic visualization of the mite, feces, or eggs from skin scrapings that are prepped with mineral oil.

Treat with permethrin 5% applied to all areas of the body from the head down and washed off after 8–14 hours. A 2nd dose in 7 days is recommended. Treat all household

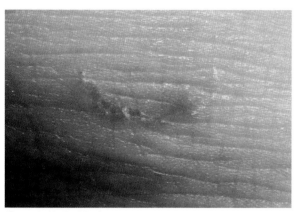

Figure 3-41: Scabies burrow

contacts simultaneously. Alternatives are crotamiton lotion or cream 10% (however, crotamiton is for scabies in adults only and is not very effective), sulfur ointment 5–10%, or lindane lotion 1% (not 1st line). Use oral ivermectin for severe or recalcitrant cases, with a repeat dose in 1 week; however, it is not approved by the FDA for this use. In nursing homes and for cases of crusted scabies (a.k.a. Norwegian scabies), a combination therapy of topical permethrin and oral ivermectin, 2 doses given 7 days apart, may be used. Oral therapy alone is also used in institutions such as when a patient is mentally impaired or when permethrin is inappropriate. Lindane has CNS toxicity—do not use during pregnancy, in infants, or in young children. Permethrin can be used in pregnancy. Precipitated sulfur is also considered safe to use during pregnancy; however, it may be less effective. Wash all linens and clothing in hot water.

Bedbugs

Bedbugs (*Cimex lectularius*; Figure 3-42) are blood-sucking ectoparasites that hide in cracks and crevices during the day and feed at night. They cause edematous pink papules that may have a central punctum. Bites are often found in groups of 3 in a linear array (breakfast, lunch, and dinner) but can be scattered (Figure 3-43). Reactions to bites can take days to develop. Symptoms can be treated with topical corticosteroids. Insects need to be eradicated from the home, which can be difficult and can require professional extermination.

Figure 3-42: Bedbug

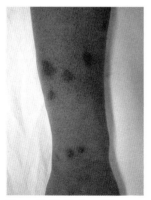

Figure 3-43: Bedbug bites

Spiders

In the U.S., the spider whose bite can cause a necrotic reaction is the recluse spider (genus *Loxosceles*). The brown recluse (*Loxosceles reclusa*) is found in the south-central U.S.; other recluse species are found along the southwestern border of the U.S. See Figure 3-44 for their distribution in the U.S.

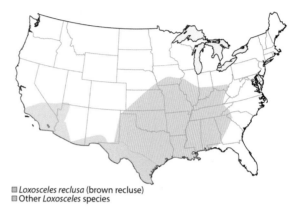

■ *Loxosceles reclusa* (brown recluse)
■ Other *Loxosceles* species

Figure 3-44: Geographic distribution of Loxosceles species spiders in 2018

Brown recluse spiders (Figure 3-45) tend to hide in woodpiles, attics, closets, and seldom-worn clothing. Adults have a leg span of ~ 25 mm, 6 eyes, and a dark violin pattern on the dorsal front portion of the body (cephalothorax); thus, they are also called "fiddleback" or "violin" spiders. The venom of brown recluse spiders contains sphingomyelinase and other substances that lyse cell walls, activate complement, and cause local necrosis.

Figure 3-45: Brown recluse spider. Note the violin pattern on the dorsal cephalothorax.

The reaction to the bite of all the recluse spiders is similar. Initially, the bite is painless; pain develops at the site 2–8 hours later. Over the next 1–2 days, a hemorrhagic blister develops that eventually progresses to a necrotic ulceration. Patients rarely have systemic symptoms such as fever, chills, nausea, or vomiting. Cutaneous loxoscelism is the term given for the ulcerative effect of the recluse bite (genus *Loxosceles*). It is the only spider that affects humans this way.

DERMATOLOGY

Because these bites are seldom infected, treatment is supportive with local wound care. They can take a week to heal. If there is obvious infection, think MRSA instead. The lesions may continue to expand for as long as 10 days, but most eventually heal spontaneously without surgical or other intervention. Other treatments (e.g., dapsone, steroids) are controversial because data on effectiveness is lacking. Dapsone is commonly used to prevent the wound from necrosing. Glucose-6-phosphate dehydrogenase deficiency is a contraindication.

Black widow spiders (Figure 3-46) are found throughout the U.S. except Alaska. The southern black widow and western black widow spiders are most commonly responsible for serious symptoms. Widow spiders hide in dimly lit, warm, dry outhouses and sheds. They are large, with leg spans of up to 40 mm. Patients usually have a recent history of outdoor activity, such as cleaning out a garage. Female spiders are twice the size of males and cause the most severe bites. A mature black widow female has a red or orange hourglass marking on the ventral surface of the abdomen.

Figure 3-46: Black widow spider. Note the red/orange hourglass on the ventral abdomen.

Black widow spider venom is a neurotoxin that causes very little local reaction, although cutaneous reactions can include erythema, edema, and piloerection. Initial signs and symptoms include pain at the site, diaphoresis, muscle cramping, chest tightness, vomiting, malaise, sweating, agitation, hypertension, and abdominal pain, which can mimic appendicitis.

Treatment includes local wound care, analgesia, and tetanus prophylaxis. Usually, all symptoms resolve within 24–48 hours. More severe cases can be treated with widow antivenin. Be aware that widow antivenin, like snakebite antivenin, can cause anaphylaxis.

Wounds from the painless bite of the brown recluse spider can take a week or longer to heal as a result of the enzymatic tissue breakdown. Wounds from the painful bite of a black widow spider releasing a neurotoxin heal more rapidly and with no tissue destruction.

CUTANEOUS ULCERS

PREVIEW | REVIEW
- Where is the preferred biopsy site of a cutaneous lesion?
- Venous ulcers are usually related to what underlying disorders?

Ulcers, defined by loss of both epidermis and dermis, can be quite challenging to diagnose and treat. They are most commonly found on the lower legs and have a vast range of causes. Biopsy and culture of ulcers can aid in ruling out neoplastic or infectious etiologies, respectively. The biopsy should be performed at the edge or margin of the ulcer rather than the center to allow for better healing and control of bleeding and to avoid a biopsy of nondiagnostic necrotic debris. The 3 most common causes are venous, arterial, and neuropathic etiologies.

Venous ulcers are commonly located on the medial malleolus and are related to venous hypertension or venous insufficiency. They typically have irregular, shallow borders and a yellow fibrinous base and may be accompanied by clinical findings of stasis dermatitis, lymphedema, varicosities, and edema. Hemosiderin deposition and/or petechiae may also be observed.

Arterial ulcers are often located on distal sites and bony prominences. The base of these ulcers may be yellow and fibrinous or dry and necrotic. Lesions are described as punched out. Surrounding skin can be shiny and devoid of hair. Peripheral pulses may be weakened or absent.

Neuropathic ulcers, like arterial ulcers, are located at pressure sites and may be described as punched out; however, they may also be surrounded by thick callus. Accompanying clinical findings include peripheral neuropathy and foot deformities.

Pyoderma gangrenosum (PG) is a neutrophilic, ulcerating disorder. Lesions start as tender nodules, papules, or pustules that progress to necrotic ulcerations with violaceous, rolled borders and a rim of erythema. PG is a diagnosis of exclusion; other causes must be worked up and ruled out. Patients can have a history of underlying disease, or it can be idiopathic. It occurs often in inflammatory bowel disease, ulcerative colitis, rheumatoid arthritis, and multiple myeloma. Other associations with PG include Sweet syndrome, Behçet disease, and Sjögren syndrome. It may be idiopathic in up to 50% of cases. Treatment includes topical steroids, systemic corticosteroids, dapsone, immunosuppressive medications, and tumor necrosis factor inhibitors. PG is worsened by trauma (pathergy), so debridement or other procedures should be avoided. For more on PG, see Pyoderma Gangrenosum on page 3-15.

There is a wide range of less common causes of cutaneous ulcers, including infection, vasculitis, physical trauma (e.g., prolonged pressure, burns, factitial), hematologic disease (e.g., sickle cell disease, α- and β-thalassemias, hereditary spherocytosis), hypercoagulable states, and vasoocclusive disease.

HAIR DISORDERS

PREVIEW | REVIEW

- What form of alopecia is from an autoimmune state?

- What is the origin of excessive hair growth that is located centrally?

- What causes excessive facial hair in women?

ALOPECIA

Androgenic alopecia results from the effect of androgens on hair follicles in genetically susceptible individuals. Androgens cause miniaturization of hair follicles and subsequent hair thinning and loss. Thinning occurs in the frontotemporal regions and vertex in men and on the central crown in women. Treatment includes topical minoxidil and oral antiandrogens, such as finasteride.

Alopecia areata (AA) is an autoimmune disease specific to hair. AA presents with discrete round patches of hair loss without scarring. It can progress to alopecia totalis (loss of scalp hair) and alopecia universalis (loss of scalp and body hair). Nails in patients with AA may have pitting in a regular or geometric pattern.

Treatment for AA depends on the age of patient, extent of disease, and duration of disease. Steroids are used intralesionally (intralesional steroid injection [ILS]), topically, or systemically.

ILS is 1st line for adolescents and adults with limited disease. Potent topical steroids are used for children < 12 years of age and those with extensive disease. They are 1st line therapy for scalp, eyebrow, and beard AA. Systemic steroids are used for those > 13 years of age and are preferred for acute disease. Topical calcineurin inhibitors can be used for scalp and eyebrow AA, but are 2nd line for beard AA. Prostaglandin analogues bimatoprost and latanoprost are used for eye lash alopecia. Minoxidil is helpful to increase the linear rate of growth and can be used alongside other treatments. Contact immunotherapy with scalene acid dibutyl ester may be helpful; however, results are not consistent.

Other systemic therapies include cyclosporine and methotrexate (MTX). In adults, Janus kinase (JAK) inhibitors may be used alone or in combination with cyclosporine and MTX.

Treatment is considered successful when all of the hair growth has returned or vellus hair is present in patches. Systemic steroids and JAK inhibitors can prevent progression to total hair loss.

Trichotillomania is a self-inflicted hair disorder and often associated with psychological stress or a personality disorder. Clinical features include irregular patches of hair loss with hair of varying lengths. Patients may also pluck hairs from other areas such as the eyebrows, eyelashes, and body.

Traction alopecia is most commonly seen in Black female patients in their 30s to 40s. It typically involves the frontotemporal regions. It results from consistent traction of the hair over years. In early stages, traction alopecia may be reversible. Over time, it becomes permanent as the hair follicles become scarred.

Telogen effluvium occurs when large numbers of hairs simultaneously enter the telogen phase and shed. This can be triggered by a pathological or physiological change in the patient's health status such as pregnancy, extreme dieting, thyroid disorder, surgery, medications, and severe stress. Diffuse hair loss occurs 4–6 months after the precipitating event. Eventual complete hair regrowth is possible, particularly if the underlying cause is eliminated.

EXCESSIVE HAIR

Hirsutism is defined as excessive body hair in areas where it is usually absent or scarce. It may be caused by increased androgens or an increased sensitivity to androgens. It may be associated with seborrhea, acne, or androgenic alopecia. It is useful to determine the source of the affecting androgens such as an ovarian source or adrenal source. The patient's pattern of hair growth can be useful. If it is centrally located, then it is likely adrenal in origin. If the hair is mostly located on the areolae and lateral neck and face, then it is likely ovarian in origin. Polycystic ovarian syndrome is the most common cause of hirsutism in women. Other etiologies include Cushing syndrome, anabolic steroids, and androgen-secreting tumors. For more information on hirsutism, see the Endocrinology section under Hormones of Reproduction.

SKIN CANCER AND PRECANCEROUS LESIONS

PREVIEW | REVIEW

- What is the metastatic potential for basal cell carcinoma?

- Squamous cell carcinoma has the highest rates of metastasis on what body areas?

- What measurement is most important when determining melanoma prognosis?

- What are the main forms of cutaneous T-cell lymphoma? Which has the worse prognosis?

DYSPLASTIC NEVI

Dysplastic nevi are "odd-looking" moles and may even look like melanomas (Figure 3-47 on page 3-28). However, most melanomas arise de novo—not in a preexisting nevus. Therefore, removing all moles does not prevent melanoma development. Closely monitor patients with these lesions, using photographic documentation. If a patient with a dysplastic nevus has 2 relatives with malignant melanoma, the patient has a 300× chance of getting malignant melanoma!

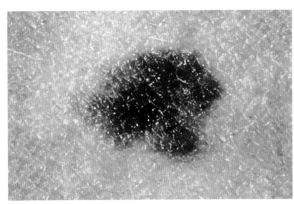

Figure 3-47: Dysplastic nevus

PREMALIGNANT SKIN CONDITIONS

Actinic keratoses are precancerous lesions that can develop into squamous cell carcinoma (SCC). Like SCC, these lesions are found on sun-exposed areas, more often in those with fair skin. These types of lesions can be treated with cryotherapy, photodynamic therapy, topical 5-fluorouracil, and topical imiquimod.

MALIGNANT SKIN CONDITIONS

Basal cell carcinoma (BCC) arises from epidermal basal cells and is the most common form of skin cancer, especially in White individuals (Figure 3-48). The usual type of BCC is characterized by translucent pearly papules, often with arborizing vessels. It often has raised borders. It spreads by local extension and, when large enough, gets a "rodent-eaten" appearance.

BCC is caused by UV radiation from sun exposure. It is typically found on sun-exposed areas, such as the head and neck, but it may appear elsewhere. Diagnose with skin biopsy to confirm pathology. BCC can be superficial

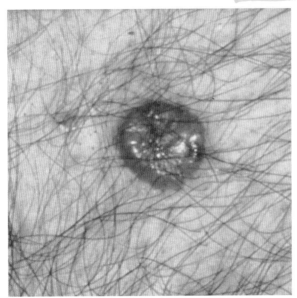

Figure 3-48: Basal cell carcinoma

or nodular. BCC can be high risk or low risk for recurrence. High-risk features include:

- Location: central face (eyelids, eyebrows, periorbital skin, nose, lips, chin, mandible), preauricular and post-auricular skin/sulci, temple, ear, genitalia, hands, feet
- Large size
- Poorly defined borders
- High-risk histology
- Occurring at site of previous radiation
- Patient use of immunosuppression

Know that the metastatic potential of BCC is < 0.1%. BCCs are usually surgically removed by excision or by Mohs surgery. However, nonsurgical treatment followed by cryotherapy or topical therapy (e.g., imiquimod, 5-fluorouracil) can be considered. Photodynamic therapy and radiation therapy are also options. Laser therapy is not recommended.

Squamous cell carcinoma (SCC): SCC develops from keratinizing epidermal cells, occurring especially in light-skinned persons from cumulative sun exposure from childhood and youth. Sun-exposed areas are at risk, especially head and neck, ears and lower lips, back of arms, forearms, and dorsal surfaces of hands (Figure 3-49). In contrast to the low metastatic potential of BCC, SCC has a 0.3–5.0% metastatic potential—and even higher when it appears on the head and neck: ear (11%) and lower lip (13%)! The metastatic rate of recurring tumors is 30%. The metastatic rate in SCC originating from scars approaches 40%.

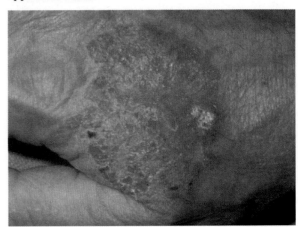

Figure 3-49: Squamous cell carcinoma

Other risk factors associated with a higher metastatic rate include size > 2 cm, depth > 4 mm, poorly differentiated lesions, and level of invasion into nerves and angiolymphatics. Risk of SCC is greater in immunocompromised hosts such as transplant patients.

Histopathology obtained from a shave biopsy confirms the diagnosis.

SCCs are generally removed with wide 4–6 mm margin local excision or Mohs surgery for high-risk lesions, depending on location and size.

SCC in situ (a.k.a. Bowen disease) is a noninvasive form of SCC that presents as small, red, scaly patches that grow slowly. The changes are confined to the epidermis and have not spread deeper into the skin; hence, "in situ." These tumors are associated with sun exposure, especially on the face, scalp, hands, and lower legs, or with HPV infection in the genital area. They are also caused by arsenic exposure. These lesions tend to grow slowly, with gradual asymptomatic enlargement over many years. SCC in situ can be treated with curettage and electrodesiccation (C&E), cryotherapy, topical 5-fluorouracil, topical imiquimod, and surgical excision. In addition, the FDA has approved photodynamic therapy.

Melanoma: This also tends to occur more commonly in light-skinned, light-haired, and freckled people with sunlight exposure, espe-cially those who had severe sunburns in child-hood (Figure 3-50). There has been a 300% increase in incidence of melanoma in the past 40 years. Other risk factors are numerous dysplastic nevi, a family history of melanoma, a high number of ordinary nevi, a congenital nevus, previous personal history of melanoma, and immunosuppression.

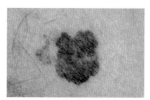

Figure 3-50: Malignant melanoma

Melanoma is more common in women < 50 years of age and in men > 50 years of age. It commonly presents on the lower legs of women and on the backs of men.

There are 4 types of melanoma: superficial spreading, lentigo maligna, acral lentiginous (palms, soles, nails, and mucosa), and nodular. Nodular is the most aggressive and is the only type that does not exhibit radial growth. Instead, it grows deeply vertical, with a high incidence of early metastasis.

Think **ABCDE** when assessing a lesion that might be malignant melanoma:

- **A**symmetry
- **B**orders are irregular.
- **C**olor variation
- **D**iameter > 6 mm is suspicious.
- **E**volving lesions are more suspicious.

General prognostic factors include age and sex of the patient (better prognosis for patients who are < 50 years of age and female), location of the lesion (improved out-comes: extremities > trunk > head and neck), and, most importantly, the depth of the lesion (deeper lesions have a poorer outcome). Other prognostic factors are mitotic index, ulceration, number of regional lymph nodes affected, site of systemic metastases, and elevated levels of LDH. Early diagnosis and excision improves prognosis and mortality, so perform excisional biopsy promptly.

Refer for an excisional biopsy (e.g., saucerization biopsy) of any suspicious lesion with a 1- to 3-mm rim of normal

skin and contiguous subdermal fat on the bottom. Punch biopsy is not recommended unless the entire lesion is removed.

A partial biopsy may result in an inaccurate diagnosis as size, symmetry, and circumscription are important histo-logic criteria when evaluating melanocytic lesions.

The American Joint Committee on Cancer's *AJCC Cancer Staging Manual, Eighth Edition* recommends a tumor size, lymph node involvement, and metastases (TNM) staging system for melanoma. Previously, the Breslow thickness (i.e., the depth of the lesion found on biopsy) alone was used.

Mohs surgery is 1st choice for melanoma in situ, lentigo maligna, as well as for melanoma of head, neck, hands, feet, pretibia, nails, and ankles.

If tumor is in situ, it can be excised with a 0.5- to 1-cm margin. If tumor depth is < 1 mm, the lesion is excised with a 1-cm, tumor-free margin. If tumor depth is > 1–2 mm, excision is with a 1- to 2-cm margin. If > 2 mm, excision is with a 2-cm margin.

In melanoma, if the depth of lesion is < 0.8 mm (0.75 is rounded up to 0.8 mm), a sentinel lymph node biopsy (SLNB) is not required.

SLNB should be discussed if the lesion has ulceration, lymphvascular invasion, a high mitotic rate, or if the patient is young. In addition, if the lesion is between 0.8 and 1 mm, discuss the option of an SLNB procedure with the patient and the surgeon, according to 2018 guidelines.

Always recommend an SLNB for patients with lesions > 1 mm in depth.

Survival rates for melanoma Stages 0, I, and II are 99%. The survival rate for Stage III is 65%. The survival rate for Stage IV is 25%.

Treatment depends on stage at diagnosis:

- Stage 0 (melanoma in situ)—excision.
- Stages I and II—excision +/– SLNB. Use lymph node mapping if SLNB+. Interferon may be recommended to reduce recurrence in Stage II.
- Stage III resectable—excision and SLNB. If SLNB is positive, use adjuvant therapy with immune check-point inhibitors (e.g., pembrolizumab, nivolumab), or CTL4 inhibitors (e.g., ipilimumab). Targeted therapy with BRAF inhibitors (e.g., vemurafenib) and MEK inhibitors is used if mutated BRAF + genes are present. Radiation can also be considered.
- Stage III unresectable, Stage IV, and recurrent mela-noma—treat as Stage III resectable plus intralesional immunotherapy (e.g., BCG and IL2 inhibitors), che-motherapy with dacarbazine, and palliative care.

Know: Dark-skinned persons also get melanoma. The lesions tend to be in acral areas (e.g., palms, soles, nail beds). Hutchinson nail sign is an important clinical clue to sub-ungual melanoma, which is typified by extension of brown or black pigment from the nail bed, matrix, and nail plate to the adjoining cuticle and proximal or lateral nail folds.

DERMATOLOGY

Mycosis fungoides and **Sézary syndrome** are the main forms of cutaneous T-cell lymphoma. Mycosis fungoides (Figure 3-51) can be mistaken for psoriasis or eczema. Sézary syndrome has peripheral blood involvement in addition to the skin manifestations and has a poorer prognosis. Patients with Sézary syndrome are often erythrodermic (erythema affecting > 90% BSA).

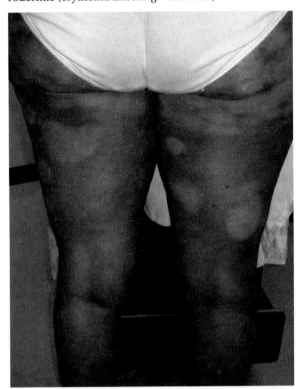

Figure 3-51: Mycosis fungoides

Paget disease of the nipple is a rare form of breast cancer; consider this diagnosis in patients with persistent unilateral oozing from the nipple and/or from eczematous plaques on the areola. It is usually due to underlying intraductal breast cancer with retrograde extension of the tumor. By far, the most common causes of an acute rash on an areola are contact dermatitis or skin irritation; consider Paget disease if there is no response to treatment.

Nevoid basal cell carcinoma syndrome (NBCCS; a.k.a. Gorlin syndrome) is an autosomal dominant disorder caused by mutations in the *PTCH1* tumor suppressor gene. Features include numerous BCCs with bifid ribs, calcification of the falx cerebri, hypertelorism, palmar and plantar pits, and bone cysts, especially of the mandible (Figure 3-52).

Children with NBCCS rarely develop medulloblastoma. Management consists of regular surveillance by a dermatologist, treatment of BCCs, and surgical excision of bone cysts. Prognosis is generally good.

Peutz-Jeghers syndrome is an autosomal dominant disorder consisting of multiple hamartomatous polyps in the GI tract and melanotic pigmentation (lentigines) on the lips and buccal mucosa. These patients are at increased risk for GI malignancy. Note that similar intraoral dark spots may occur in healthy people with dark skin and in those with primary adrenal insufficiency (a.k.a. Addison disease).

Metastases to the skin: The 5 cancers most likely to develop cutaneous metastases are lung cancer, GI cancer, melanoma, renal cancer, and breast cancer.

BLISTERING LESIONS

PREVIEW | REVIEW

- Characterize the skin findings associated with porphyria cutanea tarda (PCT).
- What type of hepatitis is associated with PCT?
- Dermatitis herpetiformis is associated with what gastrointestinal disorder?

Porphyria cutanea tarda (PCT; Figure 3-53 and Figure 3-54) is the most common type of porphyria. PCT causes hyperpigmentation, tense blisters, scaly macules, vesicles, or hemorrhagic bullae in sun-exposed areas; milia; skin fragility; and increased facial hair. PCT is caused by a congenital or acquired decreased activity of uroporphyrinogen decarboxylase (UROD), which allows a buildup of phototoxic porphyrins in the skin. Symptoms can be induced by estrogens, alcohol, hepatitis C virus infection, HIV infection, and smoking. Check for hepatitis C virus, HIV, and hereditary hemochromatosis. Whenever a patient with HCV presents with a photosensitive rash isolated to the hands, think of PCT. Lab results usually show increased serum iron, ALT, and AST. To screen, check for increased urinary coproporphyrins and uroporphyrins. Patients may have dark or pink urine.

Treatment is the same as for hemochromatosis: regular phlebotomy. Iron can inhibit the activity of UROD. By decreasing iron stores with phlebotomy, the activity of UROD increases, resulting in porphyrins being

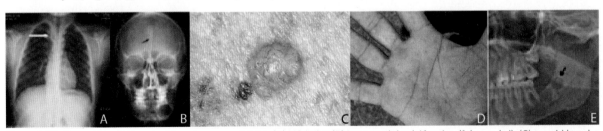

Figure 3-52: Signs of nevoid basal cell carcinoma syndrome: (A) bifid ribs; (B) intracranial calcification (falx cerebri); (C) nevoid basal cell carcinoma; (D) palmar pits (plantar pits may also occur); (E) keratocystic odontogenic tumor (mandible)

metabolized quickly, thus preventing them from building up in the skin. Antimalarials (e.g., hydroxychloroquine, chloroquine) are also effective, helping to mobilize porphyrins. They are typically used when phlebotomy is contraindicated. PCT due to hepatitis C virus infection resolves with treatment of hepatitis. Protecting skin from the sun and discontinuing aggravating agents, including alcohol and estrogen, are also indicated.

Porphyria variegata (variegate porphyria; a.k.a. South African porphyria) is called variegate because patients can present in a variety of ways. They can have acute episodes (e.g., acute intermittent porphyria [AIP]), chronic skin manifestations (e.g., PCT), or both. Patients may get blisters on sun-exposed areas and have mechanical fragility of the skin. These patients may also have abdominal pain, polyneuropathies, and mental disturbances. The symptoms are due to a deficiency of protoporphyrinogen oxidase, which leads to the build-up of excess porphyrins.

Treatment of acute attacks is the same as for AIP: glucose and hematin. Glucose and hematin theoretically work by inhibiting aminolevulinic acid (ALA) synthase and preventing the accumulation of toxic precursors. Differential diagnosis: AIP presents similarly to variegate porphyria,

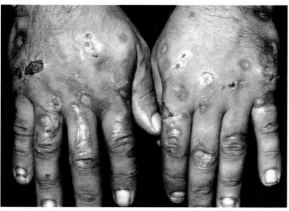

Figure 3-53: Porphyria cutanea tarda

except without the skin changes. PCT presents with the skin changes but without the neurologic/mental changes!

Epidermolysis bullosa: Congenital structural defects of the skin cause blistering after minor skin trauma such that the skin splits at the junction of the epidermis and the dermis. There are many different classifications, all of which are genetically transmitted, and each is due to a specific gene mutation. The major classifications include epidermolysis bullosa simplex (EBA), which affects the keratin genes *KRT5* and *KRT14*; junctional epidermolysis bullosa (JEB), which affects the laminin and collagen genes; and dystrophic epidermolysis bullosa (DEB), which affects the collagen 7 gene.

Nikolsky sign: Slight lateral pressure on the skin causes sloughing of the epidermis. It is positive in pemphigus vulgaris, pemphigus foliaceus, TEN, and staphylococcal scalded skin syndrome (SSSS). It is negative in bullous pemphigoid.

Bullous pemphigoid causes recurrent crops of tense, deep, intact blisters with negative Nikolsky sign (do not spread laterally with pressure). It can be locally situated, such as on the legs, and can remain there for years before spreading, or it can be generalized on the trunk, flexures, and inguinal and axillary folds (Figure 3-55). Older individuals are usually affected. The disease process is classified as a Type 2 hypersensitivity reaction and can appear similar to urticaria when it starts. It is intensely pruritic and does not commonly involve the mucosa. It has an autoimmune etiology with formation of anti-epithelial basement membrane antibodies. Diagnosis is by direct immunofluorescence of the perilesional skin, which shows linear basement membrane zone antibodies. Precipitating events include exposure to UV light, radiation therapy, and certain drugs, including furosemide, ibuprofen, captopril, and penicillamine. Therapy includes topical (mild disease) and systemic corticosteroids and immunosuppressants.

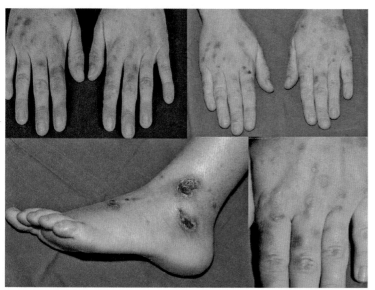

Figure 3-54: Porphyria cutanea tarda with blisters

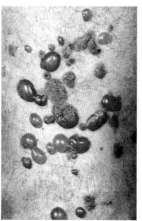

Figure 3-55: Bullous pemphigoid

DERMATOLOGY

Pemphigus vulgaris (Figure 3-56) is an autoimmune disease with intraepidermal antibodies against the desmosome desmoglein 3. This causes acantholysis (i.e., the separation of epidermal cells from each other due to decreased cohesion), which results in the formation of large, superficial, loose bullae that peel off and leave denuded skin. Nikolsky sign, which is the production of blistering through mechanical pressure at the edge of a blister, is often present. Oral mucosal involvement is common, and any cutaneous area can be affected. Lesions tend to be quite painful. Treatment of pemphigus vulgaris is similar to that of bullous pemphigoid, requiring high dose glucocorticoids but with additional rituximab for pemphigus vulgaris. Rituximab is used as 1st line treatment both to control disease severity and induce remission.

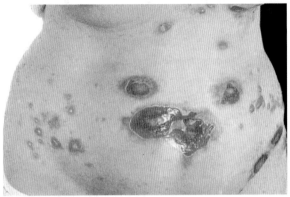

Figure 3-56: Pemphigus vulgaris

Table 3-1 summarizes key differences between pemphigus vulgaris and bullous pemphigoid.

Table 3-1: Comparison of Pemphigus Vulgaris and Bullous Pemphigoid		
	Pemphigus Vulgaris	**Bullous Pemphigoid**
Age	30–60 years	> 60 years
Rash	Flaccid bullae with mostly erosions (+ Nikolsky sign)	Tense blisters
Autoantibodies	Intraepidermal junctions	Basement membrane

Pemphigus foliaceus is caused by antibodies against the desmosome desmoglein 1 and is characterized by superficial erosions that favor the face, upper trunk, and scalp. Due to their superficial nature, vesicles are not often visualized, and clinical presentation is more consistent with crusts and scale that may be confused with impetigo. In contrast to pemphigus vulgaris, mucosal involvement is rare. Treatment is similar to that of pemphigus vulgaris, although systemic treatments are not usually necessary and the condition may be controlled with potent topical steroids only.

Stevens-Johnson syndrome (SJS) is a severe mucocutaneous reaction considered to be on the milder end of the spectrum of TEN. SJS is usually caused by medications including a variety of antibiotics, allopurinol, antiseizure medications (especially phenytoin and carbamazepine), and NSAIDs. Less commonly, SJS is associated with infections. In SJS, sloughing affects < 10% of the body surface area (BSA). Treatment requires removal of the offending drug and supportive care. Corticosteroids are controversial; use for only a very short time and prior to skin sloughing, if at all. Diagnosis is clinical + biopsy (shave or punch). For treatment, discontinue offending drug and provide supportive care in a burn unit. IVIG and systemic steroids are controversial but cyclosporine may help. For more information on SJS, see the Allergy & Immunology section under Drug Hypersensitivity Reactions.

Toxic epidermal necrolysis (TEN) is considered a variant or more severe form of SJS. It is also caused by a hypersensitivity reaction to a drug (especially allopurinol, antiseizure medications, NSAIDs, sulfas, and antibiotics). Early symptoms include fever and skin pain and tenderness out of proportion to physical findings. Like SSSS, it results in a peeling or exfoliation of large areas of skin, but it occurs at a deeper level than SSSS. By definition, sloughing affects > 30% of the BSA. Treatment requires removal of the implicated drug, aggressive skin care, and supportive care in an intensive care burn unit. Prognosis is poor with a mortality rate of up to 40%. See more on TEN in the Allergy & Immunology section under Drug Hypersensitivity Reactions.

Dermatitis herpetiformis (DH) is a skin disease where pruritic vesicular lesions appear on the extensor surfaces and the mid-to-lower back (Figure 3-57). Lesions are caused by IgA deposition in the dermal papillary tips. Given the extreme pruritus, intact vesicles are often not apparent. DH is associated with celiac disease (gluten-sensitive enteropathy). DH and celiac disease can both be treated with a gluten-free diet. Alternatively, oral dapsone can be used to treat DH but is not effective for celiac disease.

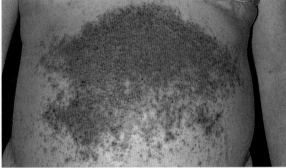

Figure 3-57: Dermatitis herpetiformis

ROUND LESIONS

PREVIEW | REVIEW

- In what age group does nummular eczema occur? How is it treated?

- What skin disorder is characterized by a "Christmas tree" pattern and a herald patch?

- What is the pathognomonic lesion for erythema multiforme? What virus is often the cause?

Granuloma annulare is an idiopathic, annular, ringworm-like lesion without scaling, commonly appearing on the distal portion of the extremities (Figure 3-58). It often occurs in children and young women. It usually is self-limited, disappearing in months to a few years. Other treatment options include topical or intralesional corticosteroids.

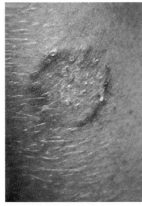

Figure 3-58: Granuloma annulare

Nummular eczema consists of small, circular (nummular = coin-shaped), pruritic lesions that are more typical on the extremities and often are associated with dry skin and atopy. The lesions are very common in older adults and have no pathologic significance. Rule out fungal infection. Treat with mid- to high-potency topical steroids.

Pityriasis rosea is a pruritic rash that is common in children and young adults. Its etiology is unknown—it may be infectious in origin (possibly human herpesvirus 6 or 7). The disease is self-limited and asymptomatic (occasionally mildly pruritic), usually lasting 4–8 weeks. Prodromal symptoms of sore throat or runny nose may be present before the rash appears.

A herald patch presents as a single, pink, oval patch, often on the trunk, and precedes subsequent pityriasis rosea lesions by 1–2 weeks (Figure 3-59). This patch is sometimes confused with tinea corporis (Figure 3-31 on page 3-21), but the 2 are not related. Subsequently, small, scaly, pruritic, papulosquamous, oval lesions with the long axis parallel to skin folds and rib lines develop in a "Christmas tree" pattern, usually on the trunk (Figure 3-60). The scale is at the periphery of the lesion and appears as a collarette (or trailing scale), unlike psoriasis, which has

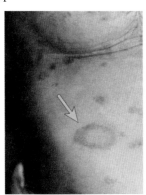

Figure 3-59: Herald patch

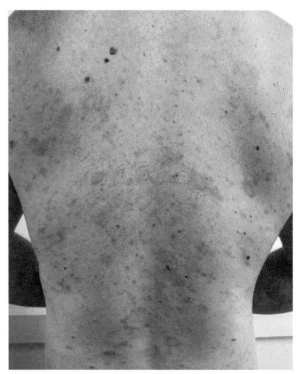

Figure 3-60: Pityriasis rosea with "Christmas tree" distribution

confluent scale over the entire plaque. Treatment is reassurance. However, topical corticosteroids, phototherapy, and/or sunlight may help. Acyclovir reduces symptoms and reduces length of disease. Pityriasis in pregnancy can cause spontaneous abortion.

Urticaria (hives) are raised pruritic papules and plaques on the skin that result from a Type 1 hypersensitivity reaction. The mast cell is the main effector cell. Mast cells have high affinity to IgE and therefore may trigger IgE-dependent allergic responses. Individual lesions of urticaria, by definition, do not last longer than 24 hours and can have smooth or irregular borders or may be annular. They are accompanied by pruritus, which often is severe. Common causes of acute urticarial (episodes occurring ≤ 6 weeks) include upper respiratory infections, drugs, and foods. 50% of patients have idiopathic acute urticaria. Chronic urticaria (episodes occurring more often than twice a week for > 6 weeks) may be associated with autoimmune disease or infection or can be idiopathic. Dermatographism is a type of urticaria due to mechanical stimuli and is characterized by whealing of the skin in response to moderate stroking. Simple dermatographism occurs in ~ 5% of the general population and is considered an exaggerated physiological response. Symptomatic dermatographism is characterized by pruritus and whealing at sites of friction and scratching. Treatment of urticaria includes avoiding triggers and aggravating factors, such as NSAIDs, aspirin, codeine, and morphine. Cooling and antiitch creams, such as those containing pramoxine, may be helpful. Antihistamines are 1st line therapy, followed by 2nd line therapies, such as systemic corticosteroids. Chronic urticaria may require immunotherapy.

DERMATOLOGY

Dermatofibromas are dome-shaped papules resulting from benign dermal proliferation. They are quite common and are most often idiopathic, but they can also be caused by trauma or bites. A "dimple sign" with central depression is often displayed secondary to lateral pressure and is specific to diagnosis. Treatment is observation only, although biopsy can be indicated if the diagnosis is in question. Multiple dermatofibromas may suggest underlying systemic disease such as immune disorders, autoimmune disease, or HIV infection, and previous and current medications should be reviewed.

Erythema multiforme consists of well-defined asymptomatic lesions varying from annular to targetoid (Figure 3-61). Palms and soles are frequently involved, and mucous membranes may be affected. These immune-mediated "target" lesions (those with 3 defined zones) are pathognomonic for erythema multiforme. Erythema multiforme is associated with HSV, *Mycoplasma*, and, much less frequently, drugs (e.g., NSAIDs, PCNs). Treatment involves antimicrobial therapy (if a causative organism, such as *Mycoplasma*, is found) or removal of an offending medication. Patients with a history of cold sores and recurrent erythema multiforme may benefit from suppressive antiviral therapy (i.e., valacyclovir, acyclovir, or famciclovir taken daily for ~ 6 months).

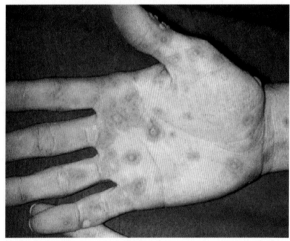

Figure 3-61: Erythema multiforme

PIGMENT CHANGES

PREVIEW | REVIEW

- Hyperpigmented areas of the axilla are associated with what underlying disease states?

- What diseases are on the short list of causes of black lesions?

- What skin discoloration occurs rarely with a polyglandular autoimmune deficiency syndrome?

HYPERPIGMENTATION

Diffuse hyperpigmentation may occur in primary biliary cholangitis (previously known as primary biliary cirrhosis), scleroderma, primary adrenal insufficiency (a.k.a. Addison disease), and hemochromatosis (patients have a grayish/bronze coloration) and with use of the cancer drug busulfan. Other causes include PCT, malabsorption and/or Whipple disease, pellagra (niacin deficiency), B_{12} deficiency, and folate deficiency. Check for metastatic melanoma in "slate-blue" patients!

Hyperpigmentation in sun-exposed areas can be caused by amiodarone, PCT, and phenothiazines. Hyperpigmentation is diffuse but darker in sun-exposed areas in pellagra, biliary cholangitis, and scleroderma. MTX can cause reactivation of sunburn.

Melasma is an acquired hyperpigmentation often seen in pregnancy or with oral contraceptive use. Diagnose based on history and clinical appearance. Hyperpigmentation occurs in sun-exposed areas of the face and is treated with varying degrees of success using skin protection from the sun and skin-lightening modalities.

Pigmented growths, such as acquired melanocytic nevi, seborrheic keratoses, and solar lentigines, are usually benign and common in the general population:

- **Nevi**—Commonly encountered nevi include:
  - Common acquired nevi are round to ovoid lesions typically measuring 2–6 mm. They are generally orderly and symmetrical.
  - Junctional nevi are macular and often darker in color, compared to compound nevi, which vary in elevation and are slightly lighter in color.
  - Dermal nevi are even more raised, often dome shaped, and lighter or more evenly pigmented. Over time, the number of nevi seen in a given patient increases and peaks by the 3rd decade of life. Indications for removing a nevus include a lesion that is changing, cosmetic concerns, irritation, and an atypical clinical appearance.

- **Seborrheic keratoses** are light brown, yellow, or dark brown macules, papules, or plaques that are waxy and "stuck-on" in appearance. They are commonly found on the face, head, neck, and back but can be located on any hair-bearing area of the body. They exhibit a familial predisposition, but sun exposure has also been implicated in their development and they are common with increasing age. Conditions associated with abrupt onset of multiple lesions followed by regression include pregnancy, erythroderma, and HIV infection. Rarely, this abrupt onset of seborrheic keratoses is associated with internal malignancy and is called the Leser-Trélat sign. Such onset should lead to investigation for a neoplasm.

- **Solar lentigines** are most commonly found in sun-exposed areas of older individuals but may also be found in younger patients after sun exposure. They are well-circumscribed, round or irregularly shaped brown macules that range from light to dark brown or black. These should be distinguished from pigmented actinic keratoses, which tend to have a rough surface, and lentigo maligna, which tends to be larger and have more pigment variation and irregularity of borders than a solar lentigo.

Peutz-Jeghers syndrome (multiple intestinal hamartomatous polyps) should be ruled out in patients with melanotic pigmentation (lentigines) on the lips and buccal mucosa.

Café au lait spots (Figure 3-62) are brown macules that occur in association with neurofibromatosis Type 1 (a.k.a. von Recklinghausen disease) and McCune-Albright disease. Café au lait spots occur in people with no disease (1 or 2 spots are normal and typical). In neurofibromatosis, 78% of patients have > 6 spots and 95% have at least 1 spot > 1.5 cm. In McCune-Albright disease, the spots have a more irregular outline and can be rather large.

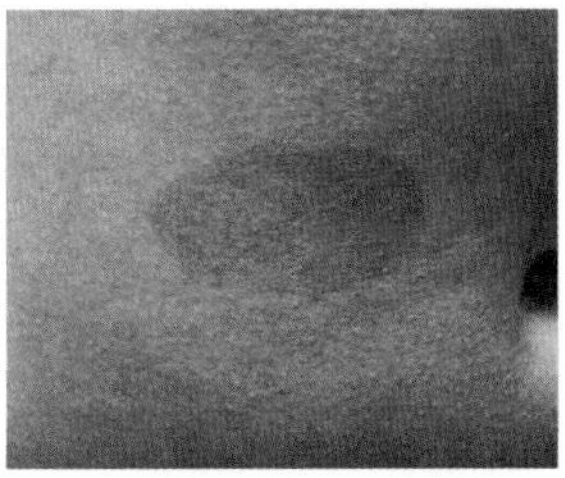

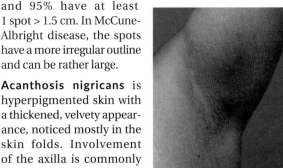

Figure 3-62: Café au lait spots

Acanthosis nigricans is hyperpigmented skin with a thickened, velvety appearance, noticed mostly in the skin folds. Involvement of the axilla is commonly shown as an example (Figure 3-63). It is rarely familial. Acanthosis nigricans is associated with:

Figure 3-63: Acanthosis nigricans

- Obesity
- Gastrointestinal malignancies
- Endocrinopathies such as diabetes mellitus, Cushing disease, hyper-/hypothyroidism, acromegaly
- Autoimmune problems

Malignant acanthosis nigricans is severe and progressive and is usually associated with gastric adenocarcinoma. It is more commonly seen on the lips, oral mucosa, and palms.

Black lesions—The etiology for black lesions is somewhat extensive, but especially consider the following:

- Rhinocerebral mucormycosis
- Anthrax
- Ecthyma gangrenosum
- Emboli to distal extremities
- Melanoma/Lentigo/Pigmented BCC
- Warfarin skin necrosis
- Necrotic spider bite
- Kaposi sarcoma

WHITE AND HYPOPIGMENTED LESIONS

Pityriasis alba is frequently seen in children and teens with atopic dermatitis. Ill-defined white macules and patches with overlying fine scale are located on the face and, occasionally, the arms. Postinflammatory hypopigmented skin changes can appear similarly after resolution of atopic dermatitis. Pityriasis alba generally improves with age,

and its appearance can be minimized with use of sunscreen and sun protection.

Tinea (pityriasis) versicolor is characterized by well-defined, hypopigmented spreading macules, usually on the upper torso and upper arms. The associated fine scale may not be observed unless the skin is stretched. It can be confirmed with use of KOH prep (Figure 3-34 on page 3-22). The associated hypomelanosis may persist for several months after eradication of the organism, but the lesions do not have scale.

Vitiligo is an autoimmune disease that causes destruction of melanocytes, resulting in depigmentation (Figure 3-64). Vitiligo usually occurs in otherwise healthy persons but can rarely occur as part of a polyglandular autoimmune (PGA) syndrome. Any of the following may be seen with a PGA: diabetes mellitus, autoimmune thyroid disease (hyper- or hypo-), Addison disease/adrenal insufficiency, hypoparathyroidism, and pernicious anemia. Any time you see a patient with vitiligo, think of these possibilities and screen appropriately!

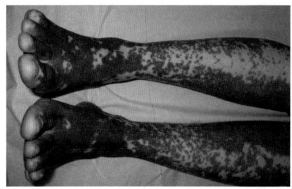

Figure 3-64: Vitiligo

Tuberous sclerosis is uncommon and autosomal dominant. It is associated with seizures, intellectual disabilities, periungual fibromas, and hypopigmented (ash-leaf) macules (Figure 3-65). You see these macules best with a Wood lamp. Adenoma sebaceum manifests in these patients as numerous midfacial papules, which are actually angiofibromas (Figure 3-66 on page 3-36).

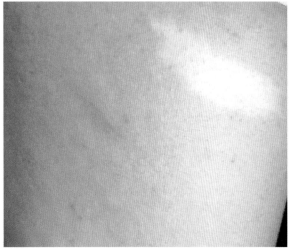

Figure 3-65: Hypopigmented (ash-leaf) macules

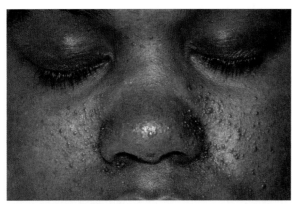
Figure 3-66: Angiofibromas

PRURITUS

PREVIEW | REVIEW

- What general measures can be used to treat itching?

Pruritus is severe itching as an effect of various conditions. It may be localized or generalized. The most common cause of pruritus in older patients is dry skin. Other causes seen across the age spectrum include:

- Hyper- or hypothyroidism
- Malignancy—think lymphoma, especially Hodgkin's, but also breast cancer.
- Iron deficiency—even if patient is not anemic
- Polycythemia vera
- Aquagenic pruritus
- Chronic kidney disease—but not acute kidney injury
- Cholestatic liver disease
- Diabetes mellitus
- HIV/AIDS

Treat pruritus first by attempting to reverse the cause. With severe systemic disorders, this often is not possible.

Treatment of the itching itself starts with general measures:

- Skin moisturization
- Covering the itchy areas to decrease trauma from scratching
- Making the environment cool and humid
- Education and psychological support to decrease stress and give the patient more control of the situation

Try topical agents if more relief is needed:

- Corticosteroid creams
- Capsaicin cream (yes, the stuff in chili peppers!). Initial burning, which occurs in the first 2–3 weeks of use, is followed by decreased pruritus. Treatment is especially effective in neuropathic disorders and with chronic kidney disease.
- Anesthetic creams
- Antihistamine creams
- Phosphodiesterase-4 inhibitors

Phototherapy is often effective for localized and systemic pruritus.

Systemic therapy is reserved for generalized pruritus not controlled by topical solutions:

- Oral antihistamines are usually the first therapy tried, but they decrease the pruritus only when it is due to histamine release, such as with urticaria or mastocytosis. Antihistamines also cause drowsiness, which can help by decreasing the perceived intensity of itching.
- Opioid receptor antagonists (naltrexone, naloxone, and nalmefene) may help in certain cases.
- Gabapentin and pregabalin are GABA (γ-aminobutyric acid) analog antiseizure medications. They appear to help with neuropathic pruritus caused by nerve entrapment.
- Thalidomide is effective, but it has a lot of side effects and is very teratogenic.
- Aprepitant is a newer, expensive drug that is being used in refractory cases.

HIV- AND AIDS-RELATED SKIN LESIONS

PREVIEW | REVIEW

- What gram-negative infection in AIDS can resemble Kaposi sarcoma?
- What cutaneous neuroendocrine tumor is more common in HIV?

Many common and uncommon skin conditions become more prevalent in HIV/AIDS:

- Infection
  - Bacterial
    - Bacillary angiomatosis (*Bartonella henselae*, the same organism that causes catscratch disease) lesions appear as vascular purple lesions that bleed easily and can be confused with Kaposi sarcoma. Treatment is with antibiotics for several months.
    - Folliculitis usually occurs in uncontrolled HIV infection and may be caused by *Staphylococcus aureus*; it improves with antiviral therapy and antibiotics. Of note, people who are HIV positive may also have eosinophilic folliculitis, which is not associated with an infectious organism.
  - Viral
    - Herpes simplex
    - Herpes zoster (shingles) is often refractory to treatment in patients with HIV/AIDS. Treat with acyclovir or famciclovir. Valacyclovir is not recommended due to its association with thrombotic

thrombocytopenic purpura (TTP) in the immunocompromised. For more on herpes zoster, see Varicella-Zoster Virus (VZV) on page 3-23.

– Condyloma acuminatum (HPV)

– Molluscum contagiosum (poxvirus)

– Oral hairy leukoplakia (Epstein-Barr virus; Figure 3-12 on page 3-8) is corrugated ("hairy") white lesions along the lateral surface of the tongue that cannot be scraped off. It improves with antiviral therapy.

– Kaposi sarcoma in HIV is frequently associated with HHV-8.

– Merkel cell skin cancer (associated with Merkel cell polyoma virus)

◦ Fungal/Yeast

– Oral candidiasis can be scraped off the tongue and mucosal surfaces.

– Folliculitis usually occurs in uncontrolled HIV infection and may be caused by *Pityrosporum orbiculare*; it improves with antiviral therapy and antibiotics.

– Disseminated *Cryptococcus* infection (Figure 3-67) is an AIDS-defining condition and may imitate molluscum contagiosum. *Cryptococcus neoformans* is a life-threatening fungal infection seen in immunocompromised patients. Cutaneous

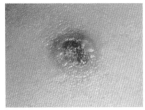

Figure 3-67: Disseminated Cryptococcus infection

lesions may present as umbilicated papules similar to molluscum in patients with HIV infection. Other lesions may be papules, pustules, nodules, ulcers, or draining sinuses. Yeast can be seen with India ink stain of the capsule or with tissue slides with mucicarmine stain. Treatment is systemic antifungals.

• Neoplastic

◦ Kaposi sarcoma, a vascular soft tissue malignancy, usually presents as < 0.5-cm, purple/red/violet/black, maculopapular lesions, which are generally concentrated on the head, neck, and lower extremities (Figure 3-68) but can also occur in the GI tract and the lung. It is common in patients with advanced HIV

Figure 3-68: Kaposi sarcoma

and improves with antiviral therapy. The CDC considers it an AIDS-defining condition.

◦ Basal cell carcinoma risk is 2–3× greater than in the HIV-negative population and occurs in regions of the body not exposed to sunlight.

◦ Merkel cell carcinoma, a neuroendocrine tumor, has a 10-fold increased incidence in HIV patients. It is associated with Merkel cell polyoma virus and is a fast-growing, painless, vascular-appearing, intracutaneous, firm nodule on sun-exposed areas. Treatment involves wide surgical excision.

• Other

◦ Xerosis (dry skin)

◦ Atopic dermatitis

◦ Eosinophilic folliculitis

◦ Seborrheic dermatitis (occurs in virtually all patients!) improves with antiviral therapy. For more information on this topic, see Seborrheic Dermatitis on page 3-2.

◦ Telangiectasias

SKIN SIGNS OF SYSTEMIC DISEASES

PREVIEW | REVIEW

• What is the significance of eruptive xanthomas?

• What is the significance of dark atrophic macules in a patient with diabetes?

DIABETES MELLITUS

Necrobiosis lipoidica diabeticorum (Figure 3-69) can be associated with diabetes in ~ 10–20% of cases. This thin, atrophic, hyperpigmented plaque, appearing on the shins, is subject to trauma and ulceration and is thought to be due to microangiopathy.

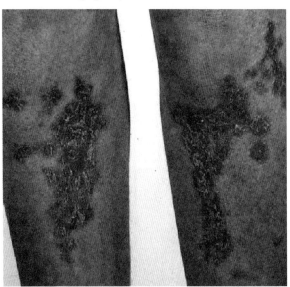

Figure 3-69: Necrobiosis lipoidica diabeticorum

Eruptive xanthomas are caused by severe hypertriglyceridemia. They are often seen in diabetic ketoacidosis, appearing abruptly as yellowish-red papules over the extensor surfaces and buttocks. These lesions resolve when the hyperglycemia is controlled.

Diabetic dermopathy ("shin spots") are dark atrophic macules; they are common and often appear on the shins. They have no clinical significance.

Acanthosis nigricans is characterized by velvety hyperpigmented patches commonly seen in intertriginous areas such as the neck, axillae, and groin. It is associated with diabetes and insulin resistance. If seen on the lips, oral mucosa, and palms, it may be malignancy related. For more on acanthosis nigricans, see Hyperpigmentation on page 3-34.

KIDNEY DISEASE

Calciphylaxis occurs in patients with end-stage kidney disease, particularly White women with diabetes and obesity and on long-term hemodialysis. Ischemic necrosis results from the calcification of dermal arterioles. Early lesions can manifest as painful erythematous nodules or livedo reticularis. Older lesions appear as indurated subcutaneous nodules with overlying retiform purpura and necrosis. They are exquisitely painful and carry a poor prognosis, especially when located proximally such as on the trunk, thighs, and buttocks. Treatment includes sodium thiosulfate, control of pain, and wound care, including debridement.

ENDOCRINE DISORDERS

Cushing syndrome: Patients with Cushing syndrome may exhibit a rounded face (moon facies), a buffalo hump, and global atrophy that may manifest as purpura, striae, cutaneous fragility, and poor wound healing.

Hereditary hemochromatosis: Patients with hereditary hemochromatosis can have diffuse bronzing of the skin (sparing the mucous membranes) that is secondary to increased melanin.

Primary adrenal insufficiency: Patients with primary adrenal insufficiency (a.k.a. Addison disease) can experience diffuse hyperpigmentation, particularly in sun-exposed areas, hair and nails, palmar creases, mucous membranes, and the axillae, perineum, and nipples. They may also note loss of pubic and axillary hair (in postpubertal women) and fibrosis of the cartilage of the ear.

RHEUMATOLOGIC DISORDERS

Gout: Patients with tophaceous gout may have deposits of monosodium urate that manifest as skin-colored to yellow-hued dermal or subcutaneous nodules or papules. They may be smooth or lobulated. The most common location for these lesions is the helix of the ear or overlying joints. They may be ulcerated or drain a chalky material.

Lupus erythematosus can have varied cutaneous findings. Acute cutaneous lupus erythematosus (ACLE) is characterized by pink, scaly, and/or edematous lesions in sun-exposed areas. A malar rash on the cheeks and nasal bridge that spares the nasolabial folds exemplifies these lesions. They heal without scarring. Erythematous scaling plaques occur on the dorsal hands and spare the knuckles.

Subacute cutaneous lupus erythematosus is characterized by annular lesions with raised red borders and central clearing in sun-exposed areas. These lesions also do not typically scar and can be seen in association with Sjögren syndrome. They are often caused by sunlight exposure and drugs, such as antihypertensive medications. The face is spared.

Lesions of discoid lupus erythematosus are commonly found on the head and neck. They are initially erythematous and indurated plaques. Chronic lesions may exhibit hypopigmentation centrally with peripheral hyperpigmentation and often leave disfiguring scarring.

Rheumatoid arthritis (RA): Patients with RA may have numerous cutaneous manifestations of their disease. More common findings include rheumatoid nodules, vasculitic lesions, pyoderma gangrenosum, and Sweet syndrome.

Sweet syndrome can resemble RA and presents with leukocytosis, fever, and tender, erythematous papules and plaques, with painful joints and nodules on the skin (see Sweet Syndrome on page 3-16).

Rheumatoid nodules are found in 20% of patients with RA and are firm, somewhat mobile papules and nodules that occur over extensor surfaces and areas of pressure or trauma. They can be asymptomatic or tender.

THE MEDSTUDY HUB: YOUR GUIDELINES AND REVIEW ARTICLES RESOURCE

For both review articles and current internal medicine practice guidelines, visit the MedStudy Hub at

medstudy.com/hub

The Hub contains the only online consolidated list of all current guidelines focused on internal medicine. Guidelines on the Hub are easy to find, continually updated, and linked to the published source. MedStudy maintains the Hub as a service to the medical community and makes it available to anyone and everyone at no cost to users.

FIGURE SOURCES

Figure 3-1: Kimberly Salkey, MD
Figure 3-2: Roymishali, CC BY-SA 3.0
Figure 3-3: James Heilman, MD, CC BY-SA 3.0
Figure 3-4: Chris 73
Figure 3-5: James Heilman, MD, CC BY-SA 3.0
Figure 3-6: Michael Sand, Daniel Sand, Christina Thrandorf, Volker Paech, Peter Altmeyer, Falk G Bechara, CC BY 2.5
Figure 3-7: Jason Reichenberg, MD
Figure 3-8: Kimberly Salkey, MD
Figure 3-9: CDC
Figure 3-10: CDC
Figure 3-11: Klaus D. Peter, Gummersbach, Germany, CC BY 3.0 DE
Figure 3-12: CDC
Figure 3-13: Kimberly Salkey, MD
Figure 3-14: Kimberly Salkey, MD
Figure 3-15: Jennifer Vickers, MD
Figure 3-16: Kimberly Salkey, MD
Figure 3-17: Doktorinternet, Wikimedia Commons, CC BY-SA 4.0
Figure 3-18: Kimberly Salkey, MD
Figure 3-19: James Heilman, MD, CC BY-SA 3.0
Figure 3-20: Kimberly Salkey, MD
Figure 3-21: Kimberly Salkey, MD
Figure 3-22: CDC
Figure 3-23: Kimberly Salkey, MD
Figure 3-24: Chris Craig
Figure 3-25: Splarka
Figure 3-26: Kimberly Salkey, MD
Figure 3-27: CDC
Figure 3-28: CDC
Figure 3-29: Aswine K. Bal et al, CC BY 3.0
Figure 3-30: CDC
Figure 3-32: CDC
Figure 3-33: Kimberly Salkey, MD
Figure 3-34: Kimberly Salkey, MD
Figure 3-35: Kimberly Salkey, MD
Figure 3-36: E van Herk, MD, CC BY-SA 3.0
Figure 3-37: F Malan, CC BY-SA 3.0
Figure 3-38: Fisle, CC BY-SA 3.0
Figure 3-39: Magnus Manske
Figure 3-40: CDC
Figure 3-41: MichaelBeckHGW, CC BY 3.0
Figure 3-42: CDC, Piotr Naskrecki
Figure 3-43: CDC, Piotr Naskrecki
Figure 3-44: MedStudy illustration
Figure 3-45: Matt Britt
Figure 3-46: Chuck Evans(mcevan), CC BY 2.5
Figure 3-47: National Cancer Institute
Figure 3-48: NIH
Figure 3-51: Jason Reichenberg, MD
Figure 3-53: Kimberly Salkey, MD
Figure 3-54: H. Jorn Bovenschen and Wynand H.P.M. Vissers, CC BY 3.0

Figure 3-55: Kimberly Salkey, MD
Figure 3-56: Kimberly Salkey, MD
Figure 3-57: Kimberly Salkey, MD
Figure 3-58: CDC
Figure 3-59: CDC
Figure 3-60: James Heilman, MD, CC BY-SA 3.0
Figure 3-61: Kimberly Salkey, MD
Figure 3-62: Jennifer Vickers, MD
Figure 3-63: DermNetNZ, CC BY 4.0
Figure 3-64: Grook Da Oger, CC BY-SA 4.0
Figure 3-65: Parisa Falsafi et al., CC BY 3.0
Figure 3-66: Herbert L. Fred, MD and Hendrik A. van Dijk, CC BY-SA 3.0
Figure 3-67: CDC
Figure 3-68: OpenStax College, CC BY 3.0
Figure 3-69: Kimberly Salkey, MD
The remaining figures are from the MedStudy archives.

DERMATOLOGY

Infectious Disease

SECTION EDITOR

Fred Arthur Zar, MD
Professor of Clinical Medicine
Program Director, Internal Medicine Residency
Director of Academic Affairs
University of Illinois at Chicago
Chicago, IL

MEDICAL EDITORS

Lynn Bullock, MD
Colorado Springs, CO

Austin D. Williams, MD, MSEd
Memorial Sloan Kettering Cancer Center
New York, NY

Table of Contents

DISEASE-BASED REVIEW

INFECTIOUS DISEASE

DISEASE-BASED REVIEW

URINARY TRACT INFECTIONS (UTIs)

PREVIEW | REVIEW

- In which 3 settings would you treat asymptomatic bacteriuria?
- What are the standard treatments for uncomplicated cystitis, complicated cystitis, uncomplicated pyelonephritis, and complicated pyelonephritis?
- What 2 subtypes of prostatitis require antibiotic therapy, and which drugs should be given?

CYSTITIS AND PYELONEPHRITIS

Epidemiology

A wide variety of organisms cause UTIs, but *Escherichia coli* and other gram-negative aerobic enterics are the most common causes. Among gram-positive organisms, *Enterococcus* is the most common genus. In the absence of a urinary catheter, *Staphylococcus aureus* is an uncommon cause of a UTI, and its presence in the urine should raise the concern that it seeded the kidney via a bacteremia from another source. Coagulase-negative staphylococci are rarely true pathogens and suggest contamination of the urine from skin flora. The one exception is *Staphylococcus saprophyticus*, which is a definite cause of cystitis but rarely a cause of pyelonephritis.

Risk factors for UTIs in women include sexual activity, spermicide and diaphragm use, pregnancy, and vaginal atrophy. UTIs are less common in men, and sexual activity is not a risk factor except in men who have sex with men. In either sex, UTIs are increased in the presence of diabetes mellitus, sickle cell disease, structural abnormalities, immunosuppression, or renal stones. UTIs are the most common nosocomial infections. Infections with urea-splitting organisms, such as *Proteus* and *Klebsiella*, are associated with urinary stones, so if these organisms are identified in the urine, order imaging tests to look for stones. *Streptococcus agalactiae* (group B strep) infections are more commonly seen in pregnancy (see the Women's and Men's Health section under Obstetrics).

Presentation

The classic symptoms of UTIs include dysuria, frequency, and urgency. Flank pain and fever are seen in ~ 50% of patients with pyelonephritis but are not common with uncomplicated cystitis.

Diagnosis

The diagnosis can be confirmed by culture growth of $\geq 10^5$ gram-negative organisms/mL of urine. Yeast or gram-positive organisms can cause infection with lower colony counts. In the presence of classic symptoms, the first episode of an uncomplicated cystitis does not require a culture prior to treatment. A positive urine culture in the absence of symptoms is not considered a UTI; it is called asymptomatic bacteriuria. In a nonneutropenic patient, the absence of pyuria has good negative predictive value toward ruling out a UTI. The presence of pyuria alone, however, is not sufficient to diagnose a UTI.

Treatment

The 1st step in determining treatment for a positive urine culture is to determine if the patient has signs or symptoms of infection. If signs or symptoms are present, it is a UTI; if not, it is asymptomatic bacteriuria. Treat asymptomatic bacteriuria under only 3 circumstances:

1) Treat pregnant women to prevent progression to pyelonephritis and to decrease maternal and fetal morbidity and mortality. Safe regimens in pregnancy include a 3-day course of trimethoprim/sulfamethoxazole (TMP/SMX; during weeks 12–36 only), nitrofurantoin (not > 38 weeks), or cephalexin.

2) Treat patients about to undergo an invasive urologic procedure.

3) Treat renal transplant recipients within the first 3 months after transplantation to decrease the risk of a symptomatic UTI, which increases the risk of rejection.

With symptomatic UTIs, the 2nd step is to determine whether the infection is in the lower tract (cystitis) or upper tract (pyelonephritis). Cystitis usually has no systemic signs of infection or flank tenderness, and fever is usually low grade if present. Pyelonephritis typically has high-grade fever (often > 102.0°F [38.9°C]) and flank pain. Sepsis may be present, and blood cultures are positive in ~ 10% of patients with pyelonephritis.

The 3rd step is to determine whether the UTI is complicated. Complicated UTIs are those that occur when there are structural anomalies, foreign bodies, prior resistant organisms, or recent antibiotic use and in patients with immunocompromise, diabetes, or pregnancy. All UTIs in men are considered complicated.

Uncomplicated cystitis can be treated based on symptoms alone and does not require a urine culture. Obtain a urine culture for all other UTIs. In cystitis, do not perform imaging of the urinary tract (ultrasound [U/S] or computed tomography [CT]). In uncomplicated pyelonephritis, perform imaging of the urinary tract only if symptoms persist after 72 hours of culture-guided therapy.

Antibiotic therapy:

- **Uncomplicated cystitis:** The treatment of choice is either a 5-day course of nitrofurantoin monohydrate/macrocrystals or a 3-day course of TMP/SMX depending on local resistance patterns (do not use TMP/SMX if there is $\geq 20\%$ resistance of *E. coli* in the community), the patient's allergy history, and whether prior antibiotics have been used. A single dose of

INFECTIOUS DISEASE

fosfomycin is a 2nd line treatment due to lower cure rates. Avoid the use of fluoroquinolones for uncomplicated cystitis because of resistance and toxicity issues (discussed in Fluoroquinolones on page 4-87).

- **Complicated cystitis or uncomplicated pyelonephritis:** Empirically treat with an oral fluoroquinolone or TMP/SMX (depending on local resistance rates) and adjust based on culture data.
- **Complicated pyelonephritis and/or hospitalized patients:** Treat with an intravenous (IV) fluoroquinolone, ceftriaxone, a β-lactam + a β-lactamase inhibitor, or ampicillin ± aminoglycoside for 7–10 days, based on local resistance rates. Adjust the antibiotic regimen based on culture data. Bacteremic patients do not require longer treatment if the bacteremia clears within 48 hours. See Catheter-Associated UTIs (CAUTIs) for more information.

Differentiate recurrent UTIs into 2 types: **relapses** (the same strain within 2 weeks of the end of prior therapy) or **reinfection** (a different strain than the initial infection). Relapses are commonly due to a persistent nidus of infection (e.g., stones, abscess, urethral/ureteral/bladder diverticula, obstruction) in the urinary tract. So, to evaluate relapses, perform a renal U/S and/or CT of the abdomen and pelvis with contrast. Reinfection is sometimes related to diaphragm use, spermicides, and sexual activity. If this is the case, consider alternative contraception, but if the reinfection is correlated with sexual intercourse, give low-dose prophylaxis (e.g., TMP/SMX 1/2 single-strength tablet, nitrofurantoin 50 mg) before or after sexual activity. If unrelated to sexual activity and the patient has < 3 episodes a year, treat the UTIs as they occur. If the patient has ≥ 3 episodes a year or ≥ 2 episodes in 6 months, consider chronic low-dose suppression for 6 months.

Complications

A perinephric abscess can occur as a complication of pyelonephritis, usually from infection with gram-negative organisms, by the direct spread of the renal infection. The diagnosis can be difficult since the symptoms are nonspecific and insidious. These include fever, chills, abdominal pain, fatigue, and weight loss. Dysuria and increased frequency are uncommon because the infection is often completely outside of the urinary tract and organisms are not entering the bladder. The patient typically has unilateral costovertebral flank pain on physical examination. Occasionally, a flank mass is palpated if the abscess is large enough.

Lab work reveals leukocytosis and elevated inflammatory markers (erythrocyte sedimentation rate [ESR] and C-reactive protein [CRP]). Pyuria may be present if the abscess communicates with the collecting system. Obtain blood and urine cultures. U/S may be the initial imaging, but a CT scan has a higher sensitivity and may show renal enlargement and inflammation with extrarenal fluid and gas collections. Perform CT- or U/S-guided percutaneous drainage for C&S testing and to therapeutically drain the abscess.

The treatment consists of empiric antibiotics directed toward Enterobacteriaceae, such as the regimens recommended for pyelonephritis (refer to Treatment on page 4-1), until the culture results are known, at which time the therapy is tailored to the culture results. If the abscess occurs in the setting of staphylococcal bacteremia, modify the selection of antibiotics and complete the entire course with IV antibiotics. The inflammatory markers help monitor the clinical status.

PROSTATITIS

Prostatitis has 4 subtypes based on symptoms, the presence or absence of bacteria, and the presence or absence of inflammation.

Type I prostatitis is acute bacterial prostatitis. The causative organisms are the same as for cystitis. Acute bacterial prostatitis typically has a very dramatic presentation, with urinary frequency, dysuria, hesitancy, perineal pain and referred penile tip pain, high-grade fevers, and chills. Bacteremia is seen in 25%. All antibiotics penetrate well into prostatic tissue during acute infection. Severely ill patients with Type I prostatitis require hospital admission and IV antibiotics (e.g., ceftriaxone). Once stable, treat patients with a total of 4 weeks of antibiotics based on the susceptibility of the organism cultured.

Type II prostatitis is chronic bacterial prostatitis. Patients with this type of prostatitis present with recurrent UTIs with the same organism (relapsing UTIs). The symptoms are less dramatic than for Type I disease; Type II presents as cystitis or persistent/recurrent bacteriuria. Penetration of antibiotics into the chronically, more mildly inflamed gland varies among antibiotic classes. Prostatic secretions are acidic, so drugs that are alkaline (i.e., fluoroquinolones, TMP/SMX) penetrate best. Give a fluoroquinolone as the 1st line treatment for Type II prostatitis and TMP/SMX as an alternative. Antibiotics are given for at least 6 weeks, but recurrences are common. If there is a recurrence, retreat the infection with 6 more weeks of a fluoroquinolone if the organism is susceptible. Consider atypical organisms such as *Ureaplasma* or *Chlamydia* in sexually active men, and treat empirically with a tetracycline if prior antibiotic failure has occurred.

Type III chronic prostatitis/chronic pelvic pain has 2 forms, Type IIIA and Type IIIB, neither of which is an infectious disease. Both forms present like Type II. Type IIIA has evidence of prostatic inflammation (white blood cells [WBCs] in expressed prostatic secretions or post–prostatic massage urine specimens) but no bacterial infection on culture. Type IIIB has neither signs of prostatic inflammation nor bacterial infection. Use α-blockers as the initial treatment, and if symptoms persist, refer to a urologist.

Type IV prostatitis is asymptomatic inflammatory prostatitis. Prostate inflammation is found incidentally when tissue is removed for another reason, such as prostate biopsy or resection. Patients do not require antibiotics.

CATHETER-ASSOCIATED UTIs (CAUTIs)

Indwelling urinary catheters are a common cause of UTIs, especially in hospitalized patients. Studies show that 23% of patients in U.S. hospitals, up to 70% of patients in critical care units, and up to 10% of patients in long-term care facilities have an indwelling urinary catheter. Consider indwelling catheters that are in place for ≤ 30 days as short term and those that are in place for > 30 days as long term. It is important (and often difficult) to distinguish between catheter-associated asymptomatic bacteriuria (CA-ASB) and a CAUTI because the former does not warrant antibiotic treatment.

Catheter-Associated Asymptomatic Bacteriuria (CA-ASB)

CA-ASB develops quickly in patients with an indwelling urinary catheter. The daily risk of acquiring CA-ASB is 3–10%, and CA-ASB is present in almost all patients after 2 weeks. In addition to catheterization, other risk factors for CA-ASB are > 50 years of age, female sex, diabetes mellitus, and errors in catheter care. Up to 80% of hospitalized patients with urinary catheters get antibiotics for a variety of infections, and this may lead to acquisition of organisms with antibiotic resistance.

Symptomatic UTIs

Anywhere from 10% to 25% of patients with CA-ASB will develop symptoms and thus have a CAUTI. CAUTIs account for 20% of all health care–associated bacteremias, and patients with CAUTIs have a mortality rate of ~ 10%.

Pathogens

E. coli is the most common pathogen. Other pathogens include *Klebsiella, Enterococcus, Proteus, Pseudomonas,* and *Candida* spp.

Proteus mirabilis infection becomes more prevalent in patients with long-term indwelling catheters. *P. mirabilis* produces urease, which alkalinizes the urine. This increases the risk of urolithiasis from struvite stones.

Diagnosis

Establish the diagnosis of CA-ASB in a patient with ≥ 10³ CFU/mL of an organism with no symptoms of a CAUTI. Catheters in place for > 2 weeks have an established biofilm, so samples collected from the catheter may reflect organisms in the biofilm but not in the bladder. The suggestion is to replace the catheter and send a sample from the new catheter to be sure the organism is present in the bladder and not just in the biofilm.

The diagnosis of a CAUTI can be made if there is no other explanation for fever, malaise, altered mental status, hematuria, or costovertebral angle tenderness. Suprapubic tenderness may also be present. If a catheter is no longer present, the patient may have dysuria, frequency, or urgency.

Pyuria in itself does not establish the diagnosis of a CAUTI because it may reflect inflammation from either the indwelling catheter or other diseases such as interstitial nephritis. By itself, pyuria is not a reason for treatment.

Treatment

Always obtain a culture prior to treatment and consider empiric therapy that accounts for local common isolates and antibiotic resistance patterns.

Permanent removal of the catheter is best; if the catheter is still clinically indicated, it should be changed when antibiotics are started.

Because a CAUTI is considered to be a complicated UTI, treatment is generally longer than for uncomplicated UTIs. There is no consensus as to the duration of treatment, but it is generally 5–21 days.

Prevention

Avoiding the use of urinary catheters is clearly the most effective way to prevent CAUTIs. Along those lines, when a catheter is in use, providers should remove the catheter as soon as possible. Automatic orders for catheter removal can reduce the occurrence of CAUTIs. Smaller catheters may be safer because they cause less trauma. There is no proven benefit with the use of antimicrobial-coated catheters or the administration of prophylactic antibiotics after catheter insertion. Avoid treatment of CA-ASB.

Some accepted indications for urinary catheters are:

- Tracking urine output in critically ill patients or during surgery
- Urinary obstruction or retention
- Perioperative use for certain surgeries
- Urologic surgery or surgery in the adjacent areas
- When giving large amounts of fluids or diuretics during surgery
- To facilitate skin healing with pressure sores or grafts in a patient who is not continent of urine (consider condom catheters instead for men)
- Patient comfort, such as hospice care

UPPER RESPIRATORY TRACT INFECTIONS (URTIs)

PREVIEW | REVIEW

- Otitis externa is usually due to which organism?
- How many days of symptoms are required to diagnose a patient with bacterial sinusitis and prescribe antibiotics?
- What are the usual causative organisms of bacterial sinusitis?
- What are some symptoms of rhinocerebral mucormycosis, and what is the best treatment?

- How can you differentiate allergic rhinitis from bacterial rhinosinusitis?
- What is the treatment for sinusitis?
- What clinical findings eliminate the need to test for group A β-hemolytic streptococcal pharyngitis?

ACUTE OTITIS MEDIA (AOM)

AOM is uncommon in adults, and its presence suggests structural anomalies or immunocompromise. It presents with ear pain and hearing loss +/– fever. Diagnose AOM by visualizing both inflammation of the tympanic membrane (erythema or purulent drainage) and fluid in the middle ear. *Streptococcus pneumoniae* is the most common infecting bacterium. Nontypeable *Haemophilus influenzae* and *Moraxella catarrhalis* are also causative agents.

Treat with amoxicillin/clavulanate if the patient has not taken antibiotics recently. Alternatives are cefuroxime, cefdinir, cefpodoxime, or fluoroquinolones if the patient has recently taken other antibiotics or if initial treatment failed. If IV treatment is needed, ceftriaxone can be used. If patients do not respond, perform tympanocentesis to obtain culture data.

OTITIS EXTERNA (SWIMMER'S EAR)

Otitis externa is also predominantly a pediatric infection. Only 5% of cases are in adults > 20 years of age. It is predisposed by trauma, foreign bodies, dermatitis, and moisture, especially from swimming (hence the term "swimmer's ear"). Otitis externa presents with pain and itching in the external auditory canal. The causative organism of otitis externa is usually *Pseudomonas aeruginosa*. Even when combined, *Staphylococcus epidermidis* and *Staphylococcus aureus* are still a distant 2nd. Treat with a topical fluoroquinolone.

Malignant (necrotizing) **otitis externa** is life-threatening infection. > 90% of patients have diabetes, and immunosuppression is another risk factor. Malignant otitis externa presents the same as otitis externa but progresses to an invasive and destructive infection of the soft tissue and bone, with the potential to invade the meninges and brain. *P. aeruginosa* is the cause in > 95% of cases. Treat the infection with IV antibiotics directed against *P. aeruginosa* (e.g., a fluoroquinolone, or antipseudomonal β-lactam), and adjust the treatment based on the culture results. Therapy is usually required for 6–8 weeks.

SINUSITIS

Sinusitis is inflammation of the paranasal sinuses.

The classification is based on the duration:

- Acute sinusitis: persists ≤ 4 weeks
- Subacute sinusitis: persists 4–12 weeks
- Chronic sinusitis: persists > 12 weeks
- Recurrent sinusitis: > 3 episodes of acute sinusitis per year

Most sinusitis stems from viral infections. Use clinical criteria (given next) to decide whether there is a likelihood of bacterial infection and thus a benefit to giving antibacterials. The pathogenesis of bacterial sinusitis is obstruction of the sinus ostia that allows bacteria that are usually transient colonizers to persist in the sinus cavity.

There are 2 clinical findings predictive of bacterial sinusitis:

1) Duration of symptoms ≥ 10 days or
2) Worsening of symptoms after an initial improvement (double sickness) that occurs after ≥ 3 days

Unless these criteria are met, most infectious sinusitis is viral, and should be treated symptomatically with nasal saline. There is no role for decongestants or antihistamines.

Fever > 102.0°F (38.9°C) with purulent drainage or facial pain for ≥ 3 days at the beginning of the illness supports the diagnosis of acute bacterial sinusitis.

The most common causative bacterial organisms of bacterial sinusitis are *Streptococcus pneumoniae*, *Haemophilus influenzae*, and *Moraxella catarrhalis* (the same 3 as for AOM). **Chronic sinusitis** can also be caused by *Staphylococcus aureus*, group A *Streptococcus*, enteric gram-negative bacilli (GNBs), *Pseudomonas aeruginosa* (especially with cystic fibrosis), and anaerobes such as *Fusobacterium* and *Bacteroides*. Cultures are difficult to interpret in this setting because patients often have received multiple courses of antibiotics, and the cultures usually represent colonization.

Fungal sinusitis (specifically mucormycosis) is seen in patients with diabetes, cancer, iron overload, and hematologic malignancies and in those receiving corticosteroid therapy. A patient with rhinocerebral mucormycosis may present with symptoms of only a sinus infection or with unilateral nasal congestion. Tissue necrosis occurs as infection spreads outside of the sinuses, with the resulting distinctive black eschar sometimes visible on the palate and/or nasal mucosa. (See the discussion on Mucormycosis on page 4-61.)

Symptoms can assist in localizing which sinus is involved. Frontal sinusitis may have headache that is worse when leaning forward (known as bowler's headache). Maxillary sinusitis sometimes presents with maxillary tooth pain, which is a very specific finding. Sphenoid sinusitis may have headache at the vertex of the skull.

Patients with chronic sinusitis commonly have > 1 symptom, including nasal congestion, alteration in smell, facial pressure or headache, and purulent rhinorrhea.

It is important to differentiate bacterial rhinosinusitis from allergic rhinitis, especially if seasonal. Both allergic rhinitis and nonallergic rhinitis with eosinophilia syndrome show a high number of eosinophils on a nasal smear. Bacterial rhinosinusitis, however, shows large numbers of neutrophils and bacteria.

Bacterial sinusitis is treated empirically, but failure to respond or frequent relapses warrant sinus cultures, which can be obtained endoscopically. Consider cystic fibrosis if *Pseudomonas* grows from a sinus culture (especially in a young adult with a history of recurrent respiratory issues).

Radiography: Sinusitis is generally a clinical diagnosis; imaging is not typically required and does not help differentiate a viral from a bacterial infection. Only perform imaging (computed tomography [CT] or magnetic resonance imaging [MRI]) for patients who fail to respond to empiric therapy or who have frequent relapses to look for a structural abnormality.

Treatment of sinusitis: If you suspect acute bacterial sinusitis based on the given criteria, start amoxicillin/ clavulanate. 2nd line drugs are the fluoroquinolones and doxycycline. (For contraindications, see Fluoroquinolones on page 4-87.) The recommended duration of therapy is 5–7 days for amoxicillin/clavulanate and 7–10 days for the 2nd line agents. Intranasal corticosteroids and saline irrigation can be used as adjunctive treatment. Intranasal decongestants and antihistamines are not useful.

Chronic sinusitis rarely responds to antibacterial therapy. An ear, nose, and throat (ENT) consultation is helpful to obtain cultures, provide surgical drainage, and correct any anatomical causes.

Treatment of rhinocerebral mucormycosis: Emergent measures, including the correction of any underlying diseases (e.g., diabetic ketoacidosis), radical surgical debridement, and lipid amphotericin B, are required. Posaconazole or isavuconazole is used after patients begin to improve on amphotericin B or in patients who cannot tolerate amphotericin B.

DEEP INFECTIONS OF THE HEAD AND NECK

Deep infections of the head and neck are named by their location and include submandibular space infections (which include infections of the sublingual and submylohyoid spaces), lateral pharyngeal space infections, and retropharyngeal space infections. An infection can spread from one space to another.

All of these infections are caused by a mixed oral flora that includes oral anaerobic bacteria. They develop from an extension of the normal oral flora into deeper locations from more superficial infections (e.g., tonsillitis leading to a peritonsillar abscess) and/or from the invasion of a high inoculum of bacteria due to poor dental hygiene. The presentation depends on which space is infected, and > 1 infection can occur at the same time (see Figure 4-1 for illustration of the various head and neck spaces). Treatment is with antibiotics directed at normal flora and surgical drainage if abscess forms.

Submandibular space infection (a.k.a. **Ludwig angina**):

- Cellulitis of the floor of the mouth and submandibular neck
- If it extends posteriorly, it can obstruct the airway.

Lateral pharyngeal space infection:

- Anterior to the sternocleidomastoid muscle
- Contains carotid artery, jugular vein, cranial nerves 9–12
- Carotid infection can lead to infected cerebral emboli.
- Jugular infection can lead to infected pulmonary emboli.
- Can be caused by *Fusobacterium necrophorum*, an anaerobic gram-negative bacteria (GNB). This is known as **Lemierre syndrome.**

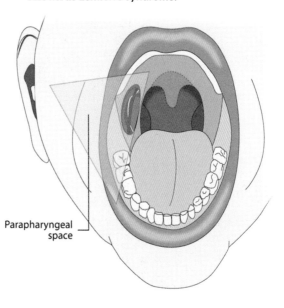

Parapharyngeal space

Submandibular space

Retropharyngeal space

Danger space

Prevertebral space

5

6

7

Parapharyngeal space

Figure 4-1: Deep infections of the head and neck

INFECTIOUS DISEASE

Retropharyngeal space infection:

- Contiguous spread from pharyngitis, tonsillitis, or other neck space
- Descends to C7–T1
- Presents with dysphagia and neck pain increased with hyperextension and possibly stridor
- Posterior to this is the danger space, so called because it extends to the mediastinum.
- Posterior to this is the prevertebral space, which is a space that extends down to the pelvis.

In an otherwise healthy patient without comorbidities, ampicillin-sulbactam or a similar antibiotic is appropriate. In a patient with extensive surgery, neoplasm, or prior antibiotic therapy, use broad-spectrum antibiotics pending the surgical culture data.

PHARYNGITIS

The majority of pathogens that cause a sore throat are viruses and are self-limited. The most common of these are rhinoviruses, coronaviruses, and enteroviruses. *Streptococcus pyogenes* (group A β-hemolytic *Streptococcus* [GABHS]) is the bacterial pathogen that causes adult pharyngitis with enough frequency to consider routine testing. The only other bacteria that cause pharyngitis amenable to treatment are *Neisseria gonorrhoeae* (pharyngeal gonorrhea) and *Corynebacterium diphtheriae* (diphtheria).

The 2012 Infectious Diseases Society of America (IDSA) guidelines for the management of group A streptococcal pharyngitis delineate which adults to test for GABHS, which diagnostic tests to perform, and who to treat based on this testing.

Use associated symptoms to assess the likelihood of GABHS vs. a viral infection. GABHS rarely infects above or below the pharynx, so having an associated cough and hoarseness is not typical. It does not inflame the nasopharynx; therefore, coryza is not seen, and it does not cause ulcerative lesions. It rarely causes conjunctivitis. Respiratory viruses can cause all of these symptoms, so the presence of these symptoms makes it unnecessary to test for or treat GABHS. Conversely, do test an adult with pharyngitis who has none of these symptoms and has a fever or swollen lymph nodes.

Initially test for GABHS via a rapid antigen-detection test (RADT). This test has a sensitivity of ~ 80% but a specificity of > 95%. Because of its high specificity, a positive test is sufficient evidence for GABHS infection to begin treatment.

Adults generally are not at high risk for streptococcal pharyngitis; therefore, a negative RADT result has a sufficient negative predictive value, and no further testing or treatment is required. However, do obtain cultures for all adults with high exposure to children and adolescents (e.g., school teachers, day care center workers) even with a negative RADT result. Regardless of which test is performed, treat only patients with a positive test result.

Treatment of GABHS infection decreases the risk of local complications (e.g., peritonsillar abscess) and rheumatic fever as long as it is given within the first 72 hours. If the RADT result is negative and clinical suspicion is low, it is appropriate to wait for a positive culture prior to treatment to avoid antibacterial treatment of viral pharyngitis. It is not clear whether treatment decreases the occurrence of poststreptococcal glomerulonephritis. Treat for 10 days with oral penicillin (PCN) or amoxicillin. Treat PCN-allergic patients with clindamycin for 10 days or with azithromycin for 5 days.

Only a few infectious diseases cause pharyngitis with a rash. These are limited to scarlet fever caused by GABHS (which presents with diffuse erythema with fine, sandpaper-like papules), acute human immunodeficiency virus (HIV, which presents with a maculopapular rash), *Arcanobacterium haemolyticum* (which presents with diffuse erythema), *Mycoplasma pneumoniae* (which presents with erythema multiforme), Epstein-Barr virus (which presents with a maculopapular rash in 30% of patients and up to 90% of patients given ampicillin), and coxsackieviruses (which present with a vesicular rash).

EPIGLOTTITIS

Infection of the epiglottis is a potentially life-threatening disease due to the possibility of airway compromise. It presents as sore throat and odynophagia but can be differentiated from pharyngitis if patients also have drooling or stridor. The base of the tongue inserts next to the epiglottis, so 50% of patients have pain with movement of the tongue and speak as if they have hot food in their mouth (referred to as the "hot potato" voice). They also may be more comfortable with neck flexion rather than extension (which is the opposite of retropharyngeal abscess). The most common infecting organism is *Haemophilus influenzae*, but there are myriad other bacterial pathogens (including *Streptococcus pneumoniae* and *Staphylococcus aureus*) and viral pathogens, and in most cases the blood and throat cultures are negative.

Diagnose epiglottitis by demonstrating inflammation of the epiglottis (Figure 4-2) with the gold standard, direct laryngoscopy (the oropharyngeal examination is often normal), or with imaging showing a swollen epiglottis on a lateral neck film (indicated by a "thumb sign") or neck CT scan.

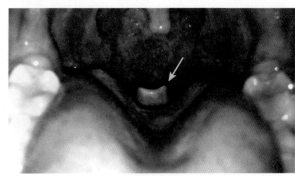

Figure 4-2: Swollen epiglottis

Treatment consists of protecting the airway immediately if there are any signs or symptoms suggestive of airway compromise and administering empiric antibiotics. Throat cultures are only obtained after airway safety is secure. Blood cultures should also be obtained. Empiric antibiotics to use are ceftriaxone plus vancomycin to treat possible methicillin-resistant *S. aureus* (MRSA).

SKIN / SOFT TISSUE, JOINTS, BONES

PREVIEW | REVIEW

- What factors determine the approach to therapy of common skin and soft tissue infections?
- What is the clinical presentation of *Mycobacterium marinum*?
- How is a prosthetic joint infection diagnosed?
- Which organism besides *Staphylococcus aureus* causes osteomyelitis in a patient with sickle cell disease?

COMMON SKIN AND SOFT TISSUE INFECTIONS

As of 2014, the IDSA recommends that skin and soft tissue infections (cellulitis affecting the deeper dermis and subcutaneous tissues) be separated into purulent and nonpurulent categories that are predictive of their microbiologic cause and best empiric treatment. Purulent cellulitis is most commonly caused by *Staphylococcus aureus*, and nonpurulent cellulitis is most commonly caused by *Streptococcus pyogenes*. The approach to management is based on the presence or absence of purulence and the severity of illness.

Patients with mild cellulitis have no associated systemic signs or symptoms. Patients with moderate cellulitis have systemic signs (e.g., fever, chills, myalgias). Patients with severe cellulitis have associated sepsis, have skin bullae or sloughing, or are immunocompromised.

Purulent Cellulitis

Incise and drain purulent cellulitis.

A **mild purulent** soft tissue infection does not require culture. Studies from 2016 show a benefit in giving a 7-day course of TMP/SMX with respect to cure, the need for repeat incision and drainage, and the spread of infection to household contacts. Doxycycline is an alternative in the sulfa-allergic patient.

Culture **moderate purulent** soft tissue infections and then give empiric therapy that targets MRSA, which is the pathogen in ~ 50% of these cases. Treat moderate infections with oral TMP/SMX or doxycycline. These inexpensive antibiotics remain active against ~ 90% of *S. aureus* strains regardless of methicillin sensitivity. Alter the treatment if needed based on the C&S report.

Culture **severe purulent** cellulitis and begin IV agents active against MRSA (e.g., vancomycin, daptomycin, linezolid) empirically.

Nonpurulent Cellulitis

The absence of pus makes obtaining cultures difficult. Treat **mild nonpurulent** cellulitis with oral agents that target *Streptococcus pyogenes*, such as penicillin, a 1st generation cephalosporin (e.g., cephalexin), or clindamycin. Because of the rapidly progressive nature of *S. pyogenes* infections, give IV therapy with the same agents or ceftriaxone to patients with **moderate** disease and obtain blood cultures.

Severe disease, especially if there is bullae formation or slough, requires immediate surgical debridement to rule out and treat necrotizing fasciitis (see Necrotizing Fasciitis) and to obtain tissue cultures along with blood cultures. Because organisms other than *S. pyogenes* can cause necrotizing fasciitis, treat empirically with vancomycin and piperacillin/tazobactam while awaiting these culture results.

Rapidly Progressive Cellulitis

A few soft tissue infections are rapidly progressive and can spread up to 1 cm/hour through infected tissue.

Necrotizing Fasciitis

Necrotizing fasciitis is a life- and limb-threatening infection that only a handful of organisms can cause. These infections can progress as rapidly as 1 cm/hour. Solitary organisms capable of doing this include group A or B *Streptococcus*, *Vibrio vulnificus*, *Staphylococcus aureus*, and *Clostridium* spp. A mixed infection with gram-negative aerobic and anaerobic organisms can also cause necrotizing fasciitis. This can occur if stool flora contaminate a pressure ulcer near the anus or as a postdelivery obstetric complication. Patients with microvascular disease from diabetes are at increased risk. When these organisms gain entrance to the fascial plane, there is little physical resistance to their lateral spread. In addition, neurovascular bundles run along the fascia, and destruction of these bundles leads to the classic symptoms that occur.

The destruction of the arterial supply of the skin causes necrosis with resultant bleb formation (often black) and sloughing. The inflammation of cutaneous nerves leads to initial extreme pain, often disproportionate to the skin appearance, that paradoxically improves as the disease progresses due to nerve destruction. If gas-forming organisms (e.g., *Clostridia*, enteric GNBs) are the cause, there can be crepitus on examination. Imaging may show fascial inflammation and/or gas, but the definitive diagnosis is made by surgical exploration, which should be done emergently to debride dead tissue and obtain cultures. Empiric broad-spectrum antibiotics are important but are only adjunctive to surgery because they do not reach the infected devascularized tissue. Repeated surgical intervention is often needed.

Erysipelas

Erysipelas is the name given to streptococcal lymphangitis characterized by well-demarcated, raised borders affecting the superficial dermis and lymphatics. Lymphatic involvement with streaks in infected limbs is common and is predisposed by lymphedema or trauma to the lymphatic system (e.g., postmastectomy in the arms, post–saphenous vein harvesting in the legs, liposuction).

Pasteurella multocida

Pasteurella multocida is a GNB that causes infection in many animals and colonizes their mouths. Transmission to humans is typically via a dog or cat bite. Initially there may be little inflammation, but a rapidly progressive, nonnecrotizing cellulitis can ensue. The overall management of bite wounds is discussed in more detail under Animal Bites. *P. multocida* is susceptible to most antibiotics. Amoxicillin/clavulanic acid is the treatment of choice. Alternative drugs include 3rd generation cephalosporins, doxycycline, and the fluoroquinolones.

UNIQUE SOFT TISSUE INFECTIONS

Vibrio vulnificus is a GNB that causes a necrotizing soft tissue infection after inoculation of saltwater into non-intact skin (e.g., skin penetrated by a fishing hook, fish spines, or an oyster shucking knife). It is common in coastal, warm, salt, or brackish water. Particularly susceptible to sepsis are those who are immunocompromised, specifically those who have chronic liver disease or hemochromatosis. It commonly causes bullous lesions. Diagnose *V. vulnificus* infection by culture, and treat with ceftriaxone with either doxycycline or a fluoroquinolone until susceptibilities are known.

Mycobacterium marinum is an acid-fast organism often called the fish tank bacillus. It causes nonhealing ulceronodular skin lesions when inoculated into the skin in people exposed to freshwater or saltwater via swimming or fish tanks. Infection can present as a single granuloma, but the organism often invades the lymphatics and can cause a series of nodular lesions along the lymphatic drainage similar to the lesions seen in sporotrichosis. It may penetrate to joints or bones. The lesions tend to localize in the distal extremities because the organism does not grow well at core body temperature. Diagnose *M. marinum* infection by biopsy and acid-fast bacilli (AFB) stain and culture. (It needs to be incubated in lower temperatures for growth.) Mild disease can be treated with a single agent (clarithromycin, doxycycline, or TMP/SMX), but severe or progressive disease is treated with a combination of clarithromycin and ethambutol or rifampin. The duration of treatment is at least 1–2 months after the lesions have resolved.

Erysipelothrix rhusiopathiae is a gram-positive rod that infects a large number of domestic and marine animals and causes a zoonotic skin infection in fish and meat handlers. The lesions are usually localized nodules, with lymphangitis occurring in ~ 25% of affected patients. Systemic disease with bacteremia is uncommon and more likely in those with alcohol use disorder. A major complication is endocarditis. Treat localized infection with oral PCN or amoxicillin. Treat diffuse cutaneous or systemic infection with parenteral penicillin, ceftriaxone, or ciprofloxacin.

SEPTIC ARTHRITIS

Joints become infected by 2 routes: direct inoculation (e.g., adjacent cellulitis, trauma, surgery) or hematogenously from another focus. Risk factors for joint infection are injection drug use, diabetes mellitus, and prior joint disease or injury (e.g., rheumatoid arthritis, trauma, surgery). By far the most common infecting organism in native joints is *Staphylococcus aureus*. It presents with the acute onset of monoarticular joint pain, swelling, and redness.

Perform joint aspiration urgently (and prior to antibiotics to increase the yield) and send for a white blood cell (WBC) count, Gram stain, and culture. Crystal disease (e.g., gout, pseudogout) can mimic and/or accompany septic arthritis, so send joint fluid for crystal analysis. Gonococcal arthritis is discussed separately under Disseminated Gonorrhea on page 4-22. Nongonococcal septic arthritis shows organisms ~ 50% of the time on Gram stain and > 95% of the time on culture if no prior antibiotics have been given. Synovial fluid usually has a WBC count > 40,000/μL (40 × 10⁹/L).

Initial therapy can be based on the Gram stain: vancomycin for gram-positive cocci or a 3rd generation cephalosporin for GNBs. The definitive therapy is based on the culture results. Treat septic arthritis typically for 3 weeks with IV antibiotics or 2 weeks with IV antibiotics followed by 1 week of oral therapy. To decrease joint damage from the organisms and the inflammatory reaction to them, perform repeat joint aspirations if fluid reaccumulates while the patient is on treatment. Endemic fungi and Lyme disease from *Borrelia burgdorferi* cause a chronic monoarticular septic arthritis (see Endemic Fungi on page 4-59 and Lyme Disease on page 4-55).

Prosthetic joint infection: Having a joint prosthesis is a major risk factor for septic arthritis. Joint infection occurs in 1–5% of prosthetic joint recipients. Manifestations are wound drainage, cutaneous erythema and warmth, prosthetic joint pain, and/or abnormal motion of the joint. Plain radiographs are helpful to diagnose prosthetic joint infection if they show a widening of the bone–cement interface, changes in the position of the prosthesis, cement fractures, a periosteal reaction, or motion of the components on stress views. Other imaging, such as bone scans, CT, MRI, and positron emission tomography (PET), are not useful in most cases. The diagnosis is definitively made by a joint aspiration; *S. aureus* and coagulase-negative staphylococci are the most commonly recovered bacteria.

There are 3 approaches to combined surgical and antibiotic therapy that attempt to preserve the joint. Incision and drainage with retention of hardware can be considered if the infection occurs within 30 days of surgery, the prosthesis is well fixed, and there is no sinus tract. In this setting, give 2–6 weeks of pathogen-specific IV antibiotics with oral rifampin if you have identified *Staphylococcus*. This can be followed by up to 6 months of oral therapy. A 1-stage procedure (incision and drainage with the exchange of prosthetic components) can be considered, especially in patients who may not tolerate 2 surgical interventions due to comorbidities. For most cases, consider a 2-stage procedure (prosthesis removal, 4–6 weeks of pathogen-specific IV antibiotics, and prosthesis reinsertion). Patients with comorbidities that place them at high risk of not tolerating surgical procedures can be tried on lifetime suppressive therapy if the organism is susceptible to oral antibiotics with high bioavailability.

OSTEOMYELITIS

Osteomyelitis is either acute or chronic, the distinction being that the latter has necrotic bone. Acute osteomyelitis is most commonly caused by *Staphylococcus aureus*. Some organisms have certain epidemiologic niches. In people who use IV drugs, *Pseudomonas aeruginosa* and *Serratia* may be causative and have a predilection for the sternoclavicular joint, symphysis pubis, and vertebrae. In the U.S., the most common etiologic agent causing osteomyelitis in patients with sickle cell disease is *Salmonella*.

Diagnosis of diabetic foot osteomyelitis has high accuracy if a solid probe is able to reach the bone on examination. Otherwise, image in order to demonstrate osteomyelitis prior to recommending bone biopsies for culture. Initial plain x-rays can be done with the understanding that radiolucency requires > 50% demineralization of the bone, and this takes weeks to occur. MRI is the most sensitive and the study of choice. Do not use bone scans because they are very nonspecific and have a very high false-positive rate.

If probing to bone or MRI is suggestive of osteomyelitis, perform cultures of the bone to confirm the diagnosis and guide antibiotic therapy. Superficial cultures are not reliable predictors of infecting organisms. Evidence of osteomyelitis on imaging and a positive blood culture are presumptive evidence of microbiologic causation.

Except for small bone disease and early prosthetic joint infection (< 30 days from insertion of the prosthesis), all necrotic bone and prosthetic material must be removed before chronic osteomyelitis can be cured with antibiotics. Erythrocyte sedimentation rate (ESR) and C-reactive protein (CRP) assays can be used to help follow the course of the disease and determine duration of treatment.

ANIMAL BITES

Animal bites create 3 specific problems:

1) Bacterial infections
2) Tetanus
3) Rabies

Bacterial infection: The risk of infection is highest from human bites, followed by cat bites and then dog bites. Causative agents can be from the animal's mouth (e.g., *Pasteurella*, streptococci, anaerobes) or inoculated from colonized skin at the bite site (e.g., *Staphylococcus aureus*). Wash and debride wounds immediately and take images if there is suspicion of joint or bone injury. Empiric antibiotic treatment is recommended for all human bites. Other bites can be observed without antibiotics unless the patient is immunocompromised, the bite is to the face or hand or is near a joint or bone, there is obvious crush injury, or there is edema (suggesting deep involvement or crush injury). Amoxicillin/clavulanate covers most of the causative organisms and is the empiric drug of choice.

Tetanus: All bites are considered tetanus-prone injuries; decide when to give prophylaxis with tetanus toxoid +/– tetanus immunoglobulin based on the patient's prior immunization history. See Approach to Tetanus Prevention on page 4-94.

Rabies: The risk of rabies from a bite and the need for the rabies vaccine +/– rabies immunoglobulin is based on the type of animal involved. This is discussed further under Rabies on page 4-27.

FEVER AND RASH

PREVIEW | REVIEW
- What are the characteristic skin lesions seen in neutropenic patients with bacteremia from *Pseudomonas aeruginosa*?
- What types of disseminated infections cause nodular lesions and fever?

OVERVIEW

The febrile patient with skin lesions can run the gamut from a benign infection to a medical emergency. Not all patients have an infectious disease as the etiology of this combination, but the approach to patients with infectious causes of fever and rash is outlined in the following topics.

LIFE-THREATENING ETIOLOGIES

A few etiologies of fever and rash constitute potentially life-threatening infectious diseases. These require urgent diagnosis and treatment and are recognized by the specific dermatologic manifestations they cause. Neutropenic patients with fever require immediate empiric antibiotics even without rash (see Febrile Neutropenia on page 4-41). Neutropenic patients with *Pseudomonas aeruginosa* bacteremia can have characteristic skin lesions known as **ecthyma gangrenosum**, which are black, necrotic, ulcerative lesions (Figure 4-3 on page 4-10). Neutropenic patients with candidemia may have a maculopapular rash as a tip-off (Figure 4-4 on page 4-10). Because it is due to hematogenous spread of the fungus, it is usually symmetrical.

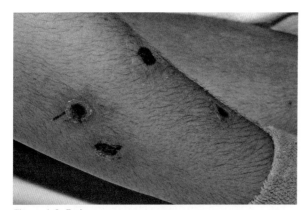

Figure 4-3: Ecthyma gangrenosum

Figure 4-4: Maculopapular rash as seen with invasive candidiasis

Petechial rash with fever can be seen from disseminated intravascular coagulation (DIC) from any cause. It also occurs without DIC from the viral hemorrhagic fevers, meningococcemia, and Rocky Mountain spotted fever (see Rocky Mountain Spotted Fever (RMSF) on page 4-53).

Disseminated varicella-zoster virus or herpes simplex virus (HSV) infection causes fever and **vesicular lesions**.

Toxic shock syndrome associated with *Staphylococcus aureus* manifests as fever, hypotension, and a diffuse, erythematous, **sunburn-like rash** (see Toxic Shock Syndrome (TSS) on page 4-45).

NON–LIFE-THREATENING ETIOLOGIES

Nodular or ulcerated nodular lesions with fever can be seen with disseminated infection from any of the endemic fungi, *Mycobacterium marinum*, other nontuberculous mycobacteria, sporotrichosis, *Erysipelothrix*, or *Leishmania* (Figure 4-5).

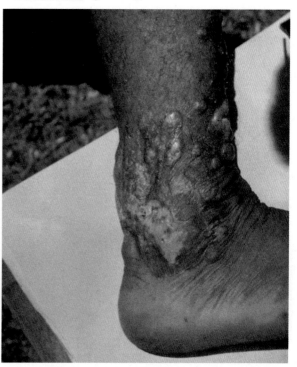

Figure 4-5: Blastomyces dermatitidis

Vesicular lesions can result from infection with the *Enterovirus* family of viruses (e.g., enteroviruses, coxsackieviruses, echoviruses) (Figure 4-6).

Pustules are seen in disseminated gonococcemia (see Figure 4-12 on page 4-22).

Secondary syphilis can produce any form of rash, with the exception of vesicles and bullae.

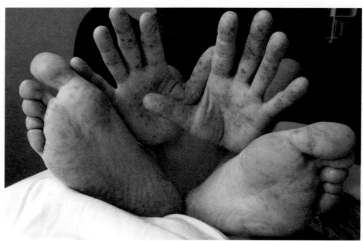

Figure 4-6: Hand-foot-mouth disease in adults

GASTROINTESTINAL (GI) INFECTIONS

PREVIEW | REVIEW

- What is the incubation period for the toxin-induced syndromes causing nausea and vomiting?

- Which findings on stool evaluation suggest invasive diarrhea?

- Know the recommendations for the prophylaxis and treatment of traveler's diarrhea.

- *Salmonella* infection is spread by which animals?

- What is a possible adverse consequence of treating infectious diarrhea due to *E. coli* O157:H7 with antibiotics?

- What is the treatment for *Shigella* infection?

- *Vibrio vulnificus* can cause severe disease in which groups of patients?

- What is the treatment for an initial episode of *Clostridioides difficile* (formerly *Clostridium difficile*) infection? What is the treatment of choice for patients with severe *C. difficile* diarrhea?

- What is the treatment recommendation for the 1st recurrence of *C. difficile* infection?

- Which infection control precautions must be used for patients with *C. difficile* diarrhea?

FOOD POISONING

Food poisoning is the common term for gastrointestinal (GI) diseases resulting from bacterial toxins, although it is sometimes extended to include all foodborne illnesses. The 3 organisms that produce illness from ingestion of toxins are *Staphylococcus aureus*, *Bacillus cereus*, and *Clostridium perfringens*.

S. aureus produces disease due to ingestion of preformed enterotoxin. Food handlers can contaminate food through improper handling and inadequate temperature controls, allowing for an increased quantity of emetogenic toxins to be ingested. The incubation period for the toxin-induced syndromes causing nausea and vomiting is 1–6 hours, so the causative meal is usually evident. Mayonnaise and cream pies are frequent culprits, although meat, eggs, and produce can be contaminated as well. The predominant symptom is vomiting that lasts < 24 hours. Vomiting with concomitant cramps and diarrhea is characteristic. Disease is self-limited, and treatment is supportive.

B. cereus grows best in starchy foods such as rice, and its spores are very heat resistant. It, too, causes vomiting within 1–6 hours but can also cause a diarrheal illness within 8–16 hours depending on which toxin it has produced. Disease is self-limited, and treatment is supportive.

C. perfringens is a bowel colonizer of almost all animals that humans ingest and has an incubation period of 8–16 hours prior to causing a watery diarrhea of 1–2 days' duration. Disease is self-limited, and treatment is supportive.

VIRAL GASTROENTERITIS

There are many viral causes of diarrhea. **Rotavirus** is the most common cause of severe diarrhea in infants; it less frequently infects older children and adults. It is easily found in the stool via an enzyme-linked immunosorbent assay (ELISA) or polymerase chain reaction (PCR) assay. **Noroviruses** (formerly known as Norwalk-like viruses) are the most common viral cause of gastroenteritis in adults. They are highly contagious (infectious inoculum of < 100 viral particles) and spread via person-to-person transmission, fomites, and food (e.g., salads, shellfish, fruit). Often called the "winter vomiting disease," noroviruses can cause outbreaks on cruise ships, in schools, and on athletic teams. Incubation period is 1–2 days. Noroviruses can be detected via reverse transcriptase polymerase chain reaction (RT-PCR) in stool samples. The treatment is supportive. There are no antivirals active against these viruses.

BACTERIAL DIARRHEA

Bacteria cause diarrhea after ingestion only if they are ingested in sufficient quantities to survive the hostile environment of the stomach and competition for nutrients with our normal microbiome, allowing them to invade the small bowel and/or colon or to produce inflammatory toxins. Detection of WBCs in the stool is a quick but variably sensitive indicator of an invasive bacterial diarrhea, with a sensitivity of 50–70% and a specificity of 50–80%. Detection of the WBC protein lactoferrin has a higher sensitivity and specificity: > 90% and > 80%, respectively.

In the U.S., *Salmonella* is the most common cause of non–toxin-related bacterial diarrhea, with *Campylobacter* being a close second, each causing ~ 1 million cases a year. Shiga toxin–producing *Escherichia coli* (enterohemorrhagic *E. coli* [EHEC]) causes ~ 200,000 cases a year, and *Shigella* causes ~ 150,000 cases a year. Since many patients are empirically treated and do not get cultures, these incidences represent significant underreporting.

Traveler's Diarrhea

This is the most common infection to occur in travelers and affects 50 million U.S. travelers to all destinations except northern Europe, Canada, Australia, and New Zealand. For those traveling to less-developed regions, the risk can approach 60%. Almost 50% of those infected are forced to change their itinerary, 20% spend 1 day in bed, and 1% are hospitalized.

The majority of infections are due to strains of enterotoxigenic *E. coli*, followed by *Salmonella*, *Campylobacter*, and *Shigella*.

INFECTIOUS DISEASE

Educate patients on how to prevent traveler's diarrhea by recommending the following:

- Avoid consumption of local, untreated water or ice, including in mixed alcoholic drinks.
- Water should be filtered or boiled for 3 minutes.
- Avoid fresh fruits that cannot be peeled.
- Even at luxury resorts, avoid uncooked vegetables, meat salads (e.g., tuna), and condiments (e.g., salsas).

Carbonated drinks without ice are okay. A good general rule: Boil it, peel it, cook it, or forget it.

Prophylactic antibiotics for traveler's diarrhea are not routinely indicated, but they are justified for those with immunodeficiencies or a history of cardiac, kidney, or inflammatory bowel disease. They are also appropriate for persons conducting important business who cannot afford to be ill. Prophylactic regimens include:

- Ciprofloxacin 500 mg daily
- Rifaximin 200 mg daily or twice a day (bid)

A fluoroquinolone (e.g., ciprofloxacin), rifaximin, or azithromycin may be given as a pretrip prescription to be taken should diarrhea occur.

For self-treatment, the patient should determine the severity of diarrhea and treat it accordingly. Mild diarrhea should be treated with aggressive oral hydration. Bismuth subsalicylate can be of benefit. Antibiotics are only required for severe disease (i.e., > 4 stools/day, high fever, or blood/pus/mucus in stools). For severe disease, prescribe one of the following:

- Ciprofloxacin 500 mg bid × 1–2 days
- Azithromycin 1,000 mg × 1 dose
- Rifaximin 200 mg 3 times a day (tid) × 3 days (for frequent stools only but not if there is high fever or blood, pus, or mucus because not systemically absorbed)

Antidiarrheals (e.g., loperamide) can be used cautiously along with the antibiotics, but an antidiarrheal should not be the only treatment in severe disease because of the risk of causing toxic megacolon.

Salmonella

S. enterica is found in the stool of many different host animals and is the only *Salmonella* species that infects humans. *Salmonella* can be spread by frozen foods (especially chicken), milk, and eggs. Baby chicks, iguanas, turtles, and other exotic pets also can be sources of infection.

An inoculum of $> 10^5$ organisms is typically required to produce disease, but fewer organisms are needed in patients on acid-suppressive drugs. After an incubation period of 1–3 days, a usually nonbloody diarrhea with fever occurs. Untreated, the fever resolves by day 3 and the diarrhea by day 7.

Diagnosis is made by culture or nucleic acid amplification test (NAAT).

Do not give antibiotic treatment routinely because it prolongs the shedding of the organism in the stool, increases antibacterial resistance, and does not shorten the course of disease. Because a small percentage of patients can have severe disease, treat patients > 50 years of age, with significant comorbid illnesses, with prosthetic materials, with significant atherosclerosis, or who are immunosuppressed. Severe exacerbations of preexistent inflammatory bowel disease can occur, so treat these patients as well. Treatment, if required, is with a fluoroquinolone, TMP/SMX, or azithromycin if susceptibilities are known. If intravenous therapy is required, use ceftriaxone.

S. enterica serotype Typhi (a.k.a. **Salmonella typhi**; formerly *S. typhi*) causes typhoid fever after ingestion of contaminated food, milk, or water. This organism is found in humans only. Infection commonly begins with fever, chills, initial constipation followed by diarrhea, leukopenia, and the appearance of classic rose spots on the trunk (Figure 4-7), which appear ~ 1 week after the fever starts. These look like little, 2- to 3-mm angiomas. Because the organism multiplies in the reticuloendothelial system, hepatosplenomegaly may develop. There may be relative bradycardia as a clue. Blood cultures are usually positive during the 1st week, followed by stool cultures and then urine cultures.

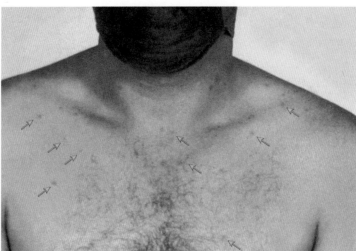

Figure 4-7: Typhoid fever with classic 2- to 3-mm "rose spots"

Treat typhoid fever with fluoroquinolone, 3rd generation cephalosporins, ampicillin, TMP/SMX, or chloramphenicol depending on the sensitivities. Carriers (those excreting the organism for > 12 months) without gallbladder disease or stones can typically be cleared with 4 weeks of fluoroquinolone administration. Chronic carriers with gallstones are at increased risk of biliary cancer.

There are moderately effective live attenuated and polysaccharide vaccines that can be given to travelers (> 2 years of age) who go outside of the usual tourist areas of Latin America, Asia, and Africa.

Campylobacter

C. jejuni and C. coli cause human disease usually from ingestion of undercooked meat—most notably poultry, as these bacteria often inhabit the lining of their intestinal tracts. Diarrhea, with cramping and often a high fever, occurs after 1–7 days. The disease is self-limited, and antibiotic therapy only decreases the duration of illness by an average of 1 day. Diagnosis is made by culture or NAAT. Treat those with severe disease or who are immunocompromised. Although resistance has been reported, most strains are susceptible to macrolides with fluoroquinolones as an alternative.

Escherichia coli

E. coli is the most common cause of bacterial diarrhea worldwide. Depending on which strain is responsible, E. coli produces diarrhea via one of the following mechanisms:

- Production of a secretory toxin (enterotoxigenic E. coli [**ETEC**]), which causes a noninflammatory watery diarrhea
- Production of a Shiga toxin (enterohemorrhagic E. coli [**EHEC**]), which causes mucosal injury and bloody diarrhea
- Invasion (enteroinvasive E. coli [**EIEC**]), which causes a watery or bloody stool. EIEC's mechanism of infection is similar to that of Shigella and causes a similar presentation
- Inducing epithelial barrier dysfunction (enteroadherrent E. coli [**EAEC**]), which causes a watery diarrhea (specifically in travelers, children, and persons infected with HIV)
- Injection of protein toxins that stimulate enterocyte secretion (enteropathogenic E. coli [**EPEC**]) causing diarrhea, usually in children, that is watery and chronic and may lead to malnutrition

ETEC is the most common cause of traveler's diarrhea. Refer to Traveler's Diarrhea on page 4-11 for information on prophylaxis and treatment.

EHEC, which is usually from serotype O157:H7, causes localized outbreaks of hemorrhagic colitis, thrombotic thrombocytopenic purpura (TTP), and hemolytic uremic syndrome (HUS), typically after eating undercooked beef or unpasteurized milk. Fever is conspicuously absent, but nausea and vomiting are common. Do not treat diarrhea caused by E. coli O157:H7 with antibiotics because killing large numbers of organisms can release large amounts of Shiga-like toxin, resulting in an increased risk of HUS development.

Shigella

Shigella spp. (S. sonnei and S. flexneri being the most common) produce Shiga toxin, causing fevers, bloody diarrhea, cramping, and tenesmus. It is the most contagious bacterial diarrhea, with an inoculum of 10 organisms being sufficient to cause disease in 50% of individuals. Thus, it is easily spread from person to person, via contaminated food, or even via flies that have had contact with infected feces. Diagnosis is made by culture or nucleic acid amplification test (NAAT).

Because of increasing resistance to fluoroquinolones, as of 2021, the CDC no longer recommends treating all patients with Shigella. Only treat patients if they are immunocompromised or have severe disease. Treatment may also be directed by local health departments to quell outbreaks. Fluoroquinolones can be used if the minimum inhibitory concentrations (MICs) show sensitivity; otherwise, use other agents based on lab-reported susceptibilities.

Yersinia

Y. enterocolitica causes diarrhea (sometimes bloody), fever, right lower quadrant (RLQ) abdominal pain (mimicking appendicitis) due to mesenteric lymphadenopathy, and sometimes sore throat due to tonsillar enlargement. Pigs are the major reservoir, and disease can occur after ingesting undercooked pork. This pathogen is siderophilic; therefore, conditions with iron overload, such as hemochromatosis and those requiring frequent transfusions (e.g., some patients with sickle cell disease), increase its pathogenicity. The use of deferoxamine also increases risk. Diagnosis is made by culture or NAAT. Treatment is typically supportive, but antibiotic therapy is warranted for invasive disease. Oral therapy is with fluoroquinolone, and for severe or systemic disease, ceftriaxone with gentamicin is recommended.

Vibrio

Vibrio spp. grow in saltwater and are transmitted via raw or undercooked seafood and shellfish, which, as filter feeders, concentrate the organism. V. cholerae O1 (which causes cholera) is occasionally found in Gulf Coast crabs but is more common in the endemic regions of Africa and Asia from contaminated water sources. The diagnosis is made clinically with the presentation of profuse watery diarrhea and significant, life-threatening volume loss. Rice-water stool is the classic descriptor; it looks like the soaking water from rice. The treatment is aggressive rehydration; without it, mortality approaches 70%. The addition of antibiotics (e.g., a fluoroquinolone, a macrolide, doxycycline) can decrease shedding in the stool and should be selected based on known regional susceptibilities or culture results.

INFECTIOUS DISEASE

The non-O1 *V. cholerae*, *V. parahaemolyticus*, and other *Vibrio* spp. are even more frequent causes of shellfish-associated diarrhea. They cause abdominal pain and diarrhea that may be bloody. Severe disease is more common in patients with cirrhosis. Treatment is supportive, and antibiotics (e.g., doxycycline, macrolides, or fluoroquinolones) are given when the disease is severe. *V. vulnificus* causes skin infections and sepsis, especially in immunocompromised patients and those with chronic liver disease. For additional information, see Unique Soft Tissue Infections on page 4-8.

Summary

With the exception of "food poisoning" and traveler's diarrhea, the initial presentation of infectious diarrhea is usually not sufficient to determine a specific etiologic organism, and stool culture or NAAT is required to make an etiologic diagnosis. Sending a stool sample for detection of lactoferrin and calprotectin is useful to suggest an invasive diarrheal pathogen. With the exception of typhoid fever, patients with mild disease should be given hydration but no empiric antibiotics. Avoid antimotility drugs unless patients are being treated with antibiotics. Treat severe disease or patients at risk for severe disease (e.g., immunocompromised patients) with a fluoroquinolone (or, for *Campylobacter*, a macrolide) unless EHEC is suspected or cultured.

DIARRHEA DUE TO *CLOSTRIDIOIDES DIFFICILE*

Microbiology, Epidemiology, and Presentation

Clostridia has been a catch-all basket for bacteria that have similar characteristics—strictly anaerobic, spore-forming, gram-positive rods. Recent findings place *C. difficile* (formerly *Clostridium difficile*) with bacteria that are far removed phylogenetically from other clostridia; thus, its name has been changed from *Clostridium difficile* to *Clostridioides* (clostridia-like) *difficile* to minimize potential confusion from a more radical name change.

Diarrhea due to *C. difficile* infection (CDI) is discussed apart from the other bacterial diarrheas due to several unique characteristics. Diarrhea during or after the administration of antibiotics is usually caused by an alteration of fecal flora (resulting in the decreased breakdown of small molecules and an osmotic diarrhea) or the promotility action of some antibiotics (e.g., macrolides); however, if the fecal flora is altered and acquisition of *C. difficile* occurs, CDI ensues. Clindamycin, cephalosporins, and fluoroquinolones are the most common precipitants of CDI. Most cases occur in health care settings, but an increasing number of cases are occurring in the outpatient setting. The use of proton pump inhibitors increases the risk.

Symptoms can develop up to 12 weeks after the antibiotics are stopped. The diarrhea is typically a watery diarrhea but may be bloody in 15% of patients. An ileus without diarrhea is common. Fever and very high peripheral WBCs can be seen and acute kidney injury may occur in severe disease.

Diagnosis

Pathogenic organisms produce 2 toxins: toxin A (an enterotoxin) and toxin B (a cytotoxin). These are used as markers for the diagnosis of *C. difficile*. The assay with the highest accuracy for detection of toxin-producing genes of the organism is the NAAT. It should be sent only on symptomatic patients because it will also be positive in carriers and they do not require treatment. This test is superior to enzyme immunoassay (EIA) used to detect the toxins themselves. Although the organism can also be cultured from the stool, this has no utility because it takes several days to grow the bacteria and many strains do not produce toxins or disease.

Initial Treatment

The IDSA clinical practice guidelines for the treatment of CDI, updated in 2021, recommend to treat **initial CDI** with fidaxomicin rather than vancomycin unless fidaxomicin is unavailable or not affordable. Initial cure rates are similar with these 2 agents, but the relapse rate with fidaxomicin is ~ 50% less than when infection is treated with vancomycin. (The 2021 American College of Gastroenterology [ACG] guidelines recommend either vancomycin or fidaxomicin as 1st line therapy but point out that the higher initial cost of fidaxomicin may be offset by lower cost of recurrence treatment, making the 2 nearly equivalent in terms of cost effectiveness.) Metronidazole is relegated to a 3rd line drug because initial cure rates with it are less than with the other 2 antibiotics. Metronidazole should not be used in patients with severe disease (a WBC count >15,000/μL [15 × 10^9/L] or a serum creatinine > 1.5 mg/dL [132.6 μmol/L]).

Fulminant disease is present when patients have ileus, megacolon, hypotension, or shock. Treat these patients with high-dose PO (by mouth) vancomycin and IV metronidazole. Give vancomycin by enema if the PO route is not an option or if there is severe ileus. Consider colectomy in patients with rising lactate levels, peritoneal signs, or sepsis.

Relapse

Relapses occur in ~ 25% of patients. Treatment for 1st recurrence:

- Fidaxomicin is the preferred agent due to its lower rate of subsequent relapses than any other agent.
- If fidaxomicin is not available or affordable, vancomycin is recommended.
- Bezlotoxumab, a monoclonal antibody directed against toxin B, should be added in patients who are at risk of severe CDI due to comorbidities or who are > 65 years of age.
- Metronidazole is not recommended.

Options for **treating subsequent relapses**:

- Fidaxomicin preferred
- Vancomycin an alternative
- Fecal microbiota transplantation (FMT)

Although FMT has a high success rate, it has been associated with transmission of multidrug-resistant fecal flora.

Prevention

Sanitizing hand gels do not prevent transmission because they do not kill the spores of *C. difficile*. Only handwashing with soap and water prevents spread. Isolate patients with *C. difficile* diarrhea in a private room and place them on contact precautions. Because the organism is found on various surfaces throughout the infected patient's room, even those who do not examine the patient should use precautions.

PROTOZOAL DIARRHEAS

Protozoal diarrheas include amebiasis, giardiasis, and several acid-fast organism infections that are discussed under Protozoa on page 4-62.

LIVER AND BILIARY INFECTIONS

PREVIEW | REVIEW

- What is the treatment for bacterial liver abscesses?
- To which 3 groups of patients should you give antibiotic prophylaxis for primary peritonitis?
- How is secondary peritonitis treated?

LIVER ABSCESS

Liver abscesses are most commonly bacterial or amebic. Amebic abscesses are discussed under *Entamoeba* on page 4-62. Patients with prolonged neutropenia can develop hepatosplenic candidiasis, in which there are numerous fungal (candidal) abscesses throughout the liver and spleen.

Bacterial liver abscesses are either due to direct bacterial spread from infection in the biliary tree (e.g., cholecystitis, cholangitis) or from transmission of gut flora to the liver from the venous drainage of the mesenteric veins through the portal vein. Many liver abscesses have no clear cause and are called cryptogenic. The microbiology is mixed fecal flora (e.g., GNBs, enterococci, anaerobes).

The presentation may initially be overshadowed by the primary infectious process. Symptoms are fever and right upper quadrant (RUQ) pain. The liver can be enlarged and tender on examination, and there may be a positive Murphy sign (arrested inspiration while performing deep right subcostal palpation).

Confirm the diagnosis by imaging, and perform aspiration to discern the microbiologic cause and guide antibiotic therapy.

Treatment of liver abscesses includes drainage and culture-guided antibiotics. Drain abscesses < 5 cm by aspiration. For larger abscesses, place and maintain a catheter until the drainage becomes minimal. Surgical intervention is required if complete drainage cannot be obtained by other means.

CHOLANGITIS

Cholangitis is a bacterial infection of the biliary tree. Entry of bacteria into bile occurs on a regular basis because the sphincter of Oddi is not a one-way valve and the duodenum is not sterile. Despite this, cholangitis does not typically ensue because biliary pressures flush organisms back into the duodenum and bile salts are bacteriostatic. Thus, a prerequisite in the vast majority of cases of cholangitis is biliary obstruction, typically from stones, benign strictures, or cancer. It may also occur post instrumentation of the biliary tree (e.g., endoscopic retrograde cholangiopancreatography [ERCP]).

The bacteriology usually shows enteric GNBs, but enterococci may also be present in 10–20% of cases.

Many patients have **Charcot's triad** of fever, RUQ pain, and jaundice. If the disease progresses, it may also include shock and altered mental status, which is known as **Reynold's pentad**. Confirm the diagnosis by imaging, which shows biliary dilation and/or obstruction.

No antibiotics reliably enter an obstructed biliary tree, so treatment includes urgent biliary drainage by ERCP, performed either percutaneously or surgically. Antibiotics are guided by the culture results of the drainage.

PERITONITIS

Infection of the peritoneal cavity can be primary or secondary. Primary peritonitis has no evident intraabdominal, surgically treatable source. Other cases are secondary, meaning they are caused by a surgically treatable source (e.g., bowel perforation).

It is critical to differentiate primary from secondary bacterial peritonitis because:

- the mortality rate is ~ 80% for patients with primary peritonitis who undergo an exploratory laparotomy and
- the mortality rate is ~ 100% for patients with secondary bacterial peritonitis who do not go to surgery.

Primary peritonitis (formerly known as spontaneous bacterial peritonitis) occurs in the presence of ascites and hypoalbuminemia. The low albumin, in addition to creating ascites, causes bowel edema, which allows the aerobic bowel flora to transmigrate (i.e., swim across) from the mucosal to the serosal surface of the bowel and enter the peritoneum. When the ascites is due to cirrhosis or nephrotic syndrome, patients have a markedly decreased ability to opsonize these organisms due to decreased complement production (cirrhosis) or loss of complement and antibodies in the urine (nephrotic syndrome). The most common causative organisms of primary peritonitis are GNBs, with *Escherichia coli* and *Klebsiella* causing the majority of cases. *Streptococcus pneumoniae* is seen as well. Anaerobes are not found.

Because of the decreased amount of opsonins, inflammation is blunted and many patients are asymptomatic. If symptoms occur, they include fever, abdominal pain, abdominal tenderness, and altered mental status, but not necessarily simultaneously. Suspect primary peritonitis in a cirrhotic patient with worsening portosystemic encephalopathy, even in the absence of symptoms. The diagnosis of primary peritonitis is made if the paracentesis fluid shows > 250 polymorphonuclear leukocytes (PMNs), the Gram stain is positive, or the culture is positive and no other cause of peritonitis is evident. This is usually a monomicrobial infection. Treat primary peritonitis empirically with a 3rd generation cephalosporin. Give antibiotic prophylaxis for primary peritonitis to 3 groups of patients who are at high risk for this disease:

1) Patients with cirrhosis and ascites if the ascitic fluid protein is < 1,500 mg/dL along with evidence of renal and/or liver failure

2) Patients with cirrhosis and a GI bleed

3) Patients with a prior episode of primary peritonitis

Use ciprofloxacin or TMP/SMX. If an oral regiment cannot be given, use ceftriaxone.

Secondary bacterial peritonitis is an infection of the peritoneal cavity due to the direct entry of bacterial flora from disruption of the integrity of the bowel. Unlike primary peritonitis, patients with secondary peritonitis almost always have abdominal pain, fever, and peritoneal signs. The ascitic fluid has a markedly elevated WBC count (often > 5,000/μL [5 × 10⁹/L]) and can be grossly purulent. Cultures are usually polymicrobial members of normal stool flora including GNBs and anaerobes. Imaging typically reveals the source of secondary bacterial peritonitis, necessitating emergency surgical intervention while administering antibiotics to cover gram-negative aerobes and anaerobes. Acceptable regimens include piperacillin/tazobactam or a carbapenem.

Peritonitis from peritoneal dialysis can also occur; this is discussed in the Nephrology section under Kidney Replacement Therapy (KRT).

INTRAABDOMINAL ABSCESS

Intraabdominal abscesses are walled-off pockets of infection that occur after secondary peritonitis but usually not after primary peritonitis. Anaerobic flora are major participants in the process. Intrabdominal abscesses typically occur after bowel perforation or appendicitis (secondary peritonitis). Abscess formation takes several days to occur and often presents itself after initial surgical and antibiotic treatment of the underlying process. Signs and symptoms include the new onset and/or recurrence of fever, abdominal pain, abdominal tenderness, and leukocytosis. The bacteriology is similar to that of secondary peritonitis, which is often a precursor, and

includes gram-negative aerobic rods and anaerobes. If an abscess is recurrent or occurs after a course of antibiotics, *Candida* and coagulase-negative staphylococci are common. This is sometimes called tertiary peritonitis. Diagnose an intraabdominal abscess by imaging, and treat it with percutaneous or surgical drainage with antimicrobial therapy. Antibiotic therapy is similar to that for secondary peritonitis (i.e., piperacillin/tazobactam or a carbapenem) but is directed at cultured organisms from the abdomen. Empiric treatment for enterococci and *Candida* species is not recommended unless these are present on prior or subsequent cultures from drainage. Multiple abscesses or abscesses due to gross fecal soiling often require repeated surgical drainage.

SEXUALLY TRANSMITTED INFECTIONS (STIs)

PREVIEW | REVIEW

- How and who do you test for gonorrhea? For chlamydia? For syphilis?

- What are the stages of syphilis, and how are they treated?

- What drugs are used to treat syphilis in pregnancy? What if the woman has an anaphylactic penicillin allergy?

- How do primary syphilis and chancroid differ?

- Discuss the clinical manifestations of lymphogranuloma venereum and granuloma inguinale.

- What are the inpatient and outpatient regimens for the treatment of pelvic inflammatory disease?

- What is the empiric treatment for cervicitis?

- What are the clinical presentations of disseminated gonorrhea?

- Which 3 tests are useful to determine the etiology of vaginitis? In what ways are these tests useful?

- Women with recurrent or recalcitrant vulvovaginal candidiasis should be tested for which 2 associated illnesses?

OVERVIEW

The incidence of STIs continues to rise despite useful screening techniques and available treatments for all of them. Thus, behavioral counseling of adolescents is a critical public health intervention, and, in 2020, the United States Preventive Services Task Force (USPSTF) recommended behavioral counseling for all sexually active adolescents and for adults at increased risk for STIs.

Most STIs are categorized into those that cause urethritis, cervicitis, and pelvic inflammatory disease (PID; i.e., gonorrhea and chlamydia) and those that cause genital ulcers (i.e., syphilis, chancroid, herpes simplex virus [HSV], lymphogranuloma venereum [LGV], and granuloma inguinale). The following discussions reflect the diagnostic and treatment guidelines recommended by the CDC in its 2015 Sexually Transmitted Diseases Treatment Guidelines.

SCREENING

General

Populations that are at increased risk for STIs include the following:

- New partner within the past 3 months
- Multiple partners within the past 12 months
- Partner who had multiple partners
- History of previous STIs (especially within the past 24 months)
- Intravenous drug use
- Recent exposure to a jail or detention facility
- Sex partner found on the internet
- Contact with sex workers
- Men who have sex with men
- Exchange of sex for drugs or money within the past year

The current screening guidelines are summarized in Table 4-1 and Table 4-2.

Gonorrhea Screening

Screening for gonorrhea is performed by NAAT testing of urine in men and a vaginal swab in women. All HIV-infected men and men who have sex with men should be tested at least annually. Men who have sex with women should be screened if they are in an at-risk group. All women < 25 years of age, or ≥ 25 years of age in an at-risk group or with HIV infection, should be screened at least annually. Women in their 1st trimester of pregnancy should be screened if < 25 years of age or in an at-risk group.

Chlamydia Screening

Screening for chlamydia has the same guidelines as for gonorrhea. It is performed by NAAT testing of urine in men and a vaginal swab in women. All HIV-infected men and men who have sex with men should be tested at least annually. Men who have sex with women should be screened if they are in an at- risk group. All women < 25 years of age, or ≥ 25 years of age in an at-risk group or HIV infected, should be screened at least annually. Women in their 1st trimester of pregnancy should be screened if < 25 years of age or in an at-risk group.

Table 4-1: Sexually Transmitted Infection Screening of Men				
	MSW HIV Negative	**MSW HIV Positive**	**MSM HIV Negative**	**MSM HIV Positive**
Gonorrhea/Chlamydia	At risk	Annual	Annual	Annual
Syphilis	At risk	Annual	Annual	Annual
HAV			Once	Once
HBV	At risk	Once	Once	Once
HCV	At risk	Once	Once	Annual
HIV	Once		Annual	

HAV = hepatitis A virus
HBV = hepatitis B virus
HCV = hepatitis C virus

HIV = human immunodeficiency virus
MSM = men who have sex with men
MSW = men who have sex with women

Table 4-2: Sexually Transmitted Infection Screening of Women				
	< 25 Years of Age	**≥ 25 Years of Age**	**Pregnant**	**HIV Positive**
Gonorrhea/Chlamydia	Annual	At risk	< 25 years of age or at risk 1st + 3rd trimester	Annual
Syphilis	At risk	At risk	< 25 years of age or at risk 1st + 3rd trimester	Annual
Trichomonas	At risk	At risk	If HIV positive	Annual
HBV	At risk	At risk	Once	Once
HCV	At risk	At risk	At risk	Once
HIV	Once	Once	Once	

HBV = hepatitis B virus   HCV = hepatitis C virus   HIV = human immunodeficiency virus

INFECTIOUS DISEASE

Syphilis Screening

Serologic testing for syphilis should be performed at least annually in men who have sex with men and men who have sex with women who are in an at-risk group. All women who are HIV infected or in an at-risk group should be tested at least annually. In addition, women in their 1st trimester of pregnancy should be tested. See Syphilis for additional information.

Hepatitis Screening

Screen for HBV by sending serum for hepatitis B virus surface antigen (HBsAg) and hepatitis B core antibody (anti-HBc) detection. Screen for HCV by sending serum for anti-HCV antibody detection. All men who have sex with men should be screened for hepatitis B at least once. Men who have sex with women should be screened once if they are HIV infected; otherwise, they should be tested only if they are in an at-risk group. Women who are in their 1st trimester of pregnancy or are HIV infected should be tested for hepatitis B. Other women should be tested if they are in an at-risk group. All adults > 18 years of age should be tested for hepatitis C once. Subsequent testing should be performed if they are HIV infected or in an at-risk group. (See the Women's and Men's Health section under Obstetrics.)

Human Immunodeficiency Virus (HIV) Screening

Screen for HIV in women during each pregnancy (see the Women's and Men's Health section under Obstetrics). The CDC also recommends HIV screening in all persons 13–64 years of age at least once. Test those outside of this age range who are in a high-risk group. High-risk individuals are considered those who use IV drugs, men who have sex with men, and those presenting for STI testing or who have a history of STIs or a new diagnosis of tuberculosis (TB). Test high-risk groups annually. Otherwise, repeat screening based on clinical circumstances.

Herpes Simplex Virus (HSV) Screening

No general screening is recommended for HSV infections.

INFECTIOUS GENITAL ULCERS

Genital ulcer diseases include syphilis, herpes simplex virus, chancroid, lymphogranuloma venereum, and granuloma inguinale (Table 4-3). Infections with 2 of these organisms are painful and they can be remembered because their names begin with "H" for "hurt": HSV and *H. ducreyi* (which can also be misspelled as duCRY as an additional reminder).

Syphilis

Treponema pallidum, a motile spirochete, causes syphilis, which is a reportable disease in the U.S. Syphilis has 3 stages. The 3rd stage has 3 forms, and 1 of the 3 forms, neurosyphilis, has 3 common manifestations (thus, it is $3 \times 3 \times 3$).

Primary syphilis presents with a painless chancre at the site of inoculation—usually genital, anal, or oral—within 3–90 days depending on the number of inoculated organisms. This may be followed by painless regional lymphadenopathy. In women, if the infection is cervical, it is often unnoticed. Even without treatment, it lasts 2–6 weeks and then resolves.

Secondary syphilis occurs 2–12 weeks later as spirochetes disseminate throughout the body. Symptoms include generalized lymphadenopathy, fever, malaise, and mucosal and/or cutaneous lesions that can mimic many other lesions ("the great imitator"). The skin lesions are macular or papular but never vesicular. They can occur on the palms and soles and are described as "nickel and dime" lesions (Figure 4-8). Condylomata lata are cauliflower-like wet lesions in the genital areas or mouth that teem with treponemes. Meningovascular disease can also occur in secondary syphilis and presents as strokes or blindness in a young person. Nonneurologic signs and symptoms resolve in 3–12 weeks, after which the disease goes into a latency period.

Table 4-3: Sexually Transmitted Infections with Genital Ulcers			
Disease	**Organism / Virus**	**Characteristic Ulcer**	**Treatment**
Syphilis	*T. pallidum*	Painless 1- to 2-cm ulcer; "punched out," clean-appearing ulcer with nonexudative base; sharp, firm, slightly elevated indurated borders	Penicillin G
Herpes genitalis	Herpes simplex	Painful grouped vesicles that rupture to form shallow, painful ulcers	Acyclovir or famciclovir or valacyclovir
Chancroid	*H. ducreyi*	Painful, shallow, soft, friable ulcer with ragged margins and a foul-smelling necrotic purulent exudate	Azithromycin or ceftriaxone or ciprofloxacin or erythromycin
Lymphogranuloma venereum	*C. trachomatis* L1, L2, or L3	Painless genital ulcer	**Preferred:** doxycycline **Alternative:** azithromycin
Granuloma inguinale	*K. granulomatis*	Painless, friable, progressive, beefy red ulcerative lesion with raised, rolled margin	**Preferred:** azithromycin **Alternative:** doxycycline or ciprofloxacin or TMP/SMX

TMP/SMX = trimethoprim/sulfamethoxazole

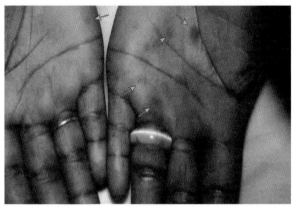

Figure 4-8: Secondary syphilis "nickel and dime" lesions

Tertiary syphilis occurs in 15–30% of untreated patients and manifests 2–30 years after initial infection. There are 3 forms:

1) **Gummatous** syphilis presents with ≥ 1 gumma, which is a noncaseating granulomatous lesion that is locally destructive.

2) **Cardiovascular** syphilis is obliterative endarteritis of the aortic vasa vasorum, which results in ascending aortic aneurysms and aortic insufficiency.

3) **Neurosyphilis** has 3 common manifestations:
   - **Chronic meningovascular syphilis** can present with brain and/or spinal cord strokes similar to meningovascular disease in secondary syphilis.
   - **Tabes dorsalis** is due to destruction of the posterior spinal cord columns, leading to the loss of position sense, lancinating pains, an abnormal foot-slapping gait, and a positive Romberg sign.
   - **General paresis** is the name given to diffuse cortical disease seen in neurosyphilis. Its numerous manifestations can be remembered with the following mnemonic derived from its name:
     ◦ **P** = defects in **p**ersonality
     ◦ **A** = reduced **a**ffect
     ◦ **R** = abnormal **r**eflexes
     ◦ **E** = **e**ye problems (Argyll Robertson pupil, which is miotic and irregular; it constricts with accommodation but does constrict to light)
     ◦ **S** = defects in **s**ensorium
     ◦ **I** = defects in **i**ntellect
     ◦ **S** = defects in **s**peech
   - Less common neurosyphilis manifestations:
     ◦ **Ocular syphilis** can involve any structure of the eye producing keratitis, uveitis, retinitis, and optic neuritis.
     ◦ **Otosyphilis** presents with hearing loss from involvement of the cochlea and/or the auditory nerve.

Latent syphilis is defined as a serology diagnostic of syphilis with no active manifestations of infection. It can occur in the 4–10 weeks between primary and secondary syphilis but is most commonly diagnosed in the much longer asymptomatic period after secondary syphilis.

Latent syphilis is divided into early latent and late latent depending on whether the last manifestations of syphilis or seroconversion to syphilis occurred within 1 year or after 1 year, respectively. This distinction arose from observational studies that showed that 90% of patients become symptomatic within the 1st year of infection.

The diagnosis of syphilis was historically based on direct visualization of the organism via dark-field microscopy of chancre exudate or cutaneous lesions of secondary syphilis; however, this is unavailable in most laboratories. Serology is otherwise required to confirm the diagnosis of syphilis. There are 2 types of serologic tests:

1) **Nontreponemal tests** (Venereal Disease Research Laboratory [VDRL] and rapid plasma reagin [RPR] tests) detect antibodies directed against the cardiolipin-cholesterol-lecithin antigen (a.k.a. reagin). These are predominantly immunoglobulin M (IgM) antibodies and are absent in ~ 1/3 of patients with primary syphilis because the disease has not been present long enough to have produced a primary IgM response. These antibodies are present in essentially all patients with secondary syphilis. 1/3 of patients with tertiary syphilis are seronegative because the IgM response has burnt out. Expect these antibodies to decline with appropriate treatment in primary or secondary disease. In late latent disease, some patients are serofast and titers do not decline with treatment.

2) **Treponemal tests** (the microhemagglutination assay for antibodies to *Treponema pallidum* [MHA-TP] and the fluorescent treponemal antibody absorption [FTA-ABS] test) detect antibodies that directly react with *T. pallidum*. These are predominantly immunoglobulin G (IgG) antibodies. The tests turn positive after 2–4 weeks and usually remain positive for life, even with treatment.

Perform a treponemal test to confirm a nontreponemal test because false-positive nontreponemal test results can occur with a variety of other inflammatory and infectious illnesses. If this sequence is followed, patients with a positive RPR test result and a confirmatory positive FTA-ABS test result are considered to have past or present syphilis.

A lumbar puncture (LP) is indicated in patients who have neurologic or ophthalmic manifestations consistent with neurosyphilis or other signs of tertiary syphilis, or serum RPR titers ≥ 1:32 or who have failed prior appropriate therapy for syphilis. The diagnosis of neurosyphilis should be made if any of the following are found in the CSF: VDRL (+), protein > 45, or WBC > 5. RPR testing should not be done on CSF because it has a lower sensitivity than the VDRL test.

RPR and VDRL titers typically decrease with treatment. Expect titers to be positive only in an undiluted specimen, or entirely negative, 1 year after treatment of primary disease, 2 years after treatment of secondary disease, and 5 years after treatment of latent disease. Most treated patients will become seronegative, but some remain seropositive despite cure.

Test all pregnant women with a nontreponemal test in the 1st trimester. If a pregnant patient is at high risk, repeat testing in the 3rd trimester and at delivery. Pregnant patients are treated with the same regimen as nonpregnant patients based on the stage of infection.

The treatment of syphilis is as follows:

- For primary, secondary, and early latent syphilis, give benzathine PCN G 2.4 MU intramuscularly (IM) × 1.
- For late latent syphilis, latency of unknown duration, and nonneurologic tertiary syphilis, give benzathine PCN G 2.4 MU IM every week × 3.
- For neurosyphilis, benzathine PCN G does not reliably cross the blood–brain barrier, so the following must be used:
  - PCN G 18–24 MU IV divided every 4 hours or continuous infusion for 10–14 days
  - Ceftriaxone 2 g/day × 10–14 days (an alternative for PCN-allergic patients; however, cross-reactive allergies may occur)

Doxycycline is an alternative for PCN-allergic patients, except for those with neurosyphilis or who are pregnant. If a patient with neurosyphilis or a pregnant patient is allergic, that patient should undergo PCN desensitization.

Herpes Simplex Virus (HSV)

HSV presents with tender, grouped vesicles on a red base (Figure 4-9) with or without regional adenopathy. Although the appearance is diagnostic, it should be confirmed with NAAT testing. Treatment is only of benefit for initial infection if given within 72 hours and for recurrent infection if given within 48 hours. Effective agents are acyclovir, valacyclovir, or famciclovir. Patients with frequent recurrences may benefit from chronic suppressive therapy.

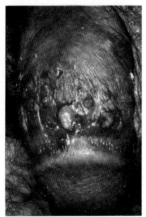

Figure 4-9: Herpes simplex

Other Infectious Genital Ulcers

Chancroid is caused by *Haemophilus ducreyi*, a small gram-negative coccobacillus. Although a much less common ulcerative STI than syphilis in the U.S., it is the most common ulcerative STI in Africa. The initial chancroid lesion transforms from a papule to a pustule to a ragged ulcer, all of which are painful, unlike the syphilis chancre. It can progress to secondary chancroid with tender inguinal lymphadenopathy (buboes), which may spontaneously drain. Spread from there (tertiary chancroid) is rare. Diagnose chancroid by the clinical appearance, and confirm the diagnosis by culture. Treat it with a single dose of azithromycin (1,000 mg) or ceftriaxone (125 mg) or ciprofloxacin 500 mg bid × 3 days.

Lymphogranuloma venereum (**LGV**) is due to 3 specific serogroups of *Chlamydia trachomatis*: LGV-1, -2, and -3. It is extremely rare in the U.S. (< 500 cases/year) but is endemic in many parts of Asia, Africa, and South America. In the 1st stage, LGV presents with a painless papule and vesicle that eventually form a clean, painless ulcer. This stage is present in only 1/3 of infected patients. Most patients present in the 2nd stage with tender inguinal masses on both sides of the inguinal ligament (a.k.a. groove sign). Diagnose LGV by the clinical appearance and NAAT. Treatment is with doxycycline for 21 days. Azithromycin is an alternative.

Granuloma inguinale (a.k.a. donovanosis) is very rare. *Klebsiella granulomatis* (formerly called *Calymmatobacterium granulomatis*) is the causative gram-negative organism that produces beefy, oozing, and paradoxically painless genital ulcers (Figure 4-10). Spread to the inguinal area produces bilateral soft tissue granulomas that look like lymphadenopathy (pseudobuboes). Diagnose the infection by its clinical appearance. Culture has a low yield, but a crushed biopsy specimen may show intracellular bacilli (**Donovan bodies**). Treatment is for at least 21 days and until all the ulcers are gone. The recommended treatment is with azithromycin. Alternatives are doxycycline and TMP/SMX.

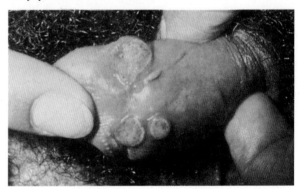

Figure 4-10: Genital lesions in granuloma inguinale

PELVIC INFLAMMATORY DISEASE (PID)

PID can be caused by *Neisseria gonorrhoeae*, *Chlamydia* (combined these make up ~ 50% of cases), or mixed genitourinary flora (aerobes and anaerobes).

Patients present with bilateral lower quadrant pain and fever +/– vaginal discharge. Physical examination commonly reveals bilateral adnexal tenderness, lower quadrant tenderness, and cervical motion tenderness. The clinical diagnosis has a positive predictive value (PPV) of only 65–90%, so use laparoscopy when the diagnosis is uncertain.

If there is no cervical discharge and cervical swabs fail to show WBCs, PID is unlikely. Test these patients for gonorrhea and chlamydia (refer to Gonorrhea Screening on page 4-17 and Chlamydia Screening on page 4-17).

Patients may have an associated perihepatitis (**Fitz-Hugh–Curtis syndrome**) with mild transaminase elevations and RUQ pain.

The CDC recommends empiric therapy for PID if a sexually active woman presents with 1 of the following findings and no other cause is identified:

- Uterine tenderness
- Adnexal tenderness
- Cervical motion tenderness

Treatment depends on whether the patient requires hospital admission. Admit patients if:

- a surgical emergency (e.g., appendicitis) cannot be excluded,
- prior oral antimicrobial therapy failed,
- they are unable to follow or tolerate an outpatient oral regimen,
- they have a high-grade fever with abdominal pain or vomiting,
- you suspect or find a tuboovarian abscess, or
- they are pregnant.

If a patient is admitted, the CDC recommends 1 of the following inpatient regimens:

- Ceftriaxone and doxycycline and metronidazole
- Cefotetan or cefoxitin and doxycycline

Most treatment regimens are designed to ensure treatment of both gonorrhea and chlamydia.

If admission is not indicated, the CDC recommends either of the following outpatient regimens:

- Ceftriaxone IM × 1 (or another 3rd generation cephalosporin), then doxycycline × 14 days and metronidazole × 14 days
- Cefoxitin IM × 1 and probenecid plus doxycycline × 14 days and metronidazole × 14 days

Follow up with patients treated for chlamydial infections with a test for cure at 3 months. The PCR test can remain positive for many weeks.

CERVICITIS

Cervicitis is usually caused by *Chlamydia* (especially if the discharge is mucopurulent) but can also be from *Neisseria gonorrhoeae*, HSV, and *Trichomonas*. Because *Chlamydia* is intracellular, you must have cervical cells for a valid smear/culture (so scrape or use a brush). A Gram stain of cervical secretions is not sensitive or specific in the diagnosis of gonococcal cervicitis (in contrast to male gonococcal urethritis). Empiric treatment for mucopurulent cervicitis is ceftriaxone 250 mg IM × 1 plus doxycycline 100 mg PO bid × 7 days. Azithromycin 1 g PO × 1 is an alternative to doxycycline. For patients with uncomplicated genital chlamydial infections, doxycycline (100 mg PO bid for 7 days) is preferred with azithromycin as a 1-g single dose as an alternative. Treat sexual partners as well.

Because of high rates of reinfection, retest all individuals diagnosed with *C. trachomatis* or *N. gonorrhoeae* for repeat infection 3 months after treatment but not as a "test of cure" (unless the patient is pregnant).

URETHRITIS

Presentation

Urethritis can be divided into gonococcal and nongonococcal infection. Endocervical, vaginal, urethral (men only), or urine specimens can be tested to detect *Neisseria gonorrhoeae*. Genitourinary infections with *N. gonorrhoeae* can be detected using culture, nucleic acid hybridization testing, and NAAT. With gonococcal urethritis, the patient virtually always has a very painful, purulent discharge. The diagnosis is confirmed by either positive culture results or the finding of gram-negative intracellular diplococci on Gram stain (within PMNs; Figure 4-11). Otherwise, consider the infection nongonococcal urethritis, which is usually due to *Chlamydia trachomatis* or, less frequently, *Ureaplasma urealyticum*, *Trichomonas vaginalis*, or HSV. For ~ 35% of cases, the cause is unknown.

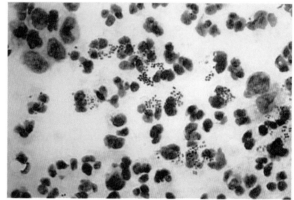

Figure 4-11: Gonorrhea (Gram stain)

Patients with nongonococcal urethritis typically have a clear urethral discharge, and a Gram stain shows WBCs and no bacteria. Gonococcal urethritis has a shorter incubation period (2–6 days vs. 1–2 weeks for chlamydia) and produces a more purulent and more productive discharge.

In all patients, perform a VDRL or RPR test and, if the result is negative, repeat it in 2 months (to allow for possible seroconversion from when blood for the 1st test was drawn). Do HIV testing for all patients with urethritis.

Consider gonococcal disease in sexually active adolescents with acute exudative pharyngitis, especially if the test results for *Streptococcus pyogenes* are negative.

Treatment

Nongonococcal urethritis: Treat with doxycycline 100 mg PO bid × 7 days. A less desirable option is azithromycin 1 g PO × 1. Levofloxacin is also an alternate antibiotic, but avoid its use in pregnant patients. Routine cotreatment for gonorrhea is no longer recommended.

Gonococcal urethritis: Resistance to penicillins, tetracyclines, and fluoroquinolones is commonly found. As a result, the CDC recommends dual therapy with ceftriaxone + azithromycin for gonorrhea infections of the cervix, urethra, and rectum, hoping that routine cotreatment might hinder the development of further antimicrobial-resistant *N. gonorrhoeae*.

Treat uncomplicated gonococcal infections of the cervix, urethra, rectum, and pharynx with a single dose of ceftriaxone and azithromycin.

For **pregnant women**, do not use fluoroquinolones or tetracyclines. Use a cephalosporin for gonorrhea and either erythromycin or azithromycin for *C. trachomatis* infection. If the pregnant patient is allergic to cephalosporins, the CDC recommends azithromycin 2 g PO × 1. Perform test of cure for pregnant women 3–4 weeks after treatment. In addition, as with all patients with documented chlamydia or gonococcal infection, pregnant women should also undergo repeat testing to evaluate for reinfection 3 months following treatment.

Always treat sexual partners of patients with either type of urethritis, even if they are not symptomatic, and always treat suspected cases immediately without waiting for culture results.

DISSEMINATED GONORRHEA

Disseminated gonococcal infection is much more common in females and typically occurs during menses because this allows the organisms on the cervix to enter the uterus and then the bloodstream. The clinical manifestations can consist of a sparse pustular dermatitis, tenosynovitis, and a septic arthritis (Figure 4-12).

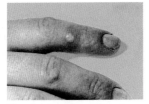

Figure 4-12: Disseminated gonorrhea skin pustule

Gram stains and cultures of skin lesions have a very low yield (25%), but if specimens are taken from genital, mucosal, and rectal sources, they have an 85% yield.

Treat patients diagnosed with disseminated gonorrhea with a 3rd generation cephalosporin. NAAT testing of the vagina should also be done to exclude chlamydia. If it cannot be excluded, give a single dose of azithromycin or levofloxacin or 14 days of doxycycline to treat possible chlamydia coinfection. After 1–2 days, patients can be switched to oral antibiotics based on susceptibilities to complete a 7-day course.

EPIDIDYMITIS

Epididymitis typically presents as unilateral testicular pain and a palpably swollen epididymis. STI pathogens are the most likely cause in sexually active men < 35 years of age. Other pathogens are usually enteric GNBs, most

commonly *Escherichia coli*. If *Neisseria gonorrhoeae* is the etiology, urethritis is usually present with the typical findings; otherwise, perform NAAT of urine for *N. gonorrhoeae* and *Chlamydia trachomatis*. Treatment of epididymitis is the same as for gonorrhea in patients at high risk for STIs. For suspected enteric rod infections, use a 10-day course of a fluoroquinolone.

Epididymitis and orchitis typically present as acute unilateral testicular pain and a palpably swollen and tender epididymis and/or testicle. This can be differentiated from a testicular torsion by Doppler ultrasound, which reveals decreased blood flow in a torsion and is usually normal in epididymitis. STI pathogens are the most likely cause in sexually active men < 35 years of age. If *Neisseria gonorrhoeae* is the etiology, urethritis is usually present with the typical findings. In this age group always perform NAAT of urine for *N. gonorrhoeae* and *Chlamydia trachomatis*. Other pathogens are usually enteric GNBs, most commonly *Escherichia coli*, and these occur more commonly from insertive anal intercourse. Treatment of epididymitis is the same as for gonorrhea or chlamydia if detected. For suspected GNB infections, use a 10-day course of a fluoroquinolone.

HUMAN PAPILLOMAVIRUS (HPV)

HPV is transmitted by direct contact and causes warts. Genital warts result in an increased risk of cervical, vaginal, vulvar, penile, anal, and oropharyngeal cancer. Virtually all cases of cervical cancer are attributable to HPV infection, with the most common types being HPV-16 and HPV-18. The strains that cause cervical cancer are usually subclinical. There's much more information on cervical cancer in the Oncology section under Cervical Cancer.

HPV vaccines protect against the most oncogenic serotypes and are recommended for all males and females at 11–12 years of age but can be started as early as 9 years of age. It is recommended that adolescents and adults 13–26 years of age who have not been fully vaccinated be vaccinated during these years.

VAGINITIS AND VAGINOSIS

Vaginitis presents with a change or increase in vaginal discharge. There are 3 major causes (in descending order of frequency): bacterial vaginosis, candidiasis, and trichomoniasis. Use a systematic approach to diagnose the etiology. See Table 4-4.

Table 4-4: Vaginitis and Vaginosis Diagnostic Tests			
	Vaginal pH	**Wet Prep**	**KOH Prep**
Bacterial Vaginosis	> 5.0	Clue cells	Amine odor
Candidiasis	< 5.0	Fungal elements	Fungal elements
Trichomoniasis	> 5.0	Trichomonads	Amine odor
KOH = potassium hydroxide			

Systematic Approach to Vaginitis and Vaginosis

Three tests on vaginal secretions/discharge can determine the etiologic agent on initial examination: pH, wet prep, and potassium hydroxide (KOH) prep.

pH: The normal vaginal pH is ≤ 4.5 and remains so with vaginal candidiasis. A pH > 4.5 is seen in bacterial vaginosis and trichomoniasis.

Wet prep (secretions placed in normal saline under microscopy): This reveals epithelial cells studded with causative organisms (i.e., clue cells) in bacterial vaginosis and trichomonads in trichomoniasis. It shows fungal elements in candidiasis.

KOH prep (secretions placed in KOH under microscopy): This yields an amine (fishy) odor in bacterial vaginosis and trichomoniasis. KOH dissolves cellular membranes and debris but not the cellulose in fungi, so it increases the yield of finding yeast forms and pseudohyphae in candidiasis.

Bacterial Vaginosis

Bacterial vaginosis results from the replacement of the normal flora such as *Lactobacillus* in the vagina with high concentrations of anaerobic bacteria (e.g., *Mobiluncus*, *Gardnerella vaginalis*). It is associated with sexual activity and the number of sexual partners. There is a thin, "skim milk," scanty, foul-smelling, nonirritating discharge that has 3 identifying features on testing:

1) Clue cells (epithelial cells with many adherent bacteria; Figure 4-13)
2) An amine (fishy) odor when mixed with KOH (positive whiff/sniff test)
3) The pH of secretions is > 4.5.

PCR testing for *Gardnerella* and testing for sialidase (an enzyme made by many of the pathogens) may also be used.

There is no cervical discharge.

Treatment is with metronidazole PO × 7 days or vaginal cream × 5 days. Alternately, give clindamycin intravaginally × 7 days. Unlike with other vaginal infectious diseases, there is no single-dose therapy.

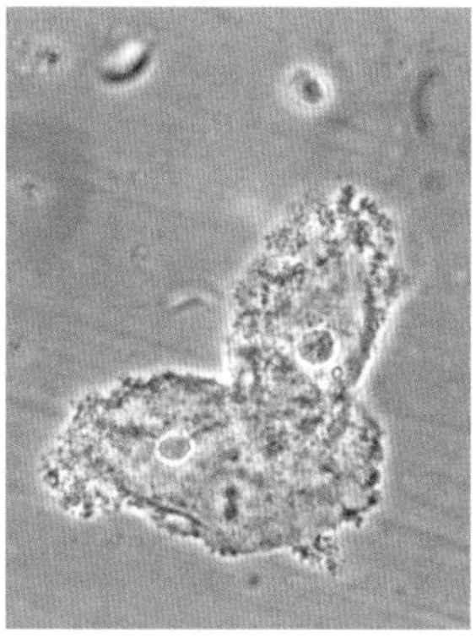

Figure 4-13: Clue cells as seen with bacterial vaginosis. Stippled appearance from being covered with bacteria

Oral metronidazole is safe in pregnancy; give this formulation instead of the gel. Bacterial vaginosis increases the risk of preterm labor if not treated orally.

Male sexual partners do not require treatment, because, although bacterial vaginosis is associated with sexual activity, it is not an STI.

Vulvovaginal Candidiasis (VVC)

VVC is almost always caused by the species *Candida albicans*. It presents with adherent white plaques on an erythematous base and is usually pruritic. Unlike the other causes of vaginitis and vaginosis, the vulva is commonly involved with redness and itching. Remember that this can be a sign of undiagnosed diabetes or HIV infection, especially if recurrent.

The treatment is as follows:

• For uncomplicated VVC in a nonpregnant patient, there are many azole vaginal creams available, several of which are over-the-counter agents. Oral fluconazole 150 mg × 1 is also highly effective.
• For recurrent VVC, weekly topical azole and oral fluconazole 150 mg 1-time doses are equally effective.
• Although systemic or topical fluconazole was previously considered safe in pregnancy, a 2016 study showed that women treated with systemic or topical fluconazole had an increased risk of spontaneous abortion and stillbirth. This does not occur with topical clotrimazole or miconazole, which are the drugs of choice for pregnant women.

Trichomoniasis

Trichomonas vaginalis, a flagellated protozoan, causes vaginitis in women. (Men can also be infected but are typically asymptomatic.) Trichomoniasis presents with a profuse, thin, frothy, yellow-green, foul-smelling discharge (which, like bacterial vaginosis, has a positive whiff test), vaginal erythema, and a strawberry cervix. Also similar to bacterial vaginosis, the pH of secretions is > 4.5. The organism can be seen on a saline prep of secretions (Figure 4-14). PCR testing, if available, is the gold standard for diagnosis.

The cure rate is higher if women are treated with PO metronidazole 500 mg bid for 7 days vs. a single PO 2-g dose. Metronidazole is safe in pregnancy. Male sexual partners should also be treated, and they should receive the single PO 2-g dose.

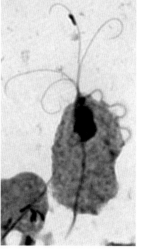

Figure 4-14: Trichomonad

CENTRAL NERVOUS SYSTEM (CNS) INFECTIONS

PREVIEW | REVIEW

- What is the clinical presentation of bacterial meningitis?
- Which organisms are the most common cause of bacterial meningitis in adults < 50 years of age?
- What is the standard empiric treatment for bacterial meningitis in adults < 50 years of age?
- To which contacts should you give prophylaxis for meningococcal meningitis?
- Empiric coverage for a patient with a spinal epidural abscess should cover which organism, specifically?
- What are acceptable empiric regimens for a brain abscess?
- Which animals are at high risk for the transmission of rabies?

BACTERIAL MENINGITIS

Untreated bacterial meningitis is a routinely fatal disease. In the U.S., there are 3 main causes of bacterial meningitis in adults:

- *Streptococcus pneumoniae* causes the majority of bacterial meningitis in all adult age groups.
- *Neisseria meningitidis* (meningococcus) is more common in young adults until ~ 25 years of age.
- *Listeria monocytogenes* meningitis begins to become more common ~ 50 years of age.

Approach to the Patient with Suspected Bacterial Meningitis

Time is of the essence in bacterial meningitis, and an organized approach to diagnosis and treatment is essential to decrease morbidity and mortality. Suspect bacterial meningitis in anyone with a fever, headache, and stiff neck.

The Kernig and Brudzinski signs have a low sensitivity (5–10%) but are highly specific (~ 95%). First obtain stat blood cultures, and then perform a lumbar puncture (LP) as soon as possible, but take caution to avoid precipitating herniation in patients who may have a space-occupying CNS lesion in certain patient groups. The following parameters are predictive of finding such lesions on a CT scan. The CT scan should be performed prior to the LP in these circumstances, but do not delay the administration of antibiotics while waiting on imaging results for patients with any of the following:

- An immunocompromised state
- Prior CNS disease
- Seizures in the last week
- Altered consciousness
- Papilledema
- A focal neurologic deficit

If a CT is performed and shows no contraindication (e.g., abscess), proceed with the LP. All patients suspected of bacterial meningitis should be given IV dexamethasone prior to empiric IV antibiotic. Dexamethasone decreases morbidity and mortality in adults with pneumococcal meningitis. Doing the LP first is ideal, but never delay the administration of antibiotics while waiting on an LP kit or CT scan result.

Cerebrospinal fluid (CSF) should have the following tests performed: Gram stain, C&S, cell count with differential, protein level, and glucose level. Rapid antigen testing is not routinely recommended because it uncommonly alters treatment. Typical findings in normal CSF vs. bacterial and viral (aseptic) meningitis are shown in Table 4-5.

Culture results are the gold standard and are positive in the majority of cases.

Antibiotics Used for Bacterial Meningitis

Because the CNS is an immune sanctuary with a decreased ability for complement and immunoglobulin to reach the site of infection, the antibiotics chosen must be bactericidal. Classes of antibiotics that are bactericidal are the β-lactams, glycopeptides, fluoroquinolones, and aminoglycosides. In addition, the drugs must be able to cross through the inflamed meninges. This presents a problem for the aminoglycosides, which, if used, may need to be given intrathecally. Selected 3rd generation cephalosporins with vancomycin should be the primary 1st line agents. Ampicillin is added for those at higher risk of *Listeria monocytogenes* due to either cell-mediated immunodeficiencies or being > 50 years of age.

	Normal CSF	Bacterial Meningitis	Viral Meningitis
WBC Count	< 5 cells/µL (0.01 × 10⁹/L) No PMNs	> 1,000 cells/µL (1 × 10⁹/L) Majority PMNs	< 1,000 cells/µL (1 × 10⁹/L) PMNs initially then monocytes and lymphocytes
Glucose Level	50–75 mg/dL (2.77–4.16 mmol/L)	Low	Normal
Protein Level	< 45 mg/dL	> 100 mg/dL	< 100 mg/dL

Table 4-5: Normal CSF vs. Bacterial and Viral (Aseptic) Meningitis

CSF = cerebrospinal fluid
PMN = polymorphonuclear leukocyte

WBC = white blood cell

Selecting Empiric Therapy

Age is the most useful predictor of the bacterial etiology of meningitis.

In adolescents and adults < 50 years of age, *S. pneumoniae* and *N. meningitidis* are the predominant organisms. Empiric therapy for this age group is ceftriaxone (which treats > 90% of *S. pneumoniae* strains and 100% of *N. meningitidis* strains) and vancomycin (which treats 100% of *S. pneumoniae* strains). If ceftriaxone-susceptible *S. pneumoniae* or the pathogen is *N. meningitidis*, the vancomycin should be stopped.

In adults > 50 years of age, *L. monocytogenes* becomes more common. This bacterium is not routinely susceptible to vancomycin and is resistant to cephalosporins, so add ampicillin empirically until the culture results are known. The CSF WBC count is lower with *Listeria* infection than with other bacterial infections, and the Gram stain is more commonly negative.

Patients with bacterial meningitis after neurosurgical procedures are at risk for staphylococcal and gram-negative aerobic infections; treat these patients with vancomycin and a 3rd generation cephalosporin.

Therapy Based on Gram Stain

Gram stain results allow for the reassessment of therapy within hours. If the CSF Gram stain results show an organism (as in the majority of bacterial meningitis cases), change the empiric therapy based on those results (Table 4-6).

Definitive Therapy

Cultures grow organisms from the CSF in the majority of patients with bacterial meningitis. Use the results of the culture and sensitivity to adjust the therapy.

Dexamethasone

Dexamethasone decreases the morbidity and mortality in adults with pneumococcal meningitis. Because > 50% of meningitis is caused by pneumococcus, start dexamethasone empirically 15–20 minutes before antibiotic administration, and continue dexamethasone treatment for 4 days if pneumococci are cultured. Discontinue dexamethasone if another causative agent is found.

PREVENTION OF MENINGOCOCCAL MENINGITIS

Give prophylaxis to close contacts of patients with meningococcal bacteremia and/or meningitis to eradicate any possible nasopharyngeal colonization, which increases the risk of subsequent development of invasive disease. Close contacts are defined as:

- persons who have spent > 8 hours within 3 feet of the index case from 7 days prior to 1 day after presentation (e.g., those who live in the patient's household, contacts at day care centers) and
- persons exposed to the patient's oral secretions (e.g., a health care worker who has intubated the patient).

Usual clinical encounters do not merit prophylaxis for health care workers.

To eradicate the carrier state, use one of the following:

- Ciprofloxacin 500 mg PO × 1 (for nonpregnant adults)
- Rifampin 600 mg PO bid × 2 days (for children and nonpregnant adults)
- Ceftriaxone 250 mg IM × 1 (for pregnant adults and children < 15 years of age)

Patients with meningococcal disease who are treated with penicillin still need to be given one of these prophylactic drugs prior to discharge because penicillin does not eradicate the carrier state. See Vaccine Schedules on page 4-93 for additional information.

Of the many serotypes of meningococcus, Serotypes A, B, C, W, and Y are the main cause of meningitis. Since 2005 there has been a conjugate vaccine against Serotypes A, C, W, and Y—MenACWY. In 2014, the FDA approved MenB vaccine against Serotype B. The MenACWY vaccine is recommended to be given at 11–12 years of age, followed by a booster at ≥16 years of age, preferable before entering college. The MenB vaccine is recommended to be given at 16–18 years of age based on shared decision making. Vaccination with both vaccines is recommended for immunosuppressed persons (e.g., asplenic, HIV infected, those with a complement deficiency, those on C5 inhibitors [eculizumab, ravulizumab]) or those at increased risk of exposure (e.g., microbiologists, travelers to endemic countries, persons exposed during an outbreak).

Table 4-6: Therapy Based on Cerebrospinal Fluid Gram Stain Results			
Gram Stain	**Likely Organism**	**Antibiotics**	**Comment**
Gram-positive cocci	*Streptococcus pneumoniae*	Vancomycin + ceftriaxone	Until ceftriaxone sensitivity is known
Gram-negative cocci	*Neisseria meningitidis*	Ceftriaxone	
Gram-positive bacilli	*Listeria monocytogenes*	Ampicillin ± gentamicin TMP/SMX if penicillin allergic	
Gram-negative bacilli	Enteric aerobe	3rd generation cephalosporin or meropenem	Cover for *Pseudomonas aeruginosa* if postneurosurgical

TMP/SMX = trimethoprim/sulfamethoxazole

INFECTIOUS DISEASE

SETTINGS TO CONSIDER NONBACTERIAL MENINGITIS

Suspect **Cryptococcus** in patients with acquired immunodeficiency syndrome (AIDS), acute lymphoblastic leukemia, or lymphoma or who use corticosteroids, and look for cryptococcal antigen in the blood and CSF.

Consider **amebic meningitis** when the patient has been swimming in freshwater lakes, ponds, or irrigation canals.

ASEPTIC MENINGITIS

The diagnosis of aseptic meningitis is based on clinical and CSF signs of meningeal inflammation (mild CSF pleocytosis and mildly elevated protein) without a clear bacterial cause based on CSF Gram stain and culture. The vast majority of these cases are due to viral infection. Patient complaints are similar to those for bacterial meningitis, although the symptoms are less acute and severe.

The viruses that cause aseptic meningitis are:

- Enteroviruses (e.g., coxsackievirus, echovirus, enteroviruses)
- Arboviruses (e.g., West Nile virus)
- HSV
- HIV

Fungal and bacterial causes of aseptic meningitis include:

- Endemic fungi
- Cryptococcal meningitis (seen in AIDS, acute lymphoblastic leukemia, and lymphomas)
- *Nocardia*
- *Mycobacterium tuberculosis*
- *Borrelia burgdorferi* (Lyme disease)

TUBERCULOUS MENINGITIS

Tuberculous meningitis causes a thick, basilar meningitis that often causes cranial nerve injury and presents with cranial neuropathy, such as a 6th nerve palsy, and CSF with a lymphocytic pleocytosis, high protein level, and very low glucose level.

LYME MENINGITIS

Lyme meningitis can cause peripheral and cranial nerve palsies, especially of the 7th cranial nerve (Bell's palsy), so think of Lyme disease or HSV infection when a patient presents with a facial nerve palsy, especially if it is bilateral. For treatment information, see Lyme Disease on page 4-55.

SPINAL EPIDURAL ABSCESS

Spinal epidural abscesses (pus between the dura and vertebrae) are caused by either hematogenous spread or local extension (e.g., from vertebral osteomyelitis or discitis). *Staphylococcus aureus* is the most common cause. Patients can present with the classic triad of fever, back pain, and radiculopathy.

On CSF analysis, a spinal epidural abscess resembles aseptic meningitis, with a moderate pleocytosis, modest protein elevation, normal glucose level, and negative result on Gram stain and culture. Obtain an MRI if any 2 of the 3 previously mentioned symptoms occur. CT is not as good as MRI because it is susceptible to bony artifacts. Obtain blood cultures. Drainage is required if technically feasible. Empiric coverage for a spinal epidural abscess includes drugs effective against staphylococci such as vancomycin. Definitive therapy is based on the blood or surgical cultures.

NEUROSYPHILIS

See the prior discussion of neurosyphilis under Syphilis on page 4-18.

BRAIN ABSCESS

Because contiguous spread from a nearby infection is the most common pathogenesis of brain abscess formation, their bacteriology often reflects organisms found in sinusitis, dental infections, and otitis media. The next most common source is via hematogenous spread from other foci, such as endocarditis, in which *Staphylococcus aureus* is often found. Common locations from hematogenous sources are the frontal, temporal, and parietal lobes via the middle cerebral artery. Postsurgical abscesses can also show *S. aureus* or GNBs.

The symptoms may be fever (absent in ~ 50% of cases), focal neurologic deficit, and/or seizures. Diagnose a brain abscess using a CT scan with contrast or MRI. If accessible, aspirate the abscess and give antibiotic treatment based on the results. An LP is contraindicated if signs of increased intracranial pressure are present, such as papilledema or focal neurologic signs. An LP rarely helps identify the infectious bacteria because the organisms are seldom in the subarachnoid space.

Treatment for brain abscess is initially empiric, followed by definitive therapy for 4–8 weeks if cultures are obtained by drainage. Give ceftriaxone + metronidazole to cover aerobes and anaerobes. If you suspect GNBs (e.g., if there is otitis media/externa), consider an agent with *Pseudomonas* coverage + metronidazole. If there was a history of bacteremia/endocarditis, a neurosurgical procedure, or penetrating head trauma, add vancomycin for MRSA. For postoperative neurosurgical patients, use ceftazidime, cefepime, or meropenem to cover hospital-related gram-negative organisms, including *Pseudomonas*.

VIRAL ENCEPHALITIS

Herpes Simplex Virus Type 1 (HSV-1)

The most common sporadic viral encephalitis is due to HSV-1. The virus enters the CNS via the trigeminal or olfactory tract following an episode of primary or recurrent HSV-1 of the oropharynx or reactivation of latent virus in the CNS without evident oropharyngeal herpes.

Disease is usually frontotemporal, and the symptoms range from alterations in behavior, seizures, cranial nerve dysfunction, and hemiparesis to alterations of consciousness, all over a period of < 1 week. Brain imaging is almost always abnormal, showing unilateral, sometimes bilateral focal cerebral inflammation. The CSF shows a lymphocytic, aseptic meningitis that is often hemorrhagic. In HSV meningoencephalitis, the CSF glucose is sometimes mildly decreased. HSV PCR of the CSF is positive > 95% of the time. Treatment is with high-dose IV acyclovir for ≥ 14 days.

Arboviral Encephalitis

The arboviruses are the most common seasonal viral encephalitides and are named after the geographic location from which they originally came (e.g., West Nile, St. Louis). They are discussed under Arboviruses on page 4-80.

Rabies

Rabies is a preventable but almost always fatal illness that is very rare in the U.S. (< 5 cases a year) but causes ~ 30,000 deaths a year worldwide. Fewer than 20 patients worldwide have survived rabies without treatment. Rabies virus is found in bats, raccoons, skunks, foxes, dogs, cats, and ferrets but not in squirrels, rats, or any other rodents. Worldwide, rabies is primarily transmitted to humans by dogs, but in the U.S., bats are the most common cause. Rabies typically presents within 1–3 months after exposure with a viral prodrome followed by encephalitis, ascending paralysis, neuropathic pain +/ sensorimotor deficits, and eventually hydrophobia, aerophobia, and delirium.

Diagnose rabies by doing all of the following because no single test has 100% sensitivity:

- Virus-specific immunofluorescent staining of a skin biopsy sample of hair follicles at the nape of the neck
- Detection of the virus from the saliva, CSF, skin, and serum by reverse transcriptase polymerase chain reaction (RT-PCR)
- Detection of antirabies antibodies in the serum and CSF

Preexposure prophylaxis is recommended for cave explorers, veterinarians, animal control workers in endemic areas, and anybody who handles bats—but not for hunters, mail carriers, or other persons.

Determine the need for postexposure prophylaxis based on the suspected animal source. Bites from bats, raccoons, foxes, and skunks are considered high risk and warrant prophylaxis. Have pet dogs, cats, and ferrets observed for 10 days, and if there are no signs of rabies, there is no need for prophylaxis. Bites from small rodents never need prophylaxis. Prophylaxis consists of human rabies immunoglobulin (HRIG)—with ~ 50% injected in the tissue around the wound and the remainder administered IM—and vaccination with the rabies human diploid cell vaccine. Give each in a separate site. If a person has been vaccinated previously, administer only a booster vaccine after a bite, not HRIG.

PRION DISEASE

Prions are proteinaceous infectious particles that lack nucleic acid and are destructive to neural tissue.

The most important prion diseases are Creutzfeldt-Jakob disease (CJD) and variant CJD (vCJD). In animals, prions cause bovine spongiform encephalopathy (formerly known as mad cow disease), which is vCJD if transmitted to humans.

CJD is almost always sporadic, but ~ 5% of cases are transmitted from person to person (e.g., corneal transplants, cadaveric human growth hormone), and very few cases are genetic. The incubation period is ~ 18 months. Patients with CJD get myoclonus and severe, rapidly progressive dementia. MRI shows diffuse cerebral disease, and electroencephalography (EEG) classically shows periodic synchronous biphasic or triphasic sharp wave complexes. An abnormal amount of 14-3-3 protein may be present in the CSF. The clinical course is one of progressive rapid deterioration, with the majority of patients dying within 6 months of diagnosis. There is no effective therapy.

vCJD is transmitted from eating meat from cattle with bovine spongiform encephalopathy. No endemic human cases of vCJD have been reported in the U.S., although some veterinary cases have been reported. Patients with vCJD have initial psychiatric symptoms and paresthesias and then ataxia and cognitive impairment. Paresis of upward gaze occurs in ~ 50% of patients. Death occurs in ~ 1 year.

INFECTIVE ENDOCARDITIS (IE)

PREVIEW | REVIEW

- What is the most common organism causing native valve endocarditis?
- What is the usual cause of prosthetic valve endocarditis > 2 months after surgery?
- What are some specific physical examination signs of endocarditis?
- How many sets of blood cultures should be drawn on a patient with suspected endocarditis?
- Which organisms cause culture-negative endocarditis?
- What 2 types of tests make up the major criteria for the diagnosis of endocarditis?
- Know the various regimens to treat endocarditis based on resistance patterns and the type of valve (native vs. prosthetic).
- List the indications for the early surgical treatment of bacterial endocarditis.

INFECTIOUS DISEASE

OVERVIEW

IE occurs on native and prosthetic valves or other endocardial surfaces. In addition, we will specifically discuss culture-negative IE and IE seen in injection drug users. These categorizations are predictive of the microbiology and hence the treatment of the disease. The previous designations of acute and subacute are no longer used. IE is universally fatal if not treated, and even with appropriate treatment there is a 15–20% in-hospital mortality rate, which approaches 40% at 1 year.

NATIVE VALVE ENDOCARDITIS (NVE)

NVE is more common on the left side of the heart and usually occurs on defective or damaged valves. It can also occur in the path of abnormal flow across a ventricular septal defect (VSD) or patent ductus arteriosus. During the past half century, the median age of onset has increased and is now ~ 60 years of age.

The most common organism infecting native valves is *Staphylococcus aureus*, followed by viridans streptococci and then enterococci. Patients with *S. aureus* endocarditis have a higher incidence of embolic phenomena and death. There is a group of organisms that causes a small percentage of IE cases. This group was previously called AACEK but, due to name changes in the first 2 organisms, is now called **HACEK**, which stands for the following:

- *H*aemophilus spp. (i.e., *H. parainfluenzae*)
- *A*ggregatibacter aphrophilus (formerly *Haemophilus aphrophilus*)
- *A*ggregatibacter actinomycetemcomitans (formerly *Actinobacillus actinomycetemcomitans*)
- *C*ardiobacterium hominis
- *E*ikenella corrodens
- *K*ingella kingae

These organisms share several commonalities: They take longer to show growth in vitro (mean of ~ 3 days), cause large vegetations with a higher risk of embolization, and are susceptible to PCNs.

Fungal endocarditis is seen in people who use IV drugs and in patients with central IV catheters.

PROSTHETIC VALVE ENDOCARDITIS (PVE)

Early PVE (occurring within 2 months of valve insertion) is usually due to inoculation of organisms during surgery, and staphylococcal species are the most common infecting organisms. PVE is harder to cure than NVE; if there is no response to the 1st round of (adequate) antibiotics, replace the valve. If acute cardiac decompensation occurs, patients need emergent surgical intervention regardless of the duration of prior antibiotics and have a mortality rate of ~ 40%.

Late PVE (occurring > 2 months after valve insertion) is caused by organisms similar to those causing NVE; however, coagulase-negative staphylococci are much more common (~ 15%). If the infecting organisms are viridans

streptococci or enterococci, the likelihood of cure with antibiotics is higher than with staphylococci. Better antibiotic treatment success is seen with porcine bioprosthesis than with metal valves.

The valve must be replaced if there is evidence of a valve ring infection, an unstable prosthesis, or myocardial penetration with abscess formation, which may manifest as new heart block or a new bundle-branch block.

HISTORY AND PHYSICAL EXAMINATION

Occasionally IE presents only with signs of embolic events, such as black toes or septic emboli to organs (e.g., embolic stroke, brain abscess, splenic infarct). It can also present as a lingering illness with nonspecific symptoms (e.g., weight loss, fevers, chills, night sweats) or heart failure due to valvular insufficiency.

Focus the history on recent potential exposures to typical organisms:

- Skin infections (staphylococci)
- Dental work (viridans streptococci)
- Genitourinary manipulation or obstruction (enterococci)
- IV catheters (staphylococci)
- Injection drug use (*S. aureus*, GNBs, or yeast)

Also look for clues to uncommon organisms, especially if the blood cultures are negative. Animal exposures predispose patients to *Coxiella*, *Bartonella*, and *Tropheryma whipplei*.

Physical examination may show the following classic stigmata, many of which are part of the Duke criteria used to diagnose endocarditis:

- Conjunctival hemorrhages
- Petechiae (conjunctival and cutaneous)
- Splinter hemorrhages (of the fingernails and toenails)
- Janeway lesions (nonblanching, painless, reddish lesions on the hands or feet due to embolic infarcts of the skin)
- Osler nodes (painful, purplish lesions on the fingers or toes due to immune complex formation)
- Roth spots (retinal hemorrhages with white centers)

These signs are seen in < 25% of cases. When found, however, they are highly specific for endocarditis. 85% of patients will have a murmur and ~ 20% a changing murmur, but these are less-specific findings.

Systemic involvement commonly includes neurologic deficits (the most common cause of death), infarctions of the spleen and kidneys, immune complex glomerulonephritis, and septic pulmonary infarction in right-sided disease.

LABORATORY EVALUATION

Blood cultures are routinely positive (> 90% of the time) for patients with IE. This is because the infection is in contact with the bloodstream.

High-grade bacteremia is a key diagnostic finding in endocarditis; draw 3 sets before starting empiric antibiotics.

Additional nonspecific laboratory abnormalities commonly seen in endocarditis include:

- Elevated erythrocyte sedimentation rate (ESR) and C-reactive protein (CRP)
- Anemia of chronic inflammation
- Leukocytosis or leukopenia
- Thrombocytopenia
- Proteinuria, hematuria, and pyuria
- Evidence of immune activation (low complement levels, cryoglobulinemia, rheumatoid factor [RF], or a +RPR test)

CULTURE-NEGATIVE ENDOCARDITIS

If all 3 blood cultures are negative, there is no history of preculture antibiotic treatment, and the patient meets the clinical criteria for endocarditis (see Diagnosis), this is called culture-negative endocarditis. Consider the following causative agents:

- Fungi
- Q fever (*Coxiella burnetii*)
- *Bartonella* spp.
- *Tropheryma whipplei*
- *Legionella pneumophila*
- *Chlamydia psittaci*
- *Abiotrophia* spp. (previously known as nutritionally deficient streptococci)

The following are the appropriate tests/procedures for each cause listed:

- Fungal blood cultures and urinary antigen testing for *Histoplasma* and *Blastomyces*
- Urine *Legionella* antigen testing
- Serologies for *Coxiella*, *Bartonella*, and *C. psittaci*
- Alerting the lab to use special culture techniques to look for *Abiotrophia*

Tissue samples from removed valves should be sent for PCR testing of as many of the organisms listed here that the laboratory can test.

ECHOCARDIOGRAPHY

In NVE, transthoracic echocardiography (TTE) has a sensitivity of 50–90% and a specificity of > 90% for the detection of vegetations. In PVE, the sensitivity drops to 36–69%. Transesophageal echocardiography (TEE) has a sensitivity and specificity of > 90% in NVE and a sensitivity of 86–92% in PVE.

The 2020 ACC/AHA Guideline for the Management of Patients With Valvular Heart Disease recommend the following indications for the use of TTE and TEE in diagnosing endocarditis:

- Use TTE as the initial test to detect vegetations.
- TEE is recommended In patients with known or suspected IE and nondiagnostic TTE results or when complications have developed or are clinically suspected or when intracardiac device leads are present.

DIAGNOSIS

The diagnosis is based on fulfillment of the **modified Duke criteria**, which include clinical, laboratory, and echocardiographic characteristics, regardless of whether a patient has native or prosthetic valves.

Definite endocarditis is diagnosed when the patient has any of the following:

- Pathologic evidence of disease
- 2 major criteria (see below)
- 1 major criterion + 3 minor criteria (see below)
- 5 minor criteria

Pathologic evidence is either visible organisms from a vegetation or valve lesion or a positive culture from the same tissue.

Possible endocarditis is diagnosed with either:

- 1 major criterion + 1 minor criterion or
- 3 minor criteria.

The 2 major criteria are:

1) **Positive blood cultures.** There are 3 ways that this criterion can be met:
   - The organism is one that typically causes endocarditis and is found in ≥ 2 blood cultures 12 hours apart. These organisms are *S. aureus* (most common) viridans streptococci, *Streptococcus bovis*, enterococci, or the HACEK organisms.
   - If the organism is not one that typically causes endocarditis, there must be ≥ 3 positive cultures or the majority of ≥ 5 cultures drawn at least an hour apart from first to last.
   - There is a single positive blood culture for *C. burnetii* (or seropositivity for *C. burnetii*). This is the only organism that meets the criterion with a single positive blood culture.

2) **Abnormal echocardiogram** with any of the following:
   - An oscillating mass on a valve or on supporting structures
   - An oscillating mass in the path of a regurgitant jet
   - An oscillating mass on an implanted device
   - An abscess
   - Prosthetic valve dehiscence
   - A new regurgitant valve by echocardiography or auscultation

The 5 minor criteria are:

1) A predisposing condition (i.e., valve disease, injection drug use)

2) Fever > 100.4°F (38.0°C)

3) Vascular phenomena (e.g., arterial emboli, pulmonary infarcts, mycotic aneurysms, stroke, conjunctival hemorrhages, Janeway lesions)

4) Immunologic phenomena (e.g., acute glomerulonephritis, Osler nodes, Roth spots, +RF)

5) A positive blood culture that does not meet a major criterion

INFECTIOUS DISEASE

Of note, *S. bovis* has recently been reclassified into 4 species: *S. gallolyticus*, *S. lutetiensis*, *S. infantarius*, and *S. pasteurianus*.

ANTIBIOTIC TREATMENT OF BACTERIAL ENDOCARDITIS

Although therapy for endocarditis is based on specific organisms, remember these 5 general concepts regarding treatment regimens:

1) Endocarditis requires bactericidal antibiotics because white cells and opsonins have difficulty penetrating to the center of vegetations, so the antibiotic must do the killing.
2) With rare exceptions, give antibiotics IV for the duration of treatment.
3) Give antibiotics at the appropriate dose to ensure bactericidal levels.
4) There are only 3 scenarios in which a 2-week duration is sufficient:
   • For viridans streptococci if an aminoglycoside is added to the regimen
   • For *S. bovis*
   • For uncomplicated right-sided *S. aureus* endocarditis
5) Treat all other organisms for a minimum of 4 weeks (Table 4-7).

Viridans Streptococi and *Streptococcus bovis*

If the viridans streptococci are susceptible to PCN, give 4 weeks of PCN G, ampicillin, or ceftriaxone (2 g/day). Adding gentamicin can reduce the duration to 2 weeks; however, keep it at 4 weeks if there is an abscess. Gentamicin is not recommended for patients with chronic kidney disease (CKD). Vancomycin can be used for 4 weeks in patients unable to tolerate the β-lactam, but it is not preferred for initial treatment.

If there is intermediate resistance to PCN, the regimen is the same except that the dose of PCN G is increased or ceftriaxone is substituted.

Prosthetic valve treatment is generally the same regimen, but the duration of treatment is lengthened.

Perform a colonoscopy if endocarditis is caused by what was formerly known as *S. bovis*, given the high prevalence of colon cancer in these patients. (*S. bovis* has been reclassified and consists of 4 species: *S. gallolyticus*, *S. lutetiensis*, *S. infantarius*, and *S. pasteurianus*.)

Staphylococcus aureus without Prosthetics

Methicillin-susceptible *S. aureus* (MSSA) left-sided or right-sided disease with emboli requires nafcillin × 6 weeks. The addition of an aminoglycoside is not recommended, because it does not improve cure rates and it increases nephrotoxicity.

Table 4-7: Treatment of Bacterial Endocarditis			
Organisms	**Susceptibility Testing**	**Drug Regimen**	**Duration**
Viridans streptococci, *Streptococcus bovis* (See reclassification of this species under Viridans Streptococci and *Streptococcus bovis*.)	PCN sensitive	PCN G, ampicillin, or ceftriaxone	4 weeks Prosthetic valve = > 4 weeks
		(PCN G, ampicillin, or ceftriaxone) + gentamicin	2 weeks
		Vancomycin (alternative)	4 weeks
	PCN intermediate	Increased dose of PCN G or ceftriaxone	4 weeks
Staphylococcus aureus or coagulase-negative staphylococci	Methicillin susceptible	Nafcillin	6 weeks Prosthetic valve = add rifampin + gentamicin
	Methicillin resistant	Vancomycin	6 weeks Prosthetic valve = add rifampin + gentamicin
Uncomplicated right-sided staphylococci	Methicillin susceptible	Nafcillin; if PCN allergic, daptomycin or vancomycin	2 weeks
Enterococci	PCN sensitive (depending on ampicillin and vancomycin susceptibilities)	(PCN G or ampicillin or vancomycin) + gentamicin	4–6 weeks Prosthetic valve = 6 weeks
	Resistant to ampicillin, PCN G, and vancomycin	Very specialized	Very specialized
HACEK		Ceftriaxone	4 weeks Prosthetic valve = 6 weeks

HACEK = *Haemophilus* spp. (i.e., *H. parainfluenzae*), *Aggregatibacter aphrophilus* (formerly *Haemophilus aphrophilus*), *Aggregatibacter actinomycetemcomitans* (formerly *Actinobacillus actinomycetemcomitans*), *Cardiobacterium hominis*, *Eikenella corrodens*, *Kingella kingae*
PCN = penicillin

Treat methicillin-resistant *S. aureus* (MRSA) endocarditis with vancomycin × 6 weeks. Alternatively, use daptomycin, especially if the vancomycin MIC is > 1 mcg/mL.

For MSSA uncomplicated right-sided disease, give nafcillin or oxacillin × 2 weeks. For patients with hypersensitivities to the nafcillin or oxacillin, cefazolin × 2 weeks can be used. Daptomycin or vancomycin × 4 weeks are acceptable alternatives for patients with anaphylactic penicillin allergy.

Treat MRSA isolates × 6 weeks with vancomycin or daptomycin only.

Staphylococcus aureus with Prosthetic Valves

For MSSA prosthetic valve disease, give nafcillin + rifampin + gentamicin for ≥ 6 weeks. For MRSA prosthetic valve disease, give vancomycin + rifampin + gentamicin for ≥ 6 weeks. Surgery is almost always indicated.

Enterococci

For native valve endocarditis, based on susceptibilities, if the organism is sensitive to PCN, give gentamicin + PCN or ampicillin or vancomycin × 4–6 weeks.

Prosthetic valve treatment is the same regimen, but the duration of treatment is lengthened to 6–8 weeks.

If the organism is resistant to PCN, ampicillin, and vancomycin, treatment is difficult and specialized, utilizing variations of linezolid or daptomycin (if sensitive) +/− imipenem/cilastatin with either ampicillin or ceftriaxone.

HACEK Organisms

Treat HACEK organisms (*Haemophilus* spp. (i.e., *H. parainfluenzae*), *Aggregatibacter aphrophilus*, *Aggregatibacter actinomycetemcomitans*, *Cardiobacterium hominis*, *Eikenella corrodens*, *Kingella kingae*) with ceftriaxone × 4 weeks. Alternatives include ampicillin-sulbactam and ciprofloxacin. If a prosthetic valve is involved, the duration of treatment is 6 weeks.

SURGICAL TREATMENT OF BACTERIAL ENDOCARDITIS

Class 1 indications for early surgery for bacterial endocarditis (defined as surgery during the initial hospitalization prior to the completion of antibiotic therapy) is indicated in the following situations:

- Heart failure from valve dysfunction refractory to medical therapy
- Resistant organisms with no available bactericidal therapy
- Development of heart block
- Development of an abscess
- Persistence of positive blood cultures or fever for > 5–7 days into therapy
- Relapse of PVE

PREVENTION OF ENDOCARDITIS

Administration of antibiotics to prevent endocarditis is only done under specific circumstances depending on whether the patient is in a high-risk group for endocarditis and if the procedure has a high risk of causing bacteremia.

The only adult patients considered to be at high risk for acquiring endocarditis are those with prosthetic cardiac material (e.g., valves, repaired cyanotic congenital heart disease) or a prior history of endocarditis.

The only procedures requiring prophylaxis are the following:

- Dental procedures that cause bleeding because of manipulation of the gingiva or periapical areas or perforation of the oral mucosa
- Respiratory tract procedures that cut through the mucosa, such as tonsillectomy or bronchoscopy with biopsy

For dental procedures:

- Give a single 2-g dose of amoxicillin 30–60 minutes prior to the procedure.
- PCN-allergic patients can receive a single dose of cephalexin, clindamycin, clarithromycin, or azithromycin.
- Those unable to take an oral medication should receive parenteral ampicillin, cefazolin, or ceftriaxone.

For respiratory tract procedures that cut through the mucosa, use the above regimens. If an active respiratory tract infection is the reason for the procedure (e.g., drainage of an abscess or empyema), use one of these antibiotics as part of the treatment regimen. If the patient is known or suspected to be colonized or infected with *S. aureus*, add anti-staphylococcal antibiotics.

CARDIAC IMPLANTABLE ELECTRONIC DEVICE (CIED) INFECTIONS

PREVIEW | REVIEW

- What are the main causes of cardiac implantable electronic device (CIED) infections?
- What is the initial imaging study if CIED is suspected?

CIED (i.e., pacemaker, implantable cardioverter-defibrillator) infections occur at a rate of ~ 1%. The infection can be limited to the tissue in which the device is placed (i.e., a pocket infection) or involve the leads within the heart, and it can occur as a result of contamination at the time of placement or from bacteremia. *Staphylococcus aureus* and coagulase-negative staphylococci are the most common organisms to cause CIED infection. Risk factors

INFECTIOUS DISEASE

include early device reoperation (posing the highest risk), a longer procedure duration, a device battery change, chronic kidney disease, and immunosuppression (either from an underlying condition or from a medication).

A pocket infection typically presents with pain, erythema, swelling, and sometimes systemic symptoms. A deeper infection presents with systemic symptoms, namely fever, chills, and right-sided endocarditis (refer to Infective Endocarditis (IE) on page 4-27).

Obtain 3 sets of blood cultures separated by at least 1 hour unless the patient is septic, in which case the cultures must be obtained sooner. Perform a TEE (not TTE) as the initial imaging modality for suspected CIED infection.

Treatment of a pocket infection consists of device removal (including leads) and initiation of empiric antibiotics to cover MRSA (e.g., vancomycin). The therapy is tailored to the causative organism once the culture results are known, and the total duration of therapy is 10–14 days. Treat a deeper device infection as you would treat endocarditis (refer to Infective Endocarditis (IE) on page 4-27).

HUMAN IMMUNODEFICIENCY VIRUS (HIV) AND ACQUIRED IMMUNODEFICIENCY SYNDROME (AIDS)

PREVIEW | REVIEW

- What is the viral set point, and what is its significance?
- Patients with immunosuppression from autoimmune deficiency syndrome (AIDS) are at risk for developing infections with which organisms?
- How is human immunodeficiency virus (HIV) infection diagnosed in the acute and chronic stages? What is the utility of measuring HIV ribonucleic acid?
- What is the significance of the CD4 count?
- Which new HIV+ patients should receive resistance testing?
- Which nucleoside reverse transcriptase inhibitor can cause the development of kidney disease?
- Which antiretroviral is teratogenic?
- What is the primary toxicity of nevirapine?
- Jaundice can occur with which antiretroviral drug?
- Which protease inhibitor (PI) is used to boost the drug concentrations of other PIs?
- What is the serious side effect of abacavir, and how can it be screened for?
- Which exposures should receive postexposure prophylaxis for HIV?

- Which pregnant women should be treated for HIV, and with what? What is the treatment goal?
- What are the symptoms of early HIV infection?
- How is *Pneumocystis jirovecii* pneumonia (PJP) best diagnosed?
- Which ancillary treatment should you give to patients who develop severe hypoxemia due to PJP?
- When should you give patients primary prophylaxis for PJP?
- What is the treatment duration for latent tuberculosis in patients with HIV/AIDS?
- How is cryptococcal meningitis diagnosed?
- What is the typical presentation of central nervous system toxoplasmosis?
- Name some of the organisms that can cause chronic diarrhea in patients with AIDS.

OVERVIEW

Changes in the treatment and management of HIV infection and associated opportunistic infections are evolving rapidly. Information on antiretroviral drugs is presented here.

EPIDEMIOLOGY

According to the CDC, as of 2019 in the U.S.:

- There were 1.2 million people living with HIV (~13% are unaware).
- There were ~ 36,740 new HIV infections that year and there has been a steady decline in new cases over the past 5 years.
- Men who have sex with men made up a disproportionate number of the cases, at 66%, as did those who identified as Black/African American, at 46%.
- Heterosexual contact was the transmission category in 24% of cases, and injection drug use was the transmission category in 7% of cases.
- Men represented 78% of cases.
- 57% of those living with HIV have undetectable viral loads thanks to ART.

HIV PATHOGENESIS

HIV pathogenesis is relevant to understanding the mechanisms of action of the antiretroviral drugs.

The HIV particle is composed of a single-stranded ribonucleic acid (RNA) core surrounded by a lipoprotein envelope. The RNA contains reverse transcriptase, which allows the RNA to be transcribed into deoxyribonucleic acid (DNA), which is then integrated into the host's genome. The cell then becomes an HIV-producing machine.

The HIV envelope glycoprotein (gp120) binds to the cluster of differentiation 4 (CD4) receptors and coreceptors (e.g., C-C chemokine receptor Type 5 [CCR5]) on helper T cells, macrophages, and monocytes. The virus must bind to both the CD4 and CCR5 molecules to fuse with the cell. After fusion, the viral core material enters the cell and is reverse transcribed into DNA that integrates into the human genome and codes for the production of more virion RNA and structural proteins. These proteins, after being cleaved by a protease, then combine with the viral RNA and bud off of the cell using the CD4 cell membrane as a new envelope. This eventually causes destruction of the CD4 cells. The CD4 cells are the major regulator cells in the body; they suppress B lymphocytes and regulate the CD8 suppressor cells.

After initial infection, the virus replicates quickly while the immune system attempts to control the infection via cell-mediated immunity. The interplay between HIV and the immune system determines what the individual's viral load will be.

The **viral set point** is the viral load that is established after a patient's immune system attempts to control the primary infection; it varies from person to person. When a patient stops ART, the virus typically rebounds to a level that is at the patient's baseline. The higher the viral set point, the faster the CD4 cells are killed and the faster the HIV progresses and the patient becomes ill if not treated.

Continued HIV replication is lytic for CD4+ cells, and B cells become dysregulated and dysfunctional and are no longer suppressed, causing a polyclonal increase in total serum immunoglobulins but with a decreased ability to create new antibodies. For this reason, infectious diseases in patients with AIDS include not only those occurring from cell-mediated immunodeficiency (e.g., *Pneumocystis* pneumonia, viruses, mycobacteria, fungi), but also those seen with humoral deficiency (e.g., pneumococcus, meningococcus, *Giardia*).

PRESENTATION

Untreated HIV has a long latent period prior to its clinical manifestations unless diagnosed in the acute stage. The acute stage is called symptomatic acute HIV infection, acute retroviral syndrome, or primary retroviral infection. The most common symptoms are rash, sore throat, headache, fever, lymphadenopathy, myalgias, and arthralgias.

The subsequent immunologic decline occurs over several years, and unless screened prior to this, the HIV infection is commonly diagnosed only when the patient presents with symptomatic disease.

SCREENING

Test all persons at least once when they are 15–65 years of age or if they have at-risk behavior outside of this age range. Repeat testing is based on their risk group:

- For high-risk populations (e.g., injection drug use, men who have sex with men, patients with prior STIs, or STI testing), screen at least annually.

- For other at-risk individuals (e.g., unprotected intercourse, partners at risk, sex for drugs/money), screen at least every 3–5 years.

- Individuals who are not at increased risk (none of the above risk factors and either not sexually active or monogamously active with an HIV-negative partner), no repeat screening is indicated unless their risk category changes or they become pregnant.

- Some clinical scenarios warrant repeat testing such as new-onset TB, recurrent *Candida* vulvovaginitis, and recurrent herpes zoster.

DIAGNOSIS

In the acute stage of HIV infection prior to the production of antibody, infection is diagnosed by looking for the HIV virus itself. In the chronic stage, HIV infection is diagnosed by demonstrating the presence of the virus or antibody to the virus. Antibody in acute infection may take up to 3–7 weeks after infection to be detectable.

The presence of HIV can also be detected with tests that measure the actual levels of HIV RNA (the viral load) by amplifying its RNA. These tests are used for initial diagnosis, to assess prognosis, and to monitor the response to ART. Current PCR assays can detect the virus as early as 5 days after infection.

The CDC 2021 Sexually Transmitted Diseases Treatment Guidelines recommend testing with a combination assay, which simultaneously tests to see if any of the following are present:

- HIV-1 antibody
- HIV-2 antibody
- HIV-1 antigen
- HIV-2 antigen

If the combination assay is positive, further testing is performed to see which specific assays are positive to detect chronic infection (antibody present) or acute infection (antigen present).

AIDS diagnosis: AIDS is diagnosed if immunosuppression leads to a CD4 count of < 200, or if one of the following opportunistic infections or malignancies occur:

- Candidiasis of the lower respiratory tract or esophagus
- Invasive cervical cancer
- Coccidioidomycosis that is extrapulmonary
- Cryptococcosis that is extrapulmonary
- Cryptosporidiosis that is > 1 month in duration
- Cytomegalovirus outside of the liver, spleen, or lymph nodes
- HIV encephalopathy
- Herpes simplex that is cutaneous for > 1 month or involving the lungs or esophagus
- Histoplasmosis that is extrapulmonary
- Isosporiasis that is > 1 month in duration
- Kaposi sarcoma

INFECTIOUS DISEASE

- Lymphoma that is either Burkitt, immunoblastic, or primary brain
- *Mycobacterium*, nontuberculous, that is extrapulmonary
- *Mycobacterium tuberculosis*, any site including pulmonary
- *Pneumocystis jirovecii* pneumonia
- Pneumonia that is recurrent
- Progressive multifocal leukoencephalopathy
- *Salmonella*, bacteremia or recurrent
- Toxoplasmosis of the brain
- Wasting syndrome

TREATMENT

Give all patients with HIV infection ART with a combination of agents. Adherence to the ART regimen is a key determinant in the degree and duration of viral suppression.

The CD4 count is an indication of how immunosuppressed the patient is at the commencement of therapy. The viral load is an indicator of how rapidly the CD4 count will continue to decline if the HIV infection is left untreated. Therapy is monitored by following the CD4 count and viral load with the goal of getting the viral load to an undetectable level, after which the CD4 count usually increases. Clinical treatment guidelines are released annually by the National Institutes of Health and can be found at: https://clinicalinfo.hiv.gov/en/guidelines/adult-and-adolescent-arv/whats-new-guidelines.

Prior to treatment, test all patients for HIV genotype resistance to antiviral drugs. Repeat testing if a patient is failing therapy, as indicated by a failure to suppress the viral load below detection when that patient is taking medications reliably. Resistance testing should also be performed in individuals who previously took ART but then stopped and now wish to start treatment again.

When the viral load is high and the CD4 count is < 100 cells/μL (0.1×10^9/L) at the initiation of ART, an **immune reconstitution inflammatory syndrome** (IRIS) can occur. There can be an exacerbation of other preexisting infections that are now unmasked, such as TB, HSV, cytomegalovirus (CMV), JC virus, VZV, HAV, HBV, and cryptococcal meningitis, because the body now has the ability to mount an immune response against these organisms. The overall risk of developing IRIS is 7–10%. If an IRIS develops, the recommendations are to continue with ART and treat the underlying opportunistic infections. In severe situations, corticosteroids can be given for a brief time. The benefit of starting ART generally outweighs the IRIS risk with 2 exceptions: active TB infection or cryptococcal meningitis. If these are present, it is recommended that ART be held until after at least 2 weeks of TB therapy and 4 weeks of cryptococcal meningitis therapy.

Antiretroviral Drugs

Summary

The classes of anti-HIV drugs are:

- Nucleoside and nucleotide reverse transcriptase inhibitors (NRTIs)
- Nonnucleoside reverse transcriptase inhibitors (NNRTIs)
- Protease inhibitors (PIs) (all names end in **navir**)
- Fusion inhibitors (FIs)
- Integrase strand transfer inhibitors (INSTIs) (all names end in **gravir**)
- CCR5 antagonists
- Attachment inhibitors
- Postattachment inhibitors

A review of these classes follows, with individual agents highlighted in Table 4-8.

Table 4-8: Antiretrovirals Used in the Management of HIV Infection				
Drug Class	**Drug**	**Use**	**Toxicity**	**Comment**
Nucleoside/ nucleotide reverse transcriptase inhibitors	Abacavir	1st line	Severe hypersensitivity reaction if HLA-B*5701+	Test for HLA-B*5701 gene prior to administration; once-daily dosing
	Emtricitabine	1st line	Rare	Cross-resistance with lamivudine; once-daily dosing
	Lamivudine	1st line	Rare	Cross-resistance with emtricitabine; once-daily dosing
	TDF; newer formulation is TAF	1st line	Renal injury and bone density loss with TDF; not seen with the newer TAF formulation; mild GI upset	Once-daily dosing
	Zidovudine	Uncommon	Marrow suppression, myopathy	Used only in those who initially responded years ago and in IV form in the perinatal care of HIV-positive mothers

Table 4-8: Antiretrovirals Used in the Management of HIV Infection (continued)

Drug Class	Drug	Use	Toxicity	Comment
Nonnucleoside reverse transcriptase inhibitors	Doravirine	2nd line	Rare	CYP interactions
	Efavirenz	2nd line	Rash, central nervous system toxicity	CYP interactions; once-daily dosing
	Etravirine	2nd line	Rash	CYP interactions
	Nevirapine	2nd line	Rash, hepatotoxicity	Initial lead-in phase with lower dose required; once-daily dosing; CYP interactions
	Rilpivirine	2nd line	Rare	Needs to be taken with food; do not use with viral load > 100,000 copies/mL
Protease inhibitors	Atazanavir (with cobicistat or ritonavir booster)	2nd line	Jaundice	Once-daily dosing; CYP interactions
	Darunavir (with or without cobicistat booster)	2nd line	Best tolerated PI	No cross-resistance with other PIs; once-daily dosing; CYP interactions
	Lopinavir (combined with ritonavir booster)	3rd line	Diarrhea, insulin resistance	CYP interactions
	Fosamprenavir	3rd line	Rash	CYP interactions
	Indinavir	3rd line	Jaundice	CYP interactions
	Ritonavir	2nd line as a booster of another PI	Diarrhea, nausea, vomiting	Used only to boost other PIs; CYP interactions
	Saquinavir	3rd line	Rare	CYP interactions
	Tipranavir	3rd line	Rash	CYP interactions
Fusion inhibitors	Enfuvirtide	Salvage if failure to suppress viral load	Local reactions	Subcutaneous administration
Integrase strand transfer inhibitors	Bictegravir	1st line	Rare	Only available in combination with emtricitabine and tenofovir alafenamide
	Dolutegravir	1st line	Rare	Blocks creatinine secretion, so can give artifactually elevated creatinine level
	Elvitegravir	1st line but bictegravir or dolutegravir are recommended	Rare	Needs to be boosted; needs to be taken with food
	Raltegravir	1st line bictegravir or dolutegravir are recommended	Rare	Twice-daily dosing, but new once-daily form approved in 2016
CCR5 antagonists	Maraviroc	2nd line	Rare	CYP interactions; twice-daily dosing
Attachment inhibitors	Fostemsavir	Salvage	Rare	Oral twice daily dosing
Postattachment inhibitors	Ibalizumab-uiyk	Salvage	Rare	IV injection every 14 days

CCR5 = C-C chemokine receptor Type 5
CYP = cytochrome P450
GI = gastrointestinal
HIV = human immunodeficiency virus
HLA = human leukocyte antigen

IV = intravenous
PI = protease inhibitor
TAF = tenofovir alafenamide
TDF = tenofovir disoproxil fumarate

INFECTIOUS DISEASE

Nucleoside/Nucleotide Reverse Transcriptase Inhibitors (NRTIs)

NRTIs are drug analogs of the deoxynucleotides needed to synthesize viral DNA. They inhibit the replication of HIV by competing with the normal deoxynucleotides. When an NRTI is incorporated into the growing viral DNA, the growing chain terminates, and that DNA cannot be incorporated into the cell's DNA or produce more HIV.

Nonnucleoside Reverse Transcriptase Inhibitors (NNRTIs)

NNRTIs work differently from NRTIs. These make the reverse transcriptase ineffective by binding to a different site on the enzyme.

Protease Inhibitors (PIs)

PIs inhibit the HIV protease enzyme that is involved with processing the final assembly of the virion. PIs are typically given with low-dose ritonavir or cobicistat, which inhibit metabolism of the drug to "boost" blood levels. This allows for increased efficacy and less frequent dosing.

Fusion Inhibitors (FIs)

FIs bind to and alter the structure of the gp41 glycoprotein on the HIV envelope, which is required for fusion of the virus with the CD4+ cell. The only one that is available is enfuvirtide. It is not a 1st line drug and is reserved for treatment of multidrug-resistant HIV infection.

Integrase Strand Transfer Inhibitors (INSTIs)

INSTIs prevent the HIV integrase enzyme from inserting HIV's reverse-transcribed DNA into an infected cell's own DNA, halting this critical step in the life cycle of HIV. They cause the most rapid decline in viral loads of any agent.

C-C Chemokine Receptor Type 5 (CCR5) Antagonists

CCR5 antagonists prevent the binding of HIV to the CCR5 coreceptor. The only one available is maraviroc. Not all HIV strains use this coreceptor, so test for this using a coreceptor tropism assay prior to considering treatment with this agent.

Attachment Inhibitors

Attachment inhibitors bind to the envelope gp120 glycoprotein and prevent it from binding to the CD4 cell surface. There is only 1 agent in this class: fostemsavir. It is indicated for those individuals failing therapy with other 1st and 2nd line drugs.

Postattachment Inhibitors

Postattachment inhibitors are monoclonal antibodies that bind to the CD4 receptor. They do not prevent HIV from binding to this receptor, but they do prevent subsequent binding to CCR5 and C-X-C chemokine receptor Type 4 (CXCR4) and thus prevent HIV from entering the cell.

Recommended Combination Regimens

According to the 2021 Guidelines for the Use of Antiretroviral Agents in Adults and Adolescents with HIV from the National Institutes of Health and 2020 recommendations of the International Antiviral Society-USA Panel, there are 4 preferred initial treatment regimens that all use an INSTI (either bictegravir or dolutegravir) and 1 or 2 NRTIs:

- Bictegravir + tenofovir + emtricitabine
- Dolutegravir + abacavir + lamivudine
- Dolutegravir + (emtricitabine or lamivudine) + tenofovir
- Dolutegravir + lamivudine

There are some recommendations that help choose the best regimen:

- Patients coinfected with HBV should receive 1 of the first 3 regimens because they contain agents that are active against this virus.
- Bictegravir should be avoided in persons who are pregnant or could become pregnant because there is insufficient safety data in that population.
- The last regimen (dolutegravir + lamivudine) has been studied only in individuals with viral loads of < 500,000 copies and no opportunistic infections, so it should be used only in that population.

Always conduct genotypic resistance testing prior to treatment but wait for results only if you are using the last regimen.

Prior to giving abacavir, test all patients for the *HLA-B*5701* allele; if positive, do not give patients abacavir. Such patients are at high risk for a severe hypersensitivity reaction.

When to Change HIV Therapy

It's time to change therapy when:

- There is virologic failure as defined as two consecutive viral loads > 200 copies/mL
- The patient becomes intolerant to ≥ 1 of the drugs

In these circumstances, base changes to therapy on resistance testing done while the patient is still taking the current regimen. Start the patient on a regimen of 3 drugs to which the virus is susceptible and that will not cross-react with side effects from prior medications. If a patient is not taking a medication reliably, the resistance testing may not show any mutations.

It is also reasonable to pursue "treatment simplification" when patients have complete viral suppression on a 3-drug regimen and there are no mutations to any of the drugs in 2-drug regimens. The drug regimens that have been shown to maintain viral suppression are 1) dolutegravir and rilpivirine; 2) a boosted PI and lamivudine; 3) dolutegravir and lamivudine; or 4) a long-acting injectable combination of cabotegravir and rilpivirine dosed every 4–8 weeks.

Preexposure Prophylaxis to Prevent Sexual Acquisition of HIV

Several studies have shown that once-daily administration of tenofovir-emtricitabine is very effective for decreasing rates of HIV transmission in high-risk populations such as men who have sex with men, patients with frequent/multiple partners, and HIV-discordant couples. In 2012, the FDA approved this combination for HIV-negative persons in such risk groups.

Postexposure Prophylaxis for Health Care Workers

Transmission of HIV from patients to health care workers is rare, with the risk from needlestick being 0.33% (1:300) and the risk from mucous membrane contact with bloody secretions being 0.09% (1:1,100). Transmission has only been documented to occur from bloody fluids and only when these fluids are injected or come into contact with nonintact skin or mucous membranes. If both of these conditions are met, vigorously wash the area with soap and water (flush the mucous membranes with saline) and give postexposure prophylaxis immediately with a 3-drug combination of 2 NRTIs plus an INSTI. This can be altered based on the index patient's HIV resistance pattern. Treatment is for 4 weeks; test the health care worker for HIV at baseline, 6 weeks, 12 weeks, and 6 months. If the index patient has an undetectable viral load, the risk of transmission is much lower than that stated above.

Pregnancy and Antiretroviral Therapy (ART)

An additional benefit of treating all pregnant women with HIV infection is reducing the risk of vertical transmission from 25% to < 1%. The vast majority of antiretrovirals are considered safe in pregnancy. The only ones that are currently not recommended are lopinavir/ritonavir, cobicistat-containing agents, etavirine, maraviroc, and enfurvitide. There are a few drugs for which there is insufficient data; these are doravirine, balizumab, and fostemsavir.

Treat all HIV-infected pregnant women with ART regardless of their CD4 level or viral load. The goal is to make their viral load undetectable. Always do initial resistance testing.

With respect to labor and delivery, give zidovudine to all HIV-infected pregnant women whose viral load is > 1,000 copies/mL as a continuous infusion during labor in addition to their current ART therapy, and deliver the baby by C-section.

EARLY HIV INFECTION

Early HIV infection is the term used for the first 6 months of infection. The majority of individuals will become ill with a flulike or mononucleosis-like syndrome that occurs 2–4 weeks after initial infection and lasts 1–2 weeks. Patients with early HIV infection present with some or all of the following:

- Fever
- Lymphadenopathy
- Pharyngitis
- Rash (usually erythematous and maculopapular with lesions on the face, trunk, or extremities; can include the palms and soles)
- Painful, mucocutaneous ulcerations involving the mouth, esophagus, or genitals
- Myalgias or arthralgias
- Aseptic meningitis

The HIV enzyme immunoassay (EIA) antibody test becomes positive at 3–7 weeks after exposure, so it is typically not positive during primary HIV infection. The diagnosis is made by assaying plasma p24 HIV antigen, which, with current assays, can detect infection as early as 5 days after the patient has acquired the virus. Give ART to all patients with primary HIV infection.

HIV / AIDS OPPORTUNISTIC INFECTIONS (OIs) AND OPPORTUNISTIC MALIGNANCIES

Introduction

OIs are caused by microorganisms that do not usually cause disease unless the host is immunocompromised. In the setting of immunosuppression, such as in HIV/AIDS, these microorganisms are able to take advantage of the weakened host, and the OIs for which a patient is at risk depends on the patient's CD4 cell count. Opportunistic malignancies are those that occur with a markedly higher frequency in HIV-infected persons.

OIs in HIV-infected persons typically present in 1 of 4 ways:

1) **Pulmonary symptoms:** dyspnea, cough, fever—think of:
   - Bacterial pneumonia
   - *Pneumocystis jirovecii* pneumonia (a.k.a. PCP; *Pneumocystis* pneumonia)
   - TB
   - Endemic fungi
2) **Systemic symptoms:** fever and wasting—think of:
   - *Mycobacterium avium* complex (MAC)
   - Cytomegalovirus (CMV)
3) **CNS symptoms:** altered mental status, focal defects, seizures—think of:
   - Cryptococcosis
   - Toxoplasmosis
   - Progressive multifocal leukoencephalopathy
   - Neurosyphilis
4) **GI symptoms:**
   - Odynophagia—think of:
     ◦ Candidiasis
     ◦ Viral infections (e.g., CMV, HSV)
   - Chronic diarrhea—think of:
     ◦ Parasitic infections (e.g., *Cystoisospora, Cyclospora, Cryptosporidium, Microsporidium*)
     ◦ Bacterial infections (e.g., *Salmonella, Shigella, Campylobacter*)
     ◦ CMV

INFECTIOUS DISEASE

Common infections and skin findings in HIV disease include:

- Persistent or recurrent seborrheic dermatitis
- Tinea infections (ringworm)
- Psoriasis
- Molluscum contagiosum
- Folliculitis
- Recurrent HSV and varicella-zoster virus
- Recurrent vaginal and oral candidiasis
- Oral hairy leukoplakia

HIV and Pulmonary Infections

Bacterial Pneumonia

Because of the successful implementation of primary and secondary prophylaxis against *Pneumocystis*, bacterial pneumonia is the most common pulmonary infection in HIV-infected persons. The presentation and bacteriology of these infections are similar to those in non–HIV-infected persons and are discussed in Immunosuppressed Patients in the Pulmonary Medicine section.

Pneumocystis jirovecii Pneumonia (PJP)

PJP (a.k.a. PCP and *Pneumocystis* pneumonia) is a fungal infection acquired via the respiratory route. This pneumonia is the 2nd most common pulmonary infection in patients with HIV and is the presenting illness in 50% of patients with AIDS. 90% of patients with PJP have a CD4 count of < 200 cells/µL (0.2×10^9/L).

Unlike bacterial pneumonia, PJP has an insidious onset of fever, shortness of breath, and dry cough that usually worsens over weeks, not days. There is minimal inflammatory response, which accounts for the lack of sputum production and the rarity of pleuritic pain.

Arterial blood gases typically show a primary respiratory alkalosis. An increased A-a gradient is common along with hypoxia. Lactate dehydrogenase (LDH) is elevated (> 400 U/L [6.68 µkat/L]), and liver transaminases are normal. The chest x-ray (CXR) usually shows a diffuse, bilateral "batwing" infiltrate, although it is sometimes lobar or unilateral. In 10–15% of patients, the CXR is normal, but a CT scan of the chest typically reveals infiltrates.

Diagnosis is made by methenamine silver stain (Figure 4-15) or immunostain of pulmonary secretions, from either induced sputum or bronchoalveolar lavage (BAL) or PCR testing of sputum samples if available.

Base treatment on disease severity. Patients with mild to moderate disease have a partial pressure of oxygen (pO$_2$) > 60 mmHg. Those with severe disease have a pO$_2$ < 60 mmHg.

Treat PJP with high-dose TMP/SMX for 3 weeks. Use oral regimens for mild to moderate disease and the IV form for severe disease. Patients with AIDS have a 15% incidence

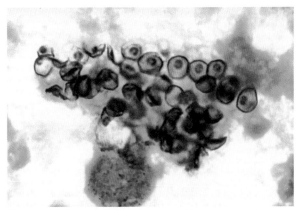

Figure 4-15: Pneumocystis pneumonia. Methenamine silver stains cyst walls black.

of sulfa allergy, so 2nd line drugs are often needed. Treat mild to moderate PJP with clindamycin + primaquine or atovaquone. Treat severe disease with clindamycin + primaquine or IV pentamidine. They appear equally effective yet pentamidine has more adverse reactions.

Give all patients with an A-a gradient ≥ 35 mmHg or a pO$_2$ < 70 mmHg glucocorticoids concurrently with antibiotics to prevent worsening respiratory failure due to the increased inflammation incited by the killing of the fungal organisms.

TMP/SMX side effects include neutropenia/leukopenia, skin rash, nausea/vomiting, and occasionally fever. TMP/SMX blocks tubular K$^+$ secretion and can cause severe hyperkalemia, especially at the high doses used to treat PJP.

Possible side effects of pentamidine use include neutropenia/leukopenia, nausea, arrhythmias, renal failure, hypoglycemia, pancreatitis, and hypotension. Long courses of pentamidine may destroy the β cells of the pancreas, causing diabetes mellitus.

Primary prophylaxis is the term used when prophylaxis is given to a patient with no prior history of the OI. **Secondary prophylaxis** is what is given when a patient has a history of previous treatment for that OI.

Double-strength (DS) TMP/SMX 1×/day is the regimen of choice with an alternative of 1 DS TMP/SMX 3×/week. Start primary prophylaxis when the CD4 count is < 200 cells/µL (0.2×10^9/L). Give secondary prophylaxis after a full course of treatment for PJP. Stop PJP prophylaxis when the CD4 count is > 200 cells/µL (0.2×10^9/L) for ≥ 3 months in response to ART.

If a patient cannot tolerate TMP/SMX, dapsone with concomitant pyrimethamine and leucovorin, aerosolized pentamidine, or atovaquone are alternative prophylactic agents. Atovaquone is more efficacious than dapsone and has a lower incidence of side effects than TMP/SMX, but it is much more expensive than the other agents. TMP/SMX also provides prophylaxis against toxoplasmosis (see *Toxoplasma gondii* on page 4-63).

Tuberculosis (TB)

Most cases of TB in HIV-infected patients are the reactivation of a prior asymptomatic infection and thus occur in those with the usual risk factors for TB (e.g., homelessness, institutionalization, IV drug misuse, birth in an endemic country). Reactivation occurs at the rate of 3–16% per year in patients coinfected with HIV and TB.

TB typically presents as a chronic pneumonia but with a presentation different from that in patients without HIV. Specifically, infiltrates can be absent or diffuse, and cavitation is uncommon. Patients can also present with an acute pneumonia, clinically similar to bacterial community-acquired pneumonia. It may also present as cervical lymph node infection, known as scrofula. Disseminated disease is more common in HIV-infected persons.

Diagnose TB in the usual fashion by demonstrating acid-fast bacilli (AFB) by smear or culture of the sputum, of a BAL specimen, a bronchial biopsy specimen, or lymph node biopsy.

Treat patients with a 4-drug regimen of isoniazid, rifampin, ethambutol, and pyrazinamide × 2 months and then narrow the regimen to isoniazid + rifampin (or rifabutin) × 4 months unless resistance is suspected or proven.

Rifampin may have to be replaced by rifabutin or other drugs in patients with HIV and TB coinfection because of extensive drug interactions with antiretroviral drugs, specifically if PIs are being used. Rifabutin dosing also needs adjustments because of these drug interactions.

See the Pulmonary Medicine section under Immunosuppressed Patients for more information on treatment.

Prevention of active TB in HIV-infected persons is facilitated by annual screening for latent infection with either a TB skin test (purified protein derivative [PPD] test) or an interferon gamma release assay (IGRA). Both can be negative in highly immunocompromised patients.

Give isoniazid for 9 months to all HIV/AIDS patients with a +PPD (> 5 mm) or +IGRA result without signs of active disease.

Endemic Fungi

Histoplasma, *Blastomyces*, and *Coccidioides* are the endemic fungi that cause pulmonary infections in HIV-infected individuals. These infections are more likely to be severe as well as to disseminate (in which case they constitute an AIDS-defining illness). These fungi are discussed individually under Fungal Infections on page 4-57.

Systemic Infections

Mycobacterium avium Complex (MAC) Infection

MAC consists of 10 species, by far the most common of which are *M. avium* and *M. intracellulare*. MAC causes a chronic pulmonary infection in immunocompetent patients. It is ubiquitous in the environment. The infection is acquired by the respiratory or GI route, and when the CD4 count drops to < 50 cells/µL (0.05×10^9/L), symptoms can occur.

In patients with HIV infection, MAC usually presents as a disseminated infection, causing a wasting syndrome with fever, weight loss, night sweats, lymphadenopathy, hepatosplenomegaly, diarrhea, and abdominal pain.

Confirm the diagnosis by culturing MAC from blood or body fluids or from biopsies of involved organs, such as the lung, bowel, and lymph nodes.

Treat MAC infection with clarithromycin (preferred over azithromycin) + ethambutol. For resistant isolates, other drugs (rifampin or rifabutin, a fluoroquinolone or an aminoglycoside) may be used.

Although it was previously recommended to give primary prophylaxis for MAC infection if the CD4 count was < 50 cells/µL, primary prophylaxis is no longer recommended since the 2018 CDC Guidelines for the Prevention and Treatment of Opportunistic Infections in Adults and Adolescents with HIV. This is because ART can usually produce a rise in CD4 counts above this level in a matter of weeks.

Cytomegalovirus (CMV) Infection

CMV infection can present as colitis with diarrhea and/or a wasting syndrome and is by far the most common cause of retinitis in HIV-infected persons (see Cytomegalovirus (CMV) on page 4-75). Less common manifestations are esophagitis and encephalitis. Most patients with these manifestations have a CD4 count < 50 cells/µL (0.05×10^9/L), which is why ART has dropped the incidence of new cases by ≥ 95%. Diagnosis is made by characteristic retinal exam (hemorrhage and vascular sheathing) or demonstration of the virus histologically in tissue or via PCR in blood. Treatment is with ganciclovir or valganciclovir. Second line are foscarnet and cidofovir. Primary prophylaxis is not recommended. Secondary prophylaxis is with valganciclovir, which can be stopped after 3–6 months if the CD4 count remains > 100 cells/µL (0.05×10^9/L).

Central Nervous System (CNS) Infections

Cryptococcus

C. neoformans and *C. gattii* are endemic worldwide. Although they cause disease in both immunocompetent and immunosuppressed individuals, most HIV-infected patients have a CD4 count of < 100 cells/µL (0.1×10^9/L) at the time of diagnosis, and the fungus commonly presents as a subacute meningitis with or without disseminated disease.

The most common presentation is a subacute meningitis or meningoencephalitis that is very different than bacterial meningitis. Subtle signs of headache, decreased mental status, personality changes, and memory loss may be the only manifestations and are due to increased intracranial pressure, not invasion of the organism. The organism may also cause pneumonia and/or skin lesions that are often umbilicated.

INFECTIOUS DISEASE

Detection of cryptococcal antigen in the CSF or serum is diagnostic and is seen in the vast majority of infected patients.

Treat cryptococcal meningitis in 3 stages:

1) Induction with liposomal amphotericin B + flucytosine × 2 weeks

2) Consolidation with fluconazole 400 mg/day for ≥ 8 weeks

3) Maintenance with fluconazole 200 mg/day for ≥ 1 year

Opening pressure is usually elevated. Repeating LP to remove CSF on a daily basis is necessary to obtain normal CSF pressures and prevent further CNS injury. If this is not possible or effective, insert CSF shunts.

If the patient presents with a cryptococcal lung infection, you must still perform an LP to investigate for meningitis, even if the patient is asymptomatic.

There is no primary prophylaxis used for this infection. Give secondary prophylaxis as part of the maintenance stage of treatment.

Because the immune reconstitution syndrome is common and can cause worsening and irreversible CNS disease, it is recommended that ART be delayed until after the induction treatment period.

Toxoplasma

T. gondii is the most common cause of focal lesions in the CNS in HIV-infected persons. Typical symptoms of toxoplasmosis are new-onset seizures, focal neurologic deficit, and/or altered consciousness. MRI (which is more sensitive) and CT show multiple ring-enhancing lesions in the gray matter and/or basal ganglia. The main differential diagnoses are primary B-cell lymphoma and brain abscesses.

Diagnose toxoplasmosis using imaging that shows typical lesions and has IgG antibody to *T. gondii*. Confirmation is by demonstrating radiographic improvement with empiric treatment. PCR testing of CSF is highly specific but has only a 50% sensitivity. A biopsy is not initially needed if imaging is typical and there is a response to therapy.

Treat toxoplasmosis with pyrimethamine and sulfadiazine. Also give folinic acid (a.k.a. leucovorin) to prevent megaloblastic anemia from the pyrimethamine. Use clindamycin in sulfa-allergic patients. Failure to respond warrants a brain biopsy.

Primary prophylaxis is indicated in patients with a CD4 count < 100 cells/μL (0.1 × 10^9/L) and a positive *T. gondii* IgG result. It is accomplished with the same regimen used for PJP prophylaxis (i.e., DS TMP/SMX 1×/day or 3×/week). Use dapsone in sulfa-allergic patients. In addition, as with primary prophylaxis against PJP, primary prophylaxis for *Toxoplasma* encephalitis can be stopped when the CD4 count is > 200 cells/μL (0.2 × 10^9/L) for 3 months.

JC Virus (JCV)

JCV is a commonly acquired asymptomatic infection. If the CD4 count drops to < 100 cells/μL (0.1 × 10^9/L), JCV can reactivate and cause a lytic infection in oligodendroglial cells that make central myelin. This results in **progressive multifocal leukoencephalopathy** (PML) which, because it is multifocal, has varied and widespread presentations. Patients experience altered mental status, motor and sensory changes, and specifically decreased visual acuity.

The diagnosis is suggested by an MRI showing multifocal demyelinating lesions in the white matter and can be confirmed by CSF PCR testing for JCV, which has a sensitivity of 70–90%.

No specific antiviral therapy is available; however, reconstitution of CD4 cells after ART can reverse some (but not all) symptoms.

Neurosyphilis

Syphilis, even if previously treated, can reactivate in patients with AIDS and cause neurosyphilis. Syphilis and neurosyphilis are treated the same, with or without HIV infection (refer to Syphilis on page 4-18).

Gastrointestinal (GI) Infections

Esophagitis

Candida albicans is the most common cause of infectious esophagitis in patients with HIV infection. Viral causes include CMV and HSV. Patients can be infected with more than one of these at the same time. Consider a coexistent viral infection if the symptoms do not improve after empirically treating the candidal infection with fluconazole. Because the response to therapy is usually dramatic, no prophylaxis for candidal esophagitis is recommended.

Diarrhea

Chronic diarrhea in patients with AIDS is commonly caused by protozoa: *Cryptosporidium*, microsporidia (includes *Enterocytozoon bieneusi* and *Encephalitozoon intestinalis*), *Cyclospora cayetanensis*, and *Cystoisospora belli* (previously known as *Isospora belli*). All of these can also infect the gallbladder and cause acalculous cholecystitis. Bacterial pathogens (e.g., *Salmonella*, *Shigella*, *Campylobacter*) cause an acute diarrhea that may persist and become chronic.

CMV is the only common viral cause of diarrhea.

Stool or bowel biopsy specimens are diagnostic and require modified acid-fast staining to detect *Cryptosporidium*, *Cyclospora*, and *Cystoisospora*. Microsporidia are seen with a modified trichrome stain. PCR assays are now available to detect all of these organisms in stool.

CMV can be diagnosed by biopsy of the ulcers or erosions during endoscopy. (Remember, if the patient has CMV colitis, check for ocular involvement.)

Treat *Cyclospora* and *Cystoisospora* infections with TMP/SMX. *Cryptosporidium* is treated with nitazoxanide. Microsporidia is treated with albendazole. ART with immune reconstitution will also hasten organism clearance. Treat *Salmonella*, *Shigella*, and *Campylobacter* infections with ciprofloxacin. Treat CMV with ganciclovir or foscarnet.

Miscellaneous Infections

Hepatitis C Virus (HCV)

Test all HIV-infected patients for HCV. Treat hepatitis C with the current well-tolerated, short-term regimens. HIV is generally treated first. Hepatitis C treatment is covered in the Gastroenterology section under Liver.

AIDS-Defining Malignancies

Although there is evidence that there is a higher frequency of many malignancies in HIV-infected persons, 4 are considered AIDS defining. These are Kaposi sarcoma, cervical cancer, high-grade non-Hodgkin lymphoma, and primary B-cell lymphoma of the brain. These are discussed in the Oncology section under Miscellaneous Cancers.

FEVER OF UNKNOWN ORIGIN (FUO)

PREVIEW | REVIEW

- What are the most common identifiable causes of fever of unknown origin (FUO)?

FUO was initially defined as documented fever on several occasions for ≥ 3 weeks with no etiology identified on routine evaluation after 1 week in the hospital. During the past 50 years, the definition has changed, and a hospital stay is no longer necessary, nor is a several-week course of investigation. Causes vary geographically due to regional exposures, diagnostic tools, and health care availability. They also differ based on the host, especially in HIV-infected persons, and in older persons. Overall, the most common identifiable causes of FUO are rheumatic diseases (e.g., rheumatoid arthritis, SLE), infections, and malignancies.

Routine evaluation must be unrevealing to diagnose FUO. This includes a history, physical, CBC with differential, comprehensive metabolic panel, blood culture, urinalysis, urine culture, and CXR.

Once FUO is established, further workup may include:

- ESR or CRP
- Serum protein electrophoresis (SPEP)
- Rheumatoid factor (RF)
- LDH
- Creatine kinase (CK)
- Antinuclear antibody (ANA)
- HIV

- TB screening
- Heterophile antibody test
- Echocardiogram
- CT scan of the abdomen
- CT scan of the chest
- Gallium or indium WBC scan

Unless a patient is clinically unstable, do not use empiric therapy in cases of FUO; patients are usually stable. Treatment is directed toward the underlying etiology once discovered. The diagnostic evaluation in up to 25% of patients with FUO fails to identify a cause; however, these patients have a good prognosis. If the initial workup is negative and the fever persists, repeat the same workup in several months.

FEBRILE NEUTROPENIA

PREVIEW | REVIEW

- What is the definition of febrile neutropenia?
- What are the empiric treatment options for the patient with febrile neutropenia? When is vancomycin included?
- In the empiric treatment of febrile neutropenia, when would you choose voriconazole over an echinocandin?

EPIDEMIOLOGY AND RISK FACTORS

Neutropenia occurs in the setting of leukemia, bone marrow transplantation, chemotherapy, exposure to drugs or toxins, and bone marrow metastasis. If infection ensues, it is usually caused by colonizing flora that enter the bloodstream across disrupted gut mucosa, via an IV catheter, or through the oropharynx into the lungs and/or sinuses.

Neutropenic sepsis can be caused by both gram-negative bacteria (GNB) and gram-positive bacteria (GPB). Of the gram-positives, the most common are *Staphylococcus aureus*, *Staphylococcus epidermidis*, and streptococcal species. Less common are *Corynebacterium* species, *Cutibacterium acnes* (previously known as *Propionibacterium acnes*), *Bacillus* species, and *Leuconostoc* species. These less-common gram-positives are important to remember because they may not be effectively treated with vancomycin. Common gram-negative organisms include *Pseudomonas* species and Enterobacteriaceae, including *Escherichia coli*, *Klebsiella* species, and *Enterobacter* species. Anaerobic bacteria are not commonly seen in neutropenic sepsis.

Fungi, such as *Candida* and *Aspergillus* species, are important pathogens in patients with prolonged neutropenia. Infections with *Fusarium* species and agents of mucormycosis can also occur.

INFECTIOUS DISEASE

The risk for infection in the patient with neutropenia is directly proportional to the degree and duration of neutropenia.

For an additional discussion of febrile neutropenia, see the Oncology section under Febrile Neutropenia.

PRESENTATION

It is important to recognize febrile neutropenia and begin emergent evaluation and empiric antibiotics. The definition of febrile neutropenia is a temperature of > 101.0°F (38.3°C) × 1 occurrence or 100.4°F (38.0°C) for 1 hour and severe neutropenia, defined as an absolute neutrophil count (ANC) < 500/µL (0.5×10^9/L) or expected to be < 500/µL (0.5×10^9/L) in the next 48 hours.

The decrease in neutrophils creates a blunted inflammatory response, so clinical signs and symptoms that localize the source of infection may be absent. Any localizing symptoms (e.g., sore throat, cough, dysuria, perirectal pain), however, are helpful in determining the source. For the physical examination, concentrate on the upper airway mucosa (looking for mucositis), teeth and periodontal tissues, eyes, and rectum. Any rash or skin ulceration/swelling is potentially significant. Portals that allow infections to enter include catheters and implants.

DIAGNOSIS

Send blood cultures immediately and obtain a CXR. Perform a urine culture if there are UTI symptoms or a bladder catheter is in place. Obtain a sputum culture if there are pulmonary signs or symptoms or if the CXR shows infiltrates. If the CXR is normal in a patient with pulmonary symptoms, obtain a CT scan of the chest. If diarrhea is present, send a stool sample for *Clostridioides difficile* toxin gene PCR testing.

Reserve LP for patients with altered mental status without an identifiable cause or other signs of meningitis. Remember that these patients are usually thrombocytopenic. There should be a low threshold for bronchoscopy for pathology, Gram stains, and bacterial/viral/fungal cultures in patients with pulmonary infiltrates. Open lung biopsy may be needed. Perform skin biopsies for pathology and bacterial and fungal smears and cultures when lesions are present.

TREATMENT

Empiric Treatment

Patients are usually treated as inpatients with intravenous antibiotics unless they are deemed unlikely to have serious illness based on scoring systems like the Multinational Association for Supportive Care of Cancer (MASCC) and the Clinical Index of Stable Febrile Neutropenia (CISNE) calculators.

According to the 2011 IDSA guidelines, when a patient with neutropenia presents with fever, the initial treatment is directed against gram-negative aerobic bacilli, including *Pseudomonas*. The 2018 IDSA clinical practice guideline update adds that oral empiric treatment can be used in patients at low risk of complications, and the regimen of choice is a combination of amoxicillin/clavulanic acid and ciprofloxacin.

Treat patients with fever and neutropenia with 1 of the following:

1) Piperacillin/tazobactam

2) A carbapenem (imipenem or meropenem)

3) Cefepime

Do not include vancomycin as part of the initial regimen unless any of the following are present:

- Hypotension or other evidence of severe sepsis
- A positive blood culture for GPB (before the organism or susceptibility is determined)
- Pneumonia documented radiographically
- Persistent fever while on empiric antibiotics
- Obvious skin infection or erythema at the site of an indwelling catheter
- A history of MRSA infection or known colonization
- Severe mucositis

If vancomycin is started, discontinue it after 2 days if there is no evidence of a gram-positive infection.

Persistent Febrile Neutropenia

If the fever and neutropenia persist after 4–7 days on empiric antibiotics (including vancomycin), begin adding empiric antifungal therapy with:

- an echinocandin (caspofungin is the only one approved by the FDA for this indication, but other echinocandins are equally effective) or
- voriconazole.

Use voriconazole instead of an echinocandin if there are pulmonary infiltrates, because voriconazole more predictably treats *Aspergillus* infection.

Prophylaxis

According to the ASCO and IDSA guidelines of 2018, prophylactic antibiotics should be given to individuals at high risk of febrile neutropenia as defined as those expected to have an ANC ≤ 100/µL (0.1×10^9/L) for > 7 days. Prophylaxis should include a fluoroquinolone and a triazole.

Septic Shock

The management of septic shock is covered in the Pulmonary Medicine section under Critical Care. The infectious disease approach is the same for each specific entity that can cause sepsis (e.g., bacteremia, UTI, pneumonia, cholangitis). Sepsis intensifies the urgency of the workup and critical care management.

NOSOCOMIAL INFECTIONS

PREVIEW | REVIEW

- Differentiate the 2 types of nosocomial pneumonias.
- Which organisms usually cause a central line–associated bloodstream infection?

OVERVIEW

Important nosocomial infections include pneumonia and central line–associated bloodstream infections (CLABSIs). UTIs and *Clostridioides difficile* infections are discussed under Urinary Tract Infections (UTIs) on page 4-1 and Diarrhea due to *Clostridioides difficile* on page 4-14. Standard precautions begin with hand hygiene but may also include gowns, gloves, and respiratory protective equipment.

PNEUMONIA

Hospital-acquired pneumonia is defined as pneumonia occurring > 48 hours after hospital admission (and that was not incubating at the time of admission). **Ventilator-associated pneumonia** is defined as pneumonia occurring > 48–72 hours after intubation. **Health care–associated pneumonia** is no longer recognized as an entity. The 2019 IDSA guidelines on the treatment of adults with pneumonia no longer recommends the term "hospital-acquired pneumonia" but rather encourages using clinical risk factors to assess the likelihood of resistant pathogens such as MRSA and *P. aeruginosa*.

Nosocomial pneumonias are almost always bacterial and have the highest mortality rate of all the nosocomial infections. They are most commonly due to gram-negative organisms and *Staphylococcus aureus*.

The diagnosis is based on a combination of findings, including a new infiltrate on chest imaging, fever, increased and purulent sputum, leukocytosis or leukopenia, and increased oxygenation requirements. Obtain sputum and blood cultures; however, note that the former can be nonspecific, especially if prior antibiotics were administered.

Major risk factors for acquisition of and infection from MRSA and *P. aeruginosa* are known prior colonization and/or antibiotics in the past 90 days. In patients with ventilator-associated pneumonia, additional risk factors are septic shock, ARDS, hospital stay ≥ 5 days, and kidney disease.

If MRSA treatment is warranted based on risk or culture results, use vancomycin or linezolid. If treatment for *P. aeruginosa* or other potentially resistant gram-negative bacilli is warranted, options include use piperacillin/tazobactam, ceftazidime, cefepime, aztreonam, meropenem, and imipenem). Adjust the antibiotics if an organism cultured from the sputum or blood is resistant to the initial therapy.

CENTRAL LINE–ASSOCIATED BLOODSTREAM INFECTIONS (CLABSIs)

Central line infections are usually due to *Staphylococcus epidermidis* and *Staphylococcus aureus*, but almost any organism can cause infection, including GNBs, *Candida* species, and *Corynebacterium jeikeium*. An IV catheter-related infection presents as sepsis without symptoms localizing to the line or as a localized infection of the subcutaneous tunnel and/or of the exit site with purulence and erythema at the site. Septic thrombophlebitis of the catheterized vein and/or right-sided endocarditis can also occur and result in septic pulmonary emboli.

When a CLABSI is suspected, obtain 2 blood cultures from 2 peripheral sites. Culturing blood through the line is no longer recommended because of an unacceptable rate of false-positive cultures resulting in unnecessary antibiotics and/or line removal. If the line is removed, culturing the tip is also no longer recommended because of a low positive-predictive value. Diagnosis of a CLABSI is made when there is no other identifiable source and ≥ 1 peripheral blood culture is positive for *S. aureus*, enterococci, Enterobacteriaceae, *Candida*, or *Bacillus* (*not B. anthracis*). For other organisms that are common skin flora, such as coagulase-negative staphylococci, *Corynebacterium*, and viridans streptococci, 2 blood cultures are required to be positive to make the diagnosis.

Once the diagnosis is made, the line should be removed except under uncommon scenarios. This is critical if the patient has sepsis, metastatic infection, endocarditis, suppurative thrombophlebitis, an associated intravascular clot, or infection of a subcutaneous tunnel or port. The following organisms also require removal to have a chance of cure: *S. aureus, P. aeruginosa*, multidrug resistance GNBs, and Candida. Long-term catheter line infections from other GNBs, coagulase-negative staphylococci, or enterococci, if uncomplicated, can be treated with the line in place; treatment should be at least 14 days from the last negative blood culture. If lines are removed, treatment is for 14 days after the last negative blood culture, or 4 weeks for *S. aureus*.

Empiric antibiotic treatment is with vancomycin alone, with the following 2 exceptions:

1) Give gram-negative coverage (that includes *P. aeruginosa*) if there is neutropenia or severe sepsis, the patient is known to be colonized with a resistant GNB, or the patient has a femoral line, which predisposes that patient to a fecal flora infection.

2) Give antifungal therapy with an echinocandin if the patient has previously been on broad-spectrum antibacterials, has > 1 site colonized with *Candida* species, has a hematologic malignancy, is on total parenteral nutrition, or has a femoral line.

Treat infections for 14 days after line removal. In cases of *S. aureus* infections of long-term catheters, give antibiotics for 4–6 weeks.

INFECTION CONTROL AND ISOLATION

Health care workers are at risk for acquisition of pathogens from patients and the environment. This topic reviews the types of precautions.

Needlesticks and HIV were discussed under Human Immunodeficiency Virus (HIV) and Acquired Immunodeficiency Syndrome (AIDS) on page 4-32. For needlesticks, obtain hepatitis B and C and HIV serologies from the index patient. The health care worker should have been vaccinated against hepatitis B; if not, administer vaccination. If the index case is positive, give hepatitis B immunoglobulin as well. Obtain the same serologies from the health care worker, and follow up with laboratory studies based on the serologic test results from the index patient and health care worker. There is no prophylaxis for hepatitis C.

Standard precautions: All health care workers must wash their hands with soap and water or gel before and after entering a patient's room. Use soap and water for *Clostridioides difficile*, norovirus, and rotavirus. Since the advent of the COVID pandemic, surgical masks should be worn at all times and N95 masks should be worn if a patient is suspected or known to have COVID infection.

In addition to the standard precautions, take the following precautions depending on the scenario:

- **Contact precautions** (gloves and gown): *C. difficile*, scabies, norovirus, MRSA colonization
- **Droplet precautions** (mask): influenza, *Neisseria meningitidis*, pertussis, coronavirus
- **Airborne precautions** (private room, negative pressure, and N95-type mask): TB, varicella, measles
- **Contact and droplet precautions:** parainfluenza
- **Contact and airborne precautions:** disseminated zoster

Isolation for *C. difficile* was discussed under Diarrhea due to *Clostridioides difficile* on page 4-14. In general, isolate patients with multiple antibiotic-resistant bacteria as appropriate for the site of infection (e.g., contact isolation, droplet isolation).

ORGANISM-BASED REVIEW

BACTERIA

PREVIEW | REVIEW

- Which antibiotics are recommended to treat skin and soft tissue staphylococcal infections?
- What is the clinical presentation of toxic shock syndrome?
- How do blood culture results differ between staphylococcal and streptococcal toxic shock?
- When should you use 2 antibiotics to treat enterococcal infections? Which drugs would you choose?
- Which patient populations are at risk for *Listeria monocytogenes*, and how do you treat *Listeria*?

- If a pathology report describes beaded, branching, mildly acid-fast, filamentous organisms, which organism is likely?
- When should you suspect *Pseudomonas aeruginosa* as a cause of infection?
- Which form of plague (*Yersinia pestis* infection) is transmitted person to person?
- Which associated symptoms are often observed with *Legionella* pneumonia?
- Which geographic locations have the most cases of tularemia?
- What are the manifestations of bartonellosis?
- Name the clinical signs and symptoms of Rocky Mountain spotted fever. Which drugs are used for treatment?
- What is Q fever? How is it treated?
- How does *Mycobacterium marinum* infection present?
- Which associated symptoms are often seen in respiratory infections due to *Chlamydia pneumoniae*?

GRAM-POSITIVE BACTERIA (GPB)

Staphylococci

Staphylococcus aureus, which on Gram stain shows cocci in grapelike clusters, colonizes the anterior nares of ~ 20% of humans, and coagulase-negative staphylococci are ubiquitous on human skin. *S. aureus* is the most common cause of **soft tissue infections** and causes purulent infections that manifest as folliculitis, furuncles (boils)/carbuncles (Figure 4-16), and impetigo. Impetigo is the most common form of skin infection caused by *S. aureus* and is characterized by "honey-crusted" lesions that ooze purulent material. It is common after minute injuries to the skin. Patients often inaccurately report a spider bite when in fact they have a staphylococcal abscess. Treatment is based on the clinical presentation. (See Common Skin and Soft Tissue Infections on page 4-7.)

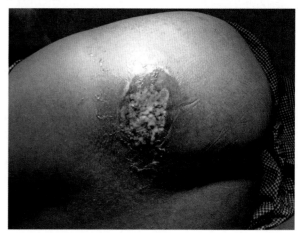

Figure 4-16: Carbuncle on buttock

S. aureus is a common cause of **bacteremia**, especially among those exposed to needles, such as people who use IV drugs, and patients who use insulin, are hospitalized, or are undergoing hemodialysis. *S. aureus* should never be considered a skin contaminant when it is seen in blood cultures. It is also a leading cause of **central line–associated bloodstream infection** (CLABSI).

Infection with *S. aureus* can also result in **toxic shock syndrome** (see Toxic Shock Syndrome (TSS)) and **staphylococcal scalded skin syndrome** (SSSS; Figure 4-17). The latter does not occur in adults unless they have chronic kidney disease because the toxin is otherwise easily excreted through the kidneys. SSSS is a desquamative dermatitis mediated by exfoliative toxins A and B. Bacteremia may or may not be present. Fever is common, and minimal friction applied to the skin results in removal of the superficial layers of epidermis (known as Nikolsky sign). The lesions are painful. Bullae are sterile when cultured, because the bacteria produce the toxin remotely.

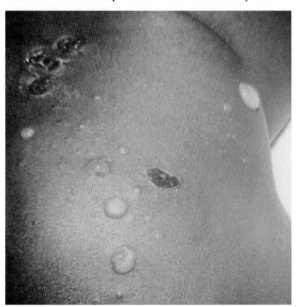

Figure 4-17: Staphylococcal scalded skin syndrome with Nikolsky sign

In addition, *S. aureus* superinfection is a common complication of influenza. *S. aureus* is also a typical cause of **osteomyelitis**.

Pathogenicity of *S. aureus* results from a variety of toxins. Only rare isolates are susceptible to PCN, and ~ 50% of isolates are methicillin-resistant *S. aureus* (MRSA) regardless of whether they are acquired from the community or in a health care setting. Methicillin resistance connotes resistance to all other β-lactam antibiotics, with the exception of ceftaroline.

General Treatment

Treatment is determined by the site and nature of the infection. If the lesion is a boil or an abscess, begin with incision and drainage and send for culture and susceptibility testing. Bacteremia and other serious *S. aureus* infections are initially treated with vancomycin until sensitivity results are available. If isolates are methicillin susceptible, then change therapy to an antistaphylococcal PCN (e.g., nafcillin) or a 1st generation cephalosporin. Otherwise, continue vancomycin. Very few cases of vancomycin-resistant *S. aureus* are reported worldwide. Additional drugs with predictable activity against MRSA include linezolid, tedizolid, tigecycline, ceftaroline, daptomycin, telavancin, dalbavancin, and oritavancin. Be aware that most of the additional drugs have no approved indication for bacteremia or serious disease.

For a boil or an abscess, begin with incision and drainage and send for culture and susceptibility testing.

Treat milder infections, including skin and soft tissue infections, with TMP/SMX or doxycycline, to which ~ 90% of strains remain susceptible, especially if known to be MRSA. Clindamycin has higher resistance rates so it should be used only if susceptibilities are known. If the infection is MSSA, use antistaphylococcal PCN or 1st generation cephalosporin

Avoid quinolones due to increasing resistance and the ability of the organism to acquire resistance while the patient is on therapy plus additional recognized toxicities. Delafloxacin was approved in 2017 with an indication for treating MRSA skin infections and is the only quinolone with reliable MRSA activity.

Toxic Shock Syndrome (TSS)

An important complication of *S. aureus* infection is TSS. Staphylococcal TSS presents with diffuse red skin (sunburn-like rash), hypotension, and fever along with ≥ 3 signs of organ system involvement: GI (e.g., vomiting, diarrhea), muscle (myalgia or elevated creatine kinase), acute kidney injury, liver (transaminase or bilirubin elevation), thrombocytopenia, or altered consciousness. Hypocalcemia can also occur. Bacteremia is uncommon. A strawberry tongue may be seen on exam, which can also be seen in scarlet fever and Kawasaki disease. The classic association is with retained tampon use during menses; however, currently the majority of cases are not related to menstruation. The majority of cases are caused by colonization of other foreign bodies (e.g., nasal packing) or *S. aureus* infection (e.g., cellulitis, pneumonia). Treatment is with fluids and pressors, source control, and antistaphylococcal antibiotics with the addition of clindamycin to inhibit toxin production.

Streptococcal TSS is the other classic form of TSS. See *Streptococcus pyogenes* (Group A) on page 4-46 for more on that topic.

Staphylococcus epidermidis and *S. saprophyticus*

S. epidermidis and *S. saprophyticus* are 2 species of coagulase-negative staphylococci that on Gram stain are seen in irregular clusters. *S. epidermidis* is usually methicillin resistant. It is the most common cause of both

INFECTIOUS DISEASE

catheter-related bacteremia and bacteremia occurring post-op when a foreign body (e.g., prosthetics [including heart valves and joints], pacemakers, shunts) is placed. Treat with vancomycin. Add rifampin and gentamicin for prosthetic valve endocarditis.

S. saprophyticus causes cystitis in women and, unlike other coagulase-negative staphylococci, is usually susceptible to antistaphylococcal PCNs and ampicillin.

Streptococcus pneumoniae

S. pneumoniae (pneumococcus) is the most common cause of bacterial meningitis and community-acquired bacterial pneumonia in adults. The former is discussed under Bacterial Meningitis on page 4-24, and the latter is discussed in the Pulmonary Medicine section under Community-Acquired Pneumonia (CAP). On Gram stain, *S. pneumoniae* appears as lancet-shaped diplococci. A history of splenectomy is a risk factor for infections due to encapsulated bacteria (e.g., *S. pneumoniae*). Remember that with influenza, there can be bacterial superinfection with *S. pneumoniae*.

Resistance to PCN occurs in ~ 5% of *S. pneumoniae* isolates, but all isolates are susceptible to vancomycin. Ceftriaxone sensitivity is > 95%. Do not use vancomycin for bacteremia unless resistance to other agents is present. Pneumonia is commonly treated with ceftriaxone or levofloxacin.

Streptococcus pyogenes (Group A)

S. pyogenes is the only group A β-hemolytic *Streptococcus* species. On Gram stain, it appears in chains. It causes the following:

- **Pharyngitis**/retropharyngeal abscess
  - The likelihood of having strep pharyngitis increases with the more Centor criteria a patient has: fever, sore throat, exudative pharyngitis, anterior cervical lymphadenopathy, absence of cough.
  - See Figure 4-18 and refer to Pharyngitis on page 4-6 for more information.
- **Scarlet fever**
  - Scarlet fever typically presents with a fine, diffuse, red rash in a patient with acute streptococcal pharyngitis (more common in children). The rash is due to streptococcal pyrogenic exotoxin.
  - Other symptoms include strawberry tongue (as seen with toxic shock syndrome [TSS]), circumoral pallor, Pastia lines (i.e., linear skin hemorrhage in the flexor skin creases of the elbow; pathognomonic for scarlet fever), and desquamation.
- **Skin infections**
  - **Impetigo** is the most common form of skin infection caused by *S. pyogenes* and is characterized by "honey-crusted" lesions that ooze purulent material. It is common after minute injuries to the skin.
  - **Erysipelas** is an acute β-hemolytic streptococcal infection of the upper dermis and superficial

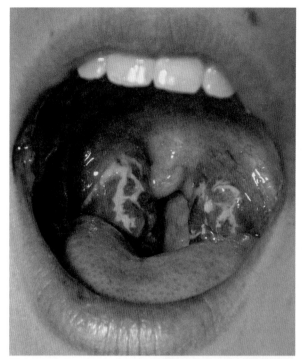

Figure 4-18: Streptococcal pharyngitis

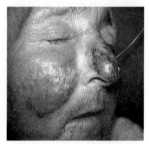

Figure 4-19: Erysipelas

lymphatics (see Figure 4-19 and Erysipelas on page 4-8). The skin is tender.
  - **Cellulitis** is a deeper infection (compared to erysipelas) of the lower dermis and the subcutaneous fat (see Common Skin and Soft Tissue Infections on page 4-7).
  - **Necrotizing fasciitis** is a rapidly progressive cellulitis that spreads along fascial planes (discussed under Rapidly Progressive Cellulitis on page 4-7). It presents with pain out of proportion to exam and may have crepitus or bullous lesions. It has a predilection to areas with decreased lymphatic drainage (e.g., after axillary node dissection or saphenous vein resection).
- **Acute rheumatic fever**
  - Acute rheumatic fever occurs only after pharyngitis—not skin infections.
  - This can be prevented with antibiotic treatment.
  - See the Cardiology section under Rheumatic Heart Disease and the Rheumatology section under Acute Rheumatic Fever (ARF) for more information.
- **Infection-related glomerulonephritis**
  - This can occur regardless of source of primary infection (i.e., pharynx or skin) and regardless of therapy.
  - See the Nephrology section under Glomerular Disease for more information.

- **Streptococcal TSS**
  - TSS can occur following minor trauma, recent surgery, or pharyngitis. Fever and pain can occur at the inoculation site, followed by hypotension.
  - In contrast to TSS related to *S. aureus*, bacteremia occurs in ~ 60% of cases of streptococcal TSS.
  - The most common entry sites are mucous membranes and skin. Chickenpox lesions can become superinfected with group A strep with bacteremia and, less commonly, toxemia. Since use of the chickenpox vaccine (released in 1995), the incidence has dropped significantly.
  - Streptococcal TSS is rapidly progressive with shock and multiorgan failure. The mortality rate is 30–60%.

This organism has yet to acquire penicillin (PCN) resistance; therefore, PCN is the drug of choice for *S. pyogenes* pharyngitis and scarlet fever.

Impetigo generally involves treatment of both *S. pyogenes* and *Staphylococcus aureus* infection, commonly with cephalexin. If methicillin-resistant *S. aureus* (MRSA) is suspected, then use clindamycin.

Treat erysipelas with amoxicillin or PCN for oral therapy and cefazolin for parenteral therapy.

Cellulitis treatment typically requires empiric coverage for both *S. pyogenes* and *S. aureus* infection if there are risk factors for MRSA. Oral therapy options include clindamycin or a combination of a β-lactam drug (e.g., amoxicillin, cephalexin) + either trimethoprim/sulfamethoxazole or doxycycline. Parenteral options include clindamycin or vancomycin. If MRSA is a low possibility, treat orally with 1st generation cephalosporin (e.g., cephalexin). Parenteral options include nafcillin, cefazolin, and clindamycin.

Treatment for necrotizing fasciitis includes immediate surgical debridement along with IV PCN and clindamycin.

Empiric therapy for strep TSS is with a β-lactam antibiotic + clindamycin. The latter is to inhibit toxin production.

Streptococcus agalactiae (Group B)

S. agalactiae (group B) is more common in older persons, especially individuals with alcohol use disorder or diabetes. It appears on Gram stain in chains. In pregnant women, *S. agalactiae* causes UTIs and is a cause of postpartum endometritis and bacteremia. It originates from a GU reservoir, although many cases of bacteremia have an unclear source. Treat with PCN or ampicillin; in PCN-allergic patients, treat with clindamycin or vancomycin.

Streptococcus dysgalactiae (Groups C and G)

Streptococci that react to Groups C and G Lancefield typing sera are considered to be a single species and 2 subspecies: *Streptococcus dysgalactiae* subspecies *equisimilis* (SDSE) and subspecies *dysgalactiae* (SDSD). They are part of the normal flora of the upper airway, skin, GI tract, and female GU tract. They can cause pharyngitis, soft tissue infection, septic arthritis, and endocarditis. They are universally susceptible to PCNs and cephalosporins. Diabetes and malignancy are risk factors.

Group D Streptococci

Group D streptococci includes 4 species previously grouped as *S. bovis* (*S. gallolyticus*, *S. lutetiensis*, *S. infantarius*, and *S. pasteurianus*) that are inhabitants of the GI tract and cause bacteremia and endocarditis. Group D *Streptococcus* bacteremia is seen in conjunction with colon cancer in 20–30% of cases; therefore, positive blood cultures from this organism without a clear origin (such as a UTI) warrant a colonoscopy.

Enterococci

Enterococci are gram-positive cocci that are difficult to distinguish from streptococci under the microscope. Like streptococci, they occur in pairs and short chains. Two species normally inhabit the intestines, with a higher amount of *Enterococcus faecalis* (95%) than *Enterococcus faecium* (5%). Thus, *E. faecalis* causes the vast majority of enterococcal infections (which include UTIs, bacteremia from lines, endocarditis, and intraabdominal polymicrobial infections). Asymptomatic enterococcal bacteriuria is managed similar to other cases of asymptomatic bacteriuria, which is generally treated only in the setting of pregnancy, those about to undergo urological procedures, and in the first 3 months after a kidney transplant.

All enterococci are resistant to cephalosporins and penicillinase-resistant PCNs. They are moderately resistant to the aminoglycosides, such as gentamicin, but these drugs are often used for synergy in the treatment of endocarditis.

E. faecium is resistant to imipenem and commonly exhibits high-level resistance to vancomycin (vancomycin-resistant *Enterococcus* [VRE]).

Single antibiotics are used to treat mild to moderate infections (UTIs and uncomplicated bacteremia) and include PCN G, ampicillin, or vancomycin, depending on sensitivities. If VRE, then additional antibiotic options include linezolid, daptomycin, and tigecycline, depending on location of the infection.

Combination treatment must be used for complicated bacteremia and endocarditis because single drugs are not bactericidal. The treatment of endocarditis is addressed in Antibiotic Treatment of Bacterial Endocarditis on page 4-30.

Listeria monocytogenes

Listeria monocytogenes, an aerobic gram-positive rod, causes infection in patients with decreased cellular immunity, such as from AIDS, lymphoma, or leukemia, and in older persons, persons with alcoholic use disorder, and pregnant women. Drugs that depress cellular immunity (e.g., glucocorticoids, transplant drugs) also increase the risk for infection.

INFECTIOUS DISEASE

Listeria is one of the most virulent foodborne pathogens, with a mortality rate of ~ 15%. It can be found in deli meats, hot dogs, milk, soft cheeses, poultry, and even fruit.

Listeria can cause neonatal meningitis via transvaginal inoculation and can affect the fetus. For this reason, pregnant women are cautioned against eating soft cheeses, unpasteurized milk, and other high-risk foods. It also causes bacterial meningitis in adults, which increases in incidence at 50 years of age.

Like enterococci, *Listeria* is resistant to all cephalosporins, so you must include ampicillin in the empiric treatment of meningitis in persons > 50 years of age, immunosuppressed patients, or neonates. Treat mild to moderate cases of listeriosis with PCN or ampicillin. Give PCN-allergic patients TMP/SMX. Although no randomized trials have been conducted, an aminoglycoside is often added to treat meningitis.

Corynebacterium diphtheriae and C. jeikeium

Corynebacterium diphtheriae (Figure 4-20) cause diphtheria. They are pleomorphic gram-positive rods that, on microscopy, may group together in patterns that somewhat resemble Chinese characters. Diphtheria is an upper respiratory infection with a gray-white **pharyngeal pseudomembrane** (Figure 4-21) that occurs along with hoarseness, sore throat, and a **low-grade** fever (< 101.0°F [38.3°C]). Toxin production causes myocarditis with heart failure and polyneuritis. Treat with erythromycin; 2nd choice is PCN, which can be given as procaine IM injections in patients who cannot take oral medications. Diphtheria equine antitoxin should be given as early as possible to inactivate the toxin prior to it binding to tissues. It is available only through the CDC.

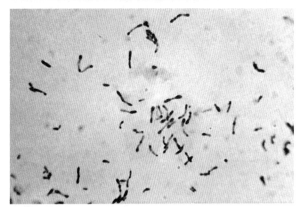

Figure 4-20: Corynebacterium diphtheriae

Corynebacterium jeikeium (JK) is a multidrug-resistant strain that colonizes and infects neutropenic patients and/or bone marrow transplant patients, where it usually causes IV catheter–related infections. Vancomycin is often the only antibiotic to which the organism is susceptible.

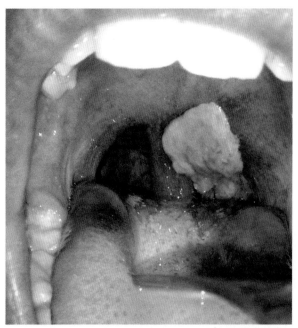

Figure 4-21: Pharyngeal pseudomembrane

Arcanobacterium haemolyticum

Arcanobacterium haemolyticum causes pharyngitis in adolescents with a desquamative scarlatiniform rash and lymphadenitis. Treat with PCN, erythromycin, or tetracycline.

Bacillus anthracis and B. cereus

Bacillus anthracis is a large, gram-positive rod that causes anthrax, a potential agent of bioterrorism.

There are 3 main clinical manifestations:

1) Cutaneous (95%)
2) Gastrointestinal
3) Inhalation (e.g., wool hides, bioterrorism)

Acquisition of the organism occurs from handling naturally contaminated hides/wool, from ingestion, or as an act of bioterrorism via maliciously contaminated sources (e.g., mail, aerosol). Unlike plague (discussed under *Yersinia* on page 4-13), anthrax is not transmitted from person to person. All forms can lead to a hemorrhagic meningitis, but this is more common with inhalation type. All persons who have or potentially have had inhalation exposure to anthrax need to be treated with 60 days of a fluoroquinolone regardless of disease manifestations.

Cutaneous anthrax starts as a **painless** papule that vesiculates and forms an ulcer (Figure 4-22), then becomes a painless black eschar, often with nonpitting, painless induration (Figure 4-23). Treat with an oral fluoroquinolone for 7–10 days.

Inhalation anthrax presents similarly to influenza, with malaise, fever, cough, and myalgias. After 2–3 days, there is a dramatic worsening of symptoms with hypoxia,

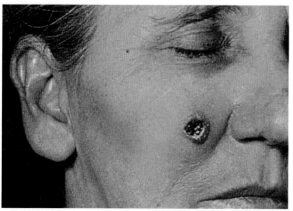

Figure 4-22: Early anthrax ulcer (painless)

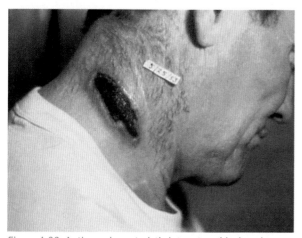

Figure 4-23: Anthrax-characteristic later-stage black eschar

hypotension, and death. Rather than causing a pneumonia, it causes a necrotizing mediastinitis that appears as mediastinal widening on imaging. Treatment is with 3 drugs for 2 weeks if meningitis has been ruled out. If meningitis is present, treatment is for at least 2 weeks and until clinical stability. Drugs should be from 1 of each of the following 3 groups: fluoroquinolone, β-lactam (carbapenem or PCN/ampicillin), and other (i.e., linezolid, clindamycin, rifampin, chloramphenicol).

GI anthrax is acquired by eating undercooked, contaminated meat. Patients get pharyngeal eschars and/or GI ulcerations.

For severe disease (disseminated and/or meningitis), there are 2 Food and Drug Administration (FDA)-approved monoclonal antibodies: obiltoxaximab and raxibacumab.

B. cereus is a close relative of *B. anthracis*. Found in the normal flora of the skin, *B. cereus* causes a benign food poisoning if its toxins are ingested. This is further discussed under Food Poisoning on page 4-11. The majority of the time when it is found in a blood culture, it is a contaminant, but on rare occasions, it is the cause of line sepsis. It can also cause endophthalmitis if inoculated into the eye by trauma, especially in contact lens wearers. It is universally susceptible to vancomycin.

Clostridioides difficile

Clostridioides difficile (*C. difficile*; formerly known as *Clostridium difficile*) is a cause of toxin-producing diarrheal illness usually precipitated by antibiotic exposure and/or health care exposures. Pathogenic organisms produce 2 toxins: toxin A (an enterotoxin) and toxin B (a cytotoxin). Almost all antibiotics can precipitate *C. difficile* colitis, but fluoroquinolones, clindamycin, and β-lactams have a higher propensity than others. Diagnosis is best made with PCR assays of the stool for the toxin B gene. Management depends on severity, but treatment typically consists of oral vancomycin or oral fidaxomicin. See Diarrhea due to *Clostridioides difficile* on page 4-14.

Clostridium

Clostridium species (there are > 100) are anaerobic, gram-positive rods that cause a wide variety of human illnesses:

- *C. difficile*, now classified as *Clostridioides difficile*, is discussed under *Clostridioides difficile*.
- *C. botulinum* produces the most potent human toxin known. It works by blocking presynaptic acetylcholine release, causing a descending motor paralysis and parasympathetic cranial nerve dysfunction that result in dilated pupils, dry tongue, and dysphagia with death from respiratory arrest if untreated. It does not enter the CNS, and thus there is no alteration of consciousness. The toxin is usually acquired via the ingestion of contaminated food (typically from people who do their own canning) but can be from a wound source. Honey is a source of infant botulism. It is the only disease other than diphtheria for which we still use an equine antitoxin. PCN is given to eradicate a wound source.
- *C. perfringens* is one of the most common causes of food poisoning in the U.S. and presents as a watery diarrheal illness with abdominal cramps similar to the enteric form of *B. cereus*. The organism itself can also cause a rapidly progressive cellulitis. See Necrotizing Fasciitis on page 4-7.
- *C. septicum* is a bowel organism, and the majority of persons with infection from this organism have an associated GI malignancy. Thus, persons with bacteremia should undergo upper and lower GI endoscopy.
- *C. tetani* produces a neurotoxin that causes tetanus. There are < 50 cases/year in the U.S. The most common form is generalized tetanus, characterized by tonic muscular contractions with interspersed intense muscle spasms. Typically, the spasms start in the jaw, known as trismus (lockjaw), before progressing to other muscle groups. There is no impairment of consciousness. Without treatment, death results from eventual respiratory failure. Manage with continuously administered neurologic blocking agents and mechanical ventilation. Human tetanus immunoglobulin is required. Metronidazole for 10–14 days is the preferred antibiotic, although PCN G is also acceptable. See Approach to Tetanus Prevention on page 4-94.

INFECTIOUS DISEASE

Clostridium species are susceptible to PCNs, cephalosporins, and clindamycin. The latter is useful when treating *C. perfringens* cellulitis to inhibit the organism's ability to produce its numerous toxins.

Nocardia

Nocardia species are aerobic, weakly acid-fast, beaded, branching, filamentous, gram-positive rods.

Nocardia species, once inhaled, usually start as a lung infection, commonly causing a thin-walled cavitary lesion. It can then cause focal brain abscesses and chronic lymphocytic meningitis. *Nocardia* species are in the soil and, if inoculated into the skin, cause nodular lesions that spread along lymphatic channels. *Nocardia* are slow growers on culture media. The usual setting is in patients with impaired cell-mediated immunity.

Treatment is high-dose sulfonamides or TMP/SMX. Susceptibility testing should be done to ensure susceptibility to these agents. In severely ill patients, imipenem or amikacin is added while awaiting susceptibilities. Minocycline can be used for sulfa-allergic patients with mild disease, but desensitization should be considered for severe disease. Treat for at least 3 months; up to 12 months may be required.

Actinomyces israelii

Actinomyces israelii is an anaerobic, gram-positive, beaded rod that causes an infection in which **yellow** sulfur-like granules can be visualized, which are actually clusters of organisms. The usual presentation of actinomycosis is cervicofacial involvement ("lumpy jaw"; Figure 4-24). *A. israelii* is part of the normal bowel flora and thus can be a participating organism in intraabdominal abscesses and pelvic inflammatory disease. Treatment is PCN, amoxicillin, or ampicillin. In PCN-allergic patients, use ceftriaxone, doxycycline, or a macrolide.

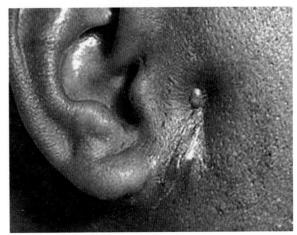

Figure 4-24: Cervicofacial involvement in actinomycosis

GRAM-NEGATIVE BACTERIA (GNB)

Neisseria

Neisseria meningitidis (meningococcus) is a gram-negative diplococcus that is carried in the human nasopharynx in 5–10% of healthy persons. It typically does not cause disease because carriers create antibodies and complement that lyse the organisms as they enter the bloodstream.

Thus, patients with complement deficiency or asplenia are especially prone to meningococcal sepsis (a.k.a. **meningococcemia**), which presents with fever, hypotension, and skin signs that vary from petechiae (early disease) to diffuse purpuric lesions and DIC (later disease). Bloodstream infection can occur with meningococcal meningitis.

The diagnosis and treatment of bacterial meningitis are discussed under Bacterial Meningitis on page 4-24.

Prophylaxis to prevent meningococcal disease is discussed under Prevention of Meningococcal Meningitis on page 4-25.

Neisseria gonorrhoeae is a gram-negative diplococcus that causes gonorrhea, which is discussed under Sexually Transmitted Infections (STIs) on page 4-16.

Moraxella catarrhalis

Moraxella catarrhalis is a gram-negative coccobacillus that causes otitis, sinusitis, and respiratory illness including exacerbations of COPD and pneumonia. All strains produce penicillinases but are usually susceptible to amoxicillin/clavulanate, 2nd or 3rd generation cephalosporin, TMP/SMX, macrolides, and fluoroquinolones.

Pseudomonas aeruginosa

Pseudomonas aeruginosa is a gram-negative bacillus (GNB) that is a ubiquitous water organism and a common cause of hospital-acquired infections. There are several clinical presentations caused by this organism:

- **Tennis shoe cellulitis and/or osteomyelitis**—*P. aeruginosa* survives in the moisture-absorbing middle layer of tennis shoes and can be inoculated into soft tissue or bone after the wearer steps on a sharp object such as a nail.
- **Otitis externa**—both benign and malignant; discussed under Otitis Externa (Swimmer's Ear) on page 4-4.
- **Ecthyma gangrenosum**—a round, indurated, necrotic lesion with central ulceration (Figure 4-25) seen in neutropenic patients with *P. aeruginosa* bacteremia.

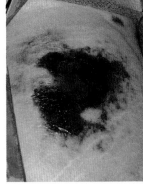

Figure 4-25: Ecthyma gangrenosum

- **Hot tub folliculitis** (hot tub rash)–from inadequately chlorinated hot tubs. This is a self-limited inflammation from *P. aeruginosa* entering the base of hair follicles in the submerged areas.

There is no single antibiotic to which all *P. aeruginosa* are universally susceptible. Therefore, it is reasonable to treat invasive infections with 2 antipseudomonal antibiotics from different classes (i.e., piperacillin/tazobactam plus a fluoroquinolone or an aminoglycoside) until you know the susceptibility pattern.

Agents with known activity against *P. aeruginosa* include:

- Carbapenems (except ertapenem)
- Aztreonam
- Fluoroquinolones (ciprofloxacin or levofloxacin)
- Aminoglycosides
- Ceftazidime or cefepime or cefiderocol
- β-Lactam/β-lactamase combinations
  - Ceftolozane/tazobactam
  - Ceftazidime/avibactam
  - Piperacillin/tazobactam
- Colistin

Enterobacteriaceae

Enterobacteriaceae is a family of aerobic GNBs that includes *Escherichia coli, Klebsiella, Proteus, Enterobacter, Salmonella, Shigella, Yersinia, Citrobacter,* and *Serratia. Salmonella* and *Shigella* are discussed under Bacterial Diarrhea on page 4-11.

Escherichia

E. coli is the most common GNB aerobe in the bowel. It is the most common cause of community- and health care–associated UTIs. It causes diarrheal disease via several mechanisms (see Bacterial Diarrhea on page 4-11): intraabdominal infection, primary peritonitis, a minority of bacterial pneumonias (typically nosocomial), a minority of endocarditis (usually on a prosthetic valve), and, rarely, osteomyelitis. Resistance to ampicillin, TMP/SMX, and quinolones is commonly > 25%, and extended-spectrum β-lactamase (ESBL)-containing organisms are becoming more prevalent. These are susceptible to carbapenems.

Klebsiella

Klebsiella pneumoniae and *K. oxytoca* are GNBs and normal flora of the bowel that can cause UTI, intraabdominal infection, primary peritonitis, and nosocomial pneumonia. All strains are resistant to ampicillin, but almost all strains are susceptible to carbapenems. Susceptibility to cephalosporins and fluoroquinolones is variable.

Some strains of *Klebsiella pneumoniae* produce carbapenemases (KPCs). These are frequently encountered in residents of nursing homes or long-term care facilities. KPCs are resistant to carbapenems and all other β-lactams. They are frequently resistant to other antibiotic

classes as well. Options for therapy can include colistin, tigecycline, or aminoglycosides, depending on the susceptibility of each strain.

Proteus

Proteus mirabilis and *P. vulgaris* are normal flora of the bowel and cause urinary tract and intraabdominal infections. They are GNBs. They produce urease, which splits urea in the urine, releasing ammonium. This creates an alkaline environment that facilitates struvite stone formation. These stones can be a nidus for recurrent UTI. *P. mirabilis* is usually susceptible to ampicillin-sulbactam, piperacillin/tazobactam, and all cephalosporin generations. Resistance to TMP/SMX is common. *P. vulgaris* is often resistant to multiple β-lactams and fluoroquinolones.

Enterobacter

Enterobacter cloacae and *E. aerogenes* are GNBs and the 2 most common species infecting humans. They are part of normal gut flora, and due to their resistance to commonly used antibiotics (e.g., ampicillin-sulbactam and cefazolin), they can become predominant species in patients receiving these drugs and cause nosocomial UTIs, pneumonia, and complicated intraabdominal infection. Both species are usually susceptible to cefepime, aminoglycosides, TMP/SMX, and fluoroquinolones.

Yersinia

Yersinia are gram-negative, rod-shaped coccobacilli that cause plague (*Yersinia pestis*) or diarrheal illnesses (*Yersinia enterocolitica* and *Yersinia pseudotuberculosis*). Wild rodents are the reservoir. *Y. pestis* is transmitted by fleas or direct contact with an infected animal, and mortality is high if not properly treated.

The **bubonic** type causes large, localized lymphadenopathy (buboes) that suppurates at the site of the inoculation. If not treated, it can lead to sepsis and death. The **pneumonic** form of plague occurs after inhalation of the organism via aerosols from infected animals or from other humans with pneumonic plague. Only a small inoculum is required, which can lead to epidemics and makes it a potential agent of bioterrorism.

Plague and tularemia present similarly (adenopathy after hunting), except that the geographic locations are different—Desert Southwest for plague vs. Arkansas, Missouri, and Oklahoma for tularemia. There is more on tularemia under *Francisella tularensis* on page 4-52.

Diagnose plague by aspirating lymph nodes or obtaining sputum specimens that reveal bipolar-staining GNBs (safety pin shape) and growth of *Y. pestis.*

Plague is 1 of 2 infectious diseases for which an aminoglycoside is the drug of choice; the other is tularemia. Streptomycin is the aminoglycoside of choice, but if it is not available, gentamicin is an acceptable alternative. 2nd line choices are tetracycline, doxycycline, or quinolones.

Ingestion of *Y. enterocolitica* and *Y. pseudotuberculosis* causes a diarrheal illness associated with abdominal pain and cramping. It can predominate in the terminal ileum with associated mesenteric adenitis in that area that mimics appendicitis. Uncomplicated illness does not require antibiotics. If complicated (i.e., associated bacteremia or extraintestinal disease), treat with a fluoroquinolone, a 3rd generation cephalosporin, or TMP/SMX.

Citrobacter

Citrobacter species (especially *C. freundii*, *C. koseri*, and *C. amalonaticus*) are GNBs that colonize the human gut and cause UTIs as their most common disease manifestation. They can be part of a polymicrobial intraabdominal abscess after bowel perforation or bowel necrosis but rarely cause other illnesses. They are universally resistant to ampicillin and 1st generation cephalosporins but are usually killed by other generations of cephalosporins, carbapenems, fluoroquinolones, and TMP/SMX.

Serratia

Serratia marcescens is a GNB found in the environment but does not often colonize the human microbiome. When it does, it can cause UTIs and nosocomial pneumonia. It can also cause bacteremia and hematogenous septic arthritis in drug users. All isolates are resistant to ampicillin and 1st generation cephalosporins but are usually susceptible to 3rd generation cephalosporins, aminoglycosides, and piperacillin/tazobactam.

Legionella

Legionella species are aerobic GNBs (but show up poorly on Gram stain) and require special media for culture (charcoal yeast extract). Obtaining a urine *Legionella* antigen is a good rapid test and should be performed on all persons with severe pneumonia. *Legionella* has > 20 known pathogenic species, but *Legionella pneumophila* causes 80–90% of human infections. *Legionella* species live within free living amoebae in standing water and enter the lungs via inhalation, causing pneumonia.

L. pneumophila causes numerous multisystem manifestations as a rule. Patients with *Legionella* pneumonia may present with diarrhea, hyponatremia, hypophosphatemia, and CNS symptoms (headache, delirium, and confusion) in addition to pneumonia.

Treat with a fluoroquinolone or a macrolide. Tetracyclines also have activity. Add rifampin for severe disease.

Brucella

Brucella is an aerobic gram-negative bacillus. *B. melitensis* causes brucellosis in goats, sheep, and camels. Other strains are *B. abortus* (cattle), *B. suis* (pigs), and *B. canis* (dogs). These are transmitted to humans via unpasteurized milk or cheese or by inhalation (work related).

Acute **brucellosis** is a nonspecific febrile disease—with night sweats (often with a foul, moldy odor), diarrhea, myalgias, arthralgias, and fatigue—that is difficult to pinpoint unless there is an occupational or travel exposure history to assist. Think "Brusmella" to help remember the association of *Brucella* with smelly sweat. If inhaled, *Brucella* pneumonia occurs. A small percentage of patients have diffuse rash, orchitis, or uveitis.

Localized infection can ensue and manifest as osteomyelitis, tissue abscesses, or endocarditis (that can initially appear culture negative because the organism takes weeks to grow).

Because cultures can take up to 6 weeks to grow, confirming the diagnosis is difficult. Diagnosis can also be made via acute and convalescent serum titers, as well as PCR.

Resistance to a single agent is common, so treatment requires 1 of the following regimens:

1) Doxycycline for 6 weeks + streptomycin for 14–21 days or gentamicin for 7–10 days
2) Doxycycline + rifampin × 6–8 weeks
3) Avoid doxycycline in pregnant persons and give rifampin + doxycycline × 6 weeks.

Francisella tularensis

Francisella tularensis is a small, gram-negative, pleomorphic bacillus that causes **tularemia**. It is found in many animals, particularly rabbits ("rabbit fever"). *Francisella* is transmitted by ticks and bloodsucking flies, but the organism can also be ingested, transmitted by contact with animal skins, or inhaled. Tularemia is seen most often in Arkansas, Missouri, and Oklahoma. It has 6 distinct forms: ulceroglandular (the most common type), glandular, oropharyngeal, oculoglandular, typhoidal, and pneumonic.

Patients with the ulceroglandular form of tularemia present with a history of sudden onset of fever, chills, myalgias, and arthralgias, as well as a single, red papuloulcerative lesion with a central eschar at the site of the tick bite. Additional symptoms can develop, based on portal of entry. Regional lymphadenopathy can develop, and these nodes can necrose and suppurate. If pneumonia occurs, it demonstrates hilar adenopathy, nodular infiltrates, and pleural effusion similar to pneumonic plague.

The diagnosis is based on the clinical and epidemiological presentation. Serologic testing for *F. tularensis* is confirmatory, but it usually takes > 2 weeks to turn positive. Culture any tissue that is apparently infected, but know that these cultures have a very low yield.

Treat with streptomycin or gentamicin. Doxycycline or ciprofloxacin can be used if the patient is not severely ill.

Bartonella henselae

Bartonella henselae (cats are the natural reservoir, especially kittens) causes **catscratch disease**. Catscratch disease has a macule → papule → pustule at the site of the infection (Figure 4-26) with painful regional lymphadenopathy.

Often the site of inoculation is no longer visible when the patient presents with lymphadenopathy. Untreated, cutaneous disease with adenopathy lasts for several months. Rarely, it causes encephalitis or endocarditis. It is a very slow-growing GNB. Treatment with azithromycin for 5 days decreases the duration of illness to a matter of weeks. Add rifampin for systemic disease.

B. henselae also causes **bacillary angiomatosis** in the immunocompromised patient (mainly in HIV-infected adults) and is characterized by vascular lesions that mainly affect the skin although they can affect other organs as well. Treat with a prolonged course (months) of azithromycin or doxycycline +/− rifampin.

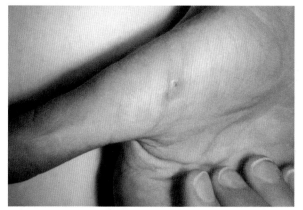

Figure 4-26: Catscratch disease primary lesion

Helicobacter pylori

Helicobacter pylori is a gram-negative, spiral, flagellated bacillus. It causes gastritis and peptic ulcer disease (PUD) and is a risk factor for adenocarcinoma of the stomach and GI lymphoma. Further discussion about *H. pylori* is in the Gastroenterology section under Stomach.

Rickettsia

Rocky Mountain Spotted Fever (RMSF)

Rickettsia rickettsii is a poorly staining gram-negative coccobacillus that causes RMSF. This tickborne disease has a 5–10% mortality rate. Classic signs and symptoms of RMSF include a rash, fever, severe headache, arthralgias (but not overt arthritis), and history of recent exposure to ticks in endemic areas (predominantly southeastern U.S.). The rash (Figure 4-27) begins on the distal extremities, involving the wrists and ankles. It then spreads within hours to the trunk, palms, and soles and progresses from maculopapular to petechial to purpuric. Patients may have diarrhea and abdominal pain.

Labs show leukopenia or leukocytosis, thrombocytopenia, hyponatremia, and increased transaminases. PT, aPTT, and fibrin split products are often increased, although the condition does not usually result in full-blown DIC.

It is important to diagnose this infection presumptively on clinical grounds (especially the distinct rash) to allow emergent treatment. The quickest confirmation of the

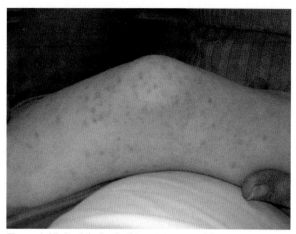

Figure 4-27: Rash in Rocky Mountain spotted fever

diagnosis is via immunofluorescent staining of a biopsy sample of a petechial lesion. Serology eventually turns positive but is often negative on presentation. PCR testing of blood is often negative early on and cannot be used to rule out the disease.

Treat with doxycycline. In patients intolerant to tetracyclines, chloramphenicol is the only other drug that has been shown to be effective.

Murine (Endemic) Typhus

Rickettsia typhi causes murine (endemic) typhus, which presents with fever, headache, myalgia, a faint rash, and transaminase elevation. In the U.S., the opossum is the reservoir, and it is transmitted by fleas that infect rats, cats, dogs, and opossums. The diagnosis is made by demonstrating the presence of IgM antibody or a 4-fold rise in IgG antibody. Treatment is doxycycline, which shortens the duration of the illness.

Coxiella burnetii

Q fever (*Coxiella burnetii* infection) is a zoonosis transmitted mainly by inhalation of the aerosol released from an infected animal. Q fever is seen in abattoir (slaughterhouse) workers and people exposed to an infected animal's products of conception during birthing. It usually presents as a flu-like febrile illness, with or without pneumonia and/or hepatitis. Headache is common. ~ 5% of infections become chronic and manifest as a fever of unknown origin or culture-negative endocarditis.

Diagnose with serology, particularly Phase II IgG (acute Q fever) and Phase I IgG (chronic Q fever). Treat Q fever with 14 days of doxycycline. Patients with endocarditis require at least 18 months of doxycycline, with hydroxychloroquine added for the duration.

Ehrlichia and Anaplasma

Ehrlichia and *Anaplasma* are small, obligate, intracellular gram-negative organisms that cause ehrlichiosis and anaplasmosis, respectively. Ehrlichiosis is called "spotless"

Rocky Mountain fever, even though ~ 30% have a rash. Like RMSF, ticks are the transmission vectors, and also like RMSF, ehrlichiosis and anaplasmosis predominantly occur in the eastern half of the U.S. (Figure 4-28 and Figure 4-29).

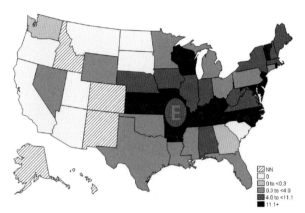

Figure 4-28: Annual reported incidence (per million population) for Ehrlichia chaffeensis, 2019

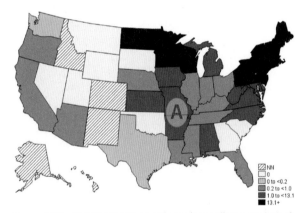

Figure 4-29: Annual reported incidence (per million population) for anaplasmosis, 2019

The 2 species of *Ehrlichia*, *E. chaffeensis* and *E. ewingii*, cause **human monocytic ehrlichiosis** (HME), mainly in Missouri and Arkansas.

Anaplasma phagocytophilum causes **human granulocytic anaplasmosis** (HGA), mainly in the Northeast and upper Midwest U.S.

Patients with either illness present similarly with fever and severe headache. Both HME and HGA can cause thrombocytopenia, leukopenia, and pancytopenia. Rash is present in ~ 30% of patients with HME but rare in patients with HGA. Definitive diagnosis is established by finding intracytoplasmic inclusions (**morulae**) in white blood cells (Figure 4-30 and Figure 4-31).

These inclusions are found within PMNs in HGA and within monocytic cells in HME. Serologies are available but require a 4-fold change in titer and thus are not useful at presentation.

Treat all patients suspected or proved to have ehrlichiosis or anaplasmosis with doxycycline just like with RMSF.

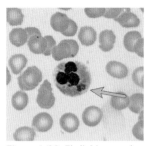

Figure 4-30: Ehrlichia morula

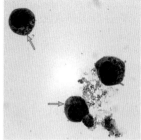

Figure 4-31: Anaplasma morula

Anaplasmosis is transmitted by the tick *Ixodes scapularis*, which can also transmit *Borrelia burgdorferi* (Lyme disease) and babesiosis. Doxycycline will be effective if coinfected with *Borrelia*, but babesiosis requires atovaquone and azithromycin.

MYCOBACTERIA

All mycobacteria are acid-fast—they do not lose their stained color when exposed to acids (red on a green background). As a rule, treat mycobacterial infections with a prolonged multidrug regimen.

M. tuberculosis is a prominent global cause of pulmonary infection and death. In addition, it can cause myriad extrapulmonary manifestations by infecting any organ. See more on TB in the Pulmonary Medicine section under Mycobacterial Infections.

Mycobacterium avium complex (MAC; a.k.a. *M. avium-intracellulare* [MAI]) causes a chronic pulmonary infection with either *M. avium* or *M. intracellulare*. Immunocompromised (especially HIV-infected) patients are at risk for disseminated disease. Older women and patients with COPD can also present with an indolent right middle lobe pneumonia (Lady Windermere syndrome). Treatment includes a macrolide (clarithromycin or azithromycin) + ethambutol and rifampin. For severe or refractory disease, aminoglycosides may be necessary. Remember that for MAC, you need a MACrolide antibiotic.

M. leprae causes leprosy. Transmission is primarily via respiratory droplets from person to person. although it can also occur from direct contact on open wounds. Armadillos serve as a reservoir of *M. leprae* in the southern U.S. The majority of the population is genetically not susceptible to infection. Presentation is with nodular, hypopigmented skin lesions, neuropathy manifested by loss of or diminished sensation, and sometimes palpable peripheral nerves. Biopsy of affected areas can demonstrate the organism with a Fite stain. PCR can also be used. The infection is further classified into **tuberculoid leprosy**, which has very few organisms (paucibacillary) due to a strong immune response, to the other extreme, **lepromatous leprosy**, which has many organisms (multibacillary) due to a very weak immune response. Treatment for tuberculoid leprosy is dapsone and rifampin for 6–12 months, and for lepromatous leprosy is dapsone and rifampin and clofazimine for 12–24 months.

M. marinum is the so-called fishtank bacillus. It causes nonhealing skin ulceration in people working with fish tanks, in addition to being associated with aquatic trauma involving saltwater. It causes strings of nodular lesions along the lymphatic channels. (Similar lesions can occur with *Nocardia brasiliensis* and *Sporothrix schenckii.*) If mild, treat with doxycycline, TMP/SMX, or clarithromycin. Treat more serious disease with clarithromycin + either rifampin or ethambutol for 1–2 months after symptoms resolve.

Other nontuberculous mycobacteria (NTM) include *M. kansasii* (pneumonia in patients with COPD) and *M. abscessus* (chronic pulmonary infections in patients with underlying lung disease).

CHLAMYDIA

Chlamydia are obligate, intracellular bacteria. *C. psittaci*, *C. trachomatis*, and *C. pneumoniae* (formerly *Chlamydophila pneumoniae*, Taiwan acute respiratory agent [TWAR]) are pathogenic in humans.

C. psittaci is found in psittacine (e.g., parrots, parakeets, macaws, cockatoos) and other birds and causes psittacosis, which presents as a community-acquired pneumonia often with splenomegaly. Any pneumonia associated with poultry contact, especially with splenomegaly, strongly suggests *C. psittaci*. (Differential diagnosis: *Histoplasma* also causes pneumonia and splenomegaly; it is found in patients with contact to bird and bat droppings; difficult to distinguish based on presentation while awaiting evaluation, but psittacosis may be more severe with onset over a shorter period of time.) Onset of psittacosis presents with myalgias, rigors, headache, and high fever—to 105.0°F (40.6°C).

C. trachomatis causes GU infections and trachoma (chronic, anterior eye infection that may lead to cataracts; found especially in Asia and Africa). ~ 5% of pregnant women have *C. trachomatis* in their genital tracts. The same *C. trachomatis* also causes neonatal pneumonia. Lymphogranuloma venereum is an STI caused by the same *C. trachomatis* but of different immunotypes. See Sexually Transmitted Infections (STIs) on page 4-16.

C. pneumoniae causes community-acquired pneumonia in adults and is acquired by person-to-person spread. Bronchospasm is particularly prominent, as is an association with early pharyngitis and laryngitis.

Treatment is with doxycycline, macrolides, or fluoroquinolones.

SPIROCHETES

PREVIEW | REVIEW

- What are the clinical presentations of leptospirosis?
- Which symptoms manifest in the various stages of Lyme disease?
- What are the treatments for Lyme disease?

SYPHILIS

Syphilis is discussed under Infectious Genital Ulcers on page 4-18.

LEPTOSPIROSIS

Leptospirosis is a spirochetal disease caused by *Leptospira interrogans* and transferred by contact with infected animals or contaminated water. It is seen in association with exposure to rodent urine. Leptospirosis is the most widespread zoonosis in the world. It is common in Hawaii (~ 50% of all U.S. cases) and can be seen after recreational water exposures (e.g., in whitewater rafters, adventure racers, surfers, swimmers, triathletes).

Leptospirosis has a wide range of signs and symptoms, from myalgias, fever, and headache (with or without aseptic meningitis) to **Weil disease** (severe hepatitis with renal failure, pneumonitis, and hemorrhagic complications).

Conjunctival suffusion (Figure 4-32) is highly specific because it is rarely seen in other infectious diseases. The hepatitis is characterized by the bilirubin being disproportionately elevated compared to the liver transaminases.

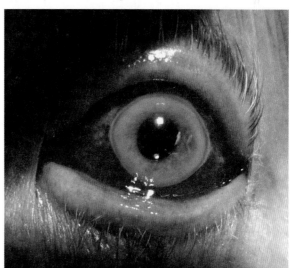

Figure 4-32: Leptospirosis conjunctival suffusion

Diagnosis is made by PCR nucleic acid detection in blood or body fluids (CSF and urine). Cultures require special media and take several days to turn positive. Serology (the presence of a single IgM titer or 4-fold rise in IgG) is helpful, but treatment should be initiated while awaiting results.

Treat with PCN or doxycycline.

LYME DISEASE

Borrelia burgdorferi causes Lyme disease. It is transmitted by the *Ixodes scapularis* tick in the mid-Atlantic, Midwest, and Northeast U.S. and by the *Ixodes pacificus* tick in California. The protozoan *Babesia* (see *Babesia* on page 4-66) and the bacterium *Anaplasma* are also transmitted by this tick so coinfection may occur.

INFECTIOUS DISEASE

Ixodes ticks have 3 stages of development: larva, nymph, and adult. Ticks transmit Lyme disease most efficiently during the nymphal stage. Nymphs are more likely to feed on humans and are rarely noticed because they are very small (< 2 mm).

Ticks require at least 36–48 hours of attachment before transmission of infection occurs. A tick found walking on the skin is not transmitting infection.

Manifestations

Stages of Lyme disease:

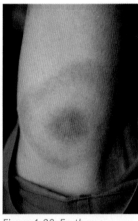

Figure 4-33: Erythema migrans

- Stage 1—early localized: **Erythema migrans** (EM) is the pathognomonic skin lesion of Stage 1 disease; it starts at the site of the bite and is a slowly spreading, circular, erythematous lesion, usually with a lighter center (Figure 4-33). Other Stage 1 symptoms include myalgias, arthralgias, fever, headache, and lymphadenopathy. ~ 50% of patients have secondary skin lesions.
- Stage 2—early disseminated: Weeks to months later, Stage 2 disease occurs with **neurologic** symptoms (i.e., lymphocytic meningitis, cranial or peripheral neuritis) and/or **heart** infection (i.e., myocarditis with transient 1st, 2nd, or 3rd degree heart block). A peripheral 7th nerve palsy (Bell's palsy) is not uncommon and, if bilateral from an endemic area for Lyme disease, is highly suggestive.
- Stage 3—late: Months to years later, Stage 3 occurs with a mono- or oligoarticular **arthritis**.
- Post–Lyme disease syndrome: After diagnosis and treatment of Lyme disease, some people experience fatigue, musculoskeletal pain, and cognitive difficulties. This used to be called chronic Lyme disease, but that term should no longer be used because it implies there is still active infection, which is inaccurate.

Diagnosis

A diagnosis can be made in 2 ways:

- presence of EM or
- Stage 2 or 3 manifestations and positive serology (an enzyme immunoassay [EIA] test, followed by a positive Western blot.

There are a few important caveats about testing for Lyme disease:

- Do not perform serology if there are no Lyme symptoms. Patients with seropositivity and no symptoms have had prior asymptomatic exposure but do not warrant and do not benefit from treatment.
- Do not perform serology in patients with EM. It is diagnostic of Lyme disease and most patients are seronegative in Stage 1.
- Reserve serology for persons from endemic areas with symptoms consistent with Stage 2 or 3 Lyme disease.

Treatment

Treatment for Lyme disease depends on the disease manifestation. According to 2020 IDSA recommendations, the drugs are either oral (doxycycline, amoxicillin, or cefuroxime) or IV (ceftriaxone).

- Treat erythema migrans or cranial neuropathy with doxycycline × 10 days or amoxicillin or cefuroxime for 14 days.
- Treat carditis manifesting as 1st degree AV block with an oral agent for 14–21 days. Higher degrees of block should be treated for the same duration, but IV therapy can be used.
- Treat meningitis or radiculopathy with oral or IV antibiotics for 14–21 days.
- Treat arthritis with an oral agent × 28 days. Recurrent or refractory arthritis can be treated with a repeat course of the same drug and duration one time only. Continued symptoms after that are not due to active infection and no further antibiotics should be given.

Although patients previously treated for Lyme disease more commonly have chronic neuromuscular symptoms (e.g., muscle and joint pain, fatigue, trouble with memory and formulating ideas—known as post–Lyme disease syndrome) than do patients never infected with *B. burgdorferi*, several studies have confirmed that there is no benefit in giving additional courses of antibiotics to these individuals.

Prevention

Because transmission does not occur until at least 36–48 hours of attachment, the best prevention is to keep ticks off the body with clothing treated with insect repellents and to find and remove the *Ixodes* tick from the skin. When in endemic areas, people should be advised to do daily tick checks and bathing. When ticks are embedded in the skin, they should be removed by grasping them with tweezers placed on their mouthparts and pulling them straight up from the skin.

Postexposure prophylaxis: Give a single dose of doxycycline 200 mg PO if an embedded tick is found on the skin and all of the following are true:

- The tick is in the nymph or adult stage.
- The tick was attached at least 36 hours and is engorged.
- The patient presents within 72 hours of tick removal.
- The local rate of tick infection with *B. burgdorferi* is ≥ 20%, such as in New England, mid-Atlantic states, and parts of Minnesota and Wisconsin.

FUNGAL INFECTIONS

PREVIEW | REVIEW

- In a febrile patient who is receiving intravenous hyperalimentation, which fungal bloodstream infection might you suspect?
- When can you disregard *Candida* as a blood culture contaminant?
- What is the treatment of candidemia when a line is present?
- Which patient population typically develops hepatosplenic candidiasis?
- Patients with candidemia should have what kind of referral?
- What are the cerebral spinal fluid abnormalities in cryptococcal meningitis?
- Initial treatment for cryptococcal meningitis includes which drugs?
- Where is *Coccidioides immitis* geographically found?
- What are the clinical presentations of histoplasmosis?
- Which tests are best for diagnosing histoplasmosis?
- What are the clinical manifestations of disseminated blastomycosis?
- Which patient groups are at risk for mucormycosis?

OVERVIEW

Fungi are divided into 2 morphologic types: **yeasts** and **molds**. There are also **dimorphs** that change from a yeast to mold, and vice versa, depending on temperature. The dimorphs are the type most likely to cause systemic disease in the nonhospitalized, immunocompetent host. The dimorphic fungi are transmitted by spores that convert to yeast at body temperature.

Some of the clinically relevant fungi include:

- *Candida* species
- *Cryptococcus* species
- *Aspergillus* species
- Endemic fungi (*Histoplasma*, *Blastomyces*, and *Coccidioides*; found in specific regions of the U.S.)
- Dermatophytes (cause tinea capitis, tinea corporis, tinea pedis, and tinea cruris)
- *Sporothrix schenckii*
- Zygomycetes (e.g., *Mucor*, *Rhizopus*, and *Rhizomucor*)

CANDIDA

Outpatient *Candida* infections are usually caused by *Candida albicans*. *Candida* species are normal flora of the mouth, bowel, and vagina, yet they uncommonly cause systemic illness.

C. albicans is by far the most common infecting genus. Other less common pathogens include *C. parapsilosis*, *C. glabrata*, and *C. krusei*. *C. auris* is an emerging multi-drug-resistant yeast with outbreaks in health care settings. Predispositions to disease include antibacterial treatment that reduces competing bacterial normal flora, immunosuppression, indwelling catheters, hyperalimentation, and uncontrolled diabetes. Disease may be localized to mucosal surfaces of the mouth (thrush), esophagus, and vagina (candidal vaginitis) or disseminate to produce endocarditis, endophthalmitis, hepatosplenic infection, or renal infection. Usually, candidemia, either from an infected vascular catheter or from overgrowth of *Candida* in the gut, is the source of dissemination to these other organ systems. Limited mucosal *Candida*, such as thrush, presents with visible whitish plaques on the oral mucosa with an underlying erythematous base. Treatment options include topical therapy (e.g., clotrimazole troches, miconazole mucoadhesive buccal tablets) or fluconazole tablets. Patients who have odynophagia and oral thrush can be assumed to have esophageal candidiasis; endoscopy is not required to make the diagnosis. These patients require systemic antifungal therapy, most commonly fluconazole. Vulvovaginal candidiasis presents as a thick, whitish discharge along with intense vaginal itching (see Vulvovaginal Candidiasis (VVC) on page 4-23).

Candidemia

Signs and symptoms of candidemia and disseminated disease are fever; rash consisting of painless, erythematous papules/pustules; visual complaints; and multiorgan involvement. *Candida* species grow readily in routine blood culture bottles. *Candida* in a blood culture should never be considered a contaminant; it represents real disease, even if the patient is relatively asymptomatic. It can take days to grow the organisms out of the blood. If the patient is ill, consider empiric antifungal treatment (e.g., in a patient with neutropenia with a prolonged fever).

Non–*albicans Candida* are common in hospitalized and immunocompromised patients. They are often resistant to fluconazole but not to echinocandins.

Treatment of candidemia includes removal of any infected catheters and administering a systemic antifungal. An echinocandin (i.e., caspofungin, micafungin, anidulafungin) is 1st line therapy in all patients, pending identification and susceptibility. Fluconazole can be considered once speciation and susceptibilities are known.

INFECTIOUS DISEASE

Chronic Disseminated Candidiasis

Chronic disseminated candidiasis (a.k.a. hepatosplenic candidiasis) is seen in patients with hematologic malignancies as they recover from a period of chemotherapy-induced neutropenia. Symptoms include fever and pain in the right upper quadrant.

Labs show increased alkaline phosphatase +/– increased transaminases and bilirubin. Contrast CT of the abdomen shows multiple small abscesses in the liver and spleen.

As with candidemia, the main therapy is an echinocandin (i.e., caspofungin, micafungin, anidulafungin).

Ocular Candidiasis

Ocular candidiasis presents with painless altered visual acuity and can be due to endophthalmitis or chorioretinitis. Disease can occur via hematogenous spread during candidemia or direct inoculation after eye surgery. Early disease (especially with chorioretinitis) can be relatively asymptomatic, so any patient who develops candidemia should have a dilated eye exam by an ophthalmologist. Approximately 10% of patients with candidemia will have ocular candidiasis.

Treat chorioretinitis without vitritis with systemic azoles (fluconazole or voriconazole). If there is azole resistance, liposomal amphotericin should be used. If there is also macular involvement, give intravitreal amphotericin B or intravitreal voriconazole. If chorioretinitis with vitritis is present, treatment may entail vitrectomy in addition to systemic and intravitreal antifungals.

Genitourinary Candidiasis

Candida can infect the bladder and kidneys as an ascending urinary tract infection, but it can also reach the kidney and then the bladder via hematogenous spread from candidemia.

Candiduria is fairly common, especially in hospital settings, and it often represents colonization, especially if the patient has had a urinary catheter.

Concern that the patient has infection and not colonization should occur if there are repeatedly positive urine cultures for *Candida* in patients with diabetes or recent urinary manipulation and in patients with systemic signs of infection. Urinalysis showing pyuria is not sensitive or specific for true infection. In the evaluation, include renal imaging with either ultrasound or CT of both the bladder and the kidneys to assess whether there is upper tract disease.

Manage asymptomatic candiduria with negative imaging by changing the urinary catheter if present. Antifungal therapy is not indicated unless the patient will be undergoing urologic manipulation.

Treat symptomatic candiduria with a systemic antifungal based on culture results. Fluconazole is preferred if the isolate is susceptible.

Lipid amphotericins are not excreted in high enough concentrations in the urine to be useful in treating *Candida* UTIs. Echinocandins are also not recommended, for the same reason. Bladder irrigation also is not recommended.

CRYPTOCOCCUS

In immunocompetent patients, *Cryptococcus neoformans* (and *C. gattii*) usually causes minimally symptomatic, self-limited infection after entering via the respiratory route. Patients can have a low-grade fever, pleuritic pain, cough, and a pulmonary infiltrate. Form of treatment depends on level of symptoms. Although it is found in pigeon droppings (similar to *Histoplasma*), most patients have no recollection of being in contact with birds. Cryptococcal pneumonia can form cavitary lesions and peripheral solid "cannon ball" lesions. Lumbar puncture is recommended in pulmonary cryptococcosis, even if without CNS symptoms, as cryptococcal meningitis may be initially asymptomatic and, if present, changes the treatment.

Dissemination is more likely with *C. gattii* in immunodeficient patients (e.g., AIDS, corticosteroid therapy, Hodgkin disease, hematologic malignancies, diabetes, after organ transplant). These patients are especially likely to get cryptococcal meningitis—the most common presentation of severe cryptococcal infection. *C. gattii* is found in northern California and the Pacific Northwest.

Suspect cryptococcal meningitis in any immunosuppressed patient who has headache +/– skin lesions and/or pulmonary lesions +/– fever. More specific meningeal symptoms (e.g., stiff neck, photophobia) are rare. Lumbar puncture commonly shows increased CSF opening pressure, usually > 200 mmH$_2$O. The rest of the spinal fluid analysis may be remarkably benign with minimal leukocytosis and protein elevation. India ink testing is relatively nonspecific and insensitive and has been replaced by cryptococcal antigen testing, which is highly sensitive and specific.

Treatment is long term and occurs in 3 stages:

1) Induction with liposomal amphotericin B + flucytosine for 2 weeks

2) Consolidation with fluconazole 400 mg/day for ≥ 8 weeks

3) Maintenance with fluconazole 200 mg/day for ≥ 1 year

Additionally, daily repeated lumbar punctures are recommended in those with increased intracranial pressure (> 200 mmH$_2$O) or with associated headache, clouded sensorium, visual/hearing loss, or cranial nerve palsies. If these do not reduce pressure, shunts are required.

Maintenance therapy in patients with AIDS should continue > 1 year if the CD4 count does not rise above 100 cells/μL or if the viral load is still detectable.

ASPERGILLOSIS

Aspergillus species are ubiquitous in the environment. *A. fumigatus* is the most commonly isolated pathogen and can cause severe infections, mostly in immunocompromised hosts. Aspergillosis can present with a spectrum of disorders spanning the following:

- **Allergic bronchopulmonary aspergillosis** (ABPA), an allergic reaction to colonization with *Aspergillus* (clinical presentation similar to asthma; more in the Pulmonary Medicine section under Interstitial Lung Diseases (ILDs)
- **Aspergilloma** (a fungus ball in a previously formed cavity; Figure 4-34)
- **Invasive aspergillosis** can be an acute destructive pulmonary process in immunocompromised patients (acute invasive pulmonary aspergillosis) or chronic in those who are immunocompromised (chronic necrotizing aspergillosis) or immunocompetent (chronic cavitary aspergillosis leading to chronic fibrosing aspergillosis).

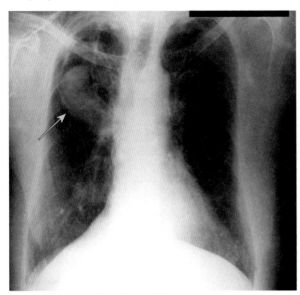

Figure 4-34: Aspergillus fungus ball

Invasive aspergillosis can be rapidly fatal and requires prompt diagnosis and treatment. Diagnose by culture of the organism in combination with lung biopsy with histologic demonstration of tissue invasion. Use caution in interpreting expectorated sputum and bronchoalveolar lavage (BAL) specimens because the organism is common in the environment and may represent colonization. Additional testing (especially if biopsy is not feasible) can include measurement of *Aspergillus* galactomannan antigen in the blood or the BAL fluid and assaying for 1,3-β-D-glucan in the blood.

Treat ABPA with steroids +/− voriconazole. Aspergillomas can be observed, but if symptomatic (hemoptysis), resect. 1st line treatment for the invasive forms of aspergillosis is voriconazole.

ENDEMIC FUNGI

The North American endemic fungi are *Coccidioides*, *Histoplasma*, *Blastomyces*, and *Cryptococcus gattii* (discussed in Cryptococcus). They have the following characteristics in common:

- They are found in specific areas of the U.S., and a patient becomes infected only after visiting or living in

the area where the organism is endemic and participating in activities that encounter the organism.
- They are acquired by inhalation.
- They most commonly cause asymptomatic or mild, self-limited pulmonary disease.
- Less frequently, they cause significant pulmonary disease requiring medical treatment.
- Least commonly, they cause disseminated disease.
- Significant pulmonary disease and dissemination are much more common in immunodeficient patients.
- Mild disease is treated with azoles. Severe disease is treated with liposomal amphotericin B.

Coccidioidomycosis

Coccidioides immitis and *C. posadasii* cause coccidioidomycosis (Figure 4-35). The spores (arthroconidia) are highly infectious at a very low inoculum.

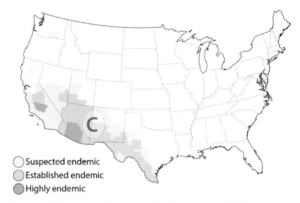

○ Suspected endemic
○ Established endemic
● Highly endemic

Figure 4-35: Geography of coccidioidomycosis, 2018

C. immitis is found in the soil of the arid southwest U.S. and northern Mexico. This disease is frequently called **valley fever** because it is endemic to the San Joaquin Valley and Death Valley.

When inhaled, the arthroconidia convert to their yeast form that, days to weeks later, causes a self-limited, flu-like illness with arthralgias, erythema multiforme, and/or erythema nodosum. Disease can result in a pulmonary "coin lesion." People at highest risk for severe infection include Asian individuals, Black individuals, pregnant women, and people with immunosuppression.

Extrapulmonary coccidioidomycosis can involve bone, skin, or the CNS. Coccidioidomycosis and ABPA are the only 2 fungal diseases that cause peripheral **eosinophilia**.

Demonstration of spherules in body fluids or tissue is diagnostic (Figure 4-36). Culture is also diagnostic, and the organism grows well on almost all media in ~ 1 week. IgM serology is available but takes 1–3 weeks to turn positive.

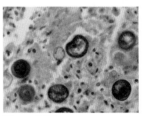

Figure 4-36: Coccidioidomycosis spherules

Most patients have self-limited disease and do not require treatment. If needed, nonmeningeal, less severe infections can be treated with fluconazole or itraconazole. Treat severe cases with liposomal amphotericin B. When treatment is indicated, continue for 6–12 weeks.

Histoplasmosis

Histoplasma capsulatum causes histoplasmosis and is found predominantly in the **M**ississippi and **O**hio River valleys (Figure 4-37).

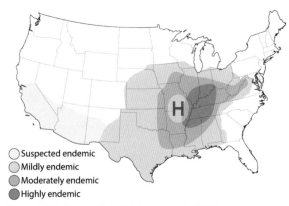

Suspected endemic
Mildly endemic
Moderately endemic
Highly endemic

Figure 4-37: Geography of histoplasmosis, 2018

H. capsulatum is especially prevalent in bat and bird droppings. Conidia or mycelial fragments are the infectious form.

Immunocompetent patients typically have a self-limited, flu-like illness with or without mild pulmonary infiltrates. *Histoplasma* can present with pneumonia, mediastinal adenopathy, superior vena caval obstruction, palate ulcers, and hepatosplenomegaly. On chest radiography, it can mimic cancer, sarcoid, or TB.

In the immunocompromised patient (especially HIV/AIDS), *H. capsulatum* can disseminate, causing a rapidly progressive sepsis and/or multisystem involvement.

Demonstration of characteristic yeast forms with narrow-based budding (Figure 4-38) that are often intracellular is diagnostic. Serum and urine antigen detection is diagnostic and has the highest yield in immunocompromised hosts and/or those with disseminated disease.

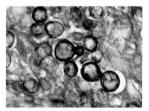

Figure 4-38: Histoplasmosis narrow-based budding

Antigen detection tests cross-react with *Blastomyces dermatitidis*, which diminishes the specificity of these tests, yet the treatments for these 2 fungi are very similar.

Acute, nonsevere pulmonary disease requires no therapy. More severe but localized histoplasmosis can be treated with itraconazole. Disseminated disease requires amphotericin B (liposomal amphotericin B preferred due to less toxicity). This is then followed by itraconazole. Duration of treatment is 12 weeks for nonsevere cases but 1 year for severe disease.

Blastomycosis

Blastomycosis is caused by *Blastomyces dermatitidis*, which, in vivo, is a broad-based budding yeast (remember the **4 Bs**: **b**lasto, **b**road-**b**ased, **b**udding).

Blastomycosis was primarily seen in states bordering the Mississippi and Ohio River basins and the basins near the Great Lakes and along the St. Lawrence River but has since expanded to cover almost all of the eastern half of the U.S. (Figure 4-39).

Figure 4-39: Geography of blastomycosis, 2018

In disseminated blastomycosis, initial infection is often asymptomatic; otherwise, it commonly presents as a flu-like illness. This can progress to a lobar pneumonia that is unresponsive to antibacterial agents. If it disseminates from the lung, it typically does so to the skin, usually causing verrucous (warty) lesions with central ulceration. Septic arthritis, osteomyelitis, and brain abscesses can also be seen.

Demonstration of the yeast form with its broad-based buds in secretions or tissue is diagnostic (Figure 4-40). Cultures require fungal media and turn positive in 1–4 weeks. Urine antigen and serum antigen are usually positive in disseminated disease, with the urine being a more sensitive test.

Treat mild to moderate disease with itraconazole. Severe or CNS disease requires liposomal amphotericin B.

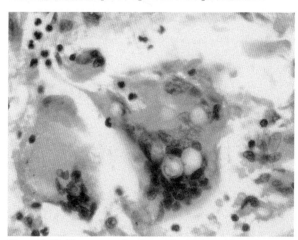

Figure 4-40: Blastomycosis; giant cell with broad-based budding

SPOROTRICHOSIS

Sporotrichosis (a.k.a. rose gardener's disease) is caused by *Sporothrix schenckii*—a ubiquitous dimorphic fungus found in soil and plants. Gardeners are prone after being pricked by a thorn. Of the 4 clinical presentations, the cutaneous and the lymphangitic (nodules form on the skin over lymph channels) types are treated with itraconazole, and the rare pulmonary and disseminated types are treated initially with lipid amphotericin B. The disseminated type is more common in those with immunodeficiency. *Mycobacterium marinum* and *Nocardia brasiliensis* cause similar lesions over lymphatic channels.

MUCORMYCOSIS

Mucormycosis (previously zygomycosis) is caused by fungi in the order Mucorales. *Mucor*, *Rhizopus*, and *Rhizomucor* are the most common species of Mucorales that cause human disease.

Rhizopus thrives in acidic and high-glucose conditions. These conditions occur in patients with iron overload on deferoxamine chelation, in patients with diabetes, and in those with primary or secondary hemochromatosis. The severely immunosuppressed are also at risk.

Disease can present as invasive pulmonary or rhinocerebral infection. **Rhinocerebral mucormycosis** presents as a black necrotic spot on the paranasal skin, nasal mucosa, or paranasal sinuses that can extend intracranially. Necrotic areas can also be seen on the hard palate. It has a poor prognosis.

Pulmonary mucormycosis presents as a necrotizing, cavitating pneumonia, similar to aspergillosis. Fungi causing mucormycosis are uniformly resistant to voriconazole, so consider mucormycosis in at-risk patients who have received voriconazole and develop new or worsening pulmonary disease.

Diagnosis is made by biopsy showing broad, nonseptate hyphae with right-angle branching that are described as "ribbon-like" (Figure 4-41).

Treat with correction of predisposing factors (e.g., diabetic ketoacidosis), aggressive surgical resection, and lipid amphotericin B. Use posaconazole or isavuconazole in those who cannot tolerate amphotericin B or for salvage therapy. The other azoles (fluconazole, itraconazole, voriconazole) do not have activity against mucormycosis.

MICROSPORIDIA

The phylum Microsporidia encompasses a large group of organisms. They are intracellular pathogens and have been recently reclassified as fungal organisms rather than protozoans. The most common microsporidia infecting humans are *Enterocytozoon bieneusi* and *Encephalitozoon intestinalis*. They most commonly cause diarrhea, though they can infect extraintestinal sites including the cornea, brain, skeletal muscle, prosthetic joints, biliary tract and gallbladder, lung, liver, and kidney. Extraintestinal involvement is rare unless the individual is immunocompromised. Water contact is a risk factor for acquisition. The diagnosis is made by demonstrating spores in the stool by trichrome, immunofluorescent, or calcofluor white staining; by PCR assay of the stool; or by biopsies from other organs. Unlike other intestinal opportunists, they are not acid fast. Bowel disease is patchy, so biopsy does not increase the yield. Albendazole is the treatment of choice but is minimally effective against *E. bieneusi*.

DERMATOPHYTES

Dermatophytes infect keratinized structures, such as skin and hair.

The names of the diseases caused by dermatophytes begin with "tinea" and end with the location of their infection: tinea corporis, tinea capitis, tinea pedis, and tinea cruris. See the Dermatology section under Skin Infections for more information.

Treat ringworm (tinea corporis) with topical clotrimazole, topical terbinafine, or undecylenic acid. If topical treatment fails, use an oral agent; the preferred ones are itraconazole and terbinafine. Infection of hair follicles (tinea capitis) requires treatment with oral agents, such as terbinafine, itraconazole, and fluconazole.

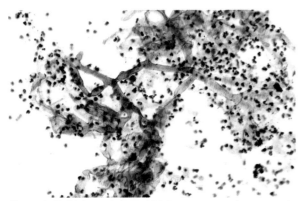

Figure 4-41: Right-angle branching in mucormycosis pneumonia

PARASITES

PREVIEW | REVIEW

- How is a *Giardia* infection diagnosed?
- What is kala azar?
- Which form of malaria is associated with banana-shaped gametocytes?
- For travel to chloroquine-resistant areas, which drugs are used for malaria prophylaxis?
- What is the presentation of *Babesia* infection?
- *Strongyloides* hyperinfection syndrome can be seen in which patient population?

INFECTIOUS DISEASE

- What is visceral larva migrans?
- What are the clinical manifestations and treatment of neurocysticercosis?

There are 2 main types of parasites, **protozoa** and **helminthic organisms**.

PROTOZOA

Protozoa are single-celled and can replicate within the body. With the exception of *Cystoisospora*, protozoa do not cause eosinophilia.

There are 3 types of protozoa:

1) Sporozoa (*Toxoplasma, Cryptosporidium, Cystoisospora* [previously *Isospora*], microsporidia, *Plasmodium, Cyclospora, Babesia*)

2) Amebas (*Entamoeba histolytica, Naegleria fowleri*)

3) Flagellates (*Giardia, Trichomonas, Trypanosoma, Leishmania*)

We classify the protozoan parasites in terms of the systems they affect (Figure 4-42).

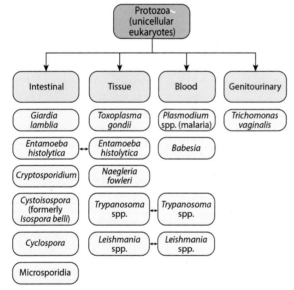

Figure 4-42: Classification of parasites — protozoa

Intestinal Protozoans

Giardia

Giardia lamblia (a.k.a. *Giardia duodenalis, Giardia intestinalis*) is an intestinal protozoan that infects the duodenum and proximal jejunum by adhering to the mucosa. Infected persons are asymptomatic in 75% of cases. Distribution is worldwide and it is the most common intestinal parasite in North America. Infection occurs through ingestion of infectious cysts from contaminated food, water, or fomites. Cysts turn into trophozoites in the gut, and look like a face with flagella legs when viewed under the microscope.

Groups of people at increased risk for *Giardia* infections include:

- Campers/backpackers (drinking unfiltered water)
- Travelers to endemic regions
- Young children in day care (and their parents)
- HIV-infected persons
- Anyone who has oral-anal sexual contact
- IgA deficiency (Remember: IgA is actively secreted across mucosal barriers, so this makes sense.)

Infection may be asymptomatic, posing infectious risk to others. If symptoms are present, they include foul, floating, watery diarrhea; sulfur-tasting burps; and flatulence associated with a malabsorption syndrome. A helpful distinguishing feature is prolonged diarrhea, with flatulence, frequently associated with weight loss. Diagnose by microscopic examination of fresh stool samples, antigen detection, or nucleic acid amplification assays, with the latter being the most sensitive. Excretion of the organism is intermittent, so up to 3 stools may be needed to make the diagnosis. Treat with a single dose of tinidazole. Nitazoxanide is also effective but is a 3-day course. Metronidazole is less effective than these 2 agents.

Entamoeba

Human amebiasis is caused by the protozoan *Entamoeba histolytica*. Distribution is worldwide, though primary burden of disease occurs in developing countries. There are 30–50 million cases per year around the world, and it is the 3rd most common parasitic disease in the U.S.; the most commonly affected population groups are persons living in institutions, immigrants, travelers, and people who have anal sex. Transmission occurs after ingestion of cysts via the fecal-oral route from food or oral-anal sexual contact. Cysts (which are viable in the environment for months) convert to trophozoites in the small bowel and then invade the colonic mucosa.

There are 3 major clinical syndromes:

1) **Asymptomatic** cyst-passing carrier state (90% of cases)

2) **Amebic colitis**: subacute (3–4 weeks) progressively worsening diarrhea with abdominal pain. 95% have bloody stools. Fever is only seen in about 1/3 of cases.

3) **Amebic liver abscess** (< 1% of cases): seeded via portal system; usually presents as subacute RUQ pain, most commonly occurs in adult men; typically a solitary abscess

Diagnosis of intestinal disease by stool for ova and parasites has been surpassed by antigen detection tests, which have in turn been surpassed by PCR testing for *E. histolytica* that have ~100% sensitivity and specificity. Amebic liver abscesses often occur in the absence of amebic colitis, so stool testing may be negative in those cases. However, ~100% of patients will have positive serologies after 1 week of illness. In serologically positive individuals, abscess aspiration is not needed unless the abscess is > 10 cm, imaging suggests imminent rupture, or there is a failure to respond to appropriate treatment. If aspirated, the fluid is thick and brown (like anchovy paste) and is made up of degenerated hepatocytes. Amebas are seen in < 20% of cases.

Treat with metronidazole or tinidazole for both forms of the disease. Although metronidazole treats amebas that have invaded, it may not kill intraluminal cysts. This must be accomplished with the administration of paromomycin, iodoquinol, or diloxanide furoate.

Cryptosporidium

Cryptosporidium parvum and *C. hominis* are acid-fast, intestinal protozoans that cause enteric infections. *Cryptosporidium* is found worldwide. Infection occurs after ingestion of oocysts, usually from fecally contaminated water. Cryptosporidium is quite hardy and unique from other intestinal pathogens in that it can be acquired after swimming in recreational, chlorine-treated water, such as swimming pools or water parks. The patient's immune response influences the severity and duration of illness, as well as response to therapy. *Cryptosporidium* typically causes watery diarrhea for 1–2 weeks in immunocompetent patients but can be quite severe and protracted in immunocompromised patients and spread to extraintestinal sites, causing cholangitis and/or acalculous cholecystitis. The most sensitive testing is accomplished through stool PCR testing, followed by (in order of decreasing sensitivity): monoclonal antibody testing, stool for trichrome staining, and stool for acid-fast staining. Therapy involves supportive care, nitazoxanide for severe or prolonged illness, and (if applicable) reduction of immunosuppression or initiation of antiretroviral therapy.

Cystoisospora belli and Cyclospora cayetanensis

C. belli (previously *Isospora belli*) and *C. cayetanensis* are 2 partial acid-fast protozoans that cause a secretory, self-limited diarrhea in immunocompetent patients and more severe chronic forms of diarrhea in patients with compromised immune systems (especially those with advanced HIV/AIDS) that can also cause cholangitis and acalculous cholecystitis. Infections occur worldwide, though more commonly in tropic/subtropic regions. Infection develops after fecal-oral ingestion of oocysts. *Cyclospora* in particular is often the cause of outbreaks related to imported fruits or vegetables. A clue to these intestinal protozoan infections is a longer duration of illness (> 1 week) than most bacterial GI infections. Diagnosis can be made via stool microscopy, aided by modified acid-fast staining and/or fluorescent monoclonal antibody staining. PCR has the highest sensitivity if available. Because excretion of oocysts is intermittent, multiple stool samples are often needed to secure a diagnosis. Treat with TMP/SMX or, in the sulfa-allergic patient, use ciprofloxacin or nitazoxanide.

Tissue Protozoans

In addition to the tissue protozoans described here, *Entamoeba histolytica* can also manifest as tissue disease (see *Entamoeba*).

Toxoplasma gondii

Toxoplasma gondii is a tissue protozoan that causes toxoplasmosis. Felines, including domestic cats, are the definitive host (i.e., the host in which the adult parasite lives); they excrete the oocysts. After oocysts are ingested by other animals, they encyst in their muscles. If undercooked muscle from these animals (mainly pigs, lambs, and cattle) or food/water contaminated by oocysts is ingested by humans, the organism excysts, and tachyzoites are released that circulate through the bloodstream and infect any nucleated cell—with a predilection for neural tissue. ~ 20% of pork and lamb and 10% of beef contain *T. gondii* cysts. Thus, consumption of undercooked meat and outdoor cat contact/ownership are modes of oral acquisition. The organism may also be transmitted vertically during pregnancy and to organ donor recipients. Infection is not uncommon in the U.S., with ~ 10% of adults demonstrating seropositivity to the organism.

There are 4 clinical settings of toxoplasmosis:

1) Immunocompetent host
2) Congenital
3) CNS
4) Ocular

Immunocompetent hosts are usually asymptomatic, but toxoplasmosis may cause fever, lymphadenopathy, and atypical lymphocytosis similar to infectious mononucleosis; pharyngitis is conspicuously absent. Diagnose by demonstrating the presence of IgM antibody. It is self-limited and requires no treatment.

If acquired during pregnancy, *T. gondii* can infect the fetus and cause **congenital toxoplasmosis,** with a combination of necrotizing chorioretinitis, hydrocephalus, intracranial calcifications, and intellectual disabilities (see the Women's and Men's Health section under Obstetrics).

CNS toxoplasmosis occurs in immunocompromised patients (particularly those with AIDS) from reactivation of previous infection. These patients present with new onset of seizures, neurologic deficit, and/or altered consciousness. Diagnosis is made by brain imaging revealing multiple, bilateral, ring-enhancing lesions with a predilection for the basal ganglia. When considering CNS toxoplasmosis, the other main differential diagnosis to consider in a patient with AIDS and ring enhancing lesions is primary CNS lymphoma (though lymphoma lesions are typically single). Because this is a reactivation disease, IgM antibody is not present—but IgG is. However, a negative IgG does not necessarily exclude infection in the immunocompromised patient because of difficulty making antibodies. Treat with pyrimethamine, sulfadiazine, and leucovorin. Substitute clindamycin for sulfadiazine in the sulfa-allergic patient.

Ocular toxoplasmosis causes retinal lesions that appear as yellow-white cotton patches, irregular scarring, and pigmentation. This can be a primary infection but can also be reactivation in the immunocompromised host. Treat with pyrimethamine and a sulfadiazine for 3 weeks.

Naegleria fowleri

Naegleria fowleri is a free-living ameba found worldwide in warm freshwater (not saltwater). It causes primary amebic meningoencephalitis, a rare and rapidly fatal disease that occurs when infested water comes in contact with nasal mucosa and the cribriform plate, usually after extensive exposure through swimming, diving, water-skiing, and surfing. The disease is rare with the risk of infection being 1 in 2.6 million exposures.

Typical cases involve a young, previously health patient, ~ 2–5 days after recreational water exposure, presenting with a rapidly progressive meningoencephalitis that is almost universally fatal within 2 weeks. Spinal fluid shows a polymorphonuclear pleocytosis and is often hemorrhagic. The diagnosis can be made by demonstrating the motile organisms on a centrifuged CSF specimen.

Because of the rarity of the disease and the high mortality rate, there are no convincing trials to determine optimal therapy, and treatment should be recommended in concert with contacting the CDC for the latest recommendations.

Trypanosoma

Trypanosoma is a tissue/blood protozoan that causes 2 distinct diseases: Chagas disease and human African trypanosomiasis.

Chagas disease is caused by *T. cruzi* and is transmitted to humans via the triatomine bug (a.k.a. reduviid bug or kissing bug). It has a large impact on health and wellness, affecting 6–8 million people worldwide with 50,000 deaths per year. It occurs primarily in Central and South America. Acute illness is nonspecific with fever, lymphadenopathy, and hepatosplenomegaly. There is an intermediate phase without symptoms, followed by a chronic phase with predominately GI (megaesophagus and megacolon) and cardiac involvement (heart failure and ventricular arrhythmias). Congenital infection occurs as well. Make the diagnosis by microscopic identification of organisms from the buffy coat of blood during acute disease and by tissue biopsy and serologies in chronic disease. Treat patients with acute illness, those with congenital infection, reactivation in immunosuppressed patients, and young patients (< 18 years of age) who are asymptomatic. Treatment is with benznidazole; 2nd line is nifurtimox. Do not treat people with advanced heart disease, those who are pregnant, or patients with multiorgan failure.

Human African trypanosomiasis, caused by *T. brucei gambiense* and *T. brucei rhodesiense*, is much less common, affecting ~ 10,000 people per year worldwide. It is transmitted by the bite of the Tsetse fly in East, Central, and West Africa. A painful chancre develops at the bite, after which organisms disseminate to lymphatics, then blood, then finally to the CNS, where neuropsychiatric symptoms and sleep disturbances can occur. Death and coma will occur if left untreated. It is important to always rule out CNS disease with a lumbar puncture. Diagnosis is made by microscopy of buffy coat or other fluids, serology study, and tissue biopsy. Treatment should be done in consultation with the CDC.

Leishmania

Leishmaniasis is caused by any of the following 4 species of the *Leishmania* protozoa: *L. donovani*, *L. tropica*, *L. mexicana*, and *L. braziliensis*. It is spread via the sand fly in tropical and subtropical regions around the world. It is characterized by a chronic, progressive course with 3 main phenotypes:

1) **Cutaneous** (painless ulcer)
2) **Mucocutaneous** (destructive lesions in oral/nasal mucosa)
3) **Visceral** (a.k.a. kala azar; hepatosplenomegaly, pancytopenia)

Of note, there is a higher susceptibility for leishmaniasis in HIV-infected patients who travel to endemic areas. Diagnosis is made by histologic examination of infected tissues for cutaneous and mucocutaneous disease, and the highest yield for visceral disease is a bone marrow biopsy. Treatment varies from observation, to local therapies, to systemic therapy, depending on the extent of disease, location of acquisition, and host immune status. Treatment regimens should be created in consultation with the CDC.

Blood Protozoans

In addition to the blood protozoans described here, *Trypanosoma* and *Leishmania* can also manifest as blood disease. They are described under Tissue Protozoans in *Trypanosoma* and *Leishmania*.

Plasmodium (Malaria)

Malaria—an acute febrile illness of varying severity caused by a blood protozoan—is a very old disease, described by ancient civilizations. There are 5 clinically relevant species within the genus *Plasmodium* (Table 4-9).

The clinical significance of malaria cannot be understated. According to the WHO World Malaria Report, there were 228 million cases of malaria with 405,000 deaths in 2019 alone. Africa carries the highest burden of disease and highest mortality, which is typically attributed to *P. falciparum*.

Table 4-9: Malaria Species Characteristics					
Species	**Fever Cycle***	**% of Cases**	**Has a Liver Stage†**	**RBCs Infected**	**Parasite Level**
P. falciparum	Tertian	48%	No	All	High
P. vivax	Tertian	51%	Yes	Retics	Low
P. ovale	Tertian	1%	Yes	Retics	Low
P. malariae	Quartan	1%	No	Old	Low
P. knowlesi	Irregular	< 1%	No	All	May be high

* Fever spikes by cycle: tertian = every other day, quartan = every 3rd day
† Liver stage requires primaquine to prevent relapse

The basic life cycle of malaria is important to consider to understand the disease. The female *Anopheles* mosquito releases sporozoites during a blood meal. Sporozoites travel to the liver and mature. *P. vivax* and *P. ovale* can form hypnozoites and "sleep" in the liver, allowing for recurrent infection unless appropriately treated. After maturation in the liver, merozoites are released into the bloodstream and continuously infect, mature, then rupture red blood cells (RBCs). In RBCs, merozoites mature into ringed trophozoites, which is the form that is typically identified on microscopy. Some merozoites in the bloodstream form gametocytes, which transmit back to uninfected *Anopheles* mosquitos and then infect additional people.

Consider malaria in any febrile traveler returning from an endemic region. Geographic hot spots include sub-Saharan Africa and tropical regions of South America, Asia, and Indonesia.

As we go through the following discussion, refer to Table 4-10.

After an incubation period of 1–12 weeks, malaria typically presents as an acute febrile illness with chills, rigors, profound fatigue, and splenomegaly. Fevers can be very high (> 40°C, 104°F) and may be spaced in regular intervals, correlating with cycles of RBC rupture. In endemic regions, due to partial immunity, symptoms can be milder or more indolent. *P. falciparum* deserves special attention because it causes the majority of severe malaria due to its ability to lodge in microvasculature and obstruct blood flow. Severe disease may manifest as cerebral malaria (seizure, coma), shock, acidosis, severe anemia, respiratory distress (ARDS), hypoglycemia, and renal failure. Anemia occurs through a combination of hemolysis and bone marrow suppression.

Diagnosis is made by microscopic analysis of blood smears. Thick blood smears analyze a larger volume of blood by lysing RBCs and looking for parasites to diagnose the diseases. Thin blood smears are used to make a species diagnosis based on the stage and appearance within intact RBCs. This then determines what initial treatment should be given and whether a "radical cure" with primaquine is needed *(P. vivax, P. ovale)*. Rapid diagnostic tests are also available that can detect antigens common to all *Plasmodium* species as well as antigens specific to *P. falciparum*.

Plasmodium falciparum

Plasmodium falciparum causes the most severe malaria and is the cause of virtually all fatal malarial infections. It has widespread chloroquine resistance.

Differentiating this species from the others is critical because *P. falciparum* causes the vast majority of the mortality attributed to malaria throughout the world. *P. falciparum* has several unique findings on blood smears that facilitate this identification: **banana-shaped**

Table 4-10: Treatment of Malaria		
	Clinical Scenario	**Treatment**
P. falciparum malaria	Artemisinins available	**Artemisinin combination therapy (ACT):** Artemisinin and lumefantrine or mefloquine or pyrimethamine-sulfadoxine
	Artemisinins not available	**Chloroquine sensitive:** chloroquine **Chloroquine resistant:** atovaquone and proguanil or any 2 of: quinine, doxycycline, clindamycin
	First trimester of pregnancy	**1st line:** Quinine and clindamycin **2nd line:** ACT
Non-P. falciparum malaria	All scenarios	**Chloroquine sensitive:** chloroquine or ACT (if available) **Chloroquine resistant P. vivax:** ACT

INFECTIOUS DISEASE

gametocytes (Figure 4-43); double chromatin knobs (giving the parasite the appearance of headphones); > 1 parasite per cell; and the number of infected RBCs being > 5%.

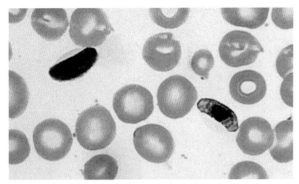

Figure 4-43: P. falciparum banana-shaped gametocytes

Treatment of *P. falciparum* was updated by the WHO in 2021 and has become simplified. All regimens should use artemisinin combined therapy (ACT)—an artemisinin drug in combination with another agent. The artemisinins have become the drugs of choice because they clear the parasitemia quicker than any other agents and kill all forms of *Plasmodia*, including the gametocytes, which decreases transmission of infection to mosquitoes, and they have a good safety profile. They have not been well studied in the first trimester of pregnancy. The 2 artemisinins available in the U.S. are artemether (PO) and artesunate (IV/IM). Artemether is in a combination tablet with lumefantrine. Oral drugs that can be used with parenteral artenusate are mefloquine or the combination pyrimethamine/sulfadoxine tablets. Drugs are given over a 3-day course.

If artemisinins are not available or tolerated, treatment for *P. falciparum* is based on the known chloroquine susceptibilities in the regions of:

• Central America west of Panama
• Haiti
• Dominican Republic
• Most of the Middle East

Infection acquired in these areas should be treated with chloroquine. Infections in all other regions of acquisition should be treated with a 2-drug regimen of either atovaquone and proguanil or any 2 of quinine, doxycycline, or clindamycin.

Non–*Plasmodium falciparum* spp.

Treatment of non–*P. falciparum* malaria is with an ACT or chloroquine. *Plasmodium vivax* chloroquine resistance exists in Southeast Asia, Ethiopia, Madagascar, and Papua, New Guinea; infection acquired in these regions should be treated with an ACT.

P. vivax and *P. ovale* remain dormant in the liver and can reactivate weeks, months, or years after initial infection. Elimination of these organisms is called a radical cure and is accomplished by the administration of primaquine or tafenoquine. These drugs can cause hemolysis in G6PD-deficient individuals so testing is required prior to administration and is contraindicated in pregnancy.

Prophylaxis

Patients traveling to malarious areas should be instructed on mosquito avoidance and given chemoprophylaxis to prevent infection. Drugs are started prior to departure to assure adequate blood levels and to detect intolerance prior to travel so that alternatives can be given. They continue after travel to assure eradication of organisms not yet released from red cells.

See Table 4-11.

In chloroquine-sensitive areas: Use chloroquine or hydroxychloroquine.

In chloroquine-resistant areas: Use mefloquine, atovaquone/proguanil, doxycycline, or tafenoquine.

Malaria in pregnancy can be particularly severe, so prevention is key. Deferment of travel is recommended. If travel cannot be delayed, emphasize mosquito avoidance and give chemoprophylaxis. Only 3 regimens are approved for administration during pregnancy: chloroquine, hydroxychloroquine, and mefloquine.

Babesia

Babesia microti is an intraerythrocytic protozoan parasite indigenous to the U.S. that causes babesiosis. Similar to malaria, it causes a febrile hemolytic anemia, and asplenic patients are at increased risk for severe disease.

Table 4-11: Malaria Chemoprophylaxis Regimens				
Drug	**Frequency**	**Pretrip Start**	**Duration Posttrip**	**Use in Pregnancy**
Chloroquine*	Weekly	1–2 weeks	4 weeks	Yes
Hydroxychloroquine*	Weekly	1–2 weeks	4 weeks	Yes
Mefloquine	Weekly	2–3 weeks	4 weeks	Yes
Atovaquone / proguanil	Daily	1–2 days	1 week	No
Doxycycline	Daily	1–2 days	4 weeks	No
Tafenoquine	Daily for 3 days, then weekly	3 days	1 week	No

*If no chloroquine resistance in area of acquisition

The organism is transmitted via the *Ixodes* tick, which is also the vector for Lyme disease and anaplasmosis. It is most prevalent in the northeast U.S. and upper Midwest, usually in summer or early autumn. The primary animal hosts are the white-footed mouse and white-tailed deer. Rare cases result from blood transfusion.

Symptoms of *Babesia* infection, which can persist for months, include fever, profuse sweats, myalgias, and shaking chills. Severe cases cause liver, renal, and neurologic failure and death. Hemoglobinuria is a predominant sign.

Diagnosis is made by a thin blood smear or PCR for *Babesia* antigens, the latter being more sensitive and specific. These may need to be repeated if tests are initially negative and there is high clinical suspicion. Serologies may be helpful with low-level parasitemia, but diagnosis should be based on a 4-fold rise and not a single titer. The presence or absence of travel to malarious areas is important for the microbiology lab because babesiosis can be misdiagnosed as malaria. *B. microti* is distinguished from *Plasmodium* by being pear-shaped or by PCR. *B. microti* occasionally form a tetrad, appearing as a **Maltese cross**. Figure 4-44 shows the *Babesia* parasites in both ring and tetrad forms.

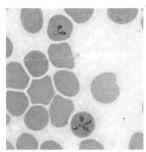

Figure 4-44: Babesia parasites in both tetrad and ring forms

Mild babesiosis infections are usually self-limited. Treat moderate infections with atovaquone + azithromycin and severe cases with clindamycin + quinine and consider an exchange transfusion.

Genitourinary (GU) Protozoans

Trichomonas vaginalis

Trichomonas vaginalis causes trichomoniasis, an STI. Treat with metronidazole for 7 days. See more about this under Trichomoniasis on page 4-23.

HELMINTHIC ORGANISMS

Helminthic organisms are multicellular worms that cause eosinophilia. Helminthic organisms consist of roundworms (nematodes) and flatworms, which are divided into tapeworms and flukes. With the exception of *Strongyloides*, helminthic organisms do not replicate in the human host.

In Figure 4-45, helminthic parasites in terms of the systems they affect.

Roundworms (Nematodes)

Roundworm (nematode) infections are listed in Table 4-12 on page 4-68.

Intestinal Roundworms

Enterobius vermicularis (Pinworm, Threadworm)

- Epidemiology: most common helminthic infection in the U.S.; humans are the only host. Occurs commonly in school-aged children and their families.
- Life cycle: Eggs (Figure 4-46 on page 4-69) are ingested and hatch in the small intestine. Gravid females migrate to the rectum and, at night, lay eggs in the perianal area. Autoinfection is possible (i.e., scratch anal area with hands and ingest eggs via contaminated hands).

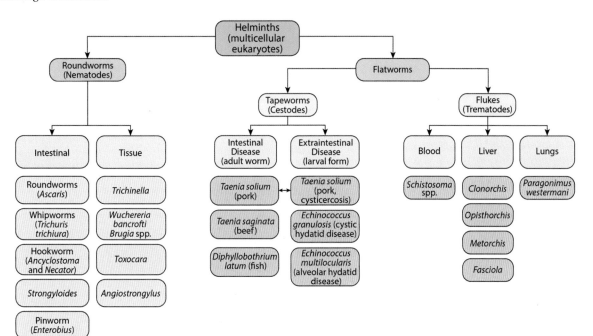

Figure 4-45: Classification of parasites—helminths

INFECTIOUS DISEASE

			Table 4-12: Roundworm (Nematode) Infections			
Species	**Common Name**	**Route of Acquisition**	**Life Cycle in Humans**	**Signs and Symptoms***	**Diagnosis**	**Treatment**
Enterobius vermicularis	Pinworm; threadworm	Ova ingestion	Eggs → hatch to adults → lay perianal eggs	Perianal itch	Tape test	Albendazole or mebendazole
Ascaris lumbricoides	Human roundworm	Ova ingestion	Eggs → larvae through lungs → swallowed → adults in bowel	PES; can obstruct bile duct or appendix	Stool ova	Albendazole or mebendazole
Trichuris trichiura	Whipworm	Ova ingestion	Eggs ingested → hatch in small intestine → mature in caecum and ascending colon → excrete eggs in stool	Diarrhea; abdominal pain; blood in stool; rectal prolapse	Stool ova	Albendazole or mebendazole
Necator americanus and *Ancylostoma duodenale*	Hookworm	Larvae enter through skin	Soil larvae → penetrates skin → through lungs → swallowed → adults attach and feed in bowel	Ground itch; CLM; iron deficiency; hypoalbuminemia	Stool ova	Albendazole or mebendazole
Strongyloides stercoralis	Strongyloidiasis	Larvae enter through skin (only spp. to autoinfect)	Soil larvae → penetrates skin → through lungs → swallowed → adults attach, mate in bowel, produce more larvae → cycle repeats	Ground itch; CLM; PES; abdominal pain; N/V/D; immunocompromised hyperinfection with multiorgan invasion and shock	Stool larvae; serology in immunocompetent	Ivermectin
Trichinella	Trichinellosis	Cysts in undercooked meat ingested	Excyst → adult releases larvae → blood → muscle	Muscle pain; high worm burdens can affect the CNS, lungs, heart, and kidneys	Muscle biopsy; serology	Albendazole with glucocorticoids
Wuchereria bancrofti, Brugia malayi, and *Brugia timori*	Lymphatic filariasis	Mosquito injects larvae	Larvae in lymphatics → adult → releases microfilaria → ingested by next mosquito	Acute fever; microfilaria in lungs cause wheezing; lymphedema	Blood smears for microfilaria; best around midnight	Diethyl-carbamazine (only available from CDC)
Toxocara canis and *Toxocara cati*	Toxocariasis, visceral larva migrans	Ova ingestion	Eggs → larvae migrate through tissues	Hepatomegaly; myocarditis; PES; eosinophilic meningitis; myalgia; ocular lesions	Serology	Albendazole
Angiostrongylus cantonensis and *Angiostrongylus costaricensis*	Rat lungworm; angiostrongyliasis	Ingestion of larvae in snails and others	Larvae enter blood → CNS or mesenteric arteries	Headache; eosinophilic meningitis or abdominal pain; N/V; GI bleed and perforation	Organisms in CSF (rare) or on bowel biopsy (rare)	No drug available; surgery for ocular complications

* If present

CLM = cutaneous larval migrans
CNS = central nervous system
CSF = cerebrospinal fluid

GI = gastrointestinal
N/V/D = nausea, vomiting, and diarrhea
PES = pulmonary eosinophilic syndrome (fleeting infiltrates, cough, wheeze, and eosinophilia)

- Presentation (if symptomatic): perianal itching
- Diagnosis: microscopic exam of transparent tape (that touched the perianal area) demonstrating eggs and sometimes female worms (Scotch tape test)
- Treatment: albendazole or mebendazole

Ascaris lumbricoides (Human Roundworm)

- Causes ascariasis
- Epidemiology: Worldwide, > 1 billion people are infected—predominantly in tropical and subtropical regions with poor hygiene. Humans are the sole host. In the U.S., 2% overall are infected (worse in the rural South), with up to 30% of young children affected in some areas.
- Life cycle: Eggs (Figure 4-47) are ingested and hatch in the small intestine; the larvae penetrate the intestinal wall and migrate to the lungs, where they mature over 10 days. Then they ascend the bronchial tree, which generates a cough reflex, and then are swallowed. They mature into adult worms in the small intestine, and eggs are excreted in the stool. Eggs can live for up to 10 years in dark, moist conditions. Worms may migrate into the biliary tree and the appendix.
- Presentation (if symptomatic): pulmonary eosinophilic syndrome (a Löffler-type syndrome) in early phase of infection, malnutrition, acute appendicitis, biliary obstruction including ascending cholangitis
- Diagnosis: microscopy, demonstrating eggs (and rarely, worms) in stool. This is usually not demonstrable until 40 days after pulmonary symptoms if they occurred.
- Treatment: albendazole or mebendazole

Trichuris trichiura (Whipworm)

- Epidemiology: Worldwide, > 1.5 billion people are infected (~ 25% of world's population), mainly children. Found in warm, moist places with poor sanitation, similar to *Ascaris*; coinfection is not uncommon.
- Life cycle: Eggs are ingested, hatch in small intestine, and mature in caecum and ascending colon where they embed in epithelial layer; eggs are excreted in stool. There is no lung stage.

- May present with eosinophilia
- Presentation (if symptomatic): chronic colitis in children, *Trichuris* dysentery syndrome (diarrhea with mucus, blood, tenesmus, abdominal pain, and rectal prolapse)
- Diagnosis: stool microscopy demonstrating eggs in stool
- Treatment: albendazole or mebendazole

Necator americanus and *Ancylostoma duodenale* (Hookworm)

- Epidemiology: *Necator* is endemic in the U.S. but can be found throughout the Americas, India, Africa, and Indonesia. *Ancylostoma* is found in the Mediterranean, Iran, India, Pakistan, China, and Southeast Asia. Acquisition requires coming into barefoot contact with larvae in the soil that have hatched from eggs excreted by humans. People walking barefoot or with open sandals in contaminated areas are at risk.
- Life cycle: Larvae penetrate the skin, migrate to the lungs and up the bronchial tree, cough reflex occurs, and then the larvae are swallowed. Once in the small intestine, they mature and attach to the intestinal wall, where they feed. Eggs are excreted in stool.
- Presentation (if symptomatic): cutaneous itching at the site of larval entry (ground itch) and serpiginous eruption along the course of the larvae's migration (**cutaneous larval migrans** [CLM]). Pneumonitis can occur during pulmonary migration, although it is less severe than that of *Ascaris*. Chronic infection leads to iron deficiency anemia from chronic GI blood loss and hypoalbuminemia in persons already malnourished. Persistent eosinophilia may also be present.
- Diagnosis: stool microscopy demonstrating eggs in stool
- Treatment: albendazole or mebendazole

Strongyloides stercoralis (Strongyloidiasis)

- Epidemiology: endemic in soil throughout tropical regions of the world and in parts of the U.S. *Strongyloides stercoralis* is the only helminthic organism that can complete its life cycle within the human body,

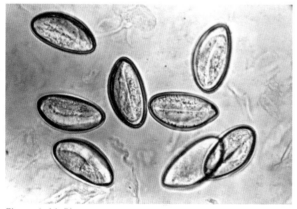

Figure 4-46: Pinworm egg

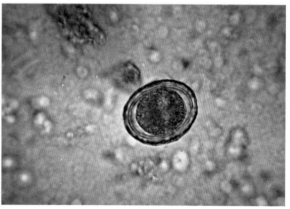

Figure 4-47: Roundworm egg

resulting in autoinfection and persistence of infection. The filariform larvae penetrate the perianal or colonic mucosa to complete the autoinfection cycle. This can lead to overwhelming worm burden in immuno-compromised patients. Patients who are immuno-suppressed, including steroid use, HTLV infection, advanced HIV/AIDS, organ or bone marrow trans-plantation, and chemotherapy, are at greatest risk for hyperinfection syndrome.

- Life cycle: Like hookworm, the *Strongyloides* larvae penetrate the skin (usually after walking barefoot on feces-contaminated ground) and migrate to the lungs. They then migrate up the tracheobronchial tree, pro-duce a cough reflex, and are swallowed. Once in the small intestine, they attach to the mucosa and mature. Adult female worms produce eggs that hatch into noninfectious rhabditiform larvae, which are mostly excreted in the stool. However, some of these noninfectious larvae convert to infectious filariform larvae while still within the small intestine. These larvae pen-etrate the wall of the colon or perianal skin to hema-togenously travel to the lung, just like exogenously introduced larvae do.

- Presentation (if symptomatic):
  ◦ Like hookworm, itching at the site of larval entry (ground itch) and a fast-moving serpiginous erup-tion along the course of the larvae's migration (larva currens) can occur; this is pathognomonic.
  ◦ Pulmonary eosinophilic pneumonitis can occur, causing a Löffler-like syndrome.
  ◦ GI symptoms include abdominal pain, nausea, vom-iting, and diarrhea.
  ◦ **Strongyloides hyperinfection syndrome** is seen in immunocompromised hosts. Those who receive high-dose steroids, and those with advanced HIV or HTLV-1 are at particular risk. This represents an augmented and accelerated autoinfection cycle. As worms migrate out of the GI tract, they can bring bacteria with them—think of this with polymicro-bial GNR bacteremia or community-acquired GNR meningitis. Perhaps counterintuitively, peripheral eosinophilia may be absent in these patients due to blunted immune response.

- Diagnosis: Larvae in the stool are diagnostic but are seen in < 50% of those infected. A higher yield is obtained by stool culture plates incubated for 2 days and demonstrating a trail of bacteria dragged along by the parasite (Figure 4-48). Serology is useful in immu-nocompetent patients. In hyperinfection syndrome, many larvae can often be seen in respiratory samples.

- Treatment: Ivermectin

Tissue Roundworms

Trichinella spp. (Trichinellosis)

- Epidemiology: ~ 10,000 cases worldwide are reported per year. *T. spiralis* is the most common *Trichinella* species in the U.S. The main sources of the disease

Figure 4-48: Strongyloides (causing a serpiginous trail around the bacterial colonies)

are undercooked wild game (e.g., bear, wild boar) and domesticated pigs (pork). In the U.S., ~ 20 cases are reported each year, although there is a much higher incidence seen on autopsy.

- Life cycle: Cysts in undercooked meat are ingested then excyst and mature into adults in the small bowel, where they release larvae that invade via the blood into the muscle, where they burrow and encyst in a muscle cell.

- Presentation (if symptomatic):
  ◦ Intestinal phase (week 1): invade small bowel mucosa, patients may experience watery diarrhea, abdominal pain
  ◦ Muscle phase (> week 1): hematogenous dissemina-tion and encystment into striated muscle; muscle pain, fevers, splinter hemorrhages
  ◦ Eosinophilia is common. High worm burdens can affect the CNS, lungs, heart (e.g., fatal cardiomyopa-thy), and kidneys.

- Diagnosis: Serology is available and turns positive after several weeks. Muscle biopsy may be performed to look for cysts. High-grade eosinophilia is almost always present.

- Treatment for mild cases is supportive. Otherwise give albendazole or mebendazole. Also give glucocorti-coids to suppress the inflammatory consequences of worm death.

Wuchereria bancrofti, *Brugia malayi*, and *Brugia timori* (Lymphatic Filariasis)

- Epidemiology: > 100 million people worldwide are infected, and 1/3 of those infected are symptomatic. These worms are transmitted via mosquito bites. Most cases occur in sub-Saharan Africa, Southeast Asia, Indian subcontinent, and Pacific islands. Epidemiol-ogy may change as countries adopt mass drug admin-istration campaigns.

- Life cycle: A mosquito introduces larvae into the skin during feeding. Larvae enter the lymphatics and mature over 9 months. Adult worms then produce microfilariae that migrate into the cutaneous blood vessels. The microfilariae are ingested by another mosquito, develop into larvae, and can be transmitted to another human.
- Presentation (if symptomatic)—primarily related to lymphatic obstruction:
  ◦ Acute infection causes a nonspecific febrile illness in a traveler (**filarial fever**) that can be similar to malaria. There may be associated tender lymphadenopathy, which is called acute adenolymphangitis.
    – **Tropical pulmonary eosinophilia** is due to microfilariae trapped in the lungs and causes nocturnal wheezing.
  ◦ Chronic infection leads to lymphatic obstruction, scarring, and severe lymphedema (**elephantiasis**).
- Diagnosis: blood smears (best obtained around midnight) to identify microfilariae from blood. Blood can also be sent for filarial antigen detection.
- Treatment: Diethylcarbamazine kills the larvae and adult worms. It must be obtained from the CDC.

Toxocara canis and *T. cati* (Toxocariasis, Visceral Larva Migrans)

- Epidemiology: *T. canis* (the dog ascarid) is more common than *T. cati* (the cat ascarid). It occurs worldwide, with a 14% prevalence in the U.S. Humans are not normal hosts for these helminths and are not a required part of their life cycle.
- Life cycle: The adult worm sheds eggs in the stool of its animal host. If humans ingest these eggs, they hatch into larvae that travel through tissue and elicit an immune response. The larvae subsequently die.
- Presentation (if symptomatic): Migrating larvae (**visceral larva migrans**) can cause injury to the liver (causing hepatomegaly), heart (causing myocarditis), lungs (fleeting pulmonary infiltrates, shortness of breath, cough, wheeze), brain (eosinophilic meningoencephalitis), muscle (myalgias), and eyes. Presentation is typically accompanied by eosinophilia.
- Diagnosis: ELISA IgG serology
- Treatment: If symptomatic organ involvement, give albendazole. Add glucocorticoids to suppress inflammation if heart or brain involvement.

Angiostrongylus cantonensis and *A. costaricensis* (Angiostrongyliasis, Rat Lungworm)

- Epidemiology: *Angiostrongylus cantonensis* is endemic in southeast Asia and tropical Pacific islands and is the most common parasitic cause of eosinophilic meningitis. *A. costaricensis* is endemic in Latin America and the Caribbean. The parasite is passed between rats and mollusks (e.g., slugs, snails) to complete its life cycle; humans are accidental hosts.

- Life cycle: *A. cantonensis* eggs found in rat stool are ingested by snails and slugs. If the snail or slug is eaten by humans, the larvae can migrate to the central nervous system, causing eosinophilic meningitis.
- Presentation (if symptomatic): *A. cantonensis* causes symptoms typical of meningitis that can be self-limiting or neuroinvasive. Headache is the most prominent symptom, and LP yields an eosinophilic inflammatory response. *A. costaricensis* causes abdominal pain, fever, and vomiting and can progress to GI bleeding and perforation.
- Diagnosis: *A. cantonensis* is rarely visualized in the CSF, so diagnose based on the presence of eosinophilic meningitis in the appropriate epidemiologic setting.
- Treatment: *A. cantonensis*—the disease is self-limited, and no antiparasitic drugs have been shown to be effective. *A. costaricensis*—antiparasitic drugs are not effective and may cause worm migration and worsening symptoms. Perform surgery for ocular complications.

Flatworms

Tapeworms (Cestodes)

Clinically important tapeworms include *Taenia solium* (pork tapeworm), *Taenia saginata* (beef tapeworm; usually asymptomatic), *Diphyllobothrium latum* (fish tapeworm; occasionally causes vitamin B_{12} deficiency because it competes with the ileum for absorption), and *Echinococcus*.

T. solium is endemic in many regions of Central and South America, sub-Saharan Africa, India, and Asia. Although it is called the pork tapeworm, humans are the definitive host. It is important to recall the life cycle of *T. solium* in order to understand the 2 manifestations of human disease it causes: extraintestinal disease (in its larval form) and intestinal disease (when it is an adult worm).

Extraintestinal Tapeworm Disease (Larval Form)

If *T. solium* eggs are ingested, they hatch in the bowel and become oncospheres that invade the bloodstream to encyst in tissues (most commonly the central nervous system) as cysticerci—causing **neurocysticercosis**. CNS cysticerci can be in the parenchyma or be extraparenchymal in the CSF, where they usually lodge in the aqueduct of Sylvius. Cysticerci are able to suppress the human host response and thus remain asymptomatic until the organism dies, when an inflammatory response ensues. The most common presentation is seizure, followed by hydrocephalus, depending on the location of cysts within the brain or ventricles. Intraocular, subarachnoid, and extra-CNS cysts occur as well.

Patients with suspected neurocysticercosis should have a head CT as well as an MRI. Diagnosis is typically made based on characteristic findings of cysts, and confirmed with serologic testing. Screen patients who will require steroids for latent tuberculosis and *Strongyloides* to

INFECTIOUS DISEASE

prevent reactivation and hyperinfection while on steroids. Prior to starting antiparasitics, do a dilated funduscopic exam to rule out intraocular disease.

Treatment is recommended in patients presenting with seizures. For < 2 viable intraparenchymal cysts, use albendazole. If > 2 intraparenchymal cysts are present, add praziquantel. Corticosteroids are recommended to reduce risk of seizures during therapy. Antiparasitic therapy is not recommended if only calcified, nonviable cysts are present—or if cerebral edema, untreated hydrocephalus, or intraocular lesions are present. These cases are typically treated with a combination of steroids and surgery, in collaboration with infectious disease and neurosurgical specialists. Cutaneous and intramuscular disease can be treated with analgesics.

Echinococcus species also cause an extraintestinal disease—**hydatid disease**—in which hydatid cysts proliferate throughout the body. It is acquired after ingesting food contaminated with feces from the definitive hosts, which are other mammals (e.g., sheep, dogs, rodents, foxes). Most cases are diagnosed in immigrants from endemic regions (i.e., Asia, Europe, South/Central America, the Middle East); hunters and veterinarians are also susceptible. The initial phase of infection is typically asymptomatic, and most people are infected as children. The liver is the most common organ affected (especially with *E. granulosus*), followed by the lungs (especially with *E. multilocularis*). The right lobe of the liver is most commonly affected, and generally presents as a single large cyst. Complications can occur due to mass effect of the cyst, cyst rupture into the biliary tree or peritoneum, or cyst infection. Ultrasound or other imaging is diagnostic and can be confirmed with a serologic test, usually ELISA. Aspiration should be performed, but open surgery is recommended for cysts that have ruptured, demonstrate hemorrhage, are secondarily infected, compress other organs, or are > 10 cm. Therapy with albendazole before and after surgery is recommended.

Intestinal Tapeworm Disease (Adult Worm Form)

If *T. solium* cysts are ingested from undercooked pork, the organism excysts and grows into the adult tapeworm in the gut (taeniasis). A person carrying a tapeworm then starts shedding eggs. Most people with a tapeworm have no symptoms. Treatment is with praziquantel.

Flukes (Trematodes)

Fluke common names are based on the part of the body in which the adult worm resides. In humans, there are blood, liver, and lung flukes. Liver and blood flukes increase risk of cancer. Table 4-13 summarizes them all.

Blood Flukes (Schistosomes)

There are 5 species of schistosomes: *Schistosoma mansoni*, *japonicum*, *haematobium*, *intercalatum*, and *mekongi*. The latter 2 species are geographically limited, uncommon, and will therefore not be discussed further.

S. mansoni is endemic to Africa, South America, and the Caribbean. *S. japonicum* is in East Asia. *S. haematobium* is found in Africa and the Middle East.

The infectious form for all species is cercariae, which are released from snails in fresh water and can penetrate intact skin. These lose their tails and become schistosomula, which migrate to the liver where they mature into motile adult flukes. From there, they swim upstream

Table 4-13: Fluke Infections						
Genus	**Common Name**	**Route of Acquisition**	**Life Cycle in Humans**	**Signs and Symptoms**	**Diagnosis**	**Treatment**
Schistosoma	Blood flukes	Cercariae enter through skin	Cercariae migrate to liver → adult fluke can then → enter mesenteric veins or vesicular plexus	Swimmer's itch, Katayama fever (fever, chills, myalgias, abdominal pain, lymphadenopathy, hepatosplenomegaly, eosinophilia), bladder cancer, portal hypertension, cirrhosis, esophageal varices	Stool ova; urine ova (*S. haematobium* only)	Praziquantel
Clonorchis, Opisthorchis, Metorchis, Fasciola	Liver flukes	Ingestion of metacercariae in raw fish; water vegetables	Metacercariae → biliary tree → adult fluke resides	Biliary obstruction, cholangiocarcinoma	Stool or bile ova	Praziquantel
Paragonimus	Lung flukes	Ingestion of metacercariae in crabs and crayfish	Metacercariae penetrate bowel → cross diaphragm to lung → adult fluke resides	Cough, hemoptysis, pleuritic pain, fever	Sputum/BAL ova, stool ova	Praziquantel

through the portal vein to spend their adult lives in their preferred venous system: *S. mansoni* in the inferior mesenteric vein, *S. japonicum* in the superior mesenteric vein, and *S. haematobium* in the vesicular venous plexus.

Initial penetration of the cercariae can produce local inflammation and itching after swimming in fresh water (swimmer's itch). If large numbers invade, an acute syndrome (**Katayama fever**) occurs 3–8 weeks after inoculation. This presents with fever, chills, myalgias, abdominal pain, lymphadenopathy, hepatosplenomegaly, and marked eosinophilia. This spontaneously resolves.

The flukes themselves do not cause symptoms, but the eggs they shed do. *S. haematobium* eggs cause inflammation and fibrosis of the bladder wall with symptoms of UTI, and they predispose to bladder cancer. *S. mansoni* and *S. japonicum* shed eggs into the portal venous system, leading to portal hypertension, cirrhosis, and esophageal varices.

Diagnose by finding the eggs in the stool or urine, depending on the species. Treat with a 1-day course of praziquantel.

Liver Flukes

Clonorchis sinensis is endemic in China and Southeast Asia. *Opisthorchis felineus* and *viverrini* are endemic in Eastern Europe and Asia. *Metorchis conjunctus* is endemic in Canada. Infection from all ensues after eating the metacercariae in raw fish, which mature to adult flukes that live in the biliary tree and can cause biliary obstruction and cholangiocarcinoma. Diagnose by finding eggs in bile (from an ERCP) or stool. Treat with praziquantel.

Fasciola hepatica is a fluke that infects livers of mammals. Its primary hosts are cattle and sheep throughout most temperate zones in the world. Eggs shed by these develop into metacercariae that encyst on nearby watercress and, if ingested, become mature flukes in the human biliary tree. The mature fluke can obstruct or migrate through the liver. Treat with triclabendazole (available through the CDC under investigational protocol) or with nitazoxanide as 2nd line. Praziquantel is not effective.

Lung Flukes

Paragonimus westermani is the human lung fluke. It is endemic in the Far East and West Africa but also is found in the Americas. It is acquired by ingestion of metacercariae in crabs and crayfish. They penetrate the duodenum into the abdominal cavity and then penetrate the diaphragm and pleura to enter the lung parenchyma, where they mature into adults that lay eggs. They are coughed up and then swallowed and defecated back into the environment. If symptomatic, the predominant symptoms are cough, hemoptysis, pleuritic chest pain, and fever. Pleural effusions, if they occur, are eosinophilic. Diagnose by finding the ova in sputum, BAL, or stool. Treat with praziquantel.

VIRUSES

PREVIEW | REVIEW

- Multinucleated giant cells can be seen with which viral infections?
- What is the most sensitive and specific method for diagnosing herpes simplex virus encephalitis?
- Which patients should receive the zoster vaccine?
- What is the clinical presentation of Epstein-Barr virus mononucleosis?
- What are the clinical symptoms of measles?
- How do you diagnose influenza A?
- Which class of drugs should be used to treat influenza A?
- What are complications of mumps in males?
- Which virus causes the "slapped cheek" rash?
- What does the bone marrow show in patients with pure red cell aplasia from parvovirus B19?
- How is West Nile virus encephalitis diagnosed?
- How does dengue hemorrhagic fever present?
- Characterize a patient with hantavirus pulmonary syndrome.

HERPES SIMPLEX VIRUS (HSV)

HSV (DNA virus) is spread person to person, usually through asymptomatic shedding. Both HSV-1 and HSV-2 cause vesicular lesions, with HSV-1 predominating in the orofacial area and HSV-2 in the genital area. If the virus is in its preferred location, it is more likely to recur.

HSV-1 causes orofacial infections in ~ 40% of the population, although the seropositivity rate is much higher. In the primary infection, the vesicular lesions and ulcers are usually localized to the oral mucosa, lips, and surrounding skin and are commonly accompanied by constitutional symptoms. Recurrent infection ulcers are typically just on the outer lip. It is possible to autoinoculate the virus, so the infection can spread, for example, from the lips to the eyes of a patient.

Recurrent HSV-1 eye infection resulting in keratitis is the most common infectious cause of blindness in industrialized nations. See the General Internal Medicine section under Ophthalmology.

Tzanck smears are performed by scraping down to the bottom of a vesicle, placing the material on a slide, then staining with either Giemsa or Wright stain. In herpes simplex and varicella-zoster virus infections, it shows multinucleated giant cells (Figure 4-49 on page 4-74). However, in current clinical practice, PCR and direct fluorescent antibody (DFA) are the most commonly used diagnostic tests and should be done to confirm the diagnosis if the clinical picture is not diagnostic.

INFECTIOUS DISEASE

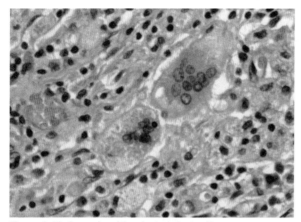

Figure 4-49: Several multinucleated giant cells

HSV-2 causes ~ 75% of HSV genital infections—the rest are due to HSV-1. The prevalence of HSV-2 is 1 in 6 people in the U.S. who are 14–49 years of age. Most cases of neonatal HSV are from intrapartum contact, so a C-section is recommended if the mother has symptoms or signs of genital herpes or has a typical prodrome at the time of delivery. HSV reactivates in 2/3 of seropositive transplant patients within 6 weeks of transplant, but this rate is drastically lower in patients receiving antiviral prophylaxis.

HSV encephalitis is the most common cause of sporadic viral encephalitis and causes the highest number of deaths due to viral encephalitis in adults. Patients with HSV encephalitis usually present with fever, altered mental status, seizures, and/or focal neurologic deficits. The virus has a predilection for the frontal and temporal lobes. Prognosis is poor, and > 60% have neurologic sequelae. MRI is almost always abnormal, potentially showing hemorrhage in the temporal lobe. Do not delay LP and empiric treatment to obtain an MRI. CSF typically shows increased protein, lymphocytic pleocytosis, and increased red cells, but it can be normal in early infection. Diagnosis of HSV by PCR in CSF is the most sensitive (98%) and specific (97%) test. False negative testing can occur early in clinical course, so if high clinical suspicion remains despite a negative test, consider repeating CSF HSV PCR 3–7 days later before stopping IV acyclovir.

HSV is one of many causes of erythema multiforme. See the Dermatology section under Round Lesions.

Treatment of HSV: Initial or recurrent mucocutaneous HSV can be treated with acyclovir PO, but this is beneficial only if treatment is given within the first 72 hours. Famciclovir and valacyclovir are similarly effective but more expensive—although they have more convenient dosing. Give acyclovir after 72 hours if the patient is immunocompromised. For HSV encephalitis, give IV acyclovir for 14–21 days. Give IV acyclovir if there is disseminated HSV (e.g., lung, skin, liver). Acyclovir (or famciclovir or valacyclovir) can also be given in low doses chronically to suppress infection in those with frequent recurrences. Use foscarnet to treat those with HSV resistant to acyclovir; ganciclovir is not used because cross-resistance is common in acyclovir-resistant strains.

VARICELLA-ZOSTER VIRUS

Varicella-zoster virus (VZV; DNA virus) causes varicella (chickenpox) when initially acquired and herpes zoster (shingles) if it recurs.

Varicella (Chickenpox)

Varicella is an airborne, highly contagious disease that causes a characteristic pruritic, vesicular eruption that comes in successive crops. On exam, skin lesions are found in various stages, from new erythematous papules to vesicles to crusted-over lesions—this is in contrast to smallpox, where lesions are all in the same stage of development (Figure 4-50).

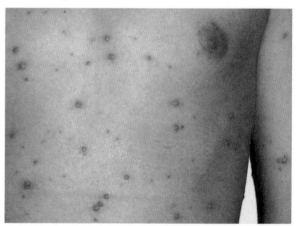

Figure 4-50: Chickenpox lesions in various stages

Patients are contagious for 1–2 days before eruption and stay contagious until the last lesion has crusted over. These pox marks do not leave scars unless superinfected or manipulated.

Patients have a characteristic prodromal phase with fever, malaise, pharyngitis, myalgias, nausea, and headache.

Varicella symptoms are usually mild in children but can be severe in adolescents and adults, especially in pregnant women, in whom pneumonia is more likely to occur.

Diagnosis is made clinically based on the classic appearance of the rash. DFA or PCR can be used for atypical-appearing rashes.

Treat all adult patients with PO acyclovir if they present within 24 hours of rash onset. This treatment decreases the number of lesions and the duration of disease. Give IV acyclovir for noncutaneous organ involvement and to patients who are immunocompromised.

Patients at increased risk of developing severe varicella infection are those who are:

- not currently immune because they have never had varicella or the vaccine,
- currently immunocompromised, or
- pregnant.

There are 2 varicella (chickenpox) vaccines on the market: a single antigen varicella vaccine and a combination measles, mumps, rubella, and varicella vaccine. Vaccination is recommended in all infants > 12 months, children, and adults who do not have immunity to varicella.

Herpes Zoster (Shingles)

Herpes zoster manifests as grouped vesicles along dermatomes with focal pain. Older age and immunosuppression (e.g., HIV) are risk factors.

Zoster is caused by reactivation of the varicella-zoster virus. After the initial infection, the virus becomes dormant and asymptomatic in sensory ganglia neurons until it is reactivated and spreads down the nerve, causing a painful eruption.

Reactivation usually has a prodromal phase with hyperesthesia and a burning, often lancinating pain over the dermatome. This is followed by the characteristic vesicular skin rash localized to that dermatome.

The most common dermatomes involved are the thoracic dermatomes simply because there are more of them. If there are > 3 dermatomes involved, or > 30 lesions outside of the primary dermatomes, it is considered disseminated zoster.

In ~ 10–20% of patients, the ophthalmic branch of the trigeminal nerve is involved, which can be sight-threatening if zoster keratitis results. Consider this in a patient with the classic vesicular lesions appearing on one side of the face anywhere on the forehead, nose, and periorbital area. This requires emergent treatment and referral.

Herpes zoster oticus (**Ramsay Hunt syndrome**) affects several cranial nerves; it presents with vesicles in the external auditory canal and tympanic membrane, along with ipsilateral facial paralysis and ear pain.

As with varicella, zoster lesions are contagious until crusted over, and they can transmit varicella. Therefore, hospitalized patients should be on contact and airborne precautions.

Rash duration is ~ 2–4 weeks. If there are any new lesions after 7–10 days, consider underlying cell-mediated immunodeficiency. Immunocompromised patients are at increased risk for dissemination, which can include internal organ involvement (e.g., CNS, lung, liver).

Postherpetic Neuralgia

Postherpetic neuralgia (PHN) is the most common complication (~ 10% overall) of zoster, and it is more likely to occur with increasing age (20% in those > 80 years of age). It can cause a stabbing, sometimes debilitating pain for many months to years. Treatment of zoster with antiviral drugs significantly decreases the incidence of this.

Treatment

If started within 72 hours of onset, antiviral therapy with acyclovir, famciclovir, or valacyclovir decreases duration of disease, severity of the initial pain, and incidence of PHN.

For pain control, tricyclic antidepressants, gabapentin, pregabalin, and lidocaine patches have some efficacy. Opiates can be useful but remain controversial due to dependency. Capsaicin cream is useful after the lesions have healed.

Adding prednisone provides no additional benefit and may prolong the course of herpes zoster in immunosuppressed patients. Tricyclic antidepressants do not decrease the onset of PHN.

Vaccination for Herpes Zoster

The most recent zoster vaccine, called recombinant zoster vaccine (RZV), was approved by the FDA in October 2017. It is a recombinant vaccine as opposed to the previous live attenuated vaccine. The Advisory Committee on Immunization Practices (ACIP) and the CDC recommend the recombinant vaccine for all healthy adults > 50 years of age. The ACIP also recommends that those who received the earlier zoster vaccine be revaccinated with the newer version.

In those 50–69 years of age, RZV has an effectiveness of 97% and 91% in preventing herpes zoster and PHN, respectively. At > 70 years of age, this falls a little to 91% and 89%. This is much better than live attenuated vaccine, with an overall effectiveness of only 50% and 75%. The longer-term immune response of RZV also appears to be much better.

As opposed to the first vaccine, with only 1 dose required, RZV requires 2 total doses repeated 2–6 months apart.

CYTOMEGALOVIRUS (CMV)

Cytomegalovirus (CMV; DNA virus) is in the herpes virus family. CMV infection in the normal population is common; 50% of the population has anti-CMV IgG antibodies by 35 years of age.

CMV infection in the immunocompetent population is usually asymptomatic, but ~ 10% have a mononucleosis-type illness with fever, sore throat, adenopathy, fatigue, and hepatitis. Unlike EBV mononucleosis, exudative pharyngitis is rare. Think of this in a mono spot–negative adult with these symptoms, especially in young or middle-aged adults, because EBV mono usually occurs more often in adolescents.

CMV is a more common infection in patients with decreased cellular immunity (e.g., posttransplant, AIDS). Pretransplant donor and recipient CMV IgG serologies are very important to guide use of antiviral prophylaxis during and after transplantation. For seronegative transplant recipients, 75% get CMV disease if the donor is seropositive. In immunosuppressed patients, there are 3 main presentations. The presentation of CMV in immunodeficient patients can range from asymptomatic CMV viremia, symptomatic CMV viremia (fever and chills with no organ-specific injury) or organ-specific infections.

CMV can cause chorioretinitis, pneumonitis, esophagitis, hepatitis, and colitis. Patients with CMV retinitis may initially complain of floaters and then gradually lose vision. CMV retinitis is distinctive; it has both retinal blanching and hemorrhage and follows along the path of the retinal arteries. Diagnosis is typically made by an ophthalmologist based on appearance. CMV esophagitis and colitis are diagnosed by endoscopy and tissue pathology.

Diagnose acute CMV infection in immunocompetent hosts by serologies, either a 4-fold rise in IgG serologies or a positive IgM. Serologies have no role in the diagnosis of CMV disease in immunosuppressed patients. CMV viremia is diagnosed by demonstrating viral DNA in peripheral blood. For tissue-invasive disease, a biopsy of the tissue involved may demonstrate cytopathic viral effects combined with positive immunohistochemical stains. Most patients with end-organ disease have an accompanying viremia, but not all.

Treat CMV infection with valganciclovir or ganciclovir. If resistant to these agents, use foscarnet or cidofovir.

EPSTEIN-BARR VIRUS (EBV)

EBV (DNA virus) causes **infectious mononucleosis**. The incubation period is 1–2 months, and it is usually acquired in adolescence through contact with others who are asymptomatically shedding the virus in their secretions (the so-called kissing disease).

The vast majority of adults have been infected, but most acute EBV infections are asymptomatic. If symptomatic, > 90% have pharyngitis, which is typically exudative. Tonsillitis, fever, lymphadenopathy, and elevated transaminases also occur. Splenomegaly is seen in ~ 50% of cases. A maculopapular rash occurs in 10–20% of symptomatic patients; however, if patients are given aminopenicillins (ampicillin or amoxicillin), up to 90% develop a similar rash. This can occur if the exudative pharyngitis is mistakenly treated as an *S. pyogenes* infection.

Symptomatic patients typically develop extreme fatigue, which can occasionally persist months after the initial symptoms disappear.

Lymphocytosis is found in acute EBV infection, usually with > 10% atypical lymphocytes on peripheral blood smear. Atypical lymphocytes (Figure 4-51) are enlarged T cells actively trying to fight EBV-infected B cells. They have abundant cytoplasm, vacuoles, and indentations of the cell membrane.

Confirm diagnosis of infectious mononucleosis with serology. Heterophile antibody titers (rapid mono test) are nonspecific antibodies that cross-react with RBCs of other mammals.

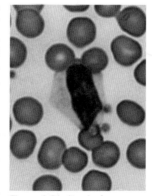

Figure 4-51: Atypical lymphocyte

They are absent ~ 25% of the time in the 1st week of illness (heterophile-negative mononucleosis). Thus, the most common cause of heterophile-negative mononucleosis of 1-week duration is still EBV. Diagnose by testing for IgM capsid antibody in these patients. Other causes of heterophile-negative mononucleosis are CMV, toxoplasmosis, acute HIV, and HHV-6 infection.

Treatment of acute EBV infection remains supportive because of its excellent prognosis and the unavailability of any antivirals active against EBV. If splenomegaly is present, patients should avoid contact sports for at least 3 weeks. Glucocorticoids are indicated only if tonsillar enlargement creates concern for impending airway obstruction.

EBV causes oral **hairy leukoplakia**, which can be seen as an early manifestation of HIV disease. These are white lesions on the lateral tongue (Figure 4-52) that, unlike thrush, do not scrape off.

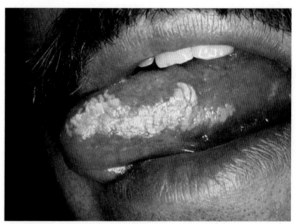

Figure 4-52: Oral hairy leukoplakia

Chronic fatigue syndrome has no proven association with EBV.

EBV is oncogenic and can result in nasopharyngeal carcinoma, non-Hodgkin lymphoma—specifically Burkitt lymphoma—and posttransplantation lymphoproliferative disorders (PTLDs).

RUBELLA (GERMAN MEASLES)

In adults, the typical rash of rubella, an ssRNA virus (a.k.a. German measles) may be preceded by up to 5 days of fever, generalized malaise, headache, sore throat, arthralgias, cough, and coryza. The illness in adults is typically a mild viral illness. Associated clinical signs include posterior cervical, postauricular, and suboccipital lymphadenopathy and an enanthem in 20% of cases (**Forchheimer sign**) characterized by soft palate petechiae and/or larger, reddish spots. Despite its mild course in adults, if acquired during pregnancy in the 1st trimester, there is up to a 90% chance that the baby will develop **congenital rubella syndrome** (e.g., deafness, cataracts, cardiac disease).

Rubella is diagnosed by demonstrating rubella-specific IgM at least 4 days after development of a rash. In pregnant persons, it can be diagnosed via PCR from nasopharyngeal swab. In infants, virus can be detected from cord blood or placenta.

Due to a successful vaccination program, rubella has been declared eliminated in North and South America but is still seen elsewhere.

RUBEOLA (MEASLES)

Rubeola (ssRNA virus) causes measles. Outbreaks continue to occur in at-risk persons who have not been vaccinated. This is one of the most contagious diseases known.

After an incubation period of 1–3 weeks with a median of 2 weeks, measles begins with a prodromal phase of fevers, malaise, and the 3Cs (cough, coryza, conjunctivitis) which lasts for 72 hours. Enanthem (mucosal rash) develops ~ 48 hours before the exanthem (cutaneous rash). These are called **Koplik spots**, described as whitish spots on an erythematous base near the molars on the inner cheeks (Figure 4-53). Exanthem lasts for ~ 72 hours and evolves rapidly. It is characterized by numerous, generalized, blanching, fine, discrete, pinkish maculopapules that begin on the face and spread down the trunk, coalesce, then disappear, generally after 3 days. The rash evolves in the same way as having paint dumped on a person's head—it drips down from the top! Convalescence with immunity occurs after resolution of the rash. If fevers persist longer, then measles-related complications should be considered.

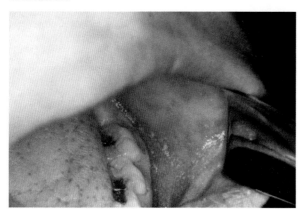

Figure 4-53: Measles; Koplik spots, small white spots that occur before the rash

If rubeola is suspected, patients should be in a room with airborne precautions. This is a reportable disease to public health authorities. Viral encephalitis occurs in 1:1,000 of these patients. Autoimmune reaction (acute disseminated encephalomyelitis) rarely occurs, and if it does, it appears ~ 2 weeks after the rash and has ~ 20% mortality and considerable morbidity. **Subacute sclerosing panencephalitis** occurs in 1:100,000 about a decade later, and it is suspected to be from a variant virus; it is universally fatal.

RETROVIRUSES

Retroviruses are ssRNA viruses:

- HTLV-1 (human T-cell leukemia virus, Type 1) causes T-cell lymphoma and tropical spastic paraparesis, a neurologic syndrome seen in Japan and the Caribbean.
- HTLV-2 causes a rare T-cell variant of hairy cell leukemia.
- HIV-1 (previously known as HTLV-3) causes AIDS.
- HIV-2 also causes AIDS and is found in West Africa and parts of the U.S.

RESPIRATORY VIRUSES

Severe Acute Respiratory Syndrome Coronavirus 2 (SARS-CoV-2)

Terminology

At the end of 2019, a novel coronavirus was detected as a cause of severe pneumonia that eventually reached global pandemic stage and has persisted into 2022. The WHO has designated the illness as coronavirus disease 2019 (COVID-19) and the virus that causes it as SARS-CoV-2.

Virology

Coronaviruses are enveloped ssRNA viruses. They bind to human tissue via their surface spike protein attaching to the angiotensin-converting enzyme 2 receptor. Like all viruses, SARS-CoV-2 mutates. The vast majority of these mutations are clinically insignificant, but others have significant effect on the severity of illness, infectivity, and/or ability to evade current treatments or immunizations. Those that have such an effect are considered as "variants of interest" by the WHO. Most of these strains have various mutations in the spike protein that effect these changes.

Transmission

SARS-CoV-2 is primarily transmitted person-to-person by inhalation of infectious respiratory droplets from other infected individuals. Infected individuals are most infectious 2 days before symptoms and up to 5 days after symptoms. Factors that increase the risk of transmission include being within 6 feet of the infected person, being indoors, the infected person being symptomatic, and having neither person wearing a mask.

For information on transmission-based precautions, see Preventive Medicine in the General Internal Medicine section.

Clinical Manifestations

Around 50% of patients infected with SARS-CoV-2 will remain asymptomatic. If symptoms occur, the typical incubation period is about 4–5 days but can be as long as 14 days. The most commonly reported symptoms are

INFECTIOUS DISEASE

cough, myalgia, rhinitis, nasal congestion, and headache. Other symptoms of an upper respiratory tract infection such as sore throat are seen in a minority of patients. Most patients are afebrile. Acute onset of alterations or loss of taste and smell occurs in up to 25% of patients. This is almost always transient; usually, there is full recovery.

The severity of illness ranges from mild (no need for hospitalization) in 80%, severe (requiring hospitalization, usually because of an oxygen requirement) in 15%, and critical (requiring ICU) in 5%. Morbidity and mortality are higher in patients who are not White, those with preexisting organ diseases, persons with immunocompromise, and older adults.

Lower respiratory involvement is usually manifested by shortness of breath and may produce an oxygen requirement with a pO_2 of $\leq$ 94%, which is the most common reason for hospitalization. An intense inflammatory reaction in the pulmonary parenchyma can lead to localized pulmonary intravascular coagulopathy and ARDS, which is the most common reason for admission to the ICU. There is a high prevalence of DVT and PE in hospitalized patients, especially those in the ICU. Pharmacologic thromboprophylaxis is recommended for all inpatients in the absence of contraindications.

Cardiac injury, as manifested by troponin elevations, has been reported in ~20% of patients. The etiology varies from direct myocardial injury, cytokine-induced inflammation of myocardium and/or small vessels, stress cardiomyopathy, and/or right heart strain (due to ARDS, pulmonary emboli).

Diagnosis

PCR testing for viral RNA from a nasal swab, saliva, or respiratory secretions is diagnostic of infection in a symptomatic patient. When used to determine asymptomatic infection after exposure, testing should be done on day 5 after exposure. Repeat testing in infected individuals is not recommended because viral RNA may persist for several weeks after infection when the virus is dead and the person is not infectious.

Prevention

Precautions

In the community, the avoidance of social gatherings, especially from persons outside of an individual's home, decreases transmission. Diligent use of hand sanitizers/hand washing is also useful. Masking an infected individual can decrease transmission to an unmasked person by ~ 90%, which can be reduced by > 95% if both people are masked. Masks in the community should be surgical masks and in health-care settings should include an N95 mask and face shield when exposure to a known or possibly infected patient is likely. Universal testing of patients and routine testing of health care workers should be used during high rates of infection in a community. Local, state, and federal guidelines should be followed with respect to the appropriate duration of isolation (when a person is known to be infected with SARS-CoV-2) or quarantined (when a person has had a significant exposure to SARS-CoV-2).

Vaccinations

There are several vaccinations available that are highly effective in preventing symptomatic illness, need for hospitalization, and death. They are discussed in COVID-19 Vaccines on page 4-94.

Pharmacologic

Many earlier and new drugs and monoclonal antibodies have shown some utility in treating COVID-19 as well as in preventing COVID-19 before or after exposure. These are discussed in Drugs for Treatment and Prevention of COVID-19 on page 4-91.

Rhinoviruses

Rhinoviruses (ssRNA viruses) are a common cause of URI in adults. They also may cause or contribute to mild community-acquired pneumonia.

Respiratory Syncytial Virus (RSV)

RSV (ssRNA virus) infections occur year-round, but more commonly during the autumn and winter. RSV infection has similar morbidity as influenza and especially affects older persons and those with immunodeficiency. It is thought to be responsible for up to 25% of excess winter season mortality that was previously attributed solely to influenza.

RSV is also an important pathogen in hematopoietic stem cell transplant recipients and lung transplant recipients. It is diagnosed by detecting RSV antigen or PCR in nasal secretions. Use ribavirin, oral or inhaled, as an antiviral therapy in immunocompromised hosts, but the efficacy is limited.

Influenza

Influenza (ssRNA virus) is a major cause of morbidity and mortality, especially in patients > 55 years of age with COPD. Annual vaccination decreases mortality.

There are 3 types of influenza viruses: influenzas A, B, and C. Subtypes of influenza A exist based on their specific neuraminidase and hemagglutinin antigens. Influenzas A and B cause the yearly epidemics of respiratory illnesses. Influenza C causes very mild symptoms, if any.

Influenza presents as an acute febrile respiratory illness with fever, cough, and myalgias. Serious complications include viral pneumonia, secondary bacterial pneumonia, rhabdomyolysis, encephalitis, and myocarditis.

A positive antigen test or PCR for influenzas A and B from nasopharyngeal swab or respiratory secretions is diagnostic. Not every patient with influenza needs antiviral therapy.

Give treatment in 3 settings:

- Those at high risk of complications (e.g., immuno-compromised; pregnancy; underlying heart, lung, liver, or kidney disease; > 65 years of age; residents of chronic care facilities; active malignancy; diabetes; morbid obesity; hemoglobinopathies; neurologic conditions causing inability to handle respiratory secretions; Native American patients; Alaska Native patients)
- Hospitalized patients
- Severe, progressive, or complicated illness

In addition, anyone outside of these high-risk groups who presents with influenza within 48 hours of onset benefits from treatment with respect to the duration of illness.

There are 3 classes of anti-flu drugs: adamantanes, neuraminidase inhibitors, and cap snatch inhibitors. Oseltamivir, a neuraminidase inhibitor, is the most commonly used. For a complete discussion of these medications, see Antiviral Agents on page 4-90.

The prevalence of antiviral resistance to any specific agent is dependent on the circulating strains. Look to CDC guidance for up-to-date information on flu resistance to antiviral drugs.

All individuals > 6 months old should receive annual influenza vaccination with one exception: previous severe allergic reaction (i.e., anaphylaxis) to influenza vaccine. A history of Guillain-Barré syndrome is a precaution to vaccination, but not necessarily a contraindication. Egg allergy is not a contraindication to vaccination. If your patient reports hives only, give influenza vaccine. If your patient reports more than urticaria (e.g., angioedema, swelling, recurrent vomiting, lightheadedness), give influenza vaccine in monitored healthcare setting with basic life support capability.

Influenza vaccines are targeted to the serotypes that are most likely to be present when the influenza season occurs. The better the antigenic match to the currently circulating virus, the better the vaccine works. The types of influenza vaccines available in the U.S. are inactivated, recombinant, and intranasal live attenuated vaccine. The inactivated vaccine also comes in a high-dose form that is more immunogenic and recommended for individuals > 65 years old. Avoid the intranasal live attenuated vaccine in immunocompromised patients, pregnant patients, and health care workers who work with immunosuppressed populations. Regardless of which is used, administer vaccines when they become available each year, which is usually in September or October.

Adenoviruses

Adenoviruses (dsDNA virus) cause upper respiratory infections and conjunctivitis more often in children than adults. When they cause pharyngitis, they cause an exudative pharyngitis that is indistinguishable from streptococcal pharyngitis; however, there is a commonly associated bilateral conjunctivitis and coryza that are distinguishing clues. Diagnose by PCR from secretions. In immunocompetent patients, the infection is self-limited.

Adenovirus is a feared virus in severely immunosuppressed populations. This includes patients who have undergone a bone marrow transplant or who have severely depleted cell-mediated immunity. Pneumonia and disseminated disease carry a very high mortality. Cidofovir can be used—though nephrotoxicity is a major concern with this drug, and dialysis may be required during its administration.

POLIOVIRUS

Poliovirus (ssRNA virus) is asymptomatic in > 90% of infections. Symptomatic cases are characterized by aseptic meningitis and an asymmetric, flaccid paralysis due to infection and destruction of anterior horn cells. It has been eliminated in the Western hemisphere and in resource-rich countries worldwide secondary to vaccination, but it is still seen in resource-poor countries, especially India. In countries in which polio has been eradicated, enterovirus 68 and West Nile virus are mimics of the disease.

MUMPS VIRUS

Mumps (ssRNA virus) occurs most commonly in winter and early spring. Although it commonly is asymptomatic, it can present with unilateral or bilateral parotitis, aseptic meningitis, and/or encephalitis. Of postpubertal males with mumps, 15–20% get epididymoorchitis, which is usually unilateral. Postinfection sterility is a rare occurrence. To differentiate mumps from bacterial parotitis, check a Gram stain of the parotid secretions. There are many WBCs and organisms in bacterial parotitis and none in mumps. Other causes of enlarged parotid glands include frequent vomiting and parotid duct stones.

PARVOVIRUS B19

Parvovirus B19 (ssDNA virus) is spread by respiratory secretions and is usually acquired early in life, commonly manifesting as **erythema infectiosum** (fifth disease) with a high fever and a "slapped cheek" appearance. Adult-acquired illness typically consists of a self-limited fever, symmetric small joint arthritis, and a lacy rash on the trunk and/or extremities (Figure 4-54).

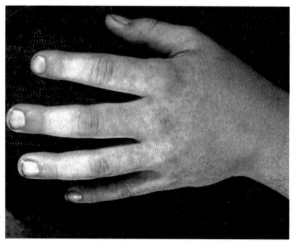

Figure 4-54: Parvovirus lacy rash

The virus infects the red cell precursors, specifically the pronormoblasts, and causes arrest of red cell maturation. This causes a halt in RBC production for the ~ 1-week duration of the infection, resulting in pure red cell aplasia. In otherwise healthy adults, this causes a drop in Hgb of 5–10%, which does not cause symptoms.

Only 3 groups of adults have any serious complications from the infection with this virus:

- Immunocompromised hosts who cannot mount an antibody response have persistent red cell arrest and develop profound anemia. These patients should receive IVIG to give passive immunity to eliminate the virus.
- Patients with chronic hemolytic anemias who rely on their reticulocytosis to maintain their Hgb levels (e.g., sickle cell disease) also become severely anemic. They should be supported with PRBC transfusions. IVIG is not indicated because they will mount their own immune response.
- In pregnant patients, if the virus is acquired during the 1st trimester, it can cause increased fetal loss due to hydrops fetalis.

Diagnose with IgM antibody assay in immunocompetent patients. In immunocompromised patients, who may not mount an antibody response, use serum PCR assay for parvovirus DNA. Bone marrow exam, if done, shows giant pronormoblasts that are also diagnostic.

There is no specific antiviral therapy for parvovirus B19.

ARBOVIRUSES

Arboviral Encephalitis

Arboviral encephalitis occurs throughout the U.S., typically in the late spring and summer. West Nile virus (WNV) is the most commonly identified arbovirus.

Arboviruses, like WNV, are named after the geographic area in which they were first found, so they carry names like La Crosse, St. Louis, Eastern equine, Western equine, Venezuelan equine, Powassan, and Colorado tick fever.

Almost all symptomatic arboviral infections have similar symptoms: fever, headache, chills, and varied severity of encephalitis or aseptic meningitis. WNV is asymptomatic in 80% of cases, but it can present as a nonspecific viral illness. Neuroinvasive disease (encephalitis, meningitis, or an asymmetric, flaccid paralysis similar to polio) occurs in only 1/150 patients. Since polio is no longer present in the U.S., test a person with a polio-like presentation for WNV. Less common presentations are tremor, myoclonus, parkinsonism, and cranial neuropathies.

Testing of patients with neurological disease should be done via sending the CSF for WNV IgM antibody. Virus concentration in the CSF is often too low for PCR to be useful.

Treatment is supportive; no specific antiviral therapy is available.

Mosquito netting, repellents, and insect mitigation help to decrease the spread of these viruses.

Dengue Virus

The dengue virus (ssRNA virus) causes a spectrum of disease ranging from asymptomatic infection to dengue fever to, most ominously, dengue hemorrhagic fever. It is the most common mosquito-borne viral disease and is seen throughout the tropics. The virus is transmitted to humans via the day-biting female *Aedes* mosquitoes, not the *Anopheles* mosquitoes that carry malaria.

There are 4 serotypes of dengue (types 1 through 4), and immunity develops to a specific serotype once infected. However, if subsequently infected with a different serotype, the infection is often more severe due to cross-reactivity and an intense cytokine response.

Dengue fever symptoms are rapid onset of high fever, markedly severe myalgias (thus the name breakbone fever), arthralgias, and headache. This may be followed by a macular red rash that covers most of the body.

Dengue hemorrhagic fever is due to a diffuse capillary leak syndrome that results in hemoconcentration, anasarca, thrombocytopenia, and spontaneous bleeding. Death due to circulatory collapse may occur; it is seen in people who have had a prior infection with a different serotype of dengue.

Diagnose by a serum IgM antibody assay. Treatment is supportive with IV fluids. No specific antiviral therapy is available. There is a vaccine that is available in high-prevalence areas but not in the U.S. It is recommended for individuals who will be in an endemic area who have already had dengue infection in an attempt to avoid a more serious 2nd infection.

Chikungunya Virus

Chikungunya is an alphavirus endemic to West Africa and transmitted by the day-biting mosquitoes *Aedes aegypti* and *Aedes albopictus*. It has been present in the U.S. since 2014. It causes an illness very similar to dengue with high fever, polyarthralgia, headache, and maculopapular rash, except arthritis and arthralgias are much more prominent with chikungunya. Diagnose by detecting virus-specific IgM (which may not appear until 5–7 days of symptom onset) or by PCR. Treatment is supportive. Mortality is rare. There is no vaccine.

Zika Virus

Zika virus (ssRNA virus) is a *Flavivirus* related to dengue, yellow fever, and West Nile virus. It was first identified in the Zika forest of Uganda in 1947, found in a rhesus monkey in a program monitoring for yellow fever. Transmitted by the *Aedes* mosquito, Zika causes symptoms in only 20% of people infected. There is evidence of male-to-female sexual transmission.

Zika virus symptoms, if they occur, include fever, rash, muscle and joint pain, and conjunctivitis. The symptoms are usually mild and self-limited. Rarely, it can cause myelitis and/or encephalitis.

In 2015, an alarming increase in the number of infants born with microcephaly was seen in Brazil. Physicians found an association between Zika infection during pregnancy and infants born with microcephaly. Subsequent studies have shown a 10–40% incidence of neurologic defects in babies born to women infected during pregnancy. Zika is also associated with Guillain-Barré syndrome. There was epidemic spread of the virus to South America, Central America, and the Caribbean in 2016, for which the WHO declared a public health emergency. As of 2019, there is no country worldwide with a Zika outbreak, but the virus is likely endemic in these new regions. Per the CDC, pregnant women and women of childbearing age should be cautioned against travel to Zika endemic regions, which include India, southeast Asia, Africa, the Caribbean, Central America, and South America. Zika has also been detected in Florida and Texas. Infected men can shed viral RNA in their semen for up to 6 months and place partners at risk.

The CDC has a reverse transcriptase polymerase chain reaction (RT-PCR) assay that can facilitate diagnosis in selected patients. There is no treatment for Zika virus. The CDC recommends prevention by avoiding insect bites.

Hantavirus

The primary reservoir for hantavirus (ssRNA virus) in the U.S. is the deer mouse. The Four Corners area of the Southwest is the area of highest concern. On the East Coast and in the Southeast, the cotton rat is the reservoir. The infection occurs when the excreta or saliva of an infected rodent is inhaled (e.g., cleaning droppings, working in a barn). No human-to-human transmission is known.

Hantavirus pulmonary syndrome (HPS) starts as a nondescript viral syndrome, often with GI symptoms. Patients then develop muscle pain, fever, headache, and cough, which quickly progresses to hypoxia, hemorrhagic pneumonia, acute respiratory distress syndrome (ARDS), and death in > 50% of cases. Laboratory findings include hemoconcentration and thrombocytopenia. Diagnose by finding IgM antibodies in the blood or CSF. No specific antiviral therapy is available.

Ebola Virus

Ebola virus (ssRNA virus)—first discovered in 1976 with an unknown reservoir, possibly fruit bats—causes episodic outbreaks of a hemorrhagic fever with severe vomiting, diarrhea, rash, and internal and external hemorrhage. Until 2014, no cases left the African continent. The 2014–2015 outbreak resulted in ~ 2 dozen cases that were exported to other continents, almost all of which involved health care workers who were in the endemic areas caring for infected persons. There have been no cases outside of the African continent since then. Presentation is similar to that of dengue hemorrhagic fever, with a > 70% mortality rate. No specific treatment has been proved effective other than supportive care.

SLOW VIRUSES

There are 2 classes of slow viruses (long incubation time):

- Normal viruses, such as papillomavirus (warts; Human Papillomavirus (HPV) on page 4-22) and polyomavirus (PML; JC Virus (JCV) on page 4-40)
- Defective viruses, such as the defective measles virus (subacute sclerosing panencephalitis; Rubeola (Measles) on page 4-77)

ANTIMICROBIAL AGENTS AND VACCINES

ANTIBACTERIAL AGENTS

PREVIEW | REVIEW

- Which antibiotics target deoxyribonucleic acid (DNA) gyrase to interrupt protein synthesis?
- Which antibiotics antagonize folic acid?
- Which classes of antibiotics affect the developing bacterial cell wall?
- What are the definitions of minimal inhibitory concentration (MIC) and minimal bactericidal concentration?
- What is the difference between concentration-dependent and time-dependent killing?
- Which type of killing do aminoglycosides exhibit?
- What is the postantibiotic effect?
- In time-dependent killing, how long should a patient's serum concentration of a drug be higher than the infecting organism's MIC?
- What coverage does ampicillin add over penicillin?
- Which organisms do extended-spectrum penicillins cover?
- 3rd generation cephalosporins are known for their additional activity against which organisms?
- Which β-lactam drug can be given to patients with a penicillin allergy?
- Which carbapenem should be avoided in those with seizures?
- What are potential complications of linezolid use?
- Which drugs inhibit the absorption of quinolones?
- The use of which class of antibiotics increases the risk of tendon rupture?

HOW ANTIBIOTICS WORK

Most antibiotics work by disrupting bacterial protein synthesis, folate metabolism, or cell wall/membrane synthesis. First, let's review protein synthesis; then, we'll tackle the mechanisms of action for specific antibiotics.

Quick Review — Protein Synthesis

Transcription: Protein synthesis requires the unwinding of DNA and having it cut and held open by DNA gyrase to be read by RNA polymerase.

RNA polymerase moves along a section of DNA to create a complementary strand of RNA, which is messenger RNA (mRNA). This occurs in the nucleus.

Translation: After transport to the cytoplasm, the mRNA is translated into a sequence of amino acids to create the desired protein product by ribosomes. mRNA attaches to the 30S ribosomal subunit, after which a 50S ribosomal subunit binds to this complex to form a 70S ribosome.

Amino acid–specific transfer RNAs (tRNAs) bring in the corresponding amino acids to make the protein.

Antibiotics That Block Protein Synthesis

Rifampin binds to RNA polymerase and blocks transcription.

Quinolone antibiotics (e.g., ciprofloxacin, levofloxacin, moxifloxacin) block the ability of DNA gyrase to reconnect the cleaved DNA strands.

Metronidazole has a similar action to the quinolones. It also affects cell membrane function.

Aminoglycosides (e.g., gentamicin, tobramycin, amikacin) bind irreversibly to the 30S ribosomal subunit and prevent the 50S subunit from attaching.

Tetracyclines (e.g., doxycycline) and **glycylcyclines** (e.g., tigecycline) bind reversibly to the 30S subunit, distorting it so that the anticodons of the tRNAs cannot align properly with the codons on the mRNA.

Macrolides (e.g., erythromycin, clarithromycin, azithromycin, fidaxomicin) bind reversibly to the 50S subunit. They prevent peptide bond formation between the amino acids and, hence, keep the 70S ribosome from forming the desired protein.

Clindamycin works similarly to macrolides.

Oxazolidinones (e.g., linezolid, tedizolid) bind to the 50S ribosomal subunit, preventing attachment to the 30S unit.

Antibiotics That Affect DNA Replication

Trimethoprim and the **sulfonamides** block the production of folic acid from *para*-aminobenzoic acid (PABA). Folic acid is required to replicate DNA.

Quick Review — Cell Wall Synthesis

Peptidoglycan is a component of bacterial cell walls. It is composed of alternating polysaccharides: *N*-acetylglucosamine and *N*-acetylmuramic acid that are cross-linked to form alternating strands that make the wall solid. Gram-negative organisms have an outer membrane outside of the cell wall.

Antibiotics That Affect the Cell Wall

A variety of antibiotics act at 1 or 2 stages of peptidoglycan synthesis. In order for an antibiotic to affect the cell wall of gram-negative organisms, the drug must pass through the outer membrane via channels called porins. Passage is affected by drug size and charge. Some gram-negative organisms have inherent resistance to certain cell wall agents because of the shape of their porins.

β-Lactams (e.g., penicillins and cephalosporins) are a class of antibiotics that interrupt formation of the bacterial cell wall. Because there is no analogous structure in human cells, people can tolerate relatively high doses.

Glycopeptide antibiotics (e.g., vancomycin, telavancin, dalbavancin, oritavancin) work by inhibiting cell wall synthesis of gram-positive organisms.

Antibiotics That Affect the Cell Membrane

Cyclic lipopeptides (e.g., daptomycin) insert into the plasma membrane of gram-positive bacteria, creating channels that allow the efflux of ions and disruption of membrane polarization. It also has a dual action on cell wall function.

Polymyxins (polymyxin B and colistin) bind to the cell membrane to create an efflux of ions and cell death.

Diagnostic Microbiology

When certain specimens are obtained (e.g., sputum, CSF, pleural, ascetic, urine), an attempt is made to directly visualize and identify the bacteria with a Gram stain before culturing it. For other samples (e.g., blood), the specimen goes directly to culture. Automated methods are now available to identify organisms in < 1 day.

Once bacterial growth is established, identification and sensitivity testing are done. Traditionally, the culture is then placed on various agar plates to identify the bacteria, and disk diffusion susceptibility is conducted to determine the minimum inhibitory concentration (MIC) and minimum bactericidal concentration (MBC) of the drug for those bacteria. Most labs currently use an automated system that performs identification and sensitivity simultaneously, usually by a microtiter method.

Disk diffusion (Kirby-Bauer) testing is used for specific, difficult-to-treat bacteria that do not grow well in the automated media or for testing with antibiotics that are not included in the standard panels.

Minimal Inhibitory Concentration (MIC) and Minimal Bactericidal Concentration (MBC)

The **MIC** is the lowest concentration of antibiotic that inhibits visible growth (visible turbidity) in vitro after 24 hours of incubation. The **MBC** is the lowest concentration of antibiotic that kills 99.9% of the bacteria.

If the MIC of a drug vs. a specific isolate is achievable in tissue based on usual dosing of the antibiotic, the organism is considered susceptible (sensitive) to the antibiotic and can be considered for treatment. All that needs to happen is for the drug to inhibit the growth of the organism, and the immune system does the rest to clear the infection.

In only a few circumstances, the goal is for the specified antibiotic to have an achievable MBC, not merely MIC. MBC is used to treat infections at sites that the immune system has trouble accessing (e.g., the center of an endocarditis vegetation, the CSF in meningitis) or when the patient is neutropenic.

General Rules of Antibiotic Use

Know these important points:

- Source control is key to treating serious infections. Examples of this are draining an abscess, removing dead tissue, and relieving a biliary or GU obstruction. Foreign bodies, lines, catheters, and devices may need to be removed.
- Pick the drug with the proper spectrum for the suspected or proven pathogen(s) and the site of infection.
- Adjust dosage for body size and clearance when appropriate.
- If the patient does not respond, consider 5 things:
  1) Is the patient getting/taking an effective drug?
  2) Is there resistance?
  3) Is there an undrained focus of infection?
  4) Is there a superinfection?
  5) Are the symptoms due to a noninfectious disease?

Concentration-Dependent Killing vs. Time-Dependent Killing

Concentration-Dependent Killing

Concentration-dependent killing means that killing increases as you increase the concentration of drug above the MIC for the bugs you are treating. This is sometimes referred to as dose-dependent killing because killing is based on concentration above MIC, not on time. Aminoglycosides and quinolones are drugs that exhibit concentration-dependent killing.

Quinolones and aminoglycosides also exhibit a **postantibiotic effect** (**PAE**). A PAE is persistent killing of bacteria even after the concentration of drug has fallen below the MIC at the site of infection. The dose-dependent killing and PAE allow these drugs to be dosed once daily, achieving a high peak concentration.

Time-Dependent Killing

In time-dependent killing, the concentration of drug above the MIC does not really matter. Instead, killing is related to how long the concentration of antibiotic remains greater than the organism's MIC at the site of infection (a.k.a. time over MIC). β-Lactams, macrolides, and glycopeptides (e.g., vancomycin) are such drugs. Aim for serum concentrations above the MIC for > 50% of the dosing interval.

Because β-lactams are time dependent, it is not important to aim for 8–10× the MIC with each dose. Instead, patients need repeated, reliable dosing intervals so they do not have prolonged periods during the dosing interval when their serum levels fall below the MIC. The clinical relevance is that with time-dependent killing, patients who miss doses risk treatment failure.

β-LACTAM ANTIBIOTICS

Overview and Development of Penicillins (PCNs)

The 1st of the β-lactam antibiotics was PCN. Its derivatives were created either to increase its spectrum of activity and/or to address developing bacterial resistance.

The development timeline of these drugs is as follows:

PCN → semisynthetic PCNs → aminopenicillins → extended-spectrum PCNs → aminopenicillins/extended-spectrum PCNs + β-lactamase inhibitors

This topic area covers the PCN-based antibiotics using the above developmental timeline.

Penicillin

Penicillin (PCN) is appropriate mainly for streptococci, sensitive enterococci, leptospirosis, *Listeria*, *Pasteurella*, and syphilis.

Staphylococci rapidly developed resistance by producing penicillinase, a β-lactamase enzyme that destroys the drug, so next came the…

Semisynthetic PCNs

Methicillin was the initial semisynthetic PCN but is no longer available. Current agents are **oxacillin**, **nafcillin**, and **dicloxacillin**, which are stable against staphylococcal penicillinase. These drugs are called semisynthetic PCNs or antistaphylococcal PCNs because they were synthesized from PCN. They are the drugs of choice for methicillin-sensitive, PCN-resistant staphylococci.

The semisynthetic PCNs lacked activity against gram-negatives, so next came the…

Aminopenicillins

The aminopenicillins are **ampicillin** and its oral formulation, **amoxicillin**. They retain the efficacy of prior PCNs but also kill many susceptible gram-negative organisms, such as *H. influenzae, E. coli, Proteus mirabilis*, and several strains of *Salmonella* and *Shigella*. Therefore, this new class added activity against urogenital and colonic bacteria. However, they are destroyed by staphylococcal penicillinase.

Unfortunately, resistance developed quickly and bacteria started producing other β-lactamases. Also, they had no activity against *Klebsiella* or *Pseudomonas*. So, the next major drug class to be developed was the…

Extended-Spectrum PCNs

Piperacillin is the currently available extended-spectrum PCN. It takes the spectrum of ampicillin and extends it to cover the more resistant GNRs, including *Pseudomonas*. Organisms created β-lactamases to this class, so the next addition to come along was the…

β-Lactamase Inhibitors

Addition of a β-lactamase inhibitor (BLI)—**sulbactam, tazobactam, avibactam**, or **clavulanic acid**—in combination with an aminopenicillin or an extended-spectrum PCN protects the PCN from β-lactamase hydrolysis.

Combinations include:

- IV ampicillin + sulbactam
- PO amoxicillin + clavulanic acid
- IV piperacillin + tazobactam (active against *Pseudomonas*)

The drugs retain the activity of the parent PCN, but they are also effective against bacteria that make β-lactamase, including most anaerobes.

Evolution of Methicillin-Resistant *Staphylococcus aureus* (MRSA)

Staphylococci eventually acquired the *mecA* gene, which encodes a change in the PCN-binding proteins that the β-lactams use to bind the bacteria. *mecA* transcription results in reduced affinity of all β-lactams for the organisms' cell walls—except for the newest 5th generation cephalosporin, ceftaroline. The staphylococci that express this gene are called methicillin-resistant staphylococci (MRSA, methicillin-resistant *S. epidermidis* [MRSE], and other methicillin-resistant coagulase-negative staphylococci).

Vancomycin, daptomycin, and linezolid effectively treat serious MRSA infections. Newer drugs with anti-MRSA activity include ceftaroline, tedizolid, oritavancin, dalbavancin, telavancin, and tigecycline; these are not for MRSA bacteremia. MRSA in skin and soft tissue infections often retains susceptibility to clindamycin, TMP/SMX, or doxycycline.

PCN Allergy

Most reported PCN allergies are not true allergic responses. PCN allergy is often incorrectly reported by patients due to recollection of nonallergic symptoms while treated in the past (e.g., diarrhea, nausea). The American Academy of Allergy, Asthma, and Immunology recommends increased use of PCN skin testing, which is safe and effective. In patients in which a PCN is the drug of choice or essential (e.g., neurosyphilis), skin testing can be performed. A negative skin test has a negative predictive value of > 95%, making an anaphylactic reaction to PCN very unlikely. If truly allergic, patients can also be desensitized. See the Allergy & Immunology section under Drug Hypersensitivity Reactions for more on drug desensitization.

Cephalosporins

Cephalosporins also contain the β-lactam ring, but are inherently penicillinase-resistant because of their structure. Cephalosporins have no activity against enterococci or *Listeria*. With the exception of ceftaroline, all methicillin-resistant staphylococci are resistant to all cephalosporins.

1st Generation Cephalosporins

1st generation cephalosporins are active against MSSA and streptococci. There is 1 parenteral form available, IV **cefazolin**, and 2 oral forms, **cephalexin** and **cefadroxil**. They are unlike PCN in that they have some coverage against community-acquired GNRs, such as *E. coli, Klebsiella*, and *Proteus*. 1st generation cephalosporins are commonly given for:

- Skin and soft tissue infections from sensitive organisms
- Surgical prophylaxis
- UTIs from sensitive organisms

2nd Generation Cephalosporins

Gram-negative coverage increases with coverage of *H. influenzae* (cefuroxime), *Moraxella, Enterobacter*, and *N. gonorrhoeae*. Pneumococcal coverage is retained. In this group, 2 drugs, **cefoxitin** and **cefotetan**, also have anaerobic coverage. These 2 drugs are used to treat:

- Pelvic inflammatory disease (PID)
- Postoperative abdominal infections

The 3rd generation cephalosporins have largely replaced the 2nd generation except for anaerobic infections, usually due to gut flora.

3rd Generation Cephalosporins

3rd generation cephalosporins are stable against most β-lactamases and have enhanced activity against pneumococci, *H. influenzae*, and *N. gonorrhoeae*. The GNR coverage is also enhanced over previous generations, so these drugs are better for the Enterobacteriaceae (*E. coli, Klebsiella, Proteus, Enterobacter*, and *Serratia*).

Remember the following facts about 3rd generation cephalosporins:

- They are great pneumococcus drugs, so they are recommended as 1st line agents for community-acquired pneumonia and meningitis in combination with vancomycin for empiric treatment.

- None of the drugs are 1st line agents for MSSA; 1st generation cephalosporins or nafcillin/oxacillin are preferred.
- None of the drugs cover anaerobes. 2nd generation cephalosporins or PCNs are better.
- **Ceftazidime** is the only 3rd generation drug that has antipseudomonal activity.
- **Ceftazidime, ceftriaxone,** and **cefotaxime** cross an inflamed blood-brain barrier. Any of these can be used as primary therapy for meningitis caused by Enterobacteriaceae.
- **Ceftolozane** was FDA approved in 2014 to treat complicated intraabdominal infections and UTIs. It is only available in combination with tazobactam.
- Cefdinir, cefixime, and cefpodoxime-proxetil are 3rd generation cephalosporins.

4th Generation Cephalosporins

Cefepime is the only 4th generation cephalosporin. Think of it as the gram-positive activity of a 1st generation cephalosporin combined with the gram-negative activity of ceftazidime (including *Pseudomonas aeruginosa*), with enhanced stability against cephalosporinases. It has limited anaerobic coverage and is commonly used for neutropenic fever.

5th Generation Cephalosporins

Ceftaroline is the only cephalosporin that treats MRSA. Think of it like vancomycin combined with ceftriaxone. It does not treat *Pseudomonas* infections.

Advanced Generation Cephalosporins

Cefiderocol is a novel cephalosporin that binds to iron. It is recognized by bacteria as a siderophore–iron complex and is actively transported through the outer membrane (think Trojan horse), where it can bind to PCN-binding proteins and halt cell wall synthesis in the same way as other cephalosporins. Gram-negative spectrum is extensive, including multidrug-resistant *Pseudomonas aeruginosa* and carbapenem-resistant Enterobacteriaceae. Gram-positive and anaerobic spectrum is limited. Cefiderocol is approved by the FDA for complicated urinary tract infections. Its therapeutic niche is treatment of infections caused by highly resistant gram-negative rods.

Addition of β-Lactamase Inhibitors

There are 4 newly approved β-lactam + β-lactamase inhibitor combinations available for extremely drug-resistant, gram-negative infections. These include the following:

1) IV ceftolozane + tazobactam

2) IV ceftazidime + avibactam

3) IV meropenem + vaborbactam

4) IV imipenem-cilastatin + relebactam

The specifics of when to use these agents should generally be discussed with an infectious disease specialist and/or antimicrobial stewardship department.

Monobactams

Aztreonam is the only monobactam with a β-lactam ring. It covers only GNBs, including *Pseudomonas*. Its spectrum is similar to aminoglycosides and 3rd generation cephalosporins. It is not active against gram-positive cocci or anaerobes. This drug can be used in patients with either a β-lactam allergy or specifically, a PCN allergy, which is its niche. It is available for intravenous or inhaled use only. The inhaled form is used to treat *Pseudomonas aeruginosa* respiratory infections in patients with cystic fibrosis.

Carbapenems

Imipenem, meropenem, doripenem, and **ertapenem** are broad-spectrum β-lactams recommended only for use in complicated infections involving multiple organisms (such as in the abdomen or the diabetic extremity with possible bacteremia), against multidrug-resistant organisms, and for empiric treatment of the critically ill.

Carbapenem Resistance

Carbapenemases are carbapenem-hydrolyzing β-lactamases that confer carbapenem resistance. Various forms of these have been identified over the last several years.

Individual Carbapenems

Imipenem covers most bacterial classes: gram-positive cocci (GPC; excluding MRSA), gram-negative rods (GNRs; including *Pseudomonas* and other resistant GNRs), and mouth and gut anaerobes (particularly *Bacteroides fragilis*). It also is effective against extended-spectrum β-lactamase (ESBL)-producing organisms.

The few organisms resistant to imipenem are:

- *Enterococcus faecium*
- *Burkholderia cepacia*
- *Corynebacterium jeikeium* (JK)
- *Stenotrophomonas maltophilia*
- *Acinetobacter* species
- MRSA

Remember that although *E. coli* and *K. pneumoniae* are typically sensitive to imipenem, the carbapenemase-producing variety can spread easily and cause major problems.

Resistance is increasingly common in *Pseudomonas* isolates, especially in those patients with recurrent infections—such as patients with cystic fibrosis.

Imipenem can lower the seizure threshold, so do not use it in patients with seizures and/or advanced-stage chronic kidney disease.

INFECTIOUS DISEASE

Imipenem is always formulated with equal amounts of cilastatin. Cilastatin is an enzyme inhibitor that impairs the metabolism of imipenem in the renal tubule, thereby increasing its half-life.

Meropenem is a similar carbapenem with a longer half-life, so there is no need for an enzyme inhibitor.

Doripenem is a carbapenem with similar activity and pharmacokinetics to meropenem.

Ertapenem is a carbapenem with convenient once-daily dosing but no activity against *Pseudomonas*. Otherwise, its spectrum is similar to the other carbapenems. It is useful for outpatient parenteral treatment, especially of diabetic foot wounds, and for abdominal, pelvic, skin, and soft tissue infections.

TETRACYCLINES

This class has activity against organisms that do not have a typical cell wall, and thus are resistant to β-lactams. These include *Mycoplasma*, *Chlamydophila*, *Ehrlichia* and *Anaplasma*, and *Mycobacterium marinum*. They are very active against the majority of *S. aureus*, including MRSA. They also have antimalarial activity.

- **Doxycycline** has replaced **tetracycline** because of its less frequent (twice daily instead of 4 times daily) dosing. It is available orally (with 100% bioavailability) as well as intravenously.
- **Minocycline** is less commonly used, is only available orally but has similar indications as doxycycline.
- **Tigecycline** is a very broad-spectrum glycylcycline (related to tetracyclines) with increased activity against enterococci, *Listeria*, and many GNRs. It is indicated to treat intraabdominal infections, community acquired pneumonia and skin and soft tissue infections. One study revealed a slight but significant increased all-cause mortality in patients receiving tigecycline so it should not be a first line agent for any of these indications. (See Glycylcyclines for more information.)
- **Eravacycline** was approved in 2018 as an intravenous agent to treat intraabdominal infections.
- **Sarecycline** was approved in 2018 as an oral agent to treat acne.
- **Omadacycline** was approved in 2018 as an oral or intravenous agent to treat community acquired pneumonia and skin/soft tissue infections.

GLYCOPEPTIDES

Vancomycin

Vancomycin is a glycopeptide antibiotic that is effective against most gram-positive organisms, including MRSA, MRSE, *Clostridium*, and *Corynebacterium*. It is a large molecule that diffuses poorly into most tissues, with only ~ 1/8 of the blood concentration reaching the site of infection. It exhibits time-dependent killing, so predose (trough) levels are measured to assure that they are ~ 8× the usual cutoff for susceptibility (2 mcg/mL), as well as to limit toxicity. For most serious infections, predose levels between 15 and 20 mcg/mL are recommended.

Clearance of vancomycin in patients undergoing hemodialysis can vary widely depending on the membranes used, so levels are needed to guide dosing.

Some strains of enterococci are vancomycin resistant (VRE). MICs are increasing in staphylococci, but vancomycin-resistant staphylococci (MIC ≥ 16 mcg/mL) are exceedingly rare. However, increases in the MIC that are still within the susceptible range (1–2 mcg/mL) can result in vancomycin treatment failure. Some experts suggest using an alternative drug to treat the infection (e.g., linezolid, telavancin, daptomycin). (Remember that daptomycin is inactive in the lungs, so use linezolid for vancomycin-resistant staphylococcal pneumonia.) It remains controversial whether to start an alternative agent as soon as the MIC is available or to wait for clinical outcome. Staphylococci with a MIC between 2 and 8 mcg/mL for vancomycin are considered to have intermediate susceptibility; use alternative drugs.

Vancomycin, when it is rapidly infused, sometimes causes **vancomycin flushing syndrome**, consisting of tachycardia, flushing, occasional angioedema, and generalized pruritus. It is an infusion rate-related phenomenon that is the result of mast cell degranulation and release of histamine. Vancomycin flushing syndrome is not a true allergy. Patients who experience this reaction can be retreated with the drug if it is infused more slowly. Pretreat these patients with H_1 blockers. Renal and ototoxicity are rare at normal doses (< 4 g/day).

The sole indication for PO vancomycin is *C. difficile* infection. IV vancomycin is not effective for *C. difficile* because it does not achieve therapeutic levels in the bowel.

Newer Glycopeptides

The FDA approved 3 glycopeptides in 2013 and 2014: **telavancin**, **oritavancin**, and **dalbavancin**. They have the same spectrum as vancomycin but have longer half-lives of 7–10 hours, 10 days, and 14 days, respectively, thus allowing for less frequent IV dosing of once daily, once weekly, or biweekly, respectively. These drugs lend themselves nicely to ambulatory treatment of infections and are FDA approved for the treatment of acute bacterial skin and skin structure infections. Telavancin is also approved for ventilator-associated and hospital-acquired pneumonia when alternatives are not appropriate. It has some cross sensitivity with vancomycin, so use caution if a known allergy exists.

OXAZOLIDINONES

Linezolid and **tedizolid** are the only oxazolidinones on the U.S. market.

They are bacteriostatic agents active against gram-positive organisms, including MRSA, MRSE, and VRE. Neither has an indication for bacteremia. They are highly bioavailable orally and come in IV and PO preparations. Linezolid is dosed twice daily, and tedizolid is dosed once daily.

These drugs are useful alternatives to vancomycin for MRSA. Tedizolid is only approved for skin and soft tissue infections.

Linezolid can cause reversible thrombocytopenia, anemia, and leukopenia especially if the patient has been taking it > 2 weeks. Tedizolid may cause this less frequently but has only been studied for short courses of therapy. Both drugs may cause a peripheral neuropathy. Both drugs can cause serotonin syndrome when used concurrently with selective serotonin reuptake inhibitors (SSRIs) and serotonin-norepinephrine reuptake inhibitors (SNRIs).

STREPTOGRAMINS

Quinupristin and **dalfopristin** are streptogramins, which are administered as a combination IV antibiotic. This compound has a narrow spectrum against certain aerobic, gram-positive organisms—specifically vancomycin-resistant *E. faecium* and MSSA—and is used when these organisms are resistant to, or patients are intolerant to, other agents. It is rarely used, given the availability of newer agents.

CYCLIC LIPOPEPTIDES

Daptomycin is a cyclic lipopeptide active against gram-positive organisms. It is a parenteral drug with a long half-life that allows once-daily dosing. It is used to treat skin and soft tissue infections, bacteremia, and right-sided endocarditis caused by MSSA or MRSA. It is reserved for resistant organisms, such as MRSA and VRE, or for patients intolerant to other drugs used for these organisms. It is also a useful drug to treat MRSA that have relatively high MICs to vancomycin.

It is inactivated by pulmonary surfactant and thus is not effective in treating pneumonia. Myopathy is a potential side effect, so monitor CK levels at least weekly during long-term use, especially in patients who are also taking a statin.

GLYCYLCYCLINES

Tigecycline is a parenteral glycylcycline that is a derivative of tetracycline. It is very broad-spectrum with activity against gram-positive organisms (e.g., VRE, MRSA), anaerobes, and GNRs. It has coverage against ESBL-producing GNRs. However, it is not active against *Pseudomonas* and has reduced activity against *Proteus* and *Providencia*.

Tigecycline is indicated for complicated skin and soft tissue infections and intraabdominal infections. Nausea and vomiting are its main side effects, occurring in > 20% of patients. There is a black box warning of increased mortality for tigecycline because certain patients, particularly those with pneumonia, did worse on tigecycline compared with other antibiotics. There is still a role for this antibiotic in multidrug-resistant infections, but it should generally be given in collaboration with infectious disease colleagues.

POLYMYXINS

Colistin is a nephrotoxic agent that was essentially replaced by the less (but definitely) nephrotoxic aminoglycosides, only to have a new niche with the advent of multidrug-resistant *P. aeruginosa* and *Acinetobacter*. Because nephrotoxicity occurs in 20–50% of patients, its use is limited to treatment of those multidrug-resistant organisms for which no other antibiotics are available and/or tolerable.

Polymyxin B is also available in parenteral and topical forms and is used for resistant gram-negatives. It is also toxic, and its use is limited as above.

AMINOGLYCOSIDES

Aminoglycosides (e.g., **gentamicin**, **tobramycin**, **amikacin**, **streptomycin**) are active against the following:

- Enteric GNRs (but not anaerobic GNRs, such as *Bacteroides fragilis*)
- *Yersinia pestis* (plague)
- *Francisella tularensis* (tularemia)
- *Pseudomonas aeruginosa*
- *Brucella* species (brucellosis)
- *Mycobacterium tuberculosis*
- *M. avium-intracellulare*

Aminoglycosides are also used to treat patients with febrile neutropenia, in combination with a 3rd generation cephalosporin or an extended-spectrum penicillin + β-lactamase inhibitor if local β-lactam resistance rates are too high to trust β-lactam monotherapy.

These drugs exhibit concentration-dependent killing and a considerable postantibiotic effect. Hence, they are best dosed once daily after a loading dose. Potential complications include ototoxicity and nephrotoxicity.

FLUOROQUINOLONES

Ciprofloxacin, **levofloxacin**, **moxifloxacin**, and **delafloxacin** are all available in IV and oral form; **Ofloxacin** is only available orally. Their oral bioavailability is from 60% to 99% (levofloxacin being the highest and delafloxacin the lowest) but is reduced by chelation with divalent cations (Mg^{2+}, Ca^{2+}) that may be components of vitamins and laxatives. Other drugs can decrease absorption (e.g., aluminum/magnesium antacids, sucralfate, ferrous sulfate). In addition, they prolong the QT interval, so you must avoid concomitant use with other QT-prolonging agents (e.g., amiodarone). Ciprofloxacin inhibits P450 enzymes and thus can have serious interactions with other medications producing elevated levels of drugs such as warfarin, theophylline, alprazolam, caffeine, clomipramine, duloxetine, ropinirole.

Fluoroquinolones all have aerobic GNR coverage, and ciprofloxacin and levofloxacin have *Pseudomonas* activity. Ciprofloxacin should not be used for empiric *S. pneumoniae* coverage. On the other hand, levofloxacin and moxifloxacin are approved for *S. pneumoniae*, which is why some refer to them as "respiratory fluoroquinolones." Although *S. aureus* may be susceptible in micro reports, resistance commonly develops during treatment, and fluoroquinolones should not be used, with the exception of delafloxacin.

Delafloxacin was FDA approved in 2017 for skin and soft tissue infections only, and the indication includes MRSA.

Moxifloxacin is less active than the others against GNRs, but it is the most active quinolone for *M. tuberculosis* and is active against most anaerobes.

There are many caveats with this class:

- Due to inhibition of tendon and bone formation, use of fluoroquinolones in individuals < 18 years of age is not recommended by the FDA, with the exception of ciprofloxacin, which is approved for 2nd line therapy in children with UTIs and patients with cystic fibrosis.
- In adults, injury to tendons (specifically the Achilles tendon), muscle, joints, and peripheral nerves can occur, especially in older persons. In addition, there is an increased risk of aortic aneurysm, aneurysm rupture, and hypoglycemia. Thus, the FDA recommends against their use as 1st line drugs for acute bacterial sinusitis, exacerbations of COPD, and uncomplicated UTIs.

MACROLIDES

There are 4 macrolides currently available: erythromycin, clarithromycin, azithromycin, and fidaxomicin.

The parent drug **erythromycin** is effective against:

- *Mycoplasma pneumoniae*
- *Chlamydia pneumoniae*
- *Campylobacter*
- Diphtheria
- Pertussis

Erythromycin has a short half-life of 2 hours and thus must be dosed several times a day. It increases intestinal motility and may cause nausea, vomiting, and/or diarrhea. It increases the concentrations of many drugs, including theophylline, cyclosporine, and warfarin.

Clarithromycin and **azithromycin** have better *S. pneumoniae* and *H. influenzae* coverage than erythromycin and have better GI tolerance. Clarithromycin is only available orally, but azithromycin comes in both IV and PO formulations. These 2 agents have longer half-lives that permit more convenient dosing— daily or twice daily for clarithromycin ($T_{1/2}$ = 3–7 hours) and daily for azithromycin ($T_{1/2}$ = ~ 3 days).

Fidaxomicin is a unique agent that is only used to treat *C. difficile* infection. It is given orally but is minimally absorbed. It has similar initial cure rates to vancomycin but its relapse rate is ~ 50% less, making it a 1st line drug for initial treatment, as well as treatment of relapses.

URINARY TRACT AGENTS

Three agents—nitrofurantoin, fosfomycin, and methenamine—are often considered together because their only indication is for the treatment of UTIs.

Nitrofurantoin has multiple mechanisms of action that disrupt protein, DNA, RNA, and cell wall synthesis; this explains why resistance is rare among species that are intrinsically susceptible, which includes most *E. coli*. All *Proteus* and most *Klebsiella* are resistant. Blood levels are not sufficient to treat pyelonephritis or systemic infections, so its use is limited to uncomplicated cystitis from susceptible strains. Toxicity is rare if kidney function is normal. It is not recommended if creatinine clearance is < 60 mL/minutes/1.73m^2 (1.00 mL/seconds/m^2). It is a 1st line drug for uncomplicated cystitis and is safe in pregnancy, except at term. It can also be used as low-dose prophylaxis of recurrent UTIs related to sexual activity in women.

Fosfomycin is a phosphonic antibiotic that has activity against most enterococci and *E. coli*, *Klebsiella*, and *Enterobacter*. For the same reasons as nitrofurantoin, it should not be used for pyelonephritis or systemic infections. It is less effective than nitrofurantoin, so it is a 2nd line agent for uncomplicated cystitis. It has the advantage of only requiring a single dose.

Methenamine is a heterocyclic antibiotic made from combining ammonia and formaldehyde. In acidic urine, formaldehyde is released, which is bactericidal to organisms. No formaldehyde is created in the alkaline environment of the blood or renal parenchyma, so toxicity is minimal. It is relegated to use in suppressing recurrent UTIs.

ANTIBACTERIALS WITH CONTRAINDICATIONS IN PREGNANCY

Nitrofurantoin is contraindicated after 38 weeks, or during labor, out of concerns for increasing the risk of neonatal jaundice and/or hemolytic anemia in the newborn.

Trimethoprim/sulfamethoxazole is contraindicated in the first trimester because it may cause neural tube defects. It is also contraindicated after 36 weeks due to increased risk of kernicterus caused by displacing bilirubin from plasma proteins.

Tetracyclines are contraindicated throughout pregnancy. As a class, these antibacterials are contraindicated due to increased risk of hepatotoxicity in pregnancy and incorporation into fetal bones/teeth with growth inhibition and/or staining. However, doxycycline does not appear to cause these issues and is considered safe when there are no alternative agents.

Fluoroquinolones are not contraindicated in pregnancy. Animal models show cartilage and bone toxicity in utero, yet human studies have not shown a similar association. Therefore, this class is not contraindicated in pregnancy, especially if there are no alternative agents.

Aminoglycosides are not contraindicated in pregnancy. The first drug in this class was associated with bilateral deafness in infants exposed during pregnancy. However, this has not been observed with other agents in this class. Therefore, aminoglycosides are not contraindicated in pregnancy, especially if there are no alternative agents and it is intended to be a short course of treatment.

ANTIFUNGAL AGENTS

PREVIEW | REVIEW

- Liposomal amphotericin B preparations are used in which circumstances? Against which fungi?
- Which candidal species are usually resistant to fluconazole?
- What are the indications for voriconazole?
- What are the indications for echinocandins?

POLYENES (AMPHOTERICIN AND NYSTATIN)

Polyenes bind to ergosterol on fungal cell walls, altering their permeability and producing cell death.

The original formulation of **amphotericin B deoxycholate** has been mostly replaced by lipid polyene formulations, echinocandins, and azoles. When given intravenously, it had many side effects: acute kidney injury, anemia, phlebitis, renal tubular acidosis, hypokalemia, and hypomagnesemia. Infusion-related chills and fevers can be severe, and hypotension can occur.

Liposomal amphotericin B preparations are less nephrotoxic and have fewer infusion-related side effects but are more expensive. Lipid preparations are better for some fungal infections, especially those that enter the reticuloendothelial system, such as cryptococcal meningitis and disseminated histoplasmosis. Lipid amphotericin B is also used to treat mucormycosis (*Mucor* and *Rhizopus*) because higher doses of the preparation can be given without nephrotoxicity. They are also used when toxicity has occurred with the amphotericin deoxycholate preparation. The very low level excreted in the urine is the reason they are not indicated in treating fungal UTIs. The original version can be used to treat fluconazole-resistant UTIs.

Topical polyene macrolides are **nystatin** and **amphotericin B**. These are effective only against mucocutaneous candidiasis. Both are also available in liquid form for oral and esophageal candidiasis.

AZOLES

Azoles work by inhibiting the synthesis of ergosterol, a necessary component of the fungal cell wall.

Ketoconazole is an oral and topical preparation that is rarely used systemically because of increasing resistance and more toxicity than other azoles. It can be used to treat refractory tinea infections. Ketoconazole is a potent P450 inhibitor and therefore has many drug–drug interactions.

Clotrimazole and **miconazole** are available in both cutaneous and vaginal (for vaginal candidiasis) preparations. Many other preparations are also available. They are also used to treat cutaneous candidiasis, tinea versicolor, and ringworm.

Fluconazole is indicated for oral and esophageal candidiasis, candidemia (for susceptible isolates), disseminated candidiasis from *C. albicans*, coccidioidomycosis, cryptococcosis, and vulvovaginal candidiasis. It has excellent penetration into the CSF. Never use fluconazole as empiric antifungal treatment in febrile neutropenic patients. *Candida krusei* is entirely resistant, and many *Candida glabrata* are resistant.

Fluconazole is a moderate P450 inhibitor and therefore has many drug–drug interactions.

Itraconazole is a triazole analog of ketoconazole that is more effective and safer. Capsules should be taken with food; a carbonated drink (acidity) helps with absorption. Always check levels when using itraconazole. Consider itraconazole for patients with non–life-threatening endemic fungal infections (e.g., histoplasmosis, blastomycosis) and sporotrichosis.

Itraconazole also is a potent P450 inhibitor and therefore has many drug–drug interactions.

Voriconazole is a triazole with an extended antifungal spectrum compared to fluconazole. Voriconazole is 1st line therapy for invasive aspergillosis—this is the most important indication to remember. It can also be used for certain resistant, invasive candidal infections with ocular involvement (azoles generally penetrate the blood–brain/blood–eye barrier), as well as other hyaline and dematiaceous mold infections. The drug can be given orally or by IV.

Major toxicity is transient, with reversible alterations in visual acuity and color vision. It happens in ~ 30% of patients 30 minutes after administration and lasts 30 minutes (30-30-30 rule). Check voriconazole serum levels whenever you are treating a serious infection because significant variations in levels occur from person to person.

Voriconazole is a potent P450 inhibitor and therefore has many drug–drug interactions.

Posaconazole is a triazole with the extended antifungal spectrum of voriconazole, with additional activity against the Zygomycetes (e.g., *Rhizopus*, *Mucor*). It is FDA approved for prophylaxis of *Aspergillus* and *Candida* infections in those with severe immunocompromised states, including prolonged neutropenia or stem cell transplant recipients with graft-versus-host disease. It is also used for treatment of oropharyngeal candidiasis (particularly infections refractory to itraconazole or fluconazole), invasive *Aspergillus*, and Zygomycetes.

Posaconazole is a potent P450 inhibitor and therefore has many drug–drug interactions.

Isavuconazole was FDA approved in 2015 for the treatment of invasive aspergillosis and mucormycosis. It is at least as good as voriconazole for the former and was found reasonably effective for the latter in an open-label study published in 2015. Drug levels do not need to be monitored. It is also a potent P450 inhibitor.

ECHINOCANDINS

Echinocandins inhibit β-1,3-glucan, an essential component of the cell walls of several fungi, including *Aspergillus*. They act very similarly and are used interchangeably. They are 1st line drugs for the treatment of severe *Candida* infections (including fungemia), as well as the 1st choice for empiric antifungal therapy in prolonged febrile neutropenia.

Caspofungin has a half-life of 30–50 hours and is dosed once daily after an initial loading dose. Caspofungin is approved for:

- Candidemia and *Candida* infections of the abdomen, peritoneum, and pleural space and fluconazole-resistant esophagitis
- Invasive aspergillosis in severely immunocompromised patients who are intolerant of lipid amphotericin B or voriconazole

Caspofungin is the only echinocandin additionally approved for invasive aspergillosis as salvage therapy. Caspofungin also has the most drug interactions. No dose adjustment is needed for renal failure.

Several drugs interfere with its metabolism: phenytoin, dexamethasone, carbamazepine, efavirenz, nevirapine, and rifampin.

Micafungin has a half-life of 11–21 hours and does not require a loading dose. It has fewer drug interactions.

Anidulafungin has a half-life of 40–50 hours and is dosed once daily after an initial loading dose. It has very few drug interactions.

OTHER ANTIFUNGALS

Flucytosine (a.k.a. 5-fluorocytosine; 5-FC) is metabolized to the antimetabolite 5-fluorouracil which competes with uracil and inhibits RNA synthesis. It is highly soluble and penetrates well into the CSF. Most *Candida* and endemic fungi are susceptible, but if used alone, drug resistance develops quickly. When combined with amphotericin B, resistance does not develop and there is a synergistic antifungal effect. This combination is used in the induction treatment of severe cryptococcosis. 5-FC can cause

serious GI, hepatic, renal, and bone marrow toxicities—the latter usually presents as neutropenia and thrombocytopenia. It is renally excreted, so a decrease in kidney function predisposes to toxic effects.

ANTIPARASITIC AGENTS

PREVIEW | REVIEW
- What are the indications for praziquantel?

Praziquantel is the only drug effective against all species of *Schistosoma*. It is effective against flukes and tapeworms. It should be used in addition to albendazole to treat neurocysticercosis caused by the pork tapeworm *Taenia solium* when > 2 cysts are present on images.

Albendazole is a 1st line drug for all nematodes (except filariasis) and cysticercosis. It is 2nd line for strongyloidiasis and schistosomiasis. Use only in nonpregnant patients.

Niclosamide is used for the treatment of tapeworm.

Pentamidine is effective against trypanosomiasis (African sleeping sickness). For *Pneumocystis*, which is a fungus and not a parasite, treat with IV or via inhalation for prophylaxis. It is not used as a 1st line drug for treatment because of the many side effects, including azotemia, leukopenia, pancreatitis, and hypo- or hyperglycemia.

Nitazoxanide is approved for treatment of *Giardia lamblia* and *Cryptosporidium parvum*.

Miltefosine is used to treat *Naegleria* and *Leishmania*. It is only available through the CDC.

Eflornithine is used to treat *Trypanosoma brucei gambiense* meningoencephalitis (sleeping sickness).

Atovaquone is used to treat babesiosis and as a 2nd line drug for *Pneumocystis*.

Nifurtimox is used to treat *Trypanosoma cruzi* and *T. b. gambiense*.

Benznidazole, an orphan drug, is used to treat *Trypanosoma cruzi*.

Ivermectin is the drug of choice for *Strongyloides* infections.

Diethylcarbamazine is the drug of choice for all forms of filariasis. It is only available through the CDC.

Triclabendazole is used to treat *Fasciola hepatica* but is not available in the U.S.

Antimalarial drugs: See *Plasmodium* (Malaria) on page 4-64.

ANTIVIRAL AGENTS

PREVIEW | REVIEW
- What are the indications for ganciclovir?

Acyclovir is a nucleoside analog used for the treatment of herpes simplex and varicella-zoster viruses. Treatment of zoster infections requires higher doses. High intravenous doses to treat herpes simplex encephalitis can crystalize in the urine, causing a microobstructive acute kidney injury that resolves with hydration.

Valacyclovir and **famciclovir** are oral antivirals that also treat herpes simplex and varicella-zoster infections. Only acyclovir is available intravenously to treat severe infections. Valacyclovir and famciclovir drugs are used primarily for less-frequent dosing of outpatients. They are more expensive than acyclovir.

Ganciclovir is used to treat cytomegalovirus (CMV) infections, which are seen most often in posttransplant patients and those with HIV/AIDS. Typical CMV infections are retinitis, encephalitis, pneumonitis, colitis, and, occasionally, severe bone marrow suppression (neutropenia and thrombocytopenia).

Valganciclovir is an oral preparation similar to ganciclovir but with better absorption, leading to blood levels comparable to IV ganciclovir.

Foscarnet is used in patients with acyclovir-resistant herpes infection or as an alternative to ganciclovir for CMV. Foscarnet toxicity includes decreases in serum K^+, Ca^{2+}, Mg^{2+}, and phosphorus along with acute kidney injury.

Cidofovir is a 2nd line drug to treat CMV infections in immunocompromised hosts.

Letermovir is used to prevent CMV infection in patients receiving hematopoietic stem cell transplantation.

Ribavirin is used as part of combination therapy for hepatitis C. It can cause significant hemolytic anemias, requiring downward dose adjustments.

Neuraminidase inhibitors are the primary drugs used to treat influenza A and B. They prevent virion release from cells by inhibiting the enzyme neuraminidase. The 3 FDA-approved drugs in this class are oseltamivir, zanamivir, and peramivir.

Cap snatch inhibitors interfere with viral RNA transcription and viral replication. These are active against influenza A and B. The one drug in this class that is FDA approved is baloxavir marboxil.

Adamantanes target the M2 ion channel protein of influenza A viruses. They are not active against influenza B. Presently, nearly all influenza A is resistant to these drugs, so they are not recommended for treatment. The two drugs in this class are amantadine and rimantadine.

See Antiretroviral Drugs on page 4-34.

DRUGS FOR TREATMENT AND PREVENTION OF COVID-19

As we discuss the drugs that have been approved or given emergency authorization by the FDA for the treatment or prevention of COVID-19, refer to Table 4-14. Guidelines are continuing to change rapidly as of 2022, so check for updates on the Infectious Diseases Society of America website: idsociety.org/practice-guideline/covid-19-guideline-treatment-and-management/.

Mechanisms of action for FDA- and EUA-approved COVID-19 drugs:

- IL-6 receptor antagonists
  - Tocilizumab
  - Sarilumab
- RNA polymerase inhibitors
  - Remdesivir
  - Molnupiravir
- Protease inhibitors
  - Nirmatrelvir/Ritonavir

Table 4-14: Infectious Diseases Society of America Suggested / Recommended Treatments					
Drug	Postexposure Prophylaxis	Ambulatory at Risk for Severe	Hospital pO^2 > 94%	Hospital pO^2 ≤ 94%	Hospital ICU
Tixagevimab/ cilgavimab	Suggested				
Nirmatrelvir + ritonavir		Suggested			
Molnupiravir		Alternative			
Remdesivir		Alternative	Suggested	Suggested	
Baricitinib				Suggested	Suggested
Tofacitinib				Alternative	
Tocilizumab				Suggested	Suggested
Sarilumab				Alternative	Alternative
Corticosteroids				Suggested	Recommended

* All listed drugs are FDA and Emergency Use Authorization (EUA) approved. All entries shown in blue were not applicable as of the June 2022 IDSA COVID-19 Treatment Guidelines update.

- Spike protein monoclonal antibody combinations
  - Casirivimab/Imdevimab (not effective against Omicron)
  - Bamlanivimab/Etesavimab (not effective against Omicron)
  - Tixagevimab/Cilgavimab
- Janus kinase inhibitors
  - Baricitinib
  - Tofacitinib

Drugs for COVID-19 Treatment

Monoclonal Antibodies

There are 2 combinations of monoclonal antibodies that are authorized for emergency use by the FDA for the treatment of mild-to-moderate COVID-19 in nonhospitalized patients who are at high risk for severe disease. The combinations are bamlanivimab + etesevimab and casirivimab + imdevimab. Both are given as a single IV infusion. They are **not** effective against the omicron strain. Another single monoclonal antibody, sotrovimab, is effective against omicron.

Antiviral Drugs

Several antiviral drugs have been effective in the treatment of COVID-19.

Remdesivir: This drug acts through inhibition of the SARS-CoV-2 RNA polymerase and is FDA approved to treat hospitalized patients with an oxygen requirement (but not on a ventilator). It decreases length of stay but not mortality. It also has a morbidity benefit in nonhospitalized individuals at high risk of progression.

Nirmatrelvir + ritonavir: Nirmatrelvir is an inhibitor of the SARS-CoV-2 protease enzyme and thus inhibits viral replication. Ritonavir has no activity against SARS-CoV-2 but inhibits CYP3A-mediated metabolism of nirmatrelvir, thus increasing its blood levels. The combination of nirmatrelvir + ritonavir is authorized for emergency use by the FDA for the treatment of mild-to-moderate COVID-19 in nonhospitalized patients who are at high risk for severe disease. This drug significantly decreases the need for hospitalization or death if given within 3–5 days of symptoms.

Molnupiravir: This drug is a nucleoside analogue that inhibits SARS-CoV-2 replication. It is authorized for emergency use by the FDA for the treatment of mild-to-moderate COVID-19 in nonhospitalized patients who are at high risk for severe disease. If given within 5 days of symptom onset, it significantly decreases the need for hospitalization or death. It is not as effective as remdesivir or nirmatrelvir + ritonavir and is not approved for use in patients < 18 years of age (may cause bone or cartilage injury) or in pregnant patients. Because of these issues, it is considered a 2nd line drug for outpatient treatment.

Antiinflammatory Drugs

Glucocorticoids: Dexamethasone is recommended for hospitalized patients with oxygen requirements and decreases mortality in patients on mechanical ventilation. In these patients it should be used in combination with either baricitinib or tocilizumab:

Baricitinib: Baricitinib is an oral Janus kinase inhibitor that decreases the signaling of proinflammatory cytokines that cause lung injury during COVID-19. It has emergency use authorization for treatment of hospitalized patients requiring supplemental oxygen—including ventilated patients—although the evidence in ventilated patients is less compelling. Ventilated patients should also be receiving dexamethasone.

Tocilizumab: Tocilizumab is an IL-6 receptor antagonist that is recommended as therapy for hospitalized patients with an oxygen requirement, including those on mechanical ventilation. Ventilated patients should also be receiving dexamethasone.

Drugs for COVID-19 Prevention

The monoclonal antibody combinations bamlanivimab + etesevimab and casirivimab + imdevimab have emergency use authorization for **postexposure** prophylaxis in persons at high risk of progression to severe COVID-19 if they are not fully vaccinated or are immunocompromised. These should not be given to patients already with symptomatic infection. These do not appear to be active against the omicron strain.

A combination injection of tixagevimab + cilgavimab has emergency use authorization for use as **preexposure** prophylaxis. Indications are for persons who have had severe reactions to vaccination that has prevented a full vaccination and booster course, or patients who have immune compromise that would limit their response to adequate vaccination.

VACCINES

PREVIEW | REVIEW

- Which vaccines contain live virus? Which patients should not receive them?

- Which vaccines are safe to administer to immunocompromised or pregnant patients?

- Which vaccines are recommended to adults and in which age groups?

- How do you decide how to prevent tetanus in a patient presenting with a wound?

VACCINE TYPES

Vaccines used solely in childhood are not discussed here.

Do not give live attenuated vaccines to immunocompromised or pregnant patients. (See the Women's and Men's Health section under Obstetrics.) **Live attenuated vaccines** include:

- MMR (measles-mumps-rubella)
- Varicella
- Zoster
- Smallpox
- Typhoid oral
- Cholera oral
- Bacille Calmette-Guérin (BCG; a.k.a. Calmette-Guérin bacillus)
- Yellow fever
- Intranasal influenza

Killed (inactivated) vaccines are safe for the immunocompromised and pregnant and include:

- Td (tetanus-diphtheria toxoid)
- Tdap (tetanus toxoid, reduced diphtheria toxoid, acellular pertussis)
- Hepatitis A
- Hepatitis B
- Polio
- Cholera (not available in the U.S.)
- Rabies
- Japanese encephalitis
- Typhoid polysaccharide
- HPV
- Pneumococcal vaccines (PPSV23 and PCV13)
- Meningococcal
- Influenza
- Varicella

VACCINE SCHEDULES

Vaccine schedules are noted here with vaccine-specific discussions to follow later in this section. The specific schedule for vaccinations changes frequently. The current schedule can be found on the web page for the Advisory Committee on Immunization Practices (cdc.gov/vaccines/schedules).

Vaccinations that are recommended for adults, according to age groups:

- **Td or Tdap:** 1 dose every 10 years. Tdap is approved for all > 7 years of age. Tdap should be given only once as an adult if the 3-dose primary childhood series has been given; after that, Td can be given. However, Tdap should be given during each pregnancy, preferably at 27–36 weeks' gestation.
- **HPV:** Initial vaccination is recommended beginning at age 9. Adults up to 26 years of age who are unvaccinated should be vaccinated with a 3-dose series.

Adults 27–45 years of age may be vaccinated based on shared decision-making.

- **Varicella Vaccine:** 2 doses, if no history of immunity or vaccination
- **Zoster Vaccine:** adults > 50 years of age; ≥ 18 years of age if immunocompromised. The recombinant vaccine has replaced the live attenuated vaccine, which was much less effective. 2-dose series, 2–6 months apart.
- **MMR:** If not immune, a single immunization should be given. Adults should be considered immune if any of the following are true:
  - Born before 1957
  - Documented receipt of MMR vaccine
  - Laboratory evidence of immunity
- **Influenza:** given annually to all persons > 6 months of age
- **Pneumococcal vaccination:** There are 4 vaccines that vary with their indications depending on age and risk of infection. The number is indicative of the number of serotypes represented in the vaccine
  - **PCV20:** Administer to all persons ≥ 65 years of age.
  - **PPSV23:** Administer to all persons ≥ 65 years of age if PCV15 or PCV13 was given previously. Administer to younger adults if at increased risk because of vital organ disease (COPD, liver disease, kidney disease, heart failure), smoking, DM, alcohol use disorder, sickle cell disease. Revaccinate every 5–10 years.
  - **PCV15:** Administer prior to PPSV23 if at increased risk because of CSF leak, cochlear implant, asplenia, immunocompromise.
  - **PCV13:** No longer routinely recommended to persons ≥ 65 years of age. Revaccination is not indicated.
- **Hepatitis A:** Administer to persons with chronic liver disease, men who have sex with men (MSM), travelers to endemic countries or adoptees from endemic countries, HIV infection, injection drug use, or undomiciled. Vaccine should also be provided for anyone desirous of immunity. Give 2–3 doses depending on vaccine selected.
- **Hepatitis B:** Administer to individuals who are health care/safety workers or have chronic liver disease, end-stage kidney disease, HIV, injection drug use, MSM, incarcerated, travel to endemic countries, or sexual exposure risk. Should also be provided for anyone desirous of immunity. Give 2 or 3 doses, depending on the vaccine selected.
- **Meningococcal polysaccharide or conjugate:**
  - **MenACWY:** Administer to individuals with asplenia, HIV infection, complement deficiency, receiving complement inhibitors, travel to endemic countries, 1st year college students in residential housing, and military recruits.
  - **MenB:** Administer to individuals 16–23 years of age based on shared decision-making.

APPROACH TO TETANUS PREVENTION

Tetanus can be prevented with the appropriate use of tetanus toxoid (Td) and tetanus immunoglobulin (TIG). The use of these depends on the type of wound and the vaccination status of the patient.

Tetanus-prone wound: Tetanus-prone wounds include crush injuries, bite injuries, dirt- or fecally contaminated wounds, puncture or missile wounds, deep penetrating wounds, wounds containing foreign bodies (e.g., wood splinters), and reimplantation of an avulsed tooth. Tetanus can be prevented based on how certain it is that patients have had the primary series of 3 injections of Td or not.

After a tetanus-prone wound, give a booster dose of Td to those who have had a primary series if they have not received Td in the last 5 years. This stimulates sufficient production of antitoxin antibodies before the tetanus toxin can travel from the wound site to the CNS.

Patients with a tetanus-prone wound who have not received the primary series or have uncertain immunization history are considered at high risk for tetanus. Give these patients Td to begin the primary series. However, since they have not had adequate prior immunization, boosting of their immune response cannot be relied upon. Therefore, these are the patients for whom tetanus immunoglobulin (TIG) is indicated.

Non-tetanus-prone wound: Persons who do not have tetanus-prone wounds (often called "clean wounds") are not at risk for tetanus from the wound. However, the patient encounter provides an opportunity to begin immunization in the previously unvaccinated or to boost immunity in people who haven't received a booster in the last 10 years. Thus, give those who have not received all 3 primary series injections of Td (or are uncertain) as many Td injections as needed to complete the 3-shot primary immunization sequence. Give a Td booster to those who have completed the primary series but have not been boosted in the last 10 years. TIG is never indicated in the management of non-tetanus-prone wounds.

Use of Tdap: When immunizing adults, Tdap instead of Td should be used once in their lifetime. This is also the immunization of choice during each pregnancy.

UNCOMMON VACCINES FOR SPECIAL SITUATIONS

Japanese encephalitis is an inactivated vaccine recommended for travelers who plan to stay an extended time in rural Asia.

Rabies vaccine is discussed under Rabies on page 4-27.

Typhoid vaccine is recommended for travelers to endemic areas. The definition of these areas should be based on the most current CDC and WHO recommendations. There is an oral attenuated live vaccine and a polysaccharide vaccine. These have efficacy rates of < 60% and, if there is continued exposure, revaccination is recommend every 3–5 years.

Polio vaccine is not routinely recommended to persons > 18 years of age. Polio vaccine is recommended for previously unimmunized travelers to endemic areas. A booster is indicated for travelers who have had only the primary vaccination and who travel to areas where exposure to the wild-type virus is likely. Only the inactivated vaccine is recommended in the U.S.

Yellow fever vaccine is recommended for travel in equatorial Africa and much of tropical South America based on the latest CDC guidelines. It is a live vaccine; therefore, do not give to immunosuppressed patients.

Cholera vaccine was approved in the U.S. in 2016 and is a live attenuated oral vaccine that can be given to adults traveling to regions with active cholera cases based on the latest CDC recommendations.

COVID-19 VACCINES

There are 3 COVID-19 vaccines used in the U.S.: 2 use mRNA technology to develop antibodies to the spike proteins of the virus (Moderna and Pfizer), and 1 uses an adenovirus vector that expresses spike proteins (Janssen). They have different age, dose, frequency, and booster recommendations (Table 4-15).

When data on all of the trials is combined, these vaccines are > 90% effective against preventing severe disease, defined as the need for hospitalization, ICU admission, or death.

Table 4-15: COVID-19 Vaccines (U.S.)				
Developer	Name	Age	Initial Doses	Booster
Pfizer	BNT162b2	≥ 5 years	0 + 21 days	5 months
Moderna	mRNA-1273	≥ 18 years	0 + 28 days	5 months
Janssen (Johnson & Johnson)	Ad26.COV2.S	≥ 18 years	0	2 months

Injection site reactions are seen in > 50% of recipients after each dose and fatigue, headache, and myalgias are each seen in ~ 25% of recipients. Vaccine-related myocarditis and pericarditis are rare but have been reported with the mRNA vaccines. Anaphylaxis is exceedingly rare, occurring in ~ 0.0005% of recipients. The Ad26.COV2.S vaccine has been associated with an autoimmune thrombotic thrombocytopenia with cerebral venous thrombosis in ~ 0.0004% of cases and a higher-than-expected number of cases of Guillain-Barré syndrome.

THE MEDSTUDY HUB: YOUR GUIDELINES AND REVIEW ARTICLES RESOURCE

For both review articles and current internal medicine practice guidelines, visit the MedStudy Hub at

medstudy.com/hub

The Hub contains the only online consolidated list of all current guidelines focused on internal medicine. Guidelines on the Hub are easy to find, continually updated, and linked to the published source. MedStudy maintains the Hub as a service to the medical community and makes it available to anyone and everyone at no cost to users.

FIGURE SOURCES

Figure 4-1: MedStudy illustration
Figure 4-2: Maxgarrett7, CC BY-SA 3.0
Figure 4-3: Kimberly Salkey, MD
Figure 4-4: CDC/ Dr. Heinz F. Eichenwald
Figure 4-5: CDC/ Dr. Lucille K. Georg
Figure 4-6: KlatschmohnAcker, CC BY-SA 3.0
Figure 4-7: CDC/ Armed Forces Institute of Pathology,
*   Charles N. Farmer*
Figure 4-8: CDC
Figure 4-9: CDC/ Dr. N.J. Flumara; Dr. Gavin Hart
Figure 4-10: CDC/ Joe Miller
Figure 4-11: CDC/ Dr. Norman Jacobs
Figure 4-12: Fred Arthur Zar, MD
Figure 4-13: CDC
Figure 4-14: Stefan Walkowski, CC BY-SA 4.0
Figure 4-15: CDC/ Dr. Russell K. Brynes
Figure 4-16: Drvgaikwad, CC BY 3.0
Figure 4-17: CDC
Figure 4-18: James Heilman, MD, CC BY-SA 3.0
Figure 4-19: CDC
Figure 4-20: CDC
Figure 4-21: Dileepunnikri, CC BY-SA 3.0
Figure 4-22: CDC
Figure 4-23: CDC
Figure 4-24: CDC
Figure 4-25: Kimberly Salkey, MD
Figure 4-26: CDC
Figure 4-27: Bal, Aswine K; Kairys, Steven W., CC BY 3.0
Figure 4-28: CDC
Figure 4-29: CDC
Figure 4-30: CDC
Figure 4-31: CDC
Figure 4-32: James Heilman, MD, CC BY-SA 3.0
Figure 4-33: CDC
Figure 4-34: CDC
Figure 4-35: MedStudy illustration
Figure 4-36: Yale Rosen, CC BY-SA 2.0
Figure 4-37: MedStudy illustration
Figure 4-38: CDC
Figure 4-39: CDC
Figure 4-40: CDC
Figure 4-41: Nephron, CC BY-SA 3.0
Figure 4-42: MedStudy illustration
Figure 4-43: CDC/ Dr. Mae Melvin
Figure 4-44: CDC
Figure 4-45: MedStudy illustration
Figure 4-46: CDC
Figure 4-47: CDC
Figure 4-48: Nathaniel Warner, MD
Figure 4-49: Nephron, CC BY-SA 3.0
Figure 4-50: Camiloaranzales
Figure 4-51: Bobjgalindo, CC BY-SA 4.0, CC BY-SA 3.0,
*   CC BY-SA 2.5, CC BY-SA 2.0, CC BY-SA 1.0*
Figure 4-52: CDC
Figure 4-53: CDC
Figure 4-54: CDC

·

Freeman Laboratory Separates in General Chemistry

precision
accuracy
random error
systematic error
blunder

Each exercise in this manual is available as a Freeman Laboratory Separate, numbered below in the order in which they appear in the manual.

The Separates are self-bound, self-contained exercises. They are 8½ inches by 11 inches in size, and are punched for a three-ring notebook. They can be ordered in any assortment or quantity at .75¢ each. Order through your bookstore, specifying number and title. (For a complete listing of other Freeman Laboratory Separates in chemistry, see the last page of this manual.)

(Price subject to change)

1209. Student Handbook: Introduction and Appendixes
1210. Mass and Volume Relationships
1212. Some Common Physical Properties of Substances
1213. Some Elementary Chemical Properties of Substances
1215. The Preparation of Pure Substances by Chemical Changes
1218. The Determination of Avogadro's Number
1222. The Molar Volume of Oxygen
1223. The Molecular Weight of a Gas
1224. The Reactivity of Metals with Hydrochloric Acid
1227. Ionic and Covalent Compounds. Ionic Reactions
1230. Hess' Law and the First Law of Thermodynamics
1300. Colligative Properties. The Molecular Weight of a Soluble Substance by Freezing-Point Depression
1231. The Rate of a Chemical Reaction. Chemical Kinetics
1233. Some Examples of Chemical Equilibrium
1234. Ionization Constants of Weak Acids
1237. Volumetric Analysis. The Titration of Acids and Bases
1239. Identification of Silver, Lead, and Mercurous Ions
1240. Identification of Ferric, Aluminum, and Zinc Ions
1241. Identification of Alkaline Earth and Alkali Metal Ions
1242. The Qualitative Analysis of Some Common Anions
1245. The Use of Paper Chromatography in the Separation of Iron(III), Cobalt(II), Nickel(II), and Copper(II) Ions
1247. Oxidation-Reduction. Electron Transfer Reactions
1249. Oxidation-Reduction Reactions and Electrochemical Cells
1250. Redox Titrations. The Oxidizing Capacity of a Household Cleanser or Liquid Bleach
1254. The Chemistry of Vitamin C

W. H. FREEMAN AND COMPANY
41 Madison Avenue, New York, NY 10010
20 Beaumont Street, Oxford, England OX1 2NQ

General Chemistry in the Laboratory

Julian L. Roberts, Jr.
J. Leland Hollenberg
University of Redlands

James M. Postma
California State University, Chico

W. H. Freeman and Company
New York

To the memory of James B. Ifft,
our friend and colleague for twenty years

Contents

Preface

This laboratory manual was written to accompany the text *General Chemistry* by Donald A. McQuarrie and Peter A. Rock, hence its title: *General Chemistry in the Laboratory*. The manual preserves the general style and format of the laboratory manuals in the Frantz/Malm series (*Essentials of Chemistry in the Laboratory*, Third Edition, *Chemical Principles in the Laboratory*, Second Edition, and *Chemistry in the Laboratory*), but adds fifteen new experiments to the repertoire available in the Frantz/Malm series.

Each experiment has an introduction that is more complete than that found in many laboratory manuals. Inevitably this introduces some redundancy but it also provides two advantages: (1) It allows each experiment to stand alone so that the order may be altered to suit the sequence of topics in any general chemistry textbook, and (2) it arouses the interest of the student because it provides a context that relates the experiment to the student's own experience. Historical notes are also included in some experiments to emphasize that the development of chemistry is the result of

human activities motivated by a desire to understand the natural world around us.

Safety Aspects. In revising old experiments and writing new ones, we have paid special attention to making each experiment safer, by devising safer procedures and by seeking to eliminate the possible exposure of students to substances that are very toxic or carcinogenic. In this effort we have been aided by Dr. Henry Feuer, Professor Emeritus of Purdue University, who made many helpful suggestions, and by the Occupational Safety and Health Administration (OSHA) guidelines. We also have profited from the continuing series edited by Dr. Malcolm Renfrew, *Safety in the Chemistry Laboratory*, published in the *Journal of Chemical Education*.

Following the recommendation of David A. Katz published in the *Journal of Chemical Education* **59**, A127(1982), we have added a safety precautions section to those experiments that present possible hazards.

A number of experiments require the use of

adequate fume hoods. In cases where the laboratory is not equipped with fume hoods we suggest that the experiment either not be performed or be performed by the instructor as a laboratory demonstration.

In our experience, the safety consciousness of students is strongly dependent on the attitudes of the laboratory instructor, and the safety precautions must be reinforced by good safety practices. No instructor should assume that students will carefully read and practice the precautions contained in the experiments. If the instructor ignores them, the students are likely to do the same.

Organization and Content. The order of experiments parallels the sequence of topics in *General Chemistry* by McQuarrie and Rock. There are 40 experiments in the manual—about 50 percent more than the number usually performed in the standard two-semester course in general chemistry. The instructor can thus choose from an ample selection those experiments that will best complement the lecture portion of the course using any general chemistry text.

In addition to the 40 experiments, there are two study assignments and an appendix on chemical nomenclature that contain laboratory exercises and problems for students to work out, either in the laboratory or as a supplement to the laboratory work. Study Assignment A might well be used as the introductory experiment because it contains a novel weighing exercise requiring the use of the analytical balance, and it introduces the student to the concepts of experimental error and graphing.

The experiments are generally designed to be completed in a three-hour laboratory period, but they vary in length. Based on your own experience, you may find that parts of some experiments may be deleted with no loss of continuity, and some experiments contain sections that are labelled as optional.

The topics covered by the experiments are listed below. (Some experiments may be listed more than once if they fit into two categories.)

Mass and Volume Relations (Experiment 1)

Chemical Formulas (Experiments 3, 6)

Gas Laws (Experiments 8, 9, 10, 11)

Electronic Structure of Atoms (Experiment 15)

Chemical Bonding (Experiment 16 and Study Assignment B)

Descriptive Chemistry (Experiments 4, 5, 16, 24, 25, 26, 27, 37, 38)

Separations (Experiments 2, 28)

Thermochemistry (Experiments 12, 13, 14)

Colligative Properties (Experiment 18)

Chemical Equilibria (Experiments 19, 20, 22, 30, 38)

Chemical Kinetics (Experiments 34, 35)

Qualitative Analysis (Experiments 2, 24, 25, 26, 27, 28)

Quantitative Analysis (Experiments 9, 11, 21, 23, 32, 33, 36, 39)

Electrochemical Cells (30, 31)

Polymer and Biochemistry (Experiments 17, 39, 40)

An experiment on separations is placed early to provide an interesting and realistic example of the power of chromatography, which is discussed in an introductory chapter in the McQuarrie/Rock text. The next group of experiments deals with chemical stoichiometry, the descriptive chemistry of oxygen and copper, and several experiments illustrating the applications of the ideal gas laws. We did not include experiments on the gas laws themselves, reasoning that the applications of the laws are intrinsically more interesting and the results less predictable.

The section on thermochemistry includes three experiments: the heat capacity of metals, the enthalpy of combustion of a vegetable oil, and Hess's law (using one of the reactions actually studied by Hess, the dilution of sulfuric acid).

The design of an experiment to accompany the chapter on the electronic structure of atoms presents a formidable challenge. Simple spectroscopes may be homemade or purchased at reasonable cost, but an appreciable investment is required to purchase the gas discharge tubes and power supplies required. We believe that this is a worthwhile investment because it gives the student a concrete experience that can be connected to the more abstract notion of electronic energy levels in atoms.

Devising simple yet non-trivial experiments to accompany the chapters on chemical bonding also presents a challenge. Experiment 16 allows the student to make simple quantitative distinctions between covalent, polar covalent, and ionic bonding by studying the conductivity of solutions containing various solutes. The role of the solvent in promoting ionic dissociation in also investigated. We have found the direct reading conductivity apparatus described in this experiment to be safe, reliable, and simple to use. Study Assignment B is an exercise in writing Lewis structures. It might be used profitably in conjunction with a laboratory exercise in which students build models of molecules using model-building kits commercially available or styrofoam balls held together by short lengths of pipe cleaner. This is very helpful in assisting students to visualize the geometry of molecules, particularly in learning to use the Valence Shell Electron Pair Repulsion (VSEPR) method to predict molecular geometry.

We felt that it was appropriate to include an experiment on synthetic polymers because of their widespread use in everyday life and the widespread ignorance of their rich and diverse chemistry. Having made the decision to include an experiment on polymers, we concluded that it should provide more than a "show-and-tell" experience for the student, so we provided a discussion of their synthesis that is more detailed than that provided in the usual general chemistry text.

Experiments 21, 23, 32, 33, 36, and 39 illustrate the chemical analysis of samples that will be familiar to students—natural waters, swimming pool water, and various commercial products that will be found in the medicine cabinet, kitchen, or laundry room. We, like other teachers, have found that students feel that the analysis of these substances is fun because they are familiar—something you can tell your roommate or family about. The analysis of swimming pool water may appear to some to be a preoccupation peculiar to the stereotypical California lifestyle. This may well be true, but we prefer to think of swimming pool chemistry as a small-scale example of a much larger and more significant public health problem—the disinfection of municipal drinking water supplies by chlorination.

Experiment 31 on electrochemical cells and electrolysis was newly written for this manual. It contains two experiments that we think students will enjoy—a study of the anodization of aluminum and an experiment illustrating electrochemical machining in which a sharpened pencil is used to make a hole in a razor blade.

Two experiments on kinetics are provided. The first introduces a number of important concepts related to chemical kinetics, and the second employs a clock reaction to determine a rate law. The particular reaction studied is the reaction of hydrogen peroxide with iodide ion, a reaction that consumes hydrogen ion but which is zero order in the hydrogen ion concentration (if the pH is greater than 3.5). This provides an intriguing surprise and gives the instructor an opportunity to discuss the connection between rate law and reaction mechanism and to point out that the rate law cannot be deduced from the reaction stoichiometry.

Finally we have included several experiments using the traditional methods of qualitative analysis to identify various cations and anions. These experiments provide a useful context for teaching descriptive chemistry and acid-base and solubility equilibria. They appeal to students because they present the challenge of an intellectual puzzle to be solved, namely, the identification of the unknown ions. They also fulfill the students' expectations that chemistry has something to do with test tubes, pretty colors, and rotten smells.

Criteria for Including an Experiment. About twenty-five of the experiments in this manual will be recognizable as reincarnations of experiments that have appeared in the Frantz/Malm series of laboratory manuals, with about fifteen being newly written for this manual. In deleting old experiments and selecting new ones, we have been mindful of the costs, both psychic and monetary, that are involved in substantially changing a particular repertoire of experiments. Most experiments in this manual use equipment that will be found in the typical student locker and reagents that will be found in the chemistry storeroom (or local supermarket). We have sought to keep costs down by minimizing reagent costs and the investment in special equipment not likely to be found in the general chemistry laboratory. Many, if not most, general chemistry laboratories are now equipped with pH meters, simple spectrophotometers, such as the popular Bausch and Lomb Spectronic 20, and voltmeters (or multimeters). In several instances (Experiments 15, 16, and 31) we have given instructions for the construction of simple homemade equipment. We anticipate, therefore, that most of the experiments in this manual will not require the purchase of special equipment or difficult-to-obtain reagents.

Beyond the practical criteria, we have particularly tried to accomplish the following: (1) Provide a repertoire of experiments that will parallel the topics usually covered in a two-semester course in general chemistry. (2) Select experiments that will illustrate important chemical principles, preferably in a quantitative fashion. (3) Assist the student in attaining a deeper insight into some aspect of the everyday world. (4) Provide an intellectual challenge to the student—some unexpected result to interpret, some unknown to be identified, or some constituent to be quantitatively determined. (5) Provide a satisfying aesthetic experience for the student by presenting an array of sights, colors, sounds, or smells. (6) Make each experiment as simple as possible without lapsing into triviality or oversimplification. It is our view that simplification is a process vital to an orderly structuring of our experience but that complexity is the spice that motivates us to probe more deeply into the nature of our world.

We will welcome the comments and suggestions of the users of this manual concerning improvements or substitutions for experiments in this manual.

Acknowledgments. We acknowledge with gratitude the invitation of W. H. Freeman and Company to write this laboratory manual, a task that was interrupted at the very beginning by the unexpected death of our friend and collaborator Dr. James B. Ifft. We also wish to acknowledge with appreciation the encouragement and patience of the editors at W. H. Freeman and Company, who helped us regroup and finish the task, and the advice and encouragement of Dr. Donald A. McQuarrie and

Dr. Peter A. Rock of the University of California, Davis.

We also express our thanks to Dr. Henry Feuer, Purdue University, who reviewed the manuscript with an eye to making the experiments safer and to Dr. Luther K. Brice, Jr., Virginia Polytechnic Institute and State University, Dr. John E. Davidson, Eastern Kentucky University, and Dr. James L. Jensen, California State University, Long Beach, each of whom reviewed the manuscript and helped us to correct errors and improve the content and organization of the experiments.

We are especially grateful to our expert typist and friend, Mrs. Eleanor Scott, who typed the final copy of the manuscript and produced the camera-ready copy for the Instructor's Manual. This is the fourth laboratory manual that she has helped us to produce.

May 1984

Julian L. Roberts, Jr.
J. Leland Hollenberg
James M. Postma

First-Day Instructions

GREETINGS

Your laboratory work is the core of your chemistry course. You have a challenging opportunity to observe many of the facts of chemistry under controlled laboratory conditions and to deduce from these observations the basic principles that constitute the foundation of the science of chemistry. This is the scientific method in action.

Here are a few brief points that will give you a good start in this course.

1. Gain self-confidence by working individually, unless the experiments demand teamwork.

2. Use your ingenuity and common sense. Laboratory directions, while quite specific, leave ample opportunity for clear-cut, logical, original, and imaginative thinking. This attitude is a prerequisite in any scientific endeavor.

3. Don't waste your time. Prepare for each experiment by studying it (both the Pre-Lab Preparation and, briefly, the Experimental Procedure) before you come to the laboratory.

4. Note beforehand any extra equipment required from the stockroom, and obtain all of it at the same time.

5. Prepare you Laboratory Report on each experiment with care. If you prepare your own report form, use a permanently bound notebook as prescribed by your instructor, preferably one with 5-mm cross rulings. Always have the data entry portion prepared in advance, and *record data directly in your final report as you obtain it.* (Data entered on scraps of paper will be confiscated.) Where calculations of data are involved, show an orderly calculation for the first set of data, but do not clutter the calculation section with arithmetic details. Likewise, think through and answer important questions that are intended to give you an understanding of the principles on which the experimental procedure is based *as you perform the experiment.*

6. Scientists learn much by discussion with one another. You may likewise profit by discussion with your classmates—but *not* by copying from them. The keystone of all science rests first on integrity. You will also profit by frequent reference to your text while working in the laboratory. (Books are generally even more reliable and complete sources of information than are your classmates!)

7. For tabular data on the properties of substances, consult one of your handbooks: the *Handbook of Chemistry and Physics* (CRC Press, Inc., Boca Raton, Florida) or *Lange's Handbook of Chemistry* (McGraw-Hill, New York).

LABORATORY PROCEDURE

Safety Rules

Familiarize yourself with the safety rules given in the Introduction. Obedience to these rules, as modified or added to by your instructor, is essential for the sake of your safety and that of others in the laboratory.

Your instructor will indicate the location and show you the proper use of the fire extinguishers, fire blanket, safety fountains or showers, and first-aid cabinet and supplies. The instructor will also tell you where to obtain safety glasses or goggles.

Laboratory Regulations

Familiarize yourself with laboratory regulations in the Introduction. It is essential that these regulations, as modified or added to by your instructor, be followed carefully.

BASIC LABORATORY EQUIPMENT AND PROCEDURES

The Laboratory Locker

Check the equipment in the locker assigned you, following the procedure described in the Introduction or as directed by your instructor. If time remains, or if your instructor so directs, read over the procedures for the handling of chemicals, use of laboratory burners, operations with glass tubing, care of laboratory glassware, and volumetric measurements of liquids.

Introduction

The chemistry laboratory can be a place of joy, discovery, and learning. It can also be a place of frustration—and danger.

Although every effort has been made to eliminate the use in these experiments of explosive, very toxic, or carcinogenic substances, there is an unavoidable hazard involved in the use of a variety of chemicals and glass apparatus. In experiments where a potential danger exists, you will find a Safety Precautions section at the beginning of the experimental procedure. Read this section very carefully before you proceed with the experiment.

Your skin and the delicate membranes of your eyes, mouth, and lungs are largely made of protein. We hope that you do not have to experience firsthand the adverse effect that even 6 M solutions—not to mention concentrated solutions—of acids and bases have on protein. The eyes are especially sensitive to acids, bases, and oxidizing agents and must be protected at all times. In addition, the open flame of a Bunsen burner presents a constant hazard to clothing and hair.

It's likely that you will experience frustration if you come unprepared to the laboratory, neglect to record important data, or frantically try to write up reports an hour before they are due. You can minimize these problems by reading the experiments carefully beforehand, noting the critical data that must be recorded, and thoughtfully considering the data while you collect it in order to avoid careless blunders.

We strongly advise you to learn and observe at all times the following laboratory rules and regulations. By doing so you will minimize the potential dangers and frustrations of laboratory work, and maximize the joy.

SAFETY RULES

These rules are designed to ensure that all work done in the laboratory will be safe for you and your fellow students. In addition to the rules listed here, your institution may have a set of rules that you will be asked to read and sign as evidence that you have read them.

Your laboratory instructor should also point out the location and demonstrate the use of various pieces of safety equipment such as fire extinguishers, fire blankets, safety showers, eye-wash fountains, and equipment for handling spills.

Finally, you should know where first-aid supplies are kept and where a telephone is located for emergencies that require paramedical, fire, or police assistance. The telephone numbers of these on- or off-campus services should be posted in a prominent place.

1. The most important rule is that *safety glasses with side panels* or *goggles* must be worn at all times in the laboratory. Ordinary prescription glasses sometimes cover only parts of the eyes and lack side panels that protect the wearer from chemical splashes that might get into the eyes from the side. For this reason, they should be covered by safety goggles. Contact lenses should not be worn in the laboratory, even under safety goggles. By themselves they offer no protection from splashes and they are considered unsafe even under safety goggles because various fumes—for instance, hydrogen chloride gas—may accumulate under the lens and cause serious injuries. If you do not wear glasses, obtain a pair of safety glasses or goggles from your chemistry stockroom. In some procedures—such as heating a crucible to dryness or evaporating an acid solution—be sure to wear safety goggles or to carry out the experiment in a hood, which is provided in most laboratories for this purpose.

If any chemical comes in contact with the eye, the most effective first aid is the immediate flushing of the eye with copious amounts of tap water. You are seldom more than a few seconds from a faucet. Continue flushing for at least five minutes and then consult a physician at once. If your laboratory is equipped with eye fountains, familiarize yourself with their use and their location.

2. Fire is a constantly present danger. Learn where the nearest fire extinguisher is and how to use it. Your laboratory should also be equipped with a fire blanket and safety shower or fountain. *If your hair or clothing should catch fire, smother the fire with a blanket or douse yourself in the shower.*

3. Minor burns, cuts, and scratches are fairly common injuries. However, you must report every such injury to your instructor, who will determine what first aid is appropriate. If you or another student must report to the infirmary or hospital,

FIGURE I-1
Exercise great care in noting the odor of a substance, using your hand to waft its vapor gently toward your face. Whenever possible, avoid breathing fumes of any kind.

be certain that someone else accompanies the injured person.

4. Bare feet are not allowed in the chemistry laboratory. Broken glass and spilled chemicals, such as concentrated acids, are all too common on the floors of chemistry labs. In addition, we recommend that bare legs, midriffs, and arms be covered with old clothing or, preferably, with a laboratory apron or coat.

5. The vapors of a number of solutions are quite potent and can irritate or damage the mucous membranes of the nasal passages and the throat. Use the technique displayed in Figure I-1 when you need to sniff an odor.

6. In many experiments, it is necessary to heat solutions in test tubes. Never apply heat to the *bottom* of the tube; always apply it to the point at which the solution is highest in the tube, working downward if necessary. Be extremely careful about the direction in which you point a tube; a suddenly formed bubble of vapor may suddenly eject the contents violently (an occurrence called *bumping*). Indeed, a test tube can become a miniature cannon. (See Figure I-2.)

7. Avoid tasting anything in the laboratory. (Poisonous substances are not always so labeled in the laboratory.) Do not use the laboratory as an eating place and do not eat or drink from laboratory glassware.

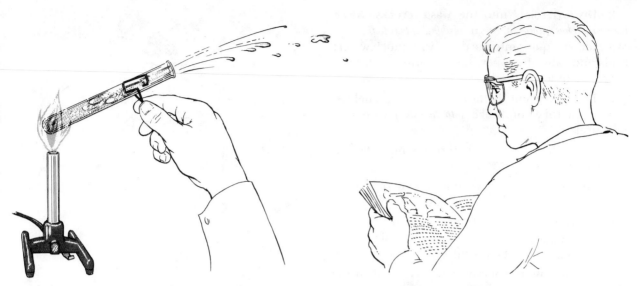

NEVER point a test tube of boiling liquid at your neighbor—it may bump.
SAFETY GOGGLES worn regularly in the laboratory will protect your eyesight.

FIGURE I-2
Two important safety precautions.

8. Perform no unauthorized experiments.

9. Never work in the laboratory alone.

10. Beware of hot glass tubing—it *looks* cool long before it can be handled safely.

11. For reactions involving poisonous gases, *use the hood*, which provides suction to remove such gases or vapors.

12. Neutralize spilled acid or base as follows: (a) acid on clothing, use dilute sodium bicarbonate solution; (b) base on clothing, use dilute acetic acid; (c) acid or base on the desk, use solid sodium bicarbonate for either, followed by water.

13. To insert glass tubing (including thermometers, long-stemmed funnels, thistle tubes, etc.) through a rubber stopper, first lubricate the tube and stopper with water or *glycerol*. Hold the tubing with a cloth *near the end to be inserted*, and insert with a twisting motion. (If you twist a long-stemmed funnel by the funnel end, it is easily broken. See Figure I-3.)

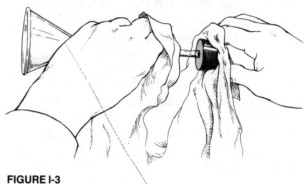

FIGURE I-3
The procedure for inserting a glass tube into a stopper. NEVER force a thistle tube or funnel into a stopper by grasping the large end. Use the stem and twist as you push. ALWAYS wrap your hands in a towel when putting a glass tube into a stopper. Moisten with water or glycerol and insert with a twisting motion.

LABORATORY REGULATIONS

These regulations are designed to guide you in developing efficient laboratory techniques and in making your laboratory a pleasant place in which to work.

1. You must read each experiment thoroughly before entering the lab. If you do not, you will waste a great deal of time (both your own and your instructor's), you may expose yourself and others to unnecessary hazards, and you will probably not obtain reliable, useful data. (You will also routinely fail all pre-lab quizzes if your instructor chooses to use them.)

2. Discard solids into the waste crocks. *Never throw matches, litmus, or any insoluble solids into the sink.* Wash down liquids into the drain with much water; acids and salts of copper, silver, and mercury are corrosive to lead plumbing.

3. Leave reagent bottles at the side shelves. Bring test tubes or beakers *to the shelf* to obtain chemicals.

4. Read the label *twice* before taking anything from a bottle.

5. Avoid using excessive amounts of reagent— 1 to 3 mL is usually ample for test tube reactions.

6. *Never* return unused chemicals to the stock bottle. You may make a mistake from which other students' experiments will suffer.

7. Do not insert your own pipets or medicine droppers into the reagent bottles. Avoid contamination of the stock solution by pouring the solution from the bottle.

8. Do not lay down the stopper of a bottle. Impurities may be picked up and thus contaminate the solution when the stopper is returned. (Hold the stopper as illustrated later in Figure I-8.)

9. Do not heat heavy glassware such as volumetric flasks, graduated cylinders, or bottles; they break easily and heating distorts the glass so that the calibrations are no longer valid. (See Figure I-4.) Test tubes may break if they are heated above the liquid level and liquid is then splashed over the hot glass. Evaporating dishes and crucibles may be heated red hot. Avoid heating any apparatus too suddenly; apply the flame intermittently at first.

FIGURE I-4
If heat is applied to the wrong type of laboratory apparatus, the outcome can be disastrous. NEVER heat a graduated cylinder or bottle.

BASIC LABORATORY EQUIPMENT AND PROCEDURES

The Laboratory Locker

Check the equipment in the locker assigned you. Refer to Figure I-5 for the identification of any unfamiliar items. Ascertain that all items are present, and examine them carefully to be sure they are in an acceptable condition. You are responsible for this equipment and will be charged for any breakage or shortage at the conclusion of the course.

The Handling of Chemicals

Some suggestions bear repeating: Be considerate of others by always bringing your container to the reagent shelf to obtain a chemical. Do not take the bottle to your desk. Maintain the purity of the chemicals in the reagent bottles. Do not withdraw more than you need, and never return any chemical to the bottle. Never contaminate the stopper by laying it down; hold it by your fingers. Do not insert your own medicine dropper into a reagent bottle or the medicine dropper from a reagent bottle down into your own test tube or solutions (Figure I-6). If necessary, clean the outside of the reagent bottle of accumulated dust, ammonium chloride, or other contaminant, rinse the neck and stopper with distilled water, and wipe dry before removing the stopper.

Some of these simple suggestions on the proper handling of solid and liquid chemicals are illustrated in Figures I-7 and I-8.

Careful observance of these suggestions will prevent the spilling of chemicals and the contamination of the stock bottles. If you do spill any chemical, clean it up completely, at once. A dirty laboratory handicaps good work.

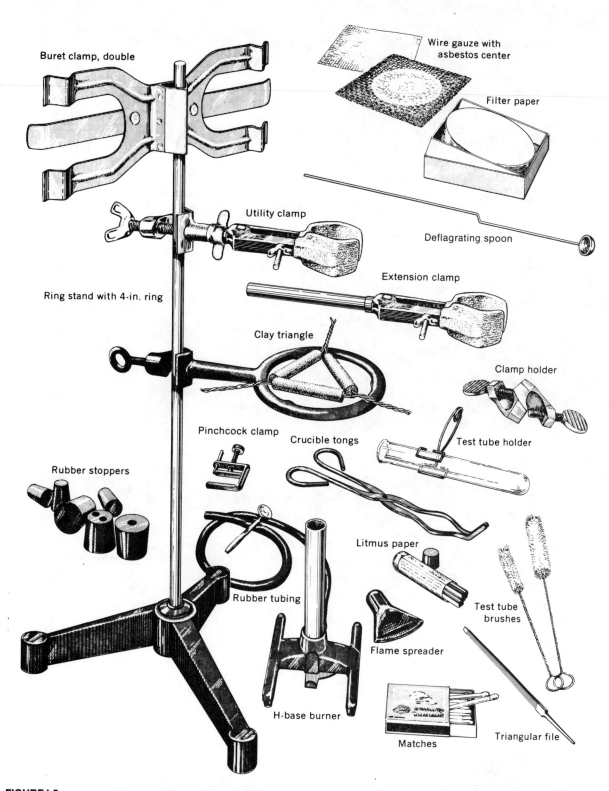

FIGURE I-5
Common laboratory equipment. [From J. W. Hagen, *Empirical Chemistry*, W. H. Freeman and
Company, San Francisco, Copyright © 1972.]

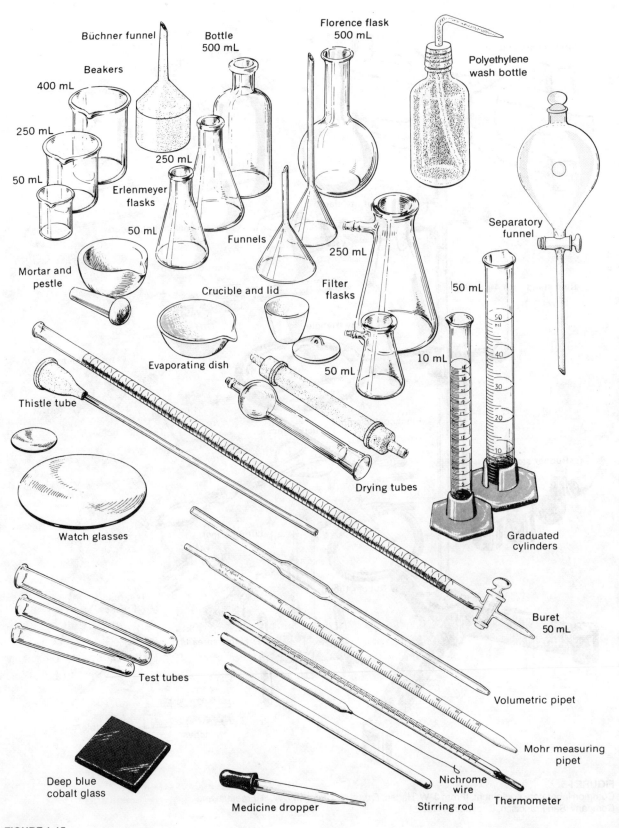

FIGURE 1-15
(continued)

When putting the contents of a
medicine dropper into a test tube

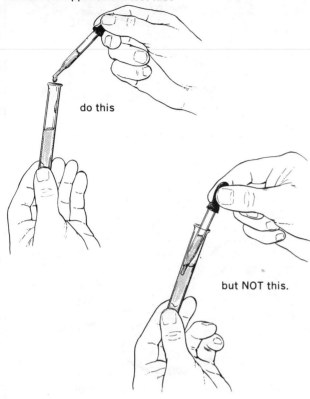

do this

but NOT this.

FIGURE I-6
The proper use of a medicine dropper.

Operations with Glass Tubing

Glass is not a true crystalline solid and therefore does not have a sharp melting point. In this respect, it more nearly resembles a solid solution or an extremely viscous liquid that gradually softens when heated. It is this property that makes glass working possible.

Soda-lime glass, made by heating a mixture of soda (Na_2CO_3), limestone ($CaCO_3$), and silica (SiO_2), softens readily at about 300 to 400°C in the burner flame. Tubing of this glass is easily bent, but because of its high temperature coefficient of expansion it must be heated and cooled gradually to avoid undue strain or breakage. *Annealing* by a mild reheating and uniform cooling is often wise. Such glass must not be laid on a cold surface while it is hot, since this introduces strains and causes breakage.

Borosilicate glass (such as Pyrex or Kimax) does not soften much below 700 to 800°C and must be worked in an oxygen–natural-gas flame or blowtorch. Because it has a low temperature coefficient of expansion, objects made of it can withstand sudden temperature changes.

Figure I-11 shows the proper way to cut glass tubing and fire polish the ends. Fire polishing smooths the sharp edges so that the glass tubing can be inserted easily into a rubber stopper without cutting your fingers. Figure I-12 shows the way to make a bend or constricted tip.

Laboratory Burners

The Bunsen burner, used for most laboratory heating, produces a cone-shaped flame, as illustrated in Figure I-9. Ordinary beakers, crucibles, and other objects to be heated are placed just above the hottest portion of the flame, which is thus allowed to spread about them. If placed down in the cold inner cone of the flame, which consists of unburned gas, the objects are not heated effectively.

The modern Fischer burner is designed to give a concentrated, very hot flame (Figure I-10). For the maximum temperature, have the gas on full pressure, and, with the air vents open, adjust the needle valve at the base (or the air cock if the compressed-air type is used) to give a short blue flame of many short cones about 0.5 cm high. The object to be heated is placed about 1 cm above the grid.

Care of Laboratory Glassware

Examine all glassware for cracks and chips. Flasks or beakers with cracks may break when heated and cause injury. Small chips in borosilicate glassware can sometimes be eliminated by fire polishing; otherwise, chipped glassware should be discarded because it is easy to cut oneself.

The recommended procedure for cleaning glassware is to wash the object carefully with a brush in hot water and detergent, then rinse thoroughly with tap water, and finally rinse once again with a small quantity of distilled or deionized water. Then allow the glassware to drain dry overnight in your locker. If you must use a piece of glassware while it is still wet, rinse it with the solution to be used.

Cleaning solution (a solution of CrO_3 or $K_2Cr_2O_7$ in concentrated sulfuric acid) is sometimes used. Such solutions should be employed in the general chemistry laboratory only under the

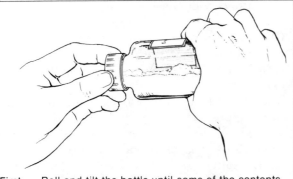

First— Roll and tilt the bottle until some of the contents enters the inside of the plastic cap.

Scoop out a little of the material with the spatula provided.

Second— Carefully remove the cap so that some of the contents remains in it.

Tap the spatula until the desired amount falls off.

Second Method

Third— Tap the cap with a pencil until the desired amount falls out.

First Method

Roll and tilt the jar until the desired amount falls out.

Third Method

FIGURE I-7
Methods for transferring powders and crystals.

REMOVING A STOPPER

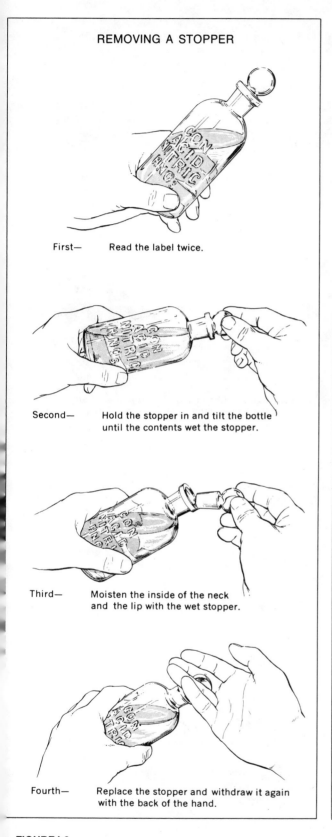

First—   Read the label twice.

Second—   Hold the stopper in and tilt the bottle until the contents wet the stopper.

Third—   Moisten the inside of the neck and the lip with the wet stopper.

Fourth—   Replace the stopper and withdraw it again with the back of the hand.

POURING A LIQUID

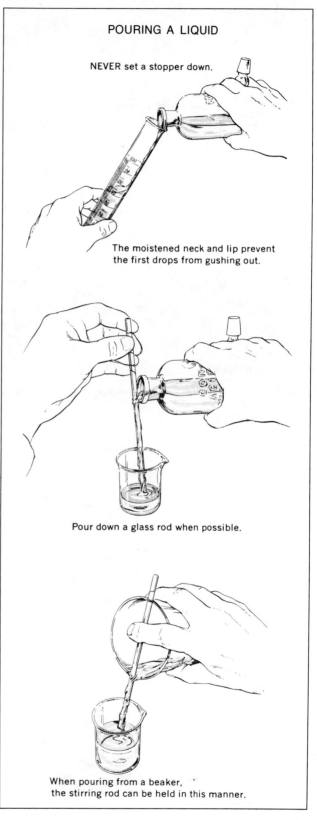

NEVER set a stopper down.

The moistened neck and lip prevent the first drops from gushing out.

Pour down a glass rod when possible.

When pouring from a beaker, the stirring rod can be held in this manner.

FIGURE I-8
Methods for transferring liquids.

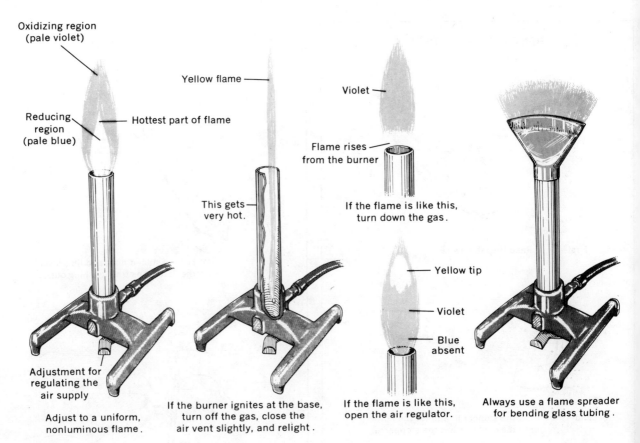

FIGURE I-9
Instructions for operating a Bunsen burner.

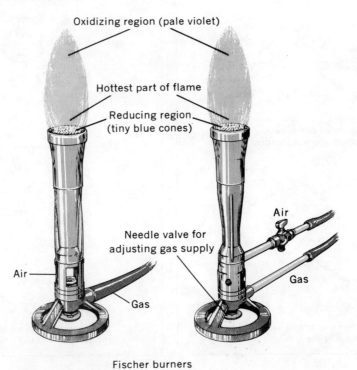

FIGURE I-10
Fischer burners.

BREAKING A TUBE

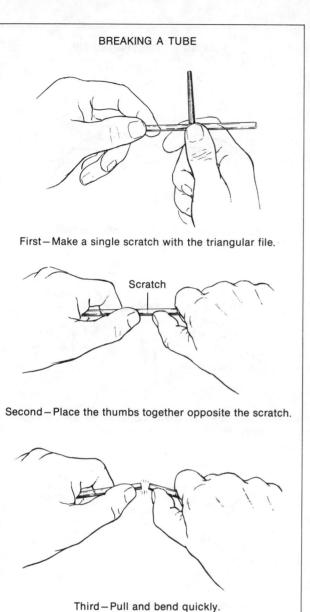

First—Make a single scratch with the triangular file.

Scratch

Second—Place the thumbs together opposite the scratch.

Third—Pull and bend quickly.

FIRE POLISHING THE END OF A TUBE

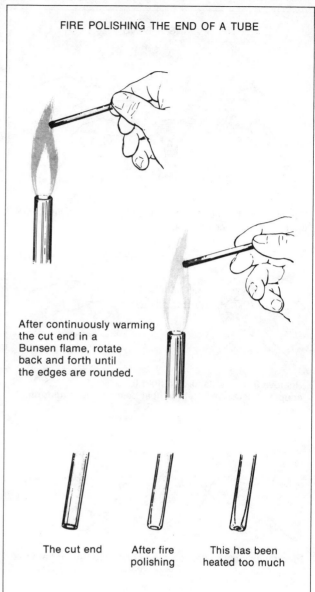

After continuously warming the cut end in a Bunsen flame, rotate back and forth until the edges are rounded.

The cut end

After fire polishing

This has been heated too much

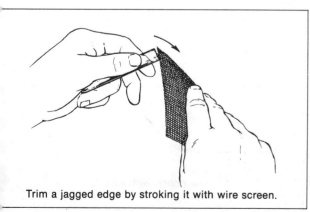

Trim a jagged edge by stroking it with wire screen.

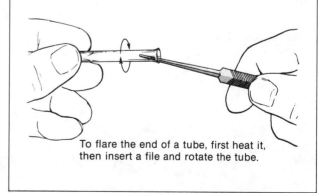

To flare the end of a tube, first heat it, then insert a file and rotate the tube.

FIGURE I-11
Some elementary manipulations of glass tubing.

MAKING A BEND

Roll the tube back and forth in the high part of a flat flame until it has become quite soft.

Remove from the flame and hold for a couple of seconds to let the heat become more uniform.

Bend quickly to the desired shape and hold until it hardens.

A good bend

Inadequate heating

Local overheating

MAKING A CONSTRICTED TIP

Roll the tube in a Bunsen flame until it softens. Don't use a flame spreader.

Allow the tube to become shorter as the walls thicken to about twice their original thickness.

Remove from the flame and after a moment pull until the softened region is as small as desired.

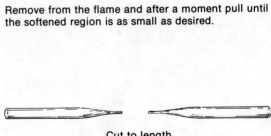

Cut to length

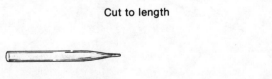

Fire polish, or file the tip

FIGURE I-12
Addtional manipulations of glass tubing.

direct supervision of the instructor, because under certain conditions the use of concentrated acids can produce noxious gases, endangering you and others nearby.

Volumetric Measurement of Liquids

Volumetric measurements of liquids are made with graduated cylinders, burets, or transfer pipets. The graduated cylinder (Figure I-13) is usually used to measure approximate volumes of liquids. Aqueous solutions wet the glass walls, forming a concave meniscus; the bottom of the meniscus is used to indicate the volume of liquid. To avoid parallax error (caused by change of observational position), your eye should always be level with the meniscus when you are making a reading. The volume is estimated to one tenth of the smallest

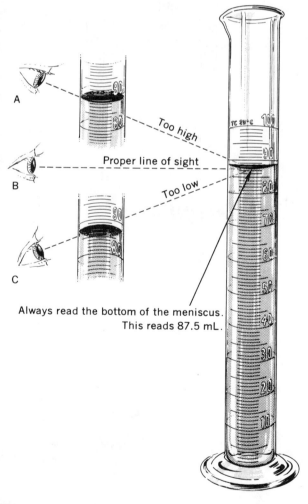

A

Too high

Proper line of sight

B

Too low

C

Always read the bottom of the meniscus.
This reads 87.5 mL.

division. The graduated cylinder is calibrated to deliver the volume that is read, and it actually contains slightly more than the volume read, thus compensating for the thin film of liquid left on the walls when the contents are poured out.[1]

The buret (Figure I-14) is used for more precise volumetric work and for titrations. If it is clean, the solution will leave an unbroken film when it drains; if drops of solution adhere to the inside of the buret, it should be cleaned with a brush, hot water, and detergent until it drains properly (see Figure I-15). Absolute cleanliness is important because the volume of a 25- or 50-mL buret can ordinarily be estimated to the nearest 0.02 mL and the error caused by a single large drop adhering to the inside of a buret causes an error of about 0.05 mL. The presence of several drops would obviously result in poor measurement of the volume delivered.

When filling a freshly cleaned buret with solution, add a 5- to 10-mL portion of the solution, being sure the stopcock is turned off, and tip and rotate the buret so that the solution rinses the walls of the buret completely. Repeat the procedure with at least two more fresh portions of solution; then fill the buret above the zero mark and clamp in a buret holder. Then open the stopcock wide to flush out any air bubbles between the stopcock and the tip of the buret. Next drain the buret below the zero mark, and take the initial reading, being careful to avoid parallax error. The smallest division on a 50-mL buret is ordinarily 0.1 mL; estimate the volume to the nearest fifth of the smallest division, or the nearest 0.02 mL.

Burets may have stopcocks made of glass, which must be periodically cleaned and lubricated as shown in Figure I-16A. Teflon stopcocks (Figure I-16B) ordinarily require no lubrication, but they may have to be cleaned if they are plugged, or adjusted if the tension nut is too tight or too loose. A drawn-out glass tip—which is connected to the buret by a short length of rubber tubing containing a round glass bead—constitutes the simple yet effective stopcock shown in Figure I-16C.

The buret is calibrated to deliver (TD) and is capable of a precision of approximately ±0.02 mL when carefully used. The tip should be small enough that the delivery time is not less than 90 s for a 50-mL buret. This allows adequate time for drainage, in order that you can obtain a proper

FIGURE I-13
The proper method of reading a meniscus to avoid parallax error.

---

[1] The abbreviation TD designates glassware that is calibrated to deliver the volume specified: for example, a 50-mL TD pipet.

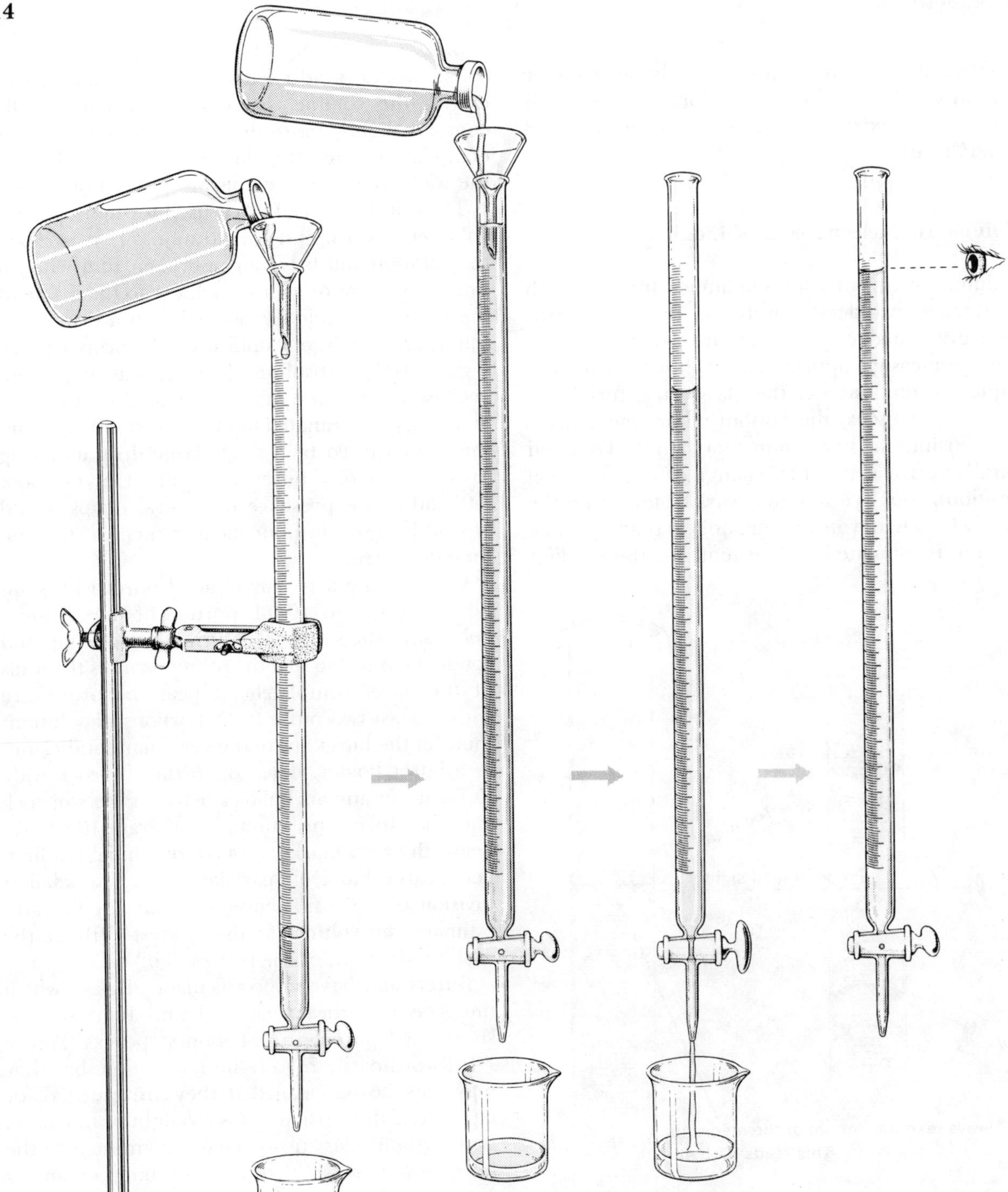

Using a small funnel, rinse a clean buret with a few milliliters of the solution. Allow the buret to drain.

Fill the buret to above the zero mark with the solution.

Open the stopcock wide for a few seconds to remove all air from the tip.

Refill to just *below* the 0.00 mark (somewhere between 0–1 mL). Take initial reading with eye level with meniscus. Do not attempt to set initial reading at 0.00 or 1.00 or any other specific reading.

FIGURE I-14
The use of a buret. [From J. W. Hagen, *Empirical Chemistry*, W. H. Freeman and Company, San Francisco. Copyright © 1972.]

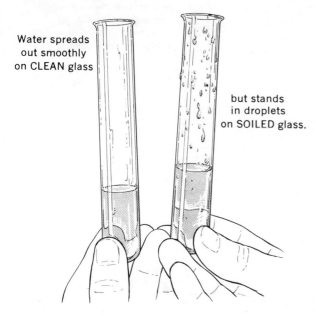

Water spreads
out smoothly
on CLEAN glass

but stands
in droplets
on SOILED glass.

FIGURE I-15
Clean and dirty glassware.

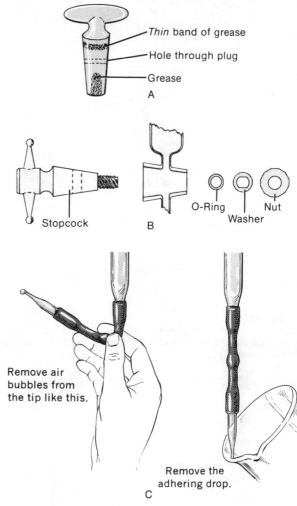

Thin band of grease

Hole through plug

Grease

A

Stopcock

O-Ring

Washer

Nut

B

Remove air
bubbles from
the tip like this.

Remove the
adhering drop.

C

FIGURE I-16
Three varieties of stopcocks. (A) A glass stopcock: To grease
a glass stopcock, remove old grease from both parts with organic
solvent; wipe dry; apply a thin film of stopcock grease as shown.
(B) A Teflon stopcock: No grease is used on a Teflon stopcock.
(C) A rubber-tubing, glass-bead stopcock: pinching the tube
near the bead allows the solution to drain from the buret.
[Parts A and B are from J. W. Hagen, *Empirical Chemistry*,
W. H. Freeman and Company, San Francisco. Copyright © 1972.]

reading. If the delivery time of your buret is faster,
wait a few seconds before taking a reading, so that
you allow the buret to drain.

Figure I-17 illustrates the recommended technique for manipulation of a buret stopcock. You
may add the solution from the buret quite rapidly
until it is close to the end point, but then you
should reduce the flow until individual drops fall
into the flask. As you add the last few drops slowly,
swirl the flask to obtain thorough mixing.

Transfer pipets are designed to deliver a single
fixed volume of liquid. The graduation mark is
located on the narrow part of the pipet to assure
precision. They come in sizes ranging from less
than 1 mL to 100 mL. They are calibrated to
deliver (TD) the specified volume if they are
handled in the prescribed manner.

Pipets are ordinarily calibrated at room temperature or close to it. In very careful work, temperature corrections are necessary if the solution
temperature is markedly different from the calibration temperature of the pipet. Fill the pipet by
placing the tip in a flask of the solution and using
a suction bulb to draw the liquid up past the
calibration mark (Figure I-18). Then slip off the
bulb and, with the forefinger, quickly seal the top
of the pipet before the solution drops below the
calibration mark. Wipe the outside of the pipet
with tissue or a clean towel, and then allow the

liquid to flow out until the bottom of the meniscus
is just at the calibration ring; to pick off the last
drop adhering to the outside of the tip, touch the
tip to the side of the flask. Then withdraw the
pipet from the flask and hold it over the vessel
into which the liquid is to be transferred. Allow
the pipet to drain in a vertical position, with the
tip against the side of the vessel. Allow 15 to 20 s
for drainage after it appears that most of the liquid
has drained out. The tip of the pipet will still
contain some liquid. Ordinarily, this has been
accounted for in the calibration and should not be

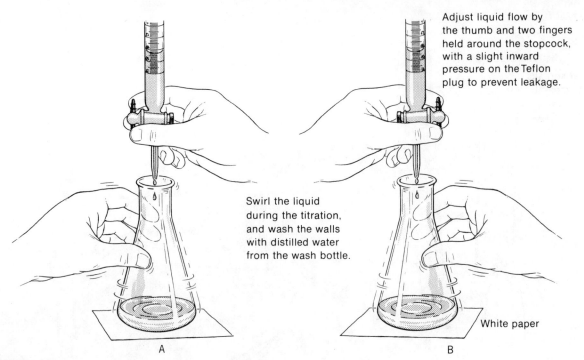

Adjust liquid flow by the thumb and two fingers held around the stopcock, with a slight inward pressure on the Teflon plug to prevent leakage.

Swirl the liquid during the titration, and wash the walls with distilled water from the wash bottle.

White paper

A   B

FIGURE I-17
Recommended technique for manipulation of a buret stopcock. Most left-handed students will manipulate the stopcock with the right hand (A), whereas most right-handed students will prefer to manipulate it with the left hand (B).

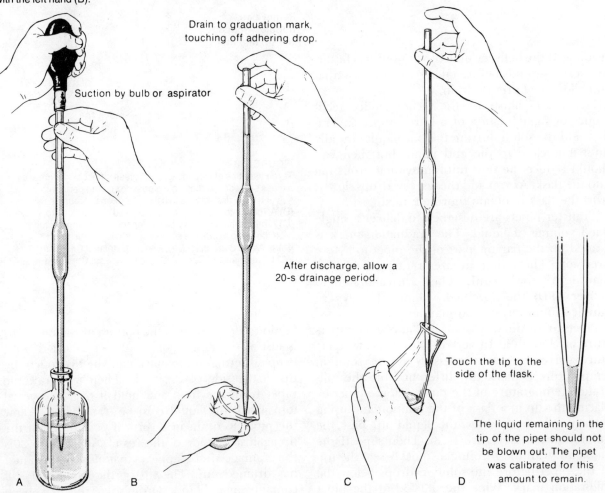

Drain to graduation mark, touching off adhering drop.

Suction by bulb or aspirator

After discharge, allow a 20-s drainage period.

Touch the tip to the side of the flask.

The liquid remaining in the tip of the pipet should not be blown out. The pipet was calibrated for this amount to remain.

A   B   C   D

FIGURE I-18
The procedure for using a transfer pipet.

blown out. (Certain types of pipets are calibrated to be blown out—most of these will have a sand-blasted ring at the top of the pipet.) Like the buret, the pipet must be scrupulously clean if precise results are to be obtained. If the pipet is still wet from cleaning, rinse with several portions of the solution to be pipetted, using the same procedure as you would for rinsing a buret.

Scientific Measurements

PURPOSE

To gain an understanding of the utility of measurements in chemistry by examining how measurements are made, what the limitations of measurements are, and how the data obtained from measurements can be presented in a useful way.

INTRODUCTION

The introduction of *quantitative* measurement brought chemistry from the magical, mystical alchemist's laboratory to the practical science it is today. In the 1600's experimenters began to measure the properties of gases in a quantitative way, and the relationship between the pressure and volume of a fixed quantity of gas was discovered and published by Robert Boyle.

It wasn't until the late 1700's, when chemists began to measure the masses of the starting materials and of the products of a reaction, that some of the fundamental laws of chemistry were recognized and stated. These include the laws of mass conservation, of definite composition, and of multiple proportions.

Such quantitative observations provided supporting evidence for the concept that matter was composed of atoms with definite masses. The ability to determine accurately the relative masses of the elements and to systematize their chemical properties led eventually to the creation of the periodic table of the elements. If you look carefully at the periodic table you will note that, with few exceptions, the elements are arranged in order of increasing atomic mass.

When quantitative measurements were made on living things, it became apparent that the processes of life were themselves chemical reactions. Measurements showed that these biochemical reactions were subject to the same laws as other chemical processes.

HOW MEASUREMENTS ARE MADE

Most quantitative measurements are operations in which two quantities are compared. An example of this practice is the simple process of measuring the length of an object by comparing it to a ruler with calibrated marks on it. The ruler itself, as it was designed and manufactured, was compared to other standards of length that are traceable to the standard unit of length agreed upon by international conventions.

The double-pan equal-arm analytical balance is another example of measurement by direct comparison. With this apparatus the mass of an object is determined by comparing it directly with a set of masses of known value. The single-pan analytical balance you may have in your laboratory also involves a comparison of masses, using the principle of substitution—an unknown mass on the pan substitutes for known masses on the beam above the pan. The point of balance occurs when the sum of the known masses that have been removed is exactly equal to the unknown mass. Figure A-1 shows how unknown and known masses are compared by means of double-pan and single-pan balances.

Time is usually measured by counting the number of periods of a system that oscillates at some natural frequency. The pendulum of a grandfather clock swings at a natural frequency. An escapement mechanism turns a toothed wheel that is connected by gears to the hands of the clock. The hands of an electric clock are driven by a synchronous electric motor supplied with alternating current of a stable frequency. A quartz digital watch measures time by counting (and subdividing) the oscillations of a tiny quartz crystal. The most accurate clocks, which serve as our fundamental time standard, are based on counting the frequency of an oscillator that is continuously compared with the frequency associated with a transition between two energy states of the electrons in gaseous cesium atoms.

From these descriptions of various timekeeping devices we see that the measurement of time is an operation in which the natural periods of various oscillating systems are compared.

Basic and Derived Units

By an international agreement reached in 1960, certain basic metric units and units derived from them are to be preferred in scientific use. The

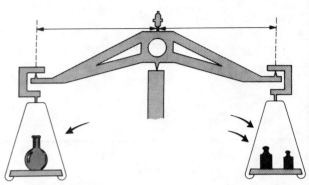
Equal-arm double-pan balance with three knife edges

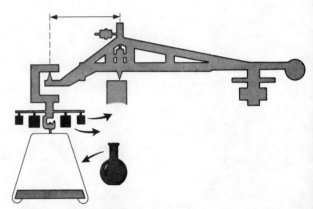
Substitution-type single-pan balance with only 2 knife edges
Constant load=constant sensitivity
Lever arm error impossible

FIGURE A-1
The upper diagram shows how masses are compared on an equal-arm double-pan balance. The lever arms of the balance must have equal lengths. The lower diagram shows how masses are compared on a substitution-type single-pan balance. Masses whose sum is equal to the unknown mass are removed from the hanger to keep the beam in equilibrium.

preferred units are known as the International System units (commonly called SI units, from the French, *Système International*). The basic units of the SI system are given in Appendix B, Table B-1.

Units obtained from the basic units are called *derived* units. The volume of a cube or rectangular box can be determined by measuring the lengths of its edges and computing the volume as the product of the three edge lengths. Thus volume is derived from length measurements and has the dimensions of length cubed, for example, cubic centimeters (cm^3). Cylindrical containers are easier to manufacture than rectangular containers, so volume is more often measured in containers such as graduated cylinders and burets. The volume of a cylinder is equal to the product of its cross-sectional area times its length. This formula allows us to use a length scale, often inscribed along the length of the cylinder, to determine volume.

THE ASSESSMENT OF EXPERIMENTAL ERRORS

Every measurement involves some measurement error. Because all generalizations or laws of science are based on experimental observations involving quantitative measurements, it is important for a scientist to take into account any limitations in the reliability of the data from which conclusions are drawn. In the following section we will discuss different kinds of errors—systematic, random, and personal error—and show how a series of measurements can give us an estimate of the precision of a measurement.

Precision and Accuracy

The limitations of both precision and accuracy will contribute to uncertainty in the measurement. The *error* in a measurement or result is the difference between the true value of the quantity measured and the measured value. The smaller the error, the closer the measured value is to the true value and the more accurate is the result. *Accuracy is a measure of the correctness of a measurement.*

Unless we have precise standards against which we can test our measurement, we often do not know the true value of a measured quantity. If we do not, we can obtain only the mean, or average, value of a number of measurements, and measure the spread or dispersion of the measurements. A measure of the spread of individual values from the mean value is the *deviation*, δ—defined as the difference between the measured value, x_i, and the arithmetic mean, $\bar{x}$, of a number, n, of measurements.

$$\delta_i = x_i - \bar{x} \qquad (1)$$

The mean value is obtained by adding all of the individual measurements and dividing by the total number of measurements:

$$\bar{x} = \frac{\sum x_i}{n} \qquad (2)$$

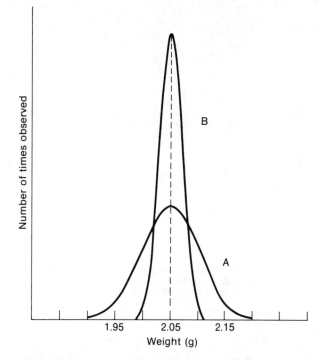

FIGURE A-2
The distribution of a number of weighings of a sample on a less precise balance (curve A), and on a more precise balance (curve B). The standard deviation for curve A is ± 0.05 g and for curve B, ± 0.02 g.

where $\sum$ represents the operation of summation.[1] The smaller the deviations in a series of measurements, the more precise the measurement is. *Precision is a measure of the reproducibility of a measurement.*

The difference between accuracy and precision is shown in Figures A-2 and A-3. Figure A-2 illustrates the distribution of a number of weighings of a sample on a less precise balance (curve A) and on a more precise balance (curve B). In this series of measurements, both balances give the same mean value, so their accuracy is the same. However, the precision of the measurement is much better for balance B, and therefore we can have more confidence in the result of that measurement.

Systematic Errors   Errors are of two general types, systematic (determinate) and random (indeterminate). A *systematic error* causes an error in

---

[1] Therefore $\sum x_i$ means to obtain the sum $x_1 + x_2 + x_3 + x_4 + \cdots$

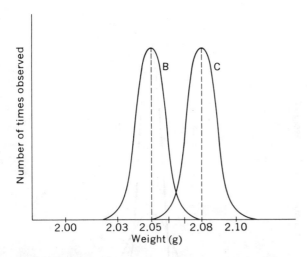

FIGURE A-3
The distribution of a number of weighings of a sample on two balances of equal precision (B and C). However, there is a systematic error in at least one of the balances.

the same direction in each measurement and diminishes accuracy, although the precision of the measurement may remain good. A miscalibrated scale on a ruler, for example, would cause a systematic error in the measurement of length.

Similarly, in Figure A-3 the result of weighings of a sample on two balances of equal precision is shown, but in at least one of the balances there is a systematic error, perhaps due to a miscalibrated weight that was used in each measurement. Ordinarily we can detect an inaccurate (but precise) measurement only by use of precision standards. Such standards are produced and tested by the National Bureau of Standards. Even if all the systematic errors in a measurement are found by careful work with precise standards, the possibility remains that the measurement will be in error because it is impossible to make any measurement with infinite accuracy.

Random Errors and Standard Deviation   If the measurement is made a large number of times, you will obtain a range of values (like those shown in Figure A-2) that is due to the *random error* inherent in any measurement. Of the random errors, small errors are more probable than large errors and negative deviations are as likely as positive ones. The resulting distribution of the measurements (like that shown in Figure A-2) is called a *normal error distribution*. The mean value of the set of measurements is the most probable value, corresponding to the center of the distri-

bution curve. The spread, or dispersion, of the results is expressed by the *standard deviation, s,* as follows:

$$s = \left[\frac{\sum (x_i - \bar{x})^2}{n - 1} \right]^{1/2} \tag{3}$$

This formula says: Sum the squares of the deviations, divide by $n - 1$, and take the square root of the result. So the standard deviation could also be called the *root-mean-square deviation*. This formula actually gives only an estimate of the standard deviation unless the number of measurements is very large (in principle, an infinite number). We must recognize that when we repeat a measurement only two or three times,[2] we are not obtaining a very large sample of measurements, and the confidence that we can place in the mean value of a small number of measurements is correspondingly reduced.

Although the formula may look forbiddingly complex, the steps are very simple. First calculate the arithmetic mean, or average, value, $\bar{x}$, of the measurements. Then subtract the mean value, $\bar{x}$, from each one of the individual values, x_i, to obtain the deviation. Square each deviation, and add all of the squares. Then divide the total by $n - 1$, where n is the total number of measurements. Finally take the square root of the result to obtain the estimate of the standard deviation. The procedure is illustrated for the calculation of the standard deviation in Table A-1.

The curves like those shown in Figure A-2 correspond to the distributions that would be obtained from a very large number of measurements. Curve A corresponds to a mean value of 2.05 g with a standard deviation of 0.05 g. Curve B corresponds to a mean value of 2.05 g with a standard deviation of 0.02 g. The standard deviation can be related to the *confidence interval*, or the range about the mean value in which one of a group of measurements may be expected to fall. If we recognize that the normal error distribution is a distribution of the probabilities of obtaining a particular measurement, we see that the probabil-

---

[2] If only two or three measurements are made, the standard deviation may be approximated by the average deviation, which is the mean value of the absolute values of the deviations, δ_i:

$$\bar{\delta} = \frac{\sum |x_1 - \bar{x}|}{n}$$

TABLE A-1
The Procedure for Calculating the Standard Deviation

Measured value* (x_i)	Deviation $(x_i - \bar{x})$	Square of deviation $(x_i - \bar{x})^2$
4.28	−0.01	0.0001
4.21	−0.08	0.0064
4.30	0.01	0.0001
4.36	0.07	0.0049
4.26	−0.03	0.0009
4.33	0.04	0.0016
$\sum = 25.74$	$\sum = 0.00$	$\sum = 0.0140$

The mean, $\bar{x} = \dfrac{\sum x_i}{n} = \dfrac{25.74}{6} = 4.29$ g

The standard deviation, $s = \left[\dfrac{0.0140}{6-1}\right]^{1/2} = 0.053$ g

The best value of the measurements is written as 4.29 ± 0.05 g.

* The measured values are those obtained from a series of six replicate measurements of the weight of a sample on a triple-beam balance.

Precision of Laboratory Operations

The precision associated with various pieces of equipment you may use in the laboratory is summarized in the following table. These uncertainties express limitations in the reading of the instruments and do not reflect systematic errors.

Instrument	Typical Uncertainty
Platform balance	± 0.50 g
Triple-beam (centigram) balance	± 0.01 g
Top-loading semimicro balance	± 0.001 g
Analytical balance	± 0.0001 g
100-mL graduated cylinder	± 0.2 mL
10-mL graduated cylinder	± 0.1 mL
50-mL buret	± 0.02 mL
25-mL pipet	± 0.02 mL
10-mL pipet	± 0.01 mL
Thermometer (10 °C to 110 °C, graduated to 1 °C)	± 0.2 °C
Barometer (mercury)	± 0.5 torr

ity of measurements occurring close to the mean will be greater than the probability of a measurement occurring far away from the mean. In fact, there is a 0.68, or 68%, probability that a given measurement will fall within plus or minus *one* standard deviation of the mean value. There is a 0.95 (95%) probability that a measurement will fall within plus or minus *two* standard deviations of the mean value. This means that for curve A of Figure A-2, we can expect that 95% of the measurements will fall between 1.95 and 2.15 g. If we were to measure the total area under the curve, we would also see that this interval of ± 2s corresponds to 95% of the area under the normal error curve. Note that we cannot make a definite prediction about any single measurement. We can only say that if we make the measurement a large number of times, we can expect that 95% of the values obtained will fall within plus or minus two standard deviations of the mean.

Personal Errors To the types of errors already described—systematic and random—we might add a third category, the personal error, or blunder. Such errors are all too common in student work. Thus if the numbers on a scale are misread, or recorded incorrectly, or if part of a solution is spilled in a titration, the result will contain an error. Careful work will not contain any blunders, and any work suspected of containing one should be repeated.

GRAPHING

In many instances the goal of making measurements is to discover or study the relationship that exists between two variables. The pressure and the volume of a gas, the volume and the temperature of a substance, or the color of a solution and the intensity of that color are examples of sets of variables that are related. As one variable changes, so does the other.

We often use graphs to visualize the relationship between two variables. If there are two variables, the graph will be a two-dimensional plot of the points that represent pairs of values of the two variables. An example of a well-drawn graph is shown in Figure A-4. You should notice that the graph has several features that help to make the meaning of the graph clear.

1. A Title: The title on a graph should be a brief but clear description of the relationship under study. Titles like "Lab Number 1" or "Volume and Temperature" are not acceptable because their meaning is clear only to those familiar with the experiment and the meaning will be lost as memory fades with the passage of time.

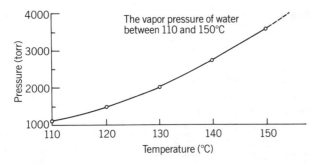

FIGURE A-4
This is an example of a well-made graph. Notice the clear title, the well-defined axes with variable names and units, the clearly marked data points, and the curve showing the observed trend and the extrapolated trend.

2. Labeled Axes: Each axis of the graph should be clearly labeled to show the quantity it represents and the units that have been used to measure the quantity. You should recognize the distinction between the quantity measured (pressure, volume, temperature, time, etc.) and the units that have been used to measure that quantity (atmospheres, liters, degrees Celsius, seconds, etc.).

It is convenient to label each axis with the name of the measured quantity followed by the units, either separating the units by a comma or enclosing them in parentheses, for example, Volume, liters or Volume (liters). Then only numbers need to appear beside each axis, and the axes are not cluttered up with the units of each variable.

3. Scales: The scale on each axis should be chosen carefully so that the entire range of values can be plotted on the graph. For practical reasons, 2, 4, 5, or 10 divisions on the graph paper should represent a decimal unit in the variable. This equivalence will make it easy to estimate values that lie between the scale divisions. For greatest accuracy and pleasing proportions, the scales selected should be chosen so that the graph nearly fills the page. Be sure, however, that no plotted points fall outside the borders of the graph.

Note that the lower left corner of the graph does not *have* to represent zero on either axis. If the range of measured values extends to zero, the latter may be a good choice; but if not, there will be much wasted space on the graph.

4. Data Points: It is good practice to mark the location of each data point with a very small dot

and then draw a small circle around the dot to make the point more visible.

5. The Curve: A smooth curve should be drawn through the points. The curve should pass as close as possible to each of the points but should not be connected point-to-point with short lines. If the relationship appears to be linear, the smooth curve should be a straight line. If the line is extended past the range of the measured values, this extension should be indicated by a dashed rather than a solid line.

Linear Relationships

Although many variables in chemical systems may be related in a complex nonlinear way, some of the relationships turn out to be direct proportions; that is, the value of one variable is a constant factor times the value of the other variable. When this proportional relationship exists, the graph of the two variables will be a straight line. An example of a linear graph is shown in Figure A-5, which is a graph of the volume of a sample of gas versus the temperature of the gas.

The *slope* of the line is the constant factor relating the two variables. The slope can be determined by using any two points on the line, as shown in Figure A-5. Note that the slope is calculated in the units of the two variables.

In Figure A-5 the point on the line where the value of the volume is zero (which is where the line crosses the temperature axis) is called the temperature *intercept*.

If a relationship exists between two variables, it is possible to estimate what the value of one variable would be for any value of the other variable by using the graph. If the point of interest lies within the range of measured values, this estimation is called *interpolation*. For example, from Figure A-4 we can determine by interpolation that at 125°C the vapor pressure of water is about 1800 torr.

If the estimation is made beyond the measured range, the process is called *extrapolation*. From Figure A-4 we can see that the vapor pressure of water at 155°C is estimated by extrapolation to be about 4000 torr.

Interpolation and extrapolation are useful techniques, but both are estimates and assume that the graph is accurate or that it extends beyond the measured values. For extrapolation, especially, this assumption may lead to incorrect conclusions.

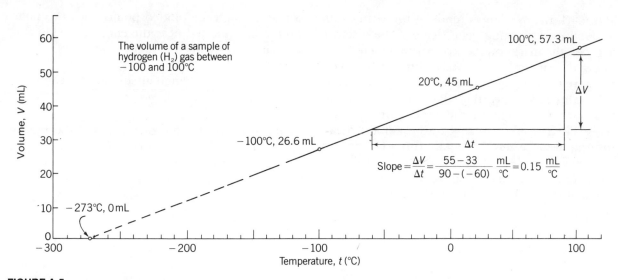

FIGURE A-5
The relation between the temperature and the corresponding volume of a sample of hydrogen gas. A direct proportion, as represented by Charles' law, $V = kT = k(t + 273)$, plots as a straight line.

EXERCISES IN MEASUREMENT

Materials and Supplies: Sets of four pennies dated 1981 and earlier and sets of four pennies dated 1983 and later, meter sticks, 30-cm metric rulers, milk cartons (quart or half-gallon size), beakers of five or six sizes, 60-cm lengths of string, fine-tipped marking pens.

1. Mass Measurement   Pennies minted in the United States in 1981 and earlier years were made from an alloy that is mostly copper. Pennies minted in 1983 and later are made of copper-plated zinc. (Pennies minted in 1982 may have either composition.)[3] Is it possible to tell the difference between these two kinds of pennies by weighing them?

Work in pairs. One student will receive from the instructor four pennies dated 1981 and earlier, and the other student will receive four pennies dated 1983 and later. Carefully check the zero on the analytical balance. Weigh and record the mass of each of the four pennies to the nearest milligram. Then put all four pennies on the pan and weigh and record the total mass of the four pennies. Also record the dates of the pennies. Finally, record the masses and dates of the four pennies weighed by your partner.

[3] Miller, J. A., "Analysis of 1982 Pennies," *J. Chem. Educ.* **60,** 142 (1983).

In your report calculate the mean (average) value and standard deviation for the masses of the pennies that you and your partner weighed. Can you tell from these data if there is a significant difference in the average mass of the two groups of pennies?

2. Volume Measurement
(a) Using a metric ruler or meter stick, measure the length of each of the three edges of a quart or half-gallon cardboard milk carton to the nearest 0.5 mm. (Ignore the irregular portion of the carton at the top.) Record these values. In your report calculate the volume of the milk carton in units of cubic centimeters, liters, and quarts.

(b) Read the volumes of partially filled 10-mL and 50-mL graduated cylinders provided by the instructor. Take care to avoid parallax error and note the position of the bottom of each meniscus as described in the Introduction. Read the value of the smaller cylinder to the nearest 0.02 mL and read the larger one to the nearest 0.2 mL. Record these values. Report the two values to the instructor. If they are not correct, the instructor will show you how to read the meniscus correctly.

3. Graphing   Using a length of string, measure the circumference of five or six different sizes of beakers. Draw the string snugly around the beaker and mark the overlapped ends of the string with a fine-tipped marking pen. Measure the distance between the marks on the string with a meter stick to get the circumference. Record this value. Now measure the diameter of each beaker. An easy way to do this is to place the edges of two books or blocks of wood against the beaker on opposite sides. Then carefully remove the beaker and measure the distance across the gap with a metric rule or meter stick. Record each diameter.

In your report make a graph of the circumferences of the beakers versus their diameters. Draw a line through the plotted points. Pick two points on the line (located near the ends of the line) and determine the slope of the line, where

$$\text{slope} = \frac{\text{change in circumference}}{\text{change in diameter}} \qquad (4)$$

Is the numerical value of the slope, the ratio of the circumference to the diameter of a circle, what you expected it to be?

Mass and Volume Relationships

PURPOSE

To become familiar with metric units of mass, length, and volume. To measure the densities of unknown liquids and solids.

PRE-LAB PREPARATION

Units of Measurement

Chemistry is distinctly an *experimental* science. The establishment of the fundamental laws and theories of the nature and behavior of matter depends on the careful measurement of various quantities—mass, volume, length, temperature, time, electrical magnitudes.

The *metric system* of units is especially convenient because it is a decimal system, like our system of numbers. The standard metric units were originally related to certain quantities in nature. For example, the meter was intended to be one 10-millionth of the distance from the North Pole to the equator along the meridian line through Paris. The first international standard meter was defined as the distance between two fine lines engraved on a bar of platinum-iridium alloy kept in a vault at the International Bureau of Weights and Measures near Paris. In 1960, a new standard was adopted by the Eleventh General Conference on Weights and Measures and the standard meter was defined to be 1,650,763.73 wavelengths of a particular orange-red line of the gas krypton-86. This standard has the advantage that it permits comparisons that are ten times more accurate than is possible with the meter bar and can be precisely reproduced so it is not subject to accidental loss or destruction, as is the meter bar.

A cornerstone of relativity theory is the notion that the speed of light is a universal constant that is the same for all observers regardless of the motion of the observer or of the source of light.

This makes it reasonable to treat the speed of light as a constant of nature and use it in conjunction with the unit of time to provide a unit of length. Because time can be measured very accurately with atomic clocks and because the speed of light is now known very accurately, the 1983 General Conference on Weights and Measures may redefine the meter in terms of the velocity of light as "the length of the path traveled by light in a vacuum during a time interval of $\frac{1}{299,792,458}$ of a second."[1]

Multiples and decimal fractions of the meter (represented as m), as well as their symbols, are listed below.

1 km	= 1 kilometer	= 1000 meters
1 dm	= 1 decimeter	= 0.1 meter
1 cm	= 1 centimeter	= 0.01 meter
1 mm	= 1 millimeter	= 0.001 meter
1 μm	= 1 micrometer	= 10^{-6} meter
1 nm	= 1 nanometer	= 10^{-9} meter

A related unit of length in common use in science is the *angstrom* ($1 \text{ Å} = 10^{-8} \text{ cm} = 10^{-10} \text{ m}$).

The kilogram was intended to be the mass of a cubic decimeter (1000 cm^3) of water. The present standard of mass is a platinum-iridium cylinder kept at the International Bureau of Weights and Measures and assigned, by international agreement, a mass of 1 kilogram. Each nation has its own metric standards, but all are based on and have been carefully compared with the originals kept in France. The U.S. copy of the international standard of mass, known as Prototype Kilogram No. 20, is housed in a vault at the National Bureau of Standards. Practically all scientists working on research and development today use metric units.

The common submultiples of the *kilogram* (kg) are the *gram* (g) and the *milligram* (mg). The terms *mass* and *weight* are often used interchangeably by scientists although they represent different concepts. Mass is defined in terms of the Paris standard kilogram; weight is a *force*, actually a mass times the acceleration due to gravity. In chemistry we are concerned primarily with mass, but because virtually all weighings in the laboratory involve the

comparison of an unknown mass with a standard mass, the operation we call *weighing* is actually a measurement of mass. This dual terminology seldom causes problems.

The volume unit is the *liter*. This is a derived unit, having the units of length cubed, $\frac{1}{1000}$ m³. It is the volume enclosed by a 1-decimeter cube. The *milliliter* (mL) is the most common volume unit in the chemical laboratory. Clearly, it is one thousandth the volume of the liter. Recently, the milliliter was redefined slightly so that $1 \text{ mL} \equiv \text{cm}^3$. (The triple equal sign means "is *exactly* equal to.")

A condensed table of the most commonly used metric units of length, mass, and volume, and their English equivalents, is included in Appendix B as Table B-1.

Precision of Measurement

When measuring physical quantities, it is important that the measuring devices be consistent with the precision desired. Thus, for a precision of 1% in the weighing of a 50-g sample, a balance that is accurate to only 0.5 g (1% × 50 g = 0.5 g) is required. For the same precision with a 1-g sample, a balance accurate to 0.01 g is necessary. In this experiment, platform balances that read to 0.1 g and graduated cylinders that can be read to about 0.2 mL should not cause uncertainty greater than about 1% in the calculated density. In a given determination, there is no point in using a greater precision for one measurement than for other measurements. Choose your measuring devices according to the precision desired.

See Study Assignment A for a more complete discussion of the treatment of experimental errors, the concept of precision, and related topics.

Density

The determination of the important physical property density requires measurements of two quantities: the mass, M, and the volume, V, of a given amount of a substance. The ratio of these quantities, or the mass per unit volume, is the *density*, written $D = M/V$. In the metric system, this ratio is expressed as grams per cubic centimeter (g/cm³) or grams per milliliter (g/mL). Study the relative densities of different substances as illustrated in Figure 1-1.

The substances displayed in the figure visually show the widely differing densities of a variety of

---

[1] Pipkin, F. M., and Ritter, R. C., "Precision Measurements and Fundamental Constants," *Science* **219**, 913 (1983).

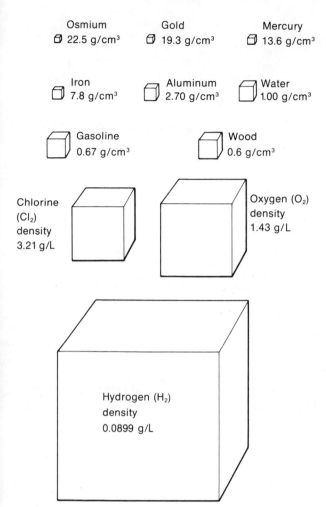

FIGURE 1-1
The relationship of density to volume. The cubes of different sizes represent the relative volumes of equal weights (about 0.2 g) of the various materials at 0°C.

and the determination of the concentration of a solute from density measurements.

An understanding of density is also important outside the chemistry laboratory. For example, the service station attendant determines the charge of an automotive battery by measuring the density (and hence the concentration) of the sulfuric acid solution in the battery. Also, a winemaker (even the amateur who makes wine at home) measures the density of the grape juice to determine whether the sugar content is sufficient for fermentation.

Measurement Techniques

Your instructor will demonstrate the correct techniques to use in reading the meniscus in a graduated cylinder and in careful weighing with the balance. See also Figures 1-2 and 1-3. For every weighing, observe the following rules and precautions:

1. Keep the balance pans clean and dry. Clean up *immediately* any chemical that is spilled.

2. *Check the rest point of the empty balance.* To do this, first be sure all movable beam weights are at their zero position. Then release the beam release (if the balance has one), cause the balance beam to swing gently, and note the central position on

compounds and elements. It is apparent that liquids and solids have much greater densities than gases. Density is also influenced by temperature. The densities of liquids and solids are affected only slightly by changes in the temperature of the substance, but gas densities are quite sensitive to temperature changes.

The measurement of density is necessary for a variety of important procedures in the science of chemistry, such as the calculation of Avogadro's number from unit-cell dimensions of crystals; the determination of the molecular weight of a substance from its gas density (see Experiment 10); the conversion of hydrostatic pressure units (see Experiment 11); the conversion from mass to volume (see Experiment 7); the measurement of densities of biopolymers in the ultracentrifuge;

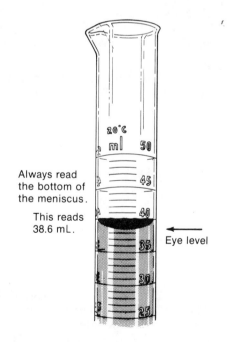

FIGURE 1-2
The proper method of reading a meniscus (curved surface of a liquid) in order to measure the volume of the liquid.

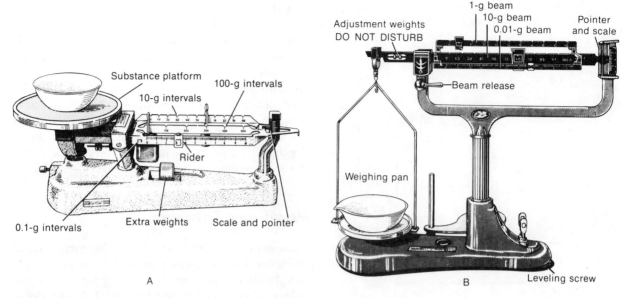

FIGURE 1-3
Laboratory balances. (A) A platform balance for weighing to the nearest 0.1 g; (B) a triple-beam balance for weighing quantities to ± 0.01 g.

the scale about which the pointer oscillates. Use this point as the reference-zero rest point in your weighings. (Never take readings with the beam and pointer at rest. Why?) If the pointer reading differs by more than two to three scale divisions from the marked zero point, have your instructor adjust the balance. *Do not change the balance adjustments yourself.*

3. Never weigh an object while it is warm; the convection currents of warm air will affect the rest point.

4. After weighing an object, return the beam weights to the zero position and restore the beam release to its rest position.

EXPERIMENTAL PROCEDURE

Special Supplies: A metric rule. Liquid samples: various organic liquids, or solutions of unknown density prepared by dissolving inexpensive soluble salts, such as NaCl or $CaCl_2$, in water. Solid samples: coarse marble chips, a coarse silica sand, pieces of metal or metal shot, roll sulfur, or other solids (do not use any powdered material).

1. *The Density of a Liquid* Weigh a clean, dry 150-mL beaker and watch-glass cover to the nearest 0.1 g, and record the weight in your experiment report. Place between 40 and 50 mL of the liquid in a graduated cylinder. Read the volume to a precision of 0.1 mL, then transfer as much of the

liquid as possible to the beaker and cover the beaker with the watch glass. Reweigh the beaker, its cover, and the contents. From these data, calculate the density of the liquid. Repeat all these measurements with a different volume of the same liquid, since the average of duplicate determinations will be more reliable, and will provide you with a check on gross errors in counting weights and reading volumes correctly.

2. *The Density of a Solid*
(a) Use the following technique to determine the density of an irregularly shaped solid. A sample will be designated by your instructor. Select 20 to 30 g of suitable-size pieces of the sample (avoiding fine powdered material), or such an amount as will give a volume increase in a graduated cylinder (see below) of a little less than 20 mL. Weigh a small beaker or evaporating dish to a precision of 0.1 g. Add the sample and weigh again. Place about 30 mL of water in the graduated cylinder and read the volume to 0.1 mL. Tilt the cylinder and slide the weighed sample pieces into it carefully, to avoid loss of water by splashing, then tap the sides to dislodge any adhering air bubbles. Again read the volume. The increase is the volume of the sample. (See Figure 1-4.) Calculate the density of the sample. If time permits, make a duplicate determination with a different weight of sample, to increase the accuracy of your determination.

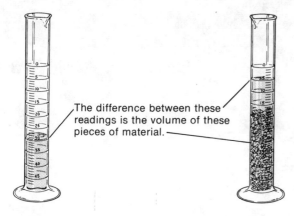

The difference between these readings is the volume of these pieces of material.

FIGURE 1-4
A method of measuring the volume of an irregularly shaped solid.

(b) *Optional.* If you wish to determine the density of a regular-shaped solid, such as a rectangular block or a cylinder, the volume can be calculated from appropriate measurements of the dimensions. The weight may be obtained directly on the balance, and the density can then be calculated. In making these measurements, note how the quality and precision of the rulers and balances you use affect the number of significant figures you retain, and hence determine the degree of precision you can expect to obtain in your answer.

Separations of Food Dyes and Plant Pigments by Paper Chromatography

PURPOSE

To become acquainted with chromatographic separation techniques by using paper chromatography to separate mixtures of food color dyes and green leaf pigments.

PRE-LAB PREPARATION

Separating two substances that have quite different physical properties is usually a simple and straightforward task. A mixture of sand and salt can easily be separated by adding water to dissolve the salt, filtering the mixture to remove the sand, and recovering the salt by evaporating the water. But what if the substances to be separated have similar physical and chemical properties? Separation of a mixture of several closely related substances presents quite a difficult problem, but the problem has been solved by the development, over the past 75 years, of a family of powerful separation techniques that collectively are called *chromatography*.

The word chromatography, formed from the Greek words *khroma*, meaning color, and *graphein*, meaning to draw a graph or to write, was coined by the Russian botanist M. S. Tswett around 1906 to describe his process of separating mixtures of plant pigments. He allowed a solution of plant pigments to percolate down a glass column of adsorbent powder where they separated into colored bands, literally a "color graph," on the powder. Even though most chromatographic methods are now used on solutes that do not produce bands of color visible to the human eye, the term chromatography is applied to any separation procedure employing the same principle as the method described by Tswett. Chromatography is widely used for qualitative or quantitative analysis or for isolation and recovery of the components of a mixture.

All forms of chromatography employ the same general principle: A mixture of solutes in a *moving phase* passes over a selectively absorbing medium, the *stationary phase*. Separation occurs because the solutes have different affinities for the stationary

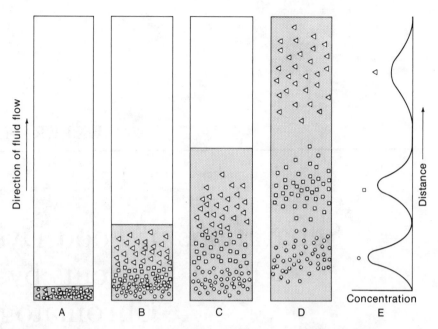

FIGURE 2-1
Schematic illustration of separation by differential migration. Parts A through D illustrate the separation of a three-component mixture by differential migration. Note that at the beginning of a separation (A), three components are clustered together at the point of sample application. As the sample migrates across the system—B through D—the three sample components are gradually separated, the fastest-moving component spending the most time in the moving fluid phase. Part E displays a smoothed plot of the concentration of each substance as a function of the distance from the origin for the distribution shown in D. [After Barry L. Karger et al., *Introduction to Separation Science,* Wiley, New York. Copyright © 1973.]

and moving phases. Solutes that have a greater affinity for the moving phase will spend more time in the moving phase and therefore will move along faster than solutes that spend more time in the stationary phase.

There are a variety of ways of achieving a flow around or through a stationary phase. In *column chromatography* small particles of the stationary phase are packed in a tube, and the moving phase (a liquid or gas) flows around the particles confined in the tube. In *thin-layer chromatography* the stationary phase is a thin layer of fine particles spread on a glass or plastic plate; in *paper chromatography* the paper itself is the stationary phase. Figure 2-1

illustrates the separation of a sample mixture as a moving liquid phase flows through a stationary phase (such as paper).

In this experiment we will employ paper chromatography. The cellulose structure of the paper (shown in Figure 2-2) contains a large number of hydroxyl groups that can form weak bonds (called hydrogen bonds) to water molecules, so the stationary phase can be regarded as a layer of water hydrogen bonded to cellulose. If the solvent is water, the moving phase is also aqueous; but if a mixture of an organic solvent is used with water, the moving phase is apt to contain a high proportion of the organic solvent.

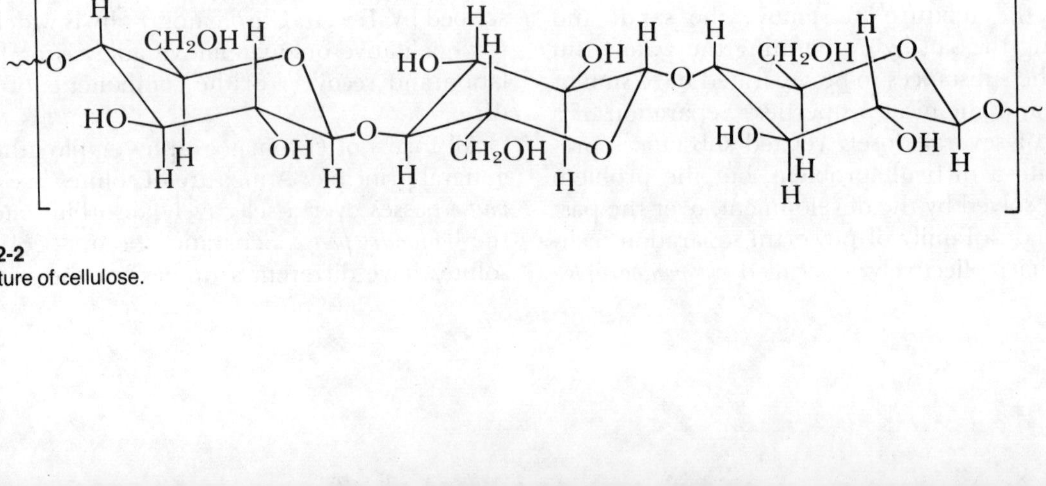

FIGURE 2-2
The structure of cellulose.

The solvents employed in paper chromatography must wet the paper so that the mobile phase will move through the paper fibers by capillary attraction. A solute in the mobile phase moves along with the solvent during the chromatographic *development* (the term used to describe the process that occurs as the solute moves along and is partitioned between two phases). As it moves, it undergoes many successive distributions between the mobile and stationary phases, the fraction of time it spends in the mobile phase determining how fast it moves along. If it spends all of its time in the moving phase, it will move along with the solvent front. If it spends nearly all of its time in the stationary phase, it will stay near the point of application.

After the chromatogram has been developed and the solutes on the paper have been located, the movement of the solute on the paper is mathematically expressed by the R_f value (called the *retention factor*), where

$$R_f = \frac{\text{distance traveled by the solute}}{\text{distance traveled by the solvent front}}$$

The distances used in calculating R_f values are measured as shown in Figure 2-3. The distance traveled by the solute is measured from the point of application to the center or densest part of the spot; the distance traveled by the solvent front is measured from the point of application to the

limit of movement of the solvent front (which must be marked immediately after the paper is removed from the developing chamber because it may be nearly invisible after the solvent evaporates).

If all conditions could be maintained constant, R_f values would be constant. However, either variations in temperature or in the composition of the solvent phase or changes in the paper can alter the R_f value. The R_f value is useful mainly for expressing the relative mobility of two or more solutes in a particular chromatographic system. The absolute R_f values may change from day to day, but their values in relation to each other remain nearly constant.

Paper chromatography can be performed on strips or sheets of paper, with the solvent being allowed to flow either upward or downward. Horizontal development may also be used, in which case the solvent is allowed to flow radially outward from the center. Two-dimensional chromatography can be used to separate complex mixtures by applying two different solvent systems. The paper is first developed in one direction, then turned by 90° and developed again in a second solvent.

Development is accomplished in the following way. First the solution containing the solutes to be separated is spotted on the dry paper—that is, a micropipet or glass capillary is used to put very small drops (microliters) of solution on the paper. Then the spots are allowed to dry and the filter paper is placed in a tightly closed receptacle containing the developing solvent, whose vapor saturates the atmosphere of the container. The paper is supported so that the developing solvent moves through the spots that have been applied. The point of application must not be immersed in the developing solvent; otherwise, the solute spots will diffuse into the solvent and be greatly diluted.

The solvent flow is allowed to continue for a fixed time or until the solvent front (the limit of wetness) reaches a specified point on the paper. Then the paper is removed, the solvent front is marked with a pencil, and the paper is dried, with the result that the separated solute spots are fixed in their position at the end of development.

If the solutes are colored, they can be readily seen on the paper. Colorless spots are located by various means. Often the paper is exposed to the vapor of a reagent (such as iodine, which makes organic compounds visible), or it can be dipped in or sprayed with a reagent that reacts with the colorless substances to form a visible spot. When placed under an ultraviolet light many substances can be located by their fluorescent glow.

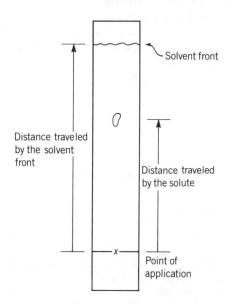

FIGURE 2-3
The movement of the solute on the paper chromatogram is expressed by the R_f value, the distance traveled by the solute divided by the distance traveled by the solvent front.

After the spots are located and their R_f values measured, they are compared with standard known materials run under the same conditions. If possible, known and unknown substances are run on the same paper. If the known and unknown compounds have the same R_f values in different solvent systems and give the same reactions with various chromogenic (color-forming) reagents, it is probable that they are identical.

Separation of FD&C Dyes

In the past few years there has been more awareness and concern about the safety of food, drug, and cosmetic (FD&C) dyes. At present only seven of these dyes are allowed in foods: reds 3 and 40, yellows 5 and 6, blues 1 and 2, and green 3. The structures of these dyes are shown in Figure 2-4 and information about them can be found in the references cited in the Bibliography. Present law does not require listing of specific dyes on labels, so there is genuine interest in dye separation and

TABLE 2-1
FD&C Dyes Present in Food Products

Food	FD&C Dye
Red maraschino cherry juice	Red 40
Red cough medicine	Red 40, Yellow 6
Red mouthwash	Red 40
Green mouthwash	Yellow 5, Blue 2
Pickle brine	Yellow 5
Orange soda	Yellows 5 and 6
Grape soda	Red 40, Blue 1

identification. These dyes are found in a variety of food products, as shown in Table 2-1.

In order to separate and identify dyes in food products it is necessary to add an extraction and concentration step like those described in the references cited in the Bibliography. In this experiment we will separate and try to identify the dyes in a concentrated form usually sold in supermarkets as assorted food colors and egg dye. This will allow us to omit the extraction and concentration step.

Separation of Plant Pigments

Green leaves of plants contain a number of natural pigments, including chlorophylls (the green pigments in plants), carotenes (yellow pigments like those found in carrots), and xanthophylls (which also have a yellow color and may be regarded as mildly oxidized carotenes). The structures of typical compounds that fall in these three categories are shown in Figure 2-5.

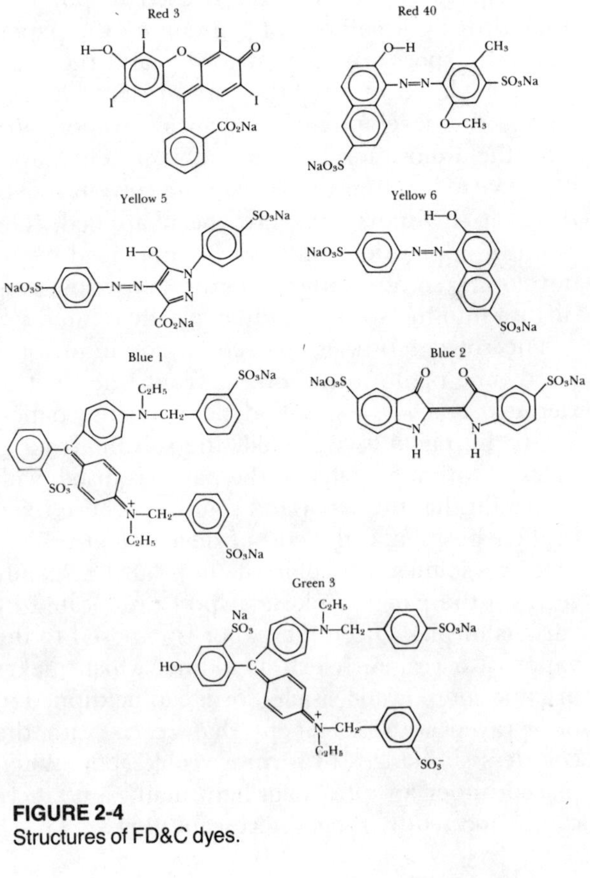

FIGURE 2-4
Structures of FD&C dyes.

EXPERIMENTAL PROCEDURE

Special Supplies: Separation of food dyes: variety of food dyes (blue, green, red, yellow) such as those sold by McCormick under the Schilling label, 11.5- × 19-cm pieces of paper cut from 46- × 57-cm sheets of Whatman No. 1 Chr. paper, centimeter rule, pencil, applicator (pointed glass rod, 0.5-mm-ID glass capillary, toothpick, or pointed matchstick), plastic food wrap, rubber band, stapler. Separation of plant pigments: fresh spinach (or other green leaves), clean sand, mortar and pestle, filter funnel and filter paper, 2.5- × 20-cm lengths of Whatman No. 1 filter paper (cut from sheets or, more conveniently, from a roll of Whatman No. 1 Chr. paper, 1 in. × 100 yards), centimeter rule, pencil, applicator, 500-mL Erlenmeyer flask with solid rubber stopper, paper clips.

Color	Name	Structure
Yellow	α-Carotene	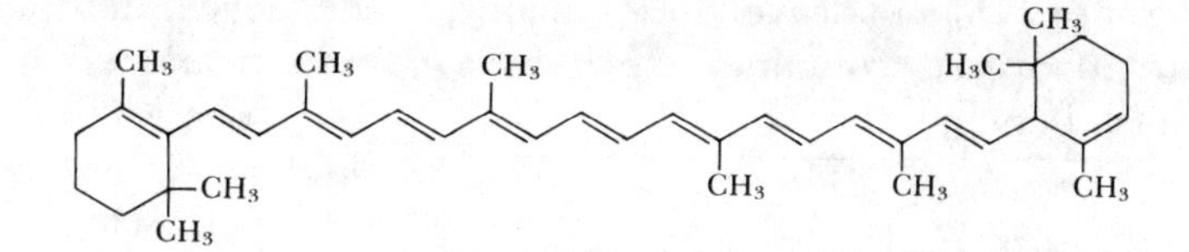
Yellow	β-Carotene	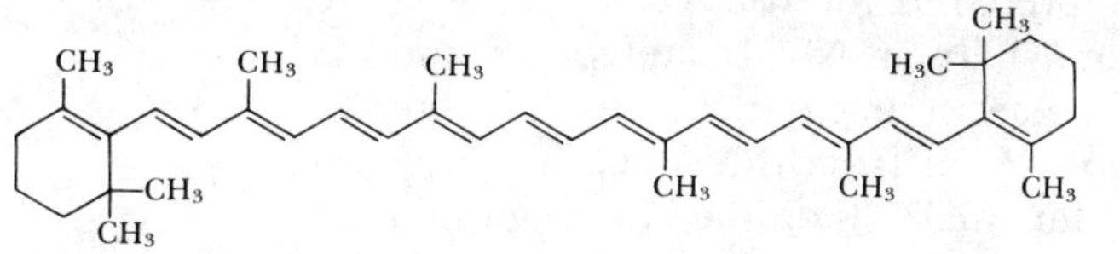
Yellow	Xanthophyll (lutein)	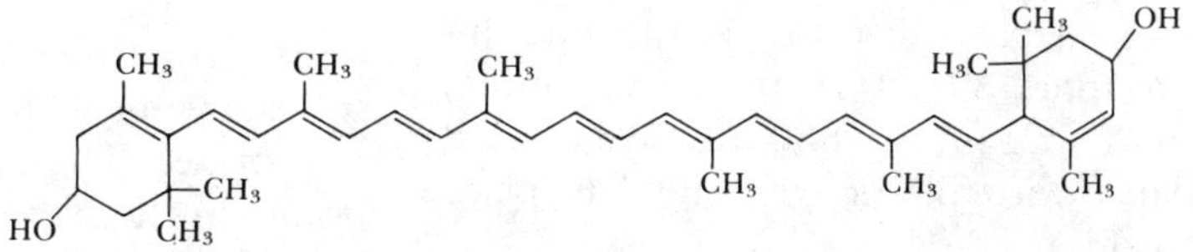
Yellow	Zeaxanthin	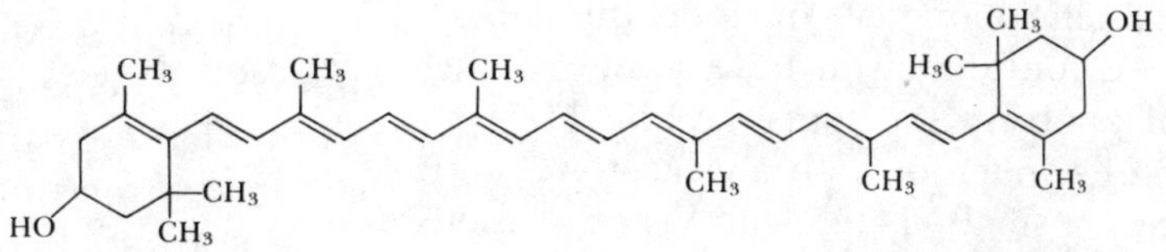
Yellow	Violaxanthin	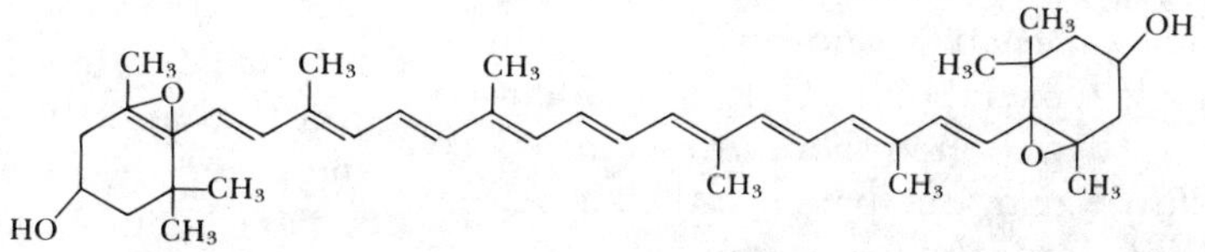
Green	Chlorophyll a (R = CH₃)	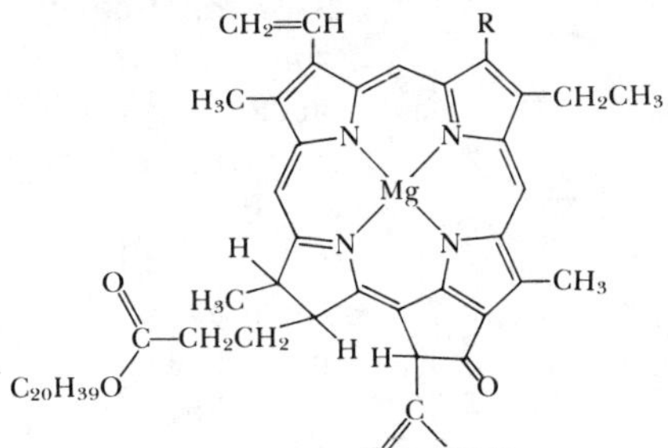
Green	Chlorophyll b (R = CHO)	

FIGURE 2-5
The structures of pigments found in green plants. The chlorophylls are catalysts for photosynthesis.

Chemicals: Separation of food dyes: developing solvent solution containing a mixture of water, concentrated aqueous ammonia, and acetone (80:10:10 parts by volume). Separation of plant pigments: methanol, petroleum ether (bp 60 to 90°C), developing solvent solution containing petroleum ether and acetone (90:10 parts by volume). To avoid the irritating fumes of concentrated aqueous ammonia and the hazard of mixing flammable solvents, these solutions should be prepared for the students in advance.

Safety Precautions: Methanol, petroleum ether, and acetone are all flammable solvents. There must be no open flames in the laboratory while this experiment is performed. To avoid exposure to the volatile vapors of these solvents, work in a fume hood. If a fume hood is not available, use an inverted funnel connected to an aspirator (as shown in Figure 5-1 of Experiment 5) to remove the methanol vapor. Do not leave these volatile solvents in an uncovered container (such as a beaker) on the lab bench.

---

1. Separation of FD&C Dyes in Food Colors   If it is not already prepared for you, cut an 11.5- × 19-cm piece of Whatman No. 1 filter paper and, with a *pencil*, draw a line parallel to the long dimension about 2 cm from the edge. Still using a pencil, put four small X's on the line, beginning 5 cm from the edge of the paper and spacing the marks about 3 cm apart. Put 70 mL of the developing solvent (water, concentrated aqueous ammonia, and acetone, 80:10:10 parts by volume) in the bottom of a clean, dry 800-mL beaker, and cover the beaker with plastic wrap held in place by a rubber band.

Get a scrap of filter paper and practice applying small (1- to 2-mm diameter) spots on the paper. When you are confident you have mastered the technique of applying the spots, lay the 11.5- × 19-cm piece of paper down on a clean towel and carefully apply a small (1- to 2-mm) spot of food color on the first X. Continue spotting the food dyes (blue, green, red, and yellow), putting a different color on each X and writing in pencil near each X a letter symbol (B, G, R, Y) to identify the color of the dye spotted there. Allow the spots to dry by gently waving the paper in the air. After they have dried, form the paper into a cylinder as shown in Figure 2-6 and staple the edges together, leaving a gap so that the edges do not quite meet.

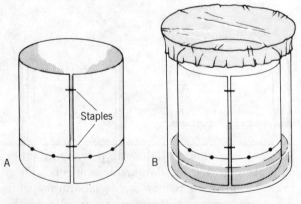

FIGURE 2-6
Form the chromatographic paper into a cylinder and staple as shown in A. Put the paper cylinder carefully into the beaker containing the solvent, and cover as shown in B.

Put the paper cylinder in the beaker containing the developing solvent, placing the spots at the bottom and taking care that the paper does not touch the wall of the beaker. *The spots of dye must be above the surface of the solvent in the beaker.* Immediately seal the beaker with plastic wrap and allow the solvent to rise to within 1 cm of the top of the paper (about 30 to 40 min). Note the position of the *solvent front* (the wet-looking leading edge of the solvent) every few minutes so that you do not let the solvent front rise all the way to the top of the paper. Also note how the spots begin to separate into bands of color as they move along.

When development is finished, remove the paper from the beaker and immediately mark the solvent front with a pencil line before the solvent evaporates. Then dry the paper thoroughly, preferably in the hood.

After the paper has dried, locate the densest part of the band for each color and draw a pencil line through it. Measure the distance (in millimeters) from the pencil line at the point of application to the densest part of the band of color, and the distance from the point of application to the solvent front. Record the values in your report. Calculate and record the R_f values for every colored spot on the paper. For each original spot of food color, describe the number of components you find and their colors. Is there a green dye in the green food color? Explain.

Pencil your name and the date on the chromatogram and turn it in with your lab report if your instructor so directs.

2. Separation of Plant Pigments   Obtain a large spinach leaf and tear or cut the leaf into small pieces. (About 10 g of any kind of plant leaves with dark green pigment or even freshly cut grass will do.) Grind the chopped-up leaf with about a teaspoon of clean sand (to break down the cell walls) in a clean mortar. Add about 25 mL of methanol and continue to grind for a minute or two. Filter the green methanol extract through filter paper in a filter funnel and evaporate the filtrate to dryness in a casserole or evaporating dish. (*Use a hot plate or steam bath in the fume hood.*)[1] The whole operation is best carried out in subdued light because exposure to sunlight or intense fluorescent light causes the chlorophyll pigments to decompose. Allow the casserole to cool to room temperature and then dissolve the dried residue

---

[1] If a fume hood is not available, see *Safety Precautions.*

in a few drops of petroleum ether. (*Caution: Petroleum ether is highly flammable; extinguish any flames in the laboratory.*)

Place 30 mL of developing solvent (petroleum ether and acetone, 90:10 parts by volume) in a 500-mL Erlenmeyer flask and stopper to prevent evaporation.

Cut a long strip of filter paper (about 20 cm long) from a roll of 1-in. width filter paper or from a larger sheet of filter paper. Handle the paper by the edges with freshly washed hands to avoid leaving oily fingerprints on the paper. Draw a *pencil* line about 2 cm from the bottom of the strip. Then, using an applicator, such as a toothpick or sharpened matchstick, carefully apply an approximately 2-mm-diameter spot on the pencil line at the center of the strip. Try not to let the spot get too wide. (If your petroleum ether solution of pigment has evaporated, add a few drops to get it back into solution.) Let the spot dry and add another spot on top of the first. Repeat this sequence until the pigment spot on the paper is a deep green color. (As many as 20 spottings may be required, depending on the concentration of pigment.)

After the last spot has dried, the strip is ready to be developed in the solvent solution contained in the Erlenmeyer flask. First carefully wipe dry the inside of the flask neck, then lower the bottom end of the strip (the end with the spot) into the solvent. (If the paper strip tends to curl, weight it at the very bottom with a paper clip.) The liquid level must *not* reach the pencil line where the spot is. (If it does, the spot will dissolve in the solvent, spoiling the separation.) Use the rubber stopper to hold the paper strip in position as shown in Figure 2-7. Let the chromatogram develop without disturbance until the solvent front reaches the neck of the flask. Then remove the paper strip, immediately mark the location of the solvent front with a pencil line, and allow the paper strip to dry in subdued light. (The pigments are gradually destroyed by exposure to sunlight or fluorescent light, which causes the colors to fade.) Make a pencil mark in the margin of the strip where the color of each spot (or band) is densest and note its color. Measure the distance (in millimeters) from the point of application to the densest part of each band and the distance from the point of application to the solvent front. Record the values in your report. Calculate the R_f value for each colored band.

The plant pigments that move most rapidly (almost with the solvent front) are the carotenes,

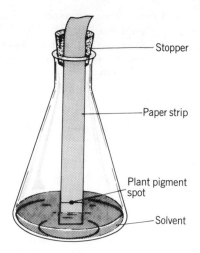

FIGURE 2-7
Apparatus for developing the chromatogram of green leaf pigments.

which are precursors to vitamin A. Then come the xanthophylls, which may not be resolved into individual yellow bands. Then come chlorophyll *a* and finally chlorophyll *b*, which appear as two distinct green bands. Identify on the chromatogram as many as of the pigments as you can, and pencil in their names on the chromatogram.

Pencil your name and date on the strip and turn it in with your lab report if your instructor so directs.

BIBLIOGRAPHY

Dixon, E. A., and Renyk, G., "Isolation, Separation, and Identification of Synthetic Food Colors," *J. Chem. Educ.* **59,** 67 (1982). Pure wool is used to extract dyes from aqueous solution, followed by thin-layer chromatography of the dyes.

Experiments in Liquid Chromatography—Separations of FD&C Dyes, 885 (April, 1979), University Marketing Division, Waters Associates, Inc., Milford, MA. This experiment describes the use of a Waters SEP-PAK C_{18} cartridge to provide a simple, convenient, and efficient dye extraction procedure, followed by analysis using thin-layer chromatography.

Furia, T. E. (ed.), *Handbook of Food Additives,* 2d ed., Vol. 1 (1973); Vol. 2 (1980); CRC Press, Boca Raton, FL. These handbooks provide information about the nature and regulatory status of food additives.

McKone, H. T., "Identification of FD&C Dyes by Visible Spectroscopy," *J. Chem. Educ.* **54,** 376 (1977).

McKone, H. T., and Nelson, G. J., "Separation and Identification of Some FD&C Dyes by TLC," *J. Chem. Educ.* **53,** 722 (1976).

Strain, H. H., "Paper Chromatography of Chloroplast Pigments," *J. Phys. Chem.* **57,** 638–640 (1953).

Strain, H. H., and Sherma, J., "Michael Tswett's Contributions to Sixty Years of Chromatography," *J. Chem. Educ.* **44,** 235 (1967). This article is immediately followed on page 238 by a translation of Michael Tswett's article, "Adsorption Analysis and Chromatographic Methods," published in 1906 in *Berichte der deutschen botanischen Gesellschaft.*

Determination of the Chemical Formula of an Oxide of Bismuth

PURPOSE

To determine the oxygen/bismuth mass ratio and the oxygen/bismuth mole ratio for a bismuth oxide prepared by heating bismuth in air. To use these data to determine the coefficients a and b in the chemical equation summarizing the stoichiometry of the reaction:

$$a\text{Bi} + \tfrac{1}{2}b\text{O}_2 \rightarrow \text{Bi}_a\text{O}_b$$

PRE-LAB PREPARATION

When you react two elements to form a binary compound it's necessary to keep track of the masses of the reactants and products in order to write a balanced chemical equation. This atom bookkeep-ing is called chemical *stoichiometry*, a word derived from the Greek words *stoikheion* (meaning element) and *metron* (to measure).

In this experiment you will make an oxide of bismuth by heating bismuth (in the form of powder) in air. (Air is a mixture of mostly nitrogen and oxygen. The fact that the product has been found to contain no nitrogen indicates that oxygen is more reactive than nitrogen with bismuth.)

We want to know two things about this compound: (1) the mass of oxygen that reacts with a given mass of bismuth, that is, the *mass ratio*, g O/g Bi, and (2) the *atom ratio*, atom O/atom Bi, and simplest chemical formula for the compound. The *mole ratio*, mol O/mol Bi, is exactly the same as the atom ratio, atom O/atom Bi, because a mole is just an Avogadro's number of the particle defined by the simplest chemical formula. Taking an Avogadro's number of particles doesn't change the ratio of oxygen atoms to bismuth atoms. We will represent the simplest chemical formula as Bi_aO_b or BiO_x, where $x = b/a$ = atom O/atom Bi = mol O/mol Bi.

There are at least two approaches we could use to determine the stoichiometry of the reaction. We could react bismuth and oxygen and analyze a sample of the pure bismuth oxide to determine the masses of bismuth and oxygen that are present. In the second approach (the one used in this experiment) we could synthesize a bismuth oxide by reacting a known mass of bismuth with an excess of oxygen. Because oxygen is a gas, there is no problem in removing the excess oxygen and weighing the bismuth oxide formed. Knowing the mass of bismuth that we started with and the mass of bismuth oxide formed, we can get the mass of oxygen in the compound by difference: grams of oxygen = grams of bismuth oxide − grams of bismuth. From these data we can easily calculate the first thing that we want to know about the compound, the mass ratio, g O/g Bi.

The second thing we want to determine is the atom ratio, atom O/atom Bi. As we pointed out, this is equal to the mole ratio, mol O/mol Bi. Determining the atom or mole ratio is more difficult than determining the mass ratio because it requires knowledge about the relative masses of Bi and O atoms. Pretend for the moment that you don't know the relative mass of a bismuth atom and an oxygen atom (put away your periodic table or table of atomic masses). This, of course, was exactly the situation of John Dalton (1766–1844) and his contemporaries in the early 1800's, who really didn't know the relative masses of the elements.

Dalton found it useful to think in terms of a model and we will do the same. Imagine that atoms are small indivisible spheres that can link together in various combinations to form compounds with a definite atom ratio that is equal to the ratio of small integers. To be specific, let's assume that bismuth and oxygen form a compound with the formula BiO_2, so that $x = b/a = \frac{2}{1} = 2.0$. The formula $Bi_{0.50}O$ is an equally correct way of writing the chemical formula but it doesn't lend itself to drawing a nice picture as BiO_2 does. We will picture the simplest particle of BiO_2 in the following way, using circles to represent the atoms.

● = bismuth, Bi   ◍ = BiO_2
○ = oxygen, O

Atoms are too small to see and count, so we can't directly determine the atom ratio by counting but we can perform the experiment we described to determine the mass ratio, g O/g Bi. How are the two ratios related? Let's write an equation in order to see the connection, making use of the dimensions of each quantity to verify that the units come out correctly:

$$\frac{2 \text{ mol O}}{1 \text{ mol Bi}} \times \frac{\text{g O/mol O}}{\text{g Bi/mol Bi}} = \frac{\text{g O}}{\text{g Bi}} \qquad (1)$$

If we multiply the mole (or atom) ratio by the ratio (*mass of a mole of O*)/(*mass of a mole of Bi*), we get the mass ratio for the compound, g O/g Bi, the quantity we will determine in the experiment.

Dalton and his contemporaries could measure g O/g Bi as you can, but they didn't know either the mole ratio, in our hypothetical example (2 mol O)/(1 mol Bi), or the ratio (*mass of a mole of O*)/(*mass of a mole of Bi*). If two of the three ratios shown in Equation (1) were unknown, how could they determine them? To be perfectly truthful there is no simple way to do this and in the early days they sometimes made mistakes. For example, Dalton knew of only one compound formed between hydrogen and oxygen, namely, water. When he believed that only one compound existed, he made the simplest possible assumption: that one atom of hydrogen reacted with one atom of oxygen. So he assumed that water had the formula HO. He knew that the mass ratio, g O/g H, in water was about 8, so in his first table of atomic weights he assigned 1 to the lightest element, hydrogen, and 8 to oxygen. It was only after many compounds had been synthesized and analyzed that inconsistencies began to show up that could only be resolved by assigning to water the formula H_2O with the result that the proper mass ratio was found to be 16 for the mass of an oxygen atom relative to the mass of a hydrogen atom.

Now uncover your periodic table or table of atomic masses and look up the values for the relative masses of bismuth and oxygen. Calculate for BiO_2 the ratio g O/g Bi from Equation (1). You should get the value 0.153 g O/g Bi. Now do a second calculation in reverse: Suppose there is an oxide of bismuth that has the composition 0.191 g O/g Bi. By rearranging Equation (1) you can calculate the mole ratio, $x = b/a$ for this compound. You should get a value of 2.5, which is equal to 5/2 so we can write the formula for this compound as $BiO_{2.5}$ or Bi_2O_5. Is there yet another bismuth oxide? Let's find out by doing the experiment.

EXPERIMENTAL PROCEDURE

Special Supplies: Size 1 (44-mm-diameter) porcelain crucibles (two per student), crucible tongs, clay triangle. Note to instructor: About 30 minutes can be saved if clean crucibles are made available that have been oven dried and cooled in a desiccator.

Chemicals: Bismuth metal powder, 100 mesh (available from Alfa Products, 152 Andover St., Danvers, MA 01923).

1. *Drying the Crucibles*   If dried crucibles are not available, obtain two clean crucibles. Place a crucible on a clay triangle supported by an iron ring as shown in Figure 3-1. Heat the crucible over a Bunsen burner adjusted to provide maximum heat. (Fischer or Meker burners are less desirable for this experiment because they are capable of heating bismuth to higher temperatures that can cause some loss of bismuth by evaporation.) Begin heating the crucible cautiously at first and then heat it strongly. The tip of the inner blue cone of the flame should be about 5 to 7 cm below the bottom of the crucible. After heating for about 10 min, shut off the burner. Allow the crucible to cool to room temperature (about 15 min).

2. *Preparation of Bismuth Oxide*   Using only crucible tongs to handle the crucible, weigh the cooled, empty crucible on the analytical balance as precisely as possible and record its mass. Place 0.4 to 0.5 g of powdered (100 mesh) bismuth metal in the dried crucible, distributing it evenly over the bottom. Reweigh the crucible plus added bismuth and record its mass. Heat the crucible containing the bismuth cautiously at first and then strongly for 15 min, again keeping the tip of the blue cone of flame 5 to 7 cm below the bottom of the crucible. Then shut off the burner. Note and record the color of the bismuth oxide as it cools.

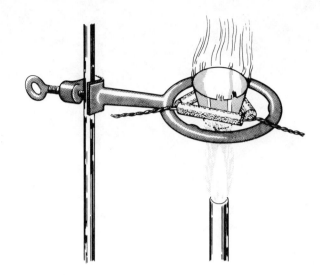

FIGURE 3-1
Setup for iron oxidation.

After the crucible has cooled at least 15 min, reweigh the crucible and contents and record the mass. (The mass will be greater because the bismuth reacts with oxygen in the air.)

Starting with a second clean crucible, repeat the entire experiment, recording the masses of the empty dry crucible, the crucible plus bismuth, and the crucible plus bismuth oxide.

After you have finished both series of measurements, give the crucibles containing the bismuth oxide to your instructor who will return them to the stockroom to be cleaned. (The residue of bismuth oxide can be removed by immersing the crucibles in warm concentrated (12 M) HCl. This should be done in a fume hood by a stockroom assistant, not by individual students.)

The Chemistry of Oxygen: Basic and Acidic Oxides and the Periodic Table

PURPOSE

To learn a method for the laboratory preparation of dioxygen, O_2. To observe the reactions of O_2 with several metallic and nonmetallic elements. To determine whether aqueous solutions of these oxides are acidic or basic. To see the relationship between acidic or basic properties of the oxides and the position of the element in the periodic table.

PRE-LAB PREPARATION

Oxygen and Life

Oxygen is one of the most abundant elements on earth. Large amounts of it are found in the molten mantle, in the crust that forms the great land masses, in the water of the vast oceans that cover most of the earth's surface, and in the gaseous atmosphere that surrounds the earth. Only in the atmosphere is oxygen found in the elemental form, primarily as the dioxygen molecule, O_2.

Dioxygen reacts so avidly with both metals and nonmetals that the presence of a large amount of free O_2 in the atmosphere raises the question: Where did all of that O_2 come from? Studies over the past 200 years have provided the general outline of the answer, but some important details are still being actively investigated. Most of the dioxygen on earth has been produced by plants, from the smallest algae to the majestic redwoods. Plants use water, carbon dioxide (CO_2), and sunlight to form carbohydrates and oxygen in a complex process called *photosynthesis*. Animals reverse the process. They react carbohydrates with oxygen inside their cells in a process called *respiration*, forming CO_2 and water. So plants and animals exist together in a grand symbiotic cycle, each supplying the others' needs. The energy involved in this biological cycle is about 30 times the amount of energy expended each year by all of mankind's machines.

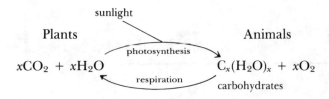

The Chemical Properties of Oxygen

To observe and understand some of the chemistry of oxygen we will first prepare some pure oxygen by catalytic decomposition of hydrogen peroxide, then react the O_2 with a variety of elements. The oxides formed will be dissolved in water and the solutions tested to see if they are acidic or basic. Ask yourself these questions while doing the experiment: (1) Is there a difference in the vigor of reaction (rate, light and heat evolved, etc.) of the different elements with oxygen that can be related to the position of the element in the periodic table? (2) Is there a relation between the acidity or basicity of the water solution of these oxides and the position of the element in the periodic table?

Acids and Bases from Oxides

If EO stands for any element combined with oxygen, the oxide may react with water to form the molecule $E(OH)_2$:

$$EO + H_2O \rightarrow E(OH)_2$$

(The number of OH groups will vary with different elements.) If the molecule $E(OH)_2$ is soluble in water, it will usually further react with water to form either hydronium ions, H_3O^+, or hydroxide ions, OH^-, depending on whether the O—H or the E—O bond breaks.

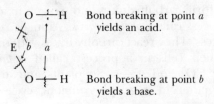

O —⋮—H   Bond breaking at point *a*
                    yields an acid.

O —⋮—H   Bond breaking at point *b*
                    yields a base.

If a proton is given up (or donated) to a water molecule (corresponding to cleavage at point *a*), we can write the reaction as

$$E(OH)_2 + H_2O \rightarrow H_3O^+ + E(O)OH^-$$

and by further dissociation

$$E(O)OH^- + H_2O \rightarrow H_3O^+ + EO_2^{2-}$$

Thus because it is a *proton donor*, the molecule formed from the oxide is an *acid*.[1]

On the other hand suppose that the E—O bond breaks at point *b*. The $E(OH)_2$ molecule then dissociates in solution to give hydroxide ion, OH^-:

$$E(OH)_2 \rightarrow E(OH)^+ + OH^-$$

$$E(OH)^+ \rightarrow E^{2+} + OH^-$$

Because it produces the *proton acceptor* OH^-, the compound is called a *base*.

If the oxide of an element forms an acid in water, it is termed an *acidic oxide* or *acid anhydride*. If the oxide in water forms a base, we speak of a *basic oxide* or *base anhydride*. To determine the formula of the anhydride of an oxy acid or base, simply subtract water to eliminate all hydrogen atoms. For example,

$$2NaOH(s) - H_2O \rightarrow Na_2O(s)$$

$$Mg(OH)_2(s) - H_2O \rightarrow MgO(s)$$

$$2B(OH)_3(s) - 3H_2O \rightarrow B_2O_3(s)$$

There are some borderline elements whose oxides are not very soluble in water, but that can display both weakly acidic and basic properties by dissolving in both strong bases and acids. Examples of these *amphoteric oxides* include SnO_2, ZnO, Al_2O_3, and PbO.

The tendency of $E(OH)_2$ to be either an acid or a base in water is controlled largely by the relative strengths of the interactions of water molecules with either H^+ and $E(O)OH^-$ or OH^- and $E(OH)^+$ and the nature of the element E. The variation in the nature of E is reflected by the position of E in the periodic table.

---

[1] A number of important acids are not derived from oxides, for example, the binary hydrides of the nonmetals: HCl, HBr, and H_2S.

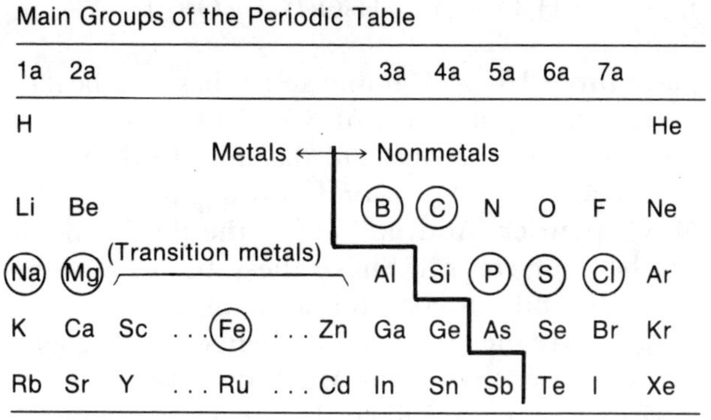

Main Groups of the Periodic Table

1a	2a				3a	4a	5a	6a	7a
H									He
			Metals ← → Nonmetals						
Li	Be				Ⓑ	Ⓒ	N	O	F	Ne
Ⓝⓐ	Ⓜⓖ	(Transition metals)			Al	Si	Ⓟ	Ⓢ	Ⓒⓛ	Ar
K	Ca	Sc	...Ⓕⓔ	...Zn	Ga	Ge	As	Se	Br	Kr
Rb	Sr	Y	...Ru	...Cd	In	Sn	Sb	Te	I	Xe

FIGURE 4-1
An abbreviated periodic table. The heavy zigzag line divides the metals from the nonmetals. The oxides (or hydroxides) of the elements that are circled will be studied in this experiment.

The elements whose oxides (or hydroxides) you will study are circled in the abbreviated periodic table shown in Figure 4-1. The heavy zigzag line in the figure approximately divides the metals from the nonmetals, so you will study a roughly equal number in each group.

Writing the Formulas of Oxy Acids and Their Anhydrides

When the acidic oxide N_2O_5 is added to water, we might expect the reaction

$$N_2O_5 + 5H_2O \rightarrow 2N(OH)_5$$

to occur. Instead, the partially hydrated oxy acid $N(OH)O_2$ is formed, which you may recognize as nitric acid when written with the more familiar formula HNO_3. Although acidic oxides seldom form fully hydrated oxy acids, it is still easy to determine the formula of the anhydride by subtracting water so as to leave no hydrogen atoms. For example, the formula of the anhydride of perchloric acid is obtained by subtracting one mole of water from two moles of perchloric acid.

$$2HClO_4 - H_2O \rightarrow Cl_2O_7$$

Do not let the conventional way of writing the formulas for nitric acid and perchloric acid as HNO_3 and $HClO_4$, respectively, mislead you into thinking that the hydrogen atoms in the acids are directly bonded to the nitrogen or chlorine atoms.

The structural formula for nitric acid might more accurately be written as $HONO_2$ or

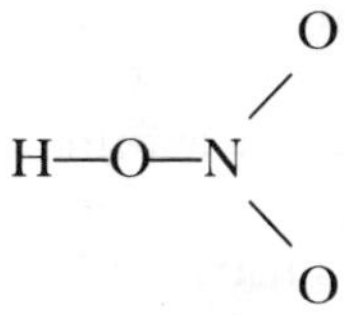

$$H-O-N \diagup\diagdown \begin{matrix} O \\ O \end{matrix} \qquad \text{nitric acid}$$

and that for perchloric acid be written as $HOClO_3$ or

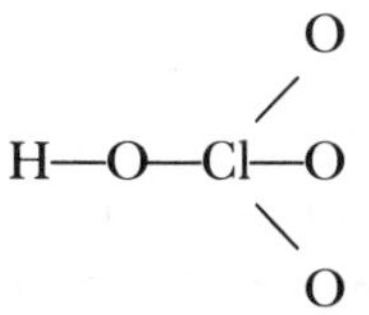

$$H-O-Cl-O \diagup\diagdown \begin{matrix} O \\ O \end{matrix} \qquad \text{perchloric acid}$$

In nearly all of the oxy acids, the hydrogen atoms that are acidic (or dissociable as protons) are bonded to oxygen atoms.

EXPERIMENTAL PROCEDURE

Special Supplies: Deflagrating spoon, six glass squares, plastic basin, six widemouthed bottles, 250-mL Erlenmeyer flask with 1-hole rubber stopper.

Chemicals: 3% (1 M) H_2O_2, 1 M $FeCl_3$, $MnO_2(s)$ (powder), Ca (metal shavings), Fe (steel wool), Mg (ribbon), P (red), S, small pieces of charcoal, universal indicator,[2] $H_3BO_3(s)$ (or $B(OH)_3(s)$), $Na_2O_2(s)$, 0.1 M $HClO_4$ (or ClO_3OH).

Safety Precautions: (a) Although we expect you to always wear safety glasses in the laboratory, it is especially important to wear them while doing this experiment.

(b) Magnesium ribbon burns so brightly that the light can damage your eyes. *Do not* stare directly at the burning ribbon. Instead, glance out of the corner of your eye to note the flame.

(c) Do not use white (or yellow) phosphorus in Part 2(e) of this experiment. It spontaneously ignites in air and is highly irritating to the skin and acutely toxic. The red form of phosphorus used in this experiment is not spontaneously flam-

---

[2] To prepare 200 mL of Yamada's universal indicator, dissolve 0.005 g thymol blue, 0.012 g methyl red, 0.060 g bromthymol blue, and 0.100 g phenolphthalein in 100 mL ethanol. Neutralize the solution to green with 0.01 M NaOH and dilute to 200 mL with distilled water. (Reference: L. S. Foster and I. J. Gruntfest, *J. Chem. Educ.* **14**, 274 (1937).)

mable but can be ignited by friction. Do not handle it with your bare hands because it is irritating to the skin.

The combustion of red phosphorus produces a choking, irritating smoke of P_2O_5. Use a fume hood for the combustion. If a fume hood is not available, the laboratory instructor will perform the experiment as a demonstration.

(d) The combustion of sulfur in Part 2(f) produces SO_2, a choking, irritating gas. Use a fume hood for the combustion. If a fume hood is not available, the laboratory instructor will perform the experiment as a demonstration.

(e) Solid sodium peroxide, Na_2O_2, is corrosive to the skin and a strong oxidizing agent. In contact with paper, it may cause the paper to ignite. It is recommended that the experiment using sodium peroxide described in Part 3 be performed by the laboratory instructor as a demonstration.

1. *Preparation of Oxygen* To observe the effect of *catalysts* (what is a catalyst?) on the rate of decomposition of hydrogen peroxide

$$H_2O_2(aq) \rightarrow H_2O(l) + \tfrac{1}{2}O_2(g)$$

place three 13- × 100-mm test tubes in a beaker or rack and put 3 mL of 3% H_2O_2 in each test tube. To the first one add 0.5 mL (10 drops) of 1 M $FeCl_3$. To the second add a pinch of solid MnO_2 powder. Add nothing to the third tube; it will be your control. Shake the tubes to mix the contents and observe the rate of evolution of oxygen. Are there any visible changes in the colors of the solutions? Does the MnO_2 dissolve or appear to react in any way? Record your observations.

Now assemble the apparatus shown in Figure 4-2.[3] Place about 4 mL of 1 M $FeCl_3$ in the 250-mL Erlenmeyer flask. Fill six 250-mL widemouthed bottles with water and invert these in the basin of water as needed. Add 200 mL of 3% H_2O_2 to the flask and replace the one-hole stopper. After about 15 s, when air has been expelled from the generator, fill the six bottles with oxygen by displacement

---

[3] Alternatively, the bottles of oxygen can be filled from an oxygen cylinder if one is available.

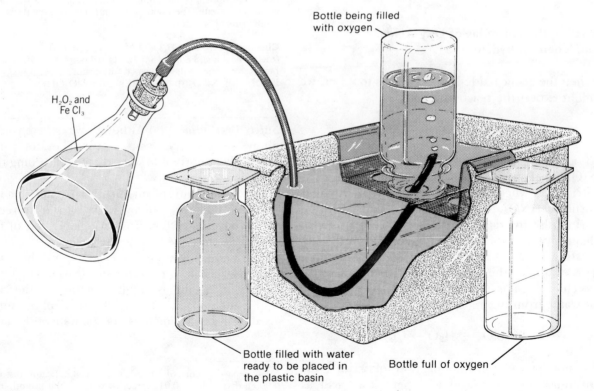

H₂O₂ and FeCl₃

Bottle being filled with oxygen

Bottle filled with water ready to be placed in the plastic basin

Bottle full of oxygen

FIGURE 4-2
Collection of O_2 prepared by catalytic decomposition of hydrogen peroxide.

of water. Leave about 5 mL of water in each bottle. As soon as each bottle is full, cover it with a glass square and place it right side up on the bench top.

2. *Preparation of Oxides* Prepare oxides of the following elements (except calcium) by burning them in the bottles containing oxygen gas, keeping the bottles covered as much as possible (see Figure 4-3). Number or label each bottle to avoid confusion. Immediately after each combustion, add 30 to 50 mL of water, replace the glass square, shake the bottle to dissolve the oxide formed, and set it aside for later use.

(a) *Magnesium.* Grip a 10-cm length of magnesium ribbon with crucible tongs, ignite it, and at once thrust it into a bottle of oxygen. (*Do not look directly at the brilliant light,* because it can injure your eyes.) *Blue*

(b) *Calcium.* Calcium metal is difficult to ignite, but burns brilliantly. Place a shaving of calcium metal in a crucible, heat it, cautiously at first and then very strongly, in the air over a Bunsen burner for 15 min. After the crucible has cooled, wash out the product with water into a beaker. *PURPLE-BLUE*

(c) *Iron.* Be sure there is a little water in the bottle to form a protective layer on the bottom. Heat some steel wool, holding it with tongs, in the Bunsen flame until it ignites, and at once thrust it into this bottle. *Green*

(d) *Carbon.* Ignite a small piece of charcoal, holding it with tongs or in a clean deflagrating spoon, and thrust the glowing charcoal into a bottle of oxygen. *Blue Green*

(e) *Phosphorus.* Carry out the ignition in a fume hood. If a fume hood is not available, your instructor will demonstrate the combustion. Put a bit of *red* phosphorus (the yellow form is too toxic) no larger in volume than half a pea in a clean deflagrating spoon. Ignite it over the burner and then thrust it into a bottle of oxygen. After the combustion dies down, reheat the deflagrating spoon (in the fume hood) to burn out all the remaining phosphorus. *Avoid breathing the residual combustion products.* *Orange*

(f) *Sulfur.* Prepare the oxide of sulfur by the same procedure that you used for phosphorus and take the same precautions (work in a fume hood). Your instructor will demonstrate this combustion if a fume hood is not available. *light pink*

3. *Acids and Bases from Oxides* To each bottle in which the oxide of an element has been formed by the foregoing procedures, and to which water

FIGURE 4-3
The use of a deflagrating spoon to burn a substance in oxygen.

has been added to form a solution, add a few drops of universal indicator solution.[4] The resulting solution color is interpreted as follows:

red orange yellow green blue indigo violet
acidic slightly acidic neutral slightly basic basic

Is there a relationship between the chemical character of the reaction product and the position of the element in the periodic table? Is there any difference between the behavior of the metal and the nonmetal oxides?

The preceding tests include representative elements from Groups 2, 4, 5, 6, and the transition metals, in the periodic table. To complete the series, let us examine an oxide or hydroxide from each of the other principal groups, 1, 3, and 7. (Why not include an element from Group 0?)

The normal *alkali oxides,* such as Na_2O, are difficult to obtain. Sodium peroxide forms when sodium burns in oxygen. The final reaction product with water, however, is the same as when Na_2O reacts with water. The extra "peroxide oxygen" is

---

[4] Iron oxide is so insoluble that the solution acidity or basicity is scarcely different from that of pure water. The effect of one or two other oxides is feeble on account of their limited solubility, but it should be sufficient to indicate the acidic or basic character of the hydroxide.

liberated as free oxygen gas. Compare the following two equations:

$$Na_2O(s) + H_2O \rightarrow 2NaOH(aq)$$

$$2Na_2O_2(s) + 2H_2O \rightarrow 4NaOH(aq) + O_2(g)$$

In a 15- × 150-mm test tube your instructor will boil a very small amount of sodium peroxide in 5 mL of water. When the solution has been cooled, test it with universal indicator. PURPLE

The *oxide of boron*, B_2O_3, is not readily available and in some forms is very insoluble. Dissolve a small amount of "boron hydroxide" in 5 mL of hot water. Cool the solution and test with universal indicator. Is this substance an acid or a base? How is the substance usually named? How is its formula usually written, $B(OH)_3$ or H_3BO_3? GREEN

The *oxides of chlorine*, $Cl_2O(g)$, $ClO_2(g)$, and $Cl_2O_7(g)$, are quite unstable. They react with water to form hydroxides. A solution of one of these, labeled 0.1 M $ClO_3(OH)$, will be available to you. Test a milliliter of this solution with universal indicator, and in your report write the formula as an acid, $HClO_4$, or base, $ClO_3(OH)$, according to your observations of its properties.

ORANGE

Chemical Reactions:
A Cycle of Copper Reactions

PURPOSE

To observe a sequence of reactions of copper that form a cycle. To gain skill in recording observations and interpreting them in terms of chemical equations. To use a simple classification scheme for grouping chemical reactions by reaction type. To practice quantitative laboratory techniques by determining the percentage recovery of the initial sample of copper.

PRE-LAB PREPARATION

To a beginning student of chemistry one of the most fascinating aspects of the laboratory is the dazzling array of sights, sounds, odors, and textures that are encountered there. Among other things, we believe that this experiment will provide an interesting aesthetic experience. You will be asked to carry out a series of reactions involving the element copper and to carefully observe and record your observations. The sequence begins and ends with copper metal, so it is called a cycle of copper reactions. Because no copper is added or removed between the initial and final steps, and because each reaction goes to completion, you should be able to quantitatively recover all of the copper you started with if you are careful and skillful. This diagram shows in an abbreviated form the reactions of the cycle of copper:

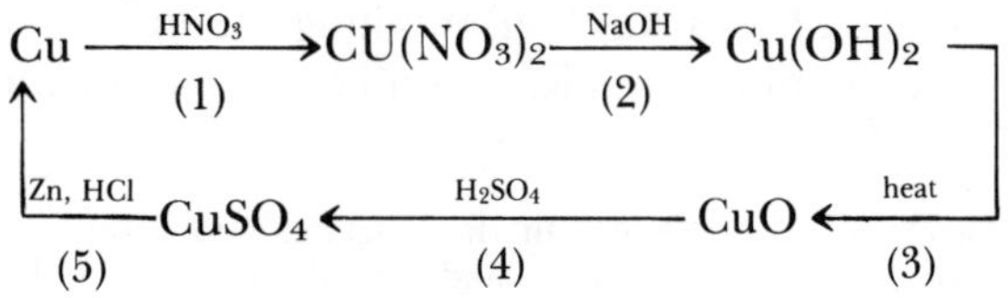

$$Cu \xrightarrow[\text{(1)}]{HNO_3} CU(NO_3)_2 \xrightarrow[\text{(2)}]{NaOH} Cu(OH)_2$$

$$\underset{\text{(5)}}{\overset{Zn, HCl}{\longleftarrow}} CuSO_4 \underset{\text{(4)}}{\overset{H_2SO_4}{\longleftarrow}} CuO \underset{\text{(3)}}{\overset{heat}{\longleftarrow}}$$

Like any good chemist, you will probably be curious to know the identity of each reaction product and the stoichiometry of the chemical reactions for each step of the cycle. Here they are, numbered so that each step of the cycle corresponds to the chemical equation with the same number:[1]

$$8HNO_3(aq) + 3Cu(s) + O_2(g) \longrightarrow$$
$$3Cu(NO_3)_2(aq) + 4H_2O(l) + 2NO_2(g) \quad (1)$$

$$Cu(NO_3)_2(aq) + 2NaOH(aq) \longrightarrow$$
$$Cu(OH)_2(s) + 2NaNO_3(aq) \quad (2)$$

$$Cu(OH)_2(s) \xrightarrow{\text{heat}} CuO(s) + H_2O(l) \quad (3)$$

$$CuO(s) + H_2SO_4(aq) \longrightarrow$$
$$CuSO_4(aq) + H_2O(l) \quad (4)$$

$$CuSO_4(aq) + Zn(s) \longrightarrow ZnSO_4(aq) + Cu(s) \quad (5)$$

These equations summarize the results of a large number of experiments but it's easy to lose sight of this if you just look at equations written on paper. You can easily be overwhelmed by the vast amount of information found in this lab manual and in chemistry textbooks. It is in fact a formidable task to attempt to learn or memorize isolated bits of information that are not reinforced by your personal experience. This is one reason why it is important to have a laboratory experience. Chemistry is preeminently an experimental science.

As you perform the experiment, watch closely and record what you see. Each observation should be a little hook in your mind on which you can hang a more abstract bit of information, like the chemical formula for the compound you are observing.

It is also easier to remember information that is organized by some conceptual framework. Observations and facts that have not been assimilated into some coherent scheme of interpretation are relatively useless. It would be like memorizing the daily weather reports when you have no knowledge of or interest in meteorology.

Chemists look for relationships, trends, or patterns of regularity in organizing their observations of chemical reactions. The periodic table is a product of this kind of thinking. It groups the elements into chemical families. Each element bears a strong resemblance to other members of the same chemical family but also has its own unique identity and chemistry.

In a similar fashion it is useful to classify reactions into different types. Several different kinds of classification schemes exist because no one scheme is able to accommodate all known reactions. A simple classification scheme we will use at the beginning is one based on ideas of *combination, decomposition,* and *replacement.*[2] Here we present an outline and some examples of this kind of classification:

A Simple Scheme for Classifying Chemical Reactions

A. *Combination reactions*
1. Simple combination of two elements to form a binary compound

$$2Na(s) + Cl_2(g) \rightarrow 2NaCl(s)$$

2. Combination of elements and/or molecules

$$CaO(s) + CO_2(g) \rightarrow CaCO_3(s)$$

B. *Decomposition reactions (often promoted by heat or light)*

$$HgO(s) \xrightarrow{\text{heat}} Hg(l) + \tfrac{1}{2}O_2(g)$$

$$NO_2(g) \xrightarrow{\text{light}} NO(g) + O(g)$$

C. *Replacement reactions*
1. Single replacement

$$2AgNO_3(aq) + Cu(s) \rightarrow 2Ag(s) + Cu(NO_3)_2(aq)$$

2. (a) Double replacement
   Formation of an insoluble salt

$$AgNO_3(aq) + NaCl(aq) \rightarrow AgCl(s) + NaNO_3(aq)$$

   (b) Neutralization (formation of a neutral un-ionized molecule)

$$HCl(aq) + NaOH(aq) \rightarrow NaCl(aq) + H_2O(l)$$

---

[1] Labels specify the states of the reactants and products: (*s*) means a solid; (*l*) means a liquid; (*g*) means a gas; and (*aq*) means an aqueous (water) solution.

[2] Donald A. McQuarrie and Peter A. Rock, *General Chemistry,* W. H. Freeman and Company, New York, 1984, Chapter 4.

As you carry out each step of the cycle of copper reactions, think about what is happening in each reaction and try to fit it into the classification scheme.

EXPERIMENTAL PROCEDURE

Special Supplies: Infrared lamps or steam baths, porcelain evaporating dish.

Chemicals: 18- to 20-gauge copper wire, concentrated (16 M) HNO_3, 3 M NaOH, 6 M H_2SO_4, 30-mesh zinc metal, 6 M HCl, methanol, acetone.

Safety Precautions: Concentrated nitric acid, HNO_3, is hazardous. It produces severe burns on the skin and the vapor is a lung irritant. When you handle it you should use a fume hood while wearing safety glasses (as always) and rubber or polyvinyl chloride gloves. A polyethylene squeeze pipet can be useful for transferring the HNO_3 from a small beaker to your 10-mL graduated cylinder. Rinse your hands with tap water after handling HNO_3.

The dissolution of the copper wire with concentrated HNO_3 should be carried out in a fume hood. If no hood is available, construct the apparatus shown in Figure 5-1 to substitute for the fume hood. The brown NO_2 gas that is evolved is very irritating to the lungs.

NaOH solutions are corrosive to the skin and especially dangerous if splashed into the eyes—*wear your safety glasses!*

Methanol and acetone are flammable and their vapors are toxic. Use them in the hood to avoid breathing the vapor and *keep them away from all open flames.*

Step 1. Cut a length of pure copper wire that weighs about 0.5 g (about a 10-cm length of 20-gauge copper wire). If it is not bright and shiny, clean it with steel wool, rinse it with water, and dry it with a tissue. Weigh it to the nearest milligram, recording the weight in your laboratory book. Coil the wire into a flat spiral, place it in the bottom of a 250-mL beaker, and—in the fume hood—add 4.0 mL of concentrated (16 M) nitric acid, HNO_3. (If a fume hood is not available, use the apparatus shown in Figure 5-1.) Record in your notebook a description of what you see. Swirl the solution around in the beaker until the copper has completely dissolved. What is in the solution

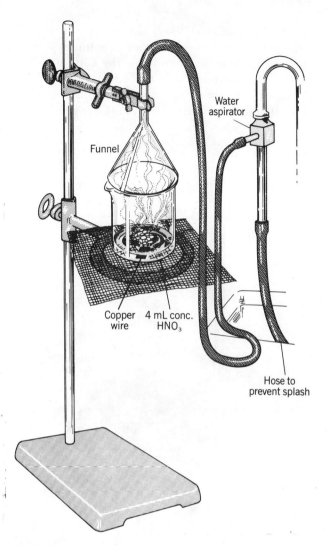

FIGURE 5-1
If a fume hood is not available, substitute this apparatus.

when the reaction is complete? After the copper has dissolved, add deionized water until the beaker is about half full. Steps 2 through 4 can be conducted at your lab desk.

Step 2. While stirring the solution with a glass rod, add 30 mL of 3.0 M NaOH to precipitate $Cu(OH)_2$. What is formed in the solution besides $Cu(OH)_2$? Record your observations in your lab book.

Step 3. Stirring gently with a glass rod to prevent "bumping" (a phenomenon caused by the formation of a large steam bubble in a locally overheated area), heat the solution just barely to the boiling point over a burner using the apparatus shown in Figure 5-2. If the solution bumps you may lose some CuO, so don't neglect the stirring. Record

Labels in figure: Water aspirator, Funnel, Copper wire, 4 mL conc. HNO_3, Hose to prevent splash

your observations. When the transformation is complete, remove the burner, continue stirring for a minute or so, then allow the CuO to settle. Then decant (pour off) the supernatant liquid, being careful not to lose any CuO. Add about 200 mL of hot deionized water, allow to settle again,

and decant once more. What is removed by this washing and decantation process?

Step 4. Add 15 mL of 6.0 M H_2SO_4, while stirring. Record your observations. What is in solution now? Now transfer operations back to the fume hood.

Step 5. In the fume hood, add all at once 2.0 g of 30-mesh zinc metal, stirring until the supernatant liquid is colorless. What happens? What is the gas produced? When the evolution of gas has become very slow, decant the supernatant liquid. If you can see any silvery grains of unreacted zinc, add 10 mL of 6 M HCl and warm, but do not boil, the solution. When no hydrogen evolution can be detected by eye, decant the supernant liquid and transfer the copper to a porcelain dish. A spatula or rubber policeman is helpful for making the transfer. Wash the product with about 5 mL of deionized water, allow it to settle, and decant the wash water. Repeat the washing and decantation. Wash with about 5 mL of methanol (*in the hood; keep away from flames*), allow to settle, and decant. Place the porcelain dish under an infrared lamp or on a steam bath or hot plate and dry the copper metal. What color is it? Using a spatula, transfer the dried copper metal to a preweighed 100-mL beaker and weigh to the nearest milligram. Calculate the mass of copper you recovered by subtracting the weight of the empty beaker from the weight of the beaker plus the copper metal.

Calculation of Percentage Recovery   Express the percentage of copper recovered as

percentage recovery

$$= \frac{\text{mass of copper recovered}}{\text{mass of copper wire}} \times 100$$

If you are careful at every step you will have recovered nearly 100% of the copper you started with.

BIBLIOGRAPHY

Condike, G. F., *J. Chem. Educ.* **52,** 615 (1975).

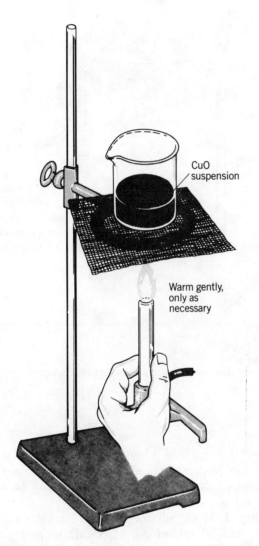

CuO suspension

Warm gently, only as necessary

FIGURE 5-2
Setup for heating $Cu(OH)_2$ to convert it to CuO.

The Reduction of Copper Oxide to Copper

The Atomic Mass of Copper

PURPOSE

To observe the reduction of copper oxide to copper metal by heating the oxide with methane (natural gas). To determine the mass ratio, g copper/g oxygen, for copper oxide, CuO. To determine the atomic mass of copper on a scale in which oxygen, O, is assigned 16.00 mass units.

PRE-LAB PREPARATION

In this experiment you will produce copper metal from copper oxide, CuO. When you do this you will be practicing on a small scale one of the oldest human arts, *metallurgy*—the art and science of extracting metals from their ores and of creating useful objects from metals.

Copper and gold were the first metals to be used, because they can be found in their native metallic state. Being malleable, they can be pounded and shaped into ornaments and implements, and their use can be traced back to Neolithic times.

Copper was probably the first metal to be isolated from its ores, and the art of copper metallurgy was known as early as 4500 BC to the people of the Vinča culture, which flourished along the Danube River in Yugoslavia, and to the people of Egypt and Mesopotamia (modern Iraq) from about 3500 BC. Egyptian copper was probably obtained by reducing the ore *malachite* from Sinai in charcoal fires. (Malachite is a basic copper carbonate; it has the formula $CuCO_3 \cdot Cu(OH)_2$.)

Although a variety of chemical arts—like metallurgy, pottery, tanning and dyeing, and brewing and winemaking—have existed for thousands of years, their practice was based not on any detailed knowledge of the elements and their chemical reactions, but on recipes that were embellished and improved as they were handed down from one generation to the next.

It was not until about 1800 that the most important ingredient appeared that set the stage for the development of modern chemistry—a useful working hypothesis about the nature of matter called the *atomic theory*. The notion of an *element* and of the smallest unit of an element, called an *atom*, gave rise to the idea that atoms might combine in various proportions to form different substances. This in turn provided an incentive to ascertain what these proportions were, thus determining a chemical formula, and to determine the relative masses of the atoms of the various elements.

By 1875 the revolution in thinking about the atomic nature of matter was nearly finished and most chemists were won over to the new atomic theory because it was so successful in interpreting what chemists observed in the laboratory.

This experiment is an example of the classic experiments used to determine the relative masses of atoms, an experiment that might have been done for the first time between 1800 and 1850. You will take a pure copper oxide, CuO, reduce it to copper by heating it with natural gas (mostly methane, CH_4), and calculate from your data the relative mass of copper and oxygen atoms. Then you will calculate the mass of a mole of copper on a scale in which 16.00 g is assigned to the mass of a mole of atomic oxygen, O.

Producing a Metal from Its Ore

The heating of a metal ore in air usually converts it to the oxide, and if this oxide is mixed with charcoal and heated to a high temperature, the carbon reacts with the metal oxide to form CO and/or CO_2, leaving behind the metal in its elemental state. An example is the reaction of iron oxide with carbon:

$$Fe_2O_3(s) + 3C(s) \rightarrow 2Fe(s) + 3CO(g)$$

In the simple classification scheme we discussed in Experiment 5, this reaction would be called a replacement reaction, the carbon replacing the metal in the metal oxide.

This type of reaction is also called a *reduction reaction* because the oxidation number of the metal is reduced from some positive value to zero in producing the free metal.[1]

---

[1] See Appendix A for an explanation of the oxidation number.

Like carbon, hydrogen gas (H_2) is a good reducing agent. For example, it will reduce silver oxide to metallic silver:

$$Ag_2O(s) + H_2(g) \rightarrow 2Ag(s) + H_2O(g)$$

What if carbon and hydrogen are combined to make methane, CH_4? Methane is the principal constituent of natural gas and is also a good reducing agent for many metal oxides. Why will we use methane rather than carbon or hydrogen as a reducing agent? First, carbon (in the form of charcoal) is a solid and to get intimate contact between the charcoal and the solid metal oxide is difficult without melting the metal oxide. Even with the addition of some other compounds to reduce the melting point, the reaction requires temperatures that are too high and equipment that is too expensive.

Hydrogen gas is effective, but we would have to either make it or buy it in steel cylinders. It's also flammable; more importantly, a mixture of hydrogen and air burns so rapidly that there is an explosion hazard unless the system is very carefully flushed to remove all air. So we will use natural gas, which is readily available and burns more slowly with air than hydrogen, so that the explosion hazard is not so great.

EXPERIMENTAL PROCEDURE

Special Supplies: 25- × 200-mm heavy-walled Pyrex ignition tube (Corning 9860 or equivalent), Pyrex glass wool, two-hole rubber stopper (to fit ignition tube), Pyrex glass tubing: one straight piece approximately 20-cm long, one 90° bend (approximately 6 to 8 cm each side), 400-grit abrasive carborundum paper, steel plate and hammer (one or two per laboratory section).

Chemicals: CuO, glycerol.

Safety Precautions: A mixture of natural gas and air can explode if ignited. Because of this element of hazard it is important that you have your instructor check and approve your apparatus on the Report sheet before you light the Bunsen burner. A heavy-walled ignition tube must be used. An ordinary test tube is likely to melt and rupture during the heating.

All of the tubing connections must fit snugly in order to prevent gas leaks. Use glycerol to lubricate the glass tubing that is to be inserted in the rubber stopper. Use a cloth towel to protect yourself should the tubing break. Ask the instructor to help by showing you how breakage can be avoided. Do *not* lubricate the rubber tubing connections or they may slip off, creating a hazard.

When heating the ignition tube, move the burner around frequently to avoid melting the tube.

Procedure

Assemble the apparatus as shown in Figure 6-1. If preformed tubing is not provided, cut a 20-cm length of tubing and fire polish both ends. Cut a 16-cm length of tubing, make a right-angle bend in it by using a flame spreader on your Bunsen burner, and fire polish both ends. After the tubing has cooled, place a drop or two of glycerin on the tubing to lubricate it. *Grasp the glass tubing near the stopper with a cloth towel to reduce the risk of breakage.* After the tubing has been inserted in the rubber stopper, wash off the glycerol, and dry the tubing

with a towel. Do not use glycerol on the rubber (or plastic) tubing. All connections and the rubber stopper must fit snugly to avoid gas leaks. When everything is ready as shown in Figure 6-1, *have your instructor check the system and approve it on your Report sheet before lighting the burner.*

1. *Weighing the Copper Oxide* Weigh the empty ignition tube, without the stopper, as precisely as possible. Record the mass of the empty tube. Then place about 1.0 g of copper oxide, CuO, in the ignition tube and weigh it again. Record this mass.

Reducing the Copper Oxide Seat the ignition tube containing the weighed sample of copper oxide firmly in place and clamp it in position. Adjust the Bunsen burner so that the air intake is closed. Turn on the gas, light the burner, and wait until a steady yellow luminous flame is present. Now the air is flushed out. Open the air intake until a hot nonluminous flame is achieved. Gradually begin warming the lower portion of the ignition tube by continually moving the flame. When the tube is very hot, place the burner so that the copper oxide is heated very strongly. Move the burner around from time to time to avoid overheating one spot and melting the tube.

Gradually the copper oxide will take on the color of metallic copper. Toward the end of the heating process, hold the burner in your hand to apply maximum heat to any remaining dark areas. The reduction normally takes 20 to 30 minutes of heating to complete. When the reaction is complete, move the burner away from the tube and close the air intake. Keep the burner on until the tube has cooled to room temperature.

2. *Weighing the Copper* After the ignition tube is completely cool, turn off the burner, remove the ignition tube, and weigh it. Record the mass.

3. *Observations on the Product* Remove the product by tapping the ignition tube over a piece of weighing paper. Gather the product into a lump on a steel plate and hammer it. Rub the lump on a piece of 400-grit abrasive carborundum paper. Does it leave a shiny metallic trace? Does it have any other metallic properties?

BIBLIOGRAPHY

Zidick, C., and Weismann, T., *J. Chem. Educ.* **50,** 717 (1973), and modification by Katz, D. A., *J. Chem. Educ.* **52,** 204 (1975).

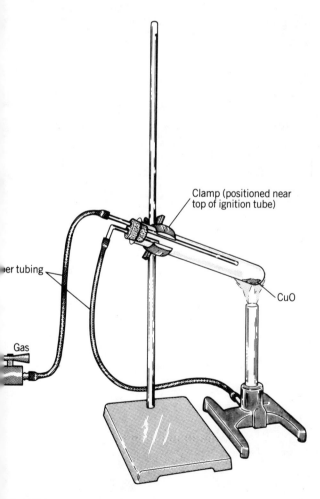

FIGURE 6-1
Setup for CuO reduction.

DATA AND OBSERVATIONS

1. Weighing the Copper Oxide

Mass of ignition tube plus copper oxide   _____ g

Mass of empty ignition tube   _____ g

Mass of copper oxide   _____ g

Instructor's approval of apparatus   _____

2. Weighing the Copper

Mass of ignition tube plus reduced copper oxide   _____ g

Mass of empty ignition tube   _____ g

Mass of copper   _____ g

3. Observations on the Product

Describe how the product looks before and after you hammer it.

Does it leave a metallic trace when you rub it on 400-grit abrasive carborundum paper? Does it have any other properties characteristic of a metal?

CALCULATIONS

4. Calculation of the Mass Ratio, g Cu/g O

From your results in parts 1 and 2 calculate the mass of oxygen in the copper oxide.

Mass of CuO   _____ g

Mass of Cu   _____ g

Mass of O   _____ g

Now calculate the mass ratio, g Cu/g O   _____

5. Calculation of the Mass of a Mole of Copper

Using the mass ratio, g Cu/g O, calculated in part 4, calculate the mass of a mole of copper, g Cu/mol Cu, assuming that there are 16.00 g of oxygen in a mole of oxygen and that a mole of copper oxide contains 1 mole of oxygen per mole of copper. (Show your calculation with the appropriate units.)

6. Calculation of the Percentage of Relative Error

Compare your result with the accepted value for the mass of a mole of copper by computing the relative error expressed as a percentage.

$$\text{percentage of relative error} = \frac{\frac{\text{g Cu}}{\text{mol Cu}}\,(\text{exp.}) - 63.55\,\frac{\text{g Cu}}{\text{mol Cu}}}{63.55\,\frac{\text{g Cu}}{\text{mol Cu}}} \times 100$$

QUESTIONS

1. If the sample is heated insufficiently, some copper oxide will not be reduced to copper metal. What effect would this have on the calculated value of g Cu/mol Cu? Explain.

2. What alternative method can you suggest to obtain copper from copper oxide? Write a balanced chemical reaction for the method you propose.

The Estimation of Avogadro's Number

PURPOSE

To make an order of magnitude estimate of the size of a carbon atom and of the number of atoms in a mole of carbon based on simple assumptions about the spreading of a thin film of stearic acid on a water surface.

PRE-LAB PREPARATION

John Dalton (1766–1844) was so taken with the notion of atomism that he never quite grasped the distinction between an atom and a molecule of an element. The most stable form of many elements, such as oxygen, hydrogen, and the halogens, is not an atom but a diatomic molecule. The belief that the smallest unit of an element must be an atom made it difficult for Dalton to accept Gay-Lussac's data about the combining volumes of gases.

The reconciliation between Dalton's theory and Gay-Lussac's data was brought about by Lorenzo Romano Amedeo Carlo Avogadro (1776–1856). He accomplished this by making the distinction between an atom and a molecule of an element and by making the hypothesis that equal volumes of gases contain equal numbers of molecules. For example, if you believe that hydrogen and chlorine are monatomic and that equal volumes of gases (at the same temperature and pressure) contain equal numbers of atoms, then one volume of hydrogen should react with one volume of chlorine to form one volume of HCl:

$$H + Cl \rightarrow HCl$$

But when you do the experiment you will find that two volumes of HCl are produced. Avogadro interpreted this result by assuming that the smallest unit of hydrogen and chlorine is a diatomic molecule, not an atom, and by writing the equation in the following way:

$$H_2 + Cl_2 \rightarrow 2HCl$$

Many subsequent experiments have proved that Avogadro's explanation was correct.

The hypothesis, published in 1811, was perhaps ahead of its time and went virtually unnoticed. More than half a century passed before Cannizzaro demonstrated the general applicability of the hypothesis in an article published in 1858 that was distributed in pamphlet form at the first international chemical congress at Karlsruhe, Germany, in 1860. The pamphlet so clearly and completely discussed atoms, molecules, atomic weights, and molecular weights that chemists were convinced of his views, which were quietly incorporated into chemical thinking. Fifty years of pondering Dalton's atomic theory had created the right moment for the acceptance of Avogadro's hypothesis. In the presentation of his views Cannizzaro gave credit to Avogadro as well as to Ampère and Dumas, and no doubt it was Cannizzaro who saved Avogadro's hypothesis from oblivion, so that today we call the number of particles (atoms or molecules) in a mole *Avogadro's number*.

How many particles are there in a mole? Avogadro never knew. A French scientist, Jean Perrin, determined the first value in 1908. He measured the vertical distribution in the earth's gravitational field of gamboge (a natural resin) particles suspended in water and obtained values in the range 5.4 to 6.0×10^{23}. After Robert Millikan determined the charge of an electron around 1915, a more accurate value was obtained by dividing the charge of a mole of electrons (the Faraday constant) by the charge of a single electron. More refined values have been obtained by accurate measurements of crystals of silicon by X-ray diffraction (division of the volume of 1 mole of silicon by the effective volume of a silicon atom yields Avogadro's number).

All of the refined measurements require sophisticated and expensive equipment and great care in experimental technique and treatment of data. The payoff is the most accurate value of Avogadro's number, N_A, that we have to date: $N_A = 6.02209 \times 10^{23}$ particles/mol. This is one of the numbers you will encounter in introductory chemistry that is worth remembering.

The mole is a fundamental unit in the International System (SI) of units. A mole of carbon is precisely 12.0000 g of carbon-12, and Avogadro's number is defined as the number of atoms in a mole of carbon-12.

In this experiment you will make an approximate (order of magnitude) estimate of Avogadro's number by determining the amount of stearic acid that it takes to form a single layer (called a *monolayer*) on the surface of water. By making simple assumptions about the way the stearic acid molecules pack together to form the monolayer, we can determine its thickness and from the thickness we can estimate the size of a carbon atom. Knowing the size of a carbon atom, we can compute its volume; and if we know the volume occupied by a mole of carbon (in the form of diamond), we can divide the volume of a mole of carbon by the volume of an atom of carbon to get an estimate of Avogadro's number. The number you get won't be accurate to within 10% or even a factor of 2, but it will enable you to estimate to within about a power of 10 the number of particles in a mole. That's better than chemists could do only 100 years ago.

Concepts of the Experiment

Matter exists in three states. The fact that a gas can be condensed to a liquid and a liquid frozen to a solid indicates that there are attractive forces between all molecules. We can schematically represent these forces at the surface of a liquid by the arrows in Figure 7-1. In the interior of the liquid the forces exerted on a given molecule are uniform in all directions. At the surface, however, it is clear that there is a net force attracting each surface molecule inward. These molecules have higher energies than interior molecules, thus giving rise to the force known as *surface tension*. It is because of this force that liquid droplets are spherical. A

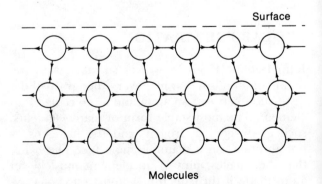

FIGURE 7-1
The molecular structure of a liquid near its surface.

spherical shape presents the least surface area for a given volume.

If our liquid is water, the surface tension is especially strong because particularly strong bonds, called *hydrogen bonds*, exist between the water molecules. These bonds arise whenever a hydrogen atom attached to a highly electronegative atom, such as oxygen, has access to an unbonded pair of electrons, such as those of another oxygen atom.

Another property displayed by water is that it is polar. Polar molecules possess a separation of charge. In ionic compounds, such as NaCl, there is a separation of a full unit charge, $Na^+ \cdots Cl^-$. Polar compounds display a partial separation of charge, denoted by a delta, δ. An arrow is used to display this charge separation. The dipole moment of a polar molecule is equal to the partial charge times the distance separating the charges, and it is represented by an arrow pointing toward the negative end of the molecule. Figure 7-2 displays the polar nature of the water molecule.

Polar molecules attract each other. The negative end of the dipole of one molecule is attracted to the positive end of the dipole of another molecule. For this reason, water dissolves formic acid, H—COOH, which has a dipole moment, but it does not dissolve butane, $CH_3CH_2CH_2CH_3$, which has a nearly uniform charge distribution. If a molecule possessing the properties of both of these molecules is brought up to the surface of water, the polar part of the molecule will be attracted to the surface and the nonpolar portion will be repelled. If the nonpolar part is much larger than the polar portion, the molecule will not dissolve in water but will simply stick to its surface. Consequently it will lower the energy of the surface water molecules and of the adhering molecules.

The molecule we will use in this experiment, stearic acid, behaves in just this way. Stearic acid has a polar end consisting of a carboxyl group, —COOH, and a large nonpolar "tail" consisting of 16 methylene groups, —CH₂—, terminating in a methyl group, —CH₃. Figure 7-3 is a reasonably accurate representation of this molecule.

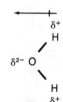

FIGURE 7-2
The water molecule.

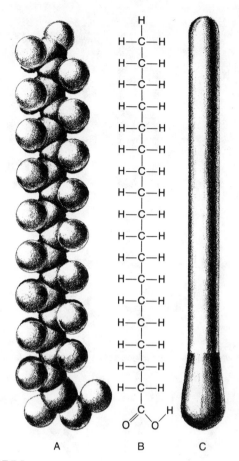

FIGURE 7-3
The stearic acid molecule. (A) Space-filling model; (B) structural formula; (C) schematic representation.

The addition of a limited number of stearic acid molecules to a water surface results in the formation of a monolayer, as illustrated in Figure 7-4. However, after the surface is covered with a monolayer of stearic acid molecules, the addition of more molecules causes the stearic acid molecules to cluster in globular aggregates. The polar heads are attracted to the polar water molecules and form a spherical surface, leaving the hydrocarbon tails pointing inward to form an "oily" interior. Figure 7-5 schematically illustrates such an aggregate.

The properties of the water surface and the stearic acid molecule permit us to perform what amounts to a titration of the water surface. We can add stearic acid molecules to the water surface until a monolayer covers the entire surface. Further addition will cause a globular lens to form on the liquid surface. At this point the stearic acid molecules are stacked on the water surface like a layer of cordwood turned on end. If we know the area of the surface of water and have a way of

New surface

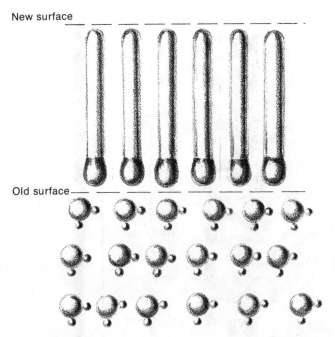

Old surface

FIGURE 7-4
Monolayer of long-chain molecules lying on top of a water surface.

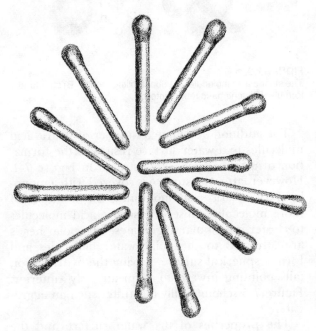

FIGURE 7-5
Globular aggregate of long-chain molecules. Such an aggregate is called a *micelle*.

measuring the volume of substance added to form the monolayer, we can calculate the thickness, *t,* of the layer. This thickness equals approximately the length of the stearic acid molecule.

As we saw earlier, this molecule consists of 18 carbon atoms linked together. If we make the simple assumption that the atoms are like little cubes linked together, the edge length of a cube of carbon is given by *t*/18. If we cube the edge length, we have estimated the volume of a carbon atom. Now we have half the data needed to calculate Avogadro's number.

The other half of the data requires no experimental work on your part. What we need is the volume of a mole of carbon. Diamond is pure carbon and the density of diamond is known to be 3.51 g/cm³. You may recall that you can calculate the molar volume of an element by dividing the molar mass (the atomic "weight") by its density. Verify this idea by looking at the dimensions of this quotient.

If we assume that diamond consists of little cubes of carbon atoms stacked together, an Avogadro's number of them would equal the volume of 1 mol. Avogadro's number results from one final step:

$$N_A = \frac{\text{molar volume (cm}^3/\text{mol)}}{\text{atomic volume (cm}^3/\text{atom)}}$$

$$= \text{number of atoms/mol}$$

EXPERIMENTAL PROCEDURE

Special Supplies: 14-cm watch glass or large Petri dish, 10-mL graduated cylinder, glass capillary pipet drawn to a fine tip (see the instructions in part 1), pure water free of surface-active materials (preferably distilled).

Chemicals: Petroleum ether (30 to 60°C b.p.) or hexane, 0.12 to 0.15 g/L stearic acid solution in petroleum ether (30 to 60°C b.p.) or hexane. The exact weight/volume concentration of this solution will be provided by your instructor. 0.1 M NaOH in 50:50 methanol/water (volume:volume, or v:v), used for washing the watch glasses.

NOTE TO INSTRUCTOR The watch glasses should be soaked in the methanolic NaOH solution in a polyethylene basin overnight or at least for an hour or two before the beginning of the laboratory period. The watch glasses should then be rinsed in distilled water before they are distributed to the students. Distilled water is better for this experiment than deionized water, because deionized water often contains organic substances leached from the organic resins used to deionize water.

Safety Precautions: Petroleum ether (or hexane) is flammable! There must be no open flames in the laboratory while this experiment is performed.

If you clean your own watch glasses by soaking them in methanolic NaOH, you must wear rubber gloves to protect your hands. As always, wear eye protection in the laboratory.

1. Preparation of Equipment and Calibration of the Dropper

Stearic acid is a solid. It is conveniently measured and applied to the water surface by dropping a solution of stearic acid in petroleum ether onto the water. The petroleum ether (a mixture of low-boiling alkanes) is insoluble in water; because it has a high vapor pressure, it rapidly evaporates, leaving a monolayer of stearic acid spread on the water surface.

Because stearic acid is one of the fatty acids present in soaps, you must not clean your watch glass with soap. Any soap, grease, or dirt present can form a film on the water that prevents the spreading of stearic acid on the surface, leading to meaningless results because not even the first drop will spread on the surface.

Obtain a 14-cm watch glass or Petri dish. If it has not been soaked in the methanolic NaOH solution described in the Chemicals section, wash it thoroughly with detergent. Rinse the detergent off completely under a full stream of cold tap water for a minute, then rinse with distilled water. Repeat the washing after each experiment, or obtain another watch glass that has been soaked in methanolic NaOH. Handle the watch glass only by the edges, being especially careful not to touch the inside of it with anything. Be particularly careful to keep your fingers (which are usually slightly greasy) off the glass.

Your instructor will demonstrate how to pull the tip of a medicine dropper out to a fine point. Alternatively, a piece of glass tubing can be pulled out, the end flared, and a rubber bulb attached. Watch your fingers. Molten glass is *really* hot and *stays* hot for several minutes.

After your dropper has cooled, calibrate it by filling it with petroleum ether. While holding the dropper vertically, count the number of drops that must be expressed into the graduated cylinder to equal 1.00 mL. The best way to do this is to fill the cylinder to a milliliter mark and then add your drops from the dropper until the meniscus reaches the next mark. Between 100 and 150 drops should be required. If fewer than 100 drops equal 1 mL,

ask your instructor for help in pulling out another capillary tip. Repeat your calibration until your results agree to within 4 to 5 drops. The angle at which you hold the dropper will affect the size of the drops. A dropper held at an angle of 45° from the vertical will usually deliver about 30% fewer drops per milliliter than the same dropper held vertically.

2. Measurement of the Volume of Stearic Acid Solution Required to Cover the Surface

Fill the clean watch glass to the brim with distilled water. Carefully measure the diameter of the water surface with a centimeter rule or meter stick. Rinse your calibrated dropper several times with stearic acid solution.

NOTE   It is important that this rinsing be carried out just before you begin adding the drops to the water surface. Otherwise, the petroleum ether will begin to evaporate, leaving behind on the tip of the capillary a more concentrated solution of stearic acid or even solid stearic acid. The first drops you squeezed out would then contain much more stearic acid per drop than the bulk of the solution.

Next, add the stearic acid solution drop by drop to the water surface, counting the drops. (Remember to keep the dropper vertical.) Wait about 5 to 10 s between drops. The solution will spread across the entire surface initially and will continue to do so until a complete monolayer of stearic acid has been produced. As this point is approached, the spreading will become slower and slower, until finally a drop will not spread out but will instead sit on the surface of the water (looking like a little contact lens). If this "lens" persists for about 30 s, you can safely conclude that you have added 1 drop more than is required to form a complete monolayer.

Thoroughly clean the watch glass (or get another one); rinse out the dropper with petroleum ether solvent, then with stearic acid solution several times; and repeat the experiment. Repeat until the results agree to within 2 or 3 drops.

BIBLIOGRAPHY

Boorse, H. A., and Motz, L. (eds.), "The Determination of Avogadro's Number," *The World of the Atom,* Basic Books, New York, 1966, Vol. 1, pp. 625–640. Describes Perrin's method.

Feinstein, H. I., and Sisson, R. F., III, "The Estimation of Avogadro's Number Using Cetyl Alcohol as the Monolayer," *J. Chem. Educ.* **59,** 751 (1982).

Henry, P. S., "Evaluation of Avogadro's Number" [by the method of Perrin], *J. Chem. Educ.* **43,** 251 (1966).

King, L. C., and Neilsen, E. K., "Estimation of Avogadro's Number," *J. Chem. Educ.* **35,** 198 (1958).

Robinson, A. L., "Metrology: A More Accurate Value for Avogadro's Number," *Science* **185,** 1037 (1974).

Slabaugh, W. H., "Determination of Avogadro's Number by Perrin's Law," *J. Chem. Educ.* **42,** 471 (1965).

Slabaugh, W. H., "Avogadro's Number by Four Methods," *J. Chem. Educ.* **46,** 40 (1969).

The Molar Volume of Dioxygen

PURPOSE

To determine the molar volume of a gas. To gain practical experience in making quantitative measurements of gas volumes, using Dalton's law of partial pressures and the ideal gas laws to calculate the volume of a gas at the standard temperature and pressure.

PRE-LAB PREPARATION

Avogadro's Law and the Molar Volume

This experiment deals with one of the most useful and important quantitative relationships involving gases—a relationship that depends on the following two ideas:

1. One mole of any substance contains the same number of molecules as 1 mol of any other substance. This is implied by the definition of a mole

as an Avogadro's number of anything (atoms, molecules, or any arbitrarily defined particle).

2. Equal volumes of all gases, under identical conditions of temperature and pressure, contain equal numbers of molecules.

These two ideas require that under identical conditions of temperature and pressure, 1 mol of any gas will occupy the same fixed volume, called the *molar volume of a gas*.

The Molar Volume at Standard Temperature and Pressure

The Ideal Gas

In this experiment we will measure the mass and volume of a sample of dioxygen gas, O_2, and from these data and the ideal gas law calculate the volume at standard temperature and pressure (STP) conditions (0°C, 760 torr); then we will calculate the volume of 32.0 g (1 mol) of dioxygen gas.

All real gases deviate more or less from the ideal behavior described by the general ideal gas law (described in the next section) because their molecules have some slight attraction for one another and do occupy some small volume of the container in which they are confined. An *ideal* gas is one in which the attractive forces between molecules are vanishingly small and in which the molecules would behave as "point masses" occupying a negligible volume compared with that of the container.

The molar volume of an ideal gas has been determined, from measurements on real gases, to be 22.414 L STP. This was done by calculating the molar volume (STP) at a series of progressively lower pressures and extrapolating to zero pressure, where the attractive forces between molecules and the volume occupied by the molecules are negligible. Most common gases, unless they have a high molecular weight or are measured quite near their condensation point (boiling point of the liquid), have molar volumes that do not deviate more than about 1% from the ideal volume at pressures around 1 atm.

Calculation of Gas Volumes

The quantity of a gas sample can be measured more easily by volume than by weight. In measuring the volume of a gas, it is also necessary to measure its temperature and pressure. Why? The separate laws relating pressure to volume, and relating either pressure or volume to absolute temperature, are

$$PV = k_1 \quad \text{and} \quad P = k_2 T \quad \text{or} \quad V = k_3 T$$

For a given gas sample, these three laws may be combined into one equation, which shows the way in which all three variables—pressure, volume, and absolute temperature—are interdependent:

$$PV = kT \quad \text{or} \quad \frac{PV}{T} = k \tag{1}$$

Since *any* two corresponding sets of PV/T measurements will be equal to k and to each other for a given amount of gas, we can write

$$\frac{P_1 V_1}{T_1} = \frac{P_2 V_2}{T_2} \tag{2}$$

This equation can be transposed to give

$$V_1 = V_2 \times \frac{T_1}{T_2} \times \frac{P_2}{P_1} \tag{3}$$

Note in Equations (2) and (3) that if the temperature is constant ($T_1 = T_2$), the inverse proportionality of pressure and volume (Boyle's law) is expressed. Likewise, for constant pressures ($P_1 = P_2$), the direct proportionality of volume and absolute temperature (Charles's law) is expressed. If any five of the quantities in Equation (2) are known, the sixth can of course be calculated by simple algebraic means.

The General Gas Law Equation

For a specific amount of any gas, Equation (1) can be restated in its most general form:

$$PV = nRT \tag{4}$$

Here, n is the number of moles of gas, and R is a proportionality constant, called the *gas constant*, that has the same value for all gases under all conditions, namely, 0.08206 L·atm·mol^{-1}·deg^{-1}. In all calculations in which this constant is employed, pressure must be expressed in atmospheres, volume in liters, and temperature in kelvins (represented by the symbol K).

As an example of the application of the general gas law where both volume and weight of a gas sample are involved, consider the following. What weight of chlorine gas, Cl_2, would be contained in a 5.00-L flask at 21°C and at 600 torr ($\frac{600}{760}$ atm) pressure? Substituting in Equation (4), transposed to give n, the number of moles, we have

$$PV = nRT \quad \text{or} \quad n = \frac{PV}{RT}$$

$$n = \frac{600/760 \text{ atm} \times 5.00 \text{ L}}{0.08206 \frac{\text{L atm}}{\text{mol K}} \times 294 \text{ K}}$$

$$= 0.164 \text{ mol}$$

and, in grams,

$$0.164 \text{ mol} \times 70.9 \frac{\text{g}}{\text{mol}} Cl_2 = 11.6 \text{ g } Cl_2$$

701.3 torr $\left(\dfrac{1 \text{ atm}}{760}\right)$

.923

24.75

Aqueous Vapor Pressure

Dalton's Law of Partial Pressures

When any gas in a closed container is collected over liquid water, or exposed to it, the water evaporates until a saturated vapor results—that is, until opposing rates of evaporation and condensation of water molecules at the liquid surface reach a balance. These gaseous water molecules contribute to the total gas pressure against the walls of the container. Thus, of all the gas molecules, if 3% are water molecules and 97% are oxygen molecules, then 3% of the total pressure is due to water vapor and 97% of the total pressure is due to oxygen. *Each gas exerts its own pressure regardless of the presence of other gases.* This is Dalton's law of partial pressures. Stated as an equation,

$$P_{\text{total}} = P_{\text{H}_2\text{O}} + P_{\text{O}_2}$$

or, if it is transposed,

$$P_{\text{O}_2} = P_{\text{total}} - P_{\text{H}_2\text{O}}$$

To illustrate Dalton's law, Figure 8-1 shows a mixture of oxygen molecules and water vapor molecules. In part B, the water molecules have been removed, but all the oxygen molecules are still present, in the same volume. The pressure has been reduced by an amount equal to the vapor pressure of the water.

EXPERIMENTAL PROCEDURE

Special Supplies: 200-mL Erlenmeyer flask with a No. 5 one-hole rubber stopper, 500-mL Florence flask with a No. 5 two-hole rubber stopper, 6- to 8-cm lengths of 6-mm-OD glass tubing, 30-cm length of 6-mm-OD glass tubing with a 90° bend 8 cm from one end, 10- × 75-mm test tube, 600-mL beaker, $\frac{3}{16}$-in.-ID rubber tubing, pinch clamp, thermometer, 500-mL graduated cylinder, barometer, analytical balance with a 150-g capacity.

Chemicals: 3% (approx. 0.9 M) hydrogen peroxide, 3 M FeCl₃.

Assemble the apparatus shown in Figure 8-2, taking care to lubricate each piece of glass tubing with a drop of glycerin and to wrap it in a towel while inserting it in the rubber stopper. (At this stage the 200-mL Erlenmeyer flask—flask A—will be empty. The solution and test tube will be added later.)

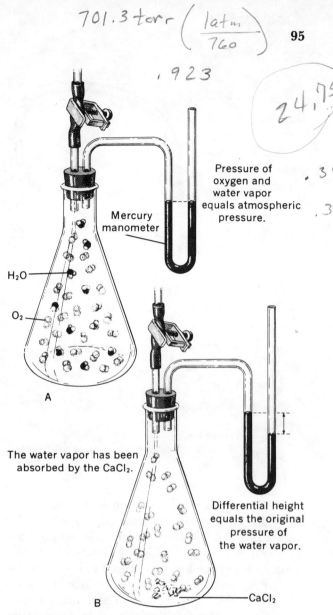

.348

.378

FIGURE 8-1
The application of Dalton's law of partial pressures when water vapor is removed from a gas mixture. Note that in this figure the gas molecules are greatly exaggerated in size.

By completely decomposing a weighed sample of H_2O_2 solution and measuring the volume of oxygen liberated at a known temperature and pressure, the molar volume of dioxygen can be determined. The reaction is the same one used in Experiment 4 to prepare oxygen:

$$H_2O_2(aq) \xrightarrow[\text{catalyst}]{\text{FeCl}_3} H_2O(l) + \tfrac{1}{2}O_2(g)$$

First measure 40 mL of 3% H_2O_2 solution in a graduated cylinder and pour it into a 200-mL Erlenmeyer flask (flask A of Figure 8-2). Next, half-fill a 10- × 75-mm test tube with 3 M FeCl₃, being careful not to get any on the outside of the

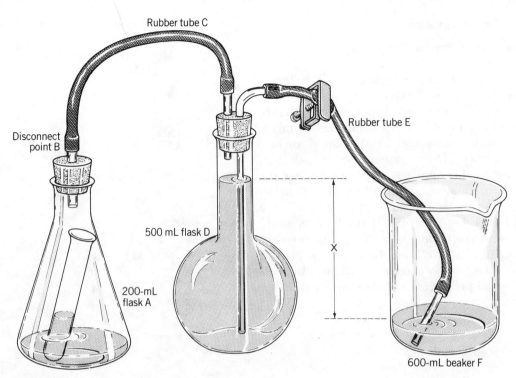

FIGURE 8-2
Apparatus for determining the molar volume of O₂.

tube. (If you spill FeCl₃ solution on the outside of the tube, rinse it off and wipe the outside of the tube dry.) Holding the 200-mL Erlenmeyer flask at about a 45° angle, slide the test tube into the flask or lower the test tube with a pair of forceps. If care is exercised, none of the FeCl₃ solution will spill. If it does spill, you must start over with a clean flask and a fresh portion of hydrogen peroxide solution.

Place the one-hole stopper, with a short length of glass tubing inserted, in the Erlenmeyer flask and seat the stopper firmly. Weigh the flask, with contents, stopper, and glass tube, as precisely as possible on the analytical balance. (The balance must have at least 150-g capacity.) Record the mass.

Fill flask D (shown in Figure 8-2) to the neck with tap water. Fill beaker F about one-third full with tap water. With the pinch clamp open, blow into rubber tube C at point B to start water siphoning into the beaker. Raise and lower beaker F to rapidly siphon water back and forth through tube E to sweep out all air bubbles. With water halfway up the neck of flask D, reconnect tube C at point B. Test the apparatus for leaks by raising beaker F as high as possible without removing the tubing from the beaker. The water level in flask

D should move a little and then remain fixed. If the water level continues to change, a leak is present. Do not proceed until the leak is fixed.

Equalize the pressures inside and outside flask D by raising the beaker until both water levels are the same. While you continue to maintain the same levels in flask D and beaker F, have another student close the pinch clamp. Pour out all of the water in beaker F, but do not dry it. Replace the tube in the beaker and open the pinch clamp. A little water will flow out, and this should be retained in the beaker. During the generation of O₂ that follows, see that the end of tube E is below the surface of the water in the beaker.

Tip the Erlenmeyer flask (flask A) carefully until the catalyst solution of FeCl₃ pours into the H₂O₂ solution. (Avoid getting any solution on the rubber stopper.) Swirl the contents of the flask to mix the reactants. Note and record any changes you see as the reaction progresses. Frequently swirl or gently shake the flask to speed the release of oxygen from the solution. After a few minutes, put your hand on the bottom of the flask. Is heat released or absorbed in the reaction?

After about 15 min, the reaction will be nearing completion. Note very carefully the water level in the beaker. Continue frequent agitation of the reaction flask. When the water level remains unchanged for at least 5 min, you can assume that the decomposition of H_2O_2 is complete.

Adjust the water levels in flask D and beaker F until they are equal. Ask another student to close the pinch clamp on tube E.

Loosen the stopper and insert your thermometer into the gas in flask A. After a minute or two, note and record the temperature. Measure and record the temperature of the gas in flask D in the same way. (In the calculations that you will make later you will take the average of these two temperatures as the temperature of the oxygen gas.)

Disconnect flask A at point B and reweigh it with its contents, rubber stopper, and glass tube. Record the mass.

Measure the volume of oxygen produced by carefully pouring the water in beaker F into a 500-mL graduated cylinder. Record the volume of water displaced by the oxygen gas. Measure and record the barometer reading and the temperature of the barometer. (The corrected barometric pressure is obtained by subtracting the temperature correction found in the *Handbook of Chemistry and Physics*. You will also need the vapor pressure of water, which can be found in Appendix B, Table B-3.)

Repeat the experiment if time permits. From your data, calculate the volume at standard temperature and pressure of 32.0 g (1 mol) of dioxygen gas, O_2.

The Composition of Air

Oxygen in Air

Carbon Dioxide in Respired Air

PURPOSE

To gain some understanding of the history of the study of air and the role of oxygen in combustion and respiration. To measure the volume percentage of oxygen in air and the volume percentage of carbon dioxide in respired air.

PRE-LAB PREPARATION

The Study of Air

In one of his notebooks the versatile artist-scientist Leonardo da Vinci (1452–1519) wrote, "Where flame cannot live no animal that draws breath can live." Like many keen observers before and after him, he noticed that air contains something vital to both combustion and respiration and, as we will see, there is a similarity between the chemical processes involved in burning and breathing.

The properties of air became the subject of intense investigation in the period 1600 to 1800. One of the first to pursue such studies systematically was the Englishman Robert Boyle (1627–1691), who was inspired by reading about Otto von Guericke's sensational experiments at Magdeburg, Germany. About 1650 von Guericke had shown that if two hollow metal hemispheres were placed base to base and the air was pumped out of the spherical interior, the pressure of the atmosphere would hold the halves together against the force exerted by two teams of six horses pulling in opposite directions.

By 1660 Boyle had published the first results of his experiments in *New Experiments: Physico-Mechanical, Touching the Spring of the Air and its Effects.* Although we mostly remember Boyle for his law that the pressure and volume of a gas are inversely related, Boyle also arrived at two other important results: (1) that air, like other material substances, has weight; and (2) that air contains a "vital quintessence" essential to animal life, although most of it serves no such purpose.

By the time 100 years had passed the study of gases (called "airs" of "elastic fluids") attracted so many practitioners scattered over the European continent and England that a term was coined to describe them. They were called *pneumatic* chemists, a word derived from the Greek word *pneuma*, meaning breath or wind.

Theories of Combustion and Respiration

During this period chemists also were struggling to understand the processes of combustion, in particular to explain how heat and light were evolved when flammable substances were burned in air. The dominant view of this period was the *phlogiston* theory, originally published by Johann Becher (1635–1682) but elaborated by his pupil Georg Ernst Stahl (1660–1734). This theory assumed that combustible substances contain an ignitable material, to which the name phlogiston (derived from the Greek *phlogistos*, meaning inflammable) was given. Charcoal, for example, was thought to be a phlogiston-rich substance. When charcoal burned in air, it was assumed that the phlogiston was released, leaving behind only ashes. Similarly, a base metal such as tin, when heated in air, was assumed to release phlogiston and leave behind an ash, or *calx* (the metal oxide).

At the time, this idea was not so unnatural or illogical as it seems to us now. We must remember that the notion that fire was a "root principle" or "element" can be traced back to the teachings of the Greek philosophers, particularly Aristotle, who suggested that there were four elements: earth, water, air, and fire. (In modern terminology we might call these "elements" by different names: solid, liquid, gas, and energy, respectively. Couched in these words the Greek ideas don't seem so strange. We might even call them reasonable conclusions, considering the state of scientific knowledge in that era.)

The phlogiston theory was described by Stahl in a book published in 1697, and it dominated the thinking and vocabulary of chemists for fully 100 years before it was overthrown, largely through the efforts of Antoine Lavoisier (1743–1794), who instigated a chemical revolution and only a few years later died by the guillotine in the social revolution that swept through France.

The ammunition that Lavoisier needed for his chemical revolution had been steadily accumulating, beginning with the experiments of Robert Boyle almost 100 years earlier. With the aid of his vacuum pump Boyle showed that sulfur and other combustible materials could not burn without air. In the years that followed, the pneumatic chemists showed that when a burning candle (or a mouse) was placed in a bell jar over a container of water, the water would rise inside the bell jar, suggesting that something in the air was being used up. It was also recognized by Jan Ingenhousz (1730–1799) that plants (with the aid of sunlight) could reverse the process, restoring the air to its normal state.

The Discovery of Oxygen

The substance in air that is necessary for combustion and respiration we know as oxygen, O_2. It was first made and described by Carl Wilhelm Scheele (1742–1786) and Joseph Priestley (1733–1804), each working independently about the same time, although Priestley's work was published before that of Scheele.

On August 1, 1774, Priestley prepared his first sample of oxygen by heating red mercuric oxide confined in a glass tube filled with mercury. To avoid having to heat the whole apparatus, he used a large "burning lens" with a diameter of about 12 in., which allowed him to focus the sun's rays on the powder inside the tube. As the mercuric oxide decomposed it produced mercury and oxygen, so the gas that formed in the tube was nearly pure oxygen.

Only two months later Priestley accompanied Lord Sherburne, by whom he was employed as a literary companion, on a trip to Paris. During this trip Priestley was invited by Lavoisier to a dinner where Priestley told him of his new discovery.

Priestley called the pure oxygen he had prepared "dephlogisticated air." This terminology was consistent with his belief in the phlogiston theory, which assumed that ordinary air becomes loaded with the phlogiston released when substances are burned in air or when animals breathe, so the air gradually becomes unfit to support combustion or respiration.

Within a year of his dinner with Priestley, Lavoisier had performed a number of experiments on his own and had written a memoir describing the results. Although Lavoisier discovered no new substances and devised no important new apparatus, he was able to utilize the work of his contemporaries (particularly Black, Cavendish, and Priestley) in conjunction with his own experiments in order to devise a completely new theory of the role of oxygen in combustion and respiration. By careful reasoning he countered all of the arguments of the phlogistonists, proposing that all of the facts could be more easily explained by assuming that when a substance such as charcoal burns it loses weight not by loss of phlogiston, but by combination of the charcoal with a substance contained in air to form a gaseous substance. Lavoisier called this gaseous product carbonic acid; we now call it carbon dioxide. Similarly, he showed, by carrying out combustions in sealed flasks, that when phosphorus was heated in air, light and heat were produced but there was no change in the weight of the sealed flask. From this result he concluded that phlogiston, if it existed, could not be a material substance.

In his studies on respiration, Lavoisier put a sparrow in a bell jar filled with air, allowing the bird to die. He observed that the air breathed by the sparrow had become very different from ordinary air: It formed a precipitate with lime water, it extinguished a burning candle, and it no longer reacted with nitric oxide as normal air does. These properties were exactly those of air in which charcoal had been burned, and from these results Lavoisier concluded that either the respirable part of the air (oxygen) is converted into carbonic acid (CO_2) as it passes through the lungs, or else an exchange takes place in which the respirable part of the air is absorbed while the lungs give out in its place nearly the same volume of carbonic acid. Later, after further measurements, Lavoisier found a discrepancy between the amounts of oxygen removed from the air and of carbon dioxide exhaled and concluded that "either a portion of the vital air (oxygen) combines with the blood, or it combines with a portion of hydrogen to form water." This is very near the modern view except that we know that the reaction takes place not just in the lungs but in all of the cells of the body.

The Roots of Modern Chemical Nomenclature

Lavoisier early recognized that his new theory would require that the useless baggage of terms and vocabulary used by the phlogistonists be discarded. A new system of chemical nomenclature was imperative. The development of this system, very like the one we use today, was supervised by Guyton de Morveau, aided by Lavoisier, Berthollet, and de Fourcroy. Their Méthode de Nomenclature Chimique was published in 1787 and soon translated into English. In it they proposed the name oxygen for the new substance discovered by Scheele and Priestley, a name derived from the Greek words meaning acid forming, because oxygen was known to form acidic substances when it reacted with carbon, phosphorus, and sulfur.

Lavoisier almost immediately began to write a textbook to illustrate the new nomenclature and to describe in detail the new theory of chemistry. This book is a landmark in chemistry, just as Newton's Principia is in mechanics. Published first in 1789 in Paris under the title Traité Elémentaire de Chimie (Elements of Chemistry), it reads like a rather old edition of a modern textbook, whereas the books on chemistry written before Lavoisier's time would be difficult for a student unacquainted with the history of chemistry to understand.

In the preface to his book Lavoisier quotes a maxim from Logic, a work by the Abbé de Condillac, which reveals why Lavoisier thought it was so important to establish a new system of nomenclature: "We think only through the medium of words.—Languages are true analytical methods.—The art of reasoning is nothing more than a language well arranged."

Respiration as Intracellular Combustion

The new theory of combustion and respiration was so compelling that by 1800 it had completely displaced the phlogiston theory. By 1875 there was little doubt that animal and plant tissues consume oxygen and release carbon dioxide (and water) in a process comparable to combustion, but it was clear that this process is not identical with the rapid and complete burning of carbon-containing compounds in a furnace. Lavoisier thought the "furnace" was in the lungs. Later the reactions were thought to take place in the blood, but we now know that the reactions take place in the cells of all living tissues, the oxygen and carbon dioxide being transported between the cells and the lungs by the circulation of the blood. Detailed studies made in the 20th century have shown that the process by which the body converts carbon- and hydrogen-containing fuels (such as carbohydrates and fats) to carbon dioxide and water involves a complex sequence of reactions that are catalyzed by types of proteins (called *enzymes*) that are made in the cells.

Measuring the Oxygen Content of Air

To measure the amount of oxygen in air we will use the same principle employed by the pneumatic chemists—a sample of air will be trapped in a glass tube along with something that uses up all of the oxygen in the tube, allowing the water to rise in the tube. Rather than use a candle or a mouse, we will employ the reaction of oxygen with iron in the form of steel wool. When conditions are arranged properly, oxygen reacts rapidly and completely with the iron, as described by the following (unbalanced) reaction (the balancing of this reaction will be left as an exercise for you):

$$Fe + O_2 + xH_2O \rightarrow Fe_2O_3 \cdot xH_2O \qquad (1)$$

This reaction is more complex than just the direct combination of oxygen with iron. It also requires the presence of water and is accelerated by acids. (The x moles of H_2O that appear on both sides of the equation indicate that the hydrated iron oxide ($Fe_2O_3 \cdot xH_2O$) that forms contains a variable amount of water.) However, the solution in contact with the iron must not be allowed to become too acidic; otherwise some hydrogen will form by the reaction

$$Fe + 2H^+ \rightarrow Fe^{2+} + H_2 \qquad (2)$$

Measuring the Carbon Dioxide in Respired Air

In some of his studies on respiration, Lavoisier employed the following reaction to remove carbon dioxide from the respired air so that he could measure the volume of other gases present (the balancing of this reaction will be left as an exercise for you):

$$CO_2(g) + NaOH(aq) \rightarrow Na_2CO_3(aq) + H_2O(l)$$

$$(3)$$

If we carry out the reaction in a system with constant volume, the absorption of the carbon dioxide gas by the sodium hydroxide solution to form the salt sodium carbonate will cause a de-

TABLE 9-1

	Composition (% by volume) of clean dry air near sea level*	Composition (% by volume) of respired air, dried to remove water†
N_2	78.09	78.1
O_2	20.94	16.4
Ar (argon)	0.93	0.9
CO_2	0.032	4.5

* From *Cleaning Our Environment: The Chemical Basis for Action*, The American Chemical Society, Washington, D.C., 1969.
† Adapted from A. White, P. Handler, and E. L. Smith, *Principles of Biochemistry*, 5th ed., McGraw-Hill, New York, 1973, Table 31-2.

crease in pressure in the closed system. This pressure decrease is a measure of the amount of carbon dioxide present in the gas.

The Composition of Clean Air and Respired Air

Table 9-1 gives the composition of clean dry air near sea level and the approximate composition of respired air (dried to remove water). The latter composition is variable, depending on how deeply the subject breathes and how long the breath is held before exhalation.

Both normal air and respired air contain water. If you know the partial pressure of water in the sample, it is easy to recalculate the values given in Table 9-1 to express the volume percentage composition in moist air by using the expression

vol % moist air

$$= \text{vol \% dry air} \times \frac{P_T - P_{H_2O}}{P_T} \quad (4)$$

where P_T is the total pressure (usually the barometric pressure) of the gas and P_{H_2O} is the partial pressure of the water. The volume percentage of water will be given by

$$\text{vol \% } H_2O = \frac{P_{H_2O}}{P_T} \times 100 \qquad (5)$$

EXPERIMENTAL PROCEDURE

Special Supplies: Oxygen in air experiment: fine (size 00) steel wool, 8-in. metal forceps, 1000-mL beaker, ring stand, two clamps, masking tape, two 20- × 150-mm culture tubes (lipless test tube), No. 6 solid rubber stopper, thermometer, barometer.

Carbon dioxide in respired air experiment: 500-mL Erlenmeyer flask with two-hole rubber stopper, plastic vial (approx. 15-mL capacity), transparent tape, 30 cm of thread, one 8-cm and one 14-cm length of 6-mm-OD glass tubing, 75-cm length of 6- to 7-mm-OD × 1- to 1.5-mm-ID glass capillary tubing, plastic or glass T-connector, $\frac{3}{16}$-in.-ID rubber or polyvinyl chloride (PVC) tubing, plastic drinking straws, two pinch (or screw) clamps, meter stick, ring stand and clamp, water-soluble dye (food coloring), thermometer, barometer.

Chemicals: Oxygen in air experiment: acetone, 1.0 M acetic acid, 0.1 M acetic acid. Carbon dioxide in respired air experiment: 6 M NaOH, mineral oil.

Safety Precautions: Oxygen in air experiment: The procedure for washing the steel wool in acetone should be carried out in a fume hood. Avoid breathing the acetone vapor or spilling it on your skin. Acetone is a flammable solvent. There must be no open flames in the hood.

Carbon dioxide in respired air experiment: Take care to moisten the glass tubing with glycerol or water and to wrap the tubing in a towel while inserting it in the rubber stopper. *Sodium hydroxide solution causes skin and eye burns. Handle with are.*

1. Oxygen in Air   Attach a strip of masking tape (on which to mark the water level) to a 20- × 150-mm culture tube (lipless test tube). Prepare a clamp and ring stand so that the test tube can be mounted, inverted, in a 1-L beaker filled with tap water. (See Figure 9-1.)

Weigh two 1.0-g portions of fine (size 00) steel wool. Do not compress the material. Your instructor will place a beaker of acetone in the hood. In addition, put 100 mL each of 1.0 M acetic acid and 0.1 M acetic acid in the hood in separate beakers. Fresh acetone and 1.0 M acetic acid are needed after two or three students have used them. The 0.1 M acetic acid should be freshly poured by each student.

Using forceps, rinse one of the pieces of steel wool in acetone for about 30 s to remove any oily material from the surface of the steel wool. Shake off the excess acetone, drain the steel wool briefly on a paper towel in the hood, and transfer it to the 1.0 M acetic acid solution. With your forceps, agitate the steel wool occasionally for about a minute. Then shake off the excess, drain on a paper towel briefly, and put the steel wool in the beaker containing 0.1 M acetic acid, agitating it for about 30 s. Using forceps, remove the steel wool and shake it vigorously to remove as much solution as possible. Then insert the steel wool in the 20- × 150-mm culture tube, pushing it to the bottom half of the tube. Do not compress the steel wool. It should be spread over most of the bottom half of the test tube.

Immediately invert the test tube and carefully lower it into the beaker of water and clamp it in

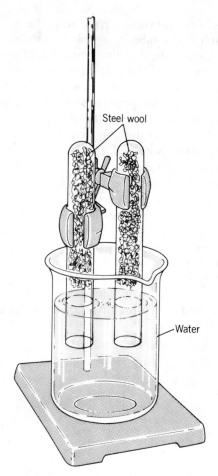

FIGURE 9-1
Apparatus for measuring the oxygen in air.

position. The mouth of the test tube must be below the water level throughout the experiment. The initial volume of air is assumed to be the total volume of the test tube (minus the volume of steel wool and adhering solution, which will be determined later).

Rinse the forceps in tap water and dry. At 5- to 10- min intervals, mark the rising water level on the masking tape. Using a second test tube, prepare the remaining piece of steel wool and carry out a duplicate run.

While you are waiting for the reaction to be completed, weigh a clean dry 250-mL beaker to the nearest 0.1 g (don't use the analytical balance). Record its mass.

When no further change in water level can be detected (usually 20 to 30 min are required), wait 5 min longer, then adjust the height of the test tube so that the water levels inside and outside the tube are the same. (When the levels are the same, the pressure inside the tube will be equal to the atmospheric pressure.) Now trap the water that has risen in the tube by pressing a rubber stopper firmly against the mouth of the tube. (The stopper should be larger than the mouth of the tube so that it does not enter the tube.) Ask a laboratory neighbor to unclamp the tube while you are holding the stopper against the mouth of the tube. Carefully transfer the water you have trapped into the previously weighed 250-mL beaker. Reweigh and record the mass of the beaker plus water. The volume of this water corresponds to the volume of oxygen that has reacted with the steel wool.

With forceps, remove the steel wool and put it in the same previously weighed beaker containing the water. Reweigh and record the mass. Finally, fill the empty test tube to the brim with water and add it to the same beaker and reweigh and record the mass again. The initial mass of the empty beaker and the subsequent three weighings will provide data from which you can calculate the total volume of the test tube, correcting for the volume occupied by the steel wool and adhering acetic acid solution.

Record the temperature of the tap water in the beaker and the barometric pressure. These data will enable you to make the necessary corrections in order to calculate the volume percentage of oxygen in moist air, a number that you can directly compare with your experimental result.

2. *Carbon Dioxide in Respired Air*   Assemble the apparatus shown in Figure 9-2, excluding the plastic vial, which will be put in the 500-mL Erlenmeyer flask later. The capillary tubing should be clamped in position so that it is standing in a 100-mL beaker containing 50 mL of water colored with a few drops of food dye to make the column of water in the capillary tubing easily visible.

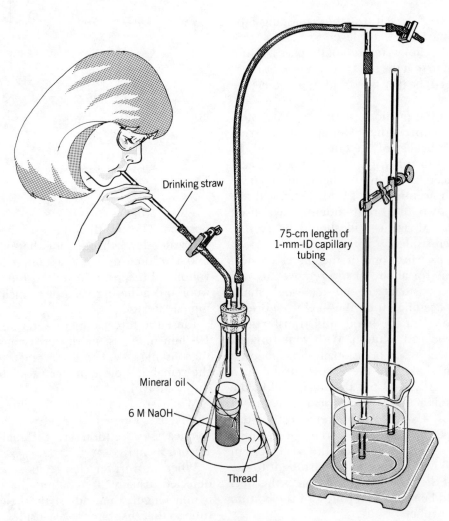

Drinking straw

75-cm length of 1-mm-ID capillary tubing

Mineral oil

6 M NaOH

Thread

FIGURE 9-2
Apparatus for measuring carbon dioxide in respired air.

Moisten the 14-cm and 8-cm lengths of 6-mm-OD tubing with a drop or two of glycerol, wrap them in a towel, and insert them into the two-hole rubber stopper. The lower end of the longer piece of tubing should be about 6 cm above the bottom of the flask when the stopper is inserted. The plastic drinking straw (used for sanitary reasons) should be connected to the longer tube in the rubber stopper. All connections must be snug and gas tight. Place the screw clamps in position.

Cut an 8-cm length of thread and tape the ends to opposite sides near the top of the plastic vial to form a bridle (see Figure 9-2). (A plastic vial is preferred because later the vial will be shaken inside the flask, and a glass vial shaken in a glass flask makes a terrible racket.) Tie another 22-cm length of thread to the center of the bridle so that the vial can be lowered without tipping into the flask. Place about 10 mL of 6 M NaOH in the plastic vial. (*Warning*: NaOH will burn your skin or eyes. Handle with care.) Pour a thin layer (5 to 6 mm) of mineral oil on top of the NaOH. Now carefully lower the vial into the Erlenmeyer flask, being very careful that the vial does not tip over. (If it tips, you must start again with a clean flask.) Drop the end of the thread inside the flask and seat the stopper firmly in place.

Open the screw clamps. With the system open, but with the end of the capillary tube immersed in the beaker of colored water, take a breath of air, hold it for a moment, and exhale completely through the plastic straw. Remove your lips from the straw and inhale. Exhale through the straw again. Repeat this process five times so that the flask is completely flushed out with respired air.

Immediately close both of the screw clamps. Measure and record the distance (in millimeters) between the top of the water column in the capillary tube and the surface of the water in the beaker.

Tip the vial inside the flask. Swirl and shake the flask gently. Periodically measure and record the height of the water column in the capillary tube. The water should rise several hundred millimeters. If it doesn't, there is probably a leak in the system.

When the water has stopped rising, measure and record the distance (in millimeters) between the top of the column of water in the capillary tubing and the water level in the beaker. Also measure and record the barometric pressure and the temperature in (or near) the flask.

The sodium hydroxide solution reacts with and completely absorbs the carbon dioxide. This causes a decrease in the pressure in the flask, so that the atmospheric pressure outside is greater than the pressure in the flask. This pressure difference forces the water in the capillary to rise. The height of the column of water in the capillary is a measure of the pressure difference and is proportional to the partial pressure of CO_2 that was in the original sample of gas. The volume percentage of CO_2 in the moist respired air is obtained by dividing the partial pressure of CO_2 by the barometric pressure. We should be careful to note, however, that some water in the respired air contained in the flask will condense because the temperature of the flask is lower than that of the lungs. The experiment measures the volume percentage of CO_2 in moist respired air at the temperature of the flask.

BIBLIOGRAPHY

Birk, J. P., McGrath, L., and Gunter, S. K., "A General Chemistry Experiment for the Determination of the Oxygen Content of Air," *J. Chem. Educ.* **58**, 804–805 (1981).

REPORT

9

**Oxygen in Air
Carbon Dioxide
in Respired Air**

NAME

SECTION   LOCKER

INSTRUCTOR   DATE

DATA AND CALCULATIONS

1. Oxygen in Air

Data   *Trial 1*   *Trial 2*

(a) Mass of steel wool (Fe) _____ g   _____ g

(b) Mass of empty 250-mL beaker _____ g   _____ g

(c) Mass of beaker + water trapped in tube _____ g   _____ g

(d) Mass of beaker + water + steel wool _____ g   _____ g

(e) Mass recorded in part 1(d) + water required to completely fill _____ g   _____ g
the tube

(f) Barometric pressure _____ torr   _____ torr

(g) Temperature of water in 1-L beaker _____ °C   _____ °C

Calculations

(h) Calculate the volume of oxygen in the moist air from the mass of water trapped in the tube [mass 1(c) − mass 1(b)] and the density of water. (Assume the density of water to be 0.997 g/mL.)

_____ mL   _____ mL

(i) Calculate the correction for the volume of the steel wool. (Assume that the density of the steel wool is 7.7 g/mL.)

$$\text{vol steel wool} = \text{g Fe} \times \frac{1 \text{ mL}}{7.7 \text{ g Fe}}$$

_____ mL   _____ mL

(j) Calculate the correction for the volume of the adhering solution. (Assume that the density of the solution is that of pure water.)

$$\text{vol soln} = \text{g soln} \times \frac{1 \text{ mL}}{0.997 \text{ g soln}}$$

where g soln = mass 1(d) − mass 1(c) − g Fe.

_____ mL   _____ mL

(k) Calculate the volume of the test tube.

$$\text{vol tube} = [\text{mass 1(e)} - \text{mass 1(d)}] \times \frac{1 \text{ mL}}{0.997 \text{ g}}$$

_____ mL _____ mL

(l) Calculate the volume of air in the tube.

$$V(\text{air}) = V(\text{h}) - V(\text{i}) - V(\text{j})$$

_____ mL _____ mL

(m) Calculate the volume percentage of oxygen in moist air.

$$\text{vol } \% \text{ O}_2 = \frac{V(\text{O}_2)}{V(\text{air})} \times 100$$

_____ % _____ %

(n) Calculate the volume percentage of oxygen in moist air from the data in Table 9-1 by using Equation (4)

$$\text{vol } \% \text{ O}_2 \text{ in moist air} = 20.94 \times \frac{P_T - P_{H_2O}}{P_T}$$

where P_T is the barometric pressure recorded in part 1(f) and P_{H_2O} is the vapor pressure of water at the temperature recorded in part 1(g). (The vapor pressure can be found in Appendix B, Table B-3.)

_____ % _____ %

(o) Calculate the relative error (as a percentage).

$$\text{percentage of relative error} = \frac{\% \text{ O}_2(\text{m}) - \% \text{ O}_2(\text{n})}{\% \text{ O}_2(\text{n})} \times 100$$

_____ % _____ %

2. Carbon Dioxide in Respired Air

Data

(a) Initial height of the column of water above the surface of the water in the beaker (before tipping the vial) _____ mm

(b) Final height of the column of water above the surface of the water in the beaker (after tipping the vial) _____ mm

(c) Barometric pressure _____ torr

(d) Temperature of the gas in the flask _____ °C

Calculations

(e) Partial pressure of CO_2. The final height of the column of water minus the initial height is equal to the partial pressure of CO_2 in millimeters of water (mm H_2O). Convert this value to an equivalent partial pressure in millimeters of mercury, mm Hg (torr) by dividing the height (in mm H_2O) by the specific gravity of mercury (13.5). (The specific gravity of mercury is the density of mercury divided by the density of water.)

$$P_{CO_2} = \text{\underline{\hspace{2cm}}} \text{ mmHg (torr)}$$

(f) Calculate the volume percentage of CO_2 in the moist respired air.

$$\text{vol \% } CO_2 = \frac{P_{CO_2}}{P_T} \times 100 = \text{\underline{\hspace{2cm}}} \%$$

(g) Compare your calculated value in part 2(f) with the approximate value from Table 9-1, corrected to account for the vapor pressure of water:

$$\text{vol \% } CO_2 = 4.5 \times \frac{P_T - P_{H_2O}}{P_T} = \text{\underline{\hspace{2cm}}} \%$$

where P_T is the barometric pressure recorded in part 2(c) and P_{H_2O} is the vapor pressure of water at the temperature recorded in part 2(d). (The vapor pressure of water can be found in Appendix B, Table B-3.)

QUESTIONS

1. If the solution used to saturate the steel wool in part 1 of the Experimental Procedure is too acidic, some hydrogen can be generated. Iron *reduces* H^+ (or reacts with H^+ in a *displacement* reaction) to form hydrogen gas: $Fe + 2H^+ \rightarrow Fe^{2+} + H_2(g)$. If this happened, would the measured volume percentage of O_2 be high or low? Explain.

2. Calculate the moles of Fe in 1.0 g of Fe (steel wool).

   Calculate the moles of O_2 in the volume of O_2 contained in the tube. (Assume that $V_{O_2} = 6$ mL at 25°C and 1 atm pressure.)

   Is the mole ratio, mol Fe/mol O_2, large enough to ensure that there is an excess of Fe above that required to react with the O_2? (See Equation (1) in the Pre-lab Preparation to determine the stoichiometric ratio required.)

3. From the volume percentage of CO_2 in clean dry air (see Table 9-1), calculate the partial pressure of CO_2 (in mm Hg) in clean dry air. (Assume that $P_T = 760$ mm Hg.) If you were to repeat the experiment to measure CO_2 in air, substituting clean dry air for the respired air, how high (in mm H_2O) would you expect the column of water to rise? (If you have time, you might try to verify this result by doing the experiment, starting with a clean flask.)

The Molar Mass of a Gas

PURPOSE

To determine the molar mass of a gas by measuring the mass of a known volume of gas at the ambient laboratory temperature and pressure as determined by a thermometer and barometer. (If ideal gas behavior is assumed, knowledge of these four quantities—mass, volume, pressure, and temperature—allows the calculation of the molar mass from the ideal gas law.) To understand the relationship between gas density and buoyancy.

PRE-LAB PREPARATION

In prior experiments we discussed Avogadro's law, estimated Avogadro's number, and determined the molar volume of oxygen. To refresh your memory, let's restate Avogadro's law: *Equal volumes of gases contain equal numbers of molecules.* This means that any time we take an Avogadro's number of molecules of a particular gas (which is the definition of 1 mol) we can expect that the volume of

gas will be the same as the volume of 1 mol of any other gas. (This expectation is, of course, subject to the usual restrictions that the gases must behave as ideal gases and that the volumes must be measured at the same pressure and temperature.) We determined the molar volume of oxygen at the standard temperature and pressure and found it to be about 22.4 L. From this result and Avogadro's law we can draw the important general conclusion that *1 mol of any gas will occupy 22.4 L STP and the mass of the gas will be the molar mass of the gas in grams.*

Of course we do not have to measure the volume of the gas at 0°C and 1 atm. We can measure the volume at any temperature and pressure and correct to the standard conditions by using the ideal gas law, $P_1 V_1 / T_1 = P_2 V_2 / T_2$, or its equivalent form, $PV = nRT$. Thus we can determine the molar mass of any gas, whether it is a permanent gas or the vapor of a volatile liquid or solid, if we can determine the mass of a known volume of the gas at a known temperature and pressure.

In this experiment we will measure the mass and volume of a sample of gas at the laboratory temperature and pressure. In principle this can be done by taking a bulb (or some other container), evacuating it so that we can get the mass of the completely empty bulb, then filling the bulb with the unknown gas, and weighing it again. The difference in masses would give us the mass of the gas, and if we measure the volume of the bulb and know the pressure and temperature of the gas, we can calculate its molar mass.

However, an evacuable glass bulb and a vacuum pump are not always available, so we are going to determine the mass of the empty container by weighing it filled with air and subtracting the mass of the air, which we can calculate if we know the volume of the container and the density of air (given in various reference handbooks). Subtracting the calculated mass of air gives the mass of the empty container, and the difference between this mass and the mass of the container filled with an unknown gas will of course give the mass of the unknown gas.

Various gases, such as helium (He), nitrogen (N_2), nitrous oxide (N_2O), carbon dioxide (CO_2), sulfur hexafluoride (SF_6), and Freons (chlorofluoromethanes), can be used in this experiment. (The use of flammable or toxic gases is not advised.)

When tanks of compressed gases are available, they are convenient, but by preparing your own sample of gas you will have an opportunity to learn some chemistry. In the Experimental Procedure, directions will be given for the preparation of carbon dioxide.

Gas Density and Buoyancy

The density of a gas is equal to its mass divided by the volume it occupies at a particular temperature and pressure. The density is directly proportional to the molecular weight, as can be seen by deriving a modified form of the ideal gas law. Let's start with the ideal gas law in the form

$$PV = nRT \tag{1}$$

where P is the pressure, V is the volume, n is the number of moles of gas, R is the gas constant, and T is the Kelvin, or absolute, temperature (K). The number of moles, n, can also be expressed as the mass of the gas, m, divided by the molar mass of the gas, M (take a moment to verify that the units are correct):

$$n = \frac{m}{M} \tag{2}$$

We can substitute m/M for n in Equation (1) and rearrange the resulting equation to obtain the density of the gas, m/V:

$$\frac{m}{V} = \frac{PM}{RT} \tag{3}$$

From Equation (3), we see that the density, m/V, is proportional to the molar mass of the gas, M.

If we fill a lightweight container, such as a balloon, with a gas that has a density much less than the density of air, we may find that when we try to weigh the balloon of gas on a balance it floats. Why is this?

The atmosphere is like an ocean of air, and when an object is immersed in air it displaces air just as your body displaces water when you jump into a swimming pool. Just as you can float in water, the balloon will float and rise in the air if the combined mass of the balloon and the gas in it is less than the mass of the air that is displaced. Since the pressure (and density) of air decreases with altitude (note the effect on density of decreasing P in Equation (3)), the balloon will expand as it rises and will either explode or stop rising when it reaches an altitude where the mass of air displaced and the mass of the balloon plus the gas are equal. You can easily observe this buoyancy effect by using a lighter-than-air gas (such as natural gas, which is largely methane, CH_4) to blow bubbles in a soap solution, and then repeating the experiment with a heavier-than-air gas (such as carbon dioxide, CO_2).

Hot-air and lighter-than-air balloonists are able to enjoy their sport by filling their balloons with a gas that is less dense than air. Hot-air balloons use propane heaters at the base of the balloon to heat air. Hot air is less dense than cold air. (Note the effect on the density of a gas of increasing T in Equation (3).) Lighter-than-air balloonists use a gas with a low molecular weight, such as helium, to obtain the necessary lower density. (Note the effect of decreasing M in Equation (3).)

The effect of buoyancy must also be considered when very accurate weighings are made, particularly for substances, such as water, that have a density less than the density of the standard weights in the balance. A sample placed on the balance pan displaces a certain amount of air. A similar effect applies to the removable weights of the balance. There will be a net effect of *buoyancy* (apparent mass less than the true mass) whenever the density of the object being weighed is less than the density of the standard weights, which are made of stainless steel for the most commonly encountered single-pan balances. (The density of stainless steel is 7.76 g/mL.)

The magnitude of the buoyancy factor is illustrated by a few examples. When water is weighed (density 1.00 g/mL), the true mass is 1.001 g when the balance reads 1.000 g. The error is -0.1% in this case. For NaCl (density 2.16 g/mL), the error would be -0.04%. For $AgNO_3$ (density 4.35 g/mL), the error is only -0.01%.

When obtaining a mass by difference, as we did in determining the molar volume of oxygen by weighing, decomposing, and reweighing a sample of dilute H_2O_2 solution, the buoyancy correction

for the water and container cancels out. In most of the experiments you will do in this laboratory the buoyancy corrections will be negligible.

EXPERIMENTAL PROCEDURE

NOTE TO INSTRUCTOR   Tell the students whether they will use compressed gases (Method A) or the gas generator shown in Figure 10-1 to generate CO_2 (Method B). If compressed gases are used, you may want to wrap the cylinders or lecture bottles with paper to conceal the identity

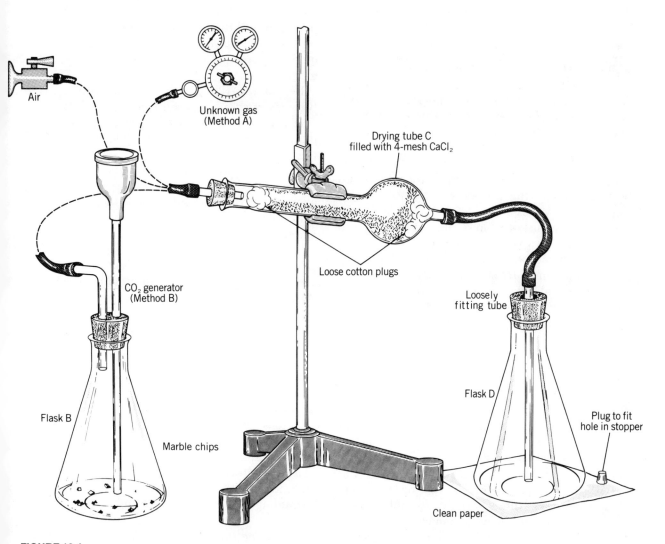

Air

Unknown gas
(Method A)

Drying tube C
filled with 4-mesh CaCl₂

Loose cotton plugs

CO_2 generator
(Method B)

Loosely
fitting tube

Flask B

Flask D

Marble chips

Plug to fit
hole in stopper

Clean paper

FIGURE 10-1
Apparatus for determining the molar mass of a gas. Flask D is filled with dry air, weighed, then filled with an unknown gas (or CO_2) and weighed again.

of the gas, and have the students identify the gas from a list of gases posted in the laboratory.

The experiment calls for first filling the flask with clean dry air. If house compressed air is not available, the flasks can be weighed filled with moist ambient air and the density of the moist ambient air calculated from the formula given as Equation (4) on page 119. Tell the students which procedure should be used.

Special Supplies: Thermometer, barometer, calcium chloride drying tube with one-hole stoppers, No. 4 one-hole rubber stopper bored out to 8-mm-diameter hole with cork or rubber stopper to plug the hole, 6-mm-OD glass tubing, cotton, $\frac{3}{16}$-in.-ID rubber tubing, ring stand and clamp, source of clean dry compressed air; nonflammable, nontoxic compressed gases in cylinders or lecture bottles if Method A is to be used. (Suitable gases include He, Ar, N_2, O_2, N_2O, CO_2, SF_6, and Freons.) If the students are to generate CO_2 by Method B, a thistle tube, a 200-mL Erlenmeyer flask with a two-hole rubber stopper, and a 6-mm-OD glass tube with a right-angle bend will be required (see Figure 10-1).

Chemicals: 4-mesh anhydrous calcium chloride, $CaCl_2$, for the drying tube; marble chips (calcium carbonate, $CaCO_3$) and 6 M HCl for CO_2 generation if Method B is to be used.

Safety Precautions: It is recommended that no toxic or flammable gases be used in this experiment. Even with this precaution it is recommended that you fill your flasks in a fume hood.

All cylinders should be chained or securely fastened so that they cannot topple, and you should be instructed in the proper way to use the gas regulators or valves.

Carefully adjust the flow rates of compressed air or unknown gas *before* connecting the tubing to the drying tube to avoid accidents resulting from sudden pressure surges.

If you assemble your own apparatus to generate CO_2, take care to lubricate the glass tubing and wrap it in a towel before inserting it in the rubber stopper.

Determining the Mass of the Flask Filled with Air The setup shown in Figure 10-1 is used to fill a flask with clean dry air. (If house compressed air is not available, the flask is weighed filled with the moist ambient air of the laboratory.) Obtain a clean and thoroughly dry 125-mL Erlenmeyer flask, preferably one that has been oven dried and allowed to cool just before it is to be used. The flask should be fitted with a one-hole rubber stopper, bored out to have a diameter about 2 mm larger than the glass tube, so that gas passing through the tube can flow out at the top through the annular space between the tube and stopper. The glass tube is connected by a section of rubber

tubing to a drying tube (C) filled with 4-mesh calcium chloride, which is protected at each end by a loose plug of cotton. Adjust the compressed-air valve to give a very gentle flow of air, then connect it to the other end of the drying tube with a short section of rubber tubing. Pass a gentle stream of dried air through flask D for at least 5 min.

Gently withdraw the glass tubing (through which you have been passing clean dry air into flask D), quickly plug the hole with a small cork or rubber stopper, and weigh this flask, including the one-hole rubber stopper and plug, to an accuracy of at least 0.001 g. Record the mass on your report sheet. (*You must use the same cork or rubber plug throughout the entire experiment, so put it in a safe place whenever it is necessary to remove it.*) After the weighing, avoid all unnecessary handling of the flask. Handle it by the rim or wrap a small piece of paper around the neck to keep greasy fingerprints off the flask. Place the flask on a clean dry square of paper to avoid contamination from the bench top.

Repeat the filling and weighing process. The two masses should agree to within 1 to 3 mg.

If compressed air is not available, use a flask that has been oven dried and allowed to cool in the ambient laboratory air. Fit it with a one-hole stopper and plug, as described above, and weigh this assembly. Then remove the stopper and plug, allow the flask to stand open to the ambient air for 10 min, put the stopper and plug back in, and reweigh.

Determining the Mass of the Flask Filled with an Unknown Gas by Using Compressed Gases (Method A) Connect a rubber tube to the outlet valve of a cylinder or lecture bottle of an unknown gas. Have your instructor adjust the flow rate to about 100 to 200 mL/min by displacement of water in an inverted graduated cylinder. Then connect the tube to the inlet of the drying tube, insert the glass tube on the outlet of the drying tube into flask D, and allow at least 1 L of gas to flow through flask D. (This will require 5 to 10 min at the recommended flow rate.) Remove the glass tube from flask D, quickly insert the plug, and weigh the flask as before. Repeat the filling and weighing operation with the same gas. The two masses should agree to within 1 to 3 mg.

Determining the Mass of the Flask Filled by Means of the Carbon Dioxide Generator (Method B) Prepare the carbon dioxide generator shown in Figure 10-1. Use a 200- or 250-mL Erlenmeyer flask that has a thistle tube[1] reaching almost to the bottom and that has a short right-angle exit tube, to be connected to the calcium chloride drying tube when you are ready to generate the gas. Place about 30 g of marble chips ($CaCO_3$) in the generator and add about 20 mL of water to cover the end of the thistle tube. Do not add acid until you are ready to generate carbon dioxide. Put flask D in position with the glass tube passing through the one-hole rubber stopper. When ready, add 6 M HCl through the thistle tube, a little at a time as needed, so as to maintain a gentle, but fairly rapid, evolution of CO_2 gas. (You may momentarily pinch the tubing between C and D and note the rate at which liquid backs up in the thistle tube, in order to estimate the rate at which gas is being generated.)

Let the generator run for at least 20 min to displace all the air in flask D by CO_2 gas. Finally, withdraw the glass tube from the flask and quickly insert the plug in the stopper. Without undue handling, weigh the flask. Repeat the filling operation again by passing CO_2 through the flask for another 10 to 15 min. Reweigh the flask. The two weights should agree to within 1 to 3 mg.

Determining the Temperature, Pressure, and Volume of the Gas   Take the temperature of the gas with a thermometer placed in the gas shortly after the last weighing. Record the barometric pressure. To measure the exact volume of the flask to the bottom of the stopper, fill the flask with water to the brim, replace the stopper, insert the plug in the stopper, and wipe off any excess water. Weigh the full flask on the platform balance to the nearest 0.5 g. (*Do not weigh the flask full of water on the analytical balance. Use a more rugged platform balance.* Note also

that milligram accuracy is not required for this weight: Why not?) How does the mass of water enable you to calculate the volume? Look up in a reference source[2] the density of dry air at the laboratory temperature and pressure. Enter all data and calculations on your report sheet.

If you filled the flask with the moist ambient air of the laboratory rather than dry air, calculate the density of the moist air from the expression

$$D(\text{g/mL}) = 0.001293 \times \frac{273}{T}$$
$$\times \frac{(P - 0.378(\text{RH})P_{H_2O})}{760} \qquad (4)$$

where D is the density in grams per milliliter of the air; T is the absolute temperature (°C + 273); P is the barometric pressure in torr (mmHg); and RH is the relative humidity. (If you don't know the relative humidity it will be sufficiently accurate to assume that RH = 0.5, which corresponds to a 50% relative humidity.) P_{H_2O} is the vapor pressure of water (Appendix B, Table B-3) at the laboratory temperature.

(Equation (4) may also be used to calculate the density of dry air. If $P_{H_2O} = 0$, the third term of the equation reduces to $P/760$.)

Equation (3) can be rearranged to yield an expression for M, the molar mass, as a function of the mass (m) of the gas, the volume (V), the pressure (P), the Kelvin temperature (T), and the gas constant, R. Calculate the molar mass of the unknown gas (or carbon dioxide), taking care that the units of R are consistent with the units of m, V, P, and T.

---

[1] If thistle tubes are not available, you may substitute a long-stemmed funnel; or you may simply use a one-hole stopper for the right-angle tubing, removing the stopper to add the acid, then quickly restoppering the flask.

[2] See, for example, *Lange's Handbook of Chemistry*, 11th ed., McGraw-Hill, New York, 1973; or the *Handbook of Chemistry and Physics*, published annually by CRC Press, Boca Raton, FL.

NAME		
SECTION		LOCKER
INSTRUCTOR		DATE

DATA AND CALCULATIONS

Data Unknown no. _____	Trial 1	Trial 2
(a) Mass of flask, stopper, and plug, filled with air	g	g
(b) Mass of flask, stopper, and plug, filled with unknown gas (or CO_2)	g	g
(c) Mass of flask, stopper, and plug, filled with water	g	g
(d) Temperature of flask	°C	°C
(e) Barometric pressure	torr	torr
(f) Density of dry (or moist) air at the flask temperature and pressure		
Reference:	g/mL	g/mL

Calculations		Trial 1	Trial 2
(g) Temperature, absolute		K	K
(h) Pressure, atm		atm	atm
(i) Volume of flask,[a] L		L	L
(j) Mass of air in flask at the start		g	g
(k) Mass of *empty* flask, stopper and plug		g	g
(l) Mass of unknown gas (or CO_2)		g	g
(m) Molar mass of gas (CO_2). Calculate from Equation (3), assuming $R = 0.08206$ L·atm·mol^{-1}·K^{-1}		g/mol	g/mol
(n) True molar mass of gas (CO_2) Reference:		g/mol	g/mol
(o) Percentage of relative error $= \dfrac{M_{calc.} - M_{true}}{M_{true}} \times 100$		%	%

[a] Why can we neglect the mass of air in the flask when obtaining the mass of the water (from which we calculate the volume of the flask), but not when calculating the mass of the carbon dioxide? Explain. If you are unable to answer this question, discuss it with your instructor before leaving the laboratory.

PROBLEMS

1. Write the equation for the reaction taking place in the preparation of carbon dioxide.

_____

2. How many moles are there in the 30.0 g of $CaCO_3$ used?

_____mol
_____

3. How many liters of carbon dioxide could be generated at standard conditions by this mass of $CaCO_3$?

_____L
_____

4. What volume would this amount of carbon dioxide occupy at ordinary laboratory conditions? (Assume 25°C and 710 torr.)

_____L
_____

5. What is the mass of a liter of each of the following gases at standard conditions? (Use no other data than atomic masses and the molar volume.)

Fluorine, $F_2(g)$ _____g

Propane, $C_3H_8(g)$ _____g

Ammonia, $NH_3(g)$ _____g
_____

6. A 1.60-g sample of impure sodium acetate was mixed with excess $NaOH(s)$ and heated in a test tube to decompose it completely according to the equation

$$NaCH_3COO(s) + NaOH(s) \rightarrow Na_2CO_3(s) + CH_4(g)$$

The evolved methane gas, $CH_4(g)$, was collected over water at 27°C and 747 torr, resulting in a volume of 320 mL of gas collected. Calculate the percentage of pure anhydrous sodium acetate, $Na(CH_3COO)$, in the sample. (*Suggestion:* Save arithmetic by using $PV = nRT$.)

_____%
_____

The Reactivity of Metals with Hydrochloric Acid

PURPOSE

To illustrate the concept of equivalent mass by determining the mass of a metal that reacts with hydrochloric acid to form 0.5 mol of hydrogen gas, H_2.

PRE-LAB PREPARATION

The Concept of Equivalent Mass

The term *equivalent mass*, as the adjective "equivalent" implies, is used to designate the relative amounts of substances that are chemically equivalent—that is, the masses of those substances that just react with or replace one another in chemical reactions. In the reaction of a metal with oxygen to form an oxide, the equivalent mass of a metal is defined as the mass of metal that reacts with

0.25 mol (8.000 g) of oxygen (O_2) gas. In this experiment, we will consider the equivalent mass of a metal to be the mass of metal that reacts with 1 mol of hydrogen ions (H^+) to produce 1 mol of hydrogen atoms or 0.5 mol of hydrogen (H_2) gas (1.008 g). The reaction is a displacement reaction in which the metal reacts with hydrochloric acid, HCl, to displace hydrogen gas. It can also be classified as an *oxidation-reduction* reaction, the metal being *oxidized* to a positively charged metal ion (*increase* in oxidation state) and the H^+ being *reduced* to H_2 (*decrease* in oxidation state). We will measure the volume of hydrogen gas produced when a weighed sample of metal is added to an excess of hydrochloric acid. A typical example is

$$Ca(s) + 2HCl(aq) \rightarrow CaCl_2(aq) + H_2(g)$$

Note that for each mole of calcium that reacts to form Ca^{2+} ions (ionic charge +2), 1 mol of hydrogen gas is formed. The equivalent mass of calcium in this reaction is therefore half its atomic mass. The equivalent mass is always either the atomic mass (for elements that form ions with ± 1 charge) or a simple fraction of the atomic mass, depending on the ionic charge of the ion produced. A general definition of the equivalent mass is therefore

equivalen mass =

$$\frac{\text{atomic mass}}{\text{change in charge on atom}} \quad (1)$$

Some elements, particularly transition metals like iron, can have more than one ionic charge in their compounds, and therefore can have *more than one possible equivalent mass*. Consider the following possible reactions:

$$Fe(s) + 2HCl(aq) \rightarrow FeCl_2(aq) + H_2(g) \quad (2)$$

$$2Fe(s) + 3Cl_2(g) \rightarrow 2FeCl_3(aq) \quad (3)$$

$$2FeCl_2(aq) + Cl_2(g) \rightarrow 2FeCl_3(aq) \quad (4)$$

In reaction (2) the change in charge is $+2$, in reaction (3) it is $+3$, and in reaction (4) it is $+1$. The corresponding equivalent masses of iron are, respectively, 27.92 (half the atomic mass), 18.62 (one third the atomic mass), and 55.85 (the atomic mass). *Thus, for elements that can have multiple ionic charges (or oxidation states) it is always necessary to specify the reaction before you can determine the equivalent mass.*

An alternative view of the definition of equivalent mass is that it is *that mass of substance that gives up or accepts 1 mol of electrons.* The defining equation then becomes

equivalent weight =

$$\frac{\text{atomic mass}}{\text{moles of electrons transferred}} \quad (5)$$

Thus, in reaction (2) iron changes from an oxidation state of 0 to oxidation state $+2$. It loses 2 mol of electrons per mole of Fe in so doing. The equivalent mass of Fe *in this reaction* therefore is

$$\frac{55.85}{2} = 27.92$$

This is the same result obtained by means of Equation (1). Verify that the equivalent masses for

reactions (3) and (4) are 18.62 and 55.85, using Equation (5).

Equation (5) emphasizes that the displacement reactions studied in this experiment can also be classified as oxidation-reduction reactions, reactions in which a transfer of electrons has caused changes in oxidation states. These concepts will be studied in greater detail in later experiments.

EXPERIMENTAL PROCEDURE

Special Supplies: Thermometer, pieces of metals (cut to size or issued as unknowns), 50-mL buret (for Method A only), fine copper wire.

Chemicals: Concentrated (12 M) hydrochloric acid, HCl.

Safety Precautions: Concentrated hydrochloric acid is a lung irritant and causes skin and eye burns. Handle with care. Dispense it in a well-ventilated fume hood. Clean up any spills immediately. Protect your hands with plastic gloves.

NOTE   The analysis samples for this experiment may be issued (1) as unknown metals, to calculate the equivalent mass, (2) as preweighed samples,[1] to calculate and report the sample mass from the known equivalent mass, or (3) as Al-Zn alloys of different compositions, to calculate the percentage composition from the known equivalent masses. Prepare the legends in your report accordingly, *before beginning the experiment.*

Your instructor will designate which of the preceding analyses and calculations you will do and which of the following alternate procedures you will follow. Method A is faster, but limits you to smaller samples, to a fixed acid concentration, and to room temperature. Method B permits larger samples and the control of both temperature and acid concentration during the reaction.

Obtain two samples of the metal to be used. Weigh these precisely on the analytical balance, at the same time taking care that the masses do not

---

[1] *To the instructor*: Samples may be preweighed by a stock assistant on a rapid single-pan balance, or, if in wire or ribbon form, cut to exact length to give a known mass, and individually coded. The student may then report the corrected volume of hydrogen as a preliminary check on his or her work, and finally the calculated equivalent mass, or the mass of the sample from the known equivalent mass.

exceed the maximum permitted, in order that you not generate more hydrogen than your apparatus can accommodate in either Method A or Method B. (For all laboratories except those at high elevation, maximum masses are, for Method A, with 50-mL buret, 0.12 g Zn, 0.032 g Al, 0.042 g Mg, 0.10 g Mn; for Method B, with 500-mL flask, 1.10 g Zn, 0.40 g Mg, 0.30 g Al, 0.90 g Mn, 0.90 g Fe, 1.90 g Sn, 1.90 g Cd.)

METHOD A

Compress the weighed samples into compact bundles, and wrap each sample in all directions with about 20 cm of fine copper wire, forming a small basket or cage, leaving 5 cm of the wire straight as a handle. This confines the particles as the metal dissolves, and also speeds the reaction.[2]

Obtain and clean a 50-mL buret. Next measure the uncalibrated volume of the buret between the stopcock and the 50-mL graduation. Measure by filling the buret with water and draining the buret through the stopcock until the liquid level falls exactly to the 50-mL mark. Then use a 10-mL graduated cylinder to measure the volume delivered when the water level is lowered to the top of the stopcock. Then pour into the buret the required amount of concentrated hydrochloric acid. Use a funnel for this addition, being careful not to allow the acid to touch your skin or clothing. Because of differences in the activity of the metals used, it is necessary to vary the amount of acid. For magnesium, use about 3 mL; for aluminum or zinc, about 20 mL; for manganese, about 7 mL. Fill the buret completely with water, slowly and carefully to avoid undue mixing of the acid. Insert the metal sample about 4 cm into the buret and clamp it there by the copper wire handle, using a one- or two-hole rubber stopper. Make certain no air is entrapped in the buret. Cover the stopper hole(s) with your finger[3] and invert the buret (Figure 11-1) in a 400-mL beaker partly filled with water. The acid, being more dense, quickly sinks and diffuses down the buret and reacts with the metal. As the H_2 is generated, it collects at the top

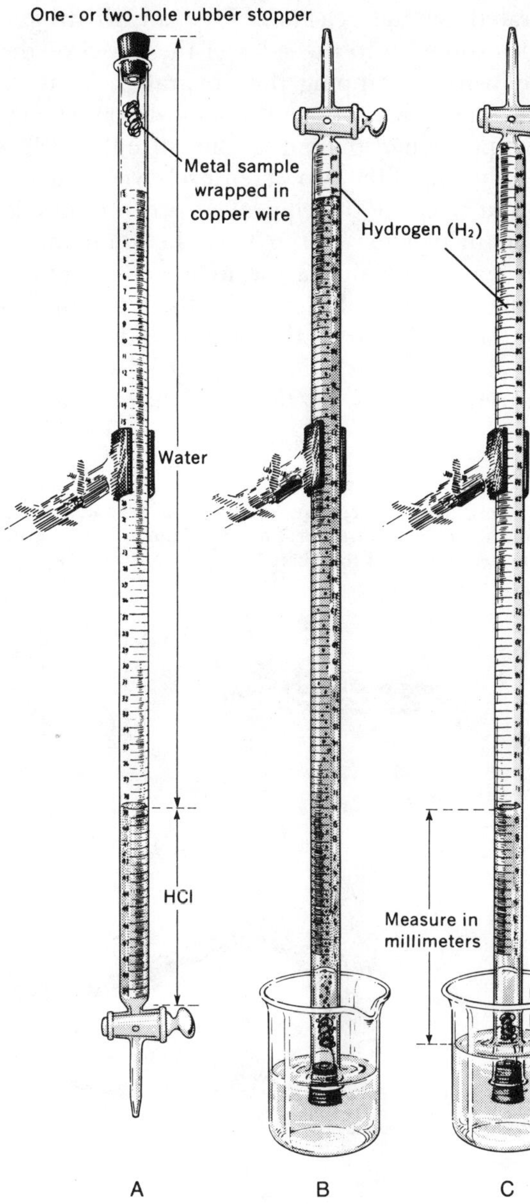

FIGURE 11-1
The appropriate volume of concentrated (12 M) HCl is added to the buret, and water is then layered on top of it until the buret is completely filled, as in A. Inversion of the buret in a beaker of water begins the reaction (B), which continues until all of the metal is gone and the buret is nearly full of hydrogen gas, as shown in C.

of the buret, expelling the HCl and water solution out the hole in the stopper at the bottom. (*Caution:* If the reaction is too rapid and the metal too close to the end of the buret, small bubbles of hydrogen may escape from the buret along with the acid solution as it is expelled. If so, repeat the experiment, using less acid.)

After complete solution of the metal, let the apparatus cool to room temperature, since heat is

---

[2] As the more active metal dissolves, it gives up electrons that move easily to the less reactive copper, where they react with hydrogen ions of the acid to form hydrogen gas. Note that the bubbles of gas form on the copper wire, and thus keep a larger surface of active metal exposed to the acid.

[3] The use of a plastic glove for this step is recommended to ensure that no acid comes in contact with your skin.

generated by the reaction. Free any hydrogen bubbles adhering to the sides of the vessel or the copper wire by tapping the apparatus. Measure the volume of gas liberated[4] and—without changing the position of the buret—measure the difference in height of the two water levels with a metric rule, and calculate the equivalent pressure in millimeters of mercury (torr). Take the temperature of the gas by holding a thermometer in contact with the side of the buret. Raise the buret up out of the HCl solution in the beaker and allow the remainder of the solution to drain down out of the buret. Allow the H_2 to escape into the atmos-

phere, flush the HCl solution down the drain with plenty of water, and discard the copper wire in the waste basket.

Obtain the barometer reading for the day. Repeat the determination with your second sample.

METHOD B

Set up the apparatus as sketched in Figure 11-2, utilizing a *500-mL flask* to contain the evolved hydrogen. The exit tube C from the test tube, connected to the flask E, must not extend below either rubber stopper (so that gas will not be trapped). The longer glass tube in the test tube should extend nearly to the bottom and should be constricted to a small capillary and bent as illustrated. The flask E is filled with water, and the

---

[4] If a 50-mL buret is used, the volume of gas liberated equals (50 minus the final buret reading) plus the volume of the uncalibrated portion of the buret.

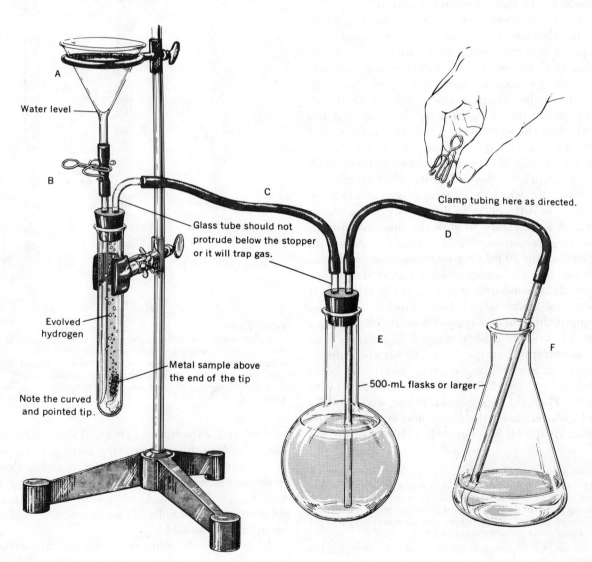

FIGURE 11-2
An alternate apparatus for the determination of the equivalent weight of a metal.

flask F is partially filled. The siphon tube D, extending to the bottom of both flasks, is also filled with water.

Place the first carefully weighed sample of metal in the 15-cm test tube, as indicated. A fine copper wire, wrapped about the sample in all directions like a cage, as in Method A, may be of some help in increasing the rate of reaction and in confining small bits of metal as it dissolves, although this is not entirely necessary. With the stopper in flask E loosened to permit air to escape, pour water into the funnel to fill completely the test tube and tubes B and C, and close clamp B. If flask E is not completely filled with water, raise flask F so that water siphons back into it, then push in the stopper in E tightly.

When all air bubbles have been thus removed from the apparatus, release clamps B and D just enough to permit the water level in the funnel to fall just to the stem top, *but no further*; then close clamp B. Now empty and drain flask F, but do not dry it, leaving tube D filled with water, and clamp D open. When all is ready, add exactly 25.0 mL of concentrated hydrochloric acid into the funnel. Release clamp B momentarily to permit a little acid to flow into the test tube and react with the metal at a moderate rate.

A volume of water equal to the volume of hydrogen generated will siphon from E to F. You can control the rate of reaction by regulating the amount of acid you add and by heating the tube gently (for less reactive metals) by a 1-in. Bunsen flame applied intermittently as needed. When all the metal has dissolved and the reaction mixture has cooled to room temperature, release clamp B to permit the acid level to fall to the funnel stem, *but no further*. Carefully measure 25.0 mL of water, add this to the funnel, and again release the clamp to let the level fall exactly to the funnel stem; then close the clamp tightly. All gas should now be displaced from the test tube and connecting tubes into flask E. If not, repeat the addition of a measured amount of water. Adjust the levels in flasks E and F by raising or lowering one of them until they are even (avoid warming the gas in E with your hands on the flask), then close clamp D tightly. Obtain the temperature of the hydrogen by removing the stopper enough to place a thermometer in flask E. Measure the volume of water in flask F by pouring it into a 500-mL graduated cylinder. This volume, minus the volumes of acid and water added to the funnel, will be the volume of the hydrogen generated. Record the barometric pressure. Repeat the determination with your second sample.

Calculation of the Experiment

Recall that the standard molar volume of any gas is 22.4 L. The volume of 0.5 mol of hydrogen gas (1.008 g) at standard conditions is thus 11.2 L, or 11,200 mL. *The equivalent mass of your metal sample therefore is that mass which will produce 11,200 mL of hydrogen gas at standard conditions from an acid.* Also note that you must consider the difference in liquid levels (Method A) and the vapor pressure of water in arriving at the correct hydrogen gas pressure.

Calculate and report your result according to the type of sample you have been given: (1) the equivalent mass of a metal (g M/equiv), (2) the mass of a preweighed sample, or (3) the percentage composition of an Al-Zn alloy. The percentage of Al in the alloy is given by

$$\text{percentage of Al} = \frac{\text{g Al}}{\text{g Al} + \text{g Zn}} \times 100$$

This requires you to know *both* the mass of aluminum (g Al) and the mass of zinc (g Zn), and you will need two independent equations to solve for the two unknown masses. These two equations may be written as

(a) g sample = g Al + g Zn

(b) $\text{vol H}_2 \text{ (STP)} = 11,200 \dfrac{\text{mL H}_2 \text{ (STP)}}{\text{equiv}}$

$$\times \left(\frac{\text{g Al}}{\text{g Al/equiv}} + \frac{\text{g Zn}}{\text{g Zn/equiv}} \right)$$

where g Al/equiv and g Zn/equiv are the equivalent masses of Al and Zn, respectively.

For your reported result, calculate the percentage of relative error given by

For your reported result, calculate the percentage of relative error given by

percentage of relative error

$$= \frac{R_{\text{calc.}} - R_{\text{true}}}{R_{\text{true}}} \times 100$$

where $R_{\text{calc.}}$ and R_{true} stand for the calculated and true results, respectively.

BIBLIOGRAPHY

Masterton, W. L., "Analysis of an Aluminum-Zinc Alloy," *J. Chem. Educ.* **38,** 558 (1961).

ρ = density
_____

ρ = 13.59 g/ml Hg

ρ = 1.00 g/ml H_2O

The Heat Capacity of Metals
The Law of Dulong and Petit

PURPOSE

To gain an understanding of the terms *heat, energy, work,* and *heat capacity.* To gain an understanding of how heat is related to molecular motion. To use a simple Styrofoam cup calorimeter to measure the heat capacity of a metal and confirm the law of Dulong and Petit.

PRE-LAB PREPARATION

The Nature of Heat, Energy, and Work What is heat? Naming something is not the same thing as understanding it, and in science a familiar name often stands for a concept that, upon close examination, proves elusive and difficult to define in a precise way.

Heat is an effect produced by the transfer of energy. We might even call it energy in transit. Energy naturally flows from warmer to cooler bodies. This is equivalent to saying that heat spontaneously passes from a hot to a cold body.

In describing heat we used another familiar word—energy—that stands for an elusive concept. What is energy? We will define it as the *capacity to produce useful work,* where work is defined as the product of *force × distance,* such as the work done in lifting a weight. The word energy was first employed in this sense by Rudolf Clausius (1822–1888), but has been traced back to the ancient Greeks (probably Aristotle), who coined the word by combining the Greek words *en* and *ergon,* meaning *at* and *work.*

Energy manifests itself in many forms. Part of the energy in coal and oxygen is released when they combine chemically to form carbon dioxide. This is called *chemical energy* and it produces heat that can be used to turn water into steam under high pressure. The energy stored in the steam is converted into *kinetic energy* by allowing the steam to expand through a turbine, causing it to rotate. The energy of motion in the rotating turbine is converted into *electrical energy* by coupling the turbine to a generator. The electrical energy distributed over wires can produce mechanical work (another form of energy), such as the shaft rotation of an electric motor, or it can be converted into heat by passing electric current through a resistor.

The rotation of the shaft of an electric motor can be used to turn a drum, winding up a cord to which a weight is attached. In raising the weight, work is done. The work done in raising the weight increases the *potential energy* of the weight. If the motor is uncoupled from the drum and the weight allowed to descend, the potential energy stored in the raised weight is converted into kinetic energy, rotating the drum as the cord unwinds. If the rotating drum is now connected by gears to a paddle wheel churning a container of water, the temperature of the water increases. The potential energy stored in the weight is converted into work, which is in turn converted into heat.

James Prescott Joule (1818–1889) used a falling weight to churn water in exactly this way to determine that there is a fixed relationship between the amount of work expended and the heat effect it produces, a quantity he called the "mechanical equivalent of heat." In modern units, 4.18 joules (J) = 1 calorie (cal) of thermal energy, where 1 calorie is the quantity of energy required to increase the temperature of 1 g of water by 1°C.

Modes of Energy Transfer   There are several ways to heat an object by energy transfer. Energy can be transferred through empty space (or vacuum) by *radiation*. You feel this effect when you turn your face to the sun on a warm spring day. Light is a form of electromagnetic radiation, and the carriers of light energy are called *photons*. Although they have no rest mass, when they are absorbed by the skin they set the atoms and molecules in the skin into motion, producing the sensation of warmth.

Heat can pass from one body to another by *convection* (movement of a fluid). If you hold the back of your hand near your mouth and exhale gently on it, you feel the sensation of warmth caused by the flow of warm air from your lungs. Finally, energy can be transferred by *conduction* through both fluids and solids. If you grasp the end of a copper rod and stick the other end in a flame, the end you are holding soon gets uncomfortably hot. The same thing happens if you spill hot coffee on yourself. The hot water heats your skin, perhaps enough to produce a painful burn.

Heat and Molecular Motion   The accumulated knowledge about the effects of heat provides a rather detailed picture of what happens when you heat (or transfer energy to) a substance. On an atomic or molecular scale, heating increases the motion of the atoms. If the atoms are linked by chemical bonds to form a gaseous molecule, we can focus our attention not on individual atoms, but on the molecule as a whole.

If we heat a gas, the individual molecules move about faster from place to place. (Their kinetic energy of *translation* is increased.)

Individual atoms in molecules are linked by chemical bonds that are "springy," constraining atoms that are bonded together to move like masses connected by springs. As the molecules are heated the amplitudes of their *vibrations* increase.

Finally, molecules can rotate about their centers of mass, and as a gas is heated the rate of *rotation* of the molecules increases.

To summarize, gaseous molecules can store energy in *translational, vibrational,* and *rotational* motions of the molecules.

What about solids such as metals? When you heat a solid metal, which consists of atoms closely packed together, the atoms, on average, are not going anywhere. An atom occupies a fixed position in the solid (unless the temperature gets too near the melting point), and when heated it just increases the amplitude of its vibration about this fixed position. Because atoms have nearly all of their mass located in a very small nucleus, they have a very small moment of inertia and therefore individual atoms have an insignificant amount of rotational energy.

Latent Heat   When you heat a substance (thus putting energy into it), will a thermometer immersed in the substance always indicate a temperature increase? Not necessarily. In some circumstances the temperature may stay constant. For example, if you drop a small piece of hot metal into a mixture of ice and water at 0°C, some ice will melt, but the temperature will remain constant until all of the ice is melted. Heat that produces a phase change such as the melting of ice (or the boiling of water) without producing a temperature change is called *latent* heat. A thermometer, therefore, can be used to measure *temperature* changes but cannot always be used to measure *energy* changes.

Heat Capacity   When you heat a substance and its temperature increases, the input of energy divided by the temperature increase is called the heat capacity. It could just as well be called the energy capacity, since the quantity has the dimensions of *energy per unit temperature change*.

The Heat Capacity of Metals and the Law of Dulong and Petit As part of a systematic study of the heat capacity of metals, Pierre Dulong (1785–1838) and his collaborator Alexis Petit (1791–1820) published in 1819 their discovery that the product of the molar mass (grams per mole) of a metal times its heat capacity (calories per gram per Celsius degree) is a constant. (This product could be called the molar heat capacity, and it is approximately equal to 6.0 cal·mol^{-1}·K^{-1}.) At the time there was no explanation of why this should be true, but this empirical result was used by Berzelius (and later by Cannizzaro) to arrive at correct atomic masses and empirical formulas for compounds of metals.

It was not until 1907 that a theory of the heat capacity of metals was published by Albert Einstein. He treated the atoms as equivalent to little oscillators and showed that the heat capacity decreases to zero as you approach zero on the absolute temperature scale, but approaches a value of $3R$ if the temperature is sufficiently high. R is the universal gas constant, which has the value 1.987 cal·mol^{-1}·K^{-1} and thus gives a predicted molar heat capacity of 5.96 cal·mol^{-1}·K^{-1}. (In measuring heat capacities, you are considering only temperature changes, so it makes no difference whether you measure these changes on the Kelvin or Celsius scale because the degree intervals on both scales are the same size.)

Heat and Enthalpy The amount of heat it takes to increase the temperature of a substance by a given amount depends on whether the heating is done under conditions of constant volume or constant pressure. If volume is constant, all of the energy goes into increasing the internal energy of the substance (increasing the motion of the atoms of the substance). If the volume is allowed to change and the pressure is constant (for example, equal to the atmospheric pressure), some work will be expended in pushing back the atmosphere and this work will require a greater amount of heat for a given temperature increase. If we represent the quantity of heat by the symbol q, we can in general say that q_P will be larger than q_V.

The heat added to a system at constant pressure is called the *enthalpy* increase (from the Greek *enthalpein*, to heat in), and changes in enthalpy are directly related to changes in temperature by the relation

$$\Delta H = q_P \tag{1}$$
$$= mC_P \, \Delta T$$

where m is the mass of the substance heated (in grams), C_P is the heat capacity at constant pressure (in calories per gram per Celsius degree), and ΔT is the temperature change. We will consistently define ΔT as the final temperature minus the initial temperature: $\Delta T = T_f - T_i$. (The temperature change ΔT will be negative if T_f is less than T_i.)

Measuring the Heat Capacity of a Metal with a Styrofoam Cup Calorimeter In this experiment we will measure the heat capacity of an unknown metal and try to identify the metal from the measured heat capacity. We will first measure the effective heat capacity of a simple calorimeter containing cool (room temperature) water by adding a known mass of hot water to it and measuring the temperature increase. Then, in a second experiment, we will add a known mass of hot metal to the calorimeter under similar conditions.

Employing the principle of the conservation of energy, we will write an equation that states that the sum of the enthalpy change of the calorimeter plus the enthalpy change of the added hot water must be zero. (The change in enthalpy of the calorimeter is equal in magnitude to the change in enthalpy of the added hot water, but they have opposite signs.) The change in enthalpy of the calorimeter will be divided into two parts: the Styrofoam cups and thermometer that make up the calorimeter, and the cool water originally present in the calorimeter. Thus,

$$\underset{\substack{\text{Styrofoam} \\ \text{cups +} \\ \text{thermometer}}}{\Delta H} + \underset{\substack{\text{cool water in} \\ \text{calorimeter}}}{\Delta H} + \underset{\substack{\text{added} \\ \text{hot water}}}{\Delta H} = 0 \tag{2}$$

In view of the definition of the enthalpy change given in Equation (1) we can rewrite Equation (2) as

$$\underset{\substack{\text{Styrofoam} \\ \text{cups +} \\ \text{thermometer}}}{(mC_P)\,\Delta T} + \underset{\substack{\text{cool water in} \\ \text{calorimeter}}}{mC_P\,\Delta T} + \underset{\substack{\text{added} \\ \text{hot water}}}{mC_P\,\Delta T} = 0 \tag{3}$$

It should be recognized that not all of the Styrofoam cups and thermometer come into contact with and are heated by the added hot water. Therefore we can determine only the *effective* product (mC_P) for the Styrofoam cups and thermometer, which we will call the *calorimeter constant*, B (calories per Celsius degree). So we will rewrite Equation (3) as

$$B\,\Delta T_C + m_C C_P\,\Delta T_C + m_{HW} C_P \Delta T_{HW} = 0 \tag{4}$$

where m_C is the mass of cool water originally in the calorimeter, ΔT_C is the temperature increase of the calorimeter and water, m_{HW} is the mass of added hot water, and ΔT_{HW} is the temperature decrease of the added hot water. These four quantities are all measured in the experiment. If in addition we know the heat capacity of water, C_P, we can solve Equation (4) to obtain the calorimeter constant, B.

A second experiment is then carried out, adding heated metal instead of hot water to the water in the calorimeter. We can write an equation similar to Equation (4) to describe the enthalpy changes in this experiment.

$$\underset{\substack{\text{Styrofoam} \\ \text{cups} + \\ \text{thermometer}}}{B\,\Delta T_C} + \underset{\substack{\text{cool water in} \\ \text{calorimeter}}}{m_C C_P\,\Delta T_C} + \underset{\substack{\text{added hot} \\ \text{metal}}}{m_{HM}C_{P,M}\,\Delta T_{HM}} = 0$$

$$(5)$$

In this experiment we measure the same four quantities (m_C, ΔT_C, m_{HM}, and ΔT_{HM}). We substitute these values and the previously determined value of B into Equation (5) and solve for $C_{P,M}$, the heat capacity of the unknown metal.

If you perform the experiments carefully, the measured value of the heat capacity will enable you to identify the unknown metal from the list of metals shown in Table 12-1.

EXPERIMENTAL PROCEDURE

Special Supplies: Hot plate, large iron ring or safety clamp, and ring stand (or burner, iron ring, metal gauze, safety clamp (or large iron ring), and ring stand), 1000-mL beaker, two 0 to 110°C thermometers (if available, use a 0 to 50°C thermometer graduated in tenths of a degree in place of one of the 0 to 110°C thermometers), fine copper wire to suspend the thermometer, two 12- to 16-oz Styrofoam cups per student, 25- × 200-mm test tubes (two to contain water and one for each unknown-metal heat capacity determination), corks or rubber stoppers to fit test tubes, beaker tongs or pliers with padded jaws, 100-mL graduated cylinder.

Chemicals: Metals (in the form of shot or pellets so that they will pour easily from a test tube), for example, aluminum, magnesium, nickel, zinc, antimony, lead.

Safety Precautions: Boiling water can cause painful and serious burns. Put a large iron ring or safety clamp around the beaker and securely fasten the ring or clamp to a ring stand, as shown in Figure 12-1A, even if you are using a hot plate. The safety clamp is even more important if you use a gas burner and ring stand to heat the water. Keep

TABLE 12-1
The heat capacity of some metals

Metal	Heat capacity ($cal \cdot g^{-1} \cdot K^{-1}$)
Magnesium	0.248
Aluminum	0.216
Iron	0.113
Nickel	0.106
Copper	0.0924
Zinc	0.0922
Silver	0.0564
Antimony	0.0495
Gold	0.0308
Lead	0.0305

the hot plate or burner and ring stand well back from the edge of the laboratory bench.

A 25- × 200-mm test tube containing 80 g of metal is too heavy to handle with an ordinary test tube holder. Use beaker tongs or ordinary pliers whose jaws have been padded by having large-diameter PVC tubing slipped over the jaws.

The thermometer used to measure the temperature in the Styrofoam cups should be suspended by copper wire from a ring stand support. (See Figure 12-1B.) If not suspended, the thermometer may tip the cups over, spoiling the measurement and possibly breaking. If the thermometer does not have a suspension ring at the top, wrap several turns of tape around the wire near the top of the thermometer.

1. *Determination of the Calorimeter Constant* Put about 700 mL of water in a 1000-mL beaker, clamp it securely in place on the hot plate or over the burner, and begin heating it to boiling. (See Figure 12-1A.) Put 30 mL of water in each of two 25- × 200-mm test tubes and place them in the beaker so that they can be heated to the temperature of boiling water.

To save time, also prepare the weighed and stoppered tube(s) containing the unknown metal(s) as described in part 2 and put them in the beaker of boiling water.

Obtain two 12- or 16-oz Styrofoam cups, put one inside the other so that they are nested, and weigh the nested cups to the nearest 0.1 g on a platform balance. Record the mass of the empty cups. Add 70 mL of water to the inner cup, reweigh, and record the mass.

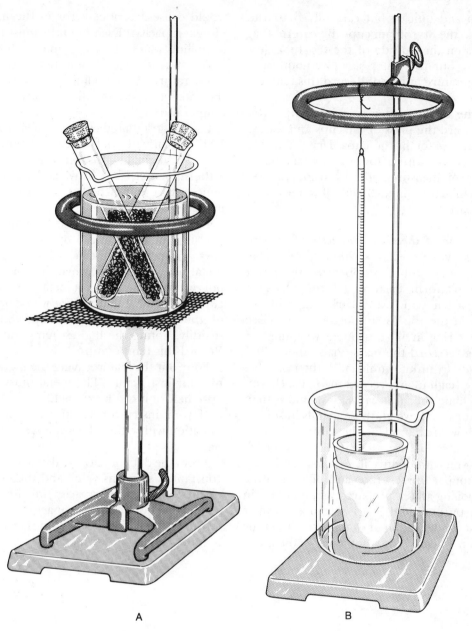

FIGURE 12-1
Apparatus for measuring the heat capacity of a metal. Samples of metal pellets are heated in the test tubes shown in A. The heated metal pellets are then poured into the Styrofoam cup calorimeter shown in B.

When the water in the 1000-mL beaker has reached the boiling point, wait 15 min longer, then stir the water in the nested cups with a thermometer (0 to 50°C graduated in tenths of a degree, if available) until a constant temperature is reached. Leave the thermometer in the cup suspended by a copper wire attached to a ring stand support. (The wire suspension will keep the thermometer from tipping the cups over and possibly breaking the thermometer. If your thermometer has no ring at the top, use tape to fasten the wire.) Record the temperature.

Determine the temperature of the boiling water with a 0 to 110°C thermometer. (*Do not place a 0 to 50°C thermometer in boiling water or it will break.*) The bulb of the thermometer should be held 2 to 3 cm above the bottom of the beaker. Record the temperature of the boiling water.

Using beaker tongs, or pliers with padded jaws, grasp the test tube containing the 30 mL of water near the top and quickly but carefully pour the hot water into the Styrofoam cups. Be careful that no hot water on the outside of the test tube gets into the cups. Stir the water steadily, noting the highest temperature attained. Record this temperature.

Remove the thermometer from the cups. Reweigh and record the mass of the cups and water.

Pour out the water in the cups. Dry the inside of the cups gently with a towel and carry out a duplicate set of measurements by using the remaining test tube containing 30 mL of water. Then proceed to part 2.

2. *Determination of the Heat Capacity of an Unknown Metal* Weigh a 25- × 200-mm test tube, fitted with a cork or rubber stopper, to the nearest 0.1 g on a platform balance. (If the platform balance has a flat pan, use a cork ring with V-grooves cut in the top to support the tube. Use the same cork ring in all subsequent weighings of the test tube.) Record the mass. Place about 80 g of a *thoroughly dry* unknown metal in the test tube, stopper it, reweigh it, and record the mass. (If you are to determine the heat capacity of more than one sample of metal, weigh these metals in similar test tubes now so that all of the samples can be heated adequately before use. Put a label on each test tube so you can identify it.

Loosely stopper the test tube and place it in the beaker of boiling water prepared as described in part 1. (The purpose of the cork or rubber stopper is to prevent condensation of water inside the tube while it is being heated. Any hot water in the metal would cause a serious error in the measurement of heat capacity.) Each test tube must be immersed in boiling water at least 15 min before the metal is transferred to the calorimeter. Determine the temperature of the boiling water with a 0 to 110°C thermometer, as you did in part 1. Record the temperature.

Using a graduated cylinder, measure out exactly 100 ± 1 mL of cool water and pour it into the nested Styrofoam cups. Stir the water gently with a thermometer ($\frac{1}{10}$°C if available) until a constant temperature is reached. Leave the thermometer in the cup suspended by a wire or string as described in part 1. Record the temperature.

Using beaker tongs, or pliers with padded jaws, grasp the test tube containing the heated metal near the top, remove the cork, and quickly but carefully pour the hot metal into the Styrofoam cups. Be careful that no hot water on the outside of the tube gets into the cups. Stir the water steadily, noting the highest temperature attained. Record this temperature.

Pour out the water, saving the metal as directed by your instructor. (The metal must be *thoroughly dried* before it can be reused.)

If your instructor so directs, repeat the determination with either the same metal or a different one.

From the data of part 1, calculate the calorimeter constant. Using this value and the data of part 2, calculate the heat capacity of the metal(s). By comparison of the heat capacity value(s) you determined with those found in Table 12-1, try to identify the unknown metal(s).

REPORT

12

The Heat Capacity
of a Metal
The Law of Dulong
and Petit

NAME

SECTION   LOCKER

INSTRUCTOR   • DATE

DATA AND CALCULATIONS

1. Determination of the Calorimeter Constant

Data	Trial 1	Trial 2
(a) Mass of empty Styrofoam cups	_____ g	_____ g
(b) Mass of cups + 70 mL water	_____ g	_____ g
(c) Mass of cups + 70 mL water + 30 mL hot water	_____ g	_____ g
(d) Initial temperature of water in the calorimeter (cups)	_____ °C	_____ °C
(e) Temperature of the boiling water bath	_____ °C	_____ °C
(f) Final temperature of calorimeter + added hot water	_____ °C	_____ °C

Calculations

	Trial 1	Trial 2
(g) Mass of cool water in cups, m_C	_____ g	_____ g
(h) Mass of added hot water, m_{HW}	_____ g	_____ g
(i) Temperature change of cool water in the calorimeter $(\Delta T_C = T_{1(f)} - T_{1(d)})$	+ _____ K	+ _____ K
(j) Temperature change of added hot water $(\Delta T_{HW} = T_{1(f)} - T_{1(e)})$	− _____ K	− _____ K

(k) Calculated calorimeter constant

The calorimeter constant, B, is calculated by rearranging Equation (4) to solve for B:

$$B = \frac{-C_P(m_C\,\Delta T_C + m_{HW}\,\Delta T_{HW})}{\Delta T_C}$$

Assume that the heat capacity of water, C_p, equals 1.00 cal·g^{-1}·K^{-1}.

_____cal/K   _____ cal/K

2. Determination of the Heat Capacity of a Metal

Unknown no(s). _____ _____

Data	Trial 1	Trial 2
(a) Milliliters of water placed in cups	_____ mL	_____ mL
(b) Mass of empty stoppered test tube	_____ g	_____ g
(c) Mass of stoppered test tube + metal	_____ g	_____ g
(d) Initial temperature of water in the calorimeter (cups)	_____ °C	_____ °C
(e) Temperature of the boiling water bath	_____ °C	_____ °C
(f) Final temperature of water + added hot metal	_____ °C	_____ °C

Calculations

(g) Mass of water in cups, m_C. Assume that the density of water is 1.00 g/mL. — _____ g _____ g

(h) Mass of added hot metal, m_{HM} — _____ g _____ g

(i) Temperature change of the water in the calorimeter $(\Delta T_C = T_{2(f)} - T_{2(d)})$ — + _____ K + _____ K

(j) Temperature change of the added hot metal $(\Delta T_{HM} = T_{2(f)} - T_{2(e)})$ — − _____ K − _____ K

(k) Calculate the heat capacity of the metal, $C_{P,M}$, by rearranging Equation (5) to solve for $C_{P,M}$. (Use the value of B determined in part 1.)

$$C_{P,M} = \frac{-\Delta T_C (B + m_C C_P)}{m_{HM}\, \Delta T_{HM}}$$

Assume that the heat capacity of water, C_P, equals 1.00 cal·g^{-1}·K^{-1}.

_____cal·g^{-1}·K^{-1} _____cal·g^{-1}·K^{-1}

(l) Using the law of Dulong and Petit and your value(s) for the heat capacities, calculate the molar mass of each metal studied.

_____g/mol _____ g/mol

(m) By consulting Table 12-1, determine the identity of each metal.

_____ _____

QUESTIONS

1. If a student used a sample of metal that was wet, several percent of the apparent mass of the metal would be water. Would the resulting measured value of the heat capacity be too high or too low? Explain.

2. A particular metallic element, M, has a heat capacity of 0.051 cal·g^{-1}·K^{-1} and forms an oxide containing 3.71 g M/g O. Using the law of Dulong and Petit, estimate the molar mass of M. Taking the molar mass of oxygen to be 16.0 g/mol, calculate the exact molar mass of M and the empirical formula of the oxide of M. Identify M by using the information in the periodic table in your lab manual.

The Enthalpy of Combustion of a Vegetable Oil

PURPOSE

To explore the idea of food as fuel and to construct a simple calorimeter for measuring the energy produced by burning vegetable oil.

PRE-LAB PREPARATION

From a strictly material viewpoint, human beings are biochemical engines that require both a fuel and an oxidant. The oxidant is oxygen in the air. The fuel is the food we eat, which consists of carbohydrates (starches and sugars), fats, and proteins plus traces of minerals, vitamins, and other substances we need for good nutrition. The big three (carbohydrates, fats, and proteins) all contain carbon and hydrogen, and most of the carbon and hydrogen we eat in our food is metabolized to carbon dioxide and water. This is equivalent to burning the food and suggests the possibility that we could measure the fuel equivalent of the food we eat by burning it in a calorimeter and measuring the energy produced as heat.

Energy Needs of the Body

What are the energy requirements of our bodies, and how do our bodies use the energy contained in the food we eat? Careful studies have shown that food energy requirements depend on factors such as age, weight, physical activity, and sex (males require about 10% more energy per kilogram of body weight than females). A surprisingly large fraction of the food we eat is required to sustain basic cell functions necessary for the maintenance of life, such as the circulation of the blood by the beating of the heart, the rhythmic contraction of the lungs in breathing, the ongoing metabolic activities of each cell, and the maintenance of body temperature. These minimum energy needs, called the *basal metabolic rate* (BMR), must be maintained before any energy can be used for physical activity or for the digestion of food.

As a rough rule of thumb, a college-age person requires about 1.0 kcal per kilogram of body weight per hour (for men) or 0.9 kcal per kilogram per hour (for women). (Problem: Verify that a young 140-lb woman would require 1375 kcal per day for her BMR. Also note that the nutritional calorie often used to express the caloric value of food portions is actually 1000 calories, or 1 kilocalorie.)

The second of the three important energy requirements is the energy required for physical activity that involves voluntary use of the skeletal muscles. This energy depends on how many muscles are involved, the amount of weight being moved, and how long the activity lasts. Contrary to popular belief, mental effort requires very little energy, although it may make you feel tired. The energy requirements for a sedentary (mostly sitting) activity like that of a typist amount to about 20% of the BMR. Light activity (such as that of a teacher or student) requires about 30% of the BMR. Moderate to heavy activity, such as that of a nurse or athlete, may require energy amounting to 40 to 50% of the BMR.

The third component of energy requirement has to do with digesting our food. When food is eaten, many cells that have been dormant begin to be active, for example, the cells that manufacture and secrete digestive juices and the muscle cells that move food through the intestinal tract. This requirement is about 10% of the total kilocalories used for BMR and physical activity.

Now let's go back and add up the daily energy requirements of our hypothetical 140-lb young woman. Her BMR requirement was about 1375 kcal/day. Assuming light activity, we will add 30% of the BMR for physical activity, or 412 kcal. Now add 10% of the sum (1375 + 412 kcal) or 179 kcal for digestion of food to get a grand total of 1966 kcal/day as her approximate requirement. Of course, these figures are based on several estimates, so her needs might fall within ±100 kcal/day of the estimated value.

Note that 70% (1375 out of 1966 kcal) of her daily food requirement is required just to sustain her BMR. If she increases her physical activity while eating the same amount, she will begin to lose weight. A deficit of 125 kcal/day brings about the loss of body fat at the safe rate of about a pound per month. (A pound of body fat is not pure fat but a mixture of fat, water, and protein, and yields about 3500 kcal when burned. A pound of pure fat would yield about 4040 kcal when burned.)

Combustion Calorimetry

The caloric content of food is determined by burning it in a closed metal calorimeter pressurized with oxygen and completely surrounded by water.

The calorimeter can be calibrated by burning a substance whose heat of combustion has been accurately determined.

The method we will employ to measure the heat (enthalpy) of combustion of a vegetable oil is similar in principle, but the calorimeter we will use is a crude version of the combustion calorimeter used for accurate scientific work.

We will construct a lamp that burns oil. The heat from the burning oil will be used to heat water and the temperature increase of the water will be a measure of the energy produced in the combustion. The enthalpy change for a sample of water that is heated from temperature T_1 to temperature T_2 is given by

$$\Delta H = mC_P \, \Delta T \qquad (1)$$

where ΔH is the enthalpy change in calories (heat absorbed by the water in this example), m is the mass of water in grams, C_P is the heat capacity (at constant pressure) in $cal \cdot g^{-1} \cdot K^{-1}$, and ΔT is the temperature change ($\Delta T = T_2 - T_1$) in Celsius degrees.

Not all of the energy released in burning the oil finds its way into the water heated in the calorimeter, so it is necessary to determine the *efficiency* of the calorimeter (the fraction of energy that is captured) by burning a substance whose heat of combustion is known. We will use 1-dodecanol, $CH_3(CH_2)_{11}OH$, whose enthalpy of combustion has been determined to be 10.1 kcal/g, to calibrate the calorimeter by burning a known mass of 1-dodecanol under the same conditions used to burn a known mass of vegetable oil. The measured enthalpy change for the vegetable oil will then be divided by the efficiency to get a corrected value that should be close to the true value for the enthalpy of combustion of vegetable oil.

$$\Delta H_{combustion} = \frac{\Delta H_{measured}}{efficiency} \qquad (2)$$

EXPERIMENTAL PROCEDURE

Special Supplies: 12-oz aluminum beverage can (cut the top out with a can opener), 20-gauge copper wire, large candle wicking (or cotton drapery cord), two 30-mL beakers, 0 to 110°C thermometer, chilled water or crushed ice, 100-mL graduated cylinder, steel wool.

Chemicals: 1-Dodecanol, vegetable oil (cottonseed, safflower, sunflower, peanut, etc.).

Using a can opener, cut the top out of a 12-oz aluminum beverage can. Mount the can vertically with a three-finger clamp held on a ring stand as shown in Figure 13-1.

From 14-cm lengths of 20-gauge copper wire form two wick holders that will fit into the mouth of a 30-mL beaker. (See Figure 13-1.) A loop at the center of the holder is needed to hold the wick in a vertical position. The holder should extend across the diameter of the beaker about one third of the way from the top. Cut two 5-cm lengths of wicking material. (Large candle wicks or cotton drapery cord are suitable wicking materials. Polyester or other synthetic materials will melt and are unsuitable.) Fit the wick holders in each 30-mL beaker and install the wicks so that they extend from the bottom to the top of each beaker. When the wicks are in place, fill one beaker to within 1.5 cm of the top with 1-dodecanol and fill the other beaker in the same way with vegetable oil. (Be careful that no oil is spilled or dribbled down the outside of the beakers, because these beakers must be accurately weighed later on.)

Light both the 1-dodecanol and vegetable oil lamps to see that they burn in a satisfactory manner. The end of the wick must not be too broad, otherwise a bushy, sooty flame will be obtained and combustion will be incomplete. If necessary, use scissors to trim the wick. The bottom of the can should be positioned about 1 cm above the tip of the flame. Blow out both flames and allow the beakers to cool to room temperature.

1. Calibration of the Calorimeter After the lamps have cooled, weigh the 1-dodecanol lamp as accurately as possible on the analytical balance and record the mass. (Be careful not to tip the beaker or spill any oil in the process.) Measure and record the room temperature.

Prepare some water that is about 10C° cooler than room temperature by mixing chilled water (from a refrigerated drinking fountain) or crushed ice with tap water. If you use ice, fill a 400-mL beaker about one-third full of crushed ice. Fill a 600-mL beaker about half full of tap water. Mix the contents of the two beakers back and forth until the ice is melted. Measure the temperature of the cold water, which should be about 10 C° lower than room temperature. Using your 100-mL graduated cylinder, measure out exactly 100 mL of the cold water and pour it into the aluminum can, being very careful not to allow any water to spill down the outside of the can. Stir the water thoroughly with a thermometer, then read the temperature to the nearest 0.2 C°, and record it.

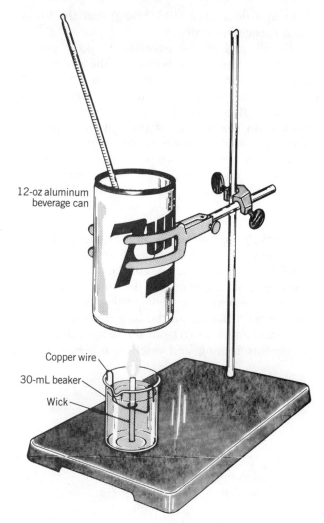

12-oz aluminum beverage can

Copper wire

30-mL beaker

Wick

FIGURE 13-1
A simple combustion calorimeter using an aluminum beverage can with the top cut out.

(There must be no ice in the water added to the can, otherwise energy would go into melting the ice rather than heating the water.)

Quickly relight the weighed 1-dodecanol lamp and place it under the can of water, carefully centering the flame under the bottom of the can. Stir the water with a thermometer and when the temperature of the water in the calorimeter has risen about as many degrees above room temperature as the initial temperature was below, remove the beaker of 1-dodecanol and blow out the flame. Keep stirring the water in the calorimeter, recording the highest temperature attained to the nearest 0.2 C°.

When the beaker of 1-dodecanol has cooled to room temperature, reweigh it, and record the mass. You now have the necessary data to calibrate the calorimeter, using the known heat of combustion of 1-dodecanol (10.1 kcal/g) and the known heat capacity of water.

At the end of the experiment, pour out the water and look at the bottom of the can. A light coating of soot is normal. If the coat is heavy, the wick should be trimmed and the measurement repeated. Between each measurement, remove the soot from the bottom of the can by scouring it with steel wool. If your instructor so directs, repeat the measurement. With care, the temperature change of the water divided by the mass change of the lamp should agree within 10% for the two trials.

2. Enthalpy of Combustion of a Vegetable Oil Record in your report the type of vegetable oil used. Weigh and record the mass of the lamp containing vegetable oil. Using exactly the same procedure as in part 1, prepare a fresh portion of cold water, put exactly 100 mL of the cold water in the calorimeter can, and carry out the temperature measurements, heating, and weighing as before. Record the initial and final temperatures of the water and the mass of the vegetable oil lamp after it has cooled to room temperature.

By assuming that the fraction of the heat captured by the calorimeter is the same for the vegetable oil lamp as for the 1-dodecanol lamp, you now have the necessary data to calculate the heat of combustion of vegetable oil. If your instructor so directs, repeat the measurements to obtain a duplicate set of values. Remember to keep the wick trimmed and to scour the bottom of the can to remove soot after each measurement.

When all of the measurements are completed, pour the unused 1-dodecanol and vegetable oil into waste recovery containers. (Do not pour the 1-dodecanol and vegetable oil back into the original stock bottles.)

Calculate the efficiency of the calorimeter from the data obtained in part 1 and the enthalpy of combustion of the vegetable oil from the measured efficiency and the data obtained in part 2.

The Enthalpy of Combustion of a Vegetable Oil	NAME _____
	SECTION _____ LOCKER _____
	INSTRUCTOR _____ DATE _____

DATA AND CALCULATIONS

1. Calibration of the Calorimeter by the Combustion of 1-Dodecanol

Data	Trial 1	Trial 2
(a) Initial mass of lamp	_____ g	_____ g
(b) Final mass of lamp	_____ g	_____ g
(c) Milliliters of water placed in calorimeter	_____ mL	_____ mL
(d) Room temperature	_____ °C	_____ °C
(e) Initial temperature of water in calorimeter	_____ °C	_____ °C
(f) Final temperature of water in calorimeter	_____ °C	_____ °C

Calculations

	Trial 1	Trial 2
(g) Mass of 1-dodecanol burned	_____ g	_____ g
(h) Temperature rise of water in calorimeter	_____ °C	_____ °C
(i) Heat absorbed by water ($\Delta H = mC_P \Delta T \times 1$ kcal/1000 cal) Assume that the density of water is 1.00 g/mL and the C_P for water is 1.00 cal·g^{-1}·K^{-1}.	_____ kcal	_____ kcal
(j) Heat produced by burning ($\Delta H = g_{\text{1-dodecanol burned}} \times 10.1$ kcal/g)	_____ kcal	_____ kcal
(k) Efficiency $= \dfrac{\text{heat absorbed}}{\text{heat produced}} =$	_____	_____

(l) Average efficiency = _____

2. Enthalpy of combustion of a vegetable oil

Data   Trial 1   Trial 2

(a) Type of vegetable oil used   _____   _____

(b) Initial mass of vegetable oil lamp   _____ g   _____ g

(c) Final mass of vegetable oil lamp   _____ g   _____ g

(d) Milliliters of water placed in calorimeter   _____ mL   _____ mL

(e) Room temperature   _____ °C   _____ °C

(f) Initial temperature of water in calorimeter   _____ °C   _____ °C

(g) Final temperature of water in calorimeter   _____ °C   _____ °C

Calculations

(h) Mass of vegetable oil burned   _____ g   _____ g

(i) Temperature rise of water in calorimeter   _____ °C   _____ °C

(j) Heat absorbed by water ($\Delta H = mC_P \Delta T \times 1$ kcal/1000 cal) Assume that the density of water is 1.00 g/mL and the C_P for water is 1.00 cal·g^{-1}·K^{-1}.   _____ kcal   _____ kcal

(k) Calculate the enthalpy of combustion per gram of vegetable oil by using the average efficiency calculated in part 1.

$$\Delta H_{\text{combustion}} = \frac{\text{heat absorbed}}{\text{average efficiency}} \times \frac{1}{g_{\text{oil burned}}}$$

  _____ kcal/g   _____ kcal/g

(l) Calculate the percentage relative error, assuming the true value for the enthalpy of combustion of vegetable oil to be 8.84 kcal/g.

$$\text{percentage of relative error} = \frac{\Delta H_{\text{comb.}} - 8.84 \text{ kcal/g}}{8.84 \text{ kcal/g}} \times 100$$

  _____ %   _____ %

QUESTIONS

1. The efficiency of the calorimeter is considerably less than 100%. Where does the heat go that does not raise the temperature of the water in the calorimeter?

2. What is the purpose of stopping the heating when the temperature of the water in the can is about as many degrees above room temperature as it started below room temperature?

3. The next time you eat a salad suppose you were to refrain from putting salad dressing on it. This would reduce your caloric intake by about the equivalent of a tablespoon (13.5 g) of vegetable oil. Based on your experimental results, how many kilocalories would this eliminate from your daily calorie intake? What percentage would this be of the 1375 kcal/day required to sustain the basal metabolic rate (BMR) of a 140-lb young woman?

Enthalpy Changes in Chemical Reactions

Hess's Law

PURPOSE

To test Hess's law that the heat of reaction is the same whether the reaction is carried out directly or in a number of steps, by measuring the enthalpy changes for the same net chemical reaction carried out by two different paths.

PRE-LAB PREPARATION

Thermochemistry deals with the thermal energy changes that accompany chemical reactions. These energy changes are usually called *heats of reaction*. When the reaction is carried out at constant pressure, the heat of reaction is called the enthalpy change, ΔH. A reaction that produces heat is said to be *exothermic*. For an exothermic reaction the enthalpy of the products is less than the enthalpy

of the reactants. If we define the change in enthalpy as $\Delta H = H_{products} - H_{reactants}$, we see that ΔH will be negative for an exothermic reaction. Conversely, if energy is absorbed from the surroundings when a reaction proceeds, the enthalpy change for the reaction will be positive and we say the reaction is *endothermic*.

Although the enthalpy change for a chemical reaction tells us whether heat will be released or absorbed, it cannot be used to determine if a reaction can spontaneously proceed. There are examples of spontaneous reactions that have either positive or negative enthalpy changes. As you study thermodynamics further you will be introduced to *entropy* and *free energy* functions, which can be used to determine if a particular reaction is possible.

A chemical reaction may also involve energy changes other than a flow of heat to or from the surroundings. For example, an electrochemical cell can produce *electrical energy* equivalent to the product of the cell voltage multiplied by the electric charge transferred to an external circuit. A chemical reaction that produces a gas must push back the atmosphere, and this mechanical *work* is another form of energy. (If the reaction is carried out in containers open to the atmosphere, the work of pushing back the atmosphere is included in the enthalpy change, ΔH.)

Enthalpy changes may be classified into more specific categories: (1) The heat of formation is the amount of heat involved in the formation of 1 mol of the substance directly from its constituent elements; (2) the heat of combustion is the amount of heat produced when a mole of a combustible substance reacts with excess oxygen; (3) the heat of solution of a substance is the thermal energy change that accompanies the dissolving of a substance in a solvent; (4) the heats of vaporization, fusion, and sublimation are related to the thermal energy changes that accompany changes in state; (5) the heat of neutralization is the enthalpy change associated with the reaction of an acid and a base.

In this experiment you will measure the heats of reaction for the following reactions:

$$H_2SO_4 \text{ (10 M)} + \text{solvent} + \text{NaOH (1 M)} \rightarrow$$

$$\text{NaHSO}_4 \text{ (0.5 M)} + H_2O \qquad (1)$$

$$H_2SO_4 \text{ (10 M)} + \text{solvent} \rightarrow$$

$$H_2SO_4 \text{ (1 M)} \qquad (2)$$

$$H_2SO_4 \text{ (1 M)} + \text{NaOH (1 M)} \rightarrow$$

$$\text{NaHSO}_4 \text{ (0.5 M)} + H_2O \qquad (3)$$

In these reactions the numbers in parentheses specify the molar concentrations of the reactants and products. Water is both the solvent and a reaction product. In order to distinguish these two roles we write H_2O when we mean a reaction product and write *solvent* when water is used to dissolve the reactants and serve as the reaction medium.

Reactions (1) and (3) can be regarded as neutralization reactions. Reaction (2) could be called a solution (or dilution) reaction, and we will call the enthalpy change for this process the *heat of solution*. Note also that if we add reaction (2) and reaction (3) we get reaction (1). Thus, reaction (1) and the sum of reactions (2) and (3) represent two different pathways by which we can get from the same initial state to the same final state.

Hess's Law

Germain Henri Hess (1802–1850) discovered the principle we now call *Hess's law*: The enthalpy change of a reaction is the same whether the reaction is carried out directly or in a number of steps. This means that the enthalpy changes for chemical reactions are additive, just like the chemical reactions themselves. If

$$\text{reaction (1)} = \text{reaction (2)} + \text{reaction (3)}$$

then

$$\Delta H_1 = \Delta H_2 + \Delta H_3 \qquad (4)$$

To state Hess's law another way, if you start at point A (enthalpy state A) and proceed to point B (enthalpy state B) by two different paths, the sum of all of the enthalpy changes along the first path will equal the sum of the enthalpy changes by the second path.

In this experiment we will measure the enthalpy changes for reactions (1), (2), and (3) and test the relation shown in Equation (4), which is a mathematical statement of Hess's law. (Reaction (2), the heat of solution of H_2SO_4, was described by Hess in his first thermochemical publication in 1840.)

Enthalpy changes are usually measured in a calorimeter, a simple version of which is shown in Figure 14-1. The purpose of the calorimeter is to isolate thermally the solution under study. All of the heat liberated (or absorbed) by the chemical reaction goes into heating (or cooling) the contents of the calorimeter.

The amount of energy (heat) required to raise the temperature of 1 g of a substance by 1 C° is called the *heat capacity* of that material. (The term *specific heat* is often used for this quantity.) The units of heat capacity are calories per gram per degree Celsius. The abbreviation for calorie is cal; 1 cal is the quantity of energy required to increase the temperature of 1 g of water by 1 C°. Heat capacities are generally measured experimentally. Knowledge of the volume and density (or the mass) of a substance, its heat capacity, and the temperature change allow us to calculate the enthalpy change of the substance according to the equation

$$\Delta H = V d C_P \, \Delta T \qquad (5)$$

Dimensional analysis of Equation (5) shows that it gives the number of calories released or absorbed:

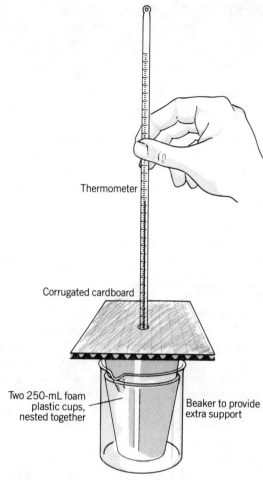

Thermometer

Corrugated cardboard

Two 250-mL foam
plastic cups,
nested together

Beaker to provide
extra support

FIGURE 14-1
A simple calorimeter for measuring the heat of a reaction.

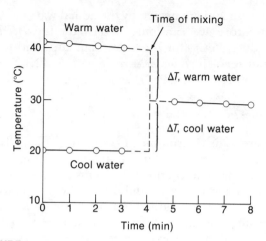

FIGURE 14-2
Typical data on temperature and time that are obtained in the determination of the water equivalent of the calorimeter.

enthalpy change (ΔH, cal)

= volume of solution (mL)

 × density of solution (g/mL)

 × heat capacity (cal·g^{-1}·K^{-1})

 × temperature change (ΔT, K)

Correction must be made for the heat absorbed or evolved by the calorimeter itself—in our case, the Styrofoam cups and thermometer that make up the calorimeter. Finally, to correct for heat leaks into or out of the calorimeter it is advisable to take a series of temperature-time readings and to extrapolate a graph of these data back to the time of mixing, to obtain a correct temperature change, ΔT K, for the reaction (see Figure 14-2).

Measuring Heats of Reaction with a Styrofoam Cup Calorimeter We will first measure the effective heat capacity of a simple calorimeter containing cool (room temperature) water, by adding a known volume of warm water to it and measuring the temperature increase. Then in three subsequent experiments we will measure the enthalpy changes for reactions (1), (2), and (3).

Employing the principle of the conservation of energy (which is a statement equivalent to the first law of thermodynamics), we will write an equation that states that the sum of the enthalpy change of the calorimeter and contents plus the enthalpy change of the added warm water must be zero. (The change in enthalpy of the calorimeter and contents is equal in magnitude to the change in enthalpy of the added warm water, but they have opposite signs.) The change in enthalpy of the calorimeter will be divided into two parts, the Styrofoam cups and thermometer that make up the calorimeter and the cool water originally present in the calorimeter. Thus,

$$\underset{\substack{\text{Styrofoam}\\\text{cups +}\\\text{thermometer}}}{\Delta H} \; + \; \underset{\substack{\text{cool water}\\\text{in the}\\\text{calorimeter}}}{\Delta H} \; + \; \underset{\substack{\text{added}\\\text{warm}\\\text{water}}}{\Delta H} = 0 \qquad (6)$$

Using the definition of the enthalpy change given in Equation (5), we can write Equation (6) as

$$\underset{\substack{\text{Styrofoam}\\\text{cups +}\\\text{thermometer}}}{(VdC_P)\,\Delta T} \; + \; \underset{\substack{\text{cool water}\\\text{in the}\\\text{calorimeter}}}{VdC_P\,\Delta T} \; + \; \underset{\substack{\text{added}\\\text{warm}\\\text{water}}}{VdC_P\,\Delta T} = 0 \qquad (7)$$

It should be recognized that only part of the Styrofoam cups and thermometer come into contact with and are heated by the added warm water. Therefore we can only determine the *effective* product, $V dC_P$, for the Styrofoam cups and thermometer—the *calorimeter constant*, B (cal/K). So we will rewrite Equation (7) as

$$B \, \Delta T_C + V_C dC_P \, \Delta T_C + V_W dC_P \, \Delta T_W = 0 \quad (8)$$

where V_C is the volume of cool water originally in the calorimeter, ΔT_C is the temperature increase of the calorimeter and cool water, V_W is the volume of added warm water, and ΔT_W is the temperature decrease of the added warm water (ΔT_W is a negative quantity). These four quantities are all measured in the experiment. If in addition we know d and C_P, the density and heat capacity of water, we can solve Equation (8) to obtain the calorimeter constant, B.

A series of three experiments is then carried out to measure the enthalpy changes for reactions (1), (2), and (3). In these experiments we mix aqueous solutions of the reactants, so water is the reaction medium and the thermal changes result from the chemical reactions that take place in solution. We can write an equation similar to Equation (8) to describe the enthalpy changes in these experiments:

$$\underset{\substack{\text{enthalpy} \\ \text{change of} \\ \text{cups +} \\ \text{thermometer}}}{B \, \Delta T_C} + \underset{\substack{\text{enthalpy} \\ \text{change of} \\ \text{solution in} \\ \text{calorimeter}}}{V_C \, dC_P \, \Delta T_C} + \underset{\substack{\text{enthalpy} \\ \text{change of} \\ \text{added} \\ \text{reactant} \\ \text{solution}}}{V_R \, dC_P \, \Delta T_R}$$

$$+ \underset{\substack{\text{enthalpy} \\ \text{of} \\ \text{reaction}}}{\Delta H_{\text{reaction}}} = 0 \quad (9)$$

In these experiments we measure V_C (the volume of reagent in the calorimeter), ΔT_C (the temperature change of the calorimeter and contents), V_R (the volume of added reactant solution), and ΔT_R (the temperature change of the added reactant solution). We will take the product of the density and heat capacity of the solutions, dC_P, to be 0.98 cal·g^{-1}·K^{-1}, nearly the same as the product for pure water.[1] Substituting these values and the previously determined value of B into Equation (9), we can solve for $\Delta H_{\text{reaction}}$, the enthalpy change for the chemical reaction. Knowing the number of moles of reactants mixed together, we can express the enthalpy change per mole of reaction.

---

[1] The density of the solutions is about 4 to 6% greater than that of pure water, but the heat capacity is about 4 to 8% less, so the product of density × heat capacity (dC_P) is nearly the same as the product for pure water (within 2%).

EXPERIMENTAL PROCEDURE

Special Supplies: Two thermometers (1 C° divisions are suitable; if available, 0.1 C° divisions will give better accuracy), four 7-oz Styrofoam cups per student for use as calorimeters (available from a supermarket), corrugated cardboard for calorimeter covers, graph paper (optional).

Chemicals: 10.0 M H_2SO_4, 1.00 M H_2SO_4, 1.00 M NaOH.

NOTE TO INSTRUCTOR Prepare the solutions in advance and store them in the laboratory so the solutions will be at the ambient temperature of the laboratory.

Safety Precautions: Sulfuric acid (H_2SO_4) and sodium hydroxide (NaOH) cause skin and eye burns. Handle with care.

---

1. *Preparation of the Calorimeters and Comparison of the Thermometers* Prepare two calorimeters, each like that shown in Figure 14-1. (Two nested cups are used to provide greater insulation.) Using a pen, label the calorimeters with a 1 and a 2. Put a piece of tape on each thermometer and label them 1 and 2 also. After comparison of the thermometers as described below, always use thermometer 1 in calorimeter 1 and thermometer 2 in calorimeter 2.

In parts 2 and 5 you will be pouring solutions from calorimeter 2 into calorimeter 1 and measuring the temperature changes. In order to measure these changes accurately, your two thermometers must agree. Usually they don't, so it is necessary to make a correction to the temperature reading on thermometer 2 so that it will agree with the temperature shown by thermometer 1. Do this in the following way: Compare your two thermometers by immersing them together in water at room temperature for 1 min and reading the temperature of each as nearly as possible to the nearest 0.1 C°. Be careful to avoid parallax in your readings (see the Introduction for a discussion of parallax). Record the two temperature readings. If thermometer 2 reads a *higher* temperature than thermometer 1, then you will correct thermometer 2 readings to conform to those on thermometer 1 by *subtracting* the difference. If thermometer 2 reads a *lower* temperature, *add* the difference to all readings on thermometer 2. This procedure arbitrarily expresses all temperatures on the scale of thermometer 1. When you record temperature readings from thermometer 2, record first the actual reading, and then in parentheses the corrected reading.

2. Determination of the Calorimeter Constant   To correct for the heat that is lost to the Styrofoam cups and thermometer that make up the calorimeter you will measure the effective heat capacity, B (cal/K), for the calorimeter. Place 50.0 mL of tap water at room temperature in calorimeter 1, and 50.0 mL of tap water that has been heated to 15 to 20 C° above room temperature in calorimeter 2. With the lids and thermometers in place, make careful temperature readings (± 0.1 C°) of each at 1-min intervals for 3 min, recording each reading. At the fourth minute, pour the warmer water quickly and as completely as possible into calorimeter 1, and continue reading and recording the temperatures read on thermometer 1 at the fifth, sixth, and seventh minutes. Correct all readings on thermometer 2 to conform to thermometer 1 and put the corrected readings in parentheses beside the actual readings recorded for thermometer 2.

Rinse and dry the cups and carry out a set of duplicate measurements. Then rinse and dry the cups in preparation for part 3.

Determine the temperatures of the two samples and of the mixture at the time of mixing by extrapolation as shown in Figure 14-2. Make the extrapolation by eye on your report form or make a graph on which you plot the temperatures of the two portions of water on the ordinate (vertical axis) and the time along the abscissa (horizontal axis).

Calculate the calorimeter constant, B, by rearranging Equation (8) to solve for B. Assume the density (d) of water to be 1.00 g/mL, and the heat capacity (C_P) to be 1.00 cal·g^{-1}·K^{-1}. Note that the units of the calorimeter constant are calories per Celsius degree. This simply measures the amount of heat required to raise the parts of the Styrofoam cups and thermometer that are in contact with the water by 1 C°. Repeat the calculation for your duplicate set of measurements and average your results. (Typical values for calorimeters of the type shown in Figure 14-1 are about 3 to 6 cal/K. A value of zero or a negative value indicates some flaw in your technique or calculations.)

3. The Heat of Solution and Neutralization of 10 M H_2SO_4 and 1 M NaOH   Place 50.0 mL of 1.00 M NaOH and 45.0 mL of water in calorimeter 1. Measure out exactly 5.00 mL of 10.0 M H_2SO_4 in a 5- or 10-mL graduated cylinder. With thermometer 1, measure the temperature of the 10.0 M H_2SO_4 and record the reading. Remove the thermometer and readjust the volume to exactly 5.00 mL, if necessary. Then rinse and dry the ther-

mometer and insert it into calorimeter 1, which contains the NaOH solution. Stir the solution gently, then read and record the temperature at 1-min intervals for 3 min as before. At the fourth minute, add the 5.00 mL of 10.0 M H_2SO_4. Stir and record the temperature at the fifth, sixth, and seventh minutes. Discard the solution and rinse and dry the cups. Carry out a duplicate set of measurements, then rinse and dry the cups in preparation for part 4.

4. The Heat of Solution of 10 M H_2SO_4   Measure 90.0 mL of water in a graduated cylinder and put it into calorimeter 1. Measure out 10.0 mL of 10.0 M H_2SO_4 in a 10-mL graduated cylinder. Measure and record the temperature of the 10.0 M H_2SO_4, using thermometer 1. Remove the thermometer and readjust the volume to exactly 10.00 mL, if necessary. Then rinse and dry thermometer 1 and place it in calorimeter 1 and gently stir. Read and record the temperature at 1-min intervals for 3 min as before. At the fourth minute, pour the 10.0 M H_2SO_4 into calorimeter 1. Continue to stir, reading and recording the temperatures at the fifth, sixth, and seventh minutes. Discard the solution, rinse and dry the calorimeter cups, and carry out a set of duplicate measurements. Rinse and dry the cups to prepare for part 5.

5. The Heat of Neutralization of 1.00 M H_2SO_4 and 1.00 M NaOH   Place 50.0 mL of 1.00 M NaOH in calorimeter 1 and 50.0 mL of 1.00 M H_2SO_4 in calorimeter 2. Put thermometers 1 and 2 in their respective calorimeters and stir gently, reading and recording the temperatures (on both thermometers) at 1-min intervals for 3 min. At the fourth minute, pour the H_2SO_4 in calorimeter 2 quickly and completely into calorimeter 1. Stir and record the temperature reading of thermometer 1 at the fifth, sixth, and seventh minutes. Discard the solution and rinse and dry the cups. Carry out a duplicate set of measurements.

Calculations   For each of the reactions in parts 3, 4, and 5, determine the temperature change for the solution in calorimeter 1 (ΔT_C) and the added reactant solution (ΔT_R) by extrapolating the temperatures to the time of mixing (see Figure 14-3). (In part 5, be careful to make the necessary corrections to the readings on thermometer 2.) Calculate the heats of reaction for parts 3, 4, and 5 by rearranging Equation (9) to solve for $\Delta H_{reaction}$. Use the average value of B (the calorimeter constant) determined in part 2. Assume that the product of the *density × heat capacity* (dC_P) for

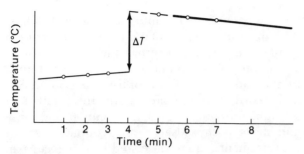

FIGURE 14-3
A time-temperature graph for a solution before and after a
chemical reaction. The temperature of the solution is measured
three times at 1-min intervals. The solution is gradually warming,
indicating that it is below room temperature. After 4 min have
elapsed, another solution, which yields an exothermic reaction, is
added, causing the temperature to rise. Temperatures are measured again at 1-min intervals, beginning at the fifth minute. The
temperature slowly falls between the fifth and seventh minutes,
indicating that the solution is now above room temperature.

each solution is 0.98 cal·mL^{-1}·K^{-1}.[2] Then calculate the enthalpy of reaction per mole for each
reaction by dividing each $\Delta H_{\text{reaction}}$ by the number
of moles of H_2SO_4 added in the reaction. (The
number of moles is calculated from V_R (L) $\times$ M
(mol/L) of the added H_2SO_4.)

---

[2] See footnote 1.

Emission Spectra and the Electronic Structure of Atoms

The Hydrogen Atom Spectrum

PURPOSE

To use a simple spectroscope to determine the wavelengths of the spectral lines emitted by excited hydrogen atoms. To show that these wavelengths fit a pattern of energy states described by a simple formula (the Rydberg equation) containing a single constant and integer quantum numbers. To show that atomic spectra can also be used qualitatively to identify elements.

PRE-LAB PREPARATION

The absorption and emission spectra of gaseous atoms of the elements do not look like the continuous rainbow-like spectrum of the heated filament of an incandescent bulb. They show instead many sharp lines with regions in between the lines where there is no emission or absorption. This provides the most convincing evidence that the electrons in

atoms do not have a continuous range of energies but only certain discrete values of energy. In reaching this conclusion, studies of the emission spectrum of the simplest atom, hydrogen, have played a crucial role.

The spectroscope, introduced by Bunsen and Kirchhoff about 1859, made possible the observation of the atomic spectra of excited gaseous atoms, and it was soon discovered that each element had a characteristic spectrum that could be used to identify the element (or to detect the presence of previously undiscovered elements). These spectral studies produced a mass of information on the spectral lines of the elements, but no real progress was made in explaining the origin of spectra until 1885, when Johann Balmer pointed out that the wavelengths of the lines of the hydrogen atom spectrum were given by a simple empirical formula containing one constant and the squares of small integers. Once this pattern of regularity was discovered, it became a challenge to human ingenuity to explain these regularities.

In 1913 the Danish physicist Niels Bohr used the notion of the quantum of energy introduced by Max Planck and the model of the nuclear atom published in 1911 by Rutherford to develop a theory of the behavior of an electron moving around a small positively charged nucleus. He used this theory to calculate the wavelengths of the spectral lines of the hydrogen atom with remarkable accuracy and showed how the regularities could be explained by assuming that energy was absorbed or emitted only when an electron passed from one energy state to another. Each energy state had an energy given by a constant divided by the square of a small integer, called a *quantum number*.

Although Bohr's theory was quite successful in interpreting the spectrum of the hydrogen atom, it was not as successful for interpreting the spectra of atoms with more than one electron. This led others, such as Erwin Schrödinger, Werner Heisenberg, and Paul Dirac, to formulate more complete theories, the first of which was published in 1926. The development of these theories after 1926 has shown that all aspects of atomic and molecular spectra can be explained quantitatively in terms of energy transitions between different allowed quantum states. (A *quantum* of energy is the smallest amount of energy that can be transferred to or from an atom or molecule. Because the energy is transferred only in packets of discrete size (called *photons or quanta*), it is said to be *quantized*.)

In this experiment you will use a simple spectroscope to measure the wavelengths of the spectral lines generated by the light energy emitted by several elements when their atoms have been excited by an electric discharge or a hot flame. After calibrating the spectroscope with the lines of mercury (whose wavelengths we will regard as known), you will measure the wavelengths of hydrogen and some gaseous nonmetal or metallic elements. The data for hydrogen will be used to construct quantitatively part of the energy diagram for hydrogen. As you do this experiment, think about the fact that you are following in the footsteps of scientific pioneers whose work ushered in the era of quantum mechanics and earned them Nobel prizes.

Waves and Diffraction

Light is electromagnetic radiation. This means that it possesses electric and magnetic properties. These properties vary sinusoidally and in phase with each other, as shown in Figure 15-1.

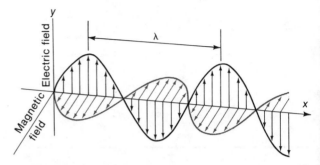

FIGURE 15-1
The electric- and magnetic-field components of a light wave.

Because only the electric part of the wave interacts with the electrons in atoms, Figure 15-1 is often simplified to the representation of Figure 15-2. The wavelength of this wave, λ, is defined as the distance between any two repeating portions of the wave. The wavelength of light visible to our eyes is 4×10^{-5} cm (blue) to 7.5×10^{-5} cm (red). Because these numbers are quite small, the units of wavelengths are often given in angstroms (Å), where 1 Å $= 10^{-10}$ m, or in nanometers (nm), where 1 nm $= 10^{-9}$ m. Demonstrate for yourself that the limits of the visible spectrum in these units are 4000 Å to 7500 Å or 400 nm to 750 nm.

Another important property of waves is frequency, ν. The frequency of a wave is the number of wavelengths that pass a given point in unit time. The units are generally number per second.

For a given wave, wavelength and frequency are not independent of each other. The higher the frequency, the smaller the wavelength. The reason for this relationship is that all light waves travel at the same velocity. This velocity is the speed of light, c, and is equal to 3.00×10^{10} cm/s. Some reflection on these three quantities (an analogy with a train in which λ = length of one car is helpful) leads to the correct mathematical expression:

$$c \text{ (cm/s)} = \lambda \text{ (cm)} \cdot \nu \text{ (s}^{-1}) \qquad (1)$$

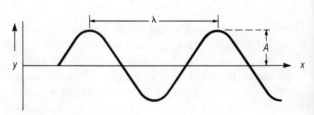

FIGURE 15-2
The amplitude (A) and wavelength (λ) of a light wave.

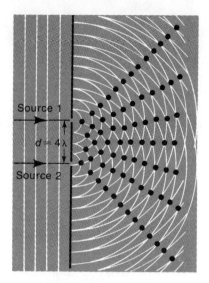

FIGURE 15-3
Diffraction of ocean waves by openings in a barrier.

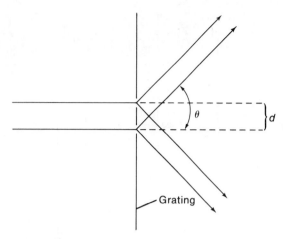

FIGURE 15-4
Diffraction of light by a transmission grating.

One of the unusual properties of waves is diffraction. All waves display this phenomenon, whether they are ocean waves, light waves, or sound waves. Perhaps you have seen ocean waves striking a small opening or several openings in a breakwater and observed the interesting patterns formed by the waves after they have passed through these openings. One pattern that you might have observed would look like the schematic diagram in Figure 15-3.

These patterns are obtained only when both the openings and the spacing, d, between the openings are of the same magnitude as λ. Thus, in order for diffraction to occur with light waves, the light must pass between slits that are very narrow and very close together. The plastic grating you will use was made from a precision-ruled metal grating in which there are 13,800 lines per inch. These gratings are of the transmission type. This means that light does not pass through the grating where the lines have been drawn but rather through the spaces between the lines.

The quantitative description of the behavior of waves on passing through slits of the appropriate size is the famous Bragg equation:

$$m\lambda = d \sin \theta \qquad (2)$$

The quantity m is a small integer having values 0, 1, 2, 3, ... The value d is the distance between the lines of the grating. The meaning of the angle θ is displayed in Figure 15-4.

The usefulness of the Bragg equation, as applied to a diffraction grating, is that it shows that the longer the wavelength is, the greater the angle of deviation, θ, will be. In all measurements made in this experiment, you will be observing the first-order, or $m = 1$, diffraction patterns. This means that if light of differing wavelengths strikes the grating, it will be bent to varying angles and in fact separated into its component wavelengths. White light consists of light of all wavelengths. The diffraction pattern of an ordinary tungsten light therefore is just a lovely rainbow. One of the first observations you should make with your spectroscope is of the light from a fluorescent lamp. In addition to the rainbow pattern observed with the tungsten lamp, you will find a bright green and a bright violet line. This is your first demonstration of the existence of line spectra of elements.

Energy Levels and Line Spectra of Elements

Our present theory of atomic structure states that electrons in an atom can possess only discrete energy values. As we noted earlier, the word quantized is used to describe discrete values. Every element has a characteristic set of energy levels. The energy-level diagram for hydrogen is given in Figure 15-5. The energy levels are characterized by an integer n, which is called the *principal quantum number*. At room temperature, most of the hydrogen atoms have energy corresponding to the $n = 1$ level, which is called the *ground state*.

If energy is supplied to a hydrogen atom in the $n = 1$ state by an electrical discharge or by heat, some of the atoms will absorb this energy and enter the $n = 2$, $n = 3$, or higher levels. These atoms having extra energy are called *excited* atoms. They can lose some of this extra energy in discrete

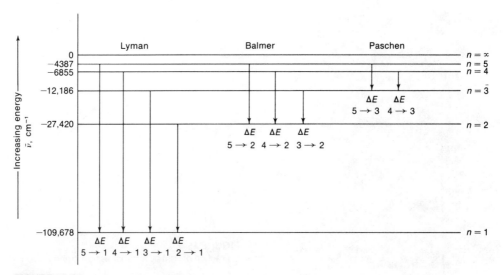

FIGURE 15-5
The energy levels of the hydrogen atom. The numbers on the left are the energy levels expressed in wave numbers. The integers on the right are the principal quantum numbers. The vertical arrows correspond to the energy differences, ΔE, between levels described by the indicated quantum numbers. The energy differences represent observable lines in the hydrogen spectrum (corresponding to the spectral transition—that is, the transition from one energy state to another state). Each of the three groups of spectral lines shown here is named for its discoverer.

amounts and drop back down to the $n = 3$ or $n = 2$ or ground state, as indicated in Figure 15-5.

The crucial question now is, How do atoms lose energy? Frequently they do so by emitting light of discrete wavelengths. It is important to note that all light is quantized in units called photons, which can be described as both particles and waves (or, indeed, as neither): in truth, they are particle-waves. Photons possess an energy proportional to the frequency of the light wave. The proportionality constant is Planck's constant, h, which has a value of 6.62×10^{-27} erg s. Thus the electron of the hydrogen atom can lose energy by emitting a photon that has an energy corresponding to the transition from n_2 to n_1, where n_2 and n_1 represent the quantum numbers of two different energy levels, and we have not specified their numerical values.

If a transition takes place between two different energy levels, n_2 and n_1, the energy difference between the n_2 and n_1 levels is related to the wavelength of the photon by the equation

$$\Delta E = E_{n_2} - E_{n_1} = h\nu = \frac{hc}{\lambda} \qquad (3)$$

The last identity is derived from Equation (1), which expresses the relationship between the velocity of light, frequency, and wavelength. The energy, ΔE, can be expressed in ergs or wave numbers, $\bar{\nu}$. *Wave number* is defined as the reciprocal of the wavelength, where λ is given in cen-

timeters. The units of $\bar{\nu}$ are reciprocal centimeters (cm^{-1}). This definition is useful because energy then is directly proportional to $\bar{\nu}$.

$$\Delta E = hc\bar{\nu} \qquad (4)$$

Sometimes, as in Figure 15-5, the product hc is divided into ΔE and the units of energy are given simply in cm^{-1}.

EXPERIMENTAL PROCEDURE

Special Supplies: Inexpensive spectroscopes like the one shown in Figure 15-6 may be purchased[1] or constructed (Method A); or a bare grating in a darkened room may be used (Method B).

---

[1] Science Kit Inc., 777 East Park Drive, Tonawanda, NY 14150, (716) 874–6020. QA Spectroscope, Catalog No. 16525 00.

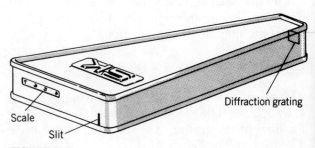

FIGURE 15-6
A hand-held spectroscope for measuring wavelengths by Method A (see text).

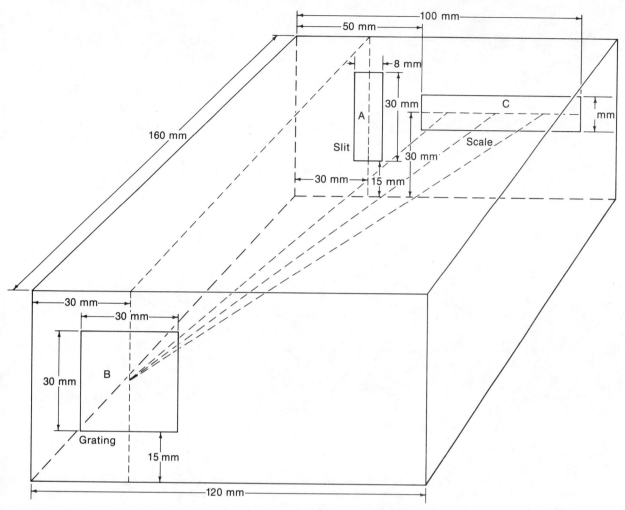

FIGURE 15-7
The construction of a hand-held spectroscope for measuring wavelengths by Method A (see text).

Method A: If the students are to construct a spectroscope like that shown in Figure 15-7, the following supplies will be needed: a cardboard box with lid (a No. 8 two-piece, set-up mailing box, 6 × 4.5 × 2.25 in., is a convenient size); spray cans of flat black paint (have the laboratory assistant spray the inside of each box with flat black paint a day or two ahead of time; this saves much time and mess); single-edged razor blade; double-edged razor blade; small piece of translucent millimeter graph paper; metric ruler; transmission-type plastic replica grating mounted in a 2- × 2-in. cardboard slide mount;[2] masking tape.

Method B: The setup shown in Figure 15-8 requires a darkened room in order to see the spectral lines, and works best with capillary-type gas discharge tubes. A Masonite grating holder and shield, constructed as shown in Figure 15-8, provide a convenient way to observe the spectra. A transmission-type plastic replica grating (see footnote 2) is taped to the grating holder. Black construction paper can be used to make a slit that is taped to the shield, which is painted flat black. A meter stick is used to measure the distance from the slit to the virtual image of the slit on the Masonite shield.

Sources: The most effective spectral sources for calibration (mercury spectrum) and examination of the emission spectra of gaseous atoms are inexpensive spectrum tubes excited by a 5000-V–7-mA-current transformer-type power supply. These are available from a number of suppliers.[3] Although more expensive, we recommend a brighter and longer-lived source for viewing the hydrogen atom emission spectrum. It is called a Balmer Gas Discharge Tube,[4] and its ends fit into standard fluorescent tube sockets, making it convenient to mount. An inexpensive power supply for this tube can be made by using a 5000-V–60-mA neon sign transformer (General Electric

[2] Edmund Scientific Co., 101 East Gloucester Pike, Barrington, NJ 08007. Card Mounted Diffraction Viewers, Container of 100, Catalog No. P-50,183.

[3] Central Scientific Co., 11222 Melrose Ave., Franklin Park, IL 60131. Catalog No. 87208-000, Spectrum Tube Power Supply/Holder. A number of different spectrum tubes are available.
Sargent-Welch Scientific Co., 7300 N. Linder Ave., P.O. Box 1026, Skokie, IL 60077. Catalog No. 2393D Spectrum Tube Power Supply/Holder. Catalog No. S-68755-30 Series Spectrum tubes.
[4] Glass Instruments Inc., 2285 East Foothill Boulevard, Pasadena, CA 91107. Catalog No. 7010 Balmer Hydrogen Gas Discharge Tube.
Central Scientific Co., 11222 Melrose Ave., Franklin Park, IL 60131. Catalog No. 87206-000 Balmer Gas Discharge Tube. Catalog No. 87201-000 Gas Discharge Tube Holder.

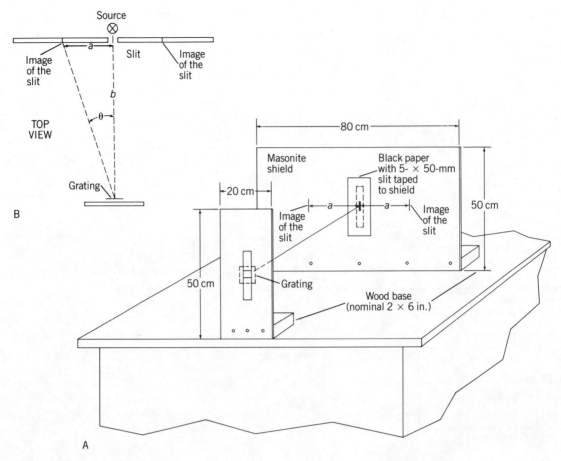

FIGURE 15-8
Plan (A) for the construction of a holder for the grating and slit for measuring wavelengths by Method B. The source and power supply are located behind the protective Masonite shield. The slit is a piece of black paper with a 5- × 50-mm aperture taped to the Masonite shield. (B) Top view of the setup.

Luminous Tube Transformer Model 9T61Y16) with an adjustable autotransformer (Variac) connected to the primary of the transformer. (The Variac is normally operated at 50 to 70 V.) Automotive spark plug wiring is used to make the connections between the secondary winding of the transformer and the spectrum tube. All exposed high-voltage connections should be covered with a heavy coating of silicone sealant.

In order to produce the spectra of different metals it is suggested that "pills," or pellets, of the metal salts be heated on the grid of a Fischer or Meker gas burner.[5] (The chloride salts of lithium, sodium, potassium, and calcium are recommended.) These can be formed with an inexpensive screw-type press of the kind used to make KBr pellets for taking infrared spectra.[6] Alternatively, a loop of Nichrome wire dipped in the metal salt and heated by a Bunsen burner may be used.

Tungsten filament bulbs and fluorescent lamps should also be available so that students can compare their spectra (see part 4 of the Experimental Procedure).

Safety Precautions: The power supplies used for the spectrum tubes are sources of high voltage that represent a danger to the unwary user. If the spectrum tube power supply or holder (or both) has exposed electrical connections, a shield like that shown in Figure 15-8 should be placed between the source and the viewer. Cut a rectangular viewing port in the shield so that the source can be viewed through the port.

A low-pressure mercury lamp puts out a large fraction of its energy in the ultraviolet (UV) 254-nm line. This, though not visible, can cause eye damage. This UV light is absorbed strongly by the lens material in eyeglasses. Do not look at the lamp without wearing glasses, and limit the calibration time to 5 to 10 min. For greater safety, a piece of ordinary window glass can be taped over the viewing port on the back of the shield to act as a UV cutoff filter.

---

[5] M. Bernard, "Spectroscopic Cation Analysis Using Metal Salt Pills," *J. Chem. Educ.* **57,** 153 (1980).

[6] Wilks Scientific Corp., 140 Water St., Box 449, South Norwalk, CT 06856. Catalog No. 019-4032 Mini-Press KBr Pellet Maker.

In order to prevent the breathing of any metal vapor (barium, for example, is toxic), the gas burners used to heat the metal salts should be placed in a fume hood.

Your instructor will tell you if you are to use spectroscopes that are already prepared or are to construct your own (Method A, Figure 15-6 or 15-7), or if you are to use a bare grating in a darkened room (Method B, Figure 15-8).

1. *Construction of a Spectroscope: Method A* If you are to construct a spectroscope like that shown in Figure 15-7, obtain a small cardboard box (6 × 4.5 × 2.25 in.) that has been sprayed on the inside with flat black paint to reduce internal reflections and make the spectra easier to observe. Noting the dimensions given in Figure 15-7, mark the positions of the holes on the outside of the box and cut out the three holes for the slit, the grating, and the scale. Cut the holes through the box and lid simultaneously, using a single-edged razor blade.

Carefully (razor blades are quite sharp) break the double-edged razor blade lengthwise in two. Tape the sharp edges facing each other to the outside of the box (at point A in Figure 15-7) with their edges 0.3 to 0.5 mm apart. (No diffraction is obtained from this slit because this opening is many times the wavelength of visible light.) Make sure that the edges of the slit are parallel to each other and perpendicular to the top and bottom of the box.

Observe the grating carefully. You will probably be able to observe some striations on the plastic surface. If you can see these reflections, mount the grating (point B, Figure 15-7) with the lines perpendicular to the top and bottom of the box. If you cannot observe these striations, close the box and hold the box with the slit pointing toward a fluorescent light. Hold the grating next to the hole at point B and observe the diffraction pattern. The orientation of the grating that produces the diffraction patterns on the right and left of the slit is the correct one. Tape the grating to the inside of the box at point B, with the grating in the correct orientation. Tape a scale cut from a piece of millimeter graph paper at point C, Figure 15-7. If too much light comes in through the scale to see the lines clearly, mask off part of the scale with tape.

Method B. The spectroscope consists of the setup shown in Figure 15-8: a source (capillary spectrum tube), a Masonite shield with a slit taped on the front, a transmission grating taped to a Masonite holder, and a meter stick. The images you see to the left and right of the slit will be virtual, not real, images of the slit (or capillary source). The slit is a 5- × 50-mm rectangular hole cut in the center of a piece of black construction paper that is taped to the front of the Masonite shield. (See Figure 15-8.)

Tape the grating to a Masonite support like that shown in Figure 15-8. (The rectangular holes, 3 × 20 cm, cut in the Masonite grating support and shield are made long in order to allow vertical adjustment of the grating and slit to match the height of the source.) Position the grating about 50 cm from the slit. (The plane of the grating must be parallel to the capillary source or slit and form a right angle with the incident light from the source as shown in Figure 15-9.)

Make sure you are wearing glasses to protect yourself from UV radiation from the sources. Turn on the mercury source and darken the room. Position your eye directly behind the grating within eyelash distance so that you are looking through the grating toward the source. Look to right and left. You should see images of the slit symmetrically displaced on both sides of the slit, corresponding to $m = \pm 1$ in Equation (2). The images on one side may appear slightly brighter because of the construction of the grating. Use the brighter side for all further measurements. If you have a good grating, you may also be able to see the second-order images ($m = \pm 2$) further displaced on both sides of the slit.

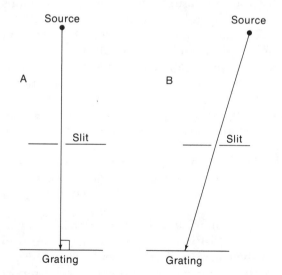

FIGURE 15-9
The angle of the incident light should be 90° with respect to the grating: (A) correct; (B) incorrect.

For each line you see in the first-order spectrum, record in your report the distance *a* (distance between the slit and the image of the slit or capillary source on the shield), measured to the nearest millimeter. (See Figure 15-8.) It may be helpful to have a lab partner place a marker such as a pencil at the apparent position of the line. Also measure and record distance *b* (the distance between the grating and the slit).

2. *Calibration of the Spectroscope*

Wear glasses at all times while observing lamps through the spectroscope to protect yourself from possible harmful UV radiation. You will use the emission lines of mercury as a "standard" to calibrate the spectroscope. Look at the spectrum of a mercury lamp. You should be able to see three or four lines. The colors and wavelengths of these lines are as follows:

Color	Wavelength, nm
Violet	404.7
Blue	435.8
Green	546.1
Yellow	579.0

Do you see any additional lines besides these four? If so, comment on them in the report form, and measure their positions on the scale.

Measure the positions of the four prominent lines on the scale as accurately as possible (nearest 0.3 mm using Method A; nearest millimeter using Method B). Record the average of several observations.

The following precautions and directions will enable you to measure reproducibly the positions of lines with hand-held spectroscopes (Method A).

(a) The lamp should be far enough away from the spectroscope (at least 25 to 30 cm) so that the direction of propagation of the light is well defined or collimated (Figure 15-10). If you do not observe this precaution, you will find that whenever you move your eye the spectral lines will appear to wander, rather than remaining stationary on the scale.

(b) The lamp should not be too far away (more than 40 cm), or the intensity of light falling on the slit will be too low for you to observe the spectrum clearly.

(c) The light must be incident on the grating at 90° (Figure 15-10) if the angle of diffraction is to satisfy the equation given previously.

On the graph paper provided in your report form draw a calibration graph of wavelength versus scale reading. Do this during your laboratory

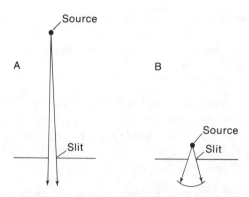

FIGURE 15-10
For the light to be well collimated when a hand-held spectroscope is used (Method A), the slit should be at least 25 to 30 cm from the source. (A) Well-collimated light; (B) poorly collimated light.

period. In the event that a good straight line is not obtained, measure the positions of the lines again.

You will use your linear graph to determine the wavelength of unknown lines by first measuring the position of the unknown line on the scale of your spectroscope; then, reading from your calibration, graph the wavelength that corresponds to the measured scale position.

3. *Observations and Measurements of the Hydrogen Spectrum*

Measure the scale position of the observable lines of the hydrogen emission spectrum. Normally at least three lines can be seen: violet, green, and red. From your measurements and your calibration graph, determine the wavelengths of these lines.

Look up the accepted literature values of the wavelengths of these lines in the *Handbook of Chemistry and Physics* (see the Bibliography). Calculate your relative error as a percentage.

Convert your values of wavelengths for the hydrogen atom spectrum to wave numbers ($\bar{\nu} = 1/\lambda$, where λ is the wavelength measured in centimeters). (The unit of wave number is proportional to energy, since $\Delta E = hc/\lambda$, where h is Planck's constant and c is the speed of light.) Each of these values should correspond to a *difference* between two energy states shown in Figure 15-5. For example, the red line of hydrogen corresponds to the difference between $-12,186$ cm^{-1} and $-27,420$ cm^{-1}, which is 15,234 cm^{-1}.

Draw that portion of the hydrogen atom energy-level diagram that you have measured, using wave numbers (in reciprocal centimeters) as units proportional to energy. Make your figure to scale on the graph paper provided.

Using the Rydberg equation,

$$\bar{\nu}\ (\text{cm}^{-1}) = R_{\text{H}} \left(\frac{1}{n_2^2} - \frac{1}{n_1^2} \right) \qquad (5)$$

calculate for each of the three lines you measured a value for the Rydberg constant, R_{H}. This constant relates the wave number ($\bar{\nu}$, cm^{-1}) of a given transition to the principal quantum numbers for the transition. The values of the quantum numbers (n_2 and n_1) for each of the lines you observed can be obtained from Figure 15-5. Keep in mind that each line you observed corresponds to a transition between two energy states. Each state has an energy and a quantum number shown in Figure 15-5.

The Ionization Energy of the Hydrogen Atom

The transition from $n = 1$ to $n = \infty$ describes the ionization of the hydrogen atom, the energy required to completely remove the electron from a hydrogen atom. The energy difference corresponding to this difference is equal to the Rydberg constant. Thus the value of the Rydberg constant in reciprocal centimeters can be read directly from Figure 15-5 as 109,678 cm^{-1}, the difference in energy between the $n = 1$ and $n = \infty$ levels.

4. *Other Uses of the Spectroscope* You will be provided with metal salts to be heated in the flame of a burner and/or other spectrum tubes containing various gaseous elements such as helium, neon, argon, or oxygen. Observe the emission spectra of the metal salts or of the gases and note and record the scale positions of the lines you see. Determine the wavelengths from your calibration graph and compare the values with literature values for the elements you observed.

Observe the spectrum of the light from a tungsten filament lamp and from a fluorescent lamp by using your spectroscope. You should see a continuous rainbow-like spectrum with both types of lamps, but the fluorescent lamp will also show some discrete lines. These lines should be familiar because you used them to calibrate your spectroscope.

BIBLIOGRAPHY

Edwards, R. K., Brandt, W. W., and Companion, A. A., "A Simple and Inexpensive Student Spectroscope," *J. Chem. Educ.* **39,** 147 (1962).

Handbook of Chemistry and Physics. Published annually by the Chemical Rubber Company, Cleveland.

Harris, S. P., "Letter to the Editor," *J. Chem. Educ.* **39,** 319 (1962).

Logan, K. R., "Some Experiments in Atomic Structures," *J. Chem. Educ.* **51,** 411 (1974).

REPORT

15

**Emission Spectra
and the Electronic
Structure of Atoms
The Hydrogen Atom Spectrum**

NAME

SECTION   LOCKER

INSTRUCTOR   DATE

OBSERVATIONS AND DATA

1. Construction of the Spectroscope

(a) Give the distance from slit to grating (Method A or Method B).   _____ mm

(b) Give the distance from center of slit to first major scale mark (Method A only).   _____ mm

2. Calibration of the Spectroscope

(a) Measure the position of the four prominent lines in the spectrum of mercury.

Color	Known wavelength (Å)	Position on spectroscope scale (mm)
Violet	4047	
Blue	4358	
Green	5461	
Yellow	5790	

(b) Comment on other lines observed.

(c) Plot wavelength (in angstroms) versus the scale reading (in millimeters) on the graph below.

3. Observations and Measurements of the Hydrogen Spectrum

(a) You should observe at least three lines in the hydrogen spectrum. If you can see an additional line, enter the data for it in the table below.

Color	Scale position (mm)	Wavelength (Å) from calibration graph	Known wavelength (Å)	Percentage error

(b) Show how you convert one of the above λ values in angstroms to the corresponding $\bar{\nu}$ in reciprocal centimeters.

(c) Convert all of your wavelengths to the corresponding wave numbers.

Your wavelength (Å)	Wave number (cm^{-1})	Literature value for wave number (cm^{-1})

(d) Calculate the Rydberg constant. Give one example showing your method of calculation.

(e) Look up the actual value of R_H and complete your percentage error for each line.

Your wavelength (Å)	Experimental value of R_H	Percentage error

4. Other Uses of the Spectroscope

(a) Record your observations of the cation emission spectra.

Salt	Color of flame	Scale position of observed lines	Wavelengths of these lines

(b) Describe the spectrum of the light from a fluorescent lamp, and try to explain what you observe. How is the element mercury involved in the operation of a fluorescent lamp?

QUESTIONS

1. Using Equation (5), the Rydberg equation, show that $\bar{\nu} = -R_H$, the Rydberg constant, for the transition $n_1 = 1$ to $n_2 = \infty$. This constant is the ionization energy of the hydrogen atom, in units of reciprocal centimeters.

---

2. The images of the lines that you see appear to be light reflected from the scale. Are the images *real*, that is, does light really fall on the scale at the point where you see the image? (*Hint:* You may want to consult an elementary physics book to answer this question. Look up the term *virtual image*.)

---

3. When you observe the spectra of the metal salts, how do you know that the emission comes from the metal atoms and not from the atoms of the anions (chlorine, for example)? Suggest one or more experiments that might provide an answer to this question.

Ionic and Covalent Compounds
Ionic Reactions

PURPOSE

To measure the electrical conductivity of a number of substances, both in the pure state and in solution, in order to see if there is any dissociation of the substances to form ions. To measure the effects of solvent properties on the dissociation of a polar substance, HCl. To measure changes in conductivity that result from the reaction of ionic substances to form products that are weakly ionized or insoluble.

PRE-LAB PREPARATION

Ionic, Polar, and Covalent Bonding

When an active metal reacts with an active non-metallic element, the latter becomes negatively charged by the transfer of one or more electrons from the metal, which in turn becomes positively charged. In general, each element tends to assume its most stable electronic configuration, with its valence electron shell filled, as in the noble gases. Using the conventional electron-dot formulas, we write, for example,

$$\text{Na} \cdot + \cdot \ddot{\underset{\cdot\cdot}{\text{Cl}}}: \rightarrow \text{Na}^+ \; :\ddot{\underset{\cdot\cdot}{\text{Cl}}}:^-$$

Such electrically charged atoms, or radicals, are called *ions*. The bonding force between ions, due primarily to the attraction of unlike electric charges, results in an *ionic bond*.

When two elements of similar electronegative character react, however, they do so by the formation of a stable electron-pair orbital, mutually shared by both of the atomic nuclei. For example,

$$\text{H} \cdot + \cdot \text{H} \rightarrow \text{H}:\text{H} \quad \text{or} \quad \text{H}_2$$

$$2\text{H} \cdot + \cdot \ddot{\text{O}} \cdot \rightarrow \text{H}:\overset{\cdot\cdot}{\underset{\cdot\cdot}{\text{O}}}: \quad \text{or} \quad \text{H}_2\text{O}$$
$$\phantom{2\text{H} \cdot + \cdot \ddot{\text{O}} \cdot \rightarrow \text{H}:}\text{H}$$

Such a bond is called a *covalent bond*. In the second example, since oxygen is more electronegative than hydrogen, the bond is quite *polar*, or *partially ionic*, in character. Note that the two types of bonds are really two extremes of a continuum—the purely ionic bond at one extreme and the purely covalent bond at the other. In between are the polar or partially ionic bonds.

Structure and Bond Type

Substances with covalently bonded atoms generally have definite molecules as the units of crystal structure.[1] Such substances, if soluble in water or other suitable solvent, give simply a mixture of electrically neutral molecules, and the solution is a nonconductor. Examples of such *nonelectrolytes* are sugar ($C_{12}H_{22}O_{11}$) and acetone (CH_3COCH_3).

Acids, bases, and *salts* possess either ionic bonds or bonds that are quite polar. As solids, the ions of such substances constitute the structural units in the crystal. When melted by heat, the ionic lattice structure is broken down and the mixture of independent ions is an electrical conductor. When these substances dissolve in water, the ions likewise separate as independently moving particles, and the solutions are electrical conductors. Accordingly, in equations throughout this manual we write the formulas of such substances in solution, or in the molten state, as separate ions. Examples of such *electrolytes* are sodium hydroxide ($NaOH$), which supplies Na^+ and OH^-, and potassium sulfate (K_2SO_4), which supplies K^+ and SO_4^{2-}.[2]

The strong, or active, acids and bases, and most salts, ionize completely in dilute aqueous solution. In solutions of weak or slightly active acids and bases, a large part of the dissolved substance is present in molecular form; thus, although the total concentration may be high, the concentration of ions is low. This accounts for their slight conductivity. Relatively insoluble salts, although regarded as strong electrolytes in that normally all of the substance that is dissolved is present in ionic form, will likewise supply only a low concentration of ions to a solution.

---

[1] Omitted from consideration here are the giant molecules, such as quartz ($SiO_2)_x$, and metal bonds and intermetallic compounds.
[2] In designating the ions of K_2SO_4, we would use the coefficient 2—for example, $2K^+$—only to designate a specific amount of the substance K^+, as when balancing an equation.

The Role of the Solvent in Dissociation Reactions

Most of the solution reactions we have studied have been in aqueous solution. However, it is important to remember that nonaqueous solvents are often used and that the dissociation of acids, bases, and salts depends very much on the properties of the solvent. For example, the dissociation of an acid involves the transfer of a proton from the acid to the solvent. Therefore the extent of dissociation of an acid will depend on the intrinsic basicity of the solvent. Although acetic acid is only partially dissociated in water, it is completely dissociated in a more basic solvent such as liquid ammonia.

The dielectric constant of the solvent and the solvation energy of ions in a solvent are also important. If two ions of opposite charge are placed in a vacuum, the force between them is given by Coulomb's law,

$$\text{force} = \frac{kq_1q_2}{r^2}$$

where k is a constant, q_1 and q_2 are the charges on the ions, and r is the distance between the centers of the ions. When the two ions are immersed in a material medium, the force between them is reduced in inverse proportion to the *dielectric constant*, ϵ, of the medium, as expressed in the equation

$$\text{force} = \frac{kq_1q_2}{\epsilon r^2}$$

Therefore the total energy expended in separating the ions will decrease as the dielectric constant increases, so that a solvent with a large dielectric constant will tend to promote the dissociation of an ionic solute more than a solvent with a small dielectric constant. The hydrocarbons (with $\epsilon < 5$) do not promote the dissociation of ionic solutes. Water (with $\epsilon \cong 80$) is a good solvent for ionic solutes.

The solvation energy is also an important factor. When an ionic solute dissociates in a solvent, the total energy of the reaction may be thought of as composed primarily of two terms: (1) the energy expended in the separation of the positive and negative ions of the crystal lattice (the *lattice energy*); and (2) the *solvation energy* liberated by the association of the ions with solvent molecules, resulting from interaction between the electric charges of the ions and the dipoles of the solvent molecules. When the solvation energy is enough to offset the energy expended in separating the positive and negative ions, the ionic solute will dissociate in the solvent.[3] A *polar* solvent, therefore, will tend to promote the dissociation of an ionic solute.

Ionic Equations

In describing a reaction in which ions are either the reactants or products, we will focus our attention on the essential changes, ignoring "spectator" ions that are not participating in the chemical reaction. This abbreviated description we will call the *net ionic equation.*

For example, the reaction of aqueous NaOH with aqueous HNO_3 could be written as

$$Na^+ + OH^- + H^+ + NO_3^- \rightarrow$$
$$Na^+ + NO_3^- + H_2O$$

which we will call the *total ionic equation.* Note that in this reaction neither the Na^+ nor the NO_3^- has reacted; both appear as separate particles on each side of the equation. They therefore may be omitted, and the equation that expresses the essential change is

$$OH^- + H^+ \rightarrow H_2O$$

Typical ionic reactions are those in which ions unite to form a weakly ionized or insoluble substance. For example, if a weakly acidic substance such as ammonium chloride, NH_4Cl, reacts with a base such as sodium hydroxide, NaOH, the net change is expressed by

$$NH_4^+ + OH^- \rightarrow NH_3(aq) + H_2O$$

A typical example of ions uniting to form an insoluble substance is expressed by the equation

$$Ca^{2+} + CO_3^{2-} \rightarrow CaCO_3(s)$$

It makes no difference whether the Ca^{2+} is derived from calcium chloride, calcium nitrate, or any other soluble calcium salt. Carbonate ion, CO_3^{2-}, could be obtained equally well from sodium carbonate, ammonium carbonate, or any soluble well-ionized carbonate salt.

Often the net result of an ionic reaction is determined by a competition between two largely undissociated substances. For example, carbonic acid, H_2CO_3, is formed when a strong acid acts on a carbonate salt:

$$CaCO_3(s) + 2H^+ \rightarrow Ca^{2+} + H_2CO_3(aq)$$

Carbonic acid readily dehydrates to CO_2 and water, so the net ionic reaction is

$$CaCO_3(s) + 2H^+ \rightarrow Ca^{2+} + CO_2(g) + H_2O$$

Thus this reaction is driven to the right by two factors: (1) the production of a very weakly dissociated substance, H_2O, and (2) the escape of volatile CO_2 gas.

The Experimental Method: Electrical Conductivity

In the experiment, we will measure the electrical conductivity of pure liquid substances and dissolved substances to determine if there is any ionic dissociation. We will also try to determine the net result of any reaction that may take place when solutions of ionic substances are mixed.

Solutions of ionic-type substances conduct the electric current by movement of their ions as influenced by the applied potential, and by reaction at the electrodes.[4] For a given applied voltage, the amount of current depends on the concentration of ions, and to a lesser extent on differences in individual ion mobilities. (Hydrogen ion has an unusually high mobility—five to eight times that of many other ions. Why?) Figure 16-1 shows a simple apparatus for the comparison of electrical conductivities.

We will compare the electrical conductivities of a number of solutions and of the products formed after certain reactions, and use the data thus obtained to interpret the character of the solutions and the course of any reactions. We will interpret these results in terms of the net ionic equation for the reaction.

---

[3] A more careful examination of the factors that determine the solubility of a solute requires the inclusion of the effect of changes in the solvent structure. The entropy change of the system is a measure of this effect, which can be strong enough that salts such as NaCl will dissolve even though the lattice energy is greater than the solvation energy.

---

[4] With alternating current (ac), the electrode reaction is diminished, and at high frequency is practically eliminated.

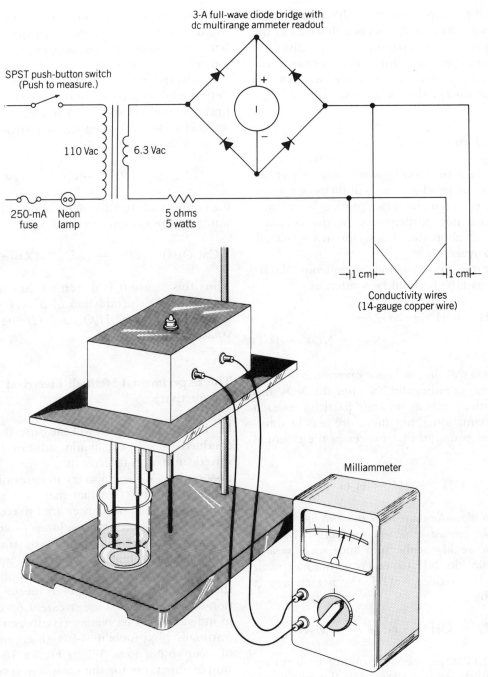

FIGURE 16-1
An apparatus for comparing the electrical conductivities of various solutions.

EXPERIMENTAL PROCEDURE

Special Supplies: Conductivity apparatus. (Use a conductivity meter or an apparatus constructed as described in the notes that follow and shown in Figure 16-1.)

Chemicals: Glacial (17 M) acetic acid, 6 M acetic acid, 0.1 M acetic acid, methanol (CH_3OH), 6 M HCl, 0.1 M HCl, toluene, anhydrous HCl in toluene produced by bubbling HCl gas through dry toluene using a glass frit gas dispersion tube, 0.1 M $HgCl_2$, 0.1 M NaOH, 0.1 M NH_3, 0.1 M H_2SO_4, 0.1 M $Ba(OH)_2$, 0.1% thymol blue indicator solution, sucrose(*s*), NaCl(*s*), $CaCO_3$(*s*) (marble chips), zinc metal (mossy).

Notes on the Construction and Use of the Conductivity Apparatus Shown in Figure 16-1

1. Build the circuit in a small aluminum chassis box, with the power cord, fuse, and pilot light on the rear, the banana jacks on the side, and the push-button switch on top. Mount the chassis box on a piece of $\frac{3}{4}$-in. plywood through which holes have been drilled to allow two pairs of 14-gauge copper wire electrodes (connected in parallel) to protrude about 15 cm. Space the wires about 1 cm apart. All but the bottom 5 cm of the copper wire should be insulated. Fasten a length of $\frac{1}{2}$-in.-OD aluminum rod on the underside of the plywood so that the apparatus can be supported by a clamp holder on a ring stand.

2. The voltage across the electrodes is about 6 V ac when the push-button switch is depressed, so be careful not to touch the electrodes while the switch is depressed. The 5-ohm, 5-watt resistor limits the current to a safe value if the electrodes are inadvertently shorted.

3. An inexpensive multimeter with a direct-current (dc) multirange ammeter provides a suitable readout. Two to four current ranges covering 50 microamperes (μA) to 300 mA will work well.

4. To make a measurement, adjust the ammeter to the highest current range (300 mA). Put enough of the test substance in a 30-mL beaker to give a depth of about 1 cm. Lower the electrodes into the beaker so that they are immersed to a depth of 1 cm. Then depress the push-button switch to get a current reading. Switch the ammeter to the most sensitive current range that can be used without driving the meter needle off scale. The solution conductivity is directly proportional to the current. Record the current reading and return the ammeter to the highest current range.

5. Rinse the electrodes with distilled water between each measurement and dry the electrodes with tissue. As an extra precaution, unplug the apparatus while cleaning the electrodes.

Safety Precautions: Mercuric chloride, $HgCl_2$, is toxic. After you have made measurements of the conductivity of 0.1 M $HgCl_2$, pour the solution into a waste bottle. *Do not pour it down the drain.* Likewise, toluene and solutions of HCl in toluene should be poured into waste containers, not down the drain.

1. *Electrolytes and Nonelectrolytes*

(a) If you will be using the conductivity apparatus shown in Figure 16-1, read over the preceding Notes describing how to use the apparatus. If you will use a commercial conductivity meter, follow your instructor's directions. When you are confident that you understand how to use the conductivity meter, measure and record the conductivity of the following *substances and/or their solutions in water* and determine if they are largely, moderately, or poorly ionized, or if they are essentially nonelectrolytes. (For an apparatus like that shown in Figure 16-1, a nonelectrolyte will give a very small current, less than a few microamperes. A completely dissociated strong electrolyte, such as 0.1 M HCl, will typically give a current of more than 100 mA.) Test the pure substance first, then add some water to it and retest. In each case, the magnitude of the current will be a measure of the conductivity of the solid or solution, indicating whether or not the substance contains ions that are free to move.

To start, test distilled (or deionized) water and tap water. What causes the difference in conductivity? Then test the following substances and their aqueous solutions: methanol (CH_3OH), glacial acetic acid (CH_3COOH), sucrose (table sugar, $C_{12}H_{22}O_{11}$), sodium chloride (NaCl), and dilute solutions only (not the pure substances) of 0.1 M HCl, 0.1 M NaOH, and 0.1 M $HgCl_2$. Be sure to dispose of the mercuric chloride, $HgCl_2$, in the waste container reserved for this purpose. Do not pour it down the drain—it is toxic.

(b) Observe the *effect of the solvent* on the ionization of HCl in toluene and in water. First test a little pure toluene (C_7H_8) in a thoroughly dry beaker, and then a solution of HCl in toluene (*already on your reagent shelf,* prepared by bubbling anhydrous HCl through dry toluene—do *not* add aqueous concentrated HCl to toluene). Then add 5 mL of deionized water to this solution, mix it well, and repeat the test with the electrodes immersed farther into the lower aqueous layer. Be sure to dispose of the toluene solutions in the waste container reserved for this purpose.

(c) Compare the *chemical* behavior of 6 M HCl and 6 M acetic acid with your conductivity data. Put three or four marble chips into each of two clean beakers. Add 6 M HCl to one beaker and 6 M acetic acid to the other. Compare the rate of evolution of CO_2 gas. Put one or two pieces of mossy zinc metal into another pair of beakers and compare the rates of evolution of hydrogen (H_2) gas when 6 M HCl and 6 M acetic acid are added. Record your observations and write balanced chemical reactions for each of the four reactions you observed.

2. Typical Ionic Reactions   Experiment with some ionic reactions to determine the nature of their products. By conductivity tests of the separate reactants and of the mixture after reaction, discover whether the acids, bases, and salts concerned are largely ionized (strong electrolytes) or only moderately ionized (weak electrolytes). For each reaction, write the total ionic equation and the net ionic equation that best describes the reaction taking place. This will require careful thinking on your part. The following procedures are suggested.

(a) 0.01 M HCl with 0.01 M NaOH.[5] These can be prepared by diluting 5 mL of each of the 0.1 M solutions to 50 mL. It is an advantage to use both pairs of electrodes connected in parallel (see Figure 16-1) by placing one pair of electrodes in

0.01 M HCl and simultaneously placing the other pair in an equal volume of 0.01 M NaOH contained in a separate beaker. Then mix the solutions, divide them into two equal portions, and again place the two solutions simultaneously in contact with the two electrode pairs. (This compensates for the dilution effect of mixing two solutions.) Why is the conductivity of the product solution lower than that of the reactant solutions?

(b) 0.1 M acetic acid, CH_3COOH, with 0.1 M NH_3.[6] As in part 2(a), test equal volumes of the separate solutions, mix them, divide the solution into two equal parts, and then remeasure the conductivity. Record your measurements.

(c) 0.1 M H_2SO_4 with 0.1 M $Ba(OH)_2$. Measure and record the conductivity of each solution by itself. Then add two or three drops of 0.1% thymol blue indicator solution to the sulfuric acid solution and add 0.1 M $Ba(OH)_2$ solution dropwise to the sulfuric acid solution while you stir. The sulfuric acid will be exactly neutralized when the indicator changes from its yellow (acid) form to its blue (basic) form. If you add too much $Ba(OH)_2$, overshooting the end point, add 0.1 M H_2SO_4 drop by drop, as you stir, until the *exact* end point—as shown by a sharp color change of the indicator—is reached. Now measure and record the conductivity of this mixture. Write balanced ionic equations to describe the reactions that take place.

---

[5] Quite dilute 0.01 M solutions are suggested so that you can interpret moderate conductivity changes more easily.

[6] Solutions of NH_3 in water are sometimes formulated as NH_4OH, called *ammonium hydroxide*. Because there is no strong evidence for the existence of such a molecule in solution, it is preferable to speak of an "aqueous ammonia solution."

REPORT 16	Ionic and Covalent Compounds Ionic Reactions	NAME
		SECTION LOCKER
		INSTRUCTOR DATE

OBSERVATIONS AND DATA

1. Electrolytes and Nonelectrolytes

(a) List the relative conductivity of each *substance* and *solution* tested, then write the formula of the individual species (molecules, ions, or both) present that account for this behavior. Star (*) those present at only low concentration.

	Conductivity	Species		Conductivity	Species
Distilled H_2O			$C_{12}H_{22}O_{11}(aq)$		
Tap H_2O			NaCl		
CH_3OH			NaCl(*aq*)		
$CH_3OH(aq)$			0.1 M $HgCl_2$		
CH_3COOH			0.1 M HCl		
$CH_3COOH(aq)$			0.1 M NaOH		
$C_{12}H_{22}O_{11}$					

(b) Explain your observations of the *effect of the solvent* on the conductivity of HCl dissolved in toluene and HCl dissolved in water.

(c) Compare your observations of the *physical and chemical behavior* of 6 M HCl and 6 M CH_3COOH with your conductivity data. Explain.

2. Typical Ionic Reactions

(a) 0.01 M HCl with 0.01 M NaOH. The relative conductivities of the solutions tested are as follows:

0.01 M HCl_____ 0.01 M NaOH_____ Mixture_____

The total ionic equation for the reaction is _____

The net ionic equation for the reaction is _____
Interpret any changes in the conductivity of the solutions, before and after mixing, in accordance with the preceding equations:

(b) 0.1 M CH_3COOH with 0.1 M NH_3. The relative conductivities of the solutions tested are as follows:

0.1 M CH_3COOH _____ 0.1 M NH_3_____ Mixture_____

The total ionic equation for the reaction is _____

The net ionic equation for the reaction is _____
Interpret any changes in the conductivity of the solutions, before and after mixing, in accordance with the preceding equations:

(c) 0.1 M H_2SO_4 with 0.1 M $Ba(OH)_2$. The relative conductivities of the solutions tested are as follows:

0.1 M H_2SO_4_____ 0.1 M $Ba(OH)_2$ _____ Mixture_____

The total ionic equation for the reaction is _____

The net ionic equation for the reaction is _____
Interpret any changes in the conductivity of the solutions, before and after mixing, in accordance with the preceding equations:

Exercises in Writing Lewis Structures

PURPOSE

To learn a procedure for drawing the Lewis structures of covalently bonded molecules (and molecular ions) and to use these structures to describe the bonding and charge distribution in the molecules.

INTRODUCTION

When atoms of elements combine with one another to form molecules like water, H_2O, or molecular ions like nitrate, NO_3^-, or ammonium, NH_4^+, the bonding can be described as a situation in which valence (outer orbital) electrons are simultaneously attracted to two or more atomic nuclei. In order for two atoms to be able to share electrons there must be vacancies in the valence orbitals of at least one atom. Covalent (shared-electron) bonds are not formed between atoms with filled valence orbitals.

A useful way of representing the arrangement of the bonding electrons in molecules and ions is to draw the Lewis structures by following the simple rules we will present here. The structures that result give a fairly accurate picture of how the electrons are arranged in the molecule.

The Lewis structure is useful for more than just a description of covalent bonding. From the Lewis structure the shape of a molecule can often be predicted. From the shape and qualitative distribution of electrons we can make predictions about the polarity of the molecule and whether or not it will have a permanent dipole. From the shape of the molecule we may also be able to deduce how the orbitals of the atoms have combined to form the chemical bonds. Although these features will not be discussed in this study assignment, you will need to be able to draw Lewis structures before you can go on to apply the valence shell electron-pair repulsion (VSEPR) rules to predict molecular shapes.

It will be helpful in learning and using the rules for drawing Lewis structures to remember the basic idea of covalent bonding: Each bond is formed by sharing a pair of electrons between two atoms. Generally, enough electron-pair bonds are formed to fill the outer orbital vacancies. For the nonmetals of the first three periods, these orbitals are the *s* and *p* orbitals, which can hold two and six electrons, respectively. Thus, the filled orbitals will accommodate eight electrons, giving rise to the *octet rule*, which states that each atom will have a share of eight electrons, with an electron configuration like that of a Group 8 noble gas. The octet rule results not so much from any special stability of the noble gas electron configuration but because bond formation proceeds until all the vacant orbitals are filled to their maximum capacity.

The exceptions to the octet rule follow from the nature of atomic orbitals as well. The hydrogen atom can share a maximum of two electrons because the filled outer 1*s* orbital contains a maximum of two electrons and quantum number restrictions dictate that 1*p* orbitals cannot exist. Elements in the third period can sometimes share more than eight electrons by making use of vacant 3*d* orbitals, whose energy lies a little above the energy of the 3*s* and 3*p* orbitals.

The rare gases normally form no covalent bonds because their atoms lack outer orbital vacancies that can be occupied by electrons from another atom. In addition, the noble gases are not good electron donors because their nuclei strongly attract their valence electrons. Thus they have little tendency to share their electrons. The heavier noble gases will form chemical bonds only with atoms—such as fluorine—that are very electronegative. They can form bonds with fluorine by making use of vacant *d* orbitals that lie at higher energies than the filled *s* and *p* orbitals. Promotion of *s* and *p* electrons to the *d* orbitals creates outer orbital vacancies, allowing the sharing of electrons and the formation of stable bonds.

A METHOD FOR WRITING LEWIS STRUCTURES

In this study assignment we will first formulate some rules for drawing Lewis structures. We will then restate each rule and discuss details of its application and possible exceptions to the rule. We will work out several examples illustrating each rule and then work out sample structures by using the rules step by step. Finally, some of the finer points will be discussed in order to ensure that the structures we draw are accurate representations of the bonding in the molecules. You should then be able to apply the rules to draw Lewis structures for molecules and molecular ions listed at the end of this study assignment.

Rules for Writing Simple Lewis Structures

1. Write the chemical formula for the molecule (or ion) and determine the total number of valence electrons in the molecule.

2. Draw the skeletal arrangement of the molecule showing single bonds connecting the atoms.

3. Assume that each bond in the skeleton requires two valence electrons (an electron-pair bond). After subtracting two electrons for each bond from the total number of valence electrons, assign the remaining electrons to give each atom an octet, or share of eight electrons.

4. If after each atom has been given a share of eight electrons, there remain additional electrons, assign the extra electrons to the central atom of the molecule.

5. If there are not enough electrons to give each atom a share of eight electrons, then form multiple bonds between atoms by moving electron pairs to form double (or triple) bonds.

RULE 1 *Determine the total number of valence electrons.*

The number of valence electrons in a molecule is simply the sum of the valence electrons of the atoms that make up the molecule. The number of valence electrons for each atom can be determined either by noting the main group to which the atom belongs or by counting across the periodic table from the left (ignoring the transition metals). Thus hydrogen in Group 1A has one electron, silicon in Group 4A has four valence electrons, all of the halogens (F, Cl, Br, and I) in Group 7A have seven, and the noble gases have eight valence electrons.

For each of the following molecules the total number of valence electrons is shown.

H_2 $(2 \times 1e^-) = 2e^-$

PCl_5 $(5e^-) + (5 \times 7e^-) = 40e^-$

CH_4 $(4e^-) + (4 \times 1e^-) = 8e^-$

H_2O_2 $(2 \times 1e^-) + (2 \times 6e^-) = 14e^-$

CO_2 $(4e^-) + (2 \times 6e^-) = 16e^-$

N_2O_4 $(2 \times 5e^-) + (4 \times 6e^-) = 34e^-$

If the molecule is a molecular ion, then the charge on the ion modifies the electron count. Because electrons have a negative charge, an electron is added to the total for each negative charge on the ion and one is subtracted for each positive charge. For each of the following molecular ions the total number of valence electrons is shown.

OH^- $(6e^-) + (1e^-) + (1e^-) = 8e^-$
(One electron has been added for the -1 charge.)

NH_4^+ $(5e^-) + (4 \times 1e^-) - (1e^-) = 8e^-$
(One electron has been subtracted for the $+1$ charge.)

NO_2^- $(5e^-) + (2 \times 6e^-) + (1e^-) = 18e^-$

SO_4^{2-} $(6e^-) + (4 \times 6e^-) + (2e^-) = 32e^-$

NO^+ $(5e^-) + (6e^-) - (1e^-) = 10e^-$

PO_3^{3-} $(5e^-) + (3 \times 6e^-) + (3e^-) = 26e^-$

$C_2H_3O_2^-$ $(2 \times 4e^-) + (3 \times 1e^-) + (2 \times 6e^-)$
$+ (1e^-) = 24e^-$

RULE 2 *Draw the bond skeleton of the molecule.*
This rule is easy to apply if the structure consists of a central atom to which the surrounding atoms are bonded, because the central atom is customarily written first. Thus the following molecules have the bond skeletons shown.

CO_2 O—C—O

NH₃
$$\begin{array}{ccc} H & & H \\ & \diagdown \diagup & \\ & N & \\ & | & \\ & H & \end{array}$$

CH_2Cl_2
$$\begin{array}{ccc} H & & H \\ & \diagdown \diagup & \\ & C & \\ & \diagup \diagdown & \\ Cl & & Cl \end{array}$$

SO_4^{2-}
$$\begin{array}{ccc} O & & O \\ & \diagdown \diagup & \\ & S & \\ & \diagup \diagdown & \\ O & & O \end{array}$$

PCl_5
$$\begin{array}{ccc} Cl & Cl & Cl \\ & \diagdown | \diagup & \\ & P & \\ & \diagup \diagdown & \\ Cl & & Cl \end{array}$$

There are some exceptions to this rule but they are easily recognized and their structures determined by noting a consequence of the rules for drawing Lewis structures: An atom will tend to form one bond for each electron it needs to fill its valence orbitals. Thus hydrogen forms only one bond and is always found on the periphery of a molecule. Group 6A atoms, such as oxygen, tend to form two bonds (two electrons are required to complete the octet). Group 5A atoms tend to form three bonds, and so on. The skeleton should be drawn so that each atom forms $8 - n$ bonds. Eight is the total capacity of the s and p orbitals, while n is the number of valence electrons that each atom has. The difference, $8 - n$, gives the number of vacancies in the valence orbitals of an atom. As we will see in the final Lewis structure, most of the time each atom will form $8 - n$ bonds.

In the following formulas the central atom is not written first, but consideration of the number of bonds that an atom is able to form will often lead to the correct bond skeleton.

Water, H_2O H—O—H   (H cannot be central if it forms only one bond.)

Hydrazine, N_2H_4
$$\begin{array}{ccc} H & & H \\ \diagdown & & \diagup \\ & N—N & \\ \diagup & & \diagdown \\ H & & H \end{array}$$

Hydrogen peroxide, H_2O_2 H—O—O—H

Hydrogen cyanide, HCN   H—C—N   or

H—N—C

Formaldehyde, H_2CO
$$\begin{array}{c} O \\ | \\ C \\ \diagup \diagdown \\ H \quad H \end{array}$$ or

H—C—O—H

Nitrous oxide, N_2O N—N—O   or

N—O—N

Ozone, O_3 O—O—O   or
$$\begin{array}{cc} O—O \\ \diagdown \diagup \\ O \end{array}$$

Propene, C_3H_6

$$
\begin{array}{ccc}
\text{H} & \text{H} & \text{H} \\
| & | & | \\
\text{C} - & \text{C} - & \text{C} \\
| & | & | \\
\text{H} & \text{H} & \text{H}
\end{array}
$$

or

$$
\begin{array}{cccc}
& \text{H} & \text{H} & \text{H} \\
& | & | & | \\
\text{H} - & \text{C} - & \text{C} - & \text{C} \\
& | & | & \\
& \text{H} & & \text{H}
\end{array}
$$

or

$$
\begin{array}{ccccc}
& \text{H} & & \text{H} & \\
& | & & | & \\
\text{H} - & \text{C} - & \text{C} - & \text{C} - & \text{H} \\
& | & | & & \\
& \text{H} & \text{H} & &
\end{array}
$$

or

$$
\begin{array}{ccccc}
& \text{H} & & & \text{H} \\
& | & & / & \\
\text{H} - & \text{C} & --- & \text{C} - & \text{H} \\
& \backslash & & / & \\
& & \text{C} & & \\
& / & & \backslash & \\
& \text{H} & & & \text{H}
\end{array}
$$

For molecules like HCN, H_2CO, N_2O, O_3, or C_3H_6, where more than one bond skeleton is possible, we will need more information about the structure of the molecule in order to draw the correct structure for the bond skeleton. (The bond skeleton of HCN is implied by the way the formula is written, and for the other molecules one of the structures may later emerge as the best one.)

Bond skeletons that have three-membered rings, such as

$$
\begin{array}{ccc}
\text{O} - \text{O} & \text{and} & \text{C} - \text{C} \\
\backslash \ / & & \backslash \ / \\
\text{O} & & \text{C}
\end{array}
$$

for ozone and propene, respectively, can often be discarded because they involve a great deal of strain or distortion of normal bond angles. In general, do not draw a structure that contains a three-atom ring unless you know that the molecule contains such a ring.

RULE 3 *Assign the remaining electrons to give each atom an octet.*

Each bond that is drawn in a skeleton represents a pair of electrons. The number of valence electrons left to assign is the total number, determined by Rule 1, minus the number of electrons required

to form the bonds in the skeleton, which is twice the number of bonds shown in the skeleton structure drawn according to Rule 2.

$$
\begin{array}{l}
\text{remaining} \\
\text{electrons}
\end{array} = \underset{\text{(See Rule 1.)}}{\text{total valence electrons}}
$$

$$
\underset{\text{(See Rule 2.)}}{- (2 \times \text{number of bonds})}
$$

It generally works best to assign the remaining electrons in pairs to each of the atoms in the skeleton structure, starting with the outer atoms and ending with the central atom. (Remember that a hydrogen atom can share no more than two electrons, not eight.) (See Table B-1.)

RULE 4 *If there are additional electrons, place them on the central atom.*

If all of the electrons are assigned by Rule 3 and each atom (except hydrogen) has a share of eight electrons, then the Lewis structure is complete. In some instances, as in the case of SF_4 in Table B-1, there are still electrons to be assigned after all octets are complete. In these cases the extra electrons are assigned to the central atoms as lone pairs. This gives the central atom an *expanded octet*.

The explanation for this violation of the octet rule is that in these instances the central atoms have a d subshell with empty orbitals that has the same principal quantum number as the s and p valence orbitals, and is thus close in energy to the s and p valence shell orbitals. The atomic orbitals from this d subshell can hold some of the electrons and thus participate in the bonding in the molecule. For molecules like PCl_5 and SF_6 the octet of the central atom must be expanded to contain all of the valence electrons of the atoms. (See Table B-2.)

RULE 5 *If there are not enough electrons to complete all of the octets, then move electron pairs to form multiple bonds between atoms.*

In the example of the O_2 molecule shown under Rule 3, there are insufficient electrons to complete each atom's octet. In such a situation, two atoms can share more than one pair of electrons between themselves, thus forming multiple bonds. If two pairs are shared between the same two atoms, a double bond is formed; three shared pairs between two atoms constitute a triple bond. Measurements of bond energies and bond lengths show that these multiple bonds are real. The atoms are more tightly bonded and they are closer together in a double bond or triple bond than in a single bond.

TABLE B-1

Molecule	Number of valence electrons	Skeleton	Remaining electrons	Complete octets
HF	8	H—F	6	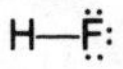 H—F̈:
H₂O	8	H—O—H	4	H—Ö—H
CCl₄	32	Cl⟍ C ⟋Cl (Cl above/below)	24	:C̈l⟍ C ⟋C̈l:
PF₃	26	F–P—F with F	20	:F̈: P—F̈: :F̈:
SF₄	34	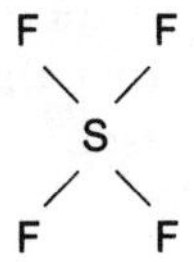 F⟍ S ⟋F	26	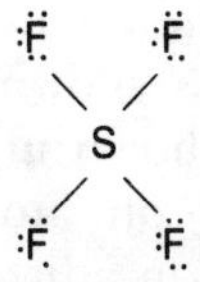 :F̈ S F̈: :F̈ F̈: (2 electrons unassigned)
O₂	12	O—O	10	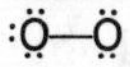 :Ö—Ö: (insufficient electrons)

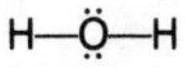

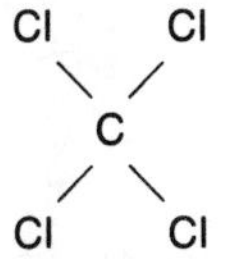

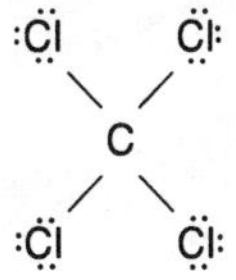

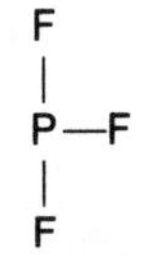

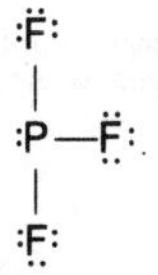

TABLE B-2

Molecule	Number of valence electrons	Skeleton	Remaining electrons	Lewis structure
SF₄	34	F⟍ S ⟋F	26	:F̈ S F̈: :F̈ F̈:
XeF₂	22	F—Xe—F	18	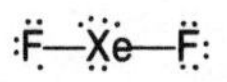 :F̈—Xe—F̈:
ICl₄⁻	36	Cl⟍ I ⟋Cl (Cl above/below)	28	[:C̈l I C̈l: :C̈l: :C̈l:]⊖

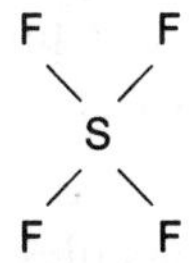

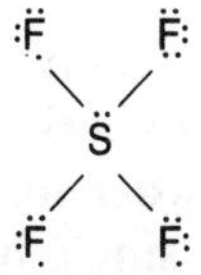

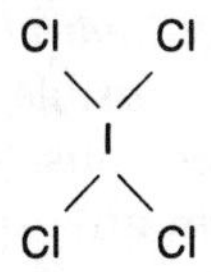

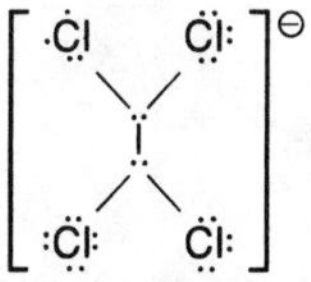

TABLE B-3

Molecule	Number of valence electrons	Skeleton	Rule 3 structure	Lewis structure*
O_2	12	O—O	$:\ddot{O}—\ddot{O}$	$\ddot{O}=\ddot{O}$
H_2CO	12	O with C below bonded to H, H	$:\ddot{O}:$ on C bonded to H, H	$:O:$ double bond to C bonded to H, H
HCN	10	H—C—N	H—C—$\ddot{N}:$	H—C≡N:

* Note that the application of the rules leads to a structure that implies that O_2 would have no unpaired electrons, whereas O_2 is known to be paramagnetic with two unpaired electrons.

In practice, to complete the octets for the structures of H_2CO and HCN shown in the discussion of Rule 2 and for O_2 shown in Rule 3, we must move some lone pairs on atoms into position between that atom and an adjacent atom with an incomplete octet. Thus for O_2, H_2CO, and HCN we complete the Lewis structures by forming double or triple bonds. (See Table B-3.)

Exceptions to the Octet Rule

Although the octet rule, based on filling each orbital vacancy so that each atom has a noble gas electron configuration, is the central rule in drawing Lewis structures, there are some instances where the best description of a molecule contains atoms that do not have an octet of electrons. A brief summary and explanation of these situations may help you to recognize circumstances when the octet rule is likely to be broken.

1. Hydrogen. For hydrogen atoms the maximum valence orbital capacity is two electrons. This is because no $1p$ orbital exists owing to quantum number restrictions.

2. Beryllium and Boron. In compounds of beryllium and boron, experiments show that when these atoms form two and three bonds, respectively, the bonds are single bonds. Thus BeF_2 and $BeCl_3$ have these Lewis structures:

$$:\ddot{F}—Be—\ddot{F}:$$

$$
\begin{array}{c}
:\ddot{Cl}: \\
| \\
B \\
\diagup \quad \diagdown \\
:\ddot{Cl} \qquad \ddot{Cl}:
\end{array}
$$

even though strict application of the rules would predict that they would have the following structures:

$$\overset{\oplus}{\ddot{F}}=\overset{2\ominus}{Be}=\overset{\oplus}{\ddot{F}}$$

$$
\begin{array}{c}
\overset{\oplus}{:\ddot{Cl}:} \\
|| \\
\overset{\ominus}{B} \\
\diagup \quad \diagdown \\
:\ddot{Cl}: \qquad :\ddot{Cl}:
\end{array}
$$

These are improbable (high-energy) electron distributions because they put positive charge on the electronegative atoms F and Cl. (In the following subsection we show how the formal charges indicated on the atoms are calculated.)

3. Expanded Octets. The central atom of some molecules may have more than an octet of electrons. This occurs in cases where the central atom has more than four atoms bonded to it, as in PCl_5 and SF_6, or where there are more than enough electrons to satisfy the octets of all of the atoms, as in XeF_2. These extra electrons are assigned to the central atom as lone pairs (Rule 4). An expanded octet can occur only in atoms that have empty d orbitals in their valence shell. (Note that $2d$ valence orbitals do not exist, so a nitrogen atom cannot have an expanded octet, whereas a phosphorus atom may.)

4. Odd-Electron Molecules. There are a few molecules that contain an odd number of electrons; NO_2 and CH_3 are examples. Molecules like these that contain an unpaired electron are known as *free radicals* and tend to be quite reactive. It is impossible to form octets from an odd number of electrons, so the Lewis structures of radicals contain an atom that has only seven electrons instead of the octet.

Formal Charge

Some of the Lewis structures that you draw will contain atoms with a formal charge; that is, if we assume that the electrons in the covalent bonds are shared equally between the atoms, there will be a net charge on some of the atoms in the structure. In the case of molecular ions like NH_4^+ and SO_4^{2-} there will inevitably be at least one atom with a formal charge, but formal charges may also exist in neutral molecules.

To determine the formal charge of each atom in a structure we divide each electron-pair bond in half and assign an electron from each bond to each of the two atoms bonded together. Counting one electron for each electron-pair bond and two electrons for each lone pair, we determine the total number of electrons assigned to each atom. We then compare this number of electrons to the number of valence electrons that the neutral atom would have. If it has one more than the number of valence electrons, we say that it has a formal charge of -1. If it is short by one electron, its formal charge is $+1$. Thus for NH_4^+ we would assign one electron from each bond to the hydrogen atoms and the others to the nitrogen atom. The nitrogen atom therefore would be assigned four electrons, one short of its normal valence of five, and the nitrogen atom would have a formal charge of $+1$. The hydrogen atoms each have one electron, their normal number of valence electrons, and thus have a zero formal charge. Note that adding all the formal charges gives the net charge of the molecular ion (or zero in the case of a neutral molecule).

$$\begin{pmatrix} \text{formal} \\ \text{charge} \end{pmatrix} = \begin{pmatrix} \text{group} \\ \text{number} \end{pmatrix} - \begin{pmatrix} \text{number} \\ \text{of bonds} \end{pmatrix}$$
$$- \begin{pmatrix} \text{number of} \\ \text{unshared electrons} \end{pmatrix}$$

Thus for the chlorate ion, ClO_3^-, the Lewis structure can be written as

and the formal charges would be

$$\text{chlorine formal charge} = \underset{\text{(group)}}{7} - \underset{\text{(bonds)}}{3} - \underset{\begin{pmatrix}\text{unshared}\\\text{electrons}\end{pmatrix}}{2} = +2$$

$$\text{oxygen formal charge} = 6 - 1 - 6 = -1$$

Again, note that addition of the formal charges on the atoms gives the net charge on the molecular ion.

We stress that the formal charge is just that: It is calculated by formal rules and may not always accurately reflect the true distribution of electron density. However, the formal charges usually correctly show the tendency of atoms to have either an excess or a deficiency of electron charge, compared to the neutral atoms.

Knowledge of the formal charges in a structure can help to eliminate an unlikely Lewis structure. In general, a good Lewis structure does not contain adjacent atoms with formal charges of the same sign. Three possible Lewis structures for the nitric acid molecule, HNO_3, are

The first structure has a $+1$ formal charge on the adjacent O and N atoms and would not be a reasonable structure for HNO_3. The other structures are better (lower-energy) representations of the bonding in nitric acid.

The $8 - n$ bond rule that was used to write the molecular skeleton is also the result of a formal counting of electrons. If an atom forms $8 - n$ bonds, it will have a formal charge of zero.

Resonance

Applying our rules for drawing Lewis structures to the substance sulfur dioxide, SO_2, gives two possible structures:

implying the existence of two different types of S—O bonds in this molecule. (A similar situation arises in the nitric acid example we discussed earlier.) Experiments show that the two S—O bonds are actually identical. The best representation of the SO_2 molecule is an average or superposition of these two structures, represented by

$$:\overset{\ominus}{\ddot{O}}{-}\overset{\oplus}{\ddot{S}}{=}\ddot{O} \leftrightarrow \ddot{O}{=}\overset{\oplus}{\ddot{S}}{-}\overset{\ominus}{\ddot{O}}:$$

These structures are called *resonance* structures. They occur whenever there are two or more Lewis structures that have identical positions for the nuclei but have different electron arrangements. Resonance structures often exist in a situation where identical atoms are bonded to the same atom and there is a double bond in the structure, but you should look for the possibility of resonance before settling on any one Lewis structure.

We emphasize that a real molecule has only one stable electron configuration. The molecule does not flip back and forth between two electron configurations, but has a configuration that is equivalent to what we would obtain by superimposing all of the resonance structures.

SUMMARY

A systematic method for drawing Lewis structures is summarized by the following procedures.

1. Determine the total number of valence electrons in the molecule.

(a) Sum the valence electrons of each atom in the molecule.

(b) Add an electron for each negative charge or subtract one for each positive charge on a molecular ion.

2. Draw the bond skeleton of the molecule.

(a) Often the central atom of the molecule is written first in the chemical formula and all other atoms are bonded directly to it.

(b) If the central atom is not written first, make use of the fact that atoms tend to form $8 - n$ bonds where n is the number of valence electrons of the neutral atom.

3. Assign the remaining electrons to give each atom an octet of electrons. H, Be, and B do not form an octet.

4. If there are more than enough electrons to give each atom an octet, place the additional electrons on the central atom to form an expanded octet.

5. If there are not enough electrons to complete all of the octets, then move lone pairs to form multiple bonds between atoms until each atom has a share of eight electrons.

6. Determine the formal charge of each atom in the resulting structure(s) and eliminate any structures with unlikely charge distributions (adjacent atoms with the same charge).

7. Look to see if there are possible equivalent resonance structures.

EXERCISES

Draw the Lewis structure(s) for each of the molecules and molecular ions listed below. Follow the procedures given in the summary at the end of the study assignment. Include the formal charges in the Lewis structures. Look for equivalent resonance structures and draw all equivalent structures.

Molecule	Number of valence electrons	Bond skeleton	Remaining electrons	Lewis structures with formal charges	Resonance structures?
CF_4					
NH_3					
OCl_2					
PO_4^{3-}					
NH_2^-					
C_2H_6					

Molecule	Number of valence electrons	Bond skeleton	Remaining electrons	Lewis structures with formal charges	Resonance structures?
C_2H_4					
C_2H_2					
CO					
XeF_4					
ClO_4^-					
BrF_6^+					
I_3^-					
NO_2^-					

Molecule	Number of valence electrons	Bond skeleton	Remaining electrons	Lewis structures with formal charges	Resonance structures?
NO_3^-					
CO_3^{2-}					
H_2O_2					
N_2O_4					
N_2H_4					
CH_3NH_2					
BrO_3^-					

QUESTIONS

1. The bond energies (the energy required to separate the molecule into atoms) and the bond lengths are shown for the molecules O_2, N_2, and Cl_2.

Molecule	Bond energy (kJ/mol)	Bond length (nm)
O_2	498	0.121
N_2	945	0.110
Cl_2	243	0.199

Draw the Lewis structures of these molecules and use them to explain the observed trends in the bond energies and the bond lengths of the three molecules.

2. The molecules PF_5 and AsF_5 exist, but the analogous molecule NF_5 does not. Why not?

3. For the molecule N_2O there are five possible Lewis structures. Three have the N—N—O bond skeleton and two would have the N—O—N skeleton.

(a) Draw the five Lewis structures.

(b) By considering the formal charges, can you suggest which structures might be eliminated?

(c) Which structures have the smallest formal charges?

(d) Because oxygen is more electronegative than nitrogen, it is more likely to have a negative formal charge. Which structure would then be the best description of N_2O?

(e) Are the structures that have the N—O—N bond skeleton resonance forms of the structures with the N—N—O skeleton? Explain.

Polymers and Plastics

PURPOSE

To introduce the chemistry and the vocabulary of polymerization reactions. To prepare some representative examples of synthetic polymers: poly(methylmethacrylate) (Lucite) by free-radical chain-growth polymerization and poly(glyceryl-phthalate) (Glyptal) by step-growth polymerization. To understand how the physical properties of linear polymers can be altered by cross-linking to form a network polymer.

PRE-LAB PREPARATION

The word *plastic* is sometimes used in a faintly derisive way to describe something that is a cheap imitation of the real thing, and most would agree that nothing offends the eye like the litter of plastic trash that seems to resist forever the ravages of sun and weather. But suppose that, sitting in our living rooms at home, we could magically remove from our bodies and our homes everything that was made with a synthetic polymer. To begin, we would find ourselves sitting nearly naked, because most of our clothing is made of fabric that contains synthetic fibers. Only if we were wearing pure cotton, wool, or silk would we have any clothing left. If we had been sitting on a comfortable couch, we would now be sitting on bare metal springs supported by a wooden frame; the polyurethane foam padding and synthetic fabric covering would be gone.

In most homes the curtains, draperies, and floor coverings would be gone. All of the paint, inside and out, would be gone. The melamine dinnerware would be gone. All of the synthetic rubber and plastic parts in our appliances and automobiles would be gone, making them inoperable. Everything held together by a synthetic adhesive would fall apart. Plastic hoses and piping for distributing water and draining wastewater and sewage would disappear. Insulation from the electric wiring would be gone; the plastic components of the wall switches would be gone. Our combs and toothbrushes would be gone.

This exercise of imagination is intended to remind us how pervasive synthetic polymers are in modern life. Yet they were largely unknown until the turn of the century, and large-scale manufacturing of synthetic polymers did not begin until the 1920's. Since then the industry has grown until it represents the largest single field in chemistry, whether measured by the percentage of chemists working in the field or by the economic importance of polymers in chemical technology and industry.

Natural polymers are also of crucial importance to living organisms. Without natural structural polymers like the *cellulose* in plants or the *proteins* that constitute the muscle and sinew of animals, no living plant or animal could stand upright against the pull of gravity. We would all be creatures of the sea, where our delicate membranes could be supported by floating in water. The *enzymes* of plants and animals that catalyze all of the vital biochemical reactions are polymers of amino acids. Finally, deoxyribonucleic acid (DNA), the very stuff of the genetic inheritance of all plants and animals, is a polymer of nucleic acids.

The term *polymer* comes from the Greek (*poly*, many + *meros*, part) and refers to a large molecule made up of many parts. *Macromolecule* is a term synonymous with polymer. Polymers are made by linking together simple molecules called *monomers* ("single parts"). If the monomers add together so that the polymer contains all of the atoms of the monomer molecules, the reaction is called *addition polymerization*. If small by-product molecules such as water are formed during the polymerization process, the reaction is called *condensation polymerization*. Some examples of polymers produced by both types of polymerization processes are shown in Table 17-1.

If a synthetic polymer is prepared from a single monomer, A, then the product is called a *homopolymer* (from the Greek *homos*, the same).

$$-A-A-A-A-A-A-A-A-$$
homopolymer

Polyethylene, polystyrene, and polytetrafluoroethylene (shown in Table 17-1) are examples of addition homopolymers. If more than one monomer is employed, the product is called a *copolymer*. Poly(ethyleneterephthalate) (shown in Table 17-1) is an example of an alternating condensation copolymer.

$$-A-B-A-B-A-B-A-B-$$
alternating copolymer

TABLE 17-1
Some representative synthetic polymers

Monomer	Repeating structural unit	Polymer name (trade name)
$CH_2=CH_2$ ethylene	$\sim(CH_2CH_2)\sim$	Polyethylene
styrene	$\sim(CH_2-CH)\sim$	Polystyrene
$F_2C=CF_2$ tetrafluoroethylene	(CF_2CF_2)	Polytetrafluoroethylene (Teflon)
$HOCH_2CH_2OH$ ethylene glycol + terephthalic acid	$OCH_2CH_2OC\text{—}C$ + $2H_2O$	Poly(ethyleneterephthalate) (Dacron)

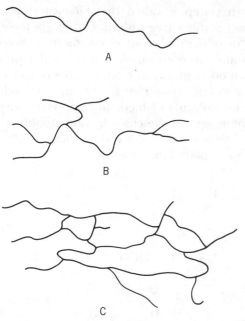

FIGURE 17-1
A schematic representation of different polymer types: (A) linear, (B) branched, and (C) network. [After M.P. Stevens, *Polymer Chemistry*, Addison-Wesley, Reading, MA. Copyright © 1975.]

Polymers can also be described as having a *linear, branched,* or *network* structure (see Figure 17-1). Network polymers are also commonly called *cross-linked polymers.* When a polymer is cross-linked, the polymer chains lose their mobility and the material will not melt or flow and therefore cannot be molded. Such polymers are said to be *thermosetting.* To make useful articles out of thermosetting polymers, the cross-linking reaction is carried out while the article is made. If all the polymer chains present are linked together, an article made with a thermosetting polymer can be considered to be one gigantic molecule!

Chain-Growth and Step-Growth Polymerization

To focus attention on the two fundamentally different ways by which monomers react to form a polymer, we will introduce the terminology *step-growth* and *chain-growth* polymerization. Most condensation polymerization reactions proceed in a stepwise fashion (called step growth). In step-growth polymerization, any time two monomer molecules collide they can react. This produces very quickly a great many small (low molecular weight) polymers, and the average molecular weight of the polymer molecules increases slowly, as shown in Figure 17-2.

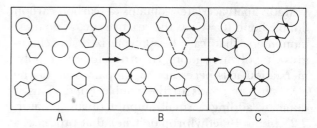

FIGURE 17-2
Step-growth polymerization: (A) unreacted bifunctional monomers; (B) 50% reacted; (C) 100% reacted. (The dotted lines show reacting monomer molecules.) [After M.P. Stevens, *Polymer Chemistry*, Addison-Wesley, Reading, MA. Copyright © 1975.]

Most addition polymerization reactions proceed by propagating from a growing chain (called chain growth). In chain-growth polymerization molecular weight increases rapidly even though large amounts of monomer remain unreacted. This is because monomer molecules cannot react directly with one another but only at the end of growing chains. This is illustrated in Figure 17-3.

We will first describe the mechanism of chain-growth polymerization used to make poly-(methylmethacrylate), a colorless *thermoplastic* solid that can be melted and formed into numerous shapes. It is sold under the trade names Lucite and Plexiglas. Then we will discuss the synthesis of Glyptal by step-growth polymerization. You will make both of these polymers and study their properties as part of this experiment.

Synthesis of Poly(methylmethacrylate) by Chain-Growth Polymerization Chain-growth reactions require an *initiator* (often loosely called a catalyst) to start the polymerization reaction. The polymerization of methylmethacrylate is an example of such a reaction. (You will carry out this reaction later, so read the description of how it works very carefully.)

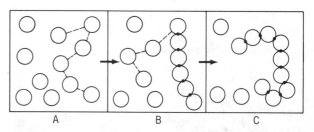

FIGURE 17-3
Chain-growth polymerization: (A) unreacted monomer; (B) 50% reacted; (C) 75% reacted. (The dotted lines show reacting monomer molecules.) [After M.P. Stevens, *Polymer Chemistry*, Addison-Wesley, Reading, MA. Copyright © 1975.]

Methylmethacrylate contains a carbon-carbon double bond (C=C) as the reactive site, as do most monomers that can be polymerized by chain-growth polymerization. In order to effect polymerization it is necessary to "unpair" one of the electron-pair bonds in the double bond. This is done by adding a small amount of an initiator, 2,2′-azobis(2-methylpropionitrile), that produces a free radical, R·.

$$(CH_3)_2—C\overbrace{{\text-}}N=N\overbrace{{\text-}}C—C—(CH_3)_2 \xrightarrow{heat}$$
$$\qquad\quad | \qquad\qquad\qquad\quad |$$
$$\qquad\quad CN \qquad\qquad\qquad\quad CN$$

2,2′-azobis(2-methylpropionitrile)

$$2(CH_3)_2—C· \quad + \quad N_2 \qquad\qquad (1)$$
$$\qquad\quad |$$
$$\qquad\quad CN$$

a free radical,   dinitrogen
    R·

When this compound is heated, the electron-pair bonds between the central carbon and nitrogen atoms break, forming a dinitrogen molecule and leaving each carbon atom with a single unpaired electron.

A molecule containing an unpaired electron is called a *free radical*. The free radicals are very reactive with double bonds, adding to one of the carbon atoms in the double bond of methylmethacrylate to form a new electron-pair bond and leaving behind a carbon atom with an unpaired electron:

$$\qquad\qquad\qquad\qquad H \quad H$$
$$\qquad\qquad\qquad\qquad | \quad\;\; |$$
$$(CH_3)_2—C· \; + \; C=C \qquad\; \rightarrow$$
$$\qquad\quad | \qquad\;\; | \quad\;\; |$$
$$\qquad\quad CN \qquad H \quad COCH_3$$
$$\qquad\qquad\qquad\qquad\qquad\quad \|$$
$$\qquad\qquad\qquad\qquad\qquad\quad O$$

R·
free-radical   methyl-
  initiator   methacrylate

$$\qquad\qquad\qquad\quad H \quad H$$
$$\qquad\qquad\qquad\quad | \quad\;\; |$$
$$(CH_3)_2—C—C—C· \qquad\qquad\qquad (2)$$
$$\qquad\qquad\quad | \quad\;\; |$$
$$\qquad\qquad\quad H \quad COCH_3$$
$$\qquad\qquad\qquad\qquad\quad \|$$
$$\qquad\qquad\qquad\qquad\quad O$$

This first step is called the *initiation* step. The product is still a free radical. (Adding a molecule with an odd number of electrons to a molecule containing an even number must yield a product with an odd number of electrons, hence still a free radical.) This free radical can in turn add to another molecule of methylmethacrylate, increasing the length of the chain by one monomer unit and of course keeping a carbon atom on the end with an unpaired electron:

$$\qquad\quad H \quad\; H \;\; H \qquad\qquad H \;\; H$$
$$\qquad\quad | \quad\;\; | \quad\; | \qquad\qquad\; | \quad\; |$$
$$(CH_3)_2—C——C—C· \quad + \; C=C \qquad\qquad \rightarrow$$
$$\qquad\quad | \quad\;\; | \quad\; | \qquad\qquad\; | \quad\; |$$
$$\qquad\quad CN \;\; H \; COCH_3 \qquad H \; COCH_3$$
$$\qquad\qquad\qquad\quad\; \| \qquad\qquad\qquad\quad \|$$
$$\qquad\qquad\qquad\quad\; O \qquad\qquad\qquad\quad O$$

$$\qquad\quad H \quad\; H \qquad\qquad H$$
$$\qquad\quad | \quad\;\; | \qquad\qquad\; |$$
$$(CH_3)_2—C——C—C—CH_2—C· \qquad (3)$$
$$\qquad\quad | \quad\;\; | \quad\; | \qquad\qquad |$$
$$\qquad\quad CN \;\; H \; COCH_3 \qquad COCH_3$$
$$\qquad\qquad\qquad\quad\; \| \qquad\qquad\qquad \|$$
$$\qquad\qquad\qquad\quad\; O \qquad\qquad\qquad O$$

Thus, the chain growth can continue from the reactive chain end until some termination reaction, such as radical coupling or disproportionation, terminates the chain. There is an increasing probability of a termination reaction occurring as the monomer is used up. We can summarize all of these steps in the following reaction scheme, in which R· represents the free-radical initiator, with the single dot representing an unpaired electron.

Initiation

$$\qquad\qquad\qquad\quad H \;\; H \qquad\quad H \;\; H$$
$$\qquad\qquad\qquad\quad | \quad\; | \qquad\quad\; | \quad\; |$$
$$R· \; + \; C=C \; \rightarrow \; RC—C· \qquad (4)$$
$$\qquad\qquad\qquad\quad | \quad\; | \qquad\quad\; | \quad\; |$$
$$\qquad\qquad\qquad\quad H \;\; H \qquad\quad H \;\; H$$

Propagation

$$\quad H \;\; H \qquad H \;\; H \qquad\quad H \;\; H \;\; H \;\; H$$
$$\quad | \quad\; | \qquad | \quad\; | \qquad\quad | \quad\; | \quad\; | \quad\; |$$
$$R—C—C· \; + \; C=C \rightarrow R—C—C—C—C· \;\; (5)$$
$$\quad | \quad\; | \qquad | \quad\; | \qquad\quad | \quad\; | \quad\; | \quad\; |$$
$$\quad H \;\; H \qquad H \;\; H \qquad\quad H \;\; H \;\; H \;\; H$$

Termination by radical-radical coupling

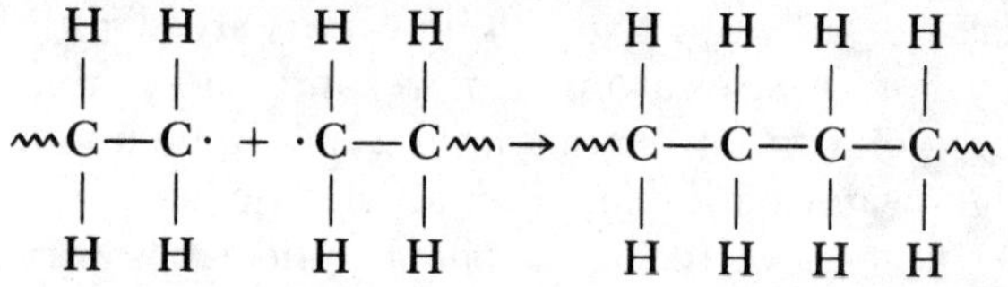

$$(6)$$

Termination by disproportionation

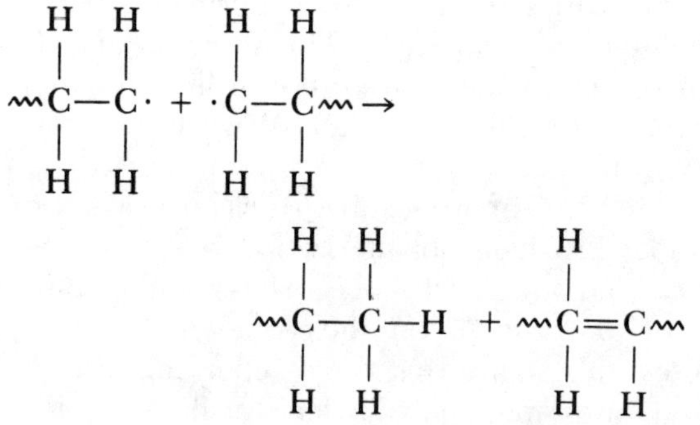

$$(7)$$

Note that the free-radical initiator, although often called a catalyst, is not a true catalyst. It gets used up in starting (or terminating) a chain, but each chain that is started can grow by adding monomer molecules one at a time until the free-radical chain is terminated, so that one initiator molecule can produce a chain containing many monomer molecules. The probability of a termination step increases as the concentration of free radicals increases; for this reason, very low concentrations of initiator are used to obtain high molecular weights. If a larger amount of initiator is used, more chains will be started, and there is a greater probability that a termination reaction will occur before the molecular weight is very high. Thus, varying the concentration of initiator is one way of controlling the average molecular weight of the polymer molecules.

Synthesis of Glyptal Resins by Step-Growth Polymerization   As an example of a polymer produced by a condensation reaction that is a step-growth reaction we will react ethylene glycol and glycerol with phthalic acid (or its anhydride) to form a linear polymer and a cross-linked network polymer that has the trade name Glyptal.

Reaction of a bifunctional alcohol with a bifunctional acid produces a linear polyester of the −A−B−A−B−A−B− type:

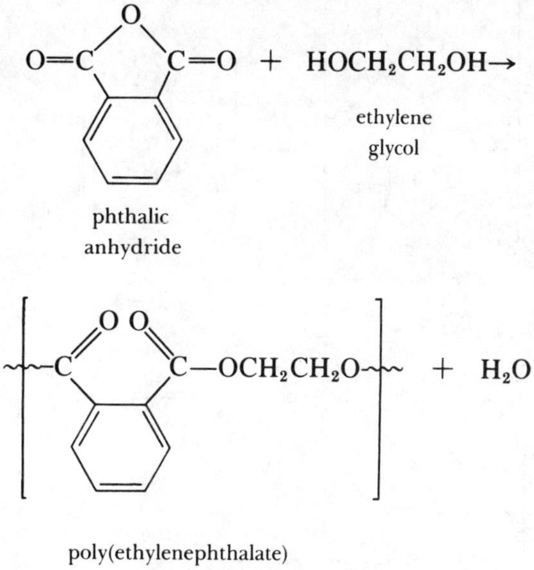

phthalic
anhydride

ethylene
glycol

$$(8)$$

poly(ethylenephthalate)

The extra —OH group of the glycerol molecule, the structure of which is shown in Equation (9), allows phthalic acid cross-links between two chains, shown schematically as

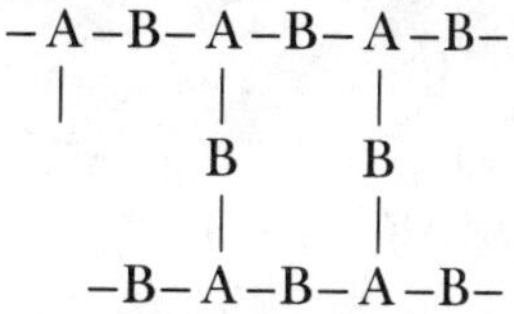

$$-A-B-A-B-A-B-$$

(A is trifunctional glycerol and B is bifunctional phthalic acid) and shown in greater detail by the chemical structures as shown on the following page.

Cross-linked compounds of this type are called *alkyd resins*, and oil-modified alkyd resins were widely used in oil-base paints until the introduction of water-based paints, which contain latex emulsions.

Sometimes both basic types of polymerization (condensation and addition) are used in making a polymer. For example, the polyester polymers used in casting resins or for forming glass-fiber-reinforced boat hulls are made by a two-step process. First, a linear polyester polymer is made by condensation, using a monomer that contains unsaturated C=C bonds. The low molecular weight polymer that is formed is then dissolved in a monomer such as styrene, which also contains C=C bonds. When the resin is used, an initiator is mixed in with it, causing cross-linking between the polyester polymer and the styrene. While still viscous, the mixture is worked into the fiberglass, which has been laid over a mold in the shape of a

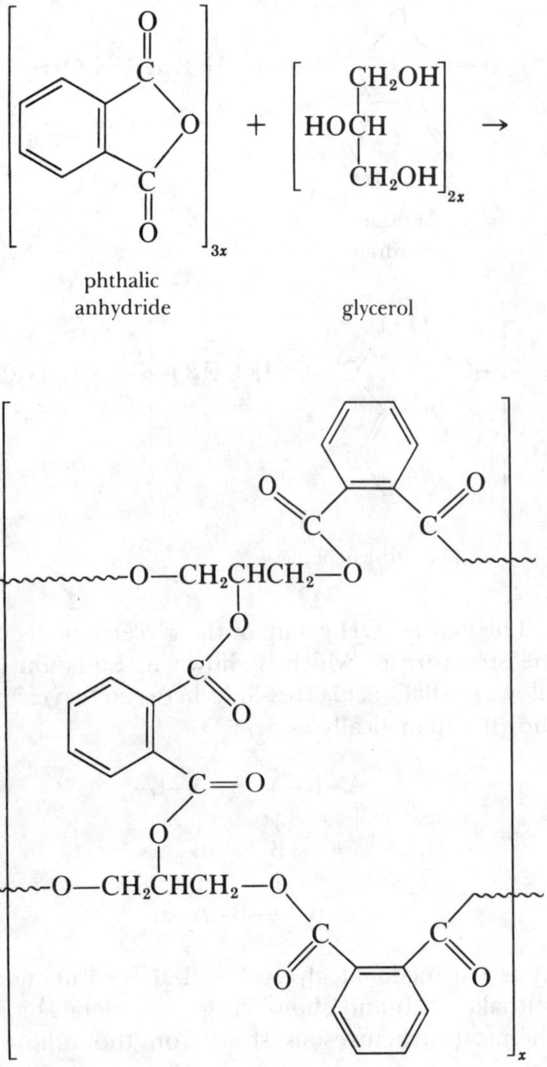

phthalic
anhydride

glycerol

poly(glycerylphthalate),
Glyptal,
a cross-linked polyester resin

$$+ \ (H_2O)_{3x} \tag{9}$$

boat hull. After the resin is cured by heating, the result is a rigid network polymer that forms a light and strong boat hull.

EXPERIMENTAL PROCEDURE

Special Supplies: 15-cm disposable glass test tubes, 30-mL polyethylene beakers, 20-cm glass stirring rods.

Chemicals: Methylmethacrylate monomer, 2,2′-azobis(2-methylpropionitrile) initiator (available from Aldrich Chemical Co.; benzoyl peroxide may be substituted), phthalic anhydride, anhydrous sodium acetate, ethylene glycol, glycerol.

Safety Precautions: Methylmethacrylate monomer is volatile and flammable. Do not heat the monomer over an open flame. The vapors are slightly toxic. For these reasons, it is recommended that the polymerization be carried out in a fume hood, using a water bath heated on an electric hot plate. If a fume hood is not available, the laboratory instructor may carry out the procedure as a demonstration.

All free-radical initiators, such as 2,2′-azobis(2-methylpropionitrile), are inherently unstable and prone to decompose. It is recommended that the small quantities used in this experiment be dispensed by the instructor. The initiator may be weighed on glassine (glazed, not ordinary) paper. Clean up *all* spills with water. Wash the glassine paper with water before discarding it.

It is difficult or impossible to clean beakers or test tubes in which polymerization reactions have been carried out. For this reason it is recommended that the polymerizations be done in disposable glass test tubes, and that the reaction mixtures be poured into small polyethylene beakers, so that the polymers can be examined later without the necessity of breaking the glass test tubes.

1. Synthesis of Poly(methylmethacrylate) (Lucite) by Chain-Growth Polymerization Have your instructor place 0.030 g of initiator (2,2′-azobis(2-methylpropionitrile) in a 15-cm disposable glass test tube. In a fume hood, add 5 mL of methylmethacrylate monomer and stir to dissolve the solid initiator. Heat the solution in a beaker of hot (near boiling) water in the fume hood. Stir the solution continuously until it becomes very viscous. Then quickly pour the viscous solution into a 30-mL polyethylene beaker. Allow it to cool, then loosen the sample and remove it. Is it flexible or brittle? Try remelting a small piece of the polymer in a glass test tube. Record what you observe. Draw a subunit of the structure of the methylmethacrylate polymer.

2. Synthesis of Glyptal Resins by Step-Growth Polymerization You will prepare linear and cross-linked polyesters. Both are examples of condensation polymers. The linear polyester is isomeric with Dacron. Prepare the two polyesters as follows: Place 3.0 g of phthalic anhydride and 0.1 g of anhydrous sodium acetate (which acts as a catalyst) in each of two 15-cm disposable test tubes. To one tube add 1.2 mL (1.3 g) of ethylene glycol, and to the other add 1.0 mL (1.3 g) of glycerol. Label the tubes so that you can distinguish them.

Clamp both tubes so that they can be heated together by a Bunsen flame. Heat the tubes gently and stir until the phthalic anhydride is dissolved and the solutions appear to boil (water is eliminated during the reaction), then continue to heat for 5 to 6 min more. (The heating should be sufficient to cause bubbling as the water escapes.) Then allow the tubes to cool and compare the viscosity of the two polymers. (If neither solution is very viscous after cooling, the reaction is incomplete. Try reheating both of the tubes for a few more minutes.) Record your observations. Draw the structure of a subunit of the linear ethylene glycol-phthalic anhydride polymer and of the network in the glycerol-phthalic anhydride polymer.

OBSERVATIONS

1. Synthesis of Poly(methylmethacrylate) by Chain-Growth Polymerization
Describe the color and texture of the polymer.

Is it thermoplastic (can it be remelted and cast?)

Draw the structure of a subunit of the poly(methylmethacrylate) polymer.

2. Synthesis of Glyptal Resins by Step-Growth Polymerization
Describe the color and texture of the polymer made with ethylene glycol.

Describe the color and texture of the polymer made with glycerol.

Compare the viscosities of the two polymers. Which is the linear polymer? Which is the network polymer?

Draw the structure of a subunit of the phthalic anhydride-ethylene glycol polymer.

Draw the structure of a subunit of the phthalic anhydride-glycerol polymer.

QUESTIONS

1. Calculate the mole ratios of the reactants for each of the two reactions in part 2:

$$\frac{\text{mol phthalic anhydride}}{\text{mol ethylene glycol}} =$$

$$\frac{\text{mol phthalic anhydride}}{\text{mol glycerol}} =$$

Why must the mole ratio be greater for the cross-linked polymer of phthalic anhydride with glycerol? (Compare Equations (8) and (9).)

2. Which of the polymers shown in Table 17-1 are *linear* polymers?

Colligative Properties

The Molar Mass of a Soluble Substance by Freezing-Point Depression

PURPOSE

To determine the molar mass of sulfur by measuring the freezing-point depression of naphthalene containing a known mass of dissolved sulfur.

PRE-LAB PREPARATION

When a nonvolatile solute is dissolved in a solvent several properties of the solvent change. Relative to the pure solvent the solution has a lower vapor pressure, a lower freezing point, and a higher boiling point. These effects are called *colligative* properties of the solution because they are linked together by a common feature: They all depend primarily on the ratio of the number of solute particles to the number of solvent particles. It makes no difference what the solute species are, whether molecules or ions, or whether they are large or small; it is the *relative number of particles* that is important.[1]

Vapor pressure lowering, freezing-point depression, and boiling-point elevation are observed for both aqueous and nonaqueous solutions. For example, a solution of a nonvolatile solute like sucrose or ethylene glycol in water shows the same kind of effects as a solution of aspirin dissolved in cyclohexanol or sulfur in naphthalene.

Practical use is made of the colligative properties of an aqueous solution of ethylene glycol by putting it in the cooling system of your automobile. Because an aqueous solution of ethylene glycol has

---

[1] These statements are quantitatively true for ideal solutions, in which the forces between molecules are small. For real solutions, except at great dilution, there is always some deviation. For polar or ionic substances this deviation may be considerable. In particular, ions cannot move independently because of the strong electric forces between them. When measuring the colligative properties, we therefore try to use as dilute a solution as will allow satisfactory experimental precision.

both a lower freezing point and a higher boiling point than pure water, the solution protects your car's cooling system against both freezing and boiling over. The boilover protection is increased by using a spring-loaded pressure cap to allow the system to operate above atmospheric pressure, because increases in pressure further raise the boiling point of the solution.

The origin of the freezing-point depression and boiling-point elevation of an aqueous solution can be understood with the aid of the phase diagram shown in Figure 18-1. The key to understanding this diagram is the lowering of the solvent vapor pressure by dissolving a nonvolatile solute in the solvent. Note that the vapor pressure curve for the solution (shown by the dotted curve) is lower than the vapor pressure curve for pure water (shown by the solid curve). Recall that the boiling point is the temperature at which the equilibrium vapor pressure equals the atmospheric pressure.

The equilibrium vapor pressure of the solvent over the solution is *less* than that of the pure solvent at the same temperature. Therefore, the solution must be heated to a higher temperature than the pure solvent in order to reach atmospheric pressure, so that the boiling point of the solution is higher than that of the pure solvent. Increasing the pressure above atmospheric pressure, as is done when you use a pressure cap on your auto radiator, raises the boiling point even further. (If you drew a horizontal line at $P = 2$ atm, it would intersect the vapor pressure curve at a higher temperature.)

When the temperature of most solutions is lowered to the freezing point, the solid that separates out is mainly pure solvent. The lowering of the vapor pressure of a solvent by added nonvolatile solute causes the equilibrium vapor pressure curve to intersect the sublimation pressure curve at a lower temperature than that for the pure solvent

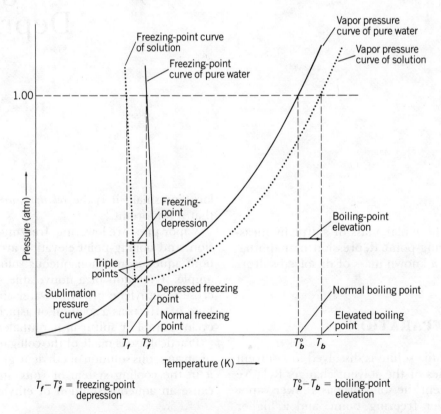

$T_f - T_f^\circ$ = freezing-point depression

$T_b^\circ - T_b$ = boiling-point elevation

FIGURE 18-1

Phase diagrams for pure water (solid line), and for water containing a nonvolatile solute (dotted line). The presence of the solute lowers the vapor pressure of the solvent. The reduced vapor pressure of the solvent gives rise to an *increase* in the boiling point of the solution relative to pure water, $T_b - T_b^\circ > 0$, and to a *decrease* in the freezing point of the solution relative to pure water, $T_f^\circ - T_f < 0$. (When the temperature of an aqueous solution is lowered to the freezing point, the solid that separates out is almost always pure ice, so the sublimation pressure curve is assumed to remain unchanged.) The extent of vapor pressure lowering is exaggerated in the diagram to show the effects more clearly.

(see Figure 18-1). The freezing-point curves for the solution and the pure solvent begin at the intersections of the sublimation pressure and vapor pressure curves, that is, at the *triple points* (shown in Figure 18-1), where all three phases (solid, liquid, and gas) simultaneously coexist. (The liquid phase is either the pure solvent or the solution containing added solute.) Therefore, the freezing-point curve for the solution lies at a *lower* temperature than the freezing-point curve of the pure solvent.

The freezing-point depression effect has several important scientific uses. It allows us to compare the freezing-point depressions of a known and unknown substance in the same solvent in order to determine the molar mass of the unknown. This type of comparison is called *cryoscopy*, the stem cryo- coming from the Greek word meaning icy or cold. In this experiment you will determine the molecular weight of sulfur dissolved in naphthalene by the cryoscopic method.

Cryoscopy is also used in the clinical laboratory to measure the total concentration of solutes in urine, making use of the fact that the freezing-point depression is proportional to the sum of the concentrations of all dissolved particles. The urine that is formed initially in the interior of the kidney has a much lower concentration of solutes than that which leaves the kidney. This is because the kidney conserves body water by recovering much of the water as the urine passes through the tubules of the kidney. This concentrating ability of the kidneys is one of its most important functions, and when the renal tubules are damaged, it is one of the first functions to be lost. Thus a cryoscopic measurement of the solute content of urine is an indication of kidney function.

Raoult's Law

The equation that quantitatively describes the vapor pressure lowering is called *Raoult's law*. It is expressed by

$$P_1 = X_1 P_1^0$$

where P_1 is the vapor pressure of the solvent above the solution, P_1^0 is the vapor pressure of the pure solvent, and X_1 is the mole fraction of the solvent in the solution. The mole fraction is a dimensionless concentration unit that expresses the fraction of the total number of molecules (or moles) that are solvent molecules:

$$X_1 = \frac{n_1}{n_1 + n_2}$$

where n_1 is the number of moles of solvent and n_2 is the number of moles of solute. This justifies the earlier statement that the colligative properties depend only on the relative numbers of solvent and solute molecules.

It is convenient in working with the colligative properties of solutions to introduce the *molality concentration scale* for solutes. We define the molality, m, of a solute as the number of moles of the solute per 1000 g of solvent.

$$\text{molality} = \frac{\text{moles of solute}}{1000 \text{ g of solvent}}$$

$$= \frac{\text{moles of solute}}{\text{kilogram of solvent}}$$

For example, a solution prepared by dissolving 1.00 mol of KCl (74.55 g) in 1.00 kg of water is 1.00 molal in KCl. The "particle molality" would be 2.00 molal, because KCl dissociates into two ions, K^+ and Cl^-.

For dilute solutions the molality is proportional to the mole fraction. Both molality and mole fraction are temperature-independent concentration scales, in contrast to the molar concentration, which changes with temperature because of expansion or contraction of the solution volume.

The Freezing-Point Depression

The equation describing the freezing-point depression is

$$\Delta T = K_f m$$

The symbol ΔT represents the freezing-point depression: $\Delta T = T_f^0 - T_f$, where T_f^0 is the freezing point of the pure solvent and T_f is the freezing point of the solution. This quantity is directly proportional to the concentration of particles expressed as the molality, m, of the particles in the solution. The proportionality constant, K_f, is called the *molal freezing-point depression constant*. By using a solute of known molar mass we can determine K_f for a particular solvent. The molality (and molar mass) of an unknown compound can then be determined by measuring the freezing-point depression of a solution of the unknown in the same solvent.

Note the phrase particle molality used in discussing the molality of an ionic solute, KCl. If the solute does not dissociate into two or more particles, the particle molality equals the molality of the solute. This will be true for the solutions we will study in this experiment, solutions of sulfur and organic compounds dissolved in naphthalene. This distinction between particle molality and solute molality is important to keep in mind. A 0.1 m KCl solution would lower the freezing point of water approximately twice as much as a 0.1 m sucrose solution. (Sucrose, ordinary table sugar, does not dissociate in water.) Does this help to explain why $CaCl_2$ is used in northern climates to melt ice on roads and sidewalks?

The freezing-point depression for a 1 m solution in water (the molal freezing-point constant) is 1.86°C, and the corresponding boiling-point rise (the *molal boiling-point constant*) is 0.52°C. The same principles apply for solutions in other solvents. For naphthalene, which we will use in this experiment, the freezing point is 80.2°C, with an ideal molal freezing-point constant of 6.9°C, and the boiling point is above 200°C, its molal boiling-point constant being unknown because it is impractical to use at this high a temperature.

These constants apply to measurements in quite dilute solution. For the more concentrated solutions (0.75 to 1 m) that we must use, the freezing-point constant may deviate slightly from the ideal value. This is the reason we shall first determine the constant under the conditions of the experiment, and then use this value for our determinations of molar mass.

Calculations of Molar Mass

Either boiling point or freezing point may be used to determine the molar mass of a soluble substance. For the latter, it is necessary only to determine the freezing point of a solution containing a known mass of the solute in a known mass of the solvent, and to compare this with the freezing point of the pure solvent, as follows.

1. Calculate the number of grams of solute per kilogram of solvent from the masses used.

2. Calculate the number of moles of solute per kilogram of solvent by dividing the measured freezing-point depression by the molal freezing-point constant.

3. Divide result 1 by result 2 to obtain the number of grams of solute per mole of solute—that is, the molar mass.

EXPERIMENTAL PROCEDURE

Special Supplies: Thermometer (1 C° divisions, or 50 to 100°C with 0.1 C° divisions if available), 27 cm of $\frac{1}{16}$-in.-diameter brass rod (brazing rod available from welding supply companies is ideal), 20- × 150-mm test tube.

Chemicals: Naphthalene, *p*-dichlorobenzene, sulfur (pulverized "roll" or "precipitated" sulfur), solid organic compounds for use as unknowns for molar mass determination, acetone or toluene solvent in plastic squeeze bottles.

Safety Precautions: Be sure to put an iron ring around the 600-mL beaker as shown in Figure 18-2. Without this protection the beaker of hot water might be tipped over, causing a severe burn.

To remove naphthalene from the test tube at the end of an experiment, remelt it in the water bath and pour the melted naphthalene into the waste container provided. *Do not pour molten naphthalene into the sink.* It will harden in the drain, clogging the drain.

To remove the last traces of naphthalene from the test tube, use a small quantity of acetone or toluene to dissolve the naphthalene. This must be done in the fume hood, far from any open flames. *Naphthalene, acetone, and toluene are all flammable.* Then dry the test tubes in the hood with a gentle stream of air. *The waste acetone or toluene should be poured into a waste container provided for that purpose, not down the drain.* It is recommended that you use a fresh test tube for each experiment, cleaning all of the test tubes at the end of the lab period.

---

1. *The Molal Freezing-Point Constant for Naphthalene* Figure 18-2 illustrates the simple apparatus required. Using a sharp razor blade, a 45° pie-shaped sector is cut longitudinally from a No. 2 one-hole rubber stopper. The split stopper easily holds a thermometer in position without danger of breakage. A circular stirrer, fashioned from $\frac{1}{16}$-in.-diameter brazing rod (or 14-gauge copper wire), is fitted through the notch at the side of the stopper.

Weigh the empty 20- × 150-mm test tube to ±0.01 g on a balance, add about 7 to 8 g of naphthalene ($C_{10}H_8$), and weigh it again. To a 13- × 100-mm test tube used as a weighing vessel, add about 1 to 1.2 g of *p*-dichlorobenzene, $C_6H_4Cl_2$ (molecular weight 147.0), and weigh this accurately to ±0.01 g.

Clamp the 20- × 150-mm test tube containing the naphthalene in a water bath (550 mL of water in a 600-mL beaker). The bottom of the test tube should be about 2 cm from the bottom of the beaker. Heat the bath to about 90°C to melt the

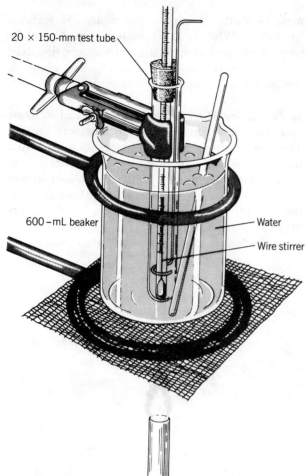

FIGURE 18-2
Freezing-point apparatus for determinations of molecular weight.

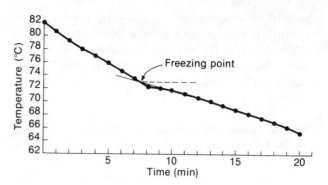

FIGURE 18-3
A typical freezing-point crystallization curve.

naphthalene. Place the thermometer and stirrer in position, with the thermometer bulb about 2 to 3 mm above the bottom of the test tube, threaded through the ring of the stirrer. This arrangement ensures good stirring around the thermometer bulb. When the naphthalene has completely melted (at about 90°C), remove the burner from beneath the water bath and stir the naphthalene gently and continuously. When crystals of solid naphthalene begin to form and the temperature is constant, read the thermometer to the nearest 0.1 C° and record this value. Reheat the water bath to melt the naphthalene, then repeat the cooling operation until you are certain of the freezing point as accurately as your thermometer can be read. When reading the thermometer, be sure to have your eye on a level with the mercury meniscus, to avoid parallax in the reading. The naphthalene should be allowed to cool in the water bath; if removed from the bath, it cools much too rapidly to obtain an accurate reading of the ther-

mometer. If the bath is heated too far above the freezing point of naphthalene, it may be quickly cooled by adding a little cold water or ice.

Now remove the stopper and attached thermometer and stirrer (avoiding loss of naphthalene) just far enough to add the sample of *p*-dichlorobenzene. Weigh the empty 100-mm test tube to obtain, by difference, the weight of the *p*-dichlorobenzene added. Heat the mixture on the water bath and stir the mixture to dissolve the solute completely. Now remove the heat and stir gently as before, and observe as accurately as possible the steady temperature at which a *small* amount of solid solvent is in equilibrium with the solution. There may be a small amount of supercooling before crystallization. Study Figure 18-3, noting especially that when a larger amount of solvent is frozen out, the remaining solution is more concentrated and therefore gives a declining freezing point. Readings therefore must be taken as soon as the first crystals appear in solution with only a very small amount of solid solvent frozen.[2] Repeat this freezing-point measurement several times by heating the solution and allowing it to cool until you are certain of this equilibrium temperature, to within 0.1 C° if possible. When you have finished the measurements, clean the tube by melting the mixture and pouring it into the waste naphthalene bottle provided. *Do not pour it into the sink.* Remove the last trace of naphthalene by dissolving it in acetone or toluene in the fume hood and drying the tube with a gentle stream of air in the hood.

From these data, calculate the molal freezing-point constant for naphthalene—that is, the change in freezing point caused by 1 mol of

---

[2] For precise determination, readings are taken every 30 to 60 s during the cooling process. A curve similar to Figure 18-3 is plotted, and the exact freezing point determined by extrapolation, as illustrated.

p-dichlorobenzene per kilogram of naphthalene. Compare your value with the literature value of 6.8 to 6.9. If sufficient time is available, repeat the determination with a fresh naphthalene sample and another weighed sample of p-dichlorobenzene.

2. The Molar Mass of Sulfur   Obtain some pulverized "roll" sulfur or "precipitated" sulfur. Using a 1.3- to 1.5-g sample of sulfur, make the freezing-point measurements for pure naphthalene and for the sulfur dissolved in naphthalene exactly as was done in part 1 for p-dichlorobenzene. From these data, calculate the molar mass of the sulfur, using the molal freezing-point constant for naphthalene determined in part 1. From the calculated molar

mass of sulfur, compute the molecular formula for sulfur. What is this formula, rounded to the nearest integer? Does it suggest that the dissolved sulfur exists as individual atoms or as a molecule containing more than one sulfur atom?

3. The Molar Mass of an Unknown Solid   Obtain from your instructor an unknown organic sample. The freezing-point measurements for pure naphthalene, and for the unknown dissolved in the naphthalene, are made exactly as was done in part 1, using a 1.3- to 1.5-g sample of unknown. From these data, calculate the molar mass of the unknown, using the molal freezing-point constant for naphthalene determined in part 1.

Colligative Properties
The Molar Mass of
a Soluble Substance by
Freezing-Point Depression

NAME		
SECTION		LOCKER
INSTRUCTOR		DATE

Sample or unknown no. _____

Data	p-Dichlorobenzene		Sulfur 2	Unknown 3
	1a	1b		
Mass of naphthalene + container	g	g	g	g
Mass of container	g	g	g	g
Mass of naphthalene	g	g	g	g
Mass of sample + test tube	g	g	g	g
Mass of test tube	g	g	g	g
Mass of sample	g	g	g	g
Freezing point of naphthalene	°C	°C	°C	°C
Freezing point of solution	°C	°C	°C	°C

Calculations	p-Dichlorobenzene	
	1a	1b
Grams of solute per kilogram of solvent	g	g
Freezing-point depression	°C	°C
Moles of solute per kilogram of solvent	mol/kg	mol/kg
Molal freezing-point constant (from these data)	$\dfrac{kg \cdot °C}{mol}$	$\dfrac{kg \cdot °C}{mol}$

Calculations	Sulfur 2	Unknown 3
Grams of solute per kilogram of solvent	g	g
Freezing-point depression	°C	°C
Moles of solute per kilogram of solvent	mol/kg	mol/kg
Molar mass of the sample	g/mol	g/mol
Percentage error, based on formula of the sample	%	%

Approval of Instructor: Your unknown is _____

Use the graph below to plot the data from one of your cooling curves as directed by your instructor.

QUESTIONS ON EXPERIMENTAL ERROR

1. If, when using an ordinary thermometer, with naphthalene as the solvent, you can be reasonably certain of the freezing-point depression to only ±0.2°C, what will be the percentage relative error in your answer due to this cause if your solution is about (a) 1 m? (b) 0.2 m?

(a) _____

(b) _____

2. Answer the same questions as in 1, if by using a more accurate thermometer and more precise technique, your freezing-point depression is known to ±0.01°C.

(a) _____

(b) _____

PROBLEMS

1. Cyclohexanol, $C_6H_{11}OH$, is sometimes used as the solvent in molecular weight determinations by freezing-point depression. If 0.253 g of benzoic acid, C_6H_5COOH, dissolved in 12.45 g of cyclohexanol, lowered the freezing point of pure cyclohexanol by 6.55°C, what is the molal freezing-point constant of this solvent?

_____

2. Since the freezing point of a solution depends on the relative number of *particles*, what would you calculate to be the freezing point of 0.1 m solutions in water of (a) NaCl, (b) $BaCl_2$? Assume that these salts are 100% ionized in solution. (Compare your answers with the actual respective freezing points: −0.348°C and −0.470°C. The difference is due to the decreased activity of the ions, largely because of their electric charges.)

(a) _____

(b) _____

3. How many grams of each of the following per kilogram of water in your car radiator are needed to give equal protection against freezing, down to −10°C? (a) Methyl alcohol, CH_3OH, b.p. 64.6°C, (b) ethyl alcohol, C_2H_5OH, b.p. 78.5°C, (c) ethylene glycol, $C_2H_4(OH)_2$, b.p. 197.2°C. In spite of higher cost, what advantage does ethylene glycol possess over the alcohols as a winter antifreeze and/or summer coolant?

(a) _____

(b) _____

(c) _____

Some Examples
of Chemical Equilibria
Le Châtelier's Principle

PURPOSE

To observe a number of interesting and colorful chemical reactions that are examples of chemical systems at equilibrium. To see how these systems respond to changes in the concentrations of reactants or products or to changes in temperature. To see that the direction of the shift in the equilibrium tends to at least partially offset the change in conditions, a principle first clearly stated by Le Châtelier.

PRE-LAB PREPARATION

Any chemical equation that describes a real chemical reaction sums up the result of an experiment (more often, several experiments). Someone had to measure out the reactants, carry out the reaction,

identify the products, and measure quantitatively the number of moles of products produced per mole of reactant consumed. The last step is the writing of a balanced chemical equation that concisely summarizes the experimental facts.

Many chemical reactions go essentially to completion, but some do not, stopping at some point of equilibrium that lies between no reaction and an essentially complete reaction. The same point of equilibrium can be attained by mixing together products or reactants, clearly indicating that chemical reactions can go either forward or backward.

Every chemical reaction is in principle a two-way reaction, but if the point of equilibrium greatly favors the reactants, we say that there is *no reaction*. If the point of equilibrium greatly favors the products, we say the reaction is *complete*. For either of these two extremes it is difficult to measure experimentally the concentrations of all of the reactants and products at equilibrium. In the first case (reactants greatly favored), the concentration

*stress
by
adding or taking
away*

of products is practically zero. In the second case (products greatly favored), no significant quantity of the reactants will be produced by mixing the products together. Thus when the equilibrium greatly favors the products, the reaction appears to go in only one direction: *reactants → products.*

Nearly every chemical reaction consumes or releases energy. (We call these, respectively, *endothermic* or *exothermic* reactions.) For these reactions, we can regard energy as if it were a reactant or product, and by adding energy to a system (by heating it) or removing energy from a system (by cooling it) we can produce a shift in the chemical equilibrium. The concentrations of reactants and products change to reflect the new equilibrium.

There is an added complication that must be considered. Not all chemical reactions are rapid. In fact, some are so slow that you might be fooled into thinking that no reaction occurs, whereas the equilibrium point when it is finally reached might greatly favor the products. The rate at which a chemical reaction reaches equilibrium will be taken up when you study the kinetics of chemical reactions.

For a reaction where equilibrium is attained, the point of equilibrium may be approached from either the side of the reactants or the side of the products, which emphasizes the dynamic nature of chemical reactions. A state of equilibrium is the point of balance where the rate of the forward reaction equals the rate of the backward reaction.

The reactions you will study in this experiment are all rapid reactions, so you will be able to observe almost immediately the effects of changing the concentration of either reactants or products. In particular you will observe that when you change the concentration of a reactant or product, the point of equilibrium shifts in a direction that tends to offset the change. This behavior can be summarized in a general principle that was first fully stated in 1884 by the French chemist Henri Louis Le Châtelier: *A chemical reaction that is displaced from equilibrium by a change in conditions (concentrations, temperature, pressure, volume) proceeds toward a new equilibrium state in the direction that at least partially offsets the change in conditions.*

This introductory experiment is designed to show qualitatively several important features of chemical equilibria. In subsequent experiments you will learn about the quantitative aspects of chemical equilibria, measuring the equilibrium constants for a variety of reactions, and making calculations of equilibrium concentrations from previously measured equilibrium constants.

EXPERIMENTAL PROCEDURE

Special Supplies: Electric hot plate, crushed ice.

Chemicals: 1 M K_2CrO_4, 3 M H_2SO_4, 6 M NaOH, 0.1% methyl orange indicator, 0.1% phenolphthalein indicator, 6 M HCl, 0.1 M CH_3COOH (acetic acid), 1 M $NaCH_3COO$ (sodium acetate), 0.1 M NH_3, 1 M NH_4Cl, 0.1 M $Fe(NO_3)_3$, 0.1 M KSCN (potassium thiocyanate), 0.15 M anhydrous $CoCl_2$ in methanol (20 g anhydrous $CoCl_2$ per liter of methanol; if only the hydrated salt $CoCl_2 \cdot 6H_2O$ is available, it must be dried before use), concentrated (12 M) HCl, saturated (5.4 M) NaCl, 0.1 M $BaCl_2$, 0.1 M $CaCl_2$, 0.5 M $H_2C_2O_4$ (oxalic acid), 0.25 M $(NH_4)_2C_2O_4$ (ammonium oxalate), 6 M NH_3.

Safety Precautions: Be careful when handling concentrated (12 M) HCl and 6 M NaOH. They cause skin and eye burns. Wear eye protection.

Take care when heating the methanol solution of $CoCl_2$. Methanol vapors are toxic and flammable, so the heating must be done by placing the test tube in a beaker of hot water at 65 to 70°C on a hot plate in the fume hood.

---

1. The Shifting of Equilibria in Acid-Base Reactions. The Common Ion Effect

(a) *The Chromate Ion-Dichromate Ion Equilibrium* Yellow chromate ion reacts with hydrogen ion to form first hydrogen chromate ion and then, by condensation and loss of H_2O, orange dichromate ion:

$$2CrO_4^{2-} + 2H^+ \rightleftharpoons$$

$$2HCrO_4^- \rightleftharpoons Cr_2O_7^{2-} + H_2O \quad (1)$$

At present, we need consider only the overall reaction,

$$\underset{\text{yellow}}{2CrO_4^{2-}} + 2H^+ \rightleftharpoons \underset{\text{orange}}{Cr_2O_7^{2-}} + H_2O \quad (2)$$

To 3 mL of 1 M K_2CrO_4 in a test tube add several drops of 3 M H_2SO_4. Mix this and observe any change. Now add several drops of 6 M NaOH, with mixing, until a change occurs. Again add H_2SO_4. Interpret the observed changes. How did the equilibrium shift in response to the added reagents, toward the formation of yellow chromate ion or toward the formation of orange dichromate ion? Explain how hydroxide ion exerts an effect, even though it doesn't appear in the overall equation.

(b) *Weak Acid-Base Indicator Equilibria* In Experiment 16 you compared the relative concentrations of molecules and ions in weak acids and weak bases. Let us now see how the chemical equilibria shift when the concentrations of these ions or molecules are changed. First we will observe the effects of strong acid and strong base on indicators, which are themselves weak acids and bases. The chemical equation for the dissociation of the indicator methyl orange can be written as

$$HIn + H_2O \rightleftharpoons H_3O^+ + In^- \qquad (3)$$

red yellow-orange

protonated HIn form

deprotonated In$^-$ form

where HIn represents the protonated (acid) form of the indicator, which is red in color, and In$^-$ represents the deprotonated (or base) form of the indicator, which is yellow-orange in color. Methyl orange indicator changes color around pH 4, which corresponds to a hydrogen ion concentration of 10^{-4} M. (For a fuller discussion of indicators and the pH scale see your text.)

Other acid-base indicators change color at a different hydrogen ion concentration. Phenolphthalein, whose acid form is colorless, changes to the pink base form around pH 9, which corresponds to a hydrogen ion concentration of 10^{-9} M.

First, in order to observe the effects of acid and base on indicators, add a drop of methyl orange to 3 mL of water. Then add 2 drops of 6 M HCl followed by 4 drops of 6 M NaOH. Repeat the experiment, using phenolphthalein indicator in place of the methyl orange. Record your observations.

(c) *Weak Acid-Weak Base Equilibria* Now we will use the indicators to observe changes involving weak acids and bases that are themselves colorless. To each of two 3-mL samples of 0.1 M CH$_3$COOH (acetic acid), add a drop of methyl orange, and then add 1 M NaCH$_3$COO (sodium acetate), a few drops at a time, with mixing. The added salt, sodium acetate, has an ion in common with acetic acid, a weak acid that dissociates in water to give acetate ion.

$$CH_3COOH + H_2O \rightleftharpoons H_3O^+ + CH_3COO^- \qquad (4)$$

Note that adding acetate ion produces a change in the color of the indicator. The color change indicates that the indicator has been changed from its acid to its base form, which in turn must mean that the hydrogen ion concentration became smaller when the sodium acetate was added. Explain your observations in terms of the equilibria shown in Equations (3) and (4). The effect on the dissociation of acetic acid that is produced by adding sodium acetate is called the *common ion* effect.

To each of two 3-mL samples of 0.1 M NH$_3$ add a drop of phenolphthalein indicator. Note and record the color. To one sample add 1 M NH$_4$Cl, a few drops at a time, with mixing. To the other add 6 M HCl, a drop at a time, with mixing. In each case, note any changes in the color and in the odor of the solution.

Write the equation for the reaction of NH$_3$ with water to form NH$_4^+$ and OH$^-$. Interpret the results in terms of the changes of H$^+$ concentration (shown by the change in color of the indicator) and the equilibrium for the dissociation of NH$_3$. Explain clearly how the equilibria shift when NH$_4^+$ ion (from NH$_4$Cl) and H$^+$ (from HCl) are added. Write the net ionic equation for the reaction of NH$_3$ with HCl.

2. *Complex Ion Equilibria* It is common for cations (especially those with $+2$ or $+3$ charge) to attract ions (or molecules with free electron pairs) to form aggregates called *complexes*. If the resulting aggregate has a net charge, it is called a *complex ion*. The composition of these complexes may vary with the proportion and concentration of reactants.

(a) *The Thiocyanatoiron(III) Complex Ion* This ion, sometimes called the *ferric thiocyanate* complex ion, is formed as a blood-red substance described by the following equilibrium equation.[1]

$$Fe^{3+} + SCN^- \rightleftharpoons Fe(SCN)^{2+} \qquad (5)$$

---

[1] For simplicity, we are using the unhydrated formulas here. This makes no difference in our equilibrium consideration, however, since water is always present at high constant concentration. With the addition of SCN$^-$ to hydrated iron(III) ion, Fe(H$_2$O)$_6^{3+}$, a substitution of SCN$^-$ for H$_2$O occurs, with possible formulas such as Fe(H$_2$O)$_5$(SCN)$^{2+}$, Fe(H$_2$O)$_4$(SCN)$_2^+$, Fe(H$_2$O)$_3$(SCN)$_3$, . . . , Fe(SCN)$_6^{3-}$.

In a 100-mL beaker add 3 mL of 0.1 M $Fe(NO_3)_3$ to 3 mL of 0.1 M KSCN. Dilute this mixture by adding 30 to 35 mL of water until the deep-red color is reduced in intensity so that further changes (to either increase or decrease the color) are easily observed. Put 5 mL of this solution in a test tube and add 1 mL (about 20 drops) of 0.1 M $Fe(NO_3)_3$. To a 5-mL portion in a second test tube, add 1 mL of 0.1 M KSCN. To a third 5-mL portion, add 5 to 6 drops of 6 M NaOH ($Fe(OH)_3$ is quite insoluble). To a fourth 5-mL portion add 1 mL of water. Put a fifth 5-mL portion in a tube to serve as a comparison for the other four test tubes. Compare the relative intensity of the red color of the thiocyanato complex in each of the first four test tubes to that of the original solution in the fifth tube. Interpret your observations, using Le Châtelier's principle and considering the equilibrium shown in Equation (5).

(b) *The Temperature-Dependent Equilibrium of Co(II) Complex Ions* The chloro complex of cobalt(II), $CoCl_4^{2-}$, is tetrahedral and has a blue color. The aquo complex of cobalt(II), $Co(H_2O)_6^{2+}$, is octahedral and has a pink color. (Figure 19-1 shows the geometry of the tetrahedral and octahedral complexes.) There is an equilibrium between the two forms in aqueous solution, and because the conversion of one form to another involves a considerable energy change, the equilibrium is temperature dependent.

$$CoCl_4^{2-} + 6H_2O \rightleftharpoons$$
$$4Cl^- + Co(H_2O)_6^{2+} + energy \quad (6)$$

Le Châtelier's principle applied to Equation (6) predicts that if energy is removed (by cooling the system) the equilibrium tends to shift toward the aquo complex, because a shift in the equilibrium to produce more aquo complex produces some energy, thus partly offsetting the change.

Put 3 mL of 0.15 M $CoCl_2$ (in methanol) into a 13- × 100-mm test tube. (Methanol is used as a solvent so that you can observe the effects of adding water.) Using a dropper, add *just enough* water to the blue methanol solution to change the color to that of the pink aquo complex. Divide the pink solution into two equal portions in two 13- × 100-mm test tubes. Add concentrated (12 M) HCl dropwise to one test tube until you observe a color change. Record your observations. Heat the test tube containing the other portion of the pink solution in a beaker of hot water (65 to 70°C) on a hot plate in a fume hood. (*Caution*: Methanol vapors are toxic and flammable. If a fume hood

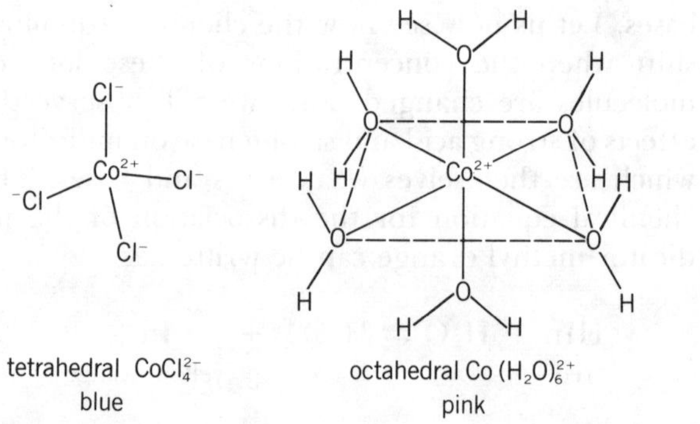

tetrahedral $CoCl_4^{2-}$
blue

octahedral $Co(H_2O)_6^{2+}$
pink

FIGURE 19-1
The cobalt(II) complexes with chloride ion and water have different molecular geometries and different colors.

is not available, use an inverted funnel connected to an aspirator (as shown in Figure 5-1) to remove the methanol vapor.) You should note a color change. (If you do not, you probably added too much water to the original methanol solution. Try again.) The color change is reversible. Cooling the solution in an ice bath will restore the original pink color. Repeat the cycle of heating and cooling to verify this. Record your observations and interpret them by applying Le Châtelier's principle to the equilibrium shown in Equation (6).

3. The Equilibria of Saturated Solutions

(a) *Saturated Sodium Chloride* To 4 mL of saturated (5.4 M) sodium chloride in a 13- × 100-mm test tube add 2 mL of concentrated (12 M) HCl. Mix, observe, and record your observations. Calculate the relative Cl^- concentrations in the original and final solutions and explain your observations in terms of the saturated solution equilibrium.

(b) *Saturated Barium Chromate* To 3 mL of 0.1 M $BaCl_2$ add 5 to 6 drops of 1 M K_2CrO_4, and then 10 to 12 drops of 6 M HCl. Record your observations. Write an equation for the reaction of Ba^{2+} with CrO_4^{2-}. Explain how the addition of HCl shifts the equilibrium of this equation.

4. Application of the Law of Chemical Equilibrium to Analytical Procedures
In qualitative analysis, Ca^{2+} is usually identified as calcium oxalate.

$$Ca^{2+} + C_2O_4^{2-} \rightleftharpoons CaC_2O_4(s) \quad (7)$$

What conditions will make the precipitation as complete as possible? Since Ca^{2+} is the unknown ion, it is desirable to drive the reaction as far as possible to the right by obtaining the maximum

$C_2O_4^{2-}$ concentration possible. Should we use a soluble salt, such as $(NH_4)_2C_2O_4$, or the moderately weak acid $H_2C_2O_4$? The dissociation equilibria are[2]

$$(NH_4)_2C_2O_4(aq) \rightarrow 2NH_4^+ + C_2O_4^{2-} \qquad (8)$$

and

$$H_2C_2O_4(aq) \rightleftharpoons H^+ + HC_2O_4^- \qquad (9)$$
$$\updownarrow$$
$$H^+ + C_2O_4^{2-}$$

Should the solution be made acidic or basic to achieve the maximum $C_2O_4^{2-}$ concentration? Test your reasoning by the following experiments.

---

[2] In writing the acid-base equilibria shown in Equations (8) and (9), we have used a shorthand notation, omitting water from the equations, and abbreviating H_3O^+ as H^+. You should not lose sight of the fact that water participates in the dissociation reaction, acting as a base (proton acceptor).

Mix 3 mL of 0.1 M $CaCl_2$ with 3 mL of deionized water, and place equal portions in two 13- $\times$ 100-mm test tubes. To one, add 0.3 mL (6 to 7 drops) of 0.5 M $H_2C_2O_4$, and to the other add 0.6 mL (12 to 14 drops) of 0.25 M $(NH_4)_2C_2O_4$. Compare the results.

To the test tube containing the $H_2C_2O_4$ mixture, add 0.5 mL (10 drops) of 6 M HCl, and mix. Explain the results. Now, to the same solution add a slight excess of 6 M NH_3 and mix. Is the precipitate that forms CaC_2O_4 or $Ca(OH)_2$? To find out if the precipitate is $Ca(OH)_2$, add a few drops of 6 M NH_3 to some diluted 0.1 M $CaCl_2$ solution. Does a precipitate form? What conclusions can you draw from this result? Explain all of your results in terms of the equilibria shown in Equations (7), (8), and (9) and the dissociation of NH_3 in water to form OH^-.

Would the acidity of the solution be of more importance in the precipitation of the salt of a strong acid or in the precipitation of the salt of a weak acid?

The Solubility Product Constant of Calcium Iodate, $Ca(IO_3)_2$

PURPOSE

To understand the relation between the molar solubility and the solubility product constant of a sparingly soluble salt. To measure the molar solubility of calcium iodate in pure water and to determine the solubility product constant. To investigate the common ion effect by measuring the molar solubility of calcium iodate in a solution containing added potassium iodate.

PRE-LAB PREPARATION

When soluble ionic compounds are dissolved in water, the solution usually contains just the ions that were present in the solid salt. For example, in a saturated solution of KNO_3, the solution contains only K^+ ions and NO_3^- ions, and the dissolved salt is completely dissociated.[1]

$$KNO_3(s) \rightleftharpoons K^+(aq) + NO_3^-(aq) \qquad (1)$$

That a salt is sparingly soluble suggests that the forces between the ions in the solid might be larger than those between the ions of very soluble salts. Many sparingly soluble salts do not completely dissociate into the ions present in the solid, but interact with one another to form aggregates, called complexes, or react with water to form new species.

---

[1] In solid KNO_3 each ion is surrounded by ions of the opposite charge. This is still largely true when the KNO_3 is dissolved in water, but the ions are farther apart and each ion is surrounded by a cluster of water molecules that are more or less tightly bound to the ion. The ions in solution are therefore said to be "hydrated" or "aquated."

For example, a saturated solution of $Ca(OH)_2$ contains $Ca(OH)^+$ ion as well as Ca^{2+} and OH^- ions, as shown by the following equilibria:

$$Ca(OH)_2(s) \rightleftharpoons Ca(OH)^+(aq) + OH^-(aq) \quad (2)$$

$$Ca(OH)^+(aq) \rightleftharpoons Ca^{2+}(aq) + OH^-(aq) \quad (3)$$

A saturated solution of $CaCO_3$ contains appreciable concentrations of HCO_3^- and OH^- as well as Ca^{2+} and CO_3^{2-} ions. Here, carbonate ion (CO_3^{2-}) reacts with water to produce bicarbonate ion and hydroxide ion as shown in the following equilibria:

$$CaCO_3(s) \rightleftharpoons Ca^{2+}(aq) + CO_3^{2-}(aq) \quad (4)$$

$$CO_3^{2-}(aq) + H_2O \rightleftharpoons HCO_3^-(aq) + OH^-(aq) \quad (5)$$

The behavior shown in Equation (5) is typical of all salts (such as carbonates, sulfides, and phosphates) in which the anion can react with H_2O to form an acid that is only weakly dissociated.

The two examples whose solubility equilibria are described by Equations (2) through (5) show that it is not always safe to make the assumption that only the ions produced by complete dissociation of the salt are present. The solubility behavior of every salt must be determined by an experimental investigation.

The Relation Between Molar Solubility and the Solubility Product Constant

Calcium iodate, the salt you will study in this experiment, has been shown to be completely dissociated in water into calcium ions, Ca^{2+}, and iodate ions, IO_3^-.[2]

$$Ca(IO_3)_2 \rightleftharpoons Ca^{2+}(aq) + 2IO_3^-(aq) \quad (6)$$

For any salt that dissolves to give just the ions originally present in the salt there is a simple relation between the molar solubility of the salt and the solubility product constant of the salt. The concentration of each ion will be equal to the molar solubility or equal to some multiple of the molar solubility.

What do we mean by the molar solubility of the salt? This quantity is just the concentration of the dissolved salt, expressed in units of moles per liter. In the calcium iodate example, the calcium ion concentration is equal to the molar solubility, and the iodate ion concentration is equal to 2 times the molar solubility. This will be true because each mole of calcium iodate that dissolves gives one mole of calcium ions and two moles of iodate ions.

If we let the symbol S represent the molar solubility of calcium iodate (in units of moles per liter), the concentrations of Ca^{2+} and IO_3^- ions will be related to S, the molar solubility, by the following equations:

$$[Ca^{2+}] = S \quad (7)$$

$$[IO_3^-] = 2S \quad (8)$$

Equation (6) shows the reaction for the dissociation of solid $Ca(IO_3)_2$ in a saturated aqueous solution. The equilibrium constant for this reaction (often called the *solubility product* constant) is written as shown in Equation (9), observing the convention that the activity[3] of the pure solid is taken to be equal to 1 so that it does not appear in the equilibrium constant expression.

$$K_{sp} = [Ca^{2+}][IO_3^-]^2 \quad (9)$$

If we substitute for the concentration of each ion its equivalent in units of molar solubility, S, by substituting Equations (7) and (8) into Equation (9), we obtain an equation that shows that there is a simple relation between the K_{sp} and the molar solubility of the salt.

$$K_{sp} = [Ca^{2+}][IO_3^-]^2 = S(2S)^2 = 4S^3 \quad (10)$$

The situation is more complicated in the case of calcium hydroxide, $Ca(OH)_2$. The equations for the dissociation of $Ca(OH)_2$ are written as shown in Equations (2) and (3) with equilibrium constant expressions given by

$$K_2 = [Ca(OH)^+][OH^-] \quad (11)$$

$$K_3 = \frac{[Ca^{2+}][OH^-]}{[Ca(OH)^+]} \quad (12)$$

---

[2] The actual composition of the solid that is in equilibrium with the ions in solution is the hexahydrate, $Ca(IO_3)_2 \cdot 6H_2O$.

[3] The effective concentration, or "activity," of a pure solid that participates in a chemical reaction does not change. By thermodynamic convention the pure solid is chosen as the thermodynamic reference state, which is equivalent to assigning the value 1.00 to the activity of the solid.

The relationship between the molar solubility, S, and the concentrations of the ions in solution is obtained by summing the species that contain Ca^{2+}:

$$[Ca(OH)^+] + [Ca^{2+}] = S \qquad (13)$$

or by summing the species that contain OH^-:[4]

$$[Ca(OH^+)] + [OH^-] = 2S \qquad (14)$$

Substitution of Equations (11) and (12) into Equations (13) and (14), respectively, with elimination of $[Ca^{2+}]$ and $[Ca(OH)^+]$ leads to the equation

$$K_2K_3 = [OH^-]^2([OH^-] - S) \qquad (15)$$

This result shows that it is necessary to know both S and $[OH^-]$ in order to have enough information to calculate K_2 and K_3.

To summarize we emphasize two important points about solubility equilibria: (a) The identity of all of the solution species in equilibrium with the solid must be determined by experiment. It is not safe to assume that all salts dissociate completely to give just the ions in the solid salt. (b) The solubility product constant can be calculated directly from the molar solubility only if the dissolved salt completely dissociates into its constituent ions, these ions neither reacting with one another to form complexes nor reacting with water.

In the case of calcium iodate, a single equilibrium describes the system, and the value of the equilibrium constant can be calculated from the molar solubility. For the other salts we described (Ca(OH)₂, CaCO₃), it requires two equilibria to describe each system, and a measurement of just the molar solubility does not provide enough information to calculate two equilibrium constants.

The Solubility of Ca(IO₃)₂ in KIO₃ Solution
The Common Ion Effect

From Le Châtelier's principle we would predict that the solubility of calcium iodate would be lower in a solution of potassium iodate, KIO₃, which is a strong electrolyte that completely dissociates in water. The hypothesis is that the addition of KIO₃

would shift the equilibrium described in Equation (6) toward the left. To test this hypothesis you will measure the solubility of calcium iodate in 0.01 M KIO₃. Under these conditions the concentrations of the ions will be related to the molar solubility of Ca(IO₃)₂ in the following way (compare Equations (16) and (17) with Equations (7) and (8)):

$$[Ca^{2+}] = S \qquad (16)$$

$$[IO_3^-] = 0.01 + 2S \qquad (17)$$

Note that all of the calcium ion must come from dissolved calcium iodate. However, the iodate ion comes from both KIO₃ and dissolved Ca(IO₃)₂. As before, we get 2 mol of iodate ions and 1 mol of calcium ions for every mole of calcium iodate that goes into solution.

The relation between the solubility product constant and the molar solubility will also be changed (compare Equation (18) with Equation (10)).

$$K_{sp} = [Ca^{2+}][IO_3^-]^2 = S(0.01 + 2S)^2 \qquad (18)$$

If we know the concentration of potassium iodate, a single measurement of the total iodate concentration allows us to calculate the molar solubility of calcium iodate and the solubility product constant.

EXPERIMENTAL PROCEDURE

Special Supplies: 50-mL buret, 10-mL volumetric pipet.

Chemicals: Standardized nominal 0.05 M Na₂S₂O₃ (sodium thiosulfate) solution, KI(s), 1 M HCl, 0.1% starch indicator solution, saturated solution of Ca(IO₃)₂·6H₂O in pure water, saturated solution of Ca(IO₃)₂·6H₂O in 0.0100 M KIO₃. The saturated solutions should be prepared a week in advance; see Notes to Instructor.

NOTES TO INSTRUCTOR As an option the standardization of the nominal 0.05 M Na₂S₂O₃ may be performed by the students if they are supplied with a solution of 0.0100 M KIO₃. The titration is performed as described for the determination of the molar solubility of calcium iodate.

The solid in equilibrium with the saturated solution of calcium iodate is the hexahydrate. We have found, however, that use of anhydrous calcium iodate to prepare the saturated solutions gives the same results. Anhydrous calcium iodate is available from a commercial supplier of laboratory chemicals (G. Frederick Smith Chemical

---

[4] Equation (14) contains the implicit assumption that the dissociation of water produces a negligible contribution to the OH^- concentration.

Co.), but a quantity of the hexahydrate sufficient for 100 students is easily prepared. Dissolve 0.5 mol (112 g) of KIO_3 in 600 mL of hot water in a liter beaker. To the hot solution, slowly add with stirring 0.25 mol of $Ca(NO_3)_2$ (or $CaCl_2$) dissolved in 200 mL water. Allow to cool. Filter off the solid on a large Büchner funnel and wash the solid with three 50-mL portions of cold water. Allow the solid to air dry or use the moist cake to prepare the saturated solutions.

The saturated solution in pure water is prepared by adding 8 g $Ca(IO_3)_2 \cdot 6H_2O$ per liter of water. The saturated solution in 0.0100 M KIO_3 is prepared by adding 2.14 g KIO_3 + 4 g $Ca(IO_3) \cdot 6H_2O$ per liter of water. Stir the solutions for at least 24 h, then allow to stand for 48 h before use. Use a siphon or some other means to provide the students with samples that are free of particles of solid calcium iodate.

Determination of the Molar Solubility of Calcium Iodate

When calcium iodate dissolves in solution, both the solid and the solution remain electrically neutral. This principle of electroneutrality requires that for $Ca(IO_3)_2$ two IO_3^- ions will go into solution for each Ca^{2+} that goes into solution. So the molar solubility can be determined by measuring either the concentration of calcium ion or the concentration of iodate ion. We will use a procedure for measuring the IO_3^- concentration that makes use of the fact that IO_3^- oxidizes iodide ion.

$$IO_3^- + 5I^- + 6H^+ \rightarrow 3I_2 + 3H_2O \quad (19)$$

The I_2 produced is in turn titrated with sodium thiosulfate.

$$I_2 + 2S_2O_3^{2-} \rightarrow 2I^- + S_4O_6^{2-} \quad (20)$$

Note from the overall stoichiometry that each mole of IO_3^- will produce enough I_2 to consume 6 mol of $S_2O_3^{2-}$. Therefore the concentration of IO_3^- ion will be given by

$$[IO_3^-], \frac{mol}{L} = \frac{mL\ S_2O_3^{2-}}{mL\ IO_3^-} \times \frac{mol\ S_2O_3^{2-}}{L}$$
$$\times \frac{1\ mol\ IO_3^-}{6\ mol\ S_2O_3^{2-}} \quad (21)$$

1. Standardization of the Sodium Thiosulfate Solution (Optional)
Use the procedure described in part 2, substituting 10.0-mL samples of 0.0100 M KIO_3 for the samples of saturated $Ca(IO_3)_2$ solution. Titrate at least two samples. Calculate the exact molar concentration of sodium thiosulfate, keeping in mind that 1 mol of KIO_3 produces enough I_2 to consume 6 mol of sodium thiosulfate. The calculated molarities for the two samples should agree within 1%.

2. The Molar Solubility of Ca(IO₃)₂ in Pure Water
Rinse a 50-mL buret with three 5-mL portions of standardized sodium thiosulfate solution (nominal concentration 0.05 M). Fill the buret and record the initial buret reading. Put 50 mL of water in a 250-mL Erlenmeyer flask. Add 2 g KI and swirl to dissolve. Record the temperature of the saturated calcium iodate solution. Then add 10.0 mL of the saturated solution to the Erlenmeyer flask. (A 10-mL volumetric pipet will give the best accuracy; if one is not available, carefully measure the volume in a 10-mL graduated cylinder.) Then add 10 mL of 1 M HCl. The solution should turn brown. Without delay, titrate the solution with sodium thiosulfate until the solution is yellow. Then add 5 mL of 0.1% starch indicator; the solution should turn blue-black. Continue the titration until you get a sharp change from blue to a colorless solution. Record the final buret reading. Repeat the titration procedure with a second sample. The volumes should agree within 0.2 mL. (A possible source of error is the air oxidation of I^- to give I_2. This will result in values that are too high if the solution is allowed to stand for too long before it is titrated.)

Calculate the concentration of iodate ion in the sample of saturated solution (see Equation (21)). The molar solubility of calcium iodate will be equal to one half the iodate concentration (see Equations (7) and (8)). Calculate the solubility product constant for calcium iodate (see Equation (10)).

3. The Molar Solubility of Calcium Iodate in 0.0100 M Potassium Iodate
Using the procedure described in part 2, titrate two 10.0-mL samples of the saturated solution of $Ca(IO_3)_2$ in 0.0100 M KIO_3. Record the temperature of the saturated solution. Record the initial and final buret readings for each titration.

Calculate the total iodate concentration as in part 2. Subtract 0.0100 M from the total concentration to obtain the concentration of iodate ion that comes from dissolved calcium iodate. Divide this result by 2 to obtain the molar solubility of calcium iodate. Is it smaller, as we predicted from Le Châtelier's principle? Calculate the solubility product constant for calcium iodate (see Equation (18)). Does the calculated value of K_{sp} agree with the value for K_{sp} calculated in part 2?

BIBLIOGRAPHY

Ramette, R. W., *Chemical Equilibrium and Analysis*, Addison-Wesley, Reading, MA, 1981, p. 109.

The Solubility Product Constant of Calcium Iodate, Ca(IO$_3$)$_2$

NAME	
SECTION	LOCKER
INSTRUCTOR	DATE

DATA AND CALCULATIONS

1. Standardization of Sodium Thiosulfate (Optional)

Volume of 0.0100 M KIO$_3$ samples _____ mL

Data	Trial 1	Trial 2	Trial 3
Volume of Na$_2$S$_2$O$_3$ titrant Final buret reading	_____ mL	_____ mL	_____ mL
Initial buret reading	_____ mL	_____ mL	_____ mL
Net volume of Na$_2$S$_2$O$_3$	_____ mL	_____ mL	_____ mL
Calculated concentration of Na$_2$S$_2$O$_3$	_____ M	_____ M	_____ M

For each trial, calculate the concentration of Na$_2$S$_2$O$_3$; show a sample calculation in the space below.

Average _____ M

2. The Molar Solubility of Calcium Iodate in Pure Water

Temperature of the saturated solution of calcium iodate _____ °C

Volume of saturated calcium iodate solution _____ mL

Data	Trial 1	Trial 2	Trial 3
Volume of Na$_2$S$_2$O$_3$ titrant Final buret reading	_____ mL	_____ mL	_____ mL
Initial buret reading	_____ mL	_____ mL	_____ mL
Net volume of Na$_2$S$_2$O$_3$	_____ mL	_____ mL	_____ mL
Calculated concentration of IO$_3^-$	_____ M	_____ M	_____ M

For each trial, calculate the concentration of IO$_3^-$; show a sample calculation in the space below.

Average _____ M

Calculate the molar solubility of $Ca(IO_3)_2$ in pure water from the average value of the IO_3^- concentration.

Molar solubility _____ mol/L

Calculate the solubility product constant, K_{sp}, for a saturated solution of $Ca(IO_3)_2$ in water. (See Equation (10).)

K_{sp} = _____

3. The Molar Solubility of Calcium Iodate in 0.0100 M Potassium Iodate

Temperature of the saturated solution of calcium iodate _____ °C

Volume of saturated calcium iodate solution _____ mL

Data	Trial 1	Trial 2	Trial 3
Volume of $Na_2S_2O_3$ titrant Final buret reading	_____ mL	_____ mL	_____ mL
Initial buret reading	_____ mL	_____ mL	_____ mL
Net volume of $Na_2S_2O_3$	_____ mL	_____ mL	_____ mL
Calculated concentration of IO_3^-	_____ M	_____ M	_____ M

For each trial, calculate the concentration of IO_3^-; show a sample calculation in the space below.

Average _____ M

Subtract the concentration of IO_3^- ion that came from the KIO_3 from the average value of the total IO_3^- concentration to get the iodate ion concentration that came from dissolved $Ca(IO_3)_2$.

Total IO_3^- concentration _____ M

IO_3^- concentration from KIO_3 _____ M

IO_3^- concentration from dissolved $Ca(IO_3)_2$ _____ M

Calculate the molar solubility of $Ca(IO_3)_2$ in 0.0100 M KIO_3 solution.

Molar solubility _____ mol/L

Calculate the solubility product constant, K_{sp}, for a saturated solution of $Ca(IO_3)_2$ in 0.0100 M KIO_3. (See Equation (18).)

$$K_{sp} = \underline{\hspace{2cm}}$$

PROBLEMS

1. Calculate the molar solubility, S, of calcium iodate in 0.020 M $Ca(NO_3)_2$, a completely dissociated strong electrolyte. (NO_3^- ion does not chemically interact with either Ca^{2+} or IO_3^-.) Assume that K_{sp} for $Ca(IO_3)_2 = 2.0 \times 10^{-6}$.

To set up the problem we can write the following equations.

$$[Ca^{2+}] = S + 0.020$$

$$[IO_3^-] = 2S$$

$$K_{sp} = 2.0 \times 10^{-6} = [Ca^{2+}][IO_3^-]^2 = (S + 0.020)(2S)^2$$

The last equation contains only one unknown, the value of S, which we would like to calculate; but S is not negligible compared to 0.020, which leaves us with a nasty equation that is cubic in S. An approach that often works in a situation like this is to rearrange the equation into a more useful form and obtain S by iteration. Thus, we can write

$$4S^2 = \frac{K_{sp}}{S + 0.020} \quad \text{or} \quad S = \frac{1}{2}\left(\frac{K_{sp}}{S + 0.020}\right)^{1/2}$$

We must find the value of S that makes both sides of the equation equal. Start first by inserting a trial value of S (say, 0.006 M) in the right-hand side of the latter equation and calculating a value for S. You will get $S = 0.00438$. For your next trial value, take something about halfway between 0.00438 and 0.006. Continue the iteration process until you calculate a value of S that is nearly the same as (within 5% of) the value you inserted on the right-hand side of the equation.

2. The molar solubility of calcium iodate in water increases with temperature about 4.5% per degree Celsius. Calculate the molar solubility at 25°C, S_{25}, by correcting your value determined at t°C, S_t, using the equation

$$S_{25} = S_t \left[\frac{2 - 0.045(t - 25)}{2 + 0.045(t - 25)} \right]$$

where t is the temperature (°C) of the saturated solution that you analyzed. Ramette (see the Bibliography) quotes the molar solubility at 25°C as 0.007976 mol/L of $Ca(IO_3)_2$. Compare your result with the literature value by calculating the percentage relative difference:

$$\text{percentage of relative difference} = \frac{S_{25} - 0.007976}{0.007976} \times 100$$

The pH Scale
Acid-Base Titrations
The Titration of Stomach Antacids

PURPOSE

To understand the meaning of pH. To measure the pH of a number of household products. To learn the difference between the H^+ concentration and the total acidity of an acid. To learn the technique of acid-base titration by using a buret to measure volume and an acid-base indicator to determine the end point of the titration. To quantitatively determine the neutralization capacity of various commercial antacid tablets.

PRE-LAB PREPARATION

A quick look in the cabinets of the kitchen, laundry, or bathroom of the average home would turn up a number of substances that are acids or bases. Acidic substances we might find include citrus juices, vinegar, carbonated soft drinks, and toilet bowl cleaners. We might also find the following substances that are bases: baking soda (sodium bicarbonate), detergents, household ammonia, chlorine-based bleaches, drain cleaners, and stomach antacid tablets.

Studies of our own body fluids would also reveal that some are acidic and others are nearly neutral or slightly basic. The contents of the stomach can be very acidic because the cells lining the walls of the stomach secrete hydrochloric acid. Human urine can be slightly acidic or basic, depending on what you may have last eaten or the state of your health. Human blood, tears, and saliva are usually just slightly basic.

Definitions of Acids and Bases

In about 1887 S. Arrhenius proposed that substances that produce hydrogen ion in water be called acids and substances that produce hydroxide ion in water be called bases. Since this early definition, the concept of an acid or base has been extended and redefined to explain more fully the terms *acidity* and *basicity* and the role of the solvent in acid-base equilibria.

J. N. Bronsted and T. M. Lowry independently proposed, in 1923, the definition of an acid as a proton donor and of a base as a proton acceptor. This definition has proved useful because it explicitly points out the role played by the solvent (often water) in acid-base chemistry. The dissociation of water is described by the equilibrium

$$H_2O + H_2O \rightleftharpoons H_3O^+ + OH^- \qquad (1)$$

$$K_w = [H_3O^+][OH^-] = 1.0 \times 10^{-14} \text{ at } 25°C \qquad (2)$$

In this equilibrium water plays the role of both an acid and a base. (Such substances are often called *amphiprotic*.) Water can act as both an acid and a base because it can form two Bronsted acid-base pairs: H_3O^+/H_2O and H_2O/OH^-.

In pure water the concentrations of H_3O^+ and OH^- are equal:

$$[H_3O^+] = [OH^-] = \sqrt{K_w}$$

$$= 1.0 \times 10^{-7} \text{ M at } 25°C \qquad (3)$$

When $[H_3O^+] = [OH^-]$, we say the solution is neutral (neither acidic or basic).

What happens when we add a little vinegar (whose active ingredient is acetic acid) to pure water? The acetic acid donates a proton to a water molecule, thus creating additional H_3O^+ ions.

$$\begin{array}{ccc} \text{O} & & \text{O} \\ \| & & \| \\ CH_3COH + H_2O \rightleftharpoons H_3O^+ + CH_3CO^- & (4) \\ (HA) & & (A^-) \end{array}$$

The equilibrium constant expression for this reaction is

$$K_a = \frac{[H_3O^+][A^-]}{[HA]} = 1.76 \times 10^{-5} \qquad (5)$$

where K_a represents the acid dissociation constant for acetic acid, a weak monoprotic acid represented by symbol HA. The anion of the acid, acetate ion, is represented by the symbol A^-. So the acetic acid acts as a proton donor and the water acts as a proton acceptor. The H_3O^+ concentration increases and the OH^- concentration must therefore decrease because their concentrations are linked by the equilibrium constant expression shown in Equation (2).

Now suppose that we add a little household ammonia to pure water. The ammonia reacts with water as a Bronsted base, accepting a proton from the water and leaving OH^- ions in solution.

$$NH_3 + H_2O \rightleftharpoons NH_4^+ + OH^- \qquad (6)$$

The equilibrium expression for this reaction is

$$K_b = \frac{[NH_4^+][OH^-]}{[NH_3]} = 1.8 \times 10^{-5} \qquad (7)$$

Note that water acts as a base (proton acceptor) with respect to acids that are stronger acids than water, and as an acid (proton donor) with bases that are stronger bases than water. The equilibria shown in Equations (1), (4), and (6) are examples of the amphiprotic behavior of water.

The pH Scale

Typical H_3O^+ and OH^- concentrations in solution range from large to very small values (from approximately 10 M to 10^{-14} M). It would be impossible to represent such a range of concentrations on a linear graph because the concentrations would either have to be compressed into an impossibly tiny length on the low end, or we would have to have an astronomically long piece of graph paper. In a situation like this, we resort to using a logarithmic scale, which assigns an equal length on the scale to each power of 10 (or decade) of the H_3O^+ concentration.

There is another important reason why a logarithmic scale is used. A hydrogen ion-sensing device called a pH meter (which employs an electrochemical cell to measure the $[H_3O^+]$) gives a voltage output that depends on the logarithm of the hydrogen ion concentration. So the deflection of the needle of the pH meter (or the digital readout) is proportional to log $[H_3O^+]$.

Therefore for both practical and theoretical reasons it is useful to define a variable called the pH, where

$$pH = -\log [H_3O^+] \qquad (8)$$

and the converse relation

$$[H_3O^+] = 10^{-pH} \qquad (9)$$

We take the symbol "p" to mean "take the negative logarithm of the quantity that immediately follows." So pK_a means $-\log K_a$, and so on. Including the minus sign in the definition is a convenience:

Most of the concentrations of interest are less than 1, so if the choice had been made to define pH as $+\log[H_3O^+]$, we would be required always to carry along a minus sign with the numerical values. However, including the minus sign in the definition of pH has one adverse consequence that is sometimes confusing. We often call the pH scale an acidity scale, but as the acidity of a solution increases, the pH decreases.

The neutral point on the aqueous pH scale (pH = 7.00 at 25°C) is a consequence of the magnitude of the equilibrium constant for the dissociation of water. (At temperatures other than 25°C in water and in other solvents, the neutral point would not be at pH 7.00.)

The Distinction Between pH and Total Acidity

If an acid completely dissociates in solution, the hydrogen ion concentration (and the pH) will be a measure of the total amount of acid in the solution. For a strong acid

$$[H_3O^+] = C \qquad (10)$$

$$pH = -\log C = pC \qquad (11)$$

where C is the molar concentration of strong acid in solution. This relation will be true for common strong acids such as $HClO_4$, HCl, and HNO_3.

But if the acid is a weak monoprotic acid, it will be incompletely dissociated and the hydrogen ion concentration (or pH) of the solution is given approximately by the expressions

$$[H^+] \cong \sqrt{K_a C} \qquad (12)$$

$$pH \cong -\log\sqrt{K_a C} = \tfrac{1}{2}pK_a + \tfrac{1}{2}pC \qquad (13)$$

where K_a is the acid dissociation constant of the weak acid and C is the molar concentration of the acid. (Take pencil and paper and derive Equations (12) and (13), consulting your text as necessary.) We see from Equations (12) and (13) that for a weak monoprotic acid, the hydrogen ion concentration is not equal to C and the pH is not equal to pC. Contrast these results with the simple expressions shown in Equations (10) and (11) for a strong acid.

Acid-Base Titrations

We can't determine the concentration, C, of a weak acid just by measuring the pH. Equation (13) shows

us that we would also need to know the dissociation constant, K_a, of the acid. But we can determine C (which we call the *total acidity* or the *stoichiometric concentration*) by measuring the amount of a strong base (such as NaOH) that is required to react completely with a sample of the acid. This is called an *acid-base titration*. The NaOH is dispensed from a buret, so if we know the concentration of the NaOH and the volume of NaOH required to titrate the acid, we can calculate the total amount of weak acid in the solution.

A plot of the pH of the solution versus the milliliters of NaOH added is called a *titration curve*. An example of a titration curve for a sample of vinegar (a dilute solution of acetic acid) titrated with NaOH is shown in Figure 21-1. Note that when the last bit of acid is titrated, the hydrogen ion concentration decreases rapidly, as shown by the dramatic increase in pH. This signals the end point of the titration.

Either a pH meter or an acid-base indicator can be used to detect the end point of the titration. An acid-base indicator is an organic dye molecule that is itself a weak acid. The acid and base forms of the indicator have different colors, so the indicator shows a color change when it goes from its acid form to its base form. The pH range where this color change takes place is governed by the dissociation constant (K_a) of the acid indicator molecule. If we represent the protonated indicator molecule by the symbol HIn, we can write the equation for the dissociation of the indicator as follows:

$$HIn + H_2O \rightleftharpoons H_3O^+ + In^- \qquad (14)$$

$$K_a = \frac{[H_3O^+][In^-]}{[HIn]} \qquad (15)$$

If we take the logarithm of both sides of Equation (15) we obtain

$$\log K_a = \log[H_3O^+] + \log\frac{[In^-]}{[HIn]} \qquad (16)$$

which we can rearrange to the following form:

$$pH = pK_a + \log\frac{[In^-]}{[HIn]} \qquad (17)$$

Now take pencil and paper and prove to yourself that Equation (17) can be obtained from Equations (8) and (16). Then prove to yourself that when

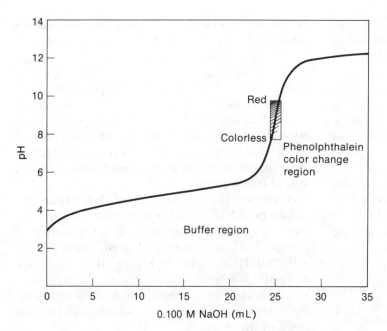

FIGURE 21-1
Titration curve for 3 mL of vinegar diluted to 25 mL in water and titrated with 0.1 M NaOH. Phenolphthalein (or thymol blue) is a suitable indicator for detecting the end point of the titration.

$pH = pK_a - 1$, $[In^-]/[HIn] = 0.1$, and that when $pH = pK_a + 1$, $[In^-]/[HIn] = 10$.

The pencil and paper exercise shows us that the indicator changes from being mostly in its acid form (HIn) to being mostly in its base form (In^-) in an interval of about 2 pH units, centered on the pK_a of the indicator. This is called the pH interval for the color change of the indicator. (Table B-5 of Appendix B gives the colors and pH intervals of a number of indicators.)

In order to have the color change of the indicator accurately signal the end point, we must choose an indicator whose pK_a is about the same as the pH at the end point of the titration, as shown in Figure 21-1. Also note that at the end point for the titration shown in Figure 21-1, the solution has a composition and pH that are identical to those of a sodium acetate solution having the same concentration.

Acid-base indicators have such an intense color that only a small amount of the indicator is necessary to produce a readily visible color. Thus the contribution of the indicator acid, HIn, to the total acidity of the solution is negligible.

Titration of Stomach Antacids

In this experiment we will determine the neutralization capacity of commercial stomach antacid tablets. These substances are bases, so direct titration would require an acid titrant. However, many of them do not readily dissolve in water and react rather slowly with acids. To circumvent this difficulty we will use a back-titration procedure. An excess of a strong acid (HCl) is added to the antacid tablet and the mixture is heated to ensure complete reaction. Some of the HCl is consumed by reaction with the antacid tablet. The antacid and HCl solution is then titrated with NaOH to determine how much HCl remains unreacted. Subtracting the amount of HCl remaining from that originally added gives the amount of HCl consumed by the antacid tablet. This gives an accurate measurement of the neutralization capacity of the antacid tablet. It also resembles the way the tablet reacts with HCl in the stomach. Typical titration curves for the back titration of antacid and HCl solutions with NaOH are shown in Figure 21-2. The indicator thymol blue (which is diprotic and therefore has two color transition regions) is a good choice for most antacids.

Antacid tablets are probably one of the most widely used self-prescribed medicines. They are taken to relieve the medically undefined conditions of heartburn or acid indigestion and sour stomach. Although this gastric distress is often attributed to excess production of HCl, sometimes the latter is not responsible for the symptoms. For instance, gastric HCl production may be less than normal in diseases such as superficial chronic gastritis and carcinoma of the stomach. The common condition heartburn is thought to be caused by regurgitation of the gastric contents into the esophagus, and acid indigestion may be merely due to overeating or an irritating food.

Television commercials stress the competition among various brands of antacids to see which has the greatest neutralization capacity, but if the pH rises too high, the entire digestive process may be

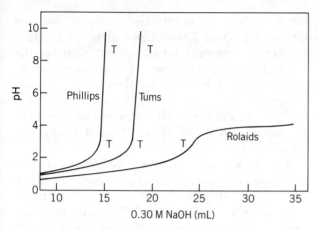

FIGURE 21-2
Titration of unreacted HCl with standardized 0.3 M NaOH after addition of 50 mL of 0.3 M HCl to various brands of antacid tablets. The indicator thymol blue has two color transitions, at the pH's shown approximately by the T's.

hindered. The digestion of proteins is catalyzed by the enzyme pepsin. The proteolytic activity of pepsin is inhibited if the pH of the stomach contents is allowed to rise any higher than the natural buffering of the proteins in the food itself would allow it to go (around pH 4). Therefore only an amount of HCl in excess of what the body of a healthy individual normally secretes following a meal should be neutralized by the antacid. Studies show that HCl produced by gastric stimulation varies widely from individual to individual, ranging from about 1 to 22 mmol of HCl per hour, but that the average figure for "excess" production is only about 10 mmol of HCl per hour greater than that of normal HCl production. Therefore one dose of an antacid product should react with no more than about 10 mmol of HCl per hour. For many people the upper limit should be less. This raises the question whether people who regularly consume the doses recommended on the labels of various antacid products are in fact interfering with normal digestion by taking doses that neutralize much more than 10 mmol of HCl or that are capable of raising the pH of the stomach contents above pH 4.

EXPERIMENTAL PROCEDURE

Special Supplies: Part 1: pH meter or pH indicators (see Chemicals); household chemicals, such as lemon juice, vinegar, carbonated soft drinks, toilet bowl cleaners (Crystal Vanish, Saniflush, etc.), baking soda (sodium bicarbonate), household ammonia, detergent powders, chlorine bleach, drain cleaners (Drano, etc.). Part 2: stomach antacids (Alka-2, Phillips tablets, Rolaids, Tums, etc.); 50-mL pipet and 50-mL buret or two 50-mL burets.

Chemicals: Part 1: universal pH indicator,[1] 0.1% thymol blue indicator, 0.1% alizarin yellow R indicator. Part 2: 0.30 M HCl, 0.30 M NaOH, 0.1% thymol blue indicator.

Safety Precautions: Part 1: Many household products are strong acids or bases. The main ingredient in many drain cleaners is sodium hydroxide; they may also contain mixtures of powdered aluminum and sodium peroxide or sodium nitrate. Household bleaches are made from chlorine and sodium hydroxide; the main ingredient in toilet bowl cleaners is often sodium hydrogen sulfate, an acid. In handling the household chemicals used in this experiment, take the same precautions as with strong acids and bases: Wear eye protection. Do not touch or handle the chemicals with your bare hands. Clean up any spills immediately.

Sometimes mixing two household products can have dangerous consequences. For example, mixing household bleach (sodium hypochlorite) with household ammonia or a strongly acidic toilet bowl cleaner can produce volatile and toxic gases. Be careful not to mix any of the household products with one another. Discard any unused materials, each by itself, in designated waste containers and not in the sink.

Part 2: If you use a bunsen burner to heat the flask of HCl containing an antacid tablet, be sure that the flask is clamped so that it cannot be overturned. A boiling hot solution splashing on you from the bench top can inflict serious burns.

1. *Measuring the pH of Household Chemicals*
Three or four household chemicals listed under Special Supplies (part 1) will be made available to you. Using a pH meter or pH indicators, determine the pH of dilute solutions of these chemicals.

Liquid household chemicals should be diluted tenfold (5 mL of liquid + 45 mL of water); make up solutions of solid household chemicals by dissolving about 0.5 g of solid in 50 mL of water.

If you use indicators to determine the pH, place 3 mL of the dilute solutions in a 13- × 100-mm test tube and add 1 drop of Yamada's universal indicator. Estimate the pH from the colors given in Table 21-1.

If the solution gives a red color with universal indicator, the pH is 4 or less. Test a separate 3-

---

[1] To prepare 200 mL of Yamada's universal indicator, dissolve 0.005 g thymol blue, 0.012 g methyl red, 0.060 g bromothymol blue, and 0.100 g phenolphthalein in 100 mL of pure ethanol. Neutralize the solution to a green color with 0.01 M NaOH and dilute to 200 mL with distilled water. (From L. S. Foster and I. J. Gruntfest, *J. Chem. Educ.* **14,** 274 (1937).)

TABLE 21-1
The colors of indicators at various pH values

Indicator		Indicator color	H_3O^+	pH
Alizarin yellow R	{	red	10^{-12}	12
		orange	10^{-11}	11
Yamada's universal indicator	{	violet	10^{-10}	10
		indigo	10^{-9}	9
		blue	10^{-8}	8
		green	10^{-7}	7
		yellow	10^{-6}	6
		orange	10^{-5}	5
		red	10^{-4}	4
Thymol blue	{	yellow	10^{-3}	3
		orange	10^{-2}	2
		red	10^{-1}	1

mL portion of the diluted solution with a drop of thymol blue indicator. If the color is red, the pH is less than 2. If the solution is orange, the pH is between 2 and 3. A yellow color indicates a pH of 3 or greater.

If the color with Yamada's universal indicator is violet, the pH of the solution is 10 or greater. In this case, test a separate 3-mL portion of the diluted solution with alizarin yellow R indicator. A yellow color indicates a pH of 10 or less. An orange color indicates a pH of about 11, and a red color indicates a pH of 12 or greater.

Consult the label of each household chemical to determine the main acidic (or basic) ingredient. Record in your report each brand name, the intended use of the product, the main acidic (or basic) ingredient, and the pH of the diluted solution. Write a balanced chemical equation that describes the Bronsted acid-base behavior in water of the main ingredient in each substance tested.

2. *Titration of Antacid Tablets* Various brands of antacid tablets will be available, such as Alka-2 ($CaCO_3$), Phillips tablets ($Mg(OH)_2$), Rolaids (sodium aluminum dihydroxycarbonate, $NaAl(OH)_2CO_3$), and Tums ($CaCO_3$). Analyze one or more brands of tablets as your instructor directs, using the following procedure. Put an antacid tablet in a small beaker and weigh the beaker and tablet on the analytical balance to the nearest milligram. Record the mass. Then transfer the tablet to a clean 250-mL Erlenmeyer flask. Reweigh the empty beaker and record the mass so that you can obtain the mass of the tablet. Put 50.0 mL of 0.300 M HCl in the flask that contains the tablet, using a pipet or buret to accurately measure the volume of HCl solution. Heat the flask to boiling on a hot plate or over a Bunsen burner. (*Caution*: If you use a Bunsen burner, clamp the flask so

that it cannot be overturned.) Gently boil the solution for about 5 min. Use a glass stirring rod, if necessary, to help break up and disperse the tablet. (*Caution*: Do not use so much force that you risk breaking a hole in the flask with the glass stirring rod.)

While the solution is boiling, rinse and fill a 50-mL buret with 0.300 M NaOH and record the initial buret reading.

Cool the solution containing the antacid to room temperature by immersing it in a container of tap water. When the solution has cooled, add 10 drops of 0.1% thymol blue indicator. The solution should appear red, indicating that the pH is less than 2. Then titrate the solution with 0.300 M NaOH until you get a color change from red to yellow. Record the buret reading. If you overrun the end point, you might observe the second color change of thymol blue, from yellow to blue, which takes place at pH 8.0 to 9.6. This can be rectified by adding a carefully measured amount of 0.300 M HCl (1 mL or less) and then carefully titrating with 0.300 M NaOH to the end point (red to yellow color change at pH 1.2 to 2.8).

Calculate the millimoles of HCl added, the millimoles of NaOH added, the millimoles of HCl that were neutralized by the antacid, and the millimoles and milligrams of the active ingredient in the tablet.

The identity of the active ingredient and the mass per tablet will be found on the manufacturer's label. Record this information in your report. Write a balanced chemical reaction for the reaction of HCl with the active ingredient in the antacid tablet. Calculate from your titration data the mass of active ingredient and compare this with the value given on the manufacturer's label. Compare the mass of the active ingredient you found with the mass of the tablet. The difference represents the mass of inert binders used in making the tablet. Calculate the milligrams of inert binder per tablet and the weight percent of inert binder.

Repeat the determination with a second brand of antacid tablet if your instructor so directs.

BIBLIOGRAPHY

Batson, W. B., and Laswick, P. H., "Pepsin and Antacid Therapy: A Dilemma," *J. Chem. Educ.* **56**, 484–486 (1979).

Breedlove, C. H., Jr., "Quantitative Analysis of Antacid Tablets," *Chemistry* **45**, 27–28 (1972).

Hem, S. L., "Physicochemical Properties of Antacids," *J. Chem. Educ.* **52**, 383–385 (1975).

Determination of the Acid Dissociation Constant of a Weak Acid

PURPOSE

To determine the acid dissociation constant of acetic acid (a weak monoprotic acid) by measuring the pH of a solution containing known concentrations of acetic acid and sodium acetate. To determine the dissociation constant of an unknown weak acid. To learn how to use a pH meter or indicators to measure the pH of a solution.

PRE-LAB PREPARATION

Acids and bases are important classes of chemical compounds. They control the pH of living systems and of many reactions carried out in the chemical laboratory. If the pH of our blood shifts by as little as 0.3 unit above or below the normal range of 7.3 to 7.5, severe illness results. Therefore, if we understand the principles of how acids and bases function, we will be better informed about the functioning of biological systems, as well as of the purely chemical systems.

In this experiment, you will study the properties of weak acids that can ionize (dissociate) to yield one hydrogen ion (proton). Such acids are called weak *monoprotic* acids. Acetic acid is a common weak acid belonging to this class. We will determine its ionization constant. We can also apply exactly the same principles to determine the ionization constant of an unknown weak monoprotic acid.

Acetic acid has the molecular formula

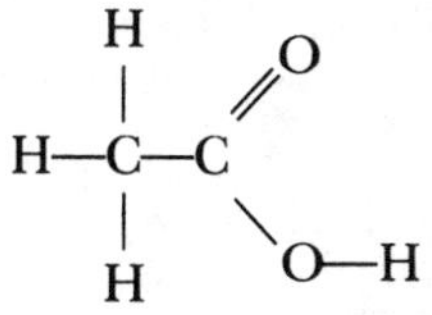

$$
\begin{array}{ccc}
& H & \quad O \\
& | & \nearrow \\
H- & C-C & \\
& | & \searrow \\
& H & \quad O-H
\end{array}
$$

The molecular formula for acetic acid is generally shortened to read CH_3COOH or $HC_2H_3O_2$. These chemical formulas are often further abbreviated to HA, where HA represents acetic acid (or any weak monoprotic acid). Then the symbol A^- stands for acetate ion, CH_3COO^-, the anion of acetic acid (or the anion of any weak monoprotic acid, HA).

The proton that dissociates in acetic acid is the one attached to the oxygen atom. The O—H bond in the acetic acid molecule is appreciably weaker than the C—H bonds, and in aqueous solution there is no significant dissociation of the hydrogen atoms bonded to carbon.

Acetic acid dissociates according to the equation

$$HA + H_2O \rightleftharpoons H_3O^+ + A^- \qquad (1)$$

The equilibrium constant expression is given by

$$K_a = \frac{[H_3O^+][A^-]}{[HA]} \qquad (2)$$

The equilibrium constant for this reaction is 1.76 $\times 10^{-5}$ at 25°C.[1] You are to measure the value of this constant in this experiment and compare your value with the previously measured value.

A straightforward way to obtain the value of K_a is to measure each of the quantities on the right-hand side of Equation (2) and carry out the indicated arithmetic. For solutions containing only the weak acid HA, the value of K_a can be determined by examining the dissociation reaction shown in Equation (1) and noting that the concentration of A^- will be equal to that of the H_3O^+ (ignoring the insignificant amount of H_3O^+ that comes from the dissociation of water). The HA concentration in the solution is equal to the *stoichiometric* concentration of HA in the solution minus the amount of HA lost by dissociation.[2] For acetic acid and most other weak acids, the amount of HA lost by dissociation is much less than the amount put into solution and thus the *equilibrium* concentration of HA is only slightly smaller than the stoichiometric concentration.

---

[1] This is the value of K_a obtained by extrapolating to zero ionic strength. In any real solution of acetic acid, the ionic strength is greater than zero, and the dissociation constant is somewhat larger.

[2] The stoichiometric concentrations of HA and A^- are calculated from the amounts of each substance that are put into the solution. However, HA and A^- can each react with water,

$$HA + HOH \rightleftharpoons H_3O^+ + A^-$$

and

$$A^- + HOH \rightleftharpoons HA + OH^-$$

so that under some conditions the actual concentrations of HA and A^- at equilibrium (which we will call the equilibrium concentrations) may not be exactly equal to the stoichiometric concentrations.

In solutions that contain both acetic acid (HA) and sodium acetate (Na^+A^-), we will show that the equilibrium concentrations of HA and A^- are approximately equal to their stoichiometric concentrations. (Similar conclusions will apply to any solution containing a mixture of a weak monoprotic acid, HA, and its salt, Na^+A^-.) The stoichiometric concentrations can be readily determined by titration or by knowledge of the quantities of HA and Na^+A^- used to prepare the solutions. If we know the stoichiometric concentrations of HA and A^-, and if the equilibrium concentrations are equal to the stoichiometric concentrations, all that remains in order to determine K_a is to measure the $[H_3O^+]$ or its derived function, the pH.

$$pH = -\log[H_3O^+]; \qquad [H_3O^+] = 10^{-pH} \qquad (3)$$

DETERMINING K_a BY THE METHOD OF PARTIAL NEUTRALIZATION

By adding sodium hydroxide to a larger amount of a weak acid we can form a mixture of the weak acid, HA, and its salt, Na^+A^-. To determine the K_a of the weak acid we must be able to calculate the equilibrium concentrations of HA, A^-, and H_3O^+. In this section we will show how to calculate the stoichiometric concentrations of HA and A^-. We will then show that the equilibrium concentrations are usually equal to the stoichiometric concentrations. In the following section we will describe how to determine the H_3O^+ concentration by using a pH meter or indicators.

To see how we can determine the stoichiometric concentrations of the acid HA and the base A^-, let's suppose that we add a known amount of NaOH to a solution containing a larger (and known) amount of HA. The reaction is

$$HA + Na^+ + OH^- \rightarrow Na^+ + A^- + H_2O \qquad (4)$$

(Na^+ ion, which appears on both sides of Equation (4), is simply a spectator ion.)

The stoichiometric amount of sodium acetate (Na^+A^-) formed is equivalent to the amount of NaOH added.

$$mol\ Na^+A^-_{formed} = mol\ NaOH_{added} \qquad (5)$$

The stoichiometric amount of HA left in solution is obtained easily by subtracting the amount of

NaOH added from the original amount of HA present in the solution.

$$\text{mol HA}_{final} = \text{mol HA}_{orig} - \text{mol NaOH}_{added} \tag{6}$$

The stoichiometric composition of the solution is precisely the same as would be obtained if we dissolved the same number of moles of acetic acid and sodium acetate as calculated from Equations (5) and (6) in the same total volume. This is why these concentrations are called stoichiometric concentrations.

Now let's see how the equilibrium concentrations of HA and A^- are related to the stoichiometric concentrations of HA and A^-. We will represent the stoichiometric concentrations of HA and A^- by a subscript zero: $[HA]_0$ and $[A^-]_0$, respectively. We will make use of two equations, one based on a material balance and the other based on a charge balance condition.

First we write the *material balance* equation that expresses the condition that the sum of the stoichiometric concentrations must equal the sum of the equilibrium concentrations:

$$[HA]_0 + [A^-]_0 = [HA] + [A^-] \tag{7}$$

This equation says that if we put known amounts of HA and A^- in solution, the sum of the stoichiometric concentrations will be exactly equal to the sum of the equilibrium concentrations. This is true because any HA that reacts with water produces A^- and vice versa, as shown by the equations in footnote 2.

The charge balance equation expresses the condition that the sum of the positive charges must equal the sum of the negative charges. This is true because the solution as a whole is electrically neutral. (All of the ions in solution must be counted, including those that come from the dissociation of water.) The *charge balance* equation for a solution containing HA and Na^+A^- dissolved in water is written as

$$[Na^+] + [H_3O^+] = [A^-] + [OH^-] \tag{8}$$

The stoichiometric concentration of A^- is exactly equal to the concentration of Na^+:

$$[A^-]_0 = [Na^+] \tag{9}$$

This is the same as saying that each mole of NaOH added to a solution containing a larger amount of HA produces a stoichiometric amount of sodium acetate given by Equation (5). Substituting $[A^-]_0$ for $[Na^+]$ in Equation (8) gives

$$[A^-]_0 + [H_3O^+] = [A^-] + [OH^-] \tag{10}$$

This result shows that the equilibrium concentration of A^- is equal to the stoichiometric concentration of A^- provided that the concentrations of H_3O^+ and OH^- are negligibly small compared to the concentration of A^-. From Equation (7) we see that if $[A^-]_0$ and $[A^-]$ are equal, $[HA]_0$ must equal $[HA]$. This illustrates the general rule that the equilibrium concentrations of A^- and HA will be equal to the stoichiometric amounts of A^- and HA calculated from Equations (5) and (6) (and divided by the total solution volume *provided that HA is not too strong an acid nor its concentration too dilute*. (As a rule of thumb, the general rule will apply whenever the stoichiometric concentrations of HA and A^- are both greater than $10^2 K_a$.)

THE MEASUREMENT OF pH

The pH Meter

All pH meters have a sensing element composed of two half-cell electrodes: a glass-membrane electrode sensitive to the hydrogen ion concentration and a reference electrode. (See Figure 22-1.) The reference electrode is often a calomel electrode. Sometimes the two half-cell electrodes are combined in a single-probe unit called a *combination* electrode. The principle of operation, however, is the same for either type. The calomel reference electrode supplies a constant potential ($E^0 = +0.24$ V versus the standard hydrogen electrode) determined by the half-reaction

$$Hg_2Cl_2 + 2e^- \rightleftharpoons 2Hg + 2Cl^- \tag{11}$$

This half-cell electrode is called a *calomel* electrode because calomel is the trivial name of the compound Hg_2Cl_2.

The $[H_3O^+]$ in the solution determines the potential of the glass electrode. The potential (or voltage) developed across the glass membrane is proportional to the logarithm of the H_3O^+ concentration ratio inside and outside the glass electrode. The pH meter measures the total cell potential across the two half-cell electrodes and displays this measurement on the scale calibrated in pH units [a logarithmic scale, as shown by

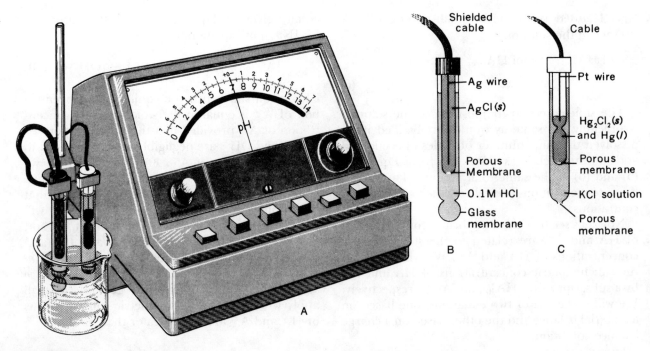

FIGURE 22-1
The pH meter and its electrodes: (A) the complete apparatus; (B) detail of the glass electrode, which is responsive to [H$^+$]; (C) detail of the calomel reference electrode.

Equation (3)]. A pH meter provides an accurate and simple method for determining the pH of a solution. In Figure 22-1, note the construction details of the glass electrode (B) and the calomel electrode (C). The thin glass bulb of the glass electrode is very fragile. Be extremely careful not to hit it against the side or bottom of a beaker.

Indicators

Indicators are a specialized class of rather large organic compounds that are weak acids or bases. They display one color when in the acidic (protonated) form and another color (or no color at all) when they are in the basic form. Organic compounds that absorb light in the visible part of the spectrum invariably contain a large number of alternating single and double carbon-carbon bonds. An example of an indicator is methyl orange, whose structures and colors are shown in Figure 22-2.

If most of the methyl orange molecules are present as HIn, the solution will be red. If most of them are present as In$^-$, the solution will be orange-yellow. Because the indicator is a weak acid, the pH of the solution determines which form predominates. We will write the equilibrium constant expression for the dissociation of HIn and then a logarithmic form of the same equation, which you should prove is correct.

$$K_a = \frac{[H_3O^+][In^-]}{[HIn]} \quad (12)$$

$$pH = pK_a + \log\frac{[In^-]}{[HIn]} \quad (13)$$

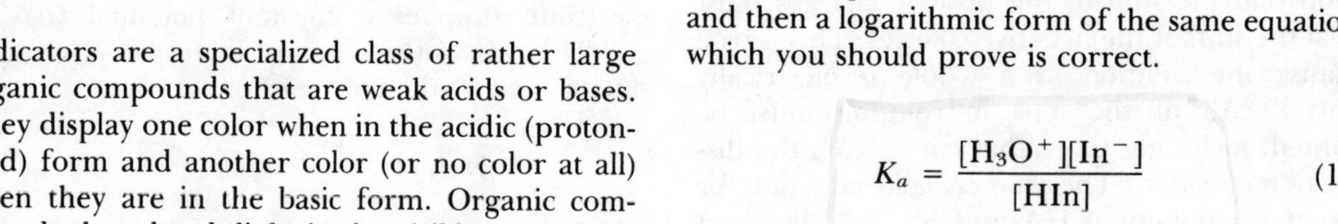

$$H_2O + (CH_3)_2\overset{+}{\underset{H}{N}}{-}\!\!\left\langle\underline{}\right\rangle\!\!-N{=}N-\!\!\left\langle\underline{}\right\rangle\!\!-SO_3^- \rightleftharpoons H_3O^+ + (CH_3)_2N-\!\!\left\langle\underline{}\right\rangle\!\!-N{=}N-\!\!\left\langle\underline{}\right\rangle\!\!-SO_3^-$$

pK$_a$ = 3.4

Acidic (HIn) form
red

basic (In$^-$) form
orange-yellow

FIGURE 22-2
The acidic and basic forms of the indicator methyl orange and their associated colors.

The pK_a of methyl orange is about 3.4. Thus at pH = 4.4, where the ratio $[In^-]/[HIn]$ = 10, about 91% of the molecules have lost a proton and the solution will be orange-yellow. At pH 2.4, where the ratio $[In^-]/[HIn]$ = 0.1, about 91% of the indicator molecules are present in the red HIn form and the solution will have a distinct reddish hue. It is important to realize that the color changes all take place in a pH interval of 2 to 4 pH units and that the pK_a of the indicator lies in the middle of this pH interval. Outside this pH range no further color changes will take place (unless the indicator has a second pH interval due to dissociation of another proton).

Table B-5 in Appendix B provides a list of a number of important indicators and the pH ranges in which their color changes occur. You will use indicators (as described in parts 3 and 4 of the Experimental Procedure) to determine the pH of a solution if no pH meter is available. Figure 22-3 demonstrates the correct technique for comparing the colors of two solutions. The test tubes should be placed next to one another and viewed lengthwise against a uniform diffuse light source.

Label the H⁺ concentration of each tube.

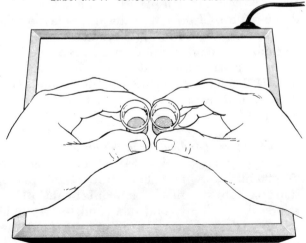

FIGURE 22-3
The correct technique for the observation and comparison of indicator colors.

Preparation of Standards and Dilution of Solutions

As we have already mentioned, it is necessary to prepare solutions of known pH to compare carefully with the colors of the unknown solution. The solutions for pH range 4 to 6 will be supplied to you. You will be able to prepare your own standard solutions for pH ranges 1 to 3. The simplest way to prepare these is to dilute solutions of 0.10 M HCl for the 1 to 3 range.

Dilutions are based on the principle that the concentration after dilution is proportional to the ratio of the original volume to the final volume of the solution. The following example, based on the first dilution you will perform, demonstrates this idea.

Example Calculate the pH of a solution prepared by diluting 5.0 mL of HCl of pH 1 to 50.0 mL.

The solution originally contained

$$5.0 \text{ mL} \times \frac{0.1 \text{ mmol } H_3O^+}{mL} = 0.50 \text{ mmol } H_3O^+$$

The symbol mmol stands for millimole and is useful when dealing with milliliter quantities of solution. The concentration of H_3O^+ in a pH 1.0 solution is of course 0.10 mol/L, or 0.10 mmol/mL.

Because only water has been added to the 5.0 mL of HCl, there must be 0.50 mmol H_3O^+ in the 50 mL of new solution and the new $[H_3O^+]$ = 0.50 mmol H_3O^+ per 50 mL solution = 0.010 M. Thus the new pH = 2.0.

A simpler but less obvious calculation is

$$[H_3O^+]_{final} = \frac{V_{orig}}{V_{final}} \cdot [H_3O^+]_{orig}$$

$$= \frac{5.0}{50} (0.10) = 0.010 \text{ M}$$

EXPERIMENTAL PROCEDURE

Special Supplies: pH meter, if available; pH 4 and 7 buffers for standardizing the pH meter. If indicators are used to measure pH, a light box with a back-lighted white translucent cover is convenient for color comparison (see Figure 22-3).

Chemicals: 1.0 M CH_3COOH, 1.0 M $NaCH_3COO$, 0.10 M CH_3COOH, 0.10 M solution of unknown monoprotic acid; 0.10 M NaOH. If the indicator method is to be employed, the following solutions will be required: 0.10 M HCl to prepare pH standards in the range pH 1 to 3. Buffer solutions (pH 4, 5, 6, and 7). Indicator solutions: orange IV (Tropeolin 00), methyl orange, bromcresol green.

1. The Dissociation Constant of Acetic Acid Your instructor will demonstrate the use of the pH meter if this instrument is available in your laboratory. If it is not, you will use indicators. (Directions for the use of indicators are given below and in parts 3 and 4.) Instructions for each method of determining approximate pH values follow.

With a pH Meter

(a) Take a 10.0-mL sample of 1.0 M acetic acid (HA) to the pH meter and measure its pH. Convert the pH value to the corresponding $[H_3O^+]$. (See Equation (3).) Think about the source of H_3O^+ and acetate ion (A^-) in an acetic acid solution, considering the equilibrium shown in Equation (1). Calculate the $[A^-]$ and $[HA]$ in this solution, and enter the values on your report sheet. Calculate the dissociation constant of acetic acid. (See Equation (2).)

(b) Repeat part 1(a), using 0.10 M HA instead of 1.0 M HA.

(c) Add 25.0 mL of 1.0 M sodium acetate (Na^+A^-) to 10.0 mL of 1.0 M HA, and mix well. Measure the pH of this solution as you did in parts 1(a) and 1(b). (Save this solution for use in part (d).) Calculate the $[H_3O^+]$ from the measured pH. Calculate the $[A^-]$ from the concentration of added Na^+A^-, taking account of the dilution when the solutions are mixed together. Similarly, calculate the $[HA]$ from the amount of HA added, taking account of the dilution. These are the stoichiometric concentrations that we showed were equal to the equilibrium concentrations if the $[H_3O^+]$ and $[OH^-]$ are negligibly small. Are they? Calculate K_a as before.

(d) Dilute 10.0 mL of the solution employed in part 1(c) with 40.0 mL of distilled water, mix thoroughly, and measure the pH with the pH meter. Calculate each concentration as before and again calculate K_a.

(e) Thoroughly mix 5.0 mL of 1.0 M Na^+A^- with 30.0 mL of 1.0 M HA. Again measure the pH of this solution, calculate the concentrations of H_3O^+, HA, and A^-, and calculate the dissociation constant of acetic acid.

With Indicators If a pH meter is not available to measure pH, the pH may be determined by means of color comparison using indicator dyes as described in parts 3 and 4. Use orange IV for part 1(a), orange IV and methyl orange for part 1(b), bromcresol green for parts 1(c) and (d), and methyl orange for part 1(e). With care, you should be able to estimate the pH value of each solution to within 0.3 to 0.5 pH unit, although the preparation of

buffers of pH 3.5 and 4.5 may be necessary to achieve this accuracy.

2. The Dissociation Constant of an Unknown Monoprotic Acid (Perform this part of the experiment if your instructor so directs.)

(a) Measure the pH of 50 ± 1 mL of a 0.10 M solution of an unknown monoprotic acid.

(b) Then add 10.0 mL of 0.10 M NaOH, stir, and determine the pH again.

(c) Finally, add 20.0 mL more of 0.10 M NaOH to the solution, stir, and measure the pH.

Calculate K_a from the first pH measurement as you did for acetic acid in part 1(a). Calculate the stoichiometric concentrations of A^- and HA after the addition of a known amount of NaOH. (See Equations (5) and (6). The number of moles of A^- and HA must be divided by the total volume of the solution to calculate the concentrations.) Determine the $[H_3O^+]$ from the measured pH. Assuming that the equilibrium concentrations of A^- and HA are equal to their calculated stoichiometric concentrations, calculate the dissociation constant, K_a, of the unknown monoprotic acid.

Repeat the calculations and determine a value of K_a from the data obtained in part 2(c), again being careful to account for the effect of dilution.

When you are finished you will have calculated a value of K_a for each of the three solutions whose pH you measured.

The Indicator Method for Measuring pH

3. The Preparation of Comparison pH Standards Use 0.10 M HCl for a pH 1.0 solution. Carefully dilute 5.0 mL of 0.10 M HCl with distilled water to a volume of 50.0 mL in a graduated cylinder, and mix this solution well to give a pH 2 solution. Then by a second tenfold dilution of 5.0 mL of the pH 2 solution, prepare a pH 3 solution. For the intermediate ranges, pH 4 to 6, standard buffer mixtures will be provided.

4. The Colors of Indicators in the pH Standard Solutions Prepare a series of six clean, labeled 13- × 100-mm test tubes. Put 5 mL of the pH 1 standard into the first tube, 5 mL of the pH 2 standard into the second tube, and so on, until you have 5 mL of each of the six pH standards (pH 1 to 6) in the six tubes. To each of these add 1 drop of orange IV indicator and mix each solution. Observe the tubes lengthwise through the solution, and describe in your report the colors that are characteristic of each pH. Keep the three or four tubes that show the color change for comparisons with tubes containing a solution of unknown pH.

Repeat the procedure with a series of 5-mL samples from pH 1 to 6 to which you add a drop of methyl orange indicator. Again carefully observe and record the colors, and keep the four labeled tubes that show the color range.

Finally, repeat the procedure once more using 5-mL samples to which you add a drop of bromcresol green indicator. Again observe and record the colors, and keep the four labeled tubes that show the color range. Enter your data in the spaces provided in the report form.

When you are finished, you should have about 12 labeled tubes showing the color ranges of the three indicators.

To determine the pH of an unknown solution, put 5 mL of the solution in each of three clean 10-cm test tubes. Put 1 drop of orange IV indicator in the first tube, 1 drop of methyl orange in the second, and 1 drop of bromcresol green in the third. By comparing the colors of these three tubes with your standards of known pH, estimate the pH of the unknown. Record this value in your report form.

The Chemistry of Natural Waters

Water Hardness by EDTA Titration

Water Softening by Ion Exchange

PURPOSE

To show how the chemical compositions of river water and seawater are largely determined by geochemistry. To measure water hardness, caused by dissolved calcium and magnesium ions, in a sample of tap water. To show how water can be softened by ion-exchange processes that replace calcium and magnesium ions with sodium ions.

PRE-LAB PREPARATION

It would be hard to imagine life without water. It is the medium in which all of the biological processes of living cells take place. Water is so essential that it can justifiably be called the most valuable of all our resources. Because we breathe oxygen, we might think that it is more essential to life, but

that is a human-centered view. Many simple organisms can live without oxygen, but no organism can live and reproduce without water.

There is a lot of water on earth (an estimated 1.4×10^{21} L), but it is mostly seawater. An estimated 97.2% is in the oceans and about 2.15% is trapped in the polar icecaps and glaciers, leaving about 0.65% of the water in the hydrosphere as the fraction on which we must rely. Our supply of fresh water would soon be exhausted except for the continual renewal of this resource by the solar-energy-driven cycle of evaporation, condensation, and precipitation as rain and snow.

The Chemical Composition of Natural Waters

In an area such as the Amazon River basin in South America, far removed from volcanic activity and the smokestacks of industry, rainwater can be very pure, containing a few dissolved substances, mainly carbon dioxide, traces of nitrogen oxides produced by lightning, and traces of NaCl. Near the sea, the rainfall will contain more NaCl. Although NaCl is not volatile, the interaction of wind and waves produces tiny droplets of seawater (called an *aerosol*) that are carried inland by the wind.

In areas near active volcanoes and in the industrialized countries, the precipitation contains appreciable concentrations of dissolved acids. These arise mostly from the combustion of fossil fuels— for heating, cooking, transportation, industrial processing, and the generation of electricity. Nitrogen oxides and sulfur dioxide (mainly from burning coal containing sulfur) are produced in the primary combustion process. These are further oxidized to nitric and sulfuric acids in a complex series of reactions that take place in the atmosphere.

Table 23-1 gives the average composition of rainfall in the northeastern United States for 88 monthly weighted ion concentrations from 17 sampling sites during the period from 1978 to 1979. These data clearly show the presence of substantial quantities of sulfuric and nitric acids. In a region where the soils lack alkaline components that can neutralize the acids, this "acid rain" produces destructive ecological effects, killing fish and other aquatic life and damaging vegetation.

The composition of river water is mainly determined by the reactions of rainwater (and water

TABLE 23-1
The average chemical composition of natural waters*

	Rainfall, northeastern United States (mmol/L)	Rivers of North America (mmol/L)	Seawater (mmol/L)
Cations			
Ca^{2+}	—	0.53	10.6
Mg^{2+}	—	0.21	54.5
Na^+	0.009	0.39	479.
K^+	—	0.036	10.2
H^+	0.072	—	—
NH_4^+	0.016	—	—
Anions			
HCO_3^-	—	1.1	2.3
SO_4^{2-}	0.028	0.21	28.9
Cl^-	0.012	0.23	546.
Br^-	—	—	0.85
F^-	—	0.008	0.07
NO_3^-	0.026	0.017	0.0001
$H_2SiO_4^{2-}$	—	0.15	—

* Quoted by J. N. Butler, *Carbon Dioxide Equilibria and Their Applications*, Addison-Wesley, Reading, MA, 1982, Chapter 5.

from melting snow) with rocks and soil as the water makes its way downhill to the sea. *Gypsum* ($CaSO_4 \cdot 2H_2O$) and *calcite* ($CaCO_3$) are commonly found in sedimentary deposits at the earth's surface. Another less stable form of calcium carbonate, *aragonite*, is found in sediments that consist mainly of the mineral skeletons of marine organisms. A relatively common mineral in ancient rocks is *dolomite*, $MgCa(CO_3)_2$. Gypsum is slightly soluble in water and all of the carbonates can be readily dissolved by water containing traces of acid. Unless the rainfall is acidic from industrial emissions, the main acid present in rainwater is dissolved CO_2, which forms a slightly acidic solution.

$$CO_2(g) + 2H_2O \rightleftharpoons$$
$$H_3O^+(aq) + HCO_3^-(aq) \quad (1)$$

In turn, the acid formed reacts with rocks containing calcium (and magnesium) carbonates.

$$H_3O^+(aq) + CaCO_3(s) \rightleftharpoons$$
$$Ca^{2+}(aq) + HCO_3^-(aq) + H_2O \quad (2)$$

The net reaction is the dissolution of calcium carbonate as given by Equation (3), which is the sum of Equations (1) and (2).

$$CO_2(g) + H_2O + CaCO_3(s) \rightleftharpoons$$
$$Ca^{2+}(aq) + 2HCO_3^-(aq) \quad (3)$$

These geochemical processes largely account for the fact that calcium and magnesium ions are the most abundant cations and bicarbonate ion is the most abundant anion in river water, as shown in Table 23-1.

By far the most abundant ionic solute in seawater is sodium chloride (see Table 23-1). This should not be too surprising, because sodium chloride (and sodium salts in general) is both abundant and very soluble. The natural hydrologic cycle, operating over eons of time, has by now washed most of the soluble sodium salts into the sea.

Water Hardness and Water Softening

In most regions of the United States water for domestic use comes mainly from rivers, lakes, and wells, and contains some dissolved salts, mostly calcium bicarbonate resulting from the reaction shown in Equation (3), with lesser amounts of sodium, chloride, and sulfate ions.

Both Ca^{2+} and Mg^{2+} ions react with soaps (the carboxylate anions of long-chain fatty acids) to form an insoluble curdy scum.

$$Ca^{2+} + 2CH_3(CH_2)_{16}\overset{\overset{\textstyle O}{\|}}{C}O^- \rightarrow$$

$$[CH_3(CH_2)_{16}\overset{\overset{\textstyle O}{\|}}{C}O^-]_2Ca^{2+} \quad (4)$$

This precipitate reduces the cleaning efficiency of soap (and leaves a ring of scum on the tub when you take a bath). Water that contains calcium and magnesium ions is called hard water, and if the water hardness is too great, it's desirable to "soften" the water by decreasing its content of calcium and magnesium.

Water softening can be done in several ways. Before the advent of synthetic detergents (which do not form insoluble calcium and magnesium salts), washing soda ($Na_2CO_3 \cdot 10H_2O$) was often added to laundry water to remove calcium ions by the reaction

$$Ca^{2+}(aq) + CO_3^{2-}(aq) \rightarrow CaCO_3(s) \quad (5)$$

Another method, called *ion exchange*, replaces calcium ion with sodium ion by using a natural or synthetic solid ion exchanger. The most efficient materials for this purpose are synthetic organic resins that have a hydrocarbon framework to which charged functional groups are chemically bound (see Figure 23-1). If the bound groups are negatively charged, the negative charge is counterbalanced by positive ions (remember the electroneutrality principle). Because the positive ions (called *cations*) are not chemically bound to the resin, they can be replaced by cations having an equivalent positive charge. Such a resin is called a *cation-exchange resin*. If the bound functional groups have positive charges, the counterions will have a negative charge and the resin is called an *anion-exchange resin*. The following equations show the ion-exchange equilibria for cation- and anion-exchange reactions.

Cation exchange (resin originally in the H^+ form):

$$2RZ\!-\!SO_3^- H^+ + Ca^{2+} \rightleftharpoons$$

$$(RZ\!-\!SO_3^-)_2Ca^{2+} + 2H^+ \quad (6)$$

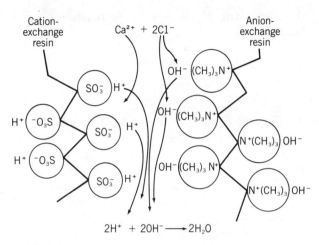

FIGURE 23-1
Deionization of a salt solution using a mixture of cation- and anion-exchange resins. The cation-exchange resin is originally in the H^+ form, and the anion-exchange resin in the OH^- form. In this example, $CaCl_2$ solution is poured into the mixed resin bed at the top. Pure water flows out at the bottom. Each Ca^{2+} ion displaces two H^+ ions and each Cl^- displaces one OH^- ion. An exactly equal number of H^+ and OH^- ions are produced, which combine to form water. The zigzag lines represent the organic polymer matrix of the resin (most often a styrene-divinylbenzene copolymer), to which the sulfonate ($-SO_3^-$) and quaternary ammonium ($-N^+(CH_3)_3$) groups are chemically bonded.

Anion exchange (resin originally in the OH^- form):

$$RZ\!-\!\overset{+}{N}(CH_3)_2OH^- + Cl^- \rightleftharpoons$$

$$RZ\!-\!\overset{+}{N}(CH_3)_2Cl^- + OH^- \quad (7)$$

(In these equations the symbol RZ represents the organic polymer matrix to which the charged groups are bound.)

If equivalent amounts of cation-exchange resin (in the H^+ form) and anion-exchange resin (in the OH^- form) are mixed together, the combination will remove all of the dissolved salts, because the H^+ produced by cation exchange exactly neutralizes the OH^- produced by anion exchange. The resulting water that emerges from the column or tank is pure *deionized* water. In many areas, deionization is a simpler and less costly alternative to distillation and is widely used for purifying water used in chemical laboratories.

In domestic water softening by ion exchange, total deionization is not necessary. Only the cations responsible for water hardness need be removed. So only a cation-exchange resin is used, usually in the Na^+ form. The ion-exchange reaction is given by

$$2RZ—SO_3^- Na^+ + Ca^{2+} \rightleftharpoons$$

$$(RZ—SO_3^-)_2 Ca^{2+} + 2Na^+ \quad (8)$$

The ion-exchange reactions are reversible. In domestic water softening systems, NaCl is used to regenerate the cation-exchange resins because it is readily available and inexpensive. The resin is flooded with the NaCl brine, which drives the equilibrium shown in Equation (8) to the left. The calcium and magnesium and excess brine are then flushed out with water, leaving the resin in the Na^+ form.

To regenerate a mixed cation–anion-exchange deionization system, it is first necessary to separate the two resins. They are then regenerated separately, the cation-exchange resin being returned to the H^+ form by treatment with a strong acid (such as H_2SO_4) and the anion resin being returned to the OH^- form by treatment with a strong base (such as NaOH).

To be suitable for use in drinking, cooking, bathing, and watering plants, water should not contain more than 500 parts per million (ppm) of dissolved solids (1 ppm = 1 mg/L). The total dissolved solids can be measured by evaporating a known volume of water to dryness and weighing the residue. (Or an approximate value can be obtained more quickly by measuring the electrical conductivity of the water, since most of the dissolved solids are ionic.)

Determining Water Hardness by EDTA Titration

The water hardness (sum of calcium and magnesium ions) is most often measured by titration, using the anion of a polyaminocarboxylic acid called ethylenediaminetetraacetic acid. This name is quite a mouthful, so it is usually abbreviated to EDTA. EDTA is a tetraprotic acid that we will represent by the symbol H_4Y. It is usually employed as the soluble disodium salt dihydrate, $Na_2H_2Y \cdot 2H_2O$, which is available in high purity. The anion, H_2Y^{2-}, reacts with Ca^{2+} or Mg^{2+} (or almost any metal ion with charge +2 or greater) to form a complex ion.

$$H_2Y^{2-} + Ca^{2+} \rightleftharpoons CaY^{2-} + 2H^+ \quad (9)$$

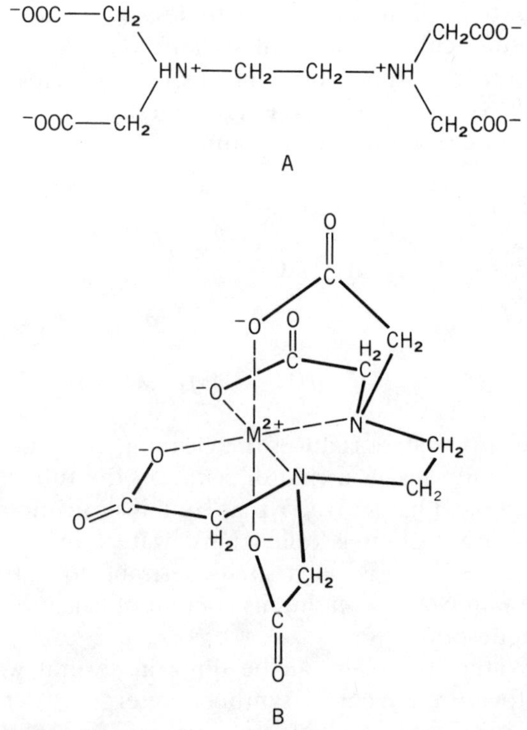

FIGURE 23-2
Structures of ethylenediaminetetraacetic acid (EDTA) and metal-EDTA chelates: (A) structure of the dianion of EDTA, H_2Y^{2-}; (B) structure of a M^{2+}-EDTA chelate, MY^{2-}.

The structures of the anion H_2Y^{2-} and the complex with a metal ion, M^{2+}, are shown in Figure 23-2. Think of the EDTA anion as surrounding a metal ion like the large claw of a crab grasping its prey. The technical term for such a complex is *chelate*, which comes from the Greek word meaning a pincer-like claw.

To determine the end point of the titration an indicator dye is added that also complexes Ca^{2+} and Mg^{2+}, forming a colored indicator-metal ion complex. As the titrant (disodium EDTA) is added it complexes the metal ions, but so long as the metal ion is in excess, the indicator-metal ion complex is still present. When precisely enough EDTA has been added to react with all of the metal, the EDTA displaces the indicator from the metal-indicator complex. This happens because the equilibrium constant for the formation of the EDTA-metal ion complex is much larger than that for the indicator-metal ion complex. This produces a reasonably sharp color change as the indicator is converted from the color of the Mg^{2+}-indicator complex (red) to that of the free (or unbound) indicator (blue). In pH 10 buffer the net reaction is described by the equation

$$HY^{3-} + \underset{\substack{Mg^{2+}\text{-indicator}\\ \text{complex, red}}}{MgIn^-} \xrightleftharpoons{pH\ 10}$$

$$\underset{\substack{\text{free indicator,}\\ \text{clear blue}}}{MgY^{2-} + HIn^{2-}} \quad (10)$$

where In^{3-} represents the indicator anion.

In this experiment you will determine the hardness of a sample of tap water by titration with EDTA. You will then treat a sample of the water with a cation-exchange resin in the sodium ion form and titrate a sample of the soft water to see how much hardness remains. You will also observe the effects of untreated and softened water on the foaming properties of a soap.

EXPERIMENTAL PROCEDURE

Special Supplies: 50-mL buret.

Chemicals: 0.0100 M $Na_2EDTA\cdot2H_2O$,[1] 0.01 M MgEDTA (prepared by mixing equimolar amounts of $Na_2EDTA\cdot2H_2O$ and $MgSO_4$), 1.5 M NH_3/0.3 M NH_4Cl buffer, Calmagite indicator[2] (0.1 g per 100 mL), 20- to 50-mesh strongly acidic (sulfonated polystyrene) cation-exchange resin in the Na^+ form (Dowex 50Wx8 or Amberlite IR-120), 0.1% soap solution (1 g/L of Ivory flake or bar soap).

1. Determination of Water Hardness by EDTA Titration (a) Rinse a clean buret with small portions of 0.0100 M EDTA ($Na_2EDTA\cdot2H_2O$, *not* the 0.01 M MgEDTA solution) and fill the buret. Add in order to a 250-mL Erlenmeyer flask: 50 $\pm$ 1 mL of tap water (this is the sample); 10 mL of 1.5 M NH_3/0.3 M NH_4Cl buffer (the reaction produces H^+, so the buffer is necessary to keep the H^+ concentration at the optimum value); about 2 mg (a pinch) of ascorbic acid (to prevent oxidation of

the indicator); 10 mL of 0.01 M MgEDTA solution;[3] 10 drops of 0.1% Calmagite indicator.

Record the initial buret reading. Titrate the solution in the flask with 0.0100 M Na_2EDTA until the last traces of red are gone and the solution is a pure blue color. The color change near the end point typically requires about 5 drops of 0.0100 M Na_2EDTA. Record the final buret reading.

Repeat the titration. The second volume should agree with the first within about 1%.

(b) Determine the indicator blank by repeating the titration procedure, substituting 50 mL of deionized water for the tap water. Record the initial buret reading. Titrate the solution with 0.0100 M Na_2EDTA (it should require only a few drops). Record the final buret reading. Subtract the volume required for the indicator blank from the volumes required to titrate the tap water samples to get the net volume of 0.0100 M Na_2EDTA required to titrate the tap water samples.

Calculate the water hardness in units of millimoles per liter. This quantity is the sum of the calcium and magnesium ion concentrations.

Water quality engineers typically express water hardness in units equivalent to parts per million of $CaCO_3$ (equal to milligrams of $CaCO_3$ per liter). Express your results in these units by assuming that the ions titrated by the EDTA were derived from $CaCO_3$.

$$\frac{mg\ CaCO_3}{L} = \frac{mmol\ Ca^{2+} + Mg^{2+}}{L}$$
$$\times \frac{1\ mol\ CaCO_3}{mol\ Ca^{2+} + Mg^{2+}} \times \frac{100\ g\ CaCO_3}{mol\ CaCO_3} \quad (11)$$

In most natural waters some magnesium ion is present, so expressing water hardness in units of milligrams of $CaCO_3$ per liter is an arbitrary convention that has been adopted for the sake of convenience (or tradition).

2. Water Softening by Ion Exchange Ion-exchange processes are usually carried out by flowing a sample down a bed of ion-exchange resin contained in a column. This procedure gives the most

---

[1] $Na_2EDTA\cdot2H_2O$ is ethylenediaminetetraacetic acid disodium salt dihydrate (also called (ethylenedinitrilo)tetraacetic acid). It is available in purity greater than 99% (from Aldrich Chemical Co. and other suppliers) and can be weighed out to make a solution whose concentration is known within 1%. If greater accuracy is desired, it can be standardized against pure $CaCO_3$ by the procedure described in part 1.

[2] Calmagite is available from Aldrich Chemical Co., Hach Co., and other suppliers.

[3] Because the indicator complexes magnesium ion more strongly than it does calcium ion, the color change at the end point will be sharper if Mg^{2+} is present. Although most natural waters will contain some magnesium ion, we deliberately add some to ensure that an adequate amount of magnesium ion will be present. It is added in the form of the MgEDTA complex so that no extra EDTA will be required to titrate the added magnesium ion.

complete exchange because as the sample solution moves down the column it is continually contacting fresh resin, which drives the equilibrium shown in Equation (8) completely to the right.

However, we will use a batch procedure because of its simplicity. To obtain near-quantitative ion exchange we will use a quantity of resin whose exchange capacity is 50 times larger than the quantity of ions to be exchanged.[4]

Another factor that tends to drive the exchange reaction (Equation (8)) toward completion is that Ca^{2+} ions, because their charge is greater than that of Na^+ ions, are more strongly attracted to the negatively charged groups bonded to the resin.

Procedure for Ion Exchange

Put 130 mL of tap water in a clean 250-mL Erlenmeyer flask. Add 5 g of dry cation-exchange resin (or 8 g if the resin is wet). Swirl the mixture in the flask for 8 to 10 min to allow time for the ion exchange to take place. Save the soft water (supernatant solution) for the following experiments.

When you have finished parts 2(a) and 2(b), pour the resin into a bottle labeled "Used Resin." *Do not pour the resin down the drain or back into the original container.* It is expensive and can be reused after regeneration.

(a) Soap Sudsing in Hard and Soft Water. Transfer 5 mL of the soft water to a clean 20- × 150-mm test tube. Measure 5 mL of tap water into a second test tube and 5 mL of deionized water into a third tube. Add exactly 5 mL of 0.1% soap solution to each of the three tubes; stopper and shake them vigorously for a few seconds. Compare the solutions for the amount and stability of the foam and for the appearance of any insoluble calcium soap. Record your observations.

(b) Efficiency of Ion Exchange. Titrate two 50-mL samples of the soft water, using the procedure described in part 1 for the titration of tap water. (Add the 0.0100 M Na₂EDTA solution dropwise. You should not have to add much, because most or all of the calcium and magnesium ions have been removed.) Calculate the percentage of water hardness removed by ion exchange.

$$\text{percentage of hardness removed} =$$

$$\frac{\dfrac{\text{mmol}}{\text{L}}(Ca + Mg)_{tap} - \dfrac{\text{mmol}}{\text{L}}(Ca + Mg)_{soft}}{\dfrac{\text{mmol}}{\text{L}}(Ca + Mg)_{tap}}$$

$$\times 100 \quad (12)$$

where the subscripts tap and soft refer to the concentrations of calcium + magnesium ions (in millimoles per liter) in tap water and soft water, respectively.

BIBLIOGRAPHY

Belcher, R., Close, R. A., and West, T. S., "The Complexometric Titration of Calcium in the presence of Magnesium. A Criticial Study," *Talanta* **1,** 238–244 (1958).

Lindstrom, F., and Diehl, H., "Indicator for the Titration of Calcium plus Magnesium with (Ethylenedinitrilo)tetraacetate," *Analytical Chemistry* **32,** 1123–1127 (1960).

McCormick, P. G., "Titration of Calcium and Magnesium in Milk with EDTA," *J. Chem. Educ.* **50,** 136–137 (1973).

---

[4] The exchange capacity is usually found on the label of the bottle of resin, expressed in milliequivalents (meq) per gram of dry resin or in milliequivalents per milliliter of resin bed. A typical value for the resin you will be using is about 1.7 meq/mL, which means that 1 mL of a packed slurry of the resin can exchange about 1.7 mmol of charge (1.7 mmol of Na^+ ion or 0.85 mmol of Ca^{2+} ion).

Chemistry of Natural Waters
Water Hardness
Water Softening
by Ion Exchange

NAME		
SECTION		LOCKER
INSTRUCTOR		DATE

DATA AND CALCULATIONS

1. Determination of Water Hardness by EDTA Titration

Data	Trial 1	Trial 2
(a) Volume of tap water sample	_____mL	_____mL
Volume of 0.0100 M EDTA titrant		
Final buret reading	_____mL	_____mL
Initial buret reading	_____mL	_____mL
Net volume of EDTA solution	_____mL	_____mL

Data	Trial 1	Trial 2
(b) Volume of deionized water (indicator blank)	_____mL	_____mL
Volume of 0.0100 M EDTA titrant		
Final buret reading	_____mL	_____mL
Initial buret reading	_____mL	_____mL
Net volume of EDTA solution (indicator blank)	_____mL	_____mL

Calculate the concentration of $Ca^{2+} + Mg^{2+}$ in the tap water sample in millimoles per liter. Be sure to subtract the net volume of the indicator blank measured in part 1(b) from the net volume measured in part 1(a). Show a sample calculation in the space below.

_____mmol/L _____mmol/L

Average _____mmol/L

Using the average value of the $Ca^{2+} + Mg^{2+}$ concentration in millimoles per liter, calculate the water hardness in units of milligrams of $CaCO_3$ per liter (parts per million of $CaCO_3$). [See Equation (11).]

Water hardness _____mg $CaCO_3$/L (ppm)

2. Water Softening by Ion Exchange

(a) Soap Sudsing in Hard and Soft Water
Compare the amount and stability of the foam produced by shaking soap solution with each of the following samples.

Tap water _____

Soft water _____

Deionized water _____

(b) Efficiency of Ion Exhange

Data	Trial 1	Trial 2
Volume of soft water sample	_____mL	_____mL
Volume of 0.0100 M EDTA titrant		
Final buret reading	_____mL	_____mL
Initial buret reading	_____mL	_____mL
Net volume of EDTA solution	_____mL	_____mL

Calculate the concentration of $Ca^{2+} + Mg^{2+}$ in the soft water sample in millimoles per liter. Be sure to subtract the net volume of the indicator blank measured in part 1(b) from the net volume measured in part 2(b). Show a sample calculation in the space below.

_____mmol/L _____mmol/L

Average _____mmol/L

Calculate the percentage of water hardness removed. [See Equation (12).]

Percentage of water hardness removed _____%

EXERCISES

1. One 10-min shower using a restricted-flow shower head (2.5 gal/min) requires 25 gal of water, and it has been estimated that each person uses about 60 gal of water a day for personal use (mostly bathing and washing). Calculate the volume of cation-exchange resin (in liters) that would be required to remove all the water hardness in the water used by one person in 30 days at 60 gal/day. Assume that the exchange capacity of the resin is 1.7 meq/mL of resin and that the water hardness is equivalent to 200 mg $CaCO_3$ per liter. (Remember that 2 meq of exchange capacity are required per millimole of $CaCO_3$.) 1 gal = 3.785 L.

2. Describe how a cation-exchange resin in the H^+ form might be used to determine the cation content of a solution containing a mixture of NaCl and KNO_3.

Identification of Silver, Lead, and Mercurous Ions

PURPOSE

To provide an overview of a general scheme for separating and identifying ten cations, to introduce the laboratory techniques used in qualitative analysis, and to begin the study of the first group of three cations, which are separated out as insoluble chloride salts: Ag^+, Pb^{2+}, and Hg_2^{2+} ions.

PRE-LAB PREPARATION

Qualitative analysis is a branch of analytical chemistry that identifies particular substances in a given sample of material. In the analysis of inorganic substances, this involves the analysis of both metallic constituents as cations and the nonmetallic constituents as anions. This and the next four experiments constitute a series in qualitative analysis. The first three deal with the identification of ten common cations, including Ag^+, Pb^{2+}, Hg_2^{2+}, Fe^{3+}, Al^{3+}, Zn^{2+}, Ca^{2+}, Ba^{2+}, K^+, and NH_4^+. The next demonstrates the identification of nine anions, NO_3^-, Cl^-, Br^-, I^-, SO_4^{2-}, SO_3^{2-}, S^{2-}, PO_4^{3-}, and CO_3^{2-}. The final experiment illustrates

a more modern separation technique, paper chromatography, by studying the separation of Fe^{3+}, Co^{2+}, Ni^{2+}, and Cu^{2+}.

Qualitative analysis has remained an important part of the laboratory experience in general chemistry for a number of years, even though the analytical methods have been replaced by sophisticated instrumental methods in practical analysis. We believe that qualitative analysis has two useful purposes: (1) it provides an ideal context for the illustration and application of the principles of ionic equilibria, such as acid-base equilibria and solubility and complex ion equilibria, and (2) it provides a logical and systematic framework for the discussion of the descriptive chemistry of the elements. Its utility aside, qualitative analysis is fun.

Organization of the Scheme for Qualitative Analysis

Of the approximately 80 metallic elements, 24 of the more common cations are usually included in the scheme of analysis. In the abbreviated scheme presented in this and the next two experiments, we will study the separation and identification of only ten cations. This permits an extensive introduction to the more commonly employed separative techniques in only three 3-h laboratory periods and obviates the need for handling the dangerous and offensive gas H_2S.

All qualitative schemes begin with the separation of Ag^+, Hg^{2+}, and Pb^{2+} ions as the chlorides. This is made possible by the low solubility products:

Metal Chloride	K_{sp}
AgCl	1.8×10^{-10}
Hg_2Cl_2	1.1×10^{-18}
$PbCl_2$	1.6×10^{-5}

These ions constitute Group 1 in most schemes of qualitative analysis.

We will not analyze for any of the eight elements generally included in Group 2. These bivalent or trivalent elements are all located near the amphoteric element dividing line of the periodic table. They are isolated as sulfides from a 0.3 M H_3O^+ solution that has been saturated with H_2S. The solubility products of the sulfides range from 10^{-26} to 10^{-93}.

Group 3 is generally separated as a mixture of sulfides and hydroxides by precipitation from an $(NH_4)_2S$ in NH_3 solution. In the abbreviated scheme employed here, Fe^{3+} and Al^{3+} are first precipitated as hydroxides and Zn^{2+} is subsequently separated as the sulfide by precipitation from an $(NH_4)_2S$ solution.

Finally, Groups 4 and 5 are separated by precipitation of the alkaline earth elements, Ba^{2+} and Ca^{2+}, as the carbonates leaving the alkali metal K^+, and the complex ion that behaves like an alkali metal, NH_4^+, in solution for individual detection.

Table 24-1 presents an overall scheme to illustrate this separation into groups. It is important for you to study this flow chart carefully so that you understand the basis for the separation into the five groups. This will be especially true if your instructor should decide to give you a general unknown containing elements from all groups.

It happens that just five steps are required for the analyses in each of the three cation experiments (Experiments 24, 25, and 26). These are sequentially numbered to assist you in constructing an overall flow chart and in the analysis of a general unknown if your instructor should provide one. In addition, flow charts are provided for each experiment. The one in Experiment 24 is completed, while those in the next two are left for your study and completion as a part of your laboratory report.

TABLE 24-1
The abbreviated scheme for the separation of ten metal ions.

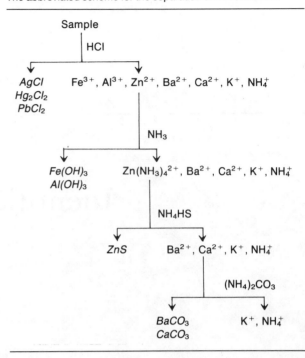

Laboratory Techniques for Qualitative Analysis

The oft-repeated admonition *keep your desk neat and orderly* will pay big dividends in time saved and in more accurate analyses. Study Figure 24-1. Keep your working space on the table top and in front of the sink clear of unnecessary equipment. Arrange conveniently the most frequently used items, such as clean test tubes, your wash bottle, stirring rods, medicine dropper, and indicator test paper, laid out on a clean towel. Keep dirty test tubes and other articles in one place. Clean and rinse these at the first opportunity so that a stock of clean equipment is always ready. Label any solutions that are to be kept for some time. *Keep your laboratory records up to date and do your thinking as you work.* To rush through experimental work, with the idea of understanding it later is an ill-advised attempt at economy of time.

The Volume of Solutions Use only the small volumes specified. You can *estimate* most volumes with sufficient precision by counting drops (15 to 20 drops per milliliter) or by estimating the height of the solution in the 10-cm test tube (capacity 8 to 10 mL). Use the 10-mL graduated cylinder only when more accurately known volumes are required.

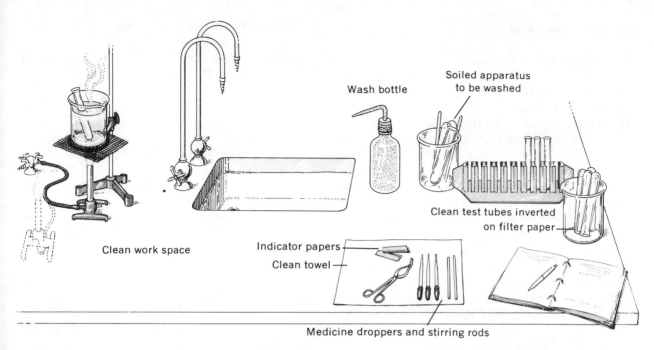

Wash bottle

Soiled apparatus to be washed

Clean test tubes inverted on filter paper

Clean work space

Indicator papers

Clean towel

Medicine droppers and stirring rods

FIGURE 24-1
Keep your laboratory work table neat and in order, with the "tools of your trade" conveniently arranged.

The Handling of Solutions   Learn to be clean and efficient. Review the sections on basic laboratory equipment and procedures in the Introduction. When mixing solutions, use a stirring rod (Figure 24-2); do not invert the test tube with your dirty thumb as the stopper. When heating solutions, avoid loss by bumping (Figure 24-3). Do not try to boil over 2 mL of solution in a 10-cm test tube; transfer larger quantities to a 15-cm test tube, a small beaker, or a casserole. Solutions in test tubes can be heated safely by immersion in a beaker of boiling water.

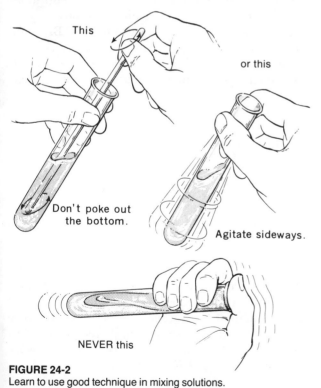

This

or this

Don't poke out the bottom.

Agitate sideways.

NEVER this

FIGURE 24-2
Learn to use good technique in mixing solutions.

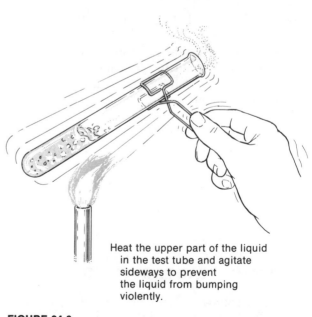

Heat the upper part of the liquid in the test tube and agitate sideways to prevent the liquid from bumping violently.

FIGURE 24-3
This will improve your technique when you heat a solution in a test tube.

Ag^+, Pb^{2+}, and Hg_2^{2+} Ions

The precipitating reagent for this group is chloride ion in an acid solution. Only three of all the common metal ions form a precipitate on the addition of this reagent: Ag^+, Pb^{2+}, and Hg_2^{2+}. The mercurous ion is not the simple ion Hg^+, but consists of two atoms held together by a covalent bond, with a double positive charge.

Ammonia solution gives different results with each of the three metal ions, as shown by the preliminary experiments that follow. The behavior of mercury salts is peculiar and needs some explanation. Mercury exhibits three oxidation states: zero in free mercury, Hg^0, $+1$ in mercurous ion, Hg_2^{2+}, and $+2$ in mercuric ion, Hg^{2+}. In some situations, the intermediate mercurous ion is unstable, part of the mercury being reduced to the metal and part being oxidized to Hg^{2+}, thus:

$$Hg_2^{2+} \rightleftharpoons Hg^0(l) + Hg^{2+}$$

When ammonia is added to mercuric chloride solution, a white "ammonolysis" product, $Hg\text{-}NH_2Cl$, is formed. This is analogous to the partial hydrolysis of $HgCl_2$ to form a basic salt. Compare the two equations

$$HgCl_2(aq) + HOH \rightleftharpoons$$
$$Hg(OH)Cl(s) + H^+ + Cl^-$$
$$HgCl_2(aq) + HNH_2(aq) \rightleftharpoons$$
$$Hg(NH_2)Cl(s) + H^+ + Cl^-$$

If mercurous chloride is treated with ammonia, part of it is oxidized to the white mercuric amidochloride, above, and part is reduced to black, finely divided mercury:

$$Hg_2Cl_2(s) + 2NH_3(aq) \rightarrow$$
$$Hg(NH_2)Cl(s) + Hg(l) + NH_4^+ + Cl^-$$

The mixed precipitates appear black or dark gray.

EXPERIMENTAL PROCEDURE

Chemicals: 1 M NH_3, 0.1 M $Pb(NO_3)_2$, 0.1 M $HgCl_2$, 0.05 M $Hg_2(NO_3)_2$, 0.1 M KBr, 1 M K_2CrO_4, 0.1 M KI, 0.1 M $AgNO_3$, 0.1 M $NaCl$, 1 M $Na_2S_2O_3$.

A. Typical Reactions of the Ions

1. *Solubility of the Chlorides* Prepare a sample of each of the three chlorides by adding 2 mL of 0.1 M $NaCl$ to 2 mL each of 0.1 M $AgNO_3$, 0.05 M $Hg_2(NO_3)_2$, and 0.1 M $Pb(NO_3)_2$. If a precipitate fails to form in any of these (why?), add 1 mL of 6 M HCl. Let the precipitates settle, decant and discard the supernatant liquid. Add to each about 2 mL of distilled water. Heat each nearly to boiling and shake. Results? Cool under the cold water tap. Results? Save for part 2.

2. *Behavior with Ammonia* To each of the three precipitates add 1 mL of 6 M NH_3. Shake these solutions to see if the precipitates will dissolve.

Compare the behavior of the Hg_2Cl_2 precipitate with ammonia with that of $HgCl_2$. To do this, add 1 mL of 6 M NH_3 to 1 mL of 0.1 M $HgCl_2$ solution.

Divide the ammoniacal solution of $AgCl$ into two unequal portions. To the smaller, add a slight excess of 6 M HNO_3. Result?

3. *Relative Solubility of Silver Salts and Stability of Complex Ions* To the larger portion of the ammoniacal $AgCl$ solution, add 1 mL of 0.1 M KBr. Result? To this, add 1 mL of 1 M $Na_2S_2O_3$ (sodium thiosulfate), and shake. The complex ion formed is $Ag(S_2O_3)_2^{3-}$. (This is the reaction of "hypo" in fixing the developed film in photography.) To this solution, add a little 0.1 M KI. From the results, you can evaluate the relative Ag^+ concentrations in the following equilibrium situations: 0.1 M $AgNO_3$, saturated $AgCl$, saturated $AgBr$, saturated AgI, $Ag(NH_3)_2^+$, $Ag(S_2O_3)_2^{3-}$. Write net ionic equations for the reactions observed and list each of the preceding in order of decreasing Ag^+

B. Analysis of a Known Solution for Ag^+, Pb^{2+}, and Hg_2^{2+}

First: Study the following Procedure for the Analysis and the flow chart on the following page, which is completed for this first group of ions. Note the precipitates obtained and the exact ions remaining in the solution. The flow chart will be a useful guide for outlining the essential separation steps and final identification tests for each ion.

Second: In your experiment report, write the net ionic equations for the reactions at each successive step of the procedure, as numbered in the flow chart. (Your instructor may require this work before issuing you an unknown.)

Flow Chart——Ag^+, Pb^{2+}, Hg_2^{2+}

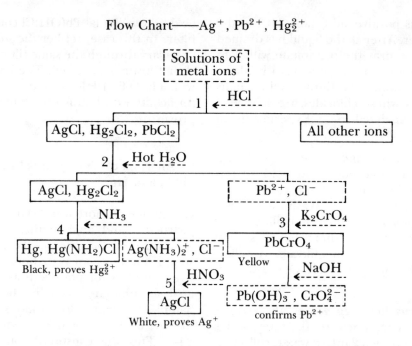

Key: *Steps* in small numerals.   *Precipitates* or *residues* in solid-line boxes.
      Reagents on broken-line arrow.   *Solutions* of ions in broken-line boxes.

Third: Prepare a known solution containing Ag^+, Pb^{2+}, and Hg_2^{2+}, and analyze this according to the Procedure for the Analysis, following your results on the flow chart. Also study the typical analysis summary (Table 24-2), which is completed for the first group, and is similar to the one you will prepare as a record of your actual observations in the analysis of your unknown solutions in part C.

Procedure for the Analysis

Precipitation of the Group. Step 1 To 3 mL of the solution to be tested, add 6 M HCl drop by drop, and mix, until any precipitation that occurs is complete. Avoid a large excess. (No precipitation indicates absence of Ag^+, Hg_2^{2+}, and of much Pb^{2+}.) Filter into a 15-mL test tube and test the filtrate for complete precipitation with a drop of

TABLE 24-2
Analysis summary of each step, observation, and conclusion for a colorless solution known to contain all three ions of the group.

Step	Sample	Reagents	Observations	Conclusions
1	Known sample	Dilute HCl	White precipitate	Ag^+, Pb^{2+}, Hg_2^{2+} (one or more) present
2	Precipitate 1	Hot H_2O	Some precipitate remains	Ag^+ and/or Hg_2^{2+} present
3	Hot H_2O filtrate	K_2CrO_4	Yellow precipitate	Pb^{2+} present, confirmed by dissolving in NaOH
4	Precipitate 2, insoluble in hot H_2O	NH_3 on the filter	Turns black	Hg_2^{2+} present
5	NH_3 filtrate	HNO_3 (excess)	White precipitate	Ag^+ present
				Summary: Ag^+, Pb^{2+}, and Hg_2^{2+} present

HCl. If the test is positive, add more HCl to the filtrate and refilter. After all the liquid has drained through the filter, spray the precipitate with 1 to 3 mL of distilled water from your wash bottle to wash it. Let this drain. (The filtrate still contains any other cations whose chlorides are soluble—and these will be analyzed for in Experiments 25 and 26.)

Test for Lead Ion. Steps 2 and 3 Heat 10 to 15 mL of water to boiling; then pour 3 to 4 mL of this water over the residue on the filter, catching the hot filtrate in a small test tube. (Wash the remaining residue by pouring 10 mL of boiling water over it, discarding these washings.) Add several drops of 1 M K_2CrO_4 to the filtrate. A yellow precipitate, soluble when 6 M NaOH is added, proves Pb^{2+}.

Test for Mercurous Ion. Step 4 To the residue from the hot water treatment on the filter, add 1 mL of 6 M NH_3 and then 2 mL of water, collecting the filtrate in a small test tube. A black residue on the filter proves Hg_2^{2+}.

Test for Silver Ion. Step 5[1] If the ammonia filtrate from the Hg_2^{2+} test is not perfectly clear, it may

---

[1] You will conduct Steps 6 to 10 in Experiment 25 and Steps 11 to 15 in Experiment 26.

be due to colloidal Pb(OH)Cl coming through the filter. In this case, refilter the solution as often as necessary through the same filter, until a perfectly clear filtrate is obtained. Then acidify the filtrate with a little 6 M HNO_3, and mix. (If in doubt, test for acidity with litmus.) A white precipitate, AgCl, proves Ag^+.

C. Analysis of Unknown Solutions for Ag^+, Pb^{2+}, and Hg_2^{2+}

Obtain one or more unknown solutions from your instructor, and analyze them by the preceding procedure. *At the same time*, keep a record of each step, including your actual observations for negative as well as for positive tests, by completing an analysis summary (with five headings: Step No., Sample, Reagents, Observations, and Conclusions) like the example for the known solution in Table 24-2. This will constitute your report for each unknown.

**Identification of Silver,
Lead, and Mercurous Ions**

NAME		
SECTION		LOCKER
INSTRUCTOR		DATE

DATA

A. Typical Reactions of the Ions

1 and 2. Solubility of the Chlorides: Their Behavior with Ammonia. In the spaces below, write the formula(s) of the principal substance(s) present (ions or molecules) when the chlorides are treated as indicated. Also indicate colors.

	AgCl	$PbCl_2{}^a$	Hg_2Cl_2
Hot water			
NH_3 (excess)			

^{a} Look up the relative solubilities of $PbCl_2$ and $Pb(OH)_2$ to help you decide whether a reaction occurs with NH_3.

3. Relative Solubility of Silver Salts and Stability of Complex Ions. Write net ionic equations for the successive reactions that take place when a $AgNO_3$ solution is treated, in turn, with HCl, excess NH_3, KBr, $Na_2S_2O_3$, and KI.

From the data above, list the following equilibrium solutions in the order of *decreasing* Ag^+ concentration in the mixture: 0.1 M $AgNO_3$, saturated AgCl, saturated AgBr, saturated AgI, $Ag(NH_3)_2^+$, $Ag(S_2O_3)_2^{3-}$.

_____ _____ _____ _____ _____ _____

B. Analysis of a Known Solution for Ag^+, Pb^{2+}, and Hg_2^{2+}

Write below, in order, the net ionic equations for *all* reactions occurring in the systematic procedure for the analysis of the ions of this group. (Some of these repeat those in part A.)

C. Analysis of Unknown Solutions for Ag^+, Pb^{2+}, and Hg_2^{2+}

Unknown no. _____   Appearance _____   Ions found _____

Unknown no. _____   Appearance _____   Ions found _____

Analysis Summary: Report your actual observations, negative as well as positive, for each step of the analysis of each unknown, and record above the ions found.

Step	Sample	Reagents	Observations	Conclusions

APPLICATION OF PRINCIPLES

After considering the observed facts listed below, arrange at the right, in order of *decreasing* Cu^{2+} concentration, the following substances: saturated $CuCO_3$, 1 M $Cu(NH_3)_4^{2+}$, saturated CuS, 1 M $CuCl_2$.

(a) Mixing $CuCl_2$ and Na_2CO_3 solutions will form a precipitate of $CuCO_3$.

(b) Passing H_2S gas into $Cu(NH_3)_4^{2+}$ solution will precipitate CuS.

(c) $CuCO_3$ solid will dissolve in NH_3 solution to form a deep blue solution.

Explain *why* you arranged the items in the order you did.

_____

_____

_____

_____

Identification of Ferric, Aluminum, and Zinc Ions

PURPOSE

To learn how to separate and identify Fe^{3+}, Al^{3+}, and Zn^{2+} ions as insoluble hydroxides or sulfides. To understand the role of buffers in controlling the H^+ and OH^- concentrations. To observe the tendency of Zn^{2+} to form soluble complexes with ammonia. To observe the amphoteric behavior of Al^{3+} as it forms an insoluble hydroxide that dissolves in excess OH^- to form a soluble hydroxy complex.

PRE-LAB PREPARATION

Reactions of Fe^{3+}, Al^{3+}, and Zn^{2+} Ions

The removal and separation of these three metal ions from our selected group of ten cations (see Experiment 24), after removal of the insoluble chlorides, depends on their distinctive behavior with NH_3 and with NaOH. Zinc ion is conveniently removed and identified by its white insoluble sulfide in a basic or slightly acid solution. The control of pH is important in all of these separations.

Buffer Action

Buffers are used to control the relative H^+ and OH^- concentrations within certain limits. These consist of weak acids or weak bases, together with their salts. Thus, in the Al^{3+} test that follows, a mixture of NH_3 and NH_4Cl is used to produce a basic solution that is much less basic than NH_3 alone. Consider the equilibrium equation, and the corresponding equilibrium constant expression

$$NH_3 + H_2O \rightleftharpoons NH_4^+ + OH^-$$

$$K_{NH_3} = \frac{[NH_4^+][OH^-]}{[NH_3]} = 1.8 \times 10^{-5}$$

Excess NH_4^+ in the mixture shifts the equilibrium to the left, resulting in a lower OH^- concentration. While 1 M NH_3 alone contains about 0.004 M OH^-, calculation shows that if NH_4Cl is added to make the NH_4^+ and NH_3 concentrations equal, the resulting OH^- concentration then will be only 1.8×10^{-5} M, a 200-fold reduction.

Likewise, if an acid solution still weaker than CH_3COOH is desired, the addition of CH_3COONa will very materially decrease the H^+ concentration, as is evident from the equilibrium

$$CH_3COOH(aq) \rightleftharpoons H^+ + CH_3COO^-$$

Sulfide Precipitation

In a solution containing the weak acid H_2S, the resulting S^{2-} concentration is very dependent on the H^+ concentration:

$$H_2S(aq) \rightleftharpoons H^+ + HS^-$$

$$HS^- \rightleftharpoons H^+ + S^{2-}$$

This fact is utilized in more complete qualitative schemes to separate the metal ions into groups by the degree of insolubility of their sulfides. In our simple scheme, precipitation of Zn^{2+} as $ZnS(s)$ in a basic NH_3 solution is satisfactory, since only alkali and alkaline earth ions remain, whose sulfides are all readily soluble.

EXPERIMENTAL PROCEDURE

Chemicals: 0.1 M $Al(NO_3)_3$, 0.1 M $Fe(NO_3)_3$, 0.1 M $Zn(NO_3)_2$, "aluminon reagent," (1.0 g/L of the ammonium salt of aurin tricarboxylic acid), saturated H_2S solution or 0.1 M NH_4HS (both freshly prepared).

Safety Precautions: H_2S gas is very toxic with a characteristic odor of rotten eggs. Perform the procedure described in "Test for Zn^{2+}. Step 10" in a fume hood. Boiling to remove H_2S should be performed in a fume hood, or you should use an inverted funnel connected to an aspirator (as shown in Figure 5-1) to remove H_2S.

A. Typical Reactions of the Ions

1. Ammonia and Hydroxide Ion Complexes Place 1-mL samples of 0.1 M $Al(NO_3)_3$, 0.1 M $Fe(NO_3)_3$, and 0.1 M $Zn(NO_3)_2$ in separate test tubes. To each add 1 drop of 6 M NH_3, then continue to add more, drop by drop, to determine whether the hydroxide precipitate first formed redissolves with excess NH_3. (*Note*: the 0.1 M $Fe(NO_3)_3$ contains excess HNO_3, which must first be neutralized before *any* precipitate appears.) Repeat these tests, using 6 M NaOH instead of 6 M NH_3. Summarize all the results in a suitable chart in your report.

2. Red Lake Formation with Al(OH)₃ The light flocculent precipitate of aluminum hydroxide is often difficult to observe. The dye called aluminon (ammonium aurin tricarboxylate) is adsorbed by the precipitate to form a characteristic red lake, which makes the identification of the aluminum hydroxide easier.

To 1 mL of water add 2 to 3 drops of 0.1 M Al^{3+} solution. Add 2 drops of aluminon reagent, then 3 to 5 drops of 6 M NH_3. Note the appearance of the precipitate. Now make the solution acid with 0.5 mL 6 M HCl, and again just basic with 6 M NH_3. Let the mixture stand a moment, and note the characteristic color and flocculation of the precipitate (which now should be red). Also note whether the solution is colored. A good red color is not obtained if the solution is too basic. Explain how the preceding treatment guarantees a very slightly basic solution.

B. Analysis of a Known Solution for Fe³⁺, Al³⁺, and Zn²⁺

First: Study the following procedure for analysis until you understand each step and the reason for adding each reagent. Then complete a flow chart for these operations, in a style similar to that of Figure 24-4. A skeleton flow chart is provided in part B of the report form: Simply insert the proper formulas of reagents, precipitates or residues, ions in solution, and so on.

Second: In your experiment report, write the net ionic equations for the reactions occurring at each step of the procedure, as numbered in the flow chart. (Your instructor may require that you do this before you receive an unknown.)

Third: Prepare a known solution containing Fe^{3+}, Al^{3+}, and Zn^{2+}, and analyze according to the procedure described in the next paragraph, following your results on the flow chart. *At the same time*, complete an analysis summary similar to Table 24-2 (a form for this summary is provided in part B of the report form).

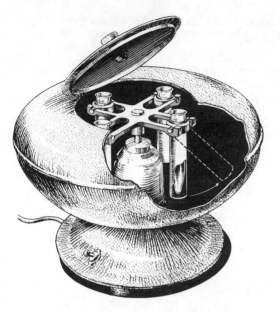

Tubes swing to dotted position when centrifuge is running.

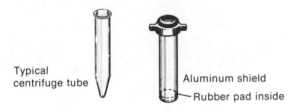

Typical
centrifuge tube

Aluminum shield
Rubber pad inside

Opposite pairs of tubes should be filled with equal
amounts of liquid to prevent excessive vibration.

FIGURE 25-1
The construction and operation of the centrifuge.

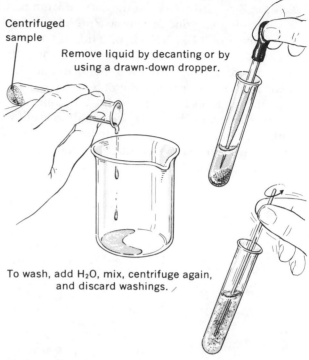

Centrifuged
sample

Remove liquid by decanting or by
using a drawn-down dropper.

To wash, add H₂O, mix, centrifuge again,
and discard washings.

FIGURE 25-2
The procedure for washing a preciptate that has been centrifuged.

Procedure for the Analysis

Precipitation of Fe(OH)₃ and Al(OH)₃. Step 6[1]   To 3 mL of the solution to be tested, add an excess (about 1 mL) of 6 M NH_3. Mix the solution, then centrifuge it. (The use of a centrifuge, if available, is more convenient for most separations of precipitate and solution. See Figures 25-1 and 25-2. *Obtain instructions from your instructor.* If filter paper is used, modify the directions accordingly.) Wash the precipitated $Al(OH)_3$ and $Fe(OH)_3$ with 1 to 2 mL of water, combining this with the filtrate, which contains any zinc as $Zn(NH_3)_4^{2+}$.

Separation and Test for Fe³⁺. Steps 7 and 8   Treat the mixed precipitate with about 0.5 mL of 6 M NaOH followed by 1 mL of water.[2] Centrifuge and wash with 1 mL of water, combining the washings with the filtrate of $Al(OH)_4^-$. Dissolve the $Fe(OH)_3$ precipitate with 1 to 3 drops of 6 M HCl, warm, if necessary, to complete the reaction, and add 2 mL of H_2O and then 1 to 3 drops of 0.1 M KSCN. A red color of $Fe(SCN)^{2+}$ proves the presence of Fe^{3+}.

Test for Al³⁺. Step 9   To the $Al(OH)_4^-$ filtrate add 6 M HCl until neutral, and then add about 0.5 mL excess. Add 1 to 2 drops of aluminon reagent, and make just basic again with 6 M NH_3. Mix this and let it stand. A flocculent precipitate, colored a characteristic red by the dye, proves the presence of Al^{3+}. If color and precipitate are indefinite, you may again make the solution acid with HCl, then basic with NH_3, to build up the NH_4^+ concentration so the solution becomes less basic.

---

[1] Directions for Steps 1 to 5 are given in Experiment 24; directions for Steps 11 to 15, in Experiment 25.

[2] If filter paper is used, add the NaOH and H_2O directly on the filter, collecting the filtrate in a test tube. The basic solution may be passed over the filter a second time for more complete solution of any aluminum as $Al(OH)_4^-$.

Test for Zn²⁺. Step 10 To the filtrate from Step 6, containing any zinc present as $Zn(NH_3)_4^{2+}$, add 1 to 3 drops of 0.1 M NH_4HS or 2 mL of saturated H_2S water. A white precipitate of ZnS proves the presence of Zn^{2+}. (When a general unknown is being analyzed, centrifuge the ZnS precipitate and save the solution for Experiment 26. Unless this solution is analyzed at once, it should be acidified with HCl and boiled in the fume hood to remove H_2S to avoid oxidation to sulfate ion and precipitation of any $BaSO_4$.)

C. Analysis of Unknown Solutions for Fe³⁺, Al³⁺, and Zn²⁺

Obtain one or more unknown solutions from your instructor, and analyze them by the preceding procedures. *At the same time,* keep a record of each step, including your actual observations for negative as well as for positive tests, by completing an analysis summary in part C of the report form.

DATA

A. Typical Reactions of the Ions

1. Ammonia and Hydroxide Ion Complexes

In the spaces provided, write the formulas of the precipitates formed, or new ions formed in solution, if any. Also indicate any characteristic colors and the like that result when each ion is treated with the reagent in the left-hand column.

Reagents	Fe^{3+}	Al^{3+}	Zn^{2+}
6 M NH_3			
6 M NH_3 (excess)			
6 M NaOH			
6 M NaOH (excess)			

2. Red Lake Formation with Al(OH)₃

Equation for the reaction of Al^{3+} with NH_3 _____

Explain how the addition, first, of an excess of HCl, then of a slight excess of NH_3, ensures that the solution will not become too basic to form a satisfactory adsorption compound of the dye with the precipitate.

B. Analysis of a Known Solution for Fe^{3+}, Al^{3+}, and Zn^{2+}

Complete the following flow chart and analysis summary for your known mixture of Fe^{3+}, Al^{3+}, and Zn^{2+}.

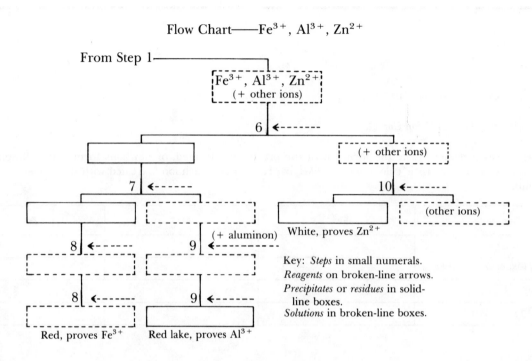

Flow Chart——Fe^{3+}, Al^{3+}, Zn^{2+}

Key: *Steps* in small numerals.
Reagents on broken-line arrows.
Precipitates or *residues* in solid-line boxes.
Solutions in broken-line boxes.

Complete the analysis summary for your *known* sample, as in Table 24-2.

Step	Sample	Reagent(s)	Observations	Conclusions
6				
7				
8				
9				
10				
			Summary	

Write below, in order, the net ionic equations for *all* reactions occurring in the systematic analysis of the ions of this group.

C. Analysis of Unknown Solutions for Fe^{3+}, Al^{3+}, and Zn^{2+}

Unknown no. _____ Appearance _____ Ions found _____

Unknown no. _____ Appearance _____ Ions found _____

Analysis Summary: Report your actual observations, negative as well as positive, for each step of the analysis of each unknown, and record above the ions found.

Step	Sample	Reagents	Observations	Conclusions

APPLICATION OF PRINCIPLES

1. A solution is 0.50 M in acetic acid, HA, and 0.25 M in sodium acetate, Na^+A^-. (With the excess of A^-, assume that the equilibrium concentration of HA equals its stoichiometric concentration.)

   (a) Write the equilibrium equation for the ionization of acetic acid.

   (b) Write the equilibrium constant expression for acetic acid ($K_{HA} = 1.8 \times 10^{-5}$).

   (c) Calculate the H^+ concentration in this buffer solution.

---

2. A solution is 1.8 M in NH_4Cl, and 0.010 M in NH_3. Will the solution be basic, acidic, or neutral? Show calculations. (With this excess of NH_4^+, assume that the molarity of NH_3 equals its stoichiometric concentration. K_b for NH_3 is 1.8×10^{-5}.)

Identification of Alkaline Earth and Alkali Metal Ions

PURPOSE

To study procedures for separating and identifying two alkaline earth cations: Ca^{2+} and Ba^{2+} ions. To learn how to use a flame test for the detection of the alkali metal cation, K^+. To learn a simple test for the detection of ammonium ion, which is grouped with the alkali metals because its salts have solubilities that resemble the alkali metal salts.

PRE-LAB PREPARATION

The elements making up the alkaline earth and alkali groups are quite similar and have many properties in common. Their compounds exhibit only one stable oxidation state; they do not form amphoteric hydroxides, being distinctly basic; and they do not readily form complex ions with NH_3 or OH^-. The separation of the alkaline earth

elements depends almost entirely on differences in the solubilities of their salts, which show a regular gradation through the periodic table. The salts of the alkali metals are almost all readily soluble. Table 26-1 will be useful in interpreting the analytical procedure.

This experiment includes the two alkaline earth ions Ca^{2+} and Ba^{2+}, the alkali ion K^+, and also NH_4^+ (whose salts are almost all soluble). We must test for NH_4^+ with a separate portion of the original unknown, since we have used it as a reagent.

Precipitation with Ammonium Carbonate

The reagent usually used to precipitate alkaline earth ions is $(NH_4)_2CO_3$. Since this is the salt of both a weak base and a weak acid, it reacts in solution to a marked extent:

$$NH_4^+ + CO_3^{2-} \rightleftharpoons HCO_3^- + NH_3$$

TABLE 26-1
Solubilities of alkaline earth salts (g/100 g H_2O, at room temperature)

	Mg^{2+}	Ca^{2+}	Sr^{2+}	Ba^{2+}
OH^-	0.001	0.16	1.74	3.89
CO_3^{2-}	0.09	0.0015	0.001	0.0018
SO_4^{2-}	35.5	0.2	0.01	0.00024
CrO_4^{2-}	138.	18.6	0.12	0.00037
$C_2O_4^{2-}$	0.015	0.0007	0.005	0.01

For this reason, we add excess NH_3 to reverse the hydrolysis and increase the concentration of CO_3^{2-}, to attain more complete precipitation.

The Separation of Barium and Calcium Ions

The following analytical procedure takes advantage of the preceding solubility differences. Note that after dissolution of the carbonate precipitate with acetic acid, barium can be effectively separated as the chromate, $BaCrO_4$, and then further confirmed by transformation to the still less soluble sulfate, $BaSO_4$. The $BaCrO_4$ dissolves in HCl because H_2CrO_4 is a somewhat weak acid and forms dichromate ion, $Cr_2O_7^{2-}$. With barium ion removed, calcium ion is easily identified, by precipitation with oxalate ion in NH_3 solution, as CaC_2O_4.

EXPERIMENTAL PROCEDURE

Chemicals: 6 M CH_3COOH, 3 M NH_4CH_3COO, 0.1 M NH_4Cl, 3 M $(NH_4)_2CO_3$, 0.1 M $BaCl_2$, 0.1 M $CaCl_2$, 0.1 M KNO_3, 1 M K_2CrO_4, 1 M $K_2C_2O_4$, 0.1 M Na_2SO_4.

A. Typical Reactions of the Ions

Instead of performing a series of separate, prescribed tests to learn the properties of the ions, proceed at once to the study of the following Procedure for the Analysis, and at the same time complete the flow chart by filling in the proper formulas of reagents, precipitates or residues, ions in solution, and so on. Compare these procedures with the data in the chart of the solubilities of alkaline earth salts, Table 26-1.

You may wish to try, on your own initiative, various test tube experiments, such as the separation of certain ions by a specific reagent, the subsequent precipitation identification tests, and the K^+ flame test in the presence of Na^+ (Figure 26-1).

B. The Analysis of a Known Solution for Ba^{2+}, Ca^{2+}, K^+, and NH_4^+

Prepare a known solution containing the ions of the group, and analyze it according to the following procedure; at the same time, prepare your own flow chart and complete it in accord with your observations. Also complete the analysis summary for this solution (part B, report form), outlining the successive steps, reagents, observations, and conclusions.

Procedure for the Analysis

Precipitation of Ba^{2+} and Ca^{2+}. Step 11[1] Start with a 3-mL sample of the solution to be tested. (If this is a general unknown, evaporate the filtrate from Step 10, Experiment 25, to a volume of 3 mL.) If your 3-mL sample is not already basic (litmus test), add 6 M NH_3 until it is basic, and then add, with mixing, 5 to 10 drops of 3 M $(NH_4)_2CO_3$. Let the mixture stand 3 to 5 minutes to complete precipitation, and then centrifuge it. Test for completeness of precipitation with further drop-by-drop additions of 3 M $(NH_4)_2CO_3$, until no further precipitation occurs. Centrifuge again if necessary. Separate the solution and save it for the K^+ test, Step 14.

Test for Ba^{2+}. Step 12 To the preceding precipitate add 5 drops of 6 M CH_3COOH, warm as needed to dissolve the precipitate, add 1 mL of water, and buffer the solution by adding 5 drops of 3 M NH_4CH_3COO. Add 3 drops of 1 M K_2CrO_4, mix, then centrifuge. If the solution is not yellow, add more 1 M K_2CrO_4, drop by drop, but avoid over 1 to 3 drops in excess. Wash any precipitate. Yellow $BaCrO_4$ indicates Ba^{2+}. (Save the solution for the Ca^{2+} test, Step 13.) This may be confirmed by adding 2 to 3 drops of 6 M HCl to dissolve the yellow precipitate, and then by adding 1 mL of 0.1 M Na_2SO_4. Centrifuge, if necessary, to see whether the precipitate is white in the yellow solution. White $BaSO_4$ proves the presence of Ba^{2+}.

---
[1] Directions for Steps 1 to 5 are given in Experiment 24, and directions for Steps 6 to 10 in Experiment 25.

Monolayer
A colored flame indicates a contaminated wire.

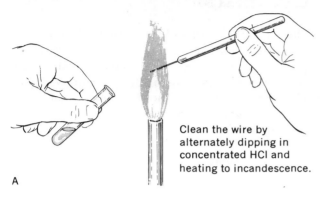

Clean the wire by
alternately dipping in
concentrated HCl and
heating to incandescence.

A

Observe through cobalt glass.

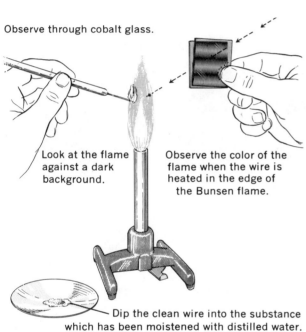

Look at the flame
against a dark
background.

Observe the color of the
flame when the wire is
heated in the edge of
the Bunsen flame.

Dip the clean wire into the substance
which has been moistened with distilled water.

B

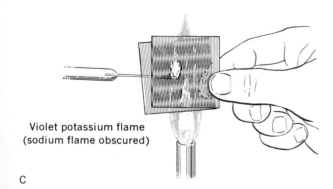

Violet potassium flame
(sodium flame obscured)

C

FIGURE 26-1
The flame test for sodium and potassium: (A) shows the procedure for cleaning the wire; (B) and (C) illustrate the steps for
observing the flame coloration.

Test for Ca^{2+}. Step 13   To the preceding yellow
solution from which the BaCrO$_4$ was removed,
add 10 drops of 1 M K$_2$C$_2$O$_4$, and then add 6 M
NH$_3$ to make the solution basic. Let stand 10 min
if a precipitate does not appear before that time.
White CaC$_2$O$_4$ proves the presence of Ca^{2+}. Further confirmation may be made by decanting the
yellow solution, adding to the residue a few drops
of 6 M HCl and 1 mL of water, to dissolve it, then
adding another drop of 1 M K$_2$C$_2$O$_4$ and again
making it basic with 6 M NH$_3$. The white precipitate of CaC$_2$O$_4$ will reappear.

Test for K$^+$. Step 14[2]   Concentrate the solution
from Step 11 (after removal of the Ba^{2+} and
Ca^{2+}) by evaporation in a porcelain dish *almost* to
dryness. Test the moist residue for potassium by
the flame test: Clean a Nichrome wire (see Figure
26-1A) by repeatedly heating it, plunging it into 5
mL of concentrated HCl in a small test tube, and
reheating it in the *hottest* Bunsen flame to brilliant
incandescence until there is only a minimum coloration to the flame. (Be sure the cleaned wire
touches nothing except your test solution after
this.) *Reduce* the flame to about 1 in. in height,
touch the wire to the moist salt or solution to be
tested, and heat it to incandescence in the colorless
flame. Because the violet potassium flame coloration lasts only a few seconds (potassium salts are
quite volatile), observe it at once. You may find it
helpful to observe the color of the flame produced
by a solution known to contain K$^+$. If sodium salts
are present, their yellow flame masks the pale-
violet potassium flame completely, and the use of
two layers of blue cobalt glass is essential to absorb
the sodium radiation so that you can observe the
potassium flame (see Figure 26-1B). Calcium salts,
if not completely removed, give an orange-red
flame.

NOTE   The potassium flame test may be carried
out, instead, on a dry sample of the original
solution evaporated almost to dryness and tested
as before. The other metal ions present, especially
if the blue cobalt glass is used, probably will not
interfere with the test.

---

[2] The potassium ion forms precipitates with several specialized
reagents. Two of these alternative tests for K$^+$ are described
in *Frantz/Malm's Chemical Principles in the Laboratory* by Roberts
and Ifft (W. H. Freeman and Company, San Francisco, 1977,
p. 341).

Test for NH$_4^+$. Step 15   This test must always be
carried out on the *original solution* or *sample*, since
ammonium salts are used as reagent throughout
the procedure.

Place 3 mL of the sample in an evaporating dish,
and make it basic with 6 M NaOH. Cover the dish
with a watch glass to the underside of which is
attached a moist strip of red litmus paper. Warm
the solution *very gently* to liberate any ammonia
present as the gas. (Avoid boiling, which would
contaminate the litmus with spray droplets of the
NaOH solution.) An even, unspotted blue color
proves ammonium ion.

C. Analysis of Unknown Solutions for Ba^{2+}, Ca^{2+}, K$^+$, and NH$_4^+$

Obtain one or more unknown solutions from your
instructor, and analyze them by the preceding
procedure. *At the same time,* keep a record of each
step, by completing the analysis summary in part
C of the report form, showing your actual observations, negative as well as positive, for each unknown.

REPORT

26

**Identification of Alkaline
Earth and Alkali Metal Ions**

NAME

SECTION   LOCKER

INSTRUCTOR   DATE

DATA

A. Typical Reactions of the Ions

NOTE: Indicate any experimental tests you have performed personally in order to be certain of the results.

1. Write net ionic equations for the reactions, *if any*, occurring when dilute solutions of the following are mixed. Write "N.R." (for "no reaction") if there is none.

(a) NH_4Cl, KNO_3, $NaOH$, heated _____

(b) $CaCl_2$, $Ba(NO_3)_2$, 1 M NH_3 _____

(c) $CaCl_2$, $Ba(NO_3)_2$, 1 M $NaOH$ _____

(d) $Ca(NO_3)_2$, K_2CrO_4 _____

(e) Mixture (d) + $BaCl_2$ _____

(f) Mixture (e) + HCl _____

(g) Mixture (f) + Na_2SO_4 _____

(h) $BaCl_2$, KNO_3, $ZnCl_2$, H_2S _____

(i) KCl, $(NH_4)_2CO_3$, $Ba(NO_3)_2$ _____

(j) $CaCO_3(s)$, NH_4Cl, 6 M CH_3COOH _____

(k) Mixture (j) + $(NH_4)_2C_2O_4$, NH_3 _____

2. On the basis of periodic table relationships, what would you predict about the general solubility (indicate "soluble," "slightly soluble," or "insoluble") of each of the following?

(a) $Be(OH)_2$ _____   (c) $Ra(OH)_2$ _____

(b) $BeSO_4$ _____   (d) $RaSO_4$ _____

3. Why does the addition of HCl dissolve such insoluble salts as $BaCrO_4$ and CaC_2O_4?

B. Analysis of a Known Solution for Ba^{2+}, Ca^{2+}, K^+, and NH_4^+

1. Complete the following flow chart in accord with your observations.

Flow Chart——Ba^{2+}, Ca^{2+}, K^+, NH_4^+

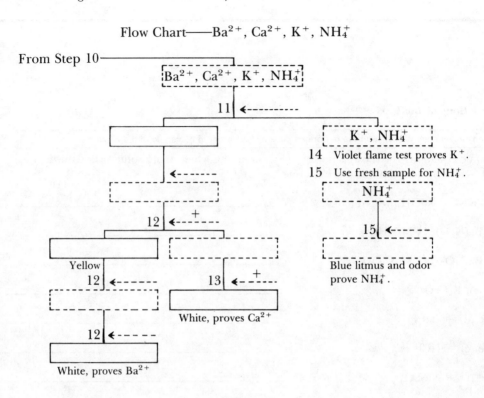

2. Complete the analysis summary for your known sample.

Appearance _____ Ions found _____

Step	Sample	Reagent(s)	Observations	Conclusions
11				
12				
13				
14				
15				
			Summary	

C. Analysis of Unknown Solutions for Ba^{2+}, Ca^{2+}, K^+, and NH_4^+

Unknown no. _____   Appearance _____   Ions found _____

Unknown no. _____   Appearance _____   Ions found _____

Analysis Summary: For your unknown samples, report below your actual observations, negative as well as positive, for each step of each analysis, and record above the ions found.

Step	Sample	Reagents	Observations	Conclusions

The Qualitative Analysis of Some Common Anions

PURPOSE

To study specific tests for detecting in an unknown sample the presence of nine common anions: nitrate, chloride, bromide, iodide, sulfate, sulfite, sulfide, phosphate, and carbonate ions.

PRE-LAB PREPARATION

The principles that are employed in the identification of metal ions can also be applied to the analysis of anions. Thus the qualitative detection of anions in a sample depends on the distinctive properties of particular ions and on the possibility of controlling experimental conditions so that a separation or identification of a given ion may be attained. In this experiment, we will explore ways to detect the presence of NO_3^-, Cl^-, Br^-, I^-, SO_4^{2-}, SO_3^{2-}, S^{2-}, PO_4^{3-}, and CO_3^{2-}.

Review thoroughly the following criteria on which the identification of an anion generally depends. (These criteria are all summarized in appropriate tables in Appendix B.)

1. Does the anion form a *precipitate* with certain cations, such as Ag^+ or Ba^{2+}, in neutral or in acidic solutions? (See Table B-8, Appendix B, for solubility rules.)

2. Is the ion the *anion of a weak or a strong acid*? (See Table B-6, Appendix B, for information on the relative strength of acids.)

3. Is the ion the *anion of a volatile acid*?

4. Can the anion act as *an oxidizing agent, a reducing agent*, or *either*? What is its relative strength as an oxidizing or reducing agent? (See Appendix B, Table B-10, for redox potentials.)

Review the descriptive chemistry of the anions we shall study in this experiment in your text as you apply the preceding criteria to the typical reactions and tests for the following anions.

Typical Reactions of Common Anions

Sulfate Ion   This ion is the anion of a *strong acid*; it forms characteristic precipitates with certain metal ions, as with barium ion:

$$Ba^{2+} + SO_4^{2-} \rightleftharpoons BaSO_4(s)$$

Other anions also form insoluble precipitates with barium ion:

$$Ba^{2+} + CO_3^{2-} \rightleftharpoons BaCO_3(s)$$

$$Ba^{2+} + SO_3^{2-} \rightleftharpoons BaSO_3(s)$$

$$3Ba^{2+} + 2PO_4^{3-} \rightleftharpoons Ba_3(PO_4)_2(s)$$

However, these are salts of *weak acids* and would all dissolve, or fail to precipitate, in an acid solution. In the presence of excess hydrogen ion, the concentration of the free anion is reduced to such a low value that the solubility equilibrium is reversed, and the precipitate dissolves or fails to form in the first place. We may therefore use barium ion in an acid solution as a test reagent for the presence of sulfate ion.

Sulfite Ion, Sulfide Ion, and Carbonate Ion   In each of these anions of *weak, volatile acids*, the free acid is formed by the addition of a strong acid:

$$SO_3^{2-} + 2H^+ \rightleftharpoons H_2SO_3(aq) \rightleftharpoons SO_2(g) + H_2O$$

$$S^{2-} + 2H^+ \rightleftharpoons H_2S(g)$$

$$CO_3^{2-} + 2H^+ \rightleftharpoons H_2CO_3(aq) \rightleftharpoons CO_2(g) + H_2O$$

The odors of sulfur dioxide (SO_2) and hydrogen sulfide (H_2S) are usually sufficient identification. Sulfite ion (SO_3^{2-}) can be oxidized to sulfate ion (SO_4^{2-}) by bromine water (Br_2) or hydrogen peroxide (H_2O_2), and then tested as the sulfate ion is tested. Sulfide ion (S^{2-}) can be further confirmed by placing it in contact with a lead salt solution on filter paper, which will result in the formation of a black deposit of lead sulfide (PbS).

The sulfite ion, which is intermediate in its oxidation state, can be reduced to free sulfur by sulfide ion, which in turn is oxidized to sulfur. The equation is

$$SO_3^{2-} + 2S^{2-} + 6H^+ \rightarrow 3S(s) + 3H_2O$$

These ions, therefore, are not likely to be found together in the same solution, particularly if it is acidic. A solution of sulfite is somewhat unstable because of its ease of oxidation by atmospheric oxygen:

$$2SO_3^{2-} + O_2(g) \rightarrow 2SO_4^{2-}$$

In the carbonate test, the evolution of a colorless, almost odorless gas when an acid is added to the sample is an indication, but not proof, that the gas is carbon dioxide. The sample must be reprecipitated as an insoluble carbonate salt, such as calcium carbonate ($CaCO_3$). When the slightly soluble carbon dioxide gas is bubbled into a neutral solution *containing calcium ion*, the weak acid that is formed, carbonic acid (H_2CO_3),

$$CO_2(g) + H_2O \rightleftharpoons H_2CO_3(aq) \rightleftharpoons 2H^+ + CO_3^{2-}$$

does not furnish a high enough concentration of carbonate ion to precipitate calcium carbonate. What would be the effect on the carbonate ion concentration if the carbon dioxide gas were bubbled into an alkaline solution instead of into the neutral one? This is the reason for using limewater, $Ca(OH)_2$, although the hydroxide is only slightly soluble, rather than some soluble calcium salt, in the carbonate ion test. The overall net ionic equation is

$$CO_2(g) + Ca^{2+} + 2OH^- \rightleftharpoons CaCO_3(s) + H_2O$$

Sulfite ion, if also present in the unknown, will interfere with the carbonate ion test, since it will liberate sulfur dioxide gas (SO_2) along with the carbon dioxide gas when the sample is acidified, and will form a calcium sulfite ($CaSO_3$) precipitate when the gases are absorbed in the limewater. (Sulfide ion, S^{2-}, would not interfere, since CaS is soluble.) To overcome this interference, it is necessary first to oxidize any sulfite ion to sulfate ion, and thus prevent the formation of any sulfur dioxide gas.

Chloride Ion, Bromide Ion, and Iodide Ion   These ions are, like the sulfate ion, the anions of *strong acids*. Their salts with silver ion are insoluble, whereas the silver salts of most other anions, which are also insoluble in neutral solution, will dissolve in acid solution. Silver sulfide (Ag_2S), however, is so very insoluble that the presence of hydrogen ion does not reduce the sulfide ion concentration sufficiently to dissolve it.

We can test for the presence of *chloride ion* in the mixed precipitate of AgCl, AgBr, and AgI by dissolving the AgCl from the still more insoluble AgBr and AgI by adding ammonia solution, thus forming the complex ion $Ag(NH_3)_2^+$ and Cl^-. When the filtrate is again acidified, the AgCl is reprecipitated:

$$AgCl(s) + 2NH_3(aq) \rightleftharpoons Ag(NH_3)_2^+ + Cl^-$$

$$Ag(NH_3)_2^+ + Cl^- + 2H^+ \rightleftharpoons AgCl(s) + 2NH_4^+$$

It is thus possible, by carefully controlling the NH_3 and Ag^+ concentrations, to redissolve the AgCl without appreciably redissolving the more insoluble AgBr and AgI. Furthermore, AgCl is white, AgBr is cream-colored, and AgI is light yellow.

The distinctive differences that enable us to separate and test for *bromide ion* and *iodide ion* in the presence of chloride ion depend on differences in their ease of oxidation. Iodide ion is easily oxidized to iodine (I_2) by adding ferric ion (Fe^{3+}), which does not affect the others. After adding dichloromethane (CH_2Cl_2) to identify (purple color) and remove the iodine, we can next oxidize the bromide ion with potassium permanganate or chlorine water solutions, absorb the bromine (Br_2) formed in dichloromethane, and identify it by the brown color produced.

Phosphate Ion   This is the anion of a moderately weak, nonvolatile acid—phosphoric acid (H_3PO_4). It is tested for by the typical method of forming a characteristic precipitate. The reagent used is ammonium molybdate solution, to which an excess of ammonium ion is added in order to shift the equilibrium further to the right. An acid solution is necessary. The equation is

$$3NH_4^+ + 12MoO_4^{2-} + H_3PO_4(aq) + 21H^+ \rightleftharpoons$$
$$(NH_4)_3PO_4 \cdot 12MoO_3(s) + 12H_2O$$

The yellow precipitate is a mixed salt, ammonium phosphomolybdate. Sulfide ion interferes with this test but can be removed first by acidifying the solution with HCl and boiling it.

Nitrate Ion   In testing for the nitrate ion, we cannot use a precipitation method, since all nitrates are soluble. Instead, two other facts are utilized. First, nitrate ion is a good oxidizing agent in an acid solution when a reducing agent such as ferrous ion (Fe^{2+}) is added:

$$4H^+ + NO_3^- + 3Fe^{2+} \rightarrow 3Fe^{3+} + NO + 2H_2O$$

Second, the nitric oxide, NO, reacts rapidly with the excess ferrous ion present to form a brown complex ion:

$$NO + Fe^{2+} \rightarrow Fe(NO)^{2+}$$

It is essential that an excess of ferrous ion be used, or the test will fail.

Summary   Table 27-1 may be of assistance to you in summarizing the behavior of the preceding negative ions with the metallic ions silver ion, barium ion, calcium ion, and lead ion.

TABLE 27-1
The behavior of some negative ions with the metallic ions Ag^+, Ba^{2+}, Ca^{2+}, Pb^{2+}

Negative ions	Metallic ions			
	Ag^+	Ba^{2+}	Ca^{2+}	Pb^{2+}
NO_3^-	Soluble	Soluble	Soluble	Soluble
Cl^-, Br^-, I^-	AgCl, white; AgBr, cream, AgI, yellow. All insoluble in HNO_3. AgCl soluble, AgBr slightly soluble, and AgI insoluble, in NH_3	Soluble	Soluble	$PbCl_2$ and $PbBr_2$, white, soluble in hot water. PbI_2, yellow, slightly soluble in hot water
SO_4^{2-}	Moderately soluble	$BaSO_4$, white, insoluble in HNO_3	$CaSO_4$, white, slightly soluble	$PbSO_4$, white, insoluble in HNO_3
SO_3^{2-}	Ag_2SO_3, white, soluble in NH_3 and in HNO_3	$BaSO_3$, white, soluble in HNO_3	$CaSO_3$, white, soluble in HNO_3	$PbSO_3$, white, soluble in HNO_3
S^{2-}	Ag_2S, black, soluble in hot, conc. HNO_3	Soluble	Soluble	PbS, black, soluble in HNO_3
PO_4^{3-}	Ag_3PO_4, yellow, soluble in NH_3 and in HNO_3	$Ba_3(PO_4)_2$, white, soluble in HNO_3	$Ca_3(PO_4)_2$, white, soluble in HNO_3	$Pb_3(PO_4)_2$, white, soluble in HNO_3
CO_3^{2-}	Ag_2CO_3, white, soluble in NH_3 and in HNO_3	$BaCO_3$, white, soluble in HNO_3	$CaCO_3$, white, soluble in HNO_3	$PbCO_3$, white, soluble in HNO_3

EXPERIMENTAL PROCEDURE

Chemicals: 0.5 M $(NH_4)_2MoO_4$, 0.1 M $BaCl_2$, saturated Br_2 water, saturated Cl_2 water, $CH_2Cl_2(l)$, 0.02 M $Ca(OH)_2$, 0.1 M $FeCl_3$, $FeSO_4 \cdot 7H_2O$, 3% H_2O_2, $Pb(CH_3COO)_2$ paper, 0.1 M KBr, 0.1 M KI, 0.1 M KNO_3, 0.03 M $AgCH_3COO$ (saturated), 0.1 M $AgNO_3$, 1 M Na_2CO_3, 0.1 M NaCl, 0.1 M NaH_2PO_4, 0.1 M Na_2SO_4, 0.1 M Na_2SO_3 (fresh), 0.1 M Na_2S (fresh).

Safety Precautions: H_2S gas is very toxic and has a characteristic odor of rotten eggs. You should avoid inhalation of H_2S in part 1 (Test for Sulfide Ion). In part 5 (Test for Chloride Ion), boiling to remove H_2S should be done in a fume hood, or you should use an inverted funnel connected to an aspirator (as shown in Figure 5-1) to remove H_2S.

The SO_2 gas produced in part 3 (Test for Sulfite Ion), is irritating and toxic and has a strong, suffocating odor. Avoid inhalation of SO_2 gas.

First: Familiarize yourself with the following test procedures, using 2-mL samples of dilute solutions of each ion to be tested. Any tests that yield unsatisfactory results should be repeated after you improve your technique.

Second: Answer the review questions and statements in the experiment report before analyzing the unknowns.

Third: Obtain one or more unknowns, and perform analyses for each of the ions, using a fresh 2-mL sample for each test.

1. *Test for Sulfide Ion* To about 2 mL of the test solution add a slight excess of 6 M HCl. You may notice an odor of H_2S; as a more sensitive test, place a piece of moistened lead acetate paper over the mouth of the test tube. Heat the test tube gently in the fume hood. A darkening of the paper indicates S^{2-} in the original solution. (If S^{2-} is found to be present, SO_3^{2-} cannot be present— why not?—and the SO_3^{2-} test may then be omitted. Note also the modification of the PO_4^{3-} test when S^{2-} is present.)

2. *Test for Sulfate Ion* To 2 mL of the test solution add 6 M HCl by drops until the solution is slightly acid. Then add 1 mL of 0.1 M $BaCl_2$ solution, or more, as needed to complete the precipitation. A white precipitate of $BaSO_4$ proves the presence of SO_4^{2-}. (Save the solution for the sulfite test.)

3. *Test for Sulfite Ion* If you noticed a sharp odor of SO_2 when the solution from the previous sulfate ion test was made acid with HCl, then SO_3^{2-} is

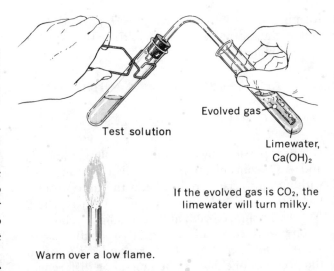

Test solution — **Evolved gas**

Limewater, $Ca(OH)_2$

If the evolved gas is CO_2, the limewater will turn milky.

Warm over a low flame.

FIGURE 27-1
The limewater test for carbon dioxide.

present. If you are in doubt, filter or centrifuge the solution to obtain a clear filtrate, add a drop or more of 0.1 M $BaCl_2$ to be sure all SO_4^{2-} is precipitated, and if necessary add more $BaCl_2$; then refilter or recentrifuge. To the clear solution, add 1 to 2 mL of bromine water to oxidize any SO_3^{2-} to SO_4^{2-}. A second white precipitate of $BaSO_4$ now proves the presence of SO_3^{2-}.

4. *Test for Carbonate Ion* Fit a 15-cm test tube with a one-hole rubber stopper and bent delivery tube (see Figure 27-1). Place about 3 mL of the test solution in this test tube. If sulfite ion (SO_3^{2-}) is present in the unknown, add 1 mL of 3% H_2O_2 to oxidize it to sulfate ion. Now insert the delivery tube into some clear limewater, $Ca(OH)_2$, in another test tube. When ready, remove the stopper just enough to add a little 6 M HCl to the test solution. Immediately close the stopper again, and heat the tube gently to boiling to drive any CO_2 gas into the limewater. Be careful not to let any of the boiling liquid escape through the delivery tube into the limewater. A white precipitate in the limewater indicates CO_3^{2-} or HCO_3^- in the test solution.

5. *Test for Chloride Ion* To a 2-mL portion of the test solution, add a few drops of 6 M HNO_3, as needed, to make the solution slightly acid. (Test with litmus paper.) Any sulfide ion present can be removed by boiling the solution for a moment in a fume hood. The free sulfur formed in the oxidation of S^{2-} by HNO_3 does not interfere. Add 1 mL of 0.1 M $AgNO_3$. (No precipitate here proves

[handwritten notes in margins: "Na2 CO3", "indicator turned brown Na2S", "Na2SO4 white cloudy precipitate"]

the absence of Cl^-, Br^-, or I^-.) Centrifuge the mixture. Test the clear filtrate with 1 drop of 0.1 M $AgNO_3$, for complete precipitation. If necessary, centrifuge again. Discard the filtrate. Wash the precipitate with distilled water to remove excess acid and silver ion. To this precipitate add 3 mL of distilled water, 4 drops of 6 M NH_3, and $\frac{1}{2}$ mL of 0.1 M $AgNO_3$. (The proportions are important, since we want to dissolve only the $AgCl$ from any mixture of $AgCl$, $AgBr$, and AgI.) $Ag(NH_3)_2^+$ and Cl^- will form. Shake the mixture well, and centrifuge. Transfer the clear solution to a clean test tube, and acidify with 6 M HNO_3. A white precipitate of $AgCl$ confirms Cl^-.

6. Test for Iodide Ion   To 2 mL of the test solution add 6 M HCl to make the solution acid. If S^{2-} or SO_3^{2-} is present, boil the solution to remove the ion. Add 1 mL of 0.1 M $FeCl_3$ to oxidize any I^- to I_2. (Br^- is not oxidized by Fe^{3+}.) Add 1 mL of dichloromethane (CH_2Cl_2), and agitate the mixture. A purple color indicates I^-. (Save the mixture for the Br^- test.)

7. Test for Bromide Ion   *If no I^- was present in the preceding mixture*, add 2 mL of chlorine water, and agitate it. A brown color in the CH_2Cl_2 layer indicates Br^-. *If I^- was present*, separate, by means of a medicine dropper, as much as possible of the preceding iodide test solution above the CH_2Cl_2 layer that contains the I_2, and place it in a clean test tube. Again extract any remaining I_2 by adding 1 mL of CH_2Cl_2, agitating the mixture, and separating the solution. The solution may be boiled a moment to remove any remaining trace of I_2. Then add 2 mL of chlorine water and 1 mL of CH_2Cl_2, and agitate the mixture. A brown color indicates Br^-.

8. Test for Phosphate Ion   First mix about 1 mL of 0.5 M $(NH_4)_2MoO_4$ reagent with 1 mL of 6 M HNO_3. (If a white precipitate forms, dissolve it by making the solution basic with NH_3, then reacidify with HNO_3.) If S^{2-} has been found in the unknown, first make a 2-mL portion of the test sample distinctly acid with HCl, boil it a moment to remove all H_2S, then add this (or a 2-mL sample of the original unknown if no S^{2-} is present) to the clear molybdate solution. A yellow precipitate of $(NH_4)_3PO_4 \cdot 12MoO_3$, appearing at once or after warming a few minutes to about 40°C, indicates the presence of PO_4^{3-}.

9. Test for Nitrate Ion   *If Br^- and I^- are absent from the unknown*, use 2 mL of test solution acidified with 3 M H_2SO_4. Add 1 mL of freshly prepared saturated $FeSO_4$. Incline the test tube at about a 45° angle, and pour about 1 mL of concentrated H_2SO_4 slowly down the side of the test tube. Be careful to avoid undue mixing. A brown ring of $Fe(NO)^{2+}$ at the interface of the two liquids indicates NO_3^-. A faint test may be observed more easily by holding the test tube against white paper and looking toward the light (Figure 27-2).

If Br^- and I^- are present in the unknown, free Br_2 or I_2 may form at the interface with the concentrated H_2SO_4 and invalidate the test. If this happens, add 4 mL of a saturated solution of silver acetate to 2 mL of the test solution, to precipitate $AgBr$ or AgI. Add a drop or two of 6 M HCl to precipitate any excess silver ion as $AgCl$. Decant the liquid into a test tube and centrifuge. Treat the clear centrifugate with $FeSO_4$ and concentrated H_2SO_4, as directed in the preceding paragraph.

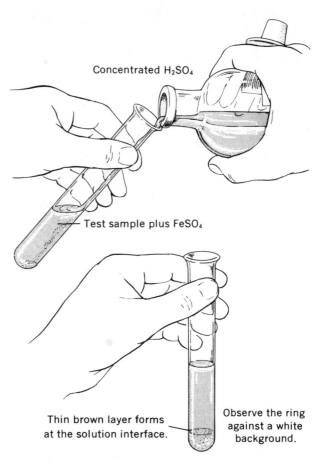

Concentrated H_2SO_4

Test sample plus $FeSO_4$

Thin brown layer forms at the solution interface.

Observe the ring against a white background.

FIGURE 27-2
The proper technique for the nitrate ion test.

The Use of Paper Chromatography in the Separation of Iron(III), Cobalt(II), Nickel(II), and Copper(II) Ions

PURPOSE

To develop an understanding of how substances can be separated by differential migration—the fundamental principle underlying all forms of chromatographic separation. To learn how the chemical properties of transition metal complexes can be adjusted by control of the acidity and of the concentration of chloride ion to achieve a separation of the metal complexes on cellulose filter paper. To identify the cations present in an unknown sample containing Fe(III), Co(II), Ni(II), or Cu(II) ions.

PRE-LAB PREPARATION

In Experiments 24 through 27 the separation and identification of a number of cations and anions were described. These separations were accomplished by selective precipitation or by the selective formation of complex ions with the use of a variety of reagents.

It would be ideal if each cation or anion formed a precipitate or colored complex with just one unique reagent. Then no prior separation would be necessary, and the addition of the proper reagent would provide a test for the presence of the sought-for ion. However, this ideal situation has not yet been attained. Consequently, simpler and more efficient methods of separation have been sought to replace the somewhat tedious methods in which precipitation is employed.

There are instrumental techniques available that can identify and quantitatively determine metal ions by their emission spectra, but these instruments are expensive and they can be used by only one person at a time. In this experiment we will use the simple, yet powerful, method of separation called chromatography, whose history and methods were discussed in Experiment 2.

Let's briefly review the important general principle employed in all forms of chromatography: A mixture of solutes in a moving phase passes over a selectively absorbing medium, the stationary phase. Separation occurs because the solutes have different affinities for the stationary and moving phases. Solutes that have a greater affinity for the moving phase will spend more time in the moving phase and therefore will move along faster than solutes that spend more time in the stationary phase. This leads to a *differential rate of migration* of solutes, which means that the solutes move at a different rate and thus become physically separated.

A solute that has no affinity for the stationary phase will move at the same rate as the molecules of solvent in the moving phase. A solute that is totally absorbed by the stationary phase and has no affinity for the moving phase will not move at all. Ideally we want to adjust the conditions of the separation so that the solutes will move along at some rate that is between these two extremes, as shown in Figure 28-1.

There are a variety of ways of achieving a flow around or through a stationary phase, as we discussed in Experiment 2. Because of its simplicity and low cost we will use paper chromatography. Paper is mainly cellulose, which contains a large number of hydroxyl (—OH) groups, so paper has a great affinity for water. (See Figure 28-2.)

The solvents employed in paper chromatography must wet the paper so that the mobile phase will move through the paper fibers by capillary attraction. The solute is first applied to the dry paper, not far from one end. Then during the chromatographic development the end of the paper nearest the spot is immersed in the solvent, which begins to flow through the paper. The solutes move along (we hope), and as they do they continually move back and forth between the moving and stationary phases. The fraction of

Direction of fluid flow

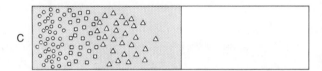

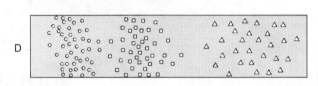

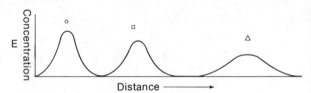

FIGURE 28-1
Schematic illustration of separation by differential migration. Parts A through D illustrate the separation of a three-component mixture by differential migration. Note that at the beginning of a separation (A), three components are clustered together at the point of sample application. As the sample migrates across the system—B through D—the three sample components are gradually separated, the fastest-moving component spending the most time in the moving fluid phase. E displays a smoothed plot of the concentration of each substance as a function of the distance from the origin for the distribution shown in D. [After Barry L. Karger et al., *Introduction to Separation Science*, Wiley, New York. Copyright © 1973.]

time they spend in the moving phase determines how fast they move along. (Look again at Figure 28-1.)

After the chromatogram has been developed, the positions of all the solutes on the paper are

FIGURE 28-2
The structure of cellulose.

located by spraying the paper with a reagent that reacts with the metal ions to form colored spots. The distance traveled by each solute is measured and the distance traveled by the moving solvent front is also measured. The ratio of these distances is the retention factor, R_f.

$$R_f = \frac{\text{distance traveled by the solute}}{\text{distance traveled by the solvent front}}$$

Our goal is to arrange conditions so that the solutes will be spread out along the paper, each with a significantly different R_f value.

After the spots are located and their R_f values measured they are compared with standard known solutes run under the same conditions. If possible, known and unknown substances are run on the same paper. If the known and unknown compounds have the same R_f values in different solvent systems and give the same reactions with various chromogenic (color-forming) reagents, it is probable that they are identical.

Separation of Fe^{3+}, Co^{2+}, Ni^{2+}, and Cu^{2+}

In separating these transition metal ions, we make use of a mixed solvent system containing water, 2-butanone, and hydrochloric acid. We may envision the stationary phase as a layer of water adsorbed or hydrogen bonded to the many hydroxyl groups contained in the cellulose molecules of the paper. The moving phase contains HCl and is rich in the less polar 2-butanone. The metal ions, ranging from water-solvated cations to anionic chloro complexes, will be distributed between these two phases. The metal ions that do not form chloro complexes, or that form only weak ones, will spend most of their time in the predominantly aqueous stationary phase. The metal ions that form chloro complexes will migrate more rapidly because they will spend most of their time in the 2-butanone-rich phase, either as neutral chloro complexes, MCl_2 or MCl_3 (where M represents a metal ion), or as protonated anionic chloro complexes, such as $HMCl_3$ or $HMCl_4$ (for example, $HFeCl_4$).

By adjusting the concentrations of HCl and 2-butanone we are able to control the composition of the metal ion complexes (and their net charges) and thus control their relative affinities for the aqueous stationary phase and organic-rich moving phase. This allows us to optimize the separation of these four metal ions.

EXPERIMENTAL PROCEDURE

Special Supplies: Whatman No. 1 paper, cut in 11- × 25.5-cm sheets; thin polyethylene film, such as Handi-wrap; rubber bands; plastic mm rulers; pencils; glass capillaries of about 0.5-mm ID; ovens or hair dryers are useful.

Chemicals: Solutions of $FeCl_3$, $CoCl_2$, $NiCl_2$, $CuCl_2$ (nitrate salts may also be used); 6 M NH_3, 0.1 M Na_2S, 7 M HCl, 2-butanone.[1] You will be provided with four metal ion solutions—one of each of Fe(III), Co(II), Ni(II), and Cu(II)—containing 5 g/L of the ion dissolved in 1 M HCl; you will also be given a solution mixture of all four of the metal ions, 5 g/L of each dissolved in 1 M HCl. Finally, you will also be provided with three unknown solutions containing one or more of the metal ions at similar concentrations.

Safety Precautions: The organic solvent (2-butanone or acetone) used in this experiment is flammable. There must be no open flames in the laboratory.

$NiCl_2$ is recognized as a carcinogen. Avoid skin contact with $NiCl_2$ solution. Wipe up any spills carefully and wash your hands thoroughly to minimize contact.

Ammonia gas is irritating to the lungs and toxic. Both 6 M NH_3 and 0.1 M Na_2S are corrosive to the skin and mucous membranes of the nose and lungs. Spraying of these two solutions on the paper chromatograms must be done in a fume hood. Take care not to inhale the mist from the sprayer, nor to get the spray on your skin. If a hood is not available, place the paper cylinder in a large beaker covered with plastic film. Cut a small 2- to 3-cm hole in the plastic film, insert the nozzle of the sprayer through the hole, and spray the paper cylinder while rotating the beaker.

Take an 11- × 25.5-cm piece of Whatman No. 1 paper and, using a pencil, draw a line parallel to the long dimension and 2 cm from the edge. Then, using a pencil, put eight small X's on the line, beginning 4 cm from the edge of the paper and spacing the marks about 2.5 cm apart.

Prepare a fresh developing solvent by putting 10.0 mL of 7.0 M HCl and 35 mL of 2-butanone in the bottom of a clean, dry 600-mL beaker, and cover the beaker with plastic wrap held in place with a rubber band.

Lay the paper down on a clean paper towel and carefully spot a tiny drop of each of the four metal ion solutions on four of the X's, beginning in the

---

[1] Acetone may be used in place of 2-butanone with only a slight sacrifice in the separation. If acetone is used, the 7 M HCl is replaced with 6 M HCl.

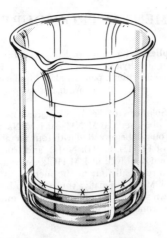

FIGURE 28-3
Preparing the samples for paper chromatography. After spotting the sample solutions on the X marks, the paper is rolled into a cylinder and stapled so that it will stand upright. Then it is placed in the beaker containing the developing solvent and the beaker is sealed with plastic wrap.

lower left corner. Use a glass capillary of about 0.5-mm internal diameter to spot the solutions. Each spot should be no larger than 3 mm. Put a tiny drop of the solution mixture (all four metal ions) on the fifth **X** and a drop of each of the three unknown solutions on the last three **X**'s.

You can expedite drying of the spots by gently waving the paper in the air. After they have dried, form the paper into a cylinder by overlapping the edges about 2 cm and fastening them together with a stapler. (See Figure 28-3.) Put the paper cylinder in the beaker containing the developing solvent, placing the spots at the bottom and taking care that the paper does not touch the wall of the beaker. (The surface of the solvent must be below the level of the spots.) Immediately seal the beaker with plastic wrap and allow the solvent to rise within 1 cm of the top of the paper (about 20 to 30 minutes). Observe the development frequently so that you do not let the solvent front rise all the way to the top of the paper. Also note the colors of the spots as they move along the paper.

When development is finished, remove the paper from the beaker and immediately mark the solvent front with a soft pencil before the solvent evaporates. Then dry the paper thoroughly. You can do so in a fume hood by gently waving the paper, or more quickly if you put the paper in an oven,[2] or if you use a hair dryer to blow a warm

stream of air over the paper. (The laboratory hot-air blower is not recommended, because it will scorch the paper unless it is used very judiciously.)

After the paper has dried, note the colors and locations of any visible spots. Then, in the hood, spray the paper lightly with 6 M NH_3. (Any kind of sprayer providing a fine mist is satisfactory.) If a fume hood is not available, use the procedure described in the safety precautions. The paper should be thoroughly moistened but not dripping wet. Visible changes in the colors of some of the spots should become observable. Note the color and location of any spots that change or become visible. (The presence of a heavy deposit of NH_4Cl salt indicates that the paper was not dried sufficiently before spraying with NH_3, so most of the HCl was not removed.)

Now dry the paper again to remove most of the NH_3 and spray with 0.1 M Na_2S solution. Brown to black spots should immediately form, and each of the four metal ions should produce a visible spot. Locate each of the spots and note its color.

Locate the densest part of the spot for each metal ion, and draw a pencil line through it. Measure the distance from the pencil line at the point of application to the densest part of the spot, and the distance from the point of application to the solvent front. Calculate the R_f values for each spot, and record on your data sheet.

Using the measured R_f values for the known solutions and the unknown solutions and the characteristic colors and intensities of the spots, identify and report the cations that are present in each of the three unknown solutions.

If time permits, run another set of chromatograms to check the reproducibility of the R_f values. Each time you repeat the experiment, make up a fresh developing solvent mixture.

You might also wish to investigate the effect of varying the HCl concentration, keeping the amount of 2-butanone and the total solvent volume constant.

BIBLIOGRAPHY

Skovlin, D. O., "The Paper Chromatographic Separation of the Ions of Elements 26 through 30," *J. Chem Educ.* **48,** 274 (1971).

---

[2] The temperature should be set at 60°C. If it is 100°C, the paper is likely to char and turn dark.

The Use of Paper Chromatography in the Separation of Iron(III), Cobalt(II), Nickel(II), and Copper(II) Ions

NAME		
SECTION		LOCKER
INSTRUCTOR		DATE

DATA AND RESULTS

1. Record your paper chromatography data below.

Distance of solvent front from point of application: chromatogram no. 1 _____ mm

chromatogram no. 2 _____ mm

Sample	Color with solvent	Color with NH_3	Color with Na_2S	Zone distance from point of application (mm)
Fe^{3+}				
Co^{2+}				
Ni^{2+}				
Cu^{2+}				
Mixture containing Fe^{3+} Co^{2+} Ni^{2+} Cu^{2+}				
Unknown no. _____				
Unknown no. _____				
Unknown no. _____				

2. Give your paper chromatograph results below.

	Fe^{3+}	Co^{2+}	Ni^{2+}	Cu^{2+}	Mixture	Unknown no. _____	Unknown no. _____	Unknown no. _____
Average R_f values of zones					Fe^{3+} Co^{2+} Ni^{2+} Cu^{2+}			

Unknown no. _____ Cations present _____

Unknown no. _____ Cations present _____

Unknown no. _____ Cations present _____

EXERCISES

1. Write an equation that represents the formation of the tetrachloroiron(III) complex, $FeCl_4^-$, from the aquo complex.

2. Write an equation that explains the formation of the blue color when Cu(II) is exposed to the vapors of NH_3.

3. Write equations for the reactions of Fe(III), Co(II), Ni(II), and Cu(II) ions with Na_2S.

4. What would you expect to happen to the R_f values of Fe(III), Co(II), and Cu(II) if you decreased the HCl concentration? Why?

5. Why is it important to have clean hands when handling chromatograms?

6. Why is a pencil used to make the points of application rather than a pen?

Oxidation-Reduction
Electron Transfer Reactions

PURPOSE

To study a number of chemical reactions that involve the transfer of electrons from a reducing agent to an oxidizing agent. To establish a qualitative chemical redox scale for seven redox couples by mixing the oxidized form of one redox couple with the reduced form of another couple and observing whether a reaction takes place. The redox couples are Cu(II)/Cu, Zn(II)/Zn, Fe(II)/Fe, H^+/H_2, Fe(III)/Fe(II), Br_2/Br^-, and I_2/I^-.

PRE-LAB PREPARATION

A Definition of Oxidation and Reduction

There is a problem in defining an oxidation-reduction, or redox, reaction as a chemical reaction that involves the transfer of electrons from the substance oxidized to the substance reduced be-cause, strictly speaking, every chemical reaction involves changes in the electron density on atoms and therefore involves charge transfer from one atom to another. Thus this definition could encompass every chemical reaction.

For this reason, some have suggested (see the Bibliography) that there is no consistent basis for distinguishing so-called oxidation-reduction reactions from other chemical reactions, other than by change in oxidation numbers; and we have pointed out that oxidation numbers are calculated by arbitrary rules and do not accurately reflect the actual distribution of charge in a molecule or polyatomic ion.

This somewhat unsatisfactory state of affairs forces us to conclude that the classification of a reaction as an oxidation reaction is somewhat artificial and arbitrary because it is based on the purely arbitrary notion of oxidation number. To be logically consistent, *we must define oxidation as an increase in oxidation number and reduction as a decrease in oxidation number.*

Only for simple reactions involving elements and their ions will there be a direct connection between the changes in oxidation number of the elements and the transfer of electrons. For example, when you put a piece of zinc metal in an aqueous solution of copper(II) sulfate, the zinc reacts with Cu^{2+} to form Zn^{2+} and Cu metal. Thus each Cu^{2+} ion has gained two electrons and each zinc atom has lost two electrons. In other words, there has been a net transfer of two electrons from a Zn atom to a Cu^{2+} ion.

Likewise, zinc goes from oxidation state 0 to $+2$, and each Cu(II) ion is reduced from oxidation state $+2$ to 0. The oxidation number of Zn has increased; we say it has been oxidized. The oxidation number of Cu has decreased; we say it has been reduced.

In the reaction of zinc with Cu^{2+}, represented schematically in Figure 29-1, zinc acts as a *reducing agent,* or *reductant,* and Cu^{2+} acts as an *oxidizing agent,* or *oxidant.*

Writing the net stoichiometric reaction as the sum of two half-reactions shows explicitly that the transfer of electrons is involved:

Oxidation half-reaction
$$Zn(s) \rightarrow Zn^{2+}(aq) + 2e^- \qquad (1)$$

Reduction half-reaction
$$Cu^{2+}(aq) + 2e^- \rightarrow Cu(s) \qquad (2)$$

Net reaction
$$Zn(s) + Cu^{2+}(aq) \rightarrow Zn^{2+}(aq) + Cu(s) \qquad (3)$$

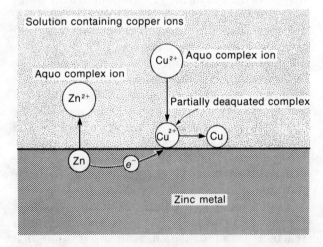

FIGURE 29-1
Direct chemical reaction of zinc with Cu^{2+}. As the zinc dissolves, Cu^{2+} is plated out on the surface of the zinc. A Cu^{2+} ion is reduced by transfer of two electrons from a Zn atom. [After J. O'M. Bockris and D.M. Drazic, *Electrochemical Science*, Barnes & Noble, New York, Figure 3.23b. Copyright © 1972.]

Note that *no electrons appear in the overall reaction.* This is why it may be sometimes difficult for you to look at a chemical reaction and try to decide whether it can be classified as an oxidation-reduction reaction. Keep this fact in mind—this decision is arbitrary. Certain conventional rules have been adopted about the definition of oxidation number. We will classify a reaction as an oxidation-reduction reaction only if there is a change in oxidation state (or oxidation number) of atoms involved in the reaction according to our previously defined rules. (These rules are summarized in Appendix A, together with some examples of how they are applied.)

The Relative Strength of Oxidizing and Reducing Agents

Oxidation-reduction processes involve a *relative competition* of substances for electrons. The stronger oxidizing agents are those substances with greater affinity for additional electrons; the stronger reducing agents are those substances with the least attraction for electrons that they already possess. Thus silver ion is a stronger oxidizing agent than is cupric ion because the reaction

$$2Ag^+ + Cu(s) \rightarrow Cu^{2+} + 2Ag(s)$$

takes place as indicated, but not appreciably in the reverse direction. That is, silver ion has a strong enough attraction for electrons to take them away from copper atoms. Similarly, copper metal is a stronger reducing agent than is silver metal, because copper releases its electrons more easily. It is possible to arrange the various oxidizing and reducing agents as "redox couples" in a series, according to their relative tendencies to gain or lose electrons. In this experiment, we shall explore such relative tendencies for a limited number of reactions.

Fluorine is one of the strongest oxidizing agents known, and lithium is one of the strongest reducing agents; therefore these two redox couples would be at opposite ends of the series, with most other redox couples falling somewhere in between. (See Figure 29-2.)

A Qualitative Chemical Redox Scale

In this experiment we establish qualitatively the relative position of a limited number of oxidation-

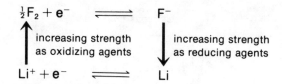

$$\tfrac{1}{2}F_2 + e^- \rightleftharpoons F^-$$

increasing strength as oxidizing agents   increasing strength as reducing agents

$$Li^+ + e^- \rightleftharpoons Li$$

FIGURE 29-2
Schematic diagram illustrating the most powerful and the weakest oxidizing and reducing agents.

reduction couples in the redox series. We will start with only three metals and their ions, and then expand our study until seven couples in all have been considered.

EXPERIMENTAL PROCEDURE

NOTE Before beginning this experiment, complete the preliminary exercise in your experiment report form, indicating as directed there the substances oxidized and reduced in the several equations given and the change in oxidation state, if any.

Chemicals: Small pieces of Cu, Zn, and Fe (in the form of wire or 5- × 15-mm strips; the Fe may be in the form of small, bright nails or steel wool); Cu (turnings), 6 M HCl, 6 M NH₃, 0.1 M CuSO₄, 0.1 M Zn(NO₃)₂, 0.1 M FeSO₄ (freshly prepared and stored in contact with powdered iron), Br₂ water (saturated solution), 0.05 M I₂ in methanol, hexane(l), 0.1 M FeCl₃, 0.1 M KBr, 0.1 M KI, 0.1 M K₃Fe(CN)₆, 0.1 M AgNO₃, 6 M H₂SO₄.

1. A Simple Redox Series for Several Metals: Copper, Zinc, Iron, and Their Ions Explore the behavior of small pieces of Cu, Zn, and Fe metals (if the iron is rusty, it should first be cleaned in 6 M H₂SO₄, then rinsed in water), putting each metal in 3 mL of 0.1 M solutions of the ions of the other metals—that is, Cu with Zn^{2+} and with Fe^{2+}, Zn with Cu^{2+} and with Fe^{2+}, and Fe with Cu^{2+} and with Zn^{2+}—to determine which metal is the strongest and which the weakest reducing agent (and which ion is the strongest and which the weakest oxidizing agent). Write equations for the reactions that occur. Note that the oxidized form of one redox couple is always mixed with the reduced form of the other couple, or vice versa. Prepare a table as directed in the report form, under part 1 of the Experimental Data.

2. The Hydrogen Ion/Hydrogen Couple Recall from previous experience, or test as needed, to prove the ability of 6 M HCl to dissolve the

preceding three metals. (Nitric acid cannot be used to test the activity of H^+, because nitrate ion is a stronger oxidizing agent than H^+ and would react first and confuse the results.) Now place the H^+/H_2 couple in its proper place in your redox series.

3. The Oxidizing Power of the Halogens First, if you are not familiar with the colors of the free halogens in hexane, add a little Br₂ water to 3 mL of H₂O and 1 mL of hexane. Mix the liquids together by shaking, and observe the color of the hexane layer floating on top. Repeat, using 0.05 M I₂ in methanol instead of Br₂ water. (Cl₂ in hexane is colorless.) Now explore the behavior of 3-mL samples of 0.1 M solutions of each of the halide ions Br^- and I^- (with 1 mL of hexane added to each), when each is treated with a little of the other free halogen—that is, Br^- with a few drops of I₂ in methanol, and I^- with a few drops of Br₂ water—to determine which halogen is the strongest and which the weakest oxidizing agent (and which ion is the strongest and which the weakest reducing agent). Write equations for the reactions that take place. Then arrange the two halogens in a separate potential series, as directed in the report form.

4. The Iron(III) Ion/Iron(II) Ion Couple Determine whether Fe^{3+} ion is a stronger or weaker oxidizing agent than I₂ or Br₂ by adding 1 mL of 0.1 M FeCl₃ to 2 mL each of 0.1 M KBr and 0.1 M KI. Add 1 mL of hexane to each, mix, and note the formation of any free halogen. To test for any reduction of Fe^{3+} to Fe^{2+}, prepare two fresh reaction mixtures, omitting the addition of hexane, and add to each a little potassium ferricyanide solution, K₃Fe(CN)₆. If Fe^{2+} is present, the deep blue precipitate of Fe₃(Fe(CN)₆)₂ will form. Write equations for any reactions in which iron(III) is reduced; note that it does not go to metallic iron. Place the Fe^{3+}/Fe^{2+} couple in its proper place in your potential series of the halogens.

5. The Reaction of the Halogens with Metals Test the ability of the halogens to oxidize metals by adding 10 mL of Br₂ water and 10 mL of 0.05 M I₂ in methanol to two different samples of one of the less active metals—some Cu turnings in a 15-cm test tube. Shake the mixtures for several minutes. If a precipitate forms, allow it to settle for a few minutes. Pour off some of each solution into separate test tubes.

Test for the formation of any halide ion by adding a few drops of 0.1 M AgNO₃ to the solutions that you poured off. Also test for the formation of any Cu(II) ion by adding 1 mL of 6 M NH_3. (Blue $Cu(NH_3)_4^{2+}$ indicates Cu(II); any AgBr(*s*) or AgI(*s*) present will not interfere with the test.) What would you conclude from the result as to the ability of other metals, such as Fe and Zn, to be oxidized by bromine or iodine?

The interaction of the Cu^{2+}/Cu and I_2/I^- couples is complicated by the fact that Cu^+, if formed, can be stabilized by the formation of an insoluble precipitate. Because of this, the reaction $2Cu^{2+} + 5I^- \rightarrow I_3^- + 2CuI(s)$ readily proceeds. The formation of I_2 is also promoted by the reaction of I_2 with I^- to form the soluble I_3^- complex ion.

6. *Summary of Data* Your experimental observations, together with the preceding data, will enable you to combine your two separate potential series into one general oxidation-reduction potential series of seven couples, which shows the relative tendencies of the various elements and ions to lose electrons. Note that each couple is written so that the change from left to right represents gain of electrons (reduction). On that table, in your report form, designate clearly which are the reducing agents, which the oxidizing agents, the end of each column that is the strongest (S), and the end that is the weakest (W).

Such a table can be expanded to include many more oxidation-reduction couples and is useful in predicting the course of many reactions. (Refer to Table B-10 in Appendix B.) In reading the table,

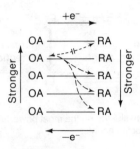

FIGURE 29-3
Tendencies for reactions between oxidizing and reducing agents. The dashed arrows indicate which reducing agent can react with a given oxidizing agent.

note that *any oxidizing agent (on the left) has the possibility of reacting with any reducing agent (on the right) that is stronger than its own reduction product—that is, that is lower in the series* (see Figure 29-3). The table makes no prediction, however, of the *rate* of a given reaction—some reactions are too slow to be practical. Again, the *concentration* of the ions in a solution has a definite effect on the tendency for reaction, in accordance with the Le Châtelier principle. This factor is considered in Experiment 30.

BIBLIOGRAPHY

Sisler, H. H., and VanderWerf, C. A., "Oxidation-Reduction: An Example of Chemical Sophistry," *J. Chem. Educ.* **57**, 42–44 (1980).

REPORT

29

Oxidation-Reduction
Electron Transfer Reactions

NAME

SECTION   LOCKER

INSTRUCTOR   DATE

PRELIMINARY EXERCISES

As a review, in the following equations for familiar reactions, underline the reducing agent once and the oxidizing agent twice. At the right, indicate the change in oxidation *per atom* for each element concerned. If there is no change, write in "no oxidation no. change."

Reaction	Element oxidized	Oxidation number increase per atom	Element reduced	Oxidation number decrease per atom
$2Al(s) + 3Cl_2(g) \rightarrow 2Al^{3+} + 6Cl^-$				
$Ag^+ + Cl^- \rightarrow AgCl(s)$				
$Mg(s) + 2H^+ \rightarrow Mg^{2+} + H_2(g)$				
$Cu^{2+} + H_2S(g) \rightarrow CuS(s) + 2H^+$				
$Ba(s) + 2H_2O \rightarrow Ba^{2+} + 2OH^- + H_2(g)$				
$3Na_2O_2(s) + Cr_2O_3(s) + H_2O \rightarrow 6Na^+ + 2CrO_4^{2-} + 2OH^-$				
$H_2O_2(aq) \rightarrow H_2O + \frac{1}{2}O_2(g)$				
$CO_2(g) + H_2O \rightarrow H_2CO_3(aq)$				
$CO_2(g) + C(s) \rightarrow 2CO(g)$				
$HCl(g) + NH_3(g) \rightarrow NH_4Cl(s)$				
$2ZnS(s) + 3O_2(g) \rightarrow 2ZnO(s) + 2SO_2(g)$				
$4H^+ + 2Cl^- + MnO_2(s) \rightarrow Mn^{2+} + Cl_2(g) + 2H_2O$				
$10H^+ + SO_4^{2-} + 8I^+ \rightarrow 4I_2(s) + H_2S(g) + 4H_2O$				

EXPERIMENTAL DATA

A Qualitative Chemical Redox Scale

1. *A Simple Redox Series for Several Metals*

Copper, Zinc, Iron, and Their Ions. Write net ionic equations for any reactions taking place between the metals and metal ions listed below (indicate any cases of no reaction).

Copper and zinc ion   _____

Zinc and cupric ion   _____

Iron and cupric ion   _____

Iron and zinc ion   _____

Copper and iron ion   _____

Zinc and iron ion   _____

Which metal is the stronger reducing agent, copper or zinc?   _____

iron or copper?   _____

iron or zinc?   _____

In the space at the right, construct an oxidation-reduction potential series for iron, copper, and zinc, and their ions. Arrange the three metals in a column at the right-hand side, with the strongest reducing agent at the bottom and the weakest at the top. To the left of each metal symbol, make a slash; to the left of the slash write the symbol for the oxidized form of the metal—for example, Cu^{2+}/Cu. You now have a brief "redox potential series."

Which is the strongest oxidizing agent: iron ion, cupric ion, or zinc ion?

Explain how this table summarizes your observations.

2. The H^+/H_2 Couple

Describe the observations that enable you to place the H^+/H_2 couple in the redox series. Also, write net ionic equations for the evidence thus obtained. Put the H^+/H_2 couple in its proper place in the redox scale you established for the metals and their ions in part 1 by adding it to the couples listed in the space on the previous page.

3. The Oxidizing Power of the Halogens

List your observations, and write net ionic equations for the reactions of the free halogens with the halide ions, in accordance with your experimental data.

Reaction	Observations	Net ionic equations
Bromine and iodide ion		
Iodine and bromide ion		

At the right, construct a potential series for the halogens and their ions, placing the strongest *reducing* agent at the *bottom* on the *right* of the series; and the strongest oxidizing agent at the *top* and on the *left*.

The strongest oxidizing agent in this series is _____ .

The strongest reducing agent in this series is _____ .

4. The Iron(III) Ion/Iron(II) Ion Couple

Write net ionic equations for the reaction of Fe^{3+} with the halide ions, in accordance with your experimental results.

Iron(III) ion with iodide ion _____

Iron(III) ion with bromide ion _____

The Fe^{3+}/Fe^{2+} couple should therefore be placed between the _____couple

and the _____couple.

5. *The Reaction of the Halogens with Metals*

Write a net ionic equation showing the results of your experiments on the reaction of Br_2 water and I_2 solution with copper.

_____

What is the experimental evidence for the above reaction products?

_____

6. *Summary of Data*

In the space at the right, construct an oxidation-reduction potential series for all seven couples studied in this experiment. Write "Oxidizing agents" and "Reducing agents" along the proper sides of the table. Indicate the position of the strongest and weakest oxidizing agents and reducing agents by placing (S) and (W) beside the formulas for these substances.

APPLICATION OF PRINCIPLES

NOTE: In answering these questions, refer to Table B-10, Appendix B.

1. In the first parentheses following each formula, write "O" if the substance may be used as an oxidizing agent, then write the formula of the reduced form. In the second parentheses, write "R" if the substance may be used as a reducing agent, then write the oxidized form. (Note that some substances may be used for either, depending on the substance with which they react.)

   Al   ( )_____ ( )_____   HBr ( )_____ ( )_____ MnO_4^- ( )_____ ( )_____

   Sn^{2+} ( )_____ ( )_____ Br_2 ( )_____ ( )_____ H_2SO_3 ( )_____ ( )_____

2. Indicate by "T" or "F" whether the following statements are true or false.

   Manganese metal can dissolve in dilute HCl.   ( )
   Tin metal will reduce Sn^{4+} to Sn^{2+}.   ( )
   Mercury metal will dissolve in nitric acid, liberating H_2 gas.   ( )
   Oxygen in moist air can oxidize Fe^{2+} to Fe^{3+}.   ( )
   Copper metal will dissolve in HNO_3 but not in HCl.   ( )
   Gold may be dissolved in 1 M HNO_3.   ( )

3. Name a substance for each of the following descriptions.

   It can oxidize Cd to Cd^{2+} but cannot oxidize Pb to Pb^{2+}. _____

   It can reduce Br_2 to Br^- but cannot reduce I_2 to I^-. _____

   It can oxidize Fe to Fe^{2+} but cannot oxidize Fe^{2+} to Fe^{3+}. _____

   It can reduce Sn^{4+} to Sn^{2+} but cannot reduce Sn^{2+} to Sn. _____

4. Hypothetical elements A, B, C, and D form the respective divalent ions A^{2+}, B^{2+}, C^{2+}, and D^{2+}. The following equations indicate reactions that can, or cannot, occur. Use these data to arrange the ion/metal couples into a short redox potential series.

$B^{2+} + D \rightarrow D^{2+} + B$

$B^{2+} + A$ (will not react)

$D^{2+} + C \rightarrow C^{2+} + D$

Electrochemical Cells

PURPOSE

To show how an electrochemical cell can be constructed based on two half-reactions that are separated so that electrons are transferred through an external circuit. To show how cell voltages are related to the concentration of the components of the cell. To show how measurements of a cell voltage can be used to calculate an equilibrium constant.

PRE-LAB PREPARATION

Electrochemistry and Everyday Life

As you read these words, nerve impulses are traveling along the optic nerves from your eyes to your brain, propagated by electrochemical discharges across the cell walls of the nerves. So important is this electrical activity that one defi-

nition of death is the cessation of electrical activity in the brain.

In our everyday lives we use electrochemical cells or their products without thinking about them. When you turn the ignition key of your car, its starter motor is powered by the current from a lead-acid battery. The chromium plate on the trim was deposited electrochemically. The aluminum in the engine parts was produced in a cell by electrolysis.

Electrochemical reactions are involved in all of these processes, which either use electrical energy to produce chemical substances or vice versa.

The Nature of Electrochemical Cells

Whenever an oxidation-reduction reaction occurs that involves two elements and their ions, there is a transfer of electrons from the substance oxidized to the substance reduced. Thus, when zinc is oxidized by cupric ion, the zinc atom loses two electrons and cupric ion gains two electrons. We can express this event as two separate half-reactions:

$$Zn(s) \rightarrow Zn^{2+} + 2e^- \quad (oxidation)$$

$$Cu^{2+} + 2e^- \rightarrow Cu(s) \quad (reduction)$$

The sum of these two half-reactions gives the net chemical reaction.

$$Zn(s) + Cu^{2+} \rightarrow Zn^{2+} + Cu(s)$$

The net (or total) reaction does not contain any electrons because all of the electrons lost by the zinc are gained by copper(II) ion. An *electrochemical cell* is simply a device used to separate a chemical reaction into two component half-reactions in such a way that the electrons are transferred through an external circuit rather than by direct mixing of the reactants. We will call the cell *self-driven* if the chemical reaction proceeds spontaneously, creating a current flow in the external circuit.

It's interesting that electrochemical cells can be constructed based on chemical reactions that we do not ordinarily regard as oxidation-reduction reactions. For example, consider the cell based on the following half-reactions:

$Ag^+(aq) + e^- \rightarrow Ag(s)$	(reduction)
$Ag(s) + Cl^-(aq) \rightarrow AgCl(s) + e^-$	(oxidation)
$Ag^+(aq) + Cl^-(aq) \rightarrow AgCl(s)$	(net cell reaction)

In this cell, the net reaction is the combination of Ag^+ with Cl^- to form AgCl, which we ordinarily think of as a precipitation reaction, not an oxidation-reduction reaction.

Or consider the cell based on these two half-reactions:

$Cu^{2+}(1M) + 2e^- \rightarrow Cu(s)$	(reduction)
$Cu(s) \rightarrow Cu^{2+}(0.1M) + 2e^-$	(oxidation)
$Cu^{2+}(1M) \rightarrow Cu^{2+}(0.1M)$	(net cell reaction)

This is called a *concentration cell,* and the net result of the operation of this cell is the transfer of Cu^{2+} from the more concentrated solution to the more dilute solution, a process that we might not even call a chemical reaction.

The message of these two examples is clear: An electrochemical cell can be based on any process that can be separated into two half-reactions that involve the transfer of electrons to or from an external circuit. The net reaction does not have to be a conventionally defined oxidation-reduction reaction. (Keep in mind that the definition of an oxidation-reduction reaction is somewhat arbitrary, as we discussed in Experiment 29, and every chemical reaction involves a redistribution of electronic charge.) In other words, chemical reactions generally involve at least partial *charge transfer* from one atom to another.

A way to carry out the reaction of zinc with Cu^{2+} in an electrochemical cell is shown in Figure 30-1. In the cell, oxidation takes place at the zinc

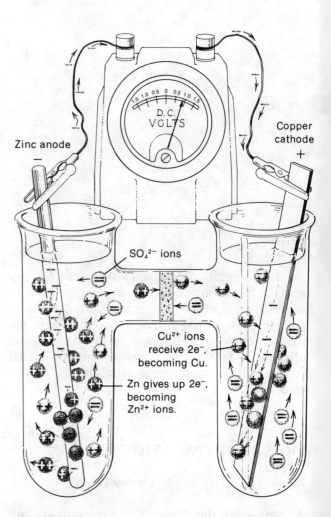

FIGURE 30-1
The Daniell cell, a simple electrochemical cell, that transforms the energy liberated by a chemical reaction into electrical energy. The electric current in the solution consists of sulfate ions moving toward the left, and of zinc(II) and copper(II) ions moving toward the right.

electrode (the anode),[1] liberating electrons to the external circuit. Reduction takes place at the copper electrode (the cathode),[1] consuming electrons coming from the external circuit. By isolating each half-reaction in its own compartment, we have arranged things so that electron transfer must take place through the external circuit made of metallic wire. It is not possible for the electrons to travel long distances through the solution because they are much too reactive, reacting rapidly with water to reduce it ($e^- + H_2O \rightarrow \frac{1}{2}H_2 + OH^-$). The current flow in solution consists of positive ions moving in one direction and negative ions in the opposite direction. This ionic current flow in solution is a direct result of the electron transfer that takes place at the surface of the electrodes. As current flows in the cell, there is a tendency for excess positive charge (in the form of Zn^{2+} ions) to accumulate in solution around the zinc anode as zinc atoms are oxidized. Likewise, excess negative charge (in the form of SO_4^{2-} ions) accumulates around the copper cathode as Cu^{2+} ions are removed from solution by reduction to copper metal. These excess charges create an electric field that causes the ions to *migrate*, positive ions (cations) migrating toward the cathode and negative ions (anions) migrating toward the anode. This migration of ions between the two compartments of the cell constitutes the cell current in the solution. To summarize, *ions are the charge carriers in solution and electrons are the charge carriers in the external circuit.*[2]

In Figure 30-1 a porous barrier (for example, a glass frit) is shown separating the two compartments of the cell. This prevents gross mixing of the solutions in the two compartments by slowing down simple diffusion, but ions can still pass through the porous barrier. If it became plugged or blocked so that no ions could pass through, current flow in the cell would cease just as if you had cut the wire in the external circuit. This could happen, for example, if reaction of ions in the two compartments produced a precipitate, because the precipitate would form right in the porous plug where the two solutions come in contact. Another point to note is that *all* of the ions in solution migrate under the influence of the electric field, even ions from an added inert electrolyte such as K_2SO_4, which are not involved in the redox reactions. Each ion moves at an average speed determined by the strength of the field and the size of the ion. Big bulky ions move more slowly (and carry a smaller fraction of the current) than small fast-moving ions.

It is important to realize that the net chemical result of the operation of the cell, shown in Figure 30-1, is exactly the same as the net stoichiometric reaction: One Cu^{2+} ion is reduced for each zinc atom that is oxidized. But there are some important nonchemical differences between the direct reaction and the reaction carried out in the cell. By using the cell, we are able to convert a fraction of the chemical energy of the reaction directly into electrical energy that can be used to do useful work (like running an electric motor). The direct chemical redox reaction wastes all of the chemical energy as *heat*—the random thermal motion of the metallic atoms and the ions in solution.

There is another practical difference in the two reactions. In the direct reaction, copper is plated out on the zinc metal as the reaction proceeds, so that after a period of time the zinc atoms get coated with a layer of copper and the reaction slows down and practically stops. In the cell, the reaction can proceed until the cell reaches equilibrium (where the cell voltage is zero). For this reaction, where equilibrium lies far to the right, current would flow until either the Zn anode is practically consumed or until practically all of the Cu^{2+} ions were plated out on the copper cathode.

The Schematic Representation of a Cell   We can always construct, at least in principle, a half-cell that corresponds to a particular redox half-reaction. For example, the redox half-reactions that take place in the Daniell cell are the following:

$$Cu^{2+} + 2e^- \rightarrow Cu(s)$$

$$Zn(s) \rightarrow Zn^{2+} + 2e^-$$

The sum of these two half-reactions gives the net chemical reaction:

$$Zn(s) + Cu^{2+} \rightarrow Zn^{2+} + Cu(s)$$

---

[1] This statement may be regarded as a definition of anode and cathode. The anode is the electrode at which oxidation takes place; the cathode is the electrode at which reduction takes place.

[2] In the wires, electrons are the charge carriers, and the flow of current in a wire consists entirely of a flow of negative charge. Since current is conventionally defined as a flow of positive charge, the conventional current flow is opposite to the electron flow. The movement of an electron in one direction in the wire is equivalent to the movement of a hypothetical positive charge in the opposite direction.

We will represent such a cell by the following diagram:

$$Zn|ZnSO_4|CuSO_4|Cu$$

in which a vertical bar (|) represents a phase boundary and the dashed vertical bar (¦) represents the boundary between two miscible ionic solutions (a liquid junction). A double dashed vertical bar (‖) will be used to represent a double liquid junction through an intermediate ionic solution called a *salt* bridge. Salt bridges are used to minimize the liquid-junction potential and to prevent mixing of the components of two half-cells.

***Cell Voltage*[3]** The *volt* is the unit of electrical potential, or driving force. The product of the voltage × the charge of the electron, e^-, is a measure of the work done when this unit electric charge is transferred from one substance to another. *The voltage of a cell—sometimes called its electromotive force or potential—is thus a quantitative value expressing the tendency of the chemical reaction occurring in the cell to take place.* The magnitude of this voltage depends on the relative strengths of the oxidizing and reducing agents used. If the oxidizing agent has an affinity for electrons that is stronger than the tendency of the reducing agent to hold electrons, the electrical potential, or voltage, is correspondingly large.

Standard Electrode Potentials Although we cannot measure a single half-cell potential, we can construct a scale of half-cell potentials by choosing a single *reference* half-cell and measuring the potential of all other half-cells with respect to it. The reference half-cell chosen is based on the half-reaction $2H^+ + 2e^- \rightleftharpoons H_2(g)$. This couple is arbitrarily assigned a potential of zero, so that the total cell voltage is ascribed to the other couple. For example, in a cell composed of the Zn^{2+}/Zn half-reaction and the H^+/H_2 half-reaction, where all species are at unit activity,[4] the potential of the cell is found to be -0.763 V, with the zinc electrode being more negative than the hydrogen electrode. This value, -0.763 V, is called the *standard electrode*

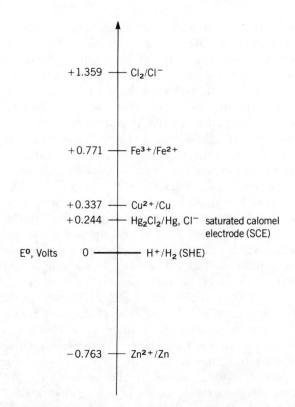

FIGURE 30-2
On the potential scale, the H^+/H_2 half-reaction is arbitrarily assigned the value zero. The zinc electrode has a voltage of -0.76 V measured against the hydrogen electrode. This value is assigned as the standard electrode potential of the Zn^{2+}/Zn couple. This procedure is analogous to measuring elevation from sea level (rather than from the center of the earth), with sea level being assigned zero in the scale of elevation. The saturated calomel electrode (SCE) is more often used as a practical reference electrode (see text).

potential for the Zn^{2+}/Zn couple (see Figure 30-2). All standard electrode potentials are the values of voltage obtained when all substances in solution are present at unit activity (approximately 1 M), all gases are at unit fugacity (approximately 1 atm pressure), and the temperature is at a fixed, convenient value, usually 25°C (see Table B-10, Appendix B).

The Standard Hydrogen Electrode (SHE) and Practical Reference Electrodes A practical hydrogen reference electrode is shown in Figure 30-3, but it is not possible to construct a standard hydrogen electrode (SHE) whose composition corresponds to the arbitrarily chosen reference state.[5] The reason for this is that the choice of the standard

---

[3] The voltmeter used to measure the cell voltage must draw only a small current from the cell, in order not to load the cell and change the concentrations at the electrode surface. The cell voltage under load will be smaller than the open-circuit voltage.

[4] The activity of an ion in solution is usually less than the molar concentration because of ionic interactions. It may be crudely thought of as the "effective concentration."

[5] See T. Biegler and R. Woods, "The Standard Hydrogen Electrode—A Misrepresented Concept," *J. Chem. Educ.* **50,** 604 (1973); and O. Robbins, Jr., "The Proper Definition of Standard EMF," *J. Chem. Educ.* **48,** 737 (1971).

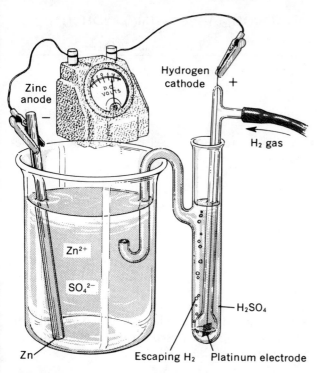

FIGURE 30-3
Hydrogen gas, adsorbed on the platinum electrode and in contact with 1 M H^+, forms the reference half-cell. When this half-cell is coupled with a Zn electrode in contact with 1 M Zn^{2+} to form the cell $(Pt)|H_2|H^+ \;||\; Zn^{2+}|Zn$, the meter indicates that the zinc electrode is more negative than the hydrogen electrode. The cell voltage will not be the same as the theoretical $E°$ (−0.76 V versus SHE for the Zn^{2+}/Zn half-reaction) because of activity and junction-potential effects.

state for an electrolyte is a solution with a concentration that is 1 molal and in which the ionic activity coefficient is also equal to unity. The standard state thus corresponds to a *hypothetical* solution (one that cannot be made in the laboratory), because the activity coefficients of real solutions are usually less than 1 for 1 molal solutions. In order to obtain a standard electrode potential (E^0), we extrapolate measured cell voltages to conditions that correspond to the standard reference state. This procedure is too cumbersome for everyday measurements, so in practice we measure cell potentials versus reference half-cells whose potentials have been very accurately determined with respect to the SHE. The saturated calomel electrode (SCE) is a popular reference electrode based on the half-reaction

$$Hg_2Cl_2(s) + 2e^- \rightarrow 2Hg(l) + 2Cl^-(\text{sat. KCl})$$

$$Hg|Hg_2Cl_2(s)|\text{sat. KCl}\|$$

$$E = 0.244 \text{ V versus SHE at } 25°C$$

One form of the saturated calomel electrode is shown in Figure 22-1 of Experiment 22. The saturated KCl electrolyte reduces liquid-junction potentials to a small and reproducible value (a few millivolts or less). Half-cell potentials measured versus the saturated calomel electrode are easily converted to the standard hydrogen electrode scale by adding +0.244 V (see Figure 30-2).

Calculating the Standard Potential of an Electrochemical Cell When two half-cells are combined to make an electrochemical cell, the standard E^0 of the cell will equal the difference of the standard half-cell potentials of the two redox couples. For example, the E^0 for the electrochemical cell formed from the half-cell couples Zn^{2+}/Zn and Cl_2/Cl^- is +2.122 V. Note that this is just the difference between the two standard half-cell potentials on the scale of redox potentials shown in Figure 30-2. The net reaction that occurs when the cell operates spontaneously is

$$Zn(s) + Cl_2(g) \rightarrow Zn^{2+} + 2Cl^-$$

Electrode Potentials and the Principle of Le Châtelier

The Effect of Concentration We have observed that the tendency for an oxidation-reduction reaction to take place is measured by the voltage created when the reaction takes place in an electrochemical cell. Thus, the electromotive force of 2.122 V created by the cell in the preceding paragraph, for the reaction

$$Zn(s) + Cl_2(g) \rightleftharpoons Zn^{2+} + 2Cl^-$$

will be attained when the reactants and products are in their standard states.

According to Le Châtelier's principle, and in accord with observed fact, an increase in the concentration (or pressure) of chlorine gas, $Cl_2(g)$, will increase the voltage of the cell. Conversely, an increase in the concentration of zinc ion, or of chloride ion, will favor the reverse process and therefore decrease the voltage.

The Nernst Equation Walther Nernst (1864–1941) introduced in 1889 the well-known equation that expresses the quantitative relationship between the voltage of a cell and the concentrations of the reactants and products,

$$E = E^0 - \frac{2.3RT}{nF} \log Q$$

where E is the measured voltage of the cell, E^0 is the standard potential as calculated from the standard electrode potentials of the half-reactions, R is the gas constant ($8.314 \ J \cdot mol^{-1} \cdot K^{-1}$), T is the temperature (K), n is the number of moles of electrons transferred per mole of net chemical reaction, F is the number of coulombs per mole of electrons (96,487), and Q is the product of the activities of the reaction products divided by the product of the activities of the reactants, the activity of each substance being raised to a power equal to its coefficient in the net chemical reaction. (The expression for Q is formulated exactly like the equilibrium constant, K, for the net chemical reaction, but the activities of reactants and products can assume any arbitrary value so that Q is not a constant.) In all of our applications of the Nernst equation, we will make the approximation that the activity coefficients are all equal to 1, replacing *activities* by *molar* concentrations and the *fugacities* of gases by their *pressures* in atmospheres. It is also convenient to remember that

$$\frac{2.3RT}{F} = 0.059 \text{ at } 25°C \text{ (298 K)}$$

Example   In the preceding reaction, we found that

$$Zn(s) + Cl_2(g)(1 \ M) \rightarrow Zn^{2+}(1 \ M) + 2Cl^-(1 \ M)$$

and $E^0 = 2.122$ V. To calculate the corresponding voltage if the $Cl_2(g)$ were at 4.0 atm, the Zn^{2+} were 0.01 M, and the Cl^- remains at 1 M we would write

$$E = E^0 - \frac{0.059}{2} \log \frac{(0.010)(1)^2}{(1)(4.0)} = 2.122 + 0.077$$

$$= 2.199 \text{ V}$$

Both the increase in the $Cl_2(g)$ pressure and the decrease in the Zn^{2+} concentration have a modest effect in increasing the voltage of the cell.

Calculating an Equilibrium Constant by Measuring the Voltage of an Electrochemical Cell

Electrochemical cells can be used to determine the equilibrium constant of chemical reactions. As an example of this let's consider a cell composed of the following half-reactions.

$$Cu(OH)_2(s) + 2e^- \rightarrow Cu(s) + 2OH^-(1M)$$

$$\underline{Cu(s) \rightarrow Cu^{2+}(1M) + 2e^-}$$

$$Cu(OH)_2(s) \rightarrow Cu^{2+}(1M) + 2OH^-(1M)$$

$$\text{(net cell reaction)} \quad (1)$$

We can represent the cell by the following schematic diagram:

$$Cu|Cu^{2+}(1M)|OH^-(1M)|Cu(OH)_2(s)|Cu \quad (2)$$

The voltage of the cell is given by the Nernst equation.

$$E_{cell} = E^0 - \frac{2.3RT}{nF} \log Q \quad (3)$$

Because $Q = 1$ for the cell represented by Equation (1) (neglecting activity coefficients), Equation (3) will reduce to $E_{cell} = E^0$.

$$Q = [Cu^{2+}][OH^-]^2 = (1)(1)^2 = 1 \quad (4)$$

$$\text{If} \quad Q = 1 \quad \text{then} \quad \log Q = 0 \quad (5)$$

Then

$$E = E^0 \quad (6)$$

If the cell is allowed to operate spontaneously, E_{cell} will gradually decrease until it reaches zero. At this point the chemical reaction has reached equilibrium and $Q = K_{eq}$, the equilibrium constant for the chemical reaction. Therefore, at equilibrium we can rewrite Equation (3) as

$$E_{cell} = 0 = E^0 - \frac{2.3RT}{nF} \log K_{eq} \quad (7)$$

which we can rearrange to

$$\log K_{eq} = \frac{E^0}{2.3RT/nF} = \frac{nE^0}{0.059} \quad (8)$$

where we have introduced the constant $2.3RT/F = 0.059$ at 25°C. This gives the interesting result that the equilibrium constant for the net chemical reaction of the cell can be calculated if we know E^0 for the cell.

For the chemical reaction of the cell we have described, the equilibrium constant is the solubility product constant, K_{sp}, for the dissociation of $Cu(OH)_2(s)$ in aqueous solution.

EXPERIMENTAL PROCEDURE

Special Supplies: Voltmeter (see following note); 9-cm lengths of 13-mm-OD glass tubing, lightly fire-polished on both ends (see Figure 30-4); cellulose dialysis tubing (cut in 3- × 3-cm pieces and stored in water 24 h before use); 12- to 15-mm lengths of $\frac{1}{2}$-in.-ID by $\frac{1}{16}$-in.-wall-thickness polyvinyl chloride (Tygon) tubing; wire or 0.5- × 10-cm strips of Cu, Zn, and Fe metal (or a large iron nail) for use as metal electrodes; 10-cm length of 20- to 22-gauge platinum or gold wire (or 0.6- × 10-cm graphite rods) for use as inert electrodes.

Chemicals: 1.0 M $Cu(NO_3)_2$, 0.10 M $Cu(NO_3)_2$, 0.10 M $Zn(NO_3)_2$, 0.10 M $FeSO_4$ (freshly prepared and stored over iron nails or powder), 0.10 M $FeCl_3$, 1 M KNO_3, Br_2 water (saturated solution), 0.10 M KBr, 0.05 M I_2 in methanol, 0.10 M KI, 6 M NH_3, 2 M Na_2S, 1 M NaOH.

NOTE For the voltage measurements in this experiment, a voltmeter with internal resistance of at least 20,000 ohms/V is recommended. The measured voltage will then approach the open-circuit voltage as only a small current (50 μA or less) will be drawn from the cell. A vacuum-tube voltmeter (or its solid-state equivalent) is even better.

For the construction of the cells in this experiment, the use of glass tubes closed with cellulose dialysis tubing is preferred. These are constructed as shown in Figure 30-4 and as described in part 1, and their use is illustrated in Figure 30-5. They are inexpensive, easily renewed, and require only a small volume of solution.

The simple classic arrangement employing two beakers or test tubes to hold the half-cells and an inverted U-tube salt bridge is also satisfactory. The salt bridge is conveniently filled with 1 M KNO_3 or NH_4NO_3 in a 1% agar gel. The resistance of a 5-mm-ID bridge made in this way is about 1,000 ohms, satisfactory for use with a voltmeter whose

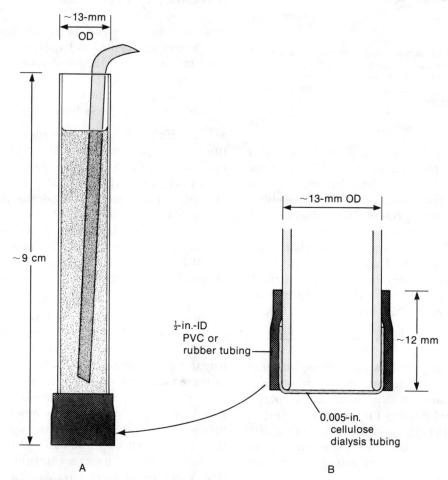

FIGURE 30-4
(A) A method of making simple metal/metal ion half-cells. (B) Detail of the construction of the ion-permeable junction.

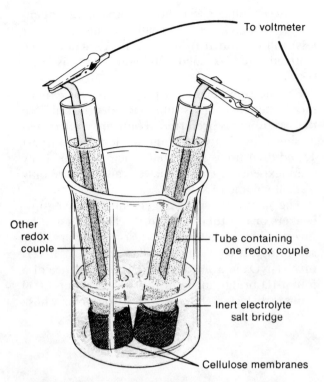

To voltmeter

Other
redox
couple

Tube containing
one redox couple

Inert electrolyte
salt bridge

Cellulose membranes

FIGURE 30-5
A simple way to make an electrochemical cell. The two redox
couples are contained in half-cell tubes closed with cellulose
membranes permeable to water and ions, but gross mixing of
the solutions is prevented. Electrical contact in solution is provided by the inert electrolyte salt bridge.

internal resistance is at least 20,000 ohms/V. If a
vacuum-tube voltmeter is used, a 50-fold higher
salt-bridge resistance could be tolerated, but it is
best to keep the cell resistance as low as possible.

An alternate arrangement, recommended in
previous editions of this manual, employs a porous
porcelain cup (3 in. tall and 1 in. in diameter),
containing one half-cell. This is placed in a 150-
mL beaker containing the other half-cell. Although
easy to use, these cups are rather expensive and
are difficult to clean when inadvertently clogged
with precipitates.

In part 1 of this experiment you will measure the
potentials of several cells composed of redox couples that you studied in Experiment 29. In part 2
you will relate Le Châtelier's principle to the effect
of concentration changes on the voltage of a cell.
In part 3 you will calculate a value for the K_{sp} of
$Cu(OH)_2$ from the measured voltage of the cell
represented by Equation (2).

Before beginning the experiments, it is necessary
to put cellulose on seven half-cell tubes if this has

not already been done. (See Figure 30-4.) Take a
3- × 3-cm piece of dialysis tubing, which has been
stored in water to keep it flexible, and center it
over the end of the tube. Soften a 12- to 15-mm
length of $\frac{1}{2}$-in.-ID Tygon tubing in hot water and
work it between your fingers until it is pliable.
Then force the tubing over the cellulose until it is
about two thirds of the way on. Now use a razor
blade to trim away excess cellulose around the top
of the tubing and slide the tubing the rest of the
way on. At the end of this operation, the cellulose
should be stretched tightly and wrinkle free across
the end of the tube. Fill the tubes with water to
check for leaks (no water should drip through, but
the membrane should be moist since water can
diffuse through it). Store the tubes in water until
you are ready to use them. When you are through
with them at the end of the laboratory period,
rinse them out and store them in water.

1. Standard Cell Potentials

In your report, rewrite the redox potential series
for the couples studied in Experiment 29 (it is part
6—Summary of the Data—of your report for that
experiment). By referring to Appendix B, Table
B-10, also enter the standard electrode potential
(E^0) of each couple you have listed.

M^{2+}/M Half-cells   For the experimental part of
this section, prepare half-cells for Cu, Zn, and Fe
by filling three half-cell tubes about three-quarters
full of 0.1 M $Cu(NO_3)_2$, 0.1 M $Zn(NO_3)_2$, and 0.1
M $FeSO_4$, and placing electrodes of the appropriate metal in each of the three half-cells. (Sandpaper
the electrodes to clean them if necessary. A large
iron nail, cleaned by immersion in a test tube of 6
M HCl, then rinsed, may be used for the iron
electrode.)

A Simple Daniell Cell: $Zn|Zn(NO_3)_2\|Cu(NO_3)_2|Cu$
To make a simple Daniell cell, place the Zn^{2+}/Zn
and Cu^{2+}/Cu half-cells you have made in a 150-
mL beaker containing 25 mL of 1 M KNO_3, which
functions as a salt bridge (see Figure 30-5). Which
of these two metals will give up its electrons more
readily? To determine the answer, connect the
metal electrodes by means of copper wire connec-
tors to the voltmeter, first with both half-cells in
the beaker, then with one half-cell removed from
the beaker. Read the meter carefully to the nearest
0.01 V, noting which electrode carries the negative
charge. (As further proof of this polarity, recall
the comparative behavior of Zn metal in Cu^{2+}

solution, and of Cu metal in Zn^{2+} solution, from Experiment 29, part 1 of the Experimental Procedure.) Explain fully all aspects of the operation of the Daniell cell, and complete a diagram of this cell in your report sheet. Be sure you understand the following: (a) What constitutes the electric current in the wire? (b) What constitutes the electric current in the solution? (c) Why must there be actual contact of the two solutions? (d) What are the chemical reactions at each electrode?

In the same manner, put the appropriate pairs of half-cells in the beaker to form the following cells:

$$Fe|FeSO_4 \| Cu(NO_3)_2|Cu$$

$$Zn|Zn(NO_3)_2 \| FeSO_4|Fe$$

Measure and record the voltage of each cell, noting carefully which electrode is positive. Save the $Zn^{2+}|Zn$ and $Cu^{2+}|Cu$ half-cells for later use.

Nonmetal Half-cells When both the oxidized and reduced form of the redox couple are water soluble, electrical contact is made by placing an inert electrode in the solution to conduct electrons to and from the external circuit. A gold or platinum wire or a graphite rod is most often used. (Graphite is somewhat porous, and this presents a problem if the electrode is to be transferred from one solution to another, because it is difficult to rinse out solution that has entered the pores.) Prepare in three small beakers or test tubes the following solutions, which contain equimolar amounts of the oxidized and reduced forms of the redox couple:

5 mL Br_2 water (sat. sol.) + 5 mL 0.1 M KBr

5 mL 0.1 M $FeCl_3$ + 5 mL 0.1 M $FeSO_4$

5 mL 0.05 M I_2 in methanol + 5 mL 0.1 M KI

(The last mixture is essentially 0.025 M in I_3^- and 0.025 M in I^-, because I_2 reacts almost quantitatively with an excess of I^- to form I_3^-.)

Now pour about 7 mL of each mixture into separate half-cell tubes. A half-cell is completed by inserting an inert electrode, preferably a gold or platinum wire. In the same way as before, a complete cell is formed by placing two half-cells in a 150-mL beaker containing 25 mL of 1 M KNO_3.

Working in this fashion, measure and record the voltages of the following cells, being sure to note which electrode is positive:

$$Au|Br_2, KBr \| Zn(NO_3)_2|Zn$$

$$Au|FeCl_3, FeSO_4 \| Zn(NO_3)_2|Zn$$

$$Au|KI_3, KI \| Zn(NO_3)_2|Zn$$

Use the same gold wire for each half-cell in turn, rinsing it in water between each measurement.

For all six cells for which you made measurements, compare the voltage of each cell (including the sign) with that calculated by combining the E^0's of the two half-cells that constitute the cell. In each case, the E^0 of a cell is obtained by algebraically subtracting one half-cell E^0 from the other. (Why is it necessary to subtract one E^0 from the other?) You will probably notice that the measured cell voltage is not precisely equal to the calculated E^0 for the cell. In your report, suggest two or three reasons why this might be so.

2. The Effect of Concentration

Place 50 mL of 0.1 M $Cu(NO_3)_2$ (or $CuSO_4$) in a 150-mL beaker along with a copper electrode. Also place the $Zn^{2+}|Zn$ half-cell you saved from part 1 in the beaker and connect the electrodes to a voltmeter. Read and record the voltage, then add with stirring about 5 mL of 6 M NH_3 to the Cu^{2+} solution until the deep blue $Cu(NH_3)_4^{2+}$ complex ion is obtained, thus reducing the concentration of $Cu(H_2O)_4^{2+}$. Read and record the voltage. Further reduce the concentration of $Cu(H_2O)_4^{2+}$ by adding, while stirring, an excess (10 mL) of 2 M Na_2S. Again read and record the voltage. Interpret the changes you observe in terms of the Le Châtelier principle.

3. Calculating an Equilibrium Constant from a Cell Voltage Measurement

Place 50 mL of 1.0 M NaOH and a clean copper strip in a 100-mL beaker. Add 5 drops of 1.0 M $Cu(NO_3)_2$ to form a precipitate of $Cu(OH)_2$ and stir the solution. Fill a half-cell tube (like that shown in Figure 30-4) about two-thirds full of 1.0 M $Cu(NO_3)_2$ and place a clean copper electrode in the tube. Place the tube in the beaker containing the precipitate of $Cu(OH)_2$, connect the voltmeter to the copper strips, and record the voltage. Which electrode is the positive electrode?

Because the concentrations of all the reactants and products in the cell are 1 M, the cell voltage will be equal to E^0_{cell}, neglecting activity coefficients. (Remember that the activity of a pure solid is defined to be 1.)

From Equation (8) you can calculate K_{sp}, the equilibrium constant for the reaction

$$Cu(OH)_2(s) \rightleftharpoons Cu^{2+}(aq) + 2OH^-(aq)$$

In using Equation (8) you must know the value of n and the magnitude and sign of E^0_{cell}. What is the value of n that appears in the half-reactions that are summed to give Equation (1)? The cell diagram is shown in Equation (2). By convention the cell voltage, E_{cell}, is defined as the potential of the right-hand electrode (the Cu strip dipping in 1 M OH^-) measured with respect to the left-hand electrode. If the right-hand electrode is the negative electrode, E_{cell} is negative. As defined by this convention, is the E^0_{cell} you measured positive or negative?

EXPERIMENTAL DATA

1. Standard Cell Potentials

A Simple Daniell Cell

Complete the diagram at the right by writing in the formulas for the composition of the electrodes and of the ions in the solutions. Place these formulas near the appropriate arrows leading into the solutions. Also indicate which electrode is the anode and which electrode is the cathode at the top.

What constitutes an electric current in a wire?

_____

Indicate the direction of these particles by drawing an arrow over each wire.

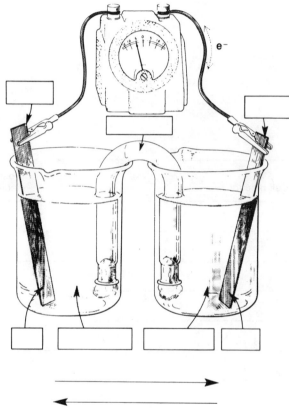

What constitutes an electric current in a solution?

_____

Indicate the direction of movement of these particles in the solution by placing their formulas on the proper arrow below the sketch.

Why must there be actual contact of the two solutions?

_____

Write the half-reaction taking place at the cathode.

_____

Write the half-reaction taking place at the anode.

_____

Write the total cell reaction.

_____

Give the experimental voltage for this cell. _____

_____

In the left-hand column on the right, rewrite the potential series for the couples studied in part 1 of the Experimental Procedure. In the right-hand column, enter the standard electrode potential for each, as obtained from Table B-10 in Appendix B. In the space below, calculate the E^0 for each cell whose voltage you measured in part 1 of the experiment. Write the calculated values in the table below. Also write the equation for each cell reaction measured in part 1. Indicate which element is the positive electrode and which the negative electrode, and give the experimental and calculated voltages in each case.

Redox series	
Couple	Volts

Cell reaction	Positive electrode	Negative electrode	Experimental voltage	Calculated voltage

Suggest two or three reasons why the measured cell voltage and calculated E^0 values might not be the same.

2. The Effect of Concentration

Record your observed voltages, and write net ionic equations for the reactions, first in NH_3, and then of Na_2S with Cu^{2+}.

Initial voltage _____

Voltage with
   NH_3 added _____ _____

Voltage with
   Na_2S added _____ _____

Explain the reasons for the effects on the cell voltage you observed when NH_3 and Na_2S were added to the $Cu^{2+}|Cu$ half-cell.

How would you adjust the concentrations of Cu^{2+} and Zn^{2+} in the cell in order to obtain the maximum voltage possible for this cell?

3. Calculating an Equilibrium Constant from a Cell Voltage Measurement

Give the magnitude of the cell voltage and indicate which electrode is positive for the following cell.

Cell voltage _____

$$Cu|Cu^{2+} \ (1M)|OH^- \ (1M)|CU(OH)_2(s)|Cu$$

Calculate log K_{sp} (and K_{sp}) using Equation (8) and your cell voltage data.

$$\log K_{sp} =$$

$$K_{sp} \ =$$

Compare your calculated value with the value for K_{sp} of $Cu(OH)_2$ given in Table B-9, Appendix B.

Suggest reasons why the value of K_{sp} that you calculated might be much larger than the equilibrium value given in Table B-9.

Electrochemical Cells and Electrolysis

Faraday's Laws

Corrosion and Passivation

PURPOSE

To observe the chemical effects produced by passing current through a cell, including the anodization of aluminum and electrochemical machining. To understand Faraday's laws, which summarize the chemical effects of passing current through a cell. To observe how an oxide layer on aluminum can provide protection against corrosion and how this protection is removed when the oxide layer is prevented from forming.

PRE-LAB PREPARATION

As we saw earlier, an electrochemical cell is a device used to separate the reactants in a chemical reaction in such a way that the electrons are transferred from one reactant to another through an external circuit rather than by direct mixing of the reactants. We will call the cell *self-driven* if the chemical reaction proceeds spontaneously, creating a current flow in the external circuit. A self-driven electrochemical cell converts the energy of a chemical reaction into electrical energy.

This process can be reversed in a *driven* electrochemical cell. That is, current can be forced to flow through a cell by using an external power source, such as a battery or dc power supply. This process of *electrolysis* can create new chemical substances that have greater chemical energy than the reactants, thereby "storing" energy. Upon demand this chemical energy can be converted into electrical energy.

The electrolysis of water is a familiar example of a driven cell, using the cell shown in Figure 31-1. Less well known is the fact that chemical energy stored in the electrolysis products (hydrogen and oxygen gases) can be directly converted into electrical energy by means of the self-driven fuel cell[1] shown in Figure 31-2.

---

[1] A *fuel cell* is any electrochemical cell whose net reaction is equivalent to the combustion of the fuel with oxygen.

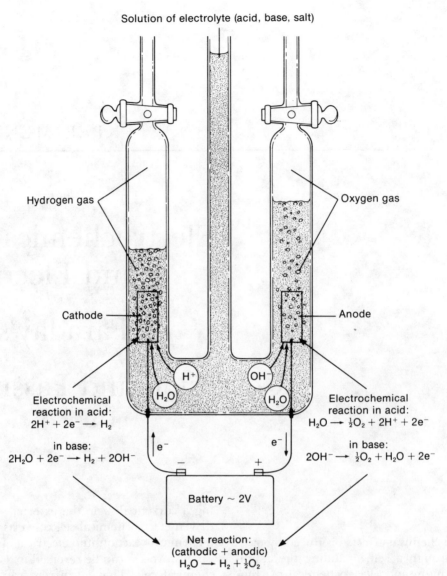

FIGURE 31-1
Production of hydrogen and oxygen by electrolysis of water in a driven cell. [After J. O'M. Bockris and D.M. Drazic, *Electrochemical Science,* Barnes & Noble, New York, Figure 1.1. Copyright © 1972.]

Several important industrial chemicals are produced by electrochemical processes. Chlorine is produced by the electrolysis of brine (NaCl) solution. Aluminum is produced by electrolysis at high temperatures of alumina (Al_2O_3) dissolved in molten cryolite (Na_3AlF_6). In these examples driven cells are used as "substance-producing" devices. Driven cells are also used in electroplating, where a thin metal layer is plated out on a conducting substrate, and in the passivation of metals like aluminum to produce a thin layer of oxide that provides a protective (and decorative) coating.

Anodization of Aluminum

In this experiment we will produce an oxide layer on aluminum by an electrochemical process called *anodization.* In some ways the process of anodizing is the opposite of electroplating. Anodic coatings, which tend to be porous, start on the outside of the surface of the metal and progress inward, but in electroplating the coating begins at the surface and begins to build outward. Anodic coatings are oxides of the metal being treated, whereas electroplated coatings are metallic coatings of a totally

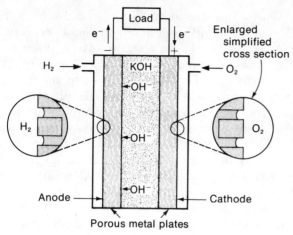

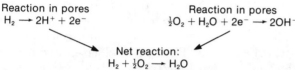

FIGURE 31-2
A scheme for obtaining electrical energy from a self-driven hydrogen-oxygen fuel cell. The net chemical reaction in the cell is equivalent to the combustion of hydrogen. [After J. O'M. Bockris and D.M. Drazic, *Electrochemical Science*, Barnes & Noble, New York, Figure 1.2. Copyright © 1972.]

different metal plated on a base metal. When a metal is to be anodized it is made the anode of the electrolytic cell, whereas a metal to be electroplated must be made the cathode of the cell.

Some metals (including Al, Be, Ti, V, Cr, Ni, and Ta) form oxide coatings that are typically continuous and adherent, thus protecting the underlying metal from corrosion and weathering. By contrast, the oxide layer that forms on iron, which we call *rust*, consists of separated iron oxide crystals that project out of the underlying iron surface and do not cover and protect it from further attack.

Clean aluminum has a stable layer of oxide about 2 nm thick after only a few minutes of exposure to air at room temperature. Oxidation at higher temperatures (350 to 450°C) in air yields surface layers of Al_2O_3 about 40 nm thick. Anodizing aluminum in an electrolyte such as dilute sulfuric acid produces much thicker coatings (10^4 nm). The outer part of the oxide layer will be porous if it is produced at high voltage or at a pH less than 7, as in this experiment. The reactions that take place during the anodization of aluminum in dilute sulfuric acid are given approximately by the following half-reactions. At the anode

$$2Al + 3H_2O \rightarrow Al_2O_3 + 6H^+ + 6e^- \quad (1)$$

At the cathode

$$6e^- + 6H^+ \rightarrow 3H_2 \quad (2)$$

Pure crystalline alumina (Al_2O_3) is an insulator. We are most familiar with alumina in the form of corundum, used as an abrasive, and as the gemstones ruby and sapphire. (A trace of chromium in the alumina gives ruby its red color, while the blue color of sapphire is produced by traces of titanium.) Increasing the thickness of the oxide layer on aluminum requires that electrons (or their vacancies) and ions move through the oxide layer. This is possible because the outer layer is somewhat porous and contains imperfections or defects that allow the ions to move more easily and because the electric field is so intense across the thin, nonporous insulating layer at the surface of the metal.

A properly anodized surface provides excellent protection against further weathering and corrosion. In addition, the more porous outer layer can absorb dyes or pigments, so the aluminum can be given a decorative color that is very durable.

Electrochemical Machining

Electrochemical machining is a less well-known example of the use of a driven cell. Here the object is not to plate out metal, but to remove metal. It is particularly useful for forming intricate shapes in hard metals that are difficult to machine by conventional techniques.

In electrochemical machining a current is passed through an electrolyte between a metal workpiece and a suitably shaped tool. The metal is made the anode and, if conditions are chosen correctly, dissolution of the metal anode will take place, mainly in the region between the metal workpiece and the tool. (See Figure 31-3.) In this experiment

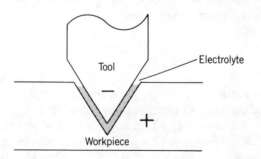

FIGURE 31-3
Electrochemical machining: The metal workpiece dissolves to form a shape complementary to that of the tool.

you will see how you can make a hole through a hard steel razor blade by using only a sharpened, soft pencil, a drop of 6 M HCl, and a dc power supply.

Faraday's Laws and Electrolysis

Michael Faraday (1791–1867) studied the effects of passing current through cells and published his findings in 1833 and 1834. His experimental conclusions have come to be known as Faraday's laws, and paraphrased in modern language they may be stated as follows. (1) The amount of chemical change produced is proportional to the total amount of charge passed through the cell. (2) The passage of an equivalent of electric charge produces an equivalent of chemical change. The quantity of electricity is usually expressed in coulombs, and can be determined experimentally by measuring the rate of flow of electricity (current in amperes, that is, coulombs per second), and multiplying this figure by the time in seconds.

$$\text{coulombs} = \text{amperes} \times \text{seconds} \qquad (3)$$

When a mole of silver (107.870 g) is deposited at a cathode, the half-cell equation

$$Ag^+ + e^- \rightarrow Ag(s) \qquad (4)$$

indicates that an Avogadro's number (6.022×10^{23}) of individual silver ions must be reduced by the same number of electrons—"a mole of electrons." The charge on a mole of electrons is

$$6.0221 \times 10^{23} \text{ electrons} \times 1.6021$$
$$\times 10^{-19} \frac{\text{coulomb}}{\text{electron}} = 96,487 \text{ coulombs} \qquad (5)$$

which is called a *faraday* and given the symbol F. When copper is plated out at the cathode, the half-cell equation

$$Cu^{2+} + 2e^- \rightarrow Cu(s) \qquad (6)$$

shows that 1 mol of electrons (1 faraday) will produce only $\frac{1}{2}$ mol of copper (63.54/2 g).

To summarize, when 1 faraday (96,487 coulombs of charge) is passed through a cell, chemical change equivalent to transfer of 1 mol of electrons (oxidation at the anode and reduction at the cathode) occurs at each electrode. This quantity of material is called 1 *electrochemical equivalent*.

Only a few electrochemical reactions are known that give a simple well-defined reaction conforming exactly to Faraday's laws. More often, an electrochemical reaction is complex, yielding several products. This may occur when more than one electron transfer reaction takes place on the electrode or when the primary products are very reactive in some side reaction. Electrochemists use the term *current efficiency* or *yield* and define these terms as the percentage of total charge that is effective in producing the desired substance. It was just these effects that made it difficult to discover these laws, which may seem self-evident to students already familiar with atomic theory. But in 1834, no modern theories of atomic structure, chemical bonding, or ionization existed, nor was anything known about the existence and properties of electrons. These laws, which eluded many who were studying electricity, should be regarded as a lasting tribute to Faraday's ingenuity and careful experimental work.

Electrochemistry and Corrosion

When it is not desired, the dissolution of a metal is called *corrosion* and much money and effort are spent in preventing or combating it. A simple example of corrosion is the dissolution of a metal in acid, where the redox processes are those shown in Figure 31-4.

Corrosion is a common affliction of automobiles in regions with cold climates, where corrosive salts are spread on the roads to melt ice. One often

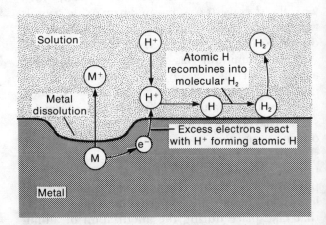

FIGURE 31-4

In corrosion, dissolution of the metal liberates electrons. If these electrons can be taken up by some other electrochemical reaction (like H_2 evolution) the metal continues to dissolve. [After J. O'M. Bockris and D.M. Drazic, *Electrochemical Science*, Barnes & Noble, New York, Figure 1.3. Copyright © 1972.]

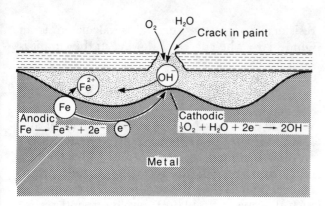

FIGURE 31-5
At a crack in the protective paint, corrosion often develops under the paint. It is the (invisible) part of the steel under the paint that becomes anodic and dissolves. Electron flow in the metal and ionic flow in the corroded area couple the two half-reactions.

observes that corrosion of the steel body is occurring *under* the paint surrounding a hole or crack in the paint that has exposed the steel. This suggests that the corrosion process is primarily electrochemical in nature, two separated half-reactions being mediated by flow of electrons in the steel (see Figure 31-5). Unless the corroded area is cleaned and repainted, corrosion will continue until the metal is rusted through over a large area.

Passivation   Some metals, like aluminum, do not display the chemical reactivity that we might expect from their position in the table of redox potentials (see Appendix B, Table B-10). This is because the surface corrosion of aluminum produces a thin very coherent layer of aluminum oxide, Al_2O_3, that effectively blocks further reaction. This is called *passivation*. If the formation of a coherent oxide layer is prevented by alloying the surface with mercury, aluminum reacts vigorously with oxygen and moisture in the air.

EXPERIMENTAL PROCEDURE

Special Supplies: 6- to 10-V, 1-A dc power supply with connecting leads terminated with alligator clips (Figure 31-6 shows the circuit diagram for a simple homemade power supply that is satisfactory); aluminum foil (heavy duty); 5- $\times$ 1.5-cm strips of heavy aluminum foil (foil of the thickness used in aluminum pie plates and baking dishes is satisfactory); red, green, or yellow Rit fabric dye (a commercial preparation readily available in supermarkets, drug stores, etc.); dc multimeter or voltmeter; soft (No. 2) pencil; pencil sharpener; sandpaper; sharp knife or single-edged razor blade; double-edged razor blade.

Chemicals: 1 M NaOH and methanol mixture (50:50 v:v), 3 M H_2SO_4, 3 M HCl, 1 M NaOH, 6 M HCl, concentrated (12 M) HCl, concentrated (16 M) HNO_3, 0.1 M $HgCl_2$, 0.1 M $CuSO_4$.

Safety Precautions: Sodium hydroxide, sulfuric acid, hydrochloric acid, and nitric acid cause skin and eye burns. Handle with care.

Make all electrical connections before turning the power supply on. Be especially careful not to short the leads of the power supply. The large current drain might damage the power supply.

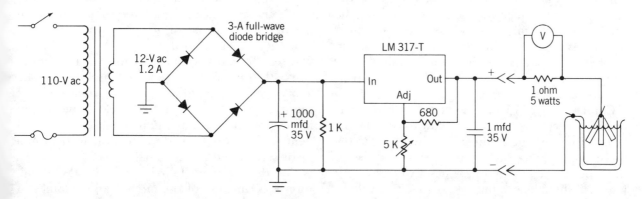

FIGURE 31-6
Circuit diagram for a homemade 1-A adjustable 1- to 10-V dc power supply. The adjustable voltage regulator is a National Semiconductor LM 317-T (Radio Shack Part No. 276-1778). The tab of the regulator must be connected to a heat sink isolated from chassis ground because the tab is connected to V_{out}. The current is measured as the voltage drop across a series 1-ohm resistor, or the 1-ohm resistor and voltmeter can be replaced by an ammeter.

Take great care not to cut yourself when using the knife or single-edge razor blade to cut a notch in the pencil. Lay the pencil flat on the benchtop while cutting the notch.

Mercuric chloride ($HgCl_2$) and cupric sulfate ($CuSO_4$) are poisonous. Try to avoid spilling any $HgCl_2$ or $CuSO_4$ solution on your hands. If you do get the solutions on your hands, wash them immediately.

---

1. *Anodization of Aluminum* Line a 400-mL beaker with a double or triple layer of folded heavy-duty aluminum foil generously cut so that the foil extends about 1 cm above the top of the beaker. This foil lining will be the cathode of the cell. Then cut three 5- × 1.5-cm strips of somewhat heavier aluminum foil (foil cut from disposable aluminum pie plates or baking pans is suitable). The aluminum foil should be clean and shiny. Degrease the foil strips by immersing them for about 30 s in 1 M NaOH and methanol (50:50 v:v), followed by a rinse of deionized water.

Put about 250 mL of 3 M H_2SO_4 in the foil-lined beaker. Make sure that the dc power supply is unplugged and switched off. Overlap the ends of the three strips of aluminum and hold them together as a unit with the alligator clip connected to the wire coming from the positive (red) terminal of the power supply. To assure the most uniform anodizing, fan out the three strips so that the lower halves of the strips do not overlap. Support the wire lead connected to the three strips by using a bit of tape to fasten the wire lead to an iron ring supported by a ring stand. Adjust the height of the iron ring so that the fanned-out strips are about half immersed in the 3 M H_2SO_4 solution. Position the beaker so that the strips are in the center of the beaker and are not touching the aluminum foil lining the beaker. In assembling the apparatus be careful not to immerse the alligator clips or lead wire in the sulfuric acid solution. Only the lower halves of the aluminum strips should be immersed.

Connect the lead from the negative (black) terminal of the power supply to the foil lining the beaker (the cathode of the cell). Then plug in the power supply and switch it on and note and record the time. If the power supply has a voltage adjust knob, it should be adjusted so that the voltage across the cell is about 6 to 10 V dc.

The current flowing in the cell may be determined by measuring the voltage drop across a resistor in series with the cell or by an ammeter in series with the cell. (See Figure 31-6.) If a series resistor is used, the current is calculated from Ohm's law. The current I flowing in the circuit is given by

$$I = E/R \qquad (7)$$

where E is the voltage drop across the resistor and R is the resistance in ohms of the series resistor.

Allow the anodization to proceed for about 15 to 20 min. Periodically record both the current and the time. When the anodization is completed, turn the power supply off, unplug it, and record the time.

While the aluminum is being anodized, a dye bath should be prepared as follows: Place 10 mL of red, green, or yellow Rit brand fabric dye in a 100-mL beaker and add 40 mL of water. Heat the solution to boiling and maintain the temperature of the dye bath near the boiling point. (*Caution:* Overheating will cause the dye solution to foam and boil over.) When the anodizing process is completed, remove the aluminum strips from the sulfuric acid solution, being careful not to touch the anodized surface. Immediately rinse the strips in water and then put *one* of them in the hot dye bath for about 10 min.

While one of the three strips is being dyed, the others are tested chemically. Put a second strip in a 20- × 200-mL test tube and add enough 3 M HCl to completely cover the strip. Place the third strip in another test tube and add enough 1 M NaOH to cover it. Observe both of the strips in the test tubes very carefully and note where tiny bubbles of H_2 first begin to form. Is it on the anodized end or the untreated end? Or at both ends simultaneously? Balance the equations shown in the report form that describe (a) the evolution of H_2 by Al in acidic and basic solution and (b) the amphoteric behavior of Al_2O_3, which dissolves in both acids and bases.

After the first strip has remained 10 min in the dye bath, remove it, rinse it well, and dry it. The anodized area should acquire the bright color of the dye while the unoxidized area should retain its original bright aluminum color. How permanent is the color? Can you wipe it off with a towel or by scratching it with your fingernail?

The thickness of the oxide layer on the aluminum is a function of the number of coulombs of charge passed through the cell. Calculate the number of coulombs from your recorded time of anodization and the current. (If the current changed slightly with time, use an average value for the current.) The number of coulombs is given

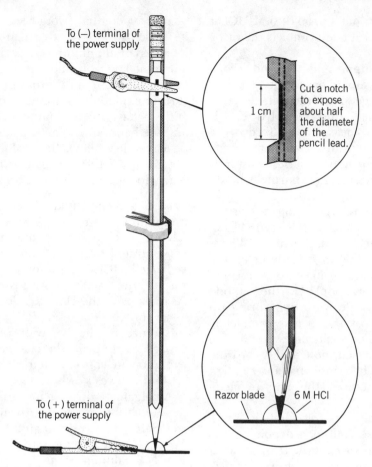

To (−) terminal of
the power supply

1 cm

Cut a notch
to expose
about half
the diameter
of the
pencil lead.

To (+) terminal of
the power supply

Razor blade   6 M HCl

FIGURE 31-7
Setup for making a hole in a razor blade by electrochemical machining using a sharpened No. 2
pencil as the tool.

by multiplying the average current (in amperes) by the time of electrolysis (in seconds).

$$Q \text{ (coulombs)} = I \text{ (A)} \times t \text{ (s)} \qquad (8)$$

Using Faraday's law, calculate the mass of aluminum oxidized, assuming the half-reaction shown in Equation (1). From this value calculate the mass of Al_2O_3 formed. Determine the total anodized area of the three strips. (Don't forget to count both sides of each strip.) Assuming that the film is pure Al_2O_3 and has a density of 4.0 g/cm^3, calculate the thickness of the film.

2. *Electrochemical Machining: Making a Hole in a Razor Blade* Obtain a soft (No. 2) pencil. With a sharp knife or single-edged razor blade cut a notch about 1 cm long near the eraser end of the pencil. Remove enough wood so that about half the diameter of the pencil lead is exposed, allowing

an alligator clip to make a good electrical contact to the pencil lead. (See Figure 31-7.) Then use a pencil sharpener (and sandpaper, if necessary) to make a fine point on the pencil. (If an ohmmeter is available, you can check the resistance between the sharpened tip of the pencil and the notch where the lead is exposed. It should be about 10 to 20 ohms.)

Obtain a double-edged razor blade. Weigh it and record the mass to the nearest 0.1 mg. Make sure that the power supply is unplugged and switched off. Connect the alligator clip coming from the positive (red) terminal of the dc power supply to one end of the razor blade and place the razor blade on a clean paper towel resting on the lab bench.

Clamp the pencil in position so that the pencil point applies enough pressure to force the blade to lie flat. (See Figure 31-7. The natural springiness of the blade provides just the right amount of contact pressure.) Then put a drop of 6 M HCl at the point where the pencil point contacts the razor blade.

Turn on the power supply and note and record the time. If the power supply has a voltage adjust control, adjust the voltage so that the voltage across the pencil and razor blade (the electrolytic cell) is about 6 V. Periodically measure and record the time and current, either with an ammeter or by reading the voltage drop across a series resistor as described in part 1. The current is normally in the range 0.15 to 0.3 A.

While the electrolysis is proceeding, watch the point where the pencil contacts the razor blade. Do you observe bubbles of gas forming? Where does the gas form—on the razor blade or on the tip of the pencil? What gas is likely to be formed on the anode (the razor blade)? On the cathode (the pencil tip)? The blade will often spring up slightly when the tip of the pencil completely pierces the blade. This normally takes 2 to 3 min. As soon as a hole is formed, note and record the time and the current. Then rinse, dry, and reweigh the razor blade to determine the mass of metal that has been removed.

If you have difficulties forming a hole in 2 to 3 min, it may be because your pencil point is too blunt or because of a poor contact. If the contact resistance is too high, the 6 M HCl electrolyte may be boiled away. If this happens, make sure the pencil point is sharp and try again in another spot after cleaning, drying, and reweighing the blade.

Determine the number of coulombs passed by multiplying the average current (in amperes) by the time of electrolysis (in seconds). Assuming the mass lost by the razor blade corresponds to the dissolution of iron according to the reaction

$$Fe \rightarrow Fe^{2+} + 2e^- \qquad (9)$$

calculate the number of coulombs corresponding to the decrease in mass of the razor blade. Then calculate the current efficiency for the dissolution of iron by dividing the coulombs corresponding to the dissolved iron by the total number of coulombs passed (ampere-seconds).

current efficiency (%)

$$= \frac{\text{coulombs to dissolve iron}}{\text{total coulombs passed}} \times 100 \qquad (10)$$

3. Passivation: The Protective Oxide Coating on Aluminum The position of aluminum in the scale

of redox potentials would lead us to believe that it should be more reactive than zinc. The apparent inertness of aluminum is caused by a thin and very adherent layer of oxide, which quickly forms on bare aluminum and protects the surface from further oxidation. In this experiment, we will look at the behavior of aluminum in concentrated acids and the behavior of amalgamated aluminum (that is, a mercury alloy). Since aluminum oxide does not form on the amalgam surface, the intrinsic reactivity of aluminum can be observed.

Procedure   Cut eight pieces of heavy-duty aluminum foil, each about 1×5 cm. Place a strip of Al foil in each of two test tubes. Pour a little concentrated nitric acid into one and a little concentrated HCl into the other. Note whether the rate of the reaction increases or decreases as the Al remains in the HCl. Recall the oxidizing properties of concentrated HNO_3 and explain the difference in the behavior of HCl and HNO_3 toward Al. Explain the change in the rate of H_2 evolution in concentrated HCl with time. (*Hint:* Al_2O_3 dissolves slowly.)

Amalgamate three strips of foil by placing them in a test tube containing 10 mL of 0.1 M $HgCl_2$ (see Safety Precautions) and 2 drops of 6 M HCl. Write an equation describing the reduction of $HgCl_2$ by aluminum in your report. After 4 to 5 min, pour off the mercuric chloride solution and rinse the amalgamated strips with distilled water. Place one of the strips in a test tube containing distilled water, a second in a test tube containing 0.1 M $CuSO_4$, and leave the third exposed to air on a clean paper towel. Use the remaining three strips of untreated aluminum foil as controls by treating them the same way as the amalgamated strips. Warm the four test tubes (two tests and two controls) in a water bath contained in a 250-mL beaker. Record your observations.

BIBLIOGRAPHY

Blatt, R. G., "Anodizing Aluminum," *J. Chem. Educ.* **56,** 268 (1979).

Doeltz, A. E., Tharaud, S., and Sheehan, W. F., "Anodizing Aluminum with Frills," *J. Chem. Educ.* **60,** 156–57 (1983).

Grotz, L. C., and Wollaston, G., "Dyeing of Anodized Aluminum," *J. Chem. Educ.* **60,** 763 (1983).

DeBarr, A. E., and Olivers, D. A. (eds.), *Electrochemical Machining,* American Elsevier Publishing Co., New York, 1968.

REPORT 31	Electrochemical Cells and Electrolysis Faraday's Laws Corrosion and Passivation	NAME	
		SECTION	LOCKER
		INSTRUCTOR	DATE

DATA AND CALCULATIONS

1. Anodization of Aluminum

Record the initial time and current and the time and current at 3-min intervals during the anodization.

Time	Current (A)
______	______
______	______
______	______
______	______
______	______
______	______
______	______

Record your observations of the experiments using the three anodized aluminum strips.

First strip immersed in dye

Second strip immersed in 3 M HCl

Third strip immersed in 1 M NaOH

Balance the following equations, which show (a) the evolution of H_2 by aluminum in acidic solution:

$$Al + \quad H_3O^+ \rightarrow \quad H_2 + \quad Al^{3+} + \quad H_2O$$

and basic solution:

$$Al + \quad OH^- + \quad H_2O \rightarrow \quad H_2 + \quad Al(OH)_4^-$$

(b) the amphoteric behavior of Al_2O_3, which dissolves in both acids and bases:

$$\text{Acid solution} \quad Al_2O_3 + \quad H_3O^+ \rightarrow \quad Al^{3+} + \quad H_2O$$

$$\text{Basic solution} \quad Al_2O_3 + \quad OH^- + \quad H_2O \rightarrow \quad Al(OH)_4^-$$

Calculate the number of coulombs of charge passed during the anodization of the aluminum using Equation (8). (Use the average current over the measured time of anodization.)

$$Q \text{ (coulombs)} =$$

Using Faraday's law, calculate the mass of aluminum oxidized and the mass of Al_2O_3 formed, assuming the half-reaction shown in Equation (1).

$$\text{g Al} =$$

$$\text{g } Al_2O_3 =$$

Measure the total anodized area (in square centimeters) of the three strips. (Don't forget to count the front and back of the strips.) Assuming that the film is pure Al_2O_3 and has a density of 4.0 g/cm^3, calculate the thickness of the film in centimeters.

2. Electrochemical Machining: Making a Hole in a Razor Blade

This experiment is short and it is suggested that you run three trials, recording the mass of the razor blade before and after each run. Also record the initial time and current and time and current at 1-min intervals during the course of the electrolysis.

Data	Trial 1	Trial 2	Trial 3
Mass of the razor blade			
Final mass	_____ g	_____ g	_____ g
Initial mass	_____ g	_____ g	_____ g
Net mass loss	_____ g	_____ g	_____ g

	Trial 1		Trial 2		Trial 3	
Time	Current	Time	Current	Time	Current	
___	___	___	___	___	___	
___	___	___	___	___	___	
___	___	___	___	___	___	
___	___	___	___	___	___	
___	___	___	___	___	___	

Closely observe the razor blade and pencil point during the electrolysis and record your observations. At which electrode do bubbles of gas form?

What gas is likely to be formed at the anode? at the cathode?

Calculate the number of coulombs of charge passed during the electrolysis using Equation (8). (Use the average value of the current.)

	Trial 1	Trial 2	Trial 3
Q (coulombs)	_____	_____	_____

Calculate the number of coulombs of charge corresponding to the decrease in mass of the razor blade, assuming that it is pure iron. Use Faraday's law and assume that the reaction is that shown in Equation (9).

Trial 1 Q (coulombs) =

Trial 2 Q (coulombs) =

Trial 3 Q (coulombs) =

Calculate the percentage current efficiency for each trial, using Equation (10).

Trial 1 Current efficiency (%) =

Trial 2 Current efficiency (%) =

Trial 3 Current efficiency (%) =

3. Passivation: The Protective Oxide Coating on Aluminum

Summarize below your observations when aluminum foil is treated with concentrated nitric and hydrochloric acids.

Write an equation describing the reduction of mercuric chloride, $HgCl_2$, by aluminum. _____

Summarize your observations when amalgamated aluminum foil is treated with water, 0.1 M $CuSO_4$, and air. How are the controls affected by the same treatment? Write equations for any reactions that occur.

QUESTIONS

1. Why does the dye adhere strongly to the anodized portion of the aluminum strip, but not at all to the aluminum surface where it was not anodized?

2. All of the coulombs of charge passed in an electrolysis must be accounted for by some chemical reaction. Suggest reasons why the calculated current efficiency in drilling a hole through a razor blade is less than 100%. Write balanced chemical reactions to account for the side reactions.

3. Why do you suppose that iron continues to oxidize (rust) until the iron is completely converted to iron oxide, whereas aluminum oxidation ceases after a thin layer of oxide forms?

Redox Titrations

The Oxidizing Capacity
of a Household Cleanser
or Liquid Bleach

PURPOSE

To show how a redox reaction (the oxidation of iodide ion to iodine) can be used for the quantitative determination of the total amount of oxidizing agent in household cleansers and liquid hypochlorite bleaches.

PRE-LAB PREPARATION

Oxidation-reduction reactions, like acid-base reactions, are widely used as the basis for the analytical determination of substances by titration.[1] In a volumetric titration, a known volume of the *titrant*, usually contained in a buret, is added to the substance being determined, called the *titrand*.

___

[1] Techniques of volumetric analysis are described in the section "Volumetric Measurement of Liquids" in the Introduction.

The conditions needed for redox titrations are the same as for any titration: The reaction between the titrant and the titrand must be rapid, stoichiometric, and quantitative; that is, the equilibrium must greatly favor the products. In addition to these basic requirements, the titrant solution must be stable, and there must be some means of determining its concentration accurately. Finally, some means of detecting the end point of the titration reaction must be available.

Oxidizing and Reducing Agents

Oxidizing agents available in pure form, such as $K_2Cr_2O_7$, may be weighed out directly to form a titrant solution of known concentration. Potassium permanganate and cerium(IV) salts are often used as oxidizing agents, but they are not pure enough to be weighed out directly, and ordinarily we must titrate them against reducing substances of known high purity (such as As_2O_3) to determine their concentrations accurately. This process is called *standardization*.

The redox potentials of several commonly used oxidizing agents are shown as follows:

$$E^0 \text{ (V)}$$

$$Ce^{4+} + e^- \rightleftharpoons Ce^{3+} \qquad +1.61$$

$$MnO_4^- + 8H^+ + 5e^- \rightleftharpoons$$
$$Mn^{2+} + 4H_2O \qquad +1.51$$

$$Cr_2O_7^{2-} + 14H^+ + 6e^- \rightleftharpoons$$
$$2Cr^{3+} + 7H_2O \qquad +1.33$$

$$I_2(aq) + 2e^- \rightleftharpoons 2I^- \qquad +0.54$$

Cerium(IV) is one of the strongest oxidizing agents available for use as a titrant, and its solutions are very stable. However, it is more expensive than either potassium permanganate, $KMnO_4$, or potassium dichromate, $K_2Cr_2O_7$. Iodine is a rather weak oxidizing agent and is most often used in indirect procedures in which iodide ion is first oxidized to iodine and then the iodine is titrated with sodium thiosulfate solution.

Most strong reducing agents are easily oxidized by the oxygen in the air. Therefore, they are not often employed as titrants. However, they are commonly employed in analysis to reduce a substance to a lower oxidation state before it is titrated with a standard solution of an oxidizing agent. Reducing agents of moderate strength, whose solutions are stable, also exist. One of these is sodium thiosulfate, $Na_2S_2O_3$, which is most often used to titrate I_2.

End-Point Detection in Redox Titrations

The most general methods of detecting the end points in a redox titration are like those used in acid-base titrations. When both the oxidized and reduced species are soluble in solution (as MnO_4^-/Mn^{2+}, for example), an inert platinum or gold electrode will respond to the redox potential of the system provided that the electron transfer processes at the electrode surface are reasonably fast, so that the equilibrium potential is established. Such an inert electrode may be used in conjunction with a suitable reference electrode in much the same way that the glass electrode is used in acid-base titrations. At the end point of the titration,

an abrupt change, of about several hundred millivolts, usually takes place in the redox potential of the system, and a voltmeter can be used to detect the change. Such a titration is called a *potentiometric redox titration*.

Redox indicators are available that function like acid-base indicators except that they respond to changes in the redox potential of the system rather than to changes in the hydrogen ion concentration. For example, the redox indicator *ferroin* is red in its reduced form, at potentials of less than $+1.12$ V. In titrations in which strong oxidizing agents, such as cerium(IV), are used, the potential jumps abruptly at the end point to potentials of greater than $+1.12$ V, and the indicator changes to its oxidized form, which is blue in color.

In some titrations, a titrant or the substance titrated acts as its own indicator. For example, the permanganate ion, MnO_4^-, is a very deep reddish-purple color, whereas the reduced product of its reaction with reducing agents in acid solution is the colorless manganese(II) ion, Mn^{2+}. Solutions titrated with standard MnO_4^- are usually colorless until the end point, then turn pink when no reducing species are left to react with the added MnO_4^-. Conversely, in the titration of iodine solutions with standard thiosulfate, $S_2O_3^{2-}$, the solutions are brown or yellow until the end point is reached, then become colorless when all of the iodine is titrated. (Also, in these titrations, starch—which forms an intense blue with I_2 and I^-—is added just before the end point, making the end point sharper and easier to detect.)

Redox Titration of the Oxidizing Agents in a Household Cleanser or Liquid Bleach

In this experiment, we will make use of two oxidation-reduction reactions to determine the oxidizing capacity of a household cleanser. To a solution containing the sample of cleanser will be added an unmeasured excess of KI, in acid solution. Oxidizing agents contained in the cleanser, such as sodium hypochlorite, oxidize the iodide ion to iodine according to the following reaction.

$$E^0 \text{ (V)}$$

$$HClO(aq) + H^+ + 2e^- \rightleftharpoons Cl^- + H_2O \qquad +1.49$$

$$2I^- \rightleftharpoons I_2 + 2e^- \qquad -0.54$$

$$HClO(aq) + H^+ + 2I^- \rightleftharpoons$$
$$I_2 + Cl^- + H_2O \qquad +0.95$$

The iodine produced in the solution will then be determined by titration with a standardized thiosulfate solution, which reduces iodine stoichiometrically according to the following reaction.

$$\begin{array}{lr} & E^0 \text{ (V)} \\ 2S_2O_3^{2-} \rightleftharpoons S_4O_6^{2-} + 2e^- & -0.09 \\ \underline{I_2 + 2e^- \rightleftharpoons 2I^-} & \underline{+0.54} \\ 2S_2O_3^{2-} + I_2 \rightleftharpoons 2I^- + S_4O_6^{2-} & +0.45 \end{array}$$

Even though the method is indirect, only one standard solution is required.

Establishing the End Point in the Iodine-Thiosulfate Titration

Starch (amylose) forms an intense blue-black complex with traces of iodine, I_2, in the presence of iodide ion, I^-; I_2 reacts with I^- to form the triiodide ion, I_3^-. This complex ion has a linear structure (I–I–I^-) that fits nicely into the helically coiled starch molecule, as shown in Figure 32-1. The formation of the starch-I_3^- complex is reversible (as is the formation of the deep blue color), and may be used as a sensitive indicator for traces of iodine in solution.

$$\text{starch} + I_2 + I^- \rightleftharpoons \underset{\text{blue}}{(\text{starch-}I_3^- \text{ complex})}$$

Iodine in concentrations as low as 10^{-6} M can be detected, provided that the concentration of iodide ion is 10^{-3} M or greater. Most iodine-containing solutions are titrated with standard thiosulfate to the disappearance of the blue color at the end point. In such titrations, the starch indicator should not be added until just before the end point, when the iodine concentration is low. If it is added too early in the titration, the formation of the blue is not as easily reversible. In practice, therefore,

withhold the starch indicator until the last tinge of yellow due to excess iodine has almost disappeared; then add the starch, and quickly complete the titration.

Iodine ion is oxidizable by air according to the reaction

$$4I^- + O_2 + 4H^+ \rightleftharpoons 2I_2 + 2H_2O$$

Although this reaction is slow in neutral solution, the rate increases with acid concentration. If an iodimetric titration must be carried out in acid solution, exclude the air if possible, and perform the titration quickly.

EXPERIMENTAL PROCEDURE

Special Supplies: Several brands of household cleansers (such as Comet, Bab-O, and Ajax) or liquid bleach containing approximately 5% sodium hypochlorite; two 50-mL burets (or one buret and one 25-mL pipet).

Chemicals: KI(s), 1 M H_2SO_4, 0.0100 M KIO_3 (potassium iodate), 3% $(NH_4)_6Mo_7O_{24}\cdot4H_2O$ (ammonium heptamolybdate) catalyst; 0.05 M $Na_2S_2O_3$ (sodium thiosulfate); starch indicator (prepare 1 L by making a paste of 1 g of soluble starch and 10 mg of HgI_2 as a preservative in about 30 mL of water; pour into 1 L of boiling water, and heat until the solution is clear; cool and store in a stoppered bottle).

Safety Precautions: Liquid bleaches containing 5% sodium hypochlorite are corrosive to the skin and eyes. Your eyes must be protected, as always, by safety glasses. Take care when handling the liquid bleach not to get the solution on your skin.

Mercuric iodide, HgI_2, which is used as a preservative in the preparation of the starch solution, is toxic. In order that students not handle HgI_2, the starch solution should be prepared ahead of time by the stockroom assistant.

---

1. *Standardization of the Sodium Thiosulfate Solution* If the approximately 0.05 M $Na_2S_2O_3$ solution has not been standardized, it may be titrated against a solution made up by dissolving pure dry potassium iodate, KIO_3, to a concentration of 0.0100 M. KIO_3 reacts with excess KI in acid solution according to the following reaction.

$$IO_3^- + 5I^- + 6H^+ \rightleftharpoons 3I_2 + 3H_2O$$

To perform the standardization, dispense 25 mL of 0.0100 M KIO_3 solution by buret or pipet into a 250-mL Erlenmeyer flask. Add 25 mL of distilled

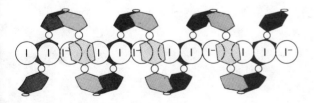

FIGURE 32-1
Starch-triiodide ion complex. The starch (amylose) molecule forms a helix with a cavity large enough to contain the triiodide ions.

water and 2 g of solid KI. Swirl the contents of the flask until the KI dissolves, then add 10 mL of 1 M H_2SO_4, and mix by swirling. A deep brown color should appear, indicating the presence of iodine. Titrate immediately with 0.05 M $Na_2S_2O_3$ solution contained in a buret until the brown fades to a pale yellow, and then add 5 mL of starch indicator solution and continue the titration until the deep blue color of the starch indicator disappears. The change from blue to a colorless solution is very sharp. Record the volume of sodium thiosulfate solution used in the titration. Repeat the procedure in a duplicate titration. In your report form, calculate the accurate concentration of the $Na_2S_2O_3$ solution.

2. Determination of the Oxidizing Capacity of a Household Cleanser or Liquid Bleach

The oxidizing agent in a household cleanser is determined by placing 50 mL of distilled water in a 250-mL Erlenmeyer flask and adding 2 g of KI, swirling the contents of the flask until the KI dissolves. Add an accurately weighed sample (about 10 g) of cleanser to the flask, and swirl to dissolve the soluble material; a residue of insoluble polishing agent contained in the cleanser will remain. Then add 25 mL of 1 M H_2SO_4, 5 drops of 3% ammonium molybdate catalyst, mix, and allow to stand for 1 to 2 min, then titrate with 0.05 M thiosulfate solution as in the standardization procedure. Record the volume of thiosulfate solution used in the titration. If time permits, make a duplicate titration. Then, if time permits, repeat the procedure, using a second brand of cleanser.

When titrating samples of cleansers that contain powdered scouring agents (and possibly dyes) the end point will be harder to see. It may be helpful to make up a sample of cleanser dispersed in the same volume of water for you to compare with the sample you are titrating so that the changes can be more easily seen.

A liquid bleach containing about 5% sodium hypochlorite can be titrated in the same manner as the cleanser using a smaller sample of about 1 g (accurately weighed). (*Caution*: Liquid bleaches are corrosive to the skin and eyes.)

From the concentration and volume of the added sodium thiosulfate solution used to titrate the different brands of cleanser, calculate the weight of oxidizing agent present, assuming it to be sodium hypochlorite, NaOCl. Express the final result as the percentage by weight of sodium hypochlorite: g NaOCl/g cleanser × 100.

If you have the time to compare two cleansers, remember that the effectiveness of a cleanser is influenced by several factors. First, the ability of a cleanser to remove food stains will be related to its oxidizing (bleaching) power. Second, its ability to remove stains from smooth surfaces is also assisted by the abrasive action of its polishing agent, which is usually pumice. Finally, detergents are also added to cleansers to provide foaming action and to emulsify greases and dirt. In your comparison, you must consider all three of these factors, as well as the cost per unit weight of the cleanser.

3. Titration of the Oxidizing Capacity of an Unknown

In this optional determination, your instructor will provide you with a sample containing an unknown amount of an oxidizing agent. Using the sample weight specified by the instructor, carry out the titration for the unknown in exactly the same manner as for the cleanser or bleach as described in part 2. Calculate the weight of oxidizing agent present, assuming it to be sodium hypochlorite, NaOCl. Express the final result as the percentage by weight of sodium hypochlorite: g NaOCl/g sample × 100.

Swimming Pool Chemistry

PURPOSE

To understand the chemical reactions that are of importance in maintaining a safe and attractive swimming pool. To analyze real and simulated swimming pool water for chlorine (hypochlorites and chloramines). To observe the effect of sunlight on the hypochlorite concentration in swimming pool water.

PRE-LAB PREPARATION

When you jump into a swimming pool you would like the water to be sparkling clear and free of objectionable odors and infectious organisms. Two kinds of treatment are required to achieve this: (1) Debris and suspended particulate matter must be continuously removed; and (2) the water must be chemically treated to kill pathogenic bacteria and algae. Proper supervision of this treatment requires daily chemical testing. Although these tests are simple to perform with the commercial test kits that are available, the basic chemistry underlying the tests often remains unexplained. A study of swimming pool chemistry will help you understand the significance of the test results and the reasons for adding various chemicals to a swimming pool.

Most present-day swimming pools, whether large municipal pools or backyard pools, use re-circulation and filtration, often coupled with mechanical skimmers, to remove debris and suspended dirt or organic matter from the water. No chemical disinfection treatment can succeed until suspended solids are removed. Suspended organic matter provides nutrients promoting the growth of bacteria and algae. Organic matter also reacts chemically with disinfecting agents, quickly lowering their concentrations to the point where they are no longer effective in killing bacteria.

The Chemistry of Chlorination

Chlorine, introduced a century ago, has remained the principal disinfectant for drinking water and swimming pools. The basic chemistry is the same in either application. When chlorine is dissolved in water it reacts quickly and completely to form hypochlorous and hydrochloric acids. The hypochlorous acid (HOCl) produced is very effective in killing bacteria and algae.[1]

$$Cl_2(aq) + H_2O \rightleftharpoons HOCl + H^+ + Cl^- \quad (1)$$

$$K_h = \frac{[HOCl][H^+][Cl^-]}{[Cl_2]} = 4 \times 10^{-4} \quad (2)$$

The ratio of hypochlorous acid to chlorine is about a million to one under the usual conditions that prevail in a swimming pool (pH 7.5, $[Cl^-] \cong$ 0.01 M).[2] Because the normal concentration of hypochlorous acid is about 1 part per million (ppm), the concentration of Cl_2 will be about 1 part in 10^{12} (1 part per trillion).

Gaseous chlorine (Cl_2) is not used by most people who maintain their own backyard pools because of the hazards of handling this very poisonous gas. However, bathers in a pool that has been properly treated with chlorine need have no fear that they will be affected by chlorine in the water. The eye irritation and chlorine-like odors that bathers often attribute to "too much chlorine" are usually caused by some other problem—a pool pH that is either too low or too high, or the presence of chloramines that result from the chlorination of dissolved ammonia.

Small swimming pools are usually chlorinated by adding sodium hypochlorite (NaOCl), calcium hypochlorite [Ca(OCl)₂], or chlorinated cyanurates (which we will discuss later). Because OCl^- is the

anion of a weak acid, it reacts with water to form OH^-.

$$OCl^- + HOH \rightleftharpoons HOCl + OH^- \quad (3)$$

Therefore the addition of hypochlorite ions makes the water more basic and tends to increase the pH of the water. (This usually requires the addition of small quantities of HCl to keep the pH at the optimum value.) Using gaseous Cl_2 as the chlorinating agent produces the opposite effect, because the chlorine reacts with water to form HCl, which tends to lower the pH. (See Equation (1).)

The Importance of pH Control

The control of the pH of a swimming pool is very important for several reasons. The first has to do with comfort. Water that is too acidic or too basic will irritate the eyes, which are normally bathed in fluid from the tear ducts that is at about pH 7.0 to 7.4. A second important reason has to do with your health. As the pool water gets more basic, HOCl is converted to OCl^- ion, and OCl^- ion is only 1% as effective as HOCl in killing bacteria.[3] Above pH 8 the effectiveness of added chlorinating agents is greatly reduced. So for the sake of comfort and health, the pH of the water must be maintained in a narrow range of about pH 7.4 to 7.6.

Hypochlorous acid is a very weak acid, so that the concentration ratio of hypochlorous acid to hypochlorite ion is determined by the hydrogen ion concentration in the pool.

$$HOCl \rightleftharpoons H^+ + OCl^- \quad (4)$$

$$K_a = \frac{[H^+][OCl^-]}{[HOCl]} = 3 \times 10^{-8} \quad (5)$$

At pH 7.5, about the optimum pH for a swimming pool, this ratio is equal to 1.0,[4] that is, there are equal concentrations of hypochlorous acid and hypochlorite ion in the water.

---

[1] Specialized cells in the body called *phagocytes* apparently also make hypochlorous acid in a reaction catalyzed by the enzyme myeloperoxidase (MPO):

$$H_2O_2 + Cl^- \xrightarrow{\text{MPO}} HOCl + OH^-$$

Phagocytes attack and destroy invading organisms, and the production of hypochlorous acid may represent a chemical defense mechanism employed by the cells to kill the invading organisms.

[2] At pH 7.5, $[H^+] = 3 \times 10^{-8}$ M. Assume that $[Cl^-] \cong 0.01$ M. By rearranging Equation (2) we obtain

$$\frac{[HOCl]}{[Cl_2]} = \frac{K_h}{[H^+][Cl^-]} = \frac{4 \times 10^{-4}}{(3 \times 10^{-8})(10^{-2})} = 1.3 \times 10^6$$

---

[3] This is attributed to the ability of the neutral HOCl molecule to diffuse through the cell walls of bacteria or algae, while the charged OCl^- ions cannot.

[4] At pH 7.5, $[H^+] = 3 \times 10^{-8}$ M. By rearranging Equation (5) we obtain

$$\frac{[HOCl]}{[OCl^-]} = \frac{[H^+]}{K_a} = \frac{3 \times 10^{-8}}{3 \times 10^{-8}} = 1.0$$

The Role of Total Alkalinity in pH Control

Maintaining the pH of a poorly buffered dilute solution within narrow limits near pH 7 can be difficult because addition of relatively small quantities of acids or bases can cause substantial fluctuations in the pH. Natural waters usually contain some bicarbonate ion, and this alkaline reserve helps to buffer the hydrogen ion concentration.

The *total alkalinity* of the water is related to the reserve of bicarbonate and carbonate ions that it contains, as well as other minor contributors such as ammonia, phosphates, and silicates. It is determined by titration with acid to the methyl orange end point (pH 4.3) where carbonates would be converted to CO_2. In water treatment practice it is normally expressed as milligrams per liter (ppm) of $CaCO_3$.[5]

The total alkalinity is normally maintained in the range 100 to 150 ppm. The main alkaline component is bicarbonate ion, and total alkalinity equivalent to 100 ppm of $CaCO_3$ would correspond to a concentration of HCO_3^- equal to 2×10^{-3} M ($10^{-2.7}$ M).

Now let's calculate the pH of a solution containing 2×10^{-3} M HCO_3^- ion in equilibrium with the partial pressure of CO_2 in the atmosphere. (This corresponds to a dissolved CO_2 concentration of about 10^{-5} M.) When these values are substituted into the equilibrium constant expression for the dissociation of CO_2 in water, we find that the pH of the water would be about 8.6, corresponding to $[H^+] = 10^{-8.6}$ M.[6]

$$CO_2(aq) + H_2O \rightleftharpoons H^+ + HCO_3^- \qquad (6)$$

$$K_{a1} = \frac{[H^+][HCO_3^-]}{[CO_2]} = 10^{-6.3} \qquad (7)$$

This pH is too high for a swimming pool, so it is necessary to add acid (usually HCl or $NaHSO_4$) in small increments to lower the pH to the optimum 7.4 to 7.6 range. When enough acid has been added to lower the pH to 7.5, about 4 to 5% of the bicarbonate has been converted to CO_2 and the dissolved CO_2 concentration increases tenfold to about 10^{-4} M. Because this is ten times larger than the equilibrium concentrations of CO_2, the excess CO_2 tends to escape slowly to the atmosphere and the pool pH tends to creep gradually back to higher pH's, so small but frequent additions of acid are required to maintain the optimum pH.

Without the alkaline reserve of bicarbonate ion, the pool pH is difficult to control. If the total alkalinity is too great (above the recommended range of 100 to 150 ppm), it can be reduced by adding acid (HCl) to the pool. If it is too low, it can be increased by adding sodium bicarbonate or sodium carbonate to the pool. The total alkalinity should be measured before attempts are made to adjust the pH to the optimum value of 7.4 to 7.6.

Stabilizing the HOCl/OCl⁻ Concentration with Cyanuric Acid

The optimum level of "free available chlorine" ($HOCl + OCl^-$) is equivalent to 1 to 2 mg/L (ppm) of Cl_2. This corresponds to a concentration of 1.4 to 2.8×10^{-5} M for the sum of $HOCl + OCl^-$. Tests have shown that on a sunny day a large outdoor pool can lose up to 90% of its $HOCl + OCl^-$ concentration in 3 or 4 h. This loss is caused by a photochemical reaction of OCl^- with the ultraviolet light from sunlight, which destroys the OCl^-.

$$OCl^- \xrightarrow{h\nu} Cl^- + \tfrac{1}{2}O_2(g) \qquad (8)$$

One of the most effective ways that has been discovered to overcome this problem is to add cyanuric acid or chlorinated cyanurates to the pool. (The optimum concentration range is 25 to 50 ppm.) Cyanuric acid is a weak acid ($pK_{a1} = 6.9$). At pH 7.5, it is mainly present as the cyanurate anion. Cyanurate absorbs ultraviolet light without decomposing, so that the photochemical destruction of OCl^- ion is greatly reduced. Cyanurate also contributes to the total alkalinity of the water, providing some buffering capacity near the optimum pH of 7.5.

It does not matter whether the cyanurate is added as cyanuric acid or as a chlorinated cyanurate salt because an equilibrium is established among the various protonated and chlorinated forms of cyanuric acid, as shown by the following equilibria.

---

[5] This can be confusing because 1 mmol of $CaCO_3$ requires 2 mmol of acid to neutralize it. Thus a water sample requiring 2 mmol of HCl per liter to titrate it to pH 4.3 would correspond to the equivalent of 1 mmol of $CaCO_3$ or 100 mg/L (100 ppm) of $CaCO_3$.

[6] Assume that $[HCO_3^-] = 10^{-2.7}$ M and $[CO_2] = 10^{-5}$ M. By rearranging Equation (7) we get

$$[H^+] = \frac{K_{a1}[CO_2]}{[HCO_3^-]} = \frac{(10^{-6.3})(10^{-5})}{10^{-2.7}} = 10^{-8.6} \text{ M}$$

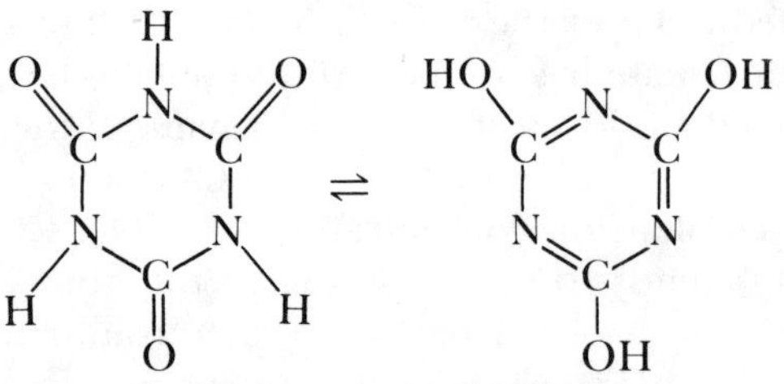

(iso)cyanuric acid
(*s*-triazinetrione)
Keto form
predominates in
the solid state.

Enol form
predominates
in solution.

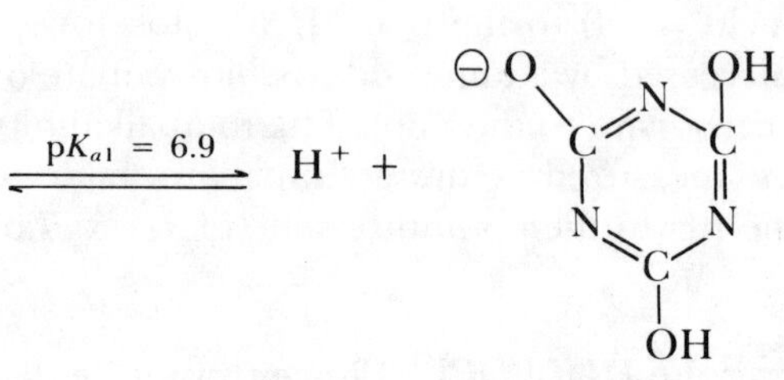

$$\xrightarrow{\text{p}K_{a1} = 6.9} \text{H}^+ +$$ (9)

anion of (iso)cyanuric acid

$$\text{Na}^+ + \qquad + 2\text{H}_2\text{O} \rightleftharpoons 2\text{HOCl}$$

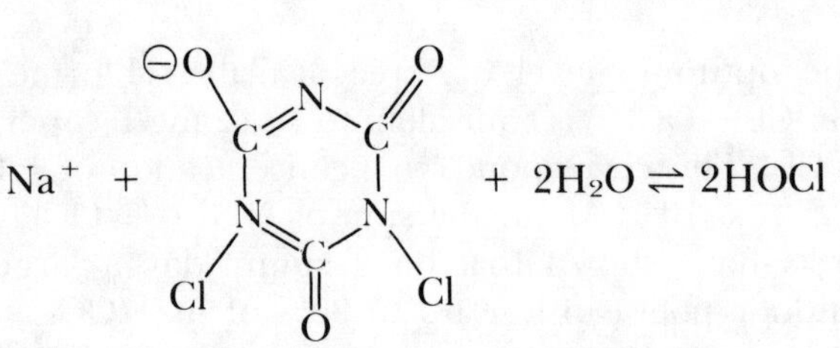

sodium dichloro(iso)cyanurate
(sodium dichloro-*s*-triazinetrione)

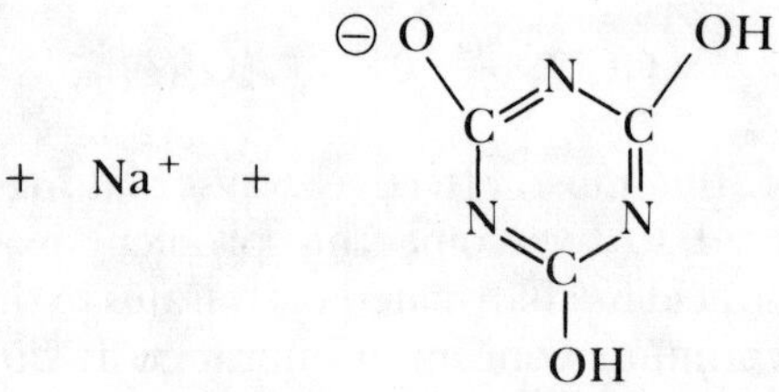

$$+ \quad \text{Na}^+ +$$ (10)

anion
of (iso)cyanuric acid

The Effects of Ammonia

Chlorination chemistry is complicated by the presence of ammonia and organic amines in swimming pool water. Mostly these come from sweat and urine. Small children are particularly likely to urinate in a pool, adding urea, which can hydrolyze to form ammonia. Nitrogen compounds add nutrients that encourage the growth of bacteria and algae. They also react with HOCl to form chlora-

mines, which are much less effective at killing bacteria than is HOCl.

$$\text{NH}_3 + \text{HOCl} \rightleftharpoons \text{NH}_2\text{Cl} + \text{H}_2\text{O} \qquad (11)$$
monochloramine

$$\text{NH}_2\text{Cl} + \text{HOCl} \rightleftharpoons \text{NHCl}_2 + \text{H}_2\text{O} \qquad (12)$$
dichloramine

The chlorine in the form of chloramines is called the *combined chlorine*. The chloramines (particularly dichloramine) are also a source of eye irritation that is often wrongly attributed to chlorine. Ammonia can be removed by treatment with five to seven times the normal dose of chlorine or hypochlorite. This is called *superchlorination* and must be done periodically to remove ammonia by a series of complex reactions whose net result is the conversion of chloramines to nitrogen gas.

$$\text{NH}_2\text{Cl} + \text{NHCl}_2 \rightarrow \text{N}_2 + 3\text{H}^+ + 3\text{Cl}^- \qquad (13)$$

A combined chlorine measurement greater than 0.2 ppm and the presence of chlorine-like odors usually indicate the presence of dichloramine and the need for superchlorination. In fact there is an axiom, "If the air above the water smells of chlorine, there is not enough chlorine in the water."

Organic amines cannot be removed by chlorination, and when the concentration of these substances gets too high, some pool water must be drained out and replaced with fresh water to lower their concentration.

Testing Swimming Pool Water

Pool water is normally tested for total alkalinity, pH, free chlorine, and cyanurates (if they are used). Currently, California and Florida require that all public swimming pools be tested for (iso)cyanuric acid. Commercial test kits for cyanuric acid are available.

Total alkalinity is measured by titration of a water sample with acid to pH 4.3. (See footnote 5.)

In most pool test kits, the pH is measured by color comparison using an acid-base indicator, after destroying all the chlorine in the sample so that it cannot bleach the indicator.

Various titration methods or color comparison methods using organic redox indicators have been proposed for measuring free and residual chlorine. The method we will use in this experiment employs an indirect titration of HOCl with Fe^{2+}, mediated by an organic redox indicator. The method works like this. Hypochlorous acid reacts with the indicator N,N'-diethyl-p-phenylenediamine (DPD) to form a red-colored product.

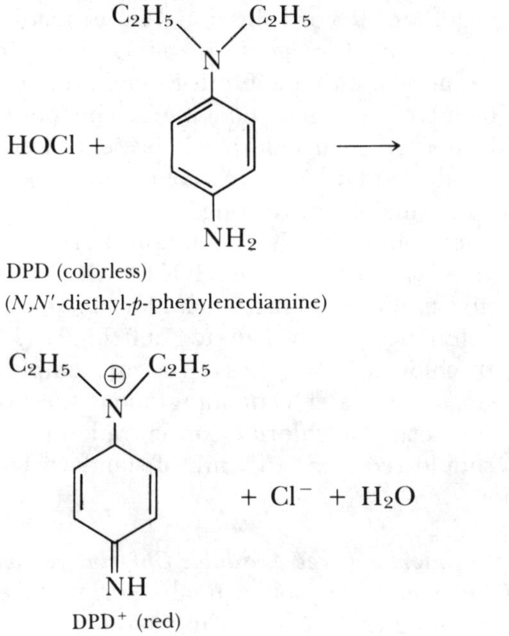

DPD (colorless)
(N,N'-diethyl-p-phenylenediamine)

$+ Cl^- + H_2O$ (14)

DPD$^+$ (red)

As the titrant, Fe^{2+}, is added it reduces the red (oxidized) form back to the colorless (reduced) form.

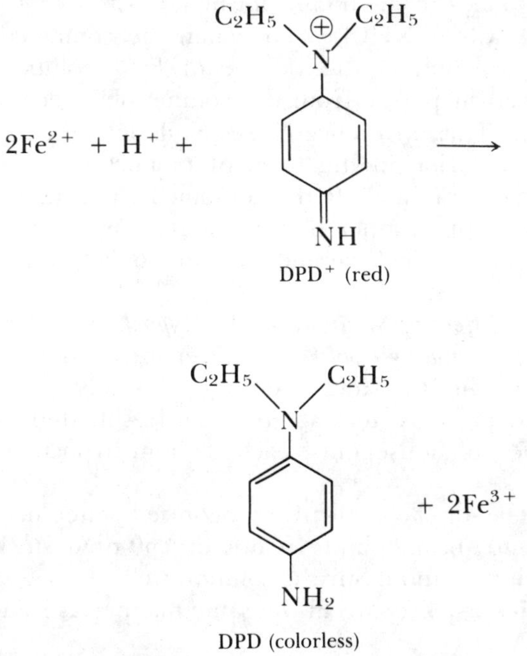

DPD$^+$ (red)

$+ 2Fe^{3+}$ (15)

DPD (colorless)

However, the reduced form of the indicator is so quickly reoxidized by HOCl that the solution remains red as long as any HOCl remains. When the last bit of HOCl is used up the end point will be signaled by a change from red to a colorless solution. The net reaction is the sum of Equations (14) and (15).

$$2Fe^{2+} + HOCl + H^+ \rightarrow 2Fe^{3+} + Cl^- + H_2O$$
                                                 (16a)

or,

$$2Fe^{2+} + Cl_2 \rightarrow 2Fe^{3+} + 2Cl^- \quad (16b)$$

The cyanuric acid concentration is estimated in pool water by measuring the turbidity of the suspended white precipitate that forms when a solution of melamine is added to cyanuric acid.

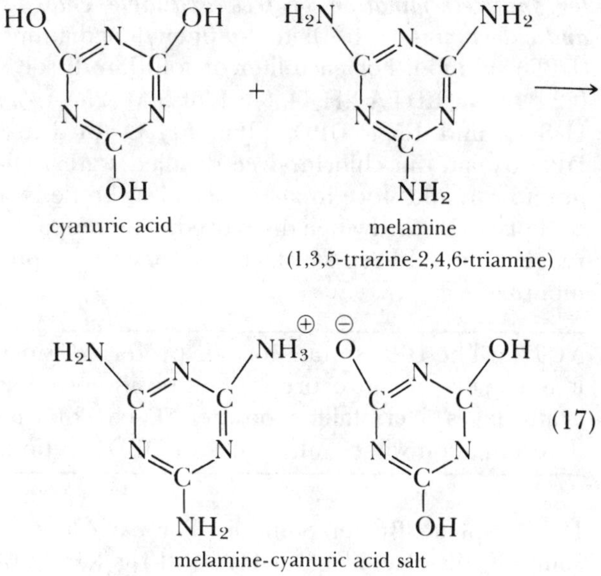

cyanuric acid   melamine
                              (1,3,5-triazine-2,4,6-triamine)

                                      (17)

melamine-cyanuric acid salt

The turbidity is proportional to the amount of cyanuric acid present. The turbidity is measured in a spectrophotometer or by measuring the depth of solution required in a standard flat-bottomed tube to obscure the image of a black **X** placed under the tube.

EXPERIMENTAL PROCEDURE

Special Supplies: 25- or 50-mL buret, 1 L of swimming pool water per student, thermometer. Optional: swimming pool test kit (tests for total alkalinity, pH, and chlorine). Test kits for cyanuric acid also are available, or the method described in part 4, employing a 0.010 M melamine/0.002 M HCl solution, can be used.

Chemicals: N,N'-Diethyl-p-phenylenediamine (DPD, $(C_2H_5)_2$ N—C_6H_4—NH_2) as the sulfate (DPD·H_2SO_4·5H_2O) or oxalate (DPD·$H_2C_2O_4$) salt; disodium ethylenediaminetetraacetate dihydrate (Na$_2$EDTA·2H_2O); disodium hydrogen phosphate, Na$_2$HPO$_4$; potassium dihydrogen phosphate, KH$_2$PO$_4$; HgCl$_2$; ferrous ammonium sulfate, Fe(NH$_4$)$_2$(SO$_4$)$_2$·6H_2O; 3 M H$_2$SO$_4$; KI(s); stock solution containing approximately 250 ppm of chlorine (freshly prepared by diluting 5.0 mL of 5% NaOCl household bleach to 1 L); optional test solution for cyanuric acid; 0.010 M melamine/0.002 M HCl (melamine is 1,3,5-triazine-2,4,6-triamine).

Safety Precautions: Diethyl-p-phenylenediamine and melamine are toxic and may cause skin irritation in sensitive individuals. Do not get these reagents on your skin.

Household bleach containing 5% sodium hypochlorite is very corrosive to the skin.

Directions for preparation of the reagent solutions for the determination of free available chlorine and chloramines: I. Diethyl-p-phenylenediamine (DPD) solution. For each liter of solution dissolve 0.2 g of Na$_2$EDTA·2H_2O, 8 mL of 3 M (25 wt. %) H$_2$SO$_4$, and 1.5 g DPD sulfate·5H_2O (or 1.0 g DPD oxalate) in chlorine-free distilled water. Dilute to 1 L and store in an amber glass bottle in a cool place. Discard when discolored. The prepared reagent should keep satisfactorily for at least one month.

NOTE The DPD sulfate form is preferred, since it is usually of more precise composition and is available as a crystalline powder. Each chlorine determination will require 5 mL of DPD solution.

II. Phosphate Buffer Solution. For each liter of solution, dissolve 24 g Na$_2$HPO$_4$, 46 g KH$_2$PO$_4$, and 0.8 g of Na$_2$EDTA·2H_2O in distilled water. Add 20 mg mercuric chloride, HgCl$_2$, to prevent mold growths. Dilute to 1 L.
III. Standard 0.00282 M Ferrous Ammonium Sulfate (Fe^{2+}) Solution. The deionized water used to prepare the solution should be bubbled with an inert gas (nitrogen or argon) or freshly boiled and cooled in order to remove dissolved oxygen. For each liter of solution dissolve 1 mL of 3 M (25 wt. %) H$_2$SO$_4$ and 1.106 g of Fe(NH$_4$)$_2$(SO$_4$)$_2$·6H_2O and dilute to 1 L. This is a primary standard and may be used for one month. Each 1.00 mL of the Fe^{2+} solution is equivalent to 0.100 mg of Cl$_2$.

Procedure The quantities given here are suitable for concentrations of total chlorine up to 4 mg/L (4 ppm). The usual sample size is 100 mL of swimming pool water. If the total chlorine exceeds 4 mg/L, use a smaller sample and dilute to 100 mL with chlorine-free distilled water.

1. *Free Available Chlorine* Fill your buret with standard 0.00282 M ferrous ammonium sulfate (Fe^{2+}) solution. Record the initial buret reading. Put 5 mL each of reagents I and II (DPD and buffer solutions) into a 250-mL Erlenmeyer flask. Add 100 mL of swimming pool water. The solution should appear red if chlorine is present. Titrate rapidly with standard Fe^{2+} to a colorless end point. Record the final buret reading.

The net volume of Fe^{2+} solution corresponds to the free available chlorine (HOCl + OCl$^-$). For a 100-mL sample, 1.00 mL of standard 0.00282 M Fe^{2+} solution is equivalent to 1.00 mg/L (1.00 ppm) of chlorine, Cl$_2$. Thus a 100-mL sample of swimming pool water containing about the optimum free available chlorine concentration (1 to 2 ppm) should require 1 to 2 mL of standard Fe^{2+} solution.

2. *Total Chlorine (Free Available Chlorine + Combined Chlorine)* To obtain total chlorine, take a fresh 100-mL sample of swimming pool water, add 5 mL of buffer, 5 mL of DPD solution, 1 g of KI, and swirl to dissolve the KI. Record the initial buret reading. Allow the solution to stand for 2 min and titrate with Fe^{2+} solution as before, until the red solution turns colorless. Record the final buret reading. The net volume of Fe^{2+} solution corresponds to the total chlorine (HOCl + OCl$^-$ + NH$_2$Cl + NHCl$_2$). To obtain the combined chlorine, subtract the volume of Fe^{2+} solution obtained in part 1 from the volume obtained in part 2. This difference corresponds to the combined chlorine in the form of monochloramine and dichloramine. (If the combined chlorine exceeds 0.2 ppm, superchlorination is recommended to remove the chloramines and ammonia.)

3. *The Effect of Sunlight on the Hypochlorite Content of Swimming Pool Water* Prepare solutions A and B using the stock 250-ppm chlorine solution provided. (This stock solution is a freshly diluted solution of household bleach, sodium hypochlorite.)
Solution A To 800 mL of deionized water in a 1000-mL beaker add 10 mL of 250-ppm stock chlorine solution. Stir the solution well.
Solution B Prepare in the same manner as solution A.

Solution C Place 800 mL of local swimming pool water in a 1000-mL beaker.

After the three solutions have been prepared, label them and analyze 100-mL samples of solutions A and B for available chlorine by the method described in part 1. (You have already analyzed solution C in part 1.) Also note and record the time. Then put solution A in your locker, protected from light. Put solutions B and C in direct sunlight. In 30 min analyze 100-mL samples of solutions A, B, and C. Record the volumes of standard 0.00282 M Fe^{2+} solution required to titrate each sample. At the time of each analysis also record the time and temperature of the solutions.

Continue analyzing samples, noting the time and temperature, every 30 min for about 2 h. As the experiment proceeds, plot the concentration of available chlorine (in parts per million) versus time on the graph provided. Plot the time accurately, since the intervals between samples may not be exactly 30 min.

4. *Optional Tests* If a swimming pool test kit is available, test samples of swimming pool water for total alkalinity, pH, chlorine, and cyanuric acid. Follow the instructions provided with the test kit.

A simple qualitative test for cyanuric acid is to add 25 mL of a solution containing 0.010 M melamine/0.002 M HCl to 25 mL of swimming pool water. Mix the solutions well. If the swimming pool water contains cyanuric acid, a white turbidity will form. This is the insoluble melamine-cyanurate salt.

If standard solutions of cyanuric acid in the range 10 to 100 ppm are available, a quantitative test can be performed by mixing equal volumes of the cyanuric acid standards and the melamine/HCl reagent. After waiting 2 to 3 min for the turbidity to develop fully, measure the turbidity (absorbance) of the standard solutions and the unknown in a spectrophotometer at 470 nm. Make a graph of absorbance versus concentration of cyanuric acid (in parts per million). From the measured absorbance of the unknown solution the concentration of cyanuric acid in the swimming pool water can be read from the graph.

Compare the test results for chlorine with the values you obtained in Parts 1 and 2. Record the test results on your report form.

BIBLIOGRAPHY

White, G. C., *Handbook of Chlorination*, Van Nostrand-Reinhold, New York, 1972.

Rutherford, D. (ed.), *Swimming Pools*, Sunset Books, Lane Publishing Co., Menlo Park, CA, 1981.

REPORT 33	Swimming Pool Chemistry	NAME	
		SECTION	LOCKER
		INSTRUCTOR	DATE

DATA AND CALCULATIONS

1. Free Available Chlorine

Volume of swimming pool water sample ______________mL

Concentration of Fe^{2+} titrant ______________M

Volume of Fe^{2+} titrant

Final buret reading ______________mL

Initial buret reading ______________mL

Net volume of Fe^{2+} soln ______________mL

Calculate the HOCl + OCl^- concentration, expressed as milligrams per liter (ppm) of Cl_2.

2. Total Chlorine (Free Available Chlorine + Combined Chlorine)

Volume of swimming pool water sample _____mL

Concentration of Fe^{2+} titrant _____M

Volume of Fe^{2+} titrant

   Final buret reading _____mL

   Initial buret reading _____mL

Net volume of Fe^{2+} solution _____mL

Calculate the total chlorine concentration ($HOCl + OCl^{-}$ + chloramines), expressed as milligrams per liter (ppm) of Cl_2.

What is the combined chlorine (chloramines) concentration, expressed as parts per million of Cl_2?

3. The Effect of Sunlight on the Hypochlorite Content of Swimming Pool Water

Record the time, temperature, and initial and final buret readings for the titration of each sample.

Data	Solution A	Solution B	Solution C
Time	_____min	_____min	_____min
Temperature	_____°C	_____°C	_____°C
Volume			
Final	_____mL	_____mL	_____mL
Initial	_____mL	_____mL	_____mL
Net	_____mL	_____mL	_____mL
Time	_____min	_____min	_____min
Temperature	_____°C	_____°C	_____°C
Volume			
Final	_____mL	_____mL	_____mL
Initial	_____mL	_____mL	_____mL
Net	_____mL	_____mL	_____mL
Time	_____min	_____min	_____min
Temperature	_____°C	_____°C	_____°C
Volume			
Final	_____mL	_____mL	_____mL
Initial	_____mL	_____mL	_____mL
Net	_____mL	_____mL	_____mL
Time	_____min	_____min	_____min
Temperature	_____°C	_____°C	_____°C
Volume			
Final	_____mL	_____mL	_____mL
Initial	_____mL	_____mL	_____mL
Net	_____mL	_____mL	_____mL
Time	_____min	_____min	_____min
Temperature	_____°C	_____°C	_____°C
Volume			
Final	_____mL	_____mL	_____mL
Initial	_____mL	_____mL	_____mL
Net	_____mL	_____mL	_____mL

In between measurements, calculate the concentration of available chlorine for the three solutions and plot the concentrations of available chlorine (in parts per million) versus time on the graph paper. Label the axes with the variable names and their units.

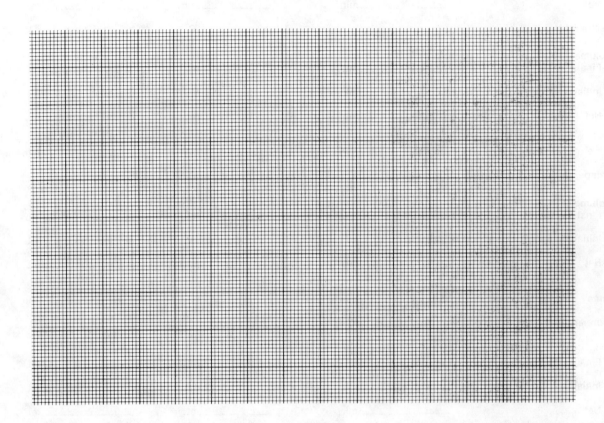

Discuss the trends you observe. Does sunlight have a measurable effect on the concentration of available chlorine?

4. Optional Tests

Describe the tests performed and the results of the tests.

Factors Affecting the Rates
of Chemical Reactions

PURPOSE

To study a number of factors that influence chemical reaction rates, including (1) concentration, (2) the nature of the chemical reactants, (3) the surface area in a heterogeneous reaction involving reacting solids and liquids, (4) the temperature of the reacting system, (5) the presence of catalysts, and (6) the effects of diffusion in a poorly mixed solution of chemical reactants.

PRE-LAB PREPARATION

At present it is safe to say that we do not yet understand in detail every factor that influences the rate of a chemical reaction. Moreover, we cannot explore in two or three hours of experimentation everything that is known about the subject, so you should regard this experiment as an introduction to several of the more important factors that influence the rates of chemical reactions.

We have omitted from this experiment the study of some factors that are known to influence reaction rates. For example, we will not discuss the effect of light on chemical reactions. (The interaction of light photons with molecules is an important subdiscipline of chemistry called *photochemistry*.) We might also discuss the effects of molecular geometry and stereochemistry, for it is well known that the shapes of molecules play an important role in affecting reaction rates. Reactions in solution are also affected by the nature of the solvent. These are all subjects you will encounter in more advanced courses in chemistry.

Measuring the Rate of a Chemical Reaction

Let's begin by defining what we mean by the rate of a chemical reaction. The simplest and most fundamental definition of reaction rate is the number of moles of reactants that disappear per unit time, or the number of moles of products that appear per unit time. According to this definition the units of reaction rate would be moles per second (mol/s).

If the volume of the reacting system is constant (or nearly constant), it is convenient to define the reaction rate in moles per unit volume per unit time, for example, $mol \cdot L^{-1} \cdot s^{-1}$. This approach allows us to measure reaction rates as changes in concentration per unit time, which is convenient when we study reactions in solution (where volume changes are usually small) or in the gas phase (where the reactants and products are confined to a reaction flask of fixed volume).

To measure the rate of a chemical reaction we must make use of some chemical or physical property of the system that allows us to determine changes in the number of moles (or concentration) per unit time. As an example, the rate of a reaction that evolves a gas can be measured by measuring the volume of gas produced per second. If a reactant or product has a characteristic color, we can measure the intensity of the color (proportional to concentration) at a particular wavelength in an instrument called a *spectrophotometer*.

Another method, one that we will use in this experiment, requires us to measure the time required for a fixed amount of a reactant to disappear. This is called a *clock* reaction and we will use this method to study the reaction of hydrogen peroxide with iodide ion.

$$H_2O_2 + 2I^- + 2H^+ \rightarrow I_2 + 2H_2O$$

The method works like this: A fixed amount of sodium thiosulfate $(Na_2S_2O_3)$ is added to the reaction mixture along with H_2O_2, KI, starch, and an acetic acid/sodium acetate buffer. (The buffer keeps the hydrogen ion concentration nearly constant.) As the hydrogen peroxide reacts with iodide ion, iodine (I_2) is produced. As the I_2 is formed it reacts very rapidly with thiosulfate ion to re-form iodide ion (thus keeping the iodide ion concentration constant).

$$2S_2O_3^{2-} + I_2 \rightarrow 2I^- + S_4O_6^{2-}$$

When the last bit of thiosulfate ion is used up, the I_2 concentration increases. In the presence of iodide ion molecular I_2 forms the triiodide complex ion,

$$I_2 + I^- \rightleftharpoons I_3^-$$

which in turn forms a dark blue-black complex with the added starch. Thus the appearance of the blue color signals that all of the thiosulfate (and a corresponding amount of H_2O_2) has been used up.

The time required for a fixed amount of thiosulfate (and H_2O_2) to react is measured. The faster the reaction, the shorter the reaction time, so the reaction rate and the reaction time are inversely related. The amount of thiosulfate is deliberately made small so that not more than 10% of the H_2O_2 reacts. Thus, during the course of the reaction the concentrations of H_2O_2, I^-, and H^+ remain nearly constant, approximately equal to their initial values. This allows us to study the effects of concentration by varying the initial concentration of one or more reactants.

Effects of Concentration

In order to react, molecules or ions must encounter one another. These encounters (or collisions) are often violent enough to produce a rearrangement of the atoms and the formation of new products. The more molecules there are per unit volume, the more likely they are to collide with one another, so increasing the concentrations of the reactants generally increases the rate of reaction. However, the dependence of reaction rate on the concentrations of the reactants is intimately linked to the reaction pathway, and in some instances an increase in the concentration of a reactant has no effect (or even a slowing effect) on the rate of reaction. Experiment 35 involves a quantitative study of the dependence of reaction rate on the concentrations of the reactants.

Influence of the Nature of the Reactants

The alkali metals all react with water. The net reaction is the same for each metal.

$$M + H_2O \rightarrow M^+(aq) + OH^-(aq) + \tfrac{1}{2}H_2$$

where M represents Li, Na, K, Rb, or Cs. The rate of reaction increases noticeably in the sequence lithium $\rightarrow$ cesium. Lithium reacts briskly, but cesium reacts violently, producing enough heat to ignite the hydrogen produced. The metals that react most rapidly have the lowest melting points and the smallest ionization potentials.

The reactions of the halogens with hydrogen show the opposite progression. The lightest element, fluorine, reacts explosively with hydrogen at room temperature, while iodine reacts slowly.

Effect of Surface Area in a Heterogeneous Reaction

In a reaction between a solid and a gas (or liquid) the reactants can get together only at the surface of the solid. The larger the surface area of the solid, the more atoms are available to react. Unmilled wheat doesn't burn very well, but when ground to fine flour and dispersed in air it forms an explosive mixture. Huge concrete grain elevators have been destroyed by the force of an explosion caused by the ignition of a mixture of air and grain dust.

Effect of Temperature

Chemical reactions involve the rearrangement of atoms into new configurations. Chemical bonds are broken and new bonds are formed. This process necessarily involves the stretching of bonds and the distortion of bond angles. This is exactly what happens when you put more energy into a molecular system. The amplitude of atom-atom stretching and bending vibrations increases, putting the atoms into a configuration where they can more easily react. In addition, the kinetic energy of the molecules increases. They move about faster, so they collide with greater force, producing the bond-length and bond-angle distortions characteristic of reacting molecules. So a molecule at a higher temperature has a higher energy and a higher probability of reacting.

Dramatic temperature effects are often observed with reactions that are exothermic. The reaction of paper with the oxygen in air is extremely slow at room temperature, but as the paper is heated it suddenly bursts into flame. The temperature at which this happens is called the *ignition temperature*. At this temperature the energy produced by the chemical reaction cannot be dissipated rapidly enough to keep the reactant from heating up. This self-heating process results in a dramatic rise in the temperature and the rate of reaction. This is characteristic of combustions and chemical explosions.

Effect of Catalysts

A catalyst increases the rate of a chemical reaction but is not permanently altered in the net chemical reaction. Catalysts generally function by interacting with one or more reactants to form an intermediate that is more reactive. In effect they change the reaction pathway so that less energy is required for the reaction to take place. Many enzyme catalyst molecules are very specific, catalyzing the reaction of a single kind of substrate molecule. Other catalysts are more general. For example, finely divided palladium metal catalyzes the rather non-specific addition of H_2 to $C=C$ bonds found in different kinds of molecules.

Effects of Diffusion and Mixing

In the gas phase, molecules are moving quite rapidly. Nitrogen molecules at room temperature have an average speed of about 300 m/s (about 650 mph). But nitrogen molecules released in a corner of a room wouldn't get to the other side in a fraction of a second. This is because they collide so often with other molecules that they must jostle their way to the other side like a person fighting through a crowd at a football game.

If it's difficult to travel rapidly in the gas phase, imagine how hard it is in a liquid, where each molecule is surrounded by a cage of molecules. Just to move a distance roughly equal to the size of a molecule requires that the molecule push and shove its neighbor out of the way. So if two different reactant solutions are not thoroughly mixed, the reaction time can be extended by minutes until the random motions of the slowly diffusing molecules produce a more uniform distribution of reacting molecules. This is an important consideration to keep in mind when studying chemical reactions in solution (or when making up a reagent solution). Thorough mixing is essential.

EXPERIMENTAL PROCEDURE

Special Supplies: Mortar and pestle, apparatus for collecting gases shown in Figure 34-1, 2.5- × 2.5-cm squares of cotton cloth (muslin).

Chemicals: 3% (0.9 M) H_2O_2, solution A (containing in the same solution 0.2 g/L starch,[1] 0.5 M CH_3COOH, 0.05 M $NaCH_3COO$, 0.30 M KI, and 0.030 M $Na_2S_2O_3$), Mg metal turnings, Ca metal turnings, 0.1% phenolphthalein indicator, marble chips, 1 M HCl, steel wool, iron nails (approx. 4 cm long), methanol, 50:50 (v:v) 2-propanol/water, 1 M $CuCl_2$, 3 M $CuCl_2$, 3 M $FeCl_3$, $KMnO_4(s)$, 0.05 M $KMnO_4$, 0.5 M $H_2C_2O_4$ (oxalic acid), 6 M H_2SO_4.

---

[1] Put 0.2 g starch in 200 mL of boiling water and heat for 5 min. Dilute the solution to about 800 mL, add the other reagents in the order given, allow to cool, and dilute to 1 L.

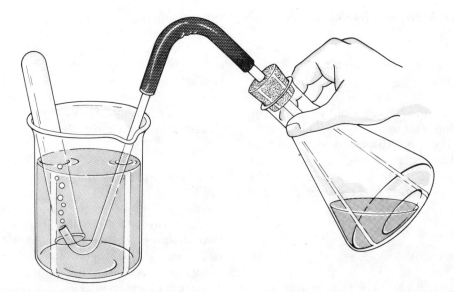

FIGURE 34-1
A simple apparatus for measuring the rate of evolution of a gas. A test tube filled with water is inverted over the gas delivery tube in the beaker and the time required to fill the test tube with gas is measured.

Safety Precautions: Part 4 of this experiment involves igniting small quantities of flammable solvents. If you follow the directions this is no more hazardous than lighting a Bunsen burner. It is recommended that the flammable solvents be kept in the fume hood, and that the requisite amounts be dispensed to you there. *There must be no open flames in the hood where the solvents are stored.* After obtaining your small amounts of solvent, you should take them to the lab bench where the experiment is to be carried out. *The containers of flammable solvents must never be taken to the lab bench.* If a fume hood is not available, the instructor should demonstrate the experiments in parts 4(b) and 4(c).

1. Effects of Concentration on Reaction Rates

Place 5 mL of solution A in a 50-mL beaker. Add 5 mL of 3% H_2O_2, mix, and note the number of seconds required for the solution to turn blue. Record the reaction time.

Repeat the procedure using 5 mL of solution A, 4 mL of water, and 1 mL of 3% H_2O_2. Record the reaction time. Is it longer? Which reactant concentrations have been changed? What is the relationship between the reaction time and the concentration of H_2O_2?

2. The Influence of the Nature of Reactants

Obtain three or four small pieces of magnesium metal turnings and about the same amount of calcium metal turnings. Add enough water to each of two 15- × 150-mm test tubes to fill them about one-third full. Place the magnesium turnings in one test tube and the calcium turnings in the other. Both of these metals are in the same chemical family of the periodic table. Which metal is more reactive with water?

To determine what gas is produced, invert an empty test tube for about 15 s over the mouth of the tube in which the metal is reacting more vigorously. Quickly move the mouth of the inverted tube near the flame of a bunsen burner. Is the gas flammable? What is the chemical composition of the gas?

Look closely at the slower-reacting metal as you agitate the test tube. Is any gas being produced? Add a drop of phenolphthalein indicator solution to each test tube containing the metals. What other product is formed besides a gas? Write chemical equations describing the reactions of the metals with water.

Is there a correlation of the reaction rates with the ionization potentials of these metals (is it easier to remove electrons from magnesium or calcium)? Which metal is the stronger reducing agent as measured by its redox potential? (See Table B-10 of Appendix B.)

3. The Influence of Surface Area in a Heterogeneous Reaction

(a) Set up the apparatus shown in Figure 34-1, using a 125-mL Erlenmeyer flask, a 13- × 100-mm test tube to collect the gas, and a large beaker or plastic basin. Fill the test tube with tap water and, holding your thumb or finger over the mouth, invert it in the beaker of water over the end of the bent gas delivery tube. Place 3 g of coarse marble chips ($CaCO_3$) in the 125-mL Erlenmeyer flask. Add 25 mL of water and then add 25 mL of 1 M HCl. Immediately insert the one-hole stopper in the flask and record the time required to fill the test tube with gas. What gas is produced?

Rinse the Erlenmeyer flask with tap water and place the used marble chips in the waste receptacle provided. *Do not discard the marble chips in the sink.* Obtain another 3 g of marble chips and with a mortar and pestle pulverize them to the size of grains of sugar. Transfer the granular material to the 125-mL Erlenmeyer flask, using a rolled-up sheet of paper as a funnel. Fill a test tube with water and invert it over the delivery tube, as before. Add 25 mL of water to the flask, followed by 25 mL of 1 M HCl, and immediately stopper. Record the time required to fill the test tube with gas. Save this apparatus for use in part 4. Is there a correlation between the surface area of the marble and the reaction rate? Write an equation describing the chemical reaction between $CaCO_3$ and HCl.

(b) Place a small iron nail (cleaned so that it is free of rust) in a 20-mm-diameter test tube. In a second 20-mm test tube place a 0.6-g ball of steel wool, using a glass rod to push it to the bottom of the test tube. Add 10 mL of 1 M $CuCl_2$ to each test tube and watch them closely. Observe and record any color changes and note in which tube they occur more rapidly. Is a new solid substance forming? What do you think it is? Agitate each test tube and feel the lower portion of the tubes. Is one tube warmer than the other? What happened to the steel wool? Would the same thing eventually happen to the nail? Write an equation describing the chemical reaction that takes place.

4. The Influence of Temperature

(a) Measure 5 mL of solution A into a test tube. Measure 4 mL of water and 1 mL of 3% H_2O_2 into a second test tube. Place both test tubes in a 250-mL beaker of warm water (50°C). After about 3 min, pour solution A and then the H_2O_2 solution into a 50-mL beaker, stir, and note the time. When the blue color appears, note and record the elapsed time. Compare the reaction time with that observed for the second reaction mixture you studied in part 1.

(b) *Ignition Temperature* Review the Safety Precautions. In a fume hood, place 10 to 20 drops of methanol in a 30-mL beaker. Remove the beaker to your lab bench. Heat the end of a glass stirring rod at the tip of the inner blue cone of a Bunsen burner until the glass starts to soften. Quickly touch the heated end to the methanol. A chemical reaction should begin easily. *Stay at arm's length from the beaker. Do not touch the beaker until it has cooled.* Describe the reaction that takes place. Write a balanced chemical equation for the reaction. Why doesn't methanol burst into flame at room temperature when exposed to air?

(c) Obtain a small square of cotton cloth (muslin) and a book of matches. (The cotton cloth should be tightly woven, about 2 to 3 cm on a side, and cleanly cut so there are no ragged edges.) Working in a hood, place about 10 mL of 50:50 v:v 2-propanol/water in a 50- or 100-mL beaker. Using crucible tongs, grasp the square by one corner and dip it into the 2-propanol/water solution. Lift the cloth and allow the excess solution to drain until no more solution drips off the cotton. Place a small watch glass over the solution in the beaker. Carry the cotton, still held in the tongs, to your lab bench. Have a lab partner light a match and bring it just near enough to the square of cotton (held in the tongs) to ignite the 2-propanol-soaked cotton. Make certain that no other person is within arm's length of the flaming cloth. When the flame dies out, carefully note the condition of the cloth. How can the 2-propanol burn without igniting the cotton?

5. Effect of Catalysts on the Rate of Decomposition of H_2O_2

Using the same apparatus as in part 3(a), place 20 mL of 3% H_2O_2 in the flask. Fill a 13- × 100-mm test tube with water and invert it over the gas delivery tube. Then add 20 drops of 3 M $CuCl_2$ to the flask, replace the stopper, continuously swirl the contents, and note and record how long it takes to fill the test tube with the evolved gas. The gas coming over first will contain some air that was present in the flask. After two or three minutes, test the gas in the Erlenmeyer flask by inserting a glowing splint into the flask. Does the gas support combustion? What is the identity of the gas?

Rinse the flask and repeat the experiment, adding only the H_2O_2 solution to the flask. Continuously swirl the contents of the flask. Is the rate of evolution of gas slower? After a few minutes' wait, you should be able to tell whether the $CuCl_2$ catalyzes the reaction.

Now fill another test tube with water and place it over the gas delivery tube. Then remove the stopper just long enough to add 2 drops of 3 M $FeCl_3$. Insert the stopper and continuously swirl the solution. Note and record the time required to fill the test tube with gas.

Rinse the flask and add to it 20 mL of 3% H_2O_2, 1 drop of 3 M $CuCl_2$, and 1 drop of 3 M $FeCl_3$, in that order. Quickly replace the stopper, continuously swirl the solution in the flask, and record the time required to fill a 13- × 100-mm test tube with gas.

Repeat the procedure using 20 mL of 3% H_2O_2, 5 drops of 3 M $CuCl_2$, and 5 drops of 3 M $FeCl_3$. Quickly stopper the flask and continuously swirl the contents of the flask. Note and record the time required to fill a 13- × 100-mm test tube with gas.

6. *The Importance of Mixing Reactants*

(a) Half-fill two 13- × 100-mm test tubes with water. Drop a small crystal of solid $KMnO_4$ into each tube. Put one tube aside in a test tube rack or beaker and let it remain undisturbed. Swirl the second tube to dissolve the crystal of $KMnO_4$. Observe the crystal in the undisturbed tube every few minutes and note how long it takes for the crystal to dissolve and for the dissolved $KMnO_4$ to spread (diffuse). Record your observations.

(b) Add 10 mL of 0.50 M $H_2C_2O_4$ to 10 mL of 6 M H_2SO_4 and mix thoroughly. Place 8 mL of this solution into each of two 15- × 150-mm test tubes. Measure out two separate 8-mL portions of 0.005 M $KMnO_4$. Add one portion of $KMnO_4$ solution to one of the test tubes containing oxalic acid, holding the test tube at a 45° angle and carefully pouring the $KMnO_4$ down the side of the test tube to avoid mixing the two solutions. Note the time. Pour another 8 mL of $KMnO_4$ into the second test tube, stopper the tube, mix by inverting the tube several times, and note the time. As the reaction proceeds, MnO_4^- will oxidize the oxalic acid to CO_2 and will itself be reduced to colorless Mn^{2+} ion. Record the time required for the solutions in the two test tubes to become completely colorless.

The Rate of a Chemical Reaction

Chemical Kinetics

PURPOSE

To determine the rate law for the reaction

$$H_2O_2 + 2I^- + 2H^+ \rightarrow I_2 + 2H_2O$$

by observing how changing the concentrations of H_2O_2, I^-, and H^+ affects the rate of reaction. To see the effect of temperature on the reaction rate. To observe the effect on the reaction rate of adding a catalyst, molybdate ion.

PRE-LAB PREPARATION

Two important questions may be asked about a chemical reaction: (1) *How far* or how completely do the reactants interact to yield products, and (2) *how fast* is the reaction? The first question, "How far?" is a question of chemical equilibrium. The study of chemical systems at equilibrium is the realm of chemical energetics, more commonly called *chemical thermodynamics*. The second question, "How fast?" is the realm of *chemical kinetics*, the subject of this experiment. For elementary reversible reactions, there is a direct relation between the equilibrium constant and the rate constants for the forward and reverse reactions. Furthermore, a study of the factors affecting the rate often gives important information about the reaction pathway or the mechanism of the chemical reaction.

In this experiment we will see how changing the concentrations of each of the reactants affects the rate and yields the rate law for the reaction. We will measure the effect of a catalyst on the rate of the reaction, and we will measure the effect of temperature on the rate of reaction. This should give you a better understanding of the particular reaction being studied and increase your understanding of the more complete discussion of these problems as presented in your text. Let us first discuss some of the problems to be considered.

TABLE 35-1
Rate expressions for different reaction paths for the overall reaction 2A + B → products

Reaction pathway*	Rate law or rate expression	Reaction order with respect to reactant A	Reaction order with respect to reactant B	Total reaction order (a + b)
PATHWAY 1: 2A + B → P	rate = $k[A]^2[B]$	2	1	3
PATHWAY 2: 2A → C (slow) B + C → P (fast)	rate = $k[A]^2$	2	0	2
PATHWAY 3: A + B → D + E (slow) D + A → E (fast) 2E → P (fast)	rate = $k[A][B]$	1	1	2

* The symbols A and B represent reactants, and P the products of the stoichiometric reaction. The symbols C, D, and E represent *chemical intermediates* that are formed in the elementary reactions. Intermediates have only a fleeting existence and do not appear as final products of the reaction.

1. *How does the concentration of each of the reacting substances affect the rate?* For a homogeneous[1] chemical reaction, it is usually possible to express the rate as an algebraic function of the concentrations of the reactants. For many chemical reactions, this algebraic function is simply the product of the concentrations of the reactants, each concentration being raised to a power called the *order* of the reaction with respect to that reactant. As an example, suppose that we have a reaction whose overall stoichiometry is

$$2A + B \rightarrow P \qquad (1)$$

and whose *rate law* can be expressed by an algebraic function of the type

$$\text{rate} = k[A]^a[B]^b \qquad (2)$$

The proportionality constant k, called the *specific rate constant*, is the rate when the concentrations of A and B are both 1 mol/L. Brackets around the symbols A and B mean "concentrations of" A and B.

Right at the beginning, we emphasize that the values of the exponents a and b that appear in the rate expression cannot be predicted from the overall stoichiometry and must be determined by experiment. In other words, *rate expressions based on the stoichiometric equation are seldom correct.* This is because the reaction pathway (or reaction mechanism) seldom involves the simultaneous collision of all reactants to yield products in a one-step reaction, which we will call an *elementary reaction.*[2] The stoichiometric equation more often represents the sum of several elementary reactions, at least one of which may be distinctly slower than the others and is therefore the rate-controlling reaction. The rate expression then corresponds to the rate for the slow step in the total reaction. Also keep in mind that in writing a rate expression like that of Equation (2) we have assumed that the rate of the backward reaction is negligible. To illustrate how the rate law depends on the reaction pathway, we show in Table 35-1 three different hypothetical reaction mechanisms, each having the overall stoichiometry 2A + B → P. The rate expression for each reaction pathway is shown, together with the reaction orders with respect to A and B, and the *total reaction order*. Note that for each reaction pathway, the sum of all the elementary reactions gives the stoichiometric equation. Note that for the first reaction pathway, where the elementary reaction is identical to the stoichiometric reaction, doubling the concentrations of A and B would

---

[1] A *homogeneous reaction* is one occurring uniformly throughout *one phase* (a solution, for example), while a *heterogeneous reaction* is one occurring at the interface of *two phases* (a solid and liquid, or gas and solid, for example). The reaction rate of the latter type depends on the extent of subdivision and surface area of the phases, and on adsorption and other phenomena.

[2] The *reaction pathway* (or *reaction mechanism*) of a chemical reaction is composed of a set of molecular reactions, which we call elementary reactions, or *steps*, and which are written just like overall chemical reactions. You must be careful in your thinking to distinguish between these elementary reactions and the stoichiometric chemical equation. Only for a single-step reaction in which the elementary reaction is identical to the overall stoichiometric reaction will the exponents appearing in the rate expression be the same as the coefficients appearing in the stoichiometric equation.

increase the rate by a factor of 8 ($2^2 \times 2^1 = 8$); for the second and third pathways, the rate would be increased by a factor of 4.

Determining the rate law is often one of the first steps in a kinetic investigation. This task can often be simplified by using a small concentration of one reactant in the presence of 50- to 100-fold larger concentrations of all the other reactants. Under these conditions, the concentrations of the reactants in excess remain essentially constant, so that the total order of the reaction is reduced to the order of the reactant present at a small concentration. For example, the first reaction mechanism shown in Table 35-1 has the rate law given by rate = $k[A]^2[B]$. If the concentration of A is made much larger than the concentration of B, the rate expression is given by rate = $k'[B]$, where $k' = k[A]^2$, the concentration of A being treated as a constant because it changes only 2 to 4% during the course of the reaction. The total third-order reaction can now be treated as a *pseudo-first-order* reaction with respect to the reactants. This is sometimes called the "swamping" technique. A related technique, called the *initial rate* method, is to measure the rate of a reaction over a period of time short enough so that less than 5 to 10% of the reactants is consumed. The reactant concentrations can be treated approximately as constants, and the reaction order with respect to each reactant can be determined by varying the concentration of only one constituent at a time and measuring the corresponding rate change.

2. *How does the temperature at which a reaction occurs affect the rate?* Figure 35-1 shows a plot of reaction rate versus temperature for three different classes of reactions. Reactions in Class I (most ordinary chemical reactions in the gas phase and in solution) show a regular exponential increase over a temperature range of 50 to 100°C. Class II behavior is typical of a combustion or explosion reaction. Class III behavior is characteristic of many enzyme-catalyzed reactions: At lower temperatures the reaction rate increases with temperature, but at higher temperatures it decreases as the configuration of the enzyme catalyst is altered and enzyme denaturation occurs. The reaction we will study in this experiment belongs to Class I, often called Arrhenius-type behavior after the chemist who proposed an explanation to account for it.

When we compare measured rates of chemical reactions in the gas phase[3] with the collision rates calculated from the kinetic gas theory, it becomes clear that only a small proportion of the many molecular collisions result in reaction. In most collisions, the molecules simply rebound like billiard balls, without change. Only molecules with the proper geometric orientation and sufficient relative momentum collide with sufficient energy to "break and make" chemical bonds, thus momentarily forming an "activated complex" and eventually forming stable products. The proportion of molecules that have a given energy can be calculated from the Maxwell-Boltzmann distribution law; this proportion increases at higher temperatures as shown in Figure 35-2. We will call the minimum net energy that the colliding molecules must possess in order to react the *activation energy,*

---

[3] We assume in this experiment that the arguments based on kinetic gas theory also apply qualitatively to chemical reactions in solution.

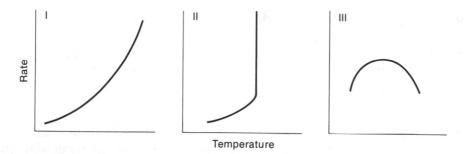

FIGURE 35-1
Effect of temperature on reaction rate. Class I: exponential (Arrhenius) behavior typical of most simple inorganic and organic reactions. Class II: typical of explosion reactions. Class III: typical of enzyme-catalyzed reactions. [After A.A. Frost and R.G. Pearson, *Kinetics and Mechanism*, 2nd ed., Wiley, New York, Chapter 2, Figure 7. Copyright © 1961.]

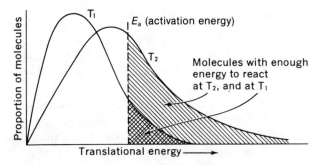

FIGURE 35-2
The Maxwell-Boltzmann distribution law. At a higher temperature (curve T_2), the total number of molecules (shaded area under this curve) with energies greater than E_a, the critical energy necessary for reaction, is much larger at temperature T_2 than at the lower temperature (curve T_1).

E_a. The situation is somewhat analogous to an attempt to roll a ball up from a mountain valley, over a pass, and down to another valley. The energy necessary to get the ball up to the top of the pass is the activation energy.

3. *How does a catalyst affect a reaction?* A catalyst is a substance that alters a reaction pathway in such a way as to decrease the activation energy requirement for the reaction. A lower activation energy for the catalyzed reaction means that at a given temperature, a larger fraction of the molecules will possess enough energy to react, and thus the catalyst increases the rates of *both* the forward and backward reactions without affecting the equilibrium constant for the reaction. Although the catalyst is not consumed in the overall reaction, it may participate in the formation of intermediates and then be re-formed in subsequent steps to produce the final products.

THE EXPERIMENTAL METHOD

In this experiment we will study the rate of oxidation of iodide ion by hydrogen peroxide, which proceeds according to the net stoichiometric reaction

$$H_2O_2 + 2I^- + 2H^+ \rightarrow I_2 + 2H_2O \quad (3)$$

By varying the concentrations of each of the three reactants (H_2O_2, I^-, and H^+) we will determine the order of the reaction with respect to each reactant and the rate law of the reaction, which is of the form

$$\text{rate} = \frac{-d[H_2O_2]}{dt} = k[H_2O_2]^a[I^-]^b[H^+]^c \quad (4)$$

where a, b, and c must be experimentally determined and are most often integers (0, 1, 2, etc.) or half-integers. We will use an acetic acid/acetate ion buffer to control the H^+ concentration at a small constant value, around 10^{-5} M. By using a solution containing known concentrations of acetic acid and acetate ion, we can readily calculate the H^+ concentration from the equilibrium constant expression for the dissociation of acetic acid, given by

$$K_a = \frac{[H^+][CH_3COO^-]}{[CH_3COOH]} \quad (5)$$

We will also examine the effect of temperature on the reaction rate and the effect of a catalyst (3.3×10^{-4} M Mo(VI)).

To measure the reaction rate we will employ a clever variation of the initial rate method. A small amount of sodium thiosulfate and starch indicator is added to the reaction mixture. Thiosulfate ion does not react at an appreciable rate with any of the reactants, but it does react rapidly with iodine, according to the equation

$$S_2O_3^{2-} + I_2 \rightarrow 2I^- + S_4O_6^{2-} \quad (6)$$

As a result, iodine is reduced back to iodide ion as fast as it is formed until all of the thiosulfate is used up. At this point the solution suddenly turns blue because the iodine concentration rapidly increases to the point where the I_2 forms an intense blue complex with the starch indicator. The time required to consume a fixed amount of thiosulfate is very reproducible, and since we measure this time, this type of reaction is often called a clock reaction.

While thiosulfate ion is present in solution, both reactions (3) and (6) are simultaneously taking place, and, by adding them together, we see that the net result in solution is given by

$$H_2O_2 + 2S_2O_3^{2-} + 2H^+ \rightarrow 2H_2O + S_4O_6^{2-} \quad (7)$$

You should be careful to note that Equation (7) expresses only the net result of the two reactions. Hydrogen peroxide is not reacting directly with $S_2O_3^{2-}$, but the result is the same as if it did, and 2 mol of thiosulfate are consumed per mole of hydrogen peroxide reacted. Knowing the amount of thiosulfate we put in the reaction mixture, we can calculate the reaction rate from the equation

$$\text{rate (mol·L}^{-1}\text{·s}^{-1}) = \frac{-d[H_2O_2]}{dt} \qquad (8)$$

which can be approximated by the expressions

$$\frac{-d[H_2O_2]}{dt} \cong \frac{-\Delta[H_2O_2]}{\Delta t} = -\frac{1}{2}\frac{\Delta[S_2O_3^{2-}]}{\Delta t} \qquad (9)$$

and

$$\text{rate} \cong \frac{1}{2}\frac{\left[\dfrac{VM_{\text{thiosulfate}}}{V_T}\right]}{\Delta t} \qquad (10)$$

where $VM_{\text{thiosulfate}}$ is the number of millimoles of thiosulfate added ($V_{\text{mL}} \times M_{\text{mol/L}}$), V_T is the total volume (in milliliters) of the reaction mixture, and Δt is the time required for all of the thiosulfate to react. (In order to make the expression for the rate of reaction a positive quantity, we insert the minus sign, because $\Delta[H_2O_2]/\Delta t$ is a negative quantity because the hydrogen peroxide concentration is decreasing with time. The factor of $\frac{1}{2}$ is inserted because hydrogen peroxide disappears half as fast as thiosulfate, as shown by the stoichiometry of Equation (7).)

Equation (8) is written as an exact differential expression, which implies the measurement of an instantaneous reaction rate, whereas we must measure the average reaction rate over a finite interval in which the hydrogen peroxide concentration changes slightly [as shown by Equation (9)]. But if only a small amount of hydrogen peroxide is consumed (say, less than 3% of the total), our rate measurement will be a very close approximation to the exact differential expression shown in Equation (8) and will accurately measure the true initial rate of reaction of the hydrogen peroxide.

Now we are in a position to understand how the thiosulfate plays an important role in the rate measurement. First, it allows us to make a simple measurement of the reaction rate by measuring the time required for a given amount of thiosulfate to be consumed under conditions where only a small fraction of the hydrogen peroxide is consumed. It also reacts rapidly with the reaction product I_2 as it forms, regenerating I^-. This keeps the I^- concentration constant and suppresses any backward reaction (the reverse of Equation (3)), so that we can be confident that we are measuring only the rate of the forward reaction.

EXPERIMENTAL PROCEDURE

Special Supplies: Buret, 5-mL graduated pipets, 10-mL graduated pipets, thermometer, timer (a digital watch or a clock with a sweep second hand is suitable). The optional standardization procedure requires the foregoing and a 1-mL pipet.

NOTE   All solutions for this experiment should be made up in high quality distilled or deionized water. Traces of metal ions, particularly copper or iron salts, catalyze the decomposition of H_2O_2.

Chemicals: 0.8 to 0.9 M H_2O_2 containing 0.001 M H_2SO_4 (the small amount of acid stabilizes the H_2O_2 solution and has a negligible effect on the rate measurements; a *fresh* 3% H_2O_2 solution of the type sold in drugstores is about 0.9 M and can be used for the H_2O_2 solution, which must be standardized, preferably on the day the solution is to be used); 0.050 M sodium thiosulfate ($Na_2S_2O_3$), 0.050 M KI, 0.050 M acetic acid/sodium acetate buffer (0.05 M in CH_3COOH and 0.05 M in $NaCH_3COO$), 0.30 M acetic acid (CH_3COOH), 0.1% starch solution (freshly made), 0.010 M Mo(VI) catalyst (containing 1.76 g/L of ammonium heptamolybdate ($NH_4)_6Mo_7O_{24}\cdot4H_2O$). The H_2O_2 standardization procedure requires, in addition, KI(s), 2 M H_2SO_4, and 3% ammonium heptamolybdate catalyst solution in a dropping bottle.

NOTE   Two students may work together advantageously in this experiment, one student mixing the solutions and the other noting the time to the exact second or fraction of a second. However, *each student should record the data* completely before leaving the laboratory, either in tabular form in the student's lab book or on the report forms.

A. Standardization of the H_2O_2 Solution

The instructor will tell you if you are to perform the standardization. For best results, the H_2O_2 solution should be standardized the same day it is to be used. The concentration should be in the range 0.8 to 0.9 M in order to yield conveniently measurable reaction times.

Procedure for Standardization   First fill a buret with 0.050 M $Na_2S_2O_3$. Then pipet exactly 1.00 mL of the approximately 0.8 M H_2O_2 solution into a 125-mL Erlenmeyer flask containing 25 mL of water.

Add 10 mL of 2 M H_2SO_4, 1 g of solid KI, and 3 drops of 3% ammonium molybdate catalyst.

Swirl until the KI dissolves and immediately titrate the brown iodine solution that forms with 0.050 M sodium thiosulfate until the brown color begins to fade to yellow.

At this point, add 2 mL of 0.1% starch indicator and titrate to the disappearance of the blue color of the starch-iodine complex. The end point is very sharp and should require 32 to 36 mL of 0.050 M Na₂S₂O₃ for the conditions specified.

Calculate the exact concentration of the hydrogen peroxide stock solution, which should be in the range 0.8 to 0.9 M.

B. Reaction Rate Measurements

Six reaction mixtures will provide the information necessary to determine the effects of the concentrations of H_2O_2, I^-, and H^+ on the rate of the reaction as well as the effect of temperature and a catalyst. Table 35-2 specifies the temperature and reagent volumes to be used for each reaction mixture.

General Instructions Make up each reaction mixture in a 250-mL beaker, adding the reactants for each reaction mixture in the order in which they appear in Table 35-2 (reading from left to right). Read and record the temperature to the nearest 0.2°C. Graduated cylinders (100, 50, and 10 mL) can be used to measure the volumes of water, buffer, KI, starch, acetic acid, sodium acetate, and catalyst. Special care should be taken to measure the volumes as accurately as possible. If you performed the standardization, the 0.050 M Na₂S₂O₃ solution can be conveniently dispensed from a buret; otherwise use a 5-mL graduated pipet. The H_2O_2 is conveniently dispensed from a 10-mL graduated pipet (or 10-mL graduated cylinder).

To avoid contamination of the reagents it is best to use a separate pipet or graduated cylinder for dispensing each solution. Put labels on them so you don't confuse them. You must be especially careful not to get any contaminant in your hydrogen peroxide stock solution. Iodide ion catalyzes the decomposition of H_2O_2 into oxygen and water, and saliva contains substances that catalyze decomposition of H_2O_2, so do not pipet any solutions by mouth. If you use pipets, draw up the solutions with a rubber bulb.

The first step in each reaction measurement is to place in a clean 250-mL beaker the specified volumes of each reagent listed on the left of the vertical line in Table 35-2. (The beakers *must* be clean. If they are not, wash them with detergent, rinse them thoroughly with tap water, then give them a final rinse with deionized water, and shake off the excess. Do not attempt to dry them with a paper towel; it may leave contamination.) The beaker now contains all the reactants except H_2O_2. The timer or stopwatch is started when the hydrogen peroxide is added (with vigorous stirring) and stopped when the solution turns blue. The final volume of each reaction mixture is 150 mL. Knowing this fact and the amount of each reactant added, you can easily compute the initial concentration of each reactant.

You will run a duplicate measurement on the first reaction mixture in order to check your technique. If time permits (and your instructor so directs), make duplicate measurements for each reaction mixture.

Inaccuracies most often arise when mistakes are made in measuring out the reactants (or forgetting to add a reactant!), or when the solution is inadequately stirred while the hydrogen peroxide is being added. You must also be careful not to get any contaminant in your hydrogen peroxide stock solution, since many substances catalyze its decomposition into water and oxygen.

TABLE 35-2
Composition of the reaction mixtures

Reaction mixture	Temperature	Water (mL)	0.05 M CH₃COOH/ CH₃COONa buffer (mL)	0.3 M CH₃COOH (mL)	0.05 M KI (mL)	0.1% starch (mL)	0.05 M Na₂S₂O₃ (mL)	0.01 M Mo(VI) catalyst (mL)	0.8 M H₂O₂ (mL)
1	R.T.*	75	30	0	25	5	5	0	10
2	R.T.	80	30	0	25	5	5	0	5
3	R.T.	50	30	0	50	5	5	0	10
4	R.T.	30	30	45	25	5	5	0	10
5	R.T. + 12	75	30	0	25	5	5	0	10
6	R.T.	70	30	0	25	5	5	5	10

* R.T. stands for room temperature.

Mixture 1. Place all reactants except H_2O_2 in a 400-mL beaker. Note and record the temperature of the solution. Arrange your watch or have your timer ready.

Then add, using a pipet, exactly 10 mL of H_2O_2 solution and stir continuously. Start the timer when half of the H_2O_2 solution has drained from the pipet and continue stirring until you are certain the solution is thoroughly mixed.

Watch the solution carefully for the sudden appearance of the blue color and stop the timer when it appears. (The total elapsed time should be of the order of 2 to 4 min.) Again note and record the temperature.

Discard the solution and rinse the beaker.

Repeat the measurement using a fresh solution. The times should agree within a few seconds.

Mixture 2. Prepare solution 2 and note and record the temperature, which should be within 0.5C° of the temperature recorded for mixture 1. (The temperature may be adjusted if necessary by cooling or heating in a water bath contained in a larger beaker.)

When the timer is ready, add 5 mL of H_2O_2 solution. Since the concentration of H_2O_2 is less than in mixture 1, you may expect that the reaction time will be at least as great as that for mixture 1.

Again, note and record the temperature at the end of the measurement.

Mixture 3. Prepare solution 3.

Note and record the temperature, which should be the same as for mixtures 1 and 2 (adjust if necessary). Note that the concentration of KI has been doubled over that contained in mixture 1, so the reaction time may be shorter.

Carry out the measurement as described for mixture 1.

Mixture 4. Carry out the measurement as described for mixture 1. This solution contains ten times as much acetic acid, therefore the H^+ concentration is ten times larger. If the reaction time is the same as for mixture 1, what does this suggest about the reaction order with respect to H^+?

Mixture 5. Prepare solution 5, which has the same composition as solution 1, and place it in a beaker of hot water.

Stir until the temperature is about 12 to 15C° above that of mixture 1, then add 10 mL of H_2O_2 solution, start the timer, and note and record the temperature.

When the solution turns blue, stop the timer and again note and record the temperature. (The average of the two readings is taken as the temperature of the reaction mixture.)

Mixture 6. This has the same composition as mixture 1, except that it contains 5.0 mL of 0.010 M Mo(VI) catalyst. Mixture 6 is adjusted to the same temperature as mixture 1, 10 mL of H_2O_2 is added, and the reaction time is recorded.

C. Interpretation of the Data

1. *Calculating the Reaction Orders* When we want to measure the order of a reaction with respect to a reactant, we vary the initial concentration of that reactant and keep constant the initial concentrations of all other reactants and the temperature.

For example, note that in reaction mixtures 1 and 2 only the concentration of H_2O_2 has been changed. (See Table 35-2.) To get the reaction order with respect to H_2O_2 we first note that the reaction rate is inversely proportional to the reaction time, Δt, as shown by Equation (10). Because we put the same amount of thiosulfate ion in each reaction mixture, the concentration terms cancel out when we take the ratio. Therefore the ratio of the reaction rates for any two reaction mixtures will be equal to the inverse of the ratio of the reaction times.

$$\frac{\text{rate}_1}{\text{rate}_2} = \frac{\Delta t_2}{\Delta t_1} \tag{11}$$

Starting with Equation (4), we can write expressions for the rates of reaction in reaction mixtures 1 and 2.

For reaction mixture 1

$$\text{rate}_1 = k[H_2O_2]_1^a \, [I^-]^b [H^+]^c \tag{12}$$

For reaction mixture 2

$$\text{rate}_2 = k[H_2O_2]_2^a [I^-]^b [H^+]^c \tag{13}$$

Dividing Equation (12) by Equation (13), we obtain an expression for the ratio rate$_1$/rate$_2$.

$$\frac{\text{rate}_1}{\text{rate}_2} = \frac{\Delta t_2}{\Delta t_1} = \left(\frac{[H_2O_2]_1}{[H_2O_2]_2}\right)^a \tag{14}$$

Note that when we write the equation for the ratio of the rates, all of the concentrations that have been held constant in the two reaction mixtures cancel out, leaving only the ratio of the concentrations of H_2O_2 (raised to the power of the reaction order, a). In addition, if the temperature is constant, the specific rate constant, k, that appears in Equations (12) and (13) will also cancel out.

Because we know the reaction times and the concentrations of H_2O_2 in reaction mixtures 1 and 2, we can calculate the unknown reaction order, a, with respect to H_2O_2. The nearest integer value of the reaction order can usually be determined by inspection, but if the logarithms of both sides of Equation (11) are taken, we can calculate a from the resulting equation.

$$a = \frac{\log(\Delta t_2/\Delta t_1)}{\log([H_2O_2]_1/[H_2O_2]_2)} \qquad (15)$$

The same method is ued to obtain the reaction order with respect to I^- (using the data for reaction mixtures 3 and 1) and the reaction order with respect to H^+ (using the data for reaction mixtures 4 and 1).

2. Effect of Temperature   In reaction mixtures 5 and 1 the concentrations of all the reactants are the same, but the temperature of mixture 5 is greater than that of mixture 1. As before, the ratio of the rates is given by the inverse ratio of the reaction times. Because all of the concentration terms are the same, they cancel out; but the specific rate constants do not cancel because the specific rate constant changes with temperature. Therefore we have

$$\frac{\text{rate}_5}{\text{rate}_1} = \frac{\Delta t_1}{\Delta t_5} = \frac{k_{T_5}}{k_{T_1}} \qquad (16)$$

where k_{T_5} and k_{T_1} are the specific rate constants at the temperatures T_5 and T_1 of reaction mixtures 5 and 1, respectively.

3. Effect of a Catalyst   Using the measured reaction times, we can calculate the ratio of the reaction rates from the data for reaction mixtures 6 and 1.

$$\frac{\text{rate}_6(\text{catalyzed})}{\text{rate}_1(\text{uncatalyzed})} = \frac{\Delta t_1}{\Delta t_6} \qquad (17)$$

How many times faster is the catalyzed reaction rate? What is the molar concentration of the Mo(VI) catalyst in the reaction mixture?

BIBLIOGRAPHY

Bamford, C. H., and Tipper, C. F. H. (eds.), *Comprehensive Chemical Kinetics*, Elsevier Publishing Co., New York, 1972, Vol. 6, p. 406. A summary discussion with references of the reaction of hydrogen peroxide with halide ions.

King, E. L., *How Chemical Reactions Occur*, W. A. Benjamin, Inc., Menlo Park, CA, 1963, pp. 36–38, 80–82.

**The Rate of a
Chemical Reaction
Chemical Kinetics**

NAME

SECTION   LOCKER

INSTRUCTOR   DATE

A. STANDARDIZATION OF THE H_2O_2 SOLUTION

If your instructor so directs, carry out the standardization procedure in duplicate.

Data		Trial 1	Trial 2
Buret readings	Final	_____	_____
	Initial	_____	_____
mL of 0.050 M $Na_2S_2O_3$	Net	_____	_____

Calculate the H_2O_2 concentration, which should be in the range 0.8 to 0.9 M. If it is outside this range consult your instructor.

B. REACTION RATE MEASUREMENTS

Make the measurement on mixture 1 in duplicate; a single measurement for the other mixtures will be sufficient. If a measurement is spoiled for any reason it should be repeated.

| Reaction mixture | Trial 1 | | | | Trial 2 | | | |
| | Time (s) | Temperature (°C) | | | Time (s) | Temperature (°C) | | |
		Initial	Final	Average		Initial	Final	Average
1								
2								
3								
4								
5								
6								

C. INTERPRETATION OF THE DATA

1. Calculating the Reaction Orders

(a) Order of the reaction with respect to hydrogen peroxide, H_2O_2

Reaction mixture	Time (s)	H_2O_2 concentration in the reaction mixture (mol/L)
1		
2		

Using Equation (15), calculate the reaction order and round off to the nearest integer.

(b) Order of the reaction with respect to iodide ion, I^-

Reaction mixture	Time (s)	I^- concentration in the reaction mixture (mol/L)
1		
3		

Using Equation (15), calculate the reaction order and round off to the nearest integer.

(c) Order of the reaction with respect to H^+

Taking K_a for acetic acid as 1.8×10^{-5} M, calculate the H^+ concentration from Equation (5) using the known concentrations of acetic acid and sodium acetate contained in reaction mixtures 1 and 4. (In mixture 4 be sure that you account for the acetic acid contained in both the buffer and the added 0.3 M acetic acid.)

Reaction mixture	Time (s)	Acetic acid concentration (mol/L)	Sodium acetate concentration (mol/L)	Calculated H^+ concentration (mol/L)
1				
4				

Show your calculations of the H^+ concentration.

Using Equation (15), calculate the reaction order and round off to the nearest integer.

2. Effect of Temperature

Reaction mixture	Time (s)	Temperature (°C)
1		
5		

Using Equation (16), calculate the reaction rate ratio for reaction mixtures 5 and 1. When the temperature is increased, does the reaction rate decrease or increase?

$$\frac{rate_5}{rate_1} =$$

3. Effect of a Catalyst

Reaction mixture	Time (s)	Mo(VI) concentration in the reaction mixture (mol/L)
1		
6		

Using Equation (17), calculate the ratio of the rates of the catalyzed and uncatalyzed reactions.

$$\frac{rate(catalyzed)}{rate(uncatalyzed)} =$$

QUESTIONS

1. Calculating the Reaction Orders

(a) From your measurements, what are the reaction orders with respect to each of the three reactants H_2O_2, I^-, and H^+?

(b) What is the rate expression (rate law) for the uncatalyzed reaction?

(c) What is the total reaction order?

(d) Is the rate law consistent with the idea that the mechanism of the reaction is $H_2O_2 + 2I^- + 2H^+ \rightarrow I_2 + 2H_2O$ (all in one step)? Why?

(e) The following reaction pathway has been proposed for the pH range 3.5 to 7:

$$H_2O_2 + I^- \rightarrow OH^- + HOI$$

$$H^+ + OH^- \rightleftharpoons H_2O$$

$$\underline{HOI + H^+ + I^- \rightarrow I_2 + H_2O}$$

Add the above equations. Do they give the overall reaction? _____

Which of the steps would be the slow, rate-determining step according to your results? _____

If the proposed mechanism agrees with the experimental rate law, does this prove that the mechanism is correct and that no other pathway is possible? _____Why not? _____

2. Effect of Temperature

From your measurements comment on the oft-quoted statement that "the rate of a chemical reaction approximately doubles for every 10 C° temperature increase."

PROBLEMS

1. Considering the volumes and the concentrations used in mixture 1, what percentage of the moles of H_2O_2 present have been consumed during the timed reaction? How does the I^- concentration change during this same time? Why?

---

2. Using Equations (10) and (12), calculate the specific rate constant, k, from your data for reaction mixture 1. [Use the integer reaction orders you determined for a, b, and c in the rate expression of Equation (12).] Compare your value with the reported value of 0.0115 $L \cdot mol^{-1} \cdot s^{-1}$ at 25°C for the uncatalyzed reaction.

---

3. It has been found that in acid solution (greater than 1 M H^+) the rate expression for the reaction of H_2O_2 with I^- is of the form rate $= k_2[H_2O_2][I^-][H^+]$ where $k_2 = 0.25$ $L^2 \cdot mol^{-2} \cdot s^{-1}$ at 25°C. Therefore the rate law over the whole range of acidity from very acid solutions to a neutral solution is given by a *two-term* rate expression:

$$\text{rate} = k_1[H_2O_2][I^-] + k_2[H_2O_2][I^-][H^+]$$

where k_1 has the value of 0.0115 $L \cdot mol^{-1} \cdot s^{-1}$ at 25°C. Compare the relative magnitudes of these two terms under the conditions employed in your rate measurements for mixture 1. (You should find that the second term makes a negligible contribution to the reaction rate at H^+ concentrations smaller than 3×10^{-4}.)

Turbidimetric Determination of Sulfate in Natural Waters

PURPOSE

To determine small concentrations of sulfate ion in natural waters or bottled drinking water by precipitating the sulfate ion with barium ion to form a turbid suspension of barium sulfate and measuring the turbidity in a spectrophotometer.

PRE-LAB PREPARATION

Natural fresh waters and bottled mineral water contain mainly calcium and magnesium cations and bicarbonate and sulfate anions. These ions come mainly from the reactions of rainwater with rocks and soil. (See Experiment 23.) Gypsum ($CaSO_4 \cdot 2H_2O$) and calcite ($CaCO_3$) are commonly found in sedimentary rocks at the earth's surface. Gypsum is slightly soluble in water and all of the carbonates can be readily dissolved by water containing traces of acid. The main acid present in rainwater is dissolved CO_2. As water containing CO_2 flows over soil containing calcium carbonate ($CaCO_3$) or dolomite [$MgCa(CO_3)_2$] the following reactions occur.

$$CO_2(g) + H_2O + CaCO_3(s) \rightleftharpoons$$
$$Ca^{2+}(aq) + 2HCO_3^-(aq)$$

$$2CO_2(g) + 2H_2O` + CaMg(CO_3)_2(s) \rightleftharpoons$$
$$Ca^{2+}(aq) + Mg^{2+}(aq) + 4HCO_3^-(aq)$$

Natural spring waters usually contain the same ions as river and lake water, but sometimes in greater concentration (about 500 mg of salts per liter). Humans apparently have become used to the taste of natural waters containing these dissolved salts. In fact, most people find the taste of distilled water or deionized water to be flat, insipid, and unappetizing.

Although mineral waters have often been touted as aids to health and digestion, there is no clear-cut evidence that the modest amount of minerals imbibed when drinking water has a significant nutritional effect.[1] Rather, it appears that drinking mineral water is a cultural pattern that has been well established in Europe for many years but that has only recently become popular in the United States. In addition to the taste provided by the dissolved carbonates and sulfates, many people like the effervescence and slightly acidic taste of carbonated mineral waters.

Some bottlers of mineral waters claim that their product comes from natural springs, but it is a common practice in the industry to start with an ordinary grade of natural water, remove all of the salts by deionization or reverse osmosis, then reconstitute the mineral water by adding controlled amounts of various salts. This gives the producer control of the uniformity and taste of the product. Moreover, it allows local production using any suitable water source. This reduces transportation costs.

The sulfate ion in most natural waters is probably of no nutritional significance for humans because we get most of the sulfur we need from our food, mainly in the form of sulfur-containing amino acids (methionine and cysteine) found in proteins. In fact, we ingest only small amounts of sulfur in the form of sulfate and the 2 to 5 g of inorganic sulfate excreted daily in the urine comes mainly from the metabolism of sulfur-containing amino acids.

Microorganisms in the soil and plants get most of the sulfur they need in the form of inorganic sulfate that is present in surface waters and soils.

Experiment 23 describes the determination of the calcium and magnesium ion content of natural waters. In this experiment you will determine the content of sulfate ion, SO_4^{2-}. Sulfate ion can be determined by precipitation with barium ion to form the very insoluble barium sulfate.

$$Ba^{2+}(aq) + SO_4^{2-}(aq) \rightleftharpoons BaSO_4(s)$$

If the amount of sulfate is sufficiently large, it can be filtered off and weighed, but this is somewhat tedious. It is also difficult to do this accurately if the sulfate ion concentration is small.

An alternative method uses the same chemical reaction, but keeps the finely divided barium sulfate precipitate in suspension. By measuring in a spectrophotometer the amount of light that passes through the turbid suspension, we can make a quantitative measurement of the sulfate ion concentration. This is done by constructing a calibration curve based on measurements of the turbidities of known concentrations of sulfate. The points are plotted to make a graph of turbidity *versus* concentration of sulfate ion. The turbidity of the unknown solution is then measured and the concentration of the unknown solution is read from the graph as shown in Figure 36-1.

The turbidity of the solutions is measured with a spectrophotometer. Figure 36-2 is a diagram of

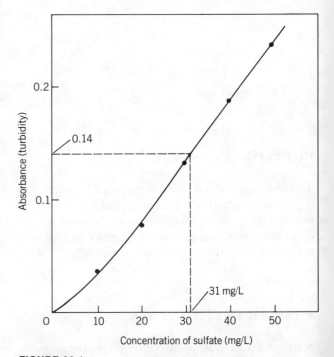

FIGURE 36-1
A calibration curve obtained by plotting the absorbance (turbidity) of suspensions of barium sulfate versus the concentration of sulfate in the samples. The measured turbidity of the unknown (0.14 absorbance units) corresponds to a concentration of 31 mg/L of sulfate in the unknown.

---

[1] The minerals in water can provide certain health benefits. Trace amounts of fluoride (approximately 1 mg/L) have been shown to provide protection against dental caries, and many communities deliberately add small amounts of fluoride to their water supplies to provide this protection.

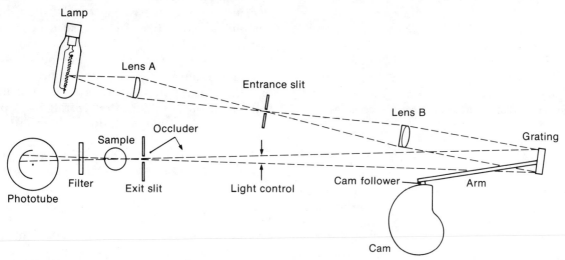

FIGURE 36-2
Schematic optical diagram of the Bausch & Lomb Spectronic 20.

the popular Bausch & Lomb Spectronic 20, which consists of a light source, an entrance slit and lenses to collimate (form a parallel beam of) the light, a reflection grating to disperse the light into its component wavelengths, an exit slit to isolate a narrow slice of the dispersed light of known wavelength, a sample cell holder, and a detector to measure the amount of light that passes through the sample.

The light detectors used in most spectrophotometers provide an electrical signal that is proportional to the radiant power (P). We may think of the radiant power as a measure of light intensity equal to the number of light photons arriving per second at the detector.

The measurement of the light absorption by the sample is made by first positioning the grating to give the desired wavelength of light. Adjust 0% next. Then a tube containing pure water is inserted in the sample cell holder and the light control (100% Transmittance Adjust Knob) is adjusted so that the meter reads its maximum value (100% Transmittance). Then a similar cell containing a turbid suspension of barium sulfate is placed in the cell holder. Because the suspension blocks or absorbs some of the light, less light will arrive at the detector. The meter reads the *transmittance*, the fraction of the radiant power that has passed through the sample. (When multiplied by 100 it is called the *percent of transmittance*, %T; see Figure 36-3.)

$$\text{transmittance, } T = \frac{P}{P_0} \quad \%T = \frac{P}{P_0} \times 100 \quad (1)$$

The probability that a photon will be absorbed at a particular point in the cell is proportional to both the *turbidity* (concentration of absorbing particles) and the number of photons per second arriving at that point. This absorption of photons causes the radiant power (P) to decline exponentially as it passes through the absorbing sample:

$$P = P_0(10^{-abc}) \quad (2)$$

where P_0 is the radiant power of the beam when

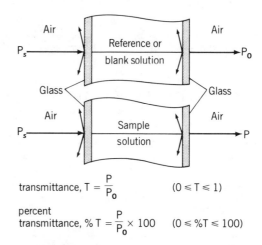

$$\text{transmittance, } T = \frac{P}{P_0} \quad (0 \leq T \leq 1)$$

$$\text{percent transmittance, } \%T = \frac{P}{P_0} \times 100 \quad (0 \leq \%T \leq 100)$$

FIGURE 36-3
The measurement of transmittance (or percentage transmittance). The radiant power from the source is P_s. When the reference or blank solution is in the cell, the radiant power that emerges from the cell is P_0. When the sample solution is in the cell, the radiant power that emerges is P. The use of a reference or blank solution compensates for reflection losses at the air/glass and glass/solution interfaces so that only absorption due to the sample is measured.

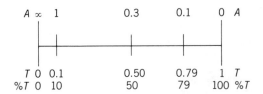

FIGURE 36-4
The relationship between absorbance (*A*), transmittance (*T*), and percentage transmittance (%*T*). The absorbance scale is a non-linear (logarithmic) scale. The transmittance scales are linear.

it enters the sample, P is the radiant power of the beam that has passed through the absorbing sample, a is a constant, b is the cell path length, and c is the concentration of the absorbing sample. Rearranging Equation (2) and taking the logarithms of both sides, we obtain a quantity, called the *absorbance*, that is proportional to the concentration (turbidity) of the sample.

$$\text{absorbance, } A = \log\frac{P_0}{P} = abc \qquad (3)$$

Many spectrophotometers have both a linear %T scale and a nonlinear (logarithmic) absorbance scale. The relationship between these scales is shown in Figure 36-4. We will define the turbidity as the apparent absorbance of the solution as given by Equation (3). With a calculator it is a simple matter to compute the absorbance from the measured %T readings.

$$A = \log\frac{P_0}{P} = \log\frac{100}{\%T} \qquad (4)$$

EXPERIMENTAL PROCEDURE

Special Supplies: Spectrophotometer (Bausch & Lomb Spectronic 20 or equivalent), spectrophotometer cells, water samples containing sulfate ion (tap water, bottled mineral water, seawater, etc.).

Chemicals: Standard solutions containing 10, 20, 30, 40, and 50 mg/L of sulfate ion, 6 M HCl, 70% w:w aqueous sorbitol solution, $BaCl_2 \cdot 2H_2O(s)$.

Safety Precautions: Barium ion is toxic. Do not touch or handle $BaCl_2 \cdot 2H_2O$ with your bare hands. Do not pipet by mouth any solutions containing barium ion. If you spill any solutions containing $BaCl_2$ or $BaSO_4$, clean up the spill immediately and rinse off your hands with tap water. Wash your hands with soap and water before leaving the laboratory.

The procedure described gives a nearly linear working curve in the range 0 to 50 mg/L (parts per million) of sulfate. Samples such as seawater that contain a higher concentration of sulfate ion may be analyzed after accurate dilution. (Seawater should be diluted 100-fold.) Most samples of river or lake water or mineral waters can be analyzed without further dilution. Concentrations of phosphate ion up to 1000 mg/L do not interfere.

1. *Measuring the Absorbance (Turbidity) of the Known and Unknown Samples* Your instructor may ask you to measure the percentage transmittance for each of the standard solutions containing 10, 20, 30, 40, and 50 mg/L of sulfate ion, or you may be assigned just one or two of them. In the latter case, you will be asked to report the measured %T values to the instructor, who will accumulate the measurements made by the class. When you make your plot of absorbance versus concentration of sulfate, use your own measurements or the average of the accumulated class measurements, as the instructor directs.

You will need a clean 20- × 150-mm test tube for each standard solution and the unknown sample. Arrange the test tubes in a test tube rack and label each tube so that it can be identified later. Each solution is prepared in the same way, as follows: Put a 10-mL sample of a standard (or unknown) solution in a test tube, add 1 mL of 6 M HCl, 5 mL of 70% sorbitol, and 1.0 g of $BaCl_2 \cdot 2H_2O$ crystals. Measure the volumes as accurately as possible using pipets or graduated cylinders. In particular, if you must use the same 10-mL pipet (or graduated cylinder) to measure out the standard and unknown water samples, make sure that you rinse the pipet at least twice with small portions of the solution before you fill it.

After you have added the reagents to each tube, stopper them with clean rubber stoppers and shake the tubes vigorously to dissolve the barium chloride. If the sample contains sulfate ion, a white turbid suspension of barium sulfate should form. Allow the tubes to stand for at least 5 min. Then read and record the percentage of transmittance (%T) for each of the solutions in a spectrophotometer at a wavelength of 470 nm. If the suspension has to stand for a particularly long time while you are waiting to use the spectrophotometer, it is advisable to shake the tube gently before you pour it into a sample cell and make the %T reading. (The added sorbitol helps to form a stable suspension of barium sulfate particles that will not rapidly settle out.)

With the Bausch & Lomb Spectronic 20 or similar spectrophotometers, the wavelength is first adjusted to 470 nm, the 0% is adjusted, and then the meter is adjusted to read 100%T when the sample cell is filled with deionized water (or a blank solution containing all the reagents described above, but with 10 mL of deionized water substituted for the 10-mL water sample containing sulfate ion). After adjusting the 100%T setting, put each solution in turn in a clean sample cell, insert the cell in the spectrophotometer, and read and record the %T for the solution. Periodically check the 0% and 100%T settings to make sure that they have not drifted. The 100%T is checked by reinserting the sample tube containing deionized water (or the blank solution).

2. *Analyzing the Data* You will need the %T measurements for each of the standard solutions and the unknown. Use either your own data or the average of the class measurements, as your instructor directs. For each solution, calculate the absorbance from the measured %T by using Equation (4). On the graph paper provided in your report form make a plot of absorbance versus concentration of sulfate ion (in units of milligrams per liter). Draw a smooth curve through the points. From the calculated value of absorbance for the unknown solution, read off the concentration of sulfate ion, as shown in Figure 36-1. If your sample had to be diluted before it could be analyzed, calculate the concentration of sulfate ion (mg/L) in the original sample.

BIBLIOGRAPHY

Verma, B. C., Swaminathan, K., and Sud, K. C., "An Improved Turbidimetric Procedure for the Determination of Sulphate in Plants and Soils," *Talanta* **24,** 49–50 (1977).

Turbidimetric Determination of Sulfate in Natural Waters

NAME

SECTION   LOCKER

INSTRUCTOR   DATE

DATA AND CALCULATIONS

1. Measuring the Absorbance (Turbidity) of the Known and Unknown Samples

Give the identity of the unknown sample (tap water, brand of mineral water, seawater, etc.). _____

Sulfate ion concentration (mg/L)	Percentage transmittance ($0 \leq \%T \leq 100$)	Calculated absorbance $A = \log(100/\%T)$
10	_____	_____
20	_____	_____
30	_____	_____
40	_____	_____
50	_____	_____
Unknown	_____	_____

2. Analyzing the Data

Using the values you determined, or the average of the class results, calculate the *absorbance* of each sample and of the unknown and tabulate the calculated values in the table for part 1. Plot the absorbance versus concentration of sulfate ion (milligrams per liter). Draw a smooth curve through the experimental points and interpolate from the graph the concentration of sulfate ion (milligrams per liter) in the unknown.

Concentration of sulfate in the unknown _____ mg/L

Plot the absorbance at 470 nm versus the concentration of milligrams per liter.

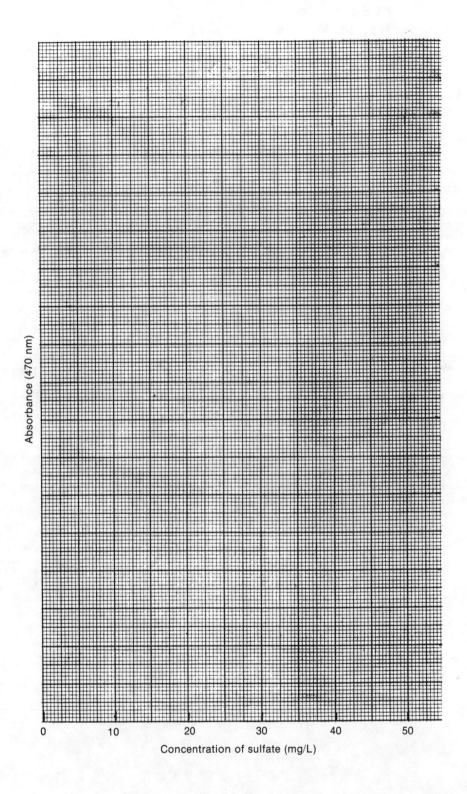

Concentration of sulfate in the unknown _____ mg/L

The Chemistry
of Some Nonmetals:
Nitrogen, Sulfur, and Chlorine

PURPOSE

To become acquainted with the chemistry of three nonmetals (nitrogen, sulfur, and chlorine) whose chemistry is representative of the elements of Main Groups 5, 6, and 7. To show that the nonmetals can exist in a variety of formal oxidation states in their compounds with oxygen and hydrogen. To understand how the chemistry of these compounds can be correlated with the electronic structures of the nonmetal elements and their positions in the periodic table.

PRE-LAB PREPARATION

The Oxidation States of Some Elements and Compounds of the Nonmetals

The oxidation states of some representative Group 5, 6, and 7 elements are shown in Figure 37-1. This chart illustrates three important points that we will discuss in the following paragraphs.

1. *Each of the elements in these groups can have many formal oxidation states.* This leads to a rich variety of compounds whose chemistry is complex in comparison with the chemistry of most metals in Groups 1 and 2.

2. *The electronic structures of the elements in the three groups place definite limits on the formal oxidation states accessible to each element.* Nitrogen, whose atoms have five valence electrons, can share these five electrons with electronegative elements like oxygen to produce a formal oxidation state as high as $+5$. It can accept a share of as many as three electrons from less electronegative elements like hydrogen to produce a formal oxidation state as low as -3. In both the $+5$ and -3 oxidation states the nitrogen atoms have a share of eight electrons (like the electron configuration of the inert gases).

Because a neutral sulfur atom has six valence electrons, the formal oxidation state of sulfur ranges from $+6$ in sulfate ion to -2 in sulfide ion. The oxidation states of chlorine range from $+7$ to -1 because a neutral chlorine atom has seven valence electrons.

Oxidizing strength →

Oxidation state	Group 5	Group 6	Group 7
+7			Cl_2O_7, $HClO_4$, ClO_4^-
+6		SO_3, H_2SO_4, HSO_4^-, SO_4^{2-}	Cl_2O_6
+5	$N_2O_5(g)$, HNO_3, NO_3^-		$HClO_3$, ClO_3^-
+4	$NO_2(g)$, $N_2O_4(g)$	SO_2, H_2SO_3, HSO_3^-, SO_3^{2-}	ClO_2
+3	$N_2O_3(g)$, HNO_2, NO_2^-		$HClO_2$, ClO_2^-
+2	$NO(g)$	$S_2O_3^{2-}$	
+1	$N_2O(g)$		Cl_2O, $HClO$, ClO^-
0	$N_2(g)$	S_8	Cl_2
−1	NH_2OH, NH_3OH^+		Cl^-
−2	N_2H_4, $N_2H_5^+$, $N_2H_6^{2+}$	H_2S, HS^-, S^{2-}	
−3	$NH_3(g)$, NH_4^+		

(Left margin, vertical: Reduction ↓ / Oxidation ↑)

FIGURE 37-1
Compounds representing a wide variety of oxidation states of three nonmetals.

We must emphasize, however, that the oxidation states are assigned to atoms by formal rules (discussed in Appendix A). *The formal oxidation number is not the actual charge on the atom as it exists in the compound.* The actual charge on the atoms of real compounds is usually a fractional charge in the range $+1$ to -1, depending on the electronegativities of the atoms. This is consistent with the electroneutrality principle, which reflects the fact that the distribution of electron density around the nuclei always adjusts itself so that large net charges on adjacent atoms are not formed. As an example, the formal oxidation state we assign to the oxygen atoms in the perchlorate ion (ClO_4^-) is -2. The chlorine atom is therefore assigned oxidation state $+7$. The net charge is given by $4(-2) + 7 = -1$. The actual partial charges have been calculated by Sanderson (see the Bibliography) to be -0.211 on each oxygen atom and -0.155 on the chlorine atom. (Verify that these sum to a net charge of -1 for the perchlorate ion.)

The addition of one electron to a neutral chlorine atom produces stable chloride ion, having an electron configuration like that of argon. (Chloride ion and argon have the same number of electrons; therefore we say they are *isoelectronic*.) In an ion like perchlorate, ClO_4^-, chlorine shares its elec-

trons with the electronegative oxygen atoms, and we can draw Lewis (electron-dot) structures that give each atom a share of eight electrons.

The Lewis structures for some of the compounds mentioned above are shown in Figure 37-2.

3. *As the formal oxidation state of the nonmetal increases in a compound, the compound will tend to be a stronger oxidizing agent.* Figure 37-1 shows this trend. The compounds at the top of the table have the largest formal oxidation number assigned to the nonmetal element and are the strongest oxidizing agents. Thus, nitric, sulfuric, and perchloric acids are all strong oxidizing agents, particularly if they are hot and concentrated.

There is also a tendency for the compounds with the most *negative* oxidation states to be good *reducing agents*. This is particularly true of NH_3 and hydrazine, N_2H_4, as well as sulfide ion, S^{2-}. However, chloride ion is not a good reducing agent, and in fact all of the chlorine compounds except chloride ion are strong oxidizing agents. This can be understood qualitatively as the effect of the increasing nuclear charge as we go from Group 5 to Group 7 elements. The increased nuclear charge makes Group 7 elements hold on to their electrons more tightly. Therefore Group 7 compounds tend to be stronger oxidizing agents.

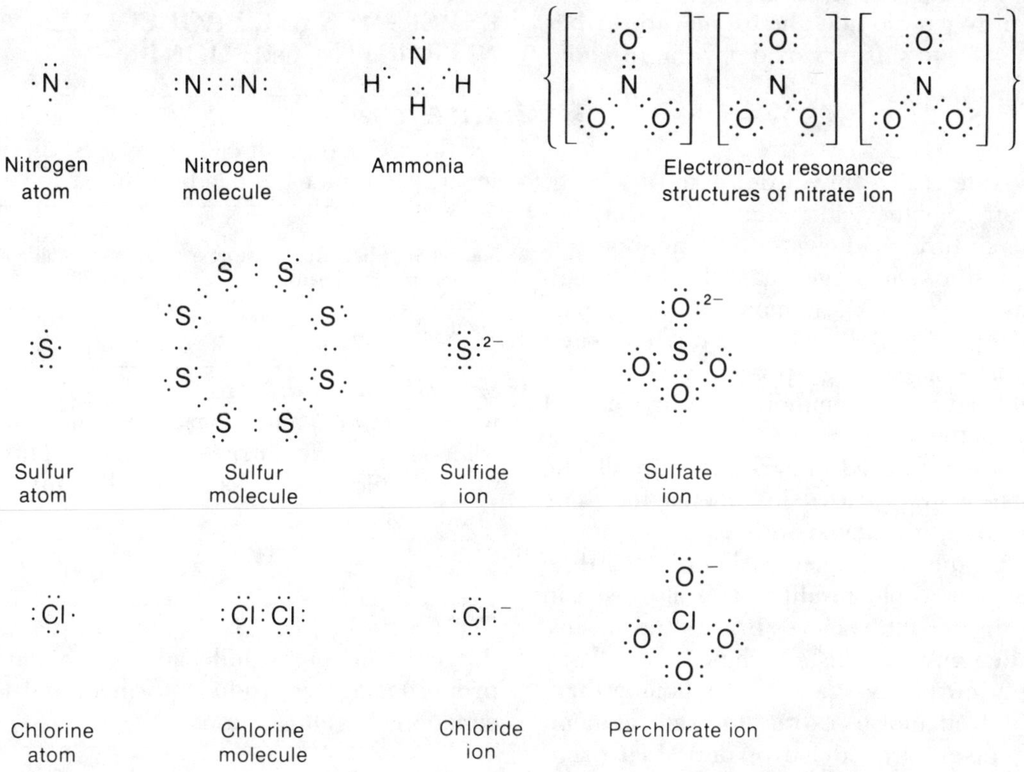

FIGURE 37-2
Electron-dot structures of three nonmetallic elements and some of their compounds.

The Chemistry of Representative Elements of Groups 5, 6, and 7

It would be impossible to explore the chemistry of all the elements in these three groups in the course of one afternoon; therefore we will choose one member of each group as representative of the chemistry of that particular group. First we will study the chemistry of some of the oxides of nitrogen, a Group 5 element, and some oxides of sulfur (Group 6) and of chlorine (Group 7).

Oxygen is so electronegative that it exists primarily in stable compounds in the formal oxidation state −2, with a few compounds (peroxides) having oxidation state −1. For these reasons we have chosen sulfur as the representative element of the Group 6 elements (chalcogens).

Similarly, we have chosen chlorine as the representative element of the Group 7 elements (halogens) rather than the first member of the series, fluorine, because fluorine is so electronegative that all stable fluorine compounds contain fluorine with a formal oxidation state of −1.

Nitrogen Oxides and Sulfur Dioxide in the Atmosphere

Nitric oxide is produced in large amounts in steel-making furnaces and by reaction of nitrogen with oxygen at high temperature in automobile engines. The nitric oxide quickly reacts with oxygen to yield nitrogen dioxide, a brownish gas. Under the action of sunlight, nitrogen dioxide can be photolyzed to give $NO + O$. The free oxygen atom can then react with oxygen to give ozone, O_3. Ozone is a lung irritant and is also very toxic to many species of pine trees. It can also react with unburned hydrocarbons in the atmosphere to yield peroxyacetyl nitrate (PAN), which is very irritating to the eyes and also damages leafy crops such as spinach.

The combustion of coal containing sulfur produces large quantities of sulfur dioxide by the reaction

$$S + O_2 \rightarrow SO_2$$

In regions in which an appreciable amount of ozone has been formed by a photochemical reaction with nitrogen dioxide, the ozone can further oxidize the SO_2 to sulfur trioxide by the reaction

$$SO_2 + O_3 \rightarrow SO_3 + O_2$$

Sulfur trioxide is the anhydride of sulfuric acid. Thus it can combine with water to produce an aerosol of sulfuric acid mist, or, if ammonia is present (produced in large quantities in agricultural areas by livestock), ammonium sulfate particles can be produced. The haze that is associated with photochemical smog apparently contains a considerable amount of ammonium sulfate as well as organic matter.

Sulfur dioxide is used in agriculture to kill the wild yeasts on grapes used in winemaking. The grapes are then inoculated with a pure strain of yeast that produces a higher quality of wine than the wild strains would produce. It is also used in bleaching dried fruit, such as apricots and raisins. One can demonstrate this bleaching action easily by taking a few petals of a red rose, boiling them in 30 mL of ethanol to extract the red pigment, acidifying the extract with a drop of 6 M HCl, and bubbling SO_2 through the solution. The solution will turn pale as the sulfur dioxide reduces the red pigment to a colorless chemical form of the pigment.

SOME CHEMISTRY OF NITROGEN COMPOUNDS

Nitrogen, the first element in Group 5, is an important nonmetal that forms compounds illustrating all the oxidation states from -3 to $+5$. In the zero oxidation state, nitrogen is particularly stable and has the electron-dot structure $:N:::N:$ The commercially important compounds are those in the -3 and the $+5$ oxidation states. Ammonia and its salts are important as soluble fertilizers. Nitric acid is an important oxidizing agent and is used in making explosives.

The electron-dot structure of ammonia is $H:\overset{..}{N}:H$, which adds a hydrogen ion to form the
H

ammonium ion $H:\overset{H}{\underset{H}{\overset{..}{N}}}:H^+$. Ammonia reacts with water to form a weak base.

When nitric acid acts as an oxidizing agent, it may be reduced to any of the lower oxidation states. Concentrated nitric acid is usually reduced to NO_2, dilute nitric acid to NO or to lower oxidation states, by very strong reducing agents.

EXPERIMENTAL PROCEDURE: NITROGEN COMPOUNDS

NOTE TO INSTRUCTOR The chemicals required for the study of each element (N, S, Cl) are listed separately under the heading for each element.

Special Supplies: Rubber stoppers and glass tubing for the two gas generators shown in Figures 37-3 and 37-4.
Chemicals: Cu (turnings), 6 M HNO_3, 3% H_2O_2, 3 M $FeCl_3$, wood splints.

Safety Precautions: Nitrogen oxides (NO and NO_2) will irritate eyes and lungs. Work in a fume hood when generating nitric oxide, NO. This experiment should not be performed if a fume hood is not available.

NOTE TO STUDENTS In your written report of this experiment, include all observations of the properties of the products formed, and write the equations for all reactions.

The Preparation of Nitric Oxide by Reduction of HNO_3 with Copper: Oxidation States $+2$, $+4$, and $+5$ Assemble the generator shown in Figure 37-3 (in a fume hood), using a 20×200 mm test tube, and place about 3 g of copper turnings in it. Prepare to collect three 15-cm test tubes of nitric oxide by displacement of water. Add 10 mL of 6 M HNO_3 to the generator, replace the delivery tube connection, and warm the test tube gently to initiate the reaction. After the air has been displaced from the apparatus and the gas bubbling through is colorless, collect two full test tubes of the gas and a third test tube about half full. Do not allow the delivery tube to remain under water while the heated test tube cools; if you do, water will be drawn into the test tube. What is the reaction for the reduction of dilute nitric acid by copper?

Test the nitric oxide in one test tube with a glowing splint to see if it supports combustion. Note the colored gas produced when the tube is exposed to the air. Write the equation for the reaction that accounts for this change.

Test the second sample of nitric oxide for solubility in water by swirling the test tube with its mouth under the water to allow contact of fresh water with the gas. Note if the water level in the test tube rises. Now take the test tube out of the water for a few seconds, and allow the oxygen of the air to react with the gas, as will be evidenced by the formation of a brown gas. Invert the test

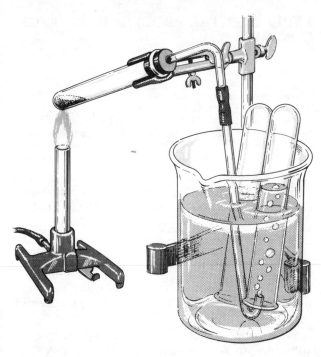

FIGURE 37-3
Apparatus for the preparation of nitrogen gas or of the oxides of nitrogen.

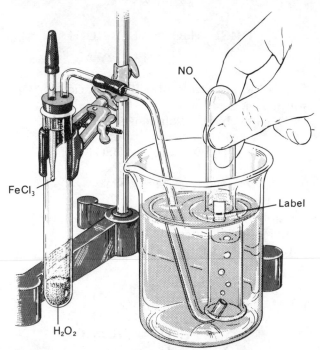

FIGURE 37-4
Generator for the preparation of a small amount of oxygen by the reaction of $FeCl_3$ with H_2O_2. This oxygen is then reacted with NO(g).

tube under the water again, and swirl it to note the solubility of the brown gas. Write the equation for the reaction occurring when this gas dissolves in water.

Mark the water level in the third test tube, which is about half full of nitric oxide, with a wax pencil or gummed label. Set up the small oxygen generator shown in Figure 37-4, placing about 10 mL of 3% hydrogen peroxide in the test tube. Draw up a few milliliters of 3 M $FeCl_3$ into the medicine dropper and replace the two-hole stopper in the mouth of the generator tube. When ready to begin generating oxygen, release a few drops of $FeCl_3$. After a brief period the $FeCl_3$ will catalyze the decomposition of H_2O_2, producing oxygen gas. After the air has been displaced from the generator, place the delivery tube under the marked test tube and allow 8 to 10 bubbles of oxygen to enter. Note whether the level of the water is lowered by the addition of oxygen. Recall that in the balanced equation for the reaction that is taking place, two volumes of nitric oxide react with one volume of oxygen to produce two volumes of nitrogen dioxide. Now swirl the test tube with its mouth under the water and note what happens to the water level as the NO_2 reacts with the water. Allow more oxygen to bubble into the tube until the gases turn brown, note the water level, and again allow the gases to dissolve in water. Repeat

the process until the water level approaches the top of the tube. Remember that excess oxygen is not soluble in water. What substances are present in the water solution in the test tube? Apply a simple test to verify your answer. What part of one of the commercial processes for the production of nitric acid does this experiment illustrate?

SOME CHEMISTRY OF SULFUR COMPOUNDS

In this experiment we study some chemical properties of some common compounds of sulfur in oxidation states -2, $+2$, $+4$, and $+6$. Sulfur is a Group 6 element with the electron configuration $1s^2 2s^2 2p^6 3s^2 3p^4$. Its electron dot structure is :S· By sharing two electrons with two hydrogen atoms it forms the covalent compound H_2S. A saturated aqueous solution of H_2S is weakly acidic and contains small concentrations of H^+ and HS^- ions. In strongly basic solutions the concentrations of HS^- and S^{2-} ions are greater.

By sharing its electrons with more electronegative elements, such as oxygen, sulfur attains positive oxidation states. In sulfur dioxide, four of the sulfur electrons are involved in bonding with oxygen:

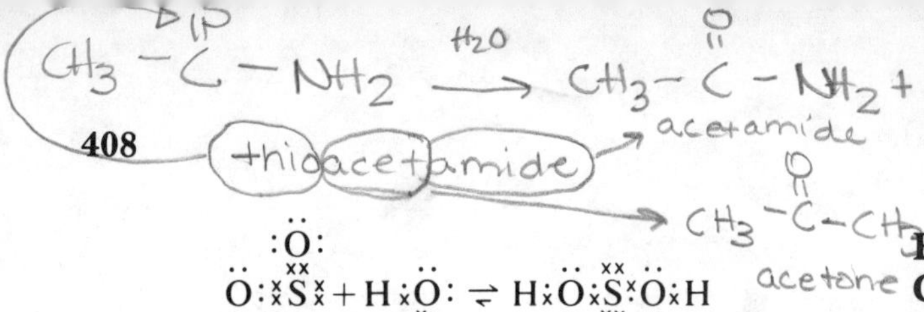

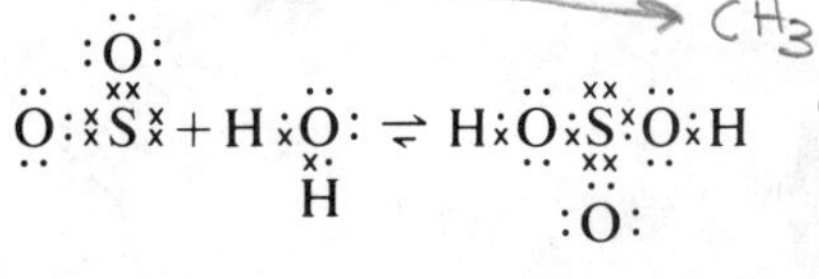

[handwritten at top of page:]

$CH_3 - C - NH_2 \xrightarrow{H_2O} CH_3 - C - NH_2 + H_2S$

thioacetamide → acetamide

$\rightarrow CH_3 - C - CH_3$ acetone

[Lewis structure diagram:]

$:\!\ddot{O}\!: + H:\!\ddot{O}\!: \rightleftharpoons H:\!\ddot{O}\!:\!\ddot{S}\!:\!\ddot{O}\!:H$

SO_2 is the anhydride of sulfurous acid, H_2SO_3, which is a weak acid, and forms some $H^+ + HSO_3^-$ ions. In basic solutions the equilibria

$$H_2SO_3 \rightleftharpoons H^+ + HSO_3^-$$

$$HSO_3^- \rightleftharpoons H^+ + SO_3^{2-}$$

are shifted to the right, to form more bisulfite and sulfite ions and water.

In sulfur trioxide all six of the sulfur electrons are involved in bonding:

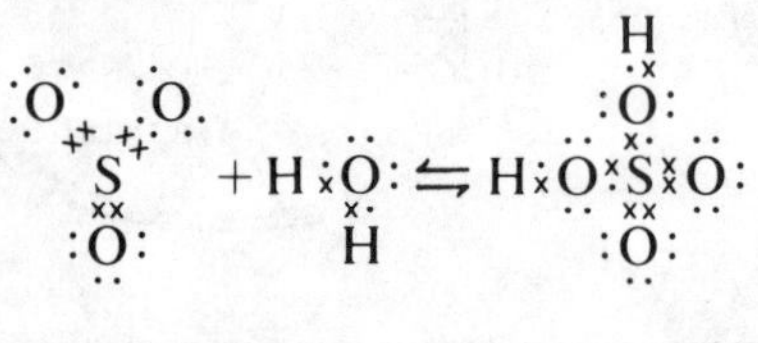

[Lewis structure diagram of SO_3 and reaction with water]

Sulfur trioxide is the anhydride of sulfuric acid, H_2SO_4, one of the most important industrial inorganic chemicals. It is a strong acid whose aqueous solutions contain large concentrations of H^+ and HSO_4^- ions. In basic solutions the SO_4^{2-} ion is the predominant species.

The electron-dot structures of sulfite, sulfate, and thiosulfate ions are represented as follows:

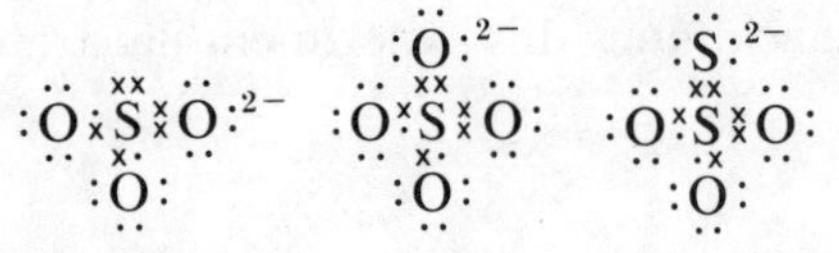

[Lewis structures]

    sulfite   sulfate   thiosulfate

Note that in the thiosulfate ion the sulfur atom that replaces the oxygen in the sulfate structure may be assigned a -2 oxidation number and that the central sulfur atom has an oxidation number of $+6$, just as it has in sulfate. The $+2$ oxidation number assigned to sulfur in thiosulfate is obtained by finding the average of $+6$ and -2: $(+6 - 2)/2 = +2$.

The experiments you perform will show that H_2SO_4 and SO_4^{2-} are mild oxidizing agents, whereas H_2S, S^{2-}, H_2SO_3, and SO_3^{2-} are reducing agents. In addition, since S^0, SO_3^{2-}, and H_2SO_3 represent intermediate oxidation states, they can act as oxidizing agents with a strong reducing agent and as reducing agents with a strong oxidizing agent.

EXPERIMENTAL PROCEDURE: SULFUR COMPOUNDS

Special Supplies: Source of H_2S gas.

Chemicals: Crushed roll sulfur, iron filings, 0.1 M $Pb(NO_3)_2$, 0.1 M $SnCl_4$, 0.1 M $Zn(NO_3)_2$, 0.05 M I_2 (0.05 M I_2/0.1 M KI), 0.1 M $Ca(NO_3)_2$, 0.1 M $BaCl_2$, 0.1 M $Ba(OH)_2$, $Na_2SO_3(s)$ (sodium sulfite), saturated Br_2 water, sugar (sucrose) crystals, pieces of Zn, Cu, NaCl(s), KBr(s), KI(s), lead acetate test paper, source of H_2S gas, 6 M HCl, concentrated H_2SO_4, 3 M H_2SO_4.

Safety Precautions: This experiment should not be performed if a fume hood is not available. Hydrogen sulfide has a noxious odor and is very toxic. Part 1 should be carried out in a fume hood.

In part 3, the addition of concentrated (18 M) sulfuric acid to NaCl, KBr, and KI should be carried out in a fume hood because the products formed (HCl, HBr, and HI) will irritate eyes and lungs.

When you are asked to note the odor of a substance, do so very cautiously. Do not stick your nose into the mouth of a test tube and inhale. Gently fan the vapor toward your nose with your hand.

NOTE TO STUDENTS In your written report, include all observations and equations for all reactions.

---

1. Sulfides and Hydrogen Sulfide: Oxidation State -2

(a) *Preparation of a Sulfide.* Mix approximately 3.5 g of iron filings with 2 g of crushed sulfur in a crucible supported on a triangle. Place a lid on the crucible, and heat with a Bunsen burner until the reaction is initiated, removing the burner and lid occasionally to note whether the reaction continues with the evolution of heat. Burn off any excess sulfur, and allow the crucible to cool. Place a small piece of the compound in a small test tube. Add a few milliliters of 6 M HCl and note cautiously the products of the reaction.

(b) *Hydrogen Sulfide as a Precipitating Agent.* Metallic sulfides, other than those of the alkali and alkaline earth metals, are sparingly soluble in water. In qualitative analysis many metal ions are identified by precipitating them as sulfides. Using the source of H_2S gas available in your laboratory,[1] saturate 3 mL of each of the following solutions with H_2S gas: 0.1 M $Pb(NO_3)_2$, 0.1 M $Zn(NO_3)_2$, and 0.1 M $SnCl_4$. Record the color and formula of each precipitate.

(c) *Hydrogen Sulfide as a Reducing Agent.* Saturate each of the following solutions with H_2S: (1) 5 mL of warm 3 M HNO_3, (2) 5 mL of 0.05 M I_2, and (3) a freshly prepared solution of H_2SO_3 made by adding a few crystals of Na_2SO_3 and a drop of 6 M H_2SO_4 to 5 mL of water. Test the vapors with moistened lead acetate paper. Note the products and write balanced equations for each reaction.

2. Sulfur Dioxide, Sulfurous Acid, Sulfite Ion: Oxidation State +4

(a) *Preparation of Sulfur Dioxide.* Since sulfur is in an intermediate oxidation state in SO_2, this compound can be prepared by oxidation of sulfides (as is done in metallurgical roasting), by oxidation of elemental sulfur, or by the reduction of hot concentrated H_2SO_4 by copper. It can also be conveniently prepared (without a change in oxidation state) from metal sulfites by the addition of an acid.

Place about 2 g of Na_2SO_3 in a large test tube. Add 6 M HCl dropwise until you can smell (*Caution!*) the odor of the gas (SO_2) given off. Now add about 15 mL of water and stir until all the solid dissolves. Save for part 2(b).

(b) *Chemical Properties of Sulfurous Acid.* Divide the solution equally among three smaller test tubes. To one portion add a few milliliters of 0.1 M $Ba(OH)_2$ until the solution is basic to litmus. What is the precipitate formed? Is it soluble in 6 M HCl added a drop at a time? (Ignore a slight turbidity, which is due to air oxidation of sulfite to sulfate.) To another portion add 5 to 6 mL of saturated bromine water, drop by drop. How do you account for the decolorization that takes place? Now add a few milliliters of 0.1 M $Ba(OH)_2$ to this test tube. What is the precipitate formed? Is it soluble in 6 M HCl?

Add a little of the third portion, a few drops at a time, to a test tube containing 5 mL of 3 M H_2SO_4 and some mossy zinc. Observe the odor of the gas, and note the precipitate formed.

3. Sulfuric Acid, Sulfates: Oxidation State +6

(a) *Physical and Chemical Properties of Sulfuric Acid.* While stirring, cautiously add a few milliliters of 18 M H_2SO_4, drop by drop, to 50 mL of tap water in a small beaker. Note the temperature change. To what do you attribute this result?

Place a few drops of 18 M H_2SO_4 on a few crystals of sugar in a small evaporating dish. Repeat the test on a small piece of paper or wood (such as a match stick). How do you explain the results?

(b) *Effect of Concentrated Sulfuric Acid.* Investigate the oxidizing strength of concentrated (18 M) sulfuric acid by adding *in a fume hood* 1 mL of concentrated H_2SO_4 to 1 g of each of the following salts in 20- $\times$ 150-mm test tubes: NaCl, KBr, and KI. Note the color of any gases evolved. (Place the tube containing KI in a beaker of hot water.) Test for acidity of the gases evolved by holding a piece of moistened blue litmus paper near the mouth of each test tube. Are any halide ions oxidized to the elementary halogens?

(c) *Solubility of Sulfates.* Add 3 mL of 0.1 M Na_2SO_4 to 3 mL each of the following solutions in separate 10-cm test tubes: 0.1 M $Ca(NO_3)_2$, 0.1 M $BaCl_2$, 0.1 M $Pb(NO_3)_2$. Test the solubility of any precipitates in dilute nitric acid by adding 1 mL of 6 M HNO_3 to each precipitate.

SOME CHEMISTRY OF CHLORINE COMPOUNDS

Higher Oxidation States of Chlorine

Chlorine and its compounds show a marked tendency to undergo self- or auto-oxidation-reduction, in which some molecules or ions of a species are oxidized to a higher state while others are reduced to the stable -1 state. This process is called *disproportionation.*

It is possible to oxidize Cl^- (oxidation state -1) to free chlorine, $Cl_2(g)$ (oxidation state 0), and then carry out a series of disproportionation reactions in which the chlorine is successively oxidized to the $+1$, $+5$, and finally the $+7$ oxidation states, as indicated on the flow chart in Figure 37-5.

(a) $Cl_2(g)$ is passed into a cold basic solution, in which it is auto-oxidized to ClO^-, and autoreduced to Cl^-. (This is the reaction that occurs in the commercial preparation of 5% NaClO bleaching solution, the bleach sold in grocery markets.)

---

[1] Consult your instructor about your best source of H_2S gas. A cylinder of the compressed gas (in a fume hood) or a Kipp generator charged with FeS and 6 M HCl (in a fume hood) is often used. A little "Aitch-tu-ess" (a commercial mixture of sulfur, paraffin, and asbestos) heated in a test tube fitted with a gas delivery tube is a convenient method.

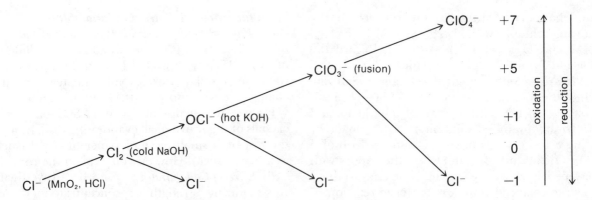

FIGURE 37-5
The interconversions of some ions containing chlorine in several different oxidation states.

(b) The ClO^- in basic solution, when heated, is further oxidized to ClO_3^-, and a portion reduced back to Cl^-. (By suitable crystallization of the salts from this solution, the commercially important oxidant $KClO_3$ or the weed killers $NaClO_3$ and $Ca(ClO_3)_2$ may be obtained.)

(c) Maintaining $KClO_3$ crystals at a temperature just above their melting point results in further auto-oxidation of the ClO_3^- to ClO_4^-, and reduces a portion of it to Cl^-. (Perchlorates are important oxidants in solid rocket fuels.)

EXPERIMENTAL PROCEDURE: CHLORINE COMPOUNDS

Chemicals: NaOCl (a commercial bleach solution of 5% NaOCl), red and blue litmus paper, 0.1 M $AgNO_3$, 6 M NaOH, 6 M HNO_3, 6 M HCl, 0.1 M KI, 0.1 M KBr, hexane (or petroleum ether, b.p. 60 to 90).

Safety Precautions: The hexane (or petroleum ether) used in part (c) is flammable. Carry out the tests for part (c) in a fume hood, making sure there are no open flames in the vicinity. Omit part (c) if a fume hood is not available.

NOTE TO STUDENTS In your written report, include all observations and equations for all reactions.

Chemical Properties of the Hypochlorite Ion Since solid NaOCl cannot be isolated easily without decomposition, we shall test portions of the solution of a commercial bleach obtained at the grocery store. It was prepared by passing chlorine into a solution of NaOH.

(a) *Litmus Reaction.* Put several drops of NaOCl solution on red and blue litmus to note its acidity or basicity. Note any bleaching effect.

(b) *Reacting to AgNO₃.* To a 3-mL portion of the NaOCl solution add 1 mL of 0.1 M $AgNO_3$. What is the precipitate? (Compare with the behavior of a drop of 6 M NaOH on 0.1 M $AgNO_3$.) Is it soluble in 6 M HNO_3, and does any other precipitate remain? Explain your observations.

(c) *Oxidizing Strength.* Place 2 mL of 0.1 M KI and 1 mL of hexane (or petroleum ether) in a test tube. (*Caution:* Work in a fume hood. Hexane is flammable. There must be no open flames nearby.) Add 5% NaOCl solution dropwise—shaking the test tube after each drop—and note any color change in the hexane layer. Is there any evidence for formation of I_2? An excess of NaOCl must be avoided because it will remove the color, owing to further oxidation of the initial product to the colorless IO_3^- ion.

Repeat this test, using 2 mL of 0.1 M KBr in place of KI. Is there any evidence for the formation of Br_2 detected by a color change in the hexane layer? Where would you place the ClO^- ion with respect to Br_2 and I_2 in a scale of oxidizing strength? Now acidify the test solution with 6 M HCl and shake, noting any color formed in the hexane layer. Does the oxidizing strength of ClO^- change when the solution is acidified?

Record all of your observations and write equations to explain the reactions.

BIBLIOGRAPHY

Sanderson, R. T., *Polar Covalence,* Academic Press, New York, 1983, p. 194.

Equilibria of Coordination Compounds

PURPOSE

To illustrate the tendency of metal ions to form coordination compounds (metal complexes) with ions and neutral polar molecules that act as electron-pair donors toward metal ions. To study metal ion complexes with ammonia, chloride ion, and hydroxide ion. To determine the equilibrium constant for the dissociation of the diamminesilver(I) complex ion, $Ag(NH_3)_2^+$.

PRE-LAB PREPARATION

The Hydration of Ions

We have already studied the most common class of coordination compounds. In Experiment 16 we noted that all ions in solution attract polar water molecules to them to form ion-dipole bonds. Thus,

the cupric ion, Cu^{2+}, does not exist as a bare ion in water but rather as the hexaaquo ion, $Cu(H_2O)_6^{2+}$. The origin of this attraction lies in the polar nature of the water molecule. Figure 38-1 shows the bent nature of the water molecule, which gives rise to the high dipole moment (a measure of the separation of charge in a molecule) of water.

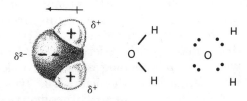

FIGURE 38-1
Three representations of the water molecule.

The bond angle formed by the oxygen atom and the two hydrogen atoms in a water molecule is known to be 105°. This is not far from the 109.5° for ideal tetrahedral coordination, and the oxygen atom in a water molecule can be viewed as having four orbitals arranged in an approximately tetrahedral fashion, two of them forming the two bonds to the hydrogen atoms and the remaining two each containing a lone pair of electrons. It is these lone pairs that are centers of excess electron density. In Figure 38-1, the symbol $\leftrightarrow$ indicates the negative direction of the dipole moment and the small delta symbols (δ) indicate where the partial charges exist in the water molecule.

The negative side of the water molecule is strongly attracted to cations. In general, the greater the charge on the cation and the larger the cation, the greater the number of coordinated water molecules. Examples are $H(H_2O)^+$, $Be(H_2O)_4^{2+}$, $Cu(H_2O)_6^{2+}$, $Al(H_2O)_6^{3+}$, $Fe(H_2O)_6^{3+}$.

Anions attract the positive side of the water molecule and are also hydrated. However, the attraction is not as large, the hydrates are less stable, and fewer water molecules are coordinated.

Coordination Compounds

These hydrates are one example of the type of substances called coordination compounds. Other neutral, but polar, molecules such as ammonia, NH_3, and also a number of ions, such as OH^-, Cl^-, CN^-, S^{2-}, $S_2O_3^{2-}$, and $C_2O_4^{2-}$, likewise can form similar very stable coordination groupings about a central ion. Such coordination compounds result from the replacement of the water molecule from the hydrated ion by these other molecules or ions when they are present in the solution at high concentration, to form a still more stable bond. The resulting coordination compound may be a positively or negatively charged ion (a complex ion), or it may be a neutral molecule, depending on the number and kind of coordinating groups attached to the central ion.

What bonding forces hold the atoms of such a complex coordination compound together? Where large differences of electronegativity are present, as in AlF_6^{3-}, these forces are largely ionic. In the majority of cases the bonding is mainly covalent, often with partial ionic character. The type of bond orbitals determines the spatial geometry, and affects the stability of a given complex. Study the examples in Figure 38-2.

Ammonia Complex Ions Some of the important ammonia complexes are the following:

$$Ag(NH_3)_2^+ \quad Cu(NH_3)_4^{2+} \quad Ni(NH_3)_4^{2+}$$

$$Au(NH_3)_2^+ \quad Cd(NH_3)_4^{2+} \quad Ni(NH_3)_6^{2+}$$

$$Cu(NH_3)_2^+ \quad Zn(NH_3)_4^{2+} \quad Co(NH_3)_6^{2+}$$

These complexes are formed by the addition of ammonia to a solution containing the hydrated cation. Ammonia molecules are bound by the cation one at a time as the concentration of ammonia increases. At low concentrations of ligand, smaller numbers of ammonia molecules may be bound. For instance, the two NH_3 molecules bound to the Ag^+ bind in successive steps. The equilibrium constant is known for each step of the following reaction sequence.

$$Ag^+ + NH_3 \rightleftharpoons Ag(NH_3)^+$$

$$K_1 = \frac{[Ag(NH_3)^+]}{[Ag^+][NH_3]} = 1.6 \times 10^3$$

$$Ag(NH_3)^+ + NH_3 \rightleftharpoons Ag(NH_3)_2^+$$

$$K_2 = \frac{[Ag(NH_3)_2^+]}{[Ag(NH_3)^+][NH_3]} = 6.8 \times 10^3$$

The equilibrium constant for the overall reaction can be obtained by the addition of the two reactions and the corresponding multiplication of their equilibrium constants.

$$Ag^+ + 2NH_3 \rightleftharpoons Ag(NH_3)_2^+$$

$$K_{formation} = K_1 K_2 = \frac{[\cancel{Ag(NH_3)^+}]}{[Ag^+][NH_3]}$$

$$\times \frac{[Ag(NH_3)_2^+]}{[\cancel{Ag(NH_3)^+}][NH_3]}$$

$$= \frac{[Ag(NH_3)_2^+]}{[Ag^+][NH_3]^2} = 1.1 \times 10^7$$

In part 5 of the Experimental Procedure, you will determine the $K_{dissociation}$ for the $Ag(NH_3)_2^+$ complex ion.[1] Because the (NH_3) is so high under the experimental conditions that are employed, the $Ag(NH_3)^+$ species may be neglected.

---

[1] The overall reaction may be written as a formation or as a dissociation, with $K_{formation} = 1/K_{dissociation}$.

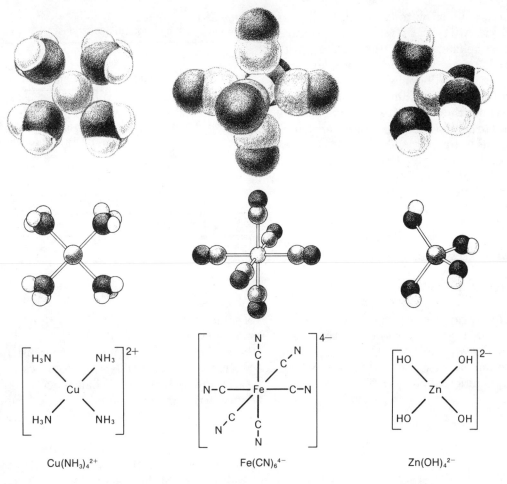

$Cu(NH_3)_4^{2+}$ $Fe(CN)_6^{4-}$ $Zn(OH)_4^{2-}$

FIGURE 38-2
Diagrams showing the spatial arrangement of the coordinating groups about a central ion in the formation of a complex ion. Above each conventional formula, the "structural formula" represents each covalent electron-pair bond by a single line. The spatial geometry is determined by the type of orbitals represented: dsp^2 (square planar) by Cu $(NH_3)_4^{2+}$, d^2sp^3 (octahedral) by Fe $(CN)_6^{4-}$, and sp^3 (tetrahedral) by Zn $(OH)_4^{2-}$. The ball-and-stick models indicate these geometric patterns more clearly, and the space-filling models in the top row portray the atoms according to their accepted ionic diameters and bond lengths.

Hydroxide Complex Ions, or Amphoteric Hydroxides
The hydroxides of most metals are relatively insoluble in water. Thus when sodium hydroxide is added to a metal ion in solution, such as lead ion, a precipitate is formed:

$$Pb(H_2O)_4^{2+} + 2OH^- \rightleftharpoons$$

$$Pb(H_2O)_2(OH)_2(s) + 2H_2O$$

or, using the simple unhydrated metal ion formula,

$$Pb^{2+} + 2OH^- \rightleftharpoons Pb(OH)_2(s)$$

By Le Châtelier's principle, excess hydroxide ion would give more complete precipitation. Instead,

the precipitate dissolves. This is explained by the tendency of lead ion to form a more stable coordination compound[2] with excess hydroxide ion:

$$Pb(H_2O)_2(OH)_2(s) + OH^- \rightleftharpoons$$

$$Pb(H_2O)(OH)_3^- + H_2O$$

or

$$Pb(OH)_2(s) + OH^- \rightleftharpoons Pb(OH)_3^-$$

---

[2] There is some uncertainty as to whether the lead hydroxide complex (and also the stannous hydroxide complex) will coordinate further to form $Pb(OH)_4^{2-}$ (and $Sn(OH)_4^{2-}$).

Other ions react similarly; for example, hydrated aluminum ion, $Al(H_2O)_6^{3+}$, reacts to form the hydroxide precipitate, $Al(H_2O)_3(OH)_3$, or, with excess OH^-, the hydroxide complex ion $Al(H_2O)_2(OH)_4^-$. Traditionally, chemists use the unhydrated formulas in ordinary chemical equations just because they are simpler, except where it is important to emphasize the hydrated structure.

The reactions to form these hydroxide complex ions are entirely reversible. The addition of acid to the above strongly basic $Pb(OH)_3^-$ solution reacts first to reprecipitate the hydroxide,

$$Pb(OH)_3^- + H^+ \rightleftharpoons Pb(OH)_2(s) + H_2O$$

and then, with excess acid,

$$Pb(OH)_2(s) + 2H^+ \rightleftharpoons Pb^{2+} + 2H_2O$$

Such metal hydroxides, which may be dissolved by an excess of either a strong acid or a strong base, are called *amphoteric hydroxides*.

The more important metal ions whose hydroxides are amphoteric are given in Table 38-1.

EXPERIMENTAL PROCEDURE

Chemicals: 1 M NH_4Cl, 1 M NH_3, 15 M (concentrated) NH_3, 6 M NH_3, 6 M $NaOH$, 6 M HNO_3, 12 M HCl, 6 M HCl, $CuSO_4 \cdot 5H_2O(s)$, 0.1 M $CuSO_4$, 0.1 M $NaCl$, 0.1 M $AgNO_3$, 0.1 M $Zn(NO_3)_2$, 0.1% phenolphthalein, alizarin yellow R, and indigo carmine indicators.

1. The Formation of Complex Ions with Ammonia To 3 mL of 0.1 M $CuSO_4$ add a drop of 6 M NH_3. Mix this. (Record your observations and write the equation for the reaction.) Continue to add NH_3 a little at a time, with mixing, until a distinct change occurs. Save this solution. Is this result contrary to the law of Le Châtelier? Obviously the OH^- concentration was increasing while the $Cu(OH)_2$ dissolved. How must the Cu^{2+} concentration have changed? Did it increase or decrease?

To learn which of the substances present in an ammonia solution (NH_4^+, OH^-, NH_3, H_2O) is responsible for the above change, try adding the following: (a) 1 mL of 1 M NH_4Cl to 1 mL of 0.1 M $CuSO_4$, (b) 2 drops (an excess) of 6 M $NaOH^3$ to 2 mL of 0.1 M $CuSO_4$, (c) ammonia gas by

[3] This provides an excess of OH^-, a much stronger base than NH_3. The strong base OH^- shows some amphoteric effect (see part 2) with cupric salts, but is far from complete.

TABLE 38-1
Some important amphoteric hydroxides

Simple ion* (acid solution)	Precipitate	Hydroxide complex ion† (strongly basic solution)
Pb^{2+}	$Pb(OH)_2$	$Pb(OH)_3^-$, plumbite ion
Zn^{2+}	$Zn(OH)_2$	$Zn(OH)_4^{2-}$, zincate ion
Al^{3+}	$Al(OH)_3$	$Al(OH)_4^-$, aluminate ion
Cr^{3+}	$Cr(OH)_3$	$Cr(OH)_4^-$, chromite ion
Sn^{2+}	$Sn(OH)_2$	$Sn(OH)_3^-$, stannite ion
Sn^{4+}	$Sn(OH)_4$	$Sn(OH)_6^{2-}$, stannate ion

* Such a highly charged ion as Sn^{4+} probably does not exist as such. In strong HCl solution, stannic salts dissolve as the chloride complex, $SnCl_6^{2-}$.
† Formerly these ions were written in the anhydrous form: PbO_2^{2-}, ZnO_2^{2-}, AlO_2^-, CrO_2^-, SnO_2^{2-}, and SnO_3^{2-}. These formulas may be derived from the hydroxide complex ion formulas simply by subtracting the appropriate number of H_2O molecules or H_3O^+ ions.

placing several crystals of $CuSO_4 \cdot 5H_2O(s)$ in a small dry beaker, and also placing at one side in the beaker a piece of filter paper moistened with concentrated (15 M) NH_3. Cover with a watch glass, and observe any changes. From this evidence, write an equation to show the formation of this new substance when excess NH_3 is added to Cu^{2+}.

To 1 mL of this cupric ammonia complex ion solution, add 6 M HNO_3 in excess. Explain the result and write the equation for the reaction.

2. The Formation of Amphoteric Hydroxides To 5 mL of 0.1 M $Zn(NO_3)_2$ add 6 M $NaOH$ by drops, with mixing, until the precipitate that first forms just redissolves. Avoid undue excess of $NaOH$. Divide this into two portions; test one portion with alizarin yellow R and the other with indigo carmine indicator. Estimate the approximate OH^- concentration (for later comparison in part 3) using the information on the color changes and pH intervals of the indicators given in Table B-5 of Appendix B. Now to one portion add 6 M HCl, by drops, until a precipitate forms (what is it?) and then redissolves as more HCl is added. Interpret all these changes as related to Le Châtelier's law, and as to the relative concentration of the various constituents (the zinc in its various forms, H^+, and OH^-), both by words and by net ionic equations.

3. The Reaction of Zinc Ion with Ammonia When ammonia is added gradually to Zn^{2+}, does the precipitate of zinc hydroxide that first forms redissolve as zincate ion, $Zn(OH)_4^{2-}$, owing to the excess base added, or does it redissolve as

$Zn(NH_3)_4^{2+}$, owing to the NH_3 molecules added? To test this point, to 3 mL of 0.1 M $Zn(NO_3)_2$, add 6 M NH_3 by drops, with mixing, until the precipitate that first forms just redissolves. Divide this mixture, test one portion with phenolphthalein and the other portion with alizarin yellow R. Estimate the approximate OH^- concentration, and compare this with the corresponding situation in part 2, where NaOH was used. (See Table B-5, Appendix B.) What can you conclude as to the possibility of forming $Zn(OH)_4^{2-}$ by adding NH_3 to a zinc salt solution? Explain. Write the equation for the equilibrium that you have verified.

4. Some Chloride Complex Ions (a) To 2 mL of 0.1 M $CuSO_4$ add 2 mL of 12 M (concentrated) HCl and then dilute this with about 5 mL of water. Write equations, and interpret the color changes you observed.

(b) To 1 mL of 0.1 M $AgNO_3$ add 3 mL of 12 M (concentrated) HCl, and then agitate this well for several minutes to redissolve the precipitated AgCl. Now dilute this with about 5 mL of distilled water. Write equations for the reactions and interpret the changes you observed, assuming that the complex formed is $CuCl_4^{2-}$.

5. The Equilibrium Constant of an Ammonia Complex Ion The dissociation of silver diammine complex ion is represented by the equilibrium

$$Ag(NH_3)_2^+ \rightleftharpoons Ag^+ + 2NH_3 \qquad (1)$$

and the corresponding equilibrium constant expression

$$\frac{[Ag^+][NH_3]^2}{[Ag(NH_3)_2^+]} = K_{dissociation} \qquad (2)$$

If you add sufficient Cl^- gradually to an equilibrium mixture of Ag^+ and NH_3, represented by

Equation (1), so that you can just barely begin precipitation of AgCl(s), a second equilibrium is established simultaneously without appreciably disturbing the first equilibrium. This may be represented by the combined equations

$$Ag(NH_3)_2^+ \rightleftharpoons Ag^+ + 2NH_3 \qquad (3)$$
$$+$$
$$Cl^-$$
$$\updownarrow$$
$$AgCl(s)$$

By using a large excess of NH_3, you can shift Equation (1) far to the left, with reasonable assurance that the Ag^+ is converted almost completely to $Ag(NH_3)_2^+$ rather than to the first step only, $Ag(NH_3)^+$. From the measured volumes of NH_3, Ag^+, and Cl^- solutions used, the concentrations of the species in Equation (1) may be determined and the value of $K_{dissociation}$ calculated.

To prepare the solution,[4] place 3.0 mL of 0.1 M $AgNO_3$ (measure it accurately in a 10-mL graduate) in a 15 × 150 mm test tube. Add 3.0 mL (also carefully measured) of 1 M NH_3. Now prepare some 0.02 M NaCl by diluting 2.0 mL of 0.1 M NaCl to 10.0 mL in your 10-mL graduate. Mix this thoroughly and note the exact volume. Then, from a medicine dropper, add it to the mixture of $AgNO_3$ and NH_3, about 1 to 1.5 mL at first, and then drop by drop until a very faint, permanent milky precipitate of AgCl remains. Return any excess NaCl from the medicine dropper to the graduate, and note the exact volume used. From these data, $K_{dissociation}$ can be calculated.

---

[4] If desired, some improvement in precision can be obtained by using larger volumes—20.0 mL each of 0.1 M $AgNO_3$ and 1 M NH_3. Then dilute 10.0 mL of 0.1 M NaCl to about 50.0 mL in your 50-mL graduate, mix this well, and note the exact volume. Add first about 15 mL, then very small portions, to the Ag^+/NH_3 mixture, stirring as you do so, until a very faint permanent milky precipitate of AgCl remains. Note the total volume of 0.02 M NaCl used.

REPORT

38

**Equilibria of
Coordination Compounds**

NAME

SECTION   LOCKER

INSTRUCTOR   DATE

OBSERVATIONS AND DATA

1. The Formation of Complex Ions with Ammonia

The net ionic equation for the reaction
of excess $CuSO_4$ with NH_3 is _____

The predicted effect on the above reaction of adding
excess NH_3 (based on Le Châtelier's principle) is   _____

List the observed results when:
  Excess NH_3 is added to $CuSO_4$ solution.   _____

  NH_4Cl and $CuSO_4$ solutions are mixed.   _____

  Excess NaOH and $CuSO_4$ solutions are mixed.   _____

  $CuSO_4 \cdot 5H_2O(s)$ is exposed to NH_3 gas.   _____

Considering the equilibrium equation $NH_3 + H_2O \rightleftharpoons NH_4^+ + OH^-$, explain which substance (NH_3, NH_4^+, or OH^-) causes the deep blue color, and give the equation for the reaction.

The observed effect, and the net ionic equation, for the reaction of HNO_3 on this deep blue solution is

2. The Formation of Amphoteric Hydroxides

The net ionic equation for the reaction
of excess $Zn(NO_3)_2$ with NaOH is _____

The predicted effect on the above reaction
of adding excess NaOH (based on Le Châtelier's principle) is _____

Explain in your own words why $Zn(OH)_2(s)$ dissolves with excess OH^-, and write the net ionic equation for the reaction.

Color with Alizarin   Indigo OH^-
yellow R _____ carmine _____ concentration _____

Explain the effect of adding a moderate amount of HCl to this strongly basic solution, and give the net ionic equation for the reaction.

What further change occurs when excess HCl is added? (Give the equation and explain.)

3. The Reaction of Zinc Ion with Ammonia

Note your observations on the addition of 6 M NH_3 to $Zn(NO_3)_2(aq)$, by drops, to redissolve the precipitate.

Color with
phenolphthalein _____

Alizarin
yellow R _____

OH^-
concentration[a] _____

Which coordination compound, $Zn(OH)_4^{2-}$ or $Zn(NH_3)_4^{2+}$, forms when Zn^{2+} reacts with excess NH_3 solution? Compare with part 2; explain fully.

The equation for the formation of this equilibrium
complex ion is therefore as follows: _____

4. Some Chloride Complex Ions

(a) Explain the successive changes observed when concentrated HCl, then H_2O, is added to a $CuSO_4$ solution; give the equations for the reactions.

(b) Explain the changes observed when concentrated HCl, then H_2O, is added to a $AgNO_3$ solution, and give the equations.

[a] Use the information on the color changes and pH intervals of the indicators given in Table B-5 of Appendix B to estimate the OH^- concentration.

5. The Equilibrium Constant of an Ammonia Complex Ion

(Indicate your calculations for each step in the spaces provided.)

Volumes of   0.1 M   1 M   0.02 M   Total

solutions: $AgNO_3$ _____NH_3 _____$NaCl$ _____volume _____

(a) Concentration of $Ag(NH_3)_2^+$

(Assume all the silver to be present as the complex ion, ignoring the trace of free Ag^+ remaining.)

_____M

(b) Concentration of Cl^-

(Ignore any trace of Cl^- removed as $AgCl(s)$.)

_____M

(c) Concentration of Ag^+

(Use the Cl^- concentration above, and the solubility product relationship, $[Ag^+][Cl^-] = 2.8 \times 10^{-10}$.)

_____M

(d) Concentration of free NH_3

(First calculate the NH_3 concentration as if none combined with Ag^+, then subtract twice the concentration of $Ag(NH_3)_2^+$ found above.)

_____M

(e) Use the values found in 5(a), 5(c), and 5(d) to calculate the value of the equilibrium constant:

_____

APPLICATION OF PRINCIPLES

1. Which reagent, NaOH or NH$_3$, will enable you to precipitate the *first-named ion* from a solution containing each of the following pairs of ions, and leave the second ion in solution? Give also the formula of the precipitate and the exact formula of the other ion in solution.

Pair	Reagent	Precipitate	Ion in solution
(a) Al^{3+}, Zn^{2+}			
(b) Cu^{2+}, Pb^{2+}			
(c) Pb^{2+}, Cu^{2+}			
(d) Fe^{3+}, Al^{3+}			
(e) Ni^{2+}, Sn^{2+}			
(f) Sn^{2+}, Ni^{2+}			
(g) Mg^{2+}, Ag$^+$			

2. When ammonia is added to Zn(NO$_3$)$_2$ solution, a white precipitate forms, which dissolves on the addition of excess ammonia; but when ammonia is added to a mixture of Zn(NO$_3$)$_2$ and NH$_4$NO$_3$, no precipitate forms at any time. Suggest an explanation for this difference in behavior.

3. Calculate the OH$^-$ concentration in (a) 1 M NH$_3$, and (b) a solution that is 1 M in NH$_3$ and also 1 M in NH$_4$Cl$^-$. (K_{NH_3} = 1.8 $\times$ 10^{-5}; see Appendix B, Table B-6.)

(a) _____ M

(b) _____ M

REPORT 38	Sheet 3	NAME

4. Suppose you are given the following experimentally observed facts regarding the reactions of silver ion.

   (a) Ag^+ reacts with Cl^- to give white AgCl(*s*).

   (b) Ag^+ reacts with ammonia to give a quite stable complex ion, $Ag(NH_3)_2^+$.

   (c) A black suspension of solid silver oxide, Ag_2O(*s*), shaken with NaCl solution, changes to white AgCl(*s*).

   (d) AgCl(*s*) will dissolve when ammonia solution is added, but AgI(*s*) does not dissolve under these conditions.

   Write equations for any net reactions in the above cases, and then, based on these observations, arrange each of the substances AgCl, AgI, Ag_2O, and $Ag(NH_3)_2^+$ in such an order that their solutions with water would give a successively decreasing concentration of Ag^+.

   (1) ______________________________ ____________

   (2) ______________________________ ____________

   (3) ______________________________ ____________

   (4) ______________________________ ____________

The Chemistry of Vitamin C

PURPOSE

To show that vitamin C (ascorbic acid) acts as a reducing agent toward iodine and other oxidizing agents. To compare the content of vitamin C in commercial tablets with the content stated on the label by the manufacturer. To determine the vitamin C content of citrus juices or other foods. To illustrate the redox chemistry of the iodate-iodide ion reaction.

PRE-LAB PREPARATION

Until late in the 19th century it was common for ships on transoceanic voyages to lose more than half their crews. The deaths were the result of the dread disease scurvy. Of those who survived, many were afflicted with massive hemorrhages, ulcerated gums, diarrhea, and exhaustion. In 1795, the British Navy ordered a daily ration of lime juice for every sailor. It was because of this measure that the nickname "Limey" was invented—but there were no more deaths from scurvy in the British Navy. (The British merchant marine considered the practice quackery, and hundreds of its

seamen perished in the course of the next 70 years before the Board of Trade passed a similar regulation, making such rations mandatory on all vessels.)

The vital antiscurvy factor in lime juice, all other citrus fruits, and nearly all fresh vegetables was not isolated until 1928. The brilliant Hungarian-born scientist Albert Szent-Györgi made the discovery, and the substance was called *hexuronic acid*. Working about the same time, American biochemist C. Glen King reported the isolation of the antiscurvy factor in crystalline form from lemon juice. In 1932–1933 hexuronic acid and the substance isolated by King were found to be identical; the substance was renamed *ascorbic acid* and it was determined to have the chemical formula $C_6H_8O_6$. Szent-Györgi received a Nobel prize in 1937 for his studies of biological oxidations and the discovery of ascorbic acid.

In 1933, the English sugar chemist W. M. Haworth reported the structure of ascorbic acid to be compound I shown in Figure 39-1. Haworth employed the standard convention for writing the structural formula of sugars with one ring. A somewhat more realistic representation of the same compound is shown as structure II in Figure 39-1.

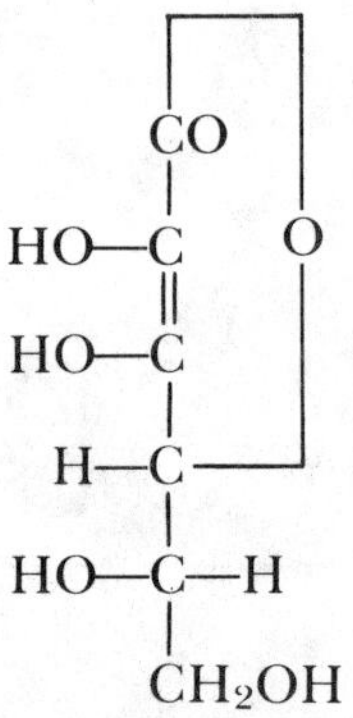

FIGURE 39-1
The structure of ascorbic acid.

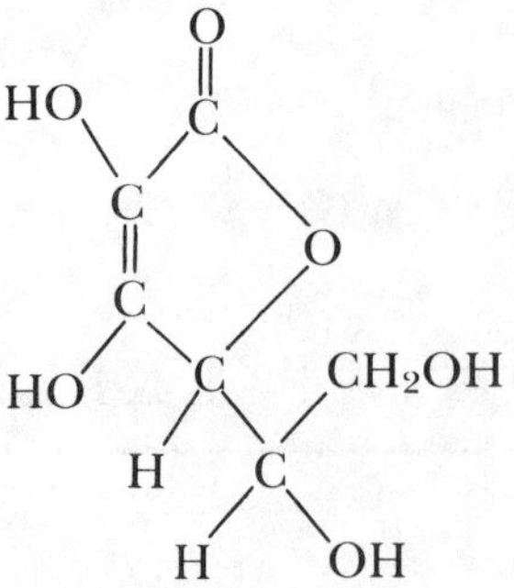

TABLE 39-1
Ascorbic acid content of foodstuffs

Ascorbic acid (mg/100 g)	Foodstuffs
100–350	Chili peppers (green and red), sweet peppers (green and red), parsley, turnip greens
25–100	Citrus juices, tomato juice, mustard greens, spinach, Brussels sprouts
10–25	Green beans and peas, sweet corn, asparagus, pineapple, cranberries, cucumbers, lettuce
Less than 10	Eggs, milk, carrots, beets, cooked meat

For many years public health organizations have recommended a minimum daily intake of ascorbic acid, now also known as *vitamin C*. The present daily dietary allowance recommended by the Food and Nutrition Board of the National Research Council is between 35 and 60 mg/day.

Linus Pauling, winner of a Nobel Prize in Chemistry and a Nobel Peace Prize, has compiled much information about vitamin C from published research papers. His small book, *Vitamin C and the Common Cold*,[1] has stimulated further work on the subject (and the idea for this experiment). Pauling surveyed a number of earlier studies on the effectiveness of this vitamin in reducing the incidence of common colds. He concluded that, if taken in sufficiently large quantities, vitamin C can dramatically curb the frequency of colds. He recommends a daily intake of between 250 mg and 10 g, depending on the size and physiology of the person. To help put the magnitudes of these numbers in better perspective, we note that the minimum daily requirements of the essential amino acids vary from 2 to 3 g/day. In this context the word "essential" means that these amino acids, like vitamin C, cannot be synthesized in the body and must be supplied from the food we eat.

It is Pauling's view that such an increased intake of vitamin C would not only offer protection against the common cold but would also have a general beneficial effect on the body's natural defense mechanisms against disease. Pauling believes that the ordinary human diet contains a suboptimal amount of the vitamin—which he describes as "a substance that participates in almost all of the chemical reactions that take place in our bodies, and is required for many of them."

This view has been disputed by other members of the scientific and medical communities.[2] It is not our intent to take sides in this dispute; rather, we intend to look at the unique chemical properties of this now famous molecule and determine the amounts of it present in some foodstuffs. Table 39-1 gives you some average values for the vitamin C contents of a variety of foods. This will help you in your selection of foods to study in part 2 of the Experimental Procedure, and it will also tell you how much you would have to eat of a particular food in order to ingest Pauling's recommended amounts. He recommends doses of ascorbic acid powder or tablets. It would be difficult to obtain such large amounts of the substance from available foodstuffs—unless you wanted to consume large quantities of green peppers daily!

Experimental Method

To determine the amount of vitamin C in a sample we will utilize one of the most distinctive features of this vitamin, its powerful reducing properties. For example, it will reduce Fe(III) to Fe(II), iodine to iodide ion, and the red redox indicator dye 2,6-dichloroindophenol to its colorless form. A method employing the latter dye was developed by C. G. King some years ago but the dye is expensive and somewhat unstable. In this experiment we will employ the reaction with iodine, generated by

[1] Linus Pauling, *Vitamin C and the Common Cold*, W. H. Freeman and Company, San Francisco, 1970. A revised and somewhat expanded version of the book was published in 1976 under the title *Vitamin C, the Common Cold, and the Flu*.

[2] E. M. N. Hamilton and E. N. Whitney, *Nutrition: Concepts and Controversies*, West Publishing Co., St. Paul, MN, 1979, p. 256.

reaction of iodate ion with iodide ion in acid solution, following a procedure described by R. W. Ramette. (See the Bibliography.)

The procedure works like this: KI, HCl (to supply H^+), and starch solution are added to a sample containing some vitamin C. Potassium iodate (KIO_3) titrant is added from a buret. As the iodate ion is added, it reacts with I^- and H^+ to form I_2.

$$IO_3^- + 5I^- + 6H^+ \rightarrow 3I_2 + 3H_2O \qquad (1)$$

Almost as quickly as it is formed the ascorbic acid reacts with the I_2.

When all the vitamin C has reacted, the concentration of I_2 begins to build up to a level where it will react with I^- to form the linear triiodide ion, I_3^-.

$$I_2 + I^- \rightleftharpoons I_3^- \qquad (3)$$

Triiodide ion combines with starch as shown in Figure 39-2 to form the starch-triiodide ion complex, which has a deep blue (almost blue-black) color. So the appearance of the blue color signals the end point of the titration.

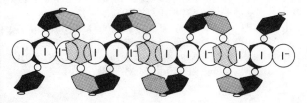

FIGURE 39-2
Starch-triiodide ion complex. The starch (amylose) molecule forms a helix with a cavity large enough to contain the triiodide ions.

EXPERIMENTAL PROCEDURE

Special Supplies: 25- or 50-mL buret; 100-mg vitamin C tablets; glazed weighing paper; mortar and pestle or food blender; cheesecloth; 150-mm-diameter funnel; citrus juices; dried breakfast drink, such as Tang; citrus fruit or other natural foodstuffs containing vitamin C. A pH meter will be required if you are going to measure the pK_a of vitamin C as an optional experiment in part 3.

Chemicals: Ascorbic acid tablets, 100 mg; 0.0100 M KIO_3 (potassium iodate); KI(s); 1 M HCl; 0.5% starch indicator solution. If you are going to measure the pK_a of vitamin C as an optional experiment in part 3, 1.00 M NaOH and 1.00 M HCl will be required.

1. *Determination of the Vitamin C Content of Commercial Tablets* Rinse and fill a buret with 0.0100 M KIO_3 solution and record the initial buret reading. Place a sheet of glazed weighing paper on the pan of an analytical balance and determine and record its mass. Then put a 100-mg vitamin C tablet on the weighing paper and reweigh. Record the mass. Is the difference in masses exactly 100 mg? Think about this and comment on it in your laboratory notebook. If you don't find anything unusual about your result, think about it again after the next step.

Put about 50 mL of deionized water in a 250-mL Erlenmeyer flask. Add the weighed tablet to the water and use a glass stirring rod to crush the tablet and dissolve the vitamin C. Vitamin C is very soluble in water, so if something remains undissolved after a minute or two of stirring the crushed tablet, it is probably a binder present in the tablet to make it more coherent. (Does this explain why a 100-mg vitamin C tablet might have a mass greater than 100 mg?)

Add 1 g of KI, swirl to dissolve, and then add 5 mL of 1 M HCl. Add 2 or 3 mL of 0.5% starch indicator and titrate with 0.0100 M KIO_3 until the appearance of a deep blue color. (As you near the end point you will get a transient blue color that quickly fades. Keep adding titrant until you get a permanent blue color.) Record the final buret reading.

Repeat the procedure with one or two more tablets, as your instructor directs. For each tablet, calculate the mass of ascorbic acid (its molecular weight, MW, is 176.13). (Your instructor may choose to collect a larger set of results from the class in order to carry out a statistical analysis of the data.) Compare the average value for the tablets you analyzed with the content stated on the label by the manufacturer.

2. Determination of the Vitamin C Content of a Foodstuff You are to determine the vitamin C content of a foodstuff you have some interest in. (*In fact, your instructor may ask you to be responsible for bringing this food to the laboratory for analysis.*) Try to obtain a sample of fresh citrus fruit, canned or frozen juices, or a breakfast drink in dry powder form (such as Tang).

Remember that if you use a highly colored food such as beets or cranberry juice, the color change at the end point will be modified and may be more difficult to see.

(a) *Juices.* Enough vitamin for an accurate titration is usually present in 50 mL of a citrus or vegetable juice. Freshly squeezed juices may be strained through cheesecloth to remove the pulp. Obtain a 150-mm-diameter funnel and support it in an iron ring with the stem of the funnel in the mouth of a 100-mL graduated cylinder. Line the funnel with 2 to 3 layers of cheesecloth, generously cut so that it drapes over the edges of the funnel. Pour the juice and pulp into the funnel. After most of the juice has run through, gather up the edges of the cheesecloth to form a sack and twist the sack to squeeze out most of the juice in the pulp.

Record the source and the volume of your sample of juice. Titrate the sample with 0.0100 M KIO$_3$, using the procedure described in part 1. (You may have to do a practice sample if the juice is highly colored.) Calculate the milligrams of ascorbic acid in the sample and divide by the sample volume to obtain the ascorbic acid content in milligrams per milliliter of juice.

(b) *Extraction from Solids.* Weigh out a sample of the solid foodstuff sufficient to contain at least 10 mg of ascorbic acid. (This would require about 1.9 mL of 0.0100 M KIO$_3$ titrant.) Record the mass of the sample. Grind the sample in a mortar and pestle or blender with 25 mL of added water. Obtain a 150-mm-diameter funnel and support the funnel on an iron ring with the stem of the funnel in the mouth of a 100-mL graduated cylinder. Line the funnel with 2 to 3 layers of cheesecloth, generously cut so that it drapes over the edge of the funnel. Gather up the edges of the cheesecloth to form a sack and twist the sack to express the juice from the pulp. If the volume is less than 50 mL, disperse the pulp in a little more water and repeat to extract as much vitamin

C as possible. The final sample should have a volume of about 50 mL.

Record the source and mass of the sample. Titrate the extract of the sample with 0.0100 M KIO$_3$, using the procedure described in part 1. Calculate the milligrams of ascorbic acid in the sample and divide by the sample mass to obtain the ascorbic acid content in milligrams per gram of sample.

3. Optional Experiments In addition to, or as an option to, part 2 you might want to think up an interesting experiment to study some aspect of the chemistry of vitamin C. Your experiment should be designed to take not more than 30 to 60 min of laboratory time. Students who have chosen to analyze a solid in part 2 will not be expected to produce as much in this part of the experiment as will those who have managed to analyze a juice sample with little or no difficulty. Some suggestions for experiments follow, but you are encouraged to try your own ideas (in consultation with your instructor).

(a) Compare fresh and reconstituted frozen orange juice for their vitamin C contents.

(b) Compare the vitamin C content of one sample of juice with a second sample of the same juice that has been heated to near boiling for 10 min, then cooled to room temperature.

(c) Compare the vitamin C content of one sample of juice with a second sample of the same juice that has had air (or oxygen) bubbled through it for 30 min.

(d) Determine the pK_a of vitamin C. In one interesting article (see the Bibliography) C. D. Hurd discusses possible reasons why ascorbic acid, although lacking a carboxylic acid group (—COOH), is still a stronger acid than acetic acid.

BIBLIOGRAPHY

Hurd, C. D., "The Acidities of Ascorbic and Sialic Acids," *J. Chem. Educ.* **47,** 481 (1970).

King, C. G., "Chemical Methods for Determination of Vitamin C," *Ind. and Eng. Chem.* **13,** 225 (1941).

Ramette, R. W., *Chemical Equilibrium and Analysis,* Addison-Wesley, Reading, MA, 1981, p. 628.

The Chemistry of Vitamin C

NAME		
SECTION		LOCKER
INSTRUCTOR		DATE

DATA AND CALCULATIONS

1. Determination of the Vitamin C Content of Commercial Tablets

Molarity of the potassium iodate (KIO_3) solution _____M

Data	Trial 1	Trial 2	Trial 3
Mass of the tablet + paper	_____g	_____g	_____g
Mass of the paper	_____g	_____g	_____g
Mass of the tablet	_____g	_____g	_____g
Volume of KIO_3 titrant			
Final buret reading	_____mL	_____mL	_____mL
Initial buret reading	_____mL	_____mL	_____mL
Net volume of KIO_3 soln	_____mL	_____mL	_____mL

Calculate the mass of ascorbic acid (MW = 176.13) in each tablet, taking account of the reaction stoichiometry shown in Equations (1) and (2). Show a sample calculation below:

Data	Trial 1	Trial 2	Trial 3
Mass of ascorbic acid	_____mg	_____mg	_____mg
		Average _____mg	

Compare the average content you determined with the content declared on the label by the manufacturer.

Are the tablets pure ascorbic acid, or is there evidence that they contain some inert material? Record your observations made when dissolving the tablets and compare the mass of a tablet with the mass of ascorbic acid found in the tablet.

2. Determination of the Vitamin C Content of a Foodstuff

Give the name of the foodstuff you analyzed. _____

Data	Trial 1	Trial 2	Trial 3
Mass of volume of foodstuff	_____	_____	_____
Volume of KIO_3 titrant			
Final buret reading	_____mL	_____mL	_____mL
Initial buret reading	_____mL	_____mL	_____mL
Net volume of KIO_3 soln	_____mL	_____mL	_____mL

Calculate the ascorbic acid content of the foodstuff (in milligrams of ascorbic acid per gram or per milliliter of sample). Show sample calculation below.

Milligrams of ascorbic acid per gram (or milliliter) of foodstuff _____

3. Optional Experiments

Carefully describe all aspects of this portion of your experiment.

Proteins and Polysaccharides

PURPOSE

To become acquainted with some of the functions of enzymes that are present in all living organisms by studying two examples of enzyme-catalyzed reactions: (1) the hydrolysis of starch by amylase in human saliva; and (2) the catalysis of hydrogen peroxide decomposition by catalase from potato.

PRE-LAB PREPARATION

There are four important classes of molecules in biological systems—proteins, polysaccharides, lipids, and nucleic acids. This experiment is designed to acquaint you with certain molecules from the first two classes.

Proteins

Proteins have numerous functions in all living systems. For example, hemoglobin transports oxygen from the lungs to myoglobin in the muscle, a variety of cytochromes cause biological oxidations, and the structural element of hair and nail is a protein. Perhaps the most important (and most amazing) of the proteins are the *enzymes*.

Enzymes are catalysts—molecules that increase the rate of a reaction. They are crucial for living organisms because without their acceleration of chemical reactions, the metabolic processes would be slowed so much that the organism would virtually cease to function. Catalysts perform such functions by lowering the activation energy, E_a, which is the minimum energy required to convert reactants to products (see Figure 40-1).

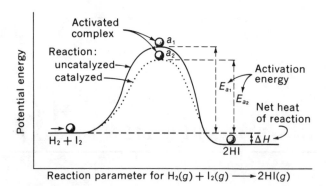

FIGURE 40-1
A potential energy diagram illustrating the meaning of the terms *activation energy* and *activated complex* as well as the effect of a catalyst and the heat of reaction.

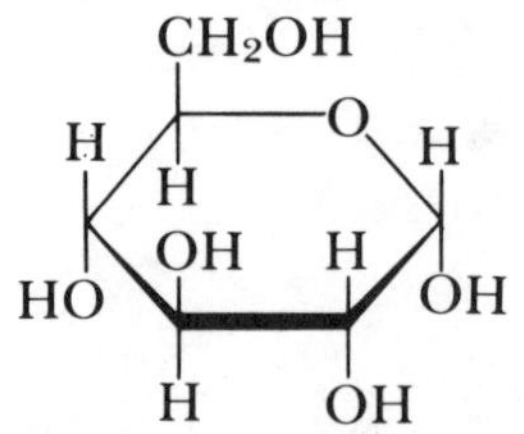

FIGURE 40-2
The structure of α-D-glucose.

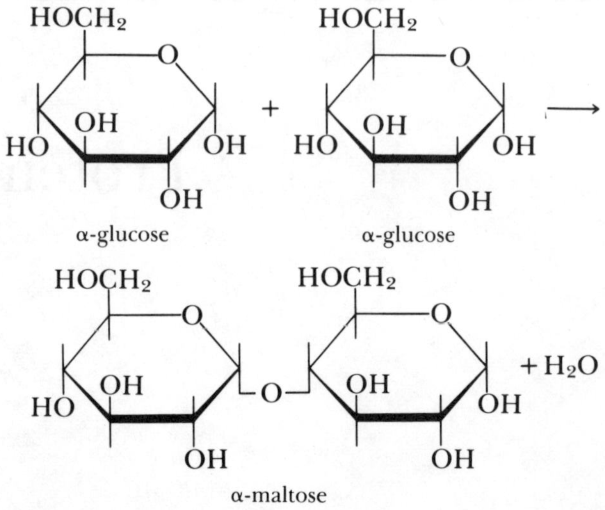

FIGURE 40-3
The formation of α-maltose from α-glucose.

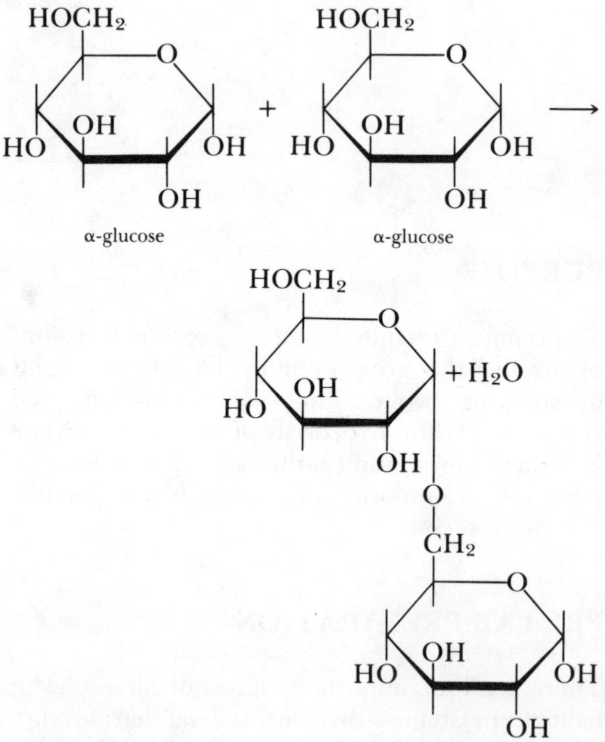

α-glucose   α-glucose

α-maltose

α-glucose   α-glucose

α-isomaltose

FIGURE 40-4
The formation of α-isomaltose from α-glucose.

Like all proteins, enzymes are large molecules composed of amino acids that are joined by peptide bonds, —NH—CO—. They have very specific three-dimensional geometries, which are responsible for their remarkable specificities. Because of their sizes and geometries, they are quite susceptible to extremes of temperature or pH, which destroy their effectiveness as catalysts.

The names of most enzymes end with the suffix -ase. The two enzymes you will study in this experiment are *amylase* from your own saliva and *catalase* from a potato.

Polysaccharides

The second class of molecules you will observe in this experiment is the polysaccharides. These molecules are polymers (or linked units) of the monosaccharides (organic compounds containing carbon, hydrogen, and oxygen in the ratio $(CH_2O)_x$, so they belong to the class of compounds known as carbohydrates). The most common monosaccharide is glucose, $C_6H_{12}O_6$. A number of monosaccharides have this formula, but only glucose has the specific configuration shown in Figure 40-2.

In Figure 40-3, glucose molecules are joined by —C—O—C— bonds, called *glycosidic linkages*, to form α-maltose. In addition to the α-maltose structure, two glucose molecules can combine to yield α-isomaltose (Figure 40-4).

Thus the possibility exists that when additional molecules of glucose are added to these dimers (*two* linked molecules) to form starch, two different polymers may be produced. The two types of structures, linear and branched, are represented schematically in Figure 40-5.

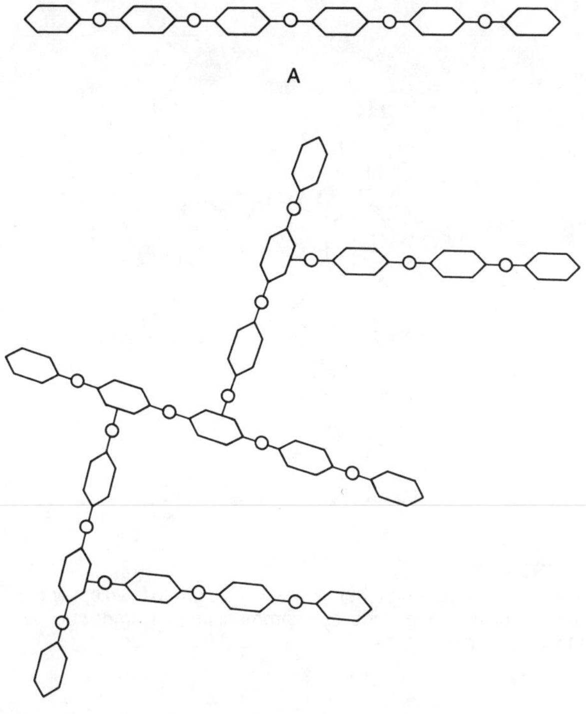

A

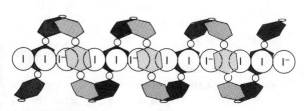

B

FIGURE 40-5
The two polysaccharides found in starch: (A) amylose; (B) amylopectin. Each unit represents a glucose molecule.

Experimental Method

In your study of the enzyme amylase you will be concerned with its action on the polysaccharides amylose and amylopectin. This action can be observed in two ways. First, we can determine the rate of disappearance of starch by studying the rate at which the blue color of a colored starch complex fades. Amylose reacts with the I_3^- ion (produced by adding I^- to a saturated solution of I_2) by forming a helix around the linear I_3^- ions, as shown in Figure 40-6. This helical compound has an intense blue color. Amylopectin forms similar complexes, which are a lighter, reddish

color. Starch contains both of these polymers. Therefore, as the amylase in saliva hydrolyzes the polysaccharides back to glucose molecules (the reverse of the reaction shown in Figure 40-3), the starch/I_3^- solution turns from a very dark blue to violet to reddish brown and finally, when there is no polymer left, to a pale yellow.

The second way to measure the action of amylase is to follow the rate of appearance of glucose molecules. A common biochemical test for the presence of most monosaccharides is Benedict's test. This test indicates the presence of reducing sugars—those monosaccharides that contain the group

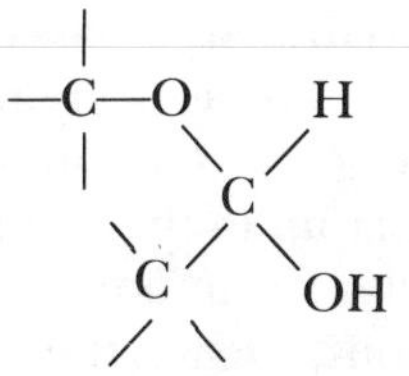

$$-\overset{|}{\underset{|}{C}}-O \overset{H}{\underset{OH}{\diagup}} \overset{}{\underset{C}{\diagdown}}$$

Reaction of this group with the citrate complex of Cu(II) in a hot alkaline solution yields gluconic acid and Cu_2O, which is rust colored and is insoluble in this solution (Figure 40-7). Thus if you observe the appearance of increasing amounts of this precipitate as the starch is converted to glucose, you will be able to follow the amylase activity.

The second enzyme you will study is catalase. Catalase is found in the tissues of most living

CH_2OH ... glucose $+2Cu(II)$ complex $\rightarrow$

CH_2OH ... gluconic acid $+Cu_2O \downarrow$ (red-brown)

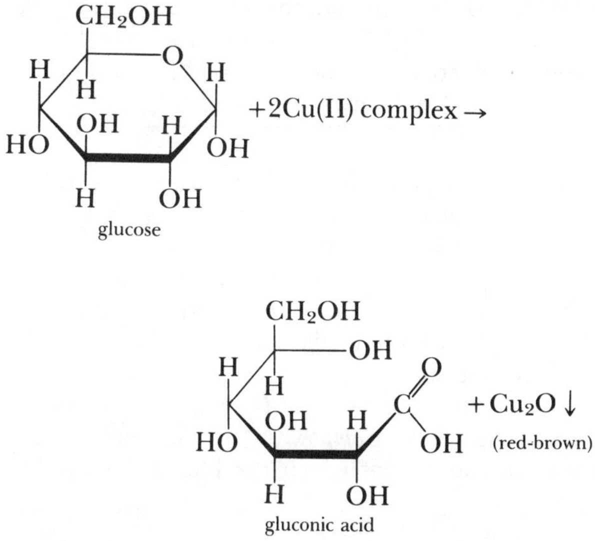

FIGURE 40-7
The formula for the reaction that takes place when Benedict's test is applied.

FIGURE 40-6
The amylose-triiodide ion complex.

organisms. Its function is to convert hydrogen peroxide to oxygen and water:

$$H_2O_2 \rightarrow H_2O + \tfrac{1}{2}O_2$$

It does this job exceedingly well. Enzymologists have tabulated turnover numbers for a variety of enzymes. This number gives the number of molecules of substrate (in this case, H_2O_2) that are converted to produce water and oxygen by each enzyme molecule per unit time. Catalase has a value of $50,000$ s^{-1} at $0°C$. Can you visualize 50,000 molecules of hydrogen peroxide diffusing to the surface of one catalase molecule and being converted to products in 1 s?

Catalase belongs to a large class of proteins called the *heme* proteins. These proteins contain heme groups—a large organic molecule called a *porphyrin ring* with an iron atom in the center (Figure 40-8). The iron atom has an important function in catalysis. When anions, such as the cyanide or sulfide ions, are added, they form a complex with the iron and totally inhibit enzymatic activity.

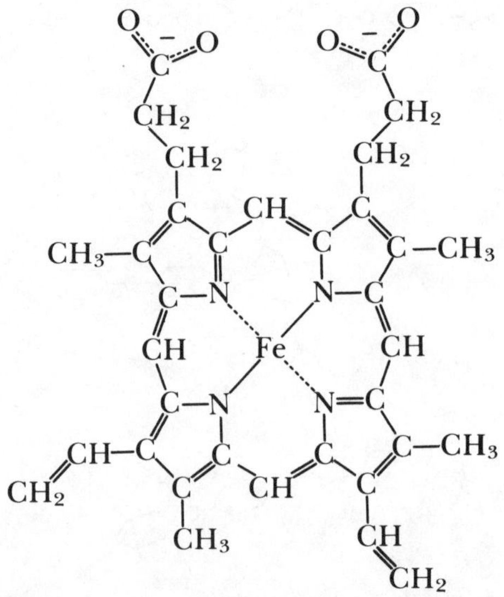

EXPERIMENTAL PROCEDURE[1]

Special Supplies: A potato; a knife; a flashlight; U-tube manometer; felt-tip pen, ruler.

Chemicals: 1% starch solution, 0.01 M KI$_3$, Benedict's reagent, 0.1 M Hg(NO$_3$)$_2$, 3% H$_2$O$_2$, 6 M (NH$_4$)$_2$S

Safety Precautions: The 0.1 M Hg(NO$_3$)$_2$ solution used in part 1(d) is highly toxic. Do not get it on your skin or in your mouth.

The 6 M (NH$_4$)$_2$S solution used in part 2(c) is toxic and corrosive to the skin. Acidification of the solution will produce very toxic H$_2$S gas.

---

1. The Hydrolysis of Starch by Salivary Amylase

(a) *Preparation of Solution of Saliva.* Spend a few minutes thinking about a T-bone steak or other delicacy of your choosing. Then transfer 2 mL of saliva to a 25-mL graduated cylinder. Dilute this fluid to 20 mL with distilled water, and thoroughly mix the solution.

(b) *Measurement of Rate of Hydrolysis by Disappearance of Starch/I$_3^-$ Complex.* You will qualitatively measure the rate at which the blue color of this

FIGURE 40-8
Structural formula for the heme group. This group is an essential component in hemoglobins, cytochromes, and enzymes such as catalase and peroxidase.

complex disappears. Four samples, as described below, will be employed:

(1) an unhydrolyzed starch solution;

(2) the same solution, hydrolyzed with saliva for half a minute;

(3) the same solution, hydrolyzed with saliva for 2 min;

(4) the same solution, hydrolyzed with saliva for 10 min.

Label four test tubes 1, 2, 3, and 4 to correspond to the four samples. Add 1 drop of the 0.01 M I$_3^-$ solution to each of the four labeled test tubes. Add 15 mL of the starch solution to a 50-mL Erlenmeyer flask.

Add 1 mL of the 1% starch solution to tube 1 and note the color.

While noting the second hand of a clock, add 1.0 mL of the saliva solution to the starch solution in the flask, and immediately swirl. At 30 s, 2 min, and 10 min after mixing, pipet 1-mL samples into tubes 2, 3, and 4, respectively. Mix and note the color of each. Compare the four colors, and describe qualitatively in your report.

(c) *Measurement of Rate of Hydrolysis by Appearance of Cu$_2$O(s).* The same concept as that in part (b) will be employed in this step, except that now you are to observe the appearance of glucose by its reaction with Benedict's solution to produce Cu$_2$O. Label the test tubes 1 through 4, as in (b). Each of

---

[1] This procedure is based in part on an experiment originally written by Professor William Jolly, University of California, Berkeley.

the numbered labels will correspond to the same time intervals. Add 5 mL of Benedict's reagent to each. Again add 15 mL of the starch solution to a 50-mL Erlenmeyer flask.

Add 1 mL of the 1% starch solution to tube 1, shake, and set it aside.

Repeat the addition of 1.0 mL of the saliva solution to the 15 mL of starch, and remove 1-mL samples after 30 s, 2 min, and 10 min. Immediately add these samples to the test tubes containing the Benedict's solution and mix. The high pH of the Benedict's reagent stops the enzymatic hydrolysis.

The Benedict's test for glucose is now completed for all four solutions. Place the four test tubes in a boiling water bath for 5 min. This "develops" the color. Note and record the relative amounts of Cu_2O precipitate. You may find a flashlight helpful to detect a small amount of precipitate. Why?

(d) *Effects of Heat and of Heavy Metals on Amylase Activity.* Add 1.0 mL of saliva solution to each of three test tubes, numbered 1 through 3, and treat them as follows:

(1) Keep as a control test tube.

(2) Heat for 5 min at 100°C in a boiling water bath. Cool to room temperature.

(3) Add 5 drops of 0.1 M $Hg(NO_3)_2$, mix, and allow to stand 10 min. (*Caution*: $Hg(NO_3)_2$ is toxic.)

Then add 5 mL of the starch solution to each test tube and thoroughly mix. After 10 min, perform the I_3^- and Benedict's tests on 1-mL samples from each test tube. (In one of the tests, the iodine color may be bleached out. Add more I_3^- solution until a color results.)

Tabulate your results on your report form, and try to explain them.

2. The Catalysis of H_2O_2 Decomposition by Catalase from Potato

(a) *Preparation of Catalase Solution.* Peel a potato and weigh out a piece that is approximately 5 g. Cut it up into small 0.5-cm cubes. Add 10 mL of distilled water to the potato pieces in a small beaker. Allow the mixture to stand for 10 min, swirling occasionally. Decant the supernatant liquid into a centrifuge tube, and centrifuge the solid matter to the bottom of the tube.

(b) *Measurement of Rate of Decomposition of H_2O_2 upon Catalysis.* Obtain the U-tube shown in Figure 40-9 and add water to it as shown. Make sure that

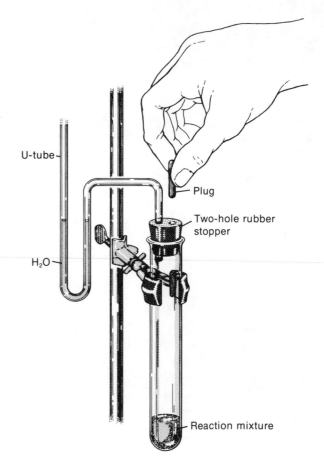

FIGURE 40-9
Apparatus for measuring catalase activity.

water does not block any other portion of the U-tube.

Transfer 2 mL of the clear supernatant potato extract from the upper part of the centrifuge tube to the test tube shown in the figure, add 3 mL of 3% H_2O_2, and swirl. After a few minutes insert the plug in the open hole of the stopper, and mark the level of water in the open end of the U-tube, using either a felt-tip pen or a small piece of masking tape. Mark the level at 1-min intervals until the water level has reached the top. Record the distance the water level moved as a function of time.

(c) *Effect of Sulfide on Catalase Activity.* Repeat part (b), but this time add a drop of 6 M $(NH_4)_2S$ and wait a few minutes before adding the peroxide. (*Caution*: 6 M $(NH_4)_2S$ is toxic and corrosive to the skin.) Again record the position of the water level as a function of time.

OBSERVATIONS AND DATA

1. The Hydrolysis of Starch by Salivary Amylase

Measurement of rate of hydrolysis by disappearance of starch/I_3^- complex

Tube	Time of hydrolysis (min)	Qualitative description of color
1	0	
2	0.5	
3	2	
4	10	

Comment on your results.

Measurement of rate of hydrolysis by appearance of $Cu_2O(s)$

Tube	Time of hydrolysis (min)	Qualitative description of amount of precipitate
1	0	
2	0.5	
3	2	
4	10	

Comment on your results.

Effect of heat and of heavy metals on amylase activity

Tube	Treatment	Results	
		I_3^- test	Benedict's test
1	Control		
2	Heated		
3	Hg^{2+} added		

Comment on your results.

2. The Catalysis of H_2O_2 Decomposition by Catalase from Potato

Measurement of rate of decomposition of H_2O_2 upon catalysis

Time (min)	Water level	Time (min)	Water level
1		6	
2		7	
3		8	
4		9	
5		10	

Make a graph plotting these data, and determine an approximate value of the rate of this reaction in the arbitrary units of centimeters per minute.

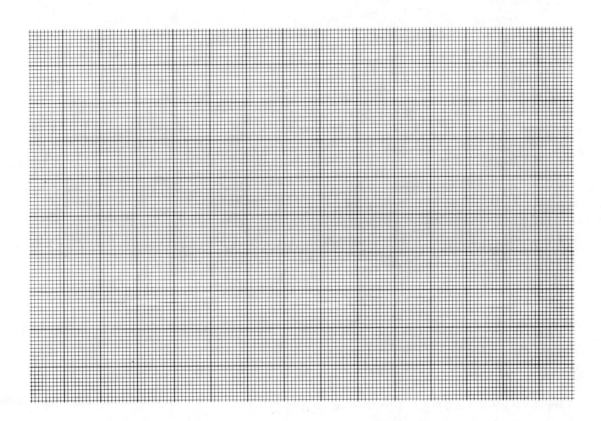

Rate _____cm/min

Effect of sulfide on catalase activity

Time (min)	Water level	Time (min)	Water level
1		6	
2		7	
3		8	
4		9	
5		10	

Again plot your data and determine an approximate value for the rate of this reaction in centimeters per minute.

Rate _____cm/min

The Language of Chemistry

The Nomenclature
of Inorganic Compounds

INTRODUCTION

This appendix provides you with a basic introduction to inorganic chemical nomenclature, and shows you how to write simple chemical formulas, using the periodic table to correlate the oxidation states (or ionic valences) of the elements. It is necessary to establish rules for naming compounds in order to avoid the massive confusion that would result if each person invented his or her own names and symbols for the elements and their compounds. The importance of this task is underscored by noting that in January 1965, *Chemical Abstracts* (a periodical that provides short summaries of all articles appearing in chemistry journals) started a compound registry index. This index contained about 6 million different chemical substances by 1983 and has been growing at the rate of 300,000 new substances each year. It is estimated that about 9 million chemical substances are known, the great majority of them being organic compounds (those containing carbon). Mastering the details necessary to name all of these substances would require a great deal of study. Fortunately, we work most of the time with a limited number of chemical substances, and therefore you will not need to learn more than a few hundred names. This task is made easier still because most of the names are established according to simple rules, and the elements are grouped in chemical families of the periodic table, those within each family bearing strong resemblances to one another. In addition, you do not have to learn all of the names at once. Just as you are able to learn the names of new friends a few at a time, you will find it easy to learn the names of new chemical substances little by little, as you encounter them.

However, one problem cannot be avoided. The grand traditions of chemistry go back several centuries, and some compounds are commonly referred to by names coined years ago, as well as by their more systematic names. Consequently, for some substances it is necessary to learn both the *common,* or *trivial,* name and the systematic name. Fortunately, the use of older common names is diminishing: For example, in industrial commerce it is common to refer to sodium carbonate (Na_2CO_3) as "soda ash," but today you are not likely to find in a chemistry laboratory a bottle of sodium carbonate labeled as soda ash.

CHEMICAL NOMENCLATURE

In many respects the best way to represent a chemical substance is to make a three-dimensional model of it, showing the arrangement of all the atoms in space and their relative sizes. This is, of course, too cumbersome most of the time, so we represent atoms and chemical substances by symbols (such as Na) and formulas (such as Na_2CO_3) and use names (such as sodium and sodium carbonate) for these symbols and formulas. We call our system of naming substances *chemical nomenclature*. In a rational nomenclature, the name of a compound would indicate (1) the elements of which it was composed and (2) the relative proportions of each element. Recent changes in chemical nomenclature have moved in this direction but still fall considerably short of this goal. Nomenclature, like language, is not static. It continually changes as needs and current usage dictate.

The standards of nomenclature are established by the International Union of Pure and Applied Chemistry (IUPAC). Since this international body must coordinate different languages and conflicting views, it is not surprising that the rules reflect a compromise; as a result, American chemists occasionally employ usages not officially sanctioned by the IUPAC rules. In this appendix we have followed the IUPAC rules[1] except those conflicting with current American usage. Most of the conflicts are minor, and the beginning student of chemistry is not likely to encounter any serious conflicts in applying the rules listed here.

---

[1] For the most recent IUPAC rules on the nomenclature of inorganic chemistry, see "Nomenclature of Inorganic Chemistry—Definitive Rules 1970," *Pure and Applied Chemistry* **28**, 1–110 (1971). Other IUPAC publications on nomenclature have been listed in the *Journal of Chemical Education* **50**, 341 (1973); **52**, 482 (1975).

CHEMICAL SYMBOLS AND FORMULAS

You may have already used chemical symbols and the formulas of substances and may have written equations for a number of chemical reactions. Now we must pause to emphasize the exact meaning and correct usage of these and other terms that constitute the unique language of chemistry.

Each element is represented by a *chemical symbol*. The symbol consists of either one or two letters, such as C for carbon and Ba for barium. Several of the elements have symbols derived from their ancient Latin names: Cu for copper from *cuprum*; Fe for iron from *ferrum*; Au for gold from *aurum*; Pb for lead from *plumbum*, and Ag for silver from *argentum*. Several elements discovered after 1780 have names derived from Latin or Germanic stems: Na for sodium from *natrium*; K for potassium from *kalium*; and W for tungsten from *wolfram*.

A *chemical formula* represents the composition of a given *substance*, which may be either an element or a compound. Thus H and O are the symbols for the elements hydrogen and oxygen, and they can also represent the atomic state of the elements, whereas H_2 (hydrogen gas) and O_2 (oxygen gas) represent the more stable molecular forms of the elements hydrogen and oxygen. When we speak of the chemical properties of oxygen, it is usually the stable molecular form of oxygen, O_2, that is meant. In this manual we will always try to specify the chemical formula of a substance in order to avoid the possibility of any confusion or misinterpretation.

A *chemical compound* is a substance formed from two or more elements, such as H_2O (water), H_2O_2 (hydrogen peroxide), or NaCl (sodium chloride).

ELECTRONEGATIVITY, OXIDATION NUMBER, AND THE PERIODIC TABLE

As you study the behavior of the elements and their compounds, you will begin to see how their properties are systematically correlated by the arrangement known as the *periodic table of the elements*. As you undertake this study assignment, you should make frequent reference to the periodic table printed on the inside front cover. Although the periodic table forms the framework for our discussion, we also need language to clothe the framework. We will begin by introducing two terms: *electronegativity* and *oxidation state*.

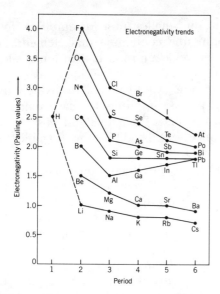

FIGURE AA-1
Electronegativity trends of the main group elements. The values
are based on those given by Linus Pauling.

Electronegativity In very simple terms, *electro-negativity is the ability of an atom to attract electrons to itself.* According to this definition, a greater electronegativity corresponds to a greater ability to attract electrons. Linus Pauling made the first important attempt to define electronegativity quantitatively and construct a scale of electronegativities of the elements. Pauling's values are shown in Figure AA-1 for the principal "a" group elements.

Note that the element fluorine is the most electronegative (4.0 on the Pauling scale) and that, in general, the most electronegative elements are in the upper right-hand corner of the periodic table. (The inert gas elements of Group 8 are excluded from this discussion because their low reactivity makes it impossible to define an electronegativity value on the Pauling scale.) We may make two generalizations about the relationship between electronegativity and the periodic table. First, in a given *period* the electronegativity increases from left to right, for example going from lithium to fluorine. This may be understood basically as the effect of increasing nuclear charge. Second, the electronegativity generally decreases in a particular group or family of elements. For example, in the Group 7a elements there is a regular decrease as you read down from fluorine to astatine. This is basically an effect of size, the valence electrons (those in the outermost, partially filled electron shells) in the heavier and larger atoms being a

further distance away from the nucleus. Although the nuclear charge increases as you read down the group, most of the effect of the increasing nuclear charge is neutralized, or "screened," by the core electrons belonging to the filled inner electron shells. In effect, the valence electrons "feel" an *effective* nuclear charge that is less than the actual nuclear charge. This screening effect tends to level off the electronegativity values of the heavier elements in a particular group.

Oxidation Number Oxidation number (or oxidation state) is an empirical concept defined by formal rules; it is not synonymous with the number of bonds to an atom, nor with the actual electronic charge (electron density) on an atom, except in the simplest cases. The oxidation number of an element in any chemical entity is the charge that would be present on an atom of the element if the electrons in each bond to that atom were assigned to the more electronegative atom. Some examples of the oxidation numbers of elements composing various compounds follow.

Compounds	Oxidation Numbers
MnO_4^-	$Mn = +7, O = -2$
ClO^-	$Cl = +1, O = -2$
NH_4^+	$N = -3, H = +1$
NF_4^+	$N = +5, F = -1$
AlH_4^-	$Al = +3, H = -1$

Note that hydrogen is assigned $+1$ in combination with nonmetals and -1 in combination with metals (metal hydrides). By convention oxygen is always assigned oxidation number -2 except in peroxides (such as H_2O_2, dihydrogen dioxide or hydrogen peroxide, or Na_2O_2, sodium peroxide), where it is assigned oxidation state -1,

$$H_2O_2 \qquad H = +1 \qquad O = -1$$

$$Na_2O_2 \qquad Na = +1 \qquad O = -1$$

or in combination with the more electronegative element fluorine, where fluorine is always assigned oxidation state -1:

$$O_2F_2 \qquad O = +1 \qquad F = -1$$

In the elementary state, the atoms have oxidation numbers of zero, and a bond between atoms of the same element makes no contribution to the oxidation number. Thus,

$$P_2H_4 \qquad P = -2 \qquad H = +1$$

but

$$P_4 \qquad P = 0$$

Difficulties in assigning oxidation numbers may arise if the elements in a compound have similar electronegativities, such as those in NCl_3 and S_4N_4.

OXIDATION STATES IN BINARY COMPOUNDS AND THEIR RELATION TO THE PERIODIC TABLE

Metals and Nonmetals   The periodic table can be roughly divided into two broad classes of elements—metals and nonmetals—by drawing a zig-zag line through the table, starting to the left of the element boron in Group 3a and running down to the left of astatine in Group 7a (as shown in the periodic table). The metallic elements lie to the left of the zigzag line and the nonmetallic elements to the right.

Binary Ionic Compounds   Compounds formed of two different elements are called *binary* compounds. Binary compounds may be approximately classified into two types: (1) covalent compounds, in which the chemical bonds are formed by sharing of the electrons, and (2) ionic compounds, in which electrons are transferred from the metal to the nonmetal to form ions. The metallic elements form positive ions (thus having a positive electric charge), and the nonmetallic elements form negative ions (having a negative electric charge). In the formation of an ionic compound, each element in its ionic form achieves the electronic structure of an inert gas. For example, when potassium reacts with oxygen, O_2, to form the compound potassium oxide (K_2O), each potassium atom loses an electron to become a potassium ion, K^+; in the process it achieves the same electron configuration as the inert gas argon. Each oxygen atom acquires two electrons to form an oxide ion, O^{2-}, which has an electron configuration like neon.

The charge possessed by an ion is sometimes called the *ionic valence*[2] because it determines the number of atoms of an element that will be con-

tained in the smallest unit (or empirical formula) of a compound containing that element. For example, the potassium ion has an ionic valence of $+1$ and the oxide ion has an ionic valence of -2: Therefore one unit of potassium oxide must contain two potassium atoms for each oxide ion, so that the number of negative and positive charges will balance exactly. Thus the formula for this oxide is K_2O.

The previously defined term *oxidation number* (or *oxidation state*) is officially approved by the IUPAC and has gradually displaced the term ionic valence. Neutral atoms of each element are by definition assigned oxidation number zero, represented by an Arabic zero (0). When one or more electrons are removed from a neutral atom, that atom becomes a positively charged ion; when one or more electrons are added to the neutral atom, it becomes a negatively charged ion. For ions containing a single atom, the ionic charge is the same as the oxidation state. The metals of Group 1a give up one electron easily to form ions of charge $+1$. Thus we assign an oxidation number (or valence) of $+1$ to the alkali metals in all of their simple binary compounds: Li^+, Na^+, K^+, Rb^+, and Cs^+. The most common oxidation state of hydrogen is $+1$. The Group 2a metals easily give up two electrons to form ions of oxidation state $+2$ in their compounds: Be^{2+}, Mg^{2+}, Ca^{2+}, Sr^{2+} Ba^{2+}, and Ra^{2+}; and the Group 3a metals give up three electrons to form ions of oxidation state $+3$ in their compounds: Al^{3+}, Sc^{3+}, and so on.[3]

All of the metal ions are given the same name as the element: Na^+ is called sodium ion; Mg^{2+} is called magnesium ion; Sc^{3+} is called scandium ion, and so on.

Like the metals, the nonmetals show strong family resemblances in their oxidation states or ionic valences. The halogens, or Group 7a elements, each tend to accept one electron to form an ion with oxidation number -1 in their simple compounds: F^-, Cl^-, Br^-, I^-. (Hydrogen atoms can also behave like the members of this group in reacting with Group 1a and 2a metals to form

---

[2] The word valence may be associated with "bond-forming capacity".

[3] Because of its high charge and small size, B^{3+} is not usually present as a simple ion, but tends to form complex ions with another element, particularly with oxygen, as in boric acid (H_3BO_3), which contains the borate ion, BO_3^{3-}. In this complex ion, the oxygen atoms are assigned oxidation state -2 so that boron is still assigned oxidation state $+3$. For the same reasons, H^+ (bare proton) does not exist as a discrete entity in solids and liquids. It is always attached to another species, for example to the water molecule (H_2O) in the hydronium ion, H_3O^+.

ionic metal hydrides in which the hydrogen has an oxidation state of -1.) An oxidation number of -2 is characteristic of the Group 6a elements in their binary compounds: O^{2-}, S^{2-}, Se^{2-}, Te^{2-}. The elements of Group 5a are assigned an oxidation number -3 in many of their compounds: N^{3-}, P^{3-}, and so on.[4] A few Group 4a ions are assigned oxidation number -4: C^{4-} and Si^{4-}. Each of these ions has an electron configuration which is like that of the inert gas element that immediately follows the element in the same period; thus F^- has the electron configuration of neon; S^{2-} has the electron configuration of argon; and so on.

Thus you can see that certain patterns or regularities correlate with the periodic table: (1) All of the elements in a particular group tend to have the same oxidation state; and (2) each element tends to achieve a stable electron configuration like that of an inert gas—the metallic elements tending to lose electrons to become positive ions and the nonmetallic elements tending to gain electrons to become negative ions.

Binary Covalent Compounds When elements in Groups 1a and 2a react with elements in Groups 6a and 7a to form simple binary compounds, it is reasonable to assume that electrons are transferred from the metallic element to the nonmetallic element to form ions. It is on this basis that we assign the ionic valence or oxidation number for these elements. However, we must recognize that as we move inward to Groups 3a, 4a, and 5a, we may assign a formal oxidation number on the basis of the assumption that the element has achieved an inert gas configuration; but we also know from extensive studies that these elements form many compounds in which the electrons are shared to form a *covalent*, rather than ionic, chemical bond. The electrons are not transferred completely from the less electronegative to the more electronegative element. In these compounds the valence can be thought of as a measure of the number of bonds that can be formed by the element. Carbon in Group 4a can share its four valence electrons to form four chemical bonds with other atoms, rather than forming an ionic carbide. In binary compounds of the nonmetallic elements the oxidation

number is assigned *in a purely formal way; it does not represent the actual charge on the atoms.* In the following examples the superscript Arabic number next to the symbol for each element indicates the oxidation number assigned to that element:

$^{(+2)}CO^{(-2)}$	carbon monoxide
$^{(+4)}CO_2^{(-2)}$	carbon dioxide
$^{(+4)}SO_2^{(-2)}$	sulfur dioxide
$^{(+6)}SO_3^{(-2)}$	sulfur trioxide
$^{(+3)}N_2O_3^{(-2)}$	dinitrogen trioxide
$^{(+5)}N_2O_5^{(-2)}$	dinitrogen pentaoxide

Note that we have assigned oxygen an oxidation state of -2 in each of these binary oxides. The less electronegative element has been assigned the oxidation state that it must have in order for the net charge on the molecule to be zero, since these are all neutral covalently bonded molecules. Note also that in these compounds the *oxidation states can be variable*: For example, sulfur has oxidation state $+4$ in sulfur dioxide and $+6$ in sulfur trioxide.

Some compounds, such as water (H_2O), ammonia (NH_3), and phosphine (PH_3), have common names that were given to them before the nomenclature of compounds was systematized, and these names are still retained.

Variable Oxidation States of Nonmetals In the foregoing discussion we stressed that metals lose electrons and the nonmetals gain electrons to form monatomic ions with an inert gas electron configuration. However, most nonmetals also form species in which the nonmetal atom is assigned an intermediate oxidation state. In these combinations the inert gas electron configuration is achieved by sharing of electrons with other atoms to form *polyatomic* species. For example, the oxidation states of carbon can range from -4 in the carbide ion, C^{4-}, to $+4$ in the compound carbon dioxide, CO_2, in which oxygen is assigned its characteristic oxidation state of -2 and carbon is therefore required to have oxidation state $+4$. Similarly, nitrogen can have oxidation states that vary from -3 in the nitride ion, N^{3-}, to $+5$ in the nitrate ion, NO_3^-. Note that the difference between the most positive and most negative oxidation states is exactly 8, because the $2s$ and $2p$ electron shells have a total capacity of eight electrons. The most positive oxidation state is obtained when all of the electrons are formally removed; the most negative when the $2s$ and $2p$ orbitals are completely filled.

---

[4] The heavier Group 5a elements As and Sb are on the borderline between the metals and nonmetals and show many metal-like properties. For this reason they are sometimes called semimetals. They do not as readily form ions with oxidation state -3 as do N and P.

SYSTEMATIC NOMENCLATURE OF SIMPLE INORGANIC COMPOUNDS

Binary Compounds

Many chemical compounds are essentially binary in nature and can be regarded as combinations of ions. Others may be treated as such for the purposes of nomenclature. The characteristic ending -ide is used for all binary compounds whether they are covalent or ionic.

Covalent Compounds   In the chemical formulas of covalent compounds, the less electronegative element is written first, followed by the more electronegative element. In the English language, the same pattern is used in naming the compounds—we name the less electronegative element first, and then the stem of the name of the more electronegative element plus the ending -ide. The Greek prefixes *mono-, di-, tri-, tetra-, penta-, hexa-, hepta-, octa-, nona-, deca-,* and so on, are used to indicate the number of atoms of each element (the prefixes in parentheses are sometimes omitted in writing the names of familiar compounds):

CO_2	carbon *di*oxide
PCl_3	phosphorus *trichloride*
PCl_5	phosphorus *pentachloride*
N_2O_4	(*di*)nitrogen *tetra*oxide
Cl_2O	*di*chlorine *mon(o)*oxide
$HCl(g)$	hydrogen chloride
$H_2S(g)$	(*di*)hydrogen (*mono*)sulfide

Cations   Monatomic cations are given the same names as their corresponding elements with no change, unless the *-ous-ic* system (to be discussed later) is used. The NH_4^+ ion, *ammonium* ion, is named as if it were a metal ion because of the saltlike properties of the ammonium salts. Examples of monatomic cations include

Li^+	lithium ion	Mg^{2+}	magnesium ion
Na^+	sodium ion	Al^{3+}	aluminum[5] ion

Monatomic Anions   The names for monatomic anions consist of the name of the element (sometimes abbreviated) and suffix -ide. Thus

Group 4a	Group 5a	Group 6a	Group 7a
			H^-, hydride
C^{4-}, carbide	N^{3-}, nitride	O^{2-}, oxide	F^-, fluoride
Si^{4-}, silicide	P^{3-}, phosphide	S^{2-}, sulfide	Cl^-, chloride
		Se^{2-}, selenide	Br^-, bromide
	As^{3-}, arsenide		I^-, iodide
		Te^{2-}, telluride	

Polyatomic Anions   Certain very stable groups of atoms are named as if they were like ions formed from nonmetal elements, and they have the binary ending -ide:

OH^-	hydroxide	N_3^-	azide
O_2^{2-}	peroxide	CN^-	cyanide
I_3^-	triiodide	NH_2^-	amide

Salts   Salts are ionic compounds formed by reaction of an acid and a base. (Note that this is a generic term, not be be confused with our everyday usage of the term for table salt, NaCl.) In simple salts consisting of a monatomic cation and a monatomic anion, we name the metal first, and then the stem of the anion plus the -ide ending:

$NaCl$	sodium chloride
CaO	calcium oxide
K_2S	potassium sulfide
$MgBr_2$	magnesium bromide
LiH	lithium hydride
BaF_2	barium fluoride

Note that the prefixes mono-, di-, tri-, and so on are not used with metals in Groups 1a and 2a, which do not show variable valence.

Metals with Variable Valence   Some metals, notably the *transition* metals (atomic numbers 22 through 30 and those below them in the periodic table), show variable oxidation states. For these elements it is necessary to distinguish their various compounds by one of the following systems:

1. In the preferred *Stock* system, the oxidation state of the metal is designated by a Roman numeral placed in parentheses just after the name of the element. This system is especially useful if the metal has more than two oxidation states and the -ous-ic system is inadequate.

$FeBr_2$	iron(II) bromide
$FeBr_3$	iron(III) bromide
VCl_2	vanadium(II) chloride
VCl_3	vanadium(III) chloride ,
VCl_4	vanadium(IV) chloride
VCl_5	vanadium(V) chloride

---

[5] This is the American spelling. In most other languages, including British standard English, it is spelled alumin*ium.*

2. In the *Ewens-Bassett* system, the charge of an ion is indicated by an Arabic numeral and the sign of the charge, in parentheses, immediately after the name of the ion:

$FeCl_2$	iron(2 +) chloride
Hg_2Cl_2	dimercury(2 +) chloride
$TlCl_3$	thallium(3 +) chloride

3. For elements having just two common oxidation states, the ending -ous is used to show the lower oxidation state, and the ending -ic, the higher.[6]

The most often encountered elements with just two common oxidation states are the following.

-ous:	Fe^{2+}	Co^{2+}	Cu^+	Au^+	Hg_2^{2+}	Sn^{2+}
-ic:	Fe^{3+}	Co^{3+}	Cu^{2+}	Au^{3+}	Hg^{2+}	Sn^{4+}

The following are names and formulas of a few corresponding compounds.

$FeBr_2$	ferr*ous* bromide
$FeBr_3$	ferr*ic* bromide
$CoCl_2$	cobalt*ous* chloride
$CoCl_3$	cobalt*ic* chloride
Hg_2O	mercur*ous* oxide
HgO	mercur*ic* oxide
$SnCl_2$	stann*ous* chloride
$SnCl_4$	stann*ic* chloride

Peroxides The O_2^{2-} ion contains two oxygen atoms with a single covalent bond between them and is given the distinguishing name "peroxide." Care must be taken to distinguish between peroxides, such as BaO_2 (barium peroxide), H_2O_2 (hydrogen peroxide), Na_2O_2 (sodium peroxide), and normal dioxides, such as MnO_2 (manganese dioxide), TiO_2 (titanium dioxide), and SiO_2 (silicon dioxide).

Trivial Names Some common binary compounds are designated by trivial names that have been assigned arbitrarily. Examples are H_2O (water), NH_3 (ammonia), PH_3 (phosphine), AsH_3 (arsine), and many carbon compounds, such as CH_4 (methane).

These names are so universally used that they are allowed by the IUPAC rules of nomenclature. In addition, because aqueous solutions of HF, HCl, HBr, and HI are acidic, they are often called by the following trivial names:

---

6 The use of the -ous-ic system is discouraged by the IUPAC rules, but it is described here because it is so firmly entrenched.

HF(*aq*)	hydrofluoric acid
HCl(*aq*)	hydrochloric acid
HBr(*aq*)	hydrobromic acid
HI(*aq*)	hydriodic acid

Ternary Compounds

Oxo Acids and Salts The oxides of the nonmetals react with water to form hydroxides that are acidic. In some cases there may be a series of oxo acids, each one containing the nonmetal in a different oxidation state. In order that these acids and their respective salts can be distinguished from one another, characteristic prefixes and suffixes are used, as illustrated below for the oxo acids containing chlorine and their salts:

OXIDATION STATE OF Cl	ACID	NAME
+1	HClO	*hypo*chlor*ous* acid
+3	$HClO_2$	chlor*ous* acid
+5	$HClO_3$	chlor*ic* acid
+7	$HClO_4$	*per*chlor*ic* acid

	SALT	NAME
+1	NaClO	sodium *hypo*chlor*ite*
+3	$NaClO_2$	sodium chlor*ite*
+5	$NaClO_3$	sodium chlor*ate*
+7	$NaClO_4$	sodium *per*chlor*ate*

This nomenclature for the oxo acids and their salts is highly traditional, and its roots can be traced back to Lavoisier (1743–1794). Unfortunately, the passage of time has revealed the great diversity of the oxo acids. Thus the prevailing system that has evolved has many limitations, not the least of which is the major feat of memory required of the student in order to distinguish the various oxo acids.

The prefix *hypo-*, Greek for under, is used to denote the lowest oxidation state of the nonmetal with the characteristic ending -ous. The prefix *per-*, from the Greek *hyper*, meaning above, is used to denote the highest oxidation state of the nonmetal. Note that for acids whose names end in -ous, the name of the corresponding salt ends in *-ite*; and for acids whose names end in -ic, the name of the salt ends in *-ate*.

Recognizing the -ic Acid The oxo acid with the nonmetal in its highest oxidation state is given the -ic ending. (But remember that the two highest oxidation states, +5 and +7, of the Group 7a oxo acids both have the -ic ending, with the prefix *per-* being added to the name of the +7 oxo acid: thus, $HBrO_3$ is called brom*ic* acid and $HBrO_4$ is called *perbromic* acid.) The following are examples of -ic acids, and their anions, listed in order of their periodic table groups.

3a	4a	5a	6a	7a
H_3BO_3	H_2CO_3	HNO_3	H_2SO_4	$HClO_3, HClO_4$
	H_2SiO_3	H_3PO_4	H_2SeO_4	$HBrO_3, HBrO_4$
		H_3AsO_4	H_6TeO_6	HIO_3, HIO_4

	Acid		Anion
H_3BO_3	boric acid	BO_3^{3-}	borate
H_2CO_3	carbonic acid	CO_3^{2-}	carbonate
H_2SiO_3	silicic acid	SiO_3^{2-}	silicate
HNO_3	nitric acid	NO_3^-	nitrate
H_3PO_4	phosphoric acid	PO_4^{3-}	phosphate
H_3AsO_4	arsenic acid	AsO_4^{3-}	arsenate
H_2SO_4	sulfuric acid	SO_4^{2-}	sulfate
H_2SeO_4	selenic acid	SeO_4^{2-}	selenate
H_6TeO_6	telluric acid	TeO_6^{6-}	tellurate
$HClO_3$	chloric acid	ClO_3^-	chlorate
$HBrO_3$	bromic acid	BrO_3^-	bromate
HIO_3	iodic acid	IO_3^-	iodate
$HClO_4$	perchloric acid	ClO_4^-	perchlorate
$HBrO_4$	perbromic acid	BrO_4^-	perbromate[7]
HIO_4	periodic acid	IO_4^-	periodate

Note that in the -ic acids the central atom is in its highest oxidation state and has an oxidation number equal to the group number.

The acids ending in -ous usually have an oxidation state of 2 less than that of the -ic acid. Shown below are the names of some of the -ous acids and their corresponding anions:

ACID		ANION	
HNO_2	nitrous acid	NO_2^-	nitrite
H_3AsO_3	arsenious acid	AsO_3^{3-}	arsenite
H_2SO_3	sulfurous acid	SO_3^{2-}	sulfite
$HBrO_2$	bromous acid	BrO_2^-	bromite

Ortho, Meta, Di Acids   The prefixes *ortho-* and *meta-* have been used to distinguish acids differing in the "content of water." The prefix *ortho-* applies to the common acid (from the Greek word meaning regular). The acid with one molecule of water less than the ortho acid is a meta acid. The acid whose formula may be derived by removing one molecule of water from two molecules of the ortho acid has

the prefix *di-*.[8] These prefixes may be applied to either -ous or -ic acids.

Some anhydrides react with water to produce acids (ortho), which may be dehydrated to form di or meta acids, such as in the following reactions and formulas.

$P_4O_{10} + 6H_2O \rightarrow 4H_3PO_4$	*ortho*phosphoric acid
$2H_3PO_4 \rightarrow H_2O + H_4P_2O_7$	*di*phosphoric acid (*pyro*phosphoric acid)
$H_3PO_4 \rightarrow H_2O + HPO_3$	*meta*phosphoric acid
H_3BO_3	*ortho*boric acid
HBO_2	*meta*boric acid
H_3PO_3	*ortho*phosphorous acid
HPO_2	*meta*phosphorous acid
$HAsO_3$	*meta*arsenic acid
H_4SiO_4	*ortho*silicic acid
H_2SiO_3	*meta*silicic acid
H_2SO_4	(*ortho*)sulfuric acid
$H_2S_2O_7$	*di*sulfuric acid (*pyro*sulfuric acid)

Metal Oxo Acids and Their Salts   When a transition metal atom is substituted for the central nonmetal atom of an oxo acid, the chemical structures and acid properties are similar, and the naming of the acids and their salts is carried on in the same spirit. The most common examples are the following.

OXIDATION STATE OF THE METAL	ACID	NAME
+6	H_2CrO_4	chrom*ic* acid
+6	$H_2Cr_2O_7$	*di*chrom*ic* acid
+6	H_2MnO_4	mangan*ic* acid
+7	$HMnO_4$	*per*mangan*ic* acid

	SALT	NAME
	Na_2CrO_4	(*di*)sodium chrom*ate*
	$K_2Cr_2O_7$	(*di*)potassium *di*chrom*ate*
	K_2MnO_4	(*di*)potassium mangan*ate*
	$KMnO_4$	potassium *per*mangan*ate*

Salts of Polyprotic Acids   When salts of polyprotic acids, such as H_2S, H_2SO_4, or H_3PO_4, are formed, one or more of the hydrogen ions may be replaced by metal ions. Several systems of nomenclature have been used in the past to differentiate between these salts. In the examples below, the first name

---

[7] Some current textbooks suggest that perbromates do not exist. But see "The Elusive Perbromates" by A. Y. Herrell and K. H. Gayer, *J. Chem. Educ.* **49**, 583 (1972).

[8] The prefix *pyro-* was formerly used.

given is the preferred name specified by IUPAC rules.

NaH_2PO_4	sodium dihydrogen phosphate[9] monosodium phosphate
Na_2HPO_4	disodium hydrogen phosphate disodium phosphate
Na_3PO_4	trisodium phosphate
NaHS	sodium hydrogen sulfide sodium bisulfide
Na_2S	sodium sulfide[10]
$NaHSO_4$	sodium hydrogen sulfate sodium bisulfate
Na_2SO_4	sodium sulfate[10]
$NaHCO_3$	sodium hydrogen carbonate sodium bicarbonate

COORDINATION COMPOUNDS

The formation of complexes is a very general phenomenon. Ions dissolved in a polar solvent attract a cluster of solvent molecules about them. Here the force of attraction is primarily that between a charged ion and the dipole created by a nonuniform electron density distribution in the polar solvent molecule. Other bonding forces may be more nearly electrostatic—such as those occurring in the formation of a complex, such as FeF_6^{3-}, in which negatively charged fluoride ions are attracted to a positively charged Fe^{3+} ion; or those occurring in a more covalent type of bonding in which a metal atom (or ion) with vacant orbitals shares the electrons donated by another atom (generally a nonmetal). The transition metal ions, because of their partially filled d electron orbitals, form numerous coordination compounds. If the product of the interaction is an ion in solution, for example $Co(NH_3)_6^{3+}$, it is generally called a complex ion. The neutral salt $[Co(NH_3)_6]Cl_3$, is generally called a coordination compound, a complex compound, or simply a complex.

---

[9] IUPAC rules recommend combining hydrogen and the name of the anion into one word, e.g., sodium dihydrogenphosphate. In American usage they are separated into two words.

[10] The di- and tri- prefixes are often omitted for Group 1a or Group 2a ions that have only one stable oxidation state.

Before we proceed to the nomenclature of coordination compounds, it will be helpful to define a number of terms that are commonly employed in the language of coordination chemistry.

1. *Ligands*: The groups attached to the central metal atom or ion in a complex are called ligands. Ligands may be monatomic or polyatomic ions or neutral molecules.

2. *Donor atom*: Within the ligand, the atom attached directly to the metal is called the donor atom. In the complex ion $[Ag(NH_3)_2]^+$, nitrogen is the donor atom of the ammonia ligand.

3. *Coordination number*: The coordination number of the central atom in a complex is the number of atoms that are directly linked to the central atom. The attached atoms may be charged, uncharged, or part of an ion or molecule. Crystallographers define the coordination number of an atom or ion in a lattice as the number of that atom's or ion's nearest neighbors. In the complex $[Cu(NH_3)_4]^{2+}$, the coordination number of copper is 4, whereas in $[Fe(CN)_6]^{3-}$, the coordination number of Fe(III) is 6. Note that the coordination number is not the same as the oxidation number (or oxidation state) of a metal atom or ion.

4. *Polydentate ligand or chelating agent*: When a molecule attaches itself to more than one coordination site of a given central metal ion to form a closed ring, it is called a polydentate (or multidentate) ligand or chelating agent. Ligands may be bidentate, tridentate, quadridentate, and so on, depending on the number of donor atoms in the ligand. Bidentate ligands, such as ethylenediamine $(H_2NCH_2CH_2NH_2)$, are very common. Polydentate ligands can surround a metal ion in a pincer-like arrangement; such ligands are called chelating agents (from the Greek word for the claw of a crab) and the complexes are called *metal chelates*.

Nomenclature of Coordination Compounds

The great number of complicated and structurally intricate complexes that arise requires a very systematic means of nomenclature. The system now in use is based largely on that which was originally devised by Alfred Werner and has been refined throughout the years. The basic IUPAC rules are summarized as follows:

1. In a coordination compound that is a salt, the cation is named first and then the anion, in accordance with usual rules of nomenclature.

2. In naming the complex, whether the complex is a cation, anion, or neutral molecule, the ligands are named before the central metal atom or ion.

3. The names of anionic ligands, whether inorganic or organic, end in *-o*. In general, if the anion name ends in *-ide*, *-ite*, or *-ate*, the final *-e* is replaced by *-o*, resulting in one of the endings *-ido*, *-to*, or *-ato*. The names of some anionic ligands are given below.

SYMBOL	ION	LIGAND
F^-	fluoride	fluoro
Cl^-	chloride	chloro
Br^-	bromide	bromo
I^-	iodide	iodo
O^{2-}	oxide	oxo
NH_2^-	amide	amido
NO_3^-	nitrate	nitrato
ONO^- (O donor)	nitrite	nitrito
NO_2^- (N donor)	nitrite	nitro
CO_3^{2-}	carbonate	carbonato
CN^-	cyanide	cyano
SCN^- (S donor)	thiocyanate	thiocyanato
NCS^- (N donor)	thiocyanate	isothiocyanato

Neutral ligands have the same names as the corresponding molecule, except for the water ligand (which is called *aquo*) and the ammonia ligand (called *ammine*). Positive ligands (which are rare) have names ending in *-ium*.

4. In the naming of coordination compounds, the ligands are named first in alphabetical order, followed by the name of the central metal atom. The multiplying prefixes *di-*, *tri-*, *tetra-*, and so on are not treated as part of the name of the ligand in determining the order of naming ligands. Thus diammine would be written before bromo. Prefixes *bis-*, *tris-*, *tetrakis-*, and so on are used before more complex ligand names such as ethylenediamine (en) and ethylenediaminetetraacetic acid (EDTA). For examples, see the list of complexes at the conclusion of this appendix.

5. The oxidation number of the central metal atom or ion is indicated in parentheses after the name of the metal. When the complex is an anion, the ending -ate is attached to the element name (or the stem) of the central metal atom. Some examples follow.

ELEMENT NAME	ELEMENT NAME IN AN ANIONIC COMPLEX
cobalt	cobaltate
chromium	chromate
lanthanum	lanthanate
manganese	manganate
molybdenum	molybdate
mercury	mercurate
platinum	platinate
zinc	zincate

The elements whose symbols are derived from their Latin names use the Latin stem name with the ending -ate, as follows:

ELEMENT NAME	LATIN NAME	ELEMENT NAME IN AN ANIONIC COMPLEX
copper	*cuprum*	cuprate
gold	*aurum*	aurate
iron	*ferrum*	ferrate
lead	*plumbum*	plumbate
nickel	*"niccolum"*	niccolate (often designated as nickelate in American usage)
silver	*argentum*	argentate
tin	*stannum*	stannate
tungsten	*wolfram*	wolframate (or tungstate)

6. In writing the *formulas* of coordination compounds, place the symbol for the central atom first, and then add those for the ligands; the formula of the whole complex is enclosed in square brackets.

The preceding rules are illustrated below by a list of complexes with names and formulas.

FORMULA	NAME
$[Ag(NH_3)_2]^+$	diamminesilver(I) ion
$[Co(NH_3)_6]Br_3$	hexaamminecobalt(III) bromide
$[Cr(H_2O)_4Cl_2]NO_3$	tetraaquodichlorochromium(III) nitrate
$K_3[Fe(CN)_6]$	potassium hexacyanoferrate(III)
$[Co(en)_3]_2(SO_4)_3$	tris(ethylenediamine)cobalt(III) sulfate
$Na_2[CrOF_4]$	sodium tetrafluorooxochromate(IV)

The Language of Chemistry
The Nomenclature
of Inorganic Compounds

NAME

SECTION   LOCKER

INSTRUCTOR   DATE

EXERCISES ON FORMULAS AND NOMENCLATURE

NOTE: These exercises will help you learn how to write correct formulas and name compounds. Check your answers, if necessary, with your instructor.

1. Name the following.

FeI_2 _____ H_2CO_3 _____

I_2 _____ $CaCO_3$ _____

$FeCl_3$ _____ Be_2C _____

$Fe_2(SO_4)_3$ _____ $SnSO_4$ _____

FeS _____ $(NH_4)_2S$ _____

NCl_3 _____ N_2O_4 _____

2. Write the correct chemical formulas.

Barium chloride _____   Ammonium sulfate _____

Stannous nitrate _____   Barium carbonate _____

Stannic nitrate _____   Sodium carbonate _____

Aluminum carbide _____   Sodium hydrogen carbonate _____

Magnesium phosphate _____   Calcium hydrogen phosphate _____

Nitrogen dioxide _____   Disulfur dichloride _____

3. Complete the following table.

Formula	Name as acid	Formula for sodium salt	Name of salt
HF			
HNO_3			
HNO_2			
HBrO			
$HBrO_2$			
$HBrO_3$			
$HBrO_4$			
H_3AsO_4		Na_3AsO_4	
$HAsO_3$			
H_3AsO_3		NaH_2AsO_3	

4. Name the following as binary compounds or as salts of polyprotic or oxo acids.

$AgHSO_4$ _____   NaHS _____

NaIO _____ $KMnO_4$ _____

$Mg_2P_2O_7$ _____ $BaSO_3$ _____

K_2HPO_4 _____ $Ca(ClO_2)_2$ _____

$Fe(NO_3)_3$ _____ $FeSO_4$ _____

P_4O_6 _____ P_4O_{10} _____

NH_4ClO_4 _____ $HClO_3$ _____

K_2CrO_4 _____ $K_2Cr_2O_7$ _____

Na_2SO_3 _____ Na_2SO_4 _____

5. Write chemical formulas for the following complex ions.

Tetrachloroferrate(III) _____

Hexanitrocobaltate(III) _____

Pentaamminechlorocobalt(III) _____

Tetraiodomercurate(II) _____

REPORT A	Sheet 2	NAME

6. Write names for the following coordination compounds.

$[Cu(NH_3)_4]SO_4$ ______________________________

$K_2[PbCl_4]$ ______________________________

$K_4[Fe(CN)_6]$ ______________________________

$[Cr(NH_3)_4CO_3]NO_3$ ______________________________

7. The spaces below represent portions of some of the main groups and periods of the periodic table. In the proper squares, write the correct formulas for the chlorides, oxides, and sulfates of the elements of Groups 1a, 2a, and 3a, respectively. Likewise, write the formulas of the compounds of sodium, calcium, and aluminum with the elements of Groups 6a and 7a. Two of the squares have been completed as examples.

Period	Group 1a	Group 2a	Group 3a	Group 6a	Group 7a
2	LiCl Li_2O Li_2SO_4		(omit sulfate)		
3				Na_2S CaS Al_2S_3	
4					
5					

Tables of Data

TABLE B-1
The International System (SI) of units and conversion factors

Basic SI units		
Physical quantity	Unit	Symbol
Length	meter	m
Mass	kilogram	kg
Time	second	s
Electric current	ampere	A
Temperature	kelvin	K
Amount of substance	mole	mol
Luminous intensity	candela	cd

Common derived units			
Physical quantity	Unit	Symbol	Definition
Frequency	hertz	Hz	s^{-1}
Energy	joule	J	$kg \cdot m^2 \cdot s^{-2}$
Force	newton	N	$kg \cdot m \cdot s^{-2} = J \cdot m^{-1}$
Pressure	pascal	Pa	$kg \cdot m^{-1} \cdot s^{-2} = N \cdot m^{-2}$
Power	watt	W	$kg \cdot m^2 \cdot s^{-3} = J \cdot s^{-1}$
Electric charge	coulomb	C	$A \cdot s$
Electric potential difference	volt	V	$kg \cdot m^2 \cdot s^{-3} \cdot A^{-1} = J \cdot A^{-1} \cdot s^{-1}$

Decimal fractions and multiples					
Factor	Prefix	Symbol	Factor	Prefix	Symbol
10^{-18}	atto	a	10^{-1}	deci	d
10^{-15}	femto	f	10	deca	da
10^{-12}	pico	p	10^2	hecto	h
10^{-9}	nano	n	10^3	kilo	k
10^{-6}	micro	μ	10^6	mega	M
10^{-3}	milli	m	10^9	giga	G
10^{-2}	centi	c	10^{12}	tera	T

Common conversion factors

LENGTH
1 ångstrom unit (Å) = 10^{-8} cm
2.54 cm = 1 inch (in.)
1 meter = 39.4 in.

MASS
453.5 grams (g) = 1 pound (lb)
1 kg = 2.20 lb
28.3 g = 1 ounce (oz, avoirdupois)

VOLUME
1 milliliter (mL) = 1 cubic centimeter (cm^3)
 (Note that the mL is now defined precisely equal to 1 cm^3.)
1 liter (L) = 1.06 quarts
28.6 mL = 1 fluid ounce

PRESSURE
1 atm = 1.013×10^5 pascal (N/m^2)
 = 760 torr (mmHg); pressure of a mercury column 760 mm or 29.92 in. high at 0°C.
 = 1.0133 bar (dyne/cm^2)
 = 14.70 lb/in^2.

TEMPERATURE
Absolute zero (K)   = − 273.16°C
       K = °C + 273.16
       °F = $\frac{9}{5}$(°C + 32)
       °C = $\frac{5}{9}$(°F − 32)

ENERGY
1 joule = 1 watt-sec = 10^7 erg
1 erg = 1 dyne-cm = $1g \cdot cm^2 \cdot s^{-2}$
1 calorie = 4.184 joule (J)
1 electron volt/molecule = 23.06 kcal/mol

TABLE B-2
Fundamental physical and mathematical constants

Physical constants		
Symbol	Name	Numerical value
N_A	Avogadro's number	6.0221×10^{23} mol^{-1}
F	Faraday constant	96,487 coulombs per mole of electrons transferred
h	Planck's constant	6.63×10^{-34} joule·s per particle
c	Speed of light (*in vacuo*)	3.00×10^8 m·s^{-1}
R	The gas constant	0.08206 L·atm·mol^{-1}·K^{-1}
		82.06 mL·atm·mol^{-1}·K^{-1}
		8.314 joule·mol^{-1}·K^{-1}
e	Charge of the electron	1.602×10^{-19} coulomb
	Volume of 1 mol of an ideal gas	
	at 1 atm	0°C = 22.41 L
	at 1 atm	25°C = 24.46 L

Mathematical constants
$\pi = 3.1416$
$\ln x = 2.303 \log_{10} x$

TABLE B-3
Vapor pressure of water at different temperatures

Temperature (°C)	Vapor pressure (torr)
−10 (ice)	1.0
−5 (ice)	3.0
0	4.6
5	6.5
10	9.2
15	12.8
16	13.6
17	14.5
18	15.5
19	16.5
20	17.5
21	18.6
22	19.8
23	21.1
24	22.4
25	23.8
26	25.2
27	26.7
28	28.3
29	30.0
30	31.8
35	42.2
40	55.3
45	71.9
50	92.5
60	149.4
70	233.7
80	355.1
90	525.8
100	760.0
110	1074.6
150	3570.5
200	11659.2
300	64432.8

TABLE B-4
Concentration of common acid and base solutions

Reagent	Formula	Molarity	Density	Percent solute
Acetic acid, glacial	CH_3COOH	17 M	1.05 g/mL	99.5
Acetic acid, dil.		6	1.04	34
Hydrocloric acid, conc.	HCl	12	1.18	36
Hydrochloric acid, dil.		6	1.10	20
Nitric acid, conc.	HNO_3	16	1.42	72
Nitric acid, dil.		6	1.19	32
Sulfuric acid, conc.	H_2SO_4	18	1.84	96
Sulfuric acid, dil.		3	1.18	25
Ammonia solution, conc. (ammonium hydroxide)	NH_3	15	0.90	58
Ammonia solution, dil. (ammonium hydroxide)		6	0.96	23
Sodium hydroxide, dil.	NaOH	6	1.22	20

TABLE B-5
The color changes and pH intervals of some important indicators

Name of indicator	pH interval	Color change	Solvent
Methyl violet	0.2–3.0	Yellow, blue, violet	Water
Thymol blue	1.2–2.8	Red to yellow	Water (+ NaOH)
Orange IV (Tropeolin OO)	1.3–3.0	Red to yellow	Water
Benzopurpurin 4B	1.2–4.0	Violet to red	20% alcohol
Methyl orange	3.1–4.4	Red to orange to yellow	Water
Bromphenol blue	3.0–4.6	Yellow to blue-violet	Water (+ NaOH)
Congo red	3.0–5.0	Blue to red	70% alcohol
Bromcresol green	3.8–5.4	Yellow to blue	Water (+ NaOH)
Methyl red	4.4–6.2	Red to yellow	Water (+ NaOH)
Chlorphenol red	4.8–6.8	Yellow to red	Water (+ NaOH)
Bromcresol purple	5.2–6.8	Yellow to purple	Water (+ NaOH)
Litmus	4.5–8.3	Red to blue	Water
Bromthymol blue	6.0–7.6	Yellow to blue	Water (+ NaOH)
Phenol red	6.8–8.2	Yellow to red	Water (+ NaOH)
Thymol blue	8.0–9.6	Yellow to blue	Water (+ NaOH)
Phenolphthalein	8.3–10.0	Colorless to red	70% alcohol
Thymolphthalein	9.3–10.5	Yellow to blue	70% alcohol
Alizarin yellow R	10.0–12.0	Yellow to red	20% alcohol
Indigo carmine	11.4–13.0	Blue to yellow	50% alcohol
Trinitrobenzene	12.0–14.0	Colorless to orange	70% alcohol

TABLE B-6
Equilibrium constants for the dissociation of acids and bases (25°C)

Compound	Dissociation reaction	K_a	pK_a
WATER			
	$H_2O = H^+ + OH^-$ (25°C)	1.00×10^{-14}	14.00
	(0°C)	0.11×10^{-14}	14.94
	(60°C)	9.61×10^{-14}	13.02
WEAK ACIDS			
Acetic	$CH_3COOH = H^+ + CH_3COO^-$	1.76×10^{-5}	4.75
Boric	$H_3BO_3 = H^+ + H_2BO_3^-$	6.0×10^{-10}	9.22
Carbonic ($CO_2 + H_2O$)	$CO_2 + H_2O = H^- + HCO_3^-$	K_1: 4.4×10^{-7}	6.35
	$HCO_3^- = H^+ + CO_3^{2-}$	K_2: 4.7×10^{-11}	10.33
Chromic	$H_2CrO_4 = H^+ + HCrO_4^-$	K_1: 2×10^{-1}	0.7
	$HCrO_4^- = H^+ + CrO_4^{2-}$	K_2: 3.2×10^{-7}	6.50
Formic	$HCHO_2 = H^+ + CHO_2^-$	2.1×10^{-4}	3.68
Hydrogen cyanide	$HCN = H^+ + CN^-$	4×10^{-10}	9.4
Hydrofluoric	$HF = H^+ + F^-$	6.9×10^{-4}	3.16
Hydrogen peroxide	$H_2O_2 = H^+ + HO_2^-$	2.4×10^{-12}	11.62
Hydrogen sulfate ion	$HSO_4^- = H^+ + SO_4^{2-}$	K_2: 1.2×10^{-2}	1.92
Hydrogen sulfide	$H_2S = H^+ + HS^-$	K_1: 1.0×10^{-7}	7.00
	$HS^- = H^+ + S^{2-}$	K_2: 1.3×10^{-13}	12.89
Nitrous	$HNO_2 = H^+ + NO_2^-$	4.5×10^{-4}	3.50
Oxalic	$H_2C_2O_4 = H^+ + HC_2O_4^-$	K_1: 3.8×10^{-2}	1.42
	$HC_2O_4^- = H^+ + C_2O_4^{2-}$	K_2: 5.0×10^{-5}	4.30
Phosphoric	$H_3PO_4 = H^+ + H_2PO_4^-$	K_1: 7.1×10^{-3}	2.15
	$H_2PO_4^- = H^+ + HPO_4^{2-}$	K_2: 6.3×10^{-8}	7.20
	$HPO_4^{2-} = H^+ + PO_4^{3-}$	K_3: 4.4×10^{-13}	12.36
Phosphorous	$H_2HPO_3 = H^+ + HHPO_3^-$	K_1: 1.6×10^{-2}	1.80
Sulfurous ($SO_2 + H_2O$)	$H_2SO_3 = H^+ + HSO_3^-$	K_1: 1.2×10^{-2}	1.92
	$HSO_3^- = H^+ + SO_3^{2-}$	K_2: 5.6×10^{-8}	7.25
CATION ACIDS—HYDRATED METAL IONS			
Aluminum ion	$Al(H_2O)_6^{3+} = H^+ + Al(H_2O)_5OH^{2+}$	1.1×10^{-5}	4.96
Chromium(III) ion	$Cr(H_2O)_6^{3+} = H^+ + Cr(H_2O)_5OH^{2+}$	1.6×10^{-4}	3.80
Iron(III) ion	$Fe(H_2O)_6^{3+} = H^+ + Fe(H_2O)_5OH^{2+}$	6.7×10^{-3}	2.17
Zinc ion	$Zn(H_2O)_4^{2+} = H^+ + Zn(H_2O)_3OH^+$	2.5×10^{-10}	9.60
WEAK BASES			
Ammonia	$NH_3 + H_2O = NH_4^+ + OH^-$	1.8×10^{-5}	4.75
Methylamine	$CH_3NH_2 + HOH = CH_3NH_3^+ + OH^-$	5.0×10^{-4}	3.3
Barium hydroxide	$Ba(OH)_2 = BaOH^+ + OH^-$	strong	
	$BaOH^+ = Ba^{2+} + OH^-$	K_2: 1.4×10^{-1}	0.85
Calcium hydroxide	$Ca(OH)_2 = CaOH^+ + OH^-$	strong	
	$CaOH^+ = Ca^{2+} + OH^-$	K_2: 3.5×10^{-2}	1.5

TABLE B-7

Equilibrium constants for the dissociation of complex ions, amphoteric hydroxides, and weak salts ($\approx 25°C$)

The formation of complex ions undoubtedly occurs in steps. It is only in the presence of a large excess of the coordinating ion or molecule that the complete, cumulative ionization constant can be used with any measure of quantitative reliability. Furthermore, the total ionic strength of the solution exerts a major influence in modifying equilibrium values. Thus, with the high concentration of ions usually present in the formation of the iron(III) thiocyanate complex ion, the calculated value of $K_{\mathrm{FeSCN2+}}$ will be increased three- to fivefold.

Compound	Dissociation reaction	K	pK
AMMINE (AMMONIA) COMPLEX IONS			
Tetraamminecadmium(II)	$Cd(NH_3)_4^{2+} = Cd^{2+} + 4NH_3$	2×10^{-7}	6.7
Tetraamminecopper(II)	$Cu(NH_3)_4^{2+} = Cu^{2+} + 4NH_3$	8×10^{-13}	12.1
Diamminesilver(I)	$Ag(NH_3)_2^+ = Ag^+ + 2NH_3$	6×10^{-8}	7.2
Tetraamminezinc(II)	$Zn(NH_3)_4^{2+} = Zn^{2+} + 4NH_3$	1×10^{-9}	9.0
HYDROXIDE COMPLEX IONS—AMPHOTERIC HYDROXIDES			
Tetrahydroxoaluminate	$Al(OH)_4^- = Al(OH)_3\,(s) + OH^-$	3×10^{-2}	1.5
Tetrahydroxochromate(III)	$Cr(OH)_4^- = Cr(OH)_3\,(s) + OH^-$	2.5	-0.40
Trihydroxoplumbate(II) ion	$Pb(OH)_3^- = Pb(OH)_2\,(s) + OH^-$	2×10^1	-1.3
Trihydroxostannate(II)	$Sn(OH)_3^- = Sn(OH)_2\,(s) + OH^-$	2.6	-0.41
Tetrahydroxozincate	$Zn(OH)_4^{2-} = Zn(OH)_2\,(s) + 2OH^-$	4×10^1	-1.6
CHLORIDE COMPLEX IONS AND WEAK SALTS			
Dichlorocadmium	$CdCl_2\,(aq) = Cd^{2+} + 2Cl^-$	2.5×10^{-3}	2.60
Tetrachloroaurate(III) ion	$AuCl_4^- = Au^{3+} + 4Cl^-$	5×10^{-22}	21.3
Trichloroiron(III)	$FeCl_3\,(aq) = Fe^{3+} + 3Cl^-$	8×10^{-2}	1.9
Dichloroiron(III) ion	$FeCl_2^+\,(aq) = Fe^{3+} + 2Cl^-$	8×10^{-3}	2.9
Chloroiron(III) ion	$FeCl^{2+} = Fe^{3+} + Cl^-$	3.5×10^{-2}	1.46
Mercury(II) chloride	$HgCl_2\,(aq) = HgCl^+ + Cl^-$	K_1: 3.3×10^{-7}	6.48
Chloromercury(II) ion	$HgCl^+ = Hg^{2+} + Cl^-$	K_2: 1.8×10^{-7}	6.74
Tetrachloromercurate(II)	$HgCl_4^{2-} = Hg^{2+} + 4Cl^-$	8.5×10^{-16}	15.07
Tin(II) chloride	$SnCl_2\,(aq) = Sn^{2+} + 2Cl^-$	5.7×10^{-3}	2.24
Tetrachlorostannate(II) ion	$SnCl_4^{2-} = Sn^{2+} + 4Cl^-$	3.3×10^{-2}	1.48
Hexachlorostannate(IV) ion	$SnCl_6^{2-} = Sn^{4+} + 6Cl^-$	$? \; 10^{-4}$	4
Dichloroargentate(I) ion	$AgCl_2^- = Ag^+ + 2Cl^-$	5×10^{-6}	5.3
OTHER COMPLEX IONS AND WEAK SALTS			
Tetracyanocadmate(II) ion	$Cd(CN)_4^{2-} = Cd^{2+} + 4CN^-$	8×10^{-18}	17.1
Thiocyanatoiron(III) ion	$FeSCN^{2+} = Fe^{3+} + SCN^-$	1×10^{-3}	3.0
Lead(II) acetate	$Pb(C_2H_3O_2)_2\,(aq) = Pb^{2+} + 2C_2H_3O_2^-$	1×10^{-4}	4.0
Triacetatoplumbate(II) ion	$Pb(C_2H_3O_2)_3^- = Pb^{2+} + 3C_2H_3O_2^-$	2.5×10^{-7}	6.60
Dicyanoargentate(I) ion	$Ag(CN)_2^- = Ag^+ + 2CN^-$	1×10^{-20}	20.0
Dithiosulfatoargentate(I) ion	$Ag(S_2O_3)_2^{3-} = Ag^+ + 2S_2O_3^{2-}$	4×10^{-14}	13.4

TABLE B-8

General solubility rules for common salts and bases

1. NO_3^-	All *nitrates* are soluble.
2. CH_3COO^-	All *acetates* are soluble, ($AgCH_3COO$ only moderately).
3. Cl^-	All *chlorides* are soluble, except $AgCl$, Hg_2Cl_2, and $PbCl_2$. ($PbCl_2$ is slightly soluble in cold water, moderately soluble in hot water.)
4. SO_4^{2-}	All *sulfates* are soluble, except $BaSO_4$ and $PbSO_4$. ($CaSO_4$, Hg_2SO_4, and Ag_2SO_4 are slightly soluble; the corresponding bisulfates are more soluble.)
5. CO_3^{2-} and PO_4^{3-}	All *carbonates* and *phosphates* are insoluble, except those of Na^+, K^+, and NH_4^+. (Many acid phosphates are soluble, such as $Mg(H_2PO_4)_2$, and $Ca(H_2PO_4)_2$.)
6. OH^-	All *hydroxides* are insoluble, except $NaOH$, KOH, and $Ba(OH)_2$. ($Ca(OH)_2$ is slightly soluble.)
7. S^{2-}	All *sulfides* are insoluble, except those of Na^+, K^+, and NH_4^+, and those of the alkaline earths: Mg^{2+}, Ca^{2+}, Sr^{2+}, and Ba^{2+}. (Sulfides of Al^{3+} and Cr^{3+} hydrolyze and precipitate the corresponding hydroxides.)
8. Na^+, K^+, NH_4^+	All salts of *sodium*, *potassium*, and *ammonium* are soluble, except several uncommon ones, such as $Na_4Sb_2O_7$, $K_2NaCo(NO_2)_6$, $(NH_4)_2NaCo(NO_2)_6$, K_2PtCl_6, $(NH_4)_2PtCl_6$.
9. Ag^+	All *silver* salts are insoluble, except $AgNO_3$ and $AgClO_4$. ($AgC_2H_3O_2$ and Ag_2SO_4 are only moderately soluble.)

TABLE B-9
Solubility product constants (18–25°C)*

Compound	K_{sp}	Compound	K_{sp}	Compound	K_{sp}
ACETATES		CHROMATES		SULFATES	
$AgCH_3COO$	4×10^{-3}	Ag_2CrO_4	2×10^{-12}	Ag_2SO_4	1.7×10^{-5}
		$BaCrO_4$	1.2×10^{-10}	$BaSO_4$	1.5×10^{-9}
HALIDES AND CYANIDES		$PbCrO_4$	2×10^{-16}	$CaSO_4$	2.4×10^{-5}
$AgCN$	10^{-16}	$SrCrO_4$	3.6×10^{-5}	$PbSO_4$	1.3×10^{-8}
$AgCl$	1.8×10^{-10}			$SrSO_4$	7.6×10^{-7}
$AgBr$	5×10^{-13}	HYDROXIDES			
AgI	8.5×10^{-17}	$Al(OH)_3$	10^{-33}	SULFIDES	
$CuCl$	3.2×10^{-7}	$Ca(OH)_2$	1.3×10^{-6}	Ag_2S	10^{-50}
Hg_2Cl_2	1.1×10^{-18}	$Cr(OH)_3$	10^{-30}	CdS	10^{-26}
$PbCl_2$	1.6×10^{-5}	$Cu(OH)_2$	2×10^{-19}	CoS	10^{-21}
PbI_2	8.3×10^{-9}	$Fe(OH)_2$	2×10^{-15}	CuS	10^{-36}
MgF_2	8×10^{-8}	$Fe(OH)_3$	10^{-37}	FeS	10^{-17}
CaF_2	1.7×10^{-10}	$Mg(OH)_2$	9×10^{-12}	HgS	10^{-50}
		$Mn(OH)_2$	2×10^{-13}	MnS	10^{-13}
CARBONATES		$Pb(OH)_2$	4×10^{-15}	NiS	10^{-22}
Ag_2CO_3	8×10^{-12}	$Sn(OH)_2$	10^{-27}	PbS	10^{-26}
$BaCO_3$	1.6×10^{-9}	$Zn(OH)_2$	5×10^{-17}	SnS	10^{-27}
$CaCO_3$	4.8×10^{-9}			ZnS	10^{-20}
$CuCO_3$	2.5×10^{-10}	OXALATES			
$FeCO_3$	2×10^{-11}	BaC_2O_4	1.5×10^{-8}		
$MgCO_3$	4×10^{-5}	CaC_2O_4	1.3×10^{-9}		
$MnCO_3$	9×10^{-11}	MgC_2O_4	8.6×10^{-5}		
$PbCO_3$	1.5×10^{-13}	SrC_2O_4	5.6×10^{-8}		
$SrCO_3$	7×10^{-10}				

* These values are approximate. The solubility is affected by the concentration of the metal ion (about 10^{-3} to 10^{-2} M, by the temperature, and by the presence of substances that cause complex ion formation or that result in rather stable colloidal suspensions. The rate of hydrolysis and precipitation is often quite slow.

TABLE B-10
Reduction potentials (25°C)*

Strongest oxidizing agents	Half-reaction	$E°$ (V)	Weakest reducing agents
	$\frac{1}{2}F_2\,(g) + H^+ + e^- \rightleftharpoons HF\,(aq)$	$+3.06$	
	$\frac{1}{2}F_2\,(g) + e^- \rightleftharpoons F^-$	$+2.87$	
	$H_2O_2\,(aq) + 2H^+ + 2e^- \rightleftharpoons 2H_2O$	$+1.77$	
	$PbO_2\,(s) + 4H^+ + SO_4^{2-} + 2e^- \rightleftharpoons 2H_2O + PbSO_4\,(s)$	$+1.685$	
	$Ce^{4+} + e^- \rightleftharpoons Ce^{3+}$	$+1.61$	
	$Bi_2O_4\,(s) + 4H^+ + 2e^- \rightleftharpoons 2H_2O + 2BiO^+$	$+1.6$	
	$MnO_4^- + 8H^+ + 5e \rightleftharpoons 4H_2O + Mn^{2+}$	$+1.51$	
	$Mn^{3+} + e^- \rightleftharpoons Mn^{2+}$	$+1.51$	
	$Au^{3+} + 3e^- \rightleftharpoons Au$	$+1.50$	
	$HClO\,(aq) + H^+ + 2e^- \rightleftharpoons H_2O + Cl^-$	$+1.49$	
	$ClO_3^- + 6H^+ + 5e^- \rightleftharpoons 3H_2O + \frac{1}{2}Cl_2\,(g)$	$+1.47$	
	$Co^{3+} + e^- \rightleftharpoons Co^{2+}$	$+1.45†$	
	$\frac{1}{2}Cl_2 + e^- \rightleftharpoons Cl^-$	$+1.3595$	
	$Cr_2O_7^{2-} + 14H^+ + 6e^- \rightleftharpoons 7H_2O + 2Cr^{3+}$	$+1.33$	
	$MnO_2\,(s) + 4H^+ + 2e^- \rightleftharpoons 2H_2O + Mn^{2+}$	$+1.23$	
	$O_2\,(g) + 4H^+ + 4e^- \rightleftharpoons 2H_2O$	$+1.229$	
	$\frac{1}{2}Br_2\,(g) + e^- \rightleftharpoons Br^-$	$+1.0652$	
	$AuCl_4^- + 3e^- \rightleftharpoons 4Cl^- + Au$	$+1.00$	
	$NO_3^- + 4H^+ + 3e^- \rightleftharpoons 2H_2O + NO\,(g)$	$+0.96$	
	$2Hg^{2+} + 2e^- \rightleftharpoons Hg_2^{2+}$	$+0.92$	

Increasing oxidizing strength (left margin) — *Increasing reducing strength* (right margin)

(continued on next page)

TABLE B-10 (*continued*)

Strongest oxidizing agents	Half-reaction	$E°$ (V)	Weakest reducing agents
	$ClO^- + H_2O + 2e^- \rightleftharpoons 2OH^- + Cl^-$	+0.89	
	$HO_2^- + H_2O + 2e^- \rightleftharpoons 3OH^-$	+0.88	
	$Hg^{2+} + 2e^- \rightleftharpoons Hg\ (l)$	+0.854	
	$O_2 + 4H^+\ (10^{-7}\ M) + 4e^- \rightleftharpoons 2H_2O$	+0.815	
	$Ag^+ + e^- \rightleftharpoons Ag$	+0.79991	
	$Hg_2^{2+} + 2e^- \rightleftharpoons 2Hg\ (l)$	+0.789	
	$Fe^{3+} + e^- \rightleftharpoons Fe^{2+}$	+0.771	
	$O_2\ (g) + 2H^+ + 2e^- \rightleftharpoons H_2O_2\ (aq)$	+0.682	
	$MnO_4^- + 2H_2O + 3e^- \rightleftharpoons 4OH^- + MnO_2\ (s)$	+0.60	
	$I_3^- + 2e^- \rightleftharpoons 3I^-$	+0.54	
	$\frac{1}{2}I_2\ (aq) + e^- \rightleftharpoons I^-$	+0.536	
	$MnO_2\ (s) + H_2O + NH_4^+ + e^- \rightleftharpoons NH_3 + Mn(OH)_3\ (s)$	+0.50	
	$O_2\ (g) + 2H_2O + 4e^- \rightleftharpoons 4OH^-$	+0.401	
	$Cu^{2+} + 2e^- \rightleftharpoons Cu$	+0.337	
	$BiO^+ + 2H^+ + 3e^- \rightleftharpoons H_2O + Bi$	+0.32	
	$HAsO_2\ (aq) + 3H^+ + 3e^- \rightleftharpoons 2H_2O + As$	+0.2475	
	$AgCl\ (s) + e^- \rightleftharpoons Cl^- + Ag$	+0.2222	
	$SbO^+ + 2H^+ + 3e^- \rightleftharpoons H_2O + Sb$	+0.212	
	$SO_4^{2-} + 4H^+ + 2e^- \rightleftharpoons H_2O + H_2SO_3\ (aq)$	+0.17	
	$Sn^{4+} + 2e^- \rightleftharpoons Sn^{2+}$	+0.15	
	$S + 2H^+ + 2e^- \rightleftharpoons H_2S\ (g)$	+0.141	
	$2H^+ + 2e^- \rightleftharpoons H_2\ (g)$	0.000	
	$O_2\ (g) + H_2O + 2e^- \rightleftharpoons OH^- + HO_2^-$	−0.076	
	$Pb^{2+} + 2e^- \rightleftharpoons Pb$	−0.126	
	$CrO_4^{2-} + 4H_2O + 3e^- \rightleftharpoons 5OH^- + Cr(OH)_3\ (s)$	−0.13	
	$Sn^{2+} + 2e^- \rightleftharpoons Sn$	−0.136	
	$Ni^{2+} + 2e^- \rightleftharpoons Ni$	−0.250	
	$Co^{2+} + 2e^- \rightleftharpoons Co$	−0.277	
	$PbSO_4\ (s) + 2e^- \rightleftharpoons SO_4^{2-} + Pb$	−0.356	
	$Cd^{2+} + 2e^- \rightleftharpoons Cd$	−0.403	
	$Cr^{3+} + e^- \rightleftharpoons Cr^{2+}$	−0.41	
	$2H^+\ (10^{-7}\ M) + 2e^- \rightleftharpoons H_2\ (g)$	−0.414	
	$Fe^{2+} + 2e^- \rightleftharpoons Fe$	−0.44	
	$S + 2e^-\ (1\ M\ OH^-) \rightleftharpoons S^{2-}$	−0.48	
	$2CO_2\ (g) + 2H^+ + 2e^- \rightleftharpoons H_2C_2O_4\ (aq)$	−0.49	
	$Cr^{3+} + 3e^- \rightleftharpoons Cr$	−0.74	
	$Zn^{2+} + 2e^- \rightleftharpoons Zn$	−0.763	
	$2H_2O + 2e^- \rightleftharpoons 2OH^- + H_2\ (g)$	−0.828	
	$SO_4^{2-} + H_2O + 2e^- \rightleftharpoons 2OH^- + SO_3^{2-}$	−0.93	
	$Mn^{2+} + 2e^- \rightleftharpoons Mn$	−1.18	
	$Al^{3+} + 3e^- \rightleftharpoons Al$	−1.66	
	$Mg^{2+} + 2e^- \rightleftharpoons Mg$	−2.37	
	$Na^+ + e^- \rightleftharpoons Na$	−2.714	
	$Ca^{2+} + 2e^- \rightleftharpoons Ca$	−2.87	
	$Sr^{2+} + 2e^- \rightleftharpoons Sr$	−2.89	
	$Ba^{2+} + 2e^- \rightleftharpoons Ba$	−2.90	
	$Cs^+ + e^- \rightleftharpoons Cs$	−2.92	
	$K^+ + e^- \rightleftharpoons K$	−2.925	
	$Li^+ + e^- \rightleftharpoons Li$	−3.045	

Increasing oxidizing strength (left margin, upward arrow)
Increasing reducing strength (right margin, downward arrow)

* The reduction potential convention recommendation by the IUPAC is used. The potentials listed are those which would be obtained for the given half-cell when measured with respect to the standard hydrogen ($H^+ - H_2$) half-cell. All species are at unit activity unless otherwise specified. Values in the table are from W. M. Latimer, *Oxidation Potentials*, 2nd ed., Prentice-Hall, Englewood Cliffs, NJ, 1952.
† Newly revised value based on the work of A. L. Rotinjan et al., *Electrochimica Acta* **19**, 43 (1974).

TABLE B-11
International atomic weights (based on $C^{12} = 12$ exactly)

Element	Symbol	Atomic number	Atomic weight	Element	Symbol	Atomic number	Atomic weight
Actinium	Ac	89	[227]*	Mercury	Hg	80	200.59
Aluminum	Al	13	26.9815	Molybdenum	Mo	42	95.94
Americium	Am	95	[243]*	Neodymium	Nd	60	144.24
Antimony	Sb	51	121.75	Neon	Ne	10	20.183
Argon	Ar	18	39.948	Neptunium	Np	93	[237]*
Arsenic	As	33	74.9216	Nickel	Ni	28	58.71
Astatine	At	85	[210]*	Niobium	Nb	41	92.906
Barium	Ba	56	137.34	Nitrogen	N	7	14.0067
Berkelium	Bk	97	[247]*	Nobelium	No	102	[254]*
Beryllium	Be	4	9.0122	Osmium	Os	76	190.2
Bismuth	Bi	83	208.980	Oxygen	O	8	15.9994†
Boron	B	5	10.811†	Palladium	Pd	46	106.4
Bromine	Br	35	79.909‡	Phosphorus	P	15	30.9738
Cadmium	Cd	48	112.40	Platinum	Pt	78	195.09
Calcium	Ca	20	40.08	Plutonium	Pu	94	[242]*
Californium	Cf	98	[247]*	Polonium	Po	84	[210]*
Carbon	C	6	12.01115†	Potassium	K	19	39.102
Cerium	Ce	58	140.12	Praseodymium	Pr	59	140.907
Cesium	Cs	55	132.905	Promethium	Pm	61	[147]*
Chlorine	Cl	17	35.453‡	Protactinium	Pa	91	[231]*
Chromium	Cr	24	51.996‡	Radium	Ra	88	[226]*
Cobalt	Co	27	58.9332	Radon	Rn	86	[222]*
Copper	Cu	29	63.54	Rhenium	Re	75	186.2
Curium	Cm	96	[247]*	Rhodium	Rh	45	102.905
Dysprosium	Dy	66	162.50	Rubidium	Rb	37	85.47
Einsteinium	Es	99	[254]*	Ruthenium	Ru	44	101.07
Erbium	Er	68	167.26	Samarium	Sm	62	150.35
Europium	Eu	63	151.96	Scandium	Sc	21	44.956
Fermium	Fm	100	[253]*	Selenium	Se	34	78.96
Fluorine	F	9	18.9984	Silicon	Si	14	28.086†
Francium	Fr	87	[223]*	Silver	Ag	47	107.870‡
Gadolinium	Gd	64	157.25	Sodium	Na	11	22.9898
Gallium	Ga	31	69.72	Strontium	Sr	38	87.62
Germanium	Ge	32	72.59	Sulfur	S	16	32.064†
Gold	Au	79	196.967	Tantalum	Ta	73	180.948
Hafnium	Hf	72	178.49	Technetium	Tc	43	[97]*
Helium	He	2	4.0026	Tellurium	Te	52	127.60
Holmium	Ho	67	164.930	Terbium	Tb	65	158.924
Hydrogen	H	1	1.00797†	Thallium	Tl	81	204.37
Indium	In	49	114.82	Thorium	Th	90	232.038
Iodine	I	53	126.9044	Thulium	Tm	69	168.934
Iridium	Ir	77	192.2	Tin	Sn	50	118.69
Iron	Fe	26	55.847‡	Titanium	Ti	22	47.90
Krypton	Kr	36	83.80	Tungsten	W	74	183.85
Lanthanum	La	57	138.91	Uranium	U	92	238.03
Lawrencium	Lw	103	[257]*	Vanadium	V	23	50.942
Lead	Pb	82	207.19	Xenon	Xe	54	131.30
Lithium	Li	3	6.939	Ytterbium	Yb	70	173.04
Lutetium	Lu	71	174.97	Yttrium	Y	39	88.905
Magnesium	Mg	12	24.312	Zinc	Zn	30	65.37
Manganese	Mn	25	54.9380	Zirconium	Zr	40	91.22
Mendelevium	Md	101	[256]*				

* A number in brackets designates the mass number of a selected isotope of the element, usually the one of longest known half-life.
† The atomic weight varies because of natural variation in the isotopic composition of the element. The observed ranges are boron, ±0.003; carbon, ±0.00005; hydrogen, ±0.00001; oxygen, ±0.0001; silicon, ±0.001, sulfur, ±0.003.
‡ The atomic weight is believed to have an experimental uncertainty of the following magnitude: bromine, ± 0.002; chlorine, ±0.001; chromium, ±0.001; iron, ±0.003; silver, ±0.003. For other elements, the last digit given is believed to be reliable to ±0.5.
Atomic weights: Courtesy the International Union of Pure and Applied Chemistry.
Bracked numbers: Courtesy the National Bureau of Standards.

Freeman Laboratory Separates in Chemistry

NOTE: When ordering Separates, please be sure to request the appropriate teacher's handbook or manual (sent free to teachers).

LABORATORY STUDIES IN GENERAL CHEMISTRY, 1001–1062
75¢ each
by FRANTZ and MALM

(These laboratory studies include most of the experiments and study assignments from the authors' two manuals CHEMICAL PRINCIPLES IN THE LABORATORY, First Edition, and ESSENTIALS OF CHEMISTRY IN THE LABORATORY, Second Edition.)

1001. Student Handbook
1003. Weighing Operations. Gravimetric Techniques
1004. Physical Properties of Substances
1005. Some Elementary Chemical Properties of Substances
1006. Analysis for Substances in the Atmosphere
1007. The Chemical Separation of a Mixture
1009. The Chemistry of Oxygen. Basic and Acidic Oxides and the Periodic Table
1010. The Formation of Salts
1011. The Activity of Certain Metals and the Stability of Their Oxides
1012. The Experimental Determination of a Chemical Formula
1013. The Formula of a Hydrate
1014. Fundamental Weight Relationships 1: Equivalent and Atomic Weights by Oxidation of the Metal
1015. Fundamental Weight Relationships 2: Equivalent and Atomic Weights by Reduction of the Metal Oxide
1016. The Properties of Gases. Relationships Among the Variables Volume, Pressure, Temperature, and Amount. *A Study Assignment*
1019. Analysis Based on the Equivalent Weight of a Metal. Ionic Valence
1020. Stoichiometric Calculations Based on Chemical Reactions. *A Study Assignment*
1021. Group Relationships in the Periodic Table
1023. Oxidation-Reduction
1024. Common Oxidizing and Reducing Agents. Balancing of Oxidation-Reduction Equations. *A Study Assignment*
1025. The Relationship of Oxidation-Reduction to Electric Cells and Electroylsis
1027. The Chemistry of Chlorine: Oxidation States −1 to +7
1031. Units of Concentration. The Volumetric Titration of Acids and Bases
1032. Volumetric Analysis—The Equivalent Weight of a Solid Acid
1034. The Equivalent Weight of Oxidizing and Reducing Agents
1036. The Molecular Weight of a Soluble Substance by Freezing-Point Depression
1037. The Preparation and Properties of Colloidal Dispersions
1038. Thermochemistry. The Heat of Reaction
1039. The Rate of Chemical Reactions. Chemical Kinetics

1040. The Rate of Chemical Reactions. Activation Energy
1041. Reversible Reactions and Chemical Equilibrium
1042. The Equilibria of Water, Weak Acids, and Weak Bases. Indicators, *pH*
1043. The Ionization Constant of Acetic Acid
1044. The Ionization Constant of Some Weak Acids
1045. Equilibria Involving Volatility, Solubility, Degree of Ionization
1046. the Equilibria Between Slightly Soluble Salts and Their Ions. The Solubility Product Constant
1048. Acid-Base Equilibria. Hydrolysis, Buffers
1049. Equilibria Involving Hard Water and Its Softening
1050. The Equilibria of Carbonic Acid and Its Salts
1051. Recapitulation of Problems on Ionic Equilibria. *A Study Assignment*
1053. An Introduction to the Qualitative Analysis of the Metal Ions. *A Study Assignment*
1054. The Silver Group
1055. The Hydrogen Sulfide Group
1056. The Ammonium Sulfide Group
1057. The Alkaline Earth and Alkali Groups
1058. The Analysis of General Unknown Inorganic Substances. The Solution of Solids
1059. Some Inorganic Preparations
1060. Introductory Organic Chemistry. Types of Compounds and Reactions
1061. Simple Biochemical Tests
1062. Some Organic Syntheses
Teacher's Manual (sent free to teachers)

LABORATORY STUDIES IN ORGANIC CHEMISTRY, 1063–1082
75¢ each
by HELMKAMP and JOHNSON

(Also available as a bound manual, SELECTED EXPERIMENTS IN ORGANIC CHEMISTRY, Second Edition.)

1063. Melting Points and Crystallization
1066. Spectra and Structure
1068. Nucleophilic Substitution Reactions
1070. Elimination Reactions
1071. Multistep Organic Syntheses I. Identification of Compounds
1072. Polymers and Polymerization
1073. Stereochemistry
1074. Triphenylcarbinol and Related Compounds
1075. Carbonyl Compounds
1076. Bimolecular Reduction of Acetone: Compounds Derived from Pinacol
1077. Aromatic Compounds: Derivatives of Nitrobenzene
1078. Heterocyclic Compounds
1079. Friedel-Crafts Reactions and Rearrangements
1080. Multistep Organic Syntheses II. Tetraphenyldihydrophthalic Anhydride
1081. Reactions of Carbonyl Compounds and Amines. Identification of a General Unknown

1082. Free Radical Reactions
Teacher's Manual (sent free to teachers)

LABORATORY STUDIES IN GENERAL CHEMISTRY, 1083–1122
75¢ each
BIRDWHISTELL and O'CONNOR, Editors

FRANTZ and MALM:
1083. Supplement to the Student Handbook, Analytical Methods and Equipment

GESSER, BADER, JAGROOP, and LITHOWN:
1084. Molecular Structure
1085. Densities of Pure Liquids and Solutions
1086. Gravimetric Analysis: Quantitative Analysis for Sulfate
1087. Quantitative Volumetric Analysis
1088. Volumetric Analysis: Determination of Sodium Carbonate in an Unknown
1089. Sources of Error—Measurement of the Gas Constant and the Molar Volume of Oxygen
1092. Vapor Pressure
1093. Viscosity
1094. Surface Tension and Contact Angle
1095. Boiling Points of Binary Systems (Siwoloboff's Method)
1097. Determination of Molecular Weight by Freezing-Point Depression
1098. The Enthalpy of Fusion of Naphthalene
1099. Heat of Solution
1100. Heat of Neutralization of an Acid and a Base
1102. *pH*, Potentiometric Titrations
1103. Conductivity
1105. Chemical Kinetics I: H_2O_2 Decomposition, Order, and Rate
1108. Chemical Kinetics: Decomposition of Benzene Diazonium Chloride
1111. Boric Acid and Its Derivatives
1112. Coordination Complexes of Iron—Preparation of Potassium Trioxalatoferrate(III)
1113. Preparation of a Polynuclear Complex—Bis(chloroacetato)copper(II)
1114. Ferrocene—An Organometallic Compound

O'CONNOR:
1116. Isolation and Study of Caffeine
1117. Analysis of Monofunctional Organic Compounds

O'CONNOR and WOELFEL:
1121. Qualitative Analysis for Certain Cations

LIPPARD:
1122. Crystal and Molecular Structure

LABORATORY STUDIES IN GENERAL, ORGANIC, AND BIOLOGICAL CHEMISTRY, 1123–1140
75¢ each
by BIRD

General Chemistry
1123. Essential Mathematical Operations
1125. A Scientific Approach
1126. Analysis by Interaction of Unknowns
1129. Hydrates
1130. Solubility and Crystallization

1131. The Empirical Formula of a Compound
1132. Relative Reactivity of Some Common Metals
1133. Acid-Base Titration
1134. Conductivity and Electrochemistry
1135. Oxidation-Reduction
1136. Anion Analysis

Organic Chemistry
1139. Organic Techniques: Melting Point and Boiling Point
1140. Organic Techniques: Crystallization and Molecular-Weight Determination

Teacher's Manual (sent free to teachers)

LABORATORY STUDIES IN GENERAL CHEMISTRY, 1151–1191
75¢ each
by HAGEN

1151. Supplement: An Introduction to Separates 1155–1191
1152. Supplement: Methods of Separation and Purification
1153. Supplement: The Measurement of Acidity
1155. The Establishment of a Chemical Equation Using the Method of Continuous Variation
1156. Writing a Chemical Equation from Titration Data
1157. The Stoichiometry of Some Reactions of Tin with Acids
1158. The Molar Combining Ratio of Copper and Sulfur
1159. Determination of the Formula of a Compound
1161. Vapor-Density Method of Molecular-Weight Determination
1162. Determination of a Molecular Weight by Freezing-Point Depression
1163. Equilibrium Vapor Pressure of a Liquid as a Function of Temperature
1165. A Study of the Reaction of Potassium Permanganate with Sodium Oxalate in Acid Solution
1167. Photometric Determination of an Equilibrium Constant
1168. Effect of Temperature on Equilibrium: Solubility Product of C_6H_5COOH
1170. Determination of an Equilibrium Constant: The Distribution of Ammonia in Chloroform and Water
1171. Determination of the Formula of a Metal Ammine Complex by Extraction and Titration
1173. Chelometric Titrations
1174. Clathrates or "Cage Compounds"
1176. Preparation and Analysis of a Complex Compound
1177. Thermal Analysis
1178. Spectra of Complexes
1179. Magnetic Properties of Complex Ions
1180. Electrochemical Cells
1182. pH Measurements
1183. Polarographic Analysis
1184. Kinetics of a Chemical Reaction: Concentration Dependence of the Reaction of Iodide with Persulfate
1185. Kinetics of a Chemical Reaction: Temperature Dependence of the Reaction of Iodide with Persulfate

1186. Kinetics of a Chemical Reaction: A Variation of Procedure
1187. Determination of the Salt Content of a Solution by Cation Exchange
1188. Separation of Four Transition Metal Ions by Means of an Anion-Exchange Resin and Preparation of an Elution Curve
1189. Methods of Separation and Purification: Simple Distillation, Fractional Distillation, Liquid-liquid Extraction
1190. More Methods of Separation and Purification: Column Chromatography of Colorless Substances in Solution, Vaporphase Chromatography with a Flame Photometer as Detector

Teacher's Manual (sent free to teachers)

LABORATORY STUDIES IN GENERAL CHEMISTRY, 1192–1208
75¢ each
BIRDWHISTELL and O'CONNOR, Editors

KEAN, BICHLMEIR, and WEST:
1192. Determination of Phosphate in Detergents
1193. Identification of an Organic Compound by Infrared Spectroscopy
1195. Gasoline Analysis by Gas Chromatography
1196. Separation of Esters from Fats and Oils

DREYER and WILLIAMS:
1197. Isolation and Characterization of Naringen from Grapefruit

GUENTHER:
1198. Atomic Weights of Silver and a Halogen

SCOTT:
1199. Protein Synthesis
1200. Amino Acid Isolation
1201. Amino Acid Separations
1202. Amino Acid and Protein Electrophoresis
1203. Amino Acid and Protein Spectrophotometry
1204. Enzymes
1205. Carbohydrate Isolation
1206. Carbohydrate Analysis
1207. Lipid Analysis
1208. The Isolation of Isoprenoid Pigments

LABORATORY STUDIES IN GENERAL CHEMISTRY, 1209–1255
75¢ each
by IFFT and ROBERTS

(Also available as a bound manual, FRANTZ/MALM'S ESSENTIALS OF CHEMISTRY IN THE LABORATORY, Third Edition.)

1209. Student Handbook: Introduction and Appendixes
1210. Mass and Volume Relationships
1211. Study Assignment: The Language of Chemistry
1212. Some Common Physical Properties of Substances
1213. Some Elementary Chemical Properties of Substances
1214. Study Assignment: Chemical

Stoichiometry. Units of Quantity and Concentration
1215. The Preparation of Pure Substances by Chemical Changes
1216. The Formula of a Compound from Experimental Data
1218. The Determination of Avogadro's Number
1220. Analysis of Substances in the Atmosphere
1221. Pressure-Volume-Temperature Relationships in Gases
1222. The Molar Volume of Oxygen
1223. The Molecular Weight of a Gas
1224. The Reactivity of Metals with Hydrochloric Acid
1225. Study Assignment: Writing Equations for Ionic Reactions
1226. Study Assignment: The Nomenclature of Inorganic Compounds
1227. Ionic and Covalent Compounds. Ionic Reactions
1228. The Chemistry of Oxygen. Basic and Acidic Oxides and the Periodic Table
1229. The Chemistry of Some Nonmetals of Groups V, VI, and VII
1230. Hess' Law and the First Law of Thermodynamics
1231. The Rate of Chemical Reactions: Chemical Kinetics
1232. Study Assignment: An Introduction to Chemical Equilibrium
1233. Some Examples of Chemical Equilibrium
1234. The Measurement of an Ionization Constant
1235. Equilibria of Coordination Compounds
1236. Hydrolysis Equilibria
1237. Volumetric Analysis. The Titration of Acids and Bases
1238. Some Inorganic Preparations
1239. Identification of Silver, Lead and Mercurous Ions
1240. Identification of Ferric, Aluminum, and Zinc Ions
1241. Identification of Alkaline Earth and Alkali Metal Ions
1242. The Qualitative Analysis of Some Common Anions
1243. Identification of Some Cations and Anions in a General Unknown
1244. Qualitative Analysis of Unlabeled Solutions: The Nine-Solution Problem
1245. The Use of Paper Chromatography in the Separation of Iron(III), Cobalt(II), Nickel(II), and Copper(II) Ions
1247. Oxidation-Reduction. Electron Transfer Reactions
1248. Study Assignment: Electrolysis and Faraday's Law
1249. Oxidation-Reduction Reactions and Electrochemical Cells
1250. Redox Titrations. The Oxidizing Capacity of a Household Cleanser
1251. Introductory Organic Chemistry
1252. Some Simple Biochemical Tests
1253. Some Organic and Biochemical Syntheses
1254. The Chemistry of Vitamin C
1255. Proteins and Polysaccharides

LABORATORY NOTEBOOK: $3.95

W. H. FREEMAN AND COMPANY
41 Madison Avenue, New York, NY 10010
20 Beaumont Street, Oxford, England OX1 2NQ